Dirk
Bogarde

Dirk Bogarde

THE COMPLETE AUTOBIOGRAPHY

A Postillion Struck by Lightning

Snakes and Ladders

An Orderly Man

Backcloth

A Postillion Struck by Lightning first published in 1977 by
Chatto & Windus Limited
Snakes and Ladders first published in 1978 by Chatto & Windus Limited
An Orderly Man first published in 1983 by Chatto & Windus Limited
Backcloth first published in Great Britain in 1986 by Viking

Published by arrangement with Chatto & Windus and The Hogarth Press, London

This edition first published in Great Britain in 1988 by

The Octopus Group Limited
Michelin House
81 Fulham Road
London SW3 6RB

ISBN 0 413 60990 1

Distributed by Methuen London Limited

Printed and bound in the United Kingdom by William Clowes Limited, Beccles

Contents

This book is for
My Father and Mother, Elizabeth,
Gareth, Tony and Lally.
With my love.

D. V. d. B.

Preface

In 1968 when I left England to live abroad, I suggested to my father that I might perhaps start to write a book about my early childhood. The severance had not been very easy, and I felt that by recalling some of the intense pleasures of the early days the break might be somewhat soothed. He agreed, but reminded me that as far as I was concerned my early family background was very hazy. He felt that I would receive little help from the Scottish side, apart from my mother, and that there was no one left on his side save for himself. Consequently, if I liked, he would start to collect as much information as he could to assist me in what, he said, would be a very lengthy task. I accepted with pleasure. It was only after his death, in 1972, that clearing up private papers in his studio I came across a packet and a cigar box labelled simply 'For Dirk'. He had been as good as his word and assembled a wide collection of diaries, letters, school reports, photographs, glass negatives, cuttings and written notes in his own hand on dates and times. It is from this carefully amassed selection from a life that this book has, in the main, been written. For the rest I have had to depend on my own memories and those of my English family and my friends.

Where it was impossible to remember a real name, I have substituted another: and also where I have felt that this might save embarrassment. Street names and some identifiable town names have likewise been altered. Otherwise the events, as I remember them, all took place as written. Although, clearly, many of the conversations have been re-constructed, these are the words we used, the phrases we used and the way we were then. Part One is a condensation of at least two summers, but Part Two is 'as it was' to the best of my recollection.

I am indebted very much to the following people for assistance with 'remembering', and for the use of their own letters and diaries: Mrs G. Goodings; Mrs A. Holt; E. L. L. Forwood; W. A. Wightman; and G. van den Bogaerde. And to Mrs Glur Dyson Taylor who was 'godmother' to the book.

To Mrs Sally Betts, who typed it, and corrected my appalling spelling, punctuation and almost indecipherable typescript, my warmest thanks and gratitude.

DIRK BOGARDE

CHATEAUNEUF DE GRASSE

A Postillion Struck by Lightning

PART ONE
SUMMER

ONE

We were almost halfway down the gully when my sister screamed and called out, 'I've found him!'

But she hadn't: it was just an old rusty can gleaming wet in the dew among the leaves. It wasn't George by any stretch of the imagination: I'd know George anywhere and he wouldn't be down the gully, of that I was pretty sure. He'd be up top, in the Great Meadow where the grass was fresh and tender, and there were hosts of dandelions which he liked.

Not in the gully, which was deep, and dry, usually, and lined with great ash and oak, and chalky along the edges full of warrens and, down at the bottom by the road, old cans and bedsteads and stoves which people dumped among the nettles. George was the kind of tortoise who thought for himself, and he would never have thought to wander so far from the house when the Great Meadow was bung full of food and surrounded the place in which he usually lived. He wasn't a complete fool.

I struggled up the side of the gully and broke through the nettles and elder bushes into the field. I was soaking with dew. Down below in the valley the first chimneys were smoking and the meadow lay still in silver light, a good hundred acres of it. It was going to be a bit of a job to find George among all that grass.

My sister was behind me, having scrambled painfully through the elder branches, whimpering from time to time. I didn't take any notice. If you said anything the least bit kind, or helpful, or sympathetic, they started to snivel, and after that cry. And you might as well have said nothing, because then they only did a whimper or two and, seeing you didn't care much, stopped. So I didn't say a thing to her. She rubbed her stung knees with a dock leaf and pushed her hair from her eyes.

'Why did we have to get up at dawn to look for him?'

'Because.'

'But because why?'

'Because it's the best time to find them. That's why.'

'To find tortoises!' she scoffed, rubbing away at her wretched knees. 'You'd think you'd been hunting them all your life.'

I started to hum and sing a bit.

'And you haven't,' she continued, 'because they come from Africa and you've never been there.'

I left her and started walking down the long slope to the valley, peering at molehills and under tussocks of ragwort, and generally trying to seem as if I had a pattern. Pretty soon she'd get windy left up there by the dark old gully and she'd come trolling and skittering down to join me.

I found a large rabbit hole, and stooped to search it. Once, a month ago, he'd got out and stuck himself in a rabbit hole in the orchard.

She wasn't far behind me now, singing a bit, and brushing the long wet grasses with her skinny brown hands. She grabbed some sorrel leaves and chewed them.

'If he gets stuck in a hole again, we'll never find him, there must be five hundred million in this field. There must be.'

I got up and dusted my hands and walked on singing my bit of humming-song. She was right, but I wasn't going to let her know that.

'We'll just have to search every single one.'

'Well I won't!' She stopped some paces behind me, waving her arms like a windmill. I walked on, looking and kicking about the big grass clumps.

'It's not my tortoise. And I'm soaking wet. My sandals are all slimy. You'll be sorry!' she screeched.

Patiently I turned and looked up at her against the morning.

'It's half yours,' I said politely, but coldly. 'Uncle Salmon gave it to us *both*. So it stands to reason that it's *ours*. Not just mine.'

She shrugged, but was silent. I stared at her. She suddenly bent and started to unbuckle her sandal. 'Well, I don't want my half of it. You've got the part with the head. That's the best part.' She sat down in the wet shaking her old brown sandal. I could see her knickers, but I didn't bother to tell her. She was so rotten.

'Well, go on home and I'll look for him alone. And when I find him I'll have both halves and you'll have to lump it.' I turned and ran away down the hill . . . in case she tried to follow. She didn't, but she screeched again.

'The head part is the most interesting part. You said so. I don't like the tail part. And if I go home alone Aleford's stallion could get me.'

I reached the edge of the meadow and threw myself on to the grass under the ash tree and lay there looking at the sky and puffing a bit. It was quite a long run down from the top.

It was only yesterday evening that I had carefully washed his shell, and then put a little olive oil on it so that it shone and gleamed like a great golden brown pebble on the beach at Birling Gap. Only yesterday that he'd had the very innermost heart of a lettuce. The pale, yellowish-whitish bit. And only yesterday that Reg Fluke told me to put a little hole in her end of the shell and fix a bit of string to it. 'Then he won't wander,' he said.

But I didn't, and here we were in the dawn, searching for him, in vain it seemed.

There was a thumping in the earth under my back, and I could hear her running. Her feet thumping along in the grass. She slithered down beside me clutching her soaking sandals and peered at me. Her long hair hung over her face, and brushed my cheek. She looked like a hideous witch-thing: she crossed her eyes at me.

'Don't!' I said in alarm. 'You'll stay like it.'

'Not that you'd care. You left me up there and the stallion might be anywhere. You just don't mind about me. I won't help you look.' She leapt to her feet and ran barefoot through the field, jumping over molehills, waving her skirts about, and singing very loudly indeed. This was not to impress me, but to frighten away Aleford's stallion, which we had never actually seen, but which we'd been told about in great detail by Reg Fluke and a boy from Woods, the butchers in the village.

And the telling was bad enough. I wasn't exactly anxious to see it myself. But I lay on, listening to her singing away in puffs and gasps as she ran furiously uphill.

The sun had been up only a little while and beside me, close to my face, so that it was actually all blurry and looked like an eagle, was a burnet-moth on a bit of grass, feeling the sun, and waiting for the dusk to come. I rolled over on my stomach and looked up the hill. She looked quite small now, leaping over the grasses, and jumping about with her long legs and the sandals held high, as if a great dog was running beside her trying to grab them.

A blackbird was singing in the ash tree and I was just wondering if there was a nest nearby when I heard her: it was rather frightening actually. She let out a terrible shriek, and then another and another as if someone was stabbing her.

I jumped up and stared. She was standing quite still, staring at the ground and holding her sandals close to her heart. Shrieking.

It must be George, and of course, he must be dead. Horribly, by the way she was yelling . . . I started to walk up the hill towards her.

'What is it? What's happened?' I called.

'Come quickly . . . come quickly . . . it's ghastly! Hurry! God's honour, it's the biggest one . . . it's the biggest! Quick.'

I ran. The wet grasses stinging my legs, and the tussocks and molehills tripping me. The yelling stopped but she was staring at me with great beseeching eyes.

'Come quickly!'

'This is as quick as I can. Is it a snake?' That was it, of course. An adder. And we'd both be bitten. 'If it's a snake,' I said, stopping immediately, 'come away. Don't stand there gawping, come away. It'll kill us. Just run.'

'It isn't a snake . . . it isn't a snake . . . it's terrible!' She hadn't moved, so I went on, rather reluctantly, but cheered that it was nothing too beastly . . . obviously not George mangled by a fox or something, otherwise she'd be snivelling. But now she was crouching in the grasses, staring at it like a mad rabbit.

Then I was beside her, my shirt had come out of the top of my shorts, and my shoes were soaking too.

'What is it? What is it then?'

When she spoke her voice was sort of roughish and very low with wonder. 'Look,' she said, and very gently parted the grasses before her. 'Look, it's the biggest mushroom in the world. Look!'

And it was. It must have been about as round as a dinner plate, quite. And it sat in a little hollow with some others around it; but they were smaller, this was a giant.

'Gosh!'

'Isn't it *huge*? It's the biggest in the world.'

'It might be a toadstool, or something.'

'Well, let's pick it and take it home and they'll tell us.'

Very gingerly I reached out and pulled the great shiny brown top . . . it smelt like a million mushrooms. It was golden brown in the sun and underneath it was pink and white, and damp. We smelt it carefully and she opened her skirt like an apron for it, and we walked breathlessly up to the house.

'It's like a beautiful parasol,' she said.

In the kitchen there was a breakfast smell. The kettle was steaming away on the Primus stove and Lally, plump in a print dress and tennis shoes, was sitting at the table buttering toast.

We stood on the brick floor looking at her, willing her to look up at us, but she went on scraping off the burnt bits and singing a song to herself. My sister deliberately dropped one sandal and then the other. Lally stopped singing and said: 'Go-and-wash-your-hands-why-haven't-you-got-your-shoes-on?' all in one breath, but still not looking up, although she must have seen us.

My sister said in her Old Maid's voice: 'We have something rather strange to show you.'

Lally looked briefly at her bulging skirt and said: 'If it's living throw it out and if it's dead likewise. Kettle's boiling.'

'It's alive and dead at the same time, sort of,' I said.

'Well, we don't want it in here, do we?' said Lally, stacking up some toast and cutting off the crusts all round. 'And I'd be pleased if you hurry up before the Prince of Wales is here.'

'It's a mushroom,' said my sister, moving across the floor with the bundle and laying it on the table among the crusts and the butter crock. 'And it's possibly the biggest in the world . . . or anyway in Sussex.' And she carefully opened her skirt and showed it.

Lally took a look and then was interested. 'Jerusalem!' she said. She always did when she couldn't think of anything else, or if you had surprised her, or if she was quite pleased but-not-going-to-show-it, or if she didn't understand clearly. And she didn't understand this. For a moment we all looked at it in dead silence.

'Well, it's big I grant you, probably wormy too. What do you want me to do with it?'

My sister removed it very gently from the cloth of her skirt and, wiping her hands together, she said: 'We could all have it for breakfast, couldn't we?'

'Fried,' I said.

'With bacon sort of,' said my sister.

'Be tough, I shouldn't doubt, you'd better ask your mother: it might be poisonous and then where should I be? Never get another job, not having poisoned a whole family. It's very large,' she said. 'Give it a good wash and we'll see.'

Well, you could tell she was impressed because she forgot to remind us to wash ourselves, and taking down the big iron frying-pan she started singing her song again.

Carefully we washed it at the big sink and smelled the fresh damp smell of it and admired the pink underneath part, and there were no worms.

It was about the best thing I've ever eaten. Cut in strips, like bacon, and fried in butter with tomatoes and a bit of ham and soft toast.

'Where did you find it then?' Lally asked.

'We were looking for George in Great Meadow and she found it.' I indicated my sister with a flick of jealousy.

'It was sort of in a little hollow place, right in the middle,' she said.

'It's a wonder Aleford's stallion wasn't about,' said Lally, wiping round her plate with a bit of bread: she said this was all right to do ever since she came to France the first time with us. Anything the French did was all right by her, which shows just how ignorant she was. 'That stallion could kick you to death with a look: there was a boy lived up at Teddington when I was your age, got kicked in the head by one. He was loopy all his life.' She cleaned the edge of her knife against the plate and stuck it in the butter. 'Any cows in the meadow?'

'Some,' I said. 'Right down at the bottom.'

'Well, you need cows and horses in the same field for mushrooms,' said Lally. 'If you don't have it that way you can't get mushrooms.'

'Why?' asked my sister.

Lally was spreading damson jam all over her toast. 'Because when you get cow dung and horse dung in the same field you get mushrooms, that's why,' she said and bit into the jam.

My sister looked white but a little scornful. 'Dung,' she said.

'DUNG, dung,' said Lally. 'You ask anyone, anyone you like. Ask Aleford or Beattie Fluke down the bottom, or the Prince of Wales. They'll all say the same thing. Dung.'

For a little time we were silent, except for the clink and scrape of knives and forks and the kettle lid plopping up and down. Sunlight streamed through the windows, across the table and the bumpy whitewashed walls.

'Do the French eat them?' I asked.

'Wee,' said Lally, nodding her head.

'Well, it must be all right for us to, I mean if they do it must be,' I said.

'They're the best cooks in the world, aren't they?' said my sister. 'So they'd be bound to know if it was all right or not.'

Lally eased up from the table and started stacking the plates. 'Can't all be right at the same time,' she said, going across to the sink and dumping them into some water. 'Can't be right all the time. Even the French. Remember one thing,' she said, taking the soap up from the shelf. 'The French eat snails too.'

We helped with the drying-up in a thoughtful silence.

We lay on our backs under the ash tree by the top of the gully and watched the crows wheeling and gliding in the wind. All around my head sorrel, buttercup and long bendy plantains shimmered and nodded. I crumbled a little empty snail shell, transparent and silvery. My sister had her eyes closed, her hands folded on her chest like a dead Plantagenet. She had the same kind of nose, poky and long; her hair was scattered with pollen.

I leant up on one elbow and sprinkled the snail shell all over her face.

She screamed and hit me with her fist.

I fell back into the grass and lay still, staring at the crows. She was mumbling and brushing her chin.

'Stupid fool,' she said.

'I merely wondered if you were feeling sick yet. That's all.'

'Well I'm not.' She lay back. 'Are you?'

'No. Not sick. Full.'

'I think Lally is a liar anyway.'

'I know she is,' I said. 'Look at the Prince of Wales.'

'What about him?'

'Well, you know: she's always saying he's coming, or she met him at the pictures, or Victoria Station. And she's always talking to him on the telephone. She says.'

'Well, that doesn't say she's a liar,' said my sister, rolling on to her stomach and squinting at the sun. 'Not like Betty Engles. She's a liar properly.'

'Why . . . I mean how do you know she is properly?'

'Because,' said my sister patiently, 'because she said her father was a millionaire and I know it's a lie.' She knelt up and picked some grass.

'How?'

'Because I saw him actually riding a bicycle.'

'Well I should think Lally is just as much of a liar as Betty Engles . . . I bet she's never even seen the Prince of Wales. And not at Victoria Station.'

'Why not Victoria Station?'

'Because to go to Sunningdale you have to leave from Waterloo.'

We lay still for a while, comforted by our proof and by the fact that we did not feel sick. After a little while I sat up and tucked my shirt into my shorts. Away across the meadow the Downs were smudged with the morning sun and a little red Post Office van went bundling along the lower road and got lost in the trees. You could just see it shining red here and there in the gaps and then it turned right up to Peachy Corner and disappeared. I got up. 'I'm going to have another look for George. Coming?'

She groaned. 'All right, coming,' she said. 'And then we'll go down to Bakers and get a bottle of Tizer, I've got threepence.' I pulled her up and we ran howling and laughing down the meadow: a linnet shot up at our feet, spiralling into the sky like a singing leaf, and as we whooped and leapt over the tussocks I could see the river sequinned with sunlight. I gave a great big shout of happiness . . . we weren't going to be sick and it was going to be a beautiful morning.

TWO

Herbert Fluke said that they weren't really canaries at all. They were ordinary sparrows dyed yellow, sometimes pink, and stuck in their cages. He said he knew because his brother Reg had a friend who used to catch them with bird-lime on twigs every year when the fair came to the village.

But I wanted one very badly. Basically because they were birds, and I worshipped birds, and also because the cages were so terribly small. They hung all round the stall in clusters . . . little square wood and wire boxes about eight by eight with chippering, tweeting little yellow, and sometimes pink, birds flittering and fluttering against the bars while you rolled pennies down a slotted thing on to numbers, or lobbed bouncy ping-pong balls into glass jars for twopence a throw. If you scored thirty or over you got a bird . . . the most you ever seemed able to score was a five or a three which together made eight, and for that, the lowest amount, you sometimes got a matchbox with a fishing set in it or a black and a pink celluloid baby with a little bath, with 'Japan' printed on their bottoms.

But sometimes people did win a bird, because I saw them. Farm boys, with tightly belted trousers and shiny hair and fat maid-girls giggling on their arms, swung a little wooden cage in their free hand as they loped and lumbered across the shadowy, trodden grass to the swings. So people did win them sometimes; and I had two and sixpence which I had pleaded, hinted, saved, and on one occasion, which I remembered with a scarlet face, thieved, from around the household. Once, when my sister and I were changing the water in the flower jar on the altar in the church by the cottage, I pinched fourpence left by a hiker in the box: and spent four days of agony before I threw the scorching and almost molten coppers wide into the barley field on the way to Berwick. A fat lot of good thieving did you.

But tonight I had two shillings and sixpence intact . . . and in coppers: we'd gone into Bakers in the village on the way and changed it all, to make it easier at the stalls. Lally's mother, Mrs Jane, was with us: tall and respectable in black with a high black hat bound round with a shiny ribbon and a big coral pin her father had brought from Naples. Lally had on her tennis shoes and socks, and a nasty blue speckly frock which she wore always when we went shopping or out on any sort of social trip, and carried the black and red shopping bag with the candles, the rice and the pound of Cheddar for old Mr Jane's supper.

My sister was wearing her shorts, and whistling like a boy, which she hoped everyone would think she was, and jingling her one and fourpence in the pockets.

'What are you going to try for?' she called above the jingle-jongle of the roundabout. 'Bet is's a canary-bird. Well, I'm going to try for one of those camels . . . a blue or a red, I don't care which, so long as it's a camel.' She hadn't bothered to wait for my answer. Naturally.

The camels, which she had envied ever since she saw them here last year, were ghastly things, covered in spangly silver paint, and with baskets on their backs to put flowers in. You had to roll pennies for them too, only the top number was eighteen.

Lally was sucking a Snofruit and in between licks singing to the music on the roundabout . . . 'I'm Happy When I'm Hiking.' And Mrs Jane was picking her way carefully through the tumbling, rushing, laughing people, very tall and black, and holding her umbrella like a diviner's rod before her. I think she was enjoying herself, but you couldn't really tell with her; she seldom smiled unless it was over some rather old and boring story of when Lally and Brother Harold were children.

The canary stall was some way off from the roundabout, and quite near the lych gate of the church. People were sitting about on the gravestones in the flickering light from the fair petting and giggling, and putting paper flowers in their hair. Mrs Jane was a bit put off by all this.

'Fancy!' she said. 'No respect for the dead at all. I'm very glad it's not me or your father as is under there on an evening like this.'

'You wouldn't know, Mother,' said Lally. She enjoyed a fair. 'And what you don't know you wouldn't care about.'

'I'd know. And your father would know for all he's deaf,' said Mrs Jane.

'Would you be a ghost by then?' my sister asked in a soppy way.

'I'm not saying what I'd be,' said Mrs Jane, pushing a large collie dog out of her way. 'But sure as there's going to be thunder tonight, I'd *know*.'

We had got to the stall, the lights and the little cages all bobbing and jingling about, and people all round the barrier shoving and counting change, and rolling pennies down the little slotted bits of wood. In the middle was a large woman with a black and white apron with a big satchel bag round her neck, and every time a coin landed on an unnumbered square she shovelled it into the bag without looking and went on calling out, 'Eight to score Thirty for a Dicky.' And all the while her eyes were scanning about the fairground as if she was looking for somewhere to go.

I rolled my first three pennies, my arms rigid with fright, my eyes concentrating on the square with 'C' marked on it. But the pennies rolled down the slotted thing and just wobbled like old bicycle wheels on to the black or white squares and the woman in the middle shovelled them up without a look. The fourth penny tumbled on to number three and my sister smirked and said, 'Ten times that and you'd have won.' And I pushed her so that she fell over a lady with a pushcart and started to whine.

'Behave yourself!' said Mrs Jane.

'You'll get a thick ear if you don't,' said Lally and gave Mrs Jane her Snofruit to hold while she helped my sister to her feet.

The fifth and sixth pennies rolled down on to a black and a white and now I only had two shillings left.

'Why don't you have a go on something else, then?' said Lally. 'You won't have anything left for the roundabouts.'

'I'll just have a few more tries,' I said, and moved round the stall to another place to bring me luck. Just in front of me my sister stood, hair across her eyes, tongue sticking out, stiff with concentration trying for her camel. Mrs Jane stood behind her like a black witch, her glasses glittering in the electric lights, and the pink pin in her hat winking and bobbing as she craned to watch.

I got a five, a three, a black, and a six. Fourteen, another black, and then my last penny wobbled across the board, teetered about for a second that seemed an hour, and finally settled just into the magic square C. But it lay cruelly exposed to all and sundry with its edge just over the line. 'Doesn't count,' cried the lady in the middle, her fat greasy hand poised over the offending coin. 'Got to be right in the centre. Jam bang in the centre!' she cried triumphantly, scooping up my coin and hurling it into her bag. 'But you got a fishing set,' she said and slung the rotten little matchbox across the squares towards me. Glumly I shoved it into my pocket and pushed my way through the people. Lally called after me, something about don't get lost and they'd be coming, but I was heavy hearted, and didn't really listen. Above the glaring lights of the fairground the swifts swung and screamed, swooping in and out of the flags and banners. The Downs were hard and blue against a copper sky, big clouds crept up, like smoke from a great fire miles away, and a little cool breeze came whiffling along, making all the lights swing and dangle, and sending paper bags and chocolate wrappings scampering and eddying about the trodden grass. People ran past laughing, with red happy faces; girls with bows in their hair and braying boys wearing paper hats. The roundabout clonked up and down and round and round the brass angels in the middle banging their cymbals together every few moments and turning their heads slowly from left to right with wide brass eyes gleaming at no-one, while the white and yellow horses, the pink pigs, and the racing, startled ostriches swung round and round petrified in enamel. Around the canopy went the words 'BROWNRIGGS PLEASURE RIDE FOR FAMILIES' blurring into a ribbon of red and gold and yellow, and I went over to the stall where you threw balls into glass jars, had three go's and won a stick of rock with Ilfracombe written through it.

Down by the dodgem cars there was a rather nasty girl with red hair and glasses. Her name was Alice McWhirter and she was new to the village. Her father was some sort of artist, and they had taken old Mrs Maiden's house up at Elder Lane, and, as far as we were concerned, they were foreigners. She had come and talked to my sister and me when we were fishing once, and, although we were as rude as possible, she wouldn't go, so we'd brought her home for tea, given her a jam sandwich, made her walk along the top of a wall by the pigsty, pushed her in the nettles and sent her home alone. But she still came back for more. Lally said she was lonely and 'an only child' and that her father was an artist and what could you expect with no mother, and we were to be better behaved to her because we had each other, our father was a journalist and we had a mother. She was awfully soft at times. And so we sort of got to know her a bit, and once she asked us to her house which was very small and untidy, and smelled of linseed oil and cooking. Her father was very tall, had a red beard and bare feet and swore at us, which was the only time he ever spoke while we were there. After we'd looked at their privy, her collection of moths, all lumped up together, dead in a jam jar, and a photograph of her mother, fat and laughing with glasses, and a pom-pom hat, who was also dead, she asked us if we'd like some orangeade. We said 'yes' and followed her up a rather rickety stairway to the bedrooms. Although it was about tea-time the beds were still unmade, and there were clothes and old shoes all over the place. One room was very small, where she slept, and the other quite large and full of paintings and leather suitcases and a dreadful old camp bed in a corner covered in dirty sheets where her father slept. On a marble-topped table there was a big white china mug which she brought over to us very carefully. 'Here you are,' she said, 'Kia Ora.' And handed me the mug. It was full and heavy. And orange. I was just about to take a sip when she suddenly threw her skirts over her head and screamed, 'Don't! It's not Kia Ora at all, it's pee!' and fell on the camp bed laughing and laughing, with her legs going all sorts of ways.

I put down the heavy white mug, and we just stood there staring at her for a bit. Suddenly my sister said, 'I'm going home' and started off down the rickety stairs with me behind her and the awful girl still laughing on her father's bed.

After that we kept out of her way and never spoke to her again, but she made friends with Reg Fluke and we sometimes met them birdnesting or down in the meadow looking for slowworms.

I stood looking at the dodgem cars clonking and bumping into each other, and the people screaming and laughing and I felt Alice McWhirter moving along towards me. She was wearing a sort of velvet dress, and her legs were bare and scratched, and her glasses shone in the lights and all the dodgem cars were reflected in them as she peered up at me. She really was frightfully ugly.

'Hellow,' she said, and smiled.

'Hello,' I said politely, but coldly to show her I had not forgotten the orangeade part.

'Reg is on number four,' she said, indicating the car with a nod of her head. 'I wouldn't go on, I'm too scared.'

I didn't say anything.

'I've got sevenpence and I'm saving if for one go on the swings and one go on the horses, only I want a cockerel,' she said, edging closer.

'I've got two shillings,' I said in a pompous voice, 'and I'm going to spend it all on rolling pennies.'

She looked amazed. 'TWO shillings! What do you want to win?' she asked, her nasty little claw-like hand clutching the dodgem rail.

'That's my affair, I wouldn't tell you,' I said, and I was just moving away when she grabbed my arm with her horrible little hand and cried: 'Look what Reg won at the rolling.' And there, in her right hand, which had been hidden behind her velvet skirt, hanging in the air between us, was a little wooden cage with a canary fluttering and beating against the wires. 'Isn't he beautiful!' she cried. 'Reg got if for four rolls!'

My heart was thudding, my mouth dry, the little cage bobbed and wobbled in her outstretched hand between us. The thing I had most longed for was in the grasp of ghastly Alice McWhirter, and Reg Fluke had got it in four rolls.

'It's very pretty,' I said. 'But the cage is too small.'

Alice McWhirter laughed a scornful laugh. 'We're going to make it a bigger one, in our garden, out of an old orange box. I know where the wire is, and we'll put in twigs and grass and things. This,' she laughed, swinging it disdainfully above her head and frightening the bird out of its wits, 'is only for fairs and travelling and that. You couldn't put them all in orange boxes!'

And then Reg Fluke was clambering over the rail, his face smiling and country-looking, and red and shiny.

'Showing you my sparrer, is she?' he asked, pulling out a dirty handkerchief and wiping his forehead. 'Cost me four rolls, that did . . . and this,' he indicated the dodgems with a jab of his head backward, 'cost me sixpence and that's me skint.'

Alice McWhirter wagged the cage about in front of my stiff face. 'I've got sevenpence you can share,' she said.

'Coconuts is sixpence for four balls,' said Reg. 'What'll you do with a penny? Save it for a pee?' He roared with laughter, and Alice McWhirter smirked away. Funny how pee kept coming up with her.

'I'll give you one shilling in coppers for it,' I said, blurting it all out. The music was very loud, the cars banging and crashing into each other. Reg's jaw was stuck open with surprise. 'How much?'

'One shilling,' I said very loudly indeed, 'in coppers.'

'For a sparrer?'

Reg took the cage from the clutching hand of Alice Mcwhirter and peered into it. The canary skittered about again, and a feather fell out.

He handed it solemnly over to me. 'Where's the bob, then?' He crammed the pennies into both his pockets, and with a wink to Alice McWhirter he pulled her off into the crowds.

My heart bursting, my face red, the cage pressed close to my chest, I shoved and pushed through the people until I caught sight, over the heads in front of me, of Mrs Jane's black hat.

'Great Heavens!' she cried, seeing me. 'You got one! Well I declare. Lally . . .' she turned and cried above the music . . . 'the boy's got his canary!'

They stood round me in a circle, the three of them, staring at my prize. My sister clasped her hands with joy, and a glimmer of liking flickered in me for her, until she said: 'It'll just wash off in the rain, all that yellow, and be an ordinary sparrow you could have got for nothing.' And hate glowed deep in the coals of my heart. Lally cuffed her head lightly and said, 'Well I daresay you've spent all your money, and Miss Know All here's got her camel, so we'd better hop, skip and jump it home.' We turned and threaded our way through the thronging fairground. The roundabout was playing 'The More We Are Together' and the little wind flapped at the legs of my shorts, and jiggled the black ribbon on Mrs Jane's hat. My heart was full, thumping with happiness. My brain reeled with all the plans for my canary – a cage next, a large cage with perches, and a jam jar full of seeding grasses; a tin tray for sand and a bowl for bathing in; and maybe, later, a mate; and nests, and babies. Oh! Lord! What joy.

Lally looked up into the dark blue of the night, and sniffed. 'Mother?' she said. 'You said there'd be thunder, and I reckon you're about right. Shouldn't wonder if we have a storm before we reached home. Good job you got your brolly.'

'Always bring my brolly everywhere,' said Mrs Jane. 'Ever since I got wetted at your Aunt Gert's Silver up at Shepperton that year. Blue crêpe it was, and I got so wet you could see my stays right through. I thought your father would do himself a hurt he laughed so much.'

We had got to the path which led to the white wood bridge across the river. Behind us the glare of the fair was like a big bonfire, the twinkling lights like embers, and the smoke from the roundabout drifting up into the night. Ahead all was dark and still, and the trees and hedge blurry shapes. The white planks of the bridge were like whales bones. It was very still again: the little wind had stopped.

My sister said: 'How much did it cost, your bird? All your two and six?'

'All,' I said flatly.

'Throwing balls or rolling?'

'I got a stick of rock throwing the balls . . . it's in my pocket. You can have it if you like.'

'I would like. Don't you then?'

'I don't mind it. It's got Ilfracombe all through it.'

'Wherever's that?'

'I don't know. Cornwall, I think.'

We were crossing the bridge now, in single file, Lally ahead, swinging the shopping bag; Mrs Jane and her umbrella; my sister holding her camel and myself. The river was low, the lights of the fair rippling faintly on the surface. No sound save our feet clonk clonking over the hollow-sounding boards, and now and then a gurgle gurgle of water round the struts.

'Struth!' said Lally suddenly. 'It's close though. Ilfracombe's in Wales by the by. And what that's got to do with Sussex rock I don't know. But those Gippos are all cheats.'

Far away, over Wilmington, was a low grumbling rumble of thunder. We had got to the path now, and our feet crunched over the gravel.

'Good job you brought that brolly,' Lally's voice came back from the dark.

'Always carry a brolly,' said Mrs Jane.

My sister was scuffing her sandalled feet, swinging her blue camel by its legs.

'I gave Reg Fluke a shilling for it,' I said in a lowish voice.

'What?' She spun round and I tripped over her.

'Get a move on you two,' called Lally, 'there's going to be a storm along any moment.'

We walked along for a bit in silence. Suddenly there was a flash of white light in the sky, and the great hump of our hill was suddenly pale green in the night. Mrs Jane gave a little cry and hurried on.

My sister did a sort of jog trot behind her, and I kept up.

'It's cheating not to have won it. I rolled for mine, and it cost ten tries,' she said.

'Buying's not cheating, and anyway I've got it, so there.'

There was another rumble of thunder over Wilmington and another and another, and we hurried in a zig-zag way along the path, across the main road and through the little iron gate into our field.

'Don't touch the gate, children!' cried Mrs Jane. 'It's iron and you might be stuck. Lally! Mark what I said to the children here, you'll be struck if you touch the gate.' We slid through the opening and up into the field: another blinding flash burst down out of the sky, lit up the whole field, grass, nettles, molehills, all suddenly faded away into utter darkness, leaving us blinded and staggering, stumbling over tussocks, and blundering into each other. My sister started to whimper and Lally was just about to shout something at her, because I heard her say 'Don't be . . .,' when a great roaring crash from the heavens descended upon us, bursting over our heads and splitting the world into a great hurling roaring blast of sound. And with it came the wind whipping through the grass and tearing through the trees in the gully. Staggering and clutching together, the four of us struggled in the dark up the hill, holding each other for some kind of protection and comfort from a world of which we seemed to be no part.

My sister was crying noisily by now, snivelling along, her beastly china camel banging my knees, while I struggled on, holding the cage tight to my chest, and wondering desperately if the canary would be dead before we reached the shelter of the house. Just as the first great plops of rain started to thud down on us we saw the lamp-lit windows ahead, and bending our heads to the wind and the now pelting rain, we pushed through the wooden gate into the orchard, along the slippery brick path and round to the kitchen door. Another great roaring raging crash tumbled about our ears and made the earth shake, as Lally fumbled with the latch and burst us all into the mellow golden light of the white-washed flint-walled kitchen. She slammed the door hard behind us, her face wet, and her hair straggling down over her eyes . . . 'Father? We're home safe and sound and the boy got his canary!'

THREE

The float suddenly started to bobble about, red and white with a bit of feather stuck through it, and then it swirled and whirled away under the surface with a grey waggling shape before it. My sister turned a somersault and landed, knees wide apart, in a clump of water mint.

'A bite! A bite! You've got a bite.'

I was swiftly, nervously, reeling it in . . . playing it gently, carefully among the weeds and trying to bring it close to the bank. It seemed to be quite a big fish . . . it was lovely and heavy at the end of my line.

'Throw it back if it's too little,' said my sister, peering down into the water, cupping her hands round her eyes in order to see to the bed of the Cuckmere; squinting, and puffing. Her hair fell over her face like an old skirt.

Gently I began to wind him up to the bank; a little breeze riffled the water and the rushes rasped and clattered like paper swords and in a second I had him flopping and wriggling on the grass. Instantly my sister was upon him, her hand round his fat white belly and the other hand wrestling with the hook – something I never very much liked doing. Taking out the hooks. She never seemed to mind at all.

'It's only gristle. That's all. It's not like lips or anything. They don't *feel* it.' Expertly she yanked the hook away and, grabbing the empty lemonade bottle, she hit him smartly and swiftly on the head. He lay glistening in the sunlight. Cool grey-green, creamy white belly. Red fins, wide glazing yellow eyes. A roach. About seven inches.

We knelt there in the grass and counted the catch of five of varied sizes. They smelt muddy and cool – and sweet. Like cucumber sandwiches.

'Will that be enough?' I asked.

'Well Jesus fed millions with five, didn't he?'

'He had bread, too. Anyway it wasn't Jesus, it was a miracle.'

'Well, whoever it was.' She got up, and started to button up the flies of her shorts. They used to be mine and were too big for her, but she was having her 'being a boy' day. 'I think it'll be enough. We'll have to FHB if it isn't that's all.' We were collecting our bits and pieces. The fish I wrapped in grasses and reeds and put into my old school satchel, and she picked up our bottle, the bait tin, and a Woodbine packet full of spare hooks, and we walked through the trees to the road.

'I think we're jolly nice going fishing specially for her,' said my sister, clambering over the rickety iron fence and opening her flies again. I laughed and hit her with the satchel, and she screamed and wobbled and fell into a bit of a ditch.

'You silly fool! I've lost the hooks now. Serves you jolly well right.' We scrabbled about in the grass and leaves in the ditch and found the Woodbine packet which I shoved into my shirt pocket.

'It's silly to push people off fences when they're climbing them,' she grumbled. 'That's how people get their legs and things broken.' She pushed through the gate and up into our field and we started to climb the hill to the cottage. The sky was high and blue and clear, with little lumpy clouds trailing about and making round black shadows on the grass. Everywhere the grasshoppers were scissoring away, and at the top of the field you could just see our highest chimney shimmering in the sun.

'But I mean,' said my sister, a bit puffed with the clamber, and holding her shorts round her waist with one hand, 'I do think it's jolly nice of us to go fishing for her just because it's Friday and she's Catholic.'

'Well I like fishing anyway.'

'I know. But it is *nice*. Why does she have to have fish because it's Friday?' She always wanted to know difficult things at difficult times.

'It's a rule,' I said shortly.

'A Bible Sort of Rule?'

'Yes.'

'I know.'

But she didn't really. We walked along in silence for a bit; well, not really silence because she was doing one of her songs and I was whistling little bits here and there, in case she thought I was puffed. Which I was. At the top of the field the cottage roof stuck up with its chimney, and then the flint walls and the two rather surprised windows in the gable looking down to the farm. Round the cottage was a rickety wooden fence with bits of wire and an old bedstead stuck in it, and some apple trees and the privy with its roof of ivy and honeysuckle and a big elderberry. The privy had no door, so you just sat there and looked into the ivy; no one could see you through it, but *you* could see them coming along the little path and so you were able to shout out and tell them not to in time. It was really quite useful. And better than a door really, because that made it rather dark and a bit nasty inside. And once a bat got in there after Lally had closed it and she screamed and screamed and had a 'turn'. So we left off the door for summer and just sort of propped it up in the winter, to stop the snow drifting and making the seats wet.

There were three seats, like the Bears'. A little low one, a medium one, and the grown-up one. The wood was white and shining where we used to scrub it, and the knots were all hard and sticking up. No one ever used the smallest one, we had the paper and old comics and catalogues for reading in that; and the medium one just had a new tin bucket in it with matches and candles for the candlestick which stood on a bracket by the paper roll, and a cardboard tin of pink carbolic.

There were lids to all the seats, with wooden handles, and they had to be scrubbed too – but not as often as the seats; which was every day and a bit boring. Sometimes at night it was rather nice to go there down the path in the dark, with the candle guttering in the candlestick, and shadows leaping and fluttering all around and the ivy glossy where the golden light caught it. Sometimes little beady eyes gleamed in at you and vanished; and you could hear scurrying sounds and the tiny squeaks of voles and mice; and once a hare hopped straight into the doorway and sat up and looked at me for quite a long time, which was fearfully embarrassing, until I threw the carbolic at him and he hopped off again.

We squeezed under the wire and into the garden and down the brick path to the kitchen. My sister was singing very loudly and happily because it felt like tea-time and we'd caught so many fish, and I joined her, because I was looking forward to seeing Angelica Chesterfield eating the fish I'd caught her and thanking me for being so polite and remembering she was a Catholic and that this was Friday.

We were making a marvellous noise when Lally appeared at the kitchen door wiping her hands in her apron. 'For the love of dear knows who shut up!' she said, her elbows covered in bubbles. 'You'll have us all arrested with that noise, anyone would think you owned the whole hill the way you carry on and your tea's on the table.' She said this all in one breath and then turned and marched back into the kitchen. 'It's rhubarb and ginger today.'

The kitchen was low and cool; white walls, pink brick floor. There was a smell of paraffin and butter and scrubbed wood and washing in the copper. Tea was scattered about the table, a plate of bread, the jam in a jar with a little white label saying Summer 1929, a big brown teapot with a blue band, cups and saucers and Minnehaha, our cat, quietly washing his face.

'What,' said Lally, after we had washed and were all seated, and she was holding her cup in two hands, her elbows on the table, blowing gently at the steam, 'what have you been up to? Nothing good I'll be bound. I said to your mother and father in my letter today, they'll be up to no good I'll be bound.' And she sucked her tea pleasantly down.

'We caught five roach for Angelica's supper this evening.' I said, spreading big lumps of ginger and rhubarb over my bread.

'Because she's Catholic and today is Friday,' said my sister.

'Fancy,' said Lally, blowing at her tea and not looking at us at all. 'Fancy it being Friday,' and settled the cup into its saucer. 'And who is going to have to take out their innards and cut off their heads and that, I'd like to know? Who has to wash them and take off the scales with a sharp knife and do all the cooking of them? Answer me that or tell the Prince of Wales if you won't tell me.' She buttered herself a piece of bread. 'And,' she said, putting on her posh voice, 'supposin' 'er 'ighness Angelica Chesterfield doesn't like muddly tasting little roach which should have been left alone in the river: supposing *that*! *Then* what do we do about 'er Catholic meal?' She took a big bite out of her bread and butter. We watched her chew away for a while. I put some sugar in my tea and said as politely as possible, 'Well, she could always have tinned salmon, couldn't she?' Lally shook her head slowly, 'No,' she said, 'no tinned salmon in this house, your father says it all comes from Japan and they put ptomaine poison in the odd tin. We don't want that do we?' She wiped her lips with the back of her hand, hit my sister a blow for swinging her feet at table and started to clatter about with the tea things.

We washed up in silence, Lally washing up, we drying and putting away. She wiped her hands and lifted my satchel off the dresser and started to take out the roach. 'Well, we'll have to make haste,' she said, breaking a longish silence and handling the fish with a practiced hand, 'because Miss Angelica Whassername will be here directly. She'll be on the six o'clock, and I've no doubt she'll want her supper sharpish after that long journey.'

The five roach didn't look much after she'd done all the innard thing and cut the heads off. She smelt them deeply, mentioned that they must be fresh, it was just the mud, and washed them under the tap and flipped them on to an old blue plate. The innards and bits we gave to Minnehaha. Lally told us to get out from under her feet.

We went out and lay on the grass. If you looked straight up you saw the blue sky and one cloud: if you looked a bit to your left you could see the grass stalks as big as bamboos and a nodding scarlet poppy as big as a duster, and if you turned your head to the right you would see my sister wrinkling her eyes and picking her nose. I hit her.

'My finger was up my nose! I could have poked my eye out.' She lashed a fist at me and I rolled over and we fell into a struggling heap, laughing and howling and trying to sit on each other. In a little while we lay spent, breathless, giggling: our faces pressed into the grass, sniffing its greenness, and feeling the sun on the back of our legs.

The Seaford bus was just rumbling into the village as we got to the Market Cross and stood waiting under the chestnut tree. It used to stop for a second outside Bakers to deliver odd packages or papers, and then it would trundle up and start reversing round the Cross so that it was pointing towards Seaford and the way it had just come. It used to arrive every evening at about six and leave again at six-thirty, and in the morning it arrived at nine-thirty and would leave again at ten and that's all it ever did. As far as we knew anyhow. Sometimes you could change buses at Polegate crossroads and go in a quite different direction, to Eastbourne, which was a very exciting thing to do. But usually we met it . . . and occasionally caught it in the morning, washed and combed with sixpence in our pockets from our father for shopping in Seaford. Which wasn't so exciting but was quite decent really because there were one or two good junk shops, and sometimes you could buy bound copies of 'Chatterbox 1884' for 2d. We used to take a picnic lunch and eat that on the beach after we had done our shopping and a bit of swimming, and then we'd have tea at the Martello Tower, which was a very curious and dampish place but where we got lovely raspberry jam tarts and sometimes lemon curd ones. Lally used to have bloater paste and toast. But my sister and I just had an American Ice Cream Soda and our tarts. Two each. And a smell of tea from the silver urns hissing on the counter, and hot butter and varnished wood. After tea we'd walk along the front a bit, have a look at the shops in Sea Street, and then back on to the bus for home.

The first person off the bus was Miss Maude Bentley in a grey wool frock and a black hat with a ribbon, and behind her, clambering down slowly as if she was being lowered on a rope, came Miss Ethel. And baskets and walking sticks which were handed down to her when she was safely on the ground by Fred Brooks the conductor. 'There you are, my darlings,' he'd call out. 'Off you go and don't get into trouble.' They were the rector's sisters and they had a little gift shop in the front room of their house. They sold writing pads and pencils and postcard views of the church and painted ones of Jesus and Mary and Mabel Lucie Attwell little girls. In the front hall, in a big china umbrella stand painted with bulrushes and yellow flags they had Lucky Dips for tuppence. You gave Miss Ethel or Miss Maude your money and then, while they watched to see you weren't cheating by squeezing the packets to tell what was inside, you could bury your two hands in the bran and fumble about for a little paper-wrapped parcel. Blue for a boy and pink for a girl. It was really a bit soppy and the prizes were rotten for tuppence. All I ever got was the three monkeys not seeing, speaking or hearing evil. That's all that boys *ever* got – except once I did see a boy get a very small penknife with a picture of 'R.M.S. Majestic' on it – but usually it was the monkeys. They must have bought millions and millions of them. We said 'Good evening', and then some more people came off and there was Angelica Chesterfield. Angelica had very, very long black hair, and long legs and long arms and a long nose. She was altogether long, and a year older than us. She wore a black knitted cap with a red pom-pom and a long blue coat and shiny London shoes with ankle straps and white socks and we all smiled stupidly at each other and then I took her suitcase and we started to walk.

'Was it a boring journey?' I asked. She smoothed her hair, moved it over her shoulders, adjusted her pom-pom and said: 'Not fearfully. Mummy put me on the train at Victoria and I had some books to look at and when we got to Seaford a lady said, "O! This is Seaford!" And I got off and said to a very nice man with a dog. "Where does the bus go from," and he said "Here," and I got on and now I've got off.' She tripped over a stone in her shiny black shoes and smiled. We turned down the lane towards the river and my sister said: 'We've thought of some lovely things to do while you are here. We've found a very creepy caravan where a witch lives, and we'll take you to a sort of cave up by Wilmington we found and we know where there's a punt and we could go along the river and pick some waterlilies.' Angelica smiled again at us, pushed her hair over her shoulder again and said: 'I like to read quite a lot.'

'Not all the time?' I said.

'Not *all* the time,' she agreed quietly, 'but I do like it.'

'But it's summer. It's holidaytime!' said my sister. 'You don't *read* on holidays.'

But Angelica smiled away and didn't say anything. We clattered across the bridge, her brown suitcase banging my legs and my heart sinking with every footfall. It was going to be a hateful week.

Lally was at the gate looking red and singing, a handful of wooden clothes pegs, and a big basket of washing in her arms. 'Well! Here's Her Highness!' she called. 'Have a good trip did you? I expect you're quite tired out and with that walk too. There's ginger beer in the kitchen and supper's at eight.'

The room where Angelica was going to sleep was through our room, through Lally's, and then through a little cupboard place. It was very small, with a bed, a chair and a table with a drawer. The window looked right down the meadow to High and Over; and on a clear day you could sometimes see the sea like a piece of silver paper. I put her suitcase on the table and said: 'We have to tell you something. If you have to go to the lav in the night it's under the bed.' Angelica went white. 'You've got the prettiest one,' said my sister reasonably. 'It's got a pheasant on the bottom.' Angelica looked nervously round the room as if she expected it to rush out from under the bed or somewhere and peck her.

My sister humped the chamber pot on to the bed and looked at it with pleasure. Angelica did a wrinkling thing with her mouth and gently pulled off her pom-pom hat. 'It's very nice,' she said flatly and smoothed her hat with her long thin fingers. I though that she was going to cry. She often did. Usually did, in fact. Once when we were all on holiday together in Wimereux she cried and moaned all day because our father and her father were going out fishing in a little boat together, and she wanted to go too. And they had to take her, and she was most dreadfully sick all day and we were jolly pleased. Because none of the rest of us were allowed to go, and she was the eldest and rotten. And here she was wrinkling up her mouth and smoothing her hat and blinking away, and I knew the tears were coming and just because of an old chamber pot.

'We caught you some fish today.'

She went on blinking. And smoothing.

'Because you're a Catholic,' said my sister.

'They aren't very big, but big enough, and Lally has cleaned them and everything.'

She stopped the blinking thing and sat on the edge of the bed.

'Thank you,' she said in a sort of twisty voice.

'Perhaps,' said my sister, 'if you go to the lav just before we go to bed you won't need to use it. And then,' she said happily, 'I can have it back.' She was holding the chamber up in the air like a tea-cup and looking at the marks on the bottom. 'Or else I'll have to use my camel I won at the fair, and it's small.'

Angelica snuffled and buried her face in her pom-pom hat.

Sitting under the apple tree was rather pleasant after that. It was a lovely tree, old and sort of leaning away from the sea winds. The bark was all rumply and covered with moss and lichens, and on one branch there was a bunch of yellowy-green mistletoe growing. And that's why it was our most favourite tree. My sister was squashing the scarlet berries from some cuckoo-spit in a tin. She squelched them round and round with an old wooden spoon. We were making Hikers' Wine. When we had squashed them into a pulp we pored them into an orangeade bottle, with the label still on, and then filled it with water. Then we used to go and leave it in the gully at a good place, and hoped that a hiker, feeling thirsty, would spot it and think how lucky he was. And of course it was deadly poison and if he drank it he'd probably die, which was fearfully funny. We had done this with about five bottles and they had all gone when we went to look the next day. The gully was full of the beastly people all clambering up in khaki shorts and green or yellow shirts, to see the smallest church in England. And we thought that Hikers' Wine might put them off. Or kill them off. And it looked exactly like orangeade . . . had the same colour, and little bits of skin and orange-sort-of-stuff swirling about in it. It was better than setting rabbit traps for them, which we did . . . but they always seemed to avoid them. Feet too big, I think.

'The trouble with her is,' said my sister, squashing away, 'that she's potty.'

'I think it's because she's a Town person . . . and because she's going to be a Nun.'

My sister stopped squashing and looked at me with a mouth like an 'O'.

'In Czechoslovakia,' I said.

'You're a fibber!'

'God's honour.'

'Who said?'

'I heard Aunt Freda tell our Mother.'

'Why is she going to be one in Czechoslovakia? Why not in Hampstead or somewhere?'

I took the tin away from here and did a bit of squashing, because they weren't quite mixed up and some of them looked like cuckoo-spit berries still.

'I don't know,' I said. 'Probably that's where you have to go to be one. Probably it's a sort of factory place where they specially make Nuns.' We cried out with laughter. The sun was getting pale and a wind came shuddering up among the grasses making the lupins bend and nod like people agreeing. From the house was a good smell of frying. We squashed the berries into a paste and started to pour them into the bottle.

'I've seen Nuns in England. In Hampstead, in the Finchley Road and on a bus,' said my sister. 'They can't all come from the same place. Anyway,' she added, pouring very carefully so that the 'muck' didn't slide down the outside of the bottle and spoil the label, 'anyway . . . they're jolly well welcome to her.'

I lay on my stomach and ate a bit of grass which tasted like liquorice. Right down at the bottom of the meadow stood a clump of cows, brown and white, all standing looking at nothing. Sometimes they stamped a foot to move the flies, or tossed their heads and mooed; their tails swung and flicked; and there they stood chewing and blinking and looking at nothing, round the little iron gate. If Lally or our mother saw them round the gate like that they turned right in the road and walked a mile and a half up the chalk road to the house. They were so frightened.

My knees were cold; I rolled over and saw that my sister had got most of the stuff into the bottle, poured some water in, and was swirling it round and round, with her tongue sticking out like an adder's.

'That's it!' she said happily and shoved the cork in with a thump of her fist.

We took it and hid it in the scullery so that it could stand all night and settle. Otherwise it just looked like a sort of soup.

But in the morning, about midday when it was hottest and the hikers were scrambling up the gully, it would look like a lovely cool bottle of orangeade left behind after a picnic. To make it look a bit like that, we used to scatter a few bits of paper about, and screw up some cake boxes and things; sometimes an eggshell or two, so that it looked more real.

And the bottles always disappeard.

We all sat round the kitchen table in the soft glow of the evening light. It was too early to light the lamps, and the pink sun outside the windows just glanced on the knives and forks and the amber handle of the brass kettle on the range.

Angelica was pale but a bit more cheerful at the sight of food. She had changed her travelling clothes and combed her hair and washed her face, because she smelled of soap, and we wondered if she'd done any more than that, caught each other's eyes and squirmed with giggles.

Lally banged the fish server against the side of the pan.

'That's enough!' she said. 'You two mind your P's and Q's or I'll take the back of my hand to you.' She knew something was up, she always did.

The roach had sort of shrivelled up a bit; not enough for us all as it happened. But *we* had pilchards on toast while Angelica picked her way through the bones of her fish. But it didn't worry us because it made us look a bit more polite, and anyway we'd eaten hundreds of roach and liked pilchards best.

'They went specially out to catch these for you, these two,' said Lally, waving her fork at us. 'So you know they must be fresh; can't abide them myself, too muddy,' she went on, 'but I must say I like a nice pilchard, for all they repeat till Thursday forenoon.' Angelica fiddled away at another bone.

'We're not actually supposed to have pilchards,' I explained, thinking she might be interested, but all she said was 'Oh.'

'Because,' I went on, cutting through a crust, 'because our father won't have anything in the house in tins.'

'He says everything in tins is Japanese and they kill people,' said my sister.

'And if you so much as open your mouth and say anything about this,' said Lally with a glinting look at us both, 'I'll fetch you a wallop on the side of your heads as'll give you both a mastoid.'

FOUR

Eggshell had a humpity back, long white hair and a black coat down to her ankles. She never spoke to us, just hurried past with her head wagging and a funny black hat like half an egg pulled down to her eyes. So we called her Eggshell.

She lived up at the top of Red Barn Hill in a wooden caravan with big wheels and a little door at one end which opened in two pieces like a stable door. The caravan was just outside a little elderberry wood right on the edge of the hill; it was painted red and the wheels were blue, but that was a long time ago, and now they were faded down to almost pale pink and grey. There was a pointy little chimney sticking out of the roof, and sometimes you could see the smoke coming out with a smell of cooking, which made her seem a bit more real and not frightening. To get to the caravan you had to go up a little path, high up the hill from the gully, and then into the elder wood, and along another little twisty path all among the rabbit burrows, and then you'd see an old rusty milk churn, a little bit of garden, about as big as a box, and the steps and door of the caravan. And that's as near as we ever got; it's as near as anyone ever got ever. Even Reg Fluke, and he's braver than I am, only got as far as that – so you can see that she *was* a *bit* frightening and of course she would be, because she was a witch.

We knew that because of the long hair and the funny hat and coat and all the cats. She must have had a hundred cats at least. Well, perhaps not a hundred exactly but really millions of them. You could see them sitting round the caravan: playing, sleeping or just sitting. And they were all colours; not only black like a witch's cat.

Once when my sister and I were up there hiding in the elders watching her, we saw her feeding them and heard, actually heard, her talking to them! That was a bit amazing really because we never heard her talk to anyone in all our lives. Just the cats. But we couldn't hear what she said; it was just a mumbling sort of sound, and she bent her way among them giving them bits of something to eat from a bag. We were a bit disappointed because, clear as clear, you could see the words 'Home and Colonial' written on the bag and that didn't seem to fit in. But my sister said it had probably been left behind by some Londoners on a picnic and she'd stolen it. I said that I didn't think it could be stolen if she had found it and they had left it behind not wanting it, and my sister said: 'Well, how do you know they didn't want it? She most likely stole it. Witches do. Remember about children. They give them to the Gipsies.' And I fell silent, remembering what I had heard. But wanting to like her anyway, witch or not, because she liked the cats.

Reg Fluke, who lived at Farm Cottages in the valley, said that his mother, Beattie Fluke, used to go and see the witch, when she was a girl, because of her chilblains. Reg Fluke was a Village Boy, and we weren't, strictly speaking, allowed to play with him because of that. 'They'll spoil your speaking ways,' said Lally, and 'They'll get you into mischief and do things you wouldn't like to tell your mother about,' which made Reg Pretty Exciting. But actually he was a bit soft in the head and we didn't want to play with him anyway.

His mother was a bit different. And she was grown up. We sometimes used to meet her outside the Magpie in the afternoon, walking a bit funnily and with a bit of a red face as if she had been running. But she was always very friendly and used to carry a big white jug full of beer home for her husband's tea. She had a squashed face like a red orange, full of little holes, and a huge fat nose and no teeth, and she laughed so much you couldn't see her eyes, which got all squeezed up and ran with tears, so that she was forever wiping them, and her nose, with the back of the hand which was not carrying the jug.

'She's a witch all right,' she roared with laughter when we asked her. 'Been a witch all her life for all she's called Nellie Wardle and had a son as went to the war. Seen her about on her broomstick many a winter's night.' We were sitting with Beattie Fluke on the river-bank, just beside the bridge. It was very hot, and she was having little sips of her husband's tea and fanning herself with her green tam o'shanter. 'When I was a girl my mother used to take me along to her for my chilblains. I can't tell you what I had to *do*, that wouldn't be very nice, now would it, but it worked a treat. Oh! she had spells for everything . . . toothache, and harvest bugs and nettle-rash and never-you-mind-what-else. There's many a lady in this village as has got a lot to be thankful for to Nellie Wardle – and they don't go round the graveyard laying no wreaths, I can tell you that!' She roared with laughter and had some more of Mr Fluke's tea.

'But she doesn't really fly, honestly Mrs Fluke?' said my sister.

Mrs Fluke lay back in the grass and started laughing so much she spilled her jug. 'Sometimes I actually seen 'er loop the loop!' she said, shaking with laughter and the tears pouring out of her screwed up eyes. 'Loop the bloody loop, right over the church with streams of fire coming out of her behind.' And she laughed until she choked and sat up slowly. For a moment the three of us looked at each other in silence, and then Mrs Fluke made a rather rude noise and said: 'I can almost see her this minute . . . with all the flames . . . twirling and twirling and twirling.' And she stopped, put her hand to her mouth with no teeth and said: 'Now you run away and play, I'm going to have forty winks.' And laying back in the grass, she put her tam o'shanter over her face and started to snore.

We walked along the path to the bridge in silence, pulling at the tall summer grasses and scuffing the stones along in front of us. Presently my sister said:

'I think she was lying. You couldn't possibly have flames coming from there, you'd get burnt.'

'And anyhow they don't fly on brooms . . . that's old fairy tale stuff. They just live in dark places with cats and do spells.'

'They *do* have cats,' agreed my sister, 'and she's got hundreds.'

'And I bet she does spells. I think Mrs Fluke was right about that because Reg said she'd told him. About the chilblain part.'

'Oh! I'm sure she's a witch, she *looks* like a witch to start with. Anyway let's make her a witch, it's more creepy like that.'

So Eggshell was a witch from then on. We leant over the bridge making spit gobs and watching them float under our feet, rather like Pooh-Sticks, only we couldn't be bothered to run to the other side to see which of us had won.

'I think she's quite *vulgar*, don't you?' my sister asked.

'Mrs Fluke? Awfully. Saying "Bloody" and making that noise. Awfully.'

A moorhen went dibble-dabbling along the sedge and, seeing us, scurried into the willows.

'Behind seems quite a rude word,' my sister said.

'I bet the Prince of Wales never says it.'

'Do you think he's got one though?' my sister asked thoughtfully. 'I don't think Kings and Queens have them.'

'How do they "go" then?' I said. 'They must have.'

'I suppose so. It's too difficult. But I do think 'behind' is quite a rude word,' she said.

I made a very big gob, sucking in my cheeks to do it, and watched it swirl slowlly down until it went splot in the water. 'Bum is much ruder,' I said.

My sister gave a shriek of delight and spun round on one foot. 'Oh! yes!' she cried. 'Bum's much ruder,' and ran away laughing up to the road.

So we decided to take Angelica to see the witch. The week was pretty dull so far. When I showed her how to blow an egg she'd had a coughing fit and we had to hit her on the back quite hard; she had been quite polite and nice, and interested in, the slow worm, but not anxious to touch it, and enjoyed a picnic in the big haystack in the yard, but hadn't liked the prickles, and come for a walk down the gully but found it damp, and generally was a Londoner. Lally said one evening that she was homesick, and that people who lived in towns usually were in the country because the quiet got them down. But my sister and

I thought that she was (a) stuck up, (b) a cissy, and (c) soft in the head. Whoever went for walks, and quite long ones, in shiny London shoes – or read in her room on hot days when the larks were up in the sky wheeling and swooping and making it all loveliness? And Holy books at that. One we saw in her room was the Life of St Theresa. And there was a picture of a droopy sort of lady in brown, holding a bunch of roses and looking up to see if it was raining.

However, we decided on the witch. And it was a wet day. Pouring wet.

Lally was folding the tablecloth and my sister was clattering the forks back into their drawer when I said,

'Let's take Angelica up to Red Barn Hill.'

'Oh! Let's!' said my sister and went to find her wellingtons in the shed. Angelica was up in her room writing her diary. That's another thing I didn't like about her, she always got out of washing up.

'She's a year older and the guest,' said Lally, taking sides.

My sister came clumping back in her wellingtons, pulling on her old mac. 'Whatever do you want to go up there for, on a dreadful afternoon like this?' said Lally, blowing hard on a spoon and polishing it on her apron.

'We want to show Angelica where the witch lives,' I said.

'Stuff and nonsense!' said Lally, huffing at another spoon. 'There's no such thing. And don't you go putting the fear of God into Angelica or you'll catch it.'

'She's got that already,' I said, pulling on my boots.

Lally shoved the spoons into the drawer, hit me on the head, and said, 'You should mind your tongue, or the Devil will fork it. You all go into the sitting-room and have a nice game of ludo or something. Or come and help me top and tail the blackcurrants.'

But we went up to Red Barn Hill, the rain dripping down our necks, and Angelica wincing along in the chalky mud in a pair of my sister's boots which were a bit too small for her long Catholic feet.

'I don't want awfully to see the witch,' she said, stepping round all the puddles she could find. 'And in any case I don't believe in them, there is no such thing.'

My sister was singing beside me plaiting a bracelet out of water grasses. She stopped singing and said, 'Oh yes there are. They nearly all got burned at the stake, but this one got away and lives up there.' She nodded her sou'wester towards the mist-shrouded hill ahead. 'They were all burned by the Catholics ages ago . . . and then got buried at crossroads with bits of wood in their hearts.' She started to sing again. Making very loud 'La la-laaaas . . .'

'You are really very silly,' said Angelica. 'The Catholics didn't do any such thing. It was just People who did it . . . and you've got it muddled up, because if they did burn them how could they put bits of wood in their hearts at the crossroads? They would not have had any heart left would they? Anyway, that was highwaymen,' she said happily.

'It was witches and it was crossroads,' said my sister.

'You've got it all muddled,' said Angelica.

'I have not got it all muddled,' said my sister, shaking rain off her face. 'It's you who are muddled. All Catholic people are muddled.'

'They are not,' said Angelica.

My sister went white with rage and brushed her face roughly with her hands as if it was covered in flies.

'My brother was going to be a Catholic once,' she said.

'Shut up!' I said.

'You were! You were! You know you were . . . you were going to be a

Catholic and then you got put off because of all the learning. And he painted a statue of Jesus and gave him black hair and a yellow beard! There you are!' she cried triumphantly. 'That's muddled if you like,' and she walked ahead in the rain, scoffing, under her breath, nodding and wagging her head like a hen.

'She's boasting and telling lies,' I said.

'I think she is a very stupid person indeed,' said Angelica, 'and I won't believe another single word she says.' We walked on in silence. It was awfully difficult trying to talk to her, she was so polite and quiet, and she used words as if they cost her money each time.

When we went up the lane into the Market Cross my sister was in a happier state of mind because she had suddenly found a penny in the fluff of her raincoat pocket and went clumping into Bakers to spend it, and very kindly she bought us all a present. A farthing humbug each. Two for her, which was fair, it was her penny, and one each for Angelica and me. I shoved mine into my mouth there and then, but I saw Angelica carefully wrap hers in a handkerchief and put it in her bloomers.

Up in the little wood everything was shrouded in mist and raindrops. The mud was chalky white, and there was no sound except our feet slithering among the elder roots; and the scuttering of a rabbit now and then.

And then, quite suddenly, there was the caravan; glistening in the wet. A little wisp of smoke coming from the tin chimney stack: shabby looking and muddy. We squatted down under a bush and watched. I could hear Angelica breathing from the clamber up the hill; her breath hung round her face like a muslin cheese bag. My sister was chewing her humbug very quietly, in case Eggshell should hear anything.

But there was no one about. No cats even. Just an old tin table with a bit of lino stuck on it, some boxes, and a chopping block, and the milk churn, all rusty. The windows were tight shut – and the door. The rain had stopped and we were getting cramp a bit. And cold.

'If we *do* see her,' said my sister in a whisper, 'let's only wait a minute and then run away quickly. Just so that Angelica can see her Very First Witch.' And she settled herself down in the dripping grasses like a broody goose.

Angelica moved a little and slid two inches down the bank. She gave a bit of a cry and hauled herself up to the bush again.

'I told you all about witches and that. I *told* you. It's silly and we'll all take cold,' she said miserably.

My sister chewed hard and swallowed quite a large piece of humbug because I heard her do a 'squeaking' noise very quietly. I was sucking mine slowly to make it last.

'All you believe in is Angels and Devils and Eternal Damnation and Purgatory and things,' she said.

'Are,' said Angelica.

My sister looked at her blankly. 'Are what?'

'It's "are" not "is".'

'But is *what*?' I asked.

'Are Angels, and the things she said just now.'

'I don't know what you mean.'

'Angels are plural. You can't be "is" Angels. You have to say "are Angels".'

'Potty,' said my sister.

And suddenly we saw Eggshell. It was very frightening; she was coming up the hill through the mist on the other side of the caravan dragging a great big piece of a tree; and there were three cats running beside her. She was wet as wet, an old sack round her shoulders and she was muttering away to the cats. You couldn't hear what she was saying, just something like, 'Tweedie, tweedie, tweedie.' And she was shaking her head from side to side and dragging at the bit of tree.

We were frozen in a little heap under the bushes. No one even breathed. Eggshell was struggling and pulling at the branch, and the cats all came skittering up to the caravan, but the branch seemed to have got caught in something and suddenly, with a cry, Eggshell fell over in the mud; her legs up in the air and the sack and her hat all twisty. We caught our breaths with horror and suddenly Angelica said: 'Help her.' And before my sister or I could stop her she was slithering down the hill to where old Eggshell was struggling to sit up.

We were very astonished. And suddenly found that we were sliding down the bank too, and the three of us stood awkwardly round the wet and muddy Eggshell, who looked up at us with fury and cried: 'What you want then?' Angelica started to try and help her up but got her arm punched for her trouble. 'You be off!' cried Eggshell. 'Leave me be.' Anyway she couldn't get up and Angelica said: 'We only want to help you. We'll pull you a bit.' And my sister and I started to tug at her soaking old coat and she was pushing us away, and eventually we all got tangled up in a bit of a smelly pile, but at least she was standing on her own two legs. She started to brush herself down and tidy her hat, pulling it right over her eyes, and mumbling away like soup boiling. I started to pull up the branch, which was actually quite heavy, and in a few moments we had got to the caravan and the cats, which were crying about the steps. Eggshell started rummaging about in the pocket of her coat, wiped her nose on the back of her hand, and took out a big iron key from a crumpled piece of rag.

Angelica said, 'Where shall we leave the wood?' and Eggshell just mumbled away and pointed under the caravan while she clambered up to the little stable door. Underneath was a big pile of sticks and logs – for her fire, I suppose – and so we lugged the branch underneath, panting and puffing and feeling a bit braver. Nothing terrible seemed to have happened. I mean she hadn't screamed at us or made a spell; anyway not that we could feel. The cats went on crying and rubbing their legs against the caravan steps and Eggshell opened the door and went in. The cats scampered after her. It was dark inside, as far as we could see that is, but there seemed to be a little iron stove-thing on one side with legs, and a bed and an old cupboard painted yellow and blue. Eggshell was rummaging about in the dark and we started to turn and go away. My sister said suddenly, 'I've swallowed all my humbug,' and we heard Eggshell call us. We turned in terror; we were just a little way down the path and she was standing on the steps with something in her hand.

'Come and look,' she said. All wet and muddy and looking terribly like a witch. 'Come 'ere.' And she offered a shape in her hands. It was a huge shell. As big as a hat. Brown spotted, with funny opened lips, like someone laughing. We went to the foot of the steps and she pushed the shell at Angelica. 'Read what it says then,' she said. 'You read what it says.'

Angelica took the shell in both her hands and we peered at the thing. 'It says Bombay,' she said politely. Eggshell came down a couple of stairs holding the little railing. 'What does it say on t'other side?' We turned it round and there was the word MOTHER.

Angelica said: 'On one side it says Bombay and on this side it says Mother.' And handed the shell back to the Witch who took it quickly. 'That's for the wood,' she said, 'fer helpin' with the wood. It's from my boy, oh a long time ago. They sent all his things. And this was fer me. It says Mother, don't it?'

We nodded. Eggshell went back up the steps slowly. The mist drifting away through the woods behind, the cats mewing. 'Tiddy, tweedie, tweedie,' she kept saying, and went into the caravan and closed the lower part of the door.

'That's fer helpin' with the wood. Now you clear off and leave me be.' She closed the top half of the door and we couldn't see her.

We turned and started to walk down the winding path through the elders.

We didn't talk much until we had got down to Sloop Lane and then my sister said we mustn't forget the paraffin and the bacon. So we went into Wildes the Grocers and got them and started back home. The rain had quite stopped, and a white sun glittered and flickered on the river. The tide was coming in and all the muddy banks were being covered with swirly water. There was a cob swan ducking about slowly and two people we didn't know were fishing.

'It's a funny thing to write on a shell,' said my sister. 'Mother and wherever it was.' She pulled off her sou'wester hat and shook her hair. 'I suppose it was a sort of present thing, like we bring our mother when we go to Eastbourne.'

'What sort of things do you mean?' said Angelica.

'Well, once we bought her a china lighthouse with "Eastbourne" written on it and a sort of shield thing. Didn't we?' she asked me. And when I agreed she rattled on skipping over the planks of the white bridge . . . 'And once we bought her a dear little china shoe, didn't we? With little blue flowers on it and it just had "Made In England" on it. But we bought it in Seaford.'

We crossed the bridge and up the path, over the main road, and through the gate into Great Meadow. The paraffin tin was rather heavy.

'I think you were very brave about the Witch,' I said. Angelica opened her mac and pulled up her sock which had slipped down. 'She's just a poor old woman with troubles of her own,' she said. 'She was very pleased we helped her. And it was rather nice to see her shell. I don't suppose many people have seen that.' My sister hummed her humming-not-listening song.

And there was the house, and the wooden fence and the privy roof and Lally pegging out some washing. She waved and called out something about the sun and trying to dry off a few things – but we weren't really listening. Angelica clambered over the fence and wandered off to help Lally with the laundry basket. My sister sniffed and swung back and forth on the gate. 'Hummm,' she said. 'Well, it's very easy not to worry about witches if you're going to be a Nun. Very easy indeed.' The gate squeaked a bit and she slipped off and helped me carry the paraffin. 'Very easy indeed it is,' she mumbled. And did a snort.

FIVE

I clonked the two buckets gently on to the kitchen floor so that the water wouldn't spill over the polished bricks. I was a bit puffed because it was quite a long way from the pump. It was my morning job to fill four buckets 'for the morning wash', as we called it . . . and then I had to do four more after lunch. My sister never had to. She just carried the milk in a white enamel can from the dairy down at the Court. It was quite a long way too; but not near as heavy as eight buckets of water.

They were still sitting at the breakfast table. Lally was talking to Angelica about her packing and some washing. My sister was building a spilly hill in the sugar bowl, dribbling sugar all over the tablecloth. Lally hit her and spilled a lot more. 'Now look what you've done, Miss Fiddler,' she cried, 'can't keep still for a minute . . . sugar all over the place, now we'll be smothered in ants. Angelica, tell your mother I couldn't get the stain out of your green cotton. If you'd come to me sooner I might have managed. But damsons is damsons and they stay.' She took up the pile of ironing and set it on the dresser. 'That's ready for you when you start packing this evening . . . and now,' she said, looking at us all, 'what are you going to do with yourselves? Angelica? What would you like to do on your Last Day?'

Angelica looked a bit startled, I suppose that Last Day sounded a bit deathly or something, but as she was the guest it was up to her to decide.

'I really don't mind,' she said helpfully.

Lally started sweeping up the breakfast things and clattering them on to a tray. 'Well make up your minds and get out from under my feet, all of you,' she said.

The sun was hot even though it was early. There was still dew on the big spikes of larkspur outside the kitchen door. We sat under the apple tree to decide. 'We could go grass sledging up at Wilmington,' said my sister. 'We make a sledge out of a big old tin tray, and put some rope on it and then we take it up to the very top of the Long Man and slide all the way down . . . right down to the Royal Oak almost . . . it's very exciting.'

Angelica didn't say anthing. She was busy plaiting three grasses together. 'Sometimes you fall off,' said my sister. 'Once He fell off and cut His knee to the bone . . . show Angelica where you cut your knee to the bone,' she said. But Angelica didn't seem interested. She stared up into the apple tree as if there was an angel there. 'It bled terribly. Or we could go to the cave or the dew pond. Only you could fall in the dew pond and if you do no one can ever get you out because it's very deep and goes to a point in the middle. We saw a drowned sheep there once. And the cave is a bit frightening. There are bats.'

Angelica said, 'I don't like bats, thank you.'

We were quite silent for a minute and then I had a good idea. 'Let's go to the church, then, and show her the altar and where the murder was. Shall we?'

My sister was on her feet in a minute and so was I and Angelica rather scrambled up and followed us down the garden path to the lane. I thought it was best just to go, otherwise we should have been there all day or something silly. And we were both rather longing for Angelica Chesterfield to go home to London and stop bothering us. We had to keep on thinking of things to amuse her. She never thought of anything herself. Only reading. And that was very dull and selfish of her.

We turned left into the lane and clambered up to the top where there was a great field of corn growing. And a little path waggling through it. And in the middle of the field, with great, huge trees all round it, was the Smallest Church in Sussex. Our house was the rectory. But all we had to do was change the water and the flowers in the vases once or twice a week. On the altar. Well, they weren't vases for flowers. Jam jars. But we put white and blue crêpe paper round them so they looked rather pretty. And my sister always picked the flowers and arranged them herself. Sitting in the sun on a gravestone singing a hymn-sounding-song.

There was a little wooden fence all round the church, with a squeaky iron gate and inside the gate was the churchyard. All the tombs and gravestones were squinty, like people standing on a ship in a storm. Leaning in all directions and covered with moss. There was no one buried there who was new. The newest one was called Anne Stacie Departed This Life 1778 aged 78. We thought that was very interesting, but Angelica didn't. The door was always open and inside there was a lovely cool feeling and a smell of floor polish and candles. It was very, very small. Sometimes the Rector, Mr Eric Bentley, came up and preached a sermon. One Sunday in the month. And we all went. And there was another for the Harvest. And then lots of people came with sheaves of corn and apples and bread and things. And it was lovely. Usually there were only about twelve or fifteen people there: it only had room for twenty anyway. And hikers used to come and people from as far away as Lewes or Polegate. It was too small inside for an organ so there was just a piano at the back and Winnie Maltravers playing hymns and singing very loudly, shaking her bun, so that we waited for it to start falling down round her shoulders, which it always did – in long grey wisps like a horse's tail.

On these days Lally wore her Best Brown and a hat with ivy leaves on it which she bought one day in Seaford. It was a bit like a pudding basin and came right down to her eyes so that she had to tilt her head backwards to read the hymn book . . . only she never wore glasses so she just sang 'la la la la' all the time, pretending she could see the tiny printing. Which, of course with that hat, she couldn't.

Our mother gave us a penny each for the collection when it came round during 'The Lord is My Shepherd' and it was interesting to see how much was in the plate to send to the African Orphans somewhere. Never very much. Because the hikers were a poor looking lot and no one ever gave more than a sixpence or a threepenny-bit. But Mr Bentley sent it all off to Africa once a month or so, with the collection from his big church in the village.

'This is the smallest church in England,' said my sister, 'and that's the altar where the murder was.' She was speaking in a rather whispery way, not because of the murder but because you do whisper in church . . . even if it is very small. Angelica had made the sign of a cross and done her bob in the aisle and then we went and sat in one of the wooden pews. There were lots of little humpty cushions covered in carpet and some rather old hymn books. Angelica picked through one but didn't seem to take any notice of the word Murder at all. My sister got a bit irritated.

'About the murder,' she said in the whispery voice, leaning very close to Angelica and putting her hand on the hymn book to stop her looking, '. . . about the murder. Well . . . it was ages ago and there was this Vicar, you see, and he had a very pretty wife and she was much younger than he was and didn't like churches and that sort of thing very much. And they were always having terrible rows and things. And one day he came into the church and found her kissing a man. Here. Right where we are sitting.' She stopped for breath and stared at Angelica. Who didn't say anything at all. Just looked back. My sister started piling the hymn books on top of each other. 'The church was much bigger in those days of course . . . huge they say.'

Angelica said, 'Who said so?'

'The people in the village. Mrs Fluke and Miss Maltravers and people. But the vicar took a candlestick from the altar and hit the man who was kissing his wife and killed him. And then he set fire to the church with the candles and they were burned to death. And that's why the church is so small. Only this bit was left.'

The pile of hymn books fell down and they scattered all over the floor so we had to grovel about looking for them and putting them back on the pew shelves.

It seemed a silly way to spend a Last Day . . . with the sun outside and Angelica not caring anyway. She was on her hands and knees under a bench and I heard her say she didn't believe it anyway. Not a word. And she crawled out and brushed down her skirt. My sister was red in the face and rather angry.

'Oh! Look! How sweet!' she said. 'I've got a holy picture, it must have come out of the books. It's so pretty, it's a lady with some roses and a heart with red spokes pointing out.' She slid it into a book and went off to look at the flowers on the altar which were looking a bit mouldy because we hadn't changed them since Angelica had come to stay. I wandered out and sat on one of the stones and peeled some moss off the word 'resteth' with a bit of twig and Angelica did her cross and bob and came out too and squinted into the sunlight.

'I don't think it's really true, that story,' she said, sitting down beside me. 'I expect it is just a legend or something, don't you?'

I said I didn't know but it was true anyway, and we'd heard it lots of times and that when they got the bodies out of the church they were just ashes and they put them into a box together and took them down in a cart to the village, all mixed together like Hundreds and Thousands, and Angelica laughed a barking laugh meaning I was silly. So I shut up. But my sister came out and lay in the grass. 'Now what shall we do?' she asked crossly. No one spoke. The day was very still. Not even a little breeze to make the poppies nod. Grasshoppers were clicking away and a pigeon was cooing up in one of the elms. It was the sort of morning for doing nothing on . . . so we just sat still. I went on picking away at 'resteth' and found 'in' under a lump of yellow lichen. My sister sat up, put her face to the sun.

'Lally said the murder was just passion. The vicar was so angry, he just hit the man with the candelstick without even thinking. He was so angry. Like when He . . .,' nodding her closed eyes towards me, 'stuck a knife in my back last Easter.'

Angelica looked at me with her mouth open, and her eyebrows went up into her fringe.

'You didn't!'

'He jolly well did. Ask him.'

'You didn't?'

I went on scratching at 'in' and moved on to 'for'.

'Yes he did. You tell her or I'll show her the place.'

'Yes I did,' I said. 'I did and I'm glad. It taught her a lesson.'

'Humph,' said my sister and opened her eyes.

'But why did you?' said Angelica.

'Because I was reading his silly old 'Larks' before he did.'

'And it was brand new and no one had looked at it before,' I said.

'But that wasn't a terrible thing to do.'

'It was to him,' said my sister. 'He stuck the knife right in, just here,' and she twisted about to show the place on her back.

'Only *I* can look at my "Larks" for the first time. I saved it up all the way from Bakers and then when we got home I had to go and get some water and while I was gone she pinched it from the table and started to read it, and she scrunched it all up.' I was shaking with anger at the thought of it and the bit of twig snapped in two.

My sister snorted with laughter and lay down on her back.

'He ran away, didn't you?' she said. 'He just ran away and hid all night under the bridge down by the river while I was practically dying.'

'You were not dying, it was a titchy little scratch. I've seen it,' I said.

Angelica suddenly got up and stood looking at us with her beaky nose. 'My mother said that you can't believe a word you say in your family. You all tell terrible stories because you are too romantic. She says it's because your mother was an actress and your father is a journalist and you just don't know what is real and what isn't.'

We both looked at her very slowly. My sister sat up. And I said, 'Well this part is true, and she has got a scar and you can ask Lally and I got a thrashing with a paint brush from my father, because actually he is an Artist, and the story about the murder is true because everyone knows it is . . . and so that's that.'

My sister got up and pulled her socks out of her sandals where they had got all ruckled. 'It's all true,' she said. 'And if you don't watch out, he might stick a knife into you too. He can do anything! . . . He once made Betty Engles climb a ladder and lit a bonfire at the bottom of it so she couldn't get down. And that's true too.' And she tossed her hair to get the grass out of it and went off down the path to the gate.

Angelica and I followed her slowly. There wasn't much to do any more. The day seemed rotten. 'I wouldn't really do anything like that,' I said. 'Only you aren't much like us, and you don't like the country much do you . . . I mean honestly?'

Angelica pushed the iron gate open and squeezed through into the lane. 'It's not the same as Hampstead,' she said. 'It's all right I suppose. But there's nothing to do.'

'But you don't like doing anything!' I said. 'You just like to read or sew or read.'

'Well, I like reading and sewing. But I don't like murders and witches and rain and all the funny things in the grass. You know . . .' She meant grasshoppers and burnet-moths and chalk blues and ladybirds and things. I really think she was more frightened of them than witches.

'Well, anyway,' I said, 'I wouldn't put a knife in you for that. God's honour.'

She winced a little bit when I said God's honour but smiled a thank-you smile, and we just went back to the cottage in silence. People are funny.

The dew had long ago left the larkspur and the sun was beating down on the fields . . . all the grasses seemed to be silver and gold . . . and far away, past High and Over, you could just see a little line of blue which was the sea at Cuckmere Haven, and just as we got to the house Lally came out with a big stone jug of ginger beer and a bowl of biscuits. 'Mademoiselle from Armentiers has been telling me you've been up to the Church and shocked the wits out of Angelica,' she said, setting the jug in the grass by the step. 'I just hope,' she said to Angelica, 'that they told you he got such a thrashing from his father that he couldn't sit down for a month of Sundays. Sticking knives in people's backs. I ask you!' she exclaimed to the sky. 'He had a very nasty evening under the old bridge, didn't you? Very nasty indeed with half the village looking for him and his sister almost bleeding to death in the kitchen. What a day. What a family. It's a wonder I keep sane at all with this lot around me.' And she stumped back into the house singing her John Boles song. Once, on her half-day, she and Mrs Jane, who was staying with us, went to the cinema in Seaford and saw somebody called John Boles singing a song called 'The Song Of The Dawn' or something . . . and that's about the only song she ever knew. But she only knew about three or four words, and like the hymn she 'la laa-ed' the rest. And we listened to her Dawn Song while she banged about in the kitchen; we drank the ginger beer in the sun.

Presently Angelica said very thoughtfully, 'I am sorry if I have been a nuisance to you.'

'You haven't at all,' I said, hoping she'd believe it.

'Well, I expect you'll be glad when I get on the bus this afternoon. You'll be glad to see the last of me. Good riddance to bad rubbish you'll say,' and she started to cry.

Quickly I put my arm round her shoulders but she shook me off in case I might knife her or something, and stared at me with weepy eyes. 'Don't!' she wailed. 'Don't touch me.' And she fumbled in her knickers for her handkerchief and blew her nose. We were silent for a bit.

'It's because I'm older than you two and I'm not much good at the country and things . . . but I do like you both, really I do. Even if you do set fire to people and knife people and frighten people with witches and murder. I do, honestly I do. I just don't show it very well.' And she started to cry again. Before I could do anything, Lally came tearing out of the house, cuffed me on the head and pulled Angelica to her.

'What's he been up to, then?' she cried. 'What have you been doing to Angelica? I can't turn my back for a minute without something happens.'

Angelica stopped snivelling and said it wasn't my fault and that she was sorry and she'd go in and start her packing before the bus left for Seaford. And so Lally took her away chattering to her like anything and I rubbed my head, it was quite a hard cuff, and went off into the garden to think things over. Just as I was going past the rasperries I heard my sister burst with laughter in the house, and Lally called out something about giving me a good wallop because no doubt I needed it – and then someone rattled a window closed upstairs. And I was alone. And in peace. And ate some raspberries and thought what a rum life it was. Down at the bottom of Great Meadow there were twelve cows all standing with their heads together round the gate in the shade swishing their tails because of the flies, and up on the side of High and Over the big White Horse shone in the sunlight. It was lovely and peaceful. I was looking forward very much indeed to the bus for Seaford.

The canary I-didn't-really-win-at-the-fair wasn't very well. Although I had made a proper cage for it out of a Lifebuoy soap box and a real cage front, and had put proper perches and a seed and water pot and things, it just seemed frightened all the time. It just jumped from one perch to another all day long, or fluttered up to the top and banged its head and came fluttering down again to lie gasping in the sand tray. Also, its feathers were a bit moulty, and where the yellow ones came out brownish ones came back. It looked a bit piebald after a time. Lally said it was a linnet and not a canary at all.

'A poor little linnet, that's what it is,' she said one evening when we were all sitting round the table trimming the lamp wicks. 'I reckon Reg Fluke was right; they just trap them with bird lime and dip them in yellow dye and sell 'em to the fair people.' She was polishing a big brass lamp vigorously and there was a nice smell of metal polish and paraffin. I was very carefully cutting round the wicks with an old razor blade and my sister was washing the chimneys in a bowl of soapy water and rinsing them at the sink. It was our Lamp Evening. A Wednesday. The middle of the week.

'I should let it go if I were you. How would you like to be cooped up in a little cage like that?' said Lally, giving the lamp an extra, final, wipe round and carrying it over to the others on the top of the copper. 'Tell you what,' she said. 'If you do, I'll see if we can't get a real canary next time we go up to Twickenham to see Mrs Jane. How would that do?' She set the lamp among the others on the copper. There were quite a lot of them altogether. The one from our bedroom, the one from hers, the three from the sitting-room and the big hanging one with honeysuckle and clover on the shade which hung over the dining-room table. While she and my sister were drying the glass chimneys, I was having a good think about the canary. It was no use to agree with Lally immediately, you had to let it simmer along a bit, otherwise if you said 'all right', or even 'perhaps' she meant that you had said 'Yes', and things got a bit muddly. So I had a bit of a think and trimmed away for a while without saying anything at all.

It was a lovely warm evening. The kitchen windows were wide open and there was a soft breeze coming over from the downs smelling of cut hay and earth, and bats flitted about in the light from the last of the sun which was slipping away behind the elms of the gully, shining red through the branches like the fire in the range at Mrs Jane's house in Twickenham. When I thought of the range and of Twickenham I had a rather nice quick feeling inside. Next to here, I liked there the best in the world. Her house was very small indeed. There was the scullery first, with the sink and the pump in a corner where we all had to wash in the mornings and last thing at night, then the kitchen which was titchy too, but very cosy, with the range and brass gas lamps and Mr Jane's little bamboo table where he had his meals alone by the range itself, and the big table where we all ate from different plates and odd patterned cups and saucers. Mrs Jane said children liked variety. Then through the kitchen was the parlour. Which we only ever went into on Sundays after lunch. The parlour was a lovely room. There was a real marble mantelpiece and a little iron fire burning and three armchairs and a settee with only one curvy end, and a big sideboard where the bowls with the eggs were kept. One bowl had 'Fresh Eggs' and the other just had 'Yesterdays'. In the middle of the sideboard there was a huge glass case with a whole family of stuffed partidges: the mother was looking very worried with her wings partly open and all the little chicks sitting underneath, and the father was standing at the back with his neck out and his beak open giving a warning. It was very pretty with lots of dried grasses and ferns and on the bottom of the case, in gold letters, it said 'Wheelers Copse 1886. G. N. Jane', which was Mr Jane's name and the place where he had shot them somewhere quite near Richmond. It was my favourite thing, apart from the giant pike in the kitchen which he caught near Teddington, and the two big jars on the mantel which were covered with bobbly blackberries and brown and red leaves.

Upstairs there were three little bedrooms. One for us, one for Lally, and one for Mr and Mrs Jane. We never went in that one though. Our room had a window over the back garden and the pear trees, two beds and a po cupboard with a candlestick. And there was one picture of a big dog looking out of a kennel with rain pouring down and it was called 'No Walkies Today'. We rather liked that.

Outside there was a little front garden with a rockery made from lumps of clinker from the gas works and a pretty little star-shaped bed in the middle full of London Pride; and at the back there was a huge, long garden full of pear and apple trees and a big greenhouse against the wall which had a vine which came from Hampton Court; and outside the back door a big walnut tree which is why the cottage was called 'Walnut Cottage'. Or rather Cottages, because there were actually two cottages joined together. Mrs Jane lived in one half and Mr and Mrs Poulter and their daughter Gooze lived in the other.

We didn't see much of Mr and Mrs Poulter, they were quite old, and just now and then I would see him pottering about in his vegetables next door, or perhaps Mrs Poulter would peg out a bit of washing. Sometimes they'd wave at us. But usually they were very quiet. I don't think that they ever spoke to Mrs Jane or Lally over the little fence which ran down the middle of the gardens, but

Gooze did quite often. Gooze was older than Lally and wore glasses and a slide in her hair which was rather short and had a fringe in front. She wore plimsolls, black and white speckles, just the same as the ones we wore for Gym at school, and a long droopy woolly with a belt. She was very pale and smiled all the time. And she hadn't got many teeth. But she was very nice, and once she called us over to the fence to show us an Oxo tin with a dead mouse in it. 'Found it in the wash-house dead,' she said. 'Now I'm going to bury 'im, Mrs Poulter can't abide mice,' and she went away laughing a lot. We thought she was rather odd. Lally said she was 'a bit thin up on top, but no harm in her', and told us that when she had asked her mother and father where she came from they told her from under a gooseberry bush. And that's why she was called Gooze.

Thinking about it all I began to hum a bit and feel happy and looking forward to something. 'When would we go to Twickenham?' I asked. Lally was just passing me, carrying the lamps on a tray into the sitting-room and she gave quite a jump. 'Goodness, you startled me. I thought you were in one of your sulks,' she said and went on into the room. 'We could go when I have my two weeks in September,' she called. 'If your mother and father say yes you could come up with me then. September for the Victoria Plums.' I collected the wicks and took the chimneys from my sister, who was busy breathing on them and polishing them up with a yellow duster. I heard Lally climbing the stairs to the bedrooms with our lamps and so I called out to her, 'All right. I'll let the canary go tomorrow morning if we can go to Twickenham in September.' My sister looked very astonished. 'Don't forget to remind her about the other canary, the one she said you could have if you go there,' she hissed. 'She might forget.' I went to the stairs and called up into the darkening rooms, 'You won't forget the canary, tho', will you?'

Lally was in her room and the door was closed so that her voice sounded far away. 'We'll see about that when the time comes. If you've done those wicks and the chimneys you'd better set the table for supper. The Prince of Wales will be here presently . . .' I went back to the kitchen and started smoothing out the tablecloth. 'She hasn't forgotten about the bird, she's just not going to say anything definite,' I said.

My sister scattered some plates about and got the pickles down and the butter and the cocoa jug. 'Well, let's let the other one go first thing in the morning, that'll remind her of her promise,' she said and smiled a smug looking smile. 'Perhaps we could get two canaries next time . . . real ones I mean. And then we could build an aviary place and have a real tree and things inside so that they could have a nest and eggs and everything. And we could sell the babies and make a lot of money, that would be nice, wouldn't it?' But I was too busy thinking about Twickenham to answer her.

Very early the next morning we took the cage out into the garden under the apple tree and I opened the door. The canary just skittered and fluttered and banged itself against the wires and Lally told us to come away and leave it alone. Which we did. And when we turned round it had gone! Just like that. It didn't fly away over the fields singing and singing for joy. Just vanished. There was nothing in the cage except a few crumbly feathers.

'I never saw it go!' said my sister. 'It must have been in a terrific hurry to escape.'

I felt quite miserable really. I had been so proud of it. But of course if it was really a dyed linnet it was better to let it go because it would never have got tame; wild birds never do in cages. My sister tried to cheer me up; she could be quite nice sometimes when she was feeling in the mood, which wasn't often; and sometimes it was because she wanted me to do something for her which she knew she couldn't do for herself. And she was in one of those moods this morning, I could feel it.

'Come on,' she said, taking my arm, 'let's go down to the gully, I've got something marvellous to show you. You will be surprised. Come on.' And because I hadn't anything else to do at that moment I went with her. We clambered up the hill outside the fence, to the top, and reached the big wood where the gully was hidden. It was cool and green and damp smelling under the trees; the sides of the gully were all big lumps of chalk with funny roots tangling about and long trails of ivy and deadly nightshade. It was quiet in there; you could just hear the wind moving about in the tops of the trees and the noise of our feet slithering in the muddy ruts of the floor.

There were voles down there, and hedgehogs too. We used to hear them at dusk squeaking and rustling about in the leaves looking for slugs. Which we thought rather disgusting. And once we found a great toad with golden eyes bulging in a little cave place in the chalk. It was almost as big as a plate and when we carried it back to the house and showed Lally she covered her face with her hands and threw the darning at us. 'Take the horrible thing away!' she cried. 'It'll give you warts you'll see. Take it out this instant.' She was really awfully silly about toads. She didn't mind anything else almost, except cows, but she was scared out of her wits by a humble, nice looking old toad.

But there weren't any toads down in the gully this morning. And we twisted along through the old cart ruts and brambles until my sister told me to stop, and there in front of me was a great pile of old tin cans and bits of bedsteads and rusty wire. It was just an old rubbish dump. Nothing exciting at all.

'I can't possibly be surprised by an old rubbish dump,' I said. 'And anyway, I've seen it before. It's been here for years and years.'

My sister was rooting about in the tins and bits of old iron bedsteads, there were tangles of old chicken wire and an oil stove with a broken door lying in a clutter of pram wheels and shards of a broken plough.

Suddenly, amidst all the clanking and clonking my sister gave a cry and called out: 'Shut your eyes. This is the surprise!' So I shut my eyes and heard her breathing and bonking and then she said I could open them and I did and there she was holding up a silly old tin box. There was nothing surprising about it at all. Just a biggish sort of biscuit tin with 'Huntley and Palmers' written on it, that's all.

'Look!' she said. 'Isn't it sweet, though?'

'It's a biscuit tin. I've seen hundreds and hundreds of them and I don't think it's a bit of a surprise.'

She came clambering over the pile of old junk holding her rotten old tin. 'But it's practically new!' she said. 'There's almost no rust on it. And it's got a nice lid which fits. It's just what I want to make my scent with.' And she set it down carefully in the muddy chalk.

'What do you mean, your scent?' I asked. She really could be very dotty sometimes, and I knew that somewhere she was getting me to do something for her. She was singing away and opening and closing the lid of her tin and tearing off the remains of the paper label.

'It's such a marvellous find. I discovered it yesterday all by myself. I was down here and I just saw it glinting in the sun, so I came all the way down, not a bit frightened really, and when I saw it I was *so* happy. Because now I can make my scent if you'll help me just a bit. All you have to do,' she said quickly in case I started to clamber up the gully and leave her in the junk heap, 'all you have to do is to knock some lovely holes in the sides, and a few on top, and then I will have a wonderful stove thing to boil up the rose petals and so on.' She sat there looking up at me, her eyes wide with pleasure. I think she could almost smell her beastly scent already.

'Then what do you do? If I do knock holes in it?' I asked.

She crossed her legs importantly and hugged herself with her skinny brown arms. 'Well,' she said thoughtfully. 'Well then when you do, I'll put it on some big stones, and then I'll make a fire inside with some logs, and put on the lid and then I'll have a stove. See? And the draught will come down through the holes and make the fire burn . . . and then it'll go up and heat the can of water and rose petals on top. And when it's all boiled it'll be scent.'

I thought about this for a time. It seemed a bit dense really; but I had nothing else to do and no money to spend down at Bakers and I was still feeling a bit miserable about the canary linnet and the empty cage. So I agreed to help her and we knocked holes in the tin with a hammer and a quite big nail. I made a sort of ring pattern on each side and a bigger one on the lid. She went off collecting the stones to set it on so that we could get a good draught under it, and gathered some dead sticks and bits of bark to start the fire. And then came the boring part really; collecting the rose petals and the flowers to boil up. We got quite a lot. And some nasturtiums and a few sweet-peas which were growing all round the privy. And then she filled a cleanish tin can with water, poured in the petals and set it on the stove.

I must say that her idea worked a bit better than I thought. But it did take rather a long time to get the fire alight and we wasted hundreds of matches and used two pages of an old comic before it started to burn, and when it did there was so much smoke that my sister started coughing and groaning with her eyes pouring with tears; she looked just like a dreadful old witch. If Angelica had been there she really would have had to believe it, Catholic or not, because she was just like one. I got fed up with the smoke, and after all it wasn't my scent and I had helped her, so after a while when the smoke was rather thick and she was still spluttering and coughing away, I went off on my own under the trees and soon reached the end of the gully which came out at the very bottom of Great Meadow near the road to the village. People said that the gully was once part of an old smugglers' road which led from a tunnel under our house and right down to the Magpie Public House in the village. Some people said that it went on from there all the way to the cliffs at Birling Gap where they landed all the rum and stuff on the beach and brought it up on ponies to our house where they hid it in the tunnel under our hall.

Once our mother was crossing the hall with a bowl of flowers to set on the sitting-room table and there was an awful crash and a screech and when we all ran into the hall there was no sign of our mother at all. Just a big hole in the floor-boards. Our father was very shocked, indeed. We all were.

'Margaret!' he yelled out, 'Margaret, what's happened, where are you?' And then far away under the hole, or so it seemed, we heard our mother's voice calling up, 'I've fallen through the floor. I'm in a hole down here.'

Our father was peering over the edge of the hole and Lally was wringing her hands and saying, 'Oh poor Lady! Poor soul! O! What'll we do?' My sister was too terrified to cry, but hearing our mother's voice was a bit reassuring.

'Margaret, are you hurt?' called our father, starting to struggle down the edge of the hole.

'No, just bruised, I think,' came our mother's voice. 'Try and get a torch or a light, it's terribly dark down here.'

Lally ran off for a torch and our father threw down a box of matches and started scrambling through the hole calling out to her all the time, 'I'm coming down, dear, I'm coming down.' It was all very exciting once we knew she wasn't dead or covered in blood. At last he was hanging by his hands and I heard our mother saying in a very muffled sort of voice, 'I've got your legs, darling,' or something and then he disappeared too. Just then Lally came back with the torch from the kitchen and gave a great cry when she saw no father and just the empty hole.

'Where's he gone?' she cried. 'Oh Lord have mercy.'

'He's down the hole with our mother.' I explained he just climbed down. We passed the torch to him, it was so deep down in the hole that just his hand came through the floor. 'Your mother's all right,' he said and took the torch and disappeared into the dark. We were a bit worried; the three of us just sat round the hole and waited. Lally was fanning herself with her hands. 'I can't take these shocks,' she said. 'They get my heart quick as a dart,' and puffed away. My sister was kneeling down, peering over the floor. All the boards were broken round the edge where our mother had gone through.

'This house is too old,' said Lally, getting some of her breath back. 'Those boards are rotten through and through, it's a wonder she wasn't killed I declare. Like bits of sponge cake they are, and covered with that rug you'd never see a sign. Too old. The whole place is too old.'

After a while we got ladders and things and helped them up again; our mother was very stiff but all right except for a big bump on her head, but she kissed us both and said there was nothing to worry about, and then our father came up looking quite excited and said the hole was a sort of tunnel all lined with bricks . . . but that it was blocked up with rubble at one end. He seemed more excited about the brick walls of the tunnel which he said were all made of very thin bricks which meant that they were Tudor, or something, or earlier. Then Lally made our mother have a lay-down, as she called it; and when there were really no bones broken and everything was tidied up we were allowed to go down ourselves.

It was very creepy. It was dark and damp and there were little puddles on the muddy floor . . . and it was quite round, like a railway tunnel, but very much smaller . . . only wide enough for two to walk side by side. It went quite a long way until the rubble started and our father said we must be beyond the cottage by now and in the Great Meadow, or nearly. Lally didn't like it much at all. She didn't even like going down the ladder to start with, and when she found an old muddy wellington boot lying in the slime of the floor she nearly had a turn and our father helped her out again and up the ladder. But it was just an old wellington, I mean nothing to do with smugglers or anything exciting like that.

After a while we had all the floor-boards mended, and people came and examined the tunnel and said that it probably started in the middle of the little church and came down under our house and then went on down the hill under the meadow to the village. But we never really found out. And in time we all forgot about it, except on winters nights when I thought we heard ghostly rumbling noises of barrels being rolled under the house. But it was only ever the wind in the elms. Anyway it was quite exciting to have a part of a real smugglers' tunnel under your own hall. Except of course that our mother could have been killed or broken her legs or something, and afterwards Lally used to walk on tiptoe crossing the hall to the sitting-room in case it all fell down again. But it never did.

SIX

At Twickenham, after Walnut Cottage, there were three other favourite places; although Walnut, with its garden and the greenhouse and a great long shed which Mr Jane used for 'pottering' in, was really the most favourite. I did like the toy shop in Church Street, the boat-yard near the bridge where we used to get punts from, Eel Pie Island, and Marble Hill.

Marble Hill was lovely. It was a big white house, not as big as Hampton Court, but white and gleaming in the sun. There was a great park all about it, and real hills which you could run up, and trees and, best of all, a lake-thing full of lilies and goldfish. Not many people used to go there. Perhaps because of the White Ladies in the lake. They were huge. Bigger than me or even bigger than our father – and they were all sitting on white rocks combing their hair, or pulling their friends out of the water. It really was very strange to look at. These big ladies, and some were gentlemen, were sort of all having a day by the seaside, only in the lake. The ones in the water, well, the parts of the ones which were in the water, were all green with slime, and they reached their hands up to the ones who were all busy combing their hair, for help.

My sister thought they were all drowning, or had fallen in among the lilies and fishes; she liked them as much as I did. But she said they were rather rude, simply because they hadn't got any clothes on, and she was worried about the gentlemen ones who wore a sort of leaf thing and were all trying to climb the white rocks. Lally said that it was a fountain and made from marble in Italy and was very famous and beautiful if you liked that sort of thing. But Mrs Jane didn't, and wouldn't really look at them, when she came sometimes with us, and just went on with her knitting in a chair.

We used to go there quite often, to get a breath of air, as Lally said, and also to meet some of her other friends who also had children with them, but much younger than we were . . . usually in prams. It was quite a long way from Twickenham and we took a bus from The Green and clambered up on the top deck and sat on the slatty seats looking over the side. It was rather like being on a boat. And sometimes, in wet weather, we had a canvas apron thing which we pulled over our knees, which made us feel very snug and safe.

From the top of the bus you could look down on people in the street, and they never knew, and also, which was more fun, you could see into people's gardens all along the way, and sometimes into their rooms. Which was very private, rather like spying. You could see people washing up, or sewing things at a machine, or having their teas, and they never ever knew that we were both watching them all. Mrs Jane said they ought to have curtains up, but that would have spoiled the fun really. It was just that they didn't know we were watching that was so interesting. Once we saw a very fat man dancing all by himself; he twirled round and round, and had his arms up in the air. I think that he was singing too, because his mouth kept on opening and shutting like a fish. We were always told it was rude to stare, but on top of a bus it was hard not to. You couldn't just look ahead all the time like Mrs Jane who was terrified that the wind would take her hat off, even though it was pinned hard into her bun. She used to get quite cross with Lally for letting us spit on the people in the street. Well, not actually spit *on* them, rather we used to drop a bit of a gobbit on the ones who had hats on. Never on people who hadn't.

'They really are getting out of hand,' she used to say to Lally. 'Why don't you stop them? It's disgusting what they're doing.'

'It's only a bit of spittle, Mother,' said Lally. 'Your hat won't blow off, you know . . . you'll have arm-ache if you go on holding on to it like that.'

'And if it does blow off? What then? It's my best you know. We aren't all made of money like some I wouldn't like to mention not half an hour from Twickenham Green. You've got spoiled in your ways, my girl. When I was in Service it took me a year to save up for a new hat . . . I am not about to forget that, my girl.' When she said My Girl to Lally we knew that she was really a bit vexed. And Lally knew it too, because she shook a fist at us and told us to stop, or else we'd get a good hiding.

Going home was rather nice too, nearly as exciting as going to Marble Hill. We got off at The Green and walked down under the chestnut trees, across the main road, and then down the street to the Cottages. They were right down at the bottom; you could see them from a long way off because of the big walnut tree and the little white fence round the clinker rockery in the front garden full of London Pride. Sometimes Mr Jane would be home first; we always knew because his bicycle was propped up against the shed in the little yard at the back through the green door.

'Father's home,' said Mrs Jane, pulling out her hat-pin and smoothing her bun, and went into the kitchen. We washed our hands at the scullery sink, a big yellow stone one, with a pump and a tin bowl and a pink cake of soap which smelled of disinfectant, combed our hair, and went into the kitchen for tea.

The kitchen was really quite small with a little window which looked out into the garden but which was so full of geraniums and wandering sailor that you could hardly see out. There was a range with a brass tap and knobs on the oven doors, a big table where we all ate, beside the staircase, and a small cross-legged bamboo table where Mr Jane ate alone by the fire. He was very deaf and didn't like having to make conversation. He hadly ever spoke at all, actually. Sometimes he said in a very rumbling voice, 'Thank you, Mother,' or 'I think I'll be going up then,' or sometimes when he found something interesting in the local paper he'd say, 'I see they're at it again.' But you never knew who they were or what they were up to. So you couldn't answer him even to be polite. No one ever seemed to talk to him really. But, sometimes, when we were in bed, we could hear Mrs Jane's voice telling him what we had all been doing during the day. We never heard him, only here, because she had to talk very loudly. Their room was next door to ours so we were able to hear everything pretty clearly. I felt rather uncomfortable and tried to make coughing noises so that she'd perhaps hear that we were awake. But she never did, and after a while I didn't bother any longer.

Over the range there was a stuffed pike and a very brown picture of two people praying in a sunset, and above our table there was a much bigger picture of ladies in night dresses lying all over a staircase with bowls of fruit and flowers scattered everywhere. The one I liked best was next to the scullery door. It was very sad. A man in a kilt with a bandaged arm was crying on a lady's shoulder, and she looked awfully pale. Or glad. Or something. But my sister and I both thought it was dreadfully sad except that there was a rather silly looking baby in it too, and we felt that rather spoiled it all. But the room, with the gas lamps flickering and the range glowing all red, was very cosy indeed and if there had to be a winter it was better to have it in the kitchen at Walnut than anywhere else.

Lally was setting the table, laying out the plates and the white cups with the gold clover leaf on them. Not Best today, because we were Family. I took down our plates; my sister had a picture of a bunch of roses on hers, and mine had a view of the pier at Worthing. We always had these special plates and washed them up ourselves afterwards.

'Your favourites today!' said Lally, bringing in a china bowl filled with freshly boiled winkles, which she placed on the table with a brown loaf of bread, butter and a scatter of hat-pins to eat the winkles with. Mrs Jane was busy filling the big blue teapot.

'I can't abide those silly little things,' she said, indicating the winkles with a nod of her head, 'too fiddly and nothing on them to fill a person. Give me a nice fat bloater any day.' She swung the kettle back over the fire and stood the teapot in the hearth to 'draw' as she called it, and set a large plate of bloaters before Mr Jane. He looked up from his paper slowly.

'What's that then?' he asked.

'It's your tea, what else,' shouted Mrs Jane kindly.

'Bloater is it?'

'That's what it is. You know you like them so don't make a fuss.'

'It's the bones,' he mumbled.

'You trim your moustache and you wouldn't have trouble with bones,' said Mrs Jane, cutting him three large slices of bread. 'Now, you be a dear soul and get them behind you and never you mind the bones. The children wanted winkles and you can't manage them with the pins and all. A bloater's filling and good,' she finished briskly. 'Won't go to the barber and won't let me use the scissors on him,' she said to Lally, '. . . and now he complains about the bones because his whiskers are too long. He's a stubborn man. Always was, and always will be, please God.'

After the winkles, which took quite a long time to eat because you had to pull them out of their shells with the hat-pins and sprinkle them with vinegar, we had home-made raspberry jam and a large piece of seedcake, and that was tea. Afterwards we all helped with the washing up in the scullery and set the crockery back on its shelves again and Lally cleared the table so that she could do some mending while Mr Jane snored quietly in his big chair, his paper over his face to keep out the light.

'When he wakes up after his nap,' said Mrs Jane, 'you can ask him to show you his bit of Zeppelin if you like. He may not feel up to it, on the other hand he may, there's no telling. But keep a sharp eye open for when he starts to stir and if he *doesn't* start to read his paper, you can ask him.'

A little while later the paper slid off his face, he rubbed his eyes, shook his head a bit, and folded his arms on his rather large stomach.

'Dropped off,' he said.

'Yes, dear soul, you did. Snoring like a grampus you were.'

'Snoring was I?' He looked vaguely curious.

'Like a grampus,' cried Mrs Jane, folding up the newspaper and putting it under a cushion. 'Now why don't you take the children out to see your bit of Zeppelin? Do you good to get a breath of fresh air . . . it isn't dark yet and it's not that far to the shed.' She was being very bossy and almost pulled him out of his chair which he clearly didn't want to leave. Muttering under his breath he took his keys off the mantelshelf, pulled his red and white spotted handkerchief tight round his neck and, pulling me gently by the hair, he went to the scullery door. He smelled nicely of cough-drops, as he always did.

'Not far to the shed!' he said grumpily.

'No it's not! You need a bit of exercise,' called Mrs Jane, stacking up his cup and saucer and plate.

'Not far to the Palace either,' he said, 'and I been there twice today on my bike. Once there and once back. I have had all the exercise I need for one day.'

'You haven't been twice to the Palace, Father, you've been there once. The next time you were coming *from* the Palace home. So it stands to reason you only *went* once. Unless you forgot something and had to go back?'

'Whether I went twice or not doesn't matter. It's the same journey whichever way. You try it, my girl,' he grumbled out of the door and I followed him out into the yard. 'Women,' he mumbled, fiddling with his keys and finding the right one he opened the shed door and the familiar smell of dust and varnish and winter onions filled the air.

The shed was long and low and dark. It was stacked with old boxes, piles of sacking, fishing nets, fishing rods, ropes of onions and shallots and sacks of corn for the hens. On one side ran a long wooden work bench with shelves above cluttered with boxes marked in white painted letters 'Screws', 'Nails', 'Washers', 'Tin Tacks' and so on, and all with their sizes after them. He was very methodical. Above the shelves hung a fox's head with its mouth open, and glassy eyes staring. He had shot it many years ago near Richmond which was where he used to do all his shooting when he was a young man. He fumbled about with some matches and lit the hanging lamp above the bench and suddenly the shed was filled with leaping shadows which came and went with the swinging of the lamp while he searched for the biscuit tin of Treasures. I knew where it was, but was much too polite to say, and anyway he liked to make it all a bit more exciting before finding it, which he did presently, and set before me on the rough wooden top of the bench. It was a fairly large tin with a scratched picture of Windsor castle on one side and the King's mother and father on the lid.

Carefully he opened it and gently shook everything out. Brass buttons, cigarette cards in neat little bundles, a tusk from a wild pig, a tooth from a shark, a set of dominoes, a bullet, some old coins, and best of all these, the bit of Zeppelin. A small ragged cross of aluminium, with blots stuck on it. I took it in my hand reverently. Although I had done this many times with him, I knew he liked me to be pleased each time.

'Potters Bar, that was. I'll never forget the night that came down.'

'All in flames?'

'Yers. Burning like a beacon . . . like a great big burning fish in the sky.' He put his fingers to his moustache to find, I thought, a lost bone from the bloater.

'Young Bert Taylor and me got pretty near to it after it was cool, and pulled this bit off as a sort of memento. It gave them Jerries a bit of a fright, that did, and they'd been dropping their bombs all over just anywhere and it served them right. Zeppelin they called it . . . a great big thing it was. You never saw such a blaze.' And then he lost interest and started pottering about in the shed. I asked him if I could take it and show my sister and he said I could but to bring it back as soon as she had seen it, he said otherwise he'd catch his death because the shed was damp, but he didn't seem to be in much of a hurry.

My sister had stayed in the kitchen because the shed gave her the creeps and once she had seen the fox snap its jaws at her, so she said, and its eyes followed her everywhere she moved. Which was silly seeing that they were glass eyes and it was only a head anyway, not a whole fox. Anyway she wasn't interested in the bit of Zeppelin.

'It's only a silly bit of twisty tin,' she said. 'How can you tell it's from a whatever it's called? It might just be a bit off an old cart or something.'

'It's from a Zeppelin and it got shot down at Potters Bar all on fire. Everyone was burned up too. It's famous,' I said.

'Well, it served them right, getting burned up, if they were Germans, and it's not the sort of thing girls like anyway. Wars and things like that. Now if it had been a dear little mouse, or a baby rabbit . . . or something *sweet* like that, well, it would be different. But it's just a soppy old bit of tin that's all and there's nothing interesting in that.' She was helping Lally to sort out some eggs to go in the bowls in the parlour next door. 'Todays' and 'Yesterdays'. Lally was marking some with a 'T' and others with a 'Y' and there was a separate little bowl with six Bantam eggs in it. These were for my sister and me. We had two each for breakfast every morning if we were lucky, with fried bread and bacon. Mrs Jane collected them all up and took them into the parlour.

'You'd better take it back to Father,' she called. 'He'll catch his death in that old shed, it's full of dust and rubbish, it'll bring on his cough again. Be a good boy and take it back, do. And tell him to come in while you're at it. Tell him I said so.'

Together, he and I shovelled all the bits and pieces back in the tin box, the buttons and the dominoes and the bit of Zeppelin. He doused the lamp, and we made our way back to the glowing kitchen and the little scullery lit by one wavering candle where we had to, both, wash our hands before we were allowed into the house again.

'There's no knowing what you have handled in that old shed,' said Mrs Jane, '. . . full of rats and mice and the dear knows what else. And Father must be tired if he *was* twice to the Palace today, although I very much doubt that, I'm sure. I'll ask him in bed later.'

'Did he go to see the King and Queen?' said my sister in a silly way, not really meaning it but just being irritating.

Lally gave a sort of sniff of laughter. 'I'll give you King and Queen, my girl. Father's been to Hampton Court . . . not the one in London . . . he goes there every day of his life and you know it, Madam. He tends the clocks and sees that they all tell the same time as each other. It's a very responsible job, you know. One day the Prince of Wales will pop in, and ask him the time and he'll be able to say, right out, "Half-past eleven", or whatever it will be, "Your Highness, and its exactly right"!' She poked away at the fire in the range, stuck on another lump of coal, fixed the slide in her hair, and took down the box of Games which sat on top of the green wooden cupboard.

'Come along now . . . we have time for one good game of Snakes and Ladders before cocoa.' And spread the board out on the table.

It was lovely and peaceful lying on the grass under the great pear tree. If you looked up through the hundreds of leaves you could just see little specks of blue sky and sometimes bits of white cloud drifting far above. It was just like being in the country and not at all in a town like Twickenham. Just across the grass was the hen run, and on the other side the place where the ducks lived, which was muddy and sploshy with water that they spilled out of the old tin bath which Mr Jane had sunk into the ground to make a little pond for them. And past, quite a long way past, them was the greenhouse with the vine. All over one wall, great glossy leaves and bunches and bunches of fat blue grapes in October. It really was like the country; and even seeing old Mrs Poulter hanging out her washing over the fence didn't spoil anything, because she was so quiet she hardly got noticed. But Mrs Jane said that it was all changing:

'Not like it was, mark my words. I remember, not so long ago, walking all the way to the Village through the fields . . . from here to Church Street . . . and now they're building rows and rows of houses all round Pope's Grove, and The Lodge is sold and they do say it's going to be a hotel or something. I never thought I'd see the day. I hope Father and I don't live to see the time when all this has to go, as go it will, mark my words, everything goes too fast nowadays . . . much too fast.' She jabbed her knitting needles into a ball of wool and started to tidy up her old straw work basket.

Lally was sewing buttons on one of my shirts when she suddenly said: 'Mother, the boy here wants a canary bird. He won one at the fair, remember, but it was a wild bird so we let it go. I promised him a real canary.' My heart leapt. She *had* remembered! I looked at her with such delight that she scowled at me and said: 'Don't you get too uppity, Sir . . . nothing settled yet. I'm only asking, that's all.' I rolled back on to the grass and closed my eyes. My heart thumping. Listening to the talking, crossing my fingers. Mrs Jane sounded a bit distant, I think she had started to walk up to the house but I heard her say: 'You better have a talk to Father . . . he knows what's what in this place. Bert Batt had some a while ago, but I don't know now, ask your Father.' I opened my eyes and stared up into the pear tree . . . she *had* remembered after all. Now all I had to do was pray.

When we were washing our hands for lunch I whispered the news to my sister who was so impressed that she wiped her hands on her shorts instead of the towel.

'I wonder if we can have *two*? One for me and one for you like I said and we can have babies and sell them and all that sort of thing? Wouldn't it be marvellous if we could?'

I said I didn't care about two as long as there was one for me because it was, after all, my canary; I had let the wild one go free so it was my reward.

'You don't get rewarded for doing kind things,' said my sister. 'Everyone knows that. But I'd help you to look after it, I promise. Oh! wouldn't it be *lovely* to have babies and nests and all that sort of thing? But wouldn't it?'

The next evening when Mr Jane came back from the Palace on his bike, had had his tea, read his paper and slept a little, Lally shouted at him about the canary and Mr Batt, and he said, yes, Mr Batt had some . . . this year's hatchings and five shillings each.

My sister covered her face with her hands and cried, 'Oh! Oh! He's only got one shilling and four coppers left.' She looked, when she took her hands away from her poky face, quite pleased. I wanted to hit her but I was too shocked by the price. I only got sixpence a week pocket money and this I had saved up for three weeks to come to Twickenham. The canary seemed a long way beyond my reach now. But I didn't let anyone see, I just went on writing in my little red note-book. I was busy writing a new play and I had to put my thoughts together so that no one could really guess what I was thinking. And the play had to be finished before we all left at the end of the week, because we were going to 'do' it on our last night as a Thank You to Mrs Jane for having us there.

'I don't think he really wants a canary now, do you?' said Lally, cheerfully cutting up a long green bean. 'I think he's got it out of his system, Mother.' I hadn't but she couldn't know that. My sister sat staring at me, Lally went on with her beans, and Mrs Jane was busy ironing. There was a nice smell of damp linen and starch, and only the clock ticking and Mr Jane snoring gently. I went on writing busily. It was all rubbish because I was only really thinking of five shillings, so I just wrote boggly boggly boggly all the time and hoped that none of them would notice.

'Got it out of your system,' said Lally, brushing all the tops and tails off the beans into a paper bag and taking the full bowl into the scullery. 'It's nice to see you with your books for a change is all I can say.' I heard the pump going and the water running in the sink and my sister calling out,

'He's writing his play for Sunday night, you see.'

'A play?' said Mrs Jane, smoothing away. 'That's nice.'

'Not this one,' said my sister, 'this one is all about bats and ghosts and things.'

'It isn't at all,' I said. She didn't know.

'I like a nice play,' said Mrs Jane. 'I haven't been to a theatre since before the Flood. Well, since a very long time ago. And I do like a nice play, especially if it's got a tune or two.'

Lally came bumbling back in with a saucepan of water and the beans and started to set them on the range with a clonk. 'Last play you went to my dear was a couple of years back when we all went up to see "Bitter Sweet", the time when Brother Harold and Ruby got married.'

Mrs Jane put down her iron and folded her arms across her pinafore. 'Of course we did,' she said. 'I'd quite forgot. Harold and Ruby got married that Thursday and then we went to His Majesty's and saw that pretty play when Mrs Williams dropped her bag of plums all over the Dress Circle! I laughed fit to burst my stays, I must say . . . what a thing to do! Still, it was a pretty play . . . and very sad too . . . wasn't it sad then Lally? As far as I can remember it was *very* sad . . . but we were all so taken with Mrs Williams' plums I can't recall very much I do admit.'

'There were some lovely tunes in that,' said Lally, 'really pretty. But what Mrs Williams was doing with plums in the Dress Circle I never shall know. A box of Cadbury's yes: plums no. I was really cross, wasn't I, Mother? Remember? Cross.'

Mrs Jane sighed deeply and went on smoothing away. 'Yes, you were, very cross as I recall, but I had to laugh . . . it was just like your father playing skittles down at the Flagstaff, the noise they made clattering everywhere.'

For a little while there was silence and then I suddenly said: 'I suppose I could go and work or something, couldn't I?'

'What for?' said Lally sharply.

'To get the money for the canary.'

'Oh! The canary . . . well . . . odd jobs do you mean?'

'Yes . . . anything.'

'You *could* I suppose . . .' She sounded vague and looked at Mrs Jane. 'He *could* do odd jobs about the place to earn a bit for his canary, couldn't he, Mother?'

'There's quite a lot to get on with here,' said Mrs Jane. 'The shed needs a good clean out, there's weeding to be done in the vegetable garden . . . I daresay we could keep you busy for threepence an hour if that's what you want?' She folded up some shirts and put the iron on a little brass stand by the range. 'Next Door said they wanted someone to whitewash the chicken shed . . . He's a bit stiff with his back, and Gooze can't hardly hold her head up let alone a whitewash brush . . . I reckon if you offered they'd be pleased to pay you for your canary.'

It was settled quite easily. I started work the next morning in our shed, carting all the boxes and sacks and bits and pieces out into the yard and getting down to a good sweep. My sister helped a bit too: she had a feeling that if she didn't she wouldn't be able to claim any of the canary when it finally came, and she hated the idea of that. But after I had made her carry down the fox's head, and some old fly papers, and lug a big bag full of rotten windfalls she pretty soon gave up, and I got on with things on my own. It was much easier, and I could still think about the play while I worked.

After the shed, which took quite a long time actually, there was the vegetable

garden and all the weeds, and after that I washed up eighty flower pots, and
cleaned them carefully ready for Mr Jane's seedlings and cuttings for the
winter. And then I went over to the Poulters and they said I could whitewash
the chicken shed; which took so long to do that I managed to earn a shilling, and
Gooze gave me two pennies which she said were really for the Collection on
Sunday but she thought that the Africans wouldn't miss two pennies just for one
week. Which was very kind of her. She was very shy, and kept twisting the belt of
her long droopy woolly cardigan, and scuffing a little hole in the grass where we
were standing. But she pushed the two warm pennies into my hand and scurried
off to her back door so that I couldn't really thank her.

On the Friday we all set off to Mr Batt's house across the Green. Lally in her
summer frock-for-Town, which was different to the one she wore in Sussex
because it had red squares all over it and she wore white ankle strap shoes and
carried a purse. But she didn't wear her hat. Because Mr Batt was a 'neighbour'
and she didn't want him to think she was just putting on airs when she came to
visit.

No. 14 Sumatra Road was not as pretty as Walnut Cottage. It was all red
brick with a pointed roof, a bay window, and a thick laurel hedge all round.
Over the green front door there was a stone lady's face, staring down with wide
eyes, surrounded by yellow brick. We didn't go into the house, but through a
side gate into the yard and then down the long garden path to the sheds at the
bottom. It really wasn't much of a garden. Not like ours at Walnut. There were
lots of old boxes and tins, a broken pram, and some washing hanging on a line.
No flowers, or trees, just some rather dead looking Michaelmas daisies and a few
rows of yellow cabbages.

Mr Batt was thin and friendly and didn't wear a collar. He took us into the
sheds through a little door – and then the magic started! The sheds were full of
cages, row upon row of them, filled with birds of all kinds. It was all very clean
and tidy, not a bit like his back garden, and he had to talk quite loudly because
of the tweeting of all the birds who were hopping about on their perches and
twittering and feeding away.

I selected a canary, bright yellow, with pink legs, who seemed to be very
cheerful and singing a lot.

'Good choice,' said Mr Batt. 'He's a bright little feller, sings like a clockwork
dickie bird. You'd think all you had to do was wind him up and let him be. But
no! Oh no! You got to look after 'im . . . feed him proper, twice a day you fill up
his seed bowl, clean water, lots of grit and a nice bit of lettuce, some chickweed,
a piece of prime apple, and a nice bit of old cuttlefish . . . then he'll sing for you
to show his thanks . . . but he ain't no clockwork dickie . . . You *sure* you'll take
care of him, otherwise I'd have to say No?'

Walking back down Sumatra Road, holding the little travelling cage, with
my real canary, after all this time, was almost more than I could bear. I daren't
speak I was so happy, and when my sister pointed out how big the conkers all
were, coming across the Green, I didn't even look. Just went walking straight on
longing to get to Walnut so that I could take him up to my room and just gaze at
him in silence. But first we had to get a packet of seed and some grit and a bit of
cuttlefish from Mrs Hicks at the Corner Shop, and then when I had paid for all
that I had only the two pence which Gooze had given me. But it was worth it.

Mrs Jane sighed a bit and said she couldn't abide birds in cages. 'It isn't
natural,' she said sadly. 'He ought to be out there flying about free.'

'Wouldn't last a minute out there, Mother. Cats 'ud get him in no time, and
anyway he comes from a foreign country, he couldn't get the proper food in the
garden . . . and think of the winter.'

'Makes no difference. Shouldn't be in a cage. Where does it come from then?'

'Madeira,' said Lally, finally as if she knew.

'That's where the cake comes from,' said my sister, showing off.

'Well, it's a long way off . . . and very hot there. So you keep him warm and don't take him up to your bedroom. He stays here in the kitchen. Where it's warm. And you can put him in the window as long as you don't knock Mrs Jane's geraniums about.'

'You mind my geraniums . . . very brittle they are . . . it's a good thing Father is deaf, though I shouldn't say it, for that twittering would drive him out of his wits . . . and me out of mine I shouldn't wonder, though I'm a patient woman, god knows . . . and don't go scattering seed about or we shall have mice.'

But really, in spite of them all being a bit difficult, people were really very nice about him, and after tea we all had a talk about what to call him, and finally decided on Madeira because that's where he came from, and Lally said it would help me with my geography if I went and looked it up on a map. Which I did: but it was very hard to find, and very small indeed when we saw it in a big bit of blue sea, just about as big as a fly-blow. And it can't have been important because it wasn't red, like India and Africa and Great Britain. But we called him that, anyway, to please Lally.

Mrs Jane didn't say much about the name. I could see she didn't think it very good for a bird.

'It's too cumbersome,' she said. 'You ought to give it a nice name like Joey or Bobby or something pretty.' She closed up the big Atlas and stuck it back on the shelf beside the Bible and three bound volumes of The Family Circle. Lally came back from the scullery with the tray of tea things and started setting them up on the shelves by the range.

'Bobby is a dog's name, and Joey is for a parrot, Mother. Madeira is *very* nice I think. Unusual.'

'Doesn't trip off the tongue,' said Mrs Jane, setting up her folding red and blue carpet chair by the fire opposite Mr Jane, who was reading his paper by the light of the gas lamp above.

'What do you think, Father?' she shouted at him, sitting into her chair and sorting through a pile of clean socks in her lap. He looked up vaguely from the paper.

'Eh?' he said.

Mrs Jane leaned towards him and shouted again. 'About Madeira. They're going to call the bird Madeira!' He looked at her in surprise and then slowly round us all.

'I don't think so, Mother,' he said eventually. 'Perhaps at Christmas. I'd rather have a nice jug of ale,' and he went back to his paper. Mrs Jane looked perplexed.

'He didn't understand me, oh dear! I wonder what he thought I'd said?' She went on sorting the socks, rolling them into neat little bundles when they hadn't got a hole or something. 'And we never got to see your play did we?' she asked. 'I expect the bird quite put it out of your mind, that's it.'

Lally said that that was it and that anyway the cottage was really too small to make a stage in, and we couldn't hang a curtain up, and anyway I hadn't written the words so we couldn't learn them but perhaps next time, and in the meanwhile we had all better start thinking about packing tomorrow for the day after we had to leave. Which filled me with sadness because we hated leaving Walnut even though it only meant going back to The Cottage and our father and mother.

'I wanted to do the play just as a sort of Thank You . . . I did forget because of the bird!' I said.

'And you would have liked it too,' said my sister sadly. 'It was all about this Lady who goes to a haunted house and gets scared out of her wits by a huge big bat and . . .' Lally cut her short:

'Don't give the story away, silly! Fancy spoiling the surprise. We'll all do it next time and that'll be fine.'

Mrs Jane sat back in her chair and started to thread a needle:

'We don't need no thanking, bless you. It's a pleasure to have you here. Oh dear! That reminds me . . . we've got Brother Harold and Ruby coming down *next* Sunday for tea with that child.' She heaved a great sigh, and Lally put an arm on her shoulder and laughed:

'Cheer up, Mother, do . . . it's only for tea and they are your flesh and blood after all.'

Mrs Jane was cross looking: 'It's just the way that Baby Dennis *will* break all my eggs so that I have to hide them in a cupboard and then he starts kicking your father! It's not natural in a child of three . . . kicks your father on the shins who has done him no harm in all the world! I don't know why Ruby doesn't take the back of her hand to him I'm sure. And my eggs . . .' She was really quite vexed and, pushing her wooden mushroom into the heel of a sock, she started darning very fast.

Mr Jane suddenly folded his paper, gave a big yawn, scratched his head and looked for a few moments at his wife in front of him, stitching away.

'Mother!' he said, searching for his handkerchief in a trouser pocket. 'Since you're on your feet, hand me down the tin of humbugs will yer . . . I just fancy one this evening.' Mrs Jane gave him a look and asked me to get the tin off the mantelpiece where it always stood under the picture of the people praying in the fields, and I handed it to him for him to choose one which always took him quite a long time although they were all exactly the same size and colour; when he found the one he wanted he sniffed it, held it to the light, and then, very carefully, put it in his mouth as if it was the first humbug he had ever tasted. Sucking at it, he offered me the tin and my sister and I had one each and then I put it on the shelf again.

'I don't know, really I don't,' said Mrs Jane. 'He really lives in a world of his own does Father. It comes of working in the silence and winding too many clocks. He doesn't pay no heed to anyone else.'

But just as I was about to get the old piece of sheet which she had given me to put over Madeira's cage at nights, I heard Mr Jane say with a mouth full of humbug: 'I think there's some old wire fronts hanging up in the shed you know. Give the boy one so he can make a cage for his bird when he gets back, be better'n that silly little box from Bert Batt.'

I was very happy and shouted, 'Thank You!' to him but he only smiled and waved his hand in the air.

'Nice little bird,' he said. 'He don't worry me because I can't hear him . . . that twittering would drive me out of my wits all day long, wouldn't it, Mother?' But he didn't wait for an answer, just closed his eyes and rolled his humbug comfortably round his mouth. Mrs Jane bit off the thread and started to roll the socks into a ball.

'He likes you two but he can't *abide* Baby Dennis . . . and no more can I, God forgive me. If only he wouldn't kick so! You go and look for that cage front tomorrow, young man, don't do it tonight with all the dust and that lying about out there. And you . . .' she said, pointing at my sister, 'when you have to leave on Sunday, don't go hiding behind his chair . . . we know you don't want to leave, and it's very kind of you, but it does upset him so. He feels sorry for a week of Sundays . . .'

But she smiled very kindly when she said it, and closed her basket.

SEVEN

In the train from Calais to Wimereux we had the whole compartment to ourselves, which was very nice indeed. There really wasn't much room for anybody else anyway. On one side sat Lally and myself and my sister . . . that was three; and opposite, sitting in a gloomy row and looking very white and rotten, were the three Chesterfield children, Angelica, Beth and Paul, and their nanny who was called Amy O'Shea and who was older than Lally and wore a grey two-piece suit and a white straw hat with a black ribbon like a man's. She was pretty ugly too. And skinny. And sat there clutching her huge handbag as if it had all their money in it. Which it didn't. Our fathers and mothers had all that. And they were coming by motor-car to Wimereux because it was more comfortable and in any case there wasn't room for us all in the O.M.

They were all looking so white and gloomy because they had all been terribly sick on the boat, which was really a bit funny because none of us were. And that made us feel very good. We had been to Wimereux quite often for holidays so we knew what to expect. Every time we got on the boat Lally would make us sit up on the deck and eat lemons. It wasn't a very nice thing to do but we did it because she said it stopped you being seasick, and the air was good for us.

So we did that. And we were never sick although Lally once said she felt queasy and hoped no one would speak to us because she'd have a terrible turn and what would we do then?

But this day everything had been lovely. Sunny, with a wind and the sea all glossy and pale and foamy like ginger beer; and gulls swinging over the funnels, and the flags streaming in the breeze. The Chesterfields all went down below to a cabin, which Lally told Amy was a Silly Thing To Do. And it was. Almost as soon as we left Folkestone Paul Chesterfield came up on deck with a white face and said that Amy had fallen down in a heap and had knocked her hat off.

When we got to the cabin she was sitting on the edge of a bunk holding her head, her hat all squint, and her pince-nez, hanging from her lapel by a little gold chain, were glinting in the sun.

'I'm taken bad!' she moaned. 'If only it would keep still for a minute I'd be all right, I'm sure. It's the floor swaying about so. Oh! What will become of us all if I'm taken queer?' Lally was very brisk indeed and ordered Angelica and Paul and Beth up on the deck, and told Amy to put her feet up and cover her eyes with a handkerchief.

Amy moaned and rolled from side to side and said No. No! Nothing would make her move and the children were to stay within her sight for she was Responsible. Angelica was sitting bolt upright like a white rabbit, and Beth just crouched in a corner holding on to the handle of the little door which led to the lavatory.

'Oh! Make it stop, dear God!' cried Amy, which made my sister and me giggle. Lally hit us sharply and said, 'What a silly thing to say, Miss O'Shea! If the good Lord stopped the boat now for you, we'd all be swinging about here for dear knows how long . . . soon as we get on the sooner we'll be on dry land.'

'I'll never see the land again. God help us all,' moaned Amy O'Shea and gave a dreadful gasp and covered her face with her handkerchief which smelled of lavender water. Suddenly Beth made a strangling sort of noise and Lally spun us both round and sent us up the stairs. We heard a splashing noise and then the door slammed shut.

We had a very nice time looking at all the people lying on the deck with big white enamel bowls beside them. They all looked very green and sad, only the sailors looked cheerful, and they were dashing about the sloping decks laughing and eating big ham rolls and sloshing water everywhere. We called out 'Bonjour!' to them all, and they all waved back and said 'Bonjour' also. It was a *very* nice feeling, as if we had always been travelling which was very good for you because, as Lally said, it broadened your mind.

In a little while we could see the long flat line of land ahead . . . and the sunshine sparkling on white sailing boats and the windows of houses in France where we were going to spend four weeks at the Hôtel d'Angleterre. Lally joined us by the rail pulling on her gloves and snapping her handbag shut, she tucked a bit of hair under her hat with the ivy leaves on it, and said: 'Miss O'Shea's in a poor way, I'm afraid. They've all been sick. But what can you expect all cooped up in that little room with no air and no lemons?'

We felt sorry for them in a vague way, but quite glad about Angelica who was really so prim that a bit of seasick would do her good. Beth, who was two years younger than Angelica, was rather a nice girl and we quite liked her. She had a freckly face and gaps in her teeth but she liked doing nearly all the things we liked doing, so she wasn't a Drawback. Paul was the youngest and Not Very Well because he had something wrong with his chest which made him very pale and quiet and he spent most of his time reading. So we didn't pay any attention to him much except to say 'Good morning, Paul,' or 'Hello, Paul,' or 'Are you having a nice day?' just things like that which he only had to say 'Yes' or 'No' to, which is what he did. And nothing more.

We watched France get nearer and nearer, and heard the boat make slowing-down noises, and the water thrashing and churning about under the propellers . . . and then we could see the great clock at Calais swing into view, and all the crooked houses; and cranes striking up into the sky, like schoolteachers' fingers. The gulls wheeled and screeched and scattered over the ginger-beery water like handfuls of rice at a wedding. And the sun glinted on the slimy green seaweedy walls of the piers while men in blue rushed all alongside throwing ropes at us, shouting and whistling. It was very exciting to feel the big ship slide slowly into her place, nudging and bumping gently at the high stone walls, and watching all the ropes growing taut to stretching point as they made us fast.

Then in a flash the gangplanks were up and we all wobbled down to stand on the cobbled road of the docks. We stood there among piles of wooden boxes smelling of fish, and still felt the land swaying a little after the movement of the ship. Lally went off into the crowd of people, looking for Amy and the Chesterfields who wouldn't leave their cabin until the ship had really stopped and everything was quite still. And then they had a terrible job getting down the gangplank because it was steep and Amy's bag, Angelica's books, and the travelling rugs seemed to all get mixed up. But eventually, pale and exhausted, they were all among the fish, and we started to make our way over to the station. It took quite a while to sort out all our luggage, find the tickets, and say 'merci' to everyone in sight: Lally said we had to because you never knew who was driving the train.

In the end we all clambered into one compartment together in the middle, just in case anything hit us in the front, or from the back, and then we were assured by Lally, we'd be completely safe and not get squashed which was often the case On French Railways.

'I do think it's exciting!' said my sister happily, but no one answered her because, with a terrific shriek of the whistle and three big jig-joggy-jerks, the train started to steam out of the station into the sunlit town.

Amy O'Shea sat bolt upright looking fearfully out of the windows to see how fast we were going, and Angelica and Beth just stared ahead. Paul went to sleep.

'He's just like the Dormouse in Alice,' whispered my sister.

Lally took off her gloves and started to count all the bits of luggage on the racks, nodding her head and counting under her breath, and suddenly we roared into a tunnel and everything was black and I heard Amy O'Shea cry out in fright but we were soon through and out into the fields and woods running quietly through lovely flat fields full of streams and little clumps of willows. There were men and women working in the fields with horses, and a girl of our age, with a flock of sheep, waved to us and we waved back like anything. Except the Chesterfields, who just sat.

The Hôtel d'Angleterre was very nice and on the promenade looking straight on to the sea. We had stayed there before so the fat lady in black, with pearls and a rose, knew us right away and kissed my sister who didn't like it much because she always used to shout at her, 'O! La belle poupéee!' which Lally said meant what a pretty doll; and my sister didn't like the doll part. She didn't look like one so it was a bit silly, but kind, I suppose.

Our room was the same one we always had, tall windows over the sea, with a balcony, a big bed for Lally and two smaller ones for us. In one corner there was a screen, and behind it was a place to wash your face and hands and another, on the floor, which was for washing your feet – which seemed a good idea because ours were always so sandy. The wallpaper was very pretty, covered in roses and lilac and there was a huge wardrobe and an armchair and a little table with three chairs for us to have our meals at.

Looking over the balcony you could see all the people on the beach, the waves flapping along the sand, and the blinds of the hotel right below. We were only on the first floor in case of a fire happening. Lally said she wasn't going to risk being any higher thank-you-very-much, which is why we always had to book the same room well in advance. It you looked to the right you could see down to the canal bridge and the spire of the church, and if you looked left you could see more hotels and then the lovely big green hump of the cliffs. There were no motors on the promenade, only bicycles, so that you could run out of the hotel down the steps, across the road, and on to the beach. It really was the nicest place in the world. Abroad.

The first thing Lally unpacked, before our suitcases even, or the big trunk, was her little wicker basket. In it she had a titchy teapot, three cups, a little tin kettle, and a very small stove-thing which she stood on a tin tray by the washbowl, with a bottle of milk and a spoon. Then she lit it, and the whole room started to smell of methylated spirits. There was a curious pale blue flame, and in almost no time at all, the tin kettle was boiling and steaming the mirror over the washplace. And then we all had a 'good strong cup of tea' on the balcony before we did anything else. Not that my sister and I wanted tea at all: but it was the rule, and we had to stick to it with Lally.

After we had unpacked almost completely, Lally went off to the W.C. across the corridor and emptied the teapot and cups down the lav while we were changing into our summer things. Sandals, shorts, and our rather silly white cotton hats which we both hated. Lally was sure that we would get sunstroke while we were shrimping, so we had to wear these awful white cotton 'hates', we called them, which pulled down right over our ears.

'With all this sun burning down on your heads they'll be boiled like a couple of eggs, sure as sure. You wear them until your mother says not. Then it's out of my hands.'

After a day or two we managed to lose them somewhere, but for the first day it was The Rule.

The Chesterfields seemed better and more cheerful, although Amy was still dressed in her two-piece with a veil round her hat to keep it in place. We all went shrimping and I caught three baby flounders and about a dozen shrimps which we kept in a bucket until we had to go back to the hotel to meet Our Parents. Lally made us throw the shrimps and the flounders back into the sea, because last year we had taken them all back to the room and filled the thing for washing your feet with sea water, some pretty seaweed, a lot of shrimps and some more baby flounders. One of us left the tap running just a little bit so that they could get oxygen, and during lunch in the big restaurant under our room, quite a large part of the ceiling fell down on some people at a table near us. There was a lot of fuss and water and plaster everywhere and it was all because the rather stupid feet-washing basin thing had overflowed and gone through the floor.

Our room was a bit of a mess too, with sand and seaweed and the flounders all plopping away on the floor gasping, poor things. I got a terrific walloping from our father and lost my Saturday franc for two weeks to help pay for the damage to the floor and the ceiling of the restaurant. Which seemed a bit unfair really, because two francs can't have been nearly enough to pay for *all* the mess. And we had to say we were sorry, in French, to the people who had got wet and covered in plaster, and also to the Lady who owned the hotel in black and pearls and a rose. And she wasn't very smiling either. At least, my sister said, she didn't grab her and call her a 'belle poupée' any more for that holiday and that it was almost worth all the punishments we had to have in order not to be frightened out of her wits on the staircase every morning. Anyway. Back we had to throw them under Lally's firm gaze, and back we all trooped to the hotel.

Our parents were very handsome we thought. More handsome than Mr and Mrs Chesterfield by far. Our father was very brown and cheerful in white trousers with a tie round his waist and a very French shirt all stripy like a sailor's, and our mother was looking very beautiful in beach-pyjams with a funny white hat called a Dough-Boy hat because it was what American sailors wore in the war and they were called dough-boys. I don't know why.

Aunt Freda had a pointed nose just like Angelica, and wore a hat with a rose and a huge brim which came so far down that all you could see was her nose sticking out and her pointed chin; she had to hold her head quite high up and backwards to see where she was going. Uncle John was rather jolly with a big belly and a pipe and always laughed a good deal. They weren't really our Aunt and Uncle but we had always known them, ever since before we were born, and so they got to be almost Family.

We all had dinner together at a huge table in one corner of the restaurant, and we were allowed a wine glass of beer or a glass of red wine with mineral water while we ate. This was a special treat this holiday for it was a sign that we were 'growing-up' and should be allowed to get accustomed to it. Lally was terribly shocked but kept herself to herself and only said how awful it was when we were getting ready for bed later. 'Starting the Rot,' she said.

Our mother said we should have an early night after such a tiring day and that tomorrow we would all go on a lovely trip to the oyster beds outside the town, and that we could go in a real coach with a horse pulling it. Which sounded very interesting.

'I thought that wine was very nice, didn't you?' said my sister from her bed in the corner, and I agreed although I thought that tomorrow I'd probably try the beer instead in spite of what Lally said about it starting the Rot.

'I don't feel a bit homesick yet, do you?' asked my sister.

'We've only been here today . . . it's too soon. It comes on later.'

'I don't think I'll *ever* be homesick here. I think it's lovely.'

'I wonder if the Chesterfields will be sick in the coach tomorrow?'

'I wonder. Fains we don't sit beside them.'

Lally called out and told us to be quiet and get to sleep or we'd all be sick in the coach with a good hiding. So we went to sleep; it seemed the best thing to do.

The Chesterfields were all sitting at the breakfast table when we got down. Amy was in a green frock but still wore her hat. She had a little book in her hand and was reading it carefully through her shining glasses.

'Reading at table indeed!' said Lally in a pretending-stern voice and setting us all round the big table. Amy closed the book and took off her glasses.

'Not actually reading, just glancing through. The tea's fresh, they just brought it in, although it's as weak as dishwater to me.'

Lally poured us all a cup and helped herself to sugar.

'I have to agree with you, Amy, dishwater it is . . . however, remember that I've always got my little supply upstairs if you ever feel the need. Nice strong Mazawattee, and a ginger snap, makes a great difference to the afternoon, I always say. What is your little book then?' You could tell she was very curious about the book because she had offered Amy her precious tea before she asked the question.

Amy picked up the book and put on her glasses again. 'It's a French phrase book. It once belonged to my father, God rest his soul, and I thought it would be useful for the children if we learned a few things to say . . . like where is the Church please? Or can you direct me to the cemeteries . . . things like that, you know? Otherwise we'd be at the mercy of foreigners wouldn't we?'

'Well for dear-knows-whose-sake!' cried Lally. 'You aren't going to take the children round all the churches and cemeteries of France are you, Amy? There are lots of nice things to see! It's morbid.'

'It's what?' said Amy.

'Morbid.'

'Morbid to learn a few phrases, is it?'

'No . . . that's all right. But morbid to dwell on cemeteries and such.'

'I'm not *dwelling* on them, I assure you. It just so happens that I have a very dear brother in one of them.' She looked rather pink in the face. 'And I've a notion to go and find him.'

Lally looked very uncomfortable and told my sister to take her elbows off the table which they weren't on. So we knew she was a bit flustered about the brother in the cemetery.

'I'm very sorry, I'm sure,' she said. 'I didn't realise that at all. Is it here?'

'It's here,' said Amy. 'Not a few miles away from this very town . . . he was hit in '17 and I just feel that I'd like to find him.'

Lally was spreading marmalade on a piece of toast. 'Well, we'll just have to ask the Porter at the desk and he'll know and then maybe we could all go and help you. That is if you'd not object I mean to say?'

Amy seemed pleased at the idea and said she didn't relish the idea of going on her own and that one day perhaps we could make an excursion, it wasn't very far away and she also believed that Miss Cavell was buried in the same place and that would be very interesting for us all. We didn't know who Miss Cavell was so I didn't really see that it could be so very interesting to go and look for two people we didn't know and had never heard about and who were dead. It was much better to be on the beach. But if Lally had offered then we had to go, for nothing would put her off once she had made up her mind or given her word.

'Fancy having to go and look at dead people when you are on holiday,' grumbled my sister when we were all standing in the lobby waiting for The Parents to come down and start the morning by going to the oyster beds. 'I think it's very silly indeed. And we don't even know them so it won't even be interesting.' But she said it in a whisper to me so no one else heard and she knew I agreed because I nodded. But it wasn't going to be today, and with any luck they might forget all about it in time.

The oyster beds were quite a way from Wimereux, along a very pretty road running straight as an arrow through lovely flat fields which rolled away for miles and miles to the sky. It was a very hot morning, and sitting up on the top of the coach-thing I could see all round me as we clip-clopped slowly along behind a bony white horse. The coach was black, and the old lady driving the horse was all in black, with a floppy bonnet on her head. Angelica and I, being the eldest and tallest, had to sit on the top beside her, one on each side, while Amy, Lally, and the other three sat squashed up inside. Our parents had gone on ahead in our father's big silver O.M. motor-car, all laughing and talking.

The sun shone down on the little streams and woods, and sent long black shadows from the tall trees along the road, across us like black bars. We could hear the birds singing, and the clip clop of the horses hooves and that's all, except for the creaking of the carriage which swayed about a bit and made Amy feel rather giddy.

Angelica sat staring ahead, holding onto the little iron rail round the seat, as if she was on a rather nasty thing at a fairground. I wished my sister was there instead because she would have much preferred it – she was very fond of horses, even the back part of them which was, sometimes, rather rude. Swaying about on top of the carriage, and feeling so happy in the sun and being so high up and looking forward to the oyster beds, I asked Angelica who the dead lady was with Amy's brother. Angelica gave me a pitying smile and pushed her pigtails over her shoulder with the hand that wasn't holding on to the iron rail.

'Miss Cavell is nothing to do with Amy's brother. She's just been laid to rest in the same place as he has. That's all.'

'But who was she? I mean why does Amy want to go and see her grave?'

'She was a very brave lady who was a nurse and a spy and got shot by the Germans,' she said, all in one breath so that I could hardly understand her, what with the swaying about and the clip clopping and creaking and the old black lady wobbling about between us. 'Was she really a spy?' I called out, wondering if I had heard her correctly.

'Yes. Yes, she was a sort of spy but she was a nice one because she was British, and the Germans hated her and shot her at dawn.'

The coach joggled about over a large pot-hole in the road and she grabbed the iron rail with both her hands and didn't seem inclined to say anything more on the subject. So I didn't say anything else either.

Suddenly the old lady made some noises to the horse, and pulled at the reins and we turned off the main road down a little rutted lane, which made the coach wobble about very alarmingly and even I had to grab the iron rail at my side lest I slipped off or fell into the old woman's lap. And then we were rolling along a quite high dyke which ran in a straight line down to the sea. On either side of us were huge square ponds, almost as big as tennis courts, and they shone and glinted in the bright sunlight like mirrors lying flat in the fields.

'The oyster beds! The oyster beds!' I cried but no one heard me inside the coach and Angelica had gone pale from the rutted road and didn't seem a bit interested.

It was very beautiful indeed. At the far end of the dyke there was a little clump of buildings like a farm, and I could see the sun shining on the silver of our father's motor-car, and streaking the sea with long lines of gold. It was very hot, and for once I was quite glad to be wearing my white cotton 'hate'.

It was a farm, an oyster farm, and as we clattered into the yard the Parents, who were all sitting at a long wooden table drinking out of little glasses, waved and cheered as if we had arrived from Africa or somewhere. They were all very jolly and helped everyone out of the coach while Angelica and I started to clamber down the sides. Angelica said she must go first and I was to wait until she got to the ground. She was just frightened that I'd see her bloomers or something. I was much too excited to see the oyster beds to bother about her old bloomers anyway.

We had a very nice time at the oyster beds, and were allowed to go with an old man who only spoke French to catch our own in a thing like a big wire shrimping net. The water in the beds was so clear, and so shallow, that you could see the oysters quite plainly, lying all over the sandy bottom, like fat buns. Some had green seaweed growing on them, some were very small indeed, and some were really very big. We carried them back to the table in a wooden bucket and the Parents cheered and seemed delighted and made us sit down together as if it was a sort of a party. Which in a way it was, all of us together and in the sunshine and so happy. Our father said that as it would be our first oysters we should be allowed a little glass of wine to have with them, and when Lally looked a bit put out, he said that it was a Celebration to have your first oyster and it was like launching a ship: you couldn't do it without a little wine.

So the glass jugs of wine arrived at the table, and lemonade for Paul, who was the youngest and didn't have wine or oysters yet, and then the big plates arrived surrounded with seaweed and piled high with the oysters all opened and sparkling in the sun. My sister went white when she saw them.

'They're raw,' she hissed.

'I know. That's how you eat them.'

'Raw?'

'Yes. Sometimes they get cooked.'

'Alive?' Her voice was almost a wail and Angelica and Beth looked at her with a start and then at the great plates of oysters before them.

'They can't be alive!' said Angelica. 'It's like being a cannibal!' Then big bowls of cut lemons and bottles of vinegar were plonked on the wooden table and all the parents started to stretch out for the food. My sister sat shocked into silence while everyone except Lally and Amy raised their glasses in a toast and cried 'Bon appetit!' No one took any notice after that, on purpose, and just got on with the eating part. Our father said to me to watch how he did it, with a fork, while Uncle John just took up the whole shell and emptied everything into his mouth.

'You don't swallow them like your Uncle,' said our father. 'You just chump them . . . that's the right way!'

Uncle John winked at me across the table. 'All a matter of personal taste, my boy . . . you swaller them or you chew them up. Aren't any rules, just personal taste!' He quickly swallowed another one. 'Food of the Gods!' he said. 'Food of the Gods!'

Lally took her fork and speared an oyster from its shell which she politely offered to my horrified sister who shook her head from side to side and covered her mouth with both her hands, watching, with wide eyes, as Lally put it into her mouth and chewed it up happily.

Seeing Lally looking so cheerful I said, 'It's the same as winkles, that's all.'

'Winkles are *boiled*.'

'Well, even if they are . . . they don't feel anything.'

'No, but I will! All crawling about inside me alive.'

'You just chew them up and then they won't.'

'Poor little things . . . that would be killing them then.'

'If our father does it it can't possibly hurt them.' She really was very silly. She stuck her fork hard into the wooden table and said:

'You haven't even *tried* one yet so how can you possibly know?'

I grabbed a fork from the pile beside me, took an oyster, put it in my mouth and ate it. Her face fell open like an old cupboard door.

'There!' I said.

'Oh, poor little thing . . . poor little thing,' she wailed; but it was the most lovely taste I had ever had. Salt, sea, slippery, sweet and cool. I chewed it with pleasure so that she would see and also so that it really would not flop about inside me. Because she had put me off a bit with that. But not off enough.

'It's lovely!' I cried to everyone as if they didn't know. 'It's lovely . . . you must eat them, it's easy and they are beautiful.'

Our father was very pleased and raised his glass to me and so did our mother who was laughing and looking pretty and happy. I could have eaten the whole plate but Lally counted out five more and that was that, but I ate them as slowly as possible to make them last, and sipped my glass of wine just like our father. I felt it was a very important day.

Later there was a big fish and then cheese and fruit, and after it was all over the Parents all got into the O.M. with many waves and kisses and drove away and we were to follow, when we felt like it, in the carriage after we had had a 'bit of a paddle' on the long sandy beach beyond the farm.

The Chesterfields went off shrimping along the edge of the sea which seemed to be feeling as lazy as we were because it just nudged the sand gently and hardly moved at all, but far away out where it ended against the sky, some big white clouds started growing into the hot blue like enormous cauliflowers. Lally was helping us with our sand castle which had a tower at each corner and a moat all round and a very big tower in the middle which we were decorating with razor-shells and little round pink ones. She stood up and dusted the sand off her hands against her skirt and looked out to sea.

'Shouldn't wonder we had a bit of a storm presently. Those clouds don't look too good to me,' and she tramped slowly up the beach to where Amy was sitting on her folding stool, which she always carried with her everywhere, reading her phrase book under a parasol.

'Did you really like those dreadful oysters?' said my sister.

'They were marvellous.'

'But I mean what did they taste like, all alive and squirmy?'

'It wasn't a bit squirmy.'

'Well . . . you know what I mean. All alive.'

'It tasted just like the smell of rock-pools.'

'How could it? Silly. You can't taste a smell!'

'You can. And they did. Exactly.'

'Tasting like a smell. I've never heard of anything so soppy.' She started to dig out a bit more of the moat under the drawbridge and a lump of wall fell down and we had to splash more water on it to hold it up, and she said: 'Well, perhaps next time I'll try one and see for myself . . . just to try, that's all, and if I don't like it I can always just spit it out, can't I?' and Lally called us to come on and start getting ready to go back, because the carriage was waiting and the clouds were getting a bit big.

'We don't want to get stuck in a storm here,' she called. 'So make haste all of you and get ready or we shall have the Prince of Wales waiting about in the hotel, and we don't want that, do we?'

While we were all drying ourselves and putting on sandals and shorts and things, and pushing each other over on the sand while we stood on one leg, Lally picked up Amy's little brown book and was rifling through it interestedly. 'Humph!' she cried 'I don't think that this is going to be much good to us, Amy . . . whatever would I want muslin for, I ask you?'

Amy was combing Paul's hair and looked rather cross. 'I don't know, I'm sure,' she said. 'My father, God rest his soul, said it was a very useful book to have with you when you were Abroad.' Lally went on rifling through the pages.

'I've no doubt it was when he came, but this is 1898 and what would I be doing in a draper's shop saying, "This muslin is too thin, have you something thicker?" . . . Goodness me! What *would* I be wanting muslin for, I ask you?'

Amy started to look rather red in the face and huffy and she pulled Paul's hair so hard that he yelled and fell over in the sand, and she had to say she was sorry and try to find the parting again. 'Oh! do hold still!' she cried. 'You really are a flibbertigibbet and no mistake.' But really she knew it was her fault because Lally had flustered her. 'You might want to use it for jelly-bags,' she said tucking Paul's shirt into his shorts and trying to fix his snake-belt which had got stuck.

'I might,' agreed Lally. 'And then I might not. But I grant you that . . . although I can't for the life of me see why.'

Amy fixed the belt and told Paul to get on his sandals and sat down rather heavily on her stool. 'There are a lot of very useful things if you look under "Travelling" and "Hospital" and "At The Station",' she said, trying to close her parasol, because a hot wind was beginning to blow and the sand was scattering all over the place and stinging our faces.

'At The Hospital,' read Lally in a laughing voice, 'my leg, arm, foot, head, elbow, nose, finger is broken! It doesn't say anything about neck, I notice, so where would that get you?'

'If your neck was broken, the dear God knows, you'd not be able to speak so that's why they left the word out . . . it stands to reason surely.'

The big clouds were starting to cover the sun, and the sands were growing dark, the sea was flat and grey looking in spite of the hot wind which was now really starting, tumbling the folded towels across the beach so that we had to run after them while Lally was still holding the book open and reading bits from it while the pages blew and flapped in her hands. 'Travelling! "The Postillion Has Been Struck By Lightning" – well!' she cried laughing. 'That wouldn't get us far today, would it?'

Amy got up off her stool and started to fold it.

'It might, my dear,' she said, 'considering the weather. We had all better be off before the Heavens open and it's a long journey back.' And she called about like an old hen for the Chesterfields and they started wandering up to the farm. We followed behind with towels and baskets and buckets and spades and a knotted handkerchief full of shells which my sister had collected, and a long wet strip of bobbly seaweed which was a present for our mother.

As we plodded up through the hot, sliding sand, I said, 'What's a postillion?' and Lally said it was a man who sat on top of the coaches in the olden days and blew a horn to tell people it was coming. 'I'm afraid we'll have to find something a bit newer for the cemetery or the dear knows where we'll all end up.'

At the farm the old lady who drove the coach was waving her arms and holding a big umbrella and pointing to the sky. It was getting darker and darker, and the big cauliflower clouds were almost right over our heads, and were heavy and purple-coloured with golden edges. As we started clambering into the coach the first plip-plots of rain fell, as big as threepenny pieces, splattering into the dusty road and pattering on the windows.

'Surely we can squeeze poor Angelica inside with us!' cried Amy; but there wasn't an inch of room with all the baskets, and buckets, towels, and shrimping nets, so we both had to climb on to the top of the coach with the old lady, who was covering herself with bits of macintosh and shoved the umbrella at me to hold over us while she pulled the reins and started off down the long dyke, through the oyster beds now all potted and spotted with fat raindrops.

It wasn't a very comfortable journey, and when we got to the rutted lane which led to the main road, the coach rolled about like a fishing boat, and everyone screamed out from inside. But the old lady was not going to wait for anyone, and she hit the horse quite hard so that we rattled and rumbled and swayed along like anything, and Angelica called out and hung on to the iron rails and the rain came pouring down, so that I couldn't hold the umbrella *and* hold on at the same time, what with the wind roaring and jiggling everything. When we reached the main road and turned on to it, the old lady slowed down a bit and the wheels went a bit smoother, and she started to try and put the old bits of macintosh round Angelica and myself, while I tried to hold the umbrella over all our heads. But it wasn't much use because I kept sticking the spokes in her eyes or hitting her on the head with the thing, so she was getting wetter and wetter and looking very cross. Suddenly there was a flash and a zig-zag of forked lightning which stabbed into the fields beside us. Angelica flung herself into the old lady's lap and I threw the umbrella on to the floor and held on to her as well; she just walloped the horse a bit harder and on we went, splashing through the rain and the great crash of thunder which roared down over us and which so frightened the horse that he galloped down the road with his ears flat to his head and the old lady waving her whip in the air.

On we rattled, with the wheels all going wobbly so that I feared one of them would presently fall off and go winging out into the ditches on either side. There was another great zig-zag of lightning just behind us and then a terrific crash of thunder. The rain was streaming down so hard that I could hardly see, but I clung on to the old lady and just hoped that if I didn't hold the iron rail I wouldn't get struck the next time there was a flash. All I could see of Angelica was one arm and a flying pigtail with a ragged red ribbon streaming in the wind. I wondered if she had been struck and was dead. But she wasn't.

And then the first houses came, and a bus, and the road got smoother and the rain became gentler and in a short time we rumbled down the Promenade towards the hotel. There was no one about. And the beaches were quite empty except for lots of tumbled deck-chairs and tents which had blown down in the storm, and now the sea was really rough and swirling and crashing round the wooden breakwaters.

In front of the hotel, under the big glass blind, we all got off the dripping coach, the horse was steaming as if he had been boiled, and Angelica didn't bother about whether I could see her knickers or not, she just scrambled down off the top looking like a drowned rat, her hair all straggly and the red ribbons untied and squiggling like red worms. Lally got out first and pulled my sister from inside, looking very red and rather cross.

'Beth and Paul have been sick,' she said flatly. 'And all over my floral. And Amy's in a bad way, too, I'm afraid. Run inside and get the keys and open the rooms, there's a good boy. We'll be up directly, just take your own things with you,' she added, shoving towels and shrimping nets and seaweed into my arms.

'A fine postillion you made,' she said. 'You didn't blow your horn once!'

'And I didn't get struck by lightning either,' I said.

'You get on up there,' said Lally, 'or you'll get struck by lightning from another direction!'

And as I hurried off up the steps with my sister hard behind me, she called out to put on the kettle and to ask the maid for an extra cup for Amy who would need it.

It was quite a long climb up the white, chalky road to the cemetery. On either side there were fields full of standing corn, green as green, and rolling away into the distance. The sky was clear and blue, with one or two little fat clouds gently drifting towards the sea which sparkled in the brilliant sunlight. A lark went whirling up like a spinning top as we passed, singing very loudly to keep us away from his nest somewhere, but there was no other sound except the whispers in the corn and Lally puffing a bit behind us.

'Don't scuff your feet!' she called out between puffs. 'There's enough dust without you making more. I'm white as Lot's wife as it is.'

Amy was walking behind with her veil pulled down all round her straw man's hat to keep off the flies, she said, and the dust of the road. She had her stool, and her big bag and a small bunch of flowers which we had stopped to buy outside the hotel when we left for the bus to the town where the cemetery was. My sister and I were a bit worried that we hadn't got any flowers to put on Amy's Brother's Grave . . . if we found him . . . but we picked quite a big bunch of poppies which were growing all along the road, to put on the gave of the Miss Cavell.

'She'll like that,' said Lally with assurance. 'She'd think it very nice of two English children to remember her and pick her some flowers.'

The gates of the cemetery were very white and tall, and made of stone. There was a big cross over them and a wall all the way round. Amy was rather pale and nervous, and we were quiet so as not to disturb her because it was a very sad thing she was doing and we did not want to get in the way. When we got inside the cemetery we all stopped. It was the biggest one we had ever seen, much bigger than the one at Teddington or even the one in our own village where we used to have the fair. It was huge. Miles and miles of little white crosses, and long green-grassy paths between them all with little black pointed trees every now and then. There weren't any flowers on many of the graves. Some had little jam jars with a few wilting daisies which looked very sad. And some had rose bushes growing beside them – which was rather nice. Here and there we could see little groups of people in black walking down the grassy paths, or a single person kneeling by a grave all alone.

'Oh dear!' said Lally, in a very low voice. 'So many; so many poor souls.' She took us both by a hand and we started to walk slowly among the white crosses looking at the names; just things like F.J. Jones, and a number and the name of the regiment and sometimes the date. But what was awful was just where it had Unknown written. Just one word. And we all wondered who they were and of course no one would ever come to see them, because they were unknown, and no one put flowers there.

Amy had a handkerchief to her face but she was peering about her and for once she looked quite nice and not irritating.

'I wonder what to do?' she said worriedly. 'There are so many, so many, and I don't know where I'd begin.'

Lally said: 'You go over to that fellow who's weeding there, I expect he belongs to the place and he'll tell you. I imagine you have to look under the O's', she said, giving Amy a little push.

Amy looked doubtful, but she opened her bag and took our her phrase book where she had marked some pages for 'Asking Directions', which she had shown us in the bus, and nervously walked up to the man who was busy weeding and when he looked up at her we all got quite a start because he only had half a face. She started to read from her book and then we heard him speak to her in real Cockney and he laughed and said he was English and what could he do for her? Well, it was a big relief, and presently, scratching his head, he took her off up one of the long grassy paths far away from us. My sister was very silent. The bunch of poppies was getting a bit droopy, and we both felt rather miserable in that quiet place with so many white crosses shining in the sun.

Lally cleared her throat and told us to cheer up. 'Goodness me! You look a couple of miseries I must say! You ought to be very happy that you're both here on such a lovely day as this, because all these poor men here died just so that you could be walking about in the sun without a care in the world. They wouldn't think you were very grateful if they could see your miserable faces, now would they? You see what it says on top of that big stone cross there? Their Sacrifice Was Not In Vain. So just you remember that. And show your manners.' She was really quite bossy, but it was only because she was feeling sad too, and didn't want to show it.

'What shall we do about Amy?' said my sister for something to say, and Lally said we were to leave her be so that she could find her brother in peace. 'It's a private thing,' she said firmly. 'So now let's go and see if we can find Miss Cavell.'

Just then, another wounded man came along and was very nice and said that he came from Herne Bay, where Lally had once spent a holiday, but he shook his head and said he didn't know a Miss Cavell. She wasn't here, he said, not as far as he knew, which was a bit disappointing. He took us all over the place and we saw some quite big graves with weeping angels and stone pots on them, but there was no one called Miss Cavell. So Lally suggested that my sister should put her flowers on one of the 'unknown' graves, just as a sign of respect for the dead. And before they died themselves.

'Amy must have got it all a bit muddled,' said Lally. 'And no one could really blame her because this was a very Trying Day for her.'

My sister put the poppies on the grave rather nervously as if someone would tell her not to, but the man from Herne Bay was very nice and said that quite a lot of people came and did that and that later on he'd try and find a little jar to put them in; he said there was probably one in his shed. Then he asked me if I would like to see something very fine, and when I said I would, he limped away up a long grassy path to a big box thing. Well, it looked like a box. It was standing at the head of a very tidy grave, and it had a glass cover. Inside the box was a beautiful uniform jacket and a cap with gold braid all over it, and the jacket had a lot of medals and buttons. It was all a bit faded by the sun, but even so it sparkled. But it looked sadder even than the crosses, all empty, and the man from Herne Bay said that it belonged to a French General or someone and that his wife had asked for it to be like this.

'Won't last long,' said Lally cheerfully. 'The moths have been at it already, not to mention the wet.'

The man agreed and said the winters there were really cruel but he thought that I'd be interested. And in a way I was. But I didn't feel particularly happy about any part of the day really. It all had a Holy and sad feeling and it was so quiet and still that not even a bird sang. Suddenly we saw Amy walking alone down the little sloping path. I think she had had a good cry, for her eyes were rather red and so was her nose, but she was making a little wavering smile as she came across the rows of crosses to us, and had put her phrase book in her bag. The man with the wounded face wasn't there any longer, so I suppose she'd found the grave and he'd left her to be private too. We all sat down on a stone seat, and waited for her to reach us, after we had said goodbye and thank you to the Herne Bay man.

It was quite nice to sit down, and the stone seat was hot in the sun, but Amy was soon standing beside us pushing her handkerchief into her pocket.

'Do you want to come and see him?' she asked.

It was just another grave like all the rest. A white cross and his name, Peter Eric O'Shea, and a number after it.

'What does Cpl mean?' asked my sister, and Amy said that he was a Corporal and very clever. 'Is he really under there?' said my sister, and Amy said she hoped so. 'And long as I know *where* he is, it doesn't feel so bad,' she said with a sigh. She stood for a minute looking out over all the crosses which surrounded us like a white sea. 'Oh the grief, dear God,' she said sadly. 'Oh the grief and the terrible waste of it all.'

And then we started off silently down the path towards the gates with the cross on the top. We kept a bit behind the two of them, looking at the names and numbers and regiments, but just as we got near the bottom, I saw Amy's head bow down and Lally slipped her hand into Amy's arm and lifted her own head high. We walked down the road quite far behind them, scuffing the dust into white clouds all round us.

There was no one to tell us not to.

EIGHT

I was sitting under the elderberry bush up by the privy, which was where I always went when I wanted to have a good 'think' with no one to disturb me, and Lally stuck her head out of a window, shook a rug very hard over the sill, and called down: 'Don't sit there like yesterday's loaf, with a shopping list as long as my arm on top of the copper and a ten shilling note, and don't forget the change. Also take the milk-can, should you see Mr Mitchell and get me a pint and a half and a small pot of cream which we'll have with the gooseberries.' She slapped the rug a few more times against the flint wall, covered the garden in dust, and went back in. She always seemed to know exactly where I'd be when she wanted me, which was very aggravating.

'I'll come too,' said my sister, pulling on her Hate. 'I'll bring a bit of sugar for the pony if we do see Mr Mitchell, and if we don't I'll eat it myself.'

We collected the milk-can, the list, the ten shilling note, and started off down the field to the gully. It was quite a long way to the village, easily two miles, so I was pretty sure that I wasn't going to have much of a 'think' that morning, which was a pity. Because something was just beginning in my head when Lally called me.

The poppies were nearly all over, and so were the buttercups; the long high hedge running down the field beside the gully was thick with Queen Anne's lace and Campion. Summer, as Herbert Fluke would say, was getting a move on. But the sun was still high and hot, and the Downs fat and green, like the bellies of horses, rounded against the sky, glossy and rippling where the wind ruffled through the thick summer grasses.

'You've got a mood on,' said my sister after a bit of a silence.

'I was just having a "think" when Lally yelled about this, and now I can't remember what it was that I was thinking, that's all.'

She was skiffling along in the white dust of the path kicking empty snail shells about.

'Was it about something lovely?'

'No. Actually. It was about a Play.'

'Oh! That!' and she lost interest. She always did. The moment I even said the very word she lost interest and went off on her own. This time she started picking a spot on her chin. I slapped her hand and she got such a shock that she dropped the milk-can and it rolled and clattered down the path and the lid flew into the hedge.

'Look what you've done! Just look! You stupid fool!' She was furious because I had shocked her, not because she'd dropped the can, and she went scrabbling about in the grasses collecting all the bits together. I went on down the hill and heard her clonking along behind me.

'It's all full of dust and leaves and things, and you could have hurt me doing that! Hitting a person and giving them a fright. I might get something terrible on my chin now and it'll be all your fault.'

'You're not supposed to pick spots, you know that.'

'I wasn't picking it. I was feeling it.'

'Same thing.'

'It's not the same thing. Now I might get ringworm just because you're in a mood.'

I didn't answer her, but started to run a bit so that she had to hurry to keep up with me. As I got to the old iron gate into the main road she suddenly made a terrible noise and I thought she might have been bitten or something because she was standing quite still just clutching her skirt with her face all screwed up.

'What's the matter?' I called.

'You're vile! You're vile!' She dropped the can into the grass and started patting her stupid skirt with both her hands. 'The sugar lumps!' she wailed. 'I've lost them . . . you made me . . . you made me when you hit me. They've gone. Now I can't feed Daisy. You're vile!'

I slammed the gate and crossed the road and left her there yowling away. But by the time I had reached the little bridge over the stream where we caught roach, she had got to me, all puffing and breathy, mumbling away about her rotten old sugar. I was glad she hadn't been bitten because I really did like her very much when she was being all right, but when she wasn't, like now about the sugar, I didn't at all. So I just started whistling and took no notice. It was the only thing to do, because I had completely forgotten what it was I was thinking about up there under the elderberry.

Mitchell's cart was standing in the shade just as we got to Sloop Lane. It had two big wheels and was painted yellow and black, and had a big silver milk churn on top with brass letters spelling out MITCHELLS DAIRY – NEW MILK all round it, and silver ladles hanging in different sizes to measure the milk. We got the pint and a half and the cream, and my sister told the stupid fat pony all about the sugar, and Mr Mitchell said he couldn't change a ten shilling note, and what did I think he was, the Bank of England? and he'd get it next time around. So we went on into the Market Square and over the cobbled road to the grocers.

Wildes was in the middle of the squre, next door to the Magpie Inn and opposite Woods the Butchers. It had two bulgy windows with lots of little panes of glass, and a front door painted black with golden letters over the top spelling the name.

Inside it was cool, and dim, and smelled of bacon and paraffin, and fresh bread. On one side was a counter with tins of tea behind and barrels of apples and dried peas and corn and walnuts in front of it. On the ceiling hung dustpans and brushes with wooden handles, rat traps, lavatory rolls threaded like beads on loops of string, and bunches of enamel mugs and saucepans which jingled and jangled in the wind when you opened the door.

On the other side was another counter with the scales, big brass ones with all the weights sparkling in a row from very big to very small like the Three Bears; and there were big blocks of butter, and white tubs of lard, and slabs of bacon and legs of ham hanging from the beams just above your head. It really was a very nice place indeed, and there was always such a lot to see that we never minded waiting about while Mr Wilde checked off the things on the list and stuffed them all into the shopping bag. At the very end of the shop, past all the barrels of apples and dog biscuits and things, there was another counter with a wire cage thing over it. This was the Post Office and Miss Maltravers, who played the organ, sat behind it looking like a ghost-lady with her wispy hair and white sleeves over her frock to keep it clean. She was always scribbling away at something, or weighing a parcel, or licking a stamp. She was very busy indeed.

'There is some post for you if you don't mind taking it up and saving the van a journey,' she called, and slid something under the cage at us. 'One's a postcard from your mother in France, says she's having a lovely time and they'll be home on Sunday, God willing, and the other's something for Miss Jane from Debenham & Freebody, a catalogue by the look of it, which seems a long way to go for a coat when Seaford is on the doorstep.'

She really was cheeky. But we didn't like to say so because she was a good friend of the Vicar's and was very churchy, what with her organ and doing the flowers and reciting poems at the Church Teas. So we just didn't say anything; except behind her back.

When we were crossing the river by the wooden bridge my sister said: 'She really is the nosiest woman in the world. She spoiled our postcard! Fancy reading someone's postcard and telling them everything in the middle of the shop! Like that time when she told Lally there was some sad news for her in a telegram and Lally went all white and she said, "I'm afraid your brother's had a little operation and he's quite poorly." Do you remember? Right in front of everyone else and Lally nearly had a turn there and then. And anyway it was only his appendicitis or something. I think she's nosy and mean.'

The postcard was of a big white church and it said: 'Having a lovely time. Home on Sunday evening. Hope you are being good. Love from Daddy and

Mummy,' and that was all, but it was very nice, or would have been if Miss Maltravers hadn't spoiled it.

'I know what we should do,' said my sister, trying not to spill the milk as we scrambled on to the main road and across it up to the iron gate. 'We should send her a postcard from Eastbourne or somewhere, and say on it "Miss Maltravers has dandruff and that's why her hair falls down all the time." That would teach her a really good lesson. It would frighten her to bits, I bet.'

It was cool in the kitchen and the table was all laid for lunch with a big jug of ginger beer waiting. Lally was very indignant.

'Jerusalem! She is a nosy parker, what's it got to do with her if I get a catalogue from Debehams, I'd like to know? I'd like to give her a piece of my mind, I really would. Drat the woman, she really gives me the pip!' But she took her catalogue and went off up to her room to have a look at it, and presently we could hear her singing away 'It Happened In Monterey' at the top of her voice, so we felt that she must have found something she liked, because she only sang songs like that when she was particularly pleased. The song was her next favourite one after 'The Song Of The Dawn' and she only liked them because this John Boles sang them and she thought he had nice legs or something funny like that. We thought he was a bit soft-looking really, and rather like Fred Brooks, the bus conductor, when she took us to Eastbourne to see a Talkie at the Palace. It was very much forbidden to go to the Pictures and our Parents always said No, but this time, while they were away, Lally had longed to go and see John Boles singing and she had taken us as a treat.

'It's deceitful, I know,' she said in the bus, 'and I shall get punished for my sins, but what else do I do? I can't leave you both outside, can I? And I've set my heart on it and it is Perfectly Suitable because it's all music and dancing and there is nothing in it to give you a fright. And it's all in colour and you can hear it too. So we'll pretend it's a treat, but if you mention it by so much as a whisper, I'll be sent packing and you'll have someone else to run errands for.'

It was very curious to sit in the dark and see all the colours and the lovely costumes, and even funnier to hear it like the wireless only much louder. But we didn't think much of John Thingummy – except he was just like Fred Brooks which annoyed Lally very much.

'If young Fred Brooks had legs like those and a voice like that he could carry me off tomorrow and I wouldn't raise a whimper!' she said, putting her hand on her hip and doing her Haughty Look.

A long time ago she had taken me to see a film in a Picture Palace in London, and it was all about a little boy who got stuck on a sinking ship in a storm. It was very thrilling and I was enjoying it very much until someone locked him in a cabin trunk just as the ship began to go down, and I got so frightened that I ate half the skip off my school cap and swallowed it. And was very sick later. 'The child is bringing up tweed and cardboard! I wonder why?' said our mother. And then Lally confessed and got a ticking off. So our mother said Never Again because I was too impressionable or something. So Lally had to go alone on her days off, except this time at Eastbourne when we were deceitful. We never told of course, and we had rather a difficult time not talking about John Whatsisname and Mexico and how they got the colours on the screen to move and sing and all at the same time. But we managed in the end, although we all felt a bit guilty about having been anyway. It didn't matter so much about the songs, I mean we could sing them quite easily all over the place because Lally had records of them which she used to play on her little black portable gramophone. So that was quite easy, and we knew all the words backwards because she only had eight records and we got very used to them.

Sometimes, in the evenings if she didn't feel like reading to us from *A Peep Behind the Scenes*, which was a terribly sad book and made us all sob like anything when it got to the part where the little girl's mother dies in the caravan in the circus and only the clown is there to hold her hand, we used to have a Little Concert. We wound up the black portable and started off always with 'It Happened In Monterey' and then 'The Song Of The Dawn' and then one or two more and always finished off with 'Spread A Little Happiness' which made us all feel cheerful. While we were listening to the concert, of course, there was a job to do. That was the trouble. You always knew when Lally said, 'What about a little cheer up, a Little Concert?' And then we had to clean the lamps, cut the rhubarb for the rhubarb and ginger jam, shell peas or something like that. I mean you never just sat there and thought about nothing or anything like that. But it was very nice and sometimes, not always, we were allowed a special treat and we put on a record called 'Laughing Gas' which was all about a man reading a Will and someone turns on the laughing gas and they all start laughing. It was terribly funny and we almost made ourselves ill. Sometimes we used to roll on the floor, it was so funny, and Lally said that we'd do ourselves a mischief but we only got hiccups. She didn't let us play it too much for that reason.

But whatever the concert was, we always ended with 'Spread A Little Happiness' and that put us all in a thoughtful mood – until we both started remembering the Gas song, and started to giggle and got sent to bed sniggering and hiccuping.

Having supper with our parents in the big room was very good. We all sat down together at the big round table. Our father did the carving and Lally served the vegetables or I did, or my sister did, and everyone was very happy and said what we had each been doing during the day.

The room was whitewashed, like the kitchen, with an inglenook fireplace which had two big wooden seats in it on each side of the fire, a polished brick floor and lots of fat wickerwork armchairs with feathery cushions. The lamp with the honeysuckle hung over the table, and there was another one near our father's chair where he could read more easily. There were lots of old jugs full of flowers, even in winter, and a clock with a boat in a storm on it and a slow swinging pendulum. This was really our Parents' private place to be, and we were only allowed there really if there were friends to tea or something, or if they had dinner with us all, otherwise we all spent our time in the big white kitchen, with the copper-fire and Minnehaha, the cat, for company. We liked it better there because we could do what we liked and it was difficult in the big room because people were reading or talking.

When our parents came back from Paris we had a chicken from The Court, and stuffing and new potatoes from the garden, and our father had brought back two big bottles of wine, and some rather smelly cheese, which he liked especially, and some mustard. So it was quite French and even Lally had a little sip of wine and everyone was very pleased to be together again.

'Hope you both behaved yourselves,' said our mother, not meaning it, and Lally said that we had been Treasures and very helpful, which always made us pleased although we knew she didn't mean that either.

'Because if not,' said our mother, 'it'll be a dreadful waste of two lovely presents from Paris.' And after dinner, when we had cleared away and helped with the washing up, we went back into the big room and there were the packages on the table, almost like Christmas.

My sister's package was, I noticed, a bit bigger than mine, but I had two to her one. And Lally had two as well. So it was all going to be fair. Lally got some stockings and a bottle of something which smelled of lemons and would make a bit of a change from Devonshire Violets; my sister had furniture for her dolls' house, and I got a wind-up racing car, blue and red, with a driver sitting inside and a paperweight thing which was a glass ball full of water and the Eiffel Tower with a little flag on top, and when you shook it hard it made a terrific snowstorm. It had 'Paris' written in blue writing on the base.

It was very nice in the big room with them both back. Even though it was very nice too with Lally and the cat, and going to the Picture Palace, which we had promised not to mention, and making jam and even having to go shopping every day almost. But it was a good comfortable feeling all being together again, and even Minnehaha came in and jumped on to my father's lap while he was reading his letters. Lally was having a very nice time talking like anything to our mother. She said she didn't count talking to children much, and missed the real Grown Ups, but all she was talking about was rotten old Miss Maltravers and being so nosy so it really wasn't different conversation, just the same as with us, but to someone else.

'She quite spoiled the children's postcard, you know. Reading it out like that.'

'I don't think she meant to be nosy,' said our mother. 'After all, anyone can read a postcard if they want to. They aren't supposed to be private, otherwise you would put them in an envelope, surely?'

Lally sniffed a bit and wouldn't give in. 'And telling everyone about my catalogue from Debenhams. *That's* cheeky, I must say!'

'But I expect that had the name printed on the outside, didn't it? So she wasn't really being nosy. After all, it is a small village, she doesn't get much fun, I imagine, or excitement for that matter.' Our mother was always very reasonable, and put like that, Miss Maltravers didn't seem to be so awful, especially if anyone could read anyone's postcard if they liked. I didn't know about that bit. But Lally was not best pleased.

'Well,' she said, gathering up all the wrapping paper from the gifts and making a neat little pile on the table, 'if she thinks it's exciting to read other people's letters, that's her business I suppose. But the next time I write off for anything, I'll tell them to put it in a plain envelope. I don't want the whole of Sussex to know I have it in mind to get a new coat for the winter, that's MY business. Come along you two . . .' she said, 'give your parents a bit of a rest and get up the wooden hill to Bedfordshire toot-sweet, it's well past time.'

The O.M. glimmered in the shade under the trees. It was beautiful, and we were all very proud of it. Our father most of all. It was his favourite thing, our mother said, next to *The Times* which is where he worked. She said he liked it better than us all put together, but we knew that wasn't true. It's just that she got a bit fed up having her hair blown all over the place when she had just had it 'done', and getting cold in the winter, and wet in the rain. The O.M. was all made of aluminium and was, our father said, an Open Tourer. It went very fast indeed, at least when he was driving it it did, and we got quite cold and wet sometimes when he couldn't be bothered to stop to put up the hood and the side windows.

My sister, Lally and I sat in the back together, under a black leather cover thing, with a separate windshield which had three sides and didn't keep the wind off us at all. We were quite warm under the black cover, but our heads poked out and got very cold, and red, so our father bought us each a leather helmet which covered us almost completely, with ear-muff things and goggles.

Lally grumbled a bit about getting her hair in a mess and one day had it all cut off, like a boy's, to save the trouble.

Our mother sat in front wrapped up in a moleskin rug, with scarves and things, but she still got terribly blown about and didn't like the car as much as we did. We all felt very swanky whizzing along in it, all silver with a lovely flying eagle on the bonnet and a very loud horn to frighten the wits out of people who were being slow, or getting in our father's way.

Sometimes, as a treat, we used to pack a big wicker hamper, load up with cups and kettles and bottles of water and a stove, travelling rugs and our father's paint-box, his easel, his stool, and his canvases and Minnehaha, and go off on a picnic somewhere far. Like Arundel, or Ashdown Forest, or Chichester: we used to leave the cottage quite early, after breakfast, and he never said where we were going, just that it was going to be a lovely place; and that was half the fun. But not for our mother. I mean she liked going on a picnic and making the sandwiches and the cold pies and things, but it was the getting there she didn't much like. Because our father would never stop if he could help it, until he wanted a little refreshment. And that could be hours and hours later. Well, nearly.

'Ulric! You really will have to stop soon.'

'Why, dear? We have just started off.'

'The children are starting to fidget.'

She could see us in her little side mirror. We couldn't do much ourselves because of our windscreen, and we couldn't shout because of the wind and the speed, and so we had to make signs so that she would see, which she nearly always did. If she didn't, Lally used to hold a big handkerchief up, so that it fluttered in the wind; she called it our Distress Signal. But still our father wouldn't stop.

'Ulric dear, please!' she would cry. We couldn't hear because of the screen, but we could jolly well tell what she was saying. And then we would reach an inn, usually one our father had chosen from a map long before we started out. It was usually the prettiest, with a garden or a lovely view, and where the beer was specially good. And we'd swerve into the courtyard and people would come out to look at the beautiful silver car from Italy, and we would all feel very pleased. Especially Lally who was longing to 'go' as much as we were.

'I do wish,' our mother would say, 'I do wish you'd listen to me.'

Our father would be very smiling and cheerful because he loved driving more than anything it seemed, especially on these picnic days, with the wind and the sun and a big glass of beer beside him.

'I do listen to you, darling, you know I do.'

'The children are not camels!'

'Well . . . it hasn't been *so* long. And now everything's all right.'

It usually was. Just. We had a packet of potato chips and American Ice Cream Sodas . . . and Lally had a shandy and we all sat in the sun and wondered where the next stop would be. Minnehaha had a collar and a lead and sat beside us spitting at any dog that was silly enough to come near.

Then off we went again, eating Rowntrees Clear Gums which our father always bought for us as a surprise, even though we knew he would do it, and he never forgot; we always pretended it was the first time. And it seemed like that on these days.

And then we had to find somewhere to stop for lunch, which was always very difficult because once our father got behind his wheel again he wanted to go almost to India before he would stop. We all used to shout and point out lovely places, with trees, and grass, and streams or woods, but he simply wouldn't listen.

'I can't stop here, it's on a corner,' he would shout over the windscreen. Or else it was on a hill going up, a hill going down, too muddy, or else we didn't see the place in time and he whizzed right past. Our mother got more and more cross, and sometimes it was nearly afternoon when we bumped on to a dusty bit of track and he found a place which was covered in old tin cans, bits of paper, or the remains of an old firesite. It was always a beastly place he chose, but he didn't seem to mind, and we all piled out and got the baskets and stove and things, and spread out the travelling rugs and cushions and tied Minnehaha to a tree or a stick or something.

It didn't really matter in the end. Especially when we had our slices of cold chicken pie, or meat loaf or whatever it was our mother had made for the day. She was a bit grumpy of course: because the ground was dirty and she usually had on a pretty white frock and had to sit carefully on the travelling rug. But our father was very happy, making a little fire from twigs and bits of log, which we didn't need because we had the stove, or going off to find somewhere he could sit and do a painting.

'Why we have to come fifty miles to sit in a rubbish heap to eat, I shall never know,' said our mother, laying out the mugs and packets of things to eat.

'We passed so *many* pretty places,' said Lally cheerfully. 'You'll never change him though, not now you won't. Give him his car and we're off no matter where. Anyway, the sun's out, and what we all need is a bit of something nice in our insides and then we'll all feel much better, and after lunch we can clear up the old tins and things and stick them in the bushes and everything will look a treat, you see.'

Going home, after tea which always tasted horrid out of Thermos flasks, in the golden light of the afternoon we were all very happy because the day, as always, had been happy too. Sometimes we stopped again at an inn for more lemonade and chips, but never more than one glass because of the Not Stopping Bit . . . but crunching up the chalky lane to the Cottage was really always the very best part. Our father drove the O.M. into a very small chalk quarry where it lived, just at the bottom of the long path up to the garden. And loaded with the baskets and hampers and rugs and the stove, we clambered up under the big elms to the wooden gate and then through the vegetable garden smelling warm in the early dusk.

Sometimes there were glow-worms glinting greenishly in the long grasses, and slow snails sliding gently across the path in the light of the torch. And the bitter-sweet scent of blackcurrant leaves filled the still summer evening as we brushed past them on the way to the kitchen door.

After the lamps were lit, the unpacking done and everything put away, and the table laid for supper in the big room, it was pleasant to slip outside and sit under the apple tree and look right down Great Meadow to the lamps sparkling in the dairy at the Court at Piggy Corner and think how nice our house must look from down there, like a lamp on a hill, with the windows glowing golden and smoke wisping from the tall chimney stack.

The dairy of the Court was right on a corner of the road, next door to the pigsties, and when we were coming back from anywhere in the O.M. we always knew just how near home we were by the smell, which is why we called it Piggy Corner. It wasn't a beastly smell, just a Farm Smell, and it always meant that we were going to turn left up the white road to the quarry and the house. And truly, coming home was about the nicest part of ever going out on a picnic.

Reg Fluke said that there was a pike in the river Ouse at Itford almost a yard long, and very fierce. He said no one had ever caught it although people had been trying and trying for years and years.

'Too wily . . . 'e knows a thing or two after all this time, I reckon. Old Hallam up at Selmeston said as 'ow once he did get 'im on his line but he fought so hard he broke it and dived away. Hallam reckons he's got about as many 'ooks in 'is jaws as he's got teeth, and I wouldn't wonder.'

It was decided that we would go and have a try oursleves. At least, he would go and try with his friend Percy Brooks, because they both had real fishing rods with reels and floats and all sorts of hooks and things, but they kindly said I could come with them as long as I brought some grub. So in a way I was quite included in the party, and I felt that it was all right to tell my sister and Lally that We were going to try for the Giant Pike in the Ouse. At first Lally was a bit put out and I was worried that she'd say No.

'Whereabouts in the Ouse, I'd like to know? It's miles away and you could fall in and then what?'

'Well . . . it's over near Beddingham, across the railway, and if I fell in Reg or Percy would get me out and it would be very exciting if we did catch it.'

I was laying the table for lunch, and she was basting a leg of lamb in the oven, kneeling on the floor with a red face, from the heat, and spooning the juice over the crackling top.

'And pray how will you get there? Beddingham's nearly at Lewes! There is no money for bus fares, you know . . . it'll take you half a day to walk.'

'We are going to go over the Downs, up past Red Barn and along the top to the Beacon and then down to the Brooks. We'll have to start early in the morning, and I've got to take the grub.'

'The what?' She looked up from the oven with raised eyebrows, the spoon in her hand, her apron all bumfley from kneeling.

'The food, I mean.'

She slammed the oven door and took the ladle over to the sink. 'They'll spoil your ways those two, you mark my words. Grub indeed! What sort of *grub*, may I ask, do you envisage?'

She was being cross, I could feel that, and she was trying to find a way of saying no without really saying no. She never wanted to actually refuse if she could help it, but it was useful if something difficult came along which was putting off a bit. Like food.

'I'll make some sandwiches, and perhaps an egg or something. I don't want much,' I said quickly, and so that she couldn't interrupt me I went on very fast and said that I would make them myself the night before, if she would let me have the egg to boil, and that I had three pence saved and could use that for some lemonade or something. I could see that she really wasn't best pleased because she banged the steamer quite hard on top of the copper, and the lid fell off and all the steam went up in the air and she cried out angrily: 'Drat the thing! What do you want to come and ask me difficult things for when I'm steaming cauliflower!'

But in the end it was all right and she said I could go, and gave me some cold lamb for the sandwiches and a new egg to boil and I did them all myself without any trouble, and with no mess. No mess was very important with Lally.

Next morning, very early, while the sun was making long thin shadows across the gully and the dew was like silver beads everywhere, I went down the brick path to meet Reg and Perce with my satchel full of sandwiches and a bottle of home-made ginger beer.

The Market Place was very quiet and still at that time in the morning; not even Mitchells Dairy was about. The shops were all closed and there was only a sleepy-looking girl sweeping the steps of the Magpie Inn. By the time we had climbed up to the top of Long Burgh Hill I was pretty well puffed out but I couldn't say much because the other two had rods and baskets and things, and I only had my satchel with the sandwiches and my bottle of ginger beer. Walking along the grassy track behind Reg and Perce up on the top there, made me feel very good. The air was still, not yet hot, and all about us lay the whole of Sussex. On the right was all the weald fading away into the misty morning in pale blue and green ridges; on the left you looked down to the sea, sparkling and winking in the sun, and Newhaven, like a toy town with red and grey roofs all jumbled together and the church spire sticking up, and beyond that the long quay poking a bent finger into the sea.

There was no sound at all, just our feet through the dew-silvered grasses and the larks; now and then sheep bleating, because this was all sheep land. And every so often we came to one of the dew ponds which people said were so deep that you got drowned in them if you slid down the sides, but Reg said that was all My Eye and that there was nothing in them except a few efts and water-boatmen, and if they were that deep why did the shepherds let the sheep drink from them, which is what they were for? Which seemed reasonable.

When we got to Firle Beacon we had a bit of a sit down. It was halfway, and Reg and Perce had an apple and I drank some of my ginger beer, and we lay in the sun listening to the sheep bells and the larks singing and the wind withering about in the gorse. At least I did. They were talking about bait and hooks and just where the exact place to find the pike was. Reg had taken off his wellingtons and I noticed that he was wearing grey socks with holes in them, but I didn't say anything and presently we packed up and started on the path again to Beddingham Hill.

By the time we reached it, and could look down over the valley below to Lewes and the castle sitting on top of the town like a piece of broken pumice stone, and Mount Caburn like a volcano, the sun was getting high and it was already warm. But they seemed very pleased because they could see the Ouse winding up the valley like a tin snake, and Reg said the tide would be in by the time we got down there. As we slithered down the steep slope to Itford Farm, Perce said that whatever I did I wasn't to come near the edge of the river bank, because the least shadow, or movement, would scare the pike away and they'd clobber me one. But since they had let me go with them, and were older than me anyway, I just held my tongue and followed them bumpily over the mole hills to the road and then across the high railway line to the river.

The pike wasn't actually *in* the river; he lived, they said, in a sort of pond thing which ran off the river and was very deep, which is why he was there at all. Because he had grown so big eating all the other fishes in the pond-bit that he had grown too big to swim out again, so he was trapped until someone hooked him.

The pond was quite large, and very weedy. The tide was coming in, rippling the clear water up towards Lewes, and the ground all round was very wet and marshy – which is why they were wearing wellingtons, I realised, because I was sopping wet already; but it didn't matter because it was so warm. Perce gave me a small jam jar with a paper lid and told me to start hunting for grasshoppers because he was going to try them on the pike.

'Get the big 'uns,' he said, starting to put his bamboo rod together. 'Don't go for the little ones, I want them big and jumping. 'E won't take 'em if they's little and not all wriggling. You can bait the hook if you like.'

I got quite a few poor old grasshoppers and a couple of beetles as well in case they would come in handy, and then I sat down, not too far away from the bank, and watched.

Well, there really wasn't very much to watch in the end. Just Reg and Perce sitting hunched up in the rushes not moving. So I opened my satchel and started to unwrap my sandwiches because I hadn't had any breakfast and I was getting quite hungry, but Reg shook a fist at me in the air, and Perce turned round and scowled, because the paper was a bit rustly and they looked very cross. So I lay back in the wettish grass and looked up at the sun and the clear shining sky. It was rather boring, I thought, and I was quite pleased when a lady came slowly walking across the field. She was tall and thin, with a long woolly, and fairish hair which looked rather wispy as if she had just washed it. She was carrying a walking stick and a bunch of wild flowers. When she saw us she stopped and shaded her eyes with her hand to see us better against the white light of the river. Reg looked very grumpily at her and went on fishing. Perce just hunched his shoulders up and didn't move, which was very rude because she was smiling a little and looked quite kind.

'Fishing?' she said in a silly way. Because what else could they be doing? Reg just looked at her and nodded his head, and Perce didn't do anything. She looked vaguely round her and said: 'I think I'm lost, I can't find the bridge.'

Reg swung his rod into the air and looked sullen. 'Up behind you, on the road,' he said gruffly, and re-cast his line so that I heard the bait plop into the still morning water.

'Thank you,' said the lady and then she held up the bunch of flowers for us all to see. No one said anything, so she turned and started walking back the way she had come, towards the bridge, stepping carefully over the mole hills and tussocks. She didn't look back and I was glad, because we had been very rude, but she hadn't spoken to me so I didn't feel I was quite to blame, and I didn't dare speak or move because of the pike and Perce's face, which was very red and cross.

'Bloomin' nuisance her. She's always about when I get here. Always up and down the river she is, like a bloomin' witch.' He reeled in his line and told me to give him another grasshopper because the one he had was drowned and not jerking any longer. While he baited the hook again we all watched her scramble up the bank to the road and then walk across the bridge swinging the stick in her hand; she was smelling her bunch of flowers and didn't look back at us again.

'A foreigner, isn't she?' said Reg.

'Londoner. From over there at Rodmell,' said Perce, skewering the biggest grasshopper onto his hook. 'They say she's a bit do-ally-tap . . . she writes books.' He swung the wriggling bait out into the still pond-like water and muttered something about never getting any peace and quiet. As the float plopped into the water and bobbed gently on the ripples from the tide, we all settled down again to fish. Which was pretty boring I was beginning to think.

So I just lay back quietly in the grasses, and watched the sky and wondered why there were so many witches in Sussex.

The bus from Seaford had just rumbled up to the Market Cross when we got back to the village, so I knew it was pretty late and that Lally would be fidgeting if I didn't hurry on up the hill to the cottage.

We hadn't caught the pike. Of course. No one really believed that we would, it was just a 'try'. Perce said that it was the pale-faced lady who put him off the whole day.

'Every time I sets meself down by that little pond-place along she comes wagging her stick and talking away to herself. Potty she is, so would anyone be living right next to a graveyard.' He was grumpy, but Reg said it was the bait we had used; next time we went, he said, we should take a bit of fresh liver or something really tempting. But Fred Brooks from the bus said that the pike was just a 'rumour', never mind what old Hallam over at Selmeston said, and that he'd been trying for the same pike ever since he was knee high to a duck, and had never had any luck, and that you'd have more luck trying to win the Irish Sweepstake than trying for the pike at Beddingham.

And that seemed to be that: so I just ambled home through the village and across the river and up the hill to the house. The sun was starting to set away behind the gully, and the shadows of the ash and oak were already quite long across the rutted path. The sun was orange-glinting on the diamond panes of glass in the cottage windows, and when I threw my arms up in the air, and stood with my legs apart, my own shadow looked very long and thin, with a tiny little head at the top, like the Long Man of Wilmington.

At the top of the gully, almost where our orchard started, a small white dog came skittering out of the bushes, barking and squealing and then dashed back again, and I knew that it was probably Mr Aleford and his brothers ferreting. And then they all came up through the hedgerow from the gully, with sacks, and a long pole with five rabbits hanging by their legs from it, and the little white dog, Tiger, leaping and jumping for pleasure. We all waved cheerfully and they went on down the hill laughing and talking. Suddenly Mr Ben turned round and called up to me, 'Hey? You lost this then?' and he threw something like a ball up in the air towards me. I couldn't catch it because I was carrying my shoes and the satchel, so it rolled rustling into the grass at my feet.

'Butterfingers!' called Mr Ben. 'Found it down the warren there, thought it must have belonged to you, reckon it got stuck in a hole and the badgers got it. Been there all summer by the look of it. Cheerio!' and he turned and went after his brothers.

It was George.

Even though it hadn't got a head or a tail or legs or anything, it was clearly George – but now he was just an empty shell looking like someone's old hat, with four holes in it. I took him up and went on up the hill.

'Will you dig a grave?' said my sister kindly, knowing I was miserable and trying to be nice. But I shook my head and finished the last bit of my gooseberry fool. Lally poured herself another cup of tea and clonked the spoon about.

'Not much point in having a funeral for just a shell,' she said cheerfully. 'It's like making a grave for a suit of clothes, isn't it? And no one would want to do that. George has been all eaten up by badgers and ants and that's that: you should have put a string on him like young Fluke told you in the first place. You should always put a string on everything you want to keep, from buttons to tortoises.'

She really seemed not to know how miserable I was, but my sister did; anyway part of it, even if it wasn't the part she liked, had been hers too . . . so she understood better.

After supper, she came down to the pump with me, and we started to wash the shell so that all the mud and chalk swirled away. But it wasn't very much good because it was all scratched and chewed up looking and made me even sadder, so I just filled the two buckets for the washing-up and we humped them, slopping water, back to the kitchen. Lally took one, and set it on the copper to boil, and took the other with her to the sink for the rinsing.

'Cheer up, you two! You'd think you'd lost a shilling and found a farthing! It's a lovely summer evening, go out and enjoy it before bedtime.'

I started to dry up a cup rather slowly while she swirled the suds about and clinked and clonked the plates and saucers onto the draining board.

'I think it feels like the end of summer now,' I said.

'Aren't we the little actor then!' said Lally, drying up a bundle of forks. 'All summers have to end sometime you know . . . can't have a summer without a good winter, can you? It stands to reason. It has to get the land ready for the next time. Can't be summer all the time.' She stacked the forks in a neat pile and started on the knives, wiping them hard against her apron before she polished them on the drying cloth.

My sister hung the cups on the dresser hooks and arranged the plates back on the little shelves.

'I mean to say!' she said suddenly. 'If there wasn't a winter whatever would happen to Christmas! Wouldn't it be simply awful with no Christmas! And you can't have a Christmas without a winter, can you? You couldn't have one in summer . . . not possibly.'

'They do in Australia,' I said grumpily but pleased I knew.

'Oh, Australia! They do everything upside down there, because they are upside down from us, everyone knows that. I expect they even play cricket on Christmas day with nuts or something.'

Lally bundled the knives and forks into a drawer, took up the tablecloth, shook it out of the window, and started to fold it, singing happily away as if she had no cares at all in the world.

Of course it didn't matter to her, really, about George; she didn't really know that I was feeling so miserable because I had been careless and let him wander and go off on his own and get eaten by badgers and so on. That was, anyway, all my fault. She just went on singing away 'Dawn With Thine Rosy Mantle' as if nothing awful had happened at all.

She even slammed the drawer shut hard, with a bang, when she put the cloth away, and sang even louder. No one cared. Not even my sister: she was mucking about with a jug of flowers on the table, so I just decided to go out into the garden and have a bit of a think, and be on my own.

It was cooler outside. The sky was flat and almost mauve-coloured. Bats swooped like little kites over the wigwams of runner beans in the vegetable garden as I wandered up to the iron gates and out into Great Meadow, holding George's shell in my hands, and wondering why everything had suddenly gone so beastly and sad-feeling.

I heard my sister rustling through the raspberry canes behind me, and the iron fence squeak as she clambered over it and lumped into the meadow. And then she was walking, quite quietly, just behind me, not saying anything, and I knew that she really was a bit sorry for me in her own peculiar way.

Up at the top of the gully, where they had all been ferreting, the grass was trodden and muddy, and there was a bit of rabbit's fur caught on a clump of thistles. But there was no sign, this evening, of any rabbits as there usually was: they had all gone.

'Is this where they found him?' said my sister in a low voice.

'Yes. They were after the rabbits.'

'Poor little things . . . what are you going to do with that then?'

I looked down at the chewed-up old shell.

'Just chuck it away, I think.'

'Into the gully?'

'Yes . . . into the gully.'

We walked slowly over to the chalky edge and looked down into the shadowing little path which ran along the bottom among all the roots and tree trunks. It looked very cold and lonely there. A blackbird blundered away worriedly into the hawthorns and then I suddenly threw the shell high up into the air: we both watched it as it made a wide arc against the fading sky and then fell swiftly into the dark branches over the gully.

For a moment there was silence and then we heard it clitter-clatter-clotter down among the leaves and stones, then everything was still again.

And that was that.

PART TWO
WINTER

NINE

In my school report for the Lent Term of 1933 Miss Polyphemus, my Housemistress, thought it necessary to observe that 'He has still to learn that life is not all cushions and barley sugar.' An odd combination of delights, one might think. However, she was right.

A small, eager, middle-aged woman, rather like a Jack Russell, she dragged me unwillingly through Mathematics, applauded wanly from a deck-chair when I muffed a catch at Cricket, and sloshed about in muddy wellingtons with a whistle in her mouth while I stood shivering with cold on the touch line during Football. I know that I tried her patience to the limits.

I hated all three. Mathematics, Cricket and, above all, Football. I found them totally illogical pursuits. I could never, and still cannot, understand why anyone should want to hit a very hard ball with a non-resistant bat high into the air so that someone else could run up and down a scrubby bit of grass until the ball is retrieved. Nor could I see, and I still cannot, the delights in kicking and hacking, and pushing, and shoving, about in mud and wet so that a small leather sphere should reach some designated area of space between two wooden poles shrouded in mist or freezing fog. As for Mathematics I simply didn't believe them.

It was no good telling me that some wise Arab, scrabbling about in the sand decided, all by himself, that Five should be Five and that twice that number should be called Ten. I couldn't accept that at all.

Miss Garlick, who took us for Botany, was marginally kinder in giving me two 'Goods' for Diligence and Apprehension, although she had to add that she wished I was 'More accurate, both in drawing and writing' and Dr Chanter, predictably Music, was glowing with two 'Very Goods' and a genial comment in a flourishing pen that I was 'Working very well indeed.' It was difficult, even for me, not to be able to learn the words of 'The Vicar of Bray' of 'Hark Hark the Lark'. The tune took a little longer.

The remainder of the report was grey. Dr Lake's final comment, in crimson ink at the bottom of the page, betrayed a good deal of suppressed irritation and weariness. 'He makes me impatient. But I am trying to be more philosophical about him. Only time will tell.' Trying, was underlined.

It just did not occur to me that what Miss Polyphemus said was not so: although I might have chosen other words than 'cushions and barley sugar'. I thought life was simply splendid. I had no reason to think otherwise. My days revolved about two pivots, if one can have two pivots. The Cottage in Sussex, and Twickenham.

Not counting my home and family which was, of course, the centre anyway. My life, as far as I could make it, was a total splendour of Summer and Constant Sunshine in which nothing unpleasant was ever allowed to happen. The fact that I was not God, and that unpleasant things *did* occur from time to time, was simply not my affair at all. I had an amazing way of setting those aside, and obliterating from my mind, and being, the things which were boring, dull or

44444444444

distressing. Like my father, I managed, quite skilfully, to set aside the disagreeable parts of life so that I coasted, cheerfully enough, from the Cottage to Twickenham without taking a great deal of notice of the things which littered that happy road. Things which, from time to time, did crack my shins or cause me a bothersome, not to say painful, stumble from my happy Seat of Grace. School, and all those who served within it, from Pupil to Teacher, was a bore and a place where one marked time until the doors opened again and one was released into Pleasures. School was Outside. And most people were Outside. And anything which was Outside was simply that. And did not affect me so far as I could help.

My family, the Cottage and Twickenham were all that mattered to me. Beyond them all else was a blank.

A sad state of affairs.

It was not that I was shielded, or cosseted, really. In fact I was not. My sister Elizabeth and I were both brought up from a very early age to fend for ourselves, to be quite self-sufficient, to work for our pleasures and physically to earn our weekly pocket money. Nothing came too easily. We were members of a young family, and they had to work hard for all they had, and we had to do the same. We lived in a world which was almost completely Grown Up. We delighted in our parents' friends who were mostly painters, writers and journalists, and found most children dull, retarded or childish. So we didn't bother with them. We didn't need them, we felt, and they got in the way. We never made close friends, or stayed at their houses ever; and seldom asked them back to ours. Unless forced by adult politeness. We liked each other better, and our father and mother and Lally provided us with all the pleasure, excitements, and delights we felt we could possibly wish for.

A very smug attitude indeed.

A rather insular life? A little ingrowing? We didn't think so. Nor do I now. It harmed no one: beyond ourselves. And it was about to change.

The Report, quoted above, was alas! only one of a number. They grew very slightly better as the terms went by; but not much. I finally 'made it' in Botany, Bookbinding, Metalwork and Drawing. Everything else was just 'V. Fair'.

My father, who had distant ideas of sending me to Fettes and then watching me proudly follow him dutifully along the dusty corridors of *The Times* until I eventually took over his chair as Art Editor in the Art Department, began, reluctantly but clearly, to realise that his dreams were just that.

The chances of my getting into the Gas, Light and Coke Company were brighter than the possibilities of my even reaching the gates of Fettes. Let alone Printing House Square.

My idleness, my backwardness, my apparent inability to grasp the fundamentals of scholastic life were blamed, possibly correctly, on the fact that I had not been sent off to a Boarding School from the start. It had been a constant battle between my parents, she refusing, he begging. I waged a neutral war. And stayed.

Time which had now been lost for twelve years had to be regained somehow. The visions of Fettes and *The Times*, though dimmed, still gleamed like an afterthought, through my father's disappointment. He did all that he possibly could to redress the wrongs. I was sent, willy nilly, to a very expensive tutor for a year in a grey stucco house in Willow Road, Hampstead.

I can only remember that it was an unpleasant shock and one which I found a little harder than usual to obliterate quite so easily from my existence. I don't, oddly enough, remember very much about it. Obliterating was still at work whatever should befall me. I don't even remember much about the Tutor except that he was very old and wore a celluloid collar and lace-up boots. There were two other boys there with me, one older and one the same age. But they were keener than I so I hardly ever spoke to them, and the eldest one was extremely busy with something rather complicated like Trigonometry. We sat round a green baize table. The Tutor at one end with an empty chair at the other. We vaguely wondered who it was for until one day a silent, elderly lady slid into it and sat there knitting during a long lecture on the Lowest Common Denominator. She only came once. Sensibly.

I spent most of my time gazing out of the window at the trees on the Heath, and the Tutor spent most of his sleeping, or speaking, in a low murmur, to the Trigonometry Boy. It was a lethal, dull, boring year. And did me no good at all. At the time. But as far as I was able I did try, although to little effect. I simply sat there planning books or poems or a new, and usually improbable, plot for a play.

Eventually, and despairingly, I was removed and sent back to the school up the hill. Where I prospered exceedingly after my time away by Producing, Writing, Directing and Acting in my own versions of 'Just William' and the other William stories. These were done during the school breaks, and my unfortunate class-mates, bullied, cajoled and sometimes even blackmailed, into playing in them, were forced to relinquish the delights of football, marbles and cigarette card swapping for the doubtful pleasures of giving highly embarrassed performances in smaller roles than mine.

It was quite clear that the entire school staff had now considered my case hopeless, and to my simple, and gratified, astonishment, I was permitted to 'do' these plays as long as they didn't interfere with the boys' working life at school.

In fact they became so popular that I even had chairs set up for the staff who actually came and watched some of the performances, thus giving me, if not the others, a first heady whiff of an Audience. Albeit they were pretty stolid and dull, they were there. And the show became For Them. Even the Headmaster vaguely approved. What else could he do?

My father by this time was now thoroughly disillusioned with me. I could sense it very well. He never made jokes any more and always seemed rather preoccupied and distant when I was in the same room with him. Lally, correctly, pointed out that he was 'disappointed' in me, that it was entirely my own fault, I had been given every chance and warning, and that if I didn't set to and pull up my socks I'd be in for a very unpleasant surprise one day. She also added that he had a great deal to worry him.

He had. After eleven years my mother suddenly found, to her despair, that she was pregnant, and life shifted imperceptibly, but firmly, into a different gear. My sister and I had noticed that she seemed to be getting rather large, and had, I remember, speculated on the very improbable fact that she might be going to have a baby. But the fact was so abhorrent to us, and we considered her so terribly old anyway, that the idea slipped easily from our narrow little minds and we thought no more about it and merely decided that she was 'putting on weight'.

She settled all that easily enough one day when we were at the top of the garden picking lilac for the drawing-room.

'I'm going to have a baby,' she said. Clearly having rehearsed it for ages.

We showed no surprise, which might have comforted her, because she went on to say that it would be quite soon, that she hoped it would be a boy and that she thought it would because it kicked so much, and that she wanted us to be very, very kind to it and love it and not make it feel that it didn't belong to us all and was loved and welcome.

Later in the Nursery, where my sister now slept alone, since Lally had one day made the disconcerting discovery during Bath Time that I was 'growing-up', we looked at each other with ashen faces and saw the future, correctly; hideous with crying and Nurses and a stranger in our midst whom we should have to like whether we wanted to or not. This would be no Other Child, no Outsider, but our very own; some eleven years late in joining.

We were bleak.

Everyone was bleak in fact. Eleven years is a long time in which to have forgotten the pattering of those blasted tiny feet. We had, we considered, all got Set In Our Ways. Well: now they were to be shifted a bit, those Ways, things were never to be quite the same again. A new phase was about to start. We all wondered, privately, how we should manage.

July 1934 was blazing. Roses opened and fell within the day, and the lawns turned rusty beige. My sister was dispatched to our grandmother in Scotland for a while so that her room, the Nursery, could become one again; this time for the Baby. I was allowed to remain at home to welcome this addition. I was, it was pointed out, the eldest and it was right and proper that I should be present in the house when he arrived. The Nursery was stripped out and painted white. A cot and armchair and small table, scales and a bath with ducks on it took the place of our battered toy boxes, book cases and a gabled dolls' house. Then came Nurse Hennessy, a broad, hefty Irish Nurse who crackled like a twig fire and was less friendly.

Lally refused to carry trays up to the Nursery until the Baby was actually born, and so a small, but deep, rift started in the family life. However, Nurse Hennessy seemed not to care and swigged down her Guinness with her lunch as cheerfully as if she had been sitting in her own Nursery sipping champagne, which, she assured us, was what she had been Accustomed to at her Other Places. Lally sipped away at her tea in the kitchen, at her table, and read *Poppies Weekly* slowly from cover to cover without saying a word. I ate with them, my mother, by this time, spending most of the day in her room lying down and feeling wretched. My father was 'at *The Times*' and I just sensed that someone had turned my egg-timer upside down and that the sand had started to run the other way. I was not at all comfortable.

One blistering Saturday when strange currents seemed to be racing through the house the brusque Doctor, who was a lady but wore a grey flannel suit with a black tie, had some urgent words with my father and I suddenly found myself walking with him through the careless weekend shoppers of Hampstead. He walked rather quickly, and I was always a little behind him, sweating and bumping into people with prams and baskets and vaguely aware that we had been sent out of the house to await the arrival of the Baby. In a florists near the Heath we spent quite a long time selecting carnations. He bought a vast bunch, choosing them individually, striped pink and white. They were my mother's favourite flower and although they reminded me of Weddings and Death these were destined for a Birth. We then went into a large Stationers and Newsagents where he slowly and thoughtfully chose tubes of oil paint, some tracing paper and a random selection of pen-nibs and bought me a copy of *Boys Own*. This surprised me more than the strange assortment of things he was purchasing for himself. *Boys Own* was very glossy and more expensive than any of the other magazines we were normally able to afford. I realised that he was not, perhaps, being as casual as he seemed. Then we walked back, in silence, down Heath Street to the rather ugly house which was my Centre. It had a high gable, fake beams and two acacia trees in the front garden.

Lally opened the door before we reached it looking rather hot and a little rumpled. But she was half smiling through her anxiety, so I knew immediately that things were more or less all right. Looming behind her in the hall, pulling on her gloves, was Doctor Findlayson, about to leave in her dark green Sunbeam parked at the gate.

'She had a hard time,' she said cheerfully. 'But she's not a girl any longer. It's a boy by the by and she'd like to see you as soon as she's ready.' She gave us both a cold smile, lit a cigarette, and went out to her car.

My father ran up the staircase. I stood and watched the doctor drive away in a hurry. A boy, I thought. Ah well . . . but mother had not died.

I sat in the window seat in the hall and waited. Unconsciously aware that I might be needed or sent for. I rifled through the glassy pages of *Boys Own* and kept one ear cocked for the awaited cry of the Baby. It was Nurse Hennessy, at the top of the stairs, who called me. Not the Baby. She was smiling and carried a white bundle.

'Come up and meet your little brother!' she cried as if we were all at a party.

It looked, from my point of view, like rabbit-offal wrapped in a shawl. I was silent with shock at the sight of this living stranger in our midst. This was the bulge in my mother's belly. This the cause of the vastly disturbed household.

The Nursery smelled of powder and methylated spirit. She unwrapped the offal and laid it in my reluctant arms.

'Hold its neck. Otherwise its head will fall off, and we don't want that, do we!' I was not altogether sure.

Small fists beat helplessly in slow motion at a bloated, scarlet, screwed-up, old man's face. The head weighed tons, the neck seemed delightfully frail. It kicked hard, and I saw the long twisting tube which still trailed from his belly. Nurse Hennessy stuffed a cigarette into her mouth and, taking up some scissors and a reel of white string, showed me how to tie 'in' this gristly worm. I was not at all over anxious to do as she suggested, but she said that I was the Eldest and that it was fitting that I should tie up the cord which had attached my brother to his mother all the time that he was growing inside her. She felt, although I rather doubted it myself, that mother would 'like this'. I didn't think she'd care one way or the other but fiddled with string and gristle and scissors until I had achieved some form of a knot.

'There!' cried Nurse Hennessy. 'Now he really is part of this World! all we have to do is wash him thoroughly and that'll rot off in two shakes of a lamb's tail.'

In my mother's room the blinds were drawn against the sun; the room was hot and smelled of hospitals. She lay, a large lump, exhausted and overheated, in the great oak bed which she and my father shared. She wore a pretty lace boudoir cap with little bows, and tried to smile in a pale way, reaching out her hand, as I came to the side of the bed.

'I hope you'll be good to him,' she said in a whispering voice. 'He was a lot of hard work, I can tell you.'

I told her, politely, for I was a little afraid of this exhausted, hot, woman who had just had a difficult time and who seemed to be almost in a dream, that I had been shown by Nurse Hennessy how to tie off my brother's cord. She smiled wearily and waved a hand vaguely in the air. 'She's a silly bitch!' she said gently. 'Brought me a soft boiled egg and toast, can you imagine what an idiot she is. For God's sake take it away and hide it. Give it to Lally and tell her to throw it away.' And she seemed to lapse into a troubled sleep and left me standing helplessly looking at the neat tray and the boiled egg.

Lally snorted and silently stuffed the lot into the sink. 'A glass of beer would do her more good, that I can tell you. But you daren't say a thing to these

Nurses.' She shoved the kettle on to the gas stove and started to lay up a small tray with the best china and a little lace cloth. From somewhere far away it seemed we heard the first cries.

Angry, defiant, furious at being late. We looked at each other with very different thoughts. She shook some sugar lumps into a china bowl. The crying went on. It was not to stop for two years.

'We thought it better,' said my mother gently a few weeks later, 'than a Boarding School. You really are a bit late for that now, and Aunt Belle adores you and you like her and she had always wanted to have you. She even wanted to adopt you ages ago when you were first born because she thought that I would not be able to bring you up properly. And a Scottish Education is what you need. It's far better than an English one. And you really have had all the chances down here and nothing seems to work. You just can't go on being a duffer, can you?'

She looked beautiful, as she always did, and calm and collected. Obviously this had all been planned before. I was to go to school in Scotland, to stay with her childless sister and her husband, to live near her family, to be brought up by strangers, even if they were Family, and to leave my Centre and my life to which I had happily become accustomed. The shock took some time to hit me. But when it did I was prostrate. Now I was no longer needed. The Baby had become the centre of the Universe. Even my sister had turned traitor and spent hours holding it and kissing it and washing it. Lally, beloved, adored, Lally was preoccupied now with getting rid of the Nurse and restoring the 'roses to your mother's cheeks' and my father, after the splendour of the amazing *Boys Own*, had retreated even further away from me than ever.

He was, evidently, putting aside the unpleasant things, as I did, and as he was good at doing. And sending me off, willy nilly, to a strange school in a strange land with strange people could surely be called 'unpleasant', even by him.

But, as Lally pointed our, boiling water and steeping great mounds of chrome nappies in a large zinc bath, I had had my chances and had failed them. The Tutor had cost a lot of money, so had the school on the Hill and the uniforms and all the rest of the stuff I had been forced to wear during Term time. Producing plays, however clever, was not going to get me to learn my sums or my spelling and all that sort of thing. What I needed, she said very kindly, was a bit of a 'pull on the reins'. And this, they all felt sure, was what Scotland and Aunt Belle and Uncle Duff and a very tough school in Glasgow would do for me.

In an emperic state of Self Pity, to which, when things go against my wishes, I am prone, I lay on my bed in my room at the top of the house and, through tear-filled eyes, said most of my farewells to the wallpaper. Blue tits smothered in wisteria. My own deathly choice. The jar of snails by my bed held no delights now. They never had in fact, frightfully boringly they only seemed to eat at night and never moved about in the daylight . . . the small altar which I had made in a corner, looked dusty and un-prayed at. It was. But today it held sudden attractions. I wondered if perhaps a prayer, even so late, would help. But I was too shattered with shock and self pity to move from the bed. I realised that no one wanted me now, and that no one cared about me. The sooner I was removed from this uncaring place the better. It might even, though this did not seem remotely possible at that time, be very interesting in Scotland. I did like my Aunt. I liked the idea of the journey there. I even liked the distant memories of my grandmother's teas and all my uncles and aunts and the odd way they all spoke and eating sticks of Edinburgh Rock. And oat cakes. And even porridge.

I might even like the school. But I felt that I could never really forgive them here for chucking me out without warning. The eldest! Ha! Now that they had a younger one I was to be put aside and dumped 'with relations' for God's sake, in a foreign land.

I knew, with savage insight, that I detested that screaming bundle of waving arms and legs on the floor below. I was even being thrown out of My Room so that my sister could have it while Lally shared the Nursery with the howling intruder. They would change the wisteria and the blue tits. Throw away my snails, muddle my books and drawings, even open my desk, and put my clothes in a different place in the house. I was in despair, a mounting wave of dislike and anger rose within me which nearly made me sick. I would never forgive that stinking, smelly, shrieking, little beast who had burst, unwelcome, into my perfect Two Pivot and Centre Life. And I didn't for over twenty years.

Before she married my father, my very beautiful mother had been an actress. She had reached her peak of success in 'Bunty Pulls The Strings' at the Haymarket in 1911. A point in history which we were never to forget. Nor were we ever allowed to forget.

All through childhood we were delighted and saddened with long recitations which she had memorised in order to Entertain The Boys from the Front. They ranged from super Show-Stoppers like 'Billy's Rose' which began: 'Billy's dead and gone to Heaven, So has Billy's sister Nell' which reduced us all to snivelling sobs long before the final stanzas to 'The Story of Dan Ma'grew' right through Hilaire Belloc and all those 'Heartless Tales For Heartless Homes'. We were entranced and delighted. When the War got into its stride she marched all over the country with Concert Parties entertaining the wounded, billed as 'Always Applauded', and fondly known to all and sundry as 'Little Madge'. Finally she went into Munitions when the War got really desperate about 1917 and went back towards London and the Theatre as soon as the Armistice was signed. Life was not easy for young actresses then, no easier than it is today, and to make ends meet she posed for Hands and Head, only, at the Slade, the St Martin's and Chelsea Polytechnic. While awaiting the Call from Cochran; which never came.

In 1920, after a famous Chelsea Arts Ball, she was given a room in someone's studio who was in Paris for three weeks. Without money, with no real roof over her head at that time, and with a group of jolly young artists and actors all in the same boat, she settled happily down to sleep off the delights and exhaustions of the Albert Hall. The young man returned from Paris, with 'flu, two weeks early. That is to say three hours after my mother had comfortably crawled into his vacant bed. She was swiftly ejected by him, and forced, since it was a strange house and she didn't know her way around it having entered it so shortly before, to spend the night huddled in the remains of her Fancy Dress, a Spanish Shawl and a borrowed mantilla, on the mat outside his room. Her anger and rage knew no bounds. However, she discovered that he was ill and stayed to nurse him. Three weeks later they were married. A honeymoon in France and then back to the same tall brick house in St George's Road, West End Lane, which my father owned and let out as rooms to his artist and writer friends. And then came The Call – from Hollywood.

Mother was asked to go to California to join the Lasky Players. Seeing herself thrusting Theda Bara from the confines of the screen, she packed a bag and signed the contract. In that order. My astonished, but cool, father said that it was either Lasky or himself; she could not have both. After days of tearful pleading, sulking, and despair, she stayed, and never ever got further West in her life than New York when she was well over fifty. She never forgot, however, and she never, totally, was able to forgive. But she was a good, properly brought up young woman, and honour was honour and the pact she made with my father lasted happily all their lives together. But the dull pain, and the vague feeling of disappointment, even un-achievement, was to remain buried away inside all her life. And all of ours.

I was born the following March. She was delighted, if vague, about it all. She has always said that I was conceived in Paris, which I do not doubt, for they travelled extensively to France in that first year of marriage, and that she was determined I should be born there. However, she muffed that too through no fault of her own, and though it was touch and go that I should be born in a taxi, they made the nursing home and I arrived at eight-thirty in the morning of March 28th, 1921. From that moment on, loving my father as much as she clearly did, she knew that she was trapped. No longer could Hollywood beckon. Well, it could; but she was never to be able to heed its call. Not that it ever did call again; but she never completely gave up hope.

My mother's background was a large Victorian Ayrshire family. Eleven children in all. She was last but three in the line. My grandfather, once a man of substance, was elegant, handsome, a gifted painter and an indifferent Actor. He was Cartoonist for a Glasgow paper, and was adored by all who met him. He wore cloaks and wide-brimmed hats, and loved my mother most of all his children for she was the 'one most like me'. Eventually, unable to bear the tremendous constrictions of a tight family life he left home and went out into the world with The Actors, joining the Neilson Terrys, the Forbes Robertsons and the Cyril Maudes and finally, kidnapping my mother from the home, she was ten, pressed her into service as his servant and companion. Together for a number of years, they toured the Provinces, coming, happily, to rest under the elegant portals of the Haymarket Theatre in 'Bunty Pulls The Strings'.

He had realised, as have done others before him, and since, that though he had a tremendous physical presence and a beautiful voice, he had not got the spark for greatness. He had started in the theatre too late in life and could not adjust, totally, to this glittering world which he so adored but felt a little lost within.

Not so his daughter Margaret. The moment she hit the Stage, at eleven or abouts, she was On. And at the Haymarket, while Grandfather played a tiny part as an old shepherd, his daughter bounced over a canvas wall as the Ingenue. Both their fates were, to some extent, sealed. After 'Bunty' closed he went sadly back to Scotland and left his daughter hooked for life. Back to the big family house in Langside, back to his resentful and by now deserted wife, who was rightfully resentful, back to his family of ten who hardly knew him and were so deeply cloaked in their own respectability that they no longer wished to.

Mother was the Lost Sheep. And although they all tried to settle her back among them, she refused to remove her lipstick, and yearned to go back to the South. Which she did pretty quickly, using the Wounded Soldiers, and her charming talent, as an excuse. Her high spirits, her jollity, her very unusual beauty and above all the great warmth of her heart and her adoration for the world at large saw to it that she never failed.

Until the night of the Chelsea Arts Ball in 1920 . . . and that can hardly be called a failure. A change of direction certainly; and I never cease to thank God that she took it.

I have said that we, as children, hardly ever made friends. This is not strictly true in the case of about four people, three of whom were at school with me, the other, a girl, who was Italian and lived in a large tumbling Roman family not very far from us. Her name was Giovanna and she was my sister's Best Friend and they went to school together at a large convent, pleasantly set in walled gardens. The other three were, strictly speaking, my Best Friends, although they might not have considered me as such. For they were seldom invited into the walls of my Centre and our friendship existed for most of the time during school.

My nearly closest friend was Jones G. C. He was called Minor to distinguish him from another Jones was was Major and who bullied me without pause, 'bumping' me on the Playing Fields, shoving powdered glass down my neck during Physics, and generally behaving in a thoroughly disagreeable way. But Jones G. C. was very quiet, a studious boy who lived in a big house in Finchley Road and kept toads and birds and wore thick hornrimmed glasses. He was as hopeless at Games as I, and was a willing participant in my Plays because he could just read his books until he had to say his lines and no one bothered him. Not even Jones Major.

Foot was very fat. As fat as any boy I ever knew. It was rumoured all over the school that the reason for his weight was not so much that he ate prodigiously, which he did, but that his testicles had failed to drop. This made him rather interesting and a great deal of time was spent at the Showers and in the Changing Rooms to verify this anatomical disaster. No one, it seems, was convinced. And no one ever actually got the chance to clearly find out, for he was as delicate in his undressing and showering as a nun. And even Jones Major didn't do very much about him. Foot ate and read a great deal. He wore thick pebble glasses, and dribbled. He also hated Games, with a dull passion, played all the fat boy parts in my plays and bored a hole with a hat-pin through his mother's bathroom door so that we could all peer at her, with one blurred eye, having her bath. I found this a rather dismal thing to do; she was as fat as he was and just as unattractive.

Trevor Roper was the third and last of my Friends. A tall vibrant boy, who more or less Designed the plays. While I did the writing and directing and casting, and all the acting if I could, he arranged the sets, the seats, the curtains, and lights when needed. He was alive, vivid and busy. Once, as a visitor to our house on a reconnaissance trip to find a suitable stage in which to perform a new play we had written in tandem, he discovered, to his delight, the big bay window in our hall, and with a flourish, which startled my mother, made swift plans to rig curtains, fix lights and turn the place into Drury Lane with a few nails and ten yards of velvet. I pointed out that there was no exiting space left and right of his Proscenium Arch. Merely wall. He airily decided that we should remove all the windows and make our exits and entrances into the garden. It seemed a logical idea to everyone but my mother.

The play was abandoned for the time being.

We made a solid group of four wandering about the grounds of the school in an inseparable block. Discussing plays and stories and who to cast as what. Until my brother was born.

Two days into shock I returned to my friends and told them of the news. They were all suitably amazed. Foot, whom we called Elephant because of his name and not because of his size strangely enough, was horrified. 'Your mother's so terribly old. I think it is disgusting. Fancy having a baby as old as that. It might have killed her!' She was, of course, very old. Exactly thirty-three. Trevor Roper found it all unpleasant and decided not to comment beyond saying that it was 'jolly hard luck' on me. And Jones G. C. looked very vague and wondered, aloud, how it could have happened.

'I know,' said Foot. 'It is all too simple, and that's why people should be more careful about where they pee.'

We all looked a little surprised; even Trevor roper was intrigued. Foot explained that all you had to do to have a baby was for the father and mother to pee together into the same chamber pot, and the baby came out of the mixture as a sort of amoeba. It didn't at all convince Jones G. C. who was very good at Botany. And although I knew, because I had been given a small book by my father and looked at the pen and ink drawings, I was not about to tell them. The book was impossible for me to understand from the written point of view, but the diagrams were simple and easy to follow and although it all rather put me off and made my sister scream when I told her up under the lilac one day, I went along with it and obliterated what I could not understand. Or chose not to understand.

I tolerated Giovanna Govoni because she was very, very nice and nearly like a boy. And although she was strictly speaking my sister's Best Friend, she was often at the house and kept out of my way so I was not disturbed. On the other hand she seemed to be interested in snails and frogs and stick-insects, and kept goldfish. Which brought her nearer to me than the fact that she spent hours with my sister looking at this absurd baby which had crashed into our midst.

There was another reason for my liking, even accepting, Giovanna as a friend. And that was her mother's cooking. When you went to their house, not unlike our own but a bit bigger with an old chestnut tree in the garden, it was not at all like going to anyone else's house I knew. Although the walls, and rooms, and even the furniture, conformed to the English Style in every conceivable way, the atmosphere within those walls was more Roman than it was London. There was always a most delicious smell of cooking. Of basil, of garlic, of rice and of olive oil. The family, Uncle Gianni and Aunt Isali plus their twin sons, Italo and Mario who were very much younger than we were, filled the house with music, laughter, screaming, and violent conversation which I found both stimulating and exciting. Coupled with the cooking smells, a great bowl of goldfish on the sitting-room mantelpiece, there was also the constant and delightful presence of Madame Chiesi; she was Giovanna's grandmother on her mother's side, a tall elegant woman from the Swiss border, who spoke no English and spent most of her time sitting in a high-backed chair, dressed in black with little white frills, sewing, knitting or making something fragile in threads and silks. I adored her, even though we never spoke a common language. She soothed frayed tempers, found the sweets when needed, scolded and laughed and spread love about her like a bounty.

Giovanna's mother, Isali, was a little younger than our mother, fair and blue-eyed, very strict and correct but always bright and busy in her kitchen making great bowls of pasta and soups filled with as many delights as a Christmas stocking. She very soon took my mother, and her kitchen, in hand and for a long time to come our house was filled with the most delicious aromas, and great cotton sacks of rice and pasta which came from as far away as Milan and Verona. Lally mournfully observed that we all ate more rice than the entire Chinese Nation, and that rice, correctly cooked and prepared, should be served with a bay leaf, honey, and a crisp golden apron. She glumly forked her way through endless Risotto alla Milanese, Rise e Bisi and Risotto Rusticos with a face like thunder and a growing weight problem.

Apart from all the laughing, quarrelling, Italians in the house with the chestnut tree, there was also Bertha.

She was German, blonde, strong, very jolly and came from Hamburg. She spoke dreadful English which delighted us all, for the Govonis spoke fluently, and smelled appallingly. However, she was kind, loved children, especially the twins, Italo and Mario, and never found anything too much for her to do. Every afternoon, wet or fine, she would stand on a rug in the middle of the garden, dressed only in an ugly black and white swimming suit, with a big tin alarm clock ticking away beside her, and do her 'Physical Exercises' much to our delight and, at first, astonishment. When the alarm went off she stopped, took three or four deep breaths, picked up the rug and the clock and marched back into the house to start the tea. It was her Strength Through Joy, she said.

We merely thought she was a bit touched in the head, and let it pass. No one else we knew put on a bathing suit and did gymnastics in the back garden with an alarm clock, and no one else we knew went on holiday with a rucksack and a collapsible kayak to canoe round the West Coast of England for their summer holidays. We were aware that she was not joking, or bragging, because she was also an ardent photographer, and one of the special joys of having Bertha home again was to go up to her very smelly little bedroom and sit on the bed amidst the debris of the rucksack and the bits of collapsible kayak, and look through all her 'snaps'. Views of Swanage, of Bournemouth Pier and Portsmouth, of cheerful groups of brown, sweaty people, waving and laughing at the camera on miles of beaches from Penzance to the Tilly Whimm Caves. She never seemed to miss a trick, and most of them delighted us. Presumably we were not the only ones meant to be delighted.

My father was the only one of us who seemed not to join in our general delight with the Italian Family. He was uncomfortable with Gianni, whom he considered to be a Blackshirt, and found the noise and hurly-burly, which so enchanted us, tiresome and unrelaxing. However, he smothered, as best he was able, these feelings, and we all managed a more or less comfortable relationship. It is unlikely that Gianni, who was a member of the Staff at the Italian Embassy, *was* a Blackshirt, if so an unwilling one. He was an Italian, and deeply proud of his country. However, none of this even remotely concerned me at the time. I had quite enough to worry me.

The resentment of my new brother was compounded by the fact that because of him and his untimely arrival, in the very middle of the summer holidays, we were unable to go, as usual, down to the Cottage. And so the long hot summer was spent sweating away in London, with occasional treks to the Heath or Kenwood for walks and 'a breath of air'. Although I hated it all, I wished for it not to end, for I knew that with the end of summer came the trip to the North, to a foreign school, to new people and to a new life which, in spite of my Aunt and Uncle's warmth and affection, I dreaded. Wisely, and with great tact, Lally said that it was time we all grew up, things had to change, and we couldn't have it all our own way. Reckoning that MY way was the best way for me I was loth to put it aside. I disliked change of any kind, and I was secretly deeply afraid of having to grow up and go off on my own, a thing I knew was bound to happen one day or another. I preferred another.

I said goodbye to Miss Polyphemus, to Miss Garlick, to Dr Chanter and to weary Dr Lake, gave Jones G. C. all my 'Just William' books and left the school on the hill for the last time.

No one seemed very sorry to see me go; they were all pretty busy getting ready for their own holidays to bother about me anyway.

Dr Lake wrote a very pleasant letter to my father saying that I was an 'amusing companion and a nice fellow', and that he wished me well. And that was that.

The summer, stuck away in London and far from my beloved gully and Great Meadow, was going to be a long, dull, time. But I realized that I'd better make the most of it.

One morning, very early, before the sun was up, the telephone rang and startled me out of sleep. The telephone was no strange device in our house. We were more than used to it attached as it was to Printing House Square. At all hours of the day or the night it rang with the news that a King had fallen off a rock, a Golden Eagle had hatched near Inverness, a Queen had been killed in a car crash, or a President had jumped out of a window.

We were never surprised by the odd items which filtered into the Nursery, and none of them appeared, at the time, to touch our golden lives. Until this one.

I heard my father answering the machine in his bedroom across the wide landing from mine. I heard him speaking for a long time . . . not hearing the words but being unmistakably aware that whatever he was being told was urgent, worrying and concerned him personally.

I lay looking at my tit-and-wisteria paper and wondered vaguely if it was anything to do with me or school. But nothing was said at breakfast, even though I could see, with a stab of surprise and alarm, that my mother had been crying.

Later, up at the top of the garden where I had built a rather rickety hut in which I painted and wrote my countless plays and stories, she came to see me.

I was making some puppets, I remember, and she vaguely admired a scrap of old brocade which I was using for a costume. 'It came from those old curtains you gave me,' I said. But she was looking sadly out of the dirty window into the garden and not listening to me.

Presently she turned round and said in a weary voice: 'I want you to listen to me very carefully. Daddy and I have to go down to Brighton immediately. It's very sudden and very urgent and we might not be home until tomorrow. You've got a new grandfather.'

TEN

Aimé Emile van den Bogaerde was a tall, dashing, handsome man with great amused eyes and a faded fortune when he met my grandmother Grace some time in the late 1880's.

I don't know very much about him, because my father hardly ever mentioned his name to us as children, and all that we vaguely knew, and it was very vague indeed, pieced together from scraps sought or heard here and there, was that he had gone to South America as an explorer and died there of yellow fever.

He came from an ancient, Catholic family which traced its origins, I am told, to Anne of Cleves, but which finally settled, at the end of the sixteenth century, near Iseghem, a small town in the centre of the orchard country of what was then the Low Countries and is now Belgium. The name, van den Bogaerde, means 'of the Orchards' and the coat of arms incorporates three fruit-laden apple trees. That the family was gently noble at its start is not in dispute; however, it apparently slipped towards the Sea (some were to become

Admirals) and the Land. From the Land they moved into Law, and my grandfather was born to a famous judge and appears to have lived the life of any other rich gentleman of his time. Part of his education was the traditional Grand Tour which he made with two tutors and an enormous Great Dane. He travelled from Brussels to Paris, Berlin, Munich, Venice, Rome and eventually, London. Liking the English, speaking their language fluently, and being rich and handsome and young, he was attracted to the County Life and spent a great deal of his time in various parts of the shires riding, hunting, shooting and generally enjoying the hospitalities of the larger country houses to which he was invited, or had 'letters of reference'.

It was while he was in Worcestershire that he met, and fell in love with, Grace Clark of that county and married her. I have always been told that the Clarks were so horrified at the idea of their golden, slender, child marrying a Foreigner that they sent her to a convent. And from there my grandfather kidnapped her and they ran away and got married. But that is legend. And I very much doubt that it happened. However, it well might have for my grandfather was an impetuous, determined man, and Grace a rather timid, gentle, creature who could just about blow her own nose for herself. But she had some will. She firmly refused to live Abroad, embraced the Catholic faith and forced him to buy a large villa in Perry Barr, then a small, pleasant village, just outside Birmingham. To be near her family one supposes. They lived very well. There are photographs of the house, many gabled, with trim lawns and great cedars, coachmen and horses, dogs and maids and my grandmother in vast hats and long silk dresses. My father was born there in 1892 and spent the first few years of his life, a solitary child, happily enough with his little pony cart, his dogs Sherry, Whiskey and Soda, and my grandfather's Great Danes. The favourite of which was called Rosé.

My grandmother, like so many converts, became more Catholic than the Catholics, if that is possible, and made my grandfather's life complicated and tiresome. There was never to be another child apart from my father, because she believed, strictly, that sex should only be accompanied by the birth of a child, and this my grandfather resented. Some time – and here I get vague because I am lost for the facts – some time in the early 1900s he went on a journey to London. He never returned to the sprawling ivy-covered villa in Perry Barr with its cedars and lawns and Converted Catholic mistress, but took ship for South America from whence he was occasionally to write, and send my father photographs of his trips up the Orinoco (he was one of the first white men ever to get as far up it as he apparently did) and from the Amazon and various seedy little villages in Brazil.

He must also have sent presents sometimes, because for many years we had a rather smelly leopard's skin, which crackled and moulted, and the upper and lower jaws of a puma which he apparently shot during one of his expeditions. It is also supposed that he tried to import orchids in abundance to England but that this venture was doomed because of a lack of knowledge of packing and that all the tubers, or bulbs or whatever they are called, were rotted and dead on arrival at Liverpool. If this is true or not I do not know: but that was how we were always told that grandfather lost his fortune. It may well be so, for in 1910 my grandmother was forced to sell up Perry Barr and move, humbly, and in her grief, to a dingy, red-brick house in Bexhill, where she lived a genteel, careful, frugal life bringing up my fatherless parent. She died there alone and bitter, while my father was in Passchendael in 1917. He said that she had died of a broken heart. A lonely, incapable, fragile woman. So, in the middle of a holocaust and at the age of twenty-three, my father to all intents and purposes became an orphan and considered that to be his lot.

It is hardly surprising, therefore, that one hot summer morning, after nearly thirty years of silence, a telephone call from a worried doctor in Brighton informing him that his father was gravely ill and wished to see him before he died, which could be at any moment, should explode like a land-mine within our household.

I have no idea what took place between my father and his own on that fateful day. It was never spoken of and we were certainly not encouraged to ask any questions. It was quite enough for us to know that we had 'found' a hitherto dead grandparent whose life, to say the very least, had been a vague shadow lost in the distance of a time unknown to us.

Later I was to find out that all through those many years he had never lost track of my father and knew every detail of his existence. He knew of his marriage to my mother, of which he did not approve because she was 'foreign', of our births, of his position at *The Times* and, clearly, of his whereabouts at all times. And even though we spent most of our lives living within a few miles of the town in which he had taken up permanent residence, he only got in touch because he feared that, finally, he was dying of pneumonia and asked the doctor, who had been sent for by his daily woman, to inform his son of that fact.

He did not die as it happened. Perhaps the sight of his son and the idea of a large family to gather around him revived him, for he shortly got better and settled back into his dingy house near the West Pier at Brighton.

When it was clear to my father that death was not to ease our new burden, he decided that we had better meet, and some weeks after the telephone call we were driven down to Brighton to see our 'dead' grandfather.

It was a faded, grubby house in a faded, grubby square. 'To Let' signs hung at every window, and children played hopscotch in the ruined patch of garden in the centre.

Inside it was dark and smelled of stale tobacco and turpentine. The ground-floor room, with a big window, was crammed with canvases, stacks of old newspapers, a huge easel, paints and brushes and a battered couch on a raised platform. The windows were thick with grime, and beside the ugly marble fireplace there were a couple of tables draped in worn American cloth, littered with saucepans and gas rings. Pots of dying herbs stood on the window-sill. We went up some dark, heavily papered, stairs.

He lay, a waxen shrivelled figure with blazing eyes and a small straggly beard, on a vast red lacquer bed in the shape of a swan, the neck and head forming the foot of the bed, the spread tail the head, and the raised wings the sides. It looked like a boat.

He stretched out a thin arm and took our hands, and smiled as we leaned to kiss him. He spoke with a heavy accent, and was delighted that we resembled him as he said.

He had established a pleasant form of rapport with my mother during the weeks, and told her how handsome we were and how handsome she was too.

'She has good eyes, you know, Ulric,' he said to my father. 'Good eyes. Probably Latin blood, I wouldn't wonder, even if she is Scotch. Remember the Spanish; they swarmed over the west coast of Scotland, and half the population were raped.' My mother laughed and he blew her a fragile kiss. 'You all probably have Spanish blood as well as Flemish! What a mixture!' He was amused. Turning to me with his fine, gaunt head, he asked me if I was clever. I was forced to admit that I was not.

'How many languages can you speak?' he asked.

'A little French,' I said. He laughed and said a little was better than none and that he spoke five fluently, including some South American Indian dialects as well.

'But you must not worry, boy,' he said gently. 'We are all very slow to develop in our family, so you have time. Do you know the family motto? Does he know it, Ulric? *Semper Viridis* . . . do you know what that means?' And when I shook my head he stroked his little straggly beard and said, 'It means Ever Green'.

Once a week, until I went to Scotland, we went down to the dirty house and saw him gradually grow stronger, and in time he was pottering, very slowly, about his dusty studio downstairs. On one occasion, swearing that he was strong enough to cook again, he sent me off with a penny to buy him four farthing eggs from a shop up the road.

'Ask for Polish eggs,' he said, 'they do me very well in an omelette.'

The herbs got watered, and my mother replaced chives and parsley and mint and sought, in vain, for his essential love, tarragon. The gas-rings blazed and he started to smoke endlessly; the smell of cooking now competed with turpentine and tobacco when we went to call.

My father realised that this state of affairs could not go on any longer. It was impossible for us to have him at home, and indeed he flatly refused the idea. So a nursing home where he could furnish his own room was sought and found near Kemp Town, and they told him firmly but gently. His rage knew no bounds. He refused to be moved and demanded to be left alone to his painting and his cooking and his own life. My father, weary of it all, shattered by the additional expense not only of a new son but a new father, gave in and, making him a small allowance which he could ill afford, left him to himself as he demanded.

He was not only impetuous and determined, but a blindingly selfish man. What happened to him in all those long years so near and yet so very far away? When did he return to England? How did he live? Why did he never make the smallest effort to reach my father or his mother, knowing, if one is to believe the facts, that he was well aware all the time of where they were, and what they were doing?

It is impossible to guess. From the moment that the letters stopped coming from South America, about 1908, until the telephone call, all remains lost in a distant past and will never, I suppose, be discovered.

It appears that for some years in England he made a modest living by painting, and selling, copies of Flemish 'masterpieces'. Usually on leather, or on secondhand canvases. Sometimes he used seamen's wooden chests, or boxes, which he picked up for shillings in the junk markets of Brighton, Worthing and Shoreham. These he covered with leather and jolly Breughel-peasants busy at their weddings, funerals and harvests. Sometimes Princes and Kings, glittering in armour, astride horses slashing at each other with swords or spears. On occasions, to vary the pace, wild groups of dead pheasants or duck hung garlanded in grapes and vines or improbable Coats of Arms.

These he covered with a special varnish which he had invented himself and which in a very short time crackled and 'aged' the paint and the leather and gave to all the patina of sepia-antiquity, as long as one didn't look too deeply. Passed off as Early Flemish, or Dutch, two galleries in London kept him gainfully occupied for some years with these curious works which as often as not ended up in America or Canada.

There still remain some excellent examples of his honesty on the walls of a big pub in Brighton and various smaller establishments along the coast, landlords of which accepted a small canvas for the walls of their private bars in exchange for a few pints of beer. Or, if he was lucky, a bottle of wine.

His 'master' was Wouvermaans. And many a second-hand canvas covered by him with rearing horses and falling soldiers may still yet be thundering about in the drawing-rooms of innumerable commercial hotels from Eastbourne to Matlock Spa.

He was, in short, a faker. And a very good one. In spite of all the languages, the travelling, the education and the family background which he had, he seems only to have made his living by deception, but after he came into our lives, or we came into his, whichever way you care to look at it, he stopped painting and scrabbling about in the junk shops and gave it up to live comfortably, if modestly, on the allowance from my unfortunate father.

I, of course, was mesmerised by him. I was happy to sit in a chair beside him in his smelly, crowded studio, looking at his stamp albums, his maps of the Amazon, faded and torn, his piles of old magazines and books, or just listen to him talking in his heavy accent about his journeys into the Andes on a mule or his astonishing voyage on a sailing ship from Lima to Valparaiso; but more than that he would not give away. And the stories had a vague not-quite-true-but-could-be quality about them which in no way diminished their delight.

He sat in a high carved oak armchair, his long bony fingers clasping the arms; his finger-nails were long like a Mandarin's, but always scrupulously clean which constantly amazed me. Sometimes in the middle of a story he would start to crack eggs and flour into a bowl and begin to cook something for his supper, a cake or biscuits: he told me that one of the wobbly tables which supported his gas-rings came from Versailles and probably belonged at one time to Marie Antoinette because there was an 'A' worked into the chipped and crumbling gesso. Lifting the tattered American cloth he would make me peer at the fine carved legs and stretchers and ask me if I could see the 'A', and sometimes I thought that I did. But I could never be sure. He said that all his Bits and Pieces came from junk shops and sale rooms when he was looking about for his work. The great red lacquer bed was from China and he felt sure that it was brought over after the Boxer Rebellion, and who was I to doubt him? All his Treasures, he said, had cost him nothing but a discerning eye, and he said that one must cultivate such a thing by watching, looking and listening, and also by always asking Why? and What? and Where? 'You must be Observant, boy. Always Observe. If you do not understand what you see, ask someone to tell you what it is . . . if they don't know, you must take books and find out. Always seek, always question, always be Interested, otherwise you will perish.'

This, strangely enough, was something which my father had inherited from him. We were always told to Look . . . to watch, to see and to listen. Even if it bored us to death at times; like Chamber Music which I hated but had to listen to very often in order to be able, later on I was told, to appreciate the great symphonies. Consequently we were curious children and delighted in finding things out for ourselves even though our frequent questioning must have seemed tremendously irritating to many of our friends. Although I detested any form of Games, and had always managed to avoid Children's Parties for fear that I should be forced to play them, I did enjoy, constantly, my father's Remember Games. In a tube train look and see how many pairs of brown shoes there are on the people opposite. How many bunions, which has a lace untied, who wears spats? And then look away at the faces above and try to fit each one out. This was a simple game to play and fun, but quite often caused offence to the unfortunate victims sitting facing one who twitched and fidgeted and stared about them under the implacable observing eyes of the child opposite.

Other games were looking in shop windows and counting the number of pots or pans with a black lid or a blue lid, how many milk jugs there were on a given row, or plates in a pile, then, making a mental list, one wandered away for a few minutes to return later and check. This caused one to give the impression that one was loitering; however it was all very good training and not easily forgotten. And although I was such a dunce at school, at these games I was more than outstanding, simply because I found detail fascinating. Of course there were never any rewards for being good at these games; it was just expected that you would be, and the reward was getting the lists as correct as possible. And it was rewarding in a strange way. Lastingly so I imagine.

The last time I went to see my grandfather at his smelly old house was just before I went up to Scotland. He was sad that I was leaving for 'so far away', as he put it, and made me promise to write to him from time to time and to send him any new stamps which might come out in that strange, to him, country. He was regretful that I was going because he had started to enjoy the family which he had cheerfully denied for so many years and feared the loneliness again. Or at least I suppose that is what it was. Also he was very anxious, suddenly, to tell me about The Family and said that I should know, and be taught, French and German so that I could go back one day to the Estates which he had left and which my unfortunate father never had the chance of seeing until 1921 or '22 when he took my mother back to Iseghem. I say 'back' which is incorrect, since he had never ever been there, however 'back' is what sounded right. Apart from a tomb in the local church and a street named after my great grandfather, very little remained of the Estates now almost surrounded by factories and urban streets. However, the chateau, which still stands today and looks much as it must have done then, was an imposing place of pale rose brick and grey stone with many shuttered windows, standing on a little hill which sloped down to a long tree-bordered lake spanned by a high, gracefully arching, white iron bridge.

Rooks cawed in the great beeches all around, and there was a screaming baby in a pram on the elegant, many-stepped, terrace. Relations were cool and polite and not about to be welcoming to the English sprig who so suddenly arrived that summer day. And my father left never to return, not to speak of it ever to me at least.

I remember in the war having 48 hours' leave after the catastrophe at Arnhem. I went to the Officers' Leave Hotel, the Palace in Brussels, wanting only to bathe and sleep for the whole two days. A very old porter helped, churlishly, to carry my sleeping-bag and haversack. In the room I fumbled for a tip and saw him looking at my name painted on the canvas of my kit-bag. He asked me, in French, where I came from and what my Christian names were. I told him, and his eyes filled with tears as he pulled off his cap and bowed gently to me, to my embarrassment and surprise. He had been my grandfather's groom at Iseghem and remembered him well.

That was the nearest I ever got to the Estates.

'When you go to this Scottish school you must study your French and German, you must be able to speak them fluently and correctly. It is easy to do, it is in your blood. I speak five, as you know, and I started to learn when I was a very small child, possibly when I was five or six. It is late for you, but you must strive. It will make you less English.'

I remember promising that I would try and he gave me a keepsake. A small metal lay figure which he had used for many years to draw from. I was sad at the apparent meanness of the gift, I was hopefully expecting a Delft jar or a rather pleasant jade frog which sat, with a coveted paperweight containing a black and yellow salamander, on the mantelshelf. However, I made do with the tin figure, which is just as well, for it is the only thing I ever received from him beyond the doubtful ability to paint, his good brown eyes, and a vague feeling of failure.

Nearly forty years later, after he had been to see 'Death In Venice', my father telephoned me here in France. Something which he had never done before. 'I was very moved indeed,' he said, 'to see my father again.'

'Well!' said Lally one evening while she was sewing Cashes labels into all my shirts. 'Now we have a new brother and a new grandfather. Whatever next, I wonder! And you mark my words, things always go in threes. They always come in threes, you see if I lie.'

Because she absolutely never ever lied to us or evaded any question, we took her very seriously. One never knew when she might be right. Sometimes, like Ilfracombe, we found out that she was wrong, and that instead of Wales on which she insisted, it was in Devon, but those were very slight irregularities. We never got fobbed off with a non-answer. We always got a Fact. Even inaccurate was better than none at all or a 'Don't bother me now I'm busy' or 'Look it up for yourself, it's in a book.' Always an answer. Even if it did mean having to check from time to time, just for safety's sake.

'Does a postillion blow his trumpet on a coach?' I asked my father. We were walking down the lane to the quarry-garage.

'Nonsense. He's the rider on the near horse if you've only got two for the coach; he's the driver.'

'What happens if he gets struck by lightning then?'

My father laughed. 'I wouldn't care to be in the coach, that's all I can say. For God's sake, turn your feet out, you walk like a penguin.'

These weren't serious inaccuracies, easily checked after all, and as Lally said, Devon and Wales were both West so we were at least in the right direction.

She had our complete confidence whatever mistakes might be made, and therefore when she said about 'coming in threes' I felt uneasy for what next might befall us. I had rather counted on the Scotland Trip as one of the three, but she seemed not to, so I worriedly awaited the final blow.

It came in the form of a letter to my father from the Aleford's Estate Manager. The Alefords owned the Court Farm and all the land around it. They had decided to retire from farming and move away. The Cottage would be up for sale at the auction in December next. The house and one acre. As a separate lot.

We had no idea, Elizabeth and I, that we did not own the Cottage. No idea that we merely rented it by the year from the rather jolly family down at the Court. It was ours completely. We had, it seemed, had it for ever and ever, and every flint and tile belonged to us. The total shock of the truth was far worse than brothers or grandfathers or even a violent change of school. To think that the Cottage was no longer ours, that in fact it never had been except for a weekly payment of seven shillings, was unthinkable. We were struck dumb with horror and grief. A grief which was silent and therefore all the more irritating to our elders. Lally was gentle and patient. She didn't mention anything about 'Three' and simply realized that our misery was too great for more than a bit of extra loving and second helpings of pudding.

'They'll find somewhere else, even nicer than the Cottage, you see,' she said with tactful ignorance. 'Remember what a lot it needs doing to it! That floor in the hall is all rotten; it needs proper sanitation, and water, and light, and the roof's bound to go in the next big storm and really I'm sure it's all for the best. You see if I lie.'

But we were listless with despair and all her cheering up was to no avail. My father was patient with our hollow-eyed sullenness and promised that he and our mother would go to the auction in December and try to buy it . . . but I knew as he spoke that it would be only a vague possibility. New brothers and schools and grandfathers cost money, even I began to realise that after a while.

In fact Lally was right about the repairs which the Cottage needed. But somehow without the old pump, without the lamps in the long winter evenings, without those solitary walks to the privy, the Cottage couldn't ever be the same again. The idea of turning on a tap in the big flint kitchen might have been delight for her but was abhorrent to me. I knew, even in my selfish and uncaring way, that things were beginning to change everywhere. Caravans had suddenly sprouted up in the fields at Cuckmere Haven. Beastly little white boxes filled with whey-faced Londoners peering through their 'cheery' orange and brown caravan-curtains. Even the Downs behind Friston and East Dean were being ploughed up for the planting of a great pine forest, and there was talk of rows and rows of cheap bungalows being allowed to scab and scar the soft dales and swards of the Seven Sisters themselves. It was all changing all right. And if the Cottage did not belong to us, if it had been a long, glorious dream and if none of it had ever really happened at all, then, so be it. Life, or rather my own life, for I tended, as usual, to see everything in terms of myself, was starting to shred away like a sail in the wind, and I was very well aware that my little boat was far too frail a craft to weather the storms which were to come. Sail-less I should be sunk or beached. Neither idea pleased me. Staring dully up at my tit-and-wisteria wallpaper, I had realised that Lally's words of some time ago were true. 'You can't have a summer without a good winter,' she had said. Winter was now.

Bishopbriggs was where the trams from Glasgow ended. Clacketting, racketting, lurching their way from Renfield Street through the black canyons of faceless tenements in Springburn, trundling through acres of blighted wasteland, scabbed with wrecked cars, rubbish tips, blackened clumps of thistle and thorn, they coasted gently into the blank granite square of what once might have been a pleasant country village. Here the small gabled houses, empty-eyed windows, draped in white lace, secret with half drawn blinds, gleamed in misty rain. Beyond slate roofs, the pointed caps of the Tips, like my sister's spilly hills of sugar only black. Dead volcanoes spotting the ruined fields. 'The Bingies', relics of a thriving pit closed since the start of the Depression.

From the terminus, the steel rails shining like swords in black granite cobbles, past a scatter of gas lit shops, up a brick alley, through a long dripping tunnel under the railway line, one arrived on 'the other side' of the town. A straggling, cold, ugly housing estate, in Avenues, Crescents, Terraces, and Drives; no Streets or Roads for the new middle classes. Flat-faced pebble-dash houses; four windows up, four below, pink-grey asbestos tiled roofs, concrete paths, creosoted picket fences and washing dripping in every back garden. All about one there was nothing to see but row upon row upon row of roofs, backed here and there by the pointed nose of a Tip or a few wind-twisted trees high on an, as yet, untouched hillock. It rained gently.

24 Springburn Terrace was the same as all its neighbours. The only way I could distinguish it for the first few months was by the fact that it stood on a corner and had a slightly larger area of garden around it with a lamp-post at the front gate. The houses were not Houses at all. They were flats. One up and one down. The down one had a front door in the centre, the up one had a front door at the side up a flight of concrete steps. Walls and the floors were made of cardboard. From the front door a long narrow passage. To the right a sitting-room, beyond that a bedroom. At the top of the narrow passage a lavatory and bath together. To the left a dining-room, beyond that the kitchen with a door

leading out into the pleasures of a wan garden. Yard more like. A hedge of Golden Elder, a few neat flower-beds, a bit of grass in the middle and in the centre of that a tall iron post for the laundry. A small world for three ill-assorted people.

Aunt Belle, my mother's elder sister, was tall, kind looking, with a patrician face and soft auburn hair flecking with grey. Her husband, Uncle Duff, was slightly shorter than she was, with thin black hair parted in the middle and glued to his head with Yardley's Hair Cream. His small black moustache looked as if it had been smudged on with coal. They welcomed me to this unprepossessing house shyly and warmly with a crackling fire and high tea.

'All boys like to eat,' said my aunt, 'so I did a Baking for you especially!' There were five different sorts of biscuit, scones, and cup cakes, as well as a Madeira Cake with candy peel on top. Sandwiches, toast, anchovy paste, and strawberry jam.

Also a canary, Joey, who lived in the window in a cage with a yellow silk frill round the base to stop the seed from scattering. Afterwards, in the sitting-room across the hall, we sat by the fire, my aunt sewing, my uncle showing me his bound volumes of Bruce Bairnsfeather's cartoons. I wondered, vaguely, where I should sleep.

About nine o'clock he went out to the kitchen to make the cocoa for supper. My aunt put aside her sewing and said I must be tired after such a long day and so many excitements. I was aware that she meant travelling, and trains and farewells and all that sort of thing. She explained gently that they had moved out of their bedroom next door so that I should have it, and that they would sleep on a Put-U-Up Settee in the dining-room.

'This is a rather small house for the three of us, but I'm sure we'll manage very well,' she said. 'It's the Depression, you know. Uncle lost everything, I'm afraid, and so we just had to cut our cloth to suit the material. It is not the sort of place we like to live in. But it'll just have to do. I don't suppose you remember the other house, do you?'

I did. Gleaming mahogany furniture, heavy and sombre, shining brass jugs filled with flowers and leaves, a piano scattered with silver frames, high windows velvet-curtained, all looking out over a soft green wooded park. Not at all like this sad, apologetic, squashed little house.

Some of the old stuff had made the swift descent from gentility to near-poverty and looked defiantly out of place in such cramped quarters. The ladder-backed chairs in the dining room, a tall mahogany bookcase, some bold chintz armchairs with anti-macassars pinned to them like maids caps, my grandfather's water-colours in thin gold frames, a set of Nashes Magazine Covers for 1918 framed in black passe-partout, and the black marble mantel-clock which thinly struck the hours and quarters.

My bedroom was a square of pink distemper. Two windows over the bleak square of garden and the dead backs of the houses beyond the ragged hedge. A one-bar electric fire, a yellow oak wardrobe with an oval mirror which reflected the entire room, a dressing chest, a dressing table and a wide yellow oak bed spread with a shining pink satin cover. In the bed a scalding aluminium hot water bottle called a 'pig' . . . and a hot brick wrapped in flannel.

I was told to use the bathroom first. A bath, a basin, a lavatory. His ivory brushes stuck together by their bristles, W.D. entwined in black on the back. The oval tin of Yardley's grease. Toothbrushes huddled in a tumbler like old men at a wedding. Izal on the lavatory paper. We said goodnight, and I lay in the dark of the wide yellow bed listening to them raking out the fire in the sitting-room and setting the china for breakfast. Then bathroom noises and the lavatory flushing twice. Pattering of feet down the corridor to the front door, a chain rattling, a bolt running home, the dining-room door closing. Silence and then the slow, low, murmur of worried conversation through the wall.

The clock struck a quarter. Ting Ting Ting. Light from the lamp-post flickered through leaf shadows on the buff paper blind. A draught waggled the cord and made the little acorn handle tap tap against the glass. In the house upstairs someone else pulled a chain and I heard a soft cataract of water and a pipe beside the wardrobe started to knock gently.

I turned into the pillows and tried to smother my blubbing.

I travelled to school every morning with Uncle Duff. We caught the eight-five. The same compartment, the same faces. Three *Glasgow Heralds*, two *Bulletins*, one *Express*. Queen Street station, an enormous inverted iron colander. Black and sooty, rife with pigeons and the smell of urine. Blazes of brilliant light here and there in the gloom from the bookstalls. Farewell to Uncle, he to his office in St Vincent Street, me to George Square and the long haul up the cobbled stone street to The School. Standing isolated in the centre of a vast asphalted playground, surrounded by high iron spikes, its red sandstone blocks rotting in the filth from the city, it resembled a cross between a lunatic asylum and a cotton mill. Faceless windows gazed blankly over the streets below. Electric lights gleamed dully even on the clearest days. A smell of chalk and concrete dust, of sulphur and soot.

Green glazed tiles, ochre distemper, red varnished wood. Cold, unloving, unloved. A Technical School for Technical People. What on earth was I doing here? I who could only just about read and write? Chosen by Uncle Duff for a 'good solid background under a progressive teaching staff', it was thoughtfully accepted by my parents as the Final Desperate Measure to try and force some learning into my addled head. They had made a swift tour of the place, dragging me in stupefied horror behind them, had outlined to the Progressive Teaching Staff what was wanted, had shaken hands in a cramped Victorian Headmaster's Study and departed with relief for the South. Leaving me to sort out the road leading to 'The Times'.

It was only a matter of days before I knew, for certain, that I was in the very worst place for my sort of complaint. I had the technical brain of a newt. Here everyone sat entranced while glum-faced teachers poured one liquid into a flask, and another liquid on to iron filings or something equally inane. They sat with tongues hanging out, and darting eyes crossing the wide blackboards following hieroglyphics which I was told were called logarithms, long division, or agreed, with eager nods, the bold assumption that 'if A equals B and C equals D thus E, F, G and X are equal to the sum total of Q'.

I never knew how many apples a farmer had left in his basket if he gave his wife two-thirds. Or how much water slipped away in an hour if the bath-plug was released and the tap dribbled at the rate of fifty drops per minute. What the Hell! I was lost. Notebooks were virginal white. Pencils unblunted. Rubbers un-rubbed. Surrounded by a class of thirty I started to observe them in preference to the impossible messages on the blackboards.

Raw-boned hulks most of them seemed. Red hair and freckles; fair hair and pigs eyes; white faces and acne. Stooped grey-flannel backs, prematurely humped, arms like gorillas stretched out along their desks: booted feet twitching for a football. Or anything to kick.

No vivid Trevor Ropers, no fat kind Foots, no bespectacled Jones G. C.'s here; these were tough, Irish-Scots, one parent away from the Pits, four years or less from the Barricades. Foreigners. And what made things harder was that I couldn't understand a word they said, nor could they understand me. A gulf had started from the very first day with the barrier of our common tongue. I was the odd man out, the Sassenach, posh, weedy, incomprehensible, alien. But I knew that because I was New, this slit-eyed raw-boned herd of bullocks was biding its time until the terror which was growing steadily within me should start to leak away, like blood in a sea of sharks. And when they scented it, they would attack. This I knew.

My desk mate – we sat two to a bench like slaves in the galleys – was called Tom. He was dark, thin, pleasant looking with round tin glasses. He showed me where to hand my cap and coat, where my locker was, where the lavatories were, the class-rooms I would use, and where to eat our lunch if we didn't go home. Which neither of us did.

A long brick shed, it was pushed into a corner of the Yard almost as an afterthought. It had a tin roof and was euphemistically called the Tuck Shop. Banks of greasy wooden tables, benches on each side, a long counter at one end with tea and coffee urns and racks of soggy hot, or cold, meat pies, sausages, cheese buns, bread and dripping and Mars Bars.

At the other end, two pin tables for the elder boys. We were not allowed to use them until we were sixteen, but everyone did anyway. In one corner a foul, stinking lavatory which was three walls with an open drain round the edges. Sluggish streams of gently steaming urine bubbled along this trough. Cigarette ends and gobs of spittle bobbed about like floats in a stream. On the walls of above the slate slabs against which we pissed, a whole holocaust of wild scribbles and obscenities, none of which I understood any better than their language.

In the other corner a cabin with doors like a stable so that one could see the feet and the top of the head of the occupant. Sometimes there were two or three pairs of feet scuffling about below the door, and the knowing shouts and bellows of laughter made me sick with apprehension, not understanding what was going on in there.

Tom used to guide me out of the Tuck Shop as often as the weather allowed and we sat, each with our bottle of Cola, a hot pie and an apple or a orange, on the low wall which ran round the dustbins watching a thousand games of football played with an old tennis ball or a rough block of wood. He talked away from time to time, and I tried to understand him, which made him laugh, and he tried to understand me, which made me laugh too. We were warm together, and I knew that I liked him, but conversation was, of necessity, limited. I did, however, glean that his father was a coal-man and that he, Tom, had won a scholarship to this unenviable school.

I was deeply impressed. Not that his father was a coal-man, but that he had been clever enough to win a scholarship and could still be so gentle, patient and kind. I liked him very much, and he became my mate.

One day when the weather was too wet to go out and eat our lunch on the dustbin wall, some of the Herd started to make muffled, smothered, giggling jokes clearly about me across the greasy tables. They were mostly the elder boys, and the younger ones were sniggering and squirming sycophantically at the jokes.

Tom suddenly stiffened with alarm and mumbled something, but before he was able to say anything more, the Herd had started to move towards me in a slow, undulating wave. With one united lunge they grabbed me and dragged me struggling in nameless terror to the lavatory at the end of the room. I heard Tom shouting, but the doors had swung closed and I was hustled into the cabin, up-ended into the lavatory pan, held firmly by my knees and legs, while someone, as if from a hundred miles down a tunnel said: 'Fuckin' posh twit.

Talking so la-di-da need your wee mouth washin' out.' Someone pulled the chain and I thought that I had drowned. Gasping and choking, vomiting like a dog on the wet slimy floor, I was told that until I learned to speak correctly this would happen again. Then they left me. I lay for an eternity, retching and gasping in a sea of filth and undigested meat pie. I thought that I would never be able to breathe again. Tears and dribble coursed down my face from the coughing and choking and the retching.

Tom helped me to clean up as best I could in the boiler room under the school. I lay on a pile of coke while he tried to apologise and wipe me down with his handkerchief and some newspaper which we had found. I stayed there hiccuping and heaving until the break bell clanged. Damp, creased and smelly I took my place in Class. No one said anything. They watched over the tops of their books or sideways from the edges of their faces. They were all quietly smiling. Through bleary eyes I looked back at them. And decided to learn to speak correctly.

For days I was in terror that I should catch some disease from my Lavatory Drowning. With some of my luncheon money – I got one and sixpence a day from Uncle Duff each morning on the train – I bought a bottle of disinfectant and, as secretly as I could, gargled and cleaned my mouth out until it was raw and blistered with whatever it was I had used. No one knew what had happened, of course, and I had a difficult job sneaking into the house and changing my filthy clothes, but managed to convince them that I had been in a fight in the rain and that was that.

Uncle Duff was quite jovial at tea that evening.

'A fight already! Well I declare! they'll make a wee man of ye yet.'

My aunt was no fool. She didn't say a word, just went on buttering her potato pancake, but I think she knew that it had been more than a fight.

For the first month or two I was bullied constantly. Being skinny, having the wrong accent, although I was doing my damnedest to correct that daily, and never joining in the break time football made me as conspicuous as a cripple. And I was accordingly treated as such, for that is really what they thought I was. Deformed, different, weak, a cissie, to be got rid of. Tom was a help, but I felt that I couldn't shelter behind him all the time, and in any case, he wasn't always with me. He had his learning to do and was frequently taking a different Class to me.

Sitting one day on the wall of the Yard (there were no benches) I got clouted on the shin by a whirling block of wood being used as a football. I yelled out in pain and fell off the wall. I was suddenly engulfed in a swirling, kicking mass of roaring footballers who dragged me across the asphalt in the direction of the lavatory. Terror loaned me desperate strength. I fought and clawed and bit and kicked and suddenly found that the crowd had pulled away and I was struggling with one sole boy, older than me, taller and stronger. His name, I think, was Bell. I don't know what happened, or how I did it, but as he swung me away from him with one arm to punch me in the face, I swung at him and hit him with all the force I could muster in the eye. He gave a great cry and fell to the ground, his face covered with his hands. I fell on top of him and went on bashing and thumping at him, but his cries grew louder and louder, and his hands flew from his face and flailed the air about his head. I saw that he now only had one eye. The other had apparently gone.

We were dragged to our feet, I stiff with terror at the pulp-face before me; he barking in a loud hoarse voice, groping about in the air, blood streaming down his face.

Whitefaced, they half carried, half led, him across to the school. I stood alone in the middle of the yard. No one moved or spoke. They stood and watched me. Somebody pointed silently to a water tap over by the wall, and they watched in little groups as I bathed my face and washed off the blood which seemed to be more his than mine. When I straightened up they had gone. I was never bullied again. Avoided for a time, but never bullied.

Naturally there was an Inquiry in the Head's office. He was a big, heavy, jovial man. Wise and aware. He knew damned well what had happened but he in no way blamed me, he merely suggested, mildly, that fighting was not what I was there for, and that he didn't want to hear another complaint about me again. I was unaware that he had had any complaints before but was grateful for his leniency. As for Bell – well, whatever I did to his eye in my terror and rage kept him in a bandage for some time. And away from the school for more than three weeks. But I didn't care; from then on I ate my hot pie in peace and found school life peaceful, if lonely.

ELEVEN

Self-preservation became my main preoccupation now. Not merely against bullying; I had got that one sorted out by some strange fluke. Not only against the isolation which my foreignness caused among my school mates. I swiftly learned a thick, and unpleasing, Glasgow accent, and was grudgingly allowed to pass as more or less one of them. However, the fact that I played no games, read during the 'breaks' rather than hacked away at lumps of wood stolen from the Woodwork Class, didn't know the difference between H_2SO_4 or 5 or 9 or whatever, and spent most of my time dreaming away plots and ideas for stories which never really got written, all these things set me clearly apart from the rest, and they resented it; and in their resentment isolated me.

I was supremely unbothered by this. For I liked none of them and preferred my own company to anyone else's, except, perhaps, for Tom whom I seldom saw apart from the hurried meat-pie at lunch on the dustbin walls.

My main self-defence was against Bishopbriggs. Not, you understand, against the town itself. It couldn't help what it was, a sordid, cold, unloving and unloved scatter of grey concrete council houses surrounding, like a belt of cement death, a grim, solid, dour little town of granite block and slate roofs. The town affected me only in so far as it was ugly, sad and apparently constantly in a drizzling rain. It was more the *life* I lived in the town which needed my defence. I found it almost impossible to realise the gentility and coldness of it without shock.

At home, among an easy-going family, we always showed our full emotions; it was, indeed, encouraged. I embraced my father nightly before going to bed, and we all touched, and liked touching, each other. Nakedness meant not having your clothes on. Going to the lavatory a normal, essential, function performed, as far as Lally was concerned, every morning after breakfast. And she wanted to know full details. Puppies, kittens, rabbits and everything else were 'born': we aided the mothers and sat entranced at the births. Everything in life was totally normal and I was quite unprepared for the opposite side of the coin, the Repressions.

The first time I offered to kiss my uncle on the cheek before I went to bed he recoiled as if I had physically assaulted him and, with a crimson face, gruffly said, 'We don't do that sort of thing here.' And offered me his hand. My aunt received her kiss as if I had threatened her. She winced uncomfortably. The Lavatory became the 'Bathroom'. You never spoke of Birth, only ever of Death. If a woman was pregnant she was 'a wee bittie under the weather'. And one was never seen in the corridor of the house in pyjamas. Always, if we had to go from bed to the 'Bathroom' a dressing-gown and slippers were obligatory. I am not blaming. This was how it was, and it was I who did not understand and so had to re-learn the rules. After all it was their house not mine. And their way of life. I would have to conform.

That settled, and accepted, the Routine had to be followed. Every weekend was planned months in advance. A constant cosy roster of relations or friends to be visited. Few ever came to our house because the change of Style had been a grave sadness to both my uncle and aunt and they preferred to keep their grief to themselves. Hence on the first Sunday of the month we went to Isa for a tinned salmon tea, where I read knitting patterns; on the second Sunday it was Aunt Teenie, who was a million years old, wore a black velvet ribbon round her throat, was blinded in one eye, and scarred dreadfully down her whole left cheek from an accident with a penknife many years ago when she had been a girl skating. She shook and trembled constantly, like a cobweb in a draught, and presided at a gigantic tea table covered with cakes and scones and home-made bread. A silver teapot smothered by a crinolined celluloid doll, its pink shiny arms held out in supplication, a simpering Madonna. A small hand-knitted pom pom hat on its head. A brass kettle steamed gently over a spirit lamp, and we ate constantly, in more or less complete silence. It was, as far as I was concerned, like force feeding a goose. Later we retired to the sitting-room lace and velvet draped, submerged in dark ferns, and while they knitted and did embroidery, the women, my uncle slept discreetly under his Sunday paper and I played eternal games of Solitaire with glass marbles on a round mahogany board.

The third Sunday in the month was usually at Meg's where we sometimes had a Smokie for High Tea, from Dundee, after which I was given a volume of photographs. The clasp would be unlocked, and I was offered a sepia world of bustles, dog carts, sailor suits and family groups of improbable strangers bug-eyed round bamboo tables.

The final Sunday was usually spent over at my maternal Grandmother's house in Langside. A long table of ten or fourteen of us, uncles and aunts, and elder cousins. Grandmamma at the head in black, a table laid as for a wedding; cakes and jams, scones and bread, tarts and sandwiches. We ate and talked of Family Matters and what had happened to us all in the month. My uncles were, without exception, handsome, dark and jolly. My aunts pleasant and kind and knitted. The cousins quiet and gently smiling. Later, in the big sitting-room upstairs, the fire was lit for Sunday and the younger of us played a new game called 'Monopoly', or else 'Snap', 'Happy Families', or 'Bezique'. My grandmamma, who ruled her house with a deceptive firmness, sat in a chintz armchair and played games of patience. The uncles read papers and were allowed to smoke there.

This routine I accepted easily. It was not at all unpleasant, and sometimes comforting to know that every Sunday was so well taken care of. Of course, in the morning, wet or fine, it was a long walk to church. We left early for the three mile walk through the gritty Estate, out into the ruined fields, and then, quite soon, the real country started and the journey was always very agreeable, even in snow or sleet. The road to Cadder, where the church was, swung up and down gentle hills, across a tumbling, rocky river, through silent beech woods. The Service was dull, slow and incomprehensible. Church of Scotland. Spartan, undecorated. None of the sweeping colours, the gilts and blues, the purples and viridians, the soaring music and the heady smell of incense to which I had grown accustomed and incorrectly associated with every church. This was white and charcoal, a place for penance not praise. I watched the sun sparkle through the branches of the trees and make dancing shadows on the white-washed walls. My aunt, inevitably, and elegantly dressed by Pettigrew and Stephens, used always to try and wear a different hat or a different costume, or coat, in the winter. She was hopeful that it would be noticed and sad when, sometimes, it was not. The Service was mostly a weekly check up on who was who and what they had been doing. It was a Social Affair, conducted with religious fervour and a great deal of kneeling and singing. But I enjoyed the walk in the country.

After lunch, which had been put in the oven while we were at our Holy Orders and Social Spying, I had to write my weekly letter home. This was thoughtfully corrected by my uncle for faults in grammar, spelling and punctuation. Should I, by mistake, miss out an interesting bit of news, such as a trip to the Orpheus Choir, or a visit to a Football Match, this was delicately inserted, even it it meant re-writing an entire page, for my uncle was at great pains that my family should know that my life in Scotland was not just one long grind of scholastic chores. In this way, of course, I had no possible chance of saying anything the least critical. And my letters were dull, dutiful, a long list of totally boring excursions and activities at school.

My parents were relieved that I had settled down so well into the family life, that I was being so warmly welcomed, and that according to the note, always appended to my letters by my uncle, my school work was improving slowly but steadily. There was, they felt, no cause for concern. Why should there be? And so, although they none of them meant to, I was gently put to one side while they went on with their affairs, and those affairs revolved mostly about the Baby and 'The Times'. When I went back on longed-for holidays, it never ever occurred to me to say otherwise; I mean that life there was simple, pleasant, and everyone was good and warm, which they were. With my usual flair for obliteration of anything unbearable, I refused to spoil the treasured days of my holiday with remembering what I had left behind me up in the bleak, melancholy North. The moment the train rumbled over the railway bridge across the river at Carlisle my heart grew wings and sang all the way down to Watford. From there joy was so heady in my breast that the sights and smells of Euston swiftly erased all traces of any aching despair or loneliness. I was a very quick recoverer.

But of course, life at home had altered subtly too. It was no longer quite the same. Lally was now in charge of my brother, and also my sister adored this living baby doll. I was not included any longer, and there was never really time for us to be together again. Gradually, over time, a thin wall of dislike and indifference grew between us, and we started the inevitable growing-away process. It was not to be healed for some years.

The Cottage too had gone. The auction had not been successful for my parents, and strangers bought it. We moved the wheel-backed chairs, the lamps, the beds and the wooden kitchen table across the valley to a smaller cottage up on the other Down at Winton Street. A collection of cottages grouped round a tithe barn and a well. It was not, and never could be, the same as the Cottage. But it was agreed that this should be only a halfway house until we found something we all liked, and which was really big enough for a now large family, where we would live for ever in the country because my father hated, with all his heart, the idea of living any longer in London. With this news at the back of his mind, the grief of losing the main pivot of my life was eased a little. I accepted. There was very little else that I could do. Holidays at Winton Street were almost, but never quite, as good as they had been: there was no gully, but still the same river, no Great Meadow, but another one almost as splendid, and the village was as near, and the same faces were still about in the lanes and fields. Sometimes I used to stand at the stile on the path down to the village and look across the valley at the soft smooth side of Great Meadow rising up to the crest of the hill and see the late sun flashing on the windows of the Cottage. Then, and then only, I got a lump in my throat and stumbled on down to the grocers.

'It's the wind!' said Lally one day, coming down with me. 'It seems to blow much harder up here than it ever did over there. Must be straight up from Cuckmere and the sea. Breathe it all in, it'll do you a power of good.'

But she knew.

After a year in Bishopbriggs things gradually began to deteriorate. Inevitably. I returned back from one holiday to find that I was no longer sleeping in the pink bedroom but on the Put-U-Up which now occupied the place of the piano in the sitting-room. The piano was in the dining-room. My uncle explained nicely that I was, after a year's wear, starting to destroy the furniture in the bedroom, that the chest of drawers, his only remembrance of his mother, was creaking badly because of the weight of the things which I placed in the drawers. Books and writing materials, as well as all my clothes. Also, far worse, the foot of the yellow oak bed had been hopelessly scratched by my long toenails. So it was decided that they should move back to their own room and I should from there on sleep on the Put-U-Up.

That the culprit, or culprits, of the scratched bed end were not my toenails, but instead the scalding aluminium 'pig' or the hot brick in flannel splitting the veneer, were unacceptable excuses.

'I have repeatedly told you about cutting your toenails,' said my uncle, 'every bath time. We are not made of money up here, you know, there's a Depression on.'

He had never ever mentioned my toenails, although he was frequently in the bathroom on Friday nights which was the allotted time of the week for my 'ablutions' as he called them. At first I had been rather surprised that he seemed to wish to brush his hair at such an odd hour in the evening, and when I, once only, locked the door, I was firmly admonished not to do so again because how could they help if the geyser blew up or I had a fainting fit suddenly? They, after all, were responsible. So no locked doors. I only minded because it was the one place where I could sing away and feel totally private without being a 'noise' either to them or the people who lived up in the house above and who, from time to time, did complain that my piano playing, pretty dreadful, by ear, and limited to a range of three melodies, 'The Wedding Of the Painted Doll', 'Always' and 'Over My Shoulder', all played very loudly with both pedals firmly down, disturbed their rest and also made it difficult to hear the Football Results on the Radio. The complaints were always very tactful and genteel. However, they *were* complaints and the piano stopped. So the bathroom seemed the next best thing musically. And also the mirror over the washbowl was useful for trying out expressions.

However, my new bed-sitting-room was pleasant enough, and we all settled down together again, although the constant worry that I refused to play all games, and had no friends, was still a source of dismay and anguish. I tried (not to play games naturally, at which I was useless and by which I was desperately uninterested), but I tried to make friends and even to bring them home to tea, which was my aunt's greatest desire. This, I suppose, to prove that I *had* friends. In desperation Tom once came all the way from his tenement in Paisley, and brought with him a slow boy called Gregg. They seemed the best two suited to our sort of house.

My aunt did a vast baking the night before and was astonished, and saddened, that Tom, in a tight blue suit, and Gregg in his Fair Isle sweater, sat for most of the meal with their hands under their thighs on the ladder-backed chairs, hardly spoke above a murmur and merely nibbled at the enormous wealth of Coburg Cakes, Soda Scones, Treacle Tarts and Fairy Cakes.

Unused to young people about them, they leant backward to be sociable and warm. But it was useless. All of us were inhibited with a deathly shyness. I hardly knew Gregg; he was usually busy in the Metalwork Class with a welding iron and solder while I battered mournfully at a copper disc beating it to death with a design of palm trees and pyramids. It was to be an ash-tray. Apart from that we hardly ever met, let alone spoke, and Tom was as out of place at a High Tea in Bishopbriggs as, he put it himself, 'a spare prick at a weddin''.

Discovering, during desperate cross-questioning, that he was studying to be an engineer, my uncle, who was one, launched into a long lecture on valves and steam compression. Tom sat mute and merely mumbled 'aye' from time to time. It was a total disaster. All the more so after they had left when my uncle found that they had, in their nervousness, picked away at the rush bottoms of the ladder-backed chairs, thereby 'ruining them for all time'.

I did not ask friends back again, although it was often suggested by my good, worried aunt.

The Summer Highlight for Bishopbriggs Society was the weekly Tennis Match held at the Club on the other side of the railway embankment. That is to say on the Right Side of Town. No one who was a member could be a member without being vetted. It was very stringent, and the waiting list was long. Naturally no one from the Estate was allowed on to the ash-courts, and nor did they ever try. I was allowed, with my aunt and uncle, because it was understood we all had 'known better days', and it was politely overlooked that we lived in the unspoken-of area.

Every Friday my aunt did a baking: it was the rule that every lady should take some of her own baking for the Club Tea. My life seemed to be governed by the Bakings as much as my aunt's. The Club House was built of varnished wood and smelled like a coffin. It had a tin roof and a veranda, a tea urn and a cupboard filled with white china cups and saucers. Each week a different lady supervised, and each week we all eagerly read the lists typed and pinned to the green baize board as to who was playing whom. The day was filled with light, high, cries of 'Good show, partner!' 'Well tried, I say!' or 'Love three all', 'My game, I think!'. The thwick and thwock of ball against gut lasted well into the evenings, for it was always light enough to play there until at least ten-thirty p.m. It grew boring sometimes, even though it was my job to retrieve, like some wretched little dog, the balls which loped and scattered about the chicken wire enclosure.

After The Tea, at which I helped to serve, and later wash up, they sat, if the weather was fine, in deck-chairs knitting and sewing until their game came up. The time passed slowly enough and I was often allowed to go home before the final game was over, to open the house and set the table for supper. I was always eager for this excuse because it meant, if I was pretty quick, that I could get back in time to put on the brown bakelite radio and just catch the nightingale singing from a Surrey wood. If it sang. It was a delicate thing to do. On with the radio, lock the front door, hang out of the window, eyes glued to the road from the tennis courts, willing, pleading, aching, for the blasted bird to sing. All Surrey flooded into the cramped, beige-and-ladder-backed room. But, as I said, I had to be quick, for apart from prudery I had learned deceit. The radio was expressly forbidden to be touched. So it was only when I had the house to myself, and played it low so that Upstairs could not hear and give me away, that I dared to put it on. And then only with a wet towel standing by, because the machine had a habit of getting warm as time went on, and the moment my uncle came back from Tennis the first thing he did was to cross the room and caress the sleek bakelite sides. Just to see. I had once been caught – the room filled with nightingales and cellos, my eyes maudlin with tears. My uncle's anger was controlled; I was being decietful and morbid. He was polite enough in a steely way and for a short time the radio was removed to their bedroom. But I managed.

Coming back from Tennis, in the after glow of the evening, if I stayed that long, which I often did, the conversations never really varied. They were always, more or less like this:

'Have you got the key, Walter?'

'No. It's McWhirter's turn this week to lock up. He's got it.'

'He wasn't playing very well today, I thought?'

'No. Not well at all. Sun in his eyes.'

'But you tossed for places surely?'

'Of course we did. He lost. Kept hitting the net.'

'Aha. Getting on, I'm afraid.'

'Aye, that's a fact.'

'Agnes's service was poor, erratic. . . .'

'Both getting on a wee bittie.'

'Oh aye. . . .'

'Ah michtie-me.'

'The Brandy Snaps went down very well. They always do. Gratifying. The cream makes it look more. Next week I'll try Molly's recipe for Soda Bread. . . .' Their voices would drift harmlessly over me, vapour trails of cloud above the Downs, to be smudged, faded, and eventually to evaporate in the gentle business of preparing the cocoa for supper.

School went ahead slowly. There appeared to be no marked improvement in my reports, and the little notes appended to the end of my letters home by my uncle, which I was not allowed to see – they were written confidentially after I had signed my name and sent love and kisses – grew steadily more pessimistic. He was doing his best to be helpful and generous, but really . . . the Boy didn't seem to be settling down, after all it was now more than a whole year. There should have been some improvement. There, apparently, was none. Except that I was doing, I thought, pretty well. I was, at least, trying. I wanted to get back to the South, and I knew that without some form of improvement in my scholastic world this would be delayed and delayed. I was there to learn, at a good Scottish School, and the sooner I learned the better. So naturally I went as hard as I could; I battered away at Metalwork making copper ash-trays and serviette-rings; I made bookends and unacceptable work boxes in woodwork; I threw cups and bowls on the potter's wheel, and I did French Translation and

Essay like no one else in the school. My English was filled with long poems and stories which were often read out to the whole, agonised, sniggering, class. My Geography was noted for the amount of space I covered, products I knew, populations I recorded, deciduous, coniferous, rain and dry belts I had assembled. I was even congratulated by teachers who smiled and were polite, and my exercise books, for these lessons, were marked well into the eighties. What was wrong?

Apparently, I was failing all the time. The fact that Maths was still incomprehensible to me, that Physics and Chemistry and Engineering were far, far beyond my meagre comprehension, seemed not to matter to me, at any rate, against the glowing reports from the few classes in which I excelled. Albeit without much competition.

An angry, hurt, letter from my father sent me off to my Altar. I had found a small burn, or brook, some miles from the Estate, deep in a beech thicket away from sight or people. When I exercised the neighbours' dogs, the neighbours from the Old Town I hasten to add – the people on the Estate didn't keep dogs, only greyhounds – I used to tramp off across the sodden fields and corrugated plough to my sanctuary. I had, one day, idly started to dam the little burn with stones and boulders, and within a short time created a splendid pool and waterfall. Then, to embellish, as I am prone to do, something which was already attractive, I started work on a small Altar which I made from shards of slate and flat stone which I collected in a bag from the shale tips round the edges of the Bingies. As I spent a great deal of my spare time by the Pool and the waterfall praying to an unheeding God for swift release back to the life I once had known, it occurred to me that He might listen better, or listen at all, if I built a bit of the appropriate furnishings. I had been taught, in my mild flirtation with Catholicism, that God could Hear You Wherever You Prayed. Just so long as you did. Well I did. Furiously and piously. However, He seemed to pass me over on zephyr wings as I lay nightly moaning in the yellow oak bed: even more so in the Put-U-Up. So I assumed that perhaps an Altar to His Glory would be more appropriate, and more obvious, to His clearly busy Eye. Also the labour which it would cost, the lugging of the slate and shards of stone, the mud and slush of the construction would surely not go unseen? With this in mind, I built a reasonable Temple to Him. Decorated with a couple of empty aspirin bottles, to hold assorted wild flowers, a tin cross made from old bottle tops and a bit of wood, and swamped with a monotony of desperate prayer, it stood, beside my burn, a model of piety and trust.

Perhaps it was the sheer boredom, the waves of self-pity, which put Him off – for whatever else happened, my mumbled pleadings and sighs fell on totally sterile ground in Heaven.

Until one day.

A shaft of thin hopeful light slit across the dullness of my existence. One Sunday, after the long effort of the Letter Home, my uncle said, with a heavy clearing of his throat and lowered eyes, that he had been, very reluctantly, forced, in his weekly note to my parents, to say that, everything being considered very carefully, it was probably better that I should be removed from School since, it was costing everyone a great deal of money and worry, and that there seemed to be no positive signs, after so long, that any good was coming from it all. He said, very politely and gently, that I had to see things that way for myself. Even my own reports were saddening; I seemed incapable of joining a team, of playing games, of making friends, or even of applying myself to the work which was set out for me to do.

In short, I was wasting everyone's time, money and patience.

The fact that I never, at any time ever, saw my school reports – they were always addressed to him, correctly, as my Guardian and he sent them on to my parents – nor ever had an discussions with anyone about them didn't seem to occur to either of us at the time. I was simply struck dumb with shock. As far as I was aware, I had worked as hard as possible and had tried my best.

The next morning, after an anguished night watching the patterns flicker on the ceiling from the Valor Perfection Stove, my uncle and I parted company as usual at Queen Street Station. At the bookstall I bought a stamp and a picture postcard on which, leaning against a pile of magazines, I wrote in pencil, 'I am very unhappy here. Please, please let me come home.' A swift Burberry'd arm shot over my shoulder and lifted it up.

My uncle's face was expressionless, a nicotined finger brushed his little moustache.

'Well now, Sonny,' he said kindly, 'why not post it?' He flipped it on to the magazines and walked away.

Dismay and guilt gave way to rising desperation. I did exactly as he said and went on to school.

It was an uncomfortable week.

Fearful of the results when this fatal correspondence would reach my unsuspecting parents I spent a lot of time walking other people's blasted dogs over to my sanctuary. Many a 'Rags' or 'Boy' or 'Bobbie' passed a bewildered hour or two while I droned away at the Altar asking for Help and some form of Direction. The latter came in a sudden surging determination which shook me like ague. If *this* is where really trying hard got you, then it was very simple. I would just not bother any longer and let the whole damned thing slide. They could all do as they liked. And so would I. I ceased praying, wrecked the Altar, opened the dam, and played truant from school as often, and as pleasurably, as I could.

It was easy. At lunch-time, instead of eating my sodden meat pie with Tom or whoever else was sitting on the dustbin wall, I just stuck my cap in my pocket, pinned a handkerchief in my Blazer pocket so that it flopped over the give-away crest on the badge, opened my collar, stuffed my tie somewhere else, and, hands in pockets, one and sixpence and a few odd coppers saved from here and there, I strolled happily down the hill from the school into the busy crowds of George Square and let Glasgow and its allure swallow me up. It was as easy as that, and no one bothered to check. At first, naturally, I was terrified. I was sure that I would be spotted and carted back to the amiable but fearsome Dr Steel. However, with no badges or colours showing, I passed for any other boy wandering about the city. I found deceit very refreshing.

Woolworths was my usual haven. Because it was warm and bright, and filled with people. Here was Life. Pushing and shoving, smiling and laughing, talking and living. Music played all day. The record counter had a constant supply of melody. To the lingering refrains of 'When The Poppies Bloom Again' I would sit on a high stool eating a Chocolate Fudge Ice Cream and beam happily at the world about me. Guiltless. It was all heady stuff.

Later, I grew bolder and went, imagine the bravery!, to the cinema alone. For sixpence, in the middle stalls with a packet of pea-nuts or a Mars Bar, I sat in my element and got two movies, all the Advertising, the Newsreel, the Forthcoming Attractions plus a pink, green and amber lit Organ Recital.

Life was *never* to be dull and drab again. I would always live like this, and the Hell with Effort, Loyalty, and 'The Times'.

It would be useful to say at this point that it was the moment when my whole future was laid before me. The great silver screen, the glamour, the glory, the guns and the chases. Camera angles, Lighting, Back Projection, Split Screen, Fade and Dissolve flew past my eyes twice a week and vanished like dreams. But I was the Original Audience for which these films were made. The refugee from worry, humdrum life, anxiety or despair. I only wanted to be bewitched, enthralled, be-glamoured. The rest of it washed away like silt in a tub. Nothing at all rubbed off at that time. My personal disillusion, even disappointment, was so great, my anger so deep, that I had fixed it clearly that I would try no more. They could come and get me and punish me in whatever way they all liked: I had given up. But until they did come to get me, or sent for me, I was going to have as pleasant a time as I possibly could. What on earth was the point in going on any longer? I had tried, and failed again. So be it.

It was, I think, at the Paramount, one matinee, that I made my first friend out of school. Tom had become more and more immersed in his Bunsen burners and retort stands, and I hardly ever saw him even for meat-pie lunches. While Gregg, after the disaster of The Tea, never spoke to me again. So apart from the dogs I walked there was no one, and I was wonderfully free, if lacking the bonds of friendship which I strangely craved since it was no longer to be had.

Even Tom was something.

The Paramount was a new, glittering Picture Palace with a deadly reputation. I had heard it spoken of in muted voices in many of the parlours to which I was bidden, or sent, for those Bakings and Teas. It was the meeting place of all the Evil in Glasgow, the Crooks and Thieves and Bookies. Any young girl going there alone, it was said, invariably ended up with a hypodermic in her bottom and a bunk in a boat at the Broomilaw awaiting the next tide down the Clyde for Morocco. Indeed the people Upstairs knew of one girl who, missing her companions, had foolishly gone in alone to see Robert Taylor and was never heard of again apart from the fact that an usherette had seen a dark-skinned man helping a young lady to a taxi from the foyer saying that she had had a 'fainting fit'. It made going to the Pictures much more interesting.

In any case I felt secure because of two things: first I was a boy, secondly I always sat in the middle of the stalls where it was lighter, and never in the shadows where, of course, anything might happen. Armed, this day, with my logic, I went to see a special showing of Boris Karloff in 'The Mummy'. I had seen it two or three times before, ages ago, bu it was still my favourite next to 'The Bride of Frankenstein'. I also saw Mr Dodd.

Mr Dodd was almost entirely beige. A beige raincoat, beige face, beige hair and freckles. He sat two or three seats away from me and smiled pleasantly all through the Forthcoming Attractions. And still I didn't know.

During the interval, when the lights went pink and green and the organ rumbled through a selection from something or other, he smiled shyly across the empty seats and I smiled back, and he moved along and came and sat beside me. He asked if I would like an ice-cream, and I said yes, and we ate together in pleasant, companionable silence. He was very polite, quiet spoken and smiled a lot; and when he took my empty ice-cream tub away from me, plus the wooden spoon and stacked it neatly into his own and tidily placed it all under his seat, he patted my leg kindly and whispered with a secret wink that I was, in all probability, playing truant from school, wasn't I? Shattered with surprise that he had so quickly found me out, I lied swiftly and said that I was 'off school' with a sprained ankle. That seemed to content him and the programme started again so that there was no need for more conversation.

It was very nice having someone to laugh at the film with, to share fear with, and to enjoy relief with all at the same time. He was very attentive and once, in a particularly creepy part he put his arm protectively round my shoulder, which I felt was very thoughtful of him indeed.

By the time the show was over it was well after six, and I realised that I would have to leave my new friend quickly and 'limp' to the station and Bishopbriggs where my aunt would be waiting to hear from me how well the rehearsals for the school play were going. My excuse, true as it happened, for the lateness of my arrival. Mr Dodd was sad, he told me his name and that I was to call him Alec, and made an appointment for us to see the film again at the end of the week before the Forthcoming Attraction took its place. I agreed with pleasure. It was to be his Treat, he said, and after we would go to Cranstons for tea but that I could still be home in time so as not to worry my aunt.

I sailed down to Queen Street Station with winged feet, no limp now, heart high with happiness. Someone at the Altar had listened after all. I had a New Friend.

Tea at Cranstons was an impressive affair at the worst of times, and this was the best. Quiet, calm, warm, sparkling with silver, white tablecloths, flowers in fluted vases, motherly waitresses in crisp aprons and little caps, and a silver stand of cakes. Mr Dodd knew his way about very well and was pleasant to everyone and anxious that I should eat as much as I could for, he said, he was a Medical Student and he knew just how much 'fuel' the working lad's mind had to have to keep it going.

It was very pleasant indeed. Although I had been there often before with my aunt on shopping expeditions, this was far more companionable. We talked at length of the film and discussed the Theatre and Plays, although I had not seen very many by that time, but the feeling of lazy companionship, of comfort and of laughter was delightful. It was as if we had known each other for years instead of hours. He told me how his mother had saved and scrimped to send him to School and then on to the Medical College where he was now studying. I asked him what kind of Doctor he was going to be and he said a Surgeon because he felt that is probably where he could do the most good. When I said that I was rather horrified at the idea of all the blood and cutting people up, he very reasonably said that I might very well feel that because I clearly had not heard the Call as he had done. I was very impressed. The conversation slid back, inevitably, to the film and he astonished me by saying that he knew exactly how mummies were bandaged and how they were embalmed; it was really very easy to do, he said cheerfully, and anyone could make a mummy if they knew how to bandage. I was overcome with curiosity and asked him more and more questions; he tried to demonstrate with his table napkin but it was too small and too thick, so he suggested that since he lived nearby and had all his books and bandages there we should go at once to his place and he could show me in a trice.

I accepted immediately; already telling my aunt the lie about the play. And I still didn't know.

His flat was a rather poky room with a kitchenette in a high block over a tobacconist and sweet shop in Hope Street. It smelled of ether and stale cigarettes and was pretty untidy, for which he apologized, pulling hurriedly at the unmade bed and taking some dirty plates and a bottle into the sink. There were books everywhere, a typewriter, old shirts, and a gas fire which plopped when he lit it. On the wall there were pictures of Rothesay Castle and two men wrestling. He opened a thick book filled with diagrams of bandaging; people were swathed in them, heads, hips, legs, wrists, arms and everything else. It was very comprehensive.

Chattering happily, he pulled a large cardboard box from under the bed and spilled rolls and rolls of blue-wrapped bandages of every size all over the floor. These, he said, were just the trick to turn me into a splendid mummy and if I would just remove my jacket and shirt and vest and sit down in that chair there he would turn me into Boris Karloff in the flick of a fly's eyelid.

I dutifully, rather shyly, did as he suggested while he started to unroll yards and yards of filmy gauzes. It was not very long before I was straight-jacketed in strips of thin cotton bandage from the top of my head to my waist, arms securely folded, in the correct position of mummies, across my chest, a small slit left for each eye so that I could hazily see through a vague fringe of white blur, a small hole left for my nostrils so that I could breathe. Otherwise I was trussed like a fowl. Taking down the oval mirror from the mantelpiece he showed me the effect which I found impressive, uncomfortable, and very restricting. I could merely manage a vague motion with my head, which didn't show, and roll my slitty eyes. I could neither see properly, nor even hear for that matter, and I was totally mute.

As he turned from replacing the mirror, and as I stood to indicate that he might now unwrap me as soon as possible, I could see that he was speaking, but only a blurred mumble came to my bandaged ears and it was with some rising degree of alarm that I found myself clutched firmly in his arms and dumped on my back in the middle of the brass bed. I tried to struggle and yell out, at least to sit up, but I was totally rigid and the only sound I made was smothered in yards and yards of thick white gauze. Putting his beige face very close to my ear Mr Dodd said that it seemed a pity not to finish the job and make me a full mummy from head to foot, that would complete the Effect.

My shoes and socks were wrenched off and thrown under the bed, then my trousers, and to my silent screams of protest, he ripped off my underpants and I was stark naked before his eager, now red-faced, gaze.

Swiftly and with the expert precision of a born embalmer, he rolled me about the bed in a flurry of bandage. I was wrapped like a parcel, rolled this way and that, on my back, on my side, every which way until I was reeling with giddiness and terror. I was wound tightly into a cocoon as a spider rolls a grasshopper. Helpless, inert, more a dummy even than a mummy, I lay rigid as Mr Dodd, his mouth stuck with safety pins, tucked in the loose ends; when this was done, and with great strength he manoeuvred me off the bed, stiff as a telegraph pole, and set me upright on cotton feet to see my reflection in the mirror of his wardrobe door. Peering desperately through the eye slits I could see that he had made a complete and thorough job. Boris Karloff wasn't half as convincing.

Unable to stand by myself I was forced to lean against the serge shoulder of my host whose face was bathed in pleasure. Surely my heart could not beat so quickly with terror and I should still live. It had leapt from my chest and now pumped and throbbed in my throat. It stopped entirely when my horrified eyes saw, pathetically thrusting through the swaddling rags, my genitals, naked and as pink and vulnerable as a sugar mouse.

Mr Dodd placed his mouth to my ear again and said that he thought he had made a very good job of things and hoped I was pleased too, and without waiting for any kind of reaction, which I would not have been able to make in any case, he swung me, like an immense skittle, into an arc of 180 degrees, so that the whole filthy little room whirled round my head, and I was back down on Mr Dodd's bed; and in Mr Dodd's hand, inches from my eyes, was a pair of scissors. I tried to faint. I heard him say that in Real Life They Cut That Off — and lay supine waiting for Death. Gently his hands caressed my helpless body, kindly he whispered that he had no intention of doing such a cruel thing for how else, otherwise, would a boy like me be able to masturbate? He said that he knew that all boys enjoyed masturbating and that he was much too good to deprive me of the rights. My mind had become a mass of solid jelly. Nothing flickered there apart from deadly terror, shame, and grief at my wickedness. I couldn't rationalise. I closed my eyes and said three or four 'Hail Mary's'.

If I prayed surely, this time, God would hear? The anxious, firm, slippery fingers caressing and annointing me splintered my whole being into a billion jagged fragments. I was only aware that if they didn't stop something terrible and horrifying would happen.

Which it did. And I knew.

The unwrapping, which followed, was a slow, forlorn, deadly affair. The wretched stuff peeled off me in long swooping swathes, littering the grubby bed and the floor around it. I had been blubbing, snivelling in a silly useless sort of way like a girl, and Mr Dodd was worried and apologetic and kept reminding me over and over again that it was all all right because he was a Medical Student and understood these things.

Dressing hurriedly, stumbling with teary cheeks and snotty nose, falling into pants and trousers, lacing up shoes, yanking up socks and fumbling with my tie, I was unable to speak or even look at the bobbing figure scrabbling about among its merchandise. He handed me a comb and I raked it through my disordered hair; he said that he would see me safely home.

We didn't speak in the train all the way to Bishopbriggs. He pointed out, as we left the train, that it was not really very late and that he would come and explain things to my aunt. In horror I said that she was ill and could not be disturbed. I led him miles across the Estate, away from where I lived, to a completely strange house where a lamp glowed through a lowered blind. He waited at the gate as I rang the bell, and just as the door opened, fortunately he turned away and was lost in the gloom. The woman who opened the door was pleasant and I apologized for making an error but she smiled and said the houses were all so alike it was no wonder. Springburn Terrace, she said, was ''way round the back'.

For some time I lived in fear that Mr Dodd would come back or find where I lived. Once, on my way to the station, I thought I saw him hovering about near the Railway Arch. But I don't think it was . . . and I never saw him ever again. Neither did I ever set foot in a cinema alone for many years to come.

A few days later a letter arrived from my father to say that my mother was coming up to Glasgow within the month. She would stay with my grandmother. And had an appointment with Dr Steel at the school for the 28th. Nothing more was said. My uncle looked uncomfortable, my aunt defensive.

What could Dr Steel say to my mother that they could not, for Heaven's sake? she wondered. It seemed a waste of good money to trail all this way for nothing. She declared that she didn't know what to make of it at all. And neither did I.

TWELVE

Neither did the irritated Dr Steel as it turned out. Or my bewildered mother for that matter. Clearly my uncle and the headmaster did not see eye to eye on the subject of my education, and while the latter admitted, with bland candour, that I was not the brightest pupil he had ever had in his Technical School but showed distinct abilities in other subjects, the former seemed to have given me up for lost.

Steel suggested that it would be the gravest folly to remove me from the place where I had already been for two years and in which I had fought to remain against quite high odds, and that for the next year I should merely concentrate on those classes which could be the most useful to me in my later life, and at which I showed some signs, at least, of promise. I was to forget Chemistry, Physics, Maths etcetera, and if I cared, only follow the courses in English, Languages, Art, and all the varied handworks from Pottery to Bookbinding. Football, Hockey and Cricket were out and I was to be left on my honour to attend whatever classes I wished.

He wondered, mildly, why I had even been sent to a Technical School in the first place and said that at the end of the year I should be enrolled into a College of Art somewhere, for my future lay in that direction and in no other as far as he could see.

My mother's worried heart lifted; mine whipped up like a kite in a gale. Both parents agreed with the wise counsel of Dr Steel and also with the College of Art part to come later. I was transported to Heaven. And removed, very tactfully, from Bishopbriggs.

Clearly my unhappy aunt and uncle had reached the end of their patience and endurance. They wanted, understandably, to return to the calm and peace of their life as it had all been before my advent into their bewildered middle-aged existence.

Nothing was said in, as they say, so many words, but a Family Gathering was called at my grandmother's house. The long and short of it was that yet another of my mother's sisters, Aunt Hester, adopted me and took me off to live with her in a different part of the city with her husband and two children, and I spent the last year of my school days in a very happy 'family atmosphere' where I was able to play the piano whenever I wished with no fear of the people Upstairs, and read every book I could lay hands on from Trollope to Austen without ever once feeling the slightest tremor of guilt that I should be dubbing my soccer boots, oiling a cricket bat, or ploughing through the miseries of Fractions or Logarithms. It nearly went to my head.

I bought a half-belted overcoat and began to talk like Ronald Colman. I graduated from 'By the Chapel in the Moonlight' to 'Sheep My Safely Graze' all by ear and with the bass pedal screwed to the floor-boards. I started to smoke 'Black Cat' cigarettes in the train coming home from school, learned to skate, and fell deeply in love with my elder cousin Jean.

The only reason that I learned to skate was because of her. I adored her with an unthinking passion, and bought Family Planning magazines which had chapters headed 'Can Cousins Marry?' 'Cousins Marrying Causes Imbecility?' When I had read all I could understand I was brave enough to mention it to her while we were skating round and round the rink at Crossmloof one evening. I have never forgotten her look of total astonishment as she pulled her steadying hand from mine and fled across the ice to a large Canadian hockey player who, covered in pads and cages and maple leaves, was her real true love.

However she agreed to accompany me to the rink from time to time, but always left me when Canada arrived for his evening match. I was sad, of course, but thought that if I was patient she would come back to me in the end. Which of course she never did. I skated miserably about the place, close to the edge, for I was not all that good on my own and her adored hand was more than just a comfort. It was a stabilizer. Together we collided round the rink with all the elegance, and overt familiarity, of mating toads. I hoped that my sad devotion would show. Which it did. In a face like a squashed muffin. I hoped that people would be moved by my nightly vigil . . . the mournful, brave boy sliding about on the perimeter while his beloved one, golden hair flying, kilts swirling, spun about centrally in the arms of a great, uncouth, goalkeeper. But no one took a bit of notice. And once, in desperation, when I did try to slide across to them and take her tiny hand, I landed flat on my back and skidded with a sickening crash on my half-belt overcoat into the barrier.

I gave it up after that. There is nothing like a public loss of dignity to restore a sense of proportion. I put away the skates and took up my pens and pencils. Warmer, safer, cheaper and, in the end one hoped, far less dangerous than a marriage between cousins.

Life had changed radically. The Late Developer was starting, and not before time, to offer tentative shoots of manhood to a singularly uninterested world. It really didn't worry me very much that no one seemed to care because I cared myself; deeply. I was enormously interested in the change, and studied myself daily with satisfaction and an awe only equal to its smugness.

I knew, of course, early on that I would never be Handsome like my uncles or one or two of the cousins. Standard Beauty was not to be my fortune. But, I reasoned, I had height, good eyes well placed, and a pleasing smile which I encouraged daily in the bathroom mirror, ranging it from Winsome to Brave. A series of exercises which, if forced to watch today, would surely make me vomit.

Even though I was hopeless at skating, at Sports of any kind or at any single thing which needed any form of co-ordination – even in my piano playing the left hand was constantly at variance with the behaviour of the right – I felt that in my half-belted overcoat, my good blue suit, a florid silk scarf pilfered from someone, and my green felt pork pie hat with a feather, I was approaching my golden future with some degree of courage and confidence.

Not to mention conceit. Nothing, up till then, had come along to freeze the tender greening shoots of my April growth, except perhaps my cousin's clear preference for a Canadian hockey playing goalkeeper. On skates. That, to me, simply showed her acute lack of sensibilities.

Perhaps for the first time in my life that third year in Scotland had at last found me 'driving my own coach'. The Postillion was on the lead horse. It was a sharply pleasurable feeling.

Of course there was always the Lightning.

During this exhilarating time changes had taken place at home. My father, more and more exhausted by the demands of 'The Times', by constant minor ailments, by his deep dislike of what he called the 'Orientals' who had suddenly invaded his Hampstead streets far from the streets of Berlin, Vienna, Munich and Hamburg, became more and more desperate to remove himself and his family far into the country away from them all and settle into 'the country house'. Pressured thus by almost constant colds and chills, delicatessens springing up in the High Street, and the growing of the storm mounting in slow-building thunder-clouds over Europe, he started his search in deadly earnest.

This eventually led us all to a big, ugly, redbrick and gabled house in three acres of overgrown gardens in the middle of a common seven miles from Lewes in Sussex.

It had been for sale for a very long time since no one wanted to attempt any work on such a hideous, sullen, uncared-for lump of tile and gargoyles, therefore he bought it cheap, ignoring protests and doubts from my unfortunate mother, and moved us all in, cat, cupboards and cooking pots, at the beginning of 1936.

I was enraptured. Enraptured by the stained glass front door, a stork standing in bulrushes, enraptured by the high rooms, the solid doors, the wide staircase, the overgrown orchard, the silted up pond with a rotting punt, the bamboo grove and the magnolias pressing glossy leaves against almost every window. But best of all, everywhere miles and miles of rolling common blazing with gorse and heather, lizards, slow worms, rabbits, a secret patch of vivid Gentians and a stark white windmill on a ridge. Never better than the Cottage but the next best thing.

In a very short time everything was stripped out: painted white from floor to attics; the stained glass door, to my regret, replaced with oak; the lawns mowed, trees felled here and there, bushes pruned and the pond, my job, cleaned, and the spring which ran through the orchard unblocked. The house, after so many years of neglect and abuse, seemed to breathe and took on a new lease of life. So did my father.

Of course all things have to be paid for. Lally decided that a total Country Life was really not for her. A couple of months in the summer, the Easter and Christmas holidays, that was acceptable. But a whole solitary existence in the middle of a common and seven miles from a reasonable town was asking too much of her patience and love. And in any case, as she pointed out, we were all growing up . . . and needed her less and less . . . whereas her parents, Mr and Mrs Jane, were getting on a little and she would be better occupied looking after them in Twickenham.

The improbable baby, now called Gareth, was already banging about on two legs and had both my adoring mother and sister to look after him. All we needed now, she said tactfully, was a nice Village Girl who would come in and take over, now that she, Lally, had set us all on the way.

She left quickly, and without sentimentality, which was not her nature; and with long and earnest promises of holidays in Twickenham she went as quietly as she had arrived in our midst all those years ago in 1925 when she came to us as a Girl Guide with a whistle and her white lanyard gleaming.

In her place a Rubens shepherdess. Elsie Brooks from Barcombe. Auburn hair, sparkling eyes, cherry red lips and a skin like gently flushed alabaster. She was eighteen and turned my head completely. She lived in a little room at the top of the house with a window which looked out on the orchard. I spent many pleasant hours crouched in the branches of a Granny Smith watching Elsie change from her Blue and White into 'something pretty' for her day off. In the half light, half shade of her room, I could see the firm rounded arms above her auburn head, the full, pale, breasts, the lips puckered in a soundless whistle. Ignorant of my yearning love, my muddled fantasies, she shoved in her Kirby-grips, buttoned up her blouse, shrugged into a coat and went off to catch the two-thirty bus from the crossroads for the excitements of Haywards Heath.

Once I summoned up the courage to ask her to let me take her photograph as she was hurrying down the drive to the front gates. Sweetly she sat on the arm of a garden seat, set her hat a little more jauntily, crossed one leg over the other and thoughtfully raised her skirt so that her pretty knee, gleaming in silk, blinded my lens. I asked her to smile, which she did, and with a jolly laugh gave me a wink before she hurried off for her bus. I was so overcome with adoration that a short time afterwards, wandering about in a haze of mumbled poetry, I walked into a tree.

What saddened me more than anything, more than the secret love in the Granny Smith, the longed-for touch for her hand at breakfast passing the sugar, the cherry lips caressing the rim of her tea-cup which I longed to feel pressed against my cheek, apart from all these delicious denials, was the fact that while I had clearly noticed her she had never, at any single moment, ever noticed me.

'Girls like older boys,' said my sister scornfully. 'You are much too young and you can't even dance or anything like that. No girl likes a boy who only builds birdcages and mucks out rabbits. You see if I'm wrong.'

I decided that I would now learn to dance.

'I have met the most delightful woman on the bus today,' said my mother happily. 'Mrs Cox. She was an actress, just like me, they live in the next village and she has three children who are just the same ages as you all. Isn't that extraordinary?'

Elizabeth and I were po-faced with disinterest. But she hurried on assuring us that we would all like each other, and that we needed to have young people about and that Mr Cox was very rich and owned the Village Hall where they put on plays twice a year. That slightly shook my indifference, but not enough to want to have to meet the wretched children. However that had been fixed. They were all, not just the ex-actress mother, but the entire family, coming to have tea with us the following week. I said that I was busy building my new Studio, and my sister said that if they came she would go and hide on the common until they left. My mother, undaunted, said we were to please ourselves. If we wished to absent ourselves from our guests she would explain why but she considered it a great pity since we all shared the same interests, were all the same ages, and also, she added, wandering off to the vegetable garden which she now cultivated, if I wanted to dance there was no better way to learn than going to the weekly 'hop' which they gave every Saturday night in their Village Hall. However if we wished to be impolite and foolish that was up to us both. Taking her trug basket and a small hand fork she left us thoughtful.

The Coxes were very pleasant. Two girls and a small boy who hardly counted because, like Gareth, he was too young. But the other two were all right. Nerine and Heather (their father also owned a Nursery Garden which grew Alpines, hence their names) liked toads and snakes, rabbits and ponds and both of them liked acting and writing. So far so good. Nerine said that the Dances were 'terrific fun' and that all I needed was a suit and a tie and that she would help me to learn in no time at all. It was arranged.

Every Saturday night I dressed carefully, clambered on to my bike and rode the three miles to Newick. The Coxes' house, 'Chez Nous', was rather grand, much bigger than ours and covered in wisteria and small diamond-paned windows. Before the Dance began we sat nervously in their sitting-room sipping chilled white wine and seltzer with Bath Olivers. I was deeply impressed. Then to the Hall next door where, on a chalked wood floor, I swooped and twirled and fell over to music played on a tall cabinet gramophone amplified through two blaring loudspeakers. This machine was called a radiogram, and no one was allowed to touch it except Mr Cox himself who arranged the records and the dances and jiggled them about magically for the 'Paul Jones' and 'The Excuse Me Dance.'

The Hall had a stage at one end with blue sateen curtains and a tall iron stove with a chimney which burned lumps of coke and made everyone choke if they danced too close to it. Around the walls droopy flags and streamers from a forgotten Christmas and little rickety card tables with plates of bridge rolls and cress sandwiches. Half time was Tea and Lemonade. The last waltz, when Mr Cox turned down all the lights, and sometimes accidentally turned them off, was at ten o'clock so that everyone could get their coats and the last bus home.

I was better at dancing than skating. At least I could move into the centre of the floor and didn't fall over as often. But I got very stuck with Slow Foxtrots and Quick Steps and really only shone when it came to the 'Valeta' or 'Roger de Coverley'. I always managed to slip out and have a Black Cat while the Latin American dancing was on; this I found too fast and difficult.

Everyone enjoyed themselves very much. The men tidy in blue suits and dance slippers, the girls in glossy silk frocks with low necklines and little puffed sleeves. We were all very hot and shiny, and laughed too much, especially during the 'Paul Jones' when one changed partners with dizzying, often tactless speed. The sweet smell of sweat, Lux Toilet Soap, French Chalk and Camp Coffee was strong stuff. The evenings always ended far too soon.

My favourite partner, because she flattered me outrageously, was Cissie Waghorn who came from Uckfield and who, though rather taller than myself, and two years older, danced beautifully and helped to teach me with patience and care – even getting me to stumble about in 'The Conga' which we all thought rather daring and new. One night, after a very spirited, if inaccurate, Thunder and Lightning Polka she told me, sitting together in a red, breathless, heap, that I had Beautiful and Expressive hands. They were, she said very seriously, an Artist's Hands and Creative. I was overcome. For days I walked about with them hanging limply at the end of my arms afraid to damage them in any way. They were, to me, thick, clumsy, stubby fingered hands. I now thought better of them and started doing more exercises, with the Smiling ones in the mirror. My sister found me, pardonably, repellent.

But little did Cissie Waghorn know that she had started a thread of fire which was shortly to consume my entire being. Not just my dangling, cold-creamed, heavily Expressive hands. Unfortunately it all went to my head, and for a long time I couldn't even lift a cup to my lips without giving it the importance of the Holy Grail. I seldom do anything in half measures.

What I yearned for now was somewhere to show off these things I had learned, the Expressive hands, the Mocking Smile, the elegance of the Slow Waltz. What better than on that blue shrouded stage at the end of the Hall?

All my life I had wanted to be an actor. All my life that is from about the age of four when, draped in a cast off curtain and an old hat with a pheasant's tail stuck in it, I had acted my own plays to myself in my room. Then came the progression, under Lally's care and interest, during the Twickenham holidays . . . and the plays my sister and I used to 'do' up in the barn near the Cottage. Tremendously ambitious plays about the sinking of the Titanic with myself as the Captain (in a sailor's cap naturally) and my unfortunate sister playing Ottoline Morrell (in a wide-brimmed hat with roses on it and a red plush table cloth). I can't think why she had to be Lady Ottoline. Perhaps because I thought that she looked like her and that Lady Ottoline must have been the kind of woman who would have been spunky enough to stay on the ship while they played 'Nearer My God To Thee'. That was *my* plot anyway. And I stuck to it.

Even at my miserable Altar near Bishopbriggs there had been a form of acting even if not in its purest sense, and late in 1936 the seal was finally set on my decision in the most obvious way imaginable.

Yvonne Arnaud was my Godmother. Not, you understand, my real Godmother: there were two or three of them floating about whom I was never to see after the ceremonial presentations of silver napkin rings and feeding spoons. Yvonne adopted Godchildren as some women adopt habits. Unthinkingly, wholeheartedly and devotedly. She never held me at any Font, nor promised to keep me to The Faith, but she never forgot a Birthday, a Christmas, even an Easter, and was more adored than anyone of the 'family blood'. She had known my parents, in the tall brick house in St George's Road days, and so I can safely claim to have been one of the earliest of the thousands of Godchildren she was to accumulate later in her life.

She arrived, or so the posters announced, on one dull day at the King's Theatre, Glasgow, with a try-out of a new farce, 'Laughter In Court'. I left a note at her hotel and was bidden to an early luncheon on Matinee day.

The suite was a Kew Gardens of bloom and blossom, Yvonne sailing towards me, arms outstretched, flowing chiffon and scarves billowing about her like the vaguest of delicious dreams; her apparent delight at seeing me, her glorious chuckle, 'But darling! You have grown *enormous*!' relaxed me and we sat down to lunch, she brimming with questions, I brimming with contentment and happiness, over-eager to answer her queries after years, it seemed, of silence, save for my moaning pleas to the Slate Altar.

'Why are you here and not at school? You *are* at school surely?'

'No. Not today . . . I mean I should be . . .'

'And you are not?'

'No. I'm playing truant.'

Wide surprised eyes; a quick crackle of Melba Toast.

'What is this Truant . . . a game. It is a game?'

I explained briefly and embarrassedly. She looked stern.

'But darling, if you do not do your lessons what will you *become*? And they will find out you know. That is deceitful and wicked of you. Do you like Spineeche? It is full of iron and very good for your teeth.'

Through smoked salmon, chicken and a raspberry ice, I confessed all; about *not* trying any longer and the stifled, bursting ambition to go away and be an actor like my mother and grandfather. The jolly smiles faded from Yvonne's eyes; she looked very serious indeed sipping her coffee.

'Have you ever tried to be an actor, my darling?'

'At school . . . in a play last term. And always at home with my sister, that's all.'

'It is not very easy, you know, but if you would like to see how *hard* it is I can show you.'

When the curtain rose on the Second Act of 'Laughter In Court' that Thursday matinee, I was in the Press Box of the Court Room Scene. 'He's too young! He's a boy,' cried a worried looking man. 'Put him at the back, darling,' said Yvonne brusquely. 'If I mix him up with the other Supers he'll look like a Juvenile Delinquent!' 'That's *exactly* what 'ee 'ees!' cried my Godmother, 'and so are most of the Press.'

The rippling whisper of that curtain going up, whatever they say and however many times they say it, is the most wonderful sound in the entire world to an actor's ears. More, even, than applause. I was sick with excitement, shaking with terror, cool as a cucumber and, for the first time ever in my whole life, I knew precisely, as if it had all happened before, where I was and, what was more important, *who* I was. I fitted. I belonged. My stupid, slothful brain burst asunder the strings of its inertia and incomprehension and started to learn. Like an engine slowly throbbing into life, my whole frame started to glow with energy and I saw the road, very clearly, stretched out before me.

I knew, there and then in that painted Press Box, that I had found my place. Like the rattling, wobbling, steel ball in a pin table, I had battered round the pins, hit a spring and shot into my little hole. Lights flashed; the score went up. No one had to tilt.

And now with my inaccurately reflecting mirror, the endless compliments from Cissie Waghorn and the total unawareness of Elsie Brooks . . . I knew that I must step upon a stage and let an audience judge what so far only I myself and one devoted dancing partner knew. And what Elsie would not fail to know when she saw it. I was ready for the World.

Readiness was tested at the end of that year, in the village hall, with the local amateur dramatic society into which I was permitted entry, although under age, as a naked slave in the second act of 'Alf's Button'. An inauspicious start. Half naked, dressed in baggy chiffon knickers, a gold turban, a squint moustache, I stood impassively, arms folded across my chest holding a paper scimitar in one hand and my terror in the other. I never moved, and no one really saw me. But there is a picture of me in the local paper to prove it all. I was cold. Frightened. Idiotic. But I had started. And nothing now was ever going to stop me.

Mr Cox, who produced, said I had Presence and Stillness. Hardly difficult the latter, as I was forbidden to move a muscle on my Turkish Staircase; as for Presence, I didn't know about that but thought that he would. Cissie Waghorn was hopeful that in the next season I might get a better part and the local paper printed my name, for the first time, in its entirety, the van and the den and all. And Lally sent me a telegram. My cup was filling, if not exactly brimming. I knew, if no one else present that memorable night did, that I was on my way. All I had to do was explain it to the family and take the next train to Victoria.

My father, when approached, looked vague, then worried, finally irritated. And said categorically No. It was no job for a man, he explained, rightly as I was later to find out; it was risky, and nearly all actors were out of work for years and years, also they were common, and in any case he had no intention, after the years of sweat and toil that had gone into whatever education I had managed to scratch together from the wreckage of all that had been offered me, of letting me follow such a lunatic, mediocre, ungentlemanly career. If career it ever was to be. I was to do as he had arranged. Finish school and start the new year as a student at the Chelsea Polytechnic and through a solid Art Education, as opposed to a solid Scottish one, prepare myself for my eventual arrival in Printing House Square.

He was immeasurably gentle, he always was, but he was firm. And we all knew in the family that when he said No it was really No. There was, as Lally had said so often, No Shilly Shally about my father. My mother on the other hand was wistful, remembering her own, and her father's world. But she took his side and endorsed what he said completely. I was on my own.

'Alf's Button' faded away gently, as did the dancing lessons under Cissie Waghorn and Nerine Cox's devoted eyes, when I discovered, by asking her directly, that Elsie Brooks couldn't dance anyway and had fallen in love with a garage mechanic in Lindfield. I went back to mucking out the rabbits and making bird-cages. I was not unduly cast down. After Scotland nothing was ever going to flatten me again. I'd wait till next year. There was time. Next year I would be sixteen, and an Art Student. Student meant, in those days, that one was Grown Up.

The farewells in Glasgow were not at all difficult. Except for Aunt Hester and her family, to whom I knew I owed so much of this new liberation of spirit, and my maternal grandfather. I was almost indecently cheerful. I seldom ever saw my grandfather during the years I lived there. Banished, as he was, to sit by the kitchen range, and sleep in a bed set into the wall with curtains all around it (a Butt and Ben they called it), the only chances of seeing him I got were when the family were resting after Sunday luncheon and the maid was out of the kitchen.

He sat in an armchair beside the big iron range, a small black and white dog at his side, his hands clasped on a stick, dozing gently. His hair was snow white, his jaw firm, his eyes clear and steady. I never ever knew why he was banished to live in the kitchen and sleep in the cook's bed and he never told me. Not that I ever asked, it must be confessed. I imagined that it was probably a form of punishment for all the wickedness of his early life with my mother when, for so many years, they had stayed away from the family house and trailed willingly all over the country with wicker hampers and bookings for Crewe, Manchester, Leeds, Birmingham, Cardiff and Liverpool, their make-up boxes in a Gladstone bag and enough money for two quarts of beer and 'digs' in a street near the Theatre. But it was never spoken of and still is not. So all this is conjecture. Our few conversations together were conducted in conspiratorial whispers lest we should be caught by one of my aunts, a maid, or worst of all, the unforgiving figure of my black-woollied grandmother.

'And what do you do with yourself, my boy?'

'Well, I write a lot. Plays mostly.'

'You like the Theatre? That's good. Of course it's in your blood. Your mother had a fine talent, a fine talent, but frittered it away in marriage. A pity.'

'I want to be an actor when I'm old enough.'

He used to chuckle, his wicked eyes opening with tired amusement: 'You'll never be Old Enough to be an Actor, my boy. Actors have to be always Young. We don't get Older, you mark my words. You will do the Classics? Those lovely, lovely words. Sheridan, Congreve; lovely things to say. I was a very acceptable Surface you know in 'Scandal', did your mother tell you? You ask her . . . very acceptable. Forbes Robertson asked me to understudy him in 'The Only Way' . . . but I missed it . . . now *there's* a role for an actor! Carton . . . do you know it? Oh! What lovely things to say. . . .'

I remember, after so many years, these words almost verbatim. Really because it was the only conversation, or topic of conversation, we ever had. Each time I spoke to him it was as if I had disturbed him in a continual ever-running band of thought. Forbes Robertson, Sheridan, the loveliness of words. It never varied. Once, when I asked him about Shakespeare (being at that time deeply into a simplified version of 'A Midsummer Night's Dream') he gruffly said that it had never come his way, and was not his 'style'. He didn't care for the blood and anxieties of the plays, he said; life was filled with that already in the streets outside, so what audience wished to be reminded of all that lay about them when they had to pay half a guinea for a good seat in order to forget?

'Give them joy and delight . . . give them lovely words and good cheer, make them laugh, and *cherish them*!' he said firmly. 'Cherish them as I cherish you, eh?' he said to the black and white dog at his knee. 'Ah! Spot! What a wealth of lovely words you have had wasted on you. He doesn't take it in, you know. Not a word.' He laughed without rancour.

He collapsed in the street one day walking with 'Spot' and died shortly afterwards in the white-tiled glare of a public ward. An actor's life.

Aunt Hester, tall, worried, continually harassed, loving, gentle as a dove, merely held me just that little bit longer in her arms at the station. Her eyes were sad.

'You'll be off in a minute. I hate farewells,' she said, and with a quick, nervous little wave, she hurried into the crowd, bumping into people. I settled back into my compartment, lit a Black Cat, and felt the train rumble over the Broomielaw Bridge. Looking out of the scummy window I watched the cranes and tugs and hulks of ships lining the sullen waters of the Clyde. I hoped never ever to see it again. And I never have.

The three years in Scotland were, without doubt, the most important years of my early life. I could not, I know now, have done without them. My parents, intent on giving me a solid, tough scholastic education to prepare me for my Adult Life, had no possible conception that the education I would receive there would far outweigh anything a simple school could have provided. Life before 1934, the Summer Life if you like, with Lally and my sister in the country and the near effortless marking-time existence at the Hampstead school, had seduced me into a totally unreal existence of constant happiness, simplicity, trust and love. What I clearly needed, and what I got, was a crack on the backside which shot me into reality so fast I was almost unable to catch my breath for the pain and disillusions which were to follow.

To be sure it was a violent break, but it did not, I trust, find me weak: amazingly the Summer Life had made me strong; the break from it and all that was to follow, astonished me but left me unsurprised, cut me but left me unbloody, bewildered me but left me unafraid. And because of it I was able to enter the new phase of life which lay ahead of me with, if not total confidence (I have never had that), at least a thick veneer of it, and with the inbuilt belief that whatever happened to me anywhere at any time, I would somehow, willy nilly, by hook or by crook, manage to survive. For myself alone if for no one else.

The enforced loneliness in which I chose to dwell was not, when all is said and done, one long trail of misery and woe and barrenness. After all I was within the confines of my 'family', my own blood. I was cared for, comfortable, well fed and looked after by people who, by their own standards, were doing their very best to assist me. I was even at times pleasured for there were trips to hear choirs, to see football matches, the Teas and Bakings, walks in the Campsie Fells and on one occasion a short holiday by the sea at Dunure. No: the life they all offered me in that alien land was reasonable, kind, uncomprehending and in many ways most generous. The fact that I rebellled against all it offered was entirely my own fault and one one else's. I *tried* to conform, but the conformation was unacceptable to us all. Compromise is a deathly weapon.

Unable to share the pleasures offered I chose to remain apart, solitary, detached. It must have been irritating and unfriendly. But that's what I did. I was desperate to preserve my Summer Life against all odds, and to some extent, to a large extent indeed, I succeeded.

But in those times of loneliness, in those solitary walks across the ruined fields, the dreadful Teas and Bakings, the reading of knitting patterns and endless games of Solitaire, I did not sit idle and let my mind float off into a vacuum. Instead I turned to my father's old teaching of the Remember Game and played it assiduously. I 'pelmanised' a million details which, one day, I felt would 'come in handy', as Lally had said so often. I looked and I watched continually. Looking and watching, as one knows, are two very different things. I watched.

My Granfather Aimé had always said, 'You must Observe. Always question.' I started to become a professional, as it were, Observer. I was unable to question for I knew that I should not receive honest answers from people who thought questioning a lack of respect for one's elders.

So I observed and from observation answered my own queries. Not always accurately, but satisfactorily enough for me at the time. At least my sluggish brain was working for itself.

From this easy, silent game, which never intruded on anyone's conversation or alarmed them, I assembled a rag bag of trinkets into which I am still able to rummage. Aunt Teenie's dreadful twitch on her poor scarred face became the twitch on von Aschenbach's face at moments of stress, in 'Death In Venice' for example; my own shyness and diffidence and loneliness at those Tennis Parties or Tea Parties became his when he arrived, alone, at the Grand Hotel des Bains. The games I played then, and the things I stole, gleaned, collected, observed, have remained with me, vividly, for the rest of my life.

At the same time I was also forced to build myself a sort of wall of protection which, until then, I had never had need of. It was unnecessary to protect myself from love, from trust, honour, warmth and companionship, all of which I had had in abundance. Now, those things were to be guarded and protected. From the moment my head hit the bottom of that lavatory pan I laid the first brick of my protection by rapidly learning a foul, but saving, Glasgow accent. The first brick went in. From that day on I didn't cease my labours, walling myself snugly into my shell slowly, deliberately and undetected.

I learned to blub without moving a muscle of my face so that even then I was not given away, and began to speak elliptically, so that whatever I said was not precisely what I meant, but nearly so. A habit to which I still, regrettably, cling, and which gets me into a good deal of trouble from time to time. However, it is a hard habit to break and one I am not very willing to try. I am still un-trusting to some degree.

Of course in the busy building of this wall I left many openings about me, so that I was able to watch, to look, to touch if I wished, and feel. But they did preclude others from getting too near and, like the winkle on the pin, pulling me outside.

And, perhaps unfortunately for me, I went on building right into adult life. An undeniably self-centred thing to do. But I am. Isolation, even from choice as in my case, incubates self-centredness like a culture. But it has been this wall, or tower really, for a wall does not necessarily contain all that it surrounds, which has allowed me to retain most of the values which I had been taught. This attitude, of course, has cost me dear at times. Living in a tower, however secure it may feel, is hardly a social attribute. It can give the impression that one is withdrawn, insular and distant. *Not* the accepted qualities for an Actor, where the very reverse is apparently required. It was said of me recently that I suffered from an Obsessional Privacy. I can only suppose it must be true. And it is doubtless because of this that I have never reached the highest peak of my profession. It held me back, mercifully, from 'playing the game' to the hilt with the Bosses, the people in power. In a profession rife with insecurity this obsessional privacy was regarded with dislike and suspicion. In the years that I made money for them the Bosses grudgingly accepted this 'fault', but as soon as I stepped out of line to change my direction and fight along with forward-looking Directors like Dearden, Losey, Schlesinger and Clayton, my general popularity waned and the box office receipts crashed accordingly. The films we made so passionately together were considered 'intellectual'. The people who had paid good money to see my Little-Boy-Looking-For-God look were *very* unimpressed, and started to stay away in droves. The films were, by and large, critical successes but box office failures. The Cinema demands that you make money for it at no matter what cost. I recall one of those over-tailored moguls, itching to 'do' his 'bob' at the Palace, saying pleasantly: 'They don't want that kind of stuff. THEY want tits and bums. Or the Burtons.' Since I was not in that category I quickly found myself unemployable. A cold wind was blowing. It was everywhere. Even the Studios were starting to crumble and close down under the almost intolerable pressures from within. By 1966 I was splendidly on the skids.

But there was a candle glowing in the window of my discomfort. Hollywood, Italy and France could, it seemed, keep me occupied with the kind of work I still wished to try to do for some considerable time. Nearing fifty, it seemed prudent therefore to follow the beckoning light from Abroad. And abroad in the first instance was personified by Luchino Visconti. My father reluctantly agreed. Either I stayed where I was and went broke, returned to the Theatre after many years absence, or tried my novice hand at Television. These alternatives seemed distinctly chilly.

'Then clear off, my dear,' he said. 'Start again. Go where they want you.'

It had not escaped our minds that 'to start again' would mean leaving England. We looked at each other bleakly. However it was not the England of my Summer Life which I should be forced to leave, it was a fast changing England. A country bent determinedly on its quiet revolution, led by people who, with avuncular joviality, constantly assured the Middle Classes that they were all doomed. And, not unnaturally, people wanted new faces; mine had been hanging about for over twenty years, and a change was needed. From all points of view, then, it seemed sensible to accept the invitations from abroad. But . . . but . . .

'Whatever you do, my dear, don't shilly shally,' said my father, pouring himself a Worthington. 'Do it neatly; mitre your corners.'

I sold my house, paid all my bills, and left. Perhaps the final bricks in my tower.

Paradise regained is an impossibility. It is not, perhaps, always even desirable; and in any case is denied to most mortals. However, I tried. With no regrets whatsoever. The day I pushed open the door of this silent, empty house, standing on its hill since 1641, sunlight slanting across the tiled floors, a vine fretworking the wide windows, another Great Meadow lying all about, I knew that, in a physical sense at least, I had at last got back to the Summer Life.

Almost intact.

THIRTEEN

A number 11 bus set me down at The Six Bells, Kings Road, and from there, just across the road, past a row of crumbling Regency houses, is Manresa Road and the Chelsea Poly. Up the broad stone steps and through the big swing doors and I had started, in my own mind, my first steps towards the Theatre. Although no one else but myself knew that.

At first it was considered, and with reason, that I was too young to attend the Poly. I was not quite seventeen. However Williamson, the Principal, had seen a folio of my 'work', that is to say examples of stage designs, costumes, and illustrations for plays which I had written but which, naturally, had not been performed. Vaguely impressed, as he himself said, by my sense of colour design and 'inventiveness', he waived the few months needed to make me as it were 'legal' and I started on my way.

Some weeks before, my patient father took me to Gamages, to a Fire Sale which he had seen advertised, and within an hour, among piles of slightly damp and smoky garments on the top floor, outfitted me in a grey tweed suit, a bottle green striped one, a sundry collection of woollen polo necked sweaters and a pair of brogue shoes, one size too large, in suede.

I was enraptured. These, and the obligatory 'smock' which we all had to wear, were to constitute my entire wardrobe for some time to come. I almost slept in the bottle green suit I liked it so much, and the brogue shoes, stuffed with a little wad of paper, gave me a stature and dignity I must otherwise have lacked. At least so I thought.

This was a very different atmosphere from the school on the Hill. No hulking lumps here itching to kick something, no shared desks, no dustbin lunches. Instead, high, airy rooms, quiet, purposeful people, sitting on stools indulging in the highest form of luxury to me, just painting, drawing and even, at times, doodling away. We signed a book on entrance to each Class and on our departure for luncheon, usually a beer and a sandwich at the Six Bells or a Lyons Tea Shop near Sloane Square – not a beer there, of course, warm tea in a thick cup, but still . . . it was not a meat pie and Cola.

The Classes were a mixed assembly of people, sexes and ages. I was astonished, and encouraged, to find that my neighbour in 'Illustration' was a woman as old as my grandmother with a smock, a floppy felt hat, a raffia bag full of paints and brushes, rubbers and pens, her sandwiches and a small flask of Brandy from which, during the morning, she would take a strengthening swig.

There were pretty girls with long blonde hair who were really not serious artists, but merely 'Finishing Orf', as they called it – and who painted endless chains of pussy cats, blue-birds or bunnies, and seldom came back after the lunch break. Others, like Erica Schwartz, were far more serious. Smocked, sandalled, rather grubby, she and her companions worked industriously in 'Design' covering yards of material with abstract patterns of blue and mauve which they then turned into skirts and shirts, and stamped about the corridors pinning notices on the Notice Board bearing large Hammers and Sickles. They, these industrious girls, and some men, also ran the Dramatic Society which I was allowed, in spite of my age, to join, so that I could help with the painting of the scenery and the making of the costumes and also to swell the chorus which used to sing 'Red Fly the Banners O!' to the tune of 'Green Grow the Rushes O!' It was all magical, exhilarating, bursting with promise. I had never, I believed, even at the Cottage, been so happy in my life before.

My first 'task' – we were usually set a 'task' at the beginning of every week to set us on a line of thought or design – was to design the cover for a book. In this particular case H. E. Bates' *The Poacher*. This of course, normally, meant that one had to read the book, or intelligently 'skip through' it in order to get at the 'essence', as it was always called. What the 'essence' was depended entirely on what one *thought* it meant. And one's work was judged accordingly. I had read the book and set to, as I so often do, without much care and preparation. My sketch book was a riot of fields, woods, dead rabbits and panoramas of Great Britain from Lulworth Cove to Ben Nevis. H. E. Bates' simple tale was illustrated, by me at any rate, as the natural history handbook of the British Isles, including every single beast which lived within them and some which did not. I was enormously impressed by my own efforts and, as usual, embellished my design with guns and traps, fishing rods, gaffing hooks and snares. I left nothing out. And nothing to the imagination. At the Wednesday Class, covered with pride and a singular lack of humility (everyone else was still at the 'blocking in stage') I offered my finished cover to our patient, calm, gentle teacher, Graham Sutherland. In his neat farmer's smock, his pale blue knitted tie, with his small dark head and steady piercing eyes, I found him the kindest and most encouraging of all the teachers at the School. He was rather frightening too, because he smiled often, spoke very little; one was never certain of what he exactly thought. And he was not about to give anything away.

Patiently this day he sat beside me, dragging up a stool to my desk, slowly he examined my startling, lurid, finished cover. Gently he explained that I might have possibly missed the point of the exercise. It was not, he said, to tell the entire story of Mr Bates on the cover, but rather to leave that to the reader to find out for himself which, after all, was the author's job. Mine, he said gently, as the designer, was to suggest to the reader what he might find beneath the wrappers; to offer him some simple, uncomplicated, symbol which he could recognize enough to tempt him to read the book. Not something which would convince him that he had read it already, or worse, that he knew what it was all about and didn't want to read it anyway.

Swiftly, economically, he drew a face, a cloth cap, some rabbits' legs, a long waving line which was clearly a field of corn, and the entire subject was before me. I apologized in a mumble. He was anxious. 'But are you *sure* you know what I mean? Simplicity, you see . . . just the suggestion. The essence. Not,' he said gently, 'a map of England with all its Blood Sports.'

I started again much cast down but already agreeing, how could I not, that he was right. But *how* to simplify . . . how to find the 'essence'? That was my problem, and eventually stealing from him shamelessly I did my design by the end of the week and got top marks.

But the discovery was magical, I mean the general discovery. Being treated as an equal, as an already proved, which I was not, artist, gave me back a great deal of ebbing courage. I drew and drew and covered page after page of sketch books with a wild assortment of ideas which I then was forced to condense, simplify, coordinate, in short . . . design. It was not, I was quick to find out mercifully, quite the same as merely 'Drawing'.

Drawing was much harder. Drawing meant, for me, the Life Class. A serious, grimy room. A wide semi-circle of stools round a battered rostrum on which reclined, or stood, in patient humility, and bored indifference, a naked woman or, at times, man. Always ugly, always thin or vastly fat, as unacceptable naked as they must have been fully clothed.

In winter they froze to liver-sausage blue in the arctic room, warmed only vaguely by a one bar electric fire, around which they huddled at the 'rests' in tatty silk kimonos – in the summer they baked and broiled under the relentless glare of the sun from the skylight windows – all for a pittance an hour. Eyes glazed with boredom, they saw past and beyond us, locked into a frozen area of numbness from which nothing save the ringing of the alarm clock, to tell them their time was up, could release them.

Although, up until then, I had never seen an entirely naked woman, I was completely unmoved. I only remember being saddened by the sight of so much ugly flesh humped so dejectedly in a bent-wood chair. I found drawing their ugliness far harder to cope with than anything else. It seemed that if I started off with a head the left foot usually ended up miles off the bottom of the page and somewhere in the region of my own feet. However much I held up my pencil to measure, as I saw the other students doing with great professionalism, I never got the proportions right, and in spite of constant rubbings-out and starting-agains, the human body defeated me entirely. I sweated on and for ageless days sat in a smaller room with some others who found it as hard as I did, studying and drawing, in vicious detail, every bone and socket in a range of dusty skeletons which hung, dangling feet and hands, from wooden gibbets, swinging forlornly in the draughts.

'Try not to bother with her too much,' said Henry Moore, who took us for Life and, later on, Sculpture. 'She's not much good really, but it's very hard to get skeletons these days. Very hard indeed. She's pretty young, this one, mid-twenties I'd say . . . died some time about 1890. You see the rib cage? All squashed up, those dreadful corsets of theirs. How did she breathe for God's sake? You see? Squashed tight. Quite useless for you really. No Form there, simply de-formed. Shocking really. But it's the best we have at the moment.' Smocked, and with a woolly tie, he too moved among his pupils quietly and gently, correcting and suggesting here and there, patient with the slow, glowing with the more advanced of us. Wanting to share his obvious delight and love of the Human Body. 'This absolute miracle of co-ordination, of muscle and bone. A brilliant conception never yet beaten,' he said.

But it took me a long time to come towards sharing his delight. And although I sat spellbound if he came to my board to tug a muscle or a joint into place, or scribbled a rapid explanation for me on the side of my disordered, erased, smudged drawing, his swathed, mostly faceless figures reminded me a little too sharply of Mr Dodd's mummies ever to re-kindle a dying interest in the Human Form. I served him better in Perspective, and he was encouraging and kind, and when I said, rather timidly, that I wanted to go in for Stage Design rather than any other form of art he set to with enthusiasm and bashed me into Vanishing Points and Source of Light until, little by little, I abandoned almost altogether Life Class and attended, as often as I could, and more often than I should, Perspective. Which is why, to this day, I can still do a remarkably good bird's eye view of the Piazza San Marco, Times Square or even Kennington Oval looking as if they had been struck by bubonic plague. My perspectives are empty. However I am very good at people leaning out of windows. That's about as far as Mr Moore, with all his patient efforts, ever got me.

If I was hopeless at Life Class I was making tremendous strides towards becoming a Playwright. The Cox family was exceedingly encouraging and

welcomed me into their family. Every evening, after I had returned from Art
School, I would cycle over to 'Chez Nous' and spend a great deal of time with
Nerine, who was soft, blonde, gentle and deeply interested in all my theories;
discussing the ideas for a new play, the plots and even the sets. We wrote poetry
together and spent hours in the depths of Rotherfield Woods talking of my
Future. We never, it seemed, ever got around to hers. And at no time did we
discuss the world around us which was steadily becoming more and more
troubled but which caused us no apparent concern. The pronoun 'I' fell rapidly
and confidently from our lips. Except that her 'I' was 'You'. Which I felt was
just as it should be. Eventually, from all this airy chatter and from all these
floating plans about my Future a play got written. It was called 'The Man On
The Bench' and starred Nerine as the Prostitute and myself as the Man. As far
as I can recall it was a very long monologue for me interrupted, only here and
there, by Nerine dressed in black satin and a feather boa. The trick was the
surprise ending when the Prostitute left in a huff and the Man fumbled about in
the skirts of his overcoat producing a white stick. Blind, you see.

Very moving. I don't quite know why I had not given the entire plot away
from the start for I fixed my eyes in a steady glazed stare at a point somewhere
beyond Ashdown Forest and never let it waver. It went on at the Village Hall
and was well received by a rather sparse audience who had other things on their
minds since, a day or so before, Germany had annexed Austria. This irritated
me more than anything else. We had a poor house, and I felt that the Message of
the play was unfairly judged. However I cheered up considerably when I
realized that within a few days I should be seventeen and Mr Cox had offered
me my first leading role in a 'real' play which was to be the September Event of
the Village.

It was decided by the all male Committee of the Newick Amateur Dramatic
Society, known as the NADS, to do an all male play With A Warning.
'Journey's End' was selected as being the most suitable – a reasonable cast, one
set, and timely in a year of mounting tensions. I was to play Raleigh. I started to
learn the French's acting edition there and then.

In the meantime the rest of life was going on in its implacable way, which in
no way affected me much until the death of beloved Mrs Jane and shortly
afterwards that of Grandfather Aimé. A slight stroke and growing incontinence
finally forced his departure from the grubby house by the West Pier into his
clean, spartan, nursing home in Kemp Town.

Enraged at being removed forcefully, as he said, he gave one of his cronies in
the Junk Trade a five pound note to strip out the house. My parents arrived to
collect him one morning as two packed vans drove away from the mouldy
square. He retained a few 'Treasures' with which to furnish his room at Kemp
Town; the rest were dispersed all over Sussex, some even landing up at
Christie's months later. There was nothing to be done, everything was perfectly
legal, and my distressed parents managed only to retrieve a Nanking jar, a
black ebony table, and a pile of National Geographical Magazines.
Grandpapa's spite had won. And it finally killed him off, loathing his Matron,
smoking like a chimney, and wilfully peeing all over his faded Aubusson. He
went almost as suddenly as he had entered, or re-entered, our lives. Singularly
unmissed and shortly forgotten.

Rehearsals for 'Journey's End' started amidst the growing tension in Europe.
Not, perhaps, the wisest of plays to attempt on the threshold of a new war –
although that did seem rather unlikely to me once I had been reassured, by
gentle Nerine, that I would not be called up until I was at least nineteen, which
gave me two years, and no war, no modern war that is to say, could possibly last

that long. Also, she had heard it said at the Red cross and in the St John's Ambulance Brigade, to which she was devoting more and more of her time, that all the German Tanks were made of cardboard and the Population were half starving, having neither milk nor meat nor butter.

My father, needless to say, did not share these opinions and was longer and longer at 'The Times' than he was at home. All about us a disturbing feeling of apprehension was stirring. People were getting restless and even starting to dig trenches in the London parks. Erica Schwartz and her friends got more and more frantic and held long urgent meetings in the Common Room and begged us all to be Conscientious Objectors, which I thought might be quite a good idea the way things were moving. One of my special new girl friends, a golden blonde with a white sports car and a father who made shoes in Czechoslovakia, one day was no longer at Class and we heard that she had suddenly been ordered back to Prague. I was very depressed because she was beautiful, rich, clever and liked me to the extent of cooking me baked beans on toast on her gas ring in a crumby little flat which she rented for fun in Jubilee Place. I was astonished that she should leave without even sending me a note for we had become, I thought, very Close Friends . . . however, she went. The Govonis had been recalled to Rome some time before, but Giovanna was sent back to stay with us for a holiday to 'keep up her English'. The telephone now rang almost constantly from Rome with worried appeals to get her back as soon as possible. My father and I drove her down to a boat at Newhaven and shoved her up the bursting gangway filled with anxious people carrying bags and suitcases. We waited on the quay until eventually a small, weeping red-headed figure fought her way to the stern waving, sobbing and crying out 'I love you. I'll never forget you. Goodbye, Goodbye.' The sirens went, gulls screeched and the packed ship moved gently away from us.

She stood there waving and waving until the ship made a slow turn to port at the end of the long jetty and bore her away, out of my sight, for twenty-three years.

My father and I were very quiet driving home through the lanes to the house. He only spoke once, when we stopped at the Chalk Pit outside Lewes for a beer. 'I can't really believe,' he said, 'that it is all going to happen again.

The rehearsals for the NADS were cancelled. No one seemed to have the heart to read through a play which was regrettably becoming more and more timely. Added to which it was difficult to get the cast together because people suddenly had extra things to do in their spare time, and Cissie Waghorn, who had a car, dragooned and bullied myself and a boy from Fairwarp called Buster into driving about the county fitting elderly people with gas marks and explaining to them the problems of Blast and Blackouts.

Influenced by all this activity and talk of a new War, and very much by 'Journey's End', I started to paint, exhaustingly, scenes from the first World War. I read every book I could lay my hands on in my father's study ranging from *All Quiet On The Western Front, The Seven Pillars of Wisdom, The War Of The Guns* to the Michelin *Guides to the Battlefields*. William Orphen, John and Paul Nash became my idols, and my bedroom was covered with reproductions of their works. I was *quite* convinced that I was painting in this fury because I was the reincarnation of a young soldier who had been killed in 1917. Nothing would budge me from the belief; the output of my work was prodigious, leading Sutherland to say that it was probably better to 'get it out of my system' and exercise my imagination. He was very patient and understanding and knew full well that no reincarnation was taking place, simply a release from too much emotionalism.

In this welter of second hand grief, anxiety, and something which was rapidly approaching self-pity, the Polytechnic closed down for the Summer Recess and, armed with my paints and brushes plus a bursting portfolio of agonizing scenes in the blazing ruins of Ypres, Albert with its leaning Virgin and sundry portions of the entire Western Front, I glumly headed for Sussex, Nerine and the fitting of yet more gas masks. I felt lost, worried and disconnected. Even though my last reports from the Art School had been glowing and highly encouraging, I felt within me the interest and love for Art slowly ebbing. I knew, instinctively, that I would never be a successful painter, for the simple reason that I did not want to be. I had no dedication but a totally God-given talent which I truthfully wished could be directed towards the main love of my life: the Theatre. And my father's sudden and extraordinary decision, already planned long before I knew anything about it, to send me off to study the process of colour photogravure at The Sun Engraving Co Ltd at Watford came like a bolt from the proverbial blue and only increased my growing despair. If I had given up the idea of the career laid down for me it was quite clear that his mind was still quietly working towards Printing House Square.

Accordingly, one hot July morning, I presented myself at the Works in Whippendall Road, was warmly welcomed, and bustled into 'digs' in an ugly terrace house in a long red brick street half a mile away. My landlady, a widow with tight yellow curls and a diamond brooch in her orange cardigan, showed me my room at the top of the stairs, hoped that I'd be 'comfy' and said that all meals would be taken in the front parlour with herself and her son, who was a coffin polisher. Tea, she said, would be very soon and she would hit the gong when it was ready. My room, floored with dead brown linoleum, had a wide double bed, a washbowl with jug and a florid brass clock on the mantel which played eight bars of 'The Sunshine Of Your Smile' at the hours and, like Bishopbriggs, struck all the quarters.

I learned absolutely nothing during my stay in the Sun Engraving Works. Not for want of teaching; people were wonderfully good and did everything they could to make me comprehend and enjoy the 'job' which I was to follow through. Colour printing was still fairly new at that time and it was my father's greatest ambition, one day, to see the picture page of *The Times* in glowing colour. It was, apart from Northcliffe and all the Astors and their Newspaper, his consuming passion. As a very small child I remember, in the studio in St George's Road, my mother standing about swathed in bolts of coloured silks while my father and Logie Baird photographed her from different rooms, I presume, with an early Television Camera. It was all very home-made and it is all rather vague in my memory. However, it was a passion which filtered into the house and into all of us, and I clearly recall the pride and excitement of seeing the first colour photograph ever taken by ordinary stage lighting in a Theatre. It was a glass plate of Pavlova dancing 'The Dying Swan' and she received it, apparently with gratitude and delight, according to her letter; that small rectangle of softly coloured glass (the second one) remained my father's most treasured possession, for it represented the culmination of years of experiment, bullying, cajoling and stubborn insistence for which he was entirely responsible.

But the love was not being transmitted to the son. Although I followed every single process from re-touching to the stapling and final folding of one wretched magazine as it came thudding off the machines, absolutely nothing whatsoever went in to my bewildered brain. I returned to the family home a little thinner, more determined than ever to try and avoid anything whatsoever to do with newspapers, and the cheerful owner of two blue budgerigars which someone in the Print Shop, who bred them, had given me. They had been in the house three days when Minnehaha, the cat, ate them: and vanished as swiftly as my father's hopes of his vision of my future.

A few nights later we drove down to Croydon Airport to meet one of his photographers who was, he hoped, on the last flight out of Prague. Standing in the dark waiting for the plane to come in he suddenly said: 'I suppose really that this is a very demanding profession. I think one really has to want to do it very much to make it work . . . I love it so much, as you know, that I wanted you to share it with me. But it is no good forcing you: I can see that it's got to be something which is in you, and it is clearly not in you. Never mind.' And that was all he ever said. A little later the plane arrived, a long lumbering corrugated iron cigar with wings. His photographer came down the gangway, tie-less, dishevelled, clutching a small case and his camera. He was very distressed.

Driving through Streatham he suddenly said: 'Christ! Oh Christ! They pulled this woman off and shoved me on. It was the last plane you see. She kept screaming and crying. I held the door against her, they were all battering at the side of the damned thing, crying, begging. I'll never forget her, I'll never forget her.'

A profession, I thought miserably, that you really have to want to do to 'make it work'.

It all stopped with Mr Chamberlain's piece of white paper, blowing in the wind, and 'Peace In Our Time'. Joy and relief were so gigantic that no one seemed to stop for a second to consider *whose* time he meant, his, or ours. But it was enough.

Back went the rehearsals of 'Journey's End' now even more potent with message. It was a tremendous success. The Hall was packed for three nights solid, and people came from as far afield as Lewes and Haywards Heath. The emotion among our audiences was tangible. My set (I had been allowed to design it) was highly accurate after my 'studies' and my own performance was warmly received. Raleigh is a cinch anyway, but I didn't know that then.

My wretched father, who detested anything which remotely reminded him of his own brutal war, was eventually dragged to see me on the final Saturday night. Sitting with my proud mother he was, he later said, very moved. Not unnaturally. But he still was not about to weaken completely on his decision about my career. An actor's life was still not discussed.

'Was I really all right?' I asked my mother.

'Yes really, you were very good indeed. I was proud.'

'But when I hit that damned plate on the table and it flew into the audience . . .'

'That was *when* I knew you could be an actor, darling, you let it go as if you had meant it to go. No one moved in the audience, you know, no one at all. You had controlled the move and made them feel that it was true, and not a mistake.'

'It really was all right?'

'That's what acting is all about,' said my mother. 'Convince yourself and convince them. Never one without the other.' She was not entirely accurate, but near enough. And without quite knowing it. 'Always Applauded' was stirring it up with a vengeance.

In October 1938 Elissa Thorburn, an elderly lady of moderate means, built and opened a theatre in a buttercup field just behind the Station and next to the Coach Terminus, at Uckfield. I had noticed, riding about the area with Nerine, the red brick form take place, but had quite thought it was to be a new factory or a building for the Public Works. It was, however, to be 'the most modern, comfortable, best designed theatre in Sussex'. Miss Thorburn had bullied and cajoled money from various sources, mostly her own, and the theatre opened with a shrill of local publicity and a performance of 'Noah', by André Obey. And she used real actors from London, not us amateurs. Except that we were asked to come along and help out by playing Crowd or small parts for which she did not pay. The First Night was splendid with the Reigning Families and anyone else who could afford the not excessively cheap price of the seats.

Unhappily Miss Thorburn had already started to alienate the Local Council by refusing to put on plays which she considered suitable only for the, what she called, Hoi Poloi . . . that is to say, no 'Rookery Nook', no 'Charley's Aunt'. It was to be 'The Dramatic Glyndebourne,' she said. And made a slight error here to start with. Never alienate your Local Councillors who consider that they are not Hoi Poloi but like a good 'Rookery Nook'; and don't choose a small market town which never even went to the local cinema except on wet Saturdays and then only if 'Tarzan' was running or the Home Team was playing Worthing at Bolton. The local councillors were bewildered by 'Noah', insulted by the unhappy phrase 'Hoi Poloi' and hated the cold, brick, functional theatre behind the Railway Station. Theatres, they reckoned, for the money that they had all contributed, should be gold and red and filled with a 'good bit of family entertainment.'

Not for them translations from the French about a Biblical figure, set in a cold warehouse. And having to wear a black tie as well in the weekday evenings was asking a bit too much all round. However they did notice that there was no central aisle, and therefore there could be an infringement of the Safety Regulations. But that point came a little later. For the moment only the anger mounted. One day, passing the theatre in as casual a way as I could manage, I found the doors open and wandered into the cool, dark, auditorium.

One working light gleamed on the stage. A tall, tweedy, woman was painting, not very well, a canvas flat. Seeing me standing among her brand new seats, only one play old, she straightened up, waving a paint-brush in my direction and told me to be off.

'Shoo!' she cried. 'Shoo!' Her hair had fallen round her face like straw; she was hot and cross. I stood. 'What do you want with me? Be off, boy!' Her anger was clear.

'I want a job,' I said.

'What kind of a job . . .?'

'I paint scenery. I'm an artist.'

'I don't need a scenic designer . . . Are you strong?'

I said I was and she told me to come across the seats and on to the stage and together we manhandled a large Austrian stove into a corner. I stayed the rest of the day there, painted a number of flats, screwed the handles on to a chest of drawers and accepted her grudging offer of a shilling an hour when I worked.

Over the next few months, in all my spare time and every weekend, I went to the Uckfield Theatre and worked with Miss Thorburn to get the place ready for the Spring Performance. It transpired that she had seen me in 'Journey's End', having used as many of the NADS as she could, to save money and 'to give them valuable experience' in the production of 'Noah'. Covered as they had been in furs and masks I had not recognised any of them, but that was not of importance. They were, I reckoned, amateurs whereas I already earned my way and was doing it as a dedication. The new production was to be 'Glorious Morning', a heavy play about a Democracy being invaded by a Fascist State. It didn't bother me one way or the other until, with one bright eye on expenses, she offered me a part and said that she would pay me five shillings a performance. The fact that I was twenty years too young for the role didn't worry either of us; however I did agree that a black leather coat, a hat and a heavy moustache, would assist me in my 'performance'. We finished off the sets, rigged all the lighting together, and by the time the Real Actors arrived from London, at the end of April, we were ready to go. Except for the rehearsals which she, as director and producer, and sole owner of her Dream, would conduct personally.

I arrived, that first morning, long before anyone else. I was excessively nervous and it was also my job to open up the theatre, arrange the stage for the reading and see that there was lavatory paper in the lavatories and a packet of Typhoo tea in the little kitchen. There were also a dozen cups and two packets of Crawford's Custard Creams. I parked my bike by the scene dock, opened the Theatre, seeing the wide beams of sunlight streak across the blue velvet seats, set the 'props' and took my copy of the play out into the buttercup field and sat under a giant oak. I felt that, as I was just about to commence my Acting Career, it might be wiser not to sit anxiously huddled on the bare stage too eagerly waiting, but to go and sit in the fields and start it all off from the peace and the calm of the country which I so loved. When they were ready, I reckoned, they'd come for me. Never be over anxious.

Someone came ruffling through the long nodding grasses behind me, whistling softly. I looked up from my script. A tall, well built, smiling man of about thirty stood before me looking oddly out of place in the buttercups dressed, as he was, in a double-breasted suit, brown suede shoes, long white cuffs with gold links and a rather faded carnation in his buttonhole. One of the actors for sure.

'Hullo,' he said. 'Do you work here?'

'Yes. At the theatre. I'm an actor.'

'So am I. I hate First Readings, don't you?'

I didn't know but agreed. He offered me a piece of barley sugar which he assured me was excellent for energy and also for the voice. We started to walk towards the Theatre, a brick box glinting in the morning sun; there were people wandering in and out of the doors. My companion started to breathe deeply, throwing his arms wide as if he was about to take off and fly over the town. I was still wearing my cycle clips and we laughed as I pulled them off and shoved them into a pocket.

'My name's Wightman,' he said. 'William, but they call me Bill. I just think I'll have a quick pee before we go in, do you know where it is?'

I told him and watched his tall, burly figure going round the side of the Theatre to the Gents.

My first counsellor and adviser had arrived.

The weeks which followed, up until the opening of the play, were filled with joys and excitements. The other actors, with the generosity of their kind, welcomed me into their midst and we all settled down as one tightly knit company. An oddity of living which only actors seem to be able to achieve. This effect of permanence in a very temporary situation.

Bill Wightman became our leader; he was always jolly, kind, patient, amused and also the possessor of a modest, but adequate, private income which he always most generously shared with us. He also had a car, which, locked into the quietness of a pretty dull, if pretty, country town, was absolutely essential and proved a much needed escape for us all to rarer places like Eastbourne, Brighton or even London. Quite apart from his own considerable personal charm, warmth and wisdom, Bill's car was the Pipe in Hamelin, if he could be called, as he was, the Piper. But he was as much sought after for his advice and counsel as any of the more obvious pleasures which he could give. Every young Actor, or Actress, is plagued by the most appalling doubts and fears and only another actor can really share or understand them.

So it was with Bill. His patience was monumental, his encouragement enormous, his good humour apparently inexhaustible, and his ear always available to listen to the problems with which we burdened him almost continually.

The play opened to critical acclaim from the local papers, and to a financial disaster. Not enough people wanted to come to a grim play about Middle Europe and the Fascists when they had narrowly avoided the problem for themselves only a few months ago. The Town was split into two groups, those who thought the Theatre was an asset to the place and those who thought a Hospital would be more useful. There were rumbles of dissent among the gentle hills of East Sussex. Talk of Rates and Taxes and Robbing the People, of Intellectuals pushing Propaganda plays in a Civic Theatre when the theatre, as everyone knew, was supposed to be there for Entertainment. There was also the vexed problem of no Centre Aisle and what would happen in a fire, they'd all like to know?

The dissent grew so strong that Miss Thorburn herself, cycling back to her cottage in Nutley one evening, was set upon by children and stoned while they all yelled 'Witch! Witch!' causing her to fall from her bike and severely cut her knee and an eye.

It didn't stop her one jot. Sitting in her study, her leg up on a stool, reading through a magnifying glass with her Good Eye, she went through countless plays searching for her next production.

My father, driven to distraction by my insistence now that I should become an Actor, with so much success clearly turning my head, arranged an audition for me at the Old Vic. I still don't know how he did it but suspect that owing to his position on 'The Times' and the help which he had given them in the past by putting in photographs of the Productions as often as he could, they felt a little blackmailed and I was summoned to the Theatre on Tuesday, August the 8th at 2.30. Armed with three 'well contrasted pieces' as demanded by the proprietors, I walked up and down the Waterloo Road mumbling away at 'Is This A Dagger?' from 'Macbeth', the whole of Blunden's 'Forefathers' which begins:

> 'Here they went with smock and crook,
> Toiled in the sun, lolled in the shade,
> Here they mudded out the brook . . .'

which I found moving, referring as it did to the Last War, and the country life I loved; and also a frightful chunk of my monologue from the play I had written for the NADS about the poor blind man on his bench. Nothing light, clearly. I don't remember, for all my terror, much about the audition except that I am sure it amused them more than impressed them, and the glittering cold eyes of Tyrone Guthrie frightened me more than anything ever before. They were, to paraphrase a description of Aldous Huxley's, 'pale blue and triangular, like the eyes peering from the mask of a Siamese cat'. But, much to everyone's astonishment, I passed, and was accepted to hold spears and carry swords and possibly play 'one of Romeo's Friends', in the forthcoming production of that play which would start rehearsals on September the 4th.

In my green Gamages suit, I ran almost all the way to Victoria, in spite of the extremely hot day, and telephoned my father at the office to tell him. He was calm and rather quiet. He said that he would write immediately to Williamson at the Chelsea Poly and hoped now that I was satisfied. He didn't say that he was.

Williamson's letter in return was regretful. He felt, he said, that I had talent far above average and that it seemed a pity to let it all go – but this meant nothing to me for I didn't even know of the letter until many years afterwards. For the time being my horizons were vast. I would start with my spears and swords and being 'one of Romeo's Friends' and bit by bit, for I was in no hurry and realized that it would be a slow process, I would eventually become one of those glorious, and honoured, people who could call themselves Classical Actors. I never wanted, then, to become a Star. I never remotely sought, as so many of my contemporaries did, my Name In Lights – I didn't want the responsibilities that would bring; all I wanted to do was to achieve respect, acknowledgement, and honour in the profession for which I longed.

If this sounds naive and dimwitted then so I was. All I can say, from all this distance, is that is what I felt and what I still feel to this day. It never changed.

My mother was, secretly, very pleased. But she hardly did more than give me a hug and remind me that my pleasure must be equalled only by the disappointment of my father who had hoped, and worked, for so long to encourage me to take over from him when his time came to retire.

Bill, in whom I now confided constantly, which must have irritated him a good deal but which he never let show, was delighted and counselled me to be patient, humble, and, above all, diligent, to work very hard and deserve the honour of having been admitted to, what he called, one of the most distinguished companies of actors in the entire world. I promised him that I would.

A few weeks before I had gone down to see him in a series of plays which were being performed in a tithe barn at Shere in Surrey. The barn was draughty, dark, up a little grassy track behind the village. The actors welcomed me into the company as if I were a member and permitted me to watch every play, and nearly every performance, free and when I liked. The plays were all rather, what the Uckfield Council Members would have called Intellectual, and so were most of the audiences, and although I was not always able to follow the plots I was vividly aware of what my grandfather in Scotland had told me sitting beside his range in the kitchen in Glasgow. The lovely words ... I revelled in the sounds and shapes of them, in the things they evoked for me, in the astonishing beauty of them.

I fed, all that season, on words as if they were my main form of nourishment: which spiritually indeed they were. Everyone, as I have said, was very friendly, but especially one actor, a youth of my own age, whose enthusiasms and excitement exactly matched my own. In a pair of wrinkled tights with a shock of wild hair, bright eager eyes and wild gestures, he sat with me on the grass outside the Barn watching the audiences arrive up the scraggy little path and spoke passionately, and fluently, of his love and his dedication for his job. We were born, we discovered, on exactly the same day of the same month of the same year – and almost to the hour. I felt, therefore, a very close affinity to him, and although he had gone much further ahead than I, for he not only acted but wrote and had written the main play of the Season, I felt that as we both so clearly held exactly the same beliefs, hopes, ideals and burning passions for our craft, that in fact we almost were twins, and given time and the chance I would one day catch him up and together we should storm the world.

'But,' he said, brushing the grass off his tights and starting towards the big stage door, 'you have to be totally dedicated. Totally. Nothing else will do here.' I wasn't absolutely sure what he meant by dedication, but his intensity was such that I clearly understood that to follow my profession correctly and successfully had to be almost a form of religion. This important encounter with Peter Ustinov was to prove the final blow to my patient father. My passion and determination were so great, that he finally capitulated, and I was offered the audition at the Old Vic.

Four days before I was due to make my way along the Waterloo Road to my first rehearsal Germany invaded Poland. My father's face at breakfast was very grave, my mother's ashen.

'I don't think that this time we'll avoid it,' he said.

Never had the sun shone so splendidly, never had the Common lain so still in a haze of heat and shimmering light. Never had the Old Vic seemed so far away.

On the Saturday evening, dressed in my green suit and a yellow polo neck shirt, I went off with Buster and Cissie Waghorn and a thin girl whose name I don't remember. We drove in Buster's car to a Road House near East Grinstead and had lager and roast lamb.

Afterwards through a sudden, crashing thunderstorm, we drove, almost in silence, all the way to Brighton. The town was deserted. Few cars, and those that were were dimmed out, few lights – it was a half blackout – no one walking. The holiday-makers had melted away. We were alone on the deserted promenade. Buster parked the car under a lamp by the King Alfred's School, and we hung over the promenade railings looking down at the black sea and then the rumbling, fading storm, moving slowly across to France. The car radio was playing softly and we started, very quietly, to dance together, cheek to cheek, holding on to each other Cissie and I, and Buster and the thin girl. Lightning flashed in great silent forks across the hot, swelling sea, the surf rustled and clawed on the shingle below, and to the gentle crackling strains of 'Deep Purple' we slowly, unhappily, shuffled into the war.

FOURTEEN

The launching of a nation into a war seemed, to me at least, remarkably like the launching of a great ship. In Scotland I had seen the slow, ponderous slide of the 534, later to be called the *Queen Mary*, as it inched down the slipway into the river. At one moment it was quite still. At the next, almost imperceptibly, it moved away from its berth, snapping poles like spaghetti, chains like cotton threads, and as it gained speed, growing ever faster, the rusty metal mass hit the water sending up a swelling tidal wave which rippled higher and higher and faster and faster across the river and engulfed the crowds on the opposite bank.

But it was all, or so it seemed, in silence. In slow motion, without the benefit of cheers, flags or bands playing. We were overawed. So it was with the start of the war, almost the same actions from start to finish.

In the first instance everything melted away. Chelsea Poly remained firmly shut; theatres, including the Old Vic, and cinemas closed; silver balloons rose gently into the air ringing London; and everyone who could, or had to, went into one Service or another. And all the lights went out.

In the eager flush I, with others of my own age, hurried to our local Labour Exchanges to volunteer, only to be told, by harassed clerks, that we would not be wanted until we had reached the age of nineteen. I had a year to go. Buster, more fortunate than I by virtue of being nineteen already, got into the RAF and was blown to bits over Kent the following summer; Cissie went off to Portsmouth and became a WREN and Nerine, trained and able, and becoming bossier and bossier as the days went by, was organizing herself very securely into the Red Cross and Ambulance Brigade. Everyone, it seemed, was busy except me.

Life was spent in a limbo of unwantedness. Until I was organized to help clear out countless empty sheds, garages, stables and barns which had been commandeered to receive the first of the sad, bewildered, evacuees who came hourly from London, lugging crying children, bursting suitcases, and stuck about with humiliating cardboard labels. These wretched women were soon taken in charge by officious, but kindly, County Ladies who bundled them off in trucks or cars to their straw-filled shelters with cups of tea and five cigarettes apiece.

Miss Thorburn's Theatre was one of the first places to be taken over, and with its seats stripped out, filled with straw, provided miserable bed spaces for a couple of hundred. Everyone who could took in their own evacuees. We had two pale, nervous, unhappy brothers who arrived one afternoon and stayed for a year.

It might seem strange, in a country so suddenly tipped into a War, that there was absolutely nothing for me to do. I was the wrong age for that moment. Limbo forced me into solitude again, painting *acres* of battle scenes from a now out of date war, and writing reams of sentimental, over-emotional, staggeringly bad poems. All of which ended in tear-drenched despair or a row of ambiguous dots. Mostly because I didn't know how to write Full Stop.

My friends were all occupied happily enough; my sister, now a groom at a stables at Scaynes Hill; my mother with the Women's Institute and other Good Works; the house filled with our glum strangers from Finsbury Park. I decided to go to London and try and find something to do there. My father, tired, harassed, overworked, accepted the suggestion with almost indecent alacrity. I had a year to go, he said, before my Call Up . . . however the war was certain to be over before Christmas so that needn't worry me, but he felt that I should use the year in trying to get work and see if I could make my way in the Theatre when, and if, they re-opened. He gave me ten shillings a week for a year and suggested that I leave as soon as possible.

Which I did. The next afternoon. With a suitcase, an extra ten shillings from my vaguely apprehensive mother, and Aunt Freda Chesterfield's telephone number in Kensington so that I could beg a bed from her until I was settled into whatever I was going to do.

To my relief they all seemed quite glad to see me go, so I arrived in an almost empty Victoria, the next afternoon, guiltless but very aware of one important factor. The night before I left, my father quietly said that a year was all he could afford, and that if I had not made my way in my chosen profession by that time, to the day, I was to return and do precisely and exactly what he said I would do. Starting as a messenger boy at *The Times*.

I had agreed, over confidently. As he was over confident that the war, so newly started, would be over and done with by the end of the next two months.

Aunt Freda lived in a Mansion Flat behind Pontings. She was warm, unsurprised, which was her nature, and said that there was a bed if I wanted it but that I'd have to find my own meals. There was always, as long as it lasted, bread, milk and cheese in the Fridge, and beyond that I was on my own. She would not, she said, make any charge, and I'd have to find my own laundry since she already had a full house. She gave me a key, half a crown, and hoped I'd manage, and said that she would mention me at Mass.

It was a strange sandbagged, almost empty, London through which I drifted. And every bit as dull and boring as it was in Sussex. No one had seen an aeroplane, or been gassed, or had a parachutist in the back yard. And as the first panic started to melt away under the strange calm, people began to return to the City and life almost came back to normal. Except for Air Raid Wardens, the gas masks, and the discomfort and indeed danger of the Black Out, nothing might have happened at all on that hot, last Saturday of Peacetime.

Total boredom and a longing for something green sent me off on a bus to Kew Gardens to see the Pagoda and perhaps look about in the Palm House. But I never got there in the end. Stopping for a moment at Kew Bridge, the bus provided a grandstand view of what appeared to be a builder's yard. Doors and windows, some scattered fireplaces, piles of junk and a girl painting a cut-out tree which was leaning against the wall of the yard. Beside this muddle of wood and canvas was a small squat building. Across the facade, in shabby letters, the words 'Q THEATRE'.

I ran down the steps, jumped off as the bus started again, and went towards a half open door into the yard. The painting girl looked up rather crossly. She was covered in blobs of green distemper and wore an old pair of navy blue trousers and a man's shirt. She was startled and hot.

'What do you want here? This is private, you know.'

'It is a theatre, isn't it?'

She looked crosser than ever. 'Yu'd better clear off . . . or else.'

'I was wondering about a job . . . that's all.'

'Well, don't bother me with your wondering, I'm busy and the office is in there.' She indicated a door which said Fire Exit and went back to her tree.

It was practically identical, this meeting, to my arrival in the dark Theatre at Uckfield; a lone woman painting a flat . . . threatening me with a paint-brush and suspicion. But I didn't think of that then. I followed her instructions blindly.

A dark, untidy corridor, with a fire extinguisher and a glass-fronted door with 'Office' painted on it. It was half open and there were voices. Just as I was about to knock, it opened and a small, hurrying little woman came out eating a cheese roll. She looked up at me mildly.

'Yes?' she finished chewing, her eyes bright and interested, the half finished roll in her hand. I said that I was wondering if there was a job going. I'd seen the yard from the top of a bus and . . . She cut me short with a wave of the cheese roll: 'Not auditioning today, dear . . . next week is all cast and we don't see anyone without an appointment . . . come again.' She started to turn away back into the Office, when I said: 'I meant painting, scenery and things. I'm an artist not an actor.'

This stopped her. She took another bite of her roll and asked me where I came from. I said from nowhere particular but had trained at the Poly and worked in Sussex and at the Uckfield Playhouse. I made it sound like the Liverpool Rep.

'What happened to the Uckfield Rep then?' she asked with a shrewd smile. 'They fire you?'

'No. They got commandeered for evacuees.'

'And you did the sets, is that it?'

I nodded. I didn't say I'd done one only. She finished her roll, licked her fingers and turned back into the office. 'You'd better come in and see my husband,' she said.

Jack and Beatrice de Leon were legendary figures in the Theatre but at that moment, in my supreme ignorance of anything which happened far from the NADS or Uckfield, I was not to know. Jack was a silver haired, handsome man, as beautiful as a Persian, immaculately dressed always, tired, often; quiet and as shrewd as he was kind. His wife, Beattie as we all grew to call her after about half an hour's talk, read his scripts, cast his plays, arranged his staff and sometimes played bits and pieces herself. Their whole life revolved about this converted skating rink in the Chiswick High Road, and to play at Q was considered to be one of the most important things for a young actor outside the immediate West End. My sudden arrival in their office that afternoon was providential. The regular set designer had walked off the day before, and with a new Show to open in a very short time and only one cross, tired, overworked girl to do it all there was indeed a job for me. I started work at the Q Theatre that afternoon on a verbal agreement of seven and six a week to help out in the scene dock, cart the props about, and do any odd jobs around the theatre which needed doing, from washing down the Gents Lavatory and calling the actors for the Curtain and the Entrances. I was, to all intents and purposes, by the grace of God and Jack and Beattie de Leon, launched.

The cross girl, who was not really at all cross when I got back to the yard, but relieved that she had someone, even someone so inexperienced, to help her, said that her name was Tanya Moiseiwitsch and that we were starting out on a musical called 'The Two Bouquets' by Herbert and Eleanor Farjeon. It was, she said, a sod with three big sets, one of them being, as she put it succinctly, 'the entire bloody Twickenham Regatta'. It was on this backcloth that I was put to work, squaring up Eel Pie Island and half the river Thames. My Twickenham. My first truly professional job. If that wasn't fate, I wondered, what was?

There really wasn't a great deal that I could do to help Tanya. She was very much more experienced than I, and as she was in the middle of the job I mostly scurried around boiling the glue, mixing the size, squaring up, and getting her cups of tea. But I had the impression that I was useful even banging in nails and stretching soggy, size-wet canvas. After a very short time my endless stream of questions started to dry up and I moved more and more about on my own.

Apart from the Scene Dock there were other jobs to be done. I bought a new toothbrush and used my old one with a tin of Brasso (supplied) to bring the taps and pipes to shining life in the Gents. No cigarette ends were ever allowed in the sweet flowing china canal of my Gents. As soon as graffiti appeared, which was not often and usually between the matinee and evening performance, I blotted them out with a wipe of distemper, polished the mirrors and swabbed down the cracked marble floor after every interval. There seemed to be quite a lot of bad aimers.

Adjacent to the Gents and opposite the auditorium was the Club Room. Q, like a number of other smaller theatres, had no licence or Bar but they were allowed to have Club Members . . . which meant a Club Room . . . which meant that if you were a Member, for very little extra per year, you were entitled to the use of the Club Room, as much drink as you could afford to consume, a snack or a meal before the Show and the month's programme of events mailed to your door. I rather think you also received a slight reduction on your seats. In any event the Club Room, presided over by fat, jolly, Vi, thrived. It was not large, about eight tables and a corner bar, a gas fire, two or three armchairs and a long couch. I carted plates about, wiped down the tables, set the salt and pepper straight, saw they were filled, emptied the ash trays and collected the 'empties', thus saving Vi a certain amount of work and assuring myself of at least one good meal a day.

If it had not been for Vi and the Club Room it is more than probable that I would have starved to death. Seven and sixpence a week, although a good deal more in 1939, was not very much. However, I managed pretty well. Aunt Freda's free bed was a godsend of course, but I didn't always use it . . . especially if we were in the middle of rehearsals when there simply wasn't time to get back to Kensington. If there was a bed in the play of the week I was particularly lucky and slept, with the mice and the creaks, on that in the Prop shop. Or even on the couch from the Second Act. Never, however, in the Club Room which Vi locked firmly every evening before she left.

I don't think that I can have looked all that clean, thinking back. I shaved in cold water in the Prop Room . . . used my own Gents, of course, and managed a bath once or twice a week when I got back to Aunt Freda's. First thing in the morning, before anyone but the milkmen were about, I was up and setting my little iron stove alight with bits of wood and paper and then heaved up the coke. Made the bed or couch on which I had slept a dreamless night, and started off down the Chiswick High Road for my breakfast. A packet of Maltesers from the local newsagent, just opened and stacking the papers for the delivery boy to collect, a packet of Woodbine, cheaper than Black Cat, and then a half bottle of milk, or a pint if I could find it, snitched from any old front door step on my way back to the theatre.

Not long ago I was asked by one of those anguished middle-aged people who seem to dominate Television interviews if there was one really 'awful, shaming, thing which I had ever done in my life and which still made me blush'. In the course of over fifty years there have been one or two. But the one single one which makes me really blush is the pinching of pints of milk and the thought of the perplexed morning faces when those doors were opened. However I reckoned that I needed it more than they did. I hadn't even got a door to open . . . let alone a doorstep or a bottle of milk idly sitting trustfully there. And I never, ever, took the only one. I took from the Rich. Those who had ordered a pint and a half or anyway two bottles. I felt that was fair.

I enjoyed waiting at table, a napkin over my arm, my hands clean, the typewritten menu offered, the little pad and pencil. All rubbish really: Vi only ever had two meals on her Menu. Grilled Gammon and Egg or Grilled Kidneys, Chops, and Two Veg. The veg depended on what she had managed to get that morning on her way to work. But it all set a 'tone', I felt, and sometimes I got a tip. Which Vi allowed me to keep. If I told her. If I didn't she never knew. It depended on the state of my week's money. Sometimes the actors would send me out to the pub next door for a bottle of Guinness or a round of sandwiches and were often very generous with a couple of pennies or even, mostly from the women, a threepenny bit . . . and all in all by the time Saturday Pay Night came along I had usually managed to break even.

As time went on I graduated more towards the actual Stage itself. Helping out the ASM, playing 'God Save The King' at the end of the Show on a scratchy old ten inch HMV . . . and on some terrifying occasions, actually 'Holding the Book' of the play in the Prompt Corner and prompting the actors who 'blew' a line. That was the nastiest part of all. The feeling of anxiety was too acute for comfort and sometimes I wondered if my own fear was affecting the actors on the stage for it always seemed to me that I had to prompt a performance more than the real ASM. Many of the plays only had a week's rehearsal, so it was a pretty nerve-racking night, a First Night at Q.

Taking the book at rehearsals was more relaxed and better for my learning. Day after day I sat through the play, in between waiting at table and swabbing down my Gents, and less and less I spent time in the Scene Dock. I was infinitely more use as, and more interested in being, general dogsbody. I was, of course, getting closer and closer to the Stage in this manner. Which was my intention. My pay packet, however, stayed firmly the same every Saturday Night. Three florins, a shilling and a sixpence. Sometimes the sixpence came in coppers.

Until one afternoon Beattie came bustling into the Club Room where I was wiping down the tables and waiting for Vi to get my lunch of left-overs out of her oven.

'Shouldn't you be on the stage, dear? It's Dress Rehearsal,' she said worriedly. I explained that one of the actors wasn't feeling well and that the rehearsal was put back half an hour.

'Oh I know all about that,' she said. 'It's the photographer's assistant isn't it?'

She hardly ever addressed small part actors by their names, but usually by the name of the role they were playing. 'Well, he's got an appendix, that's what. You know the lines, dear, don't you? There are only a couple anyway, and if you don't know them you've got plenty of time to read them up before this evening. Hop off and see if his suit will fit you; if it doesn't wear your own and carry his hat. Off you go. We're up in a couple of hours.'

Breathlessly I reported this news to my director, a red-haired young man in a wrap-around camel hair coat called Basil Dearden, who was assiduously modelling himself, with considerable success, on Basil Dean, a director noted for his brilliance, sarcasm, acidity, and apparent abhorrence of actors.

'Christ Almighty!' he said. 'Now I know there's a war on: they've started to ration the Talent!' And to my eager face he quietly said, 'Well, don't stand there, piss off and see if the blasted things fit', starting a deep friendship which only ended with his death more than thirty years later.

J. B. Priestley's 'When We Are Married' brought me, with two thin lines, a few physical miles nearer to the West End. I don't remember very much about it except that the suit did fit and that I spent over an hour making up and sitting in a real dressing-room with real lights and real actors all about me. I also had to call the Half, the Quarter, and the Acts. I felt as tinny as the Bishopbriggs clock. Too busy to be frightened, I did what I could and was allowed to stay on till the end of the Production. Quite suddenly, and as tiresomely simple as that, I became an actor proper. Although I still had the Gents and the Club Room and the errands to run for the other actors . . . but as the parts got larger, for they did as time went on, I gradually had to give up the other jobs and found that I was being paid seven and six to play quite large, for me at that time, roles. Young actors were getting hard to find easily. The war had netted quite a number already.

'There's a nice little part for you next week in "Saloon Bar",' said Beattie one day. 'You are a bit young for it but I think you'll get away with it. Alf the Pot Boy. See what you can do.' I did. And enjoyed it thoroughly and made up my mind, halfway through the week, that I would go and ask Jack de Leon for a rise. After all, I reckoned, I was now an actor with a quite respectable line of roles behind me . . . a rise was not unreasonable. But on Saturday night, my pay packet had no jingly coins inside. In terror, in case it was my Notice or something, I ripped it open and a shilling fell out on to the floor. Anxiously I scrabbled in the little buff envelope. There was one green, crackly pound note. A guinea! I'd done it.

I bought Vi a gin and lime, had a giddy whisky myself and crossed the dark street to the telephone box outside the Station. My father answered as he always did, 'Bogaerde here.' I told him what had happened. 'And next week there's a better part in a better play and if I get it they'll double the salary to two guineas.' There was a silence on the line, I heard the pips go and my father's voice saying, 'I suppose you realize that you have spent your profits. I'll tell Mother. Ring off now. Very good.' And the line went dead. But I knew that he was impressed. He was also accurate in his accounting. No more gins and whiskies, nor did I telephone them again.

The war didn't end that Christmas as so many of us had hopefully predicted, and it seemed, from where I could see, that the German tanks were hardly cardboard, and for a nation on the very brink of starvation they were doing uncomfortably well. It was an ominous, dark, waiting time. For everyone. For me it meant that Call Up loomed nearer and nearer and the chances of my making my mark in my chosen profession began to look very shaky indeed. The war, I was sure, was going to go on for ages, at least until I was over twenty-one – which was the limit I had set myself for 'success'. Not stardom, never that, but calm, assured, character-lead stuff. The kind of actor who is never out of work, always comfortably engaged, and always able to play almost any role within the wide range of Character. Never too many pressures, never too much splendour, nor too much responsibility. 'Always Applauded' would suit me very well. And when Beattie gave me my first really big role, in a revival of Priestley's 'Cornelius', I knew that I had found my exact position. Lawrence, the office boy, was what I wanted always to play. No play to 'carry', a good moment in each act – the perfect role. I enjoyed it, was good in it and liked very much the compliments which started to arrive from my fellow actors. On the last night I saw Beattie in the Club Room with her book of the week's takings. 'We had a good week,' she said. 'Funny with a serious play. But we always do well with Priestley.' As Vi came out with us, pulling on her coat and getting her torch and gas mask ready I said to Beattie: 'It was a *marvellous* week for me. I really feel now that I am a proper actor.' Beattie shot me a distant, flicker of a smile. 'Do you, dear?' she said. 'That's nice.'

We played one week at Q and then moved up north to the Embassy Theatre at Swiss Cottage and played a week there. They did an equal swap with us and so most plays had a good two weeks run before we had to start all over again. The Embassy was more of a theatre really than Q. It had a balcony and red plush and I had no responsiblities whatsoever back stage, so my week playing there, unless we were preparing the next production's set, was pretty quiet; I only had the Shows to worry me. And 'Cornelius' was, I thought, pretty well buttoned up.

It was buttoned up. So was my acting career for the time being. Beattie informed me that there was nothing 'for me' in the next three Productions but that I could carry on, if I wished, in the Gents, in the Scene Dock, and helping Vi in the Club Room. I was not over anxious. What to do? I needed advice rather quickly. Fortunately Bill Wightman had taken lodgings in a sombre yellow brick house not far away from the Embassy Theatre in Fellows Road. He was between jobs but offered me Ovaltine and chocolate digestive biscuits in his comfortable room overlooking the back gardens of Swiss Cottage. And copious advice. He agreed with me that it might be wiser to try and press ahead with the Theatre rather than go back to the Gents and boiling glue and carrying trays to more fortunate players, and suggested, very mildly, that he knew of a woman who was running a Rep Company in the country and who might be willing to give me a job. She was, he said, finding it too much of a struggle to keep going, and that he and a friend were considering making an offer to purchase the place outright thus ensuring himself a permanent job and a permanent theatre. She had not definitely made up her mind to sell, and in the meantime she was short of a Juvenile. Perhaps I should go down and see her before I committed myself to Beattie and the Gents.

The next day, after he had telephoned and made an appointment, I took the train down to Amersham in Buckinghamshire and went to meet Sally Latimer who looked at me doubtfully and asked if I could do an American accent. I lied and said yes. She asked me what else I could do, and misunderstanding her in my anxiousness, I said that I also painted sets and worked at Q and could wait at table. For twenty-two shillings a week I got the job, and as soon as 'Cornelius' closed, at the end of the week, I told Beattie and waited for the storm. There was no storm from Beattie.

'All right, dear, good luck. Remember, if you ever want to come back we'll see what we can find for you. I'm busy now dear, so let me get on with it, will you?' and she continued checking the 'pull' of a poster for the next production.

It was a little over six years later that I took her up on her generous offer. On Demob leave, in my worn Service dress, a reasonable row of campaign medals on my chest, three pips on my shoulders and ten shillings in my pocket, I stood in a line of elderly women whom she was interviewing for Char Ladies. Nothing had changed, the same rubber floor, the same smell from my old Gents, the tatty silver and black paintwork, the faded stills from 'Peg O' My Heart' and 'Abies Irish Rose' with Beattie in a bow and gingham. Nothing seemed to have altered at all since Arromanches, Arnhem, Berlin, Bombay, Singapore and Sourabaya. As I reached her, last in the line, she looked up pleasantly from her little note book.

'Hullo dear,' she said. 'Been away?'

The Amersham Rep was based in a converted grocer's shop near the station. It had no balcony, no 'flight' and a very small, narrow, stage. The Green Room and the actors' dressing-rooms, one for the men and one for the women, were down in the basement and the scene dock was a lock up garage. It was what you might call a very intimate theatre, and the atmosphere of it was more Family than Theatrical. The Front of House staff were local townspeople who worked free for the love of us, and Sally Latimer, a tough, slight, firm-jawed woman ran it with total dedication and her partner, a tall, blond-haired girl who wore flannel trousers, a blue blazer and smoked incessantly, called Caryl Jenner. We did one play a week, opening on the Monday night and starting rehearsals on the morning of the same day for the next week. It was not an unusual occurrence to find yourself rehearsing Laertes at eight-thirty a.m. and going on stage a few exhausted hours later, to open 'cold' as Maxim de Winter in 'Rebecca' with the Set being erected about your ears. But we never stopped, and the theatre was a success attracting at its height even the London Critics to some performances of New Plays including, and often led indeed, by the Emperor of them all, James Agate. It was clearly a place in which to learn, to work, and to love. I did all three.

I got Digs up the road in a semi-detached called 'Beechcroft' behind the pub, and for five and six a week received a single bed under the roof, use of the bathroom, and a hot meal after the show which was usually scrag end of neck with barley and carrots kept hot in the oven over a low gas. I was in seventh heaven. I did my American Accent, pretty frightfully, in 'Grouse in June' and started rehearsals as soon as that was over for 'Call It A Day' the week that Italy declared war and the Germans invaded Belgium and Holland. It was frighteningly clear that the cardboard tanks were making shattering progress, and by the end of the week had ripped into France and were less than two hundred miles from tranquil, unsuspecting Folkestone.

We were intermittently glued to Dodie Smith and the BBC. It didn't seem as if we had very much time left. We opened to smaller houses than usual and found the laughs rather difficult to 'get'. In an atmosphere charged with emotions of every kind, filling the air with the sullen zig-zags of summer lightning I, inevitably, fell deeply in love with my Leading Lady, a red-haired Scots girl a couple of years older than myself called Anne Deans. With a stunning lack of timeliness I announced our engagement to the astonished company during a coffee break in the Green Room on the very day that the shattered British Army started its desperate withdrawal to Dunkirk. I seem to remember that Annie was about as astonished as the Company, but was carried away by my eloquence and passion and needed, as she said, cheering up.

That evening we went down to the local equivalent of the Ritz, a chintzy, warming-panned, huddle of exposed beams and gate-legged tables called The Mill Stream, and over eggs, chips and sausage and two expensive Carlsberg Lagers celebrated my somewhat emotional announcement. I apologised for not having a ring but Annie was ahead of me and produced one, from her handbag, which belonged to her mother and which she had had the foresight to acquire just before I had collected her from her digs in White Lion Road. Slipping it on to her finger she accepted me as her future husband. I reeled with pleasure and ordered another Carlsberg Lager each.

Walking home through the blackout up the steep hill to the Recreation Grounds near which she shared two rooms with her mother, we made happy, if inaccurate, plans for our future deciding, sensibly I thought, not to get married until I was really and truly Called Up. But to go on with our Careers and announce it in the newspapers as soon as possible.

After a passionate farewell under a pollarded oak outside her front gate, I walked back to the Theatre and telephoned the news of this momentous piece of trivia to my parents who were unable to hear the telephone owing to the fact that they were both far out in the garden, standing holding hands together in the still hot night, feeling the earth trembling beneath their feet, and listening to the guns rumbling in France.

One morning while I was out 'shopping' for props for the next production (we used to go and beg and borrow anything from a grand piano to a patchwork quilt from the generous people in the neighbourhood) a telephone message arrived at the theatre asking me to call Q Theatre urgently. Feeling, I don't know why, that the message might be private and not wanting it to be heard all over the Box Office, unlike the Engagement Announcement, I went up to a call box at the station and called Q. Beattie was very calm, almost disinterested.

'They want to take the Priestley play into the West End. You know, the one you did here last season. 'Cornelius'. They want to know if you are available. I said I'd find out, dear. You'd have to start next week of course.'

I walked down the hill to the converted grocer's shop in a trance and asked Sally Latimer if she would release me from the Company, which, after a sour look and some understandable grumbles, she finally agreed to do. Annie was delighted but somewhat wistful. 'Oh dear!' she said. 'It's just like the flicks, isn't it? Where they want one half of the act and not the other . . .' But I was beyond subtleties of this kind. I had already packed the green suit, my washing bag and a 'good' pair of black shoes I had pinched from the theatre wardrobe, and as far as I was concerned had already opened in the play and caused a sensation.

Bill Wightman got me a room in his lodgings in Fellows Road. His landlady offered me the one hot meal at night, a bed under the stairs on the second floor, and said she didn't normally take actors but would make an exception because Mr Wightman had recommended me strongly. She asked for ten shillings a week, and to my astonishment, I agreed.

Miss Hanney was bossy, curious, and kind. All her lodgers, there were six of us, were 'professional' gentlemen, she said, that is to say they were Lawyers, Accountants or men who were 'good at figures'. We all sat down together, on the bong of a gong, at one big table in the front room and were served a meal of thin soup, meat and two veg, and cabinet, suet, or treacle, pudding. No one spoke much, and the only sound was the clink and clonk of the knives and forks against thick china. But I ate heartily for my daily diet was still much as it had been at Q – supplemented now and then by a sandwich in a pub or a hard-boiled egg.

The rehearsals started in the green room of the Westminster Theatre and, although I had played it at the Q and at the Embassy, it became startlingly clear that while *I* might have been tremendously enthusiastic about my performance no one seemed to be in the West End. It was not, it was felt, quite up to West End standards – and for a time it appeared that I would be given the sack. And, indeed, I would have been, had it not been for the great efforts of Ann Wilton, who had played with me at Q and felt that I did have a 'spark', as she called it.

Patiently, every day at the Lunch Break, she coached me all alone in the Green Room, encouraging me, forcing me to project, to move, even to think, listen, and time a line. She knew, as I dimly did myself, that On That Night I'd be all right. But I was holding back too much at rehearsals and no one, except herself, had the least idea of what I might possibly do. She told me bluntly that I was to be re-cast, and begged me to try harder than ever. I did. And with her help and patience finally won through.

My agonies were not unnoticed by everyone in the Company. Sometimes one of the student actors from the Mask Theatre School, who had a small part in the play, came timidly down into the Green Room and sat in the corner watching Ann's desperate efforts to force me into 'attack' . . . he was a pale, tall, blond boy with anxious blue eyes: his own shyness was so great that he too, under the irritable eyes of our director, Henry Cass, was starting to wilt and was also in danger of getting sacked. So we were both in the same boat, except that I was in a far more unpleasant position, for at least I was supposed to be a Professional Actor already, and he merely a Student. Our mutual dilemma brought us close together and although he did all that he could to breach his shyness and reserve, Paul Scofield was eventually replaced while I, thanks entirely to Ann Wilton's supreme belief and care, was coached through the whole of the rehearsals until our modestly triumphant opening on August the 24th, 1940.

If Ann Wilton taught me two of the most important lessons in the Theatre, devotion and dedication, Max Adrian, who was also in the play, taught me quite another. But not less essential or timely. Humility. Overimpressed with my modest notices in the Daily Press, and well aware that the audiences not only liked me but thought I was funny, I started, within a very few performances to attempt to take over the play from the Principals. I mugged about, invented bits of, I thought, irresistible business, extended my laughs and behaved as if I was a one-man show at the Palladium. One matinee, unable to bear my behaviour any longer, Max, who played a humbled, timid little clerk, took up a great leather ledger and brought it crashing down on my totally unsuspecting head with an infuriated cry of 'Never do that again, I say!'

Bewildered with the suddenness of the blow, the stars literally reeling about my head, I slammed into a wall and slid, winded and stunned, to the stage amidst the largest roar of delighted laughter I had ever heard in a theatre in my life. At my own expense. A salutary and necessary lesson for which I was ever grateful.

The sirens went between the shows on the following Saturday. Just before the Second House. We all excitedly clambered up to the roof and looked across the rooftops mellow in the evening sun. Far away down the river the sky was peppered with little puffs of smoke; the rattle of guns and the drone of planes carried clearly through the traffic from the street below. The All Clear had not sounded by the time the curtain rose, and by the end of the first act it was impossible to continue for the noise outside. Stephen Murray, who was playing the lead, interrupted the performance, went to the edge of the stage, and told a sparse audience that if they wished we would continue the play or else they could leave, have their money back, and we would ring down the curtain. The play continued. To our astonishment we realized that the roof above the stage was entirely made of glass through which the steadily burning sky of London was reflecting with a carmine glow. At the end of the play the audience were asked if they wished to come below to share our Shelters, great caves below the theatre which were once supposed to be Henry VIII's Wine Cellars. Crouched together, audience and Cast and one large Alsatian dog which someone had brought with them, we sat through the long night, miserable, hungry, and very aware that the war had really started at last. It was, in a strange way, almost a relief. But start it had: and the next day, after the night's toll was known, everything closed down again, and the War took charge of our lives. 'Cornelius', along with many other shows, folded for good, and I was once again back where I had started, with an ever diminishing area of opportunities.

Lying in my small bed under the stairs in Fellows Road, feeling the house shake and tremble with every near miss, I decided that it might be wiser to swallow my pride and see if Amersham would have me back: it was in the country, Annie was still there, and all told I had only been away from them for about six weeks. When my window blew in and the door slammed itself out of the room across the mahogany banisters I decided that there was no time like the present. And as soon as it was light I walked to Baker Street and got the Metropolitan Line to Amersham on the Hill.

Sally Latimer took me back. Juveniles were getting harder and harder to find, and although I was so to speak Under Sentence, I was better than nothing. I remember that at the bottom of every programme it was stated that: 'All The Actors In This Production Are Either Unfit For Military Service Or Awaiting Call Up', which made us all feel a bit second-hand. However it did stop the occasional complaining letter from patriotic Townspeople.

Annie was delighted to see me and behaved as if I had come back from Dunkirk rather than Swiss Cottage. So far the war had not touched Amersham very much: a string of bombs had fallen in an orchard up at Little Chalfont, and at nights the sky in the north east was scarlet with the flaring glow of burning London. But otherwise everything was relatively peaceful and we played to packed houses every night. I started with Caryl Jenner on the sets for 'You Never Can Tell' and Bill Wightman, who had failed in his effort to purchase the Rep from a reluctant and determined Sally, came down to play The Waiter while I played McComus in a white wig and a mass of Leichner Carmine wrinkles which gave me the appearance of something between badly laid crazy-paving and a vicious razor attack.

My money had been raised to two pounds five shillings a week and I moved out of 'Beechcroft' to an ugly bungalow in the White Lion Road where I slept in a bleak little front parlour on a camp bed surrounded by framed passe-partout signed photographs of Claude Dampier, Gillie Potter, The Crazy Gang, and George Lacy as The Dame in 'Mother Goose'. My pleasant new Landlady had clearly been on The Boards herself.

All this, of course, was in order to be a little nearer to Annie in her digs under the pollarded oak by the Recreation Fields. Our 'Romance' was becoming something of a strain, since we found it almost impossible to be on our own anywhere. I volunteered to be on almost constant duty as a Fire Watcher for the theatre, which meant that I spent the whole night in the Green Room waiting for Incendiaries to obliterate us and Annie to arrive with a Thermos of coffee, a quart of beer and a cold meat stew which we warmed up on the electric fire and ate off 'prop' plates with 'prop' spoons and forks. Hardly a conducive setting for Romance, and it was not altogether satisfactory. Neither were our perform-ances on the following days. Wan and hollow-eyed, we blundered about the stage – until Sally decided to alter the Roster and insisted, rightly, that we rested for the Theatre's sake.

After 'You Never Can Tell' it was agreed that a change of pace was needed and that we should 'do' a Revue. Everyone went to with a will and we wrote sketches and songs and pinched other people's material disgracefully, opening with a rousing number which we called 'Joan of Arc' and was, we all felt, very topical. Dressed in black berets and raincoats, for some reason best known to ourselves, and set against the wobbly backcloth of a white Eiffel Tower and a vaguely inaccurate Notre Dame which I had painted all by myself, we sang the opening bars of our Song, which went, as far as I can remember like this . . .

> '*We can hear you calling,*
> *Joan of Arc,*
> *Over the Sea,*
> *Out of the dark,*
> *To the Land of the Freeee . . .*'

Perfidious Albion all right. It made everyone feel very sad, and was hardly a rousing opening for an Intimate Revue ... nevertheless we were a success and even toured it on Sundays, when the theatre was closed, round various army camps and hospitals all over Buckinghamshire. It was patriotic, exhausting, self-indulgent, and Always Applauded. I wrote a supposedly hilarious sketch for Annie and myself called 'Doon the Watter' which was to accommodate our hardly ever used Glasgow accents, and she did a rather violent Clog Dance to the 'Petticoat Song' from 'Miss Hook Of Holland'. There were sketches and blackouts, and a plump girl from Rickmansworth did a thoughtful dance with a long cigarette holder to a scratchy recording of 'Rhapsody in Blue'. At the end the entire company assembled with many outstretched hands and wide-flung arms to a passionate rendering of 'We'll Meet Again'. Oh dear. Oh dear. But we all thought we were splendid. Perhaps we were.

After the Revue a change of pace again and a turgid piece called 'Grief Goes Over'. All I can remember is that my wife died with her baby, or having it, I can't recall, and that I was comforted, in a long sad Third Act by my mother, played by Miss Latimer herself in a fur coat and a Herbert Johnson hat, in which I was able to indulge myself in some pretty hefty masculine sobbing, wearing my father's tails borrowed for the occasion. I must admit that though I cannot remember the play I do remember thinking that I looked pretty fine in Tails, though they did not fit and Anne had to pin them together with safety-pins. The fact that I looked like a Cypriot waiter totally escaped me and I enjoyed myself nightly giving a performance of self-indulgence which would have made a Fire Eater blush. However, our sad little play was not popular, and the last Saturday night, much to my sorrow, was sparsely attended. There were a good many empty seats scattered about which, as it turned out, was just as well for me.

If Lieutenant Anthony Forwood, R.A., on leave from his Battery at Hornchurch, and slightly bored after dinner, had been able to get into the Regent Cinema for the last showing of 'Edison The Man' that Saturday night, it is fair to say that this book would have ended at the paragraph above. As it was, he bad-temperedly wandered down the hill to the Theatre and bought a seat, easily, for the last two acts of 'Grief Goes Over' and sent his card round to the dressing-room. On such frail threads hang one's destiny. Ivy who worked in Front of House came through the Green Room with a tray of empty coffee cups and the card, which she flipped through the curtained entrance to the Gents dressing-room. 'Chap out front sent this round for you,' she called. 'Says he's a representative from Al Parker the agent. He's waiting.'

The card was an ordinary visiting card. But Al Parker was no ordinary agent. At that time he was the 'chic-est' agent in London and his clients were nearly all Stars. My heart leapt. The company were impressed. Annie shot up to the stage to peer through the Curtain and have a look at the visitor while I cold-creamed my tear-ravaged face and struggled out of my father's tails.

'He's tall, blond, in full regalia,' she reported, 'and not Jewish.'

'What do you mean, regalia?' I asked.

Annie was struggling into a black lace frock because Saturday night was 'our' night together at the warming-panned Mill Stream, and she always liked to look her best on the dance floor.

'He's an officer of some sort, and Ivy says he's a local and they live up at Chalfont and are very rich or something; he's giving her a lift home in a few minutes so don't be long or we'll never get to the Mill and I'm starving.'

Someone lent me a clean white shirt and someone else a tie and in my only suit, the black stolen shoes, and clutching the card, which had impressed me by being embossed and not printed, I went up to the auditorium to meet Mr Parker's Representative who was sitting very uncomfortably, for he was over six foot, in the last seat of row A.

I was quite unprepared for the elegant splendour reclining in the too-small seat before me. Booted, breeched, tunic'd, buttons and badges glittering brightly in the meagre light of the dim auditorium, his hair shining like a halo, he extended an indifferent hand, told me his name and said that he had been in Front and thought I was 'interesting'. I sat nervously in the empty seat beside him. 'Far too young, of course, but a very strong – Quality?'

'Well . . . I'm too young, I expect, but you know . . .' He waved his vague hand somewhere in the air.

'There's a war on, I know. And the tails were frightful, of course.'

'They are my father's.'

'That's what they looked like. Have you got an agent?'

'No. It doesn't seem worth it: I'll be called up pretty soon.'

'When? I mean, how soon?'

'Next birthday. March.'

'Well . . . that gives us a little time. I represent Parker in London. I'm looking out for my own clients for after the war, if you think it's a good idea I might represent you. You need experience, of course, but you have got a . . .' again the hand waved loosely in the stale air of the theatre, 'a Quality, I suppose. Do you want to talk about it?'

I said yes very quickly and he unfolded from the seat and stood before me, a glittering figure. He murmured with a suppressed yawn that we couldn't talk here and that as his home was very near, and he was giving Ivy a lift back because she lived at the end of his lane, perhaps I'd care to come back with him, meet his grandfather and have some cocoa?

Annie was grumpy, but reluctantly agreed that I should go as long as I didn't stay long and got to the Mill Stream before the sausages ran out. She said she'd go on with the others and keep me a place at the table. Sally, unimpressed, reminded me coldly that the Set had to be dismantled before midnight because we had to start the rigging for rehearsal the next day on 'Children To Bless You'.

We dropped Ivy off at her house half way up Cokes Lane and through a misty October night bumped along a rutted drive through hundreds, or so it seemed to me, of cherry trees until we reached the low, rambling, creeper-covered house where he lived.

In the glimmer of the dimmed headlights, through wisping mist a torch bobbled among the trees and a woman in a headscarf and wellingtons waved a tin bowl at us.

'Forgot the ducks again!' she said cheerfully. 'Enjoy the show?'

We clambered out of the car and slammed doors.

'Cousin Phyllis,' he said. 'This is a chap called Bogaerde. Is there some cocoa or anything?'

Cousin Phyllis went ahead of us wagging her torch and we followed through wet grasses. In the low heavily timbered hall, she clumped off somewhere to get 'the refreshments' and my companion said that his name was Tony which would make things easier, and ushered me into the study, a snug room, down a deceptive couple of steps, a fire glowing in the grate, Staffordshire figures, and his grandfather, Pip, sitting in an armchair, late eighties, bearded, clasping a thick walking stick, one leg up on a padded stool. He was polite and warm, and I was almost immediately at my ease. We sat talking about the theatre and the War until Cousin Phyllis, chatting and eager, brought in the tray with cocoa and fruit cake and Forwood said that Herbert Farjeon was getting the Cast together for another version of his Revue, 'Diversion', at Wyndhams in a few weeks' time. There was, he said, a pretty good chance that he could get me into it, as a glorified chorus boy, if I was free and wished to do so.

I agreed immediately. He was pleasantly unsurprised. 'There is only one thing else,' he said, 'if I do get you in I would naturally wish to represent you, be your agent so to speak, after the war. Would you agree to that?'

Sitting round the study fire that evening, Pip starting to nod off, one veined hand occasionally slipping from the wooden stick, Cousin Phyllis thoughtfully sipping her cocoa, Forwood sprawled in a deep armchair hardly bothering to stifle a yawn (he had to be on duty at dawn in Hornchurch), I felt so immediately secure, the atmosphere was one of such familiar trust that it never remotely occurred to me to say anything other that 'Yes' without qualification. We shook hands, I remember, which was the only form of contract we have ever had, and shortly afterwards, full of cocoa and cake, and the warmth of the welcome, I was driven back through the orchard down to the Mill Stream where, with a very casual salute, as if this sort of thing happened every evening of his life, he dropped me in the car park and swung the car out on to the main road. For a few moments I stood in the foggy night before the blacked-out restaurant door. 'Where or When' came faintly through the latticed windows. I watched the Mercedes turn left on to the main road and roar back up the hill to the ivy-covered house at the top of Cokes Lane.

Suddenly I had an Agent. The possibility of a West End job again, and something intangible which might, or might not be . . . 'a quality'. I felt, with a burst of joy, that I owned the world, I didn't know that eight years later I should also own the house.

FIFTEEN

'A-One, A-Two, A-Three, BACK! Four, Five, Six, TURN!' The voice was a metronome, relentless, cold, mechanical, occasionally human only when it rose to a desperate cry on the words Back! or Turn! usually applied to myself. I was as graceless as a duck; the other five appeared almost balletic in comparison, probably because they had already been through it in the First Edition of the Show. I was suffering greatly from my usual complaint: lack of co-ordination. However, I bumped and staggered about and watched the others with a sense of despairing envy. Having got this far I was going to get the steps right if it killed me and everyone else concerned. A dim back room in a pub off St Martin's Lane, some mirrors, a bashed piano, the front removed, bent wood chairs insect-like round the walls, dirty coffee cups, a bald-headed man in shirt-sleeves banging out the opening number of the show. It was a Judy Garland movie, completely familiar to me: as if a dream was repeating itself. The stars, Dorothy Dickson, Bernard Miles, Edith Evans, Joyce Grenfell and the Director, Walter Chrisham, didn't come to the chorus rehearsals . . . they fitted themselves in a few days before the opening, and the whole Company only got together for the Numbers. I was in about five and both the Opening and the Finale. Not overworked; and in between fittings for a full dress Kilt, my first Tails, a bathing suit, a dinner jacket and sundry bits and pieces, I spent most of my time in the room in the pub trying to get my feet to do what the metronome voice implored them to do. It wasn't easy. I began to doubt the wisdom of Tony Forwood. I might have 'Quality' on the stage at Amersham, but it seemed not to be much in evidence half a mile from Wyndhams Theatre, Charing Cross Road.

Annie had been sceptical when I told her of my good fortune that evening at the Mill Stream. To begin with I *was* an hour late, the sausages *were* off and she felt the whole thing boded ill. Agents from the West End, she pointed out, were pretty sharp people, who seldom kept their words, and a Revue didn't seem the best place for a straight actor to begin his attempt on the West End. And if I did get the job, she asked pointedly, what would happen to her? I would be in London and she'd be stuck in Amersham on the Hill and we'd never see each other? It posed a great many problems, I could see, so I obliterated everything for the time being. I still had a whole standing Set to dismantle that night, and decided to enjoy what remained of Saturday: after all I might never hear another word from Mr Parker's Representative on his Ack Ack site in Hornchurch.

Which was where I was wrong. A few days later he telephoned to say he'd fixed it, and then a telegram arrived from Bertie Farjeon saying he was happy to welcome me to the Show, that rehearsals commenced in two weeks' time, would I please confirm soonest. Sally Latimer was understandably irritated, but agreed that I could leave at the end of the following play. Annie looked glum and said that she would try and get a job with ENSA . . . I packed my suitcase and arrived back at Fellows Road, Swiss Cottage, and repossessed my bed under the stairs.

The first rehearsal, on the stage at Wyndhams, was pretty frightening. All in our Best, Edith Evans magisterial in mink, Dorothy Dickson in fox and an Orchid, and our Director, Wally, elegant in pale blue silk. The six 'Chorus' sat on one side of the stage, the Elite on the other. We were all perfectly friendly and integrated, but everyone knew their places, and a feeling of discipline, position, and West End reigned quietly. This was no harassed Uckfield, no Rough and Tumbled Get The Show Together Amersham. This was a polished, smooth and organised as a well designed, luxurious, motor-car. Or so it seemed to me.

I was greatly heartened to find that one of the six of us was my friend in wrinkled tights from Shere, Peter Ustinov, and even happier to find that we were sharing a dressing-room together. We were the only men. The other four were girls . . . and one of them was particularly wise and understanding of my timidity and gracelessness, to such an extent that she even attempted to make herself as idiotic as I felt and was, in order to encourage me, although I well knew that she was far more experienced than she pretended. It was all done for me and I loved her very much for it. Her name was Vida Hope, and hope was exactly what she offered at every clumsy, inexperienced, rehearsal. Thus, with drums and a piano in the orchestra pit, we started out on the big adventure. I knew that I had a lot to learn and a long way to go. Never mind. Get on and do it.

Sitting there in the Stalls waiting my turn to work, watching the polished poise of Miss Dickson 'walking through' a dance routine with Wally, plotting the moves, the turns, the steps, the movement of an arm, precisely, calmly, and with complete confidence and assurance made my heart thud with excitement. I sat there every day and never missed a second of any part of the Show . . . from Irene Eisinger throwing wide imaginary shutters in a Mountain Chalet singing 'Tales From the Vienna Woods', to Joyce Grenfell making her Entrance, taking her positions, and making the Exit . . . to the most magical of all, Edith Evans, sitting under a working light on a wooden box, her mink over her shoulders, snow boots on her feet, declaring in that liquid voice of astonishing range, Queen Elizabeth's speech before the Armada. I glutted. I watched and listened constantly; all that seemed improbable was that I should ever master the A-One, A-Two, A-Three and TURN of the very ordinary Dance Routines . . . but I worked. Somewhere along the line I had been given an infinite capacity for trying, or perhaps it was Ambition.

My mother was very pleased at this turn of events, and my father forced to admit that in a little over a year I had, at least, managed to survive in my chosen profession, and with some small subsidies from himself, usually half a crown here and there when things got really tight, plus a florin and a hurried meal in her kitchen from Aunt Freda, I had managed to pay my way, supplementing my meagre income (we were not paid for rehearsals) by working in a couple of cheap restaurants near Leicester Square and pocketing the tips while clearing the tables and washing down the counters.

The only person who wasn't altogether happy with the way things had transpired was Annie. Trailing about the country from one Army Camp to another meant that she hardly ever got to London, and when she did we only seemed to manage a grabbed lunch in a pub or, on one or two occasions, tea

with Bill Wightman in his room in Swiss Cottage where we drank his hoarded
Earl Grey's, ate digestive biscuits, and asked, constantly, his advice about the
vexed problem of our Engagement. His advice one day, given with great care,
was that we should both wait until I was twenty-one . . . or until the war was
over, and until we had both gone a little further, one way or another, in our
jobs. It would be restricting and frustrating now at this moment to get married,
he thought, especially as my Call Up was imminent and who could possibly tell
how we should both feel, with so much before us, when Peace returned?

The astonishing thought that Peace would return, with Victory, at such a
dark time of the war, was unquestioned. That evening, during a fairly savage
air raid, and a pleasantly emotional supper at the Café Royal, Annie put her
engagement ring in her handbag and replaced it with a Red Indian's Head in
solid silver. As a token. We felt sad, brave, and both, I think, relieved. The next
day she went down to Borden Camp and I went on to Wyndhams to continue
with my A-One, A-Two, A-Three, TURN!

Whenever I could afford to, I went home to Sussex at the weekend to get a
couple of nights relaxed sleep. The Air Raids were now becoming a fact of life,
more and more frequent and disturbing. My window had again blown in, and
was hermetically sealed with thick black paper, and Miss Hanney, one evening
at supper, informed us all with relish that when the Private Hotel on the corner
had been hit they found one of the maids stuck all over with knives, spoons and
forks like a hedgehog. A weekend on the Common in my own house seemed
desirable; there, in my room with the McKnight Kauffers and Nevinsons and
Nashes pinned on the walls, the bits of Staffordshire I had started to collect from
barrows off the Kings Road, my sombre library of war books and pamphlets on
rearing everything from a Natter-jack Toad to a Goat gave me a great sense of
comfort and security. And the war, although constantly present with its red
waning glow in the north sky beyond the Forest at night, seemed a long way off.

In spite of all the changes the Family were still very much there. The
Evacuees had finally left, the eldest into the Merchant Navy and the younger,
miserable and lonely without his brother, packed up to risk his life again in
Finsbury Park. My mother was now in ARP as a Warden with a tin hat and full
instructions on what to do in the event of a Gas Alert. She had also mastered the
art of making Molotov Cocktails, and the shed near the garage was filled with
her collection of bottles and fuses, plus a strong smell of spilt petrol. Since the
Invasion Threat of the summer had passed somewhat, she now concentrated on
splints, bandages and hot sweet tea for shock. She was really quite enjoying her
War. Gareth was at a Dame school in Newick, wrinkled socks and a satchel;
Elizabeth groomed horses at Miss Umfreville's Stables; only my father was
absent, sleeping as he did mostly at *The Times* if the Raids were too heavy or yet
another reverse somewhere forced him to relinquish the security and peace of
his own bed. Elsie wandered about the house mournfully, her alabaster skin
dull, her eyes sad, her Mechanic in the RAF. Otherwise it was all much as it
ever had been. And yet . . .

The cold, clear, December sun slanted through the dusty windows of my
ramshackle hut up in the orchard. It was, predictably, called Trees and I had
built it with my own hands from bits of junk picked up here and there, furnished
it with a couple of chairs, a table, a marionette theatre of imposing size, shelves
for books and a glass vivarium which had once contained lizards and a grass
snake called Bill who ate them all.

Today it stood empty and forlorn. A smell of damp and rotten apples from a
great tumbled pile of windfalls in a corner, mildew on the faded carpet, books

curling limply, cobwebs draping the dusty curtains of the theatre, the vivarium cracked and empty. I picked up a forgotten copy of *Theatre World* for October '38, the pages glued together with wet, Marie Tempest and John Gielgud almost completely devoured by snails. Things weren't at all as they had been. My sister came wandering up through the lichened trees and peered through the dusty windows.

'I've been looking for you,' she said.

'What for?'

'Just looking. To see where you were, that's all.' She sat down and scraped some mud off her wellingtons with a stick. 'Doesn't it smell awful. All mouldy and horrid.'

'So do you. You smell dreadful.'

She laughed, and threw a lump of mud into the ragged garden outside. 'That's horses. I groom three, you know, and do the saddles and things.'

'It's dung,' I said. 'DUNG . . .'

'spells Dung!' she finished. 'Do you remember, Lally and the stallion?'

'Of course I do. I expect he was really quite safe, the stallion, it was only Reg who tried to frighten us out of our wits.'

'He was called Dobbin, wasn't he . . . so he can't have been all that awful.' She looked round the place. 'Isn't it sad though? All this . . . I never come here now, you know, it's too sad and creepy.'

We sat for a while in silence looking out of the door down through the trees to the little stream and the bamboo break riffling in the cool wind. Presently she got up and went to the window, pressing her face against the glass.

'Do you think you'll get killed? In the Army, I mean?' The snails had eaten right up to Marie Tempest's neck.

'I don't know. I could just as easily get killed in the Blitz. A lot of people do.'

She was playing noughts and crosses with herself in the dust. 'But the Army's different. With guns and things. I expect it'd be quick, wouldn't it? If you did get killed?'

'I hope so. Would you care?'

'Mother would.'

'But would you too, I mean?'

She crossed out a game with a stroke of her finger. 'Yes. I'd cry, I expect.'

'I hope you would. But you'd still have Gareth, wouldn't you?'

She wiped the game out with her fist in big circular movements. 'He's too little.'

'But he wears a satchel now, he'll be grown up soon.'

'It wouldn't be the same because he doesn't remember the Cottage . . .' she pulled on a pair of woollen gloves slowly pushing her fingers to the ends '. . . or the gully or Great Meadow. Do you remember Great Meadow, wasn't it lovely then . . .'

'And Lally's ginger beer! Wasn't it so lovely then . . .'

'Except you were rotten to me all the time.'

'I was not! I liked you very much indeed.'

'When you stuck the knife in me . . .'

'Oh that . . .'

'Well, I've still got the scar. Lally said it will show in an evening dress.'

We wandered out of the damp studio into the clear hard light and, dodging under the branches, walked back to the house for lunch. I took her woolly hand and she looked at me with surprise. 'I hope you don't get killed, that's all,' she said, 'because when it's all finished you might become a Film Star or something, like Lloyd Nolan or Robert Taylor and then I could come and live with you in

Hollywood and we'd have real palm trees in the garden.'

The idea suddenly cheered me up; she was being so silly that it almost made sense. I pushed her suddenly and she gave a scream and slithered about on the muddy path.

'I hate you! What did you do that for when I was being so nice to you? I might have got this coat all mucky, and it's my school one too . . . but you don't care, oh no . . . you're just vile.'

We heard Elsie through the trees banging on a tin tray with a spoon to call us in for our meal, and Rogan our terrier came bounding up the path, tongue lolling, tail wagging. I put my arm round her neck and pulled her to me. 'I'm sorry . . . I didn't mean it . . . really. I was just suddenly feeling happy again.' She shrugged me off a bit, but not much and we walked on to the house. 'It's a funny way of showing it, that's all I can say,' she said. 'It's stuffed cabbage today and there's no H.P. sauce. Oh this war! It *is* a bit of a nuisance.'

At the final run through before the dress rehearsal we heard the stick of bombs ripping down somewhere behind the theatre across St Martin's Lane. The final one, we felt sure, would hit us; on hands and knees under the Stalls we heard it, with gratitude, crash into the Hippodrome opposite. The lights flicked and went on again, we scrambled up from our graceless positions, Miss Evans straightened her hat and Peter raised his hands to catch a small disc of paper which came gently eddying down through the dusty air. He read it out aloud. 'Do Not Accept This Programme Unless The Seal Is Unbroken.' We all laughed stupidly and the rehearsal finished. Tony Forwood, who was attending this performance before he moved, the next day, to Yeovil, suggested that we all clear off and find shelter somewhere, and that if anyone wanted a lift he had a car outside and enough petrol. Miss Evans said she'd like a lift to Albany where she had a flat and we left the theatre to enter an inferno in Charing Cross Road. The whole world seemed to be on fire, the sky crimson, dust and smoke like a thick fog, the glass canopy round the theatre shattered into inch long splinters, rubble, broken branches and fire hoses everywhere. The Hippodrome was burning fiercely, people cursing, coughing and running, wires looped across the street and everywhere belching heat and smoke. Five of us piled into the miraculously untouched car standing by the curb, but by the time we had bounced and bumped to Leicester Square, past the ruins of the Café Anglais and the flaming roof of the Leicester Square Theatre, we knew that we were stuck. Wally suddenly remembered that there was a small Afternoon Drinking Club not far away in Orange Street, and rather than be buried alive in Tony's soft-top Mercedes, it was suggested that we make for its shelter. He was, he said, a member.

Streaked with dust and flakes of oily soot we clambered up a couple of flights to a discreet polished door, and were admitted, resentfully, into the calm of a dimly lit room. A thick carpet, a small bar in one corner, a white baby grand in the other. Soft, warm, safe. A pale young man in a blue angora sweater was playing 'Our Love Affair' – he looked up with polite surprise but went on, his identity bracelets gleaming softly. At the bar, brushing down the dust and bits of glass, Miss Evans ordered an Orange Juice from the slender bar man with a sun-tanned face. The rest of us had something stronger and the young man at the piano rippled into 'Run Rabbit Run' defiantly. Bombs fell intermittently, shaking the room, making a glass tank of wax lilies jerk and wobble in the blast. Eventually Miss Evans decided that she must, simply must, get back to Albany, which was, as she pointed out 'just down the road' and that she would walk since no traffic could move in Piccadilly. We went with her offering company in one form or another all of which she firmly refused, and the last we saw of her was her tall, determined figure, walking swiftly down the crimson street, until the swirling smoke and dust hid her from sight. She was back the next morning on the dot and 'Diversion' opened to a packed house and great acclaim. Apart from the Windmill up the road, we were the only theatre open for business in London.

Dressing-room number four at Wyndhams was hardly palatial, but Peter and I settled down, one on each side, and started a small salon. Rather he did. I was far too timid. He had vast energy which astonished and embarrassed me, and although he had two numbers of his own in the show, as well as doing all the bits and pieces as I did, he still found the time to write another play which he handed, sheet by sheet, to an enraptured Joyce Grenfell who sat at his feet on the cramped floor in blue velvet. People were always dropping in to see him, to talk in varied languages, argue and drink tea. It was all very Russian. Vida brought lunch from the pub next door and we had picnics which seemed to last most of the day. We were in the theatre most of the time anyway: two shows daily, three on matinées, all gauged exactly so that the audiences were well away by the time the Warning went, which it did regularly every evening between five-thirty and six. If it was hard and tiring I never knew. I was far too busy and far too happy. Although I had nothing much to do, a few lines here and there and the tag line of a not very good sketch, my days seemed filled to bursting, I was in euphoria. It came as something of a shock, therefore, one day to receive my Medical Exam Papers and a command to report at some obscure address in Brighton. A sorry undignified affair in a converted shop off North Street. Naked and ashamed, we shuffled along in a smelly line before white-coated, weary Doctors who prodded, lifted, and pressed various parts of our flinching bodies and passed us fit for duty. In one of the cheap restaurants where I cleared the tables, I had heard rumours from some of the Actors who made up most of the clientele, that the best thing to do before a medical was to drink endless cups of black coffee an hour before, thus increasing one's heartbeat, or else to swallow castor oil mixed with a certain amount of soot, which would make one cough and leave a warning sediment in the lungs for the X-rays. Neither suggestion seemed to me to be worth the risk, so I didn't bother. But that morning in Brighton in the cold, stone-floored shop, I almost wished that I had heeded my advisers. Too late. I was fit and well and returned to the show chastened but healthy.

Peter's energy being almost limitless, he also did an act in the evenings after our shows were over at a small cellar night club called 'The Nightlight' opposite the stage door of the Hippodrome. He suggested that as I found the evenings boring and dull, since the final curtain was at 5.30, I should try for an audition and get together an act for the Club. This would add to my earnings and be good experience. With a sudden spurt of imagination or something, I wrote a pretty dire monologue based on the character I had played in 'Cornelius', called 'Lawrence'. In a battered felt hat, a draggly rain coat and a tartan scarf I presented myself for my audition one morning in the empty club. It is well know that a Night Club in the morning is as near Hell as one can possibly imagine: illusions are stripped away, the sheer tattiness and ugliness of everything is laid bare. Standing on the minute stage, in my uninspired costume I went through my hastily written, hastily learned, act. I was supposed to be an Electrical Addict and did the whole monologue holding two bits of flex. The trick, if that is the word, was that at the end I put them together and blacked out the house. To immense applause, I hoped.

It must have been a pretty tough time for the Nightlight because I passed, and opened there two evenings later on a bill with Peter Ustinov, Ord

Hamilton, and a Hungarian lady who sang a song about a 'Teenie Weenie Martinee'. . . . I got paid five pounds a week. Life, apart from the Medical and the Bombs, was looking very rosy indeed.

The Nightlight was nearly always filled. It was a dark, low room below two shops, down a single winding staircase, and after the Café de Paris got hit it was closed because of the dangers it held. One bomb on the Nightlight and everyone would have perished. But while it lasted, so did I. And 'Lawrence' got polished and embellished with every exposure. Not always for his own good. Tony Forwood was delighted at my enterprise, shattered by my performance, but put it all down, charitably, to Good Experience and refused all percentages until After The War. Which from where I was standing seemed to be getting longer and longer and must surely engulf me. Which it did. One morning Peter and I, both the same age and both in the same Initial Category, went down to Charing Cross and signed up. It was a daunting moment for us both, only very slightly lightened by the fact that when we got back to the Theatre we were treated as if we had just relieved Mafeking and Vida had brought a bottle of champagne. The pleasure was increased, a few days later, by the news that we were both to be Deferred for three months because we were in the show and were helping to boost Morale. Which made me, at any rate, feel excessively important. However, May was not all that far away . . . and in one degree I was almost glad at last to know that I had to go. Everyone it seemed was in Uniform. I was beginning to feel uncomfortable and out of place in civilian clothes. A very earnest actor suggested one evening at The Nightlight that I should become a Conscientious Objector, and gave me a pile of leaflets explaining the facts. The idea of digging ditches in Scotland, of all places, of becoming a Stretcher Bearer or working for the Forestry Commission and allowing the Germans to rape my sister horrified me, and I settled for the idea of a short, undemanding, anonymous, career in the Army. The shorter the better. Preferably in the Cook House.

'You mustn't give things up, you know, ducky, when you get in,' said Vida one evening in the kitchen of the little flat in Belsize Crescent where she lived with a girl friend and sometimes cooked me a meal after the shows. 'You must go on writing and drawing, however difficult it may be. Write anywhere . . . you can always take a bit of paper and a pencil with you: don't just flop about cleaning your equipment or whatever they do in their free time . . . you must keep your mind going.' She bounced two fried slices of Spam and some potatoes on to a plate and set them before me. 'And start with poetry . . . men always do in the Army, it makes them very emotional and odd. Some of the best poetry was written in wartime you know.'

I remembered, glumly, Brooke, Blunden, Sassoon and all the others whose works I had learned by heart during my 'reincarnation' period and wondered how on earth I could ever approach such standards, and what horrors and fears I must endure in order to commit them to paper. And, as I pointed out, I felt that I would have to have someone to write to me, or for . . . I could not envisage just writing for myself.

'Well! Write to me,' she said. 'Write everything to me. I'd love it, you know that: I'd try and help you, criticize, you know . . . I used to be in Copywriting so I know a *bit* about words. Not much but something. Send me your first poem. Make it a promise now and write everything and anything which comes into your head. But put it down, ducky, get it out. Don't let it rot there . . . I know you, you're terribly lazy unless you have the incentive . . . well, it's easy. I'll be the incentive, you see.'

Walking down to Fellows Road after supper I knew that what she had said was true, and that I would try to follow her advice: I would take note books and pencils and some paints perhaps when the time came. And I'd try and join a Concert Party . . . she said they always had Concert Parties and that they would welcome a professional with open arms . . . if there wasn't one perhaps I could start one . . . first a sort of Revue . . . songs and sketches, that sort of thing, then later maybe a simple play. Which I would direct, naturally, and Star in. Thinking in this manner I felt very cheered up. The future didn't seem so daunting with these possibilities ahead and she had very generously given me herself as my Incentive, and although a raid was in progress during my long walk back, and the air lethal with red hot fragments from the Ack Ack guns on Primrose Hill, I felt happy and sure again, and protected, for she had also very thoughtfully provided me with her umbrella.

On April the 14th I left Wyndhams with Peter: our Deferment was almost up, and they had to train replacements for the show. The whole cast signed our programmes as a souvenir, and I left the theatre with a heavy heart to the strains of the Opening Number as a thin youth leaped about in my place showing signs of being far better than I had. It rose somewhat when Miss Hanney said that a Miss Deans had telephoned and would I call her back urgently the moment I got in. Annie was at Drury Lane which was the Headquarters of ENSA. She said that there was a part going in a new tour of 'The Ghost Train' and if I was out of 'Diversion' why didn't I come along and try? If I was in ENSA, she reasoned, I would almost automatically be Deferred again and this could go on for as long as the tour lasted, which was for six months at least, by which time the war was bound to be over and I needn't go. It was very persuasive. Especially as I was free, miserable and at a loose end. A couple of days later I attended a slim Audition on the stage at Drury Lane and got the part of the Juvenile with Arnold Ridley directing his own production. But I was not a good choice, and it was not the happiest of times. Cold dreary barns of theatres, long bus journeys in rain and fog, miserable hostels and endless stations. I felt even guiltier playing to uniformed troops than I had felt walking the streets of London, and by the time we got to Amesbury I welcomed the telephone call from my father, to say that I was requested to report for Military Service at Catterick Camp, Yorkshire, on May the 4th next. I wanted no further deferments. When the final curtain came down, for me, on my last performance in 'The Ghost Train' I felt a surge of joy. Someone had made a decision for me; I'd do just what I was told from now on in . . . until it was over.

Gareth said he wanted a German helmet or a coconut, depending on where I got sent. My father said that for at least twenty weeks the nearest I would get to Action of any kind would be the barrack square or assault courses on the moors. The best I'd be able to send him would be a bunch of heather or, at worst, a picture postcard of Darlington.

He was slightly amused that I had been sent to a Signals Unit. I was amazed. 'What did you put on your form when you signed up? I mean you don't know a flag from a cat's whisker! You can't even get the Home Service on the wireless. I really can't see you tapping away at Morse Code.'

'I just put "Actor" down where it said "Profession" and then the schools where it said "Education" . . .'

'Which you hardly had.'

'Well . . . I don't know *why* they sent me to a Signals Unit any more than you do. I'm told the Army is a bit funny in that sort of way.'

It was decided that, very probably, the Glasgow Technical School had tipped the scale in my favour away from the ignominious Infantry into something a little more Specialized.

'Will you try for a commission, if they ask you?' said my father, pouring the wine for my last family dinner. 'I believe it is not very fashionable among people of your age today . . . the Class thing?'

'I'll try. I mean I'd like to. It's a bit more comfortable, isn't it . . .'

He folded his napkin and slid it into a silver ring. 'That depends. Not always. It carries a good deal of responsibility. You don't come first, you realize, the men under you do. Your troop or platoon or whatever it is . . . and I never thought that you particularly cared for responsibility . . . actors don't very much, do they?' He was not being in the least unkind. Accurate. I had to agree: but assured him that a new life lay before me, and that the two years which had passed so swiftly and so filled with experiences, had opened my eyes. I would make a very determined effort to succeed somehow, whatever I had to do. I would treat the whole operation exactly as I had tried to treat the Theatre . . . with auditions, energy, elbowing and climbing; it wasn't so very different. The survival of the fittest, as with beasts, and I'd try to survive.

Strangely enough on that final evening, I really didn't think it was going to be all that difficult. One chapter had closed at Amesbury, another was about to open. I was, I felt, quite ready. He didn't seem as sure but on the other hand was happy that I had decided not to be a Conchie, as he called them, and agreed with me that with determination, hard work and a good deal of luck, anything was possible. Even an unlikely commission. I said that those were the Theatre rules. He smiled, shook his head and rang the little bell for Elsie.

We went down to the pond with the last of the wine and our glasses. It was a still, warm evening, even though it was yet so very early in the year. May bugs skimmed the surface of the water, bumping and zig zagging over the tightly closed waterlily buds which, I suddenly realized with a sharp thrust of regret, I would not see in flower, for the next time I came home it would be winter. My mother sat on the swinging hammock, a jacket about her shoulders, sewing a button, or something, on one of Gareth's shirts. Across the pond, rustling about in the new spring sedge, my sister hunted for a beast with Rogan, his tail wagging, feet splashing in and out of the water. Ripples bobbled the lily buds and we could hear her voice clear across the soft evening air: 'Ratty! Where's Ratty! Seek the rat, seek him . . .'

It was infinitely peaceful, safe, impossible to believe that at this very hour tomorrow I would be hundreds of miles away starting the process of becoming a soldier and melting my identity into a Mass. This I firmly resolved, there and then by the pond, never to do. I would keep all that these people, this place, the Cottage, Lally, and all the rest had given me, and I'd never let any of them go. They would be my salvation and my comfort if, and when, things got too hard.

My father spun his cigarette butt out across the pond. A tiny, glowing ember, arking in the dusk, a final second before extinction in the rushes.

'I expect,' he said, clearing his throat (he had been thinking too), 'they'll send you to the Far East when the time comes. But that's pretty safe really. I don't *think* we'll have much trouble there because the Americans are bound to come in with us sooner or later . . . usually later, like last time, but they'll come in, of that I'm sure. And with them there *and* Singapore, you'll have a pretty easy time. Gareth may get his coconut.'

The Far East was light million years away to me sitting there in the falling dusk. I even felt that I would prefer Yorkshire. 'Anyway,' said my father, starting to collect the cushions and empty glasses, 'your war won't be like mine. Mine was all defensive. Ten yards back and forth a year in the mud. This is an

Attacking War. I don't think you'll have much time for boredom . . . once it starts again it'll all be over before you can say Jack Robinson . . . unless I'm *very* much mistaken.' He started up the bank towards the house, calling to the dog.

My mother rolled up her sewing, closed the workbasket and pulled the jacket tightly round her shoulders.

'It suddenly gets awfully cold. It's far too early to sit out yet. But so pretty. Bring up the other cushions and that ash-tray, it will look so sordid . . .'

We walked slowly up to the house. The sky was velvet blue. A star was up. The air still. A moorhen, startled by our steps, hurried away on green legs to the water. When we got to the lawn my mother stopped and took a deep breath. 'How lovely it is!' she said. 'It's going to be a fine day tomorrow, you see. Just as well: I've got six rows of Winter Greens to get in: should have done them last week . . . never mind.' She reached out suddenly, pulled me to her and kissed me hard. 'Just you think of your poor old Ma tomorrow: I'm really past the age.' I knew that it was her way of saying goodbye. There was to be no fuss in the morning.

There wasn't. Elsie called me punctually at seven-thirty with tea and a biscuit and I lay comfortably for a moment watching the shadows of the rowan tree flicker across the ceiling. Then remembered. And fear flooded into me like a fast running tap.

There was nothing at all to pack save my washing gear, one towel, a pair of pyjamas all in an empty suitcase for the return of my Civilian Clothes, according to the bit of grey paper which had come with something called the Movement Order. In the Morning Room everyone was very bright and cheerful. My mother brilliant in a cotton summer dress. No one spoke of War, of Army or Soldiers. Breakfast was a sort of Hell.

At the car we stood about awkwardly. My father stuck the empty case into the boot: the light across the Common sharp and clear. Cobwebs dew-silvered. I said something about it going to be a perfect day for Winter Greens and climbed in. No kisses, no final embraces: my mother called out cheerfully, perhaps too loudly, 'Bye darling!' and my sister, holding Rogan in her arms, waggled one of his forelegs into a wave. I didn't look back.

Nor did I try to speak until we had passed 'The Anchor' on Scaynes Hill. Then I fumbled about and lit a cigarette.

'I'm sorry . . .' I said. My father looked troubled.

'What about?'

'Well . . . *The Times* . . . you know . . .'

'Oh that!' he sounded relieved. 'You don't have to worry about that now, my dear. Can't force people, you know. It doesn't matter.'

'But you minded?'

'Oh . . . just a bit . . .'

'Well I'll try and make up for it, in the Army . . .'

'I know you will. I don't mind what you do in life as long as you do your best. That's all that matters.'

'I promise.' We drove on through a spinney of greening larches.

'You're not worried about being killed, are you?' He sounded as if I wasn't.

'No! Goodness no . . .'

'And you know about the VD thing, naturally . . . that's as bad as any Jerry bullet . . .'

'Yes I know about that. I'll take care.'

'And keep your writing going, letters, a diary that sort of thing. I did.'

'And painting. I've slipped a tin of watercolours into my coat.'

'Excellent. There is an awful lot of sitting about in the Army, you'll find . . . fifty per cent boredom, someone said. It'll be good to have something like that to do, you'll see.'

In the train he rifled through his brief-case to find his *Times* and brought out a small green sketch-book. He chucked it across to me. 'Useful size. I had one. Just fits into your haversack or a pocket. You might find it handy.'

We parted at Victoria with no words and a rough hug. I got a taxi to Wyndhams where I left the empty suitcase with Doris at the stage door and then met Vida outside Warners. She was wearing a hat with a white rose and a veil. It didn't suit her, and she knew it. We took arms and walked down to Lyons on the corner and the 'Olde Vienna Café' which we liked because it was full of red plush gilt, and newspapers stuck on bamboo sticks. It was also cheap and you could have as much coffee as you liked if you bought a bit of gateau.

'They'll cut all your hair off, ducky, you know that of course. And to the bone because you're an Actor and you do rather look like one.' She pushed back the spotted veil laughing: 'But it'll suit you.' She touched my hand to show that she thought I was nice enough anyway.

'Given you my address, haven't I?'

'Catterick Camp, Yorks.'

'I'll know more after tomorrow. Have to change at Darlington.'

'Ghastly place. Mills and doom.'

'And then Richmond. There's a castle . . .'

She tried a bit of the gateau with a fork but it squashed and she pushed it aside.

'A theatre too. Regency but they don't use it.'

'It's not a Date or anything?'

'No. No. They store things in it. Furniture, that sort of stuff.'

'What a waste.'

'It's all a bloody waste . . .'

We sat and looked at each other. The sub-Coward dialogue faded. I tried to rally.

How long do you think the Show will last?'

She picked up the too hot coffee-pot, swore, and fumbled for her napkin to wrap round the handle. 'Another couple of months. Depends on the Raids really. Peter's in Kent, did you know? Infantry. I must say the new boy looks a bit silly in your kilts, they come down to his shins.' She stopped quickly. 'When you come back, you know, I think you ought to have a try at the Cinema. Your kind of work is just right for their what-do-you-call-it . . . Technique. It's very intimate. You might do awfully well. Do you fancy yourself as a Film Star?' She laughed as if she knew the answer.

'You've got to look like Clark Gable or someone . . .' I said. She collected her gloves and handbag from the seat beside her. 'Nonsense! Look at Wallace Beery! Or Lon Chaney! They'd snap you up. When you're marching about up there doing your drill I think you ought to have a . . well: think about it.' She made her mouth into a round O and carefully smoothed it with her finger. 'I think you'd be spiffing on the Flicks, I really do . . . with those big sad eyes of yours, ducky, you couldn't miss. *I'd* know it's because you've forgotten something, but *they'll* think it's because you've lost something . . .'

At King's Cross we pushed through a sea of khaki and blue, crying children, anxious women, trundling tea-urns, trolleys, hissing steam, and hundreds, it seemed, of men carrying empty suitcases. My lot, I thought. The Conscript Special. At Platform 10 there were three men singing 'Tipperary' and waving a bottle about and a woman passed us with a white face, weeping without expression, holding a bunch of bluebells.

Vida said: 'That's your train, isn't it?'

'Yes . . .'

'Well I'm not very good at this part. I'll just go.' I kissed her on the cheek through the veil and saw that she was crying too. Quickly she waved a hand before my mouth. 'Don't speak . . . and write . . . remember to write to me . . . the poems . . . send them to me . . .' She turned swiftly and went away. Bumping into people, fumbling in her handbag. Aunt Hester at Queen Street . . . the same wrench of sadness. All gone. I couldn't run after her.

The man at the gate looked at my bit of paper. 'Change at Darlington, sonny,' he said.

A full compartment. One elderly woman in the corner by the window, knitting something fluffy. I looked at the sketch-book which I had in my pocket. He had written on the inside cover. My initials, then 'from' and his initials, U. v. d. B. At the bottom he had put, 'With Love' and the date. A lump, large as a fist, rose unbidden to my throat. I stared out of the dirty window. Somewhere after Luton I lit a cigarette but the knitting woman said she'd vomit if I smoked and this was a Non Smoker.

I stood in the corridor leaning against the door. On both sides other men were doing the same. Hands in pockets, bodies lurching with the train, staring out at the racing fields, woods, scattered houses, billows of white smoke ripping away from the engine. No one speaking, or singing, just leaning, bodies rolling with the motion, having a 'jolly good think' as Lally used to say . . .Think. Think. Not of today, of tonight, of tomorrow, just Think. Of the good things. The partridges in the glass case at Twickenham, the Zeppelin from Potters Bar . . . Winter Greens; is she doing them now, bending between the rows . . . Not. Not *that*. Well; Great Meadow then, the way it rises high up from the road to the gate by the privy . . . the feel of wet grasses against bare legs . . . you could write a poem about that. Vida's poem. How do you write a Sonnet. 'Shall I Compare Thee To A Summer's Day . . .' How do you paint love? You can paint death and life but love? People in love, holding hands, lying with each other . . . but that's not Love. How do you paint the intangible, how do you paint all the love which I have had and which this sodding train is taking me away from . . . No! Think! Constructively. What will it be like after? When you come back. The Haymarket? His Majesty's? Maybe the Old Vic after all . . . a Star Character Actor like Edith Evans . . . there will be time, plenty of time then . . . this'll be a dream in a year or a bit . . . perhaps I *should* try the Flicks . . . be a film actor. More money. Huge money. Sometimes a hundred pounds a day even . . . will there be beds or bunks . . . or just straw on the floor or something . . . Usually bunks in the Barrack Rooms, one on top of the other, like rabbits . . . Elizabeth said that we could have real palm trees in the garden in Hollywood . . . and swimming pools too I suppose . . . Florida Palms they are called . . . Swimming pools and a Mess Hall . . . like the ones at Larkhill, Amesbury . . . like the Tuck Shop at School. But no Lavatory. Sweet God! . . . No lavatories . . . they wouldn't dunk me at nineteen would they . . . everyone has a different accent in the Army . . . a Melting Pot . . . like Hollywood. They like English accents there. You won't be dunked in the Lav. in Hollywood. Think of Ronald Colman, Leslie Howard, Dame May Whitty. . . Soldiers are equal. I wonder how soon they will let me telephone? It has started to rain. Good for the Winter Greens. . . Not that. Funny how the drops slide down the window so dreadfully slowly when the train is moving so fast. Centrifugal Force or something. See how they slip, slowly, slowly, drop by drop . . . and then stop quite still like this one . . . and as suddenly tear away and run down the window into oblivion in the sill. Like a life. My drawn reflection, behind me No Smoking: back to front it looks strange.   That's how Nosmo King found his name . . . if I'm killed let it be quick . . . not a leg or an arm or a bit of my face . . . that would muck everything up for Afterwards. Just as long as it's quick. Obliterate. Obliterate quickly . . . it's raining heavily now . . . lambs in the fields like small sodden handkerchiefs . . . high chimneys of a brick works . . . six table legs in the dark sky . . . must be Bedford. . . . Afterwards won't be a Barrack Room. That's Now. Think of Afterwards. A Dressing Room not a Barrack Room . . . a Star on the door would be quite nice . . . just imagine that. There you are, and you are just about to turn the handle and, very slowly, you go in. . . .

SIXTEEN

It was pitch dark and smelled of conditioned air and beer stains. Glitters of light slitted through the shutters. I felt my way across the room, hit a table, and pushed open the windows. Hot smoggy air came up from the Studio Yard. In front the yawning doors of A and C Stage. Six men pushing half a snow-capped mountain trundled up the yard. A woman came running down, a bundle of sequined dresses over her arm, a paper cup of coffee in her hand. To my far left, the carpenters' shop. Planks and sawdust and gilded doors leaning against the concrete walls. To my right, high up, the misty smog-smudged ridge of the hills. The great wooden sign striding the skyline, one letter missing, long since fallen. Hol-ywood.

I had arrived at last. I was there where it all started. The most oriental city on earth West of Calcutta. My heart fell with despair. Six months to go.

Joe came barging in opening doors and drawers, switching on lights, trying taps and pulling the lavatory chain. He plumped up cushions and looked round the room carefully. Hands on hips, blue jeans bursting, a gold cross round his neck winking in the thin sunlight. He jangled his identity bracelet and shrugged.

'This is a good room, you know. Masculine. All the Male Stars have rooms like this, very Butch. This one is *reely* nice, you know? They're doing you good so far. Two ice boxes you got, television, radio and a shower *and* a bath . . . that's a First Class Room. You get judged by that here, you know. If you get to have just the john and a shower and no ice box you don't *reely* rate. Not at all. This is Star Stuff. You like it?' He seemed indifferent.

It was pine panelled. Fake plaster pine panelled. Tweed carpet like old porridge. Chairs and settees covered in violent tartan. Hunting prints on the walls, a sword, a galleon in full sail, two ice boxes disguised as corn-chests, lamp shades with maps of the world on them. I found 'England' squashed up beside 'Norway', a small table with a flat bowl of plastic sweet peas and dahlias. The bathroom off. Plain, white, Butch. All very Male.

'Fine.'

'Well it's gotta be. This is what you are allocated. This is what you got. This is what you stay with. Get it? It's *reel* nice. But I'll just check something.' He was back in the bathroom turning on all the taps, pulling the plugs. He beckoned me to come in to him. In the roar of water he said, in normal tones: 'Just check we ain't got any bugging things here. If we have you gotta keep your tap closed unless you run water, get it? That blurs the tape.' He strode into the dressing room and yanked at the pictures. Henry Alkins were pushed about. No microphones. The air-conditioner above the door was pulled apart. Satisfied, he lifted the bowl of sweet peas and dahlias. They came up in his hands with a long black wire which ran down through the table-top. His face was triumphant. But the wire was unconnected. No plug at the end . . . thin twists of copper. He replaced the bowl and motioned me into the bathroom again.

'You see that? Wired. And there is another air-conditioner just over the window. Even for a *reely* good room it don't rate *two* air-conditioners.' Back he went, up on a chair and struggled with the second air-conditioner. The vented front came away in his hands revealing an empty metal box behind. There was dust and a dead moth. Worms of fabric dust . . . he scattered thoughtfully over the carpet. 'I reckon it's all been disconnected . . . when Levison was alive, every sodding room was connected to a Central Pool. So they could know if you was 'happy' or if you was 'worried about the script' or anything like that. Just so they could 'help' you if supposin' you was too shy to ask out for something . . . but I reckon that's over now. Things was different with McCarthy . . . but you seem unhooked. Just watch out, though. If you do have something reely important to say, just do it in the john. No use you taking any chances. Saul Gallows didn't want you in the Movie, you know that, a Limey with a British Accent . . . so you just gotta be careful and keep your nose nice and clean? You ain't Gay, are you?' I shook my head. He patted his crotch. 'Just thought I'd ask, that's all, most everyone is in this town . . . but we'll get on fine. There's a nice guy who tested all the girls for the part of the Countess . . . but he ain't against you. You'll like him, his name's Rod Raper . . . that's what the Studio call him . . . we just call him Al. You'll meet him I reckon. Reel nice kid. He won't hold nothing against you.'

I slumped into one of the tartan chairs and Joe jangled a bracelet, fixed the blind over the window and presently left me to my Masculine-Plaster-Panelled-Gloom.

Beside one of the map-lamps lay a large piece of paper. Cautiously I took it up and read it: Production 9678. Pre-Production Day 1. 8.00 a.m. Arrive Studio. D.R. 2. Block A. 8.30 a.m. Music Conference. Room 2456. Block C. V. Aller. Dummy piano. Playbacks. Key Board. 10.00 a.m. Make Up. Room 2784. It went on until it simply said 'Car. Main Gate. 6.30 p.m.' Trapped.

Room 2456 was dim, painted brown with a brown carpet and three pianos. The blinds were down; electric light gleamed dully on the scratched wood of the Broadwood. On one wall a faded colour photograph of Myrna Loy, on the other a View Of Naples. A tall coat and hat rack. A gramophone. Two chairs and Victor Aller. We had met briefly before at what was called a 'General Meeting To Get Acquainted'. He was to teach me the Piano and never leave my side night and day until the final Shot was in the Can. He was totally at my disposal. Small, benign. A Russian Jew with glittering rimless glasses and beautiful hands, he sat quietly at the Broadwood playing something sad. I didn't interrupt him but sat quietly in the chair beside him. He switched music and went into something extremely fast, short and vaguely familiar. He placed his hands on his knees and smiled at me.

'That's Chopsticks.'

'Oh.'

'You know it?'

'I think so . . . somewhere.'

'Everyone knows it. It's a child's exercise. Play it.'

'I have never played a piano in my life. I couldn't.'

A pause like a century.

'You gotta be Liszt.'

'I know that.'

'Liszt played piano.'

'Yes.'

'You don't dispute that?'

'No.'

'He played piano like no one else played piano.'

'I believe . . .'

'And you don't?'

'No. Never.'

'Well we gotta start then. That's what I'm here for. To teach you to play piano and fast. And like Liszt.'

'Thank you.'

'Don't thank me till I have.' He played some scales rapidly. I watched his hands, dull with fear. 'These are just scales . . . we'll have to do a lot of this, just to exercise your fingers . . . show me your span.'

'What's that?'

'Shit! Put your hands out in front of you and spread your fingers . . . that's a span.'

I did as he asked. My hands looked supplicating. They were.

'Nice span you got. You play tennis?'

'No.'

'Football?'

'No.'

'Ping pong . . . table tennis?'

'No neither.'

Another long stupefied pause. The air-conditioner hissed and throbbed.

'You play that game you have in England. With a bat and a ball . . . like rounders?'

'Cricket?'

'Yeah. Cricket. You play that?'

'No.'

'Shit.' He played another set of scales.

'And you gotta be Liszt?'

'They tell me so.'

'In five weeks we start shooting in Vienna. You going to be ready?'

'What do you think?'

'Not in a million years let alone five weeks. You got eighty-five minutes of fucking Music in this Production. Eighty-five minutes of music not including conducting Les Préludes and the Rákóczy March.'

'They said they'd use a Double for my hands. They would only shoot me in long shot or so that my hands were hidden by the key-board. That's what they said.'

'Where did they say they would use a Double?'

'They said so in London when we all first met . . . and in New York when I met the Front Office in Mr Gallows' office. We'll use a Double, they said.'

'They didn't tell *me*. They told me I was hired for six months to teach you piano, to teach you to play like Liszt and to Conduct. I got the Contract. You wanna see my contract? Six months I have. I am at your total disposal. I don't have a wife, two kids, or a cardiac condition . . . I just have you and two pianos and eighty-five fuckin' minutes of music to get into you before the end of the six months.'

'I'm sorry.'

'So'm I. Shit. A Double. No one told *me* about a Double. They said categorically you would be required to play it *all*. That's what they told me. Fuck the Front Office and Gallows. They just don't happen to be here in California. They don't know. Charles Vidor says you play and you play, I assure you.'

'Well. I'd better start. I mean, perhaps you could show me, very slowly, a bit of something I have to play . . . not Chopsticks. It's too fast.'

'So is the fuckin' 1st Concerto . . .' He started, very gently and softly to play. It was good. He played with deep feeling and tenderness. I listened and watched. Horrified. How could I ever remember where the fingers went. Which keys to use, the black or the white?

He stopped. And glittered at me.

'That's the Moonlight. That's the slowest piece you got in the whole eighty-five minutes. Try with me. Put your hands on the keys . . . look, like this . . .'

For the next half an hour he quietly and kindly told me about sharps and flats, about bass and span, about thighs, and back, about wrists and fingers, about tempo and allegro and Christ only knows what. I was stunned into voiceless silence. I grew eighty fingers, I sweated, I hit my knees but I never once hit the keys or got the right hand doing anything at the same time as the left. It was a grim half-hour. The glitter in Aller's glasses was like sheet lightning. But cold.

'You have as much co-ordination as a runaway train for Christ's sakes. . . . Do you dispute that?'

'No.'

We went on trying until my time, according to the piece of Paper, was over. I got up from my chair unsteadily. He sat in his looking stunned. His fat lower lip sticking out like a sulky baby. I thanked him and started to the door.

'Remember I'll be here all day. Right until six-thirty p.m. And then I'm available to you all evening at your hotel or here or wherever you like. I don't finish until you do. I don't leave the Studio until you do. I'm here all the time for you to practise. You got five weeks and not a chance in hell. See you later. Remember I'm here all the time, just waiting.' He started to play something slow and sad again, his head up, his eyes fixed on Myrna Loy.

Joe helped me into my trousers. Skin tight black taffeta. A white frilly shirt . . . a jacket cut like an hour-glass. We did up zips, hooks and eyes, he fixed an expert silk cravat, and tucked Kleenex round it to prevent the make-up staining the white cloth. Agony to sit down, legs stiff like a milking stool, glossy patent boots slid on, and trousers strapped under. Gloves, sixty pairs all hand made in Paris, France, were chalked and eased on to my swollen, fat fingers. He said I looked swell. I felt silly and too tight, and scared to death. It wasn't my Test we were doing . . . I already had the fatal role . . . we were testing ladies for The Countess. But I felt as terrified as if they were testing me for Cholera.

In the Make-Up Room a silent man in a white coat like a surgeon had covered me in a pink nylon robe, read a list of instructions in his hand, studied some enormous black and white blow-ups of Liszt aged twenty-seven and started to work. We didn't speak. Except once, when I said, politely and quietly, 'I never wear make-up in England.' He didn't stop covering my face with a scented sponge. 'You do in Hollywood,' he said. The final result in the mirror looked like a mad Rocking Horse. My hair had been washed and rolled in curlers and baked and combed and tinted and primped and finally covered with a thick spray of lacquer so that it moved almost independently of my head and body. A great bouffant, faintly pink, tea-cosy of a hairstyle. Liszt at twenty-seven. A mad rocking horse in a pink candyfloss wig. I was humbled to the dust. Joe didn't help by saying I looked cute . . . and when the whole paraphernalia was put together, taffeta trousers, frilly shirt, pink hair and hour-glass coat, I looked and felt like something out of an Army Drag Show. But worse.

The Test Stage was small, made of corrugated iron and concrete, and built in 1914 when the Studio first developed on the site of an Orange orchard. It was blinding, hot, and smelled of dust and wet paint. There was a quarter of a room. Flock wallpaper, gilded panels, real mahogany doors, thick carpet, bowls of plastic lilac, a piano, naturally, and a fat silk settee. They were busy hanging a chandelier when I walked onto the set and found my chair. Green canvas, my name printed across the back. Awkwardly I sat down, heart heavy, but beating like a mad yo-yo. Someone came up and shook hands and said he was Buddy and welcome to Hollywood, and a nice looking woman with rimless glasses and a stopwatch round her plump neck said her name was Connie and I looked just dreamy. I thanked her and apologized for not being able to get out of the chair because of the tightness of my pants.

'Mercy me! So British of you! Never you mind a bit. Mr Vidor won't be too long: he just went to see yesterday's Test on one of the Chopins. Do you want a cup of coffee? I'm so glad you're on the Production, I just loved you in that film about the Doctors! So English and quaint. Oh here's Mr Vidor now. I'll get you some coffee.'

Charles Vidor was shortish, sixty-ish and, as far as he was concerned, stylish. Grey spiky hair like a hedgehog. Manicured nails blushing a gentle pink. Rings glittering. A flat platinum watch. A viewfinder in gold hanging round his neck inscribed with the names of all the films he had directed with it: dressed entirely in grey. Cashmere, silk shirt, immaculate flannels, crocodile shoes, a cigarette in a long paper holder. He smiled across the quarter room, spoke to someone arranging a jar of plastic roses, slapped someone else on the back and sat down beside me in his own canvas chair.

'You look cute,' he said and patted my knee absent-mindedly.

'I feel ridiculous personally.'

'You look great, kid! Great. Like the hair. You look just like him . . . like the pictures we got up in the office . . . you seen them? You look just like him. Claude-Pierre said so too and he should know. Claude-Pierre is French from France and he's done all your costoums and he KNOWS. You know the velvet we got for your waistcoat when you play the Campanella bit cost fifty dollars a piece? Fifty dollars for a bit of Paris velvet? Can you beat that? My wife wouldn't spend that much on a bit of Paris velvet and god alone knows she *spends*. You look great.' He reached into his cigarette case and fitted another long thin cigarette into the holder.

'About the Campanella . . .'

'What about it?' He was casual and didn't meet my eye.

'Mr Aller says that I have to play the piano. You won't be using a Double.'

'That's correct.'

'But you said that you would. I can't play the piano. Or tennis or cricket, even a mouth organ.'

'Be reasonable! This is Today! Movies can't be faked now. Television brings it all close to them . . . We want you to be the first to *really* play. Everyone else had a double in the old days, but this is Today! We'll start on a close up of your head, anguish, passion, all the music registering there . . . your love for the Princess . . . your mother . . . your agony of mind over the Church . . . and then we pan down, without a cut, mind you, and see your own hands, your very own hands, actually playing the music he wrote! It'll be a sensation. So moving . . .'

'But when do I have the time to learn all this stuff. There is eighty-five minutes Aller says . . .'

'Aller is the greatest teacher in Hollywood. He taught Cornel Wilde to be Chopin. He worked on two of my last pictures, I trust him implicitly. If he says eighty-five it means he *can teach* you eighty-five minutes. And we'll have a Box Office Smash such as you have never seen before. You want to be a Movie Star? Well, you have to work for it.' He lit his cigarette and waved cheerfully across at someone else arranging yet another pot of flowers.

'Don't put the fuckin' things behind the chair, Al, they'll stick out of her head when we do the Close shot . . . move 'em to the little table by the drapes there . . . fine . . . you're a good kid.'

I sat in a state of rigid despair. There was nothing more to say; yet. I'd have to wait. Try a few more times with Aller. Connie came with coffee in paper cups, she offered sugar in paper wraps, and plastic spoons. She sat beside us on a small stool, twinkling like a Japanese lantern, all sweetness and light with the eyes of a ferret. We sipped coffee.

'What was the Test like, Mr Vidor . . . did you find your Chopin?' She swirled coffee with a pencil beaming brightly at us both.

Vidor stretched his legs thoughtfully, and smoothed his creases. The crocodile shoes shone and gleamed like Connie's eyes.

'There's one might do. Australian guy. Good looking, but I didn't like the wig. He looked faggy. You know?'

Connie nodded seriously.

'I don't want a faggy Chopin, be difficult with the George Sand . . . know what I mean? A woman with a feller's name and wearing pants . . . it could be very difficult. I got Wallis to check out some other Chopins and a few George Sands . . . maybe we'll do a couple more tests tomorrow. I can't be sold on that Australian yet.'

Connie finished her coffee. 'Maybe Make-Up or Hair could fix a different wig for him?'

'We're checking just that. He's in Hair right this minute.'

There was a slight disturbance somewhere across the quarter room. Women came huddling into the lights . . . a lot of chatter and fixing . . . in the middle of the group a small pale girl dressed in yards of blue silk with her hair plaited and an expression of sheer terror. One of the Countesses. One of the finals who would be tested that day with me. We all stood and were introduced. She was French, had flown in a day before, was sick with fright, tired, bewildered, and ready to weep. Vidor took her away gently, and talked to her kindly. His arms round her shoulders, his viewfinder hitting her breasts.

We started Testing shortly afterwards. I sitting in a chair, she arranging plastic roses on a piano. My voice seemed to come from the soles of my patent leather boots . . . hers from below the Seine. After a couple of long shots they moved in to close stuff and during the break two people walked onto the set, greeted everyone with large hand waves, hugged Vidor and, with eyes like unforgiving steel nuggets, perched themselves on two tall bar stools and watched us. Our first Audience. Tony Curtis and Jack Lemmon. No one introduced anyone, and apparently no one was about to do so. The Test proceeded before them as they sat immovable, unflinching, on the stools. It was rather like being something in a Fair Ground. Only they didn't actually chuck anything at us. It might have been better if they had. After a great deal of flower arranging, and waving of hands, and a long imploring speech at my feet, the Countess came to the end of her 'bit' . . . and we started all over again on mine. The Film Stars slid off their stools, called 'See yah!' to the crew, hugged Vidor, made a joke, roared with laughter. And left. The set went back to work. We continued.

I ate a beefsteak-tomato and some cold chicken in my Olde Worlde Male Dressing Room. Joe pottered about opening a can of beer, folding my costume, gathering together boots and button hooks. The beer tasted of thin yellow water, the tomato of water, the chicken of cold roast water. I was soggy with it all and with the day. I still had to go down and face Aller who I knew was still sitting in that hateful room waiting for me at the damned piano. Joe looked sympathetic and slid into a chair opposite me.

'Hate the Test?'

'Yes . . . everything.'

'First days are always the same kid, always the same. Even for Henry Fonda, or Gary Cooper, it's always the same. You'll be fine tomorrow when you see the stuff. And after all,' he added reasonably, 'you *got* the part. I mean it's not as if you haven't *got* the role, is it? You *got* it. They *signed* the contract. You're *IN*.'

'I'm in all right. Up to my bloody neck. Eighty-five minutes of music I've got. That's what I've got, and those bloody silly pants and gloves and this god-awful hair . . . and all the Campanella and the Moonlight and the Rhapsody . . . Jesus! Have I got it!'

Joe slid the pants on to a hanger. 'The music is different. Try. If you can't make it sure as hell they'll use a Double. Only be warned. Rod Raper, you know the one who has been Testing for you while you were in Britain, well Rod knows it all . . . the Music . . . he's been practising for weeks. And he's good, I mean good. Worse than that he's determined. I don't mean no harm to Rod . . . he's a sweet kid. We have assed about a bit, I mean he's sweet, he'll do anything. But like I said . . . he knows the Music. And he'll fit the costooms . . . he'll kill his Daddy to play this role . . . I'm just tellin' you this because Tinsel Town is a funny place . . . you can never be quite sure who's holding the knife. Get me? Try the score, shit if Rod can do it you sure as hell can. Rod came straight out of a Department Store in Dallas . . . used to sell shirts and underwear until someone asked him to model the goods one Sunday. He didn't know a piano from his asshole. About the only instrument he did know how to handle was his cock. So you can see that he's a very ambitious boy. And there's another thing you better know, though I shouldn't even mention a word.' He leaned over my crumpled form and whispered very close to my ear; there was a strong smell of 'Arpege' and collusion. 'They got a big Contract Artist standing by to take over if you screw it all up. A real nice guy . . . got a couple of good Movies behind him, and he's under Contract, he's all set . . .I shouldn't say this but you better know. They got all his measures down at Western Costume and everything would fit except maybe the boots . . . so watch it.' He straightened up and tumbled cuff links and dress studs into a small cardboard box. When he spoke again his voice was normal, for him, and flat as a steel blade. 'You better pay heed to old man Vidor. Want another beer?'

Aller was sitting in a crumpled heap reading *Newsweek*. Reluctantly we went to our pianos. And he started, again, fingering the Moonlight. I watched in anguish. Nothing seemed possible. If Rod Raper could do it, why couldn't I? We 'worked' for two hours. My hands were sweating, my arms ached, Aller's voice was dull and defeated.

'You got no co-ordination at all. It amazes me. Positively amazes me. I seen a child of four with more co-ordination than you. Do you doubt that?'

I did not.

'If it's not too personal – could you tell me how you even got this far?' I was mute.

'I'll try and give you some simple scales . . . you'll try and learn them . . . and then go over them again and again tonight on the piano in your hotel room. Maybe tomorrow something will break through. Maybe you're tired; first day after all. Now let's start with this . . . it's the simplest scale of all . . .'

La Campanella had no charm whatsoever, and by the time we got to part 2 of Rondo Capriccioso I slumped gently out of my overstuffed white tweed chair and lay, eyes closed, tears welling, on the thick white pile of my Bel Air Hotel Bungalow. Room Service hadn't cleared, and half eaten scrambled eggs stiffened in their grease, cigarette butts lay like corpses drowned in cold spilt coffee, and on the Record Player the disc revolved gently, only the hissing of the sapphire point endlessly obliterating the genius of Liszt.

Taking another record from the high pile beside his chair, Tony Forwood stepped over my recumbent form and slid it from its crackly yellow sleeve.

'Well . . . let's just hear a bit of the Etude in D Flat . . . it's slow.'

'Slow.' I was beyond help or care.

'Slower . . . it's the Theme Song, for God's sake . . .' He slid it on and moved the start button.

'I'm packing it in. Call a meeting tomorrow, with all of them, Vidor, Aller, Feldman . . . it's not too late. I'm here under false pretences. They said they'd use a Double . . . I can't do it . . . I played by ear years ago at school . . . but I can't be accurate to *one bloody note* and act all the crap they've written in five weeks. I'm packing it in . . . well get the Pan Am flight back tomorrow night. I've got five weeks to learn half Liszt's bloody output, plus all the rest.'

In despair I reached up and finished off the Hennessy bottle and shoved it upside down into the wastepaper basket. Un Sospiro droned through the room mournfully.

'I don't want to be a Movie Star! They keep asking me if I want to *be* one . . . for God's sake! I'm nearly forty! I never wanted to be one, not from the beginning . . . and always on my own terms . . . this is on their terms . . . I want to go back to those Dull Little English Movies they keep sneering about . . . maybe I *am* a late developer but it's too late to develop into something I don't want to be . . . Call Vidor tomorrow, and Feldman, call them now, tonight . . . help me!'

Wearily Tony switched off the player. I watched him hopefully, cunningly, through a haze of Hennessy and self pity, this time tomorrow I'd be on that Pan Am flight out of this monstrous place filled with monstrous, ugly, people. Carefully he slid Un Sospiro back into its yellow cover, not looking at me, preoccupied, worried, thoughtful. I knew all the danger signs.

'What is it?'

'Well . . .'

'Well what, for God's sake?'

'Well . . . no one's ever done it before . . .'

'Done what?'

'Eighty-five minutes of Classical Music . . . without a Double.'

'Oh shit! Who'll know? Who'll care?'

'You will,' he said evenly and placed the record carefully back on the pile.

Victor Aller looked up from his piano without welcome. He finished off whatever he was playing and sat silent.

'Your eyes look funny. Smog?'

'Yes . . . it's bad today.'

'When I first came here it was all Citrus orchards . . . sky was blue . . .'

'Could you go through my bit of the Campanella . . . slowly for me?'

'Sure . . . but it gets hellish fast.'

'I'll just watch . . . watch your hands . . .'

'Here we go. La Campanella . . .'

'Play it three or four times, will you . . . at that speed?'

I stood there watching those beautiful hands moving across the keys with elegance, love and confidence. He looked up at me and smiled through his glittery glasses:

'What are you doing, waiting for the lightning to strike?'

'Something like that,' I said.

Snakes and Ladders

For
Elizabeth and George

A NOTE ON THE SOURCES

My principal sources have been my note-books, diaries and letters written to my parents, during the period 1941–1947. I have also drawn on a daily journal which I have kept from 1950 to the present day, as well as scrap-books, many personal letters, and in particular a collection of about 650 letters written between 1965 and 1973 to a friend in America, and which were returned to me in accordance with her will after her death. *The Films of Dirk Bogarde* by Margaret Hinxman and Susan d'Arcy (Literary Services and Production, 1974) has also been invaluable.

ACKNOWLEDGEMENTS

I am indebted, first and foremost, to George Courtney Ward who was my personal photographer at Rank for many years. Also to Mario Tursi, for allowing me to reproduce his stills from 'Death in Venice', and to the owners of individual photographs, by whose courtesy I have reproduced many of the pictures. My gratitude to E. L. L. Forwood for taking on the Index with such care and patience, and also to Søren Fischer who traced and secured the scene written for Judy Garland. I am grateful to Miss Rosalind Toland who has waded through years of newspapers in search of information and headlines etcetera; and above all to Mrs Sally Betts, who once again, has managed to cope with my incomprehensible typescript, spelling and punctuation.

In order to save any embarrassment I have, very occasionally, used pseudonyms.

CHAPTER ONE

When I started to write the first book about the story of my life, which took me up to the age of eighteen, it was with motives which were, I suppose, rather muddled. One, certainly, was to try to discover whether or not I had any ability for writing as such, another was to occupy myself when the weather was too bad for me to work my few acres, and somewhere, buried in the midst of it, was the idea that I might be able to say something about the whole process of becoming an actor – the kind of natural instincts given one and the manner in which they were gradually developed both by myself and by the people I met along the way, so that they were ultimately fused by experience into something usable in a profession which I desperately wanted to follow. I imagined that what I had to say about myself *might* offer some clues to a new generation of would-be actors and actresses, or even to parents, who so often oppose the longing to enter a profession which is insecure, and by some people still denigrated.

One of the things which I have learned is that for a good ninety per cent of the people who want to become actors it is a mistake, and leads to poverty and unhappiness. For the other ten per cent it can be, as it has been in my case, in varying degrees, rewarding and enriching, and because I have had quite a few letters from young people as a result of the first book asking me how one does it, I have been encouraged to write most of the rest of what is inevitably something of an ego trip. Well, ego, for better of for worse, is very much involved in this business of being an actor, because we are creatures who are obliged to use our own beings as our instrument, and we tend to have to keep reassuring ourselves – and looking for reassurance – as to how good that instrument is. It tends to make us very boring as people unless we are on constant guard against a total self-preoccupation. And it has the more dangerous hazard of cutting us off from what I think to be the mainspring of all good acting, which is the minute observation of one's fellow creatures, who are really the fuel which feeds our attempts to create a living character.

So this book, the continuation of my ego trip, is also an endeavour to portray just a few of the people who have helped me to become whatever sort of an actor I may be. Living their own lives, they are also my life. In trying to compress thirty years of living into a book which may well be too long anyway, it is inevitable that many of them cannot appear, however important they may have been. Perhaps they may be only too pleased *not* to be mentioned . . . time will tell; but I, at least, am sorry. Anyway: to begin with, there was Gooley.

When we got to York the woman who had been sitting in the corner window seat, knitting something fluffy, took a couple of brown paper parcels off the rack, slung her chintz knitting bag over her arm and threaded her way carefully past our disconsolate knees. We didn't try to help her. She wrenched at the door and clambered down on to the platform without a backward look, slamming the door hard behind her. We sat in dejected silence, as we had ever since we left King's Cross. None of us had spoken throughout the journey, except the

woman, who had said that this was a Non Smoker and that if any one of us tried
to smoke she'd vomit. So we had lumbered into the corridors and lolled against
the windows, watching the rain start as the train trailed smoke across the grimy
fields of the Home Counties shortly after Watford.

Now we had creaked and huffed into York. I stared at my own reflection in
the dirty window; fist screwed into my face mottled with sooty raindrops down
the glass. A tropical disease. Cholera. Something dreadful. Mazawattee Tea
. . . Swan Pens . . . Careless Talk Costs Lives . . . Stephens Ink . . . Claudette
Colbert in . . . but the title blurred away as we jolted into movement. Air Raid
Shelter . . . Waiting Rooms . . . Gentlemen . . . we gathered speed for
Darlington.

The compartment gradually relaxed with the woman's departure. We
spread out a bit, and pulled crumpled cigarettes from pocket-squashed packets.
The air was pleasant with the hazy blue of smoke, the sweet smell of tobacco.
The youth sitting opposite me, short, thick, muscular, with greasy black hair
spiky like a wet cat's, chucked his Gold Flake into my lap. I had run out ages
ago, neurotically, in the corridor.

'Dere you are. Help yourself. Two packets in me case. Got a light?' I had, and
we lit up. He pushed the crumpled packet back into the sagging pocket of his
tired grey cardigan.

'De ould bitch! "Dis is a non smoker . . . I'll vomit." Dat's a *real* civilian now,
a real bastard civilian for youse. I know de kind. I know 'em.' He slumped down
into his corner and stared back at his reflection with hatred. The fact that we all
were, at that moment, civilians seemed to have escaped him . . . we would only
cease to be human at 23.59 hours when the barrack gates shut behind us and
our own particular Hells began. But until then we were still free. Civilian and
free. The Army waited.

Suddenly he leant across, prodding me into attention on the knee with a dirty
thumb. 'You know someting? As a matter of fact it's one of dem civilian women
like her is de reason I'm sittin' on me arse in dis fucking train at all . . . an ould
bitch, just like dat, t'in and scrawny like an ould hen. It was in dis little sweetie
shop, you see, up Charlotte Street, she was ironing or doing some fuckin' ting in
de back shop, and when she saw me picking up a few little bits and pieces like,
she let out wid such a screaming and a hollering I had to hit her hard wid de
little iron she had, to stop her, you see? And den she fell on de floor squawking
like she had seen de Resurrection so I hit her again, not much of a whack, wasn't
dat hard, just a couple of times to be sure. And would you believe it, dat evening
de papers said an ould woman had been attacked by hooligans and was near to
death.' He stared away from me out at the darkening sky. Suddenly he snorted.
'Hooligans!' He shook his wet-cat head in amazement. 'Dere was only me!'

No one took any notice of him, or showed the least interest. We all had our
own problems and worries, and I wasn't sure that he wasn't bluffing anyway
out of boredom. But he had given me his cigarette. He might offer me another
later.

'And why are you on the train then? They didn't get you?'

He looked at me with thin eyes and blew smoke down each nostril separately,
which I thought quite effective.

'Not me. Paddy Gooley? Dey never caught me for nothing. Joined the King's
bleeding army, didn't I? Took his shilling; a good boy from the Republic. Well
. . .' he squashed his cigarette stub on to the floor, 'dere was no point in hanging
around just *waiting*, now was dere?'

'Won't they catch up with you in the army even so?'

'Once I'm in, I'm in and safe, and, me darlin' boy, the first ting Gooley does

on his first leave, in twenty-t'ree weeks' time, is to slip back to me lovely
Emerald Isle with me boots and battledress, never to return. You tink I'm soft?'

He was grinning cheerfully and gave me a long slow wink as if we had both
been conspirators in the little sweetie shop. His implied acceptance pleased me.
Only I felt that I was the one who would be caught.

'You're a toff, aren't youse?' he asked suddenly.

'I don't think so, why?'

'Ach . . . you talk like one. I don't mind. What was you in Civvie Street den?'

'An actor.'

'Sweet Christ! An actor! Would I know you den?'

'I don't think so.'

'Was you ever at de Bedford, Camden Town? Or Chiswick? Dey had real
good shows dere.'

'No never. At the Q . . .'

Suspicion crept into his bashed face.

'Where's dat den?'

'Outside London really. Kew Bridge. I wasn't famous or anything.'

'Oh.' He dismissed me, and looked out at the sombre May sky. Across the
fields a woman cycled, head bowed against the rain; it was almost dark. The
man sitting beside me, older than the rest of us, leant confidentially towards me
and said in a low voice: 'I heard you say you were an actor which is very funny,
you see, because I was with the Palmers Green Light Operatic Society for quite
some time. It's funny you and I being of the same persuasion, so to speak, in the
same compartment! Only amateur status, I'm afraid, me I mean, still we did
some lovely shows there, you know, before this caper started. Last one we did
was "The White Horse Inn". A very jolly show. Lots of very hummable tunes.
A jolly show but most tasteful. *Rather* expensive.' He smiled knowingly, as one
professional to another. 'We had a bit of trouble with the boat, you know.
There's a paddle steamer type of thing, end of the Second Act, cost us a lot of
headaches, as you can imagine. But Ileen Mirren and Mrs Croft did a
remarkable job; it brought down the house. Funnel smoking, paddles turning,
all that sort of thing, really marvellous. Of course the Chorus said it made them
cough. They are for ever complaining choruses are, aren't they? Proper prima
donnas the lot of them; but I don't think anyone really noticed very much. I
must say it *was* a jolly show. I thought you'd be interested, you being an actor as
you said. Birds of a feather, you might say! Quite a coincidence really.'

He smiled at me encouragingly. I nodded and smiled back like an idiot.
Across the compartment Gooley had taken out a rosary and was ab-
sentmindedly fiddling with it, the crucifix winking in the mean blue light from
the electric light bulb in the roof. I didn't want to talk about the theatre or
acting; that had been all put aside. Now I would only think of the future and
how best to bend it to me, how to save myself in this new, daunting life which lay
a very few hours ahead. But Palmers Green wasn't going to give in easily. After
a while he asked me in a low, gruff voice, as if he was soliciting, whether I knew
Richard Tauber or Binnie Hale, and when I said no, not personally, he smiled
sadly and looked away into a past of smoking paddle steamers.

For my part, grateful for the respite, I stared out at the now dark countryside.
The gleam of wet roofs here and there, a chimney stack hard against the
scudding clouds, telegraph posts whipping past like sticks in a fence. I
remembered my father's words of only last night, at our last family dinner. 'It'll
take a bit of getting used to, of course, but it will be a good experience for you;
you may one day look back upon it all as among some of the happiest times of
your life. I know that *I* did.' And I knew that he was telling me an arrant lie. His

had been an appalling war and he suffered from it for the rest of his life. All he was doing, I knew, was jollying me along at that particular moment. Like the dentist who says this won't hurt you. No point in frightening the wits out of the patient before the operation. The operation itself would see to that.

At Darlington we had to change trains for Richmond. It seemed to be the middle of the night. The cold dank of the North, smell of gas lamps and wet concrete, of soot and oily engines; draggled shadows bumping suitcases across the crowded station, in and out of the pools of light from the blackout shades, the hiss of steam and the clatter of tea trolleys; blindly we swam through the cross currents of hunched commuters like a shoal of fish, instinctively, mindlessly, until someone in uniform at the head of the shoal halted us into a colliding huddle and directed us raggedly towards another platform and yet another train. At Richmond in a wet moor-mist, on gleaming, slippery cobbles, in a biting wind and with only torches flashing about like distracted fireflies, we stood miserably about while other uniformed men barked orders and forced us shuffling into what were called 'Alphabetical Groups' . . . all the A's and all the B's and so on. As V*, I found myself down at the far end of the long line of shuddering trucks, loaded up, tail boards slammed shut, bolts run home, tarpaulins roughly pulled down to protect us from the misty rain, and in darkness, and silence, we moved off through the night to Catterick Camp. All I knew was that we had to report to 'Lecatto Lines', and that I was suddenly very hungry. I had had nothing to eat since the morning with Vida at Lyons Corner House, when misery had doused my appetite even for a lump of squashy gateau. The truck was full, some of us standing among the knees and suitcases of the luckier ones sitting on long wooden forms, hanging on with one arm to the steel supports of the roof, empty suitcases in the other. We rumbled and bumped along twisting roads and hills for an eternity. No one spoke.

Catterick Camp was a bleak, lightless huddle of hut roofs, jagged against the steel night sky. Torches flashing at the Main Gate, sentry boxes, wire, questions shouted and answered. I heard the phrase 'New Intake' a couple of times and realised that that was what we were.

We crunched about on gleaming gravel for a time, bumping into each other, then were formed into squads and marched through the wet night to huts. Ours was up a muddy track. We slid and clambered along in the dark, snagged by bushes on either side. The hut was bleak, cold, two lamps whipping leaping shadows round the brick walls and tin roof in the draught. We were told to choose a bed site, from piles of grubby mattresses on the floor, shown where the Ablutions were, and where to put our personal possessions. Large metal two-door meat-safes evenly spaced all down each side of the cement-wet hut. 'Three biscuits each for your beds,' said a weary corporal indicating the pile of mattresses, 'and if anyone wants extra, there's straw out in the yard. Help yourselves.'

Later we were marched back down the track to the Mess Hall. A gaunt raftered shed, scrubbed tables and benches, three iron stoves smouldering sullenly down the middle, at one end a long counter with urns, mugs and bundles of knives and forks in cardboard boxes. Condensation sweated down the yellow walls.

Sitting, twenty to a table, we ate fried sausages, boiled potatoes, carrots, two slices of thick margarined bread, with a pint mug of scalding tea. In the centre of each table, a bottle of Daddies Sauce. Next to me, Palmers Green, exhausted,

---

* Van den Bogaerde, the family name.

eyes glazed, face soapstone. Opposite, a tall blond boy, cool, spruce, his mouth a coathanger of disdain.

'Won't quite do, will it? Should be organised by now . . . we'll lose the war this way. Name's Tilly, P. W., Chartered Accountant; you know Hendon Central? Thought you might.' He looked coldly round the chewing mass. 'Hope they put up the lists pretty soon, get our names down right away . . . want to avoid any mistakes, don't you think? I'm in your hut if you need any advice.'

I thanked him and told him that I was perfectly happy, wanting only to live a quiet life, giving no trouble and receiving none. He cracked a couple of knuckles loudly.

'Stay a ranker for the duration? More responsibility as an officer surely?'

'I don't *want* responsibility!'

'You'd rather stay herded together with this crowd for the rest of the war? Not me. I say! I think you friend's going to be ill.'

Back in the hut we scrabbled about laying out our mattresses, stacking suitcases on the meat-safes, sorting out washing kit and the sad relics of home in the shape of our colourful, personal, hand towels. We queued to wash hands and teeth and to urinate. The concrete floor awash with water, suds and spittle. The weary corporal shouted, 'Lights out in ten minutes, you lot,' and everyone struggled back to undress and some, not all, to drag on a sad variety of pyjamas. Then to bed. Two hairy blankets stiff as card, a round, striped, greasy bolster, clothes neatly piled beside one's head for the morning. I wound my watch and realised that it had been 14 hours since we had all said goodbye at home that morning in the bright, sharp, Sussex light. I wondered, as the lights switched off, if my mother had managed to put in her rows of wintergreens; when I'd be able to write to them; what Vida was doing at this moment? Was there a raid perhaps in London. Had my father got home from *The Times* or was he, like me, sleeping on the floor in his office, as he so often had to do? Was it warm down there, as it had been last night by the pond when we sat watching the dog snuffling about for a rat in the sedge? A great welling misery rose in my heart and swept swiftly to my throat. Tears, unwanted, salt and hot, swelled through tightly closed eyelids; I thrust my face into the greasy bolster and hoped it would smother them. My shaking only lasted a moment or two, and then I lay silent, staring into the blackness. I was more than relieved to hear, about me, that one or two other people were in the same condition. Someone coughed gently, and blew his nose. Gradually the hut became still. The cinders from the dying stove rustled into the grate. The man on the floor on my right started to snore. Someone farted. I thought it was probably Gooley.

After they had issued us with numbers, handed out sizeless new-smelling uniforms, boots made of forged iron, button sticks, gas masks and a heavy Lee Enfield rifle, plus tin helmet and camouflage net, I folded my green tweed suit from Gamages Fire Sale, the canary yellow polo necked shirt, my suede shoes a size too large, the colourful personal towel, shoved them all in the empty suitcases which had travelled with me from home, and bundled it all back. I was left with only my washing gear, a photograph of the family standing smiling by the pond, a copy of *The Oxford Book of Modern Verse* and a pile of blue notebooks ready for the Poetry which Vida felt sure, although I was much in doubt, would flood from me in the moments when, as she had put it cheerfully, 'the others were cleaning their rifles or boots'. Little did we know on those halcyon evenings at her flat during the blitz in Belsize Crescent, that when they were doing that so, indeed, should I be. Poetry waited for the quiet times in the NAAFI on Sunday afternoons after we had marched to Church, had lunch, and the rest of the day to ourselves.

I think that the very first thing which helped to break me into the life was the Haircut. For endless hours we queued in drizzling mist to be shorn like sheep. When my turn came the hefty bruiser with the clippers pronounced it as long as a girl's and asked what I'd been before. This eternal question. Unthinkingly I said that I'd been an actor. 'Aha!' cried the bruiser with relish, and shaved me down to a prickly, almost naked dome. Everyone crowded round to see; gleeful that it was not they; goading him on in his surgical efforts to reduce my morale, my appearance, and my spirit.

I remembered a rat that some of the village boys had trapped on a brick in a water tank up at the farm. They were stoning it into the water with half-bricks, it kept falling off and swimming desperately round and round the brick pile, blood running into the water, its hair sticking up like mine now, its nose split. They stoned it until it quietly gave in and floated, pink feet upwards in supplication, tail trailing, dead.

No rat I. I had to start proving, and show them what I could do. I joined in the laughter. My laughter stopped the others. I departed in a curious silence. I had learned my first psychological trick. Laugh with them at you. And then you win. As long as you can follow it up. I did by being the best boot-polisher in the squad. For one cigarette a time I offered to do it for all the others who found it difficult and, after a very short time, had enough to open a shop. I stitched on badges and 'flashes' and buttons, thanking God all the time for my training in the theatre wardrobes of 'Q' Theatre and Amersham. It was not, you understand, the most elegant of stitching, but it was able to pass muster at inspections and kept me busy in the long dull evenings while the others lay disconsolately on their beds reading *Health and Strength*, *Tit-Bits*, or just staring into space.

I never had any spare time. I excelled at Drill. Theatre training again. I enjoyed marching and about-turning, by the right and by the left. The precision of it interested me, the effort very nearly killed me; but I did it, and did it moderately well. I worked so hard in fact that every time I clambered down on to my hard bed I was almost immediately asleep. No haunting nightmares of misery assailed me. Self-preservation was strong, thanks to the theatre and a determined, sensible, family training before that.

Out on the range, scrubby heather, mist, a brick wall and rows of targets, I learned to shoot with my heavy Lee Enfield. I was determined to be best in the squad. Tilly, who was equally determined, but who could neither sew nor polish, was a comfortable second.

I was very good at everything except the one thing for which I had been sent to Catterick initially: to be a signaller in the Royal Corps of Signals. My father had been as much surprised as I myself at the arbitrary, seemingly idiotic, decision to draft me into the Signal Corps. I who had the coordination of a bursting dam and the technical intelligence of an eft. We had decided that it was probably due to the fact that I had had to state my school background on my papers and that I had attended, for some time, a highly technical school in Glasgow which may have, erroneously, given them the idea that I was qualified. At school I had been so dense that I was finally removed from all the Technical Classes and allowed to follow my own pursuits in Bookbinding, Metalwork and Pottery. Which is why,to this day, I can sew on buttons, marble paper, open tins brilliantly, and glue the handle on to a cup. Everything else had been a total mystery to me, and remained so. And so it was with Morse

Code and all the other bits and pieces which went with the Course. I was baffled, uncomprehending, lost. An although I tried to learn the handbooks as I would a play, like a parrot, the practice of the exercise left me floundering in a mess of wires, bells, batteries and code. I knew that in this instance I was utterly doomed. Polish boots I could, sew on badges, hit the inner, outer, magpie, and bull's-eye time after time with my little gun. I could throw a grenade, wash a floor, drill like a demon, pass Kit Inspection with top marks, write excellent, if mawkish, letters to a girl named Kitty who seemed to be the dominant factor in Gooley's life. But I could not perform any function, whatsoever, required by the Royal Corps of Signals. I couldn't even send the S.O.S.

So, when the time came, I volunteered for the cookhouse. And because no one knew quite what to do with me, I was left there, peeling potatoes by the barrel, scrubbing down tables and benches, bashing about in a lather of soap and swill in the tin-wash, opening tin upon tin of bully beef, liver, pilchards and plum and apple. I hoped that my diligence would not go unremarked, and that perhaps after a time they'd forget all about me and let me off the Morse Code thing and allow me to spend the rest of my war washing up. Fat chance. But for a time I was in a busy fool's paradise.

Sunday was a dreary day. After Church Parade and lunch, I wrote letters to Kitty for Gooley who was in my hut and to whom I had become very attached in spite of his violent past, and wrote reams and reams of frightful poetry in blue notebooks about Isolation, Loneliness, Shells, Death in the Mud, Barbed Wire, Larks and Cornfields. I wrote them all, without exception, like the mouse's tail poem in 'Alice'. Long wriggling columns without rhyme, or very much reason, usually ending in a single word like 'dead' or 'cigarette' or 'stench'. My war poetry, after about three weeks, was still completely second hand, and borrowed exclusively from my father's war, about which I thought I knew a great deal. It took me six years to realise I knew nothing. It was not, however, a total waste of time. Just putting words down on paper was something. Out of the welter of rubbish bits and pieces emerged, shyly, causing me great delight, and forcing my Venus pencil to even wilder efforts. It also passed the time in the grey, brown, greasy room with its scattered tables and sagging posters of the 'Night Train to Holyhead'.

Except for Tilly and Gooley, I didn't get to know anyone else very well. Because of my accent I was called, as indeed Golley had done in the train coming up, Toff, but was excused for that in some dumb way by the fact that I was good at polishing and volunteered hysterically for practically anything. Usually a frightful error. I had, I thought, my own methods for survival. Blithely unaware that there were other factors working against my conceit.

Palmers Green, my light operatic companion from the train, was not very happy. I did his boots and sewed on his flashes free. Not out of any form of generosity, because he didn't smoke and never had cigarettes, but he was, as he had pointed out a number of times, a fellow actor, and loyalty came into it. He suggested one Sunday over slopped tea in the NAAFI that perhaps we should try and start a Concert Party. It would give us something to do, and he felt sure that the lads would enjoy a bit of a sing-song or some sketches which he suggested he would write. He himself, he pointed out, with his operatic background could oblige with some renderings of familiar and well loved numbers . . . and he had two sisters who could send him all the scores and song sheets collected from his past glories at The Society. I thought it quite a good idea myself, and began to rough out a few ideas. But first we had to get people together. And then where was the stage? Not, for sure, in the NAAFI. Tilly said there was a Garrison Theatre just outside the camp, and that if we did decide to form a concert party he'd be very pleased to supervise the lighting because apart from accounting his main hobby was electricity. I might have guessed. So now there were three people ready to start things off.

We pinned a notice up one Friday evening and settled down like anglers to wait. Palmers Green became almost cheerful. Writing off to his sisters in Hammersmith for the scores and libretti, daily scanning the notice board as if it was a rat-trap. We didn't appear to be attracting anything. One or two hesitant names; someone who could play a viola; someone who was a carpenter. And then it fizzled out. After a couple of weeks I gave in and forgot all about a concert party. And then one evening Palmers Green came into my hut with an ashen face, his thin hair straggling from under his cap, his fatigues drooping round him like ectoplasm. In his shaking hand, the notice, ripped hurriedly from the board. With a smothered cough he handed it to me. Someone had drawn an enormous, detailed, erect penis, plus optimistically splendid appendages, and under it, in block letters, had printed, WE WANT TO SCREW NOT SING! I tore it up and shoved it in the stove.

'They're animals,' said Palmers Green hopelessly, 'simply animals, there's nothing you can do with people like that. Beasts, that's all. What's the use of trying to help people in life, to bring a little cheer into their lives, what's the use, I ask you?' He was distressed and near to tears as he ambled miserably across the hut. I was forced to follow him for comfort.

'It's a joke, really . . . you see. We'll put up another tomorrow.'

'They won't care. They are all obscene. It's hopeless. They'll take over the world one day, you see if I'm right.'

I leant against the door-post. 'We'll try again. Just give it time.'

He wandered down the steps. 'In my hut, you know, they all call me . . .' he screwed up his eyes and I thought he was going to cry, but they unscrewed and he said, 'Hilda.' We stood in helpless silence looking at a row of fire buckets. 'I don't know why,' he said, almost to himself, 'I try to do what I can, but it is difficult. The Morse, the marching . . . I do my best. It's just not something I'm used to at my age. Difficult to look neat in this stuff too, isn't it? Do you know,' he pulled out a handkerchief, and blew his nose hard, 'do you know, I haven't even whistled since I got here, not a note, and I was always so full of melody, little snatches here and there, really very cheery, but I just haven't the heart these days.' He shoved his handkerchief back and tried to cram the wispy hair under his cap. 'You've been very kind, very kind,' he tried a wan smile. 'I did say "birds of a feather", didn't I? Oh well, I'll be seeing you quite a bit this coming week. Cookhouse Fatigues. The Kit Inspections, you know. I don't seem to manage very well.'

I watched him wander sadly down the track in the soft June evening. It had rained all afternoon but now the sun was out, glistening in the puddles, the tin roofs of the huts shone like silver paper. Gooley and a skinny man we called Worms, because he was so thin and ate faster and more than anyone else, came down the hill. Gooley threw an affectionate arm round my shoulders.

'Come on, Toff. I'll treat you to a bromide tea. Me auntie sent a postal order yesterday.'

We walked off together, avoiding the puddles because of our polished boots, and Worms made us laugh because he said that even if they did put bromide in the tea he still felt horny every morning and woke up with an erection like a tent pole. I wondered what Palmers Green would have thought of that.

The frozen Argentinian liver came in blocks eighteen inches long and five square. It had the texture of iced sand with veins running through it like string.

This we cut into slices, tipped into boiling cauldrons, fished out after fifteen minutes, slapped into shallow tins, twenty to each, smothered in what was euphemistically called gravy, and bunged in the ovens. Then we had our breakfasts. Up since five-thirty, we ate fried eggs, left-over-potatoes, bread and marge and a mug of tea in the peace of the empty Mess Hall. A moment of luxury. I only ate liver once, ever. At seven on the dot the Army arrived, clattering blearily into the Mess, faces pink from shaving, hair, or what remained of it, sleeked with water or Brylcreem, mugs and eating-irons clutched in their fists.

We shoved the liver tins on to each table, the Daddies Sauce, the margarine-bread, and filled the mugs with bromide tea as the noise of a cattle fair mounted. For all the disadvantages of working in the cookhouse, there were excellent advantages, I found. We fed better than the others most of the time, avoided the misery of Roll Call, kit inspections and the general daily chores of the barrack room life. We also missed out on Drill for a while, which, even though I liked it, was a bit of a relief.

But best of all, I was able to avoid the absolute terror of motor bikes. This was a hazard which I had not been expecting at all. Gas, bombs, bullets, mud and discomfort, all these. But never for one single split second did it ever occur to me that I should have to sit astride a giant motorcycle and learn, not only how to drive it, but how to care for its incomprehensible guts as well. My complete lack of coordination rendered the whole enterprise of riding a bike into something as dangerous and unreasonable as crossing Niagara Falls on a rope. I could seldom start it, and the only way I could stop it was by falling off as gracefully as possible. I developed the agility of a tumbler.

For all these reasons I was happy in the cookhouse even though the work was hard, dirty and often long. But it at least sped time along and kept our minds off the submerged wreck of fear which lay just below our fragile barque of courage. The Draft. Sometimes we dared to speak of it . . . but not often. A rumour would sometimes weave a thread of chill vapour into our overtly medical conversations. We were going to Madagascar, to Iceland, to Singapore; improbably far away places, never, alas, Europe. For that was long since sealed off from us. Once someone said that they had seen hundreds of sun helmets in the Q.M's store hidden under blankets. Which meant the Tropics for certain. Africa maybe . . . even, God help us all, India! Panic, always latent, surged within each breast, until someone mentioned tits or farts and then we relaxed back into laughter, instantly banishing Madagascar.

Washing up in the tin-wash was so unpleasant that it was ranked as a punishment for anyone slack enough to have a dirty bolt to his rifle, an unblacked-out window, or a messy kit inspection. Standing at the concrete sinks, arms deep in filthy, greasy water, hands red from corrosive soda, feet soaked from the spilled swill and muck on the floors beneath us, it ranked high as disagreeable. I saw poor Palmers Green clonking and scrubbing away there, his thin hair limp with sweat, his smile, when he saw me, tremulous, his elbows raw-boned, going up and down like a wooden monkey's. For me, there was a certain satisfaction to be gained by wiping clean a battered two-handled tin, once foul with grease and caught liver or frozen kidneys, and polishing it into a brilliant shining mirror. One always felt that it might be the one to come to one's own table the next day. It never was. But one hoped. Without hope there was not the slightest possibility of surviving those initial twenty-five weeks. Some did not.

One morning, while finishing off the last of the fried bread, a man crashed into the Mess looking as if he had been hit by a falling wall. Hair staring, shirt-tails flapping, trousers, clenched in two anguished fists, sagging round his knees, braces flying like hoops, he stood barefoot, shocked. We stood up in mute surprise. He was handed a mug of tea which he waved aside and slumped on to a bench. 'There's a geezer hanging in the pisshouse.'

In the already warming June sunlight an aimless huddle of men stood about outside the latrines waiting, presumably, for Authority to arrive and settle the business. Half dressed, some with toothbrushes or washing bags, they shifted from foot to foot in the embarrassed silence reserved for death. The door of No. 8 was wide open. In the vivid shaft of sunlight which illuminated the cubicle like a pin spot, hung a man. Dressed in striped pyjamas, head on his chest, one leg twisted cruelly in the pan, the other almost kneeling on the filthy floor, a stretched figure of supplication. The cord from the cistern was as tight as a bow-string, buried deep into his livid neck, forcing his fat tongue through blue lips in a final obscene gesture at the insult of life. His hands swung gently, a ring glittered. He had messed himself. I turned suddenly away and pushed through the silent herd with its toothbrushes and washbags. Hunched against a brick wall I fought a desperate, and successful, battle to retain my breakfast. Heaving and retching, fighting down the rising nausea, I pressed my face into the rough, warm bricks. After a while it started to subside. I gasped for breath, wiping my snotty nose and the cascading tears of effort from my cheeks. In a blurred instant I saw the worried, caring face of Gooley. Gently he put out a hand and patted my shoulder.

'Silly boy, you was. You shouldn't have looked, you know. You shouldn't have looked.'

I shook my head hopelessly, brushing the muck from my face with a shaking hand. I knew damn well I shouldn't have looked. It was Palmers Green.

We prepared for the funeral with all the excitements and terrors of a First Night. Books were honed to a brilliance never before seen, even on Colonel's Inspection, badges glittered, trousers were creased like knife blades. Soap rubbed down the inside of the crease, and then ironed hard, belts blancoed, brasses shining like a Whitbread's dray horse. We were determined to do our first official Show as well as possible and to give the deceased a far better send off than he had ever had welcome.

They had asked for volunteers. Palmers Green's family, shocked and dazed, one presumed, demanded his body to be returned to them in London. Pall bearers, six, were to cart the coffin from Richmond Station along the platform to the London train. I was first, this time because of Palmers Green and the odd, unwanted bond which he had forced upon me. Tilly and Gooley came in also when they knew I was on, and a small, neat, cherubic youth called Derek. His had been one of the few signatures on our ill fated notice for the concert party, and it had written beside his name, 'Dancing, acrobatics, splits, etc.' With his wide blue eyes, pink complexion, soft blond hair, delicate voice and pleasantly defined figure, he had become a fairly frequent visitor to the Sergeants' Mess up the hill, and so no one dared to openly insult him. Behind his back was a different matter altogether. But it was felt that one false step or word with this angelic, helpless, little fellow would lead straight to a Madagascar posting or anywhere else east of Suez. Without any questions. So he was tolerated. Just about. He never got into the tin-wash or did Pack Drill at the double or anything disagreeable. We were still two short, and finally we were lucky to get Piper, who was a Christian Scientist and said that death was all in the mind so he didn't care much for the poor sod and he ought to have a fitting farewell. They were matched for height and we were off most duties for rehearsals.

For a couple of days we did our polishing and preparing, had a sort of frantic dummy run with an empty pine coffin round the Drill Yard, and one bright afternoon were loaded on to a 15 cwt truck, with Palmers Green lying boxed at our feet.

At the station, among a little group of curious citizens, there were two pale women in black, clutching handkerchiefs. The sisters from Hammersmith come to conduct him home. The coffin was hastily covered with an immense Union Jack, for which we were quite unprepared, having humped an unadorned coffin round on our shoulders during the rehearsals. On top of this, even more worrying, was placed a wreath of yellow flowers, presumably from the Royal Corps of Signals, although I couldn't see the writing on the flapping label. To add to our growing unease, sparkling away in brass and blanco in the hot sun, we became aware that there was a small flight of steps to be negotiated, and we hadn't actually rehearsed steps. However, out of sight of the mourning sisters, and without a great deal of elegance, Palmers Green was loaded on to our brave young shoulders. We immediately sagged and buckled at the knees. The shortest were in the front, Derek on the right, Grimm on the left, in the middle Gooley and Piper, behind, as we were marginally taller and therefore presumed, inaccurately, to be stronger, Tilly and myself supporting the head part of the coffin. The heaviest we supposed, and envied Derek and Grimm having only the shins and feet, so to speak, to carry.

It was an uneven stagger which brought Palmers Green towards the steps and his black clad relations from Hammersmith; he seemed rather small for his coffin. Slid about a bit, up and down it seemed, as we angled him upwards. Gooley cursing under his breath, Tilly muttering 'Steady, lads, steady,' as if we were at sea, and the sweat beading under our caps, trickling into the serge of our uniforms. Mercifully we negotiated the steps, shoulders aching, legs slightly splayed, arms locked in desperate attachment to the ever increasing weight of our lost companion. 'It's de wind,' said Gooley under his breath, and trying to catch it, 'dey say dey always blow up wid de wind after a few days. Sweet Mary! but he's a heavy bugger.'

Exhausted, blinded with a mist of sweat, breathless, we reached the entrance to the platform and started down the endless vista to the Guard's Van. Right at the end of the train, practically as far away as York. The escort marched glitteringly ahead of us, the draggle of people, plus the two black women with their handkerchiefs, trailed along on either side and then a sudden gust of wind riffled the immense Union Jack causing it to whip about like the sail of a yacht in a force nine gale. Tilly and I, separated as we were by the apparently enormous bulk of the coffin, could only see to our immediate left or, in his case, right, but we did hear the smothered cry from Derek in the front as he stumbled suddenly, swirled about in the Union Jack. We felt, all too helplessly, the wild lurch of our possession, saw the yellow wreath slither out of sight, the flag cascade in a shimmer of red, white and blue about our feet, and in spite of desperate struggles on the part of all the rest of us, Palmers Green slid inexorably, and not ungracefully, to his feet, almost upright, on the wide platform. Derek lay wrapped in the colours, with Grimm beside him and the wreath between them. I don't know what happened to the mourners. The escort broke formation and rushed to our assistance, Derek was on his feet, the flag whipped out of sight, the coffin reverently placed back on our aching shoulders and with squint caps, sweat coursing, and a Lance Corporal carrying the wreath like a suitcase we made the Guard's Van and bundled our load into the more experts hands of the L.N.E.R. An ignominious attempt at chivalry.

Riding back to Camp in the 15 cwt, we smoked nervously, wondering if we would be put on a charge or what exactly would happen. Derek was on the point of collapse most of the way, and Grimm had to bawl at him to 'belt up' at least three times before he subsided into hiccups.

'It was that bloody flag,' he said in between trying to hold his breath and count to ten as Gooley had told him. 'Whipped round my face, I couldn't see a thing, not a bloody thing, dears. Smothered I was, simply smothered. I wouldn't have done it on purpose, you all know that. I just buckled and went over. Oh the shame of it, and I've always been able to manage my skirts.' But we were all too exhausted to care. What kind of punishment was there for dropping a full coffin, we wondered? All that actually happened was that we got a severe dressing down about being slack, weak, and a disgrace to the Royal Corps of Signals from the R.S.M., who finally admonished us into shame by saying that it was the last time we'd ever be entrusted to carry a coffin again in public. Which made us wonder just how many more he was envisaging during our stay.

CHAPTER TWO

Boredom, as my father had prophesied, began to leak into life, indeed into all our lives, after a few weeks. Sitting about in the grey NAAFI with a slab of sodden cake and diluted coffee, at ringed tables under a flat light made us all depressed and stale and it was during one of these deathly evenings, with someone bashing out Ivor Novello medleys at the upright piano in the corner, that Gooley had the bright thought of starting up the abandoned concert party idea. So the notice was, once again, put up on the board and this time, to our surprised delight, or mine at any rate, we got a much better haul and auditions were started round the Upright every free evening. It seemed that almost everyone in the camp had discovered a latent talent for singing endless versions of 'I'll Walk Beside You', 'Because' and 'Ave Maria'. In stultified misery we heard them all and realised that these splendid tenors, baritones and hog-callers would only compound the boredom, not relieve it. And after one or two extra talents like conjuring, impersonations, and when Derek of the cortège had given us some pretty fancy high kicks and a couple of agonized splits, which hurt him, because, as he pointed out, he was 'not in practice', we settled for a Dramatic Society instead.

At the end of June I was promoted to Lance Corporal. And smirked with astonished pride. Someone seemed to think that I was at least showing signs of something, perhaps in leadership if not in Morse or the rest of the required activities. Slightly weighed down with the importance of my chevroned arms, I moved into the small cubicle at the end of the hut with a real bed, and assumed the responsibilities, unwittingly, for the entire Squad Hut. I lost no time in informing my father on a postcard of Richmond Castle, in heavy pencil, stiff with exclamation marks of false surprise. Overstating as usual.

The Dramatic Society flourished. We started off with a thriller, Patrick Hamilton's 'Rope'. Fairly easy since it had one set and only two parts for women, and a splendid part for me. The women's parts were willingly filled by ladies from the Officers' Quarters up the hill outside the camp who were just as bored with the Yorkshire moors as we were, and enjoyed their evenings, bringing all their friends, their knitting, thermos flasks of tea or coffee and sandwiches, imbuing the whole business with the atmosphere of a mixed Women's Institute.

We even managed a small orchestra for the intervals and the overture. Instruments were sent for from home, band parts scored, and before you could say 'Curtain Up' we were off. The play was a whacking success, so much so that we had to play it for four nights instead of only one, and travelled it about the county to less fortunate companions in arms. Bundled into trucks, with our costumes in kitbags and the band parts of 'Roses of Picardy' and 'Me and My Girl: Selections', we covered Yorkshire. There was usually a party in an Officers' Mess afterwards, with sausage rolls and small gins and limes, and warming congratulations for boosting the morale, which pleased us since the main object had been to boost our own. However, ambition had been roused and was not about to be quenched easily. I decided on another play, and before the course was over we presented a more ambitious effort in Elmer Rice's 'Judgement Day', which was an even greater success. It hardly felt like being in the army at all. If this was what it could be like, if I was crafty, I'd perhaps never have to go to Madagascar or Singapore, but might just manage to stay put and boost morale. After all, I reasoned happily, someone had to do it, why not me?

But that sort of idiocy came to an abrupt end when Tilly and I and a couple of others were sent for to be interviewed as officer material. Worriedly we cleaned and polished and blancoed days before the event, and one hot morning were summoned to our inquisition. Tilly, I noticed with regret, sparkled like a Jewish wedding. I felt sure that he would pass, he was so determined, and that I'd probably be set aside, for I looked anything but chic in my battledress, even though my brasses shone like bright deeds.

A large horseshoe table; about six or seven officers. One very tall and elegant, who made little paper darts most of the time; three or four with tabs and redder faces; and another who sat at the side of the table, crouched over his papers, wearing rimless glasses looking like Himmler's aunt. I was last to be called, on account of being 'V'. Tilly was second last and came out grim and soldierly; he gave such a smashing salute as he left the room that I feared he must have hurt himself. He about-turned and marched blindly past me, giving me no clues whatever. Sick with apprehension, I entered. There was a lot of tittle tattle over my papers; my schooling, family background, and all the rest. The thing which seemed to stick in their craws was the unacceptable fact that I had been an actor. This, I gathered, was a sign of an unstable temperament. The elegant officer who stopped making paper darts for a second asked me what I had done in London in the theatre and looked completely blank until I mentioned 'Diversion' at Wyndhams. At this he seemed to recognise something far away across the room and, staring into the breeze-block wall, he said mildly that he didn't remember seeing me. I was not fool enough not to realise that this little pleasantry could be a trap: they did this kind of thing, I had been told, to try and throw you off kilter and see your reactions. Mine, I thought, were perfectly reasonable.

'Well . . . I was in it . . . but it wasn't much. I had a few lines in a couple of numbers and a bit of a song in a kilt.'

He looked sadly at his collection of darts. 'Doesn't ring a bell.'

'Well, I don't suppose it would, Sir, I was a sort of chorus boy really.'

A sudden hush. A red-tabbed one cleared his throat and echoed 'chorus boy' as if I had said 'child molester'. I felt the earth slipping away very gradually. Chorus boys, even I could see that, were probably not officer material.

I tried to repair. 'A glorified chorus boy; not really a dancer or anything like that, you know . . .' ending helplessly.

But no one did know. They leant together and muttered away. Eventually another one, with red tabs but a younger face, asked about 'Rope' and 'Judgement Day', to my astonishment. Until I realised that everything I had ever done in my life was set down in the papers before them. There was a murmuring about 'jolly good show, boosting morale' – how that phrase cropped up with them all the time – and 'organizing powers'. My heart lifted a little and the languid officer folded another dart.

Suddenly a voice barked at me from Left Field.

'Nothing to it, of course; acting.' He was older than the others, very red-tabbed, probably a General.

'No, Sir, not really.'

'Acting's easy stuff. Girls do it.'

'Yes, Sir.' Agree with him. Clearly he's General Public.

'Done it meself . . . so I know. It's the organisation that counts.'

'Yes, Sir, that's really very hard . . .'

'Did both, you know, so I know what I'm talking about. Heard of "Aladdin"?'

'Yes, Sir.'

'Bloody good show. Did that.'

The languid officer was stilled with deference. 'You did, Sir?'

He beamed round the table having caught their full attention. 'Wrote it, played Widow Twankey, and produced it, what! Marvellous fun.'

Everyone smiled politely and he turned his jealous eyes back to me. 'Boosted morale no end, frightfully good show. Tickled 'em pink. Amritsar, 1926.'

'It must have been marvellous, Sir.'

'But acting's all twaddle, anyone can do it.'

'Yes, Sir, of course.'

For a moment he glowered at me and then barked: 'Your father!' Father, for God's sake, what about him?

'Yes, Sir?' Eager and with a pleasant filial smile.

'Art editor of *The Times*, I believe. It says so on your papers.'

'Yes, Sir.'

'Well, what exactly does the art editor do? I mean, that is to say, what is the art editor?'

'He's responsible for the picture page, all the photographs, and the arts page generally . . .'

'Takes them himself, does he? Snaps, that sort of thing?'

'Yes of course, Sir, but naturally he has hundreds of photographers of his own.'

'Naturally,' the voice was ice.

Hasten in to correct.

'He selects the photographs for the News . . . landscapes . . . all those pictures of Sussex and Scotland . . . the half-page on Saturdays. Perhaps, Sir, you saw one he did of the Isle of Wight from Ashdown Forest. It was infra-red . . .'

The elegant officer folded, very carefully, another paper dart.

'Infra-red?'

'Yes, Sir; actually he managed to save a great deal of the South Coast from ribbon-development, from things like Peacehaven . . . you know . . .'

I was talking far too much, and perhaps he liked Peacehaven. Impatience eddied in the air like a bad odour. Time was running out . . . the elegant officer gave a little laugh and said: 'All rather high quality stuff, General . . . not *Men*

Only.' There was polite laughter, and throats were cleared. I lied swiftly.

'Of course he knows all the other editors, you know; they er . . . work together really . . .'

The General looked up from my folder which he was in the act of closing gently. Like a curtain falling slowly on a play.

'Does he, indeed? Knows the editors? Of *Men Only* as well? *The Times?*'

'It's all journalism after all, Sir, they all know each other.'

'I know that!'

I stood stiffly to attention, the elegant officer leant back in his wooden chair. The General stroked his nose.

'Perhaps *The Times* might care to send us a few snaps, shall we say? To cheer up the Mess, what? Something half-page size . . . that sort of thing?'

Don't be over eager. State a fact.

'Yes, Sir, I'm sure.'

'But not landscapes of course . . . ha ha ha . . . something a little more, can we say, inspiring?'

'Of course, Sir.' Lie as hard as you can and hope to God that your unsuspecting father will come to your assistance. This is the point of no return.

Shortly afterwards I was dismissed, threw a correct salute, about-turned under the stone eyes of the RSM, and left the room, just as a small paper dart skimmed through the air and plummeted against the windows.

That evening, from a call-box outside the NAAFI, reversing the charges, I telephoned my father.

'You do know the editor of *Men Only*, don't you?'

'No.'

'Well, could you arrange to send me, oh, something like a dozen, quite big, photos of nude women? But quickly . . .'

'For your Mess?'

'No, for the Officers' Mess. I've just had my interview for an OCTU.'

The line crackled for a few seconds. 'I see.'

'Quite large, you know. And coloured if you can.'

'I'll do what I can. What is *Men Only?*'

Fourteen anxious days later Tilly and I and one other fellow saw our names on the board stating that from such and such a date were were now Officer Cadets and should put-up our white-tabs forthwith.

My father had been as good, as they say, as his word.

I had just finished Gooley's weekly letter to Kitty. It had become a firm routine over the weeks, and I sometimes felt that I knew Kitty almost as well as he did himself. It was a very intimate relationship, his and mine, for in charging me with the task of writing his passions to Cork and the girl he loved, he had placed himself confidently in my hands. In fact, after a time he simply indicated more or less what he wanted to tell her that week, and left me cheerfully to find the words (which I did, with the aid of the *Oxford Book of Modern Verse*), most of which he didn't know himself, and many of which I felt pretty sure Kitty wouldn't know either. However, he was always filled with self-pride when I read them back to him and sat in stiff amazed delight, shaking his cropped head, bemused, often moved to the point of tears.

This latest letter was the cruncher, for it was the Proposal Letter and we had spent some considerable time on its composition. He was determined that it should not sound daft, and that it should be more businesslike than poetical. 'Her Dad owns a pub, he's no fool, you know . . . Its not de pub I'm after, Toff, it's de daughter . . . get that straight and clear.' He insisted on the final lines himself, choosing, 'Be assured of my strick intentions, my darling girl, Kitty, from your respectful, hoping-to-be-accepted-husband, Patrick Gooley.' He scrawled a signature, the only thing he could actually write with any authority, and read it through slowly and carefully.

'Dat's beautiful!'

'I don't know why you don't write your own letters, for God's sake.'

'I just haven't de touch, and anyway she enjoys your letters more dan mine, she says so every time. Dat's de only ting dat worries me . . . when I leave here she'll not ge gettin' any letters and she'll likely be expecting me to talk like you write, and dat's going to be a bugger, I can tell you.' He folded the letter carefully, put it into the envelope and, with his fat tongue sticking out, laboriously printed, in his own hand, the address.

I folded my arms behind my head and looked up at the ceiling: there was a dry moth in a cobweb.

'Gooley. When you hit that old woman on the head, that time, with the iron, what did you feel? Do you remember?'

He shook his head looking vaguely worried.

'Nothing?'

'Well . . I was shit scared dey'd hear her screeching away . . . you know . . .'

'Did you think that you'd killed her? Or could have?'

'Naw! Wasn't more dan a little tap-like . . . couple of little taps . . . just to keep her quiet, you see. It was her or me, you know, and she was a ould bitch.'

'No remorse?'

'What's dat den?' He looked blank.

'Well, it didn't worry you, afterwards, I mean?'

'Mary, no! You know? I never even mentioned it on me rosary . . . not one bead did she get from me . . . after all it's her as got me into dis bloody ould army, isn't it?' He slid Kitty's letter carefully into his breast pocket, and thumped my knee. 'What's up wid you? Dere's someting worrying youse . . .'

'Well . . . the other day, you know when we were up on the exercise in the woods . . . with the dummy ammo that leaves a stain, and I got Ernie Basset in the chest . . .'

Gooley cuddled his knees happily. 'Ah wid dat last little shot our side won, didn't it den?'

'Yes, we won. But, you know I really thought that I *had* shot Basset. I thought it was real suddenly.' I could see by his eyes that he didn't know what the hell I was talking about, and I knew that I would not be able to make him understand.

'But it was just an ould exercise! It was like a game is all! What's dere to upset you about dat den?'

'It suddenly didn't seem to be a game, is what I mean. I felt sick, do you know that? When Basset just fell forward on his face out of that bush, I was sure he was dead and that I had killed him. I can't get it out of my mind, Gooley.'

He sighed with kindness, impatience and incomprehension. 'Youse daft, Toff.' He got up and went to the door of the cubicle. 'It was just de same as me and de ould woman, Toff. It's dem or you. Nothing to it,' and patting his breast pocket with the letter inside, he winked his wink and was gone.

Somewhere, buried under layers of romantic nonsense, I knew that he was right; it *was* just an old exercise, I had been on many before, but none had had this effect on me. Sitting up there in the little wood that day I was calm, serene, detached, curiously watching an ants' nest which I had thoughtlessly disturbed with a stick. I heard someone suddenly crackle through bracken, the wispy whisper of fronds against a body; heard the heavy breathing, as if that person had been running a long way; heard the little groan of effort as it buried itself into some bushes not far in front of me; saw a branch tremble violently, and then become still. Through the fretted leaves a gleam of sunlight flickered through the slender trees, glanced off a steel helmet. He was one of the enemy side; our side wore forage caps. Quite suddenly, for no apparent reason, my mouth went dry and I was frightened. Perhaps it was his almost tangible fear coming across the little clearing, perhaps the silence suddenly of the wood; still, still. Away down on the road I could faintly hear the voices of the others who had dropped out and would be sprawled about smoking. Apparently we were the last two left unaccounted for. I glanced at the magazine of my rifle. Two bullets left. I hunched back silently into the bole of a tree, bracken screening me. I think I stopped breathing.

And then I saw him. Cautiously he raised his pale helmeted face from the bush, and blindly looked about him, straight at me but unseeing. He was sweating with effort, or fear, for fear emanated from him like mist. He moved very slowly, as someone in a dream. His helmet shone in the filtered sun. He gave a little grunt of satisfaction that he was safe, and I watched as he quietly, carefully, secured his position, in the springing branches of the elder bush, lowering his gun and slowly wiping his nose with the back of his hand. My heart thudding, my body tense, I raised my gun and got him securely in my sights. A bellow of distant laughter came from the road, he instantly pulled up his gun and stiffened. I saw the clean steel of the muzzle ring, the black hole from which his bullet would speed, the trickle of sweat running down his jaw beading under his chin. For seconds we faced each other, then he relaxed a little, the muzzle dipped, he looked up into the trees and I shot him.

The report of the rifle shattered the wood and smashed my shoulder into the tree behind me. A bird went off chittering through the branches. He opened his eyes with wide surprise, his mouth in a soundless cry, and pitched forward on to his face among the branches. For a second I sat hunched, frozen with horror. It was only when he started to move that I started to shake. I recognised him immediately, Ernie Basset with red hair from H Hut. In the middle of his chest a large crimson stain from my killing bullet. He looked down at it with some consternation, and then called out to the wood loudly: 'You sod! You got me! Where are you?' Finding some hidden reserve I scrambled to my feet, surprising him, and helped him up. We walked through the trees together arm in arm. 'Didn't know you was there,' he said. 'Gave me a terrible shock, right on it did! Just like the real thing. Gave you a bloody good un, didn't I? Thought I'd lost you down by the wall there . . . Jeese, quite a thrill that . . .'

When I came to light his squashed cigarette, my hand was still shaking, and he laughed and held it firm in his two, his rifle clutched between his knees. 'Quite a little thrill,' he said.

That evening I stayed in my cubicle instead of trailing over to the NAAFI for watered coffee. It was not so much the fact that I had killed Ernie Basset which upset me, for upset I certainly was, it was the clear and blinding fact, which was uppermost in my mind, and which shocked me so deeply, that I had actually wanted to kill him. And I had enjoyed doing so, I, who never trod on a snail if I could help it, never robbed a nest of eggs, couldn't remove a hook from a fish, never said boo to a bloody goose even, had determinedly, and with pleasure, apparently, taken a man's life. Him or me. And it wasn't going to be me.

This small revelation of self knowledge nagged at me like a stone in a shoe. And if frightened me. Where had it come from, this passion, this cool determination, this almost-pleasure in an action so wildly perverse in a very late developer?

At nineteen I still behaved like a slightly retarded fifteen. It was, however, true that I was no longer a virgin. That had been seen to a year before by a slightly flaccid girl I met at Art School who was a couple of years older than I. Heavy breasted, big bottomed, with fair hair in earphones curled round her face, beads clattering between the mammoth gourds slung under her hand-printed cheese-cloth blouse, her square toes thrusting through holes in her sandals, she assaulted me, for I was too far gone on a quart and a half of light ale to do more than feebly wave my hands as she pulled down my trousers, on a very prickly rush mat in front of a plopping gas fire one evening in her so-called studio at the top of a house in Fulham.

The whole event, due to the quart and a half of ale, was all a bit hazy. I was shocked at first, but helpless, waving useless hands in the air like an overturned beetle, and then witless with terror as first the beads, the cheese-cloth blouse, the tweed skirt and a pair of yellow knickers flew about the room and she deliberately lowered herself on to my limp body spread, like a sacrifice, on the rush matting. I fought for breath. The heat from the gas fire roasting my purpling face. She raised two hefty arms and tugged at the earphones, releasing a cataract of heavy blond hair about my head like a soap-smelling tent. Confronted, as I was, with a vast black triangle only inches from my chest, I knew that I was helplessly in the hands of a cheat, hands which none the less were apparently expert, coaxing, and determined. Lost in that vast hemisphere of fleshy thighs, I orbited Mars, the Moon, Saturn and Venus, before finally coming back to earth, exhausted, sweating, blue in the face and smothered by her licking tongue, a maze of dyed fair hair, and, for some unexplained reason, most of my cardigan.

Later, after she had hauled herself off me, and padded off to her bathroom singing happily at the top of her voice as if she had just done the washing up, which in effect she had, I finished off the last of the ale, pulled up my trousers and staggered blindly about the room wondering how to get out. Her singing mingled with running taps and the flushing of the lavatory, and then she was back in the canvas-crowded room, cheerful as a bee, and told me to go and freshen up which I did, shying away from the scarlet, lopsided face I saw in the mirror over the washbowl. So that was what sex was like? Well, it was pretty good while it actually happened; it was the now part which was not so delightful.

She said her name was Constance, and laughed disdainfully as if she never could be, and told me to call her Kiki and was it the first time for me? Because she guessed it was – not that she had given me much chance anyway to prove if it had been or not. When I assented, bravely I thought, she stroked my face with stubby fingered hands, swilled the dregs of my beer and said that she'd had her eye on me ever since the play at the end of the last term. I looked at her blankly and with faint dislike which she mistook for curiosity, so she took my limp hand and pressed a kiss on my cheek. 'Those tights! In "The Miller and His Men", last term, remember?'

Repelled, but fascinated, stoat with the rabbit stuff, I returned to the ample thighs and arms of my two-toned mistress in much the same way that one returns to a restaurant or an hotel. Because you know the service and they know you.

But one day she told me, sadly, just before the lights went down for a Judy Garland film at the Royal Court in Sloane Square, that her special friend was coming back from a business trip to Morocco, and that since he was a Swede, very strong, and five years older than I was, it might be tactful to keep out of the way for a while. Which I found to my surprise I accepted with almost unseemly alacrity. She was rather expensive anyway. And heavy to move about.

And so, apart from friendly little waves across Class, and stolen, rather smothered kisses and fumbles in the lockers, we drifted apart comfortably and I went on with my interrupted journey towards the theatre. The April sprig, the late developer, was starting to put out leaves, of a sort.

But Ernie Basset, and all that he stood for, was something very different, and something which shocked me deeply. After all, sex was what everyone did, or had. But killing a man, even with a dummy bullet, and finding almost the same pleasure in release at his death, was both frightening and surely wrong?

Hunched on my blanketed bed, staring worriedly at the knot holes in the floor I began to realise, after a long time, that this was really what war was about. Killing each other. Simple as that. Him or me, you or him, it had never remotely occurred to me before. Now that it did, I would have to come to terms with it pretty quickly and put aside the romantic notions I had so firmly cherished. Now I could perhaps really understand Sassoon, Owen and the rest, and one day, not so far distant it would appear, I would have to use a real bullet against a real man, and that would be the final test of growing up, which I had delayed so long. I would put the thought of that aside until it actually came to pass. But of one thing I was perfectly certain. That when it came, I would be able to do it. It terrified me far more than it gave me courage.

Every night before going to sleep, practically without fail, I mumbled silently my prayers. A firm relic of a swiftly fading childhood. It was a sort of charm thing, rather than a religious thing. Habit rather than faith. But it also comforted me greatly, and I still do it. No set prayer, a familiar pattern of words only, beginning with 'God Bless Mother, Father, Elizabeth, Gareth . . .' and so on down to the dog. Sometimes, over-tired, exhausted from route marching, or work in the cookhouse, or even just mildly pissed on NAAFI beer I slid, without awareness, into a much older prayer which bubbled from my subconscious like a meadow spring:

'Gentle Jesus, meek and mild,
Look upon a little child,
Pity my simplicity,
Suffer me to come to Thee.'

It went on for a bit longer but I had usually, by that time, fallen asleep. Now, shuffling about my six foot by four foot cubicle, changing my boots for gym shoes in order to go over to the NAAFI for a beer, I knew that all that simplicity stuff was bunk. Innocence was melting around me like snow in the heat of the sun. I could no longer ever say that absurdly childish prayer again; all that had gone. Exit my simplicity more like. Not pity. Kiki, Palmers Green, now Ernie Basset, Innocence. Odd, I thought, growing up seems to be all exits.

Jammed at a corner table under the sagging 'Night Train to Holyhead', with a beer, I opened my much abused blue notebook and, heading the first clean page with the title 'Man in the Bush', I wrote my first poem for Vida. Straight off, in one ordered series of line and words, without corrections or additions or pencil lickings, it all fell into clean, simple shape. My muse had entered at last. I had thought that she would arrive with a crash of thunder, in a blaze of glittering light, a golden pen in one hand, my inspiration in the other. But that is not how it happens at all. As someone has said, when she comes, she comes stealing in, gently, softly, almost shyly, and taking your hand she says: 'Come and look! I have got something I want you to see.' And I had. I hoped that Vida would like the result.

Just before Lights Out, sloshing through soapy swill of the Ablutions, Gooley and his chum Worms, towels over their shoulders, washbags swinging, caught me up and we walked across the square to our hut. Gooley slung his arm round my shoulder.

'Are you better now, Toff? Was you writin' to your Ma about your problems den all dat time in de corner dere?'

'No. I wrote a poem.'

He looked patient. 'What for? A pome, for de love of God!'

'A girl I know in London.'

'Ah. A girl. Like for Kitty . . . dat sort of stuff, fancy?'

'Not very fancy, it was about killing Ernie Basset.'

'For de love of God! She'll love dat for sure. Have you told Ernie? He'd piss hisself wid laughing.'

There was a leave somewhere during the course. I don't remember much about it beyond the fact that I clambered off the bus at the crossroads in the village hung about with respirators, tin hat, kit bags and haversacks, and, I seem to think, my fateful rifle. I can't be quite sure but I have a vivid picture of my happy mother proudly marching along beside me with it slung over her shoulder, and my sister Elizabeth and Elsie, the Rubens shepherdess, humping along cheerfully, proudly, with bits and pieces of army equipment between them, as if they were fishwives marching on Versailles. And that evening, with my father, who came back from his blitz-beleaguered office at *The Times* for the special occasion, we all went up to the King's Head where I was fêted and wined as if I had won the V.C. It was all quite moving and faintly absurd. The civilians, whose war was far more uncomfortable and dangerous than mine, were enjoying themselves. It seemed a pity to spoil the fun. But I felt not-quite-right-somehow; I didn't fit. I felt taller, everyone said that I was. The women put it down to the rations we got, and the men down to the bint, as they called it, with which we appeared as far as they were concerned anyway, to be liberally supplied. Everyone was delighted that the war had made me into a man, implying that I had returned from ten months in the trenches and the Battle of the Somme. Everything, so I began to believe, was applied to their war of twenty-two years before. I was quite unable to tell them, nor did they wish to hear if I tried, that all I had seen of a war was the inside of Catterick Camp and a few acres of the Yorkshire moors. If I had grown taller it was only because I was growing up a bit, being exercised, and living a healthy life. If anything had started to make me a man it was merely a sort of rought school life. Cosseted, isolated, cared for, taught. Nothing to do with rations or with bint.

But that's the way they wanted it to be, and so let it be. I felt strangely detached, distant, like Alice after she had swallowed one of the potions. Familiar things were smaller than I had remembered; my own room, my books, pictures, sketch books, even my clothes had shrunk. The old rowan tapping as it always had done against the window, the wardrobe door creaking open spitefully, slowly, as it always had done, all these things had the ring of familiarity but from a long distance. It was rather as if I was poking about in the room of someone I had known long ago, and then but slightly. The things, the possessions, evoked memories, but hazy ones; the person that I must once have been had gone and had left behind a not very interesting collection of inanimate objects. I handled them all with careful astonishment. The white Staffordshire pug, a paperweight of the Eiffel Tower, the snow storm now long since gone dry, the tin lay figure my Grandfather had given me, legs awry, one arm missing, head squint. I set them all back exactly where they had stood, fearful lest the owner might suddenly return and find my prying into his possessions. I could not reconcile myself to the fact that I was the owner and that this room had been, was indeed, mine. I was a stranger here; I knew, certainly, that some odd metamorphosis had taken place when, finding my old, unfamiliar bed too soft, I dragged the covers on to the floor. And slept there.

It was the same a few days later when, eager, anxious to the point of rudeness, I went up to London to meet Vida. I went in uniform because I felt strange, uncomfortable, in civilian clothes, which was another surprise. We met, as we always had in the past, outside the Warner Cinema in Leicester Square, and walked arm in arm, momentarily shy of each other, down to the Olde Vienna in Lyons Corner House, where, after all, we had said our farewells together only a few months before. But that was all changed too. The place was the same, red plush, little marble tables, papers still on sticks, gateaux and thin coffee, elderly Jews sitting silently staring unseeingly across the room to Warsaw, Berlin, Vienna. It had the crushed air of a waiting room at a Consulate.

We tried to start a conversation. I looked well, she had lost weight, what was she doing, where was I going, did I like the army, had I made friends, had she seen anyone from 'Diversion', what did she really think of her poem?

'I loved it. I told you so. I mean I told you you would write something good, didn't I?' She smoothed down the cloth with a plump, generous hand.

'You always said that war made men very odd, and it was true really. It all came at once, you know. Just as I wrote it, I didn't even have to re-write or correct much, a word here and there . . . and it was for you . . . *because* of you really.'

She bowed her head very gently and went on smoothing the table cloth slowly. 'How did it get into the *Times Lit*? Was it your father?'

'No. I sent him a copy, after I sent you yours and his secretary found it and sent it over to them without telling him. I think he was a bit shocked.'

'But pleased?' She looked worried.

'Oh yes. Especially when they sent me three guineas.'

'I didn't tell you, did I, I've taken a cottage in Wiltshire for my father and mother. It was getting a bit too noisy up in Belsize Park – all the bombs. It's very small, but I go down at weekends, and when I'm not working . . .' She stopped suddenly and started to unfasten a brooch at her neck. Her eyes were full of tears. I reached across the table and offered her my hand. She went on struggling with the brooch, a tear welled and slid down her round red-lipped face. She got it off and started to examine it as if she had just found it.

'I don't know what's happened to us. You and me. I'm shy. It's idiotic, but I'm shy. I don't know what to say . . .'

I took her hand and squeezed it hard, the brooch spun across the table and lay winking its cheap light by the coffee pot. 'I'm shy too. It's all different. Isn't it strange, nothing seems to be as it was before. It's all gone, I wonder why?'

She looked up at me with swimming eyes, and made a blind reach for the glittering paste brooch. She shrugged hopelessly. 'The war, I suppose. We blame everything on the war . . . it seems to be going on and on . . . it just seems to bugger everything up. I don't know . . .'

'It can't go on for ever, honestly. I mean, after all, I haven't even gone in yet!'

A floppy joke, she smiled wanly and refastened the brooch carelessly. 'I hope you don't have to, that's all. I hope it's over by then.'

'So do I. I'm not very good at it.'

'Really not?'

'Can't do the Morse and ride motorcycles and all that stuff.'

'Well, I don't suppose the others can write poetry, can they?'

'I can't even send dit-dit-dit-da. For God's sake.'

'What's that?' She was incurious, busy repairing the eye-black which had run.

'It's the leter V. You know, dit-dit-dit-da, Beethoven. The Victory Sign.'

'Oh that!' She was weary suddenly and snapped shut her powder compact so that the dust flew up in a little cloud between us; she blew it gently across the table and started to button her coat. 'That's a hell of a long way off,' she said. 'Come on, you'd better get the bill, the big picture starts in fifteen minutes.'

There was no Gooley to welcome me when I got back to Le Cateau Lines. Tilly was there, smirking and strutting about, and old Worms who had had an exhausting time dipping his wick, as he called it, all over Wimbledon, Wandsworth and Battersea Park, but Gooley, my first real mate, had gone, as he had always promised he would from the first time we met in the train up from King's Cross. I felt a hard thrust of despair. Leave had been gloomy enough, and now with no one to laugh at the miseries of civilian life, and make comparisons in our attitudes and points of view, the future looked glum indeed. There was still a long time to go until February when the course ended. My cubicle was dank, and dusty. The *Times* calendar squint on the wall, the leave dates blocked in. I unblocked them, in so far as I blacked them out. It was over, that part, and now I settled down to the following months with something akin to despair.

I remembered our last night, Gooley and I, together in here, on the eve of our first leave. After the almost euphoric hysteria of packing kit-bags, polishing boots and brasses, and handing in the bits of equipment we would not be taking away, he came and joined me, sprawling, cigarette in mouth, across my bed.

'Who can tell, boyo, who can tell when we'll meet again? After de war, Toff, and you sitting across from me at me own bar, Kitty dere pullin' de handles and bloody great jars of Guinness slopping all over de counter! Ah de bliss of it all! Mind you, so long as I play me cards right, that is . . . de pub'll be mine, and de drinks is all on de house, I can see it now. Only, one ting, Toff,' he leant up on his elbow and wagged his cigarette butt across at me seriously, 'one ting, don't you go getting yourself killed and that. It'd be a waste, a terrible, terrible waste.' I promised, in my cracked mirror, that I'd take care.

'Better chance of survivin', Toff, if you'd only stop volunteering for every damn little ting dat comes along. Hang back a little and give the Sweet Lord a little chance to see youse . . . he can't keep his eye on us all at de same time . . . he'll lose you in de crowd . . . all dat stuff about him havin' his eyes on de sparrows is all blarney, you remember dat. And you tell dem I told you so, and I'm a good Catholic boy!'

I was struggling with the cords on my kit bag and wasn't really listening to him. He yawned heavily and eased himself off the bed and shuffled towards the door. 'Hey!' he called softly, 'catch this, you bugger!' and threw something through the air towards me. I ducked and missed the catch and it slid and scattered, glinting in the harsh light from the lamp. His rosary. 'It's not for keeps, mind; you'll give it back when you comes to Cork.' He went away whistling, his hands shoved into his pockets. I never saw him again.

Now the little dusty room seemed emptier because of remembering, and I stared miserably at the calendar which still said November. Time past. Nothing seemed good; I started unpacking slowly, cigarettes, a fruit cake in a tin, Evelyn Waugh, John Donne, a pound of winter apples from home. There was a sudden commotion through the partition in the hut. People started clapping, and cheering. I was putting everything neatly away in my locker when Worms shoved open the door, his face scarlet.

'You heard, did you?'

'What?'

'The Japs.'

'What about them?'

'They've gone and bombed some bloody harbour in Hawaii. The Yanks are in!'

CHAPTER THREE

Five and a half years later I was out; my war was eventually over and after a long and uncomfortable trip from Singapore on the *Monarch of Bermuda*, filled with anticipation, relief, and a modest sense of a modest job well done, I reached my Regimental Headquarters on a dank October morning outside Guildford, where I was issued with a pork-pie hat, a cotton-tweed suit, a pair of new black shoes, a ration book and a travel warrant for Haywards Heath. Nothing could have been more prosaic, dull, or flat. Dragging a cardboard box of ill-fitting clothing to the gates on the way to the station I was accorded my last salute from a pale young Sergeant.

'Is that all there is to it?' I asked him. 'I mean, I just go?'

He smiled a weak-tea smile. 'That's all, Sir,' and then flicking a wan eye at my thin line of ribbons he added, 'thanks for the help, Sir.' He wasn't even wearing the Defence Medal. I supposed he must have been fourteen when I joined up. Help be buggered: where, I wondered, wandering down to the station, had all those years gone? A Morris Minor stopped beside me and a man asked me if I wanted a lift. I hadn't thought about a taxi – and wasn't sure of the rate of exchange even, for I had not handled English money for a long time. We drove in silence for a while. He had assumed, correctly, that I would be going to the station.

'Been away long then?' His voice was kind, not curious.

'Not long. A couple of years.'

A woman at a crossing suddenly slapped her child, shook it angrily, and then pushed her pram hurriedly over the road.

'You'll see some changes here then, after two years.'

'I expect so.'

'People are fed up really. Can't blame them, can you? A war's a war. They don't know what to do with the peace now they've got it. All at sixes and sevens.'

So, I thought, am I. What lies ahead for me now? I don't think *I'm* all that used to a peace. Two weeks left to wear the uniform which, after five years, had given me a sense of identity, then into the cotton-tweed and then what? An interview with some headmaster in December and, if I passed, a temporary job teaching at a Prep School in, of all God-forsaken places, Windlesham. Did I want to go and sit among the pines and heather of Surrey and teach scrappy Art, History and, possibly, English to a lot of stinking little boys in grey flannel suits? And supervise their cricket, I who couldn't even buckle on my pads, or tell the bails from the ball? Was this all that I was any use for now? I was, indeed, most grateful to my brother officer who had made this temporary job even possible, for he taught, or had taught, at the same school before the war, and had put in a good word for me some months ago when I had written to him, in despair, saying that I would not, after all, make the Army my career, and would be demobilised in October without any chances of a future job, and could he suggest something for me to do. I was not, I added, ever returning to the theatre; I had been away too long, it would be impossible to try to start again; and in any case I reluctantly agreed with him that he was right when he had once said, years ago in Shrivenham where we had first met, that acting was a pansy job. So the theatre was out . . . what could I do? Windlesham and Cricket?

My silence in the car was impolite. I apologised.

'I know how you feel; at sixes and sevens yourself. Married, are you?'

'No . . . not married.'

'Just as well really. So many of them didn't last the first bloody leave; all done in hysteria, really. Sad.'

At the station he pushed a packet of five cigarettes into my hand. 'Have these, not much, might cheer you up. I can get more, don't worry. Know a girl up at the Wheatsheaf.' He drove off before I could thank him.

'I can see you been in the sun, mate,' said a porter, shoving my box and bits and pieces on to the rack. 'Where was you, Alamein then?'

'Calcutta . . . Java . . . Malaya.'

'Aha! The Forgotten Army, eh?'

'No . . . no! Nothing as brave as that.'

'Well, welcome home, though you won't get sunstroke where you're going, but I expect you'll be quite glad of that. Can't stand the heat myself, brings me out in a rash.'

Friendly, kind, solicitous; traditionally English. Like the tidy little back gardens whipping past the window. Neat, dull, familiar. Here and there a row of houses rubbled by a bomb, washing fluttering, children playing in a school-yard, a red bus turning a corner. The flat October light grey; grey as the brick houses, the autumn gardens, the pearl sky above. Through the rumble of the wheels I heard, distinctly, the bull-frogs in the lily pool outside my house in Bandoeng, the clatter and clack of the evening wind in the bamboos, the soft rustle of the frangipani leaves, and the quarrelling of the parrots, swooping low over the eaves of the house, then spiralling upwards into the lavender sky, wheeling, diving, emerald turning to ebony, as they splintered and scattered hurriedly into the gleaming leaves of the great banyan tree to roost before the swift fall of night. And then the great hush which followed; the hills across the valley gently fading from deepest blue to blackest black, the sky vermillion and in that pure stillness the urgent, angry, reminding rat tat tat tat . . . tat tat . . . tat-a-ratter of a machine gun down on the perimeter wire.

It had been a goodish war, as far as wars go. I had survived, although I still wondered, slumped as I now was, looking out at Surrey, how the hell I had. Luck most probably. That and the very early training of my sensible parents and Lally, who had always insisted that one could do anything one wanted, if one worked for it; the working was the hardest part . . . the wanting came easier; but I had worked.

When the course had finished, eventually, in February, the Royal Corps of Signals, delighted with my theatrical ventures, distressed by my lack of any technical knowledge whatsoever, even after almost half a year under their very careful eyes, bundled me off, unexpected and unwanted, like a plastic netsuke in a packet of cornflakes, to the unaware Royal Artillery who, though quick to discover my talents as an actor (I started another Dramatic Society and flogged 'Journey's End', playing Raleigh yet again), were equally quick to discover that I found guns just as incomprehensible as a field telephone, only more dangerous, so they in turn handed me on to the Infantry. Even though I had learned the handbook on the Bofors gun by heart, and was able to quote it in great chunks with the passion of a Lear, I was totally unable to do anything else with the thing, dropping dummy shells all over the place and most often on other people's feet, never, as far as I remember, on my own. I constantly jammed my fingers in the auto-loader, apologising with pain and dismay all the way to the M.O.

Defeated, therefore, once again by machines, which I came to dread and loathe for the rest of my life, I arrived at an Officer Cadets' Battle School in a wet cloud-sodden camp on the top of Wrotham Hill. There the only thing required of me was self-preservation. And since I had an extremely strong instinct for that I somehow managed to survive all the assault courses, bayonet drills, cliff-climbings up and down the quarries of Kent, and swimming, or boating, across every river and stream in the county. The fact that I couldn't swim a single stroke never daunted me. I just hung on to the nearest piece of floating matter, be it a log or a fellow cadet, and got through. My worst test of this came once at a public swimming baths in Maidstone where, in full regalia, steel helmet, boots, full kit and a clonking water-bottle on the hip, I sprang off the top board knowing that I would die. From the board the pool looked like a neat rectangle – a grave – and as I plummeted down, feet first thankfully, I knew that after this I would no longer have to try, no longer have to keep up with the best in the team, no longer have to make tremendous efforts to get myself into form as a leader of men. I no longer needed to prove anything. The angels, I had no doubt that there would be angels, could care for me from there on in; I took the sensible precaution of holding my nose. I seemed to go down a very long way, and bobbed up like an empty bottle, grabbed desperately at someone's threshing legs and was towed safely to the side. The angels receded for the time being.

I couldn't swim owing to the fact that I had once, at the age of ten, been encouraged by unknowing Lally to leap off a breakwater into the sea at Seaford. She was sure that the water was shallow and that I would love it. The water was extremely deep, the tide was coming in rapidly, and I loathed it. Floating about in the pale green gloom, a large strand of seaweed drifting gently towards me, I knew that I was a gonner and was rather surprised to find myself on my stomach some miles, it seemed, along the beach, being thumped by a fat man in a red bathing suit. I brought up most of the English Channel, and stayed at the water's edge for the rest of my life. Shrimping was as far in as I ever went.

Then at school in Glasgow, dumped in a lavatory pan by mindless classmates because I spoke with the accent of a Sassenach, I was once again immersed in roaring water and left half drowned in a sea of stale urine and floating effluvia. It was all I could do after that to take a bath. But, somehow, I got through five and half years of war without once touching a field telephone, a Bofors gun, or swimming a single stroke. I wondered if that was simply luck or deception. No matter. Here I was in one piece, with all that, sadly, behind me. Sadly, strangely enough, because in spite of all the minor, and some very major, miseries, I thoroughly enjoyed all my war and had seriously contemplated making it my full-time career when the Americans dropped the atom bomb and war, as I knew it, came to a full stop. There was no point at all being a soldier without a war to fight: like a key without a lock, a meal without salt, or Androcles without his lion.

It was borne in on me very soon at Wrotham, among the blasted trees and bomb craters of the assault course that this was my third, and possibly last, chance to win through. No Morse Code here to trouble my idiot head, no auto-loaders in which to jam my hands, just me myself and my own deep sense of Self. The only way in which I could possibly succeed in this hell hole was by being, not The Best, I could never be that, but among the first five or six. In that way I might just manage to survive. I was always among the first handful up a cliff face, over a river, through the tunnels, across the mine-fields, over the palisades, along the greasy pole and in and out of booby-trapped buildings. I went like a ferret. Panic lent me winged feet and lack of vertigo. Panic that I should have to stay behind with the slower members of the outfit who, struggling desperately over every obstacle, slipping in the mud, swirling in the swift cur-rents of the River Medway, gasping and choking, were far more dangerous than any stray bullet, coil of wire, or raging weir. A bayonet up the backside was something to dread, and most of them waved theirs around like parasols. So I let them all sink or swim as they chose and belted for dear life across acres of ravaged Kent as if the V.C. was my main objective.

In this rather shameful way I managed to clamber towards the heights of my Commission and become a fully fledged, even though unwilling, little leader of men. Which was all, in the end, that was required of me. I was given to understand that my life, in real action, would have the duration of about twenty-four hours. Which seemed to me rather a waste of effort; however, with all the supreme self-interest I could muster I felt quite sure that this unpleasing rule could only apply to the others. Never, at any time, to me.

On April 1st, 1943, a glorious, sunny, wind-whipped morning, I finally achieved greatness and marched solemnly off the parade ground at Sandhurst a fully commissioned Lieutenant. In my splendid uniform, fitted for weeks by a gentleman from Hawes and Curtis in a wooden shed near the barracks, wearing my father's Sam Browne, with the badges and buttons of the Queen's Royal Regiment flashing like the Koh-i-noor, my head held high, and before my somewhat astonished, but proud none the less, parents, I strode bravely up the stone steps preceded by a relation of the King's who rode a large white horse which defecated cheerfully when it got to the top. This was expected, and indeed hoped for, and to the strains of 'Don't Fence Me In' rather oddly chosen for the march, and a wild roar of delightd applause and cheering, I set my right foot forward to what I sincerely hoped were better things.

They took a little while coming, but I was in no great hurry. First I was sent up to the Holding Battalion, or whatever it was called, in a deserted mill in Ramsbottom, Lancashire. It was a tedious time, spent mainly in a Lloyd loom chair in the Officers' Mess, reading old copies of *The Field* and *Everybody's*. No one seemed to know what to do with me. However, I was assigned to a batman, a sturdy fellow from Bolton who worked, before the war, in a brass-foundry, and it was he, more than anyone else, who told me what to do, where to go, and when I was on duty. I have always been deeply grateful to him, and never more so than the morning he came to call me with the news that I was posted to my first assignment. I was to join an Infantry Regiment as an L.O. the next morning.

'What is an L.O., Ben?'

'Liaison Officer, I think.'

'What do they do?'

'God knows.'

'Where is the regiment? Hope to God it's not near here.'

Ben laid my gleaming Sam Brown carefully over a chair. 'How the hell do I know, sonny? Go and read the Board, it'll be in yer Mess.'

With this sensible advice, and no more, I discovered that my assignment was in a place near Redruth, which was, someone said idly over his greasy breakfast, in Cornwall. It was a long way to go to be an L.O. but one very quickly got used to that, and anywhere was better than the gloom and misery of the mill at Ramsbottom.

In an orchard, pleasantly set by a river, I was put into a tent, told we were all off to North Africa but that it was still hush-hush, and that being an L.O. meant that I should be used to send messages of a private and personal nature, rather like a pigeon, only that instead of using wings I would be required to ride a motor cycle.

Which was the silliest thing I'd ever heard in all my two years service. After a few miserable days' practice round the Cornish lanes, clutching a map and dressed as if I were about to be fired from a cannon, in breeches, boots and a too-tight crash helmet, it was deemed that I was ready for work and was given a small buff envelope marked *Secret*, a map reference which turned out to be a house in a large park which was a neighbouring Brigade Headquarters, and sent off with strict instructions that the Brigadier was to receive the envelope from my own gauntlet-gloved hands before luncheon. Or at the latest by thirteen-forty-five hours. Which was very confusing.

I didn't fall off once on my way to the HQ, but as I turned carefully into the rhododendrons lining the long drive up, thinking vaguely of 'Rebecca' and North Africa at the same time, I stalled the machine, swerved into the bushes and fell off. Quite gracefully. Since I could already see the slate roof of the house and a large bay window, I decided that I would push the thing up the hill, and give it, and myself, a bit of a rest before the journey back. However, it appeared quite immovable. I pushed, tugged, dragged the bloody thing from the bushes and, helmet askew, sweat pouring down, strove to drag it up the hill. Someone came slowly down the drive, hands on hips, and stood for a moment watching my futile efforts.

'Having trouble?'

A pleasant voice, solicitous.

'I can't start this bloody thing.'

'Apparently.'

'I simply hate the buggers . . .'

He came a little closer, hatless and smiling calmly.

'I think you'll find it's in gear.'

Shame flooded me, I cursed, slipped out of gear and started on up the hill puffing. He walked a little ahead, hands behind his back.

'Typical of the bloody army. I can't ride a motor bike and they make me an L.O. Have you ever heard of anything so idiotic . . .' We went on up, me pushing, sweat pouring, sunlight flicking through the trees, he scuffing along ahead with highly polished little boots. When we got to the front of the house, the land was flat, and I came to a halt in the gravel, thankfully. He turned at the steps to the house: 'Have you a message or something?'

'Yes . . .' I fumbled in my battledress and found the rather, by now, crumpled envelope. 'But it's for the Brigadier; I was told to deliver it personally.'

'That's what you're doing,' he said. 'I am he.'

I was told to stay to luncheon, since it was nearer thirteen-forty-five hours than it was mid-day, owing to my recalcitrant bike, and found the Mess a great deal more attractive than any of the others I had set foot in. This was a much jollier place; people laughed. Apparently my ill-delivered message, whatever it was, made everyone's spirits rise, and I was even offered a pink gin before the meal and a second helping of jam roly-poly. The Brigadier, a neat, compact little man, with reddish hair, brilliant blue eyes and a tongue like a whip when he wished to use it as such, fired questions across the table at me like balls at a coconut shy, and then disconcertingly announced that we would play a word game.

'Call it "Derivations"; invented in this Mess. We'll do a dummy-run, you'll soon pick it up. Anyone care to start?' He peered round the table under sandy brows.

A scraping of knives and forks in the sudden hush; then the I.O. cleared his throat 'The Camberwell Beauty,' he said.

The Brigadier looked thoughtful. 'Camberwell. Not Gertie Millar, is it?'

'No, Sir.'

'Well, some kind of Cabaret gel, a toe-dancer, eh?'

The I.O. shook his head.

A junior officer with a stammer took a risk.

'Some k-k-k-ind of r-r-r-r-ailway engine? like "The Flying Scot"?'

'No. Not mechanical. Animal.'

'Ah ha!' cried the M.O. happily. 'A horse, what? Derby winner, Fred Archer up?'

'Not a horse . . . six legs, I venture.'

'Got it! An insect?'

'Hot! I say, damned good! Jolly hot!'

'A butterfly?'

'Scalding, old man!'

'Derivation!' snapped the Brigadier impatiently.

'No offers?'

'Not the foggiest,' said the M.O. and helped himself to Malvern Water.

'Found there,' the I.O. was beaming. 'Cool Arbour Lane, Camberwell, 1740 something.'

The Brigadier fixed me with blue lasers. 'Got the hang of it? Stops the brain from getting soggy . . . on your toes, what? Have a think . . . but don't butt-in if someone else is playing; damned infuriating.'

Since I was quite resigned, owing to my lamentable behaviour at our meeting, to being R.T.U. or court martialled for impertinence and ignorance, I ate well and joined in the absurd game with the greatest alacrity and good humour. The condemned man having his meal with the warders. I discovered, to my astonishment, that I was as full of irrelevant knowledge and jokes as a box of crackers; it might well have been the pink gin, but I really think it was hopelessness before the drop. They were amused with my derivation of the word posh (Portside Out, Starboard Home) and seemed intrigued when I explained that the nursery song, 'Ring A Ring O'Roses' was in fact a jingle about the plague. The Brigadier's blue eyes went into slits.

'Don't follow that at all . . . why?'

'Well, er . . . the ring of roses was the red blotches the disease made on their faces, Sir.' I was nearly-overcareful about the Sir bit from now on.

'I see. What about the posies then?'

'Posies of cloves and flowers to keep the smell away, Sir.'

'Smell, was there?'

'Yes, Sir, awful.'

'And the rest? All the Atishoo Atishoo, that stuff?'

'The first symptoms of the plague, Sir.'

'And All Fall Down?'

'Well . . . dead, Sir . . . you know . . .'

'Really. Well. I see. Would somebody ring for the coffee?'

I enjoyed my lunch immensely. Six days later, in some bewilderment I must confess, I strapped up my bed-roll, folded my collapsible canvas shaving-stand, packed my books and camp bed and moved into a very small attic in the roof of Brigade Headquarters to become the unofficial A.D.C. to the Brigadier. Unofficial since there was no such post; but as I didn't know that then, and as no one told me otherwise, or cared to, and since I had enormously disliked my sagging tent in the orchard by the river, I asked no questions and simply prayed to God that I would last out this extraordinary promotion. I felt almost fondly disposed towards the khaki motor bike which had delivered me at such an opportune moment. The old thing of 'if I hadn't been there at the right moment . . .' For me, trundling up the drive that morning, pushing a stalled bike and catching, all unawares, the Brigadier on his way back from a quick pee in the bushes, was as decisive a change in my life as if the bike had heaved me over its handlebars in front of a tank.

For a week or ten days I sat proudly up front in the staff Humber, map reading us all over Cornwall and a good deal of Devon. I didn't get us lost often, and on a number of occasions got us there too early even, by taking side roads, at a frightening risk. I opened doors, stood to attention, carried the bumph without which no Staff Officer seemed complete, arranged thermos flasks of coffee with neat flasks of brandy alongside, had sandwiches ready for longer trips; I knew when to talk, and when to shut up, and how to arrange the seating at a dinner table if a visiting dignitary arrived with his A.D.C. from a neighbouring Brigade or Division. Added to which I memorised every single name that I felt would be needed in the job and a great many which only might be; a useful precaution. The training I had had as an actor, of all things, was coming in very handy, as Lally used to say. And I wasn't about to let anything slip from my joyful fingers. At last, at last, I was not a square peg. I was as round as a dowel-rod, and it seemed, I prayed deeply, that I fitted my equally round hole.

At the end of my trial session – for that's what it was naturally; no one was a complete fool; and just because I could read a map, and knew the derivation of a nursery rhyme, no one was going to risk me with anything more serious than a summer ride through the dog leg lanes of Cornwall – at the end of my trial a light remark at dinner that we were to go to London to the War Office, by road, for three days and would I please make all the arrangements, gave me hope that I had passed my test. I said, 'Yes, Sir' with a quiet confidence which I did not in the least feel, and the Adjutant, who was sitting beside me vaguely stirring his coffee, thoughtfully picked his nose.

In the last days of July, I was made up to Full Lieutenant. My kite had caught the breeze. My Brigadier took me in hand and started my training in earnest. I really do not know why: possibly he had ideas that one day he would become a General and would have need of an A.D.C., or just possibly he wanted a dog's-body to run and fetch and carry for him. I have no idea. I only knew at the time that he had given me his implicit trust and that I must, indeed wished to, honour it to the very best of my abilities. After all, I had made a pretty poor showing in the Army for the last two years. Here was something that

I could at least deal with. It was, when all said and done, an actor's job. But there was a great deal to learn. I really had had no idea how to sit a table correctly: it was he himself who, at the very beginning, scribbled vague little sketches of his table and guests and told me who should sit beside whom and why. I soon caught on and, with the help of an old copy of *Mrs Beeton* which the Mess cook slipped into my hands one afternoon on Kitchen Inspection, I was off. The tables got arranged, pretty well . . . with few mistakes; and Cabinet Pudding and Macaroni Bully Beef gave way to Chocolate Mousse and Truite aux Amandes. At first there were mild complaints but the Brigadier said everyone was getting too fat and that a little variation was essential. The Cook and I and *Mrs Beeton* did what we could to vary the monotony of the rations. It wasn't much, and sometimes was a disaster, but at least we were trying.

My absurdly boyish face was a very useful disguise. And a dangerous trap for many a Colonel or even, on a couple of occasions, a General or two. If the Brigadier wanted to find out a little bit of gossip which had so far not come his way, it was I who was set out to discover it. And after a meeting, wherever it might be, during a picnic on an exercise, a formal dinner in the Mess, or even a drink at the bar, it was my job to try and find out, in as casual a manner as possible, just what he wanted to know. I found other A.D.C.'s extremely useful for information. Usually given to bragging a little, and condescending, for they knew that my status as an A.D.C. was false, and that I had been an actor, they unwittingly fell into my traps without ever knowing they had. I didn't at all mind the patronage I often received at that time, for I knew full well what my job was, and that later in the evening I would be able to report to my Old Man and shake out a modest little packet of scraps – which only he could possibly manage to put together. It was a very successful relationship as far as that went, and I don't think that I was ever found out in my devious business. Added to which I thoroughly enjoyed it.

So intent was the Brigadier on bettering his unofficial A.D.C. that he sent me off on various courses all over the country, street fighting in Blackburn, a mortar course in Bury, a gas course at Frimley, most of which I managed to survive, if perhaps not excel in, except, unhappily as it turned out for him, one War Intelligence Course in Matlock Spa to which I reported in the October of '43 and left in the December as a fully fledged Brigade Intelligence Officer. He was pleased, I was staggered; but not very long after his pleasure gave way to white rage at breakfast when he chucked a signal across the table which said that I was to join 2nd Army Headquarters in London, directly, as an Air Photographic Interpreter. Although none of us knew it then, planning for the 2nd Front was beginning. There wasn't much he could do about it, since the order came from Montgomery himself, but he was unforgiving and when I asked permission to see him to say goodbye, and also to thank him, he refused. I left for my new, glorious job in misery. I didn't see him again until one misty October day just after the débâcle at Arnhem. There was no one I knew in the Mess in the shell-pocked red-brick château which his Brigade occupied. They were polite, if evasive, all looked rather young and new. Eventually he came into the room – we were having tea – glanced at me, sat down, crossed his shining little booted feet, milked his tea and asked me if I had enjoyed, what he called, 'your cushy job'. There was no forgiveness. He had lost too many since the Normandy landings, and made it clear. 'Won't find anyone you used to know here now; all gone. We lost more than half the Brigade. Bloody lucky for you that you got out when you did.'

There was nothing to say. Useless to try and explain that he had been my catalyst, and that even though I was still alive and in his Mess, there had been times . . . useless. I left very shortly afterwards; he was reading and didn't look up.

But there wasn't really very much point in remembering all this sort of trivia rattling through the back streets of Clapham and Wandsworth, seeing, very clearly, the present and the future through the dirty carriage window. Gooley, Catterick, the first train journey up there to that starting point. Wrotham and Shrivenham, the Brigadier and the motor bikes, assault courses, promotion, D Day and Arnhem, Berlin and the stink of dead, the hysteria of Peace on the Heath at Luneberg, Himmler lying sprawled in the bay window of a villa, a blanket over his skinny body, British Army Issue boots sticking out at five-to-nine at the end of bony ankled legs; pith helmets bobbing on the water outside Bombay, like jelly fish, a trooper sailing majestically out past us, the singing voices then across the sea in the fading tropic light, but strong with relief for all that, the voices, a swelling chorus to jeer us in . . .

> *'for we're saying goodbye to them all,*
> *the long and the short and the tall,*
> *you'll get no promotion*
> *this side of the ocean . . .'*

and five nights on another train across the stranger-continent to Calcutta. Monkeys as well as parrots in the banyan trees, Tagore's palace and the sudden monsoon, the rain falling like steel rods, iced lime juice in the sticky heat of Green's Hotel, the gentleness of the Indian, the startling, shameful, arrogance of the Memsahibs, mid-wives at the abortion of an Empire; Truman's gesture to mankind and the pulverisation of two Japanese cities, branding forever man as the descendant of the killer ape. And in the vacuum which followed, the slow trip across tropical seas in an L.S.T. to an island bent on its own self-mutilation in the name of Freedom. 'Merdeka!' the word to ring with fear through one's head for months to come. A world turned upside down, the values back to front, the oppressed rising against the oppressor, all over again, and with what results? New oppressors, new oppressed.

But now it was all over for me at any rate, the brave new world lay all about me outside the windows, the world to which I now must belong. The past was the past and all I had to worry about was now. Childhood had been easy, beautiful, a glory . . . unforgettable. Adolescence had only just started to offer the most tentative of budding shoots when the burgeoning plant was culled, bound, and trundled off in a 15-cwt truck from Richmond station into what were now quite obviously, the best years of your life. No good carrying any of this stuff about with me like a bundle of crinkled love letters. Chuck it. The hardest part was yet to come, the growing up; I was going to find it harder than anything I had ever been called upon to do.

How do you, at twenty-six, green as a frog, join the team with all the years since nineteen missing? Who would care, or have the time? Where would I go, and what would I do now? A sort of panic mounted, Windlesham, if I was lucky. Little boys in grey flannels running up and down a cricket pitch. Or I could work in a pub . . . wait at table . . . perhaps get a job in a prison even? Something with men, something with the same sort of background which I was now being forced to leave . . . could I get a job with the War Graves Commission even? Hopelessness rose in me like a fever, I wasn't ready . . . don't get into Waterloo . . . don't start my new life too quickly . . . I'm not ready, I don't know how to do it.

The man opposite, hit by my unconscious kick, woke up and blinked. I apologised and he smiled through half sleep. 'Nodded off,' he yawned and stretched his arms wide across the near empty compartment, contentedly licked round his stale mouth, belched gently and asked me where I'd been.

'The Far East.'

'I could see you had a bit of a tan . . . Burma, were you?'

'Partly . . . Malaya, you know . . .' lamely, leave it, don't ask me. Tears aren't far.

'Ah! The Forgotten Army, eh? Well, you're safely home now, sonny. Mind you, we've had our problems, oh yes! Not been easy. Dunkirk, the Blitz, and those V2s . . . shit, don't suppose you know about them, eh? And the V1s . . . very nasty . . . nearly did for us that lot did. But we won, didn't we? We muddled through . . . can't say we didn't win in the end.' He smiled again, 'Course we had Churchill, but he had to go; a bully . . . don't need a bully in peacetime.' He pulled his mackintosh and a carrier bag off the rack, and stood at the door as we rumbled into a platform. 'And,' he said with a wink, 'Waterloo's still here! But we had a bloody awful war, mark my words, we was under siege, you know . . . under siege.'

'But you weren't occupied, were you?'

He lowered the window and thrust his hand out for the handle. 'Don't follow?'

'Occupied. You weren't occupied, were you?'

He swung open the door. 'Occupied? This is Britain, mate. Good luck!' He jumped off and ran along the platform before we had finally stopped.

I collected my kit together, and the cardboard box with the black shoes and the cotton-tweed suit. I left the pork-pie hat, alone, on the rack.

If Waterloo was still there, home was not. Well, not the home that I had left five and a half years before. It was no longer the red-tiled, gargoyled, ugly, much loved house by the big pond. No more the bamboo thicket in the orchard, my tin studio called 'Trees', the magnolias, the lawns, the Granny Smiths from whose scaly arms I had often stared, hopelessly loving, concealed in leaves, at Elsie Brooks in her attic bedroom changing into something pretty for the day off with her mechanic from Lindfield; no more spreading common ablaze with summer gorse, no lizards, no gentian patch, no pond, no rotting punt. That had all since gone, sold to people who ripped down the studio, hacked down the bamboo and the magnolias, cleaned up and cemented the pond with hideous crazy paving paths, and generally opened up the place to the light, leaving the unhappy house standing baldly four square and ugly to the winds.

Home now was a small cottage, badly placed under the Downs, on a narrow lane facing south and north. That is to say the back faced south into the hill and practically never got the sun, and the front faced north across rolling plough to the station at Hassocks. It was not unlovely, just uncomfortable. But with me half across the world, Elizabeth my sister, a WREN at Portsmouth, and Gareth, now twelve, a boarder at Hurstpierpoint, the dog dead and Elsie married to her mechanic and a mother herself, it was the right size for what remained of the family.

'It is rather small, darling . . .' My mother wistful, apologetic. 'But I think you can make do in Gareth's room . . . he comes home at weekends only, you see, and then he can sleep in the telephone room on a camp bed. But you can't use the bathroom while Ulric's shaving . . . he goes up to town on the 8.25 so we have to keep everything clear for him, you see; he doesn't get back until very late. I do wish he'd retire.'

Gareth's room was very small, eight by six. A minute window looking out over the fields to Hassocks and Ditchling, a not-big-enough bed and some rather ugly bits of furniture I didn't remember. I sat on the bed and looked around the stranger's room, feeling very much as I had done in my own room on leaves long past, only in this private place there was nothing to remind me of myself. A German helmet, a jam jar full of used stamps, part of a wireless-set, coils and valves bloomed with dust, *Treasure Island, The Boy's Book of Hobbies 1912*, and handfuls of dried acorns, Sherwood Forest dormant in a Dolcis shoe-box. I didn't know the person who lived in this room any more than I knew the person sitting presently on his bed. I had been. Who was I now? Nervously, curiously, I looked for signs of myself . . . surely he must have something of mine from the days past? The Eiffel Tower was there! And the lay-figure my Grandfather had given me, legs and arms akimbo still, head pressed into its aluminium chest. In the meagre bookcase some old sketch books from Chelsea Polytechnic. I felt the pages for familiarity, riffling through them with affection. My old notebooks, filled with projects never accomplished, designs never designed, ideas long abandoned. All the help that I had been offered by Moore and Sutherland and my other teachers was intact. Sutherland's splendid Stonehenge, eight rectangles on a half sphere with a radiant sun, some of Moore's wrapped ladies helping to define form for me, they all were there still, half obliterated by crayon drawings of Spitfires, monsters, a sinking battleship, someone called 'My Pal' wearing a hat and cross-eyes, and riotous squiggles of red, yellow and green wax. The sad ruining product of an idle day and a box of crayons by my little brother.

I had no present here. I had no past here. The October day was dying in wan splendour, a flock of lapwings eddied down into the plough opposite and scuttled about busily for the last feed before night, crests rising and falling in cautious alarm. Somewhere down below I heard spoons in saucers and my mother singing. It came softly up the little staircase through the door with a Japanese flag pinned across it, which I had sent Gareth from Sourabaya, long ago. The voice was sweet, warm, gentle, a remembrance of time gone by, of rooms gone by, of places lost and other evenings. But equally a reminder, a reassurance of now; of love, of belonging, of coming home again. I went over to the little desk and started to unpack the presents I had brought back; her singing filled the house.

> *'I'll be loving you, always . . .*
> *With a love that's true . . .*
> *Always . . . .'*

'What-did-you-do-in-the-war-Elizabeth, then?'

She laughed and brushed a silk-stockinged knee with a dismissing hand. 'Nothing much, just a boring old WREN. Made a lake of cocoa, I should think.'

'Nothing brave? Firing torpedoes or something?'

'No. Nothing. The only time I ever got really upset was when I got very muddled about all that twenty-three-fifty-nine business. You know, the time thing. I never learned that ten o'clock was twenty-two hundred hours. Did you?'

'Never.'

'And I was late back from leave so I had hysterics on the platform at Haywards Heath.'

'Real hysterics?'

'Screams and sobs, it was ghastly. People thought I was having a fit. I was.'

'What happened?'

'Oh, Daddy telephoned the Head Nun, or whatever she was, and sorted it out. But it gave me a terrible turn.'

'As Lally would say.' We laughed together.

'She's married now, you know . . . terribly nice man, a footman to Lady Hedgerly. She's very happy. Are you?'

I shrugged. 'It's all so different somehow, I don't know. I miss it all. Isn't it strange?'

'I hated it all, my bit. Yours was different. What are you, a Captain or something?'

'War Substantive Captain . . . but a Major, it's difficult to explain . . .'

She lit a cigarette busily. 'Don't try, I'd never understand. But it's quite good, isn't it? Can you be a Captain in peace time?'

'They say I can.'

'But you wouldn't, would you? You'd sound like something in a Club House. What are you going to do, though?'

'That's the whole problem. I don't know.'

'Go back to the theatre thing?'

'No. Not now. Too late. I'm too old anyway. And it's a bit frivolous, isn't it? Shallow somehow. I'd feel . . .' I dried up, I didn't know what I'd feel. 'Anyway, there is this school job at Windlesham . . . I'll try that. Got to do something, I haven't a penny.'

'I'm going to get married, I think.'

I was struck dumb with shock.

She nervously pulled down her navy skirt and shook her hair round her shoulders. 'Mummy and Daddy don't know yet. Don't tell. It's not certain really.'

'It's not The Prawn, is it?' An awful wet in a Guards Regiment she had known years ago on one of my last leaves.

She snorted with scorn. 'God no!' she laughed. 'He made a pass at Mummy one night in the pub, and that was the end of that, thank you . . . ghastly creature. Do you remember his whiskers!'

'Who is this one, will I like him?'

'George, in the RAF, and you'd better. I do.'

It was a strange feeling, the two of us sitting in our uniforms, smoking with a couple of beers, in the little sitting room of the cottage. It was as if some great duster had wiped away a large chunk of our lives together, like a half-erased problem on a blackboard. The last time we had really been together she was still in her blue tweed school coat, I in my awful, but loved, green suit from a Gamages Fire Sale. And now I was talking of becoming a schoolmaster and she was talking of getting married.

I laughed aloud and she looked at me incuriously.

'George is a very nice name, you needn't laugh.'

'I'm not . . . about George. About us really.'

'What's wrong with us?'

'Nothing! Nothing's wrong. It's just so funny. You and I playing in those plays I wrote, do you remember. 'The Titanic', and pushing you off the wall into all the straw . . . Do you remember when we used Gareth as a baby and you dropped him on his head in the barn, on what you called the soft part, and we thought he'd go mad or something? Perhaps he still will; he has masses of time.'

'I remember lots of things then, Lally most of all of course, Twickenham and Mrs Jane and those lovely chocolate cakes she used to make for us . . .'

'Madeira cake.'

'I remember chocolate . . . it doesn't matter. You know I don't feel the least bit different inside, do you? I feel just the same as I always did. Isn't it awful.'

'I feel just the same too. I suppose we are supposed to be different, but I don't feel it. I feel just as silly now as I was then. Sillier.'

She sighed and went over to the window and peered out, her amrs folded over her chest, she hunched her shoulders up high as if she was cold. 'Isn't Mummy wonderful really? She's kept the garden going all the war, you know, vegetables, fruit, garlic even . . . always something; she used to eat huge garlic sandwiches all through the winters to keep well. Daddy nearly choked to death. But she never got a cold once. I wonder what happened to the time, all that time? I expect we grew up.' She sounded sad, wistful, almost as if she hoped that I would say that she was wrong. I did.

'No, I don't think we did. I haven't, I know; what worries me so much is that I have got to start doing it now, right away, and I don't know how to begin.'

She came slowly across and sat beside me, her arms still holding her body. 'But in the war, in France . . . or even, you know, in Burma or India or wherever it was. I mean that all made a difference, didn't it? There were things which happened; things which make you grow up. They say so anyway, killing people, you know. Were you frightened?'

'Yes. Very. But I didn't think fright makes much difference to it.'

She leant towards me very secretly, as she had done so often in childhood, a very private matter between us both. 'What was the most frightening thing?'

'Climbing a mill chimney in Blackburn.'

'Whatever for?' Her eyes were wide with astonishment.

'It was part of a Street Fighting Course . . . we had been doing Hand to Hand Fighting in some ruined houses, with real bullets and stuff, tiles flying, and dust . . . and at the end there was this damned chimney, about eighty or ninety feet high, with little steel spikes driven into the brickwork all the way up . . . and we had ropes, and when I looked upwards it sort of reeled against the sky and I felt sick. I think you could have refused. Some people did.'

'Why didn't you then?'

'I was too frightened not to. I didn't want to be a coward.'

'I think you must be mad, really.'

'Anyhow, when I got to the top it was about a yard wide all round and the Sergeant was covered in soot and very hearty. He made me look at the view. 'Grand view from here,' he kept saying.'

I remember that I stood clutching his arms with my shaking hands, my legs weak, as if my knees had been removed. I forced myself not to look at the great black hole to my right, but to look up where he indicated out across the filthy city cupped in its rolling endless moors and dales, far below the pale faces of those who had not come up, or those who had already reached the bottom, stared up at us like a scatter of mushrooms. When I got down I was sick. Hopelessly. But the Sergeant gave me a pat, and stuck up a thumb. I had been frightened then. But I had been far more frightened of showing that I was.

She got up suddenly and, shoving her tie into her jacket, buttoned up her little buttons. 'I'll go and give Mummy a hand with the table. She's made a meat-loaf or something with two sausage rolls she got this morning and some sage and onions. I do think she's clever; all I know is that I'm terribly frightened of growing up. I just wish I knew how to do it.' She went off into the little hall and a few minutes later I heard my mother laughing in the kitchen and the door closed.

She had only asked me about being frightened, not about terror. I thought that terror, like responsibility, and killing people which I had done, might make a difference, but it hadn't, so it seemed. And there had been terror, but I didn't want to tell her that. I didn't even, when it really came down to it, want to remind myself yet either. It was an emotion which you could, after a time, obliterate more or less for a little. Only during really bad thunderstorms would I remember Belsen, and the girl, shorn head covered in scabs, face cracked with running sores from which she carelessly waved away the April flies, who grabbed my hand and stumbled with me along the sandy tracks amongst the filth, talking, crying, singing all at the same time, pointing me out proudly as we went, her filthy striped skirt flapping, breasts swinging like empty pockets against her rib-lined chest. A Corporal, red faced and gentle, took her from me and pulled us apart, thrusting her away. She stood appalled for a moment, and then with cascading tears pressed both hands to her lips and threw me kisses until I had gone from her sight.

'Sorry, Sir,' apologetic, careful. 'Typhoid. The place is full of it . . . I reckon they'll all go.'

Outside the camp, in the pale April sun, the larches shadowy with spring, larks high above the rolling, sandy heath. Help had come, trucks and jeeps and cars still bumped slowly across the tracks through the huge wire gates into hell. I drove away.

And the wood outside Soltau . . . the dark pines and the earth below squashy, so that tent-pegs driven in slid into slime. The stench then, and the massed grave . . . legs and arms and swollen heads, the bloated, the rotten, liquefying, death beneath the pine-needles and moss. They had forced the people from the village to march past. Old men and women mostly, dragging, or carrying children. Some, the oldest, sobbed into handkerchiefs, the younger ones, white faced, spat, pointing out putrescence to unaware babies slung around their hips. Laughing, spitting into the grave, proud still, Germans.

That was terror. Because it was so completely incomprehensible. Being dive-bombed on the airfield, shot at crossing a July field of buttercups, chased by tracer-bullets at night among the dykes and ditches of Holland, getting lost in a minefield, staggering up the beach at Arromanches, seeing my very first battle casualty, a man in a kilt lying indecently sprawled among the cow-parsley, the *Daily Mirror* plastered, considerately, across his blown-away face, holding the shaking shoulders of a woman stretched out under a shattered roof, while three older women delivered a child induced by shell-blast and terror . . . they were not Terror for me, because those things, however bizarre and strange, however unexpected, were, in fact, to *be* expected in a war. Those things, because I could understand them, terrified me less than the terrors which began to emerge from a new kind of war. These things had not been in a textbook, and no one had been able to tell us that we should find them strewn along our victors' path, no one had ever said that perhaps this was what growing up entailed. If they had, I doubt very much that I would have believed them, for I tend to disbelieve anything remotely beyond my comprehension.

A limiting fault.

The light had died, the room was still. From the kitchen I could hear them clonking about, a tap running, the door opening and my mother coming into the little dining room next door; she rattled plates on to the table singing still.

'Are you hungry?' she called. 'We'll eat early tonight, won't wait for Ulric, Elizabeth has to get the eight-thirty bus back. Darling! Do put on the lights, it's so gloomy in there.'

The door shut. I put on the lamps and poured another beer. My father's portrait over the fireplace looked sternly across me to another time.

'I'm home.' I said aloud. 'You said at the beginning that I might enjoy it, and some of it I did. But I don't know what I had to go for, really, do you, now that it's over? But I'm back, and I have lost nothing much. Nothing I really regret. Nothing that I won't have a try at replacing, even adolescence. I must have gained something after all these years, but I suppose it'll take a bit of time to come through, won't it?'

Elizabeth came quietly into the room, pulling off an apron. 'Talking to yourself, my dear . . . that won't do, you haven't gone do-lally-tap, have you, like Gooze at Twickenham?' She rummaged in a large leather hand-grip and found some cigarettes. 'I suppose you'd got all lonely on your first night home . . .'

I offered her a beer, but she shook her head, and lit her cigarette blowing the smoke in a long stream towards me.

'As a matter of fact,' I said, 'I was having a bit of a chat to our father up there over the fireplace.'

She was unsurprised. 'And what were you telling him, if it's not private?'

'No. I was just telling him that it had all been a bloody waste of time, that's all.'

'God! What a dreadful thing to say.'

'And He's out too.'

'Who is?'

'God. He's all balls really.'

'But you used to be mad about God and Jesus and Mary and all that . . .'

'How does it go, do you remember? "When I was a child, I thought as a child. But now that I have reached man's estate . . ."'

'I know.' She was bored by my banality. '"I have put away childish things".'

'Growing up,' I said.

Later, when everyone had gone to bed, I sat in Gareth's little room among his dusty bits of wireless set, acorns and used stamps and sorted ruefully through my own collection of possessions and papers which I had kept with me through the years. There wasn't much; and what there was fitted into a worn crocodile briefcase which I had taken from a Japanese General later hanged for War Crimes in Java. My parents' letters in a thumbed bundle, a packet of assorted snapshots, my Identity Card and dog-tabs, polished with old sweat, a pressed daisy from the grass at Dover Castle, a Tiger's Eye ring which Harri had given me and which I had never worn, the blue notebooks in which I had written my poems for Vida, page after page filled with pencilled non-rhyming misery, and the small buff-cotton covered book, *Newnes Handy Touring Atlas of the British Isles*. This had constituted my diary and started on the first night at Catterick Camp.

It had belonged to my father, and when I ran out of pages I just inserted more so that it bulged lumpily. Every page was scattered with a wedding-confetti of figures and letters minutely inscribed with a mapping-pen and coloured inks. Every place I had ever visited, even for a night, was ringed in black on the maps, or else neatly squared if written on the extra pages when I had gone overseas. Every course I had attended, every promotion attained, every date was methodically inserted in the margins, over hill-contours, the green plains, or the blue spaces of the Irish, English and any other neighbouring sea or channel, even on the inside covers and across the Index. It was a flurry of indecipherable hieroglyphics which overlapped each other like chain mail and were as difficult to penetrate.

And in any case, what did any of these laborious entries mean now? It was all over for me, as I had been comfortingly reminded at dinner, and the past must be considered the past. I had survived after all; my war was officially done and something much worse, because I had forgotten how to manage it, was ahead. Peace.

I stuffed the little book back with the rest of the debris of time and stuck it in the bottom of the yellow-oak wardrobe. It was late anyway, and far too difficult to work out; leave it all for another time.

Which is now, thirty years or more later, up here in my workroom. The buff cover is stained, mosaicked with rings of long forgotten Bovril, tea, or beer, the spine shredding threads of cotton, cardboard corners split. Inside, however, all is pristine, hills and rivers, seas and lakes, woods and commons as bright as the day in 1906 when they were first printed, now densely annotated with the crimson, blue and green pen marks of my secret messages.

For secret is what some of them certainly appear to be. What on earth do they all mean now? For although I obviously set everything down minutely so that in some distant future I might be able to warm myself with the recollections so meticulously gathered there, I seem to have left very few clues to aid myself, and the code (why on earth did I try to use a code? Was I frightened that I, or it, might fall into enemy hands perhaps? Or was I just being unusually secretive, even for me?) seems arbitrary and to have no key that I can now remember. Some things are written in the clear; most in fact. And the dates present no problem, nor the places ringed or squared in black. 'Blackburn', for example, is easy. An arrow to the margin says 'Street Fighting Course. 30.4.43–3.5.43. Bloody. Sick after Chimney'. But then there are scatters of jumbled letters and figures. For example, 'T.T.H.PG.M. P.C.' poses a bit of a problem. This set beside 'Matlock Bath. Hydro Hotel. 26.10.43 APIS'. More understandable when you know that APIS stands for Air Photographic Interpretation Section. The other letters are the problem. The PG is isolated, without punctuation, which is presumably the start of the message. And I now remember that from the 'start' I would place the first initial of each successive word left and then right of the unpunctuated two. Arriving thus at P.G.H.M.T.P.T.C. which I decipher as pathetically, Please God Help Me To Pass This Course. Which He did. With extremely high marks, which is why I finally became a fully qualified Air Photographic Interpreter and was ordered to leave my furious Brigadier to report urgently to London. Air Photographic Interpretation (the reading of aerial photographs taken from a height of anything between 1,000 to 30,000 feet) is very much a question, in simple terms, of observation, an eye for detail, and memory. I was happily possessed, to a modest degree, of all three, due in the main, I feel sure, to an apparently witless game which my father made us play as children. In a shop window how many pots and pans, how many with lids, how many without? How many tea pots, plates with blue rims, jugs with pink roses? Make a mental list, look away for a moment or two, look back and check. In the Underground, look at the people opposite. Memorise the faces. Look at the feet. Look away. Who had the bunion, the toe-caps, the brogues, spats, lace-ups or buttons? Even the breakfast table was not spared. After a good look one closed one's eyes while he very slightly disarranged the setting. Look again. Was the label on the marmalade facing you before? Was there a lump of sugar in the tea spoon? Had the milk jug turned its back? Two or three pieces of toast in the rack?

I had no idea that this childhood game would one day prove to be the key to a life in a war; without it I would very likely have had my twenty-four hours (or whatever it was) life expectation as an Infantry Officer and that would have been that. As it was I became a moderately accomplished specialist in an extremely complicated branch of Army Intelligence for the remainder of my service. And no one was more surprised than I, or more delighted. I loved the detail, the intense concentration, the working out of problems, the searching for clues and above all the memorising. It was, after all, a very theatrical business. How many haystacks had there been in that field three weeks ago? Look back and check. Six. Now there were sixteen . . . did the tracks lead *to* them and not *away* from them? Were they made by tracked vehicles or wheeled ones? Guns, tanks or radar maybe? Or were they, after all, only haystacks, it was June . . . but the tracks led inwards. A hay cart would have been parallel and left turning-loops . . . these ended in the little stacks. Too short for tanks, too round for trucks . . . probably 88 mm guns . . . a long, silent, painstaking job.

In the high-ceilinged sitting room in a requisitioned mansion flat in Ashley Gardens, Victoria, sitting on folding chairs at rough wooden tables we were first shown a big relief map of a part of some coast-line. It stood squint on the dusty marble mantelshelf. Did any of us know where it might be? Some made guesses, no one was right. It was actually upside down we were told, could anyone say now? We twisted heads and necks and with a cheerless laugh the Briefing Officer swung his map into its correct position and before us stood the Cherbourg peninsula and all the Normandy coast. The planning of D Day had commenced.

It was not, as my Brigadier had thought, just a cushy job. To be sure at the beginning of planning I spent all my time in Ashely Gardens or hunched over maps and photographs in a servant's bedroom high in the roof of a hideous house once owned by a sauce and pickle manufacturer at Medmenham on the river. But as the time drew near for the actual assault I was moved down to Odiham RAF Station and seconded, for the duration of hostilities, to 39 Wing of the Royal Canadian Air Force. Where they went I also went, and since they operated from little landing-strips ripped out of the corn fields and orchards as near to the fighting as they could be got, life was not without interest. Preserving it being the main one.

It was a bit late for the landings as it happened. Packed and ready to leave, bad weather suddenly forced a postponement of the actual day, and worrying reports reached us from ground sources of a German Panzer Division moving, by a disastrous coincidence, into the Bayeux area which we had not expected nor discovered on our photographs, since this was a completely unexpected move. With twenty-four hours therefore in hand, and flying almost impossible because of cloud over the dropping zones, we none the less searched the new photographs which came in hourly, desperately trying to ascertain the whereabouts of this new Division. It took a good deal of time and when I was finally shoved on to a Dakota, minus my cap which I had left behind in the rush, and clutching a vast bundle of uninterpreted photographs and a small canvas kit-bag, everyone, or everyone who had survived, had landed, and after an extremely bumpy trip across the grey heaving sea, with bursts of German flak drifting below like dandelion clocks, I was set down among the trampled corn and told to dig myself a hole in a nearby hedgerow. The Flight Lieutenant who gave me this excellent advice, together with a small shovel, said that he really couldn't like the whole business *less*, but that there was some tea brewing and that as long as some idiot didn't drop a shell right into the middle of things it would be ready in a jiffy. It was a very confusing afternoon at St Suplice.

It was a pretty confusing kind of a war altogether. Fluid, sometimes dangerous, exciting, often uncomfortable but never, at any time, boring. There wasn't time for that. We never sat about, as my father's generation had had to do, trapped in waterlogged trenches staring bleakly across a hundred yards of mud to the German line for months on end. We were constantly on the move and the very nature of the work kept me fully occupied day and night, either working at the photographs which streamed into the truck hourly in fine weather, or down in the line briefing brigades, companies, platoons, sections and even individuals on the terrain and hazards they could expect to find before them during their attacks; the depth of ditches, width of streams, minefields and lines of fire. We worked shifts day and night . . . fourteen to sixteen on, ten or eight off. If we were lucky.

During what was brightly called the Rest Period I used to take my paints and brushes and go off recording what I could of that devastated summer landscape in company with my RAF counterpart, F/Lt. Christopher Greaves, an artist before the war, and together we sought some kind of relaxation from the stress in painting. Our perhaps eccentric behaviour did not go unrecognised. Owing to the fluidity of the line we were as often in front of it as in it, or behind it: generally unwittingly. Eventually the Air Ministry made us Unofficial War Artists and allowed us to continue, retaining the product of our free time as their property until the end of hostilities when it was all returned to us and we had an Exhibition at the Batsford Gallery in London, only a few weeks after the events and sights we had recorded had passed into history. But the buff *Touring Atlas* doesn't say much about this; just the long lists of names and the jumbled letters too confusing now to decipher.

The names, however, remind, as well as the forgotten ones like Ste Honorine de Ducy . . . or Caulille . . . Paris is there, Brussels, Louvain and the drenching rain and mud . . . the race towards Eindhoven and Nijmegen Bridge, hearts high that a breakthrough was in sight and that we'd all be home for Christmas. Then the catastrophe at Arnhem and the dreadful days of fury, frustration, despair and defeat which followed. The brimming dykes at Driel; helplessly staring across the wide flowing river to the burning city, the chatter and crump of machine guns and mortars, crimson tracer-bullets ripping through the night, the little huddle of Dutch civilians weeping, not for themselves, but for the few returning guests departing from what someone on the Staff had chosen to call 'a party'; scattered, ashen, straggling back desperately across the strong current hanging on to rubber dingies or anything which would float; the mouth sour with the bitter knowledge that we had lost. Ninety per cent successful they had said at Headquarters; what could a ninety per cent failure conceivably look like? The only decipherable mark I have made against Arnhem is a neat black cross. It seems fitting.

On my twenty-fourth birthday I crossed the Rhine and the curtain went up on the terrors. The first slave labourers, shaven heads, striped shirts, too weak to cheer; the ruined desolation of my ancestral town, Kleve (paradoxically a target which I had helped to select myself), the April sun in Belsen, the woods at Soltau, the empty eyed façades of thousands upon thousands of streets, and the sweet stench of rubble-buried-dead in Berlin. In Hamburg crumbling spires, twisted rusted girders silent as the mass grave it was, save for the lapping of water and the sparrows. All these are marked, and finally there is Luneberg and the capitulation on the heath. That evening, in a state of mindless euphoria, we set fire to the Mess tent and watched from a sandy hillock as it blazed into the night until all that was left were the glowing spiral-springs of six looted armchairs glowing like neon in the drifting embers. Behind us in the fire-reflection two German women stood holding silent children.

'Kaput,' said the older woman, 'Alles Kaput.' They turned and moved away through the springy heather into the dark, leaving Christopher and I alone with the cooling symbols of our own finish.

But it was not, after all, the end for me; three weeks later I was on a troop ship bound for Bombay and Calcutta to join the planning for the next invasion. Malaya . . . and, after Hiroshima, off to another war in Java . . . a civil war this time in which we were to play no part save that of Police . . . and since there were no photographs and no sorties, for we had no planes there, I was jobless until I replaced the G.O.C.'s A.D.C. who was due for demobilisation, and thus came full circle in my military career. There had been nothing brave, no gallantry, no wounds, no grievous personal losses; what you might call a comfortable war . . . but quite enough to last me a lifetime. The final entry in the buff *Atlas* is written in the clear.

'Sail Batavia. Home seven weeks. The End.'

CHAPTER FOUR

It was a tired, shabby, bomb-blasted London to which I made my nostalgic pilgrimage. However pleasant it was to be among my family once again, and it was, the changes had been too great for an immediate settling-down. I was restless, unhappy somewhere, bored truthfully. And running rapidly out of money. Hillside Cottage, cosy as it might be, was not the home in which we had all once been so young and happy, and in which our early years had been formed. I missed space, white paint, high ceilings, solid doors, the geography of hall and stairs and landing, of my father's office, the cool drawing room massed with philadelphus in June, my bedroom, private, rowan at the window, the little twisty staircase to the attics . . . above all the space and light. Now, familiar furniture in the cramped, low ceilinged rooms, was suddenly unfamiliar, and there was nothing to do at all beyond long solitary walks over the Downs to the windmills, or up to the Matsfield Arms for too many beers before lunch. And with Elizabeth, and even Gareth, away, there was no one to talk to apart from my mother, and she, busy about her small domain, admitted cheerfully that I got under her feet, so I moved listlessly from one room to another ahead of her Hoover.

Sometimes on my solitary walks up the lane to the Downs I used to meet a pleasant, pale woman pushing a pram looking almost as bored as I felt. We smiled at each other and one morning even greeted each other with something illuminating like, 'It's cold, isn't it?' or 'Might rain later', and on another occasion we actually stopped hesitantly and she said I had been away, hadn't I?, and I'd told her that I had, and she said wasn't it good that it was all over. Only I wasn't at all sure that I agreed. She pushed her baby on up the hill and I went on towards the windmills. I didn't speak to anyone else for almost a week . . . except my father when he came back, late from *The Times*. Apart from one or two passing commercial travellers in the pub, and the pleasant blonde woman in the lane, life was fairly silent for most of the day.

'That's Mrs Lewis,' said my mother, over our heavily rationed lunch (another thing I was finding it difficult to adjust to). 'She's terribly sweet, they bought that great big house at the end of the lane when the Blitz got really bad. Her real name is Vera Lynn, but you know her, surely?'

The bull frogs were croaking by the lily-pool. Below in the valley, the rice-fields lay glittering in the sun like scattered handbag mirrors among the plantations, blinding the eyes. Sitting on the little terrace of my house under the heavy speckled shade of the bougainvillaea, Harri and I sat listlessly in the Sunday heat drinking American beer from cans and listening to Vera Lynn singing, for the hundredth time of playing, 'Room Five Hundred and Four', which made her, Harri, excessively sentimental and me beerily romantic. We usually followed it with Judy Garland and 'I'm Always Chasing Rainbows' which she equally loved, a sentiment which Chopin might not have fully endorsed.

Every Sunday, when my duties permitted, and if there was no attack warning from the perimeter wire, she and I would sit together on the terrace and have our little concert in exactly the same way that Lally, my sister and I, in the distant days of the Cottage in Sussex, would have ours while we polished the lamps, trimmed the wicks, or just shelled the peas or top and tailed the gooseberries. Time lost. Time remembered. My collection of records was almost as small as Lally's had been . . . about eight or nine, looted from the already-looted bungalows and villas of the Dutch who had either been murdered in the name of Freedom or else despatched back to Holland by us, the unwilling Police Force in this sad, ravaged, island, Java. But Vera Lynn's record was the most precious since it was almost new and borrowed from an accommodating officer in 'A' Mess who had recently come out, and who swapped it for my recording of 'Great Themes From Opera' which was very much older, badly scratched by rubble and dust, since I had found it among a pile of debris and scattered papers, in the once-trim flowerbeds of a burning villa, and which we had played until we knew every note and every instrument – it took a great many years for me even to be able to bear Rossini whistled in a street.

'Room Five Hundred and Four' usually started the same old conversation off again, although I knew it would be hopeless.

'If you married me now, you'd have a British passport. We could go together.'

'No. It wouldn't do, really . . .'

'But Pearl, Helga, Nellie . . . they're all going. They'll be on the same ship with their husbands. We could be too.'

'Don't, please . . .'

'If I asked the General, now, today, he'd be able to fix things, you know he would, he's very fond of you.'

'I know . . . but don't . . .'

'It is because you are half Indonesian, isn't it?'

'The British call it half-caste.'

'But you aren't! You're only a third or whatever it is.'

'Immediately even you start to explain . . .'

'I'm not explaining! Only to you, you are so silly.'

'I'm not silly, I know what it's like, you don't. The Dutch didn't mind. We were encouraged to intermarry, it made the colony stronger. But the British do mind. I remember the British women who came here before the war, from Malaya and from India . . . polite, sometimes kind, patronising always. And they minded. I know, I was here. I was called a chee-chee.' She laughed gently and repeated it, 'a chee-chee.'

'And it's because of that only . . .'

'Not only. No.'

'Well, what else?'

'I don't think you really know what you ask. You are so romantic. You'll be bored with me in three months in England and then what would I do?'

'I love you.'

But she wasn't really listening, her eyes closed in the Sunday morning heat, her long slender fingers scrabbling gently in the pebbles of the terrace, her lovely golden skin beaded with little mists of heat-sweat.

'Pearl says that Harold and she will go to live in Lewisham. Near London. Is it pretty?'

'Lewisham? Not very, not really.'

'Will she like it?'

'I don't know.'

'And Nellie goes to Chesterfield. Is that nice too?'

'It's prettier than Lewisham, it's got a church with a twisted spire.'

She stroked her arm gently, and slid the bracelet I had given her slowly up and down. Her eyes were still closed, but she smiled. 'We have many churches with twisted spires, I don't think Nellie has ever seen them in her life. When she was fifteen she went straight to Madame Hue's . . . do you think they'll like Nellie in Chesterfield? The spires she remembers best were not on churches.'

I remember being so angry that I left her and leant over the terrace wall looking down across the uncut lawns to the banana trees and beyond.

'It's not fair of you . . . you and Nellie are not the same . . .' I was lame with anger.

'Who can tell the difference in Chesterfield? You thought we were all alike just because we offered to work for you and the Dutch girls wouldn't because you are the Enemy.'

'We aren't the Enemy!'

'The Dutch think you are. You're here as policemen . . .'

'We're here to repatriate the Dutch civilians . . .'

'They don't want to be repatriated . . .'

'I can't help that . . .'

'You let the Indonesians take over the country.'

'They want Independence.'

'And you do nothing to prevent it.'

'But how can we? It's not our business . . . we can't even fire at them until they fire on us first.'

She threw a scatter of pebbles at a long green lizard. 'So you can't blame the Dutch; you're the Enemy. But whether we worked in a Massage Parlour or were rich and had servants of our own before, as I did, we were still the same to you. Easy women.'

'Shut up! For God's sake, stop, it always ends like this . . . I can't talk to you.'

'You started it again. Is there some more beer?'

We sat for a little longer, looking out on to the shining mirrors below, the pale blind volcanoes ridging the sky far ahead, bull frogs croaking, Vera Lynn long since silenced. We were silenced too, until Kim, my Gurka batman with golden teeth, came out to say that lunch was ready, he collected the beer cans and the dish of shrimp heads, and went away.

'Put her on again, please Pip. I like so much when she says 'We never thought to ask the price, but who can bargain over Paradise . . .' It's quite good, isn't it? Awful but quite good.' She laughed and pulled her long dark hair up into a bunch on the top of her head. 'I tell you what; at your farewell party next week, after they have all gone, I'll read the tarot cards again . . . just for you. Not for me, for you. Will you let me?'

I had always refused this strange gift of hers. Everyone else I knew had let her do it, but I was too afraid always for I instinctively believed in it, as she did, and

I have never wanted to know what the future had in store for me, finding the present either pleasant enough, or difficult enough without having to be alerted to the tribulations or terrors ahead. However, miserable, irritated and angry as I was that morning, I said 'yes', and we went into lunch and I forgot about it all, immersed in self-pity, rage at not getting my own way, and six cans of thin American beer.

'I'm afraid it's one of my messes, darling,' said my mother with no apology since no apology was needed for, as I have said, she could conjure up a meal from three biscuits, a kidney, a piece of bacon rind and whatever vegetable she had been able to find in her garden, or from some generous neighbour's, or the village grocers.

'It's lovely,' I said, 'I hope there are seconds, I mean second helpings . . .'

She was gratified. 'You just dice the bacon rind, the kidney, sautè them and mix them all up with a lot of carrots. Thank God for carrots. We'd have starved to death without them.'

Vera Lynn. In my tent in the apple orchard at St Suplice, the night alive with sound; two idiots in Messerschmitts strafing us up and down, tracer bullets ripping through the leafy branches, the horizon beyond Caen white with fire, the earth shaking like a jelly with the thudding of the big guns; the Fall of Paris in that splendid, hysterical, final August week. The enormous tricolour floating gently from the Arc de Triomphe, tanks nudging about outside the Hotel Crillon like sullen carp, bullets chipping the stonework of the Cathedral, and roses, roses all the way. German faces, pale, gaunt, taut, watching as we crossed the Rhine, a toytown countryside with all the farms ablaze; slave labourers freed into the streets near Rheine, a band of shaven-headed women heaving a grand piano out of a second floor window so that it fell, with a wild jangle of wires, into a heavy white magnolia, the whole hanging for a moment in suspended motion, until everything crashed down amidst a torrent of leaves, blossom and splintered keys, the ashen-faced owners, with two small children, standing stupefied, silent beside me as slowly, their house began to burn; air raid shelters and the smell of dust, cordite and ashes. The slow swell of the Red Sea, flying fishes racing across the bows of the ship; lying naked on the decks in the sweating nights, a lifebelt for a pillow, still, save for a portable gramophone softly playing somewhere among the thousand black forms, 'The White Cliffs of Dover', from which we were slowly steaming East and to which many of us would not be returning. And through it all, always, her voice.

'Your Ration Book has been a vast help already, I got two eggs from Bannisters yesterday . . . a Welcome Home present, I imagine, but the extra butter will be such a help, and the sugar. Sylvia gave me a quarter pound she didn't need, she's awfully generous, you know.'

'When I come back from town, next week some time, do you think we might ask Mrs Lewis in for tea or something.'

'Of course. She often drops in. There isn't much to do down here, as you gather; whenever you like.'

'I'd just like to thank her really, that's all. Or do you think she'd think I was daft or something?'

My mother neatly placed her knife and fork together on her plate. 'Not that kind of woman, darling.'

Later, at the gate, she said, 'You realise that this is the first time in years that you have gone to a train and it hasn't been a farewell?'

'We never did that, did we?'

'After you had gone I did. When I was alone. I cried; but alone. It's such a messy business, and you had enough to worry you anyway.'

'You were very good and very brave . . .'

'I was, but you don't really know, you've never had a son.'

Silly, bloody, Harri. My farewell party that evening had been quite good. Nellie and her future husband Roger, Pearl and Harold, Helga and Peter, two Yanks from Shell Petrol starting up the business again, some of the Dutch staff from Radio Batavia where, for a while, I was the British announcer, playing requests and sending messages between the many prison camps all over the island.

Harri was looking tall and cool in a steel-coloured satin dress which she had had made up to a design I had done for her, by a Chinese friend in the quarter in which she lived. Her hair long and shining, the wide pewter bracelets, like cuffs, on each arm, new sandals we had bought for her from an Indian in the city.

The party started off at sundown; drinks on the terrace, Japanese White Horse whisky, looted French wine, Bols Geneva, bowls of curried chicken, prawns, rice, mangoes and a big slab of oily cheese which the Yanks had brought from their Mess. We finished, and when they had all gone, leaving only Harold from 'A' Mess and Pearl, who were to give Harri a lift home in their jeep, and me as high as a kite on Japanese White Horse, we did the tarot as I had agreed.

She was always very serious about the cards, and never drank anyway, which irritated me when I had had too much. She laid them all out as solemnly as a Mass, which, as far as she was concerned, we were attending. Pearl was a believer naturally, Harold was as high as I was and didn't really care much one way or the other. There seemed to be nothing very dreadful in store for me, or if there was she was not about to let on; she murmured something about 'Lights . . . all lights, everything is light,' and, after a long thinking pause, poking among her medieval pack, she suddenly shuffled them all together with a brisk laugh and thanked me for being so brave. Harold, I suppose out of relief, nearly broke my neck with an affectionate punch, and told Pearl to get her bits and pieces together. It was half an hour to curfew.

At the front door, waiting for the jeep, she suddenly thrust her hand over mine and crushed it hard. 'You see; it wasn't so awful, was it . . . the cards . . .?'

'No. Not awful. Unless you saw something that you won't tell me . . .'

She laughed and shook her wild hair. 'Nothing, Pip . . . nothing bad, only light I saw, and that's good I think, don't you?' She leant up and kissed me suddenly on the neck just as the headlights of the jeep swung into the forecourt.

She and Pearl climbed into the back, struggling and laughing with their long, tight skirts, Harri clutching her box of tarot cards and the little steel mesh bag we had found together in the market. Harold revved up, and she pulled my head towards her with her one free arm. 'Thank you, Pip. Next time I see you you will be in uniform.'

'I know! Tomorrow.'

'No, no, not this uniform. A different colour, different badges, a bird I think and there will be light everywhere. You see.'

Harold said, soberly, 'The big war's over now, for Christ's sake.'

'Not for Pip,' she said. 'The next time, you will see!'

The jeep lurched, swept round the lily-pond and raced off down the drive scattering gravel into the canna lilies. I stood until I heard them reach the main road, turn right, double de-clutch, and roar off towards the city. All was still. Somewhere in the house Kim was busy stacking glasses and plates; the sky shimmered with a billion winking, silent stars, up the hill in the General's house there were three lighted windows. I went to get my cap and papers, for the Nightly Report. The frogs began to agree among themselves.

I never saw her again. She didn't come to the office in the morning, or any morning following, and although I went again and again to the little Chinese kampong where she lived, no one knew where she had gone. The veranda was empty. Just the two bamboo rocking chairs, the rain-warped table, vivid sunflowers thrusting through the palings, doors and shutters locked. The Chinese smiled all the time, hands clasped, heads bobbing, shaking sadly with gold and silver smiles; no one knew where she was, or where she had gone. I left notes, but perhaps they blew away.

Trailing up to Victoria through the misty decay of an English October, my past seemed vividly clear; it was after all, only a few weeks old. My present seemed, and was, indefinite, obscure, a clutter of emotions. My future was imponderable, a long dark corridor with all the doors apparently closed, and without even the very smallest candle to light the way. Had I been thinking these thoughts aloud it would have been extremely unpleasing, since all that would have emerged would have been a high pitched wail of whining self-pity. And I was not a whit different from thousands of others who were all in the same boat; the thought, when it came, gave me no comfort. They were just The Others, and I'd never had much time for them anyway. Muffled as I was in my tattered rags of self-esteem and selfishness, my total fear of the corridor ahead, my nagging worry of my own inadequacy, I simply hadn't got the guts, slumped in my 1st Class corner of the 2.45 from Hassocks to Victoria, to hazard a guess as to what lay before me.

With my rapidly dwindling Gratuity I took a small bedroom on the Strand side of the Savoy and, thumbing eagerly through my tattered address book, began to try and make contact with the friends from before the war. It was a dreary chore. Voices, when they answered, were pleasant, surprised, glad to know I was safe and well and otherwise occupied, or on Tour, or starting a Tour, or trying, themselves, to settle down to the exhaustion of Peace. But no one actually threw their metaphorical hats in the air and invited me to endless parties. The fact was that I really had no friends from before the war; and most of them had been older than myself anyway. The Blitz had forced people to move about a good deal, and the telephone numbers either didn't reply or, if they did, were no longer the ones where my acquaintances lived.

London was as suddenly empty as Sussex – and behind the pleased voices of the few I contacted there lurked a thread of fear that I might just perhaps ask for help in getting a job. Everyone was trying to get a job; the theatre was jammed, it was always explained, with returned actors trying to get a job. The message, though infinitely tactful, was infinitely clear.

In desperation one day, for I had to find some sort of work before Windlesham's term began in January, and the theatre was, much as I disliked the idea, the only thing I knew from the past to do, I went down to Kew Bridge once again to see Beattie de Leon in her little theatre hoping that perhaps she could find me a temporary fill-in job until I went off to be a Prep School teacher. Apart from asking me, with mild surprise, if I had been away for the last six years, she said that after so long out of things I must be a bit rusty and that I should try somewhere else first, because the standard, as I must remember, was very high at 'Q'. But where else to try, I wondered?

I ate a miserable lunch in a pub near Leicester Square, bread and cheese and a half of bitter, and saw a poster announcing 'Crime and Punishment' at the New Theatre starring my friend from long before, Peter Ustinov. Since we had joined the Army together, and since he was the first actor, all those years ago at the Barn Theatre, Shere, in Surrey, to explain to me about Dedication and the Theatre and had so fired my imagination that I had gone into the profession with all the passion, faith and determination of a nun taking Holy Orders, surely he must be the one to whom I could now turn for advice. And he was presently only round the corner.

It was a rehearsal, and he had not as yet arrived at the theatre. Thinking to surprise him in my tattered, but well-pressed, uniform, I stood among the huddle of pallid fans gathered round the Stage Door. Presently a low, smart, blue sports car drove up, and parked imperiously. There was Peter himself, a little plumper, beaming genially, clutching papers and books, his hair as wild as I had remembered it from '39 . . . but successful clearly. People moved in with books and he happily signed, saw me, smiled above the scarfed heads of his fans and said cheerfully: 'Hello! If you have come to try and get a job, forget it! I can't get one for myself.' He smiled at us all, made a little joke, and strode into his theatre.

It is fortunate for me that hopelessness has usually made me extravagant and seldom suicidal. By that I mean that rather than jump off a bridge, resort to pills or an oven, I nearly always go and spend whatever I have left in my pocket on something idiotic, joyful, useless, and pleasurable, and so it was that after three or four fruitless and down-casting days in the questionable splendour of my one-bedded room on the Strand side of the Savoy, I decided to spend the last of my slender means in a final burst of epicurian delight in the Grill; and return to Sussex the next morning broke, humbled, and not too proud to borrow from my parents and just live at home.

Someone waved across the room to my single table, and blew kisses. It was Lusia Perry. I have known Lusia for so long that I don't even remember now how or where we first met. Russian, or as near Russian as makes no difference, she was dark, cheerful, loving, vivid and as comforting as the samovar which she always had steaming away in her tumbled mews flat in South Kensington where she lived with her small daughters, Natasha and Nina. There was a Mr Perry but I don't remember that I ever met him. There was tea, or baked potatoes with heaps of rock salt, or bowls of Bortsch, and always love, encouragement, and laughter and, above all, conversation. With her aliveness, her interest, her tremendous vitality and Russianism, if that is a word, she attracted people in all walks of life to her untidy, noisy, delightful mews off the Brompton Road.

And there she sat, across the Grill, waving and laughing, the eternal cigarette between her lips, beckoning me across.

'Of course you are out of work, darlink . . . everyone is.' She lit another cigarette from the butt of the last, and coughed cheerfully, 'Haven't you got an agent or something?'

'I had . . . Tony Forwood, but apparently he has given it up, now he's an actor himself.'

She laughed, and coughed again. 'Of course he has. After seven years in the Army he couldn't possibly stay in an office. He spent so much time getting jobs for total idiots at twice his salary that he decided to go back. He got married, you know, to Glynis Johns.'

'Yes, I knew; he wrote to me years ago.'

'But they've broken up. It's sad because there is a baby, a boy, did you know?'

'No. Lost touch in 1942.'

'Well, he's in London in a play . . . but he's wretched and ill, I hear . . . you should go and see him, he'd be pleased. He doesn't see anyone much now. It was a big blow, the marriage breaking up. Go and see him, and give him my love.'

Chesham Mews was just like any other fashionable mews: narrow, cobbled, faintly incestuous. Window boxes, yellow, white, pale blue, the summer's geraniums and lobelia dying into November. Spring is fashionable in a mews. Not autumn. Louvered shutters, wrought iron numerals, carriage-lamps at every primrose door.

I rang the bell three times, waited patiently, rang again. A window above opened and he looked out blearily. Hadn't shaved, pale faced, hair ruffled.

'Yes, what is it?' He had been sleeping.

'It's me.'

'Ah. Yes.'

'Came to see if you were in.'

'I've got 'flu. In bed.'

'I knew . . .'

'The key is on a string, put your hand in the letter box.'

A long, steep, flight of stairs. One smallish room. A large divan bed, some chairs, a cream painted table with a crackle-finish. Over the fireplace a Medici print of a scarlet amaryllis, a couple of Chinese tea-caddies, clothes scattered here and there, motor magazines; incongruously, a tapestried chair worked by his grandmother, claw and ball legs, squatting beside the gas-meter. He was in the bed swamped in crumpled sheets, blankets helter skelter, a pink rubber hot water bottle, cold, on the floor. He blew his nose hard on a bit of Kleenex.

'Well then.'

'Well then.'

'I have to play in the evenings, so I stay in bed all day . . . I've got 'flu.'

'Yes, I know . . . Lusia told me. You've stopped the agent business, I gather?'

He scrabbled for another Kleenex and blew his nose again.

'Yes . . . so many idiots, thought I'd do it myself. More money, less work. You just demobbed?'

'Last week . . . I'm looking for a job.'

'Everyone is. It's not easy . . . I don't know what I can do . . .' A helpless look into the middle distance.

'Marriage broken up, I gather?'

He plumped up a sagging pillow. 'Yes . . . Lusia again?'

'She knows everything.'

'So it seems. I've moved in here for a while. Give us time to sort it out; we were very happy together, but . . . well, Peace takes a bit of adjusting to, you'll see. I'm a parent too.'

'Yes . . . what time do you have to go to the theatre?'

'About six. Do you want to see it?'

'Not much. Where are you?'

'The St James. A Boy Wonder Impresario. Daubeny. Quite pleasant. Bright. Might be useful for you to meet him one day.'

'I'm leaving the theatre, I just want a job to carry me on until January. I owe the Army two hundred quid or something, they over-paid me, so they say. I'm broke. Can't go to my father after all this time and expect to be kept.'

He scratched his head and yawned.

'Have you tried Actors' Reunion yet?'

'What are they; or is it?'

'A group of ex-service people; all actors. You do an audition and if you're lucky and get a part, the Agents and Management promise to come and see what you can do and you might get something from that. If you get a part, that is. It's very hard, you must realise; the ones who didn't go in are hanging on like grim death; and suddenly thousands of people who weren't actors before discovered they had a talent in army concert parties. They're in too. A chap who has done a couple of impersonations in a troop concert, or played Elvira in "Blithe Spirit" in a prisoner of war camp, suddenly knows that he is ready for "Troilus and Cressida", or his name in lights at the Windmill. Very optimistic and totally lacking in style. You'll find it all a bit changed.'

On the crackle-topped table there was a dirty breakfast tray. I suggested that I might make a cup of tea, which I did on a sort of hot-plate in a corner kitchen, washing the cups, and chucking the sloshy tea dregs down the lavatory. It was quite like old times. I found some damp biscuits in a cupboard, a half empty packet of tea, and no milk.

He grumbled quietly. 'Biscuits are all soggy.'

'Well, they were on a plate beside an old cauliflower, that's why.'

He looked surprised. 'A cauliflower? Thought I'd had that ages ago.'

'So you're not an agent any longer then?'

'No. Too much of a sweat, filthy job, idiot people impossible to handle.'

'Where is this Reunion Theatre thing?'

'Not terribly sure. There's something about it on the desk there, among the papers and things . . . I should have a try if I were you, half London is anyway so you'll be in good company at least. And you were an actor before, it might help; most of them don't know Stage Right from Stage Left and they can't time an egg, let alone a laugh . . . try. Anyway you'll need a new agent, I'm afraid; it really is not my line.'

The audition for the Actors' Reunion Theatre, which I had the good fortune to attend a week later, was held in the Duke of York's Theatre, on the set of 'Is Your Honeymoon Really Necessary'. Although it was barely ten-thirty in the morning the theatre was full from pit to gallery and I thought that a performance must have started and that this was the Show. The fact that it was merely one solitary, monthly audition daunted me very much indeed. Forwood's depressed words of the week before became facts. Here they all were, the out of work ex-actors, clambering for a chance, looking for the break, and here I was among them. I could now no longer wear my uniform, my two weeks grace was up, and the last of my money jingled sadly in my pocket.

I decided to sit where I was in the warmth of the auditorium, and then walk back to Victoria and get a train home. Realising that it might go on for some time – how could anyone in their right senses audition an audience of nearly five hundred for a one act play for children which had a cast of barely fifteen, excluding crowds? – I took a seat on the centre aisle towards the back so that I would be able to leave for the train without disturbing whatever was going on at the time. The more ambitious had all arrived early and were packing the Stalls nearest to the stage where, at a small trestle table, amidst the stag-heads and painted beams of Ralph Lynn's farce, a small, worried, body of adjudicators sat in a self-conscious line. Someone got up and called for silence, Ladies and Gentleman, and explained that the play they were about to cast this month was a one act-er called 'The Man in the Street' and that the Director, present on the stage, would be Allan Davis, ex-The Buffs, and that he would now come among us to cast his play. It seemed to me a very dotty way of going about the business, and God knows what happened to the people who had jammed themselves into the Circle, for Mr Davis, ex-The Buffs, wasn't going to have the time to trot up there, which he very sensibly didn't.

Instead, with a spirited leap into the Orchestra Stalls, he hurried up the aisle, cast list in hand, looking for his actors. I remember that he was very spick and span and crack-regiment-looking; bright eyed, confident, a head as neat and smooth as a nine-pin, a voice, light, clear, authoritative and crisp. No wasting time . . . Up and down the Stalls he hurried, peering along every row, pencil in hand. Like a ratcatcher.

'I'm looking for Jesus now!' he cried. 'A young Jesus . . . no beards . . . smooth faced Jesus . . . anyone feel like a Jesus?' It was a rhetorical question, and no one answered. 'I've got Mary Magdalene and Joseph!' He ticked off the names as if he was checking the company stores. 'But what I need now is Jesus.' He had reached my area by this time, tripped over my feet sticking into the aisle, and when I withdrew them hastily, apologising, he grabbed my arm, pulled me to my feet and cried, 'Got him! I've got my Jesus . . . trot down there and give them your name,' and as I bewilderedly walked down to the glaring stage I heard him hurrying up into the Pit calling out for Pontius Pilate.

We rehearsed in the Dress Circle Bar for a week or so, very seriously and with intense concentration, while charladies battered about with buckets and a long thin man hoovered the carpet round our feet. Mr Davis was very particular and gave the whole horrid little playlet the importance of 'Tosca'. I can't for the life of me remember what it was all about, save that it was a play for children and had a religious flavour if not much religious fervour.

We opened one morning, at the deathly hour of eleven, in modern clothes (there were no costumes or make-up naturally) on the stag-hung, chintz-settee'd set of the current farce before a sparse audience of Agents, Managers' Assistants, Casting Directors and what were called, in those days, Talent Scouts. Sparse they might have been, but at least they had showed patriotism in coming to give the 'ex-actors' a chance. I remember that I wore my one pair of grey flannels from Whiteway and Laidlaws in Chowringhee, Calcutta, and a blue and white striped shirt which I had bought in the market in Batavia. There were hardly any lights, because there were power cuts at the time, and we were all frozen to death, and to my intense surprise I was a great success as Jesus; and after the play was over found myself jammed into a corner of the Stage Box surrounded by excited, complimentary, quacking people handing me telephone numbers and begging that I call them, all, it appeared, immediately.

In a slightly dazed state we, the cast and Mr Davis, withdrew to a pub in St Martin's Lane and had a stiff drink where he told us all how good we had been, and, leading me aside, told me that he thought I had great quality but to be careful and not let 'anything go to your head'. He needn't have worried. Though the exercise had been amusing, even in a way, stimulating, it had still not re-awakened the almost completely dormant desire for the theatre which I had allowed to slip away in the cornfields of Normandy. All I wanted was an immediate job to help me out until term time. It was uncomfortable borrowing a quid every time I wanted a drink or a packet of rationed cigarettes, from my patient, understanding, but hard up, father.

Forwood, adding up some bills, was amused and tried to give advice.

'It seems stupid not to go and see someone, if they were all so keen about your work . . . wasn't there anyone there you could deal with?'

'The lot of them sounded mad. All yelling and shoving telephone numbers at me . . . I frankly wouldn't trust one of them. I told them I really wasn't interested at all . . . there was one fellow though. Quite small, just gave me his card and said he'd be glad to advise me if I needed any help. I quite liked him. Very cool and collected . . . he just faded away, very sensible and sure.'

'He sounds you best bet then: what's his name?'

I fished about in the pocket of my Calcutta flannels. The card was crumpled. 'Frederick Joachim, an address in Regent Street.'

Forwood slid the bills into an envelope. 'I'd give him a call. He sounds all right, never heard of him, but he sounds sensible.'

Frederick Joachim's office, three floors up in a shabby building over a coffee shop at the top end of Regent Street, was the exact size of his desk. That is to say, it was about six feet by four, and contained himself, crouching in a small chair, his pleasant secretary who crouched beside him, a chair for 'The Client' and a slit of a window which faced a dark well. I asked him what he would do if there was ever a fire in the coffee shop below, and he said, very sharply, that he was an optimist.

He also said that he thought, but was not at all sure on just one performance, that I might have something but was unable to specify what exactly, and that if I cared he would try and get me a few bits and pieces and then we could all make up our minds together. He promised nothing at all, said that he was just starting out as an agent after six years as a War Reserve Policeman, and showed me his lace-up boots from the Force which, he said, were just the thing in this frightful weather. We exchanged telephone numbers and shook hands, a difficult effort, since I had to lean across the pleasant secretary and he had to hunch himself out of his chair, trapped behind his littered desk.

At first he sent me off on a round of all the Studios to meet the Casting People. Everyone was polite and kind but each asked the same question, 'What have you done recently?' and when one said nothing since 1940, except be in the Army, they all looked sadly wise and suggested, as Beattie had done, that I must be a little rusty and perhaps I should call again later after I had done a little work. Sweet Heaven! What work?

'I think,' said Freddy sipping a cup of filthy coffee in the coffee shop below his office, 'I think this thing called Television could be useful, they say it'll be very important as soon as they can get sets and things . . . but people do watch it, quite a big public, about 9,000 sets, I gather, mostly in shop windows and so on, quite large crowds. We might try that. Since they are just starting up they'll not be too choosy. I think they'd take anyone. Even you . . .'

We started on Television. And he was proved right. I got my first job, to my relief (funds were absolutely rock bottom by now, and the train fare from Haywards Heath was a killer at seven shillings return), in a television production of 'Rope' . . . the play I had started out with in Catterick all those years ago. The auditions were held in a cold room in Marylebone and I got the part of 'Granillo' – the neurotic killer, not the lead, to be sure, but I was more conscious of the salary than the billing.

'What are you going to call yourself?' Forwood asked, picking through a vegetarian salad, the cheapest meal on the menu, in the restaurant at Peter Jones, on the roof next to the Pet Department.

'I haven't thought really; I was D. v.d. Bogaerde at 'Q', sometimes.'

'Sounds awful, and they'll never get the diphthong right.'

'Well . . . . I quite like the name Simon. How about Simon and Garde. The second part after the whatever you called it.'

'Wet name, Simon. There has never been a star called Simon anything, it's weak.'

'What about de Montfort? Or Bolivar for instance? I think Simon Garde would be jolly good. Neat and simple.'

'Simple Simon. And dull.'

'Well, Dirk, then, and the rest of the name without the diphthong, it is my name in Dutch after all. Dirk Bogarde. That sounds all right, doesn't it?'

'And drop the van and the den . . . and the diphthong? It's awfully foreign to me.'

'Well . . . my grandfather's name was Forrest Niven. What about that? He was an actor too.'

'I know that. But there is a Niven already. Leads to confusion.'

I grew desperate over the salad. 'Well, it really doesn't matter. It's not for long, it won't last.'

He was reasonable. 'It might. And you can't suddenly change it in midstream. Make sure before you start.'

The chattering tide of Second Generation Harrods' voices threatened to engulf me; a grumpy waitress spilled a bowl of beetroot on the table beside us and little shrieks of 'Oh! how *too* awful . . . how *maddening*!' shattered my head.

I pushed my half-eaten vegetarian salad aside and started on the caramel cream.

'I'm going to be Dirk Bogarde and that's it; that's my new name, no one else is called that, for God's sake.'

Forwood finished the last of his shredded carrot. 'There's always Humphrey, of course . . .' he said mildly.

'He's in America and anyway he's the same family and it ends in 't' . . . and the hell with it all. These bloody women are driving me mad.'

I told Freddy that afternoon, and he pursed his lips and shook his head thoughtfully. 'Doesn't feel right . . . too harsh, you want a nice easy name that people will remember instantly. What about Paul, or Robert, or James?'

'You tell them I'm that, and not to spell it like Dick . . .'

'Ah!' said Freddy happily. 'Dick! That's the ticket! Dick is much easier than the other one: friendly.'

A few weeks later at Victoria on my way home, I bought the evening papers. And there it was for the first time . . . splendidly new, correctly spelled, under the modest Television heading, squashed between Carrol Gibbons and The News (sound only), 'David Markham and Dirk Bogarde in "Rope". A thriller.' It was a beginning again.

Freddy soon had me whizzing round London like a cotton shuttle. I went to all the Casting Directors and Studios and met Theatre Producers who showed a singular lack of interest. Forwood, one evening, arranged an interview for me backstage at the St James Theatre with the Boy Wonder called Peter Daubeny in whose play, 'But for the Grace of God' he was playing; that was a total failure. Mr Daubeny, with tight crinkled fair hair and minus an arm which he had lost in some extremely brave encounter with the Germans in North Africa, smiled almost, and turned an implacable back, his empty sleeve neatly tucked into a pocket.

At the Rank Organisation, a flourishing empire founded on flour-milling, in a palatial house in South Street which had once belonged to the Aberconways, I was interviewed for half an hour by one of the Chief Executives in her Ladyship's ex-bedroom, a vast room filled with busy typists all clustered round a giant Partners' Desk like pilot fish about a whale, at which the Executive sat in a grey suit, carnation and cigar. Helpless, I was asked to stand on a pale blue dais before him – it had obviously once supported a sumptuous bed – and told to remove my coat, jacket, waistcoat and finally my tie. Bewildered but complying, I stood before the assembled typing pool of Mighty Rank and was asked to turn around slowly, like beef on a hook. Which I did unsteadily.

'Head's too small, kid,' said Earl St John from behind his cigar. He threw a scatter of glossy photographs across the partners' desk. 'We're looking for people like that!' he said proudly indicating Stewart Granger, James Mason, Dennis Price and a sundry collection of retouched, lipsticked, hair-creamed gods.

'Nice of you to come . . . but your head's too small for the camera, you are too thin, and the neck isn't right. I don't know what it is, exactly, about the neck . . .' he squinted through money-box eyes, 'but it's not right.'

Crestfallen, with a neck-complex, not to mention a too-small head, I went back to Freddy's flat, comfort and a coffee.

'I think it's time I really packed it all in . . . it's so bloody humiliating.'

He was warmly sympathetic. 'Well . . . they know what they want, you understand. It won't be easy. Your head *is* a bit small for your body, you know, and I think your legs are too long really . . . but they want you for another Television. At Alexandra Palace, something called . . .' he riffled about in his briefcase . . . ' "The Case of Helvig Delbo". It's a war story and you would have to be a spy I think, as I said, they are just starting up again, so they'll take anyone, they aren't the least bit fussy. Perhaps your small head doesn't show up on Television. I don't know, I haven't seen anything, not having a set myself. Anyway, quite good money. You start on Monday week.' Which was just as well since Christmas was looming and term at Windlesham was not far behind.

I remember nothing whatever about 'Helvig Delbo' except that I seemed to spend a great deal of time tearing about Alexandra Palace changing my costumes and leaping up in bits of set all over the place. It was over and done with in a matter of days, it seemed, and not a ripple did it, or I, cause.

No sooner was it over than Freddy had me out on the beat again – he never let the grass grow under his War Reserve Police boots.

'You are doing very well, you know,' he said reasonably. 'You have only been demobbed a few weeks when you think of it . . . and you have already done two television shows. I know that's not very important but it is a start, and now there's another one. They want to audition you this time, it's a very serious play, I believe. I don't think it is because of your head or your neck, but they said they wanted to see you before they committed. It's really not like them, they seem quite pleased to take anyone these days. Anyway,' he brightened up a little, 'anyway, it is good money and the Male Lead . . . perhaps they want to match you for height with the female star, although I can't for the life of me see why it matters on the television since everything is just big close-ups or whatever they call them. Four-thirty, Thursday, Aeolian Hall, Bond Street . . . oh!' Suddenly he had a thought and rustled through the papers scattered all over the cramped desk. 'Tell you what, while you're there, go up and see Freddie Piffard; he runs a little theatre in the suburbs. Not much chance, but you can't tell. The play they are doing is cast already anyway, but there is no harm in your just meeting him, so that they can look you over. He's in the Aeolian Hall too . . . I'll telephone and say that you'll be coming in after the television thing. Studio 4a. Don't forget. And this is the script.'

I went down the stairs into the bitter winter sun, filled with Freddy's negatives. I wondered, vaguely crossing Regent Street, what he would sound like positive. It was an improbable vision, so I put it aside and went on down to the Tube.

It was snowing heavily when I got to the Aeolian Hall the following Thursday. However, the hall-way, guarded by a large uniformed, bemedalled, porter was warm, and having given him my name and the number of the studio where I was apparently expected, I settled down to wait on a hard bench with the floppy script from the BBC.

I noticed, as I arrived, that he did not write my name down in the ledger on his table, and that he was changing over duties with another bemedalled fellow. Shortly afterwards he came out of a doorway, changed into civilian clothes, and with a nod to his replacement, he tramped down the hall into the snow. I sat there for an hour and a half, and nothing happened at all. No one rang the telephone on the porter's table, or if they did it was not about me; people drifted in and out all the time, but I paid no attention to anyone, immersed, as I was, in the difficulties of reading a television script which contained more camera angles, it appeared, than dialogue. Eventually I plucked up courage, gave my name and studio number yet again and waited patiently while he thumbed through the ledger.

'You ain't down here,' he said in a surly manner. 'No one of that name here.'

I was patient. 'I gave it to the porter you relieved about an hour and a half ago . . . Studio 4a . . . perhaps he forgot to write it down.'

He turned back some more pages and then closed the book. 'Nothing 'ere,' he said. 'BBC was it?' He picked up the telephone and dialled something. There was a long time of unanswered ringing. He replaced it thoughtfully and looked up at the clock. 'If it was BBC Studio 4a, they've all left. Closed. They don't work after five o'clock that lot. Been a mistake, I shouldn't wonder, try again tomorrer.'

I went back to the hard bench and sat down miserably. My train from Victoria didn't go until 6.45, and it was at least warm in the liver-coloured marble hall-way. I'd wait, then walk down to Piccadilly, call Freddy about the muck-up and go home. It was just my luck to arrive at the bloody place the very moment that the damned porters were changing over. For the tenth time I opened my *Evening News* and started to read the Situations Vacant column. You never knew . . .

'You're late! You're late! You're late!' A shrill, angry, impatient female voice jerked me from the paper. She was hurrying down the staircase, coat over her shoulders flying like a banner, her reddish hair had unpinned and flew about her face like rope, she had a long, sharp nose and a cigarette stuck to the corner of her lips. 'Come along, come along! Some people have no sense of time or discipline, it seems to me . . .' Grumbling furiously, and breathless, but with the cigarette still sticking amazingly to her lip, she hurried my bewildered body up the stairs and along a corridor into a small, smoke-sour little room.

A blaze of light, a table and two chairs, people standing or lolling around the walls. 'People are so bloody casual these days.' Her voice was exasperated. 'I'm Chloe Gibson. Sit down there.' She indicated the table and one empty chair. The other chair was occupied by a slim, dark-haired girl, who smiled, offered her hand and said her name was Maureen Pook. I hadn't even taken off my coat by this time. The angry woman with the rope hair shoved a couple of sheets of typed paper before me and said crossly: 'Now; this is the end of the second act. You read "Cliff". You've done a murder, and you are confessing it to "Anna", Miss Pook here. You can have a couple of seconds to read it through, don't hurry, then we'll go. It really is bloody tiresome of people being late all the time,' she complained to the silent smoke-hazed room, lighting another cigarette from the smouldering butt glued to her lower lip. Taking a deep pull she sat down, crossed her legs, put one elbow on her knee, shoved her chin into her cupped hand and squinted at me through the smoke and her rope-straggle of hair. Her foot began to swing impatiently. 'When you're ready bang off,' she said.

For the next ten minutes or so Miss Pook and I read the scene together. It came quite easily, and since I had to do most of the talking I just ploughed on. I was flustered, irritated, cold, angry at having missed the BBC interview and frightened of missing the six-forty-five. No one interrupted us, and when it was done, I placed the loose sheets of the script neatly together on the table, and started to pull on my gloves for the walk down to the Tube.

The rope-haired woman was still sitting hunched intently, as if she was watching a cock-fight with a bet placed. Her cigarette, I noticed, had grown a long length of grey ash which spilled all over her red woollen skirt when she suddenly sprang to her feet and said briskly: 'What's your name then, after all this?' I told her and she looked angrily at a sheet of paper in her hand.

'You aren't here!' she cried accusingly. 'Your name isn't on my list!' She turned despairingly, arms thrown wide, to the room in general. 'What am I to do . . . he's not on the *list* . . . where do you come from? Who are you?'

I told her about Studio 4a and told her the agent's name and that it had all been a mistake and that I was sorry for wasting her time. She threw her list on to the table, and spun round on one leg so fast that her coat fell to the floor.

'Dear God!' she cried. 'These bloody agents . . . you're in the wrong place! We are casting a play . . . we aren't the bloody BBC . . . you are here under false pretences!' It was useless to explain to this hysterical virago about the mistake, so I just thanked Miss Pook, still patiently sitting at the table, and headed for the door. 'Anyway that part was cast weeks ago!' the angry voice zipped across the room like a ricochetting bullet. 'Weeks ago! I don't know what happens in this business. You aren't on the *list!*'

I walked slowly through driving snow down to Piccadilly underground. My feet sodden, the demob shoes as waterproof as a fishing net, my hands, in spite of the woollen gloves, wet and frozen. What I badly needed after such a wasted day was a good stiff drink, or even a cup of bottled coffee. However, all I had was the half of my return ticket to Haywards Heath, and a few coppers which I inserted into the telephone at a call box to tell Freddy of my failure.

'Afraid I screwed that all up. Missed the BBC, they forgot me or something, never saw the Piffard man you told me to, and went to the wrong room to read a play they have already cast. Terribly sorry. It's the first thing I have made a bosh of; I don't really know what went wrong.'

Freddy's voice was calm and reassuring and quite unworried. 'Never mind,' he said, 'these things happen. Fortunately . . . you've got the part.'

I was stunned in my wet shoes. The khaki woollen gloves were steaming gently. 'What part?'

'The thing you just read; they have just this minute telephoned to say they want to change their minds about the other actor and have you instead. Rehearsals start Monday morning at nine-thirty, New Lindsey Theatre, Notting Hill. Not much money, five quid. Still since you missed the BBC, you'd better accept. I think they are mad – but you never know . . . it may work out.'

Someone tapped with a coin on the glass door and made impatient signs for me to hurry up. 'Freddy . . . I've got to go . . . I'll miss my train. I don't know what to do. It's cast; and the woman was bloody rude as well; I can't make up my mind.' Freddy's voice was flat, clear and positive for the very first time. 'You take it, that's what you do. I'll call them now and say it's set. Have a nice weekend.' He rang off.

Crossing the wide underground circus, bashing into the milling throngs of commuters to Tulse Hill, Golders Green and Upminster, I found a wastepaper basket and shoved the *Evening News* and the floppy BBC script deep into its tin throat, then, unburdened, I joined the seething faceless mass and clattered down the escalator for Victoria. Entirely unaware that I was making my exit from privacy and anonymity for the rest of my life.

CHAPTER FIVE

Can a sky be the colour of opals? This one seemed to be; white, translucent with heat, little specks of green, blue and orange flicking across my tired eyes. It was not yet eight in the morning. What would it be like by noon? There was no breeze, everything still, silent, waiting, shimmering out of focus in little waves. I lay, half propped, half sprawled, against the trunk of a cusuarina tree, in the fretwork shade, where Johnny, George and a little Indian Corporal with brown teeth and a squint cap-badge had carefully set me down: my right foot hurt like fury, even though both boot and gaiter were removed, and the whole swollen lump had been carefully bandaged and eased, for some reason, into a thick, green woollen sock. An hour before Doctor Hubialla, with gentle hands, had given me a pain killing injection with a far from clean syringe.

'Is it broken?' My voice had a forced indifference.

'Oh . . . hard to tell, you know . . . could be . . . could be . . . angry swelling, I must say, but it's not broken off, is it?' He laughed cheerfully. 'Oh no, goodness me no, whatever next I say, not broken off. You still have it, don't you? But hard to say without an X-ray.' He shoved the needle into the livid ankle. 'This is not really big enough, you know.' He was apologetic. 'Came in such a hurry . . . but if you keep still, like a good fellow, we'll unscrew the plunger, fill it all up again, re-screw it in, and then Bob's your uncle, to be sure.'

He did; refilling the syringe carefully, the needle and the base still sticking awkwardly out of the swollen foot. I was beyond caring anyway, and the pain was easing. Or I thought it was. When he finished he carefully removed his cap, placed the syringe neatly inside the cap band, and shook my hand warmly.

'How did you do it? Not playing dominoes, I'll be bound.'

'I jumped out of a jeep.'

'A jeep? Ah . . .'

'It was moving quite fast.'

'Foolishness.'

'Necessary.'

'I follow. Heedless youth . . .' He left in a flurry of little bows and laughter.

Across the burned scrubby valley, the hills were opal too . . . white to grey . . . scabby thron bushes, cactus, buff-ragged rocks as high as a house, and, running like a strip of dirty bandage trailed through the scrub, the zigzag white road through the gorge along which, very soon, the first of the refugees, some thousand of them, would appear dragging along in the heat. And then, broken foot or no broken foot, I would have to scrabble down somehow and join them, and lead them painfully and slowly to the plains below – men, women, many children, goats, some sheep. Above me, slightly to my right, a baboon with matted hair the colour of dirty cornflakes defecated into the dust at my side. It spattered across my leg, and the green woollen sock. Sweat ran down my face, my neck, stinging under my chin. Flies came, humming with pleasure. The baboon threw the last of his half-eaten fruit at me and, scolding angrily, scampered into the branches which sagged and swayed with his weight. To my left the burned-out hulk of a Ford V8, tilted on its side against a boulder, smouldered acridly, thin oily smoke weaving out in to the still, breathless air, like a veil. Vultures dragged, and squabbled at something fleshy crushed into the backseat.

I heaved myself up to a more or less sitting position, and tried carefully to move my foot. The stabbing pain swamped me, and left me breathless: the injection was wearing off. I grabbed for the large piece of branch someone had given me for a crutch, and tried to haul myself to my good foot. The movement irritated the vultures who, with bloody beaks and beady eyes, battered and scrambled out of the wrecked car and lumbered, gorged, in to the air, to float gracefully away across the shimmering valley.

On the little slope below me, seeking what shade they could from a thicket of baked bamboo, the Indian troops sprawled motionless. The hard morning light winking on the brass and metal of their equipment. One of them, fanning his face with a bunch of leaves against the flies, murmured something and a ripple of laughter rose and faded in to the heat. They were still, save for the rustling bunch of leaves. Standing a little apart, incongruous in boots and breeches, Captain 'Sonny' Herkashin tapped his glittering shins thoughtfully with a swagger cane, his eyes fixed tiredly on the road across the valley. He was handsome, twenty-five, and worried. Seeing me, he called up the slope and asked me how I felt.

'Not so bad, as long as I don't put my foot to the ground.'

He looked sad. 'You resemble a stork standing there.'

'I feel like one.'

'What a business, I must say. Rotten luck.'

I hobbled down the slope towards him, sweat coursing down my throat, the green woollen foot swinging out before me like a gourd.

'It's almost nine o'clock, they should be due at any minute.' I started past him, and he offered me his arm which, in a hum of flies, I brushed aside. He was stiff with hurt.

'Stubborn chap, you really are. I was offering you help . . .'

I was immediately contrite, took his wrist and rested on my crutch. 'Sorry. Really . . . wasn't thinking.'

His brown eyes, with the faint pink whites, of all Indians, were mournful.

'I must try and do it on my own, Sonny, don't you see? I have to. Discipline, all that shit . . .' I hopped on slowly.

'Ah! Sandhurst and all that, what?'

I went on down, stubbornly, and tripped over part of a rather large ant-hill.

'Sandhurst and all that: you've got it.'

I stopped and looked back up at him standing on the little ridge. Impassive. Uncomprehending. His Sam Browne shining like conkers: suddenly he turned and walked away. I noticed he was wearing spurs and wondered if he'd trip in the sere, scraggy brush. At the bamboos he called out sharp, irritated, little orders and his Company started resentfully to straggle to their feet.

The vultures were wheeling, gliding, in the high draught from the plain. As soon as we were out of their sight they'd be down again, tugging obscenely at the muck stuffed into the back of the Ford. The valley lay before me, beige, still, and suddenly from the mouth of the gorge a low, open white roadster shot into view like a gleaming bullet. It whipped along the dusty winding bandage-road trailing a column of dust which rose into the motionless air like enormous plumes, higher and higher. Dimly through the fog, I could see a darker car following. Up on a rock behind me an English voice cursed splendidly, and someone came clattering down shouting orders beyond the reeking Ford. Captain Herkashin screamed at his Company, wagging his cane, straightening his jacket, wiping his forehead. The white car took a left turn, suddenly, and ripped across the valley floor like a toy gone wild – for a moment or two it was lost among the scrubby thorns and bushes – and then came on up towards my ridge. I stood stork-like; the dust was now so thick and so high that the sun was a crimson ball. English curses drifted back across the rocks as the white sports car slammed to a stop yards from my sagging body. She jumped out with the agility of a track-runner, trim white slacks, spotless white shirt, her initials in black on the pocket, long dark hair streaming, a ring glittering, bracelets, the buckles on her Gucci slippers flashing. She was dazzling, beautiful. Brushing hair from her forehead she came towards me smiling. The bracelets slid down to her elbow.

'Not late, am I? I told you I was a punctual woman . . . good training.' She stood hands on hips, and looked out over the dust-filled valley. 'Where are they? I mean, haven't you started yet? I haven't missed anything, I'd be furious.' She smiled a wide uncaring smile. Up on the rocks the English voices were still complaining and grumbling.

'No. We haven't started yet. I think, as a matter of fact, that Your Highness has rather mucked things up for the moment.'

She looked vaguely surprised.

'What have *I* done?'

'The dust . . .' It was thinning slowly.

'What of it?'

'Well, we can't shoot through dust; they'll have to wait until it settles.'

She shrugged impatiently. 'Oh, the cinema. I never will understand you people. But it's real, you know. There *is* dust here.'

'I know. But you can't see through it.'

A rather plump, saried lady with Bata sandals and an Instamatic camera round her neck joined us from the white car and I was presented, and bowed my head. She smiled and said that they had passed hundreds and hundreds of people and goats down the road, were they refugees? I said they were and she looked impressed. 'So many, maybe a thousand. And so tired and hot and the children crying . . . oh dear . . .'

'Well, they are supposed to be hot and tired and everything. They are supposed to be the last refugees out of Burma.'

The saried Princess giggled and put her hand politely over her mouth. 'How will they know when to start walking, I wonder?'

'We will fire a Verey Light into the sky. That's the signal.'

'But first,' said Her Highness, 'we'll wait for my dust to settle, is that it?'

She wandered up the slope in her gleaming slippers effortlessly. Captain Herkashin screamed something into the morning air and his entire Company thudded to the ground like dead grouse. He threw a salute, his eyes wild as a mad horse's, belt and buttons gleaming. Her Highness walked past the grouse pulling a long strand of hair behind her ear. She murmured something to the Captain, who by the grace of her favour, and God, relaxed his anguished posture and screamed another order, and when the Company was standing once again in a row like a triple picket-fence, they were inspected and the fat Princess in the sari started snapping away with her Instamatic. Other Princesses, and a Prince and a scatter of people had clambered out of the dark Bentley which had followed, and a faint feeling of a picnic was in the air. The dust was clearing, members of the English camera crew were presented, and then everyone took up positions for the first shot of the day. A worried-looking boy called Eric, in a thick blue serge suit from Burtons, stood ready with the Verey Pistol.

'We won't stay long . . . just see the first march of the refugees. I suppose you'll do it again and again as they always do in the films?' She was cool and matter of fact. Bored really. 'I have to get back anyway pretty soon; your party tonight. I think we have about five hundred coming, all in their traditional costumes; especially for you. They weren't frightfully pleased, but I insisted. The City Palace is only opened occasionally now, for honoured guests . . .' A bleak smile. 'So we might as well make a splash, mightn't we? It will be almost like old times again. Not quite, of course.' She smiled a vivid, accusing smile. 'Not quite, but as near as we can make it. And, anyway, it'll be the last time too . . . this time next year it will be an hotel, full of Americans all over my tennis courts.' She turned away with distaste. The Princess was photographing Eric in his blue serge suit. Up on the rocks someone yelled down: 'We can go! Dust is settled. Eric?' He nodded blindly, pistol in hand.

'I'll give you a count down. On "one" you fire, right?'

Her Highness moved a little nearer to me, on my slope, and shaded her eyes with a slender, ivory, hand. 'It'll be very beautiful tonight. I hope you'll be pleased with it all. They are working on the water pumps so that all the fountains will play, and the little canals will flow, scattered with rose petals and jasmin and marigolds. What happened to your foot, is it for the film?'

'No. I broke it yesterday jumping out of a jeep.'

Her laugh, at once derisive and unbelieving, frightened Eric, who, forgetting his position, cried out, 'Shush! . . . please!'

'Oh we're used to broken feet and every other sort of broken thing here! Polo, you remember? We have lots of wheel-chairs . . . you'll come in one of them. I'll have someone very beautiful to push you about.'

'It hurts like hell at the moment. I don't honestly think I could make the evening really. I'm terribly sorry. Can we just see how I get through today? I have to walk all the way down the valley with the damned refugees . . . I'm just terrified I'll pass out.'

She was flat. 'They have goats and sheep with them, the people in the gorge, we saw them on our way here. So no one will be walking faster than the cattle. You'll manage. And you'll manage tonight, I'm sure. A wheel-chair and Heaven knows how many nobles. All 'Our Court' . . . and all in honour of you, Sir.' Her sarcasm was pointed if faint.

Eric fidgeted; from the rocks a voice yelled down and asked me if I was ready to start moving; I was to start my descent of the hill to the valley as the head of the refugee column reached a certain tree a million miles, it seemed to me, below. There was a moment of tense silence; even the Princess with her Instamatic was still. On the morning air we heard the count down start. A thick Cockney accent began the numbers: 'Eight, seven, six . . .'

Her Highness turned slightly towards me, smiling, her eyes were very bright. 'Broken foot indeed . . . goodness me! You're British, aren't you? Well, you must show us what you can do.'

'You really must, dear. You must show us what you can do.' Chloe Gibson's voice was dull with defeat and cigarettes. Her hair, which had once hung down around her face like old rope, was scragged back into an untidy bun. She dropped her cigarette stub into the thick coffee cup where it hissed sullenly for a second before extinguishing itself in the weak dregs. Hunching her shoulders, she leaned towards me: 'I know you can do it. I knew that first evening when you came up late and read the part. I knew it . . . I *know* it. But it's the Company: they don't know. They can't judge what you are going to do. Or even if you can. It's nearly three weeks and you haven't given much of a sign, dear. Nothing. You can't go on just walking through it, the others are trying desperately hard to give performances, but it is completely and utterly impossible for them if you don't play back. You must see that?'

She was being more than reasonable, and I knew, with terror, that she was right. I was still walking through it; I hadn't even tried to give a performance. Yet. We still had another five days before opening and I was trying to save the performance until we had the costumes and the props, the real chairs, tables and the chenille curtains at the windows. Walking about on the top floor of the dingy red brick building across the street, with chalk marks on the scratched parquet floor, two or three bentwood chairs and a Watneys beer crate, didn't, for me at any rate, hold magic. I was, I thought, storing up my work until the time was ripe. All the others were hard at it making characters; Maureen even managed tears, so did Beatrice as my mother: they were able, in their actors' minds, to transform the chalk marks in to the walls and the door of the back-shop parlour as if it had the fireplace and the whole staircase down. They mimed brilliantly, teapots, beer glasses, door handles; they believed. And they obviously didn't like me much, nor, as it turned out now, did they get any help from me.

I was shattered by my selfishness, terrified by my innate shyness – this shyness which has inhibited me all my life. The wrong profession for such a malady; for malady it was which crippled me before I walked into a crowded room, theatre, restaurant or bar. But I knew, sitting at the tacky table in the Linden Cafe in Notting Hill Gate that day, that my time for timidity and selfish shyness was about up. Someone was calling my bluff. And she wasn't going to let me get away with it: her production, and her blinding faith in my capabilities, were at stake. I was at stake too. Windlesham still waited; I had not, as yet, cancelled my appointment with the patient Headmaster in the pines and heather.

She hunched and shrugged herself into her tweed coat, avoiding my assistance. 'Of course,' she fumbled about in her large, beaten, handbag, 'of course, we could always postpone things for a week . . .' She pulled a stubby bit of lipstick across her thin, cracked lips, and smacked them together as if savouring a sauce. 'Just for a week. It would give us time to re-cast you.'

My heart stopped beating altogether. I looked out through the steamy windows into the dirty snow-packed street. The red shape of a bus slowly ambled past. Re-cast. In my first theatre job in years. The utter shame overwhelmed me. I was stiff with silence. She snapped the clasp of the bag, and studied the slip of paper which was the bill for our coffees and sandwiches. 'If you would like that? The boy who was cast and went up to Newcastle with that tour is free . . . they closed in Leeds last week. It would break my heart but I must think of the Company, and my play. I know you'll understand.' She laid some money on the slip of paper, left three pennies under her cup for a tip and started for the greasy door.

I caught her up, pulling on gloves against the bitter afternoon. I couldn't speak. Crossing Notting Hill Gate, slithering among the lumps of packed, oily, snow, I kept behind her a little, watching the red tweed coat flapping, the battered bag swinging, remembering that night in the Aeolian Hall when she had hustled me up the stairs and into the little smoky room to read the play and finally to give me the part. I couldn't betray her. At the door of the grimy red brick building I took her arm. She stopped. 'What shall I do?' she asked. 'Send them home and re-cast . . . or what?'

There were icicles hanging from a burst pipe just above us. 'No . . . don't do that. Not yet. Could you, I mean would you, just let's run the play right through; from start to finish, no notes, pauses. . . all three acts . . . so I can get a run at it. Perhaps then . . .' I knew that then I'd be on trial, that I'd have to bash through, that shyness and timidity and all the rest of it would be put aside in the sheer exhilarating excitement of becoming another person. In becoming the man I was trying to play: 'Cliff'.

While they all sat about, the Company, on chairs round the wall of the beastly little room, I was sure that all they were thinking was how bad I was; inept, thin, useless: irritation and dismissal floated from their slouched bodies like a gas. Of course this was arrant nonsense; they had their own worries and problems, their own fears and doubts, as I did. But, naturally, I only considered myself. And how I felt. Not how they did. I wanted it all my way. And got it. Chloe sighed, shoved a sliding pin back into her pot-scrap-bun, and nodded doubtfully. 'I meant to do a polishing job on the Second Act. Still . . . if you think it'll help . . .' We started up the stone steps to the Rehearsal Room, slowly, her beaten-up handbag slapping the iron handrail.

The Company were assembled. Sitting round the small gas fire which blinked and popped (it was the coldest winter for fifty-three years) they looked up with no surprise. I almost expected it, because we have a cruel, and true, saying in our profession, should you be taken to lunch by your Producer, that you 'won't be with us after lunch, dear' – a sure sign of re-casting. But perhaps she hadn't told them before . . . they might not even have known anything. Perhaps I wasn't so awful. I warmed. Kenneth More, sitting in his ex-Naval overcoat, badges of rank long since ripped off, a string bag beside him with a packet of cornflakes and a pint of milk (he'd collected his rations in the break); Dandy Nichols reading the noon edition of *The Standard* to find her horoscope; Maureen Pook just sitting and smoking and warming her frozen legs; Beatrice Varley knitting with the placidity of a country nanny. How could I have doubted them? How could I have behaved so badly? Self-pity started and was smothered swiftly by Chloe chucking her coat into a corner and announcing that we would forget the polishing of the Second Act, and instead we'd run through the entire play from start to finish, no pauses, no notes, no timing. 'Just bash away at it,' she cried, as if we were all novice jockeys. 'Bash away and see what we get.'

A slightly bewildered Company got to its feet, stuffed newspapers into handbags, knitting into chintz-holdalls, and Kenny slowly removed his heavy navy blue overcoat. We started on the First Act.

At the finish, two hours later, Chloe with swimming eyes embraced us all, said nothing, and struggled into her red coat. 'There's a hell of a lot to do . . . but we still have time, thank God. Maureen, when you say "Do you see?" go below the table, not above it, so that Beatrice can play downstage . . . must see her eyes. Kenneth dear; I think you could stay a titch bit longer at the door, only a titch mind you, in the Second Act with Cliff and Anna, take the shock, see what I mean?' She rattled off orders, suggestions, pulling on gloves, tucking a tartan scarf about the scraggy hair, cigarette dangling. Eyes bright. 'Tomorrow, same time. We'll start with Act Two . . . and I'll give you notes then. What the bloody hell have I done with my lighter?'

It was dark when we reached the street. Lamps flickered . . . there was a power cut again. She shivered, pulling the red coat round her, the bag slapping. 'Oh by the by . . .' she grabbed my arm, 'pause a bit longer at the top of the stairs on your first entrance; don't milk it, just a beat longer, it'll hold.' She suddenly leaned up and gave me a rough, completely unexpected kiss. 'I knew.

I knew!' she said, and hurried off down to Holland Park.

In 1947 India at last gained her Independence, and exploded bloodily; Princess Elizabeth married a Mountbatten and tied all that up; Henry Ford and Gordon Selfridge both died; Albert Camus wrote *La Peste*, and Michael Clayton-Hutton wrote, and had produced, on February 25th, at the New Lindsey Theatre, his first play, 'Power Without Glory'. A good many other events took place as well in that year, but nothing was so impacted on my mind as that solitary event off Notting Hill Gate.

At the fall of the curtain nothing much happened. We shuffled on to the stage in a complete silence, feeling drained, unhappy, worried. Kenny murmured under his breath at the line up, 'They've all pissed off . . .' and then the place erupted. The applause and the cheering continued, after that first almost stunned silence, for so long that eventually we were all forced to take hands, on the stage, and stood grinning and laughing inanely at each other, as the curtain rose and fell. Chloe was standing in the wings in a long woollen dress. Smoking.

Up in the dressing room which Kenny and I shared on the roof, a long wooden shelf on one side, some hooks banged into the wall on the other, a washbowl crammed into a corner, we quietly removed our make-up and stared into the long, scratched mirror before us.

'I think we're a hit,' he said presently.

'They don't often do that, do they? Audiences, I mean?'

'Christ! No. Usually the other way round with a try out.'

'It's a very nice feeling is all I can say, isn't it?'

Kenny grinned into the mirror.

'Enjoy it. You may never see its like again.'

A scuffling on the stairs; the door flew open. A bright-eyed man. 'Van Thal. Pinewood Studios. Remember I saw you first!' A woman behind him pushed under his arm. 'And I saw you second!' They slammed the door and clattered away.

Kenny winked. 'Must be agents!'

We laughed together and I started to dress hurriedly. There was a reception in the Club Bar; my Father and Mother had come all the way up from Sussex, and Elizabeth from somewhere else. Kenny was being maddeningly slow. He was still wiping muck of his face, still in his underpants, calm, as ever, unhurried.

'Oh come on, for God's sake! You'll miss the party.'

He got up slowly from his wooden chair, greasy face, a lump of cotton wool in one hand, his pants slipping round his hips. He hugged me suddenly to him. 'Off you go, mate, it's your night, I'll catch you up later.'

In the excitement of the night I didn't really take in much of what he said. But somehow I did remember it. That evening I saw no further than the Club Bar of the New Lindsey, which was full to bursting with red-faced, jolly looking people. As I pushed through they clapped as if I was a dog at a Show, and some patted me on the back in the same manner. Freddy was in a corner with some people; he smiled cheerfully and raised his glass to me in a silent salute. I found my mother, and we embraced; people drew back for this moving moment of mother and son. 'Marvellous, darling!' she cried. 'Look, my mascara has all run, does it show? It hurst like hell.' My father, quiet, smiling, amused at some secret amusement (one never knew what with him), took my hand and kissed me too. 'Very good. Curious play. I've been talking to your Author. Seems very young . . .' His voice tailed away. My Author was hunched in a group by the small bar; a slight man, with blazing eyes like a lizard, a red carnation, fresh at lunchtime, a large gin and tonic. He was smiling his odd little twisted smile, which was attractive, and, tonight, kind. He winked only. I winked back, and he turned and talked to a fat hovering woman with a note pad and pencil. Elizabeth was there, in the middle of some people, splendid in a monstrous Chinchilla cape. Somebody gave me a whisky which slopped over her skirt. I apologised and started patting at it.

'Don't bother. It doesn't matter. It's old anyway.' She was happy and smiling.

'Chinchilla?'

'Sylvia loaned it to me, belonged to her mother. Stored all the war in a tin trunk in the garage but they forgot the mothballs; don't *touch* me, it comes out in handfuls.'

I hugged her to me laughing, whisky slopping unheeded, Chinchilla hairs wafting into the packed room. 'You see! I'm moulting! They'll all get hay fever or something dreadful . . . some allergy . . . I wonder what there will be left to hand back to Sylvia tomorrow?' A tall, blue-suited oaf carrying three drinks in his podgy hands pushed between us. 'How does it feel,' he roared, 'to be a Star Overnight?' He weaved his way through the pack.

Elizabeth looked quite put out. 'How frightfully rude,' she said.

Later, much later, in my small sub-let flat in Hasker Street (two rooms and a hot-plate on the landing; share of bathroom, for a quid a week), we sat together in the sitting room where I was to sleep on the divan, she to have my bed in the back room. The Chinchilla drifted hairs gently into the stuffy air. She had made some cocoa (habits die hard) in two mugs, we were both half asleep.

'What do you think it'll mean, then, all this?' She was curious, amused, not very serious.

'I don't know. Depends on tomorrow's papers and what they say really.'

'But they were awfully nice, the criticky people, weren't they? That funny woman with the hat, she was someone frightfully important. She said you were spell-binding!' She laughed, knowing much better herself. Remembering my moods and torturing, and sulks and one thing and another; sister junk. They remember everything you ever do. If they love you. 'But if it does work out, I mean, what then?'

'Well . . . we might transfer to a bigger theatre. Make more money. They might make a film out of it.'

'With you?' Her attack was sharp, pointed.

'I don't know . . . probably with Stewart Granger or someone, I don't think with me, they never use the original actor, always film stars. It's a sort of rule.'

'Oh dear! It's all ups and downs, isn't it. Like snakes and ladders.' She looked downcast, and sipped away thoughtfully. 'I'm dreadfully tired, are you? You must be, all that acting and so on. I think Daddy quite liked it, don't you? Seemed really quite impressed; for him; he had a very long talk with the Author boy. Funny creature, isn't he? So young. Sort of desperate. I think they are all a very funny lot in your profession. Do you think you could become famous? Like Charles Laughton or Michael Wilding or someone?'

I started putting a pillow case on the grubby floral cushions for my bed. 'I don't honestly know. Probably not. The people at Rank said my head was too small and my neck was all wrong.'

She looked startled, and peered up at my neck curiously. 'Your neck? Whatever is the matter with your neck? Herbert Marshall had a wooden leg, but you couldn't tell.'

I was tired now. I didn't know what would happen, all I did know was that something had happened, and that it was warm and pleasant and rewarding. So far. 'I don't know, honestly I don't. But if all went really well I suppose I might be a bit famous or something, if it lasted, and I could make a lot of money. If I was clever and all that.'

She put the cocoa mugs on to the tin tray and took them to the door. 'How much money, I mean sort-of how much?' She stood looking at me with interest. I pulled down the floral divan cover and revealed a grey-looking blanket. There were no sheets.

'A hundred pounds a week even. I don't know.'

She went out on to the landing and stacked the mugs, not clinking them so as not to wake the elderly interior decorators who lived on the ground floor. Coming back in, and closing the door gently, I saw that she was smiling contentedly to herself. 'A hundred pounds a week! Goodness! I consider that very nice indeed,' and seeing my worried face she laughed and added, 'well, I mean, just for acting it's not bad, is it? I mean it's better than a wallop . . .'

I finished it off for her, 'a wallop in the belly with a wet fish!' We laughed, tired, warmed by the childhood joke, Lally had said it was plain vulgar when we once dared to use it, and given us a cuffing.

'Much better than that!' I said.

The Press the next morning was all a Rave. That is to say we were a hit and I was 'an actor to watch' and indeed, as the podgy oaf of the night before had said, and perhaps he even wrote it, A Star Overnight. My father telephoned from *The Times* with carefully concealed pleasure and read one or two bits over the line; my mother came up with Aunt Freda and had coffee – we laughed at the caricatures of myself; and Forwood called up in the middle of it all.

'Maddening having one's friends becoming stars overnight. Are you free for some lunch?'

I wasn't. 'I have to take my mother and an aunt to lunch. I wish I were free.'

I heard him stifle a yawn. 'Never mind. But it is a very nice beginning, just don't let it go to your head.' He hung up and we all went off to Kettners. At the door there, a thin, scraggy black cat suddenly sprang across the street and, arching its back, tail like a pole, it rubbed itself hard against my legs, and then shot back into the shadow of a bombed building opposite. It was a very nice start indeed.

In the late afternoon I walked from Sloane Square down to Notting Hill with all the evening papers, which were as good as the dailies had been, and sliding over the packed snow I knew, really for the first time in my life, just how splendid it felt to have wings on your heels, and in the theatre the Company were gathered together for Second Night Notes, and in a solemn ceremonial, presented me with an inverted china pudding bowl. To put on my head to see if it still fitted. We were all extremely relieved to find that it did.

And the day after I wrote a polite, and regretful, letter to Windlesham.

Although I had more or less scooped the pool with the play, we were all of us singled out for our individual praises. My part was extremely flashy, noisy, and centre-stage for most of the time. I also had a splendid scream in the Third Act, and that is usually irresistible to both audiences and critics alike, who tend to confuse the part with the player. You really can't miss with a good yell. However, the other member of the Company who was especially singled out was a quiet, pale, sensitive girl called Mary Horn whose work was, quite simply, staggering. She got a great deal of praise but eventually, after a year or so, she withdrew from the theatre and went off to be a House-Mistress in a boys' school in Scotland. A grievous loss to the theatre.

But none of this worried me at the time naturally. I kept my money safely in a large Oxo tin in my suitcase under the bed, and knew just where I stood in the world financially. I gave my ration book to a pleasant lady called Millie in the Express Dairies at the end of the road and lived on a diet of Weetabix, Kraft cheese, H.P. sauce and an occasional apple. I washed my clothes in the washbowl in the shared bathroom and took things like sheets and pillow cases down to Hillside Cottage once a fortnight to my unfortunate mother. I brought a few bits and pieces from the cottage to stick about the anonymous furniture of my two-roomer, got a cracked lustre jug from a junk shop in Walton Street, filled it with catkins, and settled into London life, if not exactly its society.

My demob suit was wearing out, worn as it was, daily. And the shirts and slacks which I had brought from Calcutta and Singapore looked faintly dated once they were unpacked and worn in the King's Road. My father sent me off to his tailor and I got a fine grey flannel suit made, bought a neat green hat from Henry Heath, some chamois gloves from Gieves, and succeeded in looking more like a trainer of horses than a moderately successful out-of-the-West-End actor.

The play was packed nightly and we became fashionable. Everyone came to see us. Film companies, agents, talent scouts and on one memorable night, Noël Coward. Nervously we were all told to assemble on stage after the Show since The Master wished to address us individually. We stood in a short neat line of seven. I was beside Maureen and at the end of the line. I didn't hear what he said to the others, saw him kiss Beatrice, wag his finger often, and when he got to Maureen I just heard him say: 'The name Pook is disaster, change it immediately.' Maureen, shattered with nerves, said, 'It must be to something beginning with a P!' and Noël murmured gently, 'We aren't playing word games, dear.' And moved on to me. I got the finger wagged. 'Never, ever, ever take a pill, not even an aspirin before a show, and never, ever drink until after curtain-fall.' He said, in general, that we were all lovely, talented, moving and clever and thanked us.

As we wandered off to our dressing room, he shot out a very firm hand and took my elbow: 'And never, ever, go near the cinema!' and was gone into the night.

I obeyed his first commands implicitly.

Letters started to arrive from elderly Gentlemen Novelists, and odd-sounding ladies with double-barrelled names with addresses in Hampstead and South Kensington. Forwood got me a job in a Crime Film. It was hardly what you might call a part; just a policeman sitting in an office. And I was never noticed unfortunately. The uniform they gave me didn't fit and so was pinned up the front and the camera was behind me; however, I did have one line to say, 'Calling Car 2345. Calling Car 2345' into a sort of microphone, and although it starred the Attenboroughs I never met them. But it was a start, and for that one day's work I earned double my week's salary in the theatre; and coming back to Town on the bus from Islington Studios I vaguely thought how simple it was, and how much better paid, and how I could, in a very short time indeed, fill the Oxo tin and move to a larger flat than the one with the hot-plate on the landing in Hasker Street. But equally I knew that it was a flashy sort of job, and that it didn't take, or need, much talent. The theatre was at least honourable. I had a lot to learn.

Eventually the snow melted, in this extraordinary winter, and the vague signs of spring arrived and with them came Peter Daubeny, the Golden Boy Wonder I had so briefly met back stage with Forwood, and who had been singularly, or so it seemed, unimpressed with me. Mr Daubeny bought the play, which impressed him enormously, and transferred us to the West End in April. We were giddy with delight, sure of a long, long run, rich with our new West End salaries (I got ten pounds a week now), and completely overlooked the fact, or chose to ignore it if we knew it, that our theatre was miscalled the Fortune, stood opposite the Stage Door of Drury Lane, had a public right of way running through the auditorium and across the stage dating from God knew when, and was extremely difficult to get to unless you were hell bent on being there. Which, in spite of magical critics again, no one was. No one even used the public right of way, and 'Oklahoma' opened shortly after us, and filled the narrow street with steak-eating, jean-clad, healthy, Americans who all seemed to sing, dance *and* act. Confidently nursing our wounds we prophesied that we would get the overflow of those who could not obtain seats for this fantastic musical (we heard many curious stories from our dressers of people actually fainting in the Stalls and Circle from the sheer energy set before them), but there again we were miserably wrong. If you go out to see a new American musical, the first since the war, it is very unlikely that, being unable to get in you would turn your eyes across the street to our modest canopy and come in to see a tense play about the working class in South London. Forget it. And everybody did. After a very short time we slid into the eternal obscurity of the Fatal Fortune and our happy time was over. But not before Queen Mary expressed a surprising wish to see us perform, which threw us into complete panic and faint hope. Perhaps, if she liked it, we could solicit publicity from the Palace to help us fight the lusty Yanks across the street. But it didn't make a mite of difference. 'Oh What a Beautiful Morning!' became, alas, our requiem.

Apart from Royalty, someone else came before the electric lights went out for ever on our humble, modest, moving play. Ian Dalrymple, quiet, soft spoken, thoughtful, articulate, who smoked his cigarettes through paper holders and looked more like a Cambridge don than a film producer, signed me up for his next film, 'Esther Waters', showing either great courage or arrant stupidity. But he was so gentle, so persuasive, so unlike the kind of film producer I had ever expected to meet, that I was lost. Mr Coward's ultimate warning was drowned by Mr Dalrymple's charm and detailed explanations of my role of 'William Latch'.

'But what about my neck?'

He pushed his glasses up his nose and looked hard at me. 'What's the matter with your neck?'

'The Rank people say it's too thin. My head's too small. I don't look like David Farrar or James Mason.'

'I don't see anything wrong with it, your neck. Your head will soon swell anyway; and until it does we'll have your hats made by Lock and you'll be wearing stocks most of the time. I shouldn't worry This is new Cinema.' He seemed quite confident. So I decided that I should too; after all, he knew much better than I did. And wore glasses. So that when Mr Coward came to tell us all, just before we closed, that he had written marvellous parts for us all in his new play, 'Peace in our Time', mine was the only heart which sank. I knew I would have to confess.

'You remember what I told you. Never, ever, the cinema.'

'Yes.'

'You ignored my advice?'

'I didn't know that you'd written me a part.'

'You'll dine with me tonight. This is madness . . .'

It was not mentioned at the Savoy Grill – so many people came to the table that it resembled Gold Cup Day at Ascot. So we went back to his house in

Gerald Road. It was not, as he pointed out, much more than spitting distance from Hasker Street.

I was miserably shy, and walked stiffly beside him down the street and into the yard of his house. Impatiently he stood at the gate. 'Go straight ahead, that's the front door, I put on the light here.' He pressed a switch in the wall. 'I shan't jump on you. I'm not the type, and Gerald Row Police Station is immediately opposite you. Would you care for a whistle or will you merely shout?'

We talked for an age. His advice was considered, wise, careful. The cinema would ruin me, I had a great deal to offer the theatre, a whole new world was starting there now the war was over; I must be patient, loyal, devoted and learn from my new craft which had, so far, welcomed me with such warmth. Magic lay before me and he had, incidentally written me a 'walloping great part' in 'Peace'. But it was to no avail. I confessed that I had given my word to Mr Dalrymple, that I wanted to try the cinema and do the theatre as well, that my contract would allow me to do one play for six months every second year, that I had not abandoned the Proscenium Arch, merely postponed my moment. He was not at all best pleased. 'I think,' he said, 'you are being a cunt. And I am very, very, angry indeed.'

With thirty pounds a week from the Rank Organisation as a sort of holding-salary until the film started, and ten a week from the tottering play, I was richer than I imagined I'd ever be. And one day walked with great courage and my Oxo tin into an Estate Agents in Sloane Square and rented number 44 Chester Row for ten guineas a week. Furnished; with garden, three floors, and basement.

In the kitchen in the basement, with a quart of ale and a smoked haddock and mashed potatoes, and under the unbelieving, but pleased eyes, of Freddy Joachim, I signed my contract with the Rank Organisation for, at that time, seven years. In the morning I had gone along to Kettners Restaurant, found the black cat crouched in a wooden box in his bomb-site, and brought him back to S.W.1. I called him 'Cliff' after the role in the play. As Freddy and I toasted ourselves in pale ale, I chucked Cliff the haddock skin, and then started on the washing up, with Freddy drying and stacking up the plates and things on the wooden dresser. We made a comfortable, domestic scene.

'Seven years seems an eternity,' I said, wrapping up the remainder of the fish-skin and bones in newspaper.

Freddy wiped out the saucepan carefully, 'Oh! They'll probably drop you long before that, you know, the contract is renewable every year. I very much doubt if you'll last all that time. It's a fickle business, and you aren't really the right type for the cinema, you know. Of course,' he added brightly, 'this role in "Esther Waters" is what you might call a Character Part . . . probably why they picked you. You could be a very good character actor, I feel sure; but I can't remember a real cinema star who was just a character actor. They need a bit more glamour; anyway we must cross our fingers, work hard, stay modest, and hope for the best. Things change all the time, we really can't tell at the moment. Grasp the nettle, I always say.' He slid the saucepan, cleaned and shining, on to the shelf and took off the towel which he had tied round his waist as an apron. And then all the lights went out. Another power cut.

'Don't move!' I cried. 'I know where the matches are.' By the flickering light of two candles Freddy took up the contract, and placed it carefully in his briefcase. 'We don't want to lose this, do we. I must admit I really didn't expect it all to happen so soon, or even at all. You must feel very chuffed.'

'I don't know really. Chuffed or not. It's all a bit frightening, signing your life away for seven years, and all those clauses . . . I wonder if I'll even last seven years.'

He smiled his kindly smile, wrapped himself into his black coat, folded a scarf round his throat. 'These spring evenings are very chilly . . . most treacherous,' and patted my arm with an unexpected avuncularity. 'Cheer up, do! You mustn't dwell on the gloomy side tonight, it's all gone so wonderfully well so far. It's been quite a big adventure, yes, I really think that we can say that. A big adventure in a very few months, now all you have to do is work very hard, and show us all what you can do.'

Ten years later, on a scrub-covered hillside, in the centre of India, I was standing 'like a stork' on one leg, with a broken foot, a clutch of Indian Royalty behind me, an uncertain future ahead, more than thirty films in the past and a thousand refugees starting their unhappy trek along the white twisting gorge road, vultures drifting in the opal light: it was a long haul from the shabby kitchen and the crisp new contract and Freddy wrapping himself up like a parcel for the walk to Sloane Square and the Tube.

And I was still trying to 'prove', to show them what I could do. Would it ever end, this proving, this statement of determination? Wasn't it enough that I had done what I had done in spite of skinny neck, small head and a pair of too long legs? I had long since closed, with wry regret, my Oxo tin and opened an account in a high marbled hall opposite the Law Courts. I had played bookies and thugs, soldiers and sailors and pilots. Bombed Berlin. Braved a bursting dam; been various doctors, in the house, at sea, at large and in distress; suffered from amnesia, and shot a policeman. I'd even played Sydney Carton. God knows what I had not done. But my determination to prove was still insatiable, the need to show what I could do was still my driving force. Today, I realised as I started to hobble down the slope to join my thousand refugees I was heavy with despair. One had to go on doing it simply to survive, but, I wondered as I came abreast of the hot, sweating, dusty mass dragging along the road, was it really all worth it? Swinging into line with them, hopping with my crutch, with what I hoped was a noble lift of the head (to favour the main camera up above me), I could not rid myself of the thought that it was all a dreadful waste of time, effort and life. Surely there were better things to do with the years I had, so far, been given than forcing myself to prove continually?

Up on the ridge the first whisper of a breeze riffled the pink and silver sari of the fat Princess, billows of white dust swirled and eddied about our sweaty ranks. I could see the sunlight glinting on the three great cameras on their separate rocks, smoke drifting still from the wrecked car, the shimmering plain ahead. I looked, briefly behind me, and our trail seemed endless, a thousand people is a great many . . . sheep, goats, women in torn cotton prints, children dragging along, men taut-faced, sweating, some bandaged . . . an old woman with a white parasol being jostled along on a creaking cart surrounded with bundles and kettles and a clock. This had all once happened, not so long ago . . . a few years before I had signed my virgin Contract . . . this had all been real. Today we were merely re-enacting what had gone before, and what unhappily would come again one day. An exodus. And I was at the head of the column of marching souls. I was the leader, broken foot or not; I had to prove only that I could do it; and in doing that I would be showing them, even as a cinema actor with a limp, what they could do as well. Setting a good example. An absolute essential, which brooked no despairing argument.

Of course one had to go on proving: that was what one was there for. I felt a great deal better, and threw my arm round the cotton print shoulders of a hot, dusty woman. She looked up at me with flat, tired eyes and smiled; she shook her head and straightened up, and calling across the straggle to a small boy of seven or eight, she told him that it wouldn't be so far, not to dawdle, and to give Felicity a hand because she probably had a blister on her heel. We marched on, and someone not far behind, started to whistle in the blazing sun. It spread gently through the column, raggedly but clearly on the morning air, the marching became less of a straggle, more of a determined walk. Felicity's mother said, 'Do you know the words?'

The rocky walls of the gorge swelled with the sound of our voices, it drifted up to the fading cluster of Royals on the ridge; almost triumphant, pride regained, courage retrieved; a joining had taken place.

> '*I've got sixpence,*
> *Jolly jolly sixpence,*
> *I've got sixpence,*
> *To last me all my life . . .*'

Proving. Showing what one could do. That's all.

CHAPTER SIX

Numer 44 sagged dejectedly two or three houses along from a wide and deep bombsite where some pleasant artisans' cottages once had stood in neat Georgian modesty, until a land mine had hit them and scattered their yellow bricks and fragile timbers into rubble and my back garden. No. 44 had suffered from this cruel thrust of German might; cracks ran about it like inverted varicose veins, the top floor bulged heavily over the area railings, a brick pot-belly, the black and white tiled steps were badly chipped by falling debris, and the front door only closed after two good bangs. But it had a roof, and it had the garden. From the top windows you looked down on to the E. Box luxuriance of bramble, buddleia and bracken in the bomb site, and then the garden, scraggly, unkempt, cluttered with slate-shards and half bricks, a laburnum on one side, a red May on the other, and at the end, where the brick wall fended off the gardens of Cliveden Place, two giant limes which shed flowers, pollen, leaves and a thick sticky muck all through the summer. But to left and right, as well as below, one saw green; and above the green a couple of spires and the roof of the Royal Court Theatre. Not bad.

Inside, not so good; margarine yellow paint, faded cretonnes, scuffed once-elegant, neo-Georgian furniture. Curtains staccato with parrots rioting in writhing yards of peony trees. No paintings. A small engraving of Salisbury Cathedral, a black silhouette of two ladies in lacy caps taking tea. The kitchen, in the dark basement had a table covered in stained American cloth, a stove, electric wires trailing along every wall, a sink, a geyser, and a door to the area on one side and the coal cellar which ran right under Chester Row itself. There were four knives, four forks, four spoons, three saucepans and a frying-pan petrified in years of egg and bacon grease. The beds, all five in the house, had horse hair mattresses. And the lavatory was cracked and creamy with rime. But it was the first real home of my own, even though I rattled about in it like the pea in a whistle.

Millie at the Express Dairies had a sister called Rose who would 'take on another gentleman' for two hours a day starting Monday. Rose came. Small, nervous, glasses, with a floral pinny and a voice which rang through the empty house with all the melody of a gull at a fishing-port. But she washed and scrubbed, wiped-down and told me what to buy from Vim to soda, lavatory paper to extra plates, and a mat for in front of the sink. When I got back from the theatre in those long spring evenings which seem so particular to London, I took my Weetabix and cheese and a glass of beer into the ragged garden, and under the May tree, with Cliff for company and a cod's head for him, bought from Macfisheries on the way, I sat and ate and felt well content with my lot. As indeed I should have been. But what, I wondered with a twist of alarm, would happen when the cinema part of my life began in the middle of the summer? It was easy while I was in the play – a few hours per day away from my new house, patching cracks, washing walls, heaving furniture about to suit my scheme. If scheme I had. But what then? Who to look after me, run the house, tend the garden, buy the cods' heads. Sort the laundry, go to Millie for the rations?

Who but Nan?

Calcutta. She was older than I by about six years, tall, grey eyes, good hands, a generous figure. 'Ample', she used to call it, or, in a kinder manner, 'my Edwardian body'. Which it was. She wore her hair in a plait bound round her head, and had an ever ready capacity for tremendous laughter and a surge for living. She was like a crested wave, always about to tumble, full of excitement, cool, grey-green, poised, crest tilted towards whatever shore. Never quite breaking.

I first saw her in the Mess the evening I arrived after five days of travel on wooden seats from Bombay. Tagore's Palace, a low, crumbling elegant house with pillared veranda, standing in a cool wilderness of zinnias and pale lawns watered daily by unseen gardeners. In the centre of the lawns a long shallow pool skimmed by kingfishers, thrusting with the lilac lances of water hyacinth. The Mess was a high, white room; a long table in the centre, small bamboo bar in one corner, two or three rattan chairs, old copies of the air-mail edition of *The Times*, *Lilliput*, and battered *Country Life*, fans clickety-clacking slowly in the ceiling, blades wobbling, gentle air riffling the papers as they lay. She arrived suddenly through the doors flowing in long white chiffon, her hair tonight tumbling about her shoulders, in one hand a slim cigarette holder, in the other a book; the only completely unfeminine thing about her was the big Service watch on her wrist. She came straight to the bar and slid on to the stool beside me and ordered a Gin Sling.

'Are you van den Thingummy . . . or are you Wallace?' Eyes grave, mouth smiling.

'Van den Thingummy.'

'There were two of you on the Posting Order. I didn't know.' She took her glass and prodded the ice cubes with a straw.

'What is Thingummy?'

'Bogaerde.'

'Goodness! All of it? How grand. What are you called for short?'

'Pip.'

'Better. For Philip?'

'No. For 'you give me the pip' . . . my first Commanding Officer's groan every time he saw my face.'

She laughed, and bent her head, placing the book beside her on the bar.
'Were you so awful then?'

'Pretty.'

'I'm Nanette Baildon. Squadron Officer.'

'Goodness! All of it? How grand. What are you called for short?'

She snorted a laugh, choked on smoke. 'Touché! Nan.'

'Is it all right, to call you that?'

'Nan is perfect.'

I liked her very much. A large gecko ran up the wall and slid behind a picture of Their Majesties.

'I don't really know what I'm doing here actually.'

'You are Photographic? An interpreter, I mean?'

'Yes . . . ex Second Army.'

'I saw the little ribbons. Jolly. Come at the wrong time, haven't you?'

'The monsoon started as the train pulled out of Bombay Central.'

'Always the way. They want you in a hurry and then nothing. No sorties now, no flying possible for weeks in this.' She indicated the rain thudding down into the sodden Elephant Ears at the door.

'Still, the planning goes on, doesn't it? From the sorties flown?'

Her eyes widened slightly, she took the butt from her holder and squashed it out in a puddle on the bar. It hissed.

'What planning do you mean?'

'Singapore, the fall of, all that . . . I'm supposed to be working on the defences.'

'Defences! We are up to our eyes in defences, been at them for months and months; you really are late! I don't know what we'll do now. You know it's unconditional surrender for the Japs, or else, don't you? A matter of time I'd say, really. Otherwise God only knows.' She sippped her Gin Sling, clinking ice.

'It's so marvellous to see a woman in evening dress again.'

'We always wear it for dinner. Evelyn and I are the only two girls in the Mess so it rather falls on us to keep up standards, don't you think? And it's nicer.'

'Much; and you are wearing a scent?'

She looked at me steadily, grey eyes smiling.

'Clever old you. The last dregs of "Je Reviens" . . . almost squeezed the bottle dry. Do you want another drink? On me . . .'

People started to wander into the room, gruff exchanges, hand shakes, drinks all round; then hands in pockets, rocking gently on heels, laughter too loud, conversation bored and falsely jolly, straight from the showers, all of them, talcumed, scrubbed; crisp uniforms already starting to sweat slowly down the backs, under the arms; foreheads beaded. Evelyn (apparently) came in, a flutter of green silk, a white flower in her hair. Scattered applause, she bobbed a curtsey, someone handed her a drink and she waved to Nan.

'What's the book?' I turned it up on the bar, covered in coarse brown paper, the word 'Poetry' in big ink letters.

She shrugged, and her shoulder strap slid down; pulling it up gently she took the book and opened it. 'An anthology . . . poetry, prose . . . this was a poet's house so it seems appropriate . . . do you know Tagore?'

My blank face betrayed me. She hurried on, amused, confused, finding a place marked by a dead leaf.

'Do you like this?

"The yellow bird sings in their tree and makes my heart dance with gladness.

We both live in the same village, and that is our one piece of joy . . ."'

She stopped and looked up. 'Perhaps not. It's from the Bengali, of course;

perhaps not your cup of tea.'

'No! No . . . No . . . I did like it. It was just suddenly so odd. Poetry, evening dress, scent . . . civilised; I didn't expect it. I've had six weeks in a troop ship and five days and nights on a train . . . I rather expected the Japs to be hissing from every bush and tree, and that I'd have taken my cyanide pill by now.'

She closed the book gently, replacing the dried leaf to mark her place with Tagore.

'We are an awfully long way from Kohima or Rangoon here . . . Calcutta is hardly front line stuff.' There was a gentle reproof in the voice: 'I think you can breathe freely, at least for the moment. And if you like, I'll start teaching you how to enjoy Poetry. We'll try simple things, Belloc and so on . . . then Yeats, Pound . . . unless of course you have other things to do during the monsoon?'

At dinner, she at one end, Evelyn at the other, she placed me on her left in someone's place who had gone to the Hills on leave. She rang little silver bells and Bearers flitted about with tinned tomato soup and a mild curry . . .

'What did you do before?'

The usual question.

'Don't, for God's sake, ask me at dinner.'

'Why ever not? Was it something dreadful?'

'No, not dreadful. Embarrassing, that's all.'

'How curious. You must have been about ten. Can I guess?' She handed me grated coconut. 'You sold yo-yo's in Oxford Street? Trained performing fleas?'

'You're getting hot.'

'Really? In a circus? No? Something on a trapeze . . . a trainee clown?'

'You are an idiot! I was an actor.'

She laughed. 'Well, that's not so awful, is it? Owen Nares, Godfrey Tearle, Ralph Richardson, all rather respectable, I should think. Were you any good?'

'Hard to tell, they got me for this job before I could do much. Out of the cradle.'

'Well, you have plenty of time now; you can start on your Shaw and Shakespeare. And the poetry would be invaluable, stretching the mind, the Learning Mind, don't you think? Do you want cucumber? Marvellously refreshing with that . . .'

We read to each other on the cool of her veranda, and I learned blocks of Poetry and we discussed and argued while Evelyn, our chaperone, did lazy daisy stitches on cushion covers for her bottom drawer. Later I wrote a play, which had been struggling about in my mind on the journey out, miles and miles of it, which she bravely typed during the long, steamy days of rain. Sometimes there was a gentle flutter of work, but very little; and our lives started along a gentle, pleasant road together. We drove to the city and explored every market, bazaar, street and alley; joined the Saturday Club, an impossibly snobbish club, one hot morning by saying that I was Baron van den Bogaerde and that she was the Comptesse de la Vache. Improbably, but with sickening ease, we jumped a two-year waiting list and lunched in cool splendour. The Club became our Place, even though we detested most of the white clientele . . . Indians were not admitted. Apart from my Literary Education, Nan was determined that I should try to understand India and the Indian mind, and I was dragged from temple to temple, shrine to shrine and festival to festival, and in the evenings, when we rested up from MacNeice, Dorothy Wellesley, Spender and Wilde we talked about Gandhi and Congress and the Raj. It was a crammer's course. Her unashamed passion for this vast country was infectious, and I began to look about me now with clearer eyes and compassion, trying to understand as much as I could, before they threw us out.

One day, returning from the city alone (she had stayed behind to wash her hair, a tedious process because of its length), I came bearing gifts. A small bottle of 'Je Reviens' which I had discovered by chance on Chowringhee, and a pair of lovebirds in a bamboo cage.

She was not on her veranda; no one was. The mosquito nets were down, the lights on; wild dogs barked across the compound. I went over to the Mess. It was full. Silent. Only the fans clickety-clacking and a faint voice through heavy static from the bakelite radio behind the bar. I saw her standing motionless, hair in a towel, hand to her face. Evelyn in a chair, head bowed. The faces round the bar taut. There were no cheers in our Mess at the news of the atomic bomb on Hiroshima.

It was still raining on V.J. Night. We drove into the Club and dined and danced to celebrate the end, for ever we all thought, of our war. There was great euphoria in the dining room, people cheered and sang as if it was New Year's Eve. At the next table to ours a party of six wore funny hats, and a memsahib in a crepe paper wimple hit a silver salver, offered by a bearer, high into the air. 'I said mashed potatoes! Not boiled!' she shouted. The little white balls scattered about our feet. 'Christ!' she said. 'But you do grow to *loathe* Them, don't you!'

We drove home in torrential rain and struck a group of soldiers somewhere along the Barrackpore road. We turned over twice I seem to recall: Nan had a cut head, I was unhurt. There were two or three men sprawled in the muddy, roaring waters of the street. People came and took Nan back to barracks. I knew that two must be dead; but remembered, and remember now, very little. They were members of a gang of American GI deserters, known in the area, who high-jacked cars at nights. We spent weeks of misery in Court, and finally were exonerated, because witnesses had seen them link arms across the road and form a line to halt us. I had not seen them in the dark and the rain. I have never driven since.

It was decided that we should both go away on leave. To clear our minds. Whatever that meant. We took the train to Darjeeling and then up into Sikkim on stubborn mules, across the high plateau towards Tibet, which reminded us both forcibly of the Yorkshire moors and which was just as cold and uninviting. We saw dawn rise on Everest . . . the sun set slowly on the shimmering height of Kanchenjunga. In Tindzhe Dzong women hid behind the pillars in the market place horrified because Nan was wearing trousers; and somewhere else, which I have forgotten, she traded a tin of American bacon for two black agate rings, from an old man with a fluttering prayer wheel. We were hopelessly unprepared for such a trip but, like most idiots, Fortune cared for us, and we arrived back in Calcutta a month later, calm, brown, rather pompous, happy, to be welcomed in the Mess with cheers and tall John Collins's – and the news of my immediate posting to another war, in Java.

She came down to the docks with me. My exceedingly small L.S.T. was almost ready to put out for the long journey. It was the same farewell as always: the bright, uneasy chatter, the beating heart, the false bravado.

'Just remember . . .' she fiddled with the buckle of her sandal which had come undone, '. . . just remember. I'll be going home in about a month, I think . . . you have my address . . . my sister's house? Well, it's just that when you get back, if you need anything, or if there is anything I can ever do, just . . . well just . . .' the buckle came off in her hand. 'Hell! Now I'll have to hop about looking for a taxi. But I mean . . . if you want me, just give me a call . . .'

So who, but Nan?
She came right away with three suitcases and her old tin trunk, a pile of

books, and a cardboard box with a collection of doubtful Meissen, Augustus Rex, plates and saucers, and moved into the first-floor two rooms. Sitting room on the street, small bedroom over the garden, sharing the bathroom and the dark kitchen below. She had kept on her nine-to-five job because all I could offer was the accommodation and six pounds a week for housekeeping and Cliff, who took up his place in the house on the end of her bed. And we managed very well.

No more Weetabix and cheese. No more lonely suppers under the May tree. On two ration books we fared far better, and she knew a shop in Lancaster Gate where she got black-puddings and haggis and split peas and lentils and God knows what other delights. I began to eat properly, and was happy to do the washing-up in return. Walls got repainted, window boxes planted, the neo-Georgian furniture was arranged and rearranged and arranged again. I spent a lot of my time, and more money than I could afford from the Oxo tin, in junk shops up and down the King's Road; it was still, then, almost a long village street, with an ironmongers who sold hooks and bolts and pounds of nails, a haberdashers which sold woollen combinations in winter and muslin blouses in the summer, and a greengrocers spilling with cabbages, lettuce, green peppers, mud, and garlic. But the junk shops were my best place, and for a very few pounds, and often shillings, I carted back suspect Old Masters in heavy gilded frames, domes of stuffed birds shimmering with dusty feathers, cracked coffee pots and sets of odd glasses, jugs and bits of Staffordshire which, all washed and mended, suddenly gave a feeling of false richness to the sagging, margarine yellow house.

Then, just before the play finally closed, we attacked the garden, cleared all the rubble, whitewashed walls, pruned and cut and heaved the sour earth out in sacks. With the assistance of an old man with a cart and donkey whom Nan met in Elizabeth Street, we filled the place with geraniums and tobacco plants, laid out a lawn in strips of emerald turf which cost a fortune per sod, set out tubs of white daisies and fuchsias, and dined by candle light nearly every evening at a small bamboo table under the bathroom built out on two iron columns, long before anyone had ever been to Spain and learned to call a yard a patio.

'Power Without Glory' closed at the end of May due to a lack of star names on the canopy and the excessive competition from the energetic Americans across the street in 'Oklahoma'. But I was not immediately worried, nor even sad. Everyone was moving on in to Coward's new play, and I had my Contract. At the end of June the retainer money ceased and my salary began right away. I was to receive the unheard-of sum of three thousand pounds a year, with yearly options on their side to renew.

I bumped up the housekeeping, paid five pounds for an enormous 1938 Hepplewhite-style H.M.V. cabinet gramophone, with doors and lid, and decided to have a house warming party to show everything off. Including myself.

Lusia came, my catalyst from the Savoy; Freddy came, Forwood came, Chloe Gibson and all the cast came; Mr Daubeny even arrived, with a bottle of whisky and one of Vodka ('Gin is quite démodé, only sailors and servants drink it') which helped to swell the modest delights on my bar (Pimms No. 1, Pale Ale, and a bottle of Madeira from the wine shop at the corner). I wasn't that rich. Yet. My parents came from Sussex, and Elizabeth came with George from the RAF. And a bright-eyed, slender little woman came who looked rather like a blackbird with a hat and veil. Her name was Olive Dodds, the Contract Artists' Representative at Rank. My first real Official. This was the woman who was to push me, or steer me, whichever needed doing, through the Paradise-Hell of the

Cinema Jungle. She it would be who would part the thorns and brambles and strangling vines, suggest new tracks, new directions, when to move, when to lie low. She would bring me to the very brink of chasms and then dare me not to jump; to catch me on the other side, breathless.

She raised her glass of Madeira, lifted her veil, and looked around the room with its family portraits from the junk shops, bowls of flowers, worn Persian rugs, and drank to my success.

'Not what I imagined; not a Film Star's House.'

'A criticism?'

'No. A comment only. Meant kindly.'

'What did you expect?'

'Oh . . . off white . . . chromium . . . stripped pine . . . a Utrillo reproduction . . . Peter Jonesey.'

'Well, it isn't And I'm not a film star . . .'

'Yet. I'm rather afraid that you soon might be.' She cocked her blackbird head smiling gently. 'I wonder if you'll like it?'

'Won't be for ages.'

'You've got your name above the title on your first film. Technically you exist as a Star, my dear. Very good luck.' She lifted her glass and sipped gently.

'Sounds like a threat.'

'Another comment. That's all. Some people take to it like a drunk to drink, with much the same results.' She fumbled for a cigarette, I lit it for her, she blew smoke into a steady high column. 'Some others get hopelessly lost. It is not easy. Let me know if I can help. That's what I'm there for. I'm called The Shoulder. For weeping on.'

Forwood arrived one morning for coffee and said that the lease was running out on his Mews Cottage and that he was going off on Tour for four months and had nowhere to store his bits and pieces. Nan instantly offered him the top front room with the bulging wall for a pound a week, storage rate, and a few days later he moved in his Medici print of the Amaryllis, his grandmother's petit point chair, books and boxes, and a set of silver forks and spoons which Nan shoved into the kitchen. My brother Gareth, picked to play my 'son' in 'Esther Waters' and presently at a loose end, moved into the small back bedroom next to it. I bought a second-hand Sunbeam Talbot, gold, with a drop-head, and acquired a chauffeur, since I would not drive, called Bond, ex-Coldstream Guards, very tall, very fast, from an ex-Serviceman's agency. My household, including Rose of the gull-like voice, was complete, and No. 44 was bursting at its seams. I was flying. Without wings.

Giddily, like a run-amok balloon, I sailed and swirled happily into the void, no pilot in my gondola, all tielines severed, the sand bags jettisoned, filled only with hot air and the false, delirious, sense of freedom. Up I flew into a sky so dark with storms and dangers, so fraught with stresses, rumbles of distant thunder and silent flashes of lethal lightning that anyone, but myself, would have had the wit to turn back, land safely and enter a Closed Order.

But that was not my style. My adventure had begun and I really rather liked it all. There was one gentle, worrying doubt, however. Just one. Who the hell was I? More important still, what was I? Like people of an immigrant race, I was searching for my identity, although I was not at all sure what I'd do with it when, if, I found it.

So who was I suddenly? I had known, to be sure, who I had been – the brave little Captain, the hopeful novice actor – but now there was a vast vacuum and in spite of a house, a car, all my family and possessions such as they were, I belonged nowhere. Unproven, except for one modest performance in a failed play, as an actor, and worse still, in the brand new life which I had entered, quite unproven as a man.

Old friends, such as I had, began to fall away. This is something one has to get used to: they leave far quicker than you leave them. They go because you have moved ahead and they feel, usually correctly, that they are not able to keep up. As it happened I had very few old friends. Some, like Forwood, like Lusia, who had known me for many years, stayed close, because they understood the way the journey was going, and were unsurprised; but most of the others drifted away, even Vida. Uncomfortable in my new-found riches, embarrassed by my sudden new classification, so far completely undeserved, as a Film Star, they left me to get on with my new inheritance. The trouble was that I had no friends there either.

The people I had to mix with now were the established ones – they all were film stars – but they were proven. Their conversations were too hard for me to follow: I knew almost nothing of what they discussed. Having no experience of their world I desperately sought to establish myself in their eyes as someone they were sure to find interesting, delightful, clever and sophisticated. But I had no possible way of doing this except to chatter away about my war. The only thing I knew anything at all about – and no one in the world wanted to hear my stories and sagas and bragging. The war was over, the war was dead, and glazed eyes greeted my desperate efforts at self-assertion. Or was it only re-assertion? I can't be sure. But I knew that I bored them witless, and in desperation, and in fear, I started to drink too much, hoping that this would give me courage when all it gave me was a blinding hangover every morning and an over-exaggerating tongue the night before. I should have sat quietly, humbly, patiently, listening to them – they had something to teach me had I cared. Instead I beat about wildly in the seas of terror, and struck out like a drowning man at everyone who tried to come to my rescue. Including poor Nan, who was unmercifully clobbered simply because I felt I loved her well enough to do so.

A grave, and cruel, mistake.

Insecurity, that overworked word, swamped me. And swamped the new friends who leant backwards to make allowances and gave unheeded advice, which I desperately needed, and who finally moved away as determinedly as the old friends. I was very much alone for a great deal of the time. Which gave me, between beers, a good deal to think about. For thankfully, I did know that I was behaving appallingly, and I did know why. I just couldn't correct . . . or connect.

In the Studios, unable to join the top echelon, because of my own limitations, I graduated downwards in scale and made friends among the rag-tag-and-bobtail of the profession. People who would listen to my endless bleating for the sake of a double gin in the bar, or who would come to supper simply for a free meal and a shrewd feeling that they were being patronised, which most of them were.

At these suppers, which Nan prepared devotedly and constantly, after a long day's work at the office and at which she played an uncomfortable role as hostess, I happily played the role of host to my Court of small-part actors, extras, fifth-string hairdressers' assistants and noisy girls from the Publicity Pool at the Studio. I enjoyed their flattery, inaccurate gossip, false deference, and above all delighted in the respectful silences in which they patiently listened to my wild, improbable, theories about a profession of which I knew absolutely nothing. It's just that they made me feel Big. I laid down the law, in my own house, and all my trite little witticisms, if that's what they were, received bright laughter and heavy slaps on the back as someone reached again for the Vodka. Only Nan was distressed. And she did her best not to show it. Tight-lipped, but incredibly polite and charming, she served the food and drink and sought for some level of conversation in which she could safely join, in the intellectual desert of my drawing room on the second floor.

Her forced laughter, her worried eyes, her ill-concealed concern for me irritated constantly, and it was at those moments between us that I would start off on my Bore War and invent, and decorate, to astonish and gain support from my Court. My immodesty horrified her; and although I did, with little grace, assist her in the kitchen later with the washing-up, we hardly ever spoke, and indeed spoke less and less, for I would brook not the slightest criticism of my new friends. I needed their sycophancy and fed on it for my courage. And she knew only too well how dangerous this would be. I resented her wisdom, her cautions, and put it all aside furiously. I had been Small for too long, I thought. I enjoyed being Big.

So they fawned on me for my pathetic favours, borrowed money easily, invited me to grubby drinking clubs to which I went eagerly (anything now was better than sitting at 44 with the evening paper and Nan cooking a pilaff in the area), and all the time I knew that I was going the wrong way about things and desperately sought some form of balance. Even Freddy really couldn't help – he gave advice which was so sober that I immediately, and foolishly, rejected it – and Nan knew nothing of my profession, or how it worked or what it demanded. Her chief concern was that I should be happy, well fed, cosseted, loved and that she should be proud of me. Which she, blindingly, was.

Shyness has crippled me all my life; now coupled with a quite desperate desire to prove myself in my new profession, impatient for the results, I developed a cold arrogance to protect myself from the world of which I was now a part, but not truly an accepted Member. The worst, and most sickening part of each day at Pinewood was the lunch hour. I knew no one well enough to eat with. I had no set table. Like a new boy at school I sat miserably in my dressing room reading the script and not eating, or forced myself to go to the bar, which meant running the gauntlet of the great restaurant beyond which lay the bar itself and Eadie in shiny black satin who smiled at me and always talked about something. But in order to make this voyage I had to go blind and deaf and walk, like a robot, swiftly through the chattering, crowded tables, looking neither right nor left, eyes fixed in desperation on the wooden door behind which lay a temporary salvation to loneliness, with Eadie.

This caused concern among the diners. One day I was summoned by telephone to present myself at Earl St John's office at twelve-thirty. He was genial, quiet, polite. Olive Dodds was also present. Silent. My first encounter, since the days in South Street, with my Headmaster. He handed me a note wordlessly. It was a mild complaint, suggesting that perhaps Mr Bogarde might be asked not to walk through the restaurant each day as if he owned it. It was signed David Lean.

My mouth was dry, my hand shook. I apologised to Earl St John and Mrs Dodds and stayed alone in my room from then on. Until I found a way to get to the Bar through the gardens . . . which saved running the gauntlet.

One day there was a gentle knocking at my door. Two shining faces, the Attenboroughs. She with a white halo hat, smiling brightly, clutching a little purse. He with the alert, boyish smile, eager eyes, brimming confidence and infectious zeal of someone who had just seen a vision. For a blinding moment I thought that they might have been collecting for the Salvation Army.

'Hello! Just wondered if you were on your own; or simply not eating? This is

Sheila, my wife. If you are on your own we just wondered if you'd like to lunch with us? The first couple of weeks are awful; like a new school. I mean if you need any help, want to know the teachers' names, where the class rooms are, that sort of thing, we'd be delighted to help you. Or just give you lunch?'

Their kindness winded me, their thoughtfulness nearly unmanned me, it was so completely unexpected and I have cherished it always. But it was, of necessity, an oasis only. I couldn't presume on them every day, and saw to it that I did not.

One evening Forwood came to dinner with his wife, Glynis. Although they had mutually agreed by this time on a full separation after all, they were still extremely fond of each other. Nan was tremendously excited and made a splendid meal. I bought two bottles of Hock, and we lit candles. But their visit was, as it happened, not entirely social. They came to instruct, to correct, to help. I sat frozen with shock at their gentle, considered, constructive advice. I was behaving badly, they both knew why and sympathised, but I had to pull myself together pretty soon or disaster lay ahead. 'You talk too much, you exaggerate constantly, you are boring, rude and self-opinionated,' said Glynis flatly. 'And people don't like that kind of behaviour in this profession. You haven't done a single thing yet and yet you behave as if you knew it all and had nothing to learn. A little humility wouldn't be a bad thing at all. You are supposed to be a professional, try and behave like one.'

Shattered by the truth, unable to defend it, I heaved an empty Hock bottle through the enormous aquarium full of tropical fish which stood at the end of the room. Cascades of water and weed, rocks and fish shot across the floor. Mixed with my uncontrollable wine-and-anger tears. They left shortly afterwards, picking their way through the wreckage of the fish tank and the shards of my ego.

Nan came clanking up the narrow staircase wearily with the buckets.

'What I can't understand,' said Forwood a few days after this sorry episode, 'is why you just don't be yourself. Why this sudden determination to emulate Genghis Khan, for God's sake? It's a good role. I agree, but you aren't ready to play it yet . . . by a long chalk.'

'I don't know who "myself" is . . . I did once . . . you know that . . . but now it's got all muddled, and anyway being "myself" in this business won't do. They want more than that.'

'A lot of self-pitying twaddle. If you knew who you were once you can be it again. It got you through twenty-six years perfectly well. You seem to be going through a male menopause or something.'

Glynis and he started work on me as if I were an unmade bed, stripped me down to the box-springs, turned the mattress, aired the blankets and, with my unconfident, but anxious, assistance, we started to put it all back together again. Not a moment too soon. Under their wise guidance, calm advice, among their own carefully-selected friends, who to my hidden surprise neither patronised nor ignored me, I began to regain the confidence within myself which I had somehow or other lost along the line. It had all been a case of too much too soon and not being able to carry corn.

Work started on poor 'Esther Waters' proper, just after this, and that too helped to restore a sense of balance. I found that being myself, whatever that was, worked far better. I did my best to be pleasant, polite, humble and above all, with Glynis's terrible, and accurate, warning ringing constantly at the back of my mind, professional. Life became a good deal happier. At least I was just being me. And me seemed to be all right; if dull. I applied myself assiduously to the job in hand. Indeed I had to, for no one else was applying me. On the first morning of shooting on my first Epic, thirty years ago, I timidly (being myself) asked Mr Dalrymple, the director and my discoverer, what, exactly, I should do. I had never really seen a film camera before, apart from a few brief moments for make-up and costume tests in which no histrionics whatever were required on my part. Mr Dalrymple looked rather startled, and pushing his glasses high up on his nose, he said, very politely indeed: 'My dear boy! I don't know. I'm the director, you're supposed to be the actor,' leaving me nothing else to do but whistle hopelessly as I groped about for a lead line. It was the first time that I would hear this, but not the last. So, like the swimming baths at Maidstone, I held my nose and jumped, hoping that someone, or something, down in the dark water would come to my salvation.

It was fortunate indeed for me that after 'Esther Waters' I was quickly bundled into another film, and then another, leaving me no time to panic and ensuring that if the first was a disaster, which it was, there would be a second and third chance coming up. Which there was. And Rank picked up the option after the first year, increased, very modestly, the salary, and hustled me off again on a second round. It says a great deal for their patience and belief in their investment. Totally miscast in 'Waters' and lacking any screen personality whatsoever, I did not, as they hoped, come up to expectations. But by the time that this was discovered I had already played a slightly neurotic pianist in a Maugham short story, and was heavily involved in a love affair with a motor cycle for my role as a Speedway Rider. Which was nearly as dotty as anything I have ever been asked to do in the cinema. And that's saying something. I, of all people, with my horror of mechanics, machines and speed, was engaged to play the Speedway Champion of Europe. Or something. The director, standing beside a quite enormous copper and chromium bike, told me softly that he would like me to take it home, stand it in my bedroom, and love it as I would a woman.

I would have been happier with a ten foot boa-constrictor, and could have offered it far more love and affection than this harsh, gleaming, noisy machine on which I was to spend days and nights of agony, fear, and mounting hysteria. Hurtling round and round the track at New Cross Stadium, being towed by a very fast camera car, was as near as I had been to sudden death since the freedom struggles in Java. However, we got through all in one piece and the disaster of 'Esther Waters' ebbed away; I was over the first hurdle and I was beginning to enjoy myself. But it had taken time, and toll.

Nan was not enjoying herself. In this new development of my life pattern, I gradually and naturally grew into a new world, and steadily away from my life with Nan.

I rose at five-thirty every morning and arrived back at 44 well after seven p.m. While I had spent the day with amusing, interesting people, enjoying very much my new-found confidence, and starting a mild flirtation with myself on the Studio Floor which was to last me all my life and become one of the great-love-stories-of-our-time as far as I was concerned, poor Nan, slogging away in a dullish office, coping with meals, the house, Rose (who now broke things daily) shopping and rations, laundry lists and my friends who came for drinks or supper and almost always ignored her, for she was completely lost in our intensely self-absorbed conversations, found that she was being edged further and further away from the life which had seemed so promising when she first arrived.

One evening I got home a little earlier than usual. I tried to tip-toe past her sitting room (it had reached that stage by now), but she was quickly at the door.

Her smile steady.

'Your sherry's poured. I heard the car. Or there's Scotch . . .'

'Not now, I'm whacked. I'll have a bath.'

'No. Not yet, please.' She had moved into the narrow hall and blocked the way to the stairs.

'Be kind, Pip . . . it's important.'

Her room was pretty, floral prints, the Meissen bowls on the mantelshelf, flowers, all her books, Cliff asleep on a chair, drinks on the little sideboard, a fire glowing.

'It's something I've been wanting to say for a long time, and I'm a little shaky, so be patient.'

'What is it?'

'Well . . .' she fitted another cigarette into her long, black holder, 'well . . . it's not working out, is it? Our arrangement here: it's got into a bit of a mess.'

I knew what she meant and what she was going to say. I tried to swerve and avoid confrontation. 'Nan! If it's money . . . I mean housekeeping, that sort of thing . . .'

She flushed angrily. 'It's not that, Pip, don't be so damned insulting. Money! Hell . . . it's us, our attitude towards each other. Or rather yours to me.'

'What have I done?'

'I'm just a housekeeper, aren't I? Nothing more to you. Oh, I know . . .' she waved her hand towards the pretty room, 'I know I have all this; and more, I know that. But I also have pride, Pip. It's hateful of me to say so, but I have, and I'm rapidly losing it and I refuse to. There.'

We sat silent.

'I know it can't be like it was in India, I know that. Your life has changed so much, and so quickly . . . and it hasn't been easy for you. I've seen how difficult it's been, and how you have managed. But you don't need me any longer.'

'Nan! I do.'

'You don't, dear. You avoid me as much as you can now; we hardly speak at supper . . . you never come down here for a sherry like the old days. I know that you try to tip-toe past my room, you'd rather be on your own. I do see that, I do understand it, but I can't really take it any longer. I don't fit in with your friends . . . my fault . . . but I can't speak the language, I don't know what half of them are talking about, and it's always the cinema or what you did today, and I don't know what you did today because I wasn't there and you never, ever, ever tell me, do you, Pip? You don't need me because I can't help you, and I can't help you if I don't know how to . . . and if you don't tell me, or even let me share your life; all you really need is a nice comfortable lady for three quid a week, who can cook and wash and tidy things up for you.'

'Nan, Nan . . . for Christ's sake don't. It isn't like that at all, you know it.'

'It is, dear, and *you* know it. I'm not utterly stupid. I may not know anything about scripts and lights and what the hairdresser said to the make-up man, but I do know, Pip, that I have a life of my own to live, and if I stay here like this for much longer I'll be lost and we will end up hating each other for ever.' She smiled gently, and put her hand on my arm to soften the harsh truth of her words.

I was white with shock and shame.

'I wish, Pip dear, that I could say, cheer up, it doesn't matter, but you know that it does. Listen. I tell you what; you have said that you want to get out of London and live in the country . . . be nearer the Studios . . . I think that you should; it would be much wiser and healthier for you, and far less of a strain with that awful journey. But I couldn't come with you. And keep my job in Welbeck

Square . . .'

The room lay silent. Cliff suddenly yawned and stretched his legs and dozed off again. I could hear the racing ticking of her little travelling clock on the table by my chair. She lit another cigarette from the butt already in her holder. Her hand shook.

'So I think that's what we should do.' She pressed the old butt into her glass ash-tray.

'I don't honestly know what to say . . .'

'There is nothing you need to say. We have had a marvellous time together, it was exciting and fun, really it was. No regrets. But we must be very grown up and sensible and not spoil what was so good. Odd, isn't it? When one gets to these moments in life they always sound like Marie Corelli. Sorry. I'll stay on, of course, if you want me to, until you find something out of town. It would be difficult for you to break in a servant at the moment; I know the ropes and you're terribly busy. As soon as you do, give me a bit of warning so that I can get packed up. I heard of a very nice little flat near Baker Street. There is no hurry. I was just poking about, you know, quite a lot of places I can get. And I'd take Cliff, if you wouldn't mind. He's got terribly fond of me. Used to me. He'd miss his mother, wouldn't he then?' She pulled him on to her lap and buried her face in his fur.

It was a modest sign-board in the front garden of an ordinary grey-brick villa, no different at all from its Victorian neighbours on the Green. Ealing Studios. A ragged laurel hedge and, behind the house, scabby turf and three elderly fir trees, beyond them the concrete blocks of the Stages spreading through suburbia.

Ealing, although affiliated to Rank, was regarded with grave suspicion by some of the impeccably tailored members of the Front Office in the Aberconways' house in South Street. They scented anarchy on the Green, distrusted the Young Directors and Producers who they felt sure were certainly all Left if not Communists, and even though the films made a great deal of money they had a Satirical Touch, an Intellectual Flavour, which was disturbing and against all Good Family Entertainment. Indeed I was once told that when the distributors, in a line north of Oxford, saw the trade mark on the credits, Ealing Films set within a little wreath of leaves, they left the theatre in a drove and headed home. Without making a single booking. They didn't make films which the public wanted to see. So they insisted. And overlooked, conveniently, the fact that somebody somewhere wanted to see them because Ealing was extremely successful, and the cachet of working for them was very important to any actor. This point of view never changed.

However, Basil Dearden, one of the younger and brightest of the new school of directors, had sent for me, and since they, Rank, had no immediate plans to employ my services, I was despatched to the house on the Green.

Basil and I had worked together before the war when I was his rather inept Assistant Stage Manager at the 'Q' Theatre.

'You haven't changed much, have you?' Raised eyebrows, cool regard, fiddling with a pencil on his desk.

'No. I should have.'

'Yes. It's a pity. You've got a face like a baby's bottom.'

'You haven't changed much yourself. Just as bloody rude.'

'My trick. They love it.'

'Who do?'

'Bloody actors. All so puffed up. Need a kick up the arse.'

'Is that what I'm here for?'

'Could be. "The Blue Lamp"; it's about the Police Force.'

'I wouldn't think I was Copper material.'

'You aren't. You *could* play the snivelling little killer. Neurotic, conceited, gets the rope in the end.'

'That's me.'

'That's what I thought.'

'Have you seen my film work at all?'

'No. And I'm told that I am deeply enriched by that lack of experience.'

'Then why send for me?'

'Liked the play you did at the New Lindsey . . . not bad. Do you think you could do something like that? Can you keep it up, I mean? Or was it just a one off?'

'If I tried very hard.'

'You'd bloody well have to.'

'Would you help me?'

'Not much. Why?'

'I don't really know how to act for the cinema.'

'That has been made abundantly clear, I gather.'

'So I'd need help, wouldn't I?'

'If you get the part.'

'If I get the part. How do you do it . . . acting for the cinema?'

'You do the same as you do on a stage, for God's sake. Nothing different. It's a lot of bilge that you have to have a different technique for the cinema. Bilge. It's all acting. Do what you'd do in the theatre and I'll pull you down if you go over the top. All this nonsense about cinema technique! Bilge. People are trying to invent a myth. Act. It's simple. If you can.'

It was the first time anyone had ever told me what to do: suddenly doors and windows opened all about me. Light came in.

He pushed a script towards me.

'The role is Tom Riley.'

'Do you want me to do it?'

'I need a weedy type . . . and you're a Contract Artist. Rank insists that we use some of you from time to time, it's blackmail. So I haven't much choice, have I? Always on our necks to use someone out of their ruddy Charm School.'

'I'm not from their Charm School.'

'That,' said Dearden rising and hitching up his pants with an ill-suppressed yawn, 'is quite self-evident.'

'The Blue Lamp' became a legend, so to speak, within its own lifetime, providing a welter of spin-offs for years to come in the cinema and, later, in television. The Documentary Police Movie. The first of its kind in England. It also altered, for all time, my professional life. Dearden pointed me in the right direction with his illuminating, over-simplified, approach to the camera. It was the first time I came near to giving a cinema performance in any kind of depth: I think it had some light and shade, whereas the work which had gone before was cardboard and one dimensional. I have never been an extrovert actor, always an introvert; instinctive rather than histrionic, and in this semi-documentary method of working I discovered, to my amazement and lasting delight, that the camera actually photographed the mind process however hesitant it was, however awkward. It had never, of course, occurred to me before, since I had very little mind of my own; but the people I played had minds, of some sort or another, and I became completely absorbed in trying to find those minds and offer them up to the camera. I was never to be satisfied again with a one-dimension performance. And neither was the camera, which now became the centre of my whole endeavour.

If my professional life had taken a turn for the better, the same could not be said of my personal life, which limped on unhappily and awkwardly, ever since Nan had taken up frail courage to throw down her gauntlet. The gentle challenge had to be answered. I was not very well equipped to reply. I tried a new approach to our existence – driving out on picnics at the weekends in the forlorn hope that a day spent by a river, in a wood, or on a hill, would break the tensions of life at 44. Petrol rationing was still in force, and our trips were of necessity limited. And in any case they didn't work; returning to the shadows of Chester Row with a bunch of cowslips, or aching legs from a climb over Ivinghoe Beacon, did almost nothing to conceal the lightly hidden distresses and frustrations which lay beneath our apparently happy exteriors like trip wires in a mine-field. I was trapped. She was trapped. I knew that I had to get out, away from London and away from the unhappy atmosphere I had, inadvertently, created. Trying, over-hard, to make her a part of my cinema life, as she called it, failed equally. It was not her world, and in no way possible could she join it. She was a sensible, loving creature, and the mounting pressures and demands of this new life, which took us both by surprise by the rapidity of its assault, overwhelmed her. And myself.

The Indian life we had both shared so happily had all but vanished, never to return. How could it? The people we had been then we no longer were now, and never would be, ever, again. Time had marched on us, catching us unprepared and woefully unarmed. All that remained was a deep bond of mutual respect and affection. Nothing else. And even that was now in danger. So, try to protect it.

'I've found a place in the country, near the Studios. I can move in about September.'

We were down in the kitchen, she was preparing supper, her back towards me, at the sink.

'How splendid!' She took a cloth and wiped her hands. 'Let's go into the garden. I thought we might eat out this evening, it's so warm . . . the food's cold so nothing will spoil yet. Have you got your glass?'

At the bamboo table under the bathroom, set neatly, we creaked into canvas chairs. The last of the sun slanted through the big limes.

'Where is it, far? A cottage or a castle? I know you.'

'It's Forwood's family house actually, Bendrose House, near Amersham. It's empty, up for rent. He can't afford it all on his own, so if his family agrees we could go halves. He wants somewhere for his child, a sort of family base . . . seems a good idea.'

She poured herself a gin and tonic. 'Of course, there's the child. But it was a "decent" divorce, wasn't it?'

'Very. They are tremendously found of each other, just can't live together any longer. You know . . .'

The garden was very still. It trembled as a train rumbled beneath it into Sloane Square Station.

'So he wants somewhere for the boy in the holidays; they are going to share him, it's all very civilised.'

'Sounds marvellous all round.'

'Pretty big. Large garden. Unfurnished, of course.'

'You'll manage. Think of all those lovely auction rooms and second hand shops, you'll be in your element. And you'd go in September?'

'If that's all right for you?'

'Fine for me. I can use my holidays flat hunting. I have my eye on one; a dear little place, quite reasonable, and a tiny bit of garden for Cliff . . . he'd hate a real flat . . . I'm glad you told me.'

'Just had to do it, that's all . . .'

'I know.'

'And you can come down at weekends. It's big. Masses of room.'

'Lovely! And easy from Baker Street; the flat's just a few steps away. It is on the Bakerloo Line, isn't it?'

'Or Marylebone.'

'Same thing really.'

'So it wouldn't be a complete severance.'

'That would be unthinkable! Never that! Of course not . . . I'm much too fond of you. It had to happen like this, you know. I suppose I was always aware it would, deep down. It's just life, as they say, it's all a matter of ins and outs I suppose. It is, isn't it?'

'But this is just a change of route, that's all . . . direction.'

'Oh Pip dear!' She laughed gently and touched my knee. 'You are a funny one: not awfully good at looking facts in the face, are you . . . still not yet? Well, never mind, just let's call this an entrance; does that feel better?'

She took up her glass and went up the steps to the kitchen; at the top she turned and looked back. 'Such a pretty evening, that light in the trees. I had to give up two "points" for a tiny tin of sardines this morning. Would you believe it? The peace is almost as bad as the war, in little things.'

CHAPTER SEVEN

The voyage on which I had embarked with Mr Dalrymple and 'Esther Waters' in such light spirits was fraught with grave dangers. None of it, ever, was to be clear sailing, and there were moments indeed at the beginning when it looked as if it would be just a trip round the lighthouse and back to port, or, worse still, that I should be forced to founder with all hands on the hidden reef of economy. Rank was going through a very difficult period financially (and every other way) but I knew nothing of this until Olive Dodds took me quietly aside and said that owing to impossible financial problems they were going to introduce vast cuts in the economy, clear out all the dead-wood, see the wood for the trees, and try to start all over again with a neater, tighter, more manageable and less extravagant formula. To this end all the Contract Artists, to begin with, would be asked to take severe reductions in salary, otherwise, if they chose not to accept, they could annul their contracts and go free. For some, it was leaving prison.

She strongly advised me to take whatever cut was offered without question, since she felt that loyalty to the firm would not go unrecognised in the future, and that they would not forget the gesture. I was unsure. She also shoved me, against my will, into another cloth-cap and raincoat role in a film about the Irish troubles called 'The Gentle Gunman'. I said that I would certainly accept the cut if she advised it, for she knew a great deal better than I did what was afoot; but that I refused to be on the run yet again in another raincoat part. She was adamant. The film would start just as my Option Period was due, and if I was working, she reasoned, they would be less likely to chuck me out. And chuck me out, she hinted pleasantly, was just what they intended to do at the last Board Meeting. Could I afford that?

No one, as we have seen, was exactly ecstatic to have me from the very beginning; only Mr Dalrymple and she herself had felt any reason to hope that I would one day prove my worth. My record was hardly outstanding, no one was actually lighting candles to me. And worse than that, I had not made them much, if any, profit. My last effort, as she pointed out, a disastrous attempt at light comedy, had been as funny as a baby's coffin and although I argued that it had not been my fault, or my choice (the unhappy director, Val Guest, had wanted William Holden but had been forced to have me, as a Contract Artist, instead), Olive Dodds smiled her soft enigmatic smile and suggested that there were forces at work who really did want me out of the way. If I had the sense to accept her plans I might just possibly be saved from the humiliation. It was up to me.

So I accepted the cut, when it was offered, wielded with an axe rather than a penknife, accepted too the raincoated Irish killer, so that over the dangerous time of the Option Period I was to be found, had anyone so wished, being chased by more Coppers, nightly through the tunnels of Mornington Crescent Underground, and being bawled at by Basil Dearden once again.

Temporarily, at any rate, my skin had been saved by the advice of the one person in the Organisation who believed that I might, with help, one day pull it off.

It was a depressing time. Familiar faces slid away, in all departments, to fitful obscurity or television which, in those early fifties, was scooping up all the left overs from the film industry and starting to build up a force which would eventually bring us to the brink of ruin. But for the moment the Organisation, having cleared out its dead-wood, found the land clear and open and with a little more money to spend bought the rights to a best seller called 'The Cruel Sea'. Here I thought, wrongly, was a chance for me to break away from the raincoats and caps and play an Officer and a Gentleman, for there had to be one or both, in a film about the Navy. But there was not the slightest chance. I implored, I begged, I grovelled. I offered to test for any part, even if I didn't get it, just so that I would have the chance to show them that I could speak 'proper' and could therefore extend my range. I even offered to work for no money at all. Which didn't move them in the least. They insisted that I was best in working class roles, no one would believe me as a Gentleman, but that there was a nice little cameo, if I was *absolutely* determined on being in their epic, of an Able Bodied Seaman who had a 'good little moment in a lifeboat'.

Olive Dodds had done as much as possible and could help no more. I refused the Able Bodied Seaman in the lifeboat and went back to my uncertain role of Country Squire at Bendrose; but not for long. Ironically they cheerfully rented me out (they got half the salary) to a small company who offered me the part of a Wing Commander in a film about Bomber Command. He was an upper-class Wing Commander at that; never wore a raincoat and never saw a Copper. 'Appointment in London' was the first time that I actually made any kind of impression for good on the screen. The *Daily Mail* suggested that I could act with my skin, *The Graphic* said it was my finest hour, *The Telegraph* welcomed me into the front rank of English screen actors, and *Picturegoer* threw all caution to the wind and hailed me as the foremost young actor on the British screen.

But no one from the Rank Organisation ever went to see it; nor did they make any comment whatsoever. As far as they were concerned I was still Working Class League. It was a crushing blow. It was made all the worse by the deep-seated knowledge, which I had always know but put aside in my usual way, that I had an enemy at court. Earl St John, for all his charm, and he had a great deal, had never been able to overcome the overcoming of his first edict, that I had no future for the cinema, and that I was not cinema material, and he never saw reason to change his mind. A few years ago, shortly before he died, at a party in the South of France at which I was the host, he came across the bustling, noisy restaurant, greeted me warmly, one arm round my shoulder like a loving friend, and said, with the implacable smile and eyes of a baby shark caught in shallow waters, 'I said you'd never make it, kid. And you won't.'

Whether he was right or wrong is neither here nor there at this particular moment. But I did make it, albeit briefly, with Philip Leacock and 'Appointment in London'. He, with Dearden, showed me that screen acting was more to do with the head than the left profile or the capped teeth. He made me more aware than any other director up till then that it was the thought which counted more than the looks.

And the fans found me quite acceptable without my raincoat, to such an extent that the mail trebled, a fact which could not possibly have gone unnoticed by the Organisation since it kept tallies on all the mail received by their Artists, but to which they never referred. Of the hundreds of letters which were received in the Fan Mail Department in South Street, only the most apparently private or personal mail was sent on to my home. Among them one day my secretary, Val, found a glossy picture postcard with an Amsterdam postmark. 'This is something you'll have to deal with. I can't understand it.' Gabled houses reflected in a sluggish canal. On the back the once-familiar printed writing.

'I saw you again at a cinema last night. You were in the RAF. Do you remember the cards? A different uniform, different badges, a bird, and lights everywhere? You see?' It was signed Harri. There was no address.

A great deal of my time, during the war, was spent, clenched-buttocked and white-knuckled, flying through German flak in lumbering planes which, as often as not, landed nose down in extremely unsuitable terrain. I never enjoyed these journeys, and was absolutely convinced that flying, for pleasure, or anything else, would not catch on in peace time. A serious miscalculation. So it took a great deal to persuade me back on board to fly all the way to Cyprus to make my first foreign location film. The persuasion was Lewis Milestone, a legendary director whose masterpiece, 'All Quiet on the Western Front' stands as one of the ten greatest films ever made. He it was who would direct this film, and I was very happy and proud to be asked to participate. The fact that I had not much cared for the script didn't really worry me, for I felt sure that if Mr Milestone had agreed to direct it then he must also have liked what he read. Another serious miscalculation.

I discovered, far too late to cancel the flight, that he detested what he had read and demanded changes; these were promised, and he read the new material on the flight to Athens. Crossing the tarmac from the London 'plane, we were rather disconcerted to see him shredding the new material into confetti and chucking it over his shoulder into the cool Greek air.

'I don't mind,' he said, 'people carrying shit about with them in their pockets. What I do mind is that they don't know it's shit.' Lewis Milestone was a man of few words; all of them effective.

The film was called 'They Who Dare' (it was later dubbed by the Press, 'How Dare They', but we weren't to know that for a time). A commando story, based on real events in Crete. There were eight of us in the cast. Eight commando packs, under the instructions of Mr Milestone himself, were packed for us by a combat unit in Malta. They weighed ninety pounds a piece. The first time we all struggled into them we fell flat on our faces before him; Moslems in Mecca. He suggested a week's training in the Troodos mountains, while he got on with the script and we got used to the packs. For some days we crawled, sobbing and moaning, up crags, ledges, gorges, cliffs and along the sheer edges of gaping ravines into which we plummeted, with astonishing regularity, to lie crumpled and groaning among the startled goats. No one was actually killed during these activities, but many of us longed for death as a speedy relief, for we expected every sortie to the mountains to be our last. Mr Milestone (we had by now actually overcome fear of him by fear of our exercises and called him Millie to his face) had a perfectly valid point. You cannot act weight. And neither you can. But actors we were, not commandos; and it is quite hard enough to act without a pack weighing ninety pounds let alone with one dragging you constantly towards oblivion. I pointed out to him that it might be wiser, should we ever start the film, to try and finish it, all in one piece and alive, than to have to abandon it because of a couple of random deaths somewhere towards the middle of things, when the insurance people would make things difficult. So, reluctantly, the packs were lightened to sixty pounds, and although we still careened into endless ravines, apparently for ever, we managed to give the impression, anyway, of a respectable band of brave desperados, tough, rough and bloodied. The only thing we hadn't got was a script.

We never actually got one. A writer was despatched from London to assist, but Millie took a dislike to him almost instantly, set him on a high stool in the middle of his room, and walked slowly round and round him dictating his notes, until the poor man, mesmerised, like the guinea fowl with a fox who makes slow circles round their roosting tree, was overcome by giddiness, slipped from his perch, cracked his skull on the stone floor and was jubilantly returned to London. Millie didn't like being bugged; as he put it quietly in the bar later. If I give the impression that he was a monster I hasten to correct. He was not. And we all worshipped him; he was funny, scathing, hated the Front Office, and was splendidly irreverent about everything. Except his work. Even though we had not much to go on as far as a script was concerned, we all worked together with him, as a great adventure, and did the best we could. And if nothing else, and there wasn't much else alas, we all enjoyed ourselves tremendously. Anyway – I was back in the Army and consequently in my element.

He was a thick-set, heavy man, in his middle sixties at that time. And he never ever seemed to sit down, even on the roughest terrain or the highest peaks. I bought him a shooting-stick.

He accepted it gravely. His green, Russian eyes flicking about like a lizard's, suspiciously.

'What is it?'

'A shooting-stick.'

'What the hell for?'

'For you.'

'What do I shoot with it?'

'You sit on it.'

His eyes flicked across my face, narrowed. His lips pursed doubtfully.

'This thing! This tin stick! I sit on it?'

'Yes . . . look, it has two little flaps which unfold, like this, makes a seat.'

He closed his eyes thoughtfully. 'Appreciate the thought. You see the size of my ass? You want this thing to go right through me? Upwards? Head on a pike?'

He used it as a walking stick, and viewed it with dull suspicion all through the work.

After two and a half months shooting we still hadn't really got much idea of an ending for our epic. He knew that I was worried, and took action to comfort me.

'Hell! I didn't have an ending for "All Quiet" until the last minute. The Studio took the film away from me, said it was too long, too down-beat. They wanted to end it with some damned montage of thousands of marching soldiers singing some damn-fool patriotic song, flags waving, all that crap. Withdrew the money. I was sunk. There was just me and the camera crew left, in a car, coming away from the Studio with the bad news. I have never been so low in my life. A picture, and no ending. Stopped at an intersection. Rain so heavy you just couldn't see out the car. The windscreen wipers squeaking across the glass, backwards and forwards, they made a funny noise. It seemed to me like Schmetterling, Schmetterling, that's the German for butterfly . . . Schmetterling, Schemetterling, and suddenly I got it! I got the end. We turned right round and went to a butterfly farm, bought boxes of them. Found a building lot just of Sunset, in all the rain. No lights, so we used the headlamps of the car, turned them on a muddy bit of land, let the butterflies go . . . most of them flew away, but one little fellow, he just settled happily in the warmth of the lamps, flitting his wings. I reached out my hand, very gently to take him, and then he was gone. And that was the last shot of 'All Quiet on the Western Front'. Don't worry,' he grinned and thumped my knee with affection, 'we'll get an ending.'

He made a cut of his version of the film and flew off to America; the producer made his cut and between the two of them we were a catastrophe. But it had been great fun and marvellous experience. And Millie taught me one of the greatest lessons to be learned in the cinema. 'You can make a good script bad; but you can't ever make a bad script good. Never forget that.' I was to be constantly reminded of his words for years to come. It is a lesson very few have bothered to remember.

While we were struggling to find an ending for a poor script in Cyprus, Miss Betty Box, on a long and tiring journey from Scotland, left her train for a few minutes at Crewe to purchase some reading matter, magazines and a slim book, to while away the remainder of the trip to Euston. She was quite unaware that this simple action was to switch the points, so to speak, not only on her own life, but on mine and the Miller's and his men as well. By the time she had reached London she had made up her mind to buy the rights of the book, and being the most far-sighted producer in the Rank Organisation at the time, did so, had a script roughed out, and sent it to me to see if I would like to play the young student. It was called 'A Doctor in the House'.

I was not, I remember, immmediately impressed. It all seemed a bit light, the role a bit dim-witted, and every other character had funnier things to say and do. I was to be the simple Juvenile. Forwood, by now disenchanted with acting himself, although very successful, had generously renounced his own career and agreed to become my Personal Manager since I could now no longer handle my own affairs alone. He was in complete disagreement with me; here was a comedy, for the first time, which could well be an important success and lead me away from spivs and service heroes to which I was obviously becoming addicted. He urged me to accept the offer immediately before it went to someone else. Impressed by his seriousness I telephoned Miss Box and said yes.

But Miss Box, in her low and pleasant voice, confessed that there was, unfortunately, a hidden snag. Mr St John, she explained gently was strongly opposed to her choice of myself for the part. He didn't think that I could play light comedy; my metier, he said, was action stuff. I did not have the necessary charm or lightness, and he reminded her that my last effort at comedy, at his own instigation, had been a complete and total catastrophe for all concerned; especially myself. It would be disastrous to play me in such a part.

Miss Box, happily for me and my future, disagreed with him. She had a hunch it would work. So fortunately did her director, Ralph Thomas, and together they fought a quiet battle to get me, and won. There is no question in my mind whatsoever that if they had not taken this courageous stand I should never have had a career in the cinema at all; it was the absolute turning point, and by their action they secured me in my profession. A debt it is impossible to repay.

It was one of the happiest times I have ever spent in a Studio, made all the happier when, one morning, I was taken in a great bear-hug from behind and a well-remembered voice said in my ear, 'Caught you up at last!' Kenneth More. It had taken six years from the tatty dressing room in the New Lindsey Theatre to this splendid moment, made all the pleasanter eventually when he stole the picture from under all our noses. As Doctor Simon Sparrow I did surprisingly well. The film was a phenomenal success at the box office and Betty and Ralph immediately started planning sequels. Their hunch, and Olive Dodd's astute strategy, had paid off. It seemed that, at last, things were going to be all right for a time. I had proved my worth, if only modestly, and the dreaded yearly option could, more or less, be set aside. An immensely encouraging feeling, since my salary would increase comfortably each year. It was possible that I might even make the Seven Year Stretch.

No one, however, could relax, and no one did. I decided that it was perhaps now the moment for me to have for the first time in my life, a real bought-and-paid-for house of my own. I had my eye on one, not vey far away, which was empty and for sale. However, it would of course mean leaving Bendrose.

The Bendrose days were the happiest; although there were to be grander houses, greater riches, finer views, it is always to Bendrose that I look with nostalgia and happiness.

Perhaps it was because we were all so much younger then; because the calm of the countryside, after the depressed austerity of London, healed so well, or just perhaps it was because we were all content with so much less after the long strain of the war years so recently over, that even a shabby, still-rationed peace was better than anything which had gone before.

Bendrose House stood in three hundred acres of corn and mangolds surrounded by a vast cherry orchard. The estate belonged to the Forwoods, and they allowed me to rent the house and gardens at a very modest yearly rental.

Hardly to the delight and relief of the Studio Publicity Department who had already dubbed me as being uncooperative; along with the small head and the long legs and small trunk so despaired of by Earl St John, I also refused to play the game by attending premieres, escorting resting-actresses to night clubs, buying diamonds, fast cars, or fighting with waiters; I didn't even try to crash Society (a popular pastime then) by hobnobbing with minor Royalty, playing polo at Cowdray or trying to dance with Princess Margaret at Charity Balls. All the Publicity Department could scrape together was a sorry list of trivia, assembled by a harassed lady in a feathered hat one day, which stated, among other things, that I made my own lampshades, bred tropical fish, and was descended on my father's side from Anne of Cleves. Even I could see that this was hardly good news. Therefore the move from the shabby canyon of Chester Row to the elysian fields of Amersham Common was pounced upon with alacrity. I could now be given a Country Background; rolling fields, sunsets, a man of the earth, brooding solitude in the sombre plough of the Home Counties. A kind of anaemic Heathcliff. They dubbed me Lord of the Manor and only retracted a little when it was pointed out that Bendrose was not a manor nor mine, and substituted Country Squire, which anyway sounded better in a utilitarian, democratic, Socialist Britain. I was deeply relieved and brooded all over the place; anything so long as I was not forced into a black tie and the Orchid Room nightly, with a twenty pound bottle of champagne. I made the image stick.

It was not the most comfortable of houses – filled with icy draughts, twisting passages, floors on all levels and forests of dark-stained beams. The heart of the house, a modest sixteenth century cottage, stood smothered in a splendid muddle of Edwardian-Tudor extensions which ran in all directions. Forwood's grandfather, who had made it the family house, bought most of his material from builders' yards and the demolition of old houses throughout the county. Latticed windows nudged cheerfully at Georgian; four-poster beds were dismantled, cut to pieces, and formed ornate, if bewildering, fireplaces; walls were panelled with yards of cheap three-ply wood, bought in bulk from aeroplane factories after the First World War; and the kitchens lay miles from the dining room so that the food arrived frozen or spilled, since there were two floor levels to endure before arriving at the dining hatch, which fell down and jammed one's fingers every time it was raised to admit the chilling dishes. Forwood Senior bought and built expressively, and economically. One day at luncheon his wife had asked mildly what it could be she saw coming up the drive, and he replied that it was the railway station. It was. Shortly afterwards Chalfont and Latimer Station was re-erected opposite the dairy to house the hay and mangolds, proving to be a very economical barn.

On my arrival the house was empty and cobwebby, shabby, but loving, and with a van load of furniture which my father gave me from our old house in Sussex (which had been lying in store all the war) plus the bits and pieces I had got from junk shops for Chester Row, carpets and curtains bought at local village auctions, the house started to thrive again, and although it was always to be happily untidy and unplanned, it very soon became a home once more.

Bond, my driver, came from London to be odd job and handy man and to drive me to the Studios; Mr and Mrs Wally, from the Farm, came in daily, she to 'do' and he to help untangle the wilderness of the gardens; and I sought and obtained a manservant. Cook General was what I had asked for and is what I was told I had got when Catchpole arrived with his suitcase and a head of tight red wavy hair. He spent all his working time scrubbing out the kitchen and cooking cod steaks in heavy curry sauce. I don't think he knew anything else. His days off were spent entirely at the Windmill Theatre, from the first show till the last, and when he left, as leave he finally did, thankfully, glossy phototographs of ladies arrived from time to time with polite letters regretting that, 'We have no photographs of Valerie and Doves, but thought you might like to have these of Clarice and Balloons.' I couldn't send them on to him since he had left in a huff without a forwarding address.

Then came Philpot with a long record in the Merchant Navy, spick and span, and shipshape. He was carrying *The Economist* when he arrived for his first interview, so perhaps I should have been warned. Floors became decks, the twisting staircase companionways, the kitchen the galley, and he served meals, wearing a neat white apron and a Merchant Navy jacket. The meals themselves consisted mostly of corned beef in various disguises, mashed potatoes, and a rather ugly little pudding with a pink cherry on top. For the first week I let it pass, believing that I should soon wean him away from ship fare; even though rationing was still with us the diet could, I felt, be varied just a little.

Five days after he arrived I went to visit my parents, telling him to settle in and have a good clean up. Which he did. Following my instructions to the letter. On my return to Bendrose not a light shone, not a door was locked, no hens had been fed, and my open wardrobe doors revealed a softly swinging row of empty coat hangers. When they finally arrested him, in one of my suits coming down the steps of St Pancras Station, it was disheartening to discover that the nearest he had ever been to the sea, or a ship, was the Mersey ferry, and that he had spent most of his life in clink for pinching anything from a roll of linoleum to a hurrican lamp.

When I offered, rather stupidly, to stand bail for him he begged me, as one ex-serviceman to another, not to.

'I know you're a good Officer, could smell it as soon as I came aboard, but I'll only do it again, you see. It's my kick. Can't seem to get off it.' He also added, confidentially in the cell at Chesham Police Station, that he had done a shocking deal on my Rolleiflex, my dinner jacket didn't fit him, or anyone else he knew, but that he had made a tidy bit on the silver lighters and the Chelsea figures.

Loyalty for my ex-service comrades gently faded, and indeed, need never have been applied in this particular instance. So I left Philpot to the Law and sought a well-experienced Lady Cook General. Mrs Walters sped down on winged feet, slim, trim, no nonsense, late sixties, umbrella and, instead of *The Economist* a thin red volume entitled *Get to Know Jesus*.

She said that she had very good references, and I said that I had no intention of being converted to anything. With a hearty laugh she said that she was just a seeker herself and that the only thing she wouldn't brook was women pottering in and out of her kitchen. When I assured her that she would be perfectly safe, she agreed to give me a try and said that the fee I was offering was too high, she could manage on two pounds less, and that I was too extravagant by far. We made a deal, on condition that there was something to help here with the trays. 'I'm not about to carry trays from the kitchen, half a mile to the dining room, *that* I can tell you. Not at my age. You get me a nice little trolley with wheels and we'll all be as right as rain.'

For weeks to come every meal was preceded by the rumbling of tumbrils; and the shattering of falling china. Her concern for my extravagance had touched me deeply, until it became apparent that it also applied to her cooking. Dead whiting we had; tails stuffed into glazed-eyed heads, smothered in sticky white sauce and buried, comfortably, in wreaths of parsley; Lancashire hot pot, more pot than hot, shards of grey meat, swollen kidney, carrots, bullet-hard slices of blue potatoes swimming in a lake of thin gruel. One evening, returning late and hungry from London with Forwood and an old friend of his, Kay Young, she said all she could manage at that time of an evening was an egg. I lost my temper and my head and threw every tin I could lay hands upon in the larder at her. She ducked nimbly for ten minutes, while I shattered every plate and cup and saucer on the dresser, before which she was inconveniently standing.

After a glass of champagne, which she accepted cheerfully, we agreed that perhaps my irregular hours, and moods, might be tiresome for her and she left on a Green Line Bus for another post with a retired Colonel in Aylesbury.

A week later, a sullen couple of French people arrived from Lyons. They wore plimsolls, carried all their belongings in two paper bags, and took possession of the kitchen and the house which they filled with the just-remembered scents of garlic, thyme, and olive oil. Sullen they were, but cook and work they did. And Bendrose started to heave itself out of a rut and to run smoothly.

And so with excellent food at last, log fires, acres of fields in which to wander with the dogs, and assorted cats even, faded chintzes and a well-stocked drink-table, Bendrose was ready to accept its guests who came down every week-end and gave the place the feeling of a pleasant, if shabby, well-run boarding house.

We were always a mixed group; the steadies providing the solid background; these were the friends who had been summoned by Glynis and Forwood in the days of hysteria and who provided a safe and affectionate security without which I know that I could not have survived. Irene Howard, Kay Young, Michael Wilding, Jean Simmons, Michael Gough and his wife Anne Leon, Margaret Leighton and Olive Dodds; and they in turn brought other people who brought other people, and Bendrose Sundays became established.

Jessie Matthews did high kicks in the Oak Room; Gene Kelly danced up and down the staircase of an unfinished council house on a housing estate in nearby Bell Lane; Noël Coward asked me if I would like to revive his play 'The Vortex'; Elizabeth Taylor, a constantly hungry eighteen, consumed endless portions of Christmas pudding; Ava Gardner warmed her naked feet against the dogs, all of them sprawled together before the big fireplace; and Forwood brought Kay Kendall down to tea and supper one Friday evening.

'I know you aren't mad on her; she can seem rather grand, but she really is lovely, and funny, and you'd like her and she is not grand at all. It's just her manner, she's a bit unconfident really.'

I had met Miss Kendall once at the Studios and had been frightened out of my wits by her apparently Royal Manner, but as Forwood had worked with her on a film, and assured me that she was lovely I took his advice, and let her come.

She didn't seem to need confidence at all; she arrived dressed elegantly in the honey colours which she favoured and indeed she seemed as faintly condescending as before, patronising, and possessing the disdain of a Lama. It didn't really take long to discover that this was all a cover for an extremely soft centre. Forwood was right, as usual, but it was not immediately apparent.

After we had all had tea and done the walk round the gardens she thoughtfully settled herself into a deck chair and, nodding gentle approval all round, sipped her large gin and tonic. She decided to drop her Royal Manner for the role of Dorothy Adorable; which she played sickeningly well.

'What a sweet little housey pousey you have! Do you do it all yourself? So clever ... such a lot of work .. I've got a teeny weeny little flat in horrid London, too awful, and no dear little garden like this.' (There were four acres.)

'I'm a bit square, you know. Country born and bred.'

'I adore the country. So real.'

'Yes ...'

'How many rooms do you have here?'

'About, um, fifteen I think.'

'Bedrooms I mean?' She was smiling sweetly.

'Eight.'

'Oh poor little me ...' Deep sighs.

'Only one bathroom though.'

'That wouldn't matter.' Wistful look.

'Frightfully cold in the winter, full of draughts ...'

'But so near the Studios ... those ghastly morning journeys ... Ohhh ...' More sighs.

'Perfect.' Eyes closing.

'And dreadfully quiet.'

'I adore quiet.' Eyes closed dreamily.

'So do I.'

'I wouldn't utter!' Eyebrows arched like half hoops, finger to lips.

'Smelly from the farm though; cows, pigs, manure ...'

'I have no sense of taste or smell.'

'None?'

'None at all. A car crash.' Suddenly she grabbed her nose and pulled it upwards like a wild Pinocchio. 'This is all McIndoe; he only had two sorts of noses in those days, this and one other; squatter. I chose this. I look like a clown in a fright-wig ... God knows why Rank ever signed me, they can't shoot my profile.'

'But can't you taste anything at all?'

'Nothing, wifey. Someone gave me a red chilli last week somewhere ...'

'But you tasted that?'

'Just. Divine.'

'I don't believe you.'

She thrust my finger into her face.

'Wheeee! You see? No bones, all cartilage. I'm Old Mother Riley in drag.'

'He *is* in drag.'

'Well, you know ... in or out, oh dear, oh dear, what's to become of me, wifey?'

We sat there for a moment looking at each other seriously, and suddenly we burst into laughter, she laughed until the tears ran down her boneless face, and made her nose run which she wiped with the back of her hand helplessly.

'Oh dear! Poor me. I'm a ruin, a ruin ... I need someone to look after me, wifey!'

Later, as the long evening shadows crept across the lawns, I took her round the farm to see the pigs, pick some raspberries and watch the dairy being hosed and scrubbed after milking. She got her feet wet and took off her shoes to plod cheerfully after me through the vegetables and down among the hens and ducks. She found it all 'ravishing', and when we got back to the others sitting about on the terrace with their drinks, she announced that it was just what she had been looking for, and what on earth could I do with a huge house and all those rooms while she had a miserable little flat which made her depressed and lonely. Surely I could spare a teeny weeny bit of the house just for her at weekends? She'd be no trouble, she would knit a lot and do any mending, and help out with the drinks as a form of rent.

It was a bloody good act.

She moved into the double front bedroom the following Friday, with a bundle of old country clothes, her bottles of 'ox blood for her anaemia', and a small white rug for the side of her bed. She stayed, on and off, for about five years. There had never been a happier decision ever made. And it was entirely her own. Kate always made her own decisions, I was to discover. That was Bendrose.

Beel House stood in the centre of a fifty-acre ring fence. Tudor by origin it now wore its Georgian façade, and later additions, with some elegance amidst sweeping lawns and herbaceous borders; it was ten minutes' walk from Bendrose, past the piggeries, and across Finch Lane. Empty and up for sale, it stood forlorn and uncared for, one great circular bed of Ophelia roses, shabbily scattering petals, the windows cobwebbed, the terrace greening with mosses.

Standing in the shade of the two giant cedar trees which stood sentinel before its ivied West Front, I wondered how I could manage to buy it.

People who had wandered about its empty echoing rooms and dark, stone-floored kitchens, shivered at the gloom of it and said that it was a hopeless proposition. Too many rooms, nothing facing the right way, poor lighting and water systems, badly proportioned rooms and too much land to maintain. But the land joined the Forwoods' land and was excellent grazing; they thought they might extend their farm but didn't want the house. They bought the land, I bought the house and seven acres of pleasure gardens from them for the improbable sum of £4,000, and with the help of a local builder in the village and his two brothers ripped down a wing of eleven ugly rooms, tore out the kitchens, gutted the house and started from scratch, ripping down years of ivy, opening up long-blocked-in windows, and covering everything with layers of clean white paint. Beel House became manageable, bright, comfortable and my home, my first real home, for the next eight years.

We had one final family Christmas at Bendrose and moved out across the fields a week later with all my goods and chattels, the dogs, a couple of Bendrose rose bushes, but minus the sullen couple from Lyons who had become more and more sullen, refusing, on occasions, to serve at table if there were Jew or Negroes present. They went off in their plimsolls to a millionaire in Sunningdale at six times the salary and with a modest reference extolling the virtues of their cooking if not their racial charity.

We built a swimming pool, laid out a croquet lawn, turned the long-neglected tennis courts into chicken-runs and filled the enormous conservatory, which ran the entire length of the south terrace and was the only room in the house to receive any direct sun all year round, with palms, mimosa, geraniums, plumbago and heavily scented trumpet trees and an aviary of fifty tropical birds. In spite of its Victorian glamour, to me, Kate always called it the Out-Patients Department and so it remained. The sullen Lyonnais were swiftly replaced by Angnes and Hans Zwickl from Vienna, who brought a friend called Florian to tend the gardens and the vegetables, and every year, in September, we had the local gymkhana in the park when I, in tweed cap and cavalry twill, presented the cups at the end of the day. The Country Squire was fast in danger of believing his own image and changing to Lord of the Manor. It is an insidious business.

Christmas was still very much a family affair. We had a giant Christmas tree in the drawing room, my mother made all the pies and the puddings, as she always had done (except for the war years), fires blazed in every room, Hans and Florian smothered every picture, beam, and door with boughs of pine, holly and fir-cones, but the mistletoe, at my father's insistence, was hung from the brass lamp in the front hall just inside the front door so that he could smack a kiss on to the cheek of every woman who arrived. We had presents at tea-time which ran into drink time with considerable ease, and everyone dressed for dinner; candles winking on silver and glass, logs spitting, crackers, and reading the awful mottoes ... and then there was the Loyal Toast, and the one which made everyone a little thoughtful: to absent friends. Afterwards, sitting about comfortably in the drawing room, a film show, or else a word game, dancing in the wide bay window, the tree shimmering with tinsel and golden stars. So much laughter; so much sureness.

All so long ago.

Now, here on my hill in Provence, that day is almost forgotten. Perhaps a chicken for supper, dogs snoring by the fire, the Mistral whipping and clattering at the shutters, stars hard and bright above the hills, the village clock clanging out the fading day, tinnily. The theatrical splendours of those past Christmases have all long since faded; the set has been dismantled, the cast dispersed, some older, some no longer here. Which is most probably why I now choose to ignore it. Stocktaking, especially on the edge of evening, is not very amusing.

One bitter, thin-sun morning, Millie Milestone telephoned to ask if I could sit an extra couple for lunch and dinner: 'A sweet couple, just kids ... they leave for the States tomorrow, and you know what a London Sunday in February is like. They'll walk round the Park twice and cut their throats on the second Martini.' He was coming down with Akim Tamiroff and his wife Tamara, and his own wife Kendall. They all lived now in London, uncomfortable exiles from McCarthy.

The kids, as he called them, arrived in due time. Cold from the drive, pleasant, and as far as they were introduced by a vague Millie, their names were just Nancy and Alan. He was neat, tidy, dressed in a dark blue suit, glasses, and a sad nervous little smile. Nancy was bright, sparkling, blonde and pink, she laughed a lot and the day was brighter.

It was a quiet week-end. Kate was working in London on a film, and the other regulars had decided that the icy roads would be a harzard in the dark, so stayed in bed with the Sunday papers. After lunch came the obligatory walk over to the dell. We all started pulling on the old mackintoshes, scarves, gloves and wellingtons which were always kept in the downstairs bathroom, where years before the local cricket team used to shower and change after a game. It was, naturally, called the Cricket Room. Nancy said she was still frozen and preferred not to go. We stood at the windows and watched the Russians, Alan and Forwood plod away into the thin snow and failing sun.

'I don't know your names, you know ... Millie was a bit vague.'

'Well, my name is Nancy Olsen; I'm an actress, of sorts ...'

' "Sunset Boulevard"!'

'Right ... I was the girl ... and the little fellow all hunched up between Tamara and Kendall is my husband. And he's called Alan Lerner. J. He's a lyricist, he's really quite famous. Do you know "Brigadoon". "Paint Your Wagon" or perhaps "An American in Paris"? Well, those were his.'

'Ah. It seemed to me that he was something rather good in a bank.'

'A sort of clerk?' she smothered her laughter.

'Something like that. Modest, silent, good at figures ...'

'He's that all right. But I think it's that awful coat he wears.'

'And you leave for the States tomorrow?'

'Yes. Sadly. We've been here a week trying to meet with Rex Harrison, do you know him? It's very difficult ... Alan's written a show and wants him terribly badly but he won't take any notice. It's easier to ride a tiger than get a meeting fixed with Harrison.' She shrugged sadly. 'Oh well ... we tried.'

'Couldn't you wait a week? I know Rex quite well, he often comes down on Sundays, he's coming next week.'

'You talk to Alan, if he ever comes back from out there . . . we're booked out at lunch-time tomorrow. He's fed up; you know?'

In the Cricket Room, in a swirl of damp coats, scarves and muddy wellingtons, Alan accepted my apologies for thinking him something in a bank, and we all went in to tea.

'What is the Show?'

Alan was spreading a crumpet with Gentleman's Relish. He grinned a wry grin. 'You'll disapprove, I know that.'

'Come on; tell.'

'It's Shaw. A musical of *Pygmalion*. We're calling it "Lady Liza".'

Amidst cries of derision he calmly went on with his crumpet. Nancy looking a little anxious stirred her tea into a tempest.

'Disapprove! How could you! Shaw! Honestly you Americans pinch everything you can lay your hands on . . .'

'Well, why didn't the English think of doing it? It's been about for years? And it's all Shaw's dialogue, we haven't Americanised it; and we want Harrison for Higgins. Can you think of any other Higgins in the world?'

'No. Well, it's more than likely that he'll be here next Sunday, he said so. If you stayed on for a week; played it by ear, and just happened to be here for lunch next week while he was present. Very casually, you know. We won't say anything about you two at all, you'll just arrive, and then it would be up to you, wouldn't it?'

He looked across the table at Nancy doubtfully, his glasses winking in the candle-light.

'You want to risk it?'

'If you do; and I want to buy a Corgi, remember? And Dirk says he knows a kennels near Oxford, so . . .'

Tamara, sipping her tea comfortably smiled across us all: 'I'm a witch; a Russian witch. You stay. You will see.'

Rex was involved in rather a full Sunday without actually being told much about it. Millie and Kendall were there, the Tamiroffs, Peter Brook and his wife Natasha Parry (daughter of Lusia, my catalyst from the Savoy), Katie, Michael and Anne Gough. And Alan and Nancy. It was a perfectly normal Sunday. The only people absent from the obligatory afternoon walk over the fields were Rex and Alan. After tea, in the fading March light, we all gathered round the spinet in the Long Study, which was the only form of piano I possessed, and even though it was a full octave short Alan played the entire score, and sang, in a rather wavering voice, all the songs of his show, for the first time to a full audience.

Three years later, half an hour after the curtain fell on the First Night at Drury Lane, I, at Alan's request, introduced the music of 'My Fair Lady' on television, sitting by the fire in the drawing room of Beel House where, as he pointed out a small part of theatre history had started off. It was a graceful, if undeserved, gesture, for if I had not met Lewis Milestone in Cyprus all that time ago, would Alan Lerner have finally managed to meet Rex Harrison in Buckinghamshire? Tamara Tamiroff only smiled, her gentle witch's smile and, shaking her head, said that it was Fate.

At the time of this fateful lunch I had just, a few days before, finished my eighteenth picture, the second 'Doctor' film. Although the option period was now almost forgotten, only Betty and Ralph seemed to have any idea of a plan for me and although I was handing out cups at gymkhanas and playing my Squire role to the hilt, I was still just hopping about from film to film wherever I was lucky enough to be asked. It didn't make for a settled feeling; I knew that as long as the Doctor films would be made I should probably be asked to be in them, but apart from that (and they could only happen now and again) there was a clear feeling of disinterest from Above.

Looking over the smooth lawns at Beel House, I had many moments of grave doubt at the wisdom of leaving the modest comforts of Bendrose just across the fields; at least the house had not been mine, Beel was. I had not only to support myself, but a large house and a busy staff of four, plus weekly gardeners. Stupid idiot. I had probably jumped too soon; I longed to be the proud possessor of an Oxo tin again, when I at least knew, to the last halfpenny, what I had in my bank. But there were also rumbles of doubt and worry, not only in my head, but in the Aberconways' Bedroom as well. The Studio writhed with rumours of changes to be made, heads to fall, and new brooms sweeping clean. A mounting panic almost choked me; after all, no one could prove that I had actually had anything very much to do with the success of 'A Doctor in the House': the film itself was the winner, and I had shown no definite signs yet to them that I was Box Office. So now that I had gone too far and attached myself to a large country house and dependants it was fate that I should be chucked out. There was trouble at the Millers, all right, and I was convinced that my time had come. Even Olive Dodds could offer little comfort; she too, who always smiled, was now looking fairly grim, probably worrying about her own job. I only hoped that when the blow came I would be able to weather it, and spent more time than was healthy wandering round the rooms of Beel House, an anxious Camille saying goodbye to them all.

The Blow was a summons to lunch at the Dorchester to meet Mr Rank's Chief Accountant. At least that is what I understood at the time, and I experienced a slight flicker of hope; if I were to be dropped, surely Earl St John would have sent the news personally? And with pleasure. This must mean another tremendous cut in salary of such proportions that only the Chief Accountant could possibly confront me.

The confrontation with John Davis was so pleasant that I almost began to think that I might even be offered a raise in salary instead of a cut. He did, however, offer rather more than that. He started off by saying that certain changes were to be made generally, and that he was about to take a personal interest in the cinema section. He thought that I had worked exceedingly well over the years, had proved loyal and diligent, and that he was prepared to launch a campaign to involve me at the Studios for at least a couple of years, and that if I had the stamia to carry it through, he would make me into one of the biggest Stars, or biggest Box Office Attractions, Rank had ever had. How did I feel about that?

I felt fine. Could it be possible that I had, at last, a friend at court? He demanded complete loyalty, dedication and submission to the plan which he had in mind. There were already five films, in a row, some of which would be prouced by the Box-Thomas team with whom I had worked so very happily and successfully. Successfully was what he really meant. It didn't matter much about the happiness: trade is trade, money is money. The commercial cinema is both those things. There was to be no room for anything else but success, and he wanted no excuses. Mr Davis was going to be extremely tough as a boss and very demanding; he would brook no failure on my part, but he was also very correct and just, hid nothing and asked only for total commitment and faith in him. I said that he would have them. He told me that he would be available to me, at any time, for any problem or worry which I might have, and hoped that I would dine with him privately the following week so that we could start to discuss, in detail, the first project he had in mind for me, A. J. Cronin's 'The Spanish Gardener'.

On the journey back to Beel House I was pardonably, in a state of mild euphoria. The signal was green. Weights had fallen from my back to such an extent that I was literally buoyant. Now someone else, apart from the ever loyal Olive Dodds, believed that I might have a potential at Rank.

Putting thoughts of Camille deftly aside, as we turned into Western Avenue, I hazily started a plan to purchase an extra two acres of paddock from the generous, unsuspecting Forwood family. I was a quick recoverer; a little encouragement went a long, long way. It always has. I knew that I had been taken in hand and was just about to be developed – manufactured would be a better word perhaps – like a stick of seaside rock with the lettering printed all the way through right down to the last little bit. And as sweet and sickly and forgettable as that product itself. I was to be a commercial creation pure and simple; that of course was the hidden message buried in the smoked salmon and the *poulet à l'estragon*. In return for loyalty, devotion, commitment, stamina and faith I should be raised to the giddy heights of a Box Office Attraction. I had promised all these. No one, however, had mentioned the word acting. Perhaps it really didn't matter in the commercial cinema, perhaps it took too much time, and time is money etcetera . . . but what of Garbo, or Tracey? I knew from Dearden, Leacock, and a tense, harried, perfectionist called Joseph Losey with whom I had recently worked on a cheapish, unremarkable, and now unremembered film, only a few months before, that it was essential and, more than that, it was exciting. I knew that there was much more to it than what some critics cheerfully call good facial expressions. Bob Thompson, the operator on 'Doctor at Sea', he opened up unlimited vistas for me one day when he said, staring gloomily over his camera, that he didn't know how the hell I'd managed to get so far with so little camera technique.

'I know you can act all right, but you don't know how to act for the camera, do you, mate? Not much good you giving us your all with half your bleeding head off frame, your face in shadow and your back to the microphone, is it? You don't know a bloody thing about the camera, do you?'

For the rest of the film he had taught me the basics of cinema technique. Everything from lenses, to lights, to sound. I was a greedy pupil, he was a thorough tutor.

So now that all seemed safer and more secure for the first time, why not extend these lessons, work on a different plane, use a new dimension. Great opportunities to work for the camera, almost non-stop it would appear, were set before me; now was my chance to learn, and apply what I had learned: it couldn't possibly harm the box office potential because very few people would ever see what I was trying to do . . . having conquered the thin neck, small head syndrome, surely to Heaven I could conquer the acting as well? No one would stop me, for no one would know. I would be doing it for myself, so that when the miracle time had ended, as end I felt sure it must one day, I would at least be cast adrift fully equipped and armoured against a bed-sitter in Earl's Court, the pubs of Leicester Square, and supporting roles in plays for what Dearden once disparagingly called the medium of the mediocre, television. Grasp the nettle.

As we turned down towards Chalfont St Giles into the home stretch, I suddenly remembered the telegram which Noël Coward had sent me on the opening night of the revival of his play, 'The Vortex'. It was quite short. 'Don't worry,' it said. 'It All Depends On You.'

CHAPTER EIGHT

I suppose the greatest exit which we are called upon to make, or which is wished upon us, is our birth; that clumsy, uncomfortable, messy, bewildering affair which brings us often breathless into the long corridor of life leading directly, sometimes indirectly, but always inevitably, to our final supreme Exit, death.

The corridor is lined all its length with doors; some open, some just ajar, some closed. Closed; but seldom, if ever, locked. It is entirely up to us which ones we choose to try, and we are only given a certain amount of time in which to arrive at the inevitable door at the end. Nothing very original about that.

However, I have never been in too much of a hurry along the corridor. Indeed one might say that I have wandered down it overcautiously, even reluctantly on many occasions, trying deliberately to avoid the doors so temptingly set along my path. I am in no hurry to reach the end, I have no fear of it, only of the manner in which I shall have to meet it, therefore a slow, wandering, lope, with as little fuss as possible has always seemed eminently desirable. But when forced, as I have often been, I have usually chosen the door which is slightly ajar rather than the ones which stand wide with blazing light, or murky with sombre shadow, always supposing, quite inaccurately unhappily, that if I approach anything with due caution and without making too much song and dance about it, I could in Lally's words, always retreat gracefully. Complete nonsense of course. Once you are in you are in.

The two matinee tickets which Rex sent for 'My Fair Lady' seemed to provide me with a pleasingly just-ajar door. A trip to America, which I had never seen, two weeks of splendour in his house in the country, and a tempting chance to see Kate again for yet another Christmas together. The five years in which she had been a week-end lodger in Bendrose and Beel had made her very much part of one's life, her ups her downs, her sighs her moans, as Lerner so perfectly phrased it, were econd nature to me now. I had grown accustomed to her face, and missed it badly since she had upped and left to go to America and join Rex, spilling with happiness and delight, to be with him on his Royal progression and become the Queen to his King of New York. Kate, with her wit, her elegance, her beauty, her fun, her rage, her laughter; Kate gobbling handfuls of her ox blood pills for her anaemia, sobbing noisily while Bruno Walter conducted his last concert, knitting endless yards of zig-zag woollen things, trailing my father through the house one evening when, to all our amazement, her sense of smell returned for a few brief moments: 'Ulric! Wifey, I can smell your cigar! Quick, give me things to smell . . . a rose . . . the cheese . . .' in and out of rooms to find the scents so long lost, to the kitchen for garlic and lemons, burying her face deep in a great bowl of sweet-peas; in my mother's arms to savour her favourite scent, embracing us all to find again the traces of tweed, or wool, of soap, of self; tears of laughter and happiness streaming down her face. And then it was gone as suddenly as it arrived.

Her downs were as giddy as her highs. Once when I, unthinkingly, suddenly lost my patience (for she could be maddening in a completely feminine way) and sent her grumbling off to her room, Tamara Tamiroff, who was present, took my arm and chided me: 'Be kind to that little one,' she said, 'she hasn't very long here, my dear.' The constant nagging doubt, always suppressed, now so flatly stated, brought instant, and careful apology followed by swift reconciliation; with wild whoops of laughter and a most improbable Charleston danced through the hall: Kate had a fury for life.

No door, therefore, open, closed, or ajar, was difficult to enter if she was on the other side of it.

So to America I went. Forwood decided to come too. Alan Lerner had invited me to play in his projected film musical of Colette's 'Gigi', but I had three firm projects lined up in a row for the following year with Rank; so delicate manoeuvring and diplomacy would be required before I could accept the chance to work with Dietrich, Chevalier, and Audrey Hepburn (the suggested cast at that time: in the event, dates on both sides proved inflexible, and I played Sydney Carton instead). Mr Davis paid the fares, the *Mauretania* carried us there, and as dawn broke one December morning, I stood on deck and watched the flat steel waters of the still Atlantic as the first thrusts of the New World rose inch by inch slowly into the mussel-shell light of the sky.

Skyscrapers glittering in the morning light, their upper reaches hidden by the clouds, dark canyons sliding past geometrically, cars and trucks speeding like toys, lights winking, gulls wheeling, bottles, crates and cabbage leaves bobbing idly in the oily waters, piers an jetties, giant cranes, steam drifting into the white air, Christmas trees in windows, sirens blowing, dirty snow, and Alan Lerner huddled against the bitter cold at Immigration to meet us in.

'You are mad! It's much too early . . .'

'I was writing all through the night . . . I never sleep. Welcome to New York!'

'I'm overwhelmed.'

'American hospitality. And since you are godfather, it's high time you saw the child.'

A low, long, black Cadillac to Rex and Kate's borrowed house on Long Island. A white clap-board, shuttered farmhouse, set among bare trees and snowy lawns, from which George Washington once watched a battle. Logs blazing, lights gleaming, dogs leaping, Kate laughing, polished wood and fat amrchairs. Bacon and eggs, toast and Cooper's marmalade, scalding coffee, and legs still a little wobbly from six days at sea; later in the afternoon the House Lights dimming, the overture beginning, the gentle hush falling, filling one with all the long forgotten excitement of a first pantomime at the Lyceum; a long and exhilirating way to come to see a matinee . . . and Kate.

It was her Christmas. And she was determined that it should be one we would all remember. There were about eight of us, including Cathleen Nesbitt, Margaret Leighton, Forwood's son, Gareth, and Kate's ravishing sister, Kim. An enormous tree arrived, higher even than the room, decked in silver and sprayed-on frost. Holly wreaths, tied all about with scarlet ribbons and studded with candles hung at the front door and every window; boughs of fir and ivy were thrust into every nook and cranny; packets and parcels, brilliant in wrapping papers, spilled from every chair and table, the drawing room was the Fairies' Grotto in Selfridges. Music played all day, the record-player never seemed to cease, sending us all scurrying faster with yards of ribbons, evergreens, and boxes of glittering baubles for her tree. Cards were stacked on every free space, and food and drink arrived in such quantities as would have delighted Pickwick or Jorrocks and must have frightened the wits out of Rex at the cost. But he smiled bravely all about him, well pleased with Kate's delight.

She, in typical fashion, had just borrowed a large advance from the salary of her first Hollywood film which was to begin almost immediately, in order to buy everyone presents, her spending was so extravagant that one felt she must have had the entire salary plus overage in advance; not just a part. A Byron first editin in red calf for Rex, a mink-lined duffle coat, 'not the best mink, it's only a lining.' Cashmeres and gold fountain pens from Cartier's, for the rest of us, trinkets and jewels from Tiffany's to fill the stockings from Father Christmas. There was never to be such a Christmas; I don't believe there ever was. Sometimes in the hurry and rush there came a little pause. Suddenly tired Kate would crumple into a huge armchair, and legs and arms akimbo, her slow smile of pleasure lighting a tired wan face, she would ask for a drink and play, for the millionth time it seemed, her favourite record, Judy Holliday singing 'Just in Time'.

'Oh, wifey . . . I'm getting to be an old, old woman . . . oh! I am a lucky lady . . . it's Chriss'mus . . . Chriss'mus . . . and I've got all my loves about me.'

If occasionally Kate seemed weary, then I was a wreck by the end of the week. The excitements and delights were exhausting, not a moment was wasted, and not a second left idle. Our daily walks together with Rex along Jones Beach beside the leaden, December sea, in a bitter wind, did much to revive me – and the scalding plastic cups of clam chowder from the deserted cafe on the beach tasted like negus – but the nightly journeys into New York, the constant round of parties, suppers, shows and conversation gradually took their toll of the pale Country Squire from the Home Counties, and by New Year's Eve I had decided that I would do no more for a time, and stay quietly in the company of the Late Show on television. Kate was anguished.

'You can't! But you can't! It's the most important party of the year . . . the Gilbert Millers are famous for it! People murder to get invited . . . Rex begged them to invite you and now you say you'll stay at home with Doris Day! You can't, Diggie, you can't. Please come?'

I refused flatly. No more opening of doors to unsuspected delights. I had had my fair share, more than, it had been marvellous, but enough was enough.

'No. I hate parties, I always get stuck with someone's aunt who is deep into Botticelli or something . . . usually in a corner or behind a door. And no one knows me and I don't know anyone there, and I hate New Year anyway. I'll stay here, very peacefully, and watch the telly, and go to bed early. I'm dead.'

'Rex will be terribly disappointed, he went to such a lot of trouble.'

'Well, bugger the Gilber Millers . . . if they have half New York going they won't miss me.'

'But it's so rude . . .' she wailed miserably off to change.

Forwood nobly stayed behind with me and I ate a light, sensible-to-sleep-on supper and settled down to watch the telly and it was absolutely appalling. After the hundredth commercial break for toothpaste, wrapped bread, shampoo, lavatory paper and Aunt Maude's Home-Baked Deep-Frozen Apple Pie I capitulated and accepted his advice that it *was* New Year, we *were* in New York, we were invited to the grandest party in town, a car awaited us and I was being very ungracious to my extraordinarily generous host and hostess. In black tie and a certain amount of suppressed fury, hopeless at the prospect of what lay before, we skidded into the city.

We all arrived at the party together and entered the elevator just as midnight started to strike. In a wild fit of joyousness Kate threw her arms around the lift-man and we all embraced and wished each other a Happy New Year. The lift stopped right at the open door of the Gibert Millers' opulent apartment: the sound of Auld Lang Syne and cheers greeted us, and we pushed out happily, colliding with a tall, pale woman in a flowing scarlet dress who hurried into our vacated cage. As we reached for brimming glasses, Miss Garbo was borne silently from our sight forty floors to the street below.

And I was stuck with someone's aunt, a pleasant, rangy, white-haired woman of seventy, with wrap-around American teeth, who had just come back from a dig in Iran. We talked very pleasantly of shards, and artifacts, of sandstone and clay, of the total inability of the desert people to comprehend the excitement of finding a set of knucklebones, intact and in spanking condition, at a depth of fifty feet which could safely be dated to at least 44 B.C. 'Time, as Plato said, brings everything,' she cried happily. It also brought Kate speeding to my side. 'Come with me, Diggie . . . there is someone in the next room who wants to meet you.'

And there she was. Sitting in a bit of a lump in a corner, dressed in pink, hair very short, plump, jolly, laughing a great deal at something that Rubinstein was saying to her. She had a thin jade bracelet on one wrist, pearl earrings . . . the wide, brown, laughing eyes I knew so well. Kate introduced us and I kissed her quite simply on the lips. I said, 'Oh . . . I love you!' and she laughed her extraordinary chuckling laugh and said, 'Oh no! I love *you*!' and I burned a hole right through the bodice of her dress with the tip of my cigarette. Judy Garland. She gave a little scream, and then we laughed, and she pulled me down beside her and made me sit on the floor and I stayed there, on and off, for almost ten years. Almost.

'It's so good to meet you. I've seen every movie you made . . .'

'I've only been doing it for ten years.'

'I saw "Stranger Inbetween"* five single times.'

'I saw "Pigskin Parade" . . . once.'

She cried out with laughter. 'I was awful, pigtails and cutes.'

'I suppose I really went to see Betty Grable.'

'I suppose you did. 1936 . . . almost twenty years ago.'

'More. I'm loyal.'

'You are? You'll come and see me, here, at the Palace?'

'I'm sailing on Saturday.'

'You'll come Friday. I'll get you seats; now don't run away? We just met, and it's taken such a long, long time.'

'I won't run away, I promise . . . Friday.'

'And I want you real close; right up front. I hope you'll like me.'

'I will.'

She laughed, and threw her arms round my neck.

'You better, Buster. I'll be doing it for you, a Command Performance.'

'Don't you do that for all your fans?'

She was suddenly grave.

'You're my friend. An old, old friend, remember that.'

I was right up front for my Command Performance at the Palace, as close as she could place me. In the middle of the Brass Section. Rex's sister, Sylvia Kilmuir, was with us. Pale from jet lag, she had just arrived in New York that morning; I wondered how she would manage with the blasting noise. Stuffing her fingers in her ears she smiled a wink and shook her head in wry disbelief.

---

* 'Hunted' in Britain.

The theatre was almost empty.

The first half was fearful: Hungarian ladies in red boots and sparkling gypsy head-dresses urged irritated dogs over boxes and through flaming hoops; a ventriloquist with a doll on his knee which talked animatedly while he consumed glass after glass of milk; two anxious dancers revolved endlessly in a Follow Spot on roller skates to the 'Thunder and Lightning' polka. At the intermission we went into the street and smoked cigarettes.

The second half was Judy, and the theatre was suddenly full. Wise people had ignored the Hungarians and the Skaters. The lights dimmed and 'Over the Rainbow' started. Anticipation mounted, twelve youngish men leapt on to the stage carrying sequined boards on the end of long poles. They did a shaky dance, in lamé jackets, and one by one spelled out her name with happy smiles and wiggling, pointed toes; the twelfth member came in on a late beat and threw up the exclamation mark. And then she was there.

Later, sitting hunched on the steps of the corridor outside her dressing room, we held each other laughing, while unrecognising people clambered over us to reach her room. She was drenched in sweat, a shabby pink candlewick wrap, her hair spiky and wet, like Gooley's years ago at Catterick, a wet cat. Her eyeblack had run, the lips were smudged, her small hands held my arm firm as clamps.

'Was I good? Did you like me? Did you really? As good as that! You're kidding? What's the matter with the dogs and the Hungarians? I don't get to see them, they just warm up the place for me, for chrissakes; but you really did like me? Was I OK? I was what . . .? You're awful! I *couldn't* be that good . . . would it go in London? I want to bring it to London . . . how big is the Palace? As big as that . . . shit . . . the Cambridge? . . . Or they said the Princes? What do you mean you'll take care of it? You mean you'd bring me over and do the show . . . you'd take a theatre?'

'I'll take any theatre you like, but the Cambridge is a barn. Maybe the Princes would be better . . . I'll take the place and bring you over but without the Dancing Boys or the Hungarian Dancers. Just you alone.'

Her eyes were wide with disbelief and laughter, people were still clambering over us to find her. She pulled off her earrings and shoved them into the pocket of her sagging candlewick and wiped her forehead on its sleeve.

'You are mad, and I love you . . . my new impresario! But I need the warm-up. I couldn't go it alone.'

'The theatre was empty tonight until you came on . . . they were only there for the second half.'

'I know . . . but that's the way it is. I couldn't do a whole show alone! For God's sake! What do you think I am? Aimée Semple McPherson?'

'Yes.'

'You are one son-of-a-bitch. And I love you. Don't leave me now, will you? Now don't you leave me. People always go away from me, walking backwards . . . don't do that to me, will you? Promise? Just you promise me?'

Unthinkingly I made her the promise. She stared at me for a few seconds in silence and then, hugging me tightly, scrabbled to her feet and pushed through the crowd of people who had come to tell her how wonderful she was. And was. And I went into the street and joined the others and we went to the Plaza for supper.

In the deep leather chairs of the Oak Room Judy looked smaller than ever, and, rather crushed by an enormous black flat-brimmed hat, she poked about at her chicken fricassee tiredly. 'Don't talk about you bringing me into London.

Sid won't like it much . . . he's negotiating something there himself; he'd be furious if anything got in the way. We'll just leave it, huh? It was a marvellous idea, but he does all the deals, he always has, and he's very, very good at it . . . so let's forget it, okay?'

She raised her glass of white wine and looked steadily at me.

'But don't leave me, will you? You have to promise all over again.'

'All right. I promise. You want me to cross my heart?'

'Yes.'

'Cross my heart.'

'And hope to die. I'll remember that.'

We had taken Kate out to Idlewild (Rex had a matinee) to start her on the trip to California and the despairs and miseries, she expected, of Hollywood. She was bitterly unhappy about leaving, but sensible enough to know that she had mortgaged herself completely to MGM and the film by the wildly idiotic advance she had borrowed against her salary in order to buy us all the presents which had so delighted her only a few days before. Now the house, stripped of its glittering frost-sprayed tree, the ivy and the holly wreaths, the ribbons and laughter, seemed empty and chill.

She was bundled into the car, a mass of expensive luggage, a black mink coat, and for some reason which I have now forgotten, Gladys Cooper's Corgi, June, whom she was accompanying on the flight to the Coast.

While Kate sniffed and hiccupped, slumped dejectedly in a corner, June whined and moaned in her smallish ply-wood travelling cage, and we fed her handfuls of tranquillisers all the way to Idlewild which merely had the effect of making her far more energetic and angry. It was a miserable ride. At the airport we shoved Kate through the barrier for her flight, clutching a furious June in her box, her boarding card, ticket, and a slipping bundle of hastily-bought magazines for the five-hour journey. She was still sniffing and teary, and looked pale and wan, dishevelled and weary, as if she had spent a week at sea in an open boat.

'Look after Rexie, won't you, promise me? And I'll try and telephone when I get there; I can't remember if we are ahead or beind . . . oh, it's all so confusing . . .'

Watching her tall, leggy, clumsy figure humping June along to the plane it never for one moment occurred to us that this despairing, hopeless exit was leading her directly to international fame, and that when we should all meet again together she would have become a World Star.

There was a good deal more which we did not suspect.

After the show we took Rex over to the penthouse on Park Avenue which he had chosen to rent so that he could rest between shows. He was, understandably, tired and rather strained, and, after some scrambled eggs and a pot of tea, decided to go and sleep until the Second House, asking only that we should awaken him in good time. We didn't any of us speak very much; Kate had taken all the fun away with her, and we were fairly subdued, talking about politics and books back in the Long Island house until the small hours when the telephone rang and it was Kate from Los Angeles in a state bordering on hysterics, partly tears and partly helpless laughter. The Studio had found her an apartment, she didn't know where, but in a dark street; the living room was filled with Tang horses, rubber trees and reproduction Modiglianis; the bedroom looked like an Amsterdam tart's parlour, swagged and buttoned satin, scatter cushions, an immense lilac nylon teddy bear, and the ice box was filled with everything from milk to Dom Perignon.

'It's like Golders Green High Street on a wet Sunday,' she wailed. 'Right opposite the window there's an Undertaker's place wih a huge electric clock and it says, 'It's later than you think! in bright green neon . . . Diggie, I can't stay a night here!' Tears had given way to laughter. 'I'll slit my throat, wifey! Oh, I'se sick Miss Scarlett . . . help!'

Rex told her briskly to get a cab and check into the Beverly Hills Hotel even if it meant that she and June were to sleep at the pool-side, and we were all much relieved to hear that she had already contacted Minna Wallis, a much loved and capable, not to say powerful, friend of us all, who had wasted no time and had installed her there, with the cab already at the door.

We didn't know it then; but the clock opposite her window was correct.

A monstrous clattering and banging had awakened me on my very first morning in Beel House. It was barely dawn, and the sun had only just above the icing-sugar frost which sparkled on the wide lawns. The branches of the cedar trees black and silver against the lint-pink sky. A raven, seemingly the size of an eagle, was battering frantically at the dormer window of the upstairs hall. Wings wide, beak gaping, eyes brilliant with rage. Again and again he crashed and lunged at the diamond panes. The shadow loomed across the floor, flickered like a magic-lantern silhouette against the white-washed walls.

My theatrical mind instantly, and irrevocably, lined this simple moment of natural history with the supernatural, and bad omens and witchcraft proliferated all about the cold morning hall, and my head. I was convinced, on that first day, that my future in Beel House would be, as it were, cursed. Added to which I had most inconveniently been told that an elderly lady had died, quite suddenly, stuck irremovably in the guest-room bath. Here I now had proof of a lost, and indeed angry, as well she might have been, spirit come to haunt me in a most obviously Edgar Allan Poe manner. Ravens at the winter window, on my first morning. Of course it must be an omen. Of course it was perfectly absurd. Even I knew that. Somewhere. The raven was simply attacking its own reflection in the dawn light, the elderly woman could have died almost anywhere in the house; and in a house as aged as Beel it would have been most surprising if a great many other people had not died, here and there, in its rooms at one time or another. Reason tried to conquer superstition and theatricality; and succeeded. Almost. But I was never to be absolutely happy in my skin during all the years I lived there, even though they were among the most successful years of my career. If not my life.

Mr Davis's recipe for seaside rock, so lightly unfolded at a Dorchester luncheon, was speedily put into effect, and only his warning that stamina would be required caused me any great deal of surprise or worry. I needed the stamina of a vote-seeking politician coupled with that of an Everest Sherpa to survive, and to my astonishment, I had it. Film followed film, some even overlapping at times. Locations ranged from southern Spain to the Dolomites, from the Alps to Agra. I saw more of the Studios than I did of the raven-haunted house and tried, as often as was allowed, or demanded in these undemanding roles, to put all the learning I had had from the Dearden, Leacock, Losey and the Bob Thompson College of Arts and Crafts into practice. It was an exhausting if exhilarating time. My salary was increased, I celebrated my tenth year under contract, thereby allaying both my fears, and those of Freddy Joachim so long ago in the kitchen of Chester Row, and was given a private luncheon party at the Studio, a warm speech of congratulation from Mr Davis and a pair of Paul Storr sugar castors. I was almost undone.

At the same time I was now coming in for a certain amount of attention from the critics. Dismissed by a number as light weight but accepted by others, including Dilys Powell, Clive Barns, Margaret Hinxman, and Paul Dehn, I was actively encouraged. Their criticism was just exactly that; constructive, caring, and therefore strengthening. They loved the cinema, willed it to flourish, to try to be better, and their obvious love for their craft made them notable teachers.

There was also, of course, even then the Sunday-Supplement, New-Yorker Group. Schoolboys in 1939, they now emerged as an elegant shoal of piranhas savaging, on principle, practically anything which was not sub-titled. To be fair they did nod in the direction of Ealing Studios from time to time, but by and large did very little to encourage the British Cinema of the day which, with all its faults, and God knows there were some, was at least trying to exist. They offered neither true nor constructive criticism but, leaning heavily on M. Roget, provided jolly bon mots and epigrams for each other to read, filled with witty, if cruel, and often personal, observations. I accepted these attacks grudgingly enough and did my best to profit from those who gave encouragement; which is as it should be. Although I did have ideas above my station, I was quite content to bide my time for a little longer. There was still a lot to learn.

I now walked along the corridor of power (in reality a very ugly connecting link between the Admin. Block and the Executive Offices littered with junk furniture from a thousand sets, a sort of 'Bridge of Sighs with a palace on one side and a prison on the other') beside Mr Davis himself, while Earl St John walked, very delicately, just behind us. Not the sort of thing to turn one's head, but the kind of thing for which a knife is turned eventually. Although I was now under the personal supervision and advice of the Big Chief, Earl St John was still very much a figure to be reckoned with, even from five paces behind in the corridor. He was still the Studio Boss: he had great influence on whether a film would or would not, be made. He concealed his dislike, or dismay, I never knew which, but something, behind a very warm gentle, affectionate façade. Fresh red carnation, fresh-lit cigar, hidden feelings. Gently biding his time for a counter-attack.

Seaside rock, as one knows, is a sticky, insubstantial, unnourishing piece of confectionery. Meant only to be enjoyed at the moment, digested and soon forgotten. As such I prospered very acceptably. I felt that nothing more was expected of me by Rank, or would even be allowed; therefore it was with some degree of astonishment that I learned, in a very warm and personal letter from Mr Davis, that I had reached the top of the *Motion Picture Herald* poll both from Britain, my country, and also for the International Market, beating Bing Crosby, Humphrey Bogart and James Stewart. I had been top of the British Polls for the last two years, but this news was a tremendous surprise. My delight was nothing compared to the dismay and disbelief of the British Press. The *Daily Mirror* took the trouble to telephone and ask me why I thought it could possibly be me who had reached such an elevated position? It was clear from the irritated, not to say scathing voice, at the other end, that such a result must have been rigged. Either I had bought it, or had cheated in some manner. It was apparently inconceivable that I could have just won it by hard labour.

I was a bit cast down, I confess. However, a Sunday newspaper, a day or so later, left no doubt at all in anyone's mind. Milton Shulman took a whole page to express his. Referring to the 4,000 distributors who had taken part in the yearly poll he writes, or wrote: 'These experts have seriously voted Dirk Bogarde as theman who brings more money into British Box Offices than *any other Star in the world* (his italics) . . . If this poll really reflects the thinking of either the Cinema Managers or the British Public then few will mourn that cinemas have been closing at the rate of some 200 a year . . .', which seemed to place rather an excessive responsibility on my narrow shoulders. Forwood's wry comment that 'today's reviews are tomorrow's wrapping at the fishmongers' gave me little comfort, even though I knew it to be true. I suppose that I had rather hoped that someone would have said, 'Well done!' After all, they were all extremely busy flogging 'British is Best' in relation to motor cars, woollens, whisky, tweeds and sundry pieces of hardware. But not, apparently, seaside rock.

I suppose, to be truthful, it was a matter of Quantity over Quality; nevertheless it had been a long hop from the hopeless, jobless vacuum of my demobilisation leave just ten years, almost to the month, ago.

It is only fair to say at this point that during all these years Rank had always honoured my contract and permitted me to return to the theatre from time to time.

I made these sorties in order to stretch myself and to make contact again with a living audience; they proved to be rather a mistake and they were not altogether happy experiences.

The plays I chose to do were not simple ones, being written by master writers like Anouilh, Coward, Betti, Boussicault, but they provided exhilarating escapes from the platitudes of so many of the film scripts of the day. The audiences, in the main, however, came to see the Film Star and not the Play, something which had never remotely occurred to me, and each performance became an exhausting, and extended, Personal Appearance, during which every entrance and exit was greeted by the hysterical screams and moans reserved today for pop singers; and the alarming chants, during the performance, of 'We love you, Dirk!' or, if I was unwise enough to let exasperation show, even more threateningly, 'We put you where you are!', destroyed the play, dismayed my fellow actors, and distressed me to such an unforeseen extent that every theatrical appearance became an ordeal.

Things finally reached a head during a matinee in Cardiff when the Scene Dock doors eventually gave way and cascaded a dishevelled, screaming, horde of young women across the stage hotly pursued, it appeared, by half the City Police Force. Helmetless.

In 1956 I lost my nerve and reluctantly abandoned the theatre for good. So deep was my fear of ridicule that later, in the summer of '61 when Laurence Olivier asked me to join him in the opening season at Chichester Theatre, suggesting that I might 'do Hamlet or some such thing', I funked the honour and probably the greatest chance I had ever been offered really to learn my craft. Hoist by my own petard. So that to reach the top in the cinema did do something at least to alleviate my loss of the theatre.

I wondered if Gooley knew and was amused in his bar in Cork. If Kitty, Worms, or smug Tilly, cared. The only thing I knew with certainty was that Palmers Green, had he not decided to leave the scene so early, would have been very chuffed, as he would have called it; and that rather cheered me up. I was to stay there for the next four or five years, and in the Top Ten until 1964, presumably closing a further 2,000 cinemas in the process.

Mr Davis's recipe became ever more ambitious; a spectacular adventure story in the Canadian Rockies, a costly remake of 'A Tale of Two Cities', later to be advertised in Amercia as 'To Men and a Girl in Turbulent Paris', and a tragic love story all set in exotic India – all of them happily to be made with Miss Box and Mr Thomas. It was all very encouraging, and after them we would look even further afield. Any script I cared to do they would be willing to consider.

'You can have any Star you want to play opposite you from anywhere in the world,' he announced one evening at dinner, 'anyone you like. We'll bring them over.'

I suggested Judy Garland.

'I meant a Star,' he said kindly. She hadn't made money since 'Summer Stock', in 1950 . . . too long.

Finding the scripts was bad enough; they had to conform to Family Entertainment which made choice limited. When a very young John Osborne shyly brought me a copy of his play 'Look Back in Anger' down to Beel one wet Sunday afternoon to see if there was a possible film in it, the Studio returned it a week later with a polite, if strained note, stating that I should try to remember that the cinema was a Visual Art and that there was altogether too much dense dialogue in the enclosed manuscript. When I hopelessly submitted a book called *Saturday Night Sunday Morning*, Earl St John gave me a splendid lunch in his private, pine-panelled office, and, after he had lighted his cigar, asked me, gently, how I imagined that anyone could consider making a film which began with a forty-year-old woman inducing an abortion in a hot bath?

So off we all went to India and made a 'never the twain shall meet' kind of film during which I broke my foot and fought a long and bitter battle to prevent the Studio tacking on a happy ending. Eventually after a good deal of strained politeness, a play-safe compromise was reached. It made a great deal of money and suddenly, out of the blue, Anthony Asquith arrived with a beautiful script by Rattigan on Lawrence of Arabia.

Although this could, under no circumstances, be termed Family Fun, to my delighted astonishment the Studio agreed. (Looking back from this distance it might just have been a ploy to shut me up.) This was to be no monumental epic, rather the straightforward, if there could be such a term applied to such a man, story about Lawrence, starting in Uxbridge and ending with his still-unexplained death on the lonely country road to Clouds Hill. I had never, in my life, wanted a part, or script, so much. Asquith spent a lot of time helping me to put aside my very serious doubts about my ability, my physical resemblance (nil) and my acceptability in such a role. Locations were found and King Feisal offered us his entire army.

Mr Davis insisted that an hour should be cut from the three-hour running time; this was reluctantly agreed to, and Script Conferences started daily, almost hourly. Wig fittings, costume fittings and intensive research now occupied my time entirely. I thought of nothing else but the man I was to represent, which was a word that Puffin Asquith and I agreed on mutually rather than the word 'be'. I could never 'be' Lawrence, but we both felt that it could be possible to offer a portrait of the man to a public generally in ignorance of his stature. I read every book available on his work and life, wrote to his friends, received warm and encouraging letters in return, especially from Geoffrey Woolley who even sent me unpublished letters and a mass of deeply considered information, and quite lost my own identity in what the Americans call a period of total immersion.

So lost was I in preparation and absorption that I took little, if any, notice of what was going on around me: all I could think of was the strange blond wig which was slowly, and carefully, taking shape in Make-Up, and the probable starting date in the desert of April 7th. I didn't take any notice at all of what was happening about the Studios, which is why I was so completely unprepared for Olive Dodds's cool, impersonal, business-voice on the telephone on Friday, March the 14th at six-thirty precisely to announce that 'Lawrence' was now off. And please would I report to Mr St John's office at the Studios on the following Monday morning at eleven am promptly. She could say no more, she regretted;

the Office was closing for the week-end.

Puffin and his producer, de Grunwald, and all the production team were still, at this moment in the Middle East with the King. They returned the next morning, happily unaware of catastrophe until they met it physically in the form of Earl St John himself at the airport as they arrived in and he was busy meeting a flight from New York. Across the crowded hall he told them casually that the film was no longer operative and would they come to his office on the Monday morning at ten o'clock.

At the meeting they were each accorded half an hour, told it was definitely off but, as far as I know, were never ever given a reason. When my turn came, just as de Grunwald had hurried out past me with an ashen face and without a greeting, Earl St John, beaming pleasantly, offered me a chair and a book which he placed in my unresponsive hands and asked me, earnestly, to consider as an alternative to 'Lawrence'. He gave no reason for the cancellation whatsoever. I looked at the book. It was a jolly comedy set on board a Cruise Liner.

'But, Earl . . . we turned this down a year ago.'

'I'm aware of that. But we still own the rights. You could change your mind.'

'We've made it already, it's the same formula as "Doctor at Sea".'

'And that made a tidy fortune; you can't beat a well-tried formula, kid. Girls, lovely locations in the Mediterranean, a comic cook, there's a Dowager too. Can you imagine Maggie Rutherford in a lifeboat with a tiara?'

No one ever mentioned 'Lawrence' again. I never knew, and still do not know, what stopped the plans so suddenly a few weeks before shooting. Neither, if I remember, did Puffin or anyone else connected with the production. Was it a matter of politics? Did someone somewhere object to the exposing of a very private man? Was the strange, still unexplained, ending to his life a forbidden area? The lonely road, a black car, two school boys, skid marks . . . was this a silence to be kept for ever? Or did someone know that the situation in the Middle East at that moment was to lead to the assassination of King Feisal, his heir and his Prime Minister in the middle of July? Or, simply, did the Studio go cold, fearing the high cost? Mr Davis kept firmly out of it all and only in a letter, months later, confided that he himself had been too distressed to even speak of it at the time. Whatever happened, 'Lawrence' did not go as a film, although Rank, who still owned the copyright, permitted Rattigan to re-work it as a play, which opened subsequently under the title of 'Ross' with Alec Guinness giving a moving performance. But my door, pushed at, closed sharply. It was my bitterest disappointment. However, Puffin was not one to be downcast for long. We had worked so hard and so long together on the project that the idea of full abandonment was unthinkable, and he set his mind towards another objective which could serve us well enough, Shaw's 'The Doctor's Dilemma', which an American Studio, MGM, offered to finance and distribute.

Mr Davis gave me the necessary permissions, and the saddened team who had fought so long to bring 'Lawrence' to the screen swung back into business on a very different level. It was not, however, thankfully, a jolly romp on a Cruise Liner; someone else did that while I steered myself, with Puffin's help, towards the despised Art Cinema circuit, much to Earl St John's amusement.

'The public,' he said one evening at dinner in my house, 'will confuse it with one of the real "Doctor" films you made for us, kid. They'll feel cheated, you wait and see. They don't want to pay good money to watch you croaking about with TB in an attic! Who does, for chrissakes? And once they find you've cheated them it'll be downhill all the way.'

Later on, just as Hans brought in the coffee, he rose a little unsteadily to his feet and turned towards the fireplace.

'Earl, dear!' cried his pretty wife helplessly. 'Whatever are you doing?'

He rolled his cigar slowly and deliberately to the other side of his mouth. 'Trying to put my host's goddamned fire out, that's what,' he said.

But he was right. The British public did feel cheated, and as soon as they found out that I was not playing the adorable, twinkling Dr Simon Sparrow, they stayed firmly away from Shaw, and apart from some kind comments from a few of the critics, the film slid into obscurity. Not, however, in America, where they were ready for the Art Theatre Snob Stuff, and MGM, delighted with their modest investment, financed us all again to do another subject together. I was invited to go and work in Hollywood, which this time, after many refusals in the past, I accepted. I realised, almost subconsciously, that the recipe for the manufacturing of seaside rock after two or three years was wearing thin unless I agreed to continue in the old formulas which, as Earl had pointed out, were well tried and seldom failed. It seemed the right time to make a change. I was nearly forty.

'The one thing that you simply have to remember all the time that you are there,' said Olivia de Havilland just before I left, 'is that Hollywood is an Oriental city. As long as you do that you might survive. If you try to equate it with anything else you'll perish.'

There was a scatter of photographers wearily popping flashlights at the airport, the smog, through diluted white sun, stung my eyes, a girl with red plastic boots, a tall hat with a plume, a braided satin jacket tight across her enormous breasts and a smile like a silent scream, offered me a cellophane-wrapped basket of oranges and said, 'Hi, Dirk! I'm Mary-Paul-Jayne, welcome to California!'

The hotel was a scatter of pseudo-Spanish bungalows around a vast kidney-shaped pool, amidst hibiscus, banana palms, carmine bougainvillaea and a constant soaking mist from thousands of water-sprinklers buried in the plastic grass. There were also humming birds, two swans on a stream, and the street on which it was set was called Charing Cross Road.

The bungalow allotted to me was filled with flowers, baskets of yet more fruits in stiff yellow cellophane, packets of nuts, pretzels, bottles of drink, and a deep canyon-like gloom. Everything was off-white. Chairs, carpets, walls, lampshades even the logs in the fake Louis fireplace. There were screens at every window to keep out the bugs, and the lintel between my bedroom door and the lounge was splintered violently down its entire length, ripped into jagged pieces, as if someone had used a dagger or an axe to force and entry. A four-inch shard of wood rammed into my hand and I bled like a stuck pig.

My fist wrapped in an off-white towel I dialled the desk clerk.

'Yeh?'

'Um . . . it's about the bedroom door here.'

'So?'

'It won't close. The lintel is smashed.'

'The what?'

'Lintel.'

'Where are you?'

I told him.

'Who are you?'

I told him my name. A long silence . . . rustling sounds, eventually a tired voice. 'We don't have you listed here.'

'I must be listed here. I'm here. In your bungalow.'

'You with a firm? Colgate or something? You with Sunkist-Krispies?'

'Columbia Pictures.'

'Oh . . . you the British actor, right?'

'Right. And the lintel is smashed . . .'

'Yeh . . . I don't rightly know what a lintel is; what number did you say?' Again I told him.

'Ah. Yeh . . . okeydokey . . . that's the Lana Turner Suite . . . you say the door's smashed?'

'That's right, can you fix it or move me?'

'Can't do a thing; Sunday, you know. How about a coffee or juice or something? We'll get it fixed Monday morning for sure.'

I sucked the wound mournfully; staring across the room through the cellophane fruit and bottles of imported gin. Under a plastic rubber tree, a wide dummy piano keyboard glistened. Beside it a foot-high pile of records in neat, crackly, orange covers.

'What do you suppose that all is?'

Forwood picked up a disc and turned it to the light.

'Concerto No. 1 in E Flat. Liszt.' He placed it neatly back on top of the pile. 'Your music, I imagine.'

'A foot high? All that . . . they said they were using a double.'

'Well, you'll have to know the music, even if they do . . .'

The telephone rang.

'Hello? Hello?' a breathless, whispering voice.

'Who do you want?'

'You're British, aren't you?' the voice gasped softly.

'Yes.'

'I heard you talking by the pool a while back . . . I'm British, I need help. Help me.'

'Where are you?'

'It's my feet, oh God! My feet . . .'

'What do you want?'

'I'm next door, across your patio . . . help me. They've strung me up by my feet, from the ceiling . . . my feet . . . I'm hanging here; help me, please help me.'

I hung up swiftly.

Forwood looked curious. 'Who was it?'

'A man hanging by his feet in the next bungalow.'

'Call the desk clerk.'

The same tired voice. 'Can't do anything about the lintel today, I told you . . .'

'There is someone in the next bungalow who needs help urgently.'

'Which bungalow?'

'Across from mine. He just called. He's British.'

'Oh God, again . . . they're crazy in there. Was he drunk?'

'Strangling.'

'Okeydokey, we'll take care of it.'

We looked at each other dully across the off-white room. 'I think,' I said, 'I'd like to go home.'

A week later I was more determined; I had done costume tests, make-up tests, acting tests with sundry people hoping to be cast as Countesses, George Sand, Chopin and my Mother. I had also been faced with the prospect of having to learn eighty-five minutes of piano music accurately enough for my hands to be examined by the giant Cinemascope camera, within five weeks. Since I couldn't even play a Jew's harp with any degree of confidence this was a severe challenge. My music coach, a gentle, gifted, Russian with rimless glasses and thirty years experience of music, called Victor Aller, sadly shook his head and pronounced it impossible.

An urgent meeting to request my immediate withdrawal from this débâcle was demanded and resignedly agreed to. The cast was all assembled, Charles Vidor the director, Victor Aller, Mr Goetz, the producer, Forwood, and my extremely gentlemanly, calm, and pleasant American agent, Charles Feldman. And all the Top Brass. I was assured that it had never happened before in Columbia, and was I sure I knew what I was doing? I knew all right; I was going home as soon as possible. Before the meeting Vidor asked me to go to his office to have a 'final little chat, just to see if we can't come to some arrangement . . . this is a desperate step you're taking.'

Rubber trees again, a small Renoir, a Manet with poppies, air-conditioning, Mr Vidor, a symphony in grey and cream, cashmere and silk, alligator shoes winking like glass boats. His desk neat and tidy. A copy of the script, a telephone with fifty extension buttons, a photograph of Liszt aged twenty-five, a swatch of red and yellow suede, an onyx pen holer.

'This is a terrible state of affairs, kid . . . terrible.' He shook his spiky white cropped head and pulled out a deep drawer on his right. There were four, chilling, Martinis, each with a twist of lemon. He offered me one, and when I refused sipped his own with worried eyes fixed on Manet's poppies.

'I hope you'll be reasonable . . . just think of all the people who have been working so hard for you for months. Researchers, musicians, writers. The little people who work on the sets with such care and love. The costoom people, hours and hours they've spent designing just for you . . . 35,000 dollars worth of costooms we have, all authentic, all his stuff. . . so dedicated, so devoted . . . all for you.' In my silence he took another Martini, dribbles of condensation puddled his grey leather desk-top. 'You know we have five million dollars invested in you, kid?' The question was gentle, mild, there was no rebuke.

'Yes. I know.'

He was startled, but only showed it by the trembling of his glass. 'You know?'

'They told me in New York. They said that five million dollars was on my shoulders.'

'They said five? Not three?' He was anxious.

'No. They said five.'

He finished his Martini, a hint of satisfaction.

'Just because of a little bit of music, you know, it doesn't seem fair to throw all this away?' He waved the empty glass gently round the air-conditioned room and the grey leather desk.

'Everyone told me in London we'd use a double. I simply can't do what you ask me to do. You must re-cast and let me go back to Europe.'

'Be reasonable, please. So many heads could fall . . . you want that?'

The Executive Office was on the top floor. The cast assembled, uneasily, all in dark suits, a convention of coroners. A *Fiscus Benjamina* wept motionless in one corner, an iced-water machine bubbled occasionally. Papers were shuffled, seats creaked, Victor Aller stared dully at the deep pile carpet, his lips pursed, glasses winking. Someone behind a vast desk cleared his throat comfortably.

'What seems to be the trouble, Mr Bogaarde?'

'I'm here under false pretences. You engaged me to play Liszt and presumably play a piano. I cannot do this. At the first meeting I had at the Connaught in London I explained this point carefully, and it was accepted, it was agreed then that a double would be used for the piano work and that I would merely do my job as an actor. Since it is now deemed necessary that I must do both, I must ask you to release me from the contract, and re-cast. There has not been very much publicity so far; at this stage I can simply announce that I was not able to perform my duties and so have withdrawn. It is very simple . . .'

The man behind the desk smiled a cosmetic smile.

'I suggest it is more than that. I suggest that you are not too happy with your Co-Star . . .'

'I refute that. I am extremely fond of Miss Capucine, she is absolutely charming.'

'Then you dislike Mr Vidor . . .'

'Not at all. He has been very kind and sympathetic . . .'

'The script then; you say you don't agree with the story line.'

'Not true.'

He leaned across the desk and killed the smile.

'There has been an item to this effect in the last five editions of the *Los Angeles Times* . . . we have already bought out two whole morning editions . . . how do you account for that?' His eyes were lasers.

'I can't account for it at all. I have never spoken to a member of the Press.'

He turned to the room at large, expansive hands.

'Gentlemen, didn't Mr Goetz here have to buy out two entire morning editions of the *Los Angeles Times* because of some very, very unattractive comments made by Mr Bogaarde about the script, Mr Vidor and Miss Capucine's height being too tall for him by a good ten inches. Isn't that a fact?'

Mr Goetz agreed. 'But I do not think that Mr Bogarde voiced those opinions.'

'Then who the hell did? Khrushchev?'

Mr Feldman now leaned forward quietly.

'We have been very distressed by these paragraphs, we have checked on them, and it would seem that they were all written, and despatched, by the Front Office in New York. My client has had no contact whatsoever with any member of the Press since his arrival here in Los Angeles. Front Office do not wish his participation in this motion picture, they would prefer he be replaced by a Contract Artist from Columbia, as you well know; Mr Goetz and Mr Vidor have fought long and hard to have him for their project, because they believe he is emotionally capable of such a role.'

The man behind the desk took the top off his fountain pen, and snapped the clip nervously with his fingers. He swivelled suddenly like a bird of prey on the hunched figure of Victor Aller.

'You are the music coach on this production, right?'

'Right.'

'You coached Cornel Wilde to play Chopin, right?'

'Right. But Cornel Wilde could play tennis.'

An aching stillness.

'What the hell has tennis got to do with the piano?'

'A matter of coordination. Cornel Wilde could swim, ride horseback, play tennis and squash.'

'So?'

'So my pupil here can't even play "Happy Families".'

'He lacks, er, coordination, I take it?'

'Completely.'

'How long will it take you to teach him to play piano?'

Victor Aller sat upright; courage flooded his weary, stocky, frame. 'If my pupil had just one degree of coordination, which he has not, if he had one iota of understanding for the piano, which he had not, I could probably get him to learn, and to play, the first eight bars of the Moonlight Sonata, the very simplest piece in the repertoire chosen for this motion picture – if you gave me one thousand years.'

I heard an ambulance bell far away on Hollywood Boulevard, the elevator rattle down to a lower floor; the man at the desk stared worriedly at Mr Vidor.

'Charlie . . . say, can we compromise? We are too deep in. He can fake the long shots, you come in close over the keyboard for the rest, we use a double for the hand inserts. OK?'

It was agreed. My heart plummeted. We left in a draggle and stood in silence waiting for the elevator. I said I'd walk down, Victor Aller came with me. He mopped his brow with a handkerchief.

'That's the first inquisition I ever attended in this town in over thirty years; I feel sick to my stomach.'

'You were very brave, thank you.'

'You shouldn't bring your good British manners here; they don't want 'em.'

'Anyway, than you for speaking the truth.'

'They don't like the truth here, that's another thing, the truth's dangerous.'

'I know . . . it could have meant your job, that's why I said "thank you".'

'Shit. Sometimes it's nice to tell the truth once in a while.'

'You are a very good friend.'

He laughed mirthlessly, paused and removed his glasses, and wiped them carefully on his tie.

'Well, you got plenty of time to find out . . . plenty of time . . .' he settled the glasses back on his nose and hurried on down the concrete steps, '. . . like one thousand years.'

CHAPTER NINE

Back in the Lana Turner Suite with its squashed porridge carpet, Forwood steadily played through the entire foot-high pile of records required for the film, while I sprawled, numb with misery and full of Hennessy and self-pity, half in and half out of one of the porridge tweed armchairs, staring hopelessly at the splintered woodwork of the unmended lintel. After an hour and a half of sonorous organs, crashing cymbals and a run-amok piano, I slid into a heap on the floor and begged most earnestly to be carried to the next flight for London.

Forwood carefully replaced 'Fantasy on Verdi's Rigoletto' in its crackly new orange paper sleeve, and took my empty glass; and bottle.

'Come on. Stop whining. They've made a compromise . . . you only have to play from the back. And it's a dummy keyboard, not a real piano . . .'

'Oh God help me . . . but I still have to play the exact keys . . . it's got to be musically accurate.'

'No one has ever done it before, of course, you know.'

'Done what?'

'Played eighty-five minutes of piano music *without* a double.'

'Oh shit! Who'll know? Who'll even care?'

'You will.'

'I can't do it! I have no coordination; you heard what Aller said. He should know, he's been teaching the piano for years and years . . .'

Forwood blew some dust off the plastic rubber tree.

'Seems a bit undignified finally coming all this way to a place which you have avoided for so long and letting it beat you; a kind of Dunkirk retreat; without valour.'

Victor Aller and I worked together in a dank brown sound-proofed room with a picture of Myrna Loy on one wall and a view of Naples on another for twelve to fourteen hours a day. Every day, with Sunday afternoons off for rest. By the time we got to Vienna, one month later, I played my part of Liebestraum No. 3 before 'all the Crowned Heads of Europe' including half the Court and many hangers on, in the ballroom at Schönbrunn Palace. With the camera on my hands. It had not, as Aller had predicted, taken a thousand years after all, and although it was a slow piece we had made a start, and with his patience and devotion, Forwood's unending encouragement and Capucine's constant loving support (she was never to miss a single performance all through the weary seven months of work), plus ten to twelve hours work at the keyboard daily, including all day on Sundays latterly, I lost three stone in weight but managed to get through all the pieces selected for me to play, ending up eventually with the major chunk of No. 1 in E Flat with entire orchestra in the Cuvillies Theatre, Munich, accurately enough and with some degree of Lisztian panache; it brought the house to its feet voluntarily, and the orchestra applauded beaming brightly. Aller turned his back and burst into tears. I had no retreat without valour; and although I frequently choked to death on the dialogue, I almost began to enjoy my steady walk to the piano in every palace, church, concert hall and drawing room from Bayreuth to the Hungarian border.

How I did it I do not know nor ever will. I invented a private code for the keys which only I could comprehend, leaving Aller mystified but pleasantly amazed as he corrected posture, wrists, thighs, back, feet, head and every form of musicianly behaviour. One piece of behaviour which vexed us considerably was the blood. After so many days, weeks and hours of practice, my fingers were inclined to split from time to time, leaving sensationally blodd-splattered keys for the eager eye of the Cinemascope camera to delight in. During the Campanella there was a veritable cascade, which although quite inaccurate for a pianist, even one as passionate as Lovable Liszt, pleased the Studio Chiefs enormously since it proved that I had worked hard for my money and that audiences would be quite electrified by such intensity. I very much doubt that they were. However, I had done it; that is what mattered to me. Capucine and Aller both felt that God had leaned out of Heaven for a while, and although I seriously doubted that He had the time to spare, I was bound to agree, in private, that He might perhaps have sent a friend along. It was the nearest thing to a miracle that I have ever personally encountered.

The full story of the making of this unhappy epic is so distressing that it cannot, yet, be written. Although I managed, eventually, to overcome my lack of coordination, it was a grinding and profoundly unhappy experience. After the first three weeks of shooting, Charles Vidor died of a heart attack in his hotel bedroom and the film foundered like a holed galleon. Capucine, Aller, Forwood and myself, now a solid block of four, were overwhelmed with relief. Not so much at Vidor's untimely death – although his apparent illness before made all our lives unbearable, particularly Capucine's whose first film this was

– as the fact that everyone was convinced that the whole sorry mess must surely be abandoned before any more money was spent, any more tears were shed, or any more people were humiliated. Surely now there would be calm and a chance for the survivors to move quietly away from the wreckage. No more candy-floss hair styles, no more appalling dialogue to struggle with, no more oaths or yells sent ripping across the bewildered Austrian technicians and small-part actors. 'Don't give me that goddamned "lampshade" look, Kraut!'; above all no more endless piano practice long into the night in the Bristol Hotel room which had seemed now to become my tomb.

For the first two or three days, while a shattered Hollywood decided what to do, Cap, Aller, Forwood and myself drove into the countryside, walked in the woods, dined nightly at Sacher and, arms linked in delight, sang our way through the spring streets of Vienna. We did not, I regret to say, behave with the respect normally reserved for sudden death, although Cap and I did at least go to the lying-in-state of our late director in the mortuary, taking flowers (one could hardly take champagne), and were about the only two to do so. But relief was short-lived. Almost as soon as Mr Vidor was frieghted aboard a K.L.M. flight to Los Angeles, another flight arrived bearing a tired, but encouraging, George Cukor who arrived determined to hold the sagging epic together, bearing Osbert Sitwell's *Life of Liszt* firmly clutched for us all to see in his hand. A flicker of hope dawned amidst our well-concealed despair. Perhaps Mr Cukor could make some changes in the script? Perhaps he could even read? He could do both. And did.

Mr Cukor had dealt with the very greatest all his working life, the Barrymores, Hepburn and Tracey, Garbo, Garland and many others: he was not about to be dismayed by taking over a shipwreck with an almost, to him, unknown crew. He was a working professional from the tip of his fingers to the crown of his splendid head, and he expected and demanded no less from us. He rallied our forlorn band together swiftly; giving each one of us a private pep talk outlining the way that he would now steer our drifting barque. He was rightly appalled by my own performance, 'a mincing tailor's dummy' he cried furiously, and sent my heart soaring by the detailed ideas he had for a complete re-working of Lovable Liszt. He also, as it happened, had a total love of, and dedication to, Kate Kendall with whom he had recently worked on 'Les Girls'. This slender bond of mutual love and respect was a great asset at the uneasy beginning of our partnership, and the laughter we shared together talking of Kate's idiocies eased him into wary confidence and me into total trust.

Under his determined authority we all began to come alive, costumes were altered to the correct period, actors re-cast where needed, sets modified, a general feeling of enthusiasm began to flow and Capucine found it possible to laugh again. The only thing he couldn't do much about was the script, although he did manage to clear up quite a number of 'Hi! Liszt . . . meet my friend, Schubert, he's a pal of Chopin's'. Which was a relief. However, none of us was under any illusion that we were making anything more than a big Hollywood standard. We just tried harder to make it work better, and Cukor was even able to make me realise that a line like 'Pray for me, Mother!' was possible if you managed to believe it, and that nothing whatsoever should be done on a screen unless you made it interesting, from closing a door, crossing a room, to reading a letter. And so, finally, we ended the location work in the Cuvillies Theatre in Munich, I now weighing seven stone with bleeding fingers and eighty minutes of piano music behind me and a lasting and binding friendship with Cukor and gratitude for his teaching.

The modest house I rented in Hollywood had a swimming pool, two eucalyptus trees and a staggering view of Los Angeles swarming across its dusty plain below. Life was more tolerable here than in the Lana Turner Suite and seemed all the better because the light was now glimmering softly at the end of the long, long tunnel. I still spent hours at the piano, but Aller often sat by the pool reading a paper in the sun, tapping his feet, and the pressure was not nearly as great as it had been before; I was working up for my final concert, the 6th Rhapsody – it had originally been cut out as being too complicated, but after the successes of the European tour it was reinstated. After that nothing bad could happen again, I felt sure. I was nearly through; the Studio were very pleased with me, it had even been said that the moment the film opened in New York, the following July they planned, I'd be a World Star, and the Coroners, whenever I met them, actually put their arms affectionately round my shoulders, and said I was doing just great, kid. Which was very comforting, knocking forty. I even allowed myself to think, for the first time, of Beel House, and wondered what the new dahlia beds which Florian and Hans had planted by the pool must look like now, since this was the first week of September. I realised wistfully that I'd not see them before the frosts came; however, maybe next year. There was always time.

It was almost dawn when the telephone rang, that urgent, desperate sound which drags you from the deepest moment of sleep. In the dim room I groped about for the thing, heard the bell stop and Forwood's voice from his room down the long corridor. I lay very still. In the flint sky beyond the eucalyptus trees a thin wavering thread of crimson in the east. I knew what had happened even before he had opened my door.

'It's Kate.' He was a silhouette.

'When?'

'A few hours ago.'

'I see.'

'Leukaemia.'

'Yes.'

'Rex with her.'

'Who called?'

'Annie Leon. She and Mike have been at the hospital with him.'

'How good of them; good friends . . .'

'She never knew . . .'

'No.'

He closed the door quietly. The crimson thread in the sky gently split and became two, then three and then a whole shimmering mass, tangled silks spilled into the sky above the hazy sprawl of the city far below. The leaves of the tree hung still, thin fingers; no point now in thinking about Beel, or dahlia beds or frost; the bright one had gone, and another day, but without her, was breaking.

Her death was not unexpected. For some time a small group of us, Kenny More and his wife Billie, the Goughs and others had been growing increasingly alarmed and distressed by the subtle and insidious changes in her health. One day, the summer before, playing croquet at Beel she quite suddenly collapsed and sat shivering and pinched, humped into a corner in the Out-Patients Department.

'I'm so cold, wifey . . .'

'There's a cool wind.'

'But it's June.'

'Unpredictable weather in England, darling.' I wrapped her heavy mink round her.

She smiled wanly: 'I'se sick, Miss Scarlett . . .'

'I'll get your medicine.'

As she sipped slowly at her large glass of Guinness with a double Port, the only thing which ever seemed to bring some immediate energy back, she stared with wide troubled eyes out across the sun-flecked lawns.

'Do you think I've got something dreadful, Diggie? And they won't tell me.'

'Balls! Of course you haven't, don't be such an idiot . . . you've probably got the curse or something.'

She laughed a bit, and shook her head gently. 'I've got something . . .'

Our mounting distress was compounded by the fear that Rex did not know that something was gravely wrong. But he did know. He had known, for certain from the doctors, on that unhappy day long ago, when we had bundled her off to Los Angeles with Gladys Cooper's Corgi and had made him scrambled eggs between the shows. He had decided then with extraordinary courage to keep the facts to himself, and that on no account was Kate ever to get the very slightest hint that her life was measured out to the very last day. It was never mentioned by any of us, and the only cause for doubt which she might have had was when the *Sunday Express* decided to print in a banner headline on the Entertainments page after her last important work, 'Will Kay Ever Film Again?' Proving that there is always a market for private grief.

Rex asked us to arrange a memorial service for her in Hollywood at the same time as one was held in London and New York. As a mark of respect, three major studios closed down for two hours in Hollywood so that people could attend the service in the little English church of St John's, an extraordinary gesture of love and respect for a woman who had only ever made a single film in that Oriental city. Gladys Cooper read the eulogy, I funked it I regret to say, and George Cukor had a splendid magnolia standing at the altar, which was planted later on in the gardens of the Actors' Home in North Hollywood as a green and flourishing memorial to a vivid, joyful, all too short, life.

A few weeks later 'Liszt' finally ended and I accepted to replace Montgomery Clift in a film which was to be made in Italy opposite Ava Gardner, almost immediately. I had no urgent desire, now, to return to Beel, in fact I was not even sure that I wanted to see it ever again and resolved, on the long flight over the Pole to Europe, that I would put it on the market and find somewhere else to live.

I had only been on the Italian-Hollywood film a very few days before I realised that Mr Clift had shown remarkable sagacity in withdrawing from the production. Spanish Civil War and Gentle-Priest-Loves-Tart-With-Heart etc. We started off, mercifully free from Studio interference, in a semi-documentary style, no make-up, grainy, real – which pleased me after the theatricalities of Liszt, and Ava, burdened by the absurd label, 'The World's Most Exciting Animal', was equally happy. Hair scraped back, skin shining, in a cheap floral dress, she made a perfect foil to my shabby cassocked Priest. For a little time we thought we could be 'bucking the system'. But after the first ten days' rushes had been viewed by an astonished, not to say shocked, Hollywood, we were ordered to re-shoot and gloss everything up. Ava was bundled into a wardrobe by Fontana and I was tidied up generally. The title 'La sposa Bella' was suddenly altered to 'Temptation' and finally, incomprehensibly, to 'The Angel Wore Red'. We spent a considerable time freezing to death in a Catania slum. Nunnally Johnson, our gentle director, grew sadder by the day, and finally Ava and I lost heart and threw in the sponge helplessly; you *couldn't* buck the system. As far as I know the film never even got a showing on television. Our attempt at realism had angered the bosses who wanted passion and sacrifice in blazing

Madrid and our desperate attempts at a compromise failed miserably. However, we were handsomely paid, because of all the retakes they kept on insisting upon, and Christmas found me finally released from the burden, exhausted, but moderately rich, in Rome.

I decided to have an enormous family Christmas to obliterate at least some of the disappointments which had enabled me to afford such a gesture. My father and mother flew in from London; Capucine and my gentlemanly agent, Charles Feldman, of whom she was exceptionally fond, flew in from Los Angeles; Glynis, ever loyal, came all the way from Sydney where she was filming; and her son Gareth came from Prep School with Irene Howard as a chaperone. It was a splendid family effort. Turkey, holly, mistletoe, presents galore, and the loyal toast proposed by my father at the end of dinner. Afterwards we all went on to a night club and danced until four in the morning. Kate, we all felt, would have approved enormously.

'Well! Would you believe it!' said my father when we all arrived back at the Hassler. 'The bar is still open. I think we should have just a little night cap after such a strenuous day.'

Charlie Feldman, Forwood and I, led by my determined father, headed for the empty bar, leaving the women to go on up to bed.

'A most successful Christmas, I think,' said my father chucking a log on to the dying embers of the fire. He raised his glass towards me: 'I drink to your continued success, my dear.'

'Depends what you mean by success, but thank you.'

'Well . . . twelve years must count for something, surely?'

'Quantity rather than Quality. I've made thirty films and a lot of money.'

'You've made more money than I have ever seen in my life. I brought you all up on two thousand five hundred pounds a year. I never earned more. On *The Times* one is supposed to have private means, only I didn't; it was a struggle but I think it was a success in the end.'

'But, Pa, you had personal satisfaction from your work, didn't you?'

'Of course!' he looked surprised. 'Don't you?'

'Not much. I've done an awful lot of junk over the years; and this last year has been even worse. They may be successful in terms of money at the box office, but they don't actually fulfil anyone much, apart from the producers.'

'I think,' said Charles, 'that he's kicking against entertainment movies. But that's what the cinema was invented for, you know. To entertain.'

'And what do you think they should do?' said my father, stretching in his chair.

'Disturb, educate, illuminate.'

My father snorted cheerfully. 'We get quite enough of that in the newspapers and things. I like a good flick. I don't think I want to be disturbed, as you call it; but perhaps that's a question of age. I must say I like a good comedy you know; Charlie Chaplain, Laurel and Hardy, Will Hay, that sort of thing. Don't you think that people should have a laugh sometimes? You sound very worthy to me.'

'No, of course I do! I'd love to make a good comedy Cukor, Billy Wilder, Lubitsch, Robert Hamer. I enjoyed the "Doctor" films, but there isn't much scope in England for sophisticated comedy nowadays.'

'Oh well. That doesn't go down very well in Uckfield or Burgess Hill, I'm afraid. Your people must know what they're up to surely?'

'Anyway I have a nasty feeling that it is all going to change quite soon; the kind of films I've been making are going to be swept away by television and by people like Bill Haley and Elvis Presley. There is a new audience on the way, and not for the stuff I make.'

'You do sound depressed! And after such a splendid day!'

'Look; if these two epics fail, which I personally think they will, then I am in serious trouble. They are old-fashioned movies, I don't believe that the kids, as they call them, will give a tuppenny damn about them. I think that my days o success, as you call it, are numbered. It's been a good innings; but if I don't catch the trolley I'm for it.'

My father looked very bewildered indeed. 'Tote!' he said to Forwood, his eyebrows raised in disbelief. 'Is that really so? You're his Manager, what does he mean?'

'What he means,' said Forwood slowly and carefully, 'I think, is that he has never given a great performance in a great film; good ones in bad films, excellent ones in medium ones, poor ones in appalling ones, but never a spellbinding, commanding performance in anything. He's worked hard, is highly competent, sometimes interesting, often watchable, but really nothing more than a very successful film star; and he wants more, and feels that he can be more. But the subjects haven't been there; the climate isn't right yet. But it is changing, and when it comes he is frightened that he may not be able to convince the new directors that he is anything more than just a pretty face . . . and perhaps he's not . . . do you follow me?'

'No,' said my father shortly. 'It sounds quite like one of his reports from school: not very encouraging. But in spite of that he had made something of his life, isn't being a successful film star enough?'

'No.' I said.

'Well . . . I think you're all taking it much too seriously. It's been a very successful time, I'd have said. I don't know what anyone could possibly want more.' He set his glass carefully on the table and got to his feet. He leant down and kissed the top of my worried head. 'It's been a splendid time, splendid day too; I'm off to bed now. As far as Mother and I are concerned we are very proud of you, and I think that you have been a very lucky fellow indeed.'

I watched him thread his way carefully across the empty bar; suddenly he stopped and patted his pocket. 'My key isn't on the table, is it?'

'Mother's got it.'

'Of course! You've really made me quite muddled.' He went on towards the lift.

A cat ran hurriedly down the Spanish Steps, shadowy, deserted under the pale lamps. The wind was soft and cool, traffic lights winked red, amber, green unheeded on the empty Via Sistina, below me a giant Christmas tree shimmered and rustled in the hush before morning, the golden star at its peak, nodding and swaying gently. A star. How could I explain it to him? No wonder he was muddled, I was as muddled myself. I now lived in an alien world, as unlikely and unfamiliar to him, and the rest of my family, as a walk on Mars. A world in which all the standards and beliefs we had been brought up to respect as right and honourable were almost completely redundant and which, if one did try to observe them, tripped you up more often than they ever secured you.

'It's rude to point!' Lally used to say, rude to stare, to laugh or to comment on someone else's appearance or disabilities, at all times and with no allowable exceptions; it was right and proper to consider other people's feelings above one's own no matter what. This we had had drummed into us from the very earliest days, and it was so ingrained in me that it came as a major shock to discover on my rise towards the giddy elevation to the canopy of the Odeon, Leicester Square, that these rules did not, seemingly, apply to public property like politicians, jockeys, footballers, boxers, murderers, the entire Royal Family and its appendages, and above all to film stars. We, I understood fairly quickly, were immune from any form of respect, like the clown who gets water squirted in his face, or the polar bear in a tutu dancing in the ring to a whip. By placing ourselves from choice, apparently, in the glare of the spotlight we had automatically forfeited our privacy and, for the most part, our lives. We belonged to the mass just as much as their three-piece suite belonged to them, and were treated, for the most part, with the same easy familiarity. Stage actors, one gathered, were a little more distant, due perhaps to the saving distance between audience and player created by the proscenium arch. The cinema, however, threw you right into their laps, and hopefully, for some, their arms. The intimacy of the close-up destroyed any possible illusion of apartness, and only the excessive riches one was supposed to accrue – yachts, servants, swimming pools and mansions – made one in any way different. In fact they merely created something more desirable, desirable because, in fact, deeply concealed beneath the cosy owning was a constant longing for the unattainable. The Dream.

It had never at any time remotely occurred to me that one day I might become part of the Dream, that for a number of years in fact I would be the Dream. It was the last thing I had wanted, and the last thing that my father, or the family, could come to terms with.

'Can't understand it at all, my dear,' he had said, his eyes bright with amusement. 'They must all be bonkers!' Some of them were. But by the time I had really discovered that, I had succumbed to being bonkers, as he put it, myself.

Audiences, one gathered, liked the performances I gave, even if they left me dissatisfied and keenly aware that I should do better, and so I was a success. Rank were pleased because I made money with the films, most of them, and that was their yardstick to everything; the cinema was big business. So. If this success secretly caused me distress, despair and disillusion at times, the reaction of my family had been comforting, for they simply didn't believe it and, apart from being slightly bewildered and amused, accepted it calmly with a vague sense of disbelief. Which had a very stabilising effect on me. My family life, which I cherished above all things, was never in any way altered; they and it were the ballast which had helped to carry me on a pretty long journey. We all went on much as we had done before my gentle climb upwards, except that I had made something out of my life and this gave them all the greatest pleasure. But my father was too wise a creature to come to terms with it seriously. It in no way diminished the pleasure he took in the modest perks, as he used to call them, which came his way. Trips to Venice or Malaga, St Moritz or New York; lazy afternoons sketching on Long Island, or surfing at Biarritz; choosing the best clarets and burgundies he could find in hotels and restaurants all over Europe, and even tonight he had made his toast to the Queen in Rome. But he simply brushed aside the reasons for these pleasures. As far as he was concerned it was all really nothing but a bit of a lark.

My mother, on the other hand, had taken it rather more in her stride, as she takes most things, eagerly and unthinkingly. After all, she pointed out, it was all perfectly natural since I took after her, and had she not married so young and decided to have me, she herself would have been a famous star, for had she not been on the point of going to Hollywood when my father shattered her dream for ever by explaining that she had made a contract with him, and not Mr Lasky? Wistfully she languished in England bringing up her family, doing her best to hide the disappointment. Not altogether successfully. So when the time came she delighted in fluttering about like an elegant dragonfly, in the warm periphery of my spotlight; it was as near as she ever got to the silver screen which she had so coveted.

Elizabeth, now married to George and a mother of two, was altogether less sure. We had grown up so closely together, shared so much of life, that she could not be so easily swayed by screaming fans in the streets, police escorts, and the curious fact that on some occassions during public appearances it had been deemed necessary at times for me to have my flies sewn up as a protection from my more ardent followers.

'My dear, I just can't take it seriously, that's all. I'm awfully sorry if it sounds rude or something . . . you know . . . but it's all so dotty, isn't it? I mean why you of all people? Really! It doesn't make sense to me at all. It's really rather disgusting, in a way, I mean when you think of it.'

'You mean like being sick on a bus?'

'Well . . . not as awful as all that . . . but pretty vile really. It isn't even as if it was a very important thing to be, is it? A film star?'

'It isn't.'

'Well then; like a surgeon, or scientist, a composer even, you know. Goodness; you must feel *awful* really.'

But generally we had managed, over the years, to weather this strange metamorphosis together, although I could only guess at the silent stresses and strains they must have endured; for it is no great pleasure to be on the fringe of the famous; and their privacy and anonymity were constantly invaded by idle chatter and envious gossip which inevitably, it seems, surrounds what is euphemistically called today a celebrity.

To a closely-knit, loving family who wished and indeed expected to keep their lives quite undisturbed and above all private, it sometimes came as a bit of a jolt. But I was never reproached. Lally, however, with her usual excellent sense and awareness of what was what, kept out of it all entirely; she was delighted for me, if what I had was what I wanted, but she wished no part of it herself. She preferred to carry on with her own life, her own family, and her own affairs, and as always kept herself to herself. Very wisely.

I envied her her wisdom and tidiness of mind. How could I be wise? Know when and how to make the jump. To have less, like my father, but to have more, as he had in self-fulfilment and pride in his work. I knew that he was right. I had been very, very lucky in the twelve years. It had been a totally unexpected achievement, if achievement it could be called, it had even started off with a mistake that cold, snowy day in the Aeolian Hall, but I couldn't kick against that. Here I was, thirty films behind me, popular, highly paid, and constantly in work, something most actors would willingly give up everything in life to have. And yet I was deeply unsatisfied under all the glitter and gloss, unfulfilled, and almost, it had to be faced, ashamed of the position I had reached.

Why? I had been manufactured to entertain people, that was all, and apparently I had done just that. I should have no pretensions. That was my function. So why go on trying to prove things? Was there anything left to prove really? Only the one nagging doubt that I could act. But since no one really cared much about that except myself, what did it matter? And if I cared all that much, all I ad to do was to get my release from Rank, clear off back to the theatre, and start all over again if I could.

All I wanted, I supposed, was respect in my work, but how could I possibly achieve that by playing spaniel-eyed priests or Liszt in a fright-wig? The theatre, I knew, terrified me and could not satisfy me now; I had fallen completely under the spell of the cinema, the technical work. The camera excited me by its apparent awareness of anything which I wished to impart to an audience mentally; it was my friend never my enemy, for some unexplained reason; there was a rapport between us which exhilarated me. Dearden had seen this, Losey and Asquith, so too had Cukor, and I revelled in the intensity of concentration which it demanded and I gave it until I was almost ill with exhaustion; and because I very often fell desperately short of what I had hoped I was doing, I wanted to go on and on until one day I would be able to sit down and say, 'Ah! That's it! That's what I meant it to be.'

But how long would my opportunities hold out? Where could I find the subject which would really allow me to apply everything I had so far learned? I leaned my head against the cold glass of the window watching the light rise on Rome. St Peter's, a tin jelly mould shimmering in the first glow of day. A sudden flight of starlings swirling into the grey sky, a soaring comma . . . below me the day staff were beginning to arrive, *prego*-ing themselves cheerfully up the hotel steps. I pulled the shutters to and went to bed. Next week a new decade would begin; perhaps things would change.

But they didn't; at first. I was sent off to Spain to play a Mexican bandit sheathed in black leather, riding a white horse, carrying a white cat, and belting everyone in sight with a silver-topped riding crop. It wasn't much fun; it was the last picture in Mr Davis's recipe, and the last I was to make for Rank under his protection.

Shortly afterwards the Liszt Bio opened in America and, after seven excellent weeks in New York, died the death everywhere else. The same thing happened in London, and in spite of a great publicity campaign in which Columbia discreetly suggested that Capucine and I would announce our engagement at the Press Reception, of all unlikely places, it floated down the river of no return. The Spanish Priest and Tart With Heart film, as I said, never even got shown on television. One way or another a depressing start. What it all proved, without much doubt, was that I had failed in America. My work, or personality, or whatever you care to call it, was unacceptable to American audiences. The American audiences like meat and potatoes, one lady critic told me in New York, which, unhappily for me, I was not. A piano was not, obviously, quite enough. The blame was neatly laid on my shoulders. But never, at any time, by my producer Bill Goetz, who with his enchanting wife, Eadie, remained staunchly loyal and undismayed. A rare and heart-warming event in Tinsel Town.

But everything which Dolly Rubin had warned me about during a supper at Sardi's in New York, months before, came to pass.

The telephone, which had rung almost daily from California asking me how it felt 'to be a Star' after the first seven weeks at Radio City, stopped abruptly. Columbia, who had eagerly been negotiating to buy out my contract from a delighted Rank Organisation, just faded gently away like a dispersing morning-fog. And two producers of repute, to whose children I had very happily become godfather, were suddenly no longer available when I called.

Dolly was a tough, bright, rather short Estonian with an accent which could crush rocks. She was something important to do with Publicity for the Liszt film. After a hellish day of interviews with the Press, which was known as 'Total Exposure', we had gone for Eggs Benedict to Sardi's.

'How do you think we're doing?' I was really too tired to care.

'Fine. Just great.' She snapped a pretzel. 'Wanna know what I *really* think. Off the record? It's old fashioned. The movie. I don't think the kids'll go for it.

It's pre-war, for God's sake. Know what I mean?'

'And if it fails at the box office?'

'You'll fail too. Remember this, honey; it isn't great acting that gets you up there as a Star, it's great grosses. Nothing more and nothing less. That old chestnut about being only as good as your last movie is absolutely true.' She leant across the table and tapped my hand. '*Absolutely*. If this movie makes it you'll be offered every role from Mary Magdalene to Stalin . . . never mind you don't look like them, they'll fix it so you do because you'll be bankable, they can sell you. This is a Consumers' Market. When you don't sell they don't buy, not the Prodoocers, not the Exhibitors, not the goddamned audiences. Maybe one near-miss is allowable, but two is curtains. You can be the greatest goddamned "King Lear" Broadway ever saw, but if you don't come off the screen and bring in the shekels they can't give you away with a packet of Mary Baker Cake-Mix. I bin here a long, long time, sweetie; I know. It is a mathematical formula you could remember from Aunt Dolly, and it all starts with the letter B. Box Office equals Big Name equals Bankability, anything else equals Bankrupt.' She forked her frozen spinach into a neat green hillock.

'Get it? The facts of life.'

So, to be fair, I had been expecting this all to happen, but when it did it was not the most agreeable of feelings. However, as George Cukor said, when a thing doesn't go, then the hell with it: just say, 'Well; it didn't go' and get on with life. Much easier said than done. A door had closed for me rather firmly. I had made my exit from the Hollywood scene with as much dignity as possible, and I was comforted by the fact that every exit has to have an entrance, although I was not absolutely sure now where this might be. Well aware of Mr Presley, of James Dean with his sullen youth-identification, of Brando with his power and force, of the new generation who were now following a different piper in Hamelin, I was supremely aware that the kind of work I did, and the kind of actor I was, was doomed. I had to take action pretty soon, and drastically.

To this end I sold Beel House, which I had come to dislike more and more since Kate's death, to my other catalyst, Basil Dearden, and moved into a vast stone and marble edifice near Beaconsfield which I got cheap since it had been a Children's Home for years and no one knew what to do with all the partitioning, frosted glass, and red crosses everywhere.

But just before I left Beel for ever, Kate's bedroom had its final guest. Judy Garland arrived unexpectedly, slightly amazed herself at her own daring, since she had come from Los Angeles quite alone for the first time in her life, with, as she said, 'a real purse with real money in it! I'm so excited.' The last time we had met was in my house in Hollywood; then she was fat, ill, moved in a trance, and those wide brown eyes were almost buried in a white puffy face. But now here she was eating a vast breakfast, laughing and giggling, pretty, plump I suppose, but no longer fat, and back on form and ready to go.

'I'm planning a concert, just two nights, at the Palladium, and you'd better be there, but first of all I'm going to Rome . . . can you imagine? All alone, no Sid, no family. I'm having such a ball! And I'm going to look about for a house in London to live in for ever. We are all coming over; no more Hollywood, no more Hell. I'm better now, cured by a wonderful doctor, and I know just where I'm at.'

It was a wonderfully happy time. We went for long drives into the country, Chipping Campden, Burford, Lechlade, King's Stanton, Oxford, places she had never seen and most times had never heard of. We walked with the dogs; sat in the sun; talked and laughed. She was without doubt, I suppose, the funniest woman I have ever met. We seemed, in that July, to laugh endlessly.

'Oh! I'm so happy, you know that?' She put her arms round my neck.

'You sound happy, I know it.'

'You want to know why?'

'Why?'

'Because you are my new friend, Kate brought you to me, that night ages ago . . . you made me a promise, remember? You'd not leave me, remember that promise?'

'I do.'

'And I trust you.'

'That's a very serious statement.'

'It's supposed to be goddamned serious, trust is. I don't have too much of it in my life, you know that. I spend most of my time groping about in the dark like Helen Keller, feeling faces to find someone to trust, to be safe with.'

She ran her fingers lightly over my face. 'I found you. Now don't you go and leave me; all I have in all this world is Sid and my family, I love them and I trust them, but no one else in all this stinking world, except you.'

'That's a heavy burden.'

'You can carry it. I'll help you along.'

'All right; you promise me that. You'll help me along.'

'And you be at the Palladium.'

'Same show? Hungarians with dogs and ventriloquists?'

'Oh you! Now just you stop that! I need the warm-up.'

'You don't. And you don't need those Dancing Gentlemen to spell out your name. They all know who you are.'

'I need the warm-up, I've always had a warm-up . . . I know this part better than you do, Buster.'

'How many songs do you know by heart?'

She looked vaguely round the Out-Patients Department, playing thoughtfully with a pearl earring.

'Songs? You mean words of the songs, lyrics?'

'Yes . . . how many?'

'Oh . . . I dunno . . . maybe two hundred, could be. Why?'

'Just sing them all.'

She looked up in amazement and burst into laughter. 'All of them! Are you out of your mind?'

'Just you and a whopping big orchestra and just go on singing.'

'Until the cows come home?'

'Until they let you go; as long as they ask for more.'

'You mean start cold? Cold! And just sing?'

'A tremendous overture, and just you in a spotlight. Cold.'

Her eyes were suddenly interested.

'Not a spotlight . . . a pin spot . . . maybe a follow spot crossing the stage . . .'

'Whatever kind of spot you want. And take a big place, a huge place, Madison Square Garden, a football stadium.'

'I know!' she was laughing now. 'I'll take the Metropolitan and be like the wife in "Citizen Kane"! You want to kill me for ever?'

'You said that you trust me? Well, I tell you it would work.'

'Honey,' she poured out a small glass of Blue Nun, poked the ice cubes with her finger. 'Honey, I played the Met. I played every goddamned Opera House in the U.S.A.; and I filled them, I am always a sell-out. But I've been terribly, terribly sick. That hepatitis nearly killed me and I have to go back to work and earn some money, I can't take any kind of risk, believe me . . . I do the show-I-know-how.'

'Then make a change, do it alone.'

'I'm not Samson, for God's sake! I'm not that strong. I'm Fay Wray in "King Kong", remember? I just holler. And I can't holler for two long hours.'

'Try.'

'You are a shit. My best friend and you want to ruin me . . . I'm going to see Kay Thompson in Rome, I love her and I trust her too. I'll maybe kick it around with her.'

She moved into a pretty house in Chelsea with the family, and started to settle down to what she called just being a housewife; and although she was often to be seen shopping for her groceries up and down the King's Road, the food she served was mainly from Fortnum and Mason; if she was worried about anything as sordid and incomprehensible to her as money, she never showed it, and the time was happy.

At the Palladium at the end of August she did her show alone. For the first time. Halfway through she had a spot turned on me, to my misery, and forced me to go up on stage and sit at her feet while she sang a song which she knew I loved above all the others. 'It Never Was You'. It was a calculated piece of show business . . . and she knew it. I sat humbly at her feet, she sang softly and sweetly, one arm round my shoulder, but when she finished, and while the crash of applause brought down the plaster, she kissed me and said: 'You see, I can; thank you.'

That show and the second one she did were triumphs. She was radiant, reborn, sure. Once she said to me: 'You know something? It's so damned lonely up there. I'm so alone, so afraid. Just before it starts you have everyone around you, telling you you're great, doing your hair, making up your face, mending your pants, kissing you, telling you they love you, touching you (I hate to be touched), building it all up for you, giving you wine, giving you pills, getting you on to your feet so you'll be ready to go on . . . they take you right to the side of the stage, all touching, kissing, whispering, encouraging . . . they have the towel, the glass of water, the hair spray, all the goddamned paraphernalia, and they know the "Take". And then you go out there and you are absolutely, absolutely, alone. Suddenly you are *alone*. It is the most awful feeling in the world. And that's how it's always been, and that's how it always will be . . . alone.'

'But then it gets better?' I said.

'Sure it gets better; the moment I open my mouth. You know once at the Hollywood Bowl a damned great moth, yes a moth!, flew right in there!'

Her eyes were wide with remembered horror.

'What did you do?'

She shrugged slightly. 'Oh . . . I parked it . . . what else? But I'm so sure, you know, that one day they'll find me out.' She suddenly burst out laughing, shaking her head. 'You know, I can't really sing, not really; I holler, like I said. Oh sure, I'm no Deanna Durbin, now she really can't sing, and that silly horse, Jeanette MacDonald, yakking away at wooden-peg Eddy with all that glycerine running down her Max Factor! I have a voice that hurts people where they think they want to be hurt, that's all . . . and I can't act a row of beans either; I'm just me. And I'm so damned scared they'll all find out one day. Can you imagine the pleasure everyone will have? But just now I feel what the hell! I feel good! I feel great! I am great, and I love you.'

For Judy then, another start, for me, at that time, another move from Beel House to the stone and marble Children's Home, now gutted, redecorated, and far too opulent and rich for my present position of almost complete limbo.

It was Christmas again, another house full, the same cast as the year before in
Rome, and my gloom and foreboding of that Christmas were in no way
relieved. However, there were presents to wrap, a tree to decorate, a job my
father had done every year since I was born and which he still took extremely
seriously. Wreathed in yards of tinsel he sat on the top of a ladder fixing
glittering balls among the branches, and fitting barley sugar candles into
holders. The telephone rang, it was Basil Dearden. My heart sank, I thought
he'd found something wrong with the plumbing at Beel.

'No . . . nothing wrong, thanks, we're very comfortable. Melissa is spending
a fortune, of course, putting in a new bathroom, stripping the panelling all over
the house . . . and planning an Italian Garden where the old tennis court was.'

'Oh good. I thought the central heating had blown up.'

'No, it's working. I gather the Liszt epic did though?'

'You gather correctly.'

'And the other two. My spies tell me the bandit thing is a sod.'

'Could be. I haven't seen it.'

'Getting a bit old for leather knickers, aren't you?'

'I'm beginning to think so.'

'A bad run really . . . anything planned for next year?'

'Nothing . . . you got anything planned?'

'Sent you a script over this afternoon, by messenger. Might interest you.
Read it over the holiday and let me know, OK?'

'I'll try . . . got a full house here, family.'

'You may not like it. No one else does. Everyone we offered it to has turned it
down. You're our last chance.'

'Thanks. What's it about, paedophilia?'

'No. But our first choice said that it would prejudice his chances of a
Knighthood.'

'What is it? The October Revolution?'

'No. Homosexuality, actually. Middle-aged married man with a yen for a
bloke on a building site.'

'Can you make a film about that?'

'Rank have said they'll distribute, the lawyers say there's nothing wrong
libel-wise; just wanted to wash their hands after reading it.'

'It gets better and better.'

'Better still. An accountant read it for costing and said he felt he should have a
gargle.'

'Must have read it aloud.'

'Must have. If it's any comfort we don't call anyone a queer, homo, pouf,
nancy or faggot.'

'What the hell do you call them then?'

Basil's voice was silky.

'Inverts.'

My father was struggling at the top of the tree trying to fix the fairy on top. A
little pink angel with wings and benevolent wand. He came slowly clambering
down the steps, puffing a bit. 'Jolly hot work this tree business. I think a nice
little sip of one of your Worthingtons would be just right now. What's the
matter?'

'Pa . . . would you mind if I made a rather, difficult film . . . I mean difficult
in the moral sense; serious stuff?'

'I don't think I quite follow you. Political do you mean?'

'Homosexual.'

He pulled out his handkerchief and mopped his brow gently; had a sip of his beer. 'Oh my dear boy, we get so much of that sort of thing on television. Mother and I find it dreadfully boring, all those doctors and psychiatrists bumbling on. Now if you want to do something really serious, why on earth don't you do *The Mayor of Casterbridge*?'

'Well, you remember what I said in Rome last year?'

'Yes, I do. I do. Something about disturbing. I can't really remember . . .'

'Yes, disturb, educate, that sort of thing.'

'You know I must confess that I really didn't understand what you were talking about. Got into a bit of a muddle, I seem to recall. Personally I think there are quite enough people doing that all over the place without your having to do it in the local fleapit, but that's up to you. Just remember that mother and I live in a small village, we have to get on with our neighbours, not always easy. Try not to do anything which would embarrass *her*, people are so narrow, you know. That's all I have to say.'

Forwood and Capucine were laying cloths on the long tables in the hall ready for the evening party. He looked up.

'Who was on the telephone?'

'Dearden. He's sending a script over. It's a bit of a problem one.'

'Oh. Why?'

'Married man with a secret passion.'

'What's the problem there?'

'The passion is another bloke.'

'I don't see the problem,' said Capucine. 'My God! You English. You think that nothing happens to you below your necks.'

'And in any case,' said my father settling comfortably down into his chair, I've told him that I think he ought to do *The Mayor of Casterbridge*.'

But I did 'Victim' instead, and played the barrister with the loving wife, a loyal housekeeper, devoted secretary and the Secret Passion. It was the wisest decision I ever made in my cinematic life.

It is extraordinary, in this over-permissive age, to believe that this modest film could ever have been considered courageous, daring or dangerous to make. It was, in its time, all three.

To start with, very few of the actors approached to play in it accepted; most flatly refused, and every actress asked to play the wife turned it down without even reading the script, except for Sylvia Syms who accepted readily and with warm comprehension. The set was closed to all visitors, the Press firmly forbidden, and the whole project was treated, at the beginning, with all the false reverence, dignity and respect usually accorded to the Crucifixion or Queen Victoria. Fortunately this nonsense was brought to a swift end by one of the chippies yelling out, 'Watch yer arse, Charlie!' to a bending companion, and we settled down to work as if it was any other film. Except that this was not.

Janet Green's modest, tight, neat little thriller, for that is all it was fundamentally, might not have been Shaw, Ibsen, or Strindberg, but it did at least probe and explore a hitherto forbidden Social Problem, simply, clearly, and with great impact for the first time in an English-speaking film. It was refused a Seal of Approval in America for being too explicit and it was many years before Hollywood even dared to tread the same path with any truth or honour. Some critics complained that it was only a thriller with a message tacked on rather loosely; but the best way to persuade a patient to take his medicine is by sugaring the pill – and this was the only possible way the film could have been approached in those early days. Whatever else, it was a tremendous success, pleasing us and confounding our detractors. The countless letters of gratitude which flooded in were proof enough of that, and I had achieved what I had longed to do for so long, to be in a film which disturbed, educated, and illuminated as well as merely giving entertainment. I had been fortuitously pointed in the right direction again, just in time. This time the door I had chosen to enter was not just ajar . . . it had been wide with a blaze of light and I was not to retreat ever again.

Incredibly, the fourteen-year-old image was almost instantly shattered. The fans, that is those who thought that being queer meant having a head cold or the belly ache, whirled away like chaff in a gale. They were bored by the subject I had chosen, felt betrayed that I had, as they said, gone serious, and had admitted my age; and in any case they had heard a different sound on the wind, the sound of the sixties – Youth. Elvis Presley led a whole generation away from my kind of old-fashioned cinema; television gave them all they needed in the way of visual entertainment. What they wanted now was music, a new beat, a new sound, a new believing and new identification with themselves, and they got it from him . . . and while he was leading them out of the fifties, five young Liverpudlians in Hamburg were waiting to grab them and remove them from sight for ever. The kids were leaving Hamelin, and although half-hearted attempts would be made to lure them back they would pay no heed, and I would have to learn to play my new pipes and go off on my own.

It would be a great deal easier, I thought, than learning to play a piano.

CHAPTER TEN

Another serious miscalculation on my part. It was far harder. After the failure of my Hollywood ventures, and the equal failure of my attempts as a Mexican bandit on a white horse, a cool, not to say chilling, wind rustled down the long corridor of power which I had once so blithely walked in august company. Now I was alone there; not often accompanied. No longer by Mr Davis at least, of whom, sadly, for he had been a good friend, I now saw very little. Dolly Rubin's words echoed in the solitude. Bluntly, Rank had no plans for me in the foreseeable future, and suggested that I have a look round for subjects myself which might be of interest to us both. Which I knew would be extremely unlikely.

I owned, at this time, the rights to John Osborne's play, 'Epitaph for George Dillon' and had spent a considerable sum of money having it scripted as a film. This I carried to Earl St John who pronounced it downbeat and negative and that was that. Despairingly I asked for release from my contract, not out of pique, but from a steadily mounting sense of hopelessness. I was determined to break into a new kind of cinema, they were equally determined not to.

Freddy Joachim, after a long and happy partnership felt that I was being both impetuous and childish. Which perhaps I was, but his very gentleness and caution and innate sense of fair play were paper swords in a duel with an adversary, for this is how I now openly considered St John, armed with steel. My release was refused, but I heard growing rumours that plans were afoot to seel the remainder of my contract elsewhere. Which they had a perfectly legal right to do if they wished. I was in a state bordering panic, and bitterly resented the idea that after so many years loyal work I should be offered up like a packet of the Miller's own flour. Freddy and I agreed to differ on the subject, and after fourteen happy years we parted company in a warm and friendly manner.

I was still determined to obtain my release but neither Forwood nor myself was capable of negotiations which were, to say the least of it, strained and dangerously fused. Robin Fox and Dennis van Thal, who had a thriving agency, agreed to take me on and help me in the uncomfortable struggle. Eventually, under pressure, Earl St John agreed to let me go, immediately, on condition that I surrender a large amount of money due to me by contract which I could ill-afford. John Davis, in a final gesture of goodwill overruled this and in return I offered to make a film for them at a later date at a much reduced salary. Accordingly a handout was drawn up for the Press, which merely stated that 'at the request of Dirk Bogarde, the Rank Organisation has not exercised the option on his contract with them'. After fourteen years, twice the amount of time I had expected even in my most optimistic dreams, I was released. Nobody waved goodbye. Nor did they telephone any more. It was like a protracted armistice, except that it had finally been a compromise rather than a battle. But I was free at last.

For the time being I rattled round my vast stone edifice like a glass marble; Elizabeth's husband George, now running a very successful business as a tree surgeon and garden consultant, spent hours with his team of men laying out the long-neglected borders, making a vast lagoon with water-lilies and fountains, wrenching up brambles and overgrown rhododendrons and planting walks and alleys; I was very busy hunting for specimen plants, costly shrubs, and old-fashioned roses, spending capital with nothing coming in; if I felt optimistic, Forwood felt the reverse.

'It always amazes me that just when you should be pulling in you expand. Every time there is a crisis you buy a palace; you have no savings, no work in the future and there's George hacking about out there like Capability Brown, and you playing a latter-day Linnaeus.'

'That's what I have always done. Something will happen.'

'You'll end up in a debtors' prison, that's what'll happen.'

'I'm spending my own money, for God's sake.'

'You're spending your tax reserve money, my boy.'

'Well, they can bloody well wait . . . they've taken a hell of a chunk of my loot already.'

'They don't wait, they sit in their bungalows in Hillingdon and Edgware planning how to give you the chop. Their wives haven't got a mink coat, so why should you?'

'I haven't got a mink coat.'

'Don't be so blood dense, you know what I mean. If you don't get a job in a couple of months you'l have to sell up. Right away.'

Judy arrived suddenly one morning, pale, tired and under stress, a few weeks after the end of a marathon concert tour of America ending with a final show at Carnegie Hall which had proved to be one of the greatest peaks of her career.

She came alone *again*, no Sid and no family. There was a tighter edge to her now; sure, trim, confident, harder, but exhausted.

'I want to sleep for days. Unwind. Heal. I'm dead. I've come to hide. No one knows where I am . . . I had to get away from them all, they try to tear me apart.'

The healing started after lunch. She refused to go to bed and instead insisted on a drive into the country which always seemed to relax her better than almost anything else. To Pangbourne, Henley, along the river as far as its source. She sat curled in the back of the car, in slacks and a sweater, impracticable little taffeta boots, her face pale, hands trembling but her eyes delighting in the tumbling blossoms of the orchards, lambs in the fields, the 'houses with hay on their roofs' and the soothing peace of May in England. By the time we had got back to The Palace, after tea by the river at Sonning, she was nothing to do with the harassed, pale, tired woman of the morning. In the evening, round the fire in the Study, she handed me a packet almost shyly.

'This is what I really came to do; to bring you this. I hope you'll like me. No dancing boys, no Hungarians.'

Two blue transparent records. No labels. Side One, Side Two. The matrix of the Carnegie Hall concert. 'You wouldn't come, so I brought it to you . . . you know there were two empty seats waiting there for you until the end of the overture . . . just in case you made it.' She sat on the floor beside my chair, her head on my knee, the dogs sprawled beside her, once or twice she squeezed my leg hard during key moments, or clapped her hands and cried with laughter at her own version of 'San Francisco'. Just before the final number, 'Chicago', she stopped the record.

'You hear my voice? I had almost gone. I was dead beat . . . they wanted more and more . . . they wouldn't let me go, you can hear? And then when I got to this last song I knew I'd not get through, I couldn't get the breath . . . and then something fantastic happened; I want you to listen. Right after the first verse, when I sing . . . 'And you will never guess where' . . . right there, in the silence, one voice from way, way out in the dark, called out 'Where?' . . . right on beat . . . and he saved me. I took it from him and I went, brother I went! I have tried ever since to find out who he was . . . where he was . . . to thank him. Do you believe in God?'

'Sometimes, not often.'

'Well . . . God sent this voice . . . you listen.'

Although she had said that no one knew where she was, the telphone was almost constantly busy, and one afternoon there was a call for her from California. We were all sitting on the terrace having tea, I saw her come through the study windows, her arms outstretched; she beckoned, and I went to her. She put her arms round me, eyes smiling, tears brimming, lips trembling.

'It was the Coast. Stanley Kramer. He wants me to do a movie . . . with Burt Lancaster.'

'And?'

'It's about retarded children; I said yes. Now do you believe in God?'

'No. But I believe in Stanley Kramer.'

She punched me, and laughed. 'Oh you! You are so damned British, I hate you!'

'When does it start?'

'I have to leave at the end of the week.'

It was a good, happy week. Although she was still tired, still restless, not yet able to sleep, she was happy, funny as always and above all excited at the near prospect of the film. On her last evening we gave a great party for her; she made out a list, and everyone she asked accepted. She had never looked prettier, never been in such form, she was having a really magical time and was the most immaculate hostess. After supper, in the fading light of the summer sun, everyone sat round the grand piano and she and Noël Coward sang for their suppers. She knew all Noël's lyrics, which pleased him greatly, from 'Mrs Worthington' to the entire score of 'Bitter Sweet', and 'If Love Were All', which they sang as a duet, brought the packed room roaring to its feet. It was a shimmering evening; and Noël was the last to leave sometime in the very early hours. I got into bed about five, just as the first light was rising above the trees, under my pillow a note from her. It read in part:

'. . . What you have given me is something I will never be able to explain to you, ever. I honestly don't know what I would have done without you. You always give me pride in myself and belief in myself . . . and that's the loveliest gift of all. How I will ever repay you, Heaven knows!

Thank you for my shining new life. I won't fail you, and you have made it impossible for me to fail myself. God bless you.

for ever,
Judy.'

Alas.

If the telephone rang constantly for Miss Garland it now hardly ever rang for me. Sitting slumped with a guinness amidst my playing fountains and tossing rhododendrons I became very well aware of the sudden shift in my status. Rank had been a superb umbrella; however much I might have railed and complained against it. Now the elements hit me full on the head. No weekly cheque, no future plans, no capital. Apart from the tax reserves which I was steadily eating into like a termite.

One morning Hans and Agnes announced, in floods of tears, that The Palace was far too big for them to handle on their own and that after ten happy years in my service they now felt it was time to move elsewhere and in consequence had accepted the offer of a job with a millionaire in Florida. We were all suitably distressed . . . but Florida was Florida, and Beaconsfield and no capital was, to say the least of it, alarming. I was dragging my anchor; clearly The Palace had to go.

I made a brilliant decision on the third Guinness, staring into the night-scented-stock and bee-ridden lupins; I would sell up, and with the capital hopefully obtained, purchase a small farm and retire to work on the land for ever. No more cinema, no more theatre, peace and self-containment. I would, I thought, get Elizabeth and George (he was obviously good at land and farms and that sort of thing) to join me; give them a cottage, and together we would run the Elysian fields, and go to market, milk, collect eggs, plough, reap and sow, and lead the simple unrushed life of the land. I was immensely cheered by the idea of Elizabeth already in a gingham poke bonnet churning the butter; of the children, Mark and Sarah, on the hay wain, of ample teas and suppers round the scrubbed table in the lamp-light: the simple family life.

I took up a bundle of old *Country Life*'s and started to thumb through them in a happily bucolic state, secure in having made a firm decision at last. And Dennis van Thal called, almost at that moment, to say that he had managed to get me a film, at a much reduced salary, and that I'd better grab it while I could. Poke bonnets and hay wains slide from my grasp and I was shortly bobbing about off the coast of Spain in a three-masted schooner, being beastly to my crew and ordering everyone in sight to submit to the cat-o'-nine-tails, while Alec Guinness slapped his thigh from time to time in a grey wig which looked remarkably like a tea-cosy.

It was not a very distinguished affair, and apart from the enormous pleasure of being with Alec, a patient and generous actor if ever there was one, it was nothing, I think, which either of us greatly enjoyed. But it brought in a little loot, and thus, secured temporarily, a breathing space which I spent trailing about Kent and Sussex searching for the farm which would provide me with my kind of Mary Webb-Stella Gibbons-Thomas Hardy existence. Elizabeth in her poke bonnet simply would not leave my mind, although her immediate reaction to it had been less than exuberant.

'We are really very comfortable in Rustington, dear. I mean, what *sort* of farm, and where? It's very flattering of you, I'm sure, but George has got quite a big firm now, he's pretty busy; and I don't know anything about butter or cows . . . and the children can't ride about on hay wains all the year through, can they? Isn't it only in June or something?'

However, I would not be daunted and found a farm in a perfect setting not far from Edenbridge, which was up for auction. It had a tumbled-down timbered house, five cottages and four hundred acres with a river running through, starred by marsh-marigolds. I was determined to have it. All the money which I had spent on restoring The Palace, lagoons, fountains and smooth lawn walks, paid off, and I sold it privately, extremely well, and thus armed with a comforting cushion against immediate disaster sent poor Forwood off to the auction for the farm which he speedily obtained for me but without the five important cottages, which were all sold for enormous prices, singly, to stockbrokers and junior architects who would, in due time, smother them in high-gloss paint, William Morris papers, London lampposts and wishing wells and sell them at vast profit. I was left with a derelict farm-house, a huddle of barns, and four hundred acres. Ruin stared me in the face, and Elizabeth in gingham faded swiftly from sight for ever. I put it straight back on the market and sold it for the price I had paid to a neighbouring farmer and with a deep sigh of relief came sadly down to earth; homeless.

Although The Palace was technically sold, I did not have to give possession until April, and by the grace of God and Irene Howard, who was then casting at MGM, I found myself in a modest little Army-Comedy-Drama and stamped through the coldest winter for years with army boots and a cockney accent. It was a fortuitous move. The film was made entirely on location all over Essex, Surrey and Kent; each time we reached an area it was desperately combed for an alternative to The Palace. Day after day, as I slid and shivered through snow drifts rallying my brave soldiery, Forwood trailed wanly about with Estate Agents and too-eulogistic catalogues of Home Counties Tudor, until one morning he found me lying, frozen, n a barn near Ewhurst buried in straw eating a hard-boiled egg at the lunch break.

'It's not a farm; but it's pretty marvellous.'

'Where is it?' I was numb with cold and past caring.

'Just up the hill there, staggering view. I can run you up in the car now.'

'I can't come and see a house like this, covered in mud and plastic blood . . . this filthy uniform . . .'

'I think you should. It's exactly what you want . . .'

It was. And I moved into Nore six weeks later.

Judy had been in a cinematic limbo, so to speak, since 'A Star Is Born' which she made in 1954 with George Cukor. Apart from a small role in 'Judgement at Nuremberg', and the recent film with Kramer, she had not faced a camera for seven years. Now, with her shining new life, the stresses and strains were once more appearing like cracks in a patched-up wall. She was finding life difficult to handle and telephoned three or four times a week from New York, always about four or five in the morning my time. She couldn't sleep, and feared the dark; she wanted, and often got, constant reassurance, although I can't believe I ever made a great deal of sense blurred with sleep as I was. Sometimes she was on form and happy, but mostly she was depressed, worried, or planning wild All-Star-Concerts for the Kennedys, whom she much admired, or earthquake victims in Peru or Persia; these problems were harder to deal with at four in the morning.

'What time is it with you?' her voice careful, worried.

'Five am, you beastly woman.'

'Oh! I waked you!'

'Doesn't matter . . . I have to get up soon anyway, it's a Studio day.'

'Have you ever heard about a script called "The Lonely Stage"?'

'No . . . why?'

'Well there is one and they want me to do it; in London.'

'I heard rumours, didn't know the title. So?'

'It stinks.'

'Well, say "no" then.'

'But it's a good idea. The idea is good. The dialogue is just yuccky.'

'What's it about if it's so good?'

There was a pause, she laughed ruefully.

'This big, big Star goes to London to do a concert at the Palladium and finds the man who got away . . . It's about me; I guess somebody has read my lyrics.'

'Well, get a new writer and see how you feel then.'

'Would you do it with me?'

'Play the one who got away?'

'Sure.'

'Of course I would. You know that. But I know they want an American star.'

'Why for chrissakes! He's supposed to be British.'

'Box Office.'

'Don't give me that. I'll do it if you say yes. Yes?'

'Yes.'

There was a pause again, crackle noises: 'I love you very much,' she said. And hung up.

She got to work pretty quickly, for a very few days later I was asked if I would care to do a film with Miss Garland. Although there was no script ready yet, would I take it on trust? I agreed, providing that it did not interfere with a film I was discussing with Dearden for July, 'The Mind Benders'. The spokesman assured me warmly that the Garland film would commence in early May and that I would be well finished by June, since my role was not long. Miss Garland was the star. I would have plenty of time. Little did he know.

We all embarked, unwittingly, on a brakeless roller-coaster which, reaching its final peak, roared down ricketing and racketing, exploding us all into smithereens at the end.

Although the script, when it arrived finally, was a professional workmanlike job, well constructed and not quite as bad as Judy had led me to believe, I knew from her present state of depression and indecision (for she now telephoned me nightly, filled with doubts and fears and an unreasoning dislike of her part as written) that something would have to be done quickly or we would all be in for a very bumpy ride. I implored the producers not to show it to her when she arrived in England.

'But we have made a number of changes according to her wishes.'

'If you show her that she'll turn right round and go back to the States. I know Judy, and I know her present mood.'

'Well, what do we do? This is the script she agreed.'

'I think she agreed only the story line. If you let me have a day or two I could try and re-write some of the stuff she has to say; but don't show it to her until I have talked with her.'

They agreed, worriedly. Her present mood was frantic. Panicked by marital trouble in New York, she was in terror that the children, Liza, Lorna and Joe, would be forcibly removed from her, so she shoved them on to a flight in such haste that Liza arrived in London in slacks and a shirt with a bundle of odd garments clutched in her arms and Judy immediately sought to have them all made wards of the British Court. It was not the calmest way to start a very difficult assignment. To compound the problems which she had to face she was hurried to a foul little house in Sunningdale which the Company had rented for her for the duration of the film, adjacent to the golf course, because they thought she liked to play golf. This was a grave error and only served to make her feel that they were amateur idiots, since her affection for golf at a time like this was nil to say the least.

'Who do they think they've hired? Babe Zaharias?'

She eventually found a house in Hyde Park Gardens and moved in just before we started work. She was tired, frightened, and quite alone. Now at the top of her career again, after years in a limbo of illness and despair, and box office failure, she was unsure and unequipped to handle things for herself; van Thal willingly took over her domestic problems which were many, while I tried to assist her with the professional ones. The script was the first. Someone, idiotically, had already shown it to her and it caused immense distress. She was trusting no one from now on in. The storm was in the wind.

The firs day at the Studio, make-up tests only, was not so bad. The crew, handpicked for such an august Star, were delighted and proud to be working with her. She was charming, funny, easy, and almost gay. It all seemed, on the surface, as if things would settle down. In her dressing room, later, massed with flowers and crates of Blue Nun, cards of good wishes and boxes of Bendkics chocolates, she shut the door firmly and announced that she was leaving . . . immediately . . . and slammed into the bathroom.

'You can't leave. You have a contract, darling. We're in.'

'I'm not in . . . it won't be the first contract I've broken. I can't play this crap. They promised changes: they failed.'

She was sitting on the closed lavatory seat, always her place of refuge in moments of shattering panic, a glass of Blue Nun clinking in her hands, her face pale, drawn, body shaking, looking small, ill and hopeless. For an hour I sat on the edge of the bath and reasoned with her; she wouldn't budge. Just shook her head slowly at every suggestion, at every gentle argument I brought forward. Finally, in desperation, I read her the first scene which we were to play and which I had entirely re-written. She stopped her head-shaking and sat listening; then reached out and took the pages and started to read them aloud with me. She laughed a couple of times, put down the Blue Nun; we went over it two or three times . . . she was suddenly, immediately, worryingly, happy.

'Hey! It's good . . . did you do all this?'

'Yes.'

'It's really funny . . . don't you think Atlantic City would be funnier than Wilmette? They're both *awful*, but Atlantic City . . . I can make that funny . . . let's do it again. With Atlantic City instead.'

We started shooting a day later at the Palladium. She was happy, in marvellous voice, nervous, excited; it was her first big number in the film, 'Hello, Blue Bird'. I had given her a blue bird brooch in sapphires; she was in her familiar dressing room, surrounded by an adoring company of Make-Up and Hair people; she was literally, at eight in the morning, bubbling with pleasure. She held the brooch tightly in a small closed fist.

'We'll be a new team, you and I. Won't it be great!' She was sparkling.

'Gaynor and Farrel!'

'Macdonald and Eddy!'

'I don't sing . . .'

'The Lunts!'

We held each other laughing, promising each other our futures.

At twelve-thirty she was on her way to hospital in an urgently clanging ambulance. We had started as we had, obviously, intended to go on.

'But why? Why, darling? What did you do it for . . . it was such a good beginning.'

'It was a lousy beginning.' Unrepentant, unashamed, pale, two days later.

'What went wrong? Was it me? Something I did?'

'No . . .' She twisted a spit-curl int place in the mirror and stuck it to her cheek. 'Something *he* didn't do.'

'Who?'

'Neame, our so darling director. He didn't even say "thank you" when I finished the number, he didn't say anything. Just "Marvellous, Judy darling".' She mocked a very British accent. ' "Marvellous, Judy darling". Christ!'

'That's not so. He was thrilled by what you did, we all were, everyone was, you must know that, you must have felt it?'

'I don't "feel" things. I need to be told; OK? Confidence. Who the hell does he think I am, Dorothy Adorable? I'm a goddamned star . . . I need help.'

'Darling, you'll have to get used to the way we all work here. It's not the same as the States, we don't use the exaggerations, great, greatest, the best. It's all a bit cooler. If you don't understand that you'll get hurt; we don't get hysterical very often.'

She shrugged and pulled on a show angrily. 'That damned British understatement, the stiff upper lip . . . well, it won't do for Frances Gumm.'

'Who the hell's that?'

For a moment she looked at me in the mirror with a face of white stone. Then it cracked, and she started to smile a little, she reached out her hand and took mine. Not facing me directly. Ashamed suddenly, aware of bad behaviour. In the wrong. I pressed her hand hard. She lowered her head.

'It's me. Frances Ethel. Isn't it awful?'

'Well, Frances Ethel, just remember that Neame had one hell of a day . . . he had to clear the Palladium by four-thirty for the evening show there . . . he was under pressure and first days shooting are frightening for everyone.'

She withdrew her hand gently. 'Just you tell Neame he'd better watch out for me. *I* get scared, he think he's the only one? I need help and trust. I don't trust him. I want him off the production.'

She didn't have him off; but she never trusted him again and the first serious crack was opened, never to be more than very temporarily repaired. It was a very uncomfortable situation for Ronnie Neame, and he behaved impeccably with the patience and care of a saint. He was helpful, enthusiastic, and agreeable to all the re-writes I did for our scenes together. He did everything possible to make her happy and secure and lavished her with praise, justified always, but she never quite bent towards him again, even though after our first few scenes together she was patently thrilled by her work and was giving a quite superb performance. For a little time we settled down; writing every evening and every week-end. Sometimes she came down to Nore and made brilliant suggestions, funny, real, moving, and although she never wrote a word herself, she sat in my office all the time, smoking, sleeping, keeping close, awaiting each page as it came off the machine, reading it aloud, rejecting some words or phrases, offering better alternatives. It was a marvellous, happy combination. We honed and polished and rehearsed continually, avidly, so that when we eventually got to the take it was smooth and precise, spinning along on ball bearings. Spirits everywhere rose; her work was proving to be the best she had ever done, and she knew it.

'I'm good aren't I?' She was humble, happy, sure.

'Gooder than you've ever been.'

'You didn't see "A Star is Born" . . . not really, they hacked it to bits, George Cukor and I have never ever seen it . . . do you know that? They mutilated it. Do you remember that scene I did in the dressing room with Bickford, about a ten-minute monologue? Remember? Well . . . could you write me something like that for the end of this thing? A long scene, all about . . . all about . . .' she fished slowly in the air seeking words, 'all about what it means to be Jenny Bowman.' Her name in the film.

'I'm not sure that I know all about what it means to be Jenny Bowman.'

'Sure you do . . . she's me. You know that, don't you? She's really me. And you know me all right, Buster. That line you wrote that you say to the kid . . . remember? "Jenny gives more love than anyone but takes more love than anyone can possibly give." Remember that?' she chuckled happily wickedly. 'I reckon you know; and I'll always help you out with a real Garland-line when you get stuck. I'm full of goodies!'

But the good times grew fewer and fewer as Judy got later and later, or sometimes didn't even arrive at all for work. We used to sit about from eight-thirty, in dull, depressed heaps; the crew played cards and drank endless cups of tea; the guts were slipping out of the production. We were losing so many work days that I realised that the film I wanted so much to make with Dearden, and to which I had wholeheartedly committed myself, was in jeopardy. I would never, at this rate, make the Start Date and they would probably have to recast.

'Judy . . . you know I have to start another film in July?'

'So?'

'Well with all these delays . . .'

'Don't you start blaming me! I've been sick . . .'

'I know, but just remember that I only have seven weeks' work on this . . . you have ten, if I can't finish my part in that time I'll just have to leave.'

'You can't.'

'I have a contract with the other people. Signed.'

'Break it.'

'I don't want to. I want to do the film desperately.'

She turned from the mirror, we always seemed to have these discussions in her portable dressing room on the set, and looked me straight in the eye.

'When you leave, lover, I leave. Finish. Right?'

'But you can't . . . for God's sake . . .'

'Don't tell me what I can't do! Everyone tells me what I can and can't do . . . I do what I want to do . . . and I don't want to shoot one bloody frame on this stinking mess after you have gone. When you leave for your oh-so-marvellous movie, I leave on the first flight for L.A. . . . don't you forget it!'

'I've always promised I'd never ever lie to you, right?'

'Right.'

'But I'm leaving at the end of my seven weeks.'

'Then we won't have a movie, will we?' She pulled off her earrings slowly and put each one carefully on the tray before her.

'You won't have a movie. This is your movie, no one else's. We've got the big scene to do; you want to do it, you know that, so far this is the best work you have ever done, better perhaps than "Star". It's your time; your career, I promise you I'll never fail you, but you must promise me to not fail yourself . . . please?'

Darling, be a good girl and come back again . . . please.'

'Don't you good girl me, for godssake! They hate me out there. Have you seen those loving Cockney faces full of "good girl"; they hate me. I feel the hate.'

'They don't, they don't; they're working for you all the way . . . you know that.'

She swivelled round on her chair and took my hands suddenly. 'You really, really want to do this damned movie of yours?'

'I do.'

'What's it about?'

'Deprivation of the senses.'

'In English?'

'Brainwashing. It's a new, terrible weapon.'

'Someone used it on me.'

'They used it on the American troops in Korea. No one knows much about it yet.'

'I do, all about it. I invented it; Louis B. Mayer invented it. My loving damn agents "Frick" and "Frack" invented it. There is nothing I don't know about it, do you hear? Nothing I don't know about your terrible new weapon. *I've* been so brainwashed I'm Persil White all through.' She burst into tears and I held her very tightly. Above her shoulder I saw my own face reflected in the mirror; it was Persil White as well.

At Canterbury; a one-day location at the cathedral started well. She met the Red Dean and made him laugh, posed for the Press. At the lunch break an ashen faced wardrobe-mistress hurried from her caravan, her costume bundled in one arm, shoes in the other. 'She's not working any more; you never heard such language.' Grim-faced producers, the director, a covey of assistants; one or two blazered choir-boys hoping for an autograph. Despair wafting like smoke from a dying bonfire.

In her caraan, curtains drawn, light filtered, a litter of clothes, papers, a fallen vase of carnations, water dripping on the cheap linoleum. Judy hunched at her dressing table in a green silk kimono; hair a ruin, make-up wiped roughly off a white, anguished face. In front of her a tin tray with a wrecked salmon mayonnaise.

'What's wrong, pussy cat?'

'Get out . . . get right out.'

'You were so happy this morning.'

'Now I'm not.'

'My fault?'

'You know damned well . . .'

'I don't . . . what is it?'

'I wanted you to stay tonight in Folkestone . . . I booked you a room; Liza, Lorna, Joey, all of us together. Just one night, one happy, lovely night . . .'

'I can't, darling, I told you. I have to get back by eight.'

'You told me. The only thing I have ever asked of you.' She started to weep silently. 'Tonight, there's a full moon, did you know? A full moon, we could have all gone along the beach together, along the shore, in the moonlight, peaceful, calm, I need calm. The kids want to go. I want to go. Just one time and you refuse.'

'I told you why.'

'They were all looking forward to it . . .' she suddenly took her knife from the tray and stabbed me in the arm. I grabbed her wrist and we fell, in a sprawling heap together among the sodden carnations and the tumbled tray of salmon mayonnaise. 'I hate you! I hate you!' She struggled and heaved, the knife still tight in her fist, I twisted her wrist and she cried out suddenly. Somewhere the knife clattered. I was across her, heavy; she fought for breath.

'Say you hate me . . . say you hate me.'

'I don't.' I still held her twisted wrist firmly. She moved under me, her free hand scrabbling in the debris. A fork suddenly thrust against my cheek, under the right eye.

She stared up in the gloom. 'This can do as much damage. Say you hate me, I know you hate me, they all do, hate me . . .'

Gently I leant down and kissed her face; she crumpled, sobbing un-controllably, her arms around me, clutching like a drowning child. I helped her up and we stood in the ruins of her lunch and the water from the fallen flowers, standing together until the pain had eased, then I gently put her from me, smoothing her straggling hair, wiping her nose with my finger.

'You are all snotty . . . disgusting.'

She half laughed, pushed the hair from her face, her eyes wide, streaming, filled with pain.

'How long will it take to make you presentable; an hour?' She wiped her mouth with the back of a hand, shrugged the kimono over her shoulders. 'About; wheel them in.'

Outside the sun was so brilliant that I could only just see the anxious huddle, a few discreet paces from the caravan; Neame was twisting and untwisting a white plastic spoon.

'She'll work,' I said. I suddenly realised that I was still wearing my hat, that there was a splatter of mayonnaise on my tie. Wisely they stood aside and no one followed me, blindly I wlked into a tree; and knocked myself out.

We had one week, one final week which she did for me, of complete, unforgettable magic. She was on time every day, her work was brilliant, we tore into the scenes and she blasted off the screen. My final day was our big scene. We started together rehearsing in her dressing room at eight-thirty. No one came near us. She had wanted to play it sitting down, not to move; I wrote it so that she had sprained an ankle and was carted, drunk, to St George's Hospital. She sat in a chair, I knelt at her feet. We rehearsed for six hours, with half an hour for a sandwich, in the cramped little caravan. At four-thirty we went on to the floor and shot the entire scene just once. It lasted eight minutes and was one of the most perfect moments of supreme screen-acting I have ever witnessed. I shall never see its like again. She never put a foot wrong, not an effect was missed, the overlaps, the stumbling, the range, above all the brilliance of her range. The range was amazing; from black farce right through to black tragedy, a cadenza of pain and suffering, of bald, unvarnished truth. It had taken us three days to write; she passed every line as I set it down, 'warts,' she said, 'and all'; it took six hourse to rehearse, eight minutes to shoot, and when it was over one of the crew walking across from the stage was stopped by one of his fellows.

'What,' said the man, 'happened on your stage today?'

'A miracle,' said Bob.

A miracle it was indeed; in that last week of June, we shot twenty minutes of screen time and, more or less, finished off the main bulk of our work together. Judy was quite aware of what she was doing. She gave me the week in order that I could go off to do my 'damned movie' as she called it, knowing full well that she would then be on her own to finish off the film which she so detested. The following week only a few seconds were shot, and she behaved unkindly and uncontrolledly, falling, in one instance, in a bathroom, cracking her head

badly, necessitating, yet again, hospital treatment. Once more she tried to fire
the patient, unhappy Neame, and finally, on Black Friday the 13th of July she
walked off the film and that was that. I still had one or two small pick-up shots
to do with her, and was forced to do them with a double, wigged, and dressed in
her clothes. The miracle, though gigantic, was finally over. With my
completion of the seven weeks' work, in my acceptance of the film with Dearden
to which I had been fully committed, I could no longer stay at her side and she
felt completely rejected. In a hostile atmosphere, untrusting and by now quite
unloved, she was unable to contain her terror and her unhappiness; her private
life lay about her like a pillaged room, there were court cases, and a bitter
struggle to retain her children whom she adored above all things, but I could no
longer heed the urgent summonses by telephone, nor could I make her
understand that my duty, if one dared use such a word, now lay with Dearden
and a new, extremely involving film.

'You are walking away from me,' she cried in anguish, 'you are walking
away, like they all do . . . walking away backwards, smiling.'

Useless to try to explain; there was no way now that I knew to help her. All I
did know was that being with her, working with her, loving her as I did, had
made me the most privileged of men.

And later, when one had added up the total of this unhappy summer's sum,
the result was, tragically, a loss. 'The Mind Benders', the film with Dearden,
was too far ahead of its time. No one knew very much about brainwashing; no
one really believed that it was possible, nor, apparently, did they wish to. If they
had ever heard of Gary Powers, or had known the appalling effects on the GI
prisoners in Korea, if they had known then, what they know today, about
psychiatric treatment of political dissidents, maybe we might have fared a little
better; but they didn't, alas, and one headline which blared, 'Bogarde Thriller
Is Shabby and Nasty' summed up the general reaction. Another thumping
failure in my brave new effort to disturb, illuminate and educate. Someone was
on the wrong track; it depressed me deeply that all the signs pointed towards
myself.

And when finally the stuck-together, patched-up version of 'The Lonely
Stage' opened it was, in the main, received with superlatives by a loyal, loving,
Garland Press. Although they all disliked the woman's-magazine story, which
we had already known it to be, they praised Judy unstintingly, deservedly. One
of the, at the time, leading critics, awash with what Judy called 'spastic Garland
mania' overstepped himself slightly: 'There is one drunk scene,' he wrote, 'with
Bogarde which mixes laughs with tears with such expert timing that I felt like
raising my hat to the script-writer. I am told, in fact, that this one scene which
did not go according to the script. Halfway through it Judy suddenly realised
that this might well be a moment from her own life. The real Judy took over
from the cinema heroine. She started to make up her own lines. Just you listen to
them,' he sagely counsels his readers, 'they are spoken from unhappy memories.
Bogarde could only lean back, feed in a word here and there and let the camera
move in on someone re-enacting an experience of her very, very own.' Three
days writing, six hours rehearsal.

'Golly!' she said, laughing with pleasure at the idiocy. 'It only goes to show
they don't *really* know . . . but we must have been very, very good.' She had
flown in from New York with a vast enourage of hangers-on, American Press
and our now ebullient producers. It was the most amazing First Night I have
ever witnessed. I picked her up at the Savoy, pushed her into the car, leaving her
Empty Suits and Frilly Shirts aghast on the pavement, and together, quite

alone, we drove slowly round London, all pain forgotten; all happiness ahead. At the cinema the crowds were dense, shouting, cheering, loving her, rocking the car with wild abandon, grabbing to touch her, tears streaming, voices screaming, hands outstretched as if to heal . . . to touch . . . to be healed. She was radiant, moved deeply, in tears herself. Afterwards we danced together at the reception; 'We were good, you know that? Really good . . . we are a team.'

'Gaynor and Farrel.'

'Garland and Bogarde.' She laughed and hugged me.

'Do you mind if I take first billing?'

'No . . . your privilege, ladies first.'

'G is before B, isn't it?'

'Now it is.'

'Oh! I'm so happy . . . and you were such a bastard to me all the time . . . so mean! How could you have been so mean when I love you so much; you better be sweet to me the next time around, Buster!'

But there was not to be a next time. If the film was a critical succes, it was a public disaster, crumbling away like a piece of old lace. In Guildford, three days after it opened, they ripped down the posters and announced the revival of a well-tried British comedy about vintage cars. We were off. It is hard to tell why. Maybe the story was too sickly, maybe the new awful title, 'I Could Go On Singing', which the producers changed in a fit of panic on the day of the Press Show itself, misled audiences into thinking that it was a straight Garland musical which it obviously was not. Maybe Judy, playing so close to the truth of herself, distressed her fans. Whatever it was, it sank without trace. But she, happily, was unaware of this at the time. She flew back to America after the premier to be present as her daughter, Liza, set her own course towards the dizzying roller-coaster of the lonely stage.

It is almost extraordinary to discover that a great many other things were taking place in 1962, one was so hermetically sealed in a globe of self-absorption that they passed almost unnoticed or not even noticed at all. Algeria and Uganda became independent, the Russians sent arms to Cuba, Charles Laughton died, someone tried to assassinate President de Gaulle, they built a Hilton Hotel in Park Lane, France and England decided to build Concorde and, somewhere in April a much-loved and respected friend from many years, Daniel Angel, telephoned from Rome. It was a pleasant surprise, but so apparently ordinary that, like the rest of events, it too almost might have gone unnoticed. Almost.

'Enjoying your new house then?' He was laughing.

'Only been in a week or two. It seems fine.'

'You move about more than fleas on a dog . . . who are you dodging? Creditors?'

'Any time now. Where are you, Danny?'

'Rome . . . trying to set up a deal, usual thing, know what I mean? Got a very old friend of yours here, wants to say hello. Hang on . . .' There was a pause, then a weary, well-remembered voice.

'Hulloo . . . how are you?' No interest in the question really, barest good manners.

'You dn't sound very happy, anything wrong?'

'No. Just bored. Bored and tired and not working. It's been a long time since *we* worked; about ten years?'

I had first met Joseph Losey ten years before, on a bitter winter afternoon at the Studio. I knew nothing about him save that he was an American refugee from McCarthy, a director of talent, that his assumed name, for security reasons was Victor Hanbury, and that he was setting up a small budget film and was hopeful that I could be interested to play in it; my presence, it was explained, would help him to increase, if not double, his budget. I was not truthfully interested. Tired after making three films in a row, uncertain of this director with an assumed name and a not very good script I agreed, at least, to let him show me some of the last film he had made before he had had to leave Hollywood and the witch-hunt. I hope that I was not patronising; I know that I was not enthusiastic at the time.

It was freezing in the small theatre where the film was projected. I was alone, since he preferred to walk about outside in the slush like an expectant father, and quite unaware of the importance for him, then, of my acceptance or not of his work. After twenty minutes I knew, without any doubt whatsoever, that the one person I wanted to work with most was kicking his heels in the car-park in a long blue overcoat waiting for my verdict. We watched the rest of the film together in silence – it was called 'The Prowler' – and after, in the Studio Bar, he started to outline for me the ideas he had for the hackneyed little thriller which neither of us liked but which he knew we could use as a base to move from. Alexis Smith willingly agreed to join us, taking an incredible risk for an American actress in those days of McCarthy, and so became my first Hollywood leading lady. The modest budget was therefore, predictably, doubled, and in high heart we all set off.

The result, after weeks of uncomfortable work in a run-down little studio where we had to fire a gun to frighten away the sparrows from the Sound Stage before every Take, was not, perhaps the greatest of our careers, but it had served to form a bond of respect and affection which was to last a lifetime. And it taught me, very early on, in line with Dearden and Leacock, that there was a magical, untapped, untrodden world awaiting in the cinema. I had managed in my Corridor of Power years, and with the willing assistance of Olive Dodds, to get him a contract with Rank; for which he eventually forgave me; his stay there not being of the happiest or most successful, although it did help a little to settle som problems for him, we unhappily had never worked together again. His weary, flat, affectionate voice, that morning from Rome, was sunlight through fog.

'What are you doing in Rome?'

'Finishing off a job.'

'Happy with it?'

'I think so. Can't tell. It was a sweat. Good, ultimately.'

'What next, something fun?'

'What the hell is fun? Do you know?'

'Just asking. Nothing then?'

'Nope. You?'

'A film with Judy Garland. Then something with Dearden.'

'You'll never get rich that way.'

'I'm trying.'

He laughed gently. 'So you're unavailable then, I take it?'

'Not after the Dearden thing. Then there's a big, big void. I'm on my own now. No Rank . . . free . . .'

'Happy?'

'Chilly. I wish we could find something to do together again . . .'

'And I. But what?'

'Joe. Joe, remember that book you found, ages ago? A slight thing, novella more than a novel. You thought it might make a film when we were doing

'Sleeping Tiger'.

There was a long pause, when he answered his voice was not quite as flat.

'You mean the Robin Maugham thing? About the man-servant?'

'"The Servant". That's it. What about that? Do you think it's still available?'

'I don't know, let me check it out. But Christ! You're too old now to play the boy.'

'I know that, but I could produce it or something with you, couldn't I?'

'Producers have to be bright. Anyway . . . let me check it . . . I'll call you later.'

When he called it was to say that the book was still available, that it had been bought by someone, scripted by Harold Pinter, abandoned, and that for a certain sum we could secure the rights; he didn't like the present version, had had long discussions with Pinter and they had found a new formula together. If, he said, I was really serious he would start negotiations right away.

'Of course I'm serious; could I produce it with you?'

'God no. I've got a producer, you can play the servant.'

'No, we need someone like Ralph Richardson . . .'

'I need a movie name; they tell me you are what is laughingly called "hot", so you play the servant; we won't get finance otherwise, yes or no? There's a lot of work to do.'

'Yes, of course. When will there be something to read?'

'Not in time for you to change your mind. Late summer, after you have gotten through with being a movie star. I'll keep in touch.'

The bay of Cannes lay before me, blue, still, calm in the September sun. The sand was hot, the beer iced, the rattan shades slatted shadows across the pages and made it difficult to read; it was difficult enough anyway (I had never read Pinter before), but I knew instinctively, which is how I have always worked, that what I presently held in my sandy hands on the hot morning beach, was not merely a script, but rather a key. The key to a door in my long corridor which only awaited the courage of my turning; and keeping to my dangerous track.

CHAPTER ELEVEN

Elizabeth came and squatted down beside me, spilling a handful of bulbs into my lap. 'Those are the last, no more. November is a bit late for tulips, isn't it? Shouldn't it be October or something?'

'Better late than never; didn't have the time. Actually I forgot really.'

She got up and stretched, swivelling to look out over the fish pool through the bar chestnuts. 'I'm so stiff. Getting old. I do think it's pretty here, the prettiest house you've ever had. The last place, The Palace, was a bit film starry; not really you, if you know what I mean.'

I pushed in the last of the bulbs, raked the earth over them, wrote 'Carrara' on the wooden marker and got up.

'Everything is white.'

'It's the White Garden, that's why.

'I expect you forgot them because of all that business in Cuba. I was so frightened, I wouldn't even listen to the News.'

'Perhaps that's why.'

'It really was nearly war, wasn't it? I don't think I could have managed another one, could you? I mean so soon after.'

'No. I had enough last time.'

'I was thinking of the children, and George, not so much myself this time.'

We stood together and looked down across the Weald. To the right Chanctonbury Ring; far, far away, like a slit in the canvas of the sky, Shoreham Gap, glinting. Magpies stalked importantly, like judges, through the stubble across the sunken lane. It was cool, still, white doves clattered down in a covey and bobbed gently to each other.

She sighed; almost a laugh. 'I don't think I could have. Do you remember how worried we both were about growing up; after ours? I didn't think I'd know how to do it.'

'I remember. Took me a long time.'

She put her arm round my shoulder and scuffed the November leaves into flurries. 'Do you think we have now? Oh, I know I have. That hotel in Hove we ran, for Allied ex-Service men, a sort of rehabilitation centre really; our first job after we got married. You know how hard it was to start again. George and I did all the cooking, and the boilers: we couldn't get help, one old woman who came in sometimes. We were doing the beds, cleaning, cooking, washing up. I'd never ever had to do anything like that before. Sheltered little thing. I grew up all right. I felt so old at the end of it that I was just like that lady in the Shangri La thing; you know, the one who turned to dust in the end . . . she was so terribly old really? That was just how I felt. Dust.'

I pulled her down the steep bank, among the leaves and we started up towards the house through the chestnut walk.

'I was so thick,' I said, 'That I tried to be an adolescent all the time; to recapture what I had never really had. Very boring for people who had to deal with a twenty-six-year-old eighteen. Do you know what I mean?'

'No. Not really. You were pretty awful sometimes; isn't it funny that we didn't actually grow up in the war, just when you'd expect it, with all the killing and bombs and things. It all happened in the peace; not what you imagine really.' She stopped suddenly and scrabbled about in the leaves for some conkers and put them in her pocket. 'They're for Mark, champion conker killer . . . or something idiotic. Conkers on a bit of string. Isn't it silly? We grow up but we don't much change do we, inside I mean. I'd quite like to play conkers again; you were awfully good, weren't you? Champion as well. I look at the children, I look at George, look at myself in the mirror and I know I've only got older. I don't suppose we'll ever really grow up truthfully, I mean like real people, do you?'

'Don't suppose so. Don't know, don't care now.'

We reached the oak gate leading on to the ribbon-smooth lawns, worm casts like Pontefract cakes, neat box hedges, the house glowing in the winter sun. She clambered on to the gate and sat there, brushing dried earth from her hands; I heaved myself up beside her.

'I was saying to Pa the other evening that I think I could put my roots down here, you know.'

She looked vaguely across the lawns. 'Your roots?'

'Yes . . . for good.'

'Have you got a super job coming or something?'

'In January, perhaps. A film by Pinter; with Losey.'

'The Red Indian-looking man?'

'Yes.'

'Will you get lots of money?'

'No. Nothing really, it's a small budget.'

'How much?' Always deadly curious.

'Seven thousand pounds, about.'

She looked at me with surprise, her eyes smiling. 'Seven thousand pounds? That's all you'll make?'

'About . . . it's a difficult film, no one wants to do it, you know.'

'Do you?'

'We all do . . . yes, of course . . . more than anything. But the money-men don't want to.'

'Why don't they want to make it then?'

'It's not commercial, they won't risk the loot.'

'Will anyone ever go to see it, if you do make it?'

'Not many perhaps . . . it's difficult, you know.'

'Don't keep on saying 'you know' – I don't.'

'Sorry.'

'You must be dotty.'

'Why?'

'Well. . .' She polished a conker briskly on her sleeve. 'You say you think you can put your roots down here. how can you for seven thousand pounds in a film no one wants to make and no one will go to see? Of course, you're dotty! Why don't you do something like, oh I don't know, "Cleopatra" or something.' She laughed and her breath wisped into the till morning air. 'It really isn't very sensible, is it? I mean if you do want to put down roots or whatever you call it.'

I slid off the gate and it wobbled, she dropped her conker to hold on.

'Don't do that! You are vile! I could have fallen off easily. Now I've lost Mark's best conker.' She clambered down beside me, searching for in in the cropped grass. 'If you want to be in that kind of film you ought to live in a little flat like the one you had in Hasker Street. With two suitcases.' She found the conker and caught me up walking towards the house. 'You shouldn't have all this. It's silly.' She waved her arms wide, embracing lawns, hedges, dovecote, house.

'Shut up!'

She threw the conker high in the air, waited for it to fall, caught it.

'I don't think you have grown up,' she said flatly.

But I did, I think. The four films which I made with Losey between '62 and '66 saw to that. Each one was a bitter, exhausting, desperate battle. It never got any better; only Losey's obstinacy, determination, belief, optimism and unflagging courage managed to get us through; that coupled with a crew who also believed and a growing company, as he called it, of actors who were also prepared to put money second to career. In order to get any of these films made we all had to work for very modest salaries with the vague promises of percentages which we were seldom to see. No one got rich, in any possible degree from these enterprises. But we were enriched in our values; and that is what mattered most to us all; however, our values at no time matched the values of the Distributors or the Money. As Losey said, 'The Money isn't even smart, even about money.' But we fought, and we fought, until eventually they beat us in the battle between Art and Profit; and Art is the ugliest word you can use in their limited vocabulary.

We wrestled 'The Servant' to the screen. It was on and off with the frequency of a conjuror's hat. If I had found Pinter's script difficult to read, then the Distributors and Money found it utterly incomprehensible and shied away from it like frightened horses, but a series of odd coincidences gave us courage.

With myself set to play the servant, Losey knew that he must bolster my name in such a delicate enterprise with a sound female one. He had in mind a new and very exciting girl called Sarah Miles. She, we both knew, was the ideal choice. But, it appeared, others had the same ideas about her, and she was greatly in demand. It seemed unlikely that she would accept such a modest assignment. She read it, said she liked it but . . . One night I switched on the television to watch the News and, quite by chance, tuned into the wrong channel. A small one-act play of not much interest except for the sudden astonishing appearance of a young man who was instantly, beyond any shadow of doubt, the one actor we had to have for the third, exceptionally difficult part. I had never seen nor heard of him before. His name was Maurice Oliver. I called Losey, who hung up to watch, and our mutual agent, Robin Fox who was, as it happened, watching already. Since Maurice Oliver was in fact James Fox, and his own son. Losey agreed that Oliver-Fox was ideal-looking, but was worried that his inexperience (this was his first acting role as it happened) might be a strain on such a complicated, subtle, part.

We were starting. And then the slender hopes were dashed when we learned that Sarah Miles was now committed to a more commercial project for a great deal more money than we could ever hope to pay her. Even though, at this juncture, we had no money; only high hopes. Not quite enough. Once again the conjuror doffed his hat, the film folded its timorous wings, and settled down with a dull thump. Without her we were lost. Not only was she the only conceivable actress for the part, she was also the only bait we had to offer the Money.

Some days later, much against my wishes, and only under constant prodding from Forwood, I was forced, and that is the word, to attend an important premiere and go to the supper which was to follow. Something which I absolutely detested. I found my own premieres bad enough but someone else's intolerable. Forwood insisted that it would be the gravest of ill-manners not to accept the invitation which came from an extremely powerful producer who had, quite recently, been making polite overtures about a couple of not-very-interesting but commercial subjects. I was made to see, eventually, that I was not in the position to play the role of recluse at this juncture, nor to refuse the offered hand. So I went. It was a tedious event except for one fact, which made it depressing as well. In the seats in front of me were Sarah Miles and the golden-haired Fox boy. Together. Coincidence of a saddening kind. The supper which followed was the usual affair of many round tables and rounder producers and money-men, but at the table to which I was bidden I found myself, surprisingly, beside Joseph Losey, more of a stranger at this kind of junket than I myself. We smiled wanly, and spoke little. Both of us depressed. Forwood on the other hand was sitting at a table some distance away and found himself beside Sarah Miles, whom he did not know, except by sight. Across from him, to his mild astonishment, was Fox. He decided to meddle.

'It's awfully sad that you can't do "The Servant",' he said. 'You'd be marvellous.'

Sarah looked vaguely surprised. 'I simply long to do it! What do you mean?'

'But I hear you are committed elsewhere?'

'No . . . no that's all nonsense. I love "The Servant", I'm mad about it, really.' She nodded her head across the table to Fox. 'And wouldn't he be super as "Tony"!' she said happily.

'That's who we want for Tony.'

'I don't believe it! How marvellous! Oh! Goodness . . . he's my very best friend.'

'I think,' said Forwood, 'that we ought to go and have a word with Mr Losey . . . he's sitting over there.'

The next morning, at half past ten, we all met together in my apartment at the Connaught, and over coffee and Bloody Marys 'The Servant' unfolded its wings again, Losey was back in battle, successfully tested the boy, and I had once again been steered towards another door.

With Sarah we eventually got some money; not much, but a start. We also had, therefore, a distributor. One important part remained to be cast, and I suggested a much underestimated actress called Wendy Craig who had played a very minor role with me in the ill-fated Dearden film, 'The Mind Benders'. Thus we had the cast. But not the final, ready-to-shoot with money. Robin Fox, now rather heavily committed in the project, much to his surprise, with a son and three clients busting to start, one memorable afternoon at the Connaught, made a swift, desperate, and final telephone call to Leslie Grade; who came to the rescue and provided the necessary cash. Losey has called Mr Grade noble, I cannot better the word. After the weeks and weeks of battle and strain, of high hope and shattering disappointment almost hourly, Losey was a weakened man, and exactly one week after we started shooting on our film he collapsed, in the coldest winter we had had for years with pneumonia.

'It's a bitch. Got to stay put until I'm better. Maybe three or four weeks: and that's that. I'm sorry.' His voice was weak, whispery, agonised.

'But, Joe . . . surely we can do something?'

'Nothing. What can we do? They'll abandon; never wanted to make it in the first place, this is an excellent chance; collect the insurance money and forget all about it. If often happens.' He was so weak that he could hardly speak, and I could hardly hear him, but I did hear the softest word which he managed to add.

'Unless . . .'

'Unless what?'

'Could you take over?'

'And direct?'

'Yes. . . I could give you instructions by telephone. I've worked a lot of it out.'

The next day, with a thudding heart and a willing, loyal cast and crew, I nervously picked up his baton, and were off again.

For ten days, with almost hourly calls to Losey's bedside for explicit and detailed instructions which he never failed to give, however ill, we carried on with the film. My authority and decisions were never doubted, my suggestions examined and either accepted or, otherwise, discussed and modified, I never strayed from Losey's style, and the work went along at a good pace. They did not abandon. I was immeasurably proud, not of myself, ever, but of the crew and cast who so eagerly moved to help a man they greatly respected, almost revered in fact, who lay so despairingly ill and whose super-human efforts and beliefs now seemed to be in jeopardy. It was one of the most extraordinary expressions of loyalty and devotion that I have witnessed in this sometimes tawdry profession; and when he broke the rule, yet again, by staggering back to the Studio far too soon, gaunt, grey, painfully weak, the heartfelt applause which greeted his arrival was deeply moving. He is not, however, a sentimental man. Lying on an iron bed, wrapped in blankets and a long woollen scarf which

Wendy Craig had bought for him, smothered in hot water bottles and attended by a slightly bewildered, and ignored, nurse, he got on with the job. The only concession he made to his state of health was that we were asked to refrain from smoking since it made him cough. That evening, again breaking doctor's orders, he attended, with me, a full running of all the material which I had shot during his absence. He made no comment, other than hoicking and spitting into a steadily mounting pile of paper handkerchiefs, and was eventually led by his worried nurse through the bitter February wind to his car. 'See you tomorrow,' he croaked, and was driven away.

Every film which I had made before this, with very few exceptions, was timed by a stop-watch. That is to say, every look, every move, every gesture even, every speech and even a run-along-a-busy-street was ruled by the vicious, staggering move of the stop-watch hand. Films cost money. Time is money. Waste, even intelligent waste, was not tolerated. I remember being politely taken to task by a producer because I had made a move (crossing a room and looking from a window, merely that) last one minute four seconds instead of the laid-down time of thirty-six seconds which had been allotted me. I had overrun time . . . if I continued to play in this manner, he explained kindly enough, the film would run another fifteen minutes, which would mean serious editing problems, something else would have to be cut, otherwise the film would run too long and not fit its time-slot which had all been carefully worked out, I gathered, by a lady called Barbara-Jo in an office in Hollywood, California, some months before. Barbara-Jo, sitting at her desk, reading her script, decided with a press of her steel button, just exactly how long a totally unknown person would take to do the things required of him or her set down by the script. There was no time for human error, for a developing emotion, for inspiration. It was all set down and sealed. Timed to the last split-second. Pre-packaged behaviour. So we speeded things up a little, and any time required for thought was neatly erased. One developed the habit and tried to accommodate to it as best one could, playing against the text sometimes, walking with the lines, to save time, and so on. It was a soulless piece of machinery, but it fitted the film into its slot in the programme and allowed the audiences to catch the last bus home.

With Losey there was none of this. No frantic cry from the Script Girl that a scene, a move even, had overrun its time; it was a sublime luxury. Not a form of self-indulgence (that is to be avoided at all costs, it is both false and ugly to watch) but an exhilarating form of developing someone else, of letting another person, so to speak, inhabit the empty vessels of one's body and mind. Under Losey's shrewd, watching eye, and with Bumble Dawson's simple, brilliant, designs for the clothes he would wear and live in, we started together to build the character of Barrett.

It is important to make it clear at this juncture that a brilliant designer, and Bumble was one of the very best, has a great deal to do with an actor's performance. I am an actor who works from the outside in, rather than the reverse. Once I can wear the clothes which my alter-ego has chosen to wear, I then begin the process of his development from inside the layers. Each item selected by her was carefully chosen by Losey, down to the tiepin: a tight, shiny, blue serge suit, black shoes which squeaked a little, lending a disturbing sense of secret arrival, pork-pie hat with a jay's feather, a Fair Isle sweater, shrunken, darned at the elbows, a nylon scarf with horses' heads and stirrups. A mean, shabby outfit for a mean and shabby man.

For me the most important element of the wardrobe are always the shoes. From the shoes I can find the walk I must use; from the walk comes the stance, since naturally the spine is balanced on the feet. From the stance the shoulders may sag or become hunched, the neck might be thinly erect, or slip suggestively to one side or the other, the arms hang or are braced. In the chosen clothes one's body starts to form another's; another person walks and breathes in the shabby, serge suit. The whole is carried by the softly squeaking shoes. Thus the shape is arrived at; the physical frame.

Next the detail. Brylcreemed hair, flat to the head, a little scurfy round the back and in the parting, white puddingy face, damp hands (arms which hand loosely often have damp hands at their extremities, I don't know why). Glazed, aggrieved eyes, and then the walk to blend the assembly together. These details are always obtained from observing other people; an extension of my father's childhood game of 'Pots and Pans'. Always examine, question, the little things which go to make up human behaviour. The nervous ticks, the throbbing vein, the sudden flush of pleasure or anger, the unaware habits under stress. Ask what makes a man use this behaviour, analyse why he does, try to trace it back to a source. A complicated game; but one which has proved invaluable. Barrett's hair came from poor Philpot who ransacked Bendrose and went to clink. His walk I took from an ingratiating Welsh waiter who attended me in an hotel in Liverpool. The glazed and pouched eyes were those of a car-salesman lounging against a Buick in the Euston Road, aggrieved, antagonistic, resentful, sharp; filing his nails. No make-up, ever.

With my paraphernalia assembled under Losey's approving eye, with a superb text from Pinter handed to me as a gift, Barrett was ready to exist, there was almost nothing left to do but wind him up and set him off to work.

Like all the greatest directors, Losey never tells one what to do, or how to do it. Ever. Only what not to do. Which is very different. You give him your character and he will watch it develop, encouraging or modifying, always taking what is offered and using it deftly. You only know that you have done it to his ultimate satisfaction when he says, 'Pring!' at the end of a take. There is no waste of chatter, no great in-depth discussions about motivation, no mumbo-jumbo about identification, soul, or truth. You get on with it. Coward's famous advice years ago to an actor still holds good. 'Just learn your lines, dear,' he said, 'and don't bump into the furniture.'

With Pinter the same applies. We never, at any time either on 'The Servant' or on the later, and far more complicated 'Accident', sat in huddled readings of the text having it explained or trying to find what was 'meaningful'. Pinter's scripts are honed and polished along before they reach the actor's hand, and what he intends, or doesn't intend, becomes abundantly clear and lucid the instant one starts to work. His writing, at least as far as I have personally been privileged to experience it, reminds me of a beautifully laid-out scenic model railway. A start and an end. Tunnels and level-crossings, gradients, cuttings, little stations and smaller halts, signals all the way. The whole track laid and set out with the precision of a master jeweller. Pinter doesn't give you instructions like a packet of instant minestrone. The instructions are implicit in the words he offers so sparingly for his characters to speak. There is a popular and far too widely-held belief among many actors, and directors too (not to mention critics) that Pinter writes pauses. I don't think that he does. But I do think that he is one of the few writers who are brilliant in the text they *don't* write. His pauses are merely the time-phases which he gives you so that you may develop the thought behind the line he has written, and to alert your mind itself to the dangerous simplicities of the lines to come; it is an exhilarating experience, and given all these factors it is almost, and I repeat carefully, almost, impossible to go wrong.

As well as discovering the time for thinking or thought, with Losey one also discovered the values of texture. The textures of things; of wood, of metal, of glass, of the petals of a flower, the paper of a simple playing card, of snow even, and fabric. Plaster wood, however well combed does not feel like wood, neither does it photograph like wood; nylon is not silk, fibre glass is not steel, a canvas door does not close with the satisfying sound or weight of mahogany. All these apparently trivial items, or obvious if you like, add up to an enorous whole. Even if the audience is not immediately aware, it is subliminally aroused and its emotions feel the truth. It is real. And the actor feels the reality. It is, of course, totally cinematic not theatrical. In the theatre almost nothing must be real. It is reality extended; an actor must act the weight of mahogany when he closes his canvas door, his style is larger than life and must be of necessity, for he has to reach both the man in the Stall seat as well as the man in the back of the Gallery.

Because of the distance between himself and his audience the stage actor must project reality. Reality itself seldom reaches beyond the Orchestra Pit. The camera is a magnifying glass, and it betrays the theatre technique cruelly; a number of theatre actors, either out of fear or ignorance, despise the cinema and all its technicalities. And it very often shows. I committed the same error all those years ago when I got that one day's work on a film with the Attenboroughs, and derided a job which earned me three times the amount I was paid in the theatre for just sitting about looking like a policeman. Nothing to it, I thought cheerfully, any fool can do it. And fool can. But not any fool can make it work. One just has to go on trying and proving, sometimes for years. For the intense love of it.

It was the intensity of this love which started us all off on the battle to get 'The Servant' off the ground. And we managed. It was, however, quite another thing to get it shown when we finally finished. No one wanted this effort, no one was even prepared to give it a single showing. Obscure, obscene, too complicated, too dark, too slow, and naturally too uncommercial. Even the slight of obscenity didn't help it; it was removed from our hands and placed on the Distributors' shelves to gather dust like a poor wine. It seemed that the whole endeavour had not paid off, the courage had been in vain, the money, such as there had been, was lost, written off as a company loss. We set it aside as experience. It was to be the first example only.

Elizabeth was no fool; what was the point in making films which no one would show and to which very few people would come if they did? This *was* a form of self-indulgence which I could ill-afford. Surely, if my dedication was so intense, I should behave like a novice Buddhist, crop my hair, clothe myself in saffron and sandals and offer my begging bowl for physical sustenance. Or, less romantically, clear out of Nore, take a small flat and move in with a couple of suitcases. In that way I could just about manage to sit it out and wait for the Art Film of my heart to arrive, if it ever did again, instead of facing ruin sitting amidst a splendour of exposed oak beams, Meissen china and the best collection of dud eighteenth-century paintings the man from Christie's said he'd ever seen. But I had, I discovered to my shame, become very attached to the better things of life. The distance between Chester Row and Nore was an ocean. I liked my exposed oak beams and dud collection; I liked the life I lived. I liked travelling first class; and what was more, both my friends and my family liked it too.

The same old group from Bendrose had now come deeper into Sussex, bringing with them the same sense of security and affection. I had lost no one on the way and had gained many. Irene and Glynis, Margaret Leighton, David

Oxley, the Goughs, and Gareth Forwood who rightly considered every house as his home in between terms at Ludgrove or Millfeld, Daphne and Xan Fielding, Moura Budberg and Bumble Dawson, who were now joined by a younger, newer group who joined the team on Sundays. John Standing and his wife Jill Melford, Sarah and Noel Harrison and all their children, James Fox and Sarah Miles, Sybil and Jordan Christopher, Boaty Boatwright and others. No one tremendously grand; real friends to provide real stability.

Every month, for two or three days, I moved into the Connaught where I had a more or less permanent suite, and from there the business and the more social life was conducted. It was altogether a more elegant, and convenient setting for the other side of the life I chose to live. Here the deals were made, here the contracts were argued, here the Americans were feted as they preferred. Here status was symbolised. At Nore we sat around the fire, ran movies in the cinema at nights, read the papers, talked endlessly and walked miles across the fields with dogs and raincoats and a varied assortment of boots and stout sticks. At the Connaught it was dark suits and head waiters; duty in an elegant form.

This, if I altered my life to accommodate the Art Cinema, would all have to go. So too would the travelling which both I and my family had now grown to enjoy so well: Venice, Rome, New York, Vienna, Athens, Paris – they came with me to all points – and even Elizabeth willingly left her sink, family and the Hoover for the wistful pleasures of Budapest or the more obvious ones of Cannes, and my brother Gareth, the late arrival in the family, presently a trainee cutter at Pinewood, joined us for holidays. In those days we drove many thousands of miles across Europe, flew and sailed across oceans, and forged a pattern of discreet, one hopes, luxury all the way. The Gritti in Venice, Hassler in Rome, the Lancaster in Paris, the Bristol in Vienna, the Plaza in New York, car to the gangplank of the *Elizabeth*, flowers in the State Rooms, the one particular table reserved always in the corner of the Verandah Grill. It was the Grand Life and I enjoyed every moment of it. The only problem was having to earn the money which this sybaritic life demanded. And it demanded a lot.

So I compromised. Reluctant to let slip these undoubted pleasures, I decided on a sort of sandwich existence: Commercial Products which would provide the money to enable me to make the uncommercial Art film if and when it arrived. I saw no other way out, for the pickings, on both sides, were now getting thin on the ground.

In accepting this deadly weapon, compromise, I knew that I had once again broken one of the rules which Noël Coward had brandished at me like a stick, sitting in the Oak Room at Bendrose, just when the first flickers of succes were beginning to kindle my wood. He had waved his finger angrily across the room and said, 'Whatever you do, theatre or cinema, never, never, never compromise!' But there was no other way that I could see. 'The Servant' lay in its dust. Surely therefore it was wiser to accept the chances which were being offered here and there to raise yet another eyebrow, a trademark with which I seemed to have saddled myself, as the cheerful, commercially acceptable 'Doctor' . . . and a long line of semi-romantic heroes which I knew I could play on the top of my un-Brylcreemed head? In any case I was existing at that time in a compromise world in the cinema. No one knew which way to jump. Aware of those pipers in Hamelin, frightened by declining box-office receipts, the directors and producers themselves were compromising. Trying to add serious undertones to perfectly ordinary subjects and nervously congratulating themselves that they were keeping abreast of the new trend. Although their roots were far too deep down to alter anything; they knew almost nothing of the new trend, and were unable to implement it even if they did. Wallowing in compromise we steered a desperate course for the rocks. I was unhappily a passenger; I could not complain since I had purchased my own ticket.

Losey, on the other hand, was not prepared to let his work lie on shelves, or to compromise. From time to time he rescued his stack of tins and we had showings of the film for selected people in private screening theatres for which he, or we, paid the rent. Afterwards the reaction from these groups gave him so much confidence that he grew bolder and carried his packages to Paris were Florence Malraux set up screenings for influential people, and people began to talk; favourably. Eventually, after eight months of battle and trailing about like commercial travellers selling a brand of soap which nobody, including the owners, believed in, fortune came in the shape of Arthur Abeles, then head of Warner bros in Europe. With a spare week to fill at his vast theatre in Leicester Square he ran a pile of rejected films to try and fill the gap. 'The Servant' was the one he chose. A gentle man, more like a writer or an artist than a hard-headed American film tycoon, we could not have fallen into more sensitive hands. Amazed at the stupidity of his fellows, passionate about the film, he announced that we were to open after all. It was an unbelievably lucky chance.

I was in my Dressing Room, changing out of my costume to go and lunch, when Arnold Schulkes, my Stand-in for many years, banged at the door with the entire London Press in his arms.

'Brought you these; the first reviews.' He never gave anything away.

'All right? A slating or what?'

'Not a slating, no. Bloody fantastic.'

'All of them?'

'All . . . every one. Good, isn't it? After all this time? *The Times* is on top, read it first I would. After all you are family-connected, you might say; right?'

They lay before me, the verdicts on our work. A jury returned. I locked the door and leant against it with *The Times* and read slowly and carefully all the way through, slowly sliding down until I was squatting on my hanches, my back hard against the primrose paint. The last two paragraphs of John Russell Taylor's review were difficult to read because of tears. But I got the point. The moment which I had never thought would come had come at last. The moment when, sitting down, albeit squatting on Mr Rank's brown Wilton, I would be able to say, 'Ah! That's it! That's what I meant it to be.' And I said it aloud to relish the sounds of the thought-of words; not only for myself, indeed not that, but for all of us. Blearily I got to my feet and clumped across to the dressing table where Arnold had left the rest of the papers. The large lamp-framed mirror reflected a woeful image. Tall boots, green tights, frilly shirt, pink-smeary face, neatly waved hair on top of which coyly rested, at a jaunty angle, a Robin Hood hat stuck with a fistful of black cockerel's tails. What the hell did I look like? What was I doing? Compromising, said the reflection. 'Right!' I said aloud. 'Compromise comes to a full stop. Whatever happens. From now on.'

Brave words. And they were brave words which blazed, in scarlet neon, from the façade of Warner's Cinema that night. Finally we had all made it; it remained to be seen how long we would stay, but at least we had got there. A far cry from the times when I had waited for Vida, or she had waited for me, outside this very same building, during the blitz when we would march off together through the crumping bombs to toast and beans at Lyons Corner House or, if we were better off that night, to the Café Royal for unrationed venison and steamed cauliflower. An equally far cry from 'Rope' in Catterick and thimble-gins-and-limes in the officers' messes; I had pushed open a great many doors along the way since then. But time, as they say, is all relative and this was only one battle won.

At the big party later which I gave in the Connaught drawing room, the air was splendid with the scents of success. The Press had hailed the film as nothing other than a masterpiece, James Fox as the star of the future, and Losey no more nor less than a master. Standing watching him across the crowded room he looked, I thought, more like a weary don at a Speech Day. Surrounded by congratulating students, glass tightly in both hands, head bowed to listen to constant questions and praise, flushed with the pleasure he was so good at concealing. My heart rose with delight at his quiet triumph.

'What chances do you think it's got outside London?' I asked Theo Cowan, who, as always throughout my long career with Rank, had never left my side at receptions of this kind. He was Head of Publicity when I had started off with 'Esther Waters' and had steered me through the early days of Image Building, skilfully getting me through the inanities of judging Beauty Queens, opening swimming pools in civic centres, giving bouquets to the Most Glamorous Grannies of Hull or Gipsy Hill and helping me to deal with the not-always-enthusiastic Press at innumerable press-shows after innumerable near misses. always genial, always alert, always the kindest of men and the shrewdest, he had finally left Rank when I did and started out on his own. 'The Servant' was his first assignment, so he too was in at his own form of baptism. His opinions, when sought, were always honest, usually devastating in their accuracy. Losey trusted his judgement implicitly.

'Slender, I'd say.' He had almost finished an entire plate of smoked salmon sandwiches.

'That's what worries me, and worries Joe. If this fails outside we won't ever get another penny to do anything again,' I said.

'Well, it's difficult to say, you know; audiences are changing quickly now . . . it's exciting, the film, sexy enough, good exploitation stuff there; but it's a fickle world, what pleases the critics usually bores the provincial audience stiff. Just have to keep our fingers crossed; at least we did it, didn't we?'

I embraced my parents and took them across to meet Losey. His glass was empty. I refilled it and he took it automatically raising it only for a moment towards me in a silent toast just as Basil Dearden slowly, and gracefully, knelt at his feet.

'I am kneeling,' said Dearden, 'as you will note, in respect and homage to you.'

Losey looked slightly embarrassed and smiled his gentle smile. 'I really wish you wouldn't, Basil, you are too far away . . .'

'Just tell me, I ask in all sincerity, how can I make a film like this?'

'Oh for God's sake! You could . . .'

'How would I go about it? How should I even start?'

Losey took a slow sip of his vodka. 'I can't answer while you are down there.' Basil rose and faced him squarely. 'Well, how would I? How should I start . . . you must know?'

Losey grinned happily. 'Sure I know. Shall I tell you? Well; first of all you take your son away from Eton, sell all Melissa's furs, get rid of the house and the pool, get rid of the cars, pack a couple of suitcases and move into a small flat and think things over. That's the only way I know, Basil . . . no overheads; just the film.'

'Uncompromising chap,' said my father as we went across to the bar-table. 'I suppose that's right; takes a lot of courage, I should think.'

'Too much for me all at once. Elizabeth said the same thing . . . I know they are right, of course . . .'

'You told me, my dear, that Christmas in Rome, that you wanted to be more than just a film star, didn't you?'

'Yes.'

'Well, isn't this the chance you wanted? You said something about catching a tram-car or something, I didn't really understand.'

'No, Pa, trolley.'

'Oh well; whatever it was, it seems to me that you have caught it now, surely?'

'Not surely, no.'

'What's the difficulty?'

'Staying on,' I said.

Hanging on would have been more accurate, for hanging on it was. Although we were swamped with awards and prizes and an enormous amount of Press coverage on both sides of the Atlantic and in Europe too, the film was, eventually, only a satisfactory success commercially, and the struggle to make the kind of films we both wanted to grew harder than easier. 'King and Country' was made in eighteen days for a total sum of £85,000. This Daniel Angel, who had been responsible for the telephone call from Rome with Losey which had sparked the whole thing off, guaranteed us and, presumably lost, for although we once again reaped a generous harvest of accolades and awards galore everywhere, and even sold it to television all over the world, it never made a profit and the film is, to this day, apparently still in the red.

Prestige doesn't pay the rent; not even on a small flat.

'This is not going to be a prestige picture,' said John Schlesinger at lunch the first time we ever met. 'By that I mean there is no money, and really no one wants to make it much except me and the girl and Joe Janni. We're calling it "Darling" . . .'

'Who is the girl?'

'Oh, you wouldn't know her, just starting; brilliant, that's been the problem. We can't find a man to play the second role. Gregory Peck's turned it down already. They all have. Everyone we wanted.'

It was almost a repetition of the conversation I had had three years ago with Dearden about 'Victim'. I was to be last chance again.

'But who is the girl?'

'Called Julie Christie, she's marvellous; huge future.'

'Well, do you want me to do it or not?'

He looked at me thoughtfully across his vichyssoise, spoon poised. 'You're so frightfully *soigné* . . . you know . . .' He waved the spoon worriedly, not very much liking what he saw.

'Well, it's only because I'm wearing a suit, for God's sake. And I've brushed my hair. I can be quite un-*soigné*, or whatever you call it.'

'But this character is a telly interviewer; rather intellectual; Hampstead, baggy flannels, a couple of kids. Shaggy, brilliant. A sort of Robert Kee; he's also supposed to be Jewish but we can give that a miss.'

'Well, I'll do it. I want to work with you and I want to work with Christie.'

'Have you ever seen her?'

'On telly, in a space fiction thing. But she's The Young. I want to be with the young.' He looked mollified and took the compliment for himself. 'Well, thank you . . . we'd just have to tweed you up a bit. We've got to have *someone*.'

'I like the script and I'll do it; what more do you want, if I'm last chance?'

He shrugged sadly and went on with his soup. 'We really did need a *big* name to bolster hers at the box office. Unknown, you see. An American name would be perfect. If you do it we won't, of course, get the backing we'd need. Never mind. If you want to we could do some tests next week.'

'Not acting tests? For God's sake! Surely I've done enough.'

He waved his spoon across the table again. 'No. No. Not acting . . . we'll manage that somehow. Tweedy tests. Try to make you look . . .' He paused and took a sip of his wine. 'Well . . . un-*soigné*, I suppose, dear.'

In the final event I wore my old gardening clothes, washed my hair, and bought a lot of knitted ties from the Stonehenge Woollen Industries shop. And got the part. Julie was glorious. A gift. We were joined immediately. She lived in a noisy flat in Earl's Court and slept on a lilo mattress. One morning (we were working in Paddington Station) she confessed that, during the night, it had sprung a leak and she was sleeping on the floor with a tribe of stray cats which she had rescued. She might therefore be rather tired. She had seen a proper bed, very expensive, she explained, but it was a big brass one with bobbles and bars in a junk shop in the King's Road, and as soon as she could, she'd save enough to buy it. Meanwhile she had asked someone to go and get her some puncture patches from a garage near the station. While she went off to have a pee in the Ladies, Forwood wrote out a modest cheque for the bedstead, and I did one for the matress with a little left over for the blankets, always supposing that she needed them. Which seemed more than possible. We put them in her handgrip and she was surprised to find them rummaging through later for an apple.

'What's this then?'

'For the bed and the mattress.'

She smiled happily and bit her apple. 'Ta,' she said. She was absolutely adorable, and taught me more about ad-libbing than anyone else in the business; she could ad-lib and overlap endlessly, so I had to learn; self-protection. It was a very happy film although, predictably, we ran out of money halfway through and no one really believed in it except for the people who were actually involved in it. Joseph Janni, our producer, came sadly into my room one evening at the end of work. Face putty, his eyes hooped with fatigue. 'Disaster,' he murmured sitting dejectedly on the arm of a chair. 'I've mortgaged everything; car, flat, stocks and shares, everything except Stella, my wife. Can you help us? Will you accept a cut in salary and defer your deferments?' The reluctant backers sat glumly through the daily rushes; no big American name, an unknown girl and an, almost, unknown director. They also thought the story was, in the good old Wardour Street word, downbeat. Anything that didn't have a happy ending had to be downbeat.

'She's got a face like the back of a bus,' said one of them unhappily at a screening of the first week's work. 'She looks just like a feller! Look at that jaw . . . she could play bloody football.' He swivelled round in his seat, and appealed miserably to Forwood, 'Don't you agree? She's dead ugly.'

'I think she's the nearest thing I've seen to Brigitte Bardot,' said Forwood. The anxious monkey face before us was blank. 'You think she's sexy!'

'Very. She'll be a big, big star.'

The monkey face looked in bewilderment at its partner who removed his cigar and blew a smoke ring into the dead air of the projection theatre.

'You heard what the gentleman said.' He dispersed the ring with a polite cough. 'I must be losing my wits. Sexy? It's all going mad.'

But the news had spread that something remarkable was happening on 'Darling'. David Lean, at that time casting his epic of Pasternak's 'Dr Zhivago' asked to see film on both Julie and myself. Losey allowed me to send a reel of 'King and Country' and Julie got Schlesinger to send a bit of her best work. We waited, naturally curious, to hear the results of our exam. Julie heard that she was hired, on the lawns of Skindles in Maidenhead where we were doing some location work. She was sitting in a tweed suit and pearls, for her role, and reading Karl Marx in paperback. She came from the telephone quietly and serene.

'What happened?'

She opened Karl Marx and smoothed the pages. 'I've got Lara. Rather good. But they want me to get out of this little picture . . . said it wasn't important and that I should get to Madrid as soon as possible and start working on the part; they say,' and she closed her book and slammed it on to the grass, 'I could get an Oscar for it; that I should leave John and all this . . .'

'And so . . .'

'And so what?' Her eyes were filled with tears of outrage. 'I told them stuff Lara or wait.' She pushed a hairpin which had slipped loose back into her bun. 'They'll bloody have to wait. Leave this? Leave John, all this? What kind of a business is this?'

'Not lovely.'

'Did you hear anything?' She was cautious, gentle, knowng anyway.

'No. Nothing.'

In the event she won the Oscar. For 'Darling', the little film, and rocketed to stardom in Hollywood. All she ever got out of 'Zhivago', as far as I know, was a theme song.

Losey and I worked together again on two more films in succession, 'Modesty Blaise' which was nearly a compromise between commercialism and intellect and which, to my mind, but not to his, never quite succeeded, and finally in 1966 the most exhausting, exciting and valuable work we ever did together, Pinter's 'Accident'. A perfectly hand-crafted piece of work from the first shot to the last and quite the most exacting work I had ever had to do on a screen. Once again the part had not been intended for me, but for another actor, and once again by some strange fluke I got the chance; and took it.

The work in those years with Losey gave me the self-respect in my work which I had never dared even hope for and strengthened my somewhat shaky belief that I must never again compromise no matter what the cost. But although my belief had been strengthened all right, it did not mean, sadly, that othr forces far beyond one's control, would not cause it to bend; it is unrealistic to try and make films for a minority audience in a business which is geared above all things towards a mass audience. After we had finished 'Accident', the most difficult and perhaps the most successful of our endeavours together, Losey and I found, regretfully, that the *boucle était bouclée:* we had used ourselves up; there was nothing more for us to say together; weary, drained almost, and to some extent disillusioned, we realised that we must separate for a time and go our own ways; even the Press was finally beginning to hint that our work together was becoming incestuous. We both of us, in our very different ways, knew also, for all our high intentions, that we should eventually be forced to have to bend a little in order to survive, but in the bending, I think we believed that we should be able to bring the same integrity to the commercial-compromises, should they arise, which we had brought to our own high endeavours in the past. I think that we did, as it happened; but the emotional cost was high.

On the last morning of shooting on 'Accident', Arnold brought me my usual egg-and-bacon sandwich for breakfast. He tidied round the room a bit, laid out *The Times* and *The Guardian* and poured me a mug of coffee from his always-steaming coffee pot.

'Sad day today,' he said.

'Yes; sad day.'

'But I've just had some interesting news.'

'Oh.'

'You know Zelda? Zelda Barron?'

'Of course.'

'She's doing Production Secretary on the new Jack Clayton film.'

'So, good for her.'

'Good for us too.'

'What do you mean, Arnold, I'm tired.'

'She read the script last night, says it's a real beauty. "Our Mother's House".'

'And?'

'And there's a smashing part for you in it.'

'Does Jack Clayton know, by an chance?'

'No. Hasn't a clue. Hasn't cast it. We thought you'd be perfect.'

'You and Zelda?'

'Sure, she's going to suggest you at lunch time when she sees Jack. He's lovely.'

'Maybe, but he might have his own ideas, Arnold, he'd have asked me if he'd wanted me.'

'Hasn't thought of you! That's the point. It's our idea.'

'Arnold! For the love of God. You can't go begging parts for me!'

'We've both got to live, Governor, and I've got a kid to think of.'

'Yes, but you can't do this; it might be terribly embarrassing. He may hate the idea, he's probably got someone in mind you two don't know anything about.'

'Hasn't got anyone in mind. Told Zelda. Dead worried. Super part too. Just what you want after all these neurotic blokes. Cockney dad with eight kids. Right up your street. All on location in a house in Croydon; you'll love it.'

He was absolutely right; I did. Clayton was highly amused by this unethical approach, but we talked it over and he seemed to think that Arnold and Zelda might be right.

'Not a very attractive role . . . shifty, seedy, and you have to face a whole gang of kids all on your own, there is no one else in the film, and they are pretty tough, but if you'd like to have a try?'

On my first morning in the gloomy house in Croydon I was in a bit of a funk. Eight pairs of eyes, ranging from five to fourteen, gazed at me solemnly. Not a smile, no welcoming grin even. In the little caravan in the scrubby front garden which I had given to change in there was a jam jar stuffed with privet and some wilting Michaelmas daisies. Under it a note. 'Let's hope you are as good as you're cracked up to be. You'd better be. Sincerely; The Children.'

I loved every second of the film which was one of the happiest I have ever made. The children were fantastic, good actors, kind, funny, devoted and professional. Clayton was a demanding, challenging, exciting director. We were all locked into a make-believe world which I found hard to break away from even at the week-end.

Perhaps we all got too lost in our Croydon existence too isolated, too immune. For although we had all passionately believed and loved what we had set out to make together, no one else did. And the film was a failure. A distinguished failure to be sure, but failure none the less, it doesn't much matter about the adjective used. At the Venice Festival our hopes, reasonably high, were very soon damned by faint praise and light applause. Walking back from the cinema to the hotel the air was sweet, the night soft, the moon riding over a flat, silver Adriatic. And I hoped never to see Venice again. Clayton and I could not ease each other's distress very much. It is hard indeed to laugh off the severing of a limb, and so acute was our sadness that that is what it felt like to us.

Even on the third or fourth glass of champagne we still tasted ashes, surrounded as we were by the noisy, happy audience who had attended our funeral and now seemed intent on turning it into an Irish wake.

Full of brave self-pity it is hardly surprising that I paid scant attention to the people all around me laughing and talking; instead I immersed myself in a deep and useless conversation with Clayton trying to work out, far too late, just where we had all gone wrong; so immersed was I that I quite failed to notice my future standing at the bar watching me. Luchino Visconti.

The chestnut candles, I saw, were almost ready to flower, the leaves below like small spread hands. A ring dove cooed above our heads.

'It hasn't come to that, surely?' I said.

'It surely has, it would appear.' Forwood pushed open the gate and we walked up to the house slowly.

'Television commercials? Finally . . .' I was stiff with alarm.

'There is nothing else, is there?'

'Well, there are some scripts in the office . . .'

'You refused them all.'

'They are all dreadful, that's why.'

'Well, no one has exactly been banging on the door for some time, have they?'

'So why should I go and do a telly commercial . . . there's no panic.'

'No money is a sort of panic, I should have thought.'

'Well I'm buggered if I'm going to go running up and down the Spanish Steps in a pair of sun-glasses just because no one had asked me to do a film for a year.'

'You'll be buggered if you don't.'

'But why? You said the other day that the account was very healthy. You said so clearly.'

'It is. But ninety per cent of what you have goes for tax.'

'And what's left after that?'

'You'll have eight thousand pounds left.'

'I see.'

'Look; I absolutely respect your No Compromise rule, believe me. But you can't afford it any longer, that's the fact of the matter.'

'What shall I do . . .? I'm lost.'

'Go to Rome, do the telly thing, it's a lot of money, and they have agreed never to show it in England, and have a look round. You've been asked to work there often enough; no one wants you here, it seems, there are hardly any Studios left anyway, the Unions have seen to that. Start again; somewhere else.'

I looked hopelessly round the gardens, the wind shaking the apple trees, the Downs hard against the early April sky.

'I can't chuck this all up, the family, England. I can't, it's been too long.'

Forwood stooped down and pulled a long straggly plantain from the path. 'You're right. Far too long. Something's got to give.'

CHAPTER TWELVE

The Hassler hadn't changed in eight years, I can't imagine why I thought that it would; all good hotels, like the Connaught or the Lancaster or the Hassler never change. Everyone gets a little older over the years, they re-lay the carpets from time to time, re-paint a room, but otherwise everything is much as it was. Which is why one returns. Via Sistina still ran away to the left of my window, the Trinita dei Monti rose, crumbling, to the right, a little fig plant growing from a crack in the belfry now almost a sapling, and below flowed the Spanish Steps up and down which I was shortly to run, showing my elegance in sun-glasses, and my lack of pride in everything else I was doing. The only immediate change that I could see now was that instead of a rustling Christmas tree with a glittering star on top, giant azaleas in Tuscan pots tumbled down the wide steps, a splendid cascade of magenta, pink, and white. It was May; no longer cold December although my mood, for want of a better word, was still much as it had been then, strengthened, but still one of bewildered perplexity.

The last time I had stood here I had coveted the dream of making a change in my cinematic existence and was desperate that the changing patterns swirling all around me like marsh gas will o' the wisps would lead me into a smothering bog; I had longed for self-respect in my work. Well; in the eight-years' interval I had fortunately achieved this, but how odd it was that it should lead me back to Rome, where, as someone once pointed out, all roads end (rather than lead), in the cinema of the day, and where I was about to become more commercial than ever before. Advertising sun-glasses for an American company. There was an irony somewhere. But if my dreams had to end where they had begun there seemed no pleasanter place for the quiet finale than this city jumbled below in umber, terracotta, saffron and blazing white; St Peter's still hung serenely in the sky, the jelly mould almond green against the hard, clear blue. Familiar, reassuring; a great deal better than Earl's Court. The Eternal City; only proving my own transience.

I ran up and down the steps twenty or thirty times, inanely smiling, blacked-out by the sun-glasses which successfully concealed my face, mute, since I spoke no word, sweltering in a flannel suit and new shoes which slipped on the polished stone. It didn't take very long, and was less shameful than I had imagined, and when I was back in the cool of the suite, and had changed into a shirt and slacks, Forwood came in and announced that while I had been labouring so too had he; or meddling might be a better phrase, for it had only meant a few well-placed telephone calls about the city to say, casually, that I was there. Not what I was doing, but just that I was, well, about, if anyone cared.

Since the work Losey and I had done together a number of people in the Italian cinema did care, and I had only refused all the offers which temptingly came because I was loth to leave England, frightened to work in a foreign country and, truthfully, distrustful. Also, an important fact, the scripts, or the dialogue to be exact, of practically every subject offered was an appalling

Dirk Bogarde

mixture of Hollywood and literal translation. Hollywood because all the scripts
were translated by Roman refugee Americans, and literal translation because
some bewildered secretary had sat at a desk with a dictionary and laboriously
worked it all out. Since the Italians use a great many words to say anything at
all, or nothing, the scripts were thicker than *Whitaker's Almanack*, and as dense as
Bradshaw. So I had declined.

'There is a new revision of that "Macbeth" thing which you got from
Visconti,' said Forwood, being English in the Roman heat with a pot of tea. 'I
said that you might have time to read it again, if they wished, before you left. I
did not commit you,' he added quickly, seeing my alarm.

'The first script was pretty dreadful. The part was so wet. I'm really not very
interested.'

He slopped the detestable tea-bags into an ash tray. 'Well, just read it . . .
maybe they've made some changes; no skin off your nose if you still say "no".
Where do you want to eat tonight? Passeto?'

It was a much better version as it happened. I almost rather liked it. The part
was still wet; Macbeth is, I have always thought, unless in a Master's hands.
However, this version was clearly based on the Krupp family, and the parallel
was intriguing. So, it had to be faced, was Visconti, even though, at this
moment, he was slightly in the shadows softly cast by Fellini's rising moon. I
agreed that we should meet and discuss the project before again rejecting it out
of hand. It would have been a high-handed thing to do; and I had absolutely no
intention of making another commercial, for no matter what, ever.

I offered to go and see Signor Visconti at his office whenever he so wished. I
should have known better, of course; Signor Visconti did not possess an office
nor would he, it appeared, have been seen dead in one; the message would,
however, be relayed to him, could I repeat my name once again?

Just as I was about to leave for Passeto, hand on the light switch, a telephone
call to say that Signor Visconti was dining in my part of the city and would find
it possible to come to my hotel; would I please expect him within twenty
minutes? And he drank, they assured me confidentially, Johnny Walker Black
Label and soda water. No ice.

He was punctual, taller than I had imagined, immaculately groomed for his
later appointment, steel hair, dark, steady eyes, weary but alert, beautiful
hands which he waved towards his companion, a slight man in grey flannel, *his*
hands primly folded before him, like a cardinal in mufti.

'Signor Notarianni; he will translate.'

He wandered slowly to the windows and looked out. 'Molto bene . . . c'est
charmant . . . calm . . . eh, Notarianni? Molto bello . . .' He took his whisky
and we sat in a sort of semicircle. He raised his glass. 'Cin Cin.' We drank in a
restrained silence.

'You like the new scenario, eh?'

'It is much better than before.'

His falcon's eyes were immediately hooded, he leant back in his chair.

'Once it was enough if I asked an actor to work with me; enough, you know?
To be with Visconti. But now . . .,' he shrugged resignedly, 'now they all
demand a script to read.' He picked up the blue-covered copy and weighed it in
his hand. 'They do not like the part, they do not like the words, they do not like
not anything. They do not know.' He clattered it on to the table as if he had
found it sullied in a lavatory. 'You imagine I will make this . . . merde? Vous
comprenez le mot merde, j'imagine?'

'Oui.'

'Pas très jolie. Not polite. Pas du tout polite. But it is so. I do not shoot that.

Never. Is for the actors to refuse, for the American agents to understand, for the financiers to read and give us money.' He sighed and stared at me solemnly. 'But you think is better this new merde, eh?'

'Much.'

'You think the role of Friedrich is good.'

'No, truthfully no. He is so . . . wet, still.'

The eyebrows raised fractionally. He turned to the Cardinal. 'Non capisco . . .'

'Morbido,' murmured the Cardinal, his eyes on the floral carpet.

'Ah so!' Visconti took a long drink from his glass, and placed it on the table by the blue folder. 'Macbeth, you know this man? He is . . . morbido also? Macbeth is weak, a weak man, is Lady Macbeth who is the strong one. Is true, is not true?'

'True.'

'Ecco! So?' His eyebrows questioned more than his word.

'I have to play so many weak men.'

'Maybe you play them well? "Accident" is weak, the man Stephen, and the Pappa with all the children; Clayton's so beautiful film.'

' "Our Mother's House"?'

'Certo! The Pappa is weak, but is different weakness. You have a big range; "Il Servio" is weak, I am right?'

'Weak-strong . . . yes.'

'Non capisco.'

'Si, said the Cardinal quickly.

Visconti opened his arms wide to the whole of Rome. 'So? Is a problem to be a weak man? I must have a *strong* actor to play a weak man, not a weak actor. I have Lady Macbeth for you . . . molto forte, stupenda . . .'

'Who?'

'Thulin. Ingrid Thulin. You know her work?'

'Yes.'

'You like this work?'

'Yes, very much. Is it sure, Thulin?'

He looked at the Cardinal questioningly. The Cardinal nodded his head slowly. 'Since this morning we have Thulin,' he said.

Visconti raised his glass to his lips. 'Ah! Bene . . . bene. Signatura?'

'Si, si,' assented the Cardinal comfortably. 'Signatura.'

'I asked this Vanessa Redgrave to be my Lady Macbeth . . . but she too did not like the scenario.' He shrugged again, spread his hands as if to count his nails. 'Finally, it is good, I think. Too tall for you. Friedrich would be weak *and* short. Not good.'

'No,' I agreed, 'not good. When do you start to shoot?'

'We will shoot all in English. Very terrible for me, I cannot understand, but we must be international.' His voice heavy with sarcasm. 'And we will work all in Germany . . . very terrible for me, I am Italian you know, in Essen, in Unterach, in all the places where it happened. It will be molto pericoloso.'

'Yes, Signor, but when?'

'When I have found my Friedrich finally. Then.'

'I will be him.'

I heard Forwood clear his throat softly.

Visconti made a little nod in my direction. 'Molto bene,' he said.

Later in Passeto Forwood smiled across the table and laid his fork on his plate.

'You didn't waste much time.'

'No . . . it was instant. The moment he came into that room I knew. I don't know quite what I knew. But I did. He had such power about him. Like an Assyrian bull, a Tartar Prince, something tremendous.'

'He is a Prince.'

'I know that; but it was a feeling of such determination, such assurance, I know he knows what he is doing. It's very . . .' I pushed th salt cellar about the table hunting for the word which I could not find . . . 'very un-domestic, very un-Gerrard's Cross. Do you know what I mean?'

'I do. I don't know if anyone else would.'

'Royal. I suppose.' The salt cellar tumbled and hit my glass. 'A sort of Emperor really.'

'I understand actors very well,' he had said on his third Black Label and soda. 'Actors are surface. I prefer to use people in my work. People who become the personage on the screen. Most actors are surface creatures. Self-absorbed. Is not for me. In opera yes; that is different. You saw Callas in my "Traviata", certo? Ah no? So . . . generally actors are like horses; you know? I was a trainer; you must be very, very careful with them . . . if they are to win for you. When they leave the travelling box some will come down very confidently, head high, eyes wide, very sure . . . others step very timid down, they test the ground, scent the air, ears flat, unsure, nervous, very tense . . . you must take the greatest care of him. He must be controlled, loved, treated very, very gently for he will win the race . . . usually he will win; but you must be aware all the time; a director is like a trainer, ecco . . . actor is like a horse.' He had smiled for the first time suddenly. 'You do not mind to be a horse?'

'Not if it means that you expect me to "become" instead of to act only?'

'I expect you to become Friedrich . . . not put him on like a coat . . . it is too easy . . . not real . . . I think that you become in all the work I see of you . . . which one is the one you think is best? We play a little game now? Which part you feel you had become?'

'Stephen in "Accident".'

'Exact. Certo. Parfait. Why?'

'Because he was absolutely nothing to do with the man I am. I will speak slowly.'

'Please.'

'When we finished, after three months' work, I was dead. Really dead. We stopped shooting by the river at Oxford one afternoon. At three o'clock I was still him, still Stephen; at three-thirty it was over and he had gone. My body and my mind were a vacuum; he had left. I could not return to myself. I drove to my home and I wept like a small boy for the man I had lost. I put all the clothes he wore in a suitcase and locked them away; it took me many weeks to get back to my body. I'm sorry, I bore you.'

He shook his fine great head vigorously, 'Not bore. Not bore. It is correct. Is what I want. So.' He rose and looked at his Cardinal, who had looked at his watch unreproachfully. 'So. We go now . . .' He put out his hand. 'You remember one thing very important. I make the cinema like I make my operas. It is big, how I work, bigger than life . . . it is very hard but it is my way. This film . . .' he waved his hand disdainfully towards the blue-covered script, 'this merde is "Götterdämmerung", that is opera, no? Grand opera, like Germany in 1932. You will go to Essen, you will see the Krupp house, what folie! Quelle horreur! You will see the house in which you lived. You will become. You will be poor, morbido, Friedrich. It will be amusing, no? Ciao, Bogarde.' He had smiled quietly and I saw him to the elevator and in a trance had gone to dinner.

Plans were rapidly altered, and I stayed on in Rome longer than I had intended. Fittings, make-up tests, the deal itself; all this took time. It was May and the film was to commence in early July. Just time enough for me to go back to England and make the arrangements to be away from home until October at least; I would miss the summer, but a summer in Rome would not be untenable, especially since I would be working at something I really wished to do; dragging my heels around Sussex, weeding the shallots, removing tendrils from the sweet peas, bedding out gernaiums, picking mint and playing cheerful host on Sundays had started to lose its pleasure. (Ingrid Bergman, staying at Nore while she was playing in 'A Month in the Country' at Guildford, was constantly amused by my evening walk down to the vegetable gardens to pick the mind for supper. As she set off for her theatre, so I set off for my mint bed. It became, for both of us, a symbol of unemployment . . . a far more agreeable phrase than just out of work and one which we have used together ever since.)

There were many other more exciting and stimulating things to do – like going to the Krupp villa in Essen, as appalling as he had suggested, and meeting Joseph Strick, a devoutly esoteric director, who arrived the day before I was due to leave Rome with a first script of Lawrence Durell's 'Alexandria Quartet' which he persuaded me to do with him, playing the role of Pursewarden. It would start, he said, in November in Tunis; then studio work in Paris, and Anouk Aimée had already agreed to be his Justine.

After so much indifference in England this attention went, slightly, to my head. I had not had a single offer from a British Studio, apart from the job I did with Jack Clayton which Arnold and Zelda had so cunningly contrived for me, since 'Accident' with Losey in 1966. It would appear that I had overstayed my welcome there to some degree, and nineteen years was a long time in which to have stayed anywhere. Too long. I had been exceedingly fortunate; I had had my training and had chosen my path. I was unable to go backwards now; the doors had all shut behind me, but the corridor went on and other doors were flying open in the welcome which was being extended to me now from Abroad. The temptation was much too strong to resist; the alternatives were unattractive, and the British film industry was showing such distressing signs of malaise that it could only be a matter of time before a final diagnosis would prove the malady to be terminal and the only thing that I could possibly be asked to do was to attend at its funeral; a prospect which filled me with the keenest sadness after such a long, fortunate, battling innings.

I had worked as hard as I knew how to help the industry. I had not exactly bled it white, and with Losey, Dearden, Clayton and earlier with Asquith, we had tried to give the audiences a better meal, so to speak. The fact that our audiences now were feeding at the breast of television and could not accept our richer diet was our bad luck. But at least we had tried; nothing wrong with trying until you fail. I was nearly fifty; I had overstayed my time; the only future I could see for me now was Abroad.

'Do you see what I mean?' I must have sounded desperate because Forwood stopped eating and looked up, he cupped his ear with one hand.

'Speak up. When in Rome . . .'

'Do you see what I mean? About leaving . . .'

'Yes. Yes, I do. But just because you have got two films to do in Foreign Parts doesn't seem to constitute a good reason for tearing up your roots and emigrating . . .'

'I think it does, it's not just two films in Foreign Parts either. There's another to follow if I like with Fliano. Resnais has asked me to work for him; Jean Renoir and Truffaut; all abroad. Now Visconti and Strick. It is going to my head; I want to work. I want to work with these directors. Do you realise that the last thing I was asked to do in England was a half-hour narration for the Forestry Commission?'

Forwood poured another glass of Valpolicella. 'Point taken,' he said.

A day or two later we drove home through a deceptively calm France; for just below the surface of this smiling May lay the possbility of a civil war. The Students were marching, barricades going up, shops closing, and the streets of almost every major city seemed strangely deserted and dead. A long, hot Sunday. In Paris there was a silence which was almost tangible. Little traffic, few people, the sound of pigeons' wings and hurrying feet along almost empty boulevards. A breath held; Alain Resnais sitting at a small table at the Café du Rond Point, almost entirely alone, waiting for me. We had made the arrangement to meet some days before to discuss the possibility of a film which he wanted to make, and which we had been trying to get financed by an American company for months, 'The Adventures of Harry Dickson'. Now the finance had come through finally; but Alain, staring at his coffee, felt that the steam, as he put it, had gone out of his ambition. He had had to wait too long, make too many idiotic compromises for our future bosses, so that, now the money was available, he felt that he could no longer face the challenge.

'I will not compromise to the extent which they demand. No. I cannot do it now . . . it is finished you understand?' I did, of course, but was sad. It would have followed 'Justine' and was a part which I longed to play above all others especially since Resnais, as he said, had written it for me.

'I have here a letter for Vanessa Redgrave, she has been so kind and patient to wait, will you give it to her in London, we have no post now with the events of these weeks. I think she will understand too. Explain to her for me.'

I took the letter, declined his offer to cross the river and come, as he said, 'to see history being made; the Students are fighting for their existence two kilometres from here.' I left him standing on the pavement, tall, slightly stooped, a shabby raincoat, his red scarf, an airline holdall slung over his shoulder, the legend peeling: BOAC. He waved slightly as the car moved out into the thin traffic. He looked infinitely sad; infinitely worried. I put the letter for Vanessa Redgrave in my passport and we headed for calais. And managed to catch the last ferry across the Channel before the strikes finally closed France.

Driving up through Ashford Forwood said that perhaps, with things as they were now in France, I had better think again about moving there to live. We agreed that since I would be working almost immediately, and for a lengthy time, in Italy, it would be wiser to rent a house outside Rome, and see how it went. But first of all, and irrevocably, I would go ahead and put the English house on the market while I was away. I'd tell no one, apart from my parents, and perhaps the staff, Antonia and Eduardo who had taken over from the much-loved Hans and Agnes, and who, for their own futures must be admitted into he plans, for they would, I hoped, come with me when I left for Italy. I had about five weeks to go before Visconti would need me; there would be a great deal to do.

There is an army saying that the camp tailor knows more about troop movements than the Chiefs of Staff; and sooner. The same thing applies to theatrical costumiers. From them, after standing mutely for five days, amidst a welter of half-finishes suits and coats, being pinned and chalked and offered endless cups of lethal espresso's in Tirelli's in Rome, I was informed that Visconti, whom I had not met since the one evening long ago, it seemed, at the

Hassler when I agreed to this enterprise, now wished my physical body presented to him, for one single shot, by ten o'clock tomorrow morning. Since it was already three-thirty in the afternoon I was in some degree of panic.

'But where are they?'

'Salzburg. Very pretty.'

'How do I get there?'

'We have the plane tickets; Düsseldorf and you change for Munich then a car . . .'

'But I was told not for three weeks.'

'Changed his mind; tomorrow ten o'clock.'

'I have nothing to wear; no costume is ready.' I threw a despairing hand about the cluttered, stuffy room, hung about with half-finished hacking jackets, coats and evening clothes.

'Ah si, si . . . all you will need is raincoat. And here he is; is only a big shot. Just your head. All is ready. Tirelli is always ready. Never later.'

But I sure as hell was going to be late for my first day's work with Visconti. Something I felt absolutely sure he would not tolerate. How could I get myself on and off planes to bloody Salzburg; I had never moved a step unaccompanied either by Theo Cowan or Forwood ever since I had waltzed into this monstrous business. I was not about to do it now.

We drove. Packing two suitcases in the space of fifteen minutes, we left the Hassler holding all the rest of the stuff, and headed for Salzburg. It was a fiendish drive through the night with a four-hour stop-over in Trento, and a dawn start the next day. One hour late, that is to say at eleven o'clock in the morning, we drew up, dusty, exhausted, anxious and hot, at the door of the elegant hotel which was Visconti's headquarters. The manager was extremely polite; certainly this was the right place, and Signor Visconti was staying there; I could not possibly be late, he added in a hushed voice, since Signor Visconti was still asleep and would not be awake until at least four in the afternoon. He had attended the first night of Von Karajan's 'Don Giovanni' the night before, and had also worked very hard at the film. There was no cause for me to be distressed by my lateness, since no one would work today because it was a rest day. He suggested that I might like to see my room, regretfully in the annex, because the place was completely full on account of the Festival, and that my chauffeur was accommodated in a small room in a pension up the hill.

White with exhaustion and anger I went to see my annex room. A small place under the eaves, overlooking the garage-wash area. The manager shrugged his shoulders sadly and said he regretted the situation, but for one night only . . . One night! At this rate how many nights would there be? Who was in charge, what had gone wrong, why had I been dragged through the night for absolutely no good reason? I was seething with anger, and shaking with fear. My first work in a strange country . . . not a good indication of things to come.

The day passed slowly. Salzburg is just another city when all is said and done, and apart from an exhibition of Egon Schiele there was nothing much to see. Or that I, in my present mood, cared to see. By the time I had returned to the hotel Visconti had, like Box or Cox, left for some unknown destination. He would not be returning for dinner. There was no note, no explanation, no form of contact. I might just as well have still been in Rome; probably he thought that I was. We walked, Forwood and I, forlornly up the hill behind the too-elegant hotel, found a small bar with high wooden settles, a juke-box and a pretty waitress in a swirling dirndl who brought beer, wine, and piled plates of wurst and röesti. Life seemed a little more tolerable. Until the next day when the same procedure took place. Signor Visconti was asleep, and would be until four in the afternoon;

he could not be disturbed.

'This is very curious behaviour,' I said. 'Perhaps he doesn't know I am here?'

'He must do . . . he must have seen the car outside . . . the management have told him . . . he's just being an Emperor; is that what you called him?'

'Well, if he makes no sign this evening by six, or whenever he gets up, I'm off; we leave for Rome and pack the whole business in. I don't mind forgetfulness so much but I won't tolerate sheer bloody rudeness.'

At precisely six that evening I went down to the bar; no sign of life, but a scattering of laughter from the garden beyond. I stepped out on to a gravel path and walked, rather self-consciously, towards a collection of elegant cages clustered around the trunk of a giant lime. there were golden pheasant, quail, a toucan; casually I looked through the wires across the lawns towards the terrace. Sitting around a large table in the evening sun, Visconti and his court; the Cardinal from the evening at the Hassler, five or six others listening to him, agreeing, clapping politely at some gentle joke, laughing, sipping cool drinks from long glasses, relaxed, casual, quite unaware that I was hovering furiously behind two blue macaws in the aviary.

'I'll give it another five minutes,' I murmured to one, who clambered inquiringly down the wire to the piece of twig I offered. 'Five minutes, and if nothing happens straight back to Rome and England.'

But there was a slight pause suddenly in the laughter at court. Someone looked across to the aviary, a bending of heads, and just as I was about to leave and cross the lawn towards the annex the Cardinal came loping worriedly across, hand outstretched, the other buttoning nervously his immaculate jacket.

'Ah! Buona sera . . .' Saved by the bell.

They made room at the table, and drinks were ordered, but no explanation was offered beyond the fact that they had done some good work already, and that tomorrow I would do one single shot and then be free.

'Is very simple,' said Visconti. 'Just a close-up. You see your brother-in-law in bed with a boy, you are shocked, you shoot him, poum! poum! then you close the door. Is all. Then to Rome again; very simple, eh? A good beginning for you.'

I was still angry and I confess bewildered, but remained exceedingly British and cool, and when he invited us to join them all at dinner in Salzburg I declined, politely, and said that I preferred to eat up the hill. He looked curious. 'Up the hill? There is up the hill here, restarant?'

'No, a little trattoria; very small, very ordinary, quite simple.' We said goodnight and walked thoughtfully back to the annex.

There was a wedding party in the little bar up the hill, the bride red-faced and shy in white, swigging down pints of beer, the bridegroom tightly stuffed into a blue suit, a massive crimson carnation matching his complexion. Children ran about the room in wrinkled socks, laughing and rolling beer mats, bouncing balloons; someone sang a rousing song to an accordion, the waitress hurried through the throng balancing steins of beer and plates of sausage. It was warm, relaxed, noisy and cheerful; through the smoke and clattering children I suddenly saw one of the faces from Visconti's table, as he saw me. He came directly to the table, elegant in grey silk, politely he stood to attention.

'Herr Bogarde, Herr Visconti sends me to ask if there is room at your table perhaps?'

'Of course . . . plenty . . .'

'He will be here directly.' The elegant young man clicked his heels and left. Two minutes later (he had clearly been outside in the car), Visconti entered with the court. Dressed in dinner jackets and with extreme elegance and care they made an impressive picture. The waitress hustled extra chairs about the table, threw plates down and hurried off to the kitchens. A child nearby burst a red balloon. Visconti removed his jacket and sat down beside me in his braces. He was grinning happily.

'I like,' he said, indicating the wedding and the blasting accordion. 'You like too?'

I nodded. He patted my shoulder comfortably and, taking up my glass, finished my wine.

Unterach was dressed all over in scarlet, black and white. Banners and swastikas fluttered all about the cuckoo-clock village on the placid lake, the streets were thronged with laughing, jolly, blond young men, clumping over the cobbles in their jackboots, brown shirts and breeches; belts and holsters sparkling in the sun. Girls in dirndls and modest blouses, hung on their arms, singing and smiling at the memory of a time they never knew, and the elders happily held their babies up to clutch the sailing banners and have their photographs taken by fat lederhosened fathers. A spirit of festivity was everywhere, and the villagers were enjoying it all; they were making a lot of money out of the Italian film company, and reliving a past of which they now remembered they were very proud. No one was in the least distressed, except for one unhappy tourist driving throuh in his Ford Taunus on the way to somewhere else, who, trapped in recreated history, had a minor heart attack and was carted waxen-faced to the nearest clinic; this evinced much laughter since he was Jewish, but he shortly recovered and, I was informed with much laughter by a jolly lady in the pharmacy, fled back to Zurich. I detested the smiling little village.

I did my first shot for Visconti at the end of the morning. They were in a hurry to get out of the small hotel in which they had been working for some weeks . . . and I was hustled, in my raincoat, to the door of the bedroom in which they were shooting.

'All you must do,' said Visconti quietly, 'is open the door; you see the wicked Konstantin in the bed with a boy. Orribile! Orribile! You fire. Paum! Paum! Paum!, make a little look retreat, close the door. Is very easy . . . capisci?'

On his cry of 'Actione!' I threw open the door, stared at Konstantin and his lover, suggested by a large apple crate with an X chalked on it . . . did my shooting and the look, and left. There was a silence. The door opened. Visconti stood there, cigarette in hand, one finger rubbing his chin. 'You do again, this time you are smiling? Capisci?'

I repeated the process. Smiling . . . I did it Nervously, Ruthlessly, Sardonically, Coldly, and eventually with tears streaming down my face with Regret and Grief. Or whatever he had demanded in his low voice. I opened the door and shot Konstantin and his chalk-mark lover, six very different times, all within twelve minutes. The tears had taken a few moments to prepare. Visconti printed all six and strode off to his lunch at the hotel in the square. He said nothing. OK. So now I was through and could return to Rome. Albino Coca, his right-hand man, and chief assistant, caught me up crossing the cobbled streets, threading our way between the laughing Nazi children. He put his arm round my shoulder like an old friend.

'Six prints. Is amazing for Visconti . . . usually only one or two perhaps . . . but six, and all different, he prints all! Amazing. He like what you do. I know, I work always with him. He is very surprised, I can tell. Very good.' He squeezed my arm tightly, smiling.

'He didn't look very pleased; is that normal?'

'Ah si, si . . . he says nothing. Not ever; but I can tell.'

'Well, bully for you.'

'Scusi?'

'I suppose it's his way; what do I call him on the set? Visconti? Sir? Signor?'

Albino thought for a moment. 'You must call him Visconti, for sure; not Sir, is very military, I think, eh? Fascisti?'

'I always call my directors Sir. It is simpler and quicker.'

'Not Visconti . . . but never, never, never call him Luchino. That is very private name. Personal. No one calls him that on the film, ever. Remember.'

The hotel was full, the restaurant, on a terrace over the lake like a ballroom. I found a small table with dirty plates and an empty wine glass. Suddenly, as I was about to sit, the Cardinal appeared at my side, smiling deferentially, hands clasped: 'Please! To come . . .' I followed him through the tables to where Visconti sat in splendour round a white cloth sipping his wine and eating from a plate of beetroot salad. He motioned me to sit beside him, smiled at Forwood and indicated another place. He beamed genially about him.

'Some wine? The house wine is delicate . . . not too heavy. You like trout, Forellen blau? Some Kartoffel Salat? Molto bene.'

I shook my head. 'No, Visconti, no . . . some wine . . . not food yet.'

He raised his hand in mock surprise, laying it gently on my own. 'My God! So formal! Visconti! La la la . . . Luchino! Everyone calls me that! Capisci?'

I didn't return to Rome. Preferring to stay and watch him working, to see how he did it, and what he demanded. It was all very quiet, hardly a word was ever spoken. He never moved from his chair; instructions were given in a soft voice to Albino and relayed to the players or to the large crowd. It was an absorbing experience, and I stayed at his side, daily, sitting in a canvas chair, for the next three weeks. We hardly spoke, there was never any need to, he knew what I was doing and instinctively knew why; he was serene and happy, and together we developed what can only be described as, for want of a better phrase, a form of mental shorthand or even telepathy. I was the pupil. He became my Plato or my Socrates . . . although he would have scorned me had I told him.

However; all was not well elsewhere. By the end of the three weeks working on the Night of the Long Knives and sundry other pieces, we had spent all the money available. The German Finance had been suddenly withdrawn without warning because they considered that we were making an anti-German film. The locals grew tired of our presence, had fearsome battles with the Italian crew, whom they considered to have let them down as allies in the war, and put up the prices for everything from a glass of Coca Cola to a reel of thread. The battles were physical. The laughing Brown Shirts beat the living daylights out of the tight-shirted, and too-tight-trousered Italians, trapping them at nights, after dark, in small bars or walking through the bannered streets. At Visconti's suggestion the Italians bought up all the cheap tourist rings in the local jewellers shops, crammed them on to every available finger of each hand and thus armed with knuckledusters gave as good as they had got; and more.

We left the ugly little smiling village and headed to the next set-piece in Düsseldorf. Here we were locked in our hotels, the equipment and the film impounded, until the bills had been settled, and all cables to Rome were unanswered. The film was on and off again constantly. We sat about in dejected heaps with our luggage packed and the feeling that we were a broke variety troupe whose agents had abandoned them. The Cardinal flew about trying to find money, and Visconti, after rising late, lunched daily in regal splendour since he was paying out of his own pocket, as indeed, was I. Eventually some money came, we did the work needed and thankfully headed back to Italy.

The main set at the studio in Cinecitta was the ground and second floor of the Krupps' villa at Essen, the Villa Hügel. Complete. All of it. In all the years that I had worked in the cinema I had never seen a set like it. The great main hall, rooms leading off, Music Room, Drawing Room, Library, a great gallery with an immense staircase, and off that too, more and more rooms, all furnished, crammed with flowers, real fireplaces in which blazed real logs, and antique furniture of great worth and beauty. Tapestries, as well as faux Titians and Rubens, covered every spare inch of space, and every detail, from pencils and magnifying glasses in the vast library, to family photographs in silver frames and a half-finished piece of needlework lying, as if hurriedly put aside, in a huge armchair in the small Study, were in place. The flowers, fresh twice a day because the heat of the lamps caused them to wilt, were dozens and doznes of white lilies and deep crimson roses. 'Gladioli are bourgeois flowers . . . for yachts in St Tropez . . . remove them. And no mixed flowers, it is vulgar to mix flowers, and the Krupps would know that; they were tinkers originally, but they had great pretentions towards "comme il faut". We do not make mistakes.'

Standing in awe in the midst of my villa, I realised immediately why we had gone broke. It must have cost thousands and thousands. It had. And more was to come. The entire place was carpeted, wall to wall, up and down stairs, in dark brown. Visconti, on the first morning of his inspection, with not one single cent left in the bank and some of the film still impounded at the airport in Düsseldorf for non-payment of bills, tapped his foot gently on the acres of carpet, shook his head gently, and said, 'No'. In appalled horror his designers and assistants and production staff, trailing behind him as if he was indeed an Emperor, implored him to explain. It was very simple. There was a *muffled* sound through the villa . . . no sound of feet clacking onpolished wood, no sense of urgency would be heard, hurrying feet, running feet, frightened feet, stealthy feet. It was ruin to the atmosphere, it must be relaid, immediately with wood: parquet flooring, polished, shining, cold. The floor must play the music of fear.

It did. It took six men five days to rip up and relay, in oak and beech wood blocks, the two floors and staircase of the house. And Visconti was right. Now the house rang with a clear, cold steel sound. Of course. It caused a tremendous scandal in Rome; and everyone prophesied ruin for the film. They were nearly right. With the cost of the floors and the cost of the flowers and costumes alone, Losey and I could have made 'King and Country' twice. But this was Visconti. The attention which he paid to the smallest detail was incredible. Always I had been brought up in the cinema to believe that they would never see it. They being the much maligned audience. This was the direct opposite of Visconti's theory which was that they would all see it, feel it, smell it; and they were not to be cheated. Fires were fires, and burned from real logs. The meals we ate at the dinner scene, which went on for three solid weeks in sweltering heat in the studios which were not air-conditioned, were cooked and brought in by Alfredo's in Rome. Wood was wood, never plaster, and wood was wood indeed. Silk was also silk. I had leaned texture from Losey; but this was really texture, and if Visconti's excesses sometimes seemed self-indulgent he never, at any time, excused them. Save by example. The old man I must kill with my small revolver lay propped up in his vast walnut bed. The room softly lit, the sheets and pillows, vast and of the finest silk, he lay white and ashen, his veins green as malachite, raised across hands and arms, like tributaries of the Amazon. A dinosaur for dying. Visconti took up a pint plastic bottle of real blood (bought from a local Accident Clinic) and with careful aim sprayed the venerable corpse, his silken sheets, his pillows, his nightgown of finest lawn, the bed even, walls and carpets. It was a cavern of blood.

'Visconti! It is too much surely? Excessive?'

He looked at me from beneath his craggy brows, alefully, as if I had questioned his pedigree. With a swift movement he threw the plastic squeezy-bottle into my astonished grasp.

'You are English, Bogarde? You must know your heritage . . . Shakespeare? You know your text to "Macbeth" . . . you remember, "who would have thought the old man to have had so much blood in him?", is a line from "Macbeth"? I am correct? Not excessive, Elizabethan perhaps. I tell you, I make opera in the cinema. Macbeth is opera, this death is opera. Ecco, capisci, Bogarde?'

But on occasion this desire for texture took up a great deal of time; and that, coupled with the on and off situation, grabbing money in small parcels whenever possible to pay for the excesses like the dozens of roses and lilies, the exact beautiful Art Deco jars to hold them, and his alarming rages if they were not immediately available, put the shooting time of the film in a frightful mess. My looming commitment to Mr Strick in Tunis bothered no one but myself; Visconti was, I feel sure, convinced that when the moment came for me to pack up on his opera and fly to 'Justine' I would refuse, and stay on in Rome ignoring my future assignment. It was a repeat of 'The Lonely Stage' situation, and I grew increasingly nervous as each day's delay continued either in a search of ready cash or else of a particular object with which to decorate a scene. I would arrive at Cinecitta every morning at seven-thirty in the hopes that work would proceed. Very often it did not. Sometimes there was no Visconti to be seen, and no one dared to telephone him to ask why. So I was often handed the instrument, after someone in the office had bravely dialled the number of his country house at Castelgondolfo, and asked to find out why.

'No one has paid me one single lira for two weeks. I do not work. Where are you?'

'At the Studio.'

'Come to the house, is better here by the pool, Rampling is here too, she has not been paid. We do not work today.'

I would then relay the news to the worried crew members and go to Castlegondolfo where Charlotte Rampling and one or two others of the cast not immediately woking nor yet paid would be sitting in rather hopeless heaps round the pool. Visconti would be happily working away at something in his study. Charlotte, whose big break this was – Visconti had chosen her for his film because 'she has the beautiful eyes of tragedy . . . she can be one day a big, big star . . . it is her decision, not mine: mine to have her, but hers to take the chance', – was naturally depressed. No work, no money, and what, we all wondered, would happen if the film was, like so many before it, quite suddenly abandoned? It was a possibility which seemed to go with the kind of pictures I had elected to make. A haunting.

'Luchino, you know I have to leave for Tunis in a few days?'

'Tunis! What for Tunis?'

'For another film. "Justine".'

'Non possible. We do not finish this yet! How to Tunis and this not finished?'

'I'll have to leave you and come back after I finish "Justine".'

'When you finish, you think?'

'After Christmas.'

'Ayee! Is now October! What do I do, Bogarde . . . you leave? We have one big, big scena, in the steel works, is essential, is not possible to go.'

But go I had to. He was very philosophical in the end. He would have to shoot what he could of the film which remained without me, and then settle down until I could be released from Mr Strick. So be it. He would wait.

'But we must have a little party before you go. You must show your respects to the troupe, is very important. Some beer, some sandwiches, I will arrange. Very simple.'

The night of the farewell party, my beer and sandwich 'thank you' to the troupe, I arrived at the studio canteen at the appointed hour to find it dark, chairs stacked, a cool wind whipping through the pines in the shaggy gardens. A night watchman said that the party was being held on the set of the villa. Visconti had staged my party for me. Lights blazed from every corner of the immense set, fires crackled, a bar ran the length of one room, and the entire cast and crew was present, dressed in their best frocks and suits, all laughing and applauding as I walked, bewildered, to the high-backed chair in the centre of the great hall where Visconti sat smiling brightly and offered me a brimming glass of champagne.

'Is such a 'orribile place, the studio canteen, no? And we have this, all this, free; and the party is so big, everyone had come to honour you.' He meant himself, but no matter. I accepted the wine and the compliment intended. 'It is Krug, non-vintage,' he said, looking at my worried face. 'Beer is not right for this kind of parting.'

It was a night of great happiness and also great sadness. I hated the idea of leaving them all tomorrow; we had fought such a tremendous battle together, from Unterach onwards, that I wanted to be there to the end. However, that was not possible; I would have to put 'Götterdämmerung', for myself at least, into cold storage. At eleven-thirty, an enormous cake arrived in the shape of the dreadful, ornate villa, and amidst cries of delight and much applause I was presented with a cigarette case inscribed by every member of the unit. The gesture brought me to the edge of tears, it was so entirely unexpected, and Visconti, in his great chair, nodded smiling and demanded a little speech which I made, appallingly, in ractured Italian, with a very full heart.

It had been a splendid party, we all agreed. All that remained for me to do was to pick up the bill. Which rocked me gently when it arrived the next morning at the Hassler just before I left for Tunis. It had all been most tactfully done, Visconti had smiled only, waved a vague hand and called, 'Ciao, Bogarde' as we parted, and I was left to walk alone through the night, under the sighing parasol pines to my car. He knew how to handle his horses.

Arnold was at the airport at Tunis to meet me. The sun sparkled on the blinding white city, on the dusty roads, on the walls of livid bougainvillaea. Rome was only forty-five minutes away by air, but already lost to me.

We settled into the car for the journey to the hotel on the beach where I would stay during the location. Arnold was full of news, but first of all, after a separation of some months, wanted mine.

'How's the family, Dad? Your Mum?'

'Oh fine . . . how's June? And your boy?'

'Great . . . he's almost talking. Visconti all right?'

'The greatest ever. I miss him.'

Arnold stared out of the window at some passing camels. 'You will, gov, you will. It is all a bit of a cock up here.'

'Oh God! Not another?'

'This is the revised script.' He handed me a fat package. 'And there is one other thing which will make you happy, I hate to tell you, but we have to go to Hollywood for the studio work. Not Paris.'

'What!'

'Changed their minds. L.A. now.'

'I can't go to Hollywood! I haven't finished the Visconti thing . . . there is a week's work left to do.'

'You'll have to fly back from lovely L.A., that's all.'

In the dusty road a small boy thrashed a plodding donkey.

'What about Mr Strick, is he all right?'

Arnold lit a cigarette and blew smoke steadily ahead of him. 'He's a nice man. A bit lost: they've only been working a week. It's early days. You know; it's a funny thing, do you know the aggregate age of the camera crew is three hundred?'

'The aggregate what?'

'The age. Is about three hundred and I'm not kidding. Everyone is into sixty knocking seventy . . . maybe more even. Goldie, now he's really nice, told me he already bought a double-plot at Forest Lawn. Cost him a bomb. It's on a hillside, see? No seepage. You pay more to stay dry. The Sound Mixer can't get around too well so they push him and his equipment about on a cart.' He spun the spent match through the open window. 'Trouble is they made the thing too wide for the doors, so he had to stay outside the Sets mostly and can't get to see the action. It's all a bit weird. Most of them did their first Movies with Constance Talmadge and the Gish Sisters. You're in for a few surprises, Gov.'

'I have already had a few.'

He laughed nervously: 'Oh well . . . that's Show Business.'

Hollywood has always been praised for its extraordinary efficiency. A German inheritance? It does not work, alas, outside the city itself. We were a lost rabble. Nothing was just exactly what it should be. Except for Mr Strick who was calm, apparently genial, and enthusiastic even though little of Mr Durrell remained in the revised-from-Hollywood script. Anouk Aimée was wan and sad for most of the time, since she had suddenly realised, too late, that her decision to accept 'Justine' had most probably been, for one reason or another, a serious error of judgement on her part, and was now feeling abandoned and lonely; she had brought her two cats with her from Paris to keep her company and fed them on fillet steak which angered the waiters in the hotel who had to make do with chick-peas. Everyone got some form of Tunis stomach; the company flew in Jumbo loads of American Press weekly, whom we had to entertain and deal with socially in the 'fabled city of Tunis' while they watched, with some degree of boredness, and eye irritation from the constantly blowing dust, the shooting of this 'great saga of literature'; and I shortly discovered that none of my costumes fitted nor were right for the seedy character of Pursewarden with which I was trying, against all these odds, to come to terms. I was swamped by the gravest misgivings.

After four incredible, unorganised, miserable weeks we were flown off to lovely Los Angeles just in time for Christmas, and a total overhaul. That is to say, Mr Strick was replaced by George Cukor, the four weeks' work in Tunis was all scrapped, and everything started from scratch again. Cukor, once again stepping into the breach, employed three Literature students from nearby U.C.L.A. to sift through all four books which comprised Mr Durrell's masterpiece, and had restored, to what characters remained, some of the original dialogue, so that at least one felt one was speaking the writer's written word; it gave a little courage in a sagging epic. Cukor, as ever filled with boundless enthusiasm, struggled and fought and began wresting shape into the soggy mass. But the Studio, now alerted to the early disaster in Tunis too late, sliced the budget and applied the brakes; we were also constantly trapped by the idiotic rules of Old Hollywood. Forbidden, because of the Decency Laws or something, to use real children in the Children's Brothel, we were forced to employ elderly dwarfs instead, swathed in veils or strategically placed back to camera. Most of the sets looked like the Coffee Shop in the Tunis Hilton; everything was clean and neat; and even wretched Michael York was forced to wear a flesh-coloured pair of briefs for his seduction scene on a beach, and striped flannel pyjamas when he was in bed. Hollywood's decadent, fabled Alexandria had all the mystery, allure and sin of Derry and Toms' roof garden.

None of this was Mr Cukor's fault, perhaps the most cultured and erudite of all Hollywood directors. It was the Studio system to which he was, of necessity, bound. He had generously taken over an established production and just had to make do with what he found, and although he found some pretty rum things he made do marvellously, although he constantly longed to return to Durrell's books and remove the whole benighted effort out to Alexandria itself and shoot it all there. However, this was not to be; we struggled on under his blazing enthusiasm, his infectious love of the cinema, his boundless energy and quite extraordinary capacity for teaching. He wanted one to learn, and by Heaven, one learned. He swept us all along on a glorious wave of mounting excitement and determination, it was really very much like working with Visconti. The same dogged battles for perfection as far as it could possibly be achieved. And sometimes he was fighting against immense odds, and the perfection which he sought became ever harder to accomplish. There were some incredibly awful bits of original casting which he was powerless to change, and half his vibrant energies were spent in bullying, cajoling, pleading and encouraging perform- ances of one kind and another out of these wooden, self-indulgent method actors. However, in spite of these harrowing vicissitudes, he fought bravely on, with the enthusiastic assistance of the splendid Philippe Noiret and Anna Karina, and we took every opportunity which he offered, and he was prodigal, to profit from his experience and knowledge.

'How nice it would be,' he once said ruefully, 'if some time, somewhere, you and I could do a whole picture together right from the beginning!' It was a compliment to cherish, but, alas! we were never able to manage it. And so we worked on into a wet, fog-shrouded, December.

But Christmas was coming, and after it I would be that much nearer to my return to Italy. Visconti sent constant sad little notes asking me when I thought I could come, and reminding me sternly that he had an Opera, a real one, to stage in Milan and that nothing should come in the way of it . . . please would I ask Hollywood and Mr Cukor, whom he much admired, to hurry a little?'

No one wanted to hurry away more than I did. It was a forlorn Christmas when it finally came, spent in pouring rain; the plastic Christmas trees dripped and sagged along every street, absurd and vulgar among the palms, and 'Jingle Bells' blared from speakers at every corner. Down on Wilshire Boulevard there was a small cage of reindeer, rhinestone in their antlers, coats dyed pink and hoofs gilded. They stood huddled in the rain in mute subjection while the pink puddled round their shabby golden hoofs, and the rhinestones scaled off like shining scabs.

'Happy Yuletide,' cried my chauffeur as he dropped me at the hotel on Christmas Eve. 'I don't wish you a Happy Christmas on account of this is a Jewish Town and they don't care for the connotation; so it's Yuletide; saves a lot of feelings; we don't have Christmas here.'

In the bungalow, set amidst sodden palms and the squelching lawns of the hotel garden, a log fire crackled in the sitting room, a handful of cards cluttered the mantelshelf. Robins, a Mickey Mouse with plastic eyes, Tower Bridge in a blizzard. Arnold came in with presents and we had a beef stew for supper, cooked in the kitchenette, with a couple of bottles of Nappa Valley Beaujolais and watched the first men round the moon trying, agonizingly, to fire their motors and break away from its orbit. Which they did eventually; as they came round from the far side of the moon a low, and relieved, voice was heard to say, 'Let it be known that Santa Claus does exist!' which put all the idiocy and vulgarity of Hollywood firmly into perspective.

It was still raining the next morning when we drove down to Noël and Sarah Harrison's house to deliver presents to their horde of children. They lived in a kind of mini ranch house up a dank, shadowy canyon, feet deep in thick brown mud, with two horses steaming miserably behind a split-rail fence, and flickering fairy lights looped mournfully round the dripping porch. Sarah was lying full length on a settee, covered in a rug, wearing green velvet and a long fox stole. She also had Hong Kong 'flu and a very high temperature; the children ripped packages apart and hit each other, and Noël, dressed for Katmandu and clinking and clonking with chains and lumps of Tibetan jade, opened gallon jars of Californian wine which he poured into hand-blown glass goblets capable of holding, at least, three goldfish apiece. Firelight gleamed on the knotty-pine walls, the beaming children's faces and the exhausted, fevered one, of their pretty mother who coughed and streamed apologetically into a steadily mounting pile of paper handkerchiefs and her black fox stole. But the Christmas Spirit, helped enormously by the gallon jars, prevailed and reached a splendid peak with the arrival of Lionel Bart dressed in early Carnaby Street and cowboy boots with a car load of Pretty People all bearing gifts and contagious good humour. We left, in the gathering afternoon, to the beat of 'Lucy in the Sky with Diamonds' at full blast; the horses, up to their withers in mud, hung despondent heads over the split-rail fence in the still-teaming rain.

There was a party that evening at George Cukor's elegant house high up a hillside road. It was set in a walled garden, lofty columns, ivy, white marble figures shadowy in the heavy mist, ilex and magnolia. Inside, polished wood and shining silver, a great bowl of punch, the scent of pot-pourri and beeswax, flowers in profusion, books, paintings, elderly smiling maids in black, neat white aprons crackling, deep old chairs and gentle, amusing conversation. Proudly he showed us all a gift he had received, a kind of bird made out of pine-cones and nuts, which we all dutifully admired, since the donor was present, wondering privately what on earth he would do with it in a house so clearly unsuited to its rustic quaintness. One of his dogs, however, settled its future neatly, by eating it entirely, half an hour later, thus saving Mr Cukor a good deal of anxiety.

Driving back through the wet night I was happy that I had spent such a day with good friends in their own homes, it had given me a feeling of security and strength which I had needed, for much earlier, before setting off for the Harrisons, I had learned that I no longer had a home. The house in England had been sold. I had telephoned my father in traditional Sussex quite early that morning.

'Merry Christmas! I suppose you are only just starting over there aren't you? We're nearly over it here. Mother's just putting a little capon in the over for supper.'

'Just starting here. It's raining and cold.'

'Never! But good about the moon-business, wasn't it? Extraordinary!'

'Yes, marvellous. All well with you? Any news from the house?'

'We're quite fit, thanks. Antonia and Eduardo are very well, and all the dogs and things . . . no messages this week . . . Judy Garland called a couple of times, she said she couldn't reach you in Rome and didn't know where you were . . . by the way there is one thing; you remember the people I told you about who liked the house last week? Well, they want it. No conditions; accept the price and want possession as soon as possible. Mid-February too early for you?'

'I don't know. I still have to finish here, then go back to Italy to finish that. It might fit. Is it definite do you think?'

'Absolutely. I think they've signed their contracts and so on. They know they'll have to wait a little for you to pack up. Otherwise . . .'

'Well, look; I'll call you from Rome as soon as I get there in a week or two, but say mid-February should be all right definitely. Mother well?'

'Fine. A bit of a cold, just sniffles really, it's the weather here. So I'm to say mid-February for certain, right?'

'Yes. I'll need a week to pack the place up, you see.'

How odd, I had thought, to pack up England. In a week.

'Funny feeling; not having a home any more.' I was looking for spoons and knives. Forwood was boiling eggs in the kitchenette for Christmas Dinner.

'It's what you wanted.'

'Yes, I know . . . but now . . . feels odd. Possession mid-February. Rather soon.'

I started to lay the table with the hotel cutlery; Arnold was coming in to eat with us; they don't have egg cups in America so we were using tea cups; it all seemed a bit upside down, like the rest of the hideous place. The salt was damp, the bread wrapped, the white-plastic-frosted tree with all its scarlet ribbons stood dejectedly in the corner where the delivery-boy had left it two days before. It bore a label which said, in florist's writing, 'Hi there! Happy Yuletide. Have Yourself fun!' We didn't know who had sent it; probably no one.

'Do you think we could make February . . . all the packing; removal vans?'

'Don't know. You want two eggs or one?'

'One. I'll have a bit of cheese.'

'You'll have to get your arse up from here pretty quickly,' he said.

Fifteen mornings later we landed, ashen with jet lag, stale air, the in-flight movie and hours of taped Victor Sylvester, at Rome. The Cardinal was there to greet me, freezing in the bitter wind, huddled in a fur coat, neat little gloved hands clasped in eternal prayer.

'Visconti is in Spoleto; is quite near the place we shoot the Steel Works, but not today, not tomorrow, maybe three days' time.'

'But I have raced across the world to get here for tomorrow!'

He spread the doe-skinned hands apologetically. 'He changes his mind again . . . you have a good rest . . . two, three days we will be making the scene.'

Later in the day, furious and fatigued, we drove through the snowy hills of Italy to Spoleto; the hotel was warm, modern, small and ugly. Albino smiling happily in the bar.

'So good to see you! Notarianni has told you we don't work tomorrow? Maybe two, three days . . .'

'But why? I left California yesterday I think . . . to be here in time . . . what has happened? Money?'

Albino was gentle. 'No, no, not money, now we have all we need; they like the film. eccellente! Bravo, the Warner Brothers say, bravo! Now we relax a little;

we wait for one of the other actors to come from Milano. He is very tired, all
week he is in a play . . . and the other actor, he must come from Berlin . . . he is
also in a play . . . very fatigued. We work in a day or two, you rest, you will see,
all is well.'

'Where is Visconti now?'

Albino looked miserably at the terrazzo floor. Then he looked up, put his
hand on my arm, to break the news gently. 'In there; but please by very quiet,
he is working very hard, not to disturb, anyone . . . please . . . do not trouble
him?'

In there was a small, dark room. In there he sat. Alone amidst a sea of small
metal chairs, in the dark, watching television. I crept in and settled beside him
in a chair. It creaked. He looked up, anger reflected in the flickering blue light
from the set. He suddenly saw me, anger flicked to a small smile. He put a finger
to his lips.

'Ciao, Bogarde. You stay with me? Certo . . . not to speak . . .' He was
whispering, his voice hoarse with the effort. 'Not to speak. Is the Eurovision
Song Contest . . . very exciting. United Kingdom is bad, France is bad, now is
Denmark; poor. Maybe Italy will win? Capisci?'

CHAPTER THIRTEEN

The removal vans trundled slowly down the long drive in a flurry of sleet and
snow-showers, leaving the house empty, bare and strangely silent after the long
racketing week of packing and crating-up of one's life.

Elizabeth had come to stay for the final week to comfort; and to assist
Antonia with a woman's hand, to fold blankets, sort sheets and pillowcases, and
also to make endless cups of tea, on the hour, hourly, for all the removal men
who accepted them with gratitude when they were not busy swigging the last of
the vodka, sherry and whisky from the decanters which huddled forlornly on a
tin tray in the stripped Drawing Room.

And now she too had left, taking with her an odd assortment of house plants,
one howling Siamese cat, a cage of tropical finches fluttering, and Candy, the
ageing English mastiff who knew (only too well by her hooped eyes and
drooping tail) that something cataclysmic was afoot, and that she too would be
shortly starting a new life elsewhere, and how would she manage?'

We were left, my parents, Antonia and Eduardo, Forwood, George and the
ever-loyal Arnold, sitting in exhausted heaps on the window-sills of the empty
Staff Sitting Room, drinking beer out of Italian-Spode breakfast cups, waiting
for the arrival of the new owners so that I could hand over the keys, a formality I
could well have done without.

The house was cold, dead, a shell now that its life was packed and trailing off
to a warehouse near Victoria to await a new beginning. Somewhere a tap
dripped; agreed fixtures and fittings left, a drum of Harpic and a brush in the
downstairs cloakroom, telephone directories neatly stacked, a list of local
traders pinned to a cupboard in the kitchen, a box of keys labelled
'Greenhouses', 'Garage', 'Linen Cupboards', a long-forgotten cigarette burn

on the wooden shelf in the Boot Room.

The gardens were bleak; fine snow drifting, bare branches riding harshly against a grey sky; urns, statues, tubs all long since removed by George; goldfish motionless in the fish-pool under then ice.

'You're not saying goodbye?' Arnold in a duffle coat beside me, anxious, pale, tired.

'Christ, no. Did that ages ago. Just checking, that's all.'

George came down the path pulling on gloves. 'Well; I'll be getting back now; before it gets too thick, it tends to drift up on the hill, don't want to get stuck with all that fragility in my van.'

I walked up with him, helped him slam the doors on terracotta, marble, lead, and a sundry collection of garden implements. We shook hands warmly, he started up his engine and with a quick wave turned out into the lane and went off after the rest of the house. I watched him go; wondering when next I'd see the Drummer Boy, the saucer urn from Crystal Palace, the camellia pots . . . and where? He pulled in sharply, after two hundred yards, to let a metallic-blue Rolls inch past gently towards the house. The new owners.

'Here they come,' said my father. 'Well, I think Mother and I will just get off now, leave you to it. She's been saying goodbye to Antonia for ten minutes, both in floods of tears. Women, really; must say I don't like this moment myself.'

'It's not as bad as all that, Pa, you know . . . I mean it's not as if it was my ancestral home, I haven't lived here for generations upon generations, it's not my heritage I'm leaving as some people have to, my roots never got that far down, you know, in the end. I don't quite know what I should have done if that had been the case . . . I'd rather not think, I suppose. And remember I'm leaving of my own free will. Before anyone lowers the portcullis. It's not too late to start again. Just.'

He rubbed his nose with a gloved finger thoughtfully. 'Suppose you're right. Well, good luck anyway, we'll come out and see you as soon as you say; when you're settled. April? May perhaps, when it's still coolish . . . Mother doesn't like the heat, you know. Not Rome heat anyway. Mother! Come along, dear, we'll be in the way if we don't get along now.'

They drove away just as the Rolls stopped, pale blue, shimmering in the steel light. Doors slammed; the woman was wearing snow boots and a leopard coat, thin blond hair, clutching a lavender poodle in a jewelled collar.

'Hope we didn't interrupt anything?' She let the poodle down gently on to the gravel path where it squealed and shivered and cocked its leg nervously against the front door. 'Look at him! Marking his territory already.' The woman laughed merrily and put out a diamond hand.

Forwood and I, with Antonia and Eduardo in the Rolls, Arnold hard behind in the Simca with all our luggage, left the house and drove up the hill, through the darkening afternoon, past the barns surrounded by softly bleating sheep huddled under the big oaks against the swirling flakes, which lay upon their fleece like powdered glass, and turned left out on to the main road. The journey had begun. We none of us looked back.

It was almost like a sailing; the room was crammed with flowers and the heavy scent of white hyacinths from Losey, daffodils from Irene, roses and roses, a wanton thrusting of early yellow tulips from someone else . . . notes, messages, cards and letters stacked, bottles chilling in beading silver bearing labels; 'Bon Voyage'.

'All we need,' said Forwood tiredly, 'are the streamers . . .'

In a collision of suitcases in my room I wondered exhaustedly which and what to unpack. A month here at the Connaught, to rest, one though hopefully, from the long year of packing and unpacking before the final effort and final severance. First things first; I lugged a handgrip into the bathroom and set out shampoo, razor, toothbrush, lotions; from the window I could just see, under the tall lamppost, that the snow was settling in Carlos Place.

From the azaleas in early May on the Spanish Steps, the industrial sun of Essen and Düsseldorf, painted reindeers in California, bougainvillaea blazing in Sidi Bou Said, the blinding heat of Visconti's Steel Mills in Terni, the soft bleating of the sheep recently as we passed them on the hill . . . it had been a long time, a long way, many voyages; but perhaps the longest and most daunting was ahead. I would use this month to relax and prepare, just sleep perhaps.

But that was not possible. Every day was filled with luncheons, suppers, dinners, drinks and various entertainments. The generosity and love of one's friends was overwhelming. Everyone wanted to have a farewell party; and everyone did. The engagement book was steadily filled for days, even weeks, in advance.

Ten days after arriving in London I was desperately planning to leave it; a surfeit of affection, wine, food and too many late nights. One morning I looked through the crammed book and made a sudden and firm decision; this would be the last day of all. After the planned luncheon I would pack up and just clear off and head for Italy.

It was an amusing, decorative final luncheon. Kathleen Tynan, Caroline Somerset, Patrick Lichfield, Angelica Huston, a representative gathering of loving, if all-unsuspecting, friends, and when they had finally left, promising to meet again within a few days, I telephoned Arnold and alerted him to be ready with the Simca to drive down to Dover that evening, and called my father.

'We're leaving, tonight, try and get an early boat tomorrow morning.'

'A bit sudden, isn't it? Thought you had another couple of weeks?'

'On my knees; if I don't go now I'll never go. It means I can't get down to see you and Mother; do you mind?'

'Goodness, no! Don't you worry about us; we'll see you very soon anyway wherever you land up, I mean unless it's somewhere like Turkey.' His laughter cheerfully unbelieving.

'No. Rome . . . it'll be Rome I think for a while, to try it for size.'

'Well, have a word with Mother, and don't worry about us.'

'You are sure you wouldn't come with me? Follow in a month or so?'

A little pause.

'No, my dear; as I said, we're both a bit too old now; might have said yes ten years ago . . . but we'd be pretty lost, you know; all our friends are here, the ones who remain . . . I'd miss the Rose and Crown in Fletching and my Worthington . . .'

'I'm sure you could get Worthington in Rome.'

'No, off you go; good luck, and God bless you. Get some in for me though; I'll need a little strength after the journey.'

'Get some what?'

'Worthington, of course . . . you are dense!'

We were the first two cars in the queue at the Customs shed next morning for the first boat across. The night before at dinner in the local hotel we had made the final plans for our journey. Arnold would leave us at Arras and go by way of Macon, we to Paris; and the next night, all things, and the slightly aged Simca, being equal, we would meet up again at the Hotel de l'Europe in Avignon, then to Genoa and on to Rome; it all seemed perfectly straightforward. The Customs official, a tall gaunt man, his arms wrapped around him for warmth in the bitter wind, leant down and said good morning.

'Wonder if you'd mind stepping out, sir; bit chilly, but I'd like to have a little chat, if you don't mind.'

I stood beside him in the dirty shed, gulls wheeling and crying, wind whipping a flag taut, scraps of torn paper eddying in a corner.

'All yours, is it, Sir?'

'Yes . . . both cars.'

'Quite a lot of luggage, eh?'

'Yes; a lot.'

'How much money are you carrying, sir?'

'Three hundred and fifty pounds.'

'That would be all, would it?'

'That's all.'

'And the other gentlemen?'

'We have three hundred and fifty between us all.'

He wandered to the back of the Simca and peered in.

'Record player, I see. Spare tyres?'

'For the Rolls. Expensive in Italy.'

'Going on a little holiday?'

'No.'

'Ah . . . what are you going for then, sir, with all this luggage?'

'Ever.'

He stood and looked at me impassively, his coat tails whipping around his legs, arms still wrapped.

'I see. Thank you, sir.' The barrier went up and we started the cars.

In the shuddering British Rail cabin, grey as the morning, one tartan rug on the bunks, I replaced the papers and passports in the briefcase, gave Arnold his, and rang the Stewards' bell for something hot to drink.

'Aren't you coming up top?' Arnold looked worried, huddled in his sheepskin.

'What for? It's bitter.'

'To see them go . . .'

'The white cliffs?'

He shrugged, and sat on the bunk.

'You go up if you want to, Noldie. I've done it so often before.'

So often before. With Lally and Elizabeth for holidays from as early as I could remember, sitting on deck eating lemons against seasickness, on Lally's stern advice, repeating the phrases she thought we might need on the other side – 'Bonjour', 'Merci', 'Le Doublevey Sey, s'il vous plait' – watching the gulls swoop and glide behind us on the wake, smoke stream away from the black and red funnel, the water all about us like foaming ginger beer. We hadn't ever looked behind then; no last looks, no silly waving, 'Full Steam Ahead!' Lally used to cry happily. Ahead to Abroad, to adventure, a return rather than a parting. And that's how I would think of it today in the sullen light; not a severance, a beginning.

The London flight was on time when we got to the check-in at Fiumicino; Arnold was pretty silent all the way down in the car. No one felt much like speaking.

'I wish you'd let me stay a bit longer; just to see you settled in somewhere.' He stared miserably out of the window.

'No, don't even think of it, we'll manage . . . got three houses to see today.'

'Just don't like leaving like this. It doesn't feel right.'

He checked in his baggage, a small handgrip. I handed him the presents which he'd bought for June and his child. A bottle of Chianti, a long sausage in a net bag, a wind-up police car with flashing lights.

'I'm going to miss you, Gov. Miss you bad.'

'I am too. It's the only thing I really feel guilty about; leaving you, Noldie.'

He rallied swiftly. 'Aw Hell! We had a good innings though, didn't we? Fifteen years . . . a long time . . . couldn't ask for much more, could we?'

We walked together towards Immigration, no sense in hanging about.

'Maybe when we're all settled you could come out for a holiday . . . bring June and Aidan? In the summer – have a real relax . . .'

'Sure. I'll miss all those early morning calls though; the bacon sandwiches. Always had the coffee ready, didn't I? In my little percolator.'

'You'll be doing it for someone else soon, you see.'

We stopped at the barrier, he rummaged for his passport and boarding card.

'No. Not me . . . I don't want to stand in for anyone else now. Try and get my ticket on the Floor somewhere. Assistant . . .'

'Give June my love.'

'I will; and take care, right?'

'Sure.'

'It was a really *great* time,' he said and turned away abruptly.

Rome seemed, then, to be full of ladies who ran Estate Agencies, or at least worked in them, and I got to know a varied selection of both the ladies and the properties which they had on offer to rent. All pretty awful.

An elderly Russian Princess, dressed as if for a tough shoot in the Highlands, and with an inaccurate, not to say completely erroneous knowledge of my station in life, implored me round a number of decaying palazzos in the hills and ornate villas on the Appia Antica, promising that the central heating would be mended, the pools made watertight, the furniture returned, and that the views, on clear days were incredible . . . all the way to Frascati or even further. That these sad villas lay in vast, unkempt gardens amidst mouldering columns and crumbling putti, that they were cold, damp and neglected and often furnished as if by a mad Maharaja left naked with a cheque book in Drages or Maples, never caused her a moment's care or worry. Everything, she insisted, could be done by tomorrow – and quite clearly, from the neglect and disarray of most of them, never was. Although I continued to insist that my funds were very modest, and that I only wanted a very small house with a swimming pool if possible, not as a luxury but as a dire necessity in summer in Rome, and that it should be as easily run and compact as possible, I still had to make fruitless journeys into the smart areas of the city, or up into the hills, where wreathed in mists and scrofulous with damp, yet another rusting, crested gate was thrown open and warrens of rooms and corridors explored.

Signorina Dora was a little easier to convince, and far less grand; her agency was small and seemed to cater for a more modest client. The flats she offered were often small, foul, in dark streets, or high blocks, and had all been used for one kind of a business or another. Usually one kind. She didn't do houses very often. She was a wan girl, bleached blonde hair with an angry black parting, plastic alligator boots and a fur coat which moulted in the rain. She chewed thoughtfully at her pencil and made copious notes, a telephone glued into the crick of her neck, Italian streamng from her lips like bullets from a Tommy gun. Eventually she hung up, ran her hand wearily through the harsh blonde hair and pushed an address towards me.

'It is north of the city, not chic, very not chic. Via Flaminia; not a good address. The big cemetery is there, Prima Porta. Molto doloroso, eh, va bene. It has what you want, is empty, is cheap, has telephone, pool . . . and you must pay the gardener.'

Villa Fratelli was twelve kilometres out of Rome on a small hill stuckall over with parasol pines, mimosa, magnolia. Below it lay a clutter of squatters' houses, apparently built overnight, from blocks of porous tufa. Bilious yellow, tin roofs, an open sewer running through the dirt streets, dumped cars, a football pitch, television aerials, enormous refrigerators incongruously standing in the muddy yards linked to the main electricity cable by meters of tangled wire. There was one Bar with green walls, striplights and a pin table; a butcher, a baker, and a shop which sold Kodak film and wedding enlargements or confirmation photographs in vivid colour. Otherwise there was nothing much there apart from a few scrawny chickens, starving dogs, and an old man who rode about in an invalid car with a musical box, a monkey and no legs.

The villa, when you finally reached it through the unmade roads and dank tufa houses, was not so bad. Surrounded by a walled garden, with stout wooden gates, it was a modern reproduction of a casa colonica . . . and commanded the most marvellous views; from the upper windows. It was cool, light and not depressing. A good swimming pool in the garden, reasonable kitchen, sparse furniture, most of it awful, but it was cheap and it was in the country; if you ignored the sprawl of suburban Rome below the hill. There was even an empty chicken run, and a small vineyard. I made arrangements to re-visit and finalise it the following day and hurried back to Rome to warn the Princess.

'Where is this villa?' she said darkly, the commission slipping through her anxious fingers. 'Near Prima Porta! Dio! Not possible . . . you can not live near Prima Porta! only dead people are there . . . no one goes to that part of the city except on the day of the dead. It is appalling, dangerous, and not chic . . . I have all arrangements made for you to see Palazzo Gondoli . . . is divine, is the house of our Ambassador to Uruguay . . . is ravishing. 2,000 dollars a month. You come now. Immediately.'

'But I have seen the Palazzo, Princess, it is too big, too grand and too expensive for me . . .'

'We can make an arrangement, maybe they take 1,800 . . .'

'But it overlooks the city dump yard.'

'No. No. Is not true!'

'I've seen the trucks, big trucks dumping the rubbish. The fires . . . you can see it from the gardens clearly.'

'Ha!' she cried cheerfully. 'Only when you stand up!'

Villa Fratelli belonged, as might seem reasonable, to Signora Fratelli, a newly widowed lady, of considerable charm, reduced circumstances, and lost hopes. She was about thirty, pretty, vivacious when she was not melancholy, which was all the time now, and smart in a last-year's-model kind of way. Something had distressed her greatly in the past, and she was not about to relinquish her grief easily. Her husband, she told me the first day we met, had been a very handsome man, very brave and dashing; if not particularly bright about finance, he was extremely good about guns and hunting which had led to his tragic death, by falling from a low flying aircraft, a Piper Cub she thought, attempting to shoot his first zebra in Kenya. He had unhappily lost balance and had fallen into the galloping herd below. Without having fired a shot. She herself was told the dreadful news while sitting on a Nile steamer floating gently towards Luxor and unsuspected widowhood. It had destroyed her. The house which they had built together was now too full of memories, so she had ripped out the furnishings, save for a few odds and ends, and put it on the market. The last, and indeed they had been the first, tenants, were an American family, very friendly, with many children. They were employed at NATO and he had been posted away suddenly; so the house was free. Would I care to rent it, or buy it? It didn't matter much one way or another.

I rented it for a year, and paid the slightly astonished Signorina Dora her first deposit. Capucine and Julie Christie, both of whom happened to be working in Rome just then, lost no time in having a look at it and both pronounced it acceptable if bleak.

'You need masses of flowers and cushions everywhere!' they said, and later sent both to prove it.

Two days later Signora Fratelli came up and did the inventory, which took very little time, since there was really very little left to check. Some ashtrays from local Roman restaurants, beds with straw mattresses, some chairs, a large refectory table too heavy to cart away, and a dining-room suite of spartan simplicity and ugliness. There were no sheets, naturally, and no electric light bulbs. Little things had to be found; like knives and forks, and something to cook in.

'Ah! Si . . . I forget. I will find at the casa de Mamma where now I live alone . . . you understand.'

She showed me how to work the central heating, where the water main was turned off or on, how to empty and fill the pool, and that the gardener's name was Peppino and that he had been in the service of her mother's family for fifty years. He was now, she thought, about eighty and useless. 'The gardens,' she indicated them with a sad shrug, 'we had so many plans to make it pretty . . . but God was unkind,' implying that what was left was for me to get right.

It was a wilderness of red earth, clumps of frosted oleanders, long-dead geraniums, and a scrappy piece of grass outside the drawing room which might, once, have been a lawn. The tall pines dropped their needles endlessly, the magnolias shed enormous rusty leaves, the raspberry canes were a thicket. Through an overgrown hedge lay Peppino's province, the vegetable garden where he grew tomatoes, onions, asparagus and ragged rows of beans in a vague haphazard way. Down at the bottom, the empty chicken run. All about the mimosa, pines, twisted olives, and at their feet, a cobalt carpet of voilets scenting the March air. There was plenty of time; as soon as the house was livable I'd start on the garden with Peppino, useless or not.

Signora Fratelli drove off in her small red car, a list of promises in her hand which I hoped she would remember, but already expected her not to; I was, after all, quite used to Italy.

Eventually, with a certain amount of pressure from Signorina Dora, bits and pieces of missing inventory returned to the villa, and by the time that Eduardo and Antonia arrived to join me from Valencia, where they had been waiting, the place was almost a going concern. At least one could eat, sleep and cook in it, and they were delighted by the views all around, by the simplicity of the house, and by the fact that they could go to Mass anywhere they liked within minutes of the slummy village below.

Peppino proved to be willing, kind, and eager to help. Ignored for years by the Fratellis, hardly spoken to by the American family from NATO, he clumped after me through his domain, chattering in incomprehensible Italian, apparently explaining what he could do with a few packets of seed, some encouragement, and a new spade and fork. His smelly little shed, in which he spent his siesta, beside the chicken run, was the centre of his life and his domain.

A sagging bed, a wooden chair and table, Gina Lollobrigida on one wall and a Milan football team on the other, the beams wreathed with drying chillis, pomodori and onions. We shred a glass of repellent house wine and I promised him the tools he needed, and Antonia willingly agreed to cook him a meal daily in return for baskets of fresh fruits and vegetables, providing that he stopped hurling bricks at the cringing little dog, rib cage showing, foreleg smashed and bloody, with bone sticking out, riddled with worms and heaving with ticks, which haunted us day and night. He explained that it had been the property of the Americans who had bought it the year before as a puppy for Christmas for the children; and that when they left, apparently in a great hurry, they abandoned it, with two cats, now gaunt and starving, to fend for themselves, leaving him a small amount of money to buy them food. Since he reckoned that he needed the food far more than the beasts, he had spent it (compassion for animals is not in the Pope's recipe for Holy Salvation); and most of the day chucking stones and bricks at the bewildered animals which refused to leave. I determined to find a vet to come out and painelssly destroy the three of them. They would obviously be a problem when Candy eventually arrived from England. In the event the vet wormed and mended everybody, which cost a fortune I had not budgeted for (I was on a tight rein here), and the house now had three more occupants who took over the place as a right. Under Antonia's loving eye and gentle care, they prospered well. The dog was called Labbo, the cats Prune and Putana. Villa Fratelli was complete.

Elizabeth was our first staying guest in the ugly Blue Guest Bedroom.

'I admit the wallpaper is a bit dizzy-making, my dear, but still . . .'

Blue roses and sweet peas writhed across walls, ceiling, curtains, bedspread and the one upholstered chair which Prune had claimed as his; the floor was of blue shining tiles.

'It's a bit like sleeping in a knitting-bag or something.'

'Signora Fratelli calls it her bower.'

'Her what?'

'Bower . . . I think it was her room.'

'How peculiar. Hope he doesn't come back haunting people in his safari hat, I'd really have a frightful turn if he did; perhaps I should have brought old Candy after all . . . oh dear.'

It had been the original intention that she would accompany Candy from England; but she had come alone, finally deciding that a mastiff was, at nine, too old to make the trip in a small cage, and that it would be far better off in the cooler climate of Sussex with her own family. She arrived instead with a pile of much needed bed linen, custard powder, Bisto, and three pudding bowls which Antonia said she could not possibly manage without; and was much impressed with the villa and the gardens, which were already starting to show promise, since Peppino and I spent hours attacking weeds and thick red clay, pruning, planting and mowing, making large compost heaps and dribbling beans and peas into long carefully-measured trenches. As the spring wore on more and more people started to arrive, Rome was a very busy place, and all roads seemed to cross there, even if they did not always end there, as I had been told. Eventually Villa Fratelli became just like Bendrose, Beel and Nore, with much the same cast, all coming out for holidays or long week-ends. Xan and Daphne, Moura, Irene, Gareth, the Lerners, Bumble and so on. The Blue Room was hardly ever without occupants. With the pool at the edge of the terrace, the Frascati wine in barrels, the soft spring sun of Italy, and three excellent meals from Antonia it was a happy temptation; instead of feeling a lost, wistful immigrant I was once again in the bosom of my friends, or they were in mine, whichever way you put it, and all that seemed to have happened was that the set and background had changed but little else.

One of the things which I surprised myself discovering was the sheer delight of marketing. Something I had not been able to do for over twenty years. In England it had been impossible to walk about in shops or streets alone; I was always accompanied by Forwood or Theo Cowan to ward off the inevitable scatter of curious people who would constantly follow me about from place to place making life sadly uncomfortable. Eventually I resigned the business of shopping at all, hating the stir it always caused which irritated both me and the shopkeepers. People were never rude intentionally, merely unthinking, and it was just better to keep out of the way. I never carried money in my pockets, Forwood paid for everything, and for many years I never even signed a cheque; this was done at a much higher level by a group of black-pin-striped gentlemen who were my accountants and lawyers and so on. Life was totally unreal in this direction, even in the village where I lived, unless I was very careful and went about looking like a tramp. Now to be able to wander among the towering piles of fruits, fish and flowers in the market at Ponte Milvio every morning at eight o'clock, alone and unheeded, was a delight that I had almost completely forgotten. Daily I would return to Antonia's kitchen with baskets of fresh green beans, artichokes, new potatoes the size of bantams' eggs, loaves of still-warm bread, kilos of gleaming coral-pink prawns, bunches of amber grapes, arms full of carnations and heavy-scented stocks. No one asked for autographs, pulled my clothes or asked for signed photographs for relations. If I was recognised it was always politely, with a smile, a salute, or sometimes even an offered flower. And if, after the exertions of bargaining with Elsa at the fish-stall, I went into a bar for a coffee, no one asked me to come outside and put up my fists to impress the woman they were with, which had been a frequent hazard before in pubs from Chiddingfold to Bristol. I naturally found it all very refreshing and even exhilarating to feel so free. I inevitably came to grief in the supermarkets, which for the first time in my life I now entered bravely with my trolley and clattered up and down the aisles plundering like Attila the Hun arriving back at the villa with a varied assortment of goods ranging from tinned beans, toilet rolls and pot-scrubbers to a five-foot cactus in a plastic pot. Having money in my pockets was a serious problem for the accountant, Forwood, who, after a few hysterical weeks of my assaults on Super-Romano or Standa, managed to bring my polka down to a slow foxtrot, if not a complete halt. The first showing, in private of 'Götterdämmerung' now retitled 'La Caduta degli Dei', managed to do that quite well.

I was deeply impressed with the tremendous scale and theatricality of the film, of the breadth of Visconti's vision ad work and of all the performances save for my own. Clearly I had done what I could with the role of 'Friedrich', but what I had done was not, perhaps, quite enough. He still remained wet; this was not, I hasten to add, entirely my fault. Visconti admitted that he was eventually the villain of the piece, because he had decided to favour the second plot-line rather than the first; and had hacked most of the big set-piece scenes between Ingrid Thulin and myself out of the picture in favour of those of the incestuous son and his mother – which was the line he wished to pursue in his story. The fact that so much that had been strong was now eliminated, and that what was left was mostly played on the back of my head, rather diminished the effects which I had tried, successfully, I thought at the time, to achieve. Milestone had said years ago that you could make a good script bad but that you could never make a bad one good. It applied also to the parts. Now I learned the hard way.

'You are sad, Bogarde. Va bene . . . but I change my mind, is my privilege, no? I make this not just the story of the Macbeths, it is the story also of the corrupted youth . . . so . . . we have to cut. Already the film is four hours; too long! And you will agree,' he smiled when he said it, 'that you give the best back-to-camera performance that has ever been seen!'

'But the big scene in my study, the one with Ingrid in the salon, the one after I have done the first murder . . . all gone, Luchino?'

'All gone . . . were perfect, molto bello, molto, molto; but they distracted the story from the boy. He must be the pivot, not Friedrich, they had to go.'

He looked sad enough for me to doubt his sureness; I tried once again.

'And the big scene, walking through the house all alone. The big terror scene?'

'Ah! said Visconti, holding up a warning hand. 'In that you were not good. Orrible. Troppo Mozart and not enough Wagner . . . capisci?'

But at least I was proud of the film and prouder still that, however wet, I was in it. It had not been a wrong decision; just a lesson in tactics and acting.

At dinner that night, in his house on Via Salaria, among white-gloved footmen, sparkling crystal, and excited and congratulating company, he became Emperor Supreme knowing that the smell of the film was good, and that the great efforts he had made had not, apparently, been in vain; leaning across the gleaming cloth, he placed his hand gently on my arm, 'Salute!' he said warmly. 'The Friedrich you have given me is the Friedrich I wanted; not so happy for you . . . but happy for me. And one day, you will see, I will give you a present. I will not forget; it will be a present, not a reward. Remember.' He raised his glass and took a sip of his wine. 'I drink to that, Bogarde.'

In the early part of June my parents arrived, and settled into the Blue Room, my father ravished by the brilliant light all about him, armed with sketch books and boxes of paints; my mother bewildered by the smells of pine and roses, the dizzying sun, the squalor of the squatters' village below the hill, and the splendours of the city itself, spent a great part of the day, however, in the kitchen, discovering, with Antonia, the mysteries of pasta, which the latter had learned to make herself.

'Aren't women funny?' said my father, squinting over his easel at the hills. 'Came all this way to see Rome and she spends all her time in the kitchen and says she hates cooking. Funny lot. Odd.'

'As long as she's happy.'

'What else could she be? This lovely place. I suppose this is all quite usual for you, isn't it? Breakfast on the terrace, the light through the pines, those cricket things singing away.'

'No. Not usual. But cherished. I'm not even getting used to it yet.'

'How many suitcases did you bring?' He raised gentle white eyebrows, mildly, and went back to his hills.

'Ah. You remembered! More than two, I'm afraid, and the Rolls, and a record player and books, and all of this is a bit more than a flat. But it is a start in the right direction; I wouldn't go back now, I can manage this much quite easily . . . somewhere warm, simple, easy to run.'

He unscrewed a tube of paint carefully. 'I think it was a good move.'

'You don't mind that I left?'

'Left? Goodness no . . . an Englishman's right still. As long as it makes you happy. I feel it wasn't just work, was it? A bit political?'

'A bit; yes.'

'If they lose the next election?'

'They'll get back. I just hope they manage it better than we all did.'

He mixed some colour on his china palette. 'We didn't do so badly . . .'

'We think that. But the kind of life we though we were fighting for in our wars was all the past really. The things we knew were worth keeping have all become class symbols now. They'll never come back. *We* finished in '39; I know that.'

He mixed a little yellow busily. 'I suppose so. You'll be honourable, won't you? Wherever you finally settle. Become a resident, you know. You won't just flit about . . . evade things?'

'No. Never.'

'Because I wouldn't like that.'

'I promise you.'

He turned away suddenly and cleared his throat; his face furrowed in concentration. 'I can't ever get the right green for olives. How did Cézanne do it? And Bonnard? It's not green it's blue, not blue it's silver, not silver it's, I don't know, I can't get it. Mother says all my olive trees look like broccoli. It *is* a worry.'

'I'm thinking that if I start pulling out of the acting now, it would be a good idea. I never really wanted this to happen as it did. It was too much and too soon and too fast. I hate the struggling for power, the pushing and shoving, the battles to try and do anything decent . . . it's too much of a fight now; I'm not a starry-eyed idiot any longer. I don't think I ever was. Lost the glitter a long time ago.'

'What would you do . . . write or something? Painting again?'

'No, write. I want to start my book . . . I've done the first three chapters already up here. About Elizabeth and me and the Cottage.'

'I've been looking out stuff for you as I proised. School reports, letters, that sort of thing. They might be helpful one day . . . What about money, can you manage?'

'If I was very, very frugal and lived carefully.'

He laughed at the word frugal and flicked me a shrewd look.

'No Antonia, no Eduardo, no Rolls of course; a small house like this, small amount of land. I'd manage I think.'

He brushed a ladybird off his paper, and applied a little brush of green. 'It's *just* green, isn't it? What do you think? Green, not *olive* green.'

'But not here in Italy. I think I'd go over to France. Wiser in the long run.'

'Italy's always been a bit of a mess,' he laughed shortly. 'Charming people but all a bit volatile, not awfully stable really.' He started carefully blocking in a tree.

Forwood came across the terrace with bottles and glasses, my father looked up in relief. 'A little refreshment? Splendid . . . I'm having a dreadful time with my olives again.'

Forwood set everything down on the table. 'Margaret is about to be instructed into the mysteries of a real Bolognese sauce. She didn't know there were chicken livers in it, or that you pound pine nuts for a *pesto*.'

My father snorted. 'She'll have a hell of a job getting pine nuts in Haywards Heath, I can tell you. You've heard Dirk's plans for becoming an old man, I suppose?'

'Yes; I rather think he means it this time. He could manage; carefully. Maybe do one film now and again, just to keep the bank happy. We'll see.'

In the evening, after dinner, we sat out under the trees among the fireflies, the frogs chanting down in the field below the house, a warm wind rustling through the pines scattering needles into the pool.

'What about film work though?' said my father. 'Wasn't there something with Jean Renoir? Now *his* father could mix the green I want. Used it in all his paintings, that olive green I can't get, Margaret, you know? Renoir found it.'

'And Renoir lost it,' I said. 'I mean the film, well he didn't lose it, but after the troubles in France last year everything got rather set aside. But there is a lot of work here; mostly commercial stuff, historical, police, adventure stuff, nothing I want to do. I'm not going back to that ever again. Not those films.'

'Oh dear!' said my mother. 'What a pity.' She lit a cigarette, a sudden spear of vermillion light among the fireflies. 'I think you are very snobbish about those kind of films as you call them. I don't know where you get it from; not *me*. If I had had half the chances you have had . . .' She dropped her lighter into her handbag and snapped it shut. 'I'd have adored to have done the things you have; I just didn't have the chance.' She leant back in her cane chair and it creaked a little. My father took up his brandy and patted her knee kindly.

'Now, Margaret, we don't want to go through all that again, dear, you had a very good career as a wife and a mother. Did it quite brilliantly. Very good mother, dear.'

She smoothed down her skirt and sighed. 'Yes I know, Ulric, don't patronise. But it wasn't the career I had intended. Never mind, I won't bore you all with me again . . . I have my memories, you know. But we did have such lovely times on those films. All the places you took us to. Padua, I'll never forget, darling Padua; and that funny place, what was it called, where people sat in hot mud all day and you made a frightful fuss because the food was so bad in the hotel that belonged to the man who built Big Ben?'

'Abano Terme. Yes, the trips were fun, but the films really weren't; for me.'

'Margaret dear, the man didn't own the hotel, he only lived there years ago when it was his private house. You've got it muddled.'

'I'm not muddled! It's the same thing, isn't it? I don't know why you have to make everything so complicated, you two . . . it's no fun really; it's negative thinking.'

Forwood laughed in the soft blue light. 'Trouble with your son is that whenever he's not working he becomes negative. He's very positive when he is working though.'

My mother reached for her glass and took a thoughtful sip. 'Well, I think he's been damned lucky, if you ask me,' she said. 'And that's positive.'

They were both right. I remembered the conversation a few weeks later going down in the evening to feed Peppino's fifteeen white pullets which now occupied the hen-run. Not working made one introspective, slightly neurotic, and certainly negative. The temptation to accept, just one, of the fat scripts which now cluttered the small room I used as an office, was very great. They were all commercials there would be no battles to get them off the ground . . . but the very thought of playing yet another light weight, another bantering hero, another elegant Englishman, filled me with dread. I had made a definite decision which had very possibly cost me dear; I must stick to it, pick the mint and feed Peppino's chickens, do the daily marketing, amuse the team who came to stay, chill the wine, and try, in between the chores, to get on with my writing; I was finding it pleasanter to look backwards rather than look forwards. A danger signal which I chose to ignore.

The fifteen pullets came cluttering round me as I went into the run, craning necks, leaping, flapping scrawny unfledged wings. I scattered the corn and kitchen bits in a wide arc and saw Peppini running towards me through the pines, holding his battered hat with one hand, the other waving a piece of paper.

'Telegrammo! Telegrammo!' he cried and thrust it folded through the wire. He didn't stop, and with profuse, if unintelligible, excuses turned round and ran back down the hill towards his train to Viterbo, still holding his hat.

I sat on the upturned bucket, kicked a chicken bone among the cannibal hens, and opened it. 'Thinking of you. Stop. Desperately sorry about Judy. Stop. Know how much you loved her. Stop. Hope she has found her rainbow now.' The signature was one I vaguely knew. Past tense. Past tense. The pullets blurred before me. The triteness hurt as deeply as my own knowledge of failure. I had broken the promise I had made her and turned my back. I hadn't walked away facing her smiling as she feared, I had done a far worse thing, I had left her and closed the door behind me. Rejection. What crueller weapon could I have found to use. And why? The demands had been too many and too strong for me to support; she had gone her own way, as she always said that she would, and I had determined to go mine. As she spiralled slowly downwards into her particular black well of despair and fear, I had ignored the outstretched hands imploring help. How can one halt a blazing meteor in its fall? It was no consolation; I walked up to the villa filled with shame, but also filled with a fury at the waste, the sheer bloody waste, of a husked-out, rejected, once glorious life destroyed by the cinema.

At least fury was positive, so positive indeed that when Visconti telephoned an hour later he knew that I was angry.

'You don't want to speak to me?' His voice was mild.

'No, I love to speak to you.'

'You sound molto furioso. You are ill?'

'No. Forgive me; a telegram with bad news, personal. Nothing . . .'

'Ah! I have bad news too. From the Warner Brothers in America. They like very much our film but they wish to make more cuts in it than I agreed. They will butcher me, my work, everything for the dollar. I hate this business: it is always the money. Will the film be understood in Wisconsin? If you do not make money you are rejected like robaccia, capisci?'

'Yes, very well.'

'Can you make me an English lunch perhaps? This week? I will bring my very nice cousin, Ida Cavalli. You will like her and she will like some Pudding Inglese. Is possible? I want to speak with you also . . .'

Antonia's reputation for making an English trifle was almost the main reason that Visconti ever braved the dangers of the journey from Via Salaria to the via Flaminia. He ate it in great quantities making Antonia's cheeks flush with sheer delight. But he hated the journey always. 'Ecco! You must drive through Inferno to find Paradiso, only an Englishman would have found this house. It is a miracle!'

They arrived for lunch a few days later, as if they had crossed China in a cart. Dusty, unbelieving, exhausted. We had a splendid lunch and spoke mostly about the wickedness of Warner Brothers and the cuts they wished to make in the film. Contessa Cavalli was a plump, cheerful, chain-smoking woman of about the same age as Visconti. She coughed constantly, wheezed like a bellows and spoke perfect Nanny-English. 'I have emphysema, it is fatal,' she said with great good nature, 'but they tell me it will take a long time, and so why do I worry? And therefore I don't We can't have Mr Glumm about the house, can we? We must all die one day.' She rummaged in her bag for her cigarettes and handed Visconti a small, wrapped packet, which she found there apparently by mistake.

'This is yours?' she asked him. He took it in one hand and weighed it carefully.

'No. Is for Bogarde here.' He placed it by my hand on the table. 'A present; not for anything, but for the Pudding Inglese, certo . . . for that.'

I took it, wrapped in ribbon, a gold and black paper. 'You should give this to Antonia perhaps, she makes the trifle.'

He laughed and pulled the almost empty glass dish towards him: 'I take a little more Ida? You will have a half with me?' But she refused, laughing at his gluttony, and as he started to eat I held in my hands a paperback copy of *Death in Venice.*

'You know it?' He was smiling over his spoon.

'Yes, ages ago.'

'We make a film together, you and me. You like?'

'Yes. When?'

'Spring, I think, March maybe; maybe early summer. Venice is difficult later with tourists. I must have the light of the sirocco.'

'It is sure? Certain?'

He laughed and placed his spoon neatly in his bowl. 'No, not certain. For *me* is certain, but there are many problems. There is money, it will be expensive; it is difficult, only one man, one beautiful child; is not Box Office, you see? I must speak with the Warner Brothers, maybe if I say yes to some more cuts they will say yes to this. But you will be von Aschenbach?'

'Yes. No conditions. Am I too young?'

'Why? He says no age, after fifty only. You know it is about Mahler, Gustav Mahler? Thomas Mann told me he met him in a train coming from Venice; this poor man in the corner of the compartment, with make-up, weeping . . . because he had fallen in love with beauty. He had found perfect beauty in Venice and must leave it in order to die. If you ever look upon perfect beauty, then you must die, you know that? Goethe. There is nothing else left for you to do in life. Eh! We will shoot from the book as Mann has written it, no script. You will trust me this time?'

'I trust you.'

'I watched you the first day in "La Caduta degli Dei", remember? You made six shots for me all different, the first day? No dialogue, just the mind. I saw. And I knew that I had found my actor. Voilà! I promised you a present, I drank to it, and now you accept it. Molto bene, but you must do nothing else whatever until we do it. Promise? No Fliano, no Resnais, you wait for me only? Capisci?'

'Positive. I'll wait for you as long as you ask.'

He nodded approvingly and pushed his bowl away from him. 'You must start right away to learn. You must hear all the music of Mahler, everything. Play it and play it. We make a study of solitude, of loneliness, if you hear the music you will understand, and you must read, and read, and read the book. Nothing else. You must live the book. I will tell you nothing finally. You will know. Because Mann and Mahler will have told you; listen to what they say and you will be prepared for me. When the time comes.'

Which was anybody's guess. It might be never at all. There was every possibility of that. But I was now working. I had nearly ten months, if there was a possibility of starting in March, to prepare. The negativity which had so irritated my poor mother was now replaced by an active positivity which would have exhausted her. I though how strange it was that everything was slipping into shape gently after all. If Forwood hadn't forced me to run up and down the Spanish Steps in a pair of somebody's eyeshades; if Arnold and Zelda hadn't suggested me to Jack Clayton and Visconti had not been present that night in Venice; if I hadn't spoken to a blue macaw in a cage in Salzburg – but there were too many ifs in life. Like the doors, one must not question them; accept them and never regret them. And there was a very long way to go before anything could be certain. But I must reject that thought too and do as I was told to do; prepare myself so that if the time came I should be ready.

Closing the gate on the mint fields for the time being I took up the corn bucket and the kitchen stuff and wandered up in the evening sun to the hen-run. Sitting on the upturned bucket among the scrabbling pullets where I had heard of her death made me feel nearer; she had taught me more about loneliness than anyone else I had ever know.

I didn't see Visconti again for a long time. Nor did I expect to. He went off to his castle in Ischia to prepare. I spent the rest of the summer driving about looking at houses for sale with the fading idea of living in Italy permanently, fading because the prospects were always poor rather than good, and the astounding amount of bribery and corruption which seemed to be a regular part of the life disconcerted me deeply. It appeared that you could do almost anything if you knew who to speak to and absolutely nothing if you did not.

Every transaction, from registering one's car, leasing a villa, applying for a *carte de séjour*, receiving a parking ticket or obtaining a table in a restaurant was accompanied always by a flurry of paper money, or surrogate contracts. Nothing was above board, nothing ever seemed to be exactly what it was. This, coupled with the agonizing poverty crushed against quite nauseating and overt richness, made me miserably apprehensive and aware that this, apparently, smiling, sunny, extrovert country was marking time before catastrophe. I had gone through one cruel and bloody war of Liberation in Java as a soldier: I had no wish, if it could be avoided, to repeat the experience in Italy as a middle-aged civilian. Once was quite enough.

I made up my mind that as soon as the premiere of 'La Caduta degli Dei' was over, in October, I would leave for France and see what possibilities lay there.

It was a very grand premiere indeed. The Barberini Cinema had been closed and redecorated especially for the event. Visconti and I took our places in the front row of the balcony in a theatre smothered with a million pink and white carnations and an audience composed of all Rome society and the entire Government, in lounge suits in deference to Visconti's apparent political sympathies. He claimed to me to be Communist but I found it hard to accept the fact among the palaces, Picassos, footmen and cooks and the splendour and abundance of his living style. So I placed him vaguely Left, which irritated him constantly and made him promise that one day he would explain it all to me. For the moment none of that mattered. The film was received as a masterpiece, and at the finale, as the lights came up in the vast auditorium, Fellini leapt from his seat in the stalls and facing us, he saluted Visconti with a great cry of 'Il maestro! Il maestro!' which brought the entire audience to its feet cheering and applauding and Visconti to his, modestly bowing in his dark grey suit and neat blue tie. He smiled but never moved a muscle, suffused with quiet triumph. Rome had restored its Emperor.

CHAPTER FOURTEEN

I suppose it is fair to say that I fell hopelessly in love with Simone Signoret the very first time I clapped eyes on her in a modest Ealing film called 'Against the Wind' some time during the period that I lived in Chester Row and was attempting my own passage into the cinema. I placed her then on the very peak of the profession, and as far as I am concerned she has never budged from it and I still love her dearly. For many years we were often not more than paces apart; my table at the Colombe d'Or in St Paul de Vence was just across from hers summer after summer, year after year, whenever we managed to get there. But we never spoke, nor did we ever recognise each other by nod or smile. There was no reason indeed why she ever should, but every reason that I might. However, apart from an occasional slow, considering, look out of those extraordinary eyes, the years passed in total silence; and I was left to worship from a discreet distance over the *gigot* or *loup de mer grillé*.

One day in the early sixties, with a hangover of the most punishing dimensions, I lay flat on my back in the sun beside the swimming pool, too weak to move, too ill to sit up, just wishing to be left alone and for the world to stop swinging about my aching head. A shadow fell across my face. And stayed there. Reluctantly I opened my eyes to the blazing light and saw, immediately above me, a pair of ravishing brown legs and two motionless fists. In the right a large Bloody Mary, in the left a packet of Marlboroughs clutched, an enormous gold bracelet glinting in the sun. I recognised the accessories and attempted to sit, but the voice bade me stay where I was.

'Don't move,' it commanded. 'I may not stay long.'

At seven in the evening, as the staff were setting up the tables on the terrace for dinner, we finished luncheon together; it had to be a long luncheon to bridge the many years which we had spent sitting apart, she at her table under the big fig tree, me at mine a little along the wall under the oranges. We had, and still do have, a great deal to talk about.

The one thing I finally became absolutely positive about, living in Italy, was exactly where I wished to live in France. I stuck the point of a compass into the village of St Paul de Vence and measured a half arc in pencil towards the south in a radius of about twenty kilometres. I had got to know and love this area, and a great deal beyond and above it, intimately, through Michael Powell with whom I had, in the early fifties, made a film based on the extraordinary exploits of Patrick Leigh-Fermor during the war in Crete. Mickey knew every hamlet, track, crag and olive grove. Together we had explored them and I had quickly grown to share his passion for the calm and peace which lay not so far beyond the cruelly ravaged coast. In this gentle, undulating, wooded land as yet almost untouched by the rotting fingers of the prospective property tycoons, I determined to seek and acquire my house. St Paul, once so sweet and calm and lost, except to a fortunate few, when I first came to it at the end of the forties, was now, in 1969, slowly but inexorably turning itself into a kitschy ruin of faux art galleries, Provençal boutiques, Vietnamese restaurants, and tarty little shops selling postcards, hideous porcelain, olive-wood salad bowls and key-rings.

Only the Colombe d'Or managed to stand aloof from this onslaught of quaintness, remaining a small, bright island around which all the flotsam and jetsam of package tours and coach trips ebbed and surged hourly, red-skinned, hot, smelling of suntan oil and *pommes frites*. Yvonne and Francis Roux who own it, were patient and polite and listened to my plans with no shred of astonishment, merely shaking their heads thoughtfully, if sadly, insisting that what I wanted (a small, tumbled down old mas or shepherd's house in a few isolated acres for very little money) simply no longer existed in the area of the village. Everything had been bought and converted, the land was almost the highest priced in all Europe per square metre, and I would have to search well down into my compass-inscribed permiter to avoid tremendous prices, swimming pools, macadamed drives, wrought iron, or Manniken-Pis and storks in every garden; the dreadful attributes of Paris-rustic, well-heeled New Jersey, Frankfurt, or Bexley Heath.

Since M. Roux had been born in the village and knew his way about things extremely well, I saw absolutely no reason to doubt their word. But Simone was ever brave, ever courageous, and at this present time a little bored with picking mint. She said that she would come with me on the journeys I would take, and offered herself as guide and translator, since my French was almost limited to the phrases which Lally had taught us years ago and those, I felt, were hardly enough to deal with plumbing, contracts, rights of way, electricity and septic tanks. This was indeed generous of her, and we all set out confidently on a course of house-hunting.

Simone's presence, alas, was a mixed blessing. Although she dealt fearlessly, vocally, and expediently with rights of way, septic tanks and land boundaries with the agents, the householders fell back in awe and delight at her presence and brought out the bottles of Marc, or Cognac and endless cups of coffee. The social delights tended to obscure, rather, my desperate search in the limited time I had for my next, and I hoped, final abode in the soft hills of Provence. We visited many possibilities that November, none of them remotely acceptable.

Eventually, with time rapidly running out, I took another look at my map with a weary eye and discovered, almost by chance, that the pencil line of my perimeter neatly bisected a small village on its southernmost tip in which lived a much admired actress Yvonne Mitchell. Indeed she had been the recipient of the very first fan letter I had ever written in my life. She had lived there for over six years. How on earth could I have forgotten? Surely she must know the region pretty well and perhaps even know of something for sale, or someone who could advise me? Of one thing I was perfectly certain: Yvonne would know exactly what I was after. And she did. Indeed she did; and knew of a house, quite remote, near a village which had almost entirely been by-passed. It had, she thought, quite a bit of land, would need restoration, but not, she said firmly, at the price which I envisaged. For that, all I could hope for would be a studio flat with a small balcony in one of the new blocks which were spreading like white fungus along the coast from Juan-les-Pins to Antibes. However, she agreed to call the owners, whom she knew slightly, and see if they would consider selling. They were anxious to move into Nice because the land was becoming too much for them and their children were now growing up and should be nearer scholls and so on; although the place was not actually on the market she had a feeling that a fair price might tempt them. The next evening she telephoned to say that they would consider selling, and the price they were asking. Which was rather more than half my savings; she assured me that it was reasonable, that the family had owned the house for more than four hundred years, that they were very distinguished and honourable, and that if I really did wish to settle in that part of France it was the ideal place for me.

It was. It stood three sides full to the winds; the north sheltered by a high hill and wood of ancient oaks; the east had the sea far below as a distant border, shimmering white in the November sun; to the west rose the seven hundred metre hump of the Bois de la Marbrière which would help to deflect the mistral which roared down from the Rhone Valley from time to time; and to the south the terraced land fell steeply to the plain and the wooded hills which rose eventually towards the craggy line of the Estoril range. Twelve acres of long abandoned vine and jasmine fields surrounded it, and four hundred venerable olive trees sheltered it from view, an uncompromising, stone-built, pink-tiled, shepherd's house, approached by a long rutted track. Above the front door leading directly into the stone sink and tiled-floored kitchen was a stone with the date deeply incised upon it. 1641. I knew that I had arrived.

The next day I went again, taking Simone (there were no householders to be bewitched; they had very discreetly vanished), and we were shown round the house by a plump girl listlessly sweeping out a shed. There was much to be done. But there were a lot of possibilities. Simone approved of the rough-cast walls, the tiled floors, the great oak beams, and a large photograph of Che Guevara pinned to the wall in the only, rather small, sitting room upstairs. Below were just stables and the kitchen with its immense open fireplace. She pronounced herself satisfied, said the place was 'une vraie maison', and that, knowing my obsession for privacy and solitude, she didn't think I need look further. I knew that I didn't, and by the following January the house and its land were mine to do as I pleased. I made arrangements to move in immediately after 'Death in Venice' was finished, some time in mid-summer, and for various alterations to be made in that time. I knew that living there would be a great challenge both financially and physically, but beyond that I had no doubts whatsoever. Yvonne Mitchell had secured me my foreseeable future.

It really would be refreshing to report that preparations for 'Death in Venice' went ahead smoothly, calmly and confidently. The reverse, alas, is true; it was all perfectly normal. We had to fight, cajole, push and batter to get Mr Mann's classical work even near a screen. Money, naturally, was the first problem; this was finally more or less overcome (we thought) by a grant, modest enough, from the Italian State. But we needed a great deal more.

'La Caduta degli Dei' (now re-titled 'The Damned' for English-speaking countries) was a tremendous success in America with eulogistic Press reports and highly encouraging attendances in the cinemas. We were the hit of the season and Visconti put it down to the fact that New York was a predominantly Jewish city (as were many of its critics) and the film was splendidly anti-German. Whatever the true facts we were successful, the only thing you need to be in America, and they offered to back his next venture. On certain conditions. First I must be replaced by one or other of two British players who, at that time, brought in a great deal more money to the box office than I did. Or ever would. This Visconti refused outright, insisting, to their bewilderment, that I was exactly like a pheasant hanging by its neck in the game larder, ready and perfect for the pot. They eventually agreed but promptly halved the budget which they had originally offered. Visconti still refused to yield me up, and settled for half-money.

Secondly, they insisted, or tried to insist, that Tadzio, the boy, should be played by a girl. This, they declared, would be far more acceptable to American audiences; if the story was left exactly as Thomas Mann had written it, it could only possibly mean one thing in that shining new country: 'a dirty old man chasing a kid's ass.' Visconti heard them out in a stunned silence. 'But if I change Tadzio to a little girl, and we call her Tadzia, you seriously believe that American audiences would be prepared to accept that?'

'We certainly do.'

'You do not think that in America they mind child molestation?'

There was, he told me, a nervous pause and then the spokesman bravely shook his head and said that they didn't see it like that.

'Mister Visconti, we do not envisage that kind of problem. We are not as degenerate here as you are in Europe,' he said comfortably. Vietnam was still to come.

'This is a search after purity and beauty,' said Visconti. 'Surely people will recognise that? They have been reading the book for many years. Even in America.'

The battle went on for almost a week; and finally, reluctantly, suspiciously, they capitulated on both points; and Visconti flew back from New York victorious, battered. There was not enough money to make the film exactly as he had planned unless everyone concerned with the project would accept severe cuts in their salaries. He himself said that he would accept no fee whatsoever. nd did not. Setting an example which was impossible to ignore. I accepted the salary offered by an extremely embarrassed producer (Visconti quite properly always avoided personal confrontations over money) of 40,000 dollars for five months' work (plus a large percentage of which, to this very day, I have never seen a cent).Silvana Mangano, who played the lady of the pearls, Tadzio's mother, waived her salary altogether, working only for her hotel expenses, and the rest of the troupe from the great Pasquale de Santis to the set decorators accepted equivalent reductions. It was more important to us all that the film was made; and buoyed by our cooperation Visconti set out, in an immense fur hat and a pair of seal-skin boots, to search for his Tadzio in the northern capitals.

He found him right away, on the first day of his search, in Stockholm. A slim, pale, blond boy of thirteen, Björn Andresen, who had been brought to the auditions by an ambitious grandmother and who was, in spite of a strong predilection for black Bubble Gum and The Beatles, the ideal choice. Anyone else was unthinkable; although Visconti, always a man of honour, carried out the rest of the tour from Copenhagen to Helsinki and only signed Andresen at the very last moment so as not to disappoint the many eager parents and children who flocked to his presence in the hopes of landing the part. Björn was not immediately impressed by the idea himself, but once it was promised that he would receive at least enough money from the modest salary that was offered him to be able to purchase an electric guitar and a motor bike he accepted, and the perfect Tadzio was ours.

We were on our way. Except for one very minor-major matter which seemed to cause Visconti not the least shred of concern. The rights to the subject. He was so sure that he would be able to secure them with no trouble at all, since he knew the Mann family well and was convinced that no one else would even want to attempt such a difficult proposition, that he simply never bothered to find out if they were free or not. Robin Fox telephoned from London four weeks before we were due to start work and very politely suggested that, if Visconti really did want to go ahead, mightn't it be a good idea to check the rights? He had heard from a fellow agent in New York that they did in fact belong to someone else, who planned not only to play von Aschenbach, but to write the script himself, direct it and produce it. A one man band. He had owned them for some long time and was not about to give an inch.

Consternation filled the quiet, elegant rooms of via Salaria when Forwood and I, after an urgent request for an appointment, arrived one evening with the news and came face to face with an ashen Visconti. The first time, and indeed the last, until his illness some years later, that I was ever to see him shattered into helplessness. At first he absolutely refused to believe that our news was correct or that Robin Fox knew what he was talking about and it was only by forcing him, almost physically, to lift his receiver and call the agent in New York that we succeeded in making him realise that the appalling rumours, as he had insisted on calling them, were in fact true. He hadn't even known how to dial New York, and when this was done for him, and when he had spoken at some length, the silence which followed his replacing of the receiver was frighteningly eloquent.

For a few moments he stared helplessly before him, one hand toying with a small ball of lapis lazuli, the other nervously flicking a Cartier lighter. 'It is true. True what they tell you. This dreadful thing. Orribile! He bought the rights long ago . . . but he does not set the film up . . . now he waits patiently like a tiger in the grass. What to do? Quel catastrophe! I am helpless; what can I do . . . eyee!'

It was distressing to see him sitting slumped in his great velvet chair among the Picassos, Klimts, Schieles and glittering bric-a-brac, his greatest plans in ruins about him like an exploded house of cards. Despondently we drove back to the villa on the hill near the cemetery with leaden hearts. 'Death in Venice' was clearly lost.

But Visconti rallied swiftly after our departure and three days later we were summoned back to via Salaria and a triumphant, if disgusted, victor explained in confidence that, after a long and bitter altercation on the telephone to America, followed by numerous vitriolic cables, in which he had threatened the unfortunate owner with ever possible kind of indignity and a 'great mischief in all the newspapers of the world which I will make personally,' he managed to buy him out. For a vast sum. The rights were now ours. But at such a cost; the already slender budget had further been depleted. Visconti's over confidence had cost us all dear. There was even less to work with now four weeks before starting, and strict and even savage econimies had to be made. I for one lost my entire wardrobe which had been meticulously planned down to the last button and hook eye, and made do with a couple of old second-hand suits, a too small evening jacket, and hats and shoes which Piero Tosi, the designer of the film and probably the most brilliant of them all, had somehow found for me from stock in the enormous wardrobe at Tirelli; but the crowd, so important to the film, and all carefully handpicked by Visconti himself, had to be halved and on it went, one slashing cut after another to try and balance up the shaking budget. But we were all cheerful in spite of this, and felt confident that once we really started, help, if we needed it, would come from somewhere. Although not one of us dared to consider where that somewhere could possibly be.

I, after all, was well used to working under duress and actually found that it increased the intensity of concentration. I spent the next three weeks reading and re-reading the book, and going through the unmitigated hell of having a nose built to resemble Mahler's own. This entailed hours of lying prone while plaster of Paris was poured over my face, two straws shoved up my nostrils so that I could breathe, and then anxious days of fitting the plastic model made to fit over my own nose. Once all that was done we had to start the packing up of

Villa Fratelli – taking the cats to the photographer in the village who promised them a home, sorting out the possessions which we had all of us accumulated in the year, and trying to placate Peppino who wept silent tears in his little shed with Gina Lollobrigida, his hat twisted in his fist, his face buried in the crook of his arm, even the sight of two months' salary failing to get him to raise his head. Signora Fratelli mistrustfully checked her very inadequate inventory, told us to leave the keys under a flower pot in the garden, and accordingly one dark, bitter March morning, exactly one year to the day that I had arrived there, we all drove away in convoy again, much as we had left the house in England, but this time for Venice; and with the addition of an extra passenger, since Labbo, the abandoned dog, had now become so much a part of life that to leave him would have been unthinkable.

Equally unthinkable to cart him round the hotels of Venice for five or six months, and to this end Visconti, who was deeply attached to the beast whom he called Poverino, sought and found a small house with an acre of garden which he persuaded his friends the Volpi's to allow me to rent, assuring them that though I was, unfortunately, a cinema actor, he could guarantee that I would not wreck it, turn it into a bawdy house, or receive any members of the Press there. This having been solemnly agreed to, and accepted, we all moved into Ca'Leone, a ravishing eighteenth-century house which, although cold, damp and often flooded, stood in an acre of flowering gardens on the lagoon immediately joining the gardens of the Redentore. We were all ravished by its calm and tranquillity, by the many arched colonnades, secret little piazzas, vines and trees, white walls, and elegant simple furnishings. The only one who actively disliked the whole project, acreage and trees included, was the dog. Ca'Leone was to become my evening sanctuary from the exhausting problems which beset 'Death in Venice' daily.

The first, I suppose, was the matter of Mahler's nose. It fitted perfectly and looked exactly as it should. After three hours of make-up on the very first morning of work, dressed in the old second-hand suit we had found, and from which I had hastily removed a tailor's lable bearing the date of its making, April 1914, lest Visconti reject it out of hand as being four years ahead of the story, my button boots and the uncompromising felt hat, I looked, in the mirror at least, very like Mahler himself. Visconti was in raptures.

'Ah!' he cried, clasping his beautiful hands. 'Ah! My Mahler! My Mahler!'

The only problem was that I was quite unable to move my head or face. Embalmed as I was in three hours' work of plastic, wax and glue, the very slightest movement caused the nose to crack immediately round the edges, from which oozed an extremely unbecoming fluid. The perspiration, which had gathered between my own unhappy member and its plastic and rubber addition, trickles implacably from the fissures which appeared every time I moved a muscle even to speak, and slid inexorably down my chin, beading there like crystal warts.

The groans of anguish which emanated both from Visconti and the unhappy Mauro, my make-up man, were as nothing to my own distress. It was impossible to use the nose; without it, I knew, I would have no character. I would be reduced just to my old familiar face, of which I was exceedingly weary, peering out from a baggy, brown suit. Although Visconti stubbornly insisted that we go ahead in the Mahler mould, I equally insisted that the only way I could go through the film under those conditions was in a wheel chair bolted by the neck to the headrest. It would, I felt, be at least a still performance. Eventually it was decided that Silvana mangano's make-up man, a retired gentleman of great experience who had agreed to leave his peaceful retreat in Tuscany to work again for his adored Mangano, should be the one to give the casting vote as to whether the nose could or could not be made workable. He pronounced it, after a good ten minutes close and agonising inspection, as impossible and sadly left the room.

There was a dreadful silence. So still was the small room in the Hotel des Bains where I was dressing that I could hear the gulls crying across the gardens, and the sea flat-lapping softly against the distant sands. Visconti sighed, lit a new cigarette and stared out of the windows; Mauro turned to the wall and leant against it, his tears quietly falling; Forwood looked stoically over my shoulder into the mirror, and I wrenched the sticky mess from my face and dropped it onto the waste-paper basket. Visconti quite suddenly slammed the window and looked at his watch.

'In one half an hour you must come downstairs to the big Saloon, we will have a glass of champagne there for the good luck. The Press are waiting, many friends are there to wish us success. At 2 o'clock we will make the first shot of the picture; it is necessary for the insurance people. Ciao.'

He and Mauro left the room and closed the door. I stared at my crumpled reflection. I looked exactly like a depraved choir-boy with bags under his eyes and a badly running nose. Mann and Mahler had never been so far away.

'What shall I do?' I was relieved at least to hear that my voice had broken.

'Difficult. You'll have to start from scratch again.'

'I have half an hour, I gather.'

'Well, you'll have to hurry up, won't you? Start thinking him.'

'But I just look like myself. They will all expect Mahler, that's what they've been told.'

Forwood was fingering through a small box of moustaches which Mauro had left behind in his grief. He handed me one at random. I stuck it on; it was bushy, greyish, Kipling. In another box of buttons, safety pins, hair grips, and some scattered glass beads he disentangled a pair of rather bent pince-nez with a think gold chain dangling. I placed the hat back on my head, wrapped a long beige woollen scarf about my neck, took up a walking stick from a bundle of others which lay in a pile, and borrowing a walk from my paternal grandfather, heavily back on the heels, no knee caps, I started to walk slowly round and round the room emptying myself of myself, thinking pain and loneliness, bewilderment and age, fear and the terror of dying in solitude. Willing von Aschenbach himself to come towards me and slip into the vacuum which I was creating for his reception.

And he came, not all at once, but in little whispers . . . bringing with him the weight of his years, the irritability of his loneliness, the tiredness of his sick body, and stiffly he went out into the long, long corridor which lead to the great staircase, walking heavily, thumping firmly with the stick for confidence, frighteningly aware of the rising sounds of voices and laughter from below, some idea of tears behind the glittering, pinching pince-nez. At the top of the staircase he stopped suddenly, one shaking hand holding the cool mahogany rail, trying to square the sagging shoulders which emphasised his agonising shyness; below, the hall seemed jammed with people he didn't know and had never seen before. Arrogance slid in like a vapour; carefully, firmly, no longer shaking now, he started to descend towards them, head held as high as it would go, legs as firm as they would allow, hand lightly touching the rail for moral support. There was a sudden hush in the crowded room. Faces swiftly turned upwards towards him, pink discs frozen. He continued slowly down, allowing himself the barest smile of German superiority. From a long way away he suddenly heard Visconti's voice break the almost unbearable stillness. 'Bravo!

Bravo!' it cried. 'Look, look, all of you! Look! Here is my Thomas Mann!'

I led a curiously isolated and protected existence for the next five months. I seldom, if ever, joined in with the troupe, or the other players, or met Visconti, or anyone else for that matter, socially; my life was in a state of limbo. Daily I sat alone on the Lido beach in my little cabana aloof and distant, silent and yearning as von Aschenbach himself. Indeed I had absolutely no doubt that I was him, and the exterior shell of my normal body was only the vessel which contained his spirit. My main objective at this time, which was understood and respected by everyone around me, was to remain in total, exhausting, concentration at all times and under all circumstances in order to contain this spirit which was so completely alien to myself. It was a fragile thing; I was constantly terrified that he would at one moment or another slip away from me. But he stayed. Eventually, even in the peace of Ca'Leone, alone in my garden massed now with nodding spikes of white hollyhocks, or walking through the silent piazzas of the city after I had changed into jeans and a tee-shirt, I still retained his walk and mannerisms which might have surprised anyone who didn't know that I walked as a man possessed without consciousness of the present world.

My relationship with Visconti was extraordinary. We were fused together in a world of total silence. We seldom spoke, and never ever about the film. We sat a little apart from each other, admitting each other's need for privacy, but never much more than a metre away. Incredibly we had no need of speech together. We worked as one person. I knew, instinctively, when he was ready, he knew when I was. We worked very much on sign language; a raising of eyebrows from him signified that all was set when I was. Should I shake my head, then he would sit again, and light another cigarette until such time as I felt myself in condition, and then I would touch his arm and walk towards the lights. We hardly ever shot two takes of anything – occasionally he would murmur, 'Encora' and we would do it again – but that was all that was ever said and it happened very few times.

Our behaviour startled the occasional stranger to the set. An American female photographer, forced upon us by our American bosses, haunted us for a few days, and was dispirited and furious at the same time, at our total lack of co-operation, which must, I suppose, have seemed rude to her. One day, in a bitterly sarcastic whisper I heard her remark that she had just heard us say 'good morning' to each other . . . right beside her.

'They've stopped feuding!' she said triumphantly.

Feuding! I told Visconti with a wry smile, and he patted my hand comfortably: 'Non capisce matrimonio, hey?' And it was a marriage indeed. We had never, at any time, discussed how I should attempt to play von Aschenbach; there were no discussions at all about motivation or interpretation. He chose the three suits I should wear, the two hats, the three ties, all my luggage and the shabby overcoat and scarf – and he had chosen me. Apart from that not a word was spoken. Once, just before our departure from Rome, I requested him to give me just half an hour to discuss the role. He grudgingly agreed and, telling me to help myself to wine on the table beside him, asked me how many times I had read the book. When I told him at least thirty, he advised another thirty and that was that; nothing more was ever said.

I think that the only direct instruction he ever gave me was one morning when he requested that I should stand upright in my little motor-boat at the exact moment that I felt the mid-day sun strike my face as we slipped under the great arc of the Rialto bridge. I did not know why I had to make this specific movement at such a precise time until I saw the final film with him some months later, and it was only then, too, that I realised he had been choreographing the entire film, shot by shot, blending all my movements to the music of the man he had wanted to embody the soul of Gustav von Aschenbach. Gustav Mahler.

The partial withdrawal from ordinary life was not, when all is said and done, as depressing as it might seem. Although I moved about in a sort of trance for most of the time I did manage to attempt some kind of normality on Sundays, the one day we had free, and Ca'Leone with Antonia and Eduardo at the helm welcomed carefully chosen, and sympathetic, guests – Kathleen Tynan, Rex Harrison, Alan Lerner, David Bailey, Alain Resnais and his wife Florence, Penelope Tree and Patrick Lichfield with all his cameras, and others who were understanding of what has been called my obsessional privacy and who allowed me to wander off back to the attendant shade of von Aschenbach whenever the need arose, without question.

Nor was I absolutely unaware of things which went on around my solitary figure sitting in the cabana on the beach. I noticed, casually, one day, that some of the troupe, carpenters, the script girl, an assistant property man for example, were walking about wearing neat little squares of white paint, no bigger than a postage stamp. I didn't pay very much attention, but after three or four days, and an ever-increasing amount of little white squares appearing on people's arms or legs or, once, on a forehead, I asked Mauro what was happening. His very evasiveness gave me a worrying clue. They were testing some kind of make-up. The more I took notice the more I saw that the patches were being worn on the most sensitive areas of the skin. It was a worrying clue because of all the things which I had to face in the film the thing which frightened me most was the actual, final, death scene, which I knew I would find difficult, and which I also knew Visconti was keeping to the very end of the work in Venice. Clearly that moment was upon us. They were testing special make-up because the one I would have to use must be a total death mask: it was to crack apart slowly, symbolising decay, age, ruin and the ultimate disintegration of a man's soul. But I kept silent, as was my habit, and merely watched with mounting terror the daily proliferation of little white patches among the troupe. Whatever they were using (or Mauro was trying to invent) was going to be both unpleasant, and possibly from the amount of care being taken, dangerous. The bolt hit me one morning, heavy and hot with the sirocco; the sea grey and flat, the wind spinning burning grains of sand across the beach, the heat almost insufferable. Visconti's perfect weather for his grand finale. I was told that today, towards four in the afternoon when the light would be exactly right, I should have to play the final death scene. In the make-up room Visconti was quiet, firm, and very gentle.

'Today is the perfect light, you see . . . the real sirocco . . . it will help you . . . the heat; you are sick now, and old; remember what Mann has said, you will have lips as ripe as strawberries . . . the dye from your hair will run . . . when you smile to Tadzio, your Summoner, your poor face will crack, and then you will die . . . I tell you all this because when you have the make-up on your face you will not be able to speak, it will be dead as a mask . . . we only do one take for that reason . . . it is hard like a plaster.'

'But what is it?'

'The make-up? Very good. We have tested very much. All will be well, you will see.'

He left me to Mauro who held in his hand a fat silver tube of a white substance which, when he applied it, immediately burned like fire and started to stiffen. It was too late to protest; for two hours I sat immobile while the stuff was plastered and smoothed to my wretched face. Before he had gone too far I was able, just, to implore him not to use it round my eyes, for from the intensity of the burning I was sure that it would blind me; he nodded sagely, and continued his work implacably. When it was finished I looked like a Japanese puppet. I was carried into a car and driven down to the beach lest the least movement should cause the by now iron-hard mask to crack or chip before the cameras turned. Two strong men carried my inert body across the burning, copper sand to the deck-chair placed ready for my demise. I had thought, foolishly, that the beach would be deserted and that tact would have been used to remove any idle bystanders frm my eye-line. Not so. Twenty feet away from my electric chair, for that is how it felt to me, ranged a line of eager spectators all seated comfortably under umbrellas, all with Instamatics, Nikons, Leicas and even, I noticed miserably, one pair of binoculars. In the very centre of this array sat Visconti himself, the host to his invited guests from Milan, Rome and Florence, who, led by Alida Toscanini, had been offered the great privilege of witnessing the final shot of his film. They all looked very jolly and relaxed, sipping cool drinks. If comparisons with the Coliseum flashed into my mind they could be forgiven. Someone removed my hat and fixed, with dexterity, a small plastic sac of black dye . . . this was to break with the heat generated under my hat, when the moment came, and would run down my painted face. I noticed hopelessly that someone had placed three long pieces of bamboo cane in the sand before me. One quite near, one further away, the third five metres out into the leadened sea. Albino, leaning close to my ear, whispered that the first cane marked the position of the fight between Tadzio and Jaschiu; the second would represent Tadzio after he had broken away; and the third his ultimate position in the sea beckoning to me, and pointing out an immensity of rich expectations.

Since I could not speak, let alone breathe (it is exhausting to breathe only through one's nose for any length of time) for fear of cracking the scalding mask, I was able simply to reply by hand movements and when Albino asked me in a deferential whisper, a priest giving the last rites, if I was ready, I drew the figure 5 with one finger on my knee. This he interpreted as five minutes, correctly, so that I could prepare. The silence was intense. The visitors were stiff now with apprehension. I could hear the hot wind flipping the little frills of the sheltering umbrellas; somewhere miles away a child laughed. I looked at the three markers, felt the heat rising within my body, my heart racing, the blood surging, and raised my hand for the cameras. We had three to cover this supreme moment and I never even heard Visconti's accustomed cry of 'Actione!'

Back in the make-up room Mauro was beside himself with joy, slapping his thighs, hitting the walls with the flat of his hand, brushing tears of happiness and triumph from his glowing eyes. Everything, as far as he was concerned, had worked. The hair dye had run perfectly, the face had cracked, the strawberry red lipstick had smeared, my tears had coursed through the wreckage; it had been splendid. Apparently the dying bit had been all right too.

We worked for an hour with soap and water, a palette knife, cold cream, petrol, and a pair of blunt scissors to remove the white make-up. My face, when parts of it emerged, was crimson and blistered, burned like a severe scalding. 'Tomorrow will be better; you see. We put some pommade on; you will sleep, all finished by tomorrow morning. Is sure.' Mauro was highly encouraging.

'What was it?'

He picked up one of the many squashed tubes which littered the table before me. 'Is the idea of me, Mauro! Is English preparation, very save, is English, made in England, must be safe for you.'

I took the flattened tube from his hand. He had carefully scraped off most of the label. All that remained were the words '—ghly Inflammable. Keep away from eyes and skin'. It was a preparation used for removing oil stains from fabric.

We finished shooting on August 1st in a plum orchard high up a mountain outside Bolzano, precisely at lunch time. There was no celebration; after five months of work, six days a week and mostly between the hours of two am and seven am, in order to catch the dawn light, a substitute for the overcast light of the sirocco, and also to avoid the traffic and tourists of daytime Venice, we were all far too exhausted even to think of celebrating anything except the fact that we had actually, amazingly, finished the project. Visconti and I shook hands in silence; I had my hair cut, changed into jeans and a shirt and went to take my leave of him in the local village Pensione, where, in spite of everything, he was starting his lunch.

'You eat nothing, Bogarde?'

'No, thank you. I'm all packed now. Cars ready.'

'You drive to Provence now? Is long, no?'

'Twelve hours about . . . we'll stop in Cremona . . .'

'And you have Poverino, certo . . .'

'Sure. He's very happy. Hated Venice.'

'You take him from his country, poor Poverino . . .'

'He'll like France. There are twelve acres.'

Deliberately he cut himself a thin slice of sausage and removed the skin. 'So now you both become Frenchmen. One English, one Italian. Avventuroso!' He pulled out a chair beside him and patted the rush seat. 'Sit down, one little moment. Good. Now.'

He closed his eyes for a moment. 'I am thinking to make the Proust, *La Recherche*. You know this?'

'Yes. A long time ago.'

'But you like?'

'Of course.'

'I am thinking in my head of Olivier for Charlus, good eh? You must think of Swann perhaps, yes?'

'But not for a long time surely?'

'Ah no, maybe two years. Who can tell, there is much work to do first.'

'Because I want to stop acting now for a few years.'

His eyebrows rose in chevrons of polite surprise.

'To stop? How so?'

'Had enough. I'm nearly fifty. I've done fifty-five films. Basta.'

'But you came to Europe to work, you told me.'

'I know. But during this film I came to a decision. I don't know if I am good in it, or if it is good, how can I? But I do know that whatever happens it marked the peak for me in work. The summit. Where do you go from the summit but down?'

He laughed suddenly and punched my arm. 'I am on a summit too, Bogarde. I go on to another one; I do not descend! To do Proust maybe . . . or *The Magic Mountain*, you would like this? Another Mann, I go on, I have many summits to reach and I am sixty; we have much we can do together, more to say, eh?'

'Yes; but today I know I finished one part of my life, in a few moments I will start off to begin a new part in a new country. It is not easy. I want time to settle, to think, to rest. Maybe two or three years. I am now out of the competition, I don't want to fight any more. Resnais has brought me a beautiful script, the Marquis de Sade in the Bastille. Poetry, beauty, but he will never get the finance, it will be the old battles all over again; one man in a cell! Who will care? If it was one man in a cell with two naked women and whips then they will care. But the fight we have had with the Americans to make our film has made me revolted. No more. I stop. It was the finish for me. I know what their Press will do to us; you remember the man from Chicago?'

He brushed the wooden table thoughtfully, cupping a pile of crumbs into his hand and spilling them into his plate.

'Ah, the Press,' he snapped his fingers, 'you live by the Press, you will die by the Press. They say I am losing touch . . . that I shoot only the surface of the emotions, that I am degenerate, that I am operatic! They say so stupid things. They have only theory not practice, they cannot construct only criticise, and if they find something they do not comprehend they get angry and destroy like children! Pouf! You must think nothing of them. They do not *risk*, nothing ever. How can they know, eh? Callas risks. Stravinsky, Seurat, Diaghilev all risked; even *we* risk. All true creators must. Think only of the people for whom we work. The audiences. They understand, they know, they encourage. You see.'

'Well, for the moment I have had enough; today I finish. I'm not "retiring" exactly, but I will no longer seek employment from now on.'

'You are just tired old horse, eh? No more race.'

'Exactly. No more racing. I don't want to try to win anything any more.'

'So you go out to grass; excellent. But you will come to me if I call you, for a little lump of sugar?'

'Of course I will, in time . . .'

'Ah yes, in time. There is much to think about. Maybe, you know, we even do the life of Puccini. Opera! Really Opera. The Press will comprehend that at least. You think of Puccini too in your shepherd's house. We have many possibilities together, I think. But we have not finished yet with Mr Mann, you know, there is still work to do. Looping for the sound, I think. Not much, some.'

'Of course. When will you know? How soon will ou see all the work, the first assembly of "Death in Venice"?'

He broke a piece of bread and kneaded it thoughtfully. He never, ever, saw the daily work on the film, relying only on the great de Santis, his cameraman, who did, for assurance that everything was as it should be; with five months work to look at I was sure it would be an age before he could give me a verdict on our joint effort which had started in such turmoil and which had ended so peacefully just now under the plum trees. He took a sip of his wine, wiped his lips carefully and smiled suddenly at me.

'Ah! You do not know; but I have already seen nearly all, nearly all, just not the last three or four days is all. You did not know, hey?'

'No. And . . . I mean . . . is it all right, Luchino?'

He folded his hands carefully before him on the woden table. 'You look for compliments, that is it?'

'No, Christ no . . .'

'Your work transcends anything that I even remotely dreamed of.' He suddenly took my head and kissed me roughly on both cheeks. 'Go away!' he commanded and turned back to his lunch.

It was a long, and silent, journey down the valley to Brescia and Cremona in the blistering afternoon sun. The dog slept trustingly in the small space available to him left by a junkshop of coats, books, typewriters, plastic bags and an ornate silver-plated salver, a gift from the troupe on parting. Forwood doubtless had his own problems; the furniture vans from England would arrive within thirty-six hours, Antonia and Eduardo would be arriving shortly at Nice airport after their brief holiday in Spain to join us, for six months only, in order to settle us into the new house. He was also probably mourning the loss, months before when we left Villa Fratelli, of the Rolls which had been shipped back to England and sold, since the tax on such a car in France would have been prohibitive; and, anyway, who could use a Rolls up and down a goat-track? The big cut-down had started. And although it was far away from the two-suitcase small-flat syndrome, it was a determined start on a different way of life, and one to which, under the waves of fatigue, I was eagerly looking forward. Fatigue had smothered reaction so far. I was not yet in the desperate state which the ending of 'Accident' had induced; no tears on this journey for the departed von Aschenbach, for he had not lingered long. His hair had tumbled greyly about my heels under Mauro's ruthless scissors, his buttoned boots I had seen being tied together, labelled and thrown into a vast wicker hamper by Maria in the wardrobe room; she had bundled up his white suit and battered panama hat, tied them roughly with string, and sent them to follow, reserving only, at the last moment, with gentle Italian insight, the pair of steel-rimmed spectacles which, wordlessly, she had slipped into the pocket of my jeans jacket. When the last dyed lock of hair had fallen, when Maria slammed shut the lid of the hamper and wrestled with the padlock, I knew, for certain that he had gone. It was not so much a hamper which had closed but another door. And how nearly I had turned my back on that door in the gardens by the aviary of blue macaws so long ago in Salzburg. Notarianni loping anxiously across the evening lawns buttoning up his jacket: 'Buona sera . . .' Just in time.

I knew, clearly, that 'Death in Venice' was, for me at any rate, the culmination of years of work and training, of learning from and striving under such teachers as Dearden, Leacock, Ralph Thomas, Asquith, Cukor, Milestone, Losey, Clayton and Schlesinger, a not inconsiderable fraternity, which had prepared me for the hardest job I had ever had to do. Apparently I had satisfied Visconti and since he appeared to me to be the Emperor of my profession I was content.

I had not seen even a millimetre of the work we had done together; I must rely on his word. Perhaps eventually we should be savaged by the Press, for we had attempted to film an unfilmable, it was said, minor masterpiece, and that was always a dangerous, precocious, thing to do. The slightest degree of failure would mean disaster. But my instinct told me that whatever happened to it finally, it could have a deep and lasting effect upon the audiences who might come to see it . . . at least in Europe. In America one could not be sure; generally their culture is so very different from ours, the barrier of the common-tongue so firmly in place, the nuance, diplomatically, intellectually and above all conversationally, so despairingly extinct, the dislike and fear of degenerate Europe so strongly imbedded, that there we might easily be destroyed.

I had remembered the man from a big Chicago newspaper eventually managing to corner Visconti in a stinking alley while we were setting up a shot. Hot, sweating, furious at having been avoided, he attacked like an Evangelist, his pencil and pad shaking with righteous anger. 'Look, I came all this way . . . I even passed up the really *big* picture they're doing in Padua with Loren and Mastroianni just to try and give you a *break* . . . and what is this? You say you don't care about publicity! You refuse to see me . . . I came from Chicago . . . we can do you a lot of good in our columns . . . you be careful . . . this is a very, very dangerous subject you are making, I understand . . . just who the hell are

you making it for, Mister Visconti?' He sat back in his canvas chair fanning
himself with his note pad, a hot toad.

Visconti raised his eyes slowly, looked at me with a little smile, deliberately
patted my hand, 'For Bogarde and myself,' he said pleasantly.

Chicago left shortly after, and wrote nothing. I had laughed aloud at the
splendid conceit. But now it was all over, and I, sitting speeding towards my
brave new life, was too tired, drained and, it had to be admitted, apprehensive
for the future which lay ahead. However, of one thing I was now very certain; I
would never go back into competition again. The doors along the corridor
could all remain closed as far as I was concerned, I would not push one, nor
venture again towards them, however tempting they might seem. I would wait
until they were opened for me; until someone came out and literally dragged me
protestingly in. I was no longer curious, anxious to prove, seeking; I had, it
seemed to me, reached a point beyond which I now no longer wished to explore.
What I had been taught, what I had done eventually with that teaching, what I
had worked for had, as far anyway as I was concerned, at last been achieved; I
did not think that I could better myself. I would happily go out to grass now, as
Visconti had said. But if one day he, or Resnais or some other magic piper as yet
unknown to me called, I should, most likely, follow. For me now the game, for
such is what it had all been really, was almost over. But not quite.

Forty years ago, in her little parlour in Twickenham while Elizabeth and I
had placed the cups and saucers after supper tidily back on the dresser, Lally
would take down the box of games from the mantelshelf. 'One last game of
snakes and ladders before we go up the wooden hill to Bedfordshire!' she would
say. The board would be laid out on the bamboo table before the glowing
range, the counters and dice scattered, and in the honey-glow of the hanging
lamp we would be off. Up the ladders and down the dreadful snakes we would
go, tongues hanging out with the intense concentration of willing the dice to
tumble with the numbers which we needed; and then one of us would hit the
base of the tallest ladder and whizz right up to the top of the board a few squares
only away from the one marked WIN. And this was the most dangerous part.
For lying in wait was the tip of the tail of the longest snake who would lead you
terrifyingly all the way down to START again. A three and a one, or a double
two, and you were lost.

It seemed to me that afternoon on the road to Cremona, Genoa, the frontier
and France that this was just exactly where I had now got to in this dangerous
game of ups and downs and that the next throw of the dice would be decisive. It
was a game of chance, not skill, and although I might close my eyes, cross my
fingers or murmur a couple of Hail Mary's, only fate could possibly decide on
which square I should land eventually . . . the one with the snake's tail or the
other marked WIN. I tried to comfort myself with the thought that it was no
good worrying, there was nothing much I could do about it anyway; Judy's
song from long ago came back to me:

> But it's all in the game,
> and the way you play it,
> and you've gotta play the game
> . . . . you know . . .

An Orderly Man

For
E.L.L. Forwood

ACKNOWLEDGEMENTS

I am indebted to Chatto & Windus Ltd for allowing me to use extracts from their letters written to me. Also to Mrs G. Goodings, Mrs A. Holt, and the executors of 'Mrs X's' estate in America.

As always, most particularly, to Mrs Sally Betts who has managed to make some order out of my typescript in record time.

D.v.d.B.

ONE

I am an orderly man. I say this with no sense of false modesty, or of conceit. It is a simple statement of fact. That's all. Being orderly, as a matter of fact, can be excessively tiresome and it often irritates me greatly, but I cannot pull away. I sometimes think that I would far prefer to live slumped in some attic amidst a litter of junk, dirty underclothing, greasy pots and pans, paints and canvases strewn about everywhere, an on-the-point-of-being-discarded mistress weeping dejectedly on the stairs, fungus on the walls, and an enormous overdraft at the bank or, better still, absolutely no money at all. Unvarnished, music-less, Puccini.

But it just wouldn't work for me. I have to live in an orderly manner; I'd tidy up the attic in a flash, scrub the pots and pans, stack the canvases, exterminate the fungus, label the paints and send the mistress back to her mother. Or husband. And keep what money I had, as frugally as a miser, in a sock beneath my mattress. Orderly is what I am. You only have to see my plate at table, when I have dealt with asparagus, kippers or an artichoke, to know this: neat bundles of chewed stalks; bones and skin precisely laid aside in immaculate little blocks; tidy piles of leaves stacked as carefully as Dresden saucers.

All this is done quite unconsciously. I am not aware that I discard my rubbish in so fastidious, not to say elegant, a fashion. It simply happens. There they are. No scattered heaps of detritus or masticated vegetable matter. Neat, tidy, organized packets on a pristine platter. I often wonder, why? I look with quiet astonishment at my contribution to the dustbins.

What instinct makes me behave in this extraordinary fashion? Is it something which I have inherited from my father: a man who was always correct, contained, persistent and fully planned all his life? Or is it some hideous subconscious fault which a psychiatrist would hold against me as a sign of some monstrous flaw in my otherwise apparently serene make-up. God knows. But it is always there, and it has ruled my life from my earliest days. Precision, order, plan.

I live, and I must live, according to a pattern which I have made for myself, and fill it in with great care. I take grave risks with it, of course: bend it, turn it, sometimes even turn it quite over, re-arrange it, re-design it, but it is always within its frame, just as a stained-glass window is bounded by the strong pillars of its stone arch.

If a risk seems to me to be too dangerous (that is one which might shatter the whole amazing fabric itself), then I swiftly modify the risk and find another way to go about the alteration, seeking a less satisfying, less exciting, but far safer way of placing the bright fragments of life. No Nicholson or Sutherland am I: rather a Burne-Jones or Millais. In short, I am not abstract, I am realist. I think.

Often pinched by doubt.

But, after all, one cannot, at sixty-two, look back down the corridor of one's life and not have *some* doubts about the journey one has made. The doors which one opened are now all closed. The doors one did not dare to open remain shut. The corridor is dark; only ahead is lighter. So one turns and proceeds in that direction. To go back is madness. To turn left or right, at this stage, is both exhausting and dangerous.

However, there was not the least shadow of a doubt in my mind when we crunched gently up the rutted track towards this house one golden November day twelve years ago. Not the very slightest. From the moment that we turned off the narrow road up the lane between giant olive trees and wound up the hill among spiky amber grasses, jutting rocky outcrops, crimson brambles, sparkling little springs of crystal water in verdant bog, all under a sky the colour of Fabergé's blue enamel, I knew that the track was the right track and that my pattern was intact. And that the house, framed in its saffron vine and a large orange and lemon tree, was just about to fit into that pattern as smoothly and effortlessly as a foot into a well-worn slipper. After months of trailing about France, and before that most of Italy, I knew that I had found my ideal without once having set a toe across its threshold. It was instinctively, physically, and most important, spiritually, the exact fragment which I needed to complete my orderly pattern. There it was, glowing brightly in the sun. Waiting for me to embrace it and fit it into my life. Which I did.

Fitting *myself* into it proved, on the other hand, to be quite another matter. Crossing the threshold that morning for the very first time, I discovered that the ground floor consisted of three separate quarters. A kitchen with a vast canopied fireplace, a stone sink in one corner and a set of dusty sequinned drums and a music stand set in the centre of the tiled floor. Next door, down a couple of steps, two lofty stables, one for sheep, one for carts.

On the second floor, arrived at by a curving slate staircase, a sitting-room with an upright piano and a photograph of Che Guevara; beyond it three small bedrooms and a pitch dark bathroom. On the same level, just beside Mr Guevara, a door led up two steps into a sort of black pit, which had a stove and a sink and could have held two people in a grave emergency, and one in extreme discomfort. Above all this, running the length of the entire house, was a vast room which had recently been the hay loft. That's all. I admired the circular windows in the hay loft and the view from them of the massed olives below, and the sea shining some way off like a sheet of silver paper. I was instantly in love.

If the house did not quite contain the accommodation which I knew I should require for this permanent abode, it did contain the space. In my mind I rapidly decided that the ground floor should be opened up to form one enormous fifty-foot room, retaining the kitchen part, arching through the separating stable walls. The ceilings were all, most fortunately, on the same level; the floors rather attractively, I thought, on differing ones. Where the stable door was, presently swinging in the gentle autumn wind, I would have a window made. I should retain the canopied fireplace, convert the hay loft, put in an extra bathroom, and come to terms with the black pit at some later date. The house had limitless possibilities, only my bank balance was restricting. So I must go carefully at the start, and with the invaluable help of Mr Loschetter, my architect, and a rough set of scribbled sketches in his notebook, the ideas conceived between us all rapidly became almost-possibilities. Almost fact indeed. Loschetter nodded sagely and assured me that, as long as I did not desire a swimming-pool, marble stairs, plate-glass windows, wrought iron, and central heating throughout, it need not cost me a fortune. I asked only that the house be made large enough within its walls to provide the accommodation I required and that it should, above all else, retain the character which five hundred years had bestowed upon it. The arches which we would make through the downstairs walls must be irregular, the floors not completely level, the windows must be in sympathy with the ones which already existed, and the plaster must have the texture of centuries instantly imposed upon it. He was suddenly relieved and almost affable. He later confessed that he had heard that I was in 'the movies' and expected to have to gut the house, build a sauna and a swimming-pool, and string Venetian lanterns from every ceiling. When I asked him what he would have done had I insisted on these bits of kitsch, he said sharply that he would have 'quitted the job'.

He stayed, thankfully, and promised that everything would be perfectly ready and in order by the time I arrived back from my work on 'Death in Venice' in Italy, which was soon to start. He had no qualms, a splendid workforce of well-trained craftsmen, understood my sympathetic feelings for the house, would only use the most ancient of materials, and assured me that I could have every confidence in him. I had It was all very orderly. Just what I wanted.

Except that I had not yet got it. A small point; but important.

From that day in November until the middle of January the battle to secure the house raged. The Bank of England stumbled about, blind to the fact that I was desperately anxious lest some other person might make an offer right away and move in. Papers and forms wandered through the air between London and Rome, where I was at that time living in a rented villa above a slum village, and I drove desperately across Italy almost weekly to show good faith and to re-assure the doubting owner that I was serious and all would be well. Eventually, after a great deal of desperate haggling, battling, pleading and struggle, the money was released from the vaults and the house was within my grasp. Numb with relief, I then went into the French phase. That is to say, I discovered that my limited knowledge of that language was of no use at all when it came to dealing with the French law, taxes, the rights of way, plumbing, septic tanks, boundaries and, above all, I speedily learned, something called French Logic. An example? Well: you are ill in bed and wish to have it re-made lying, as you are, in a rumple of sheets and discomfort. The nurse, if she is French, will explain politely that she obviously cannot remake your bed as you are at the moment occupying it. French Logic. My sense of order was constantly outraged, and I was thrown daily into a state of anguish and disarray, from which I was sure I would never recover.

Fortunately I realized, very quickly indeed, that I simply had to come to terms with things as they presently stood, and to tread my new path with calmness, caution, humility and, above all, patience, love and tolerance. If I were to live the rest of my life out in France, as I sincerely hoped I would, and yet still behave as if I were living in England, then I would very shortly come to grief.

I had seen it happen to so many exiles who had made the journey before me. Lonely, isolated, wistful, clinging in desperation to shrinking pensions, the BBC World Service, old London newspapers and the enervating company of the other expatriates at bridge and cocktail parties. That was no sort of life: one might just as well have gone to live in Sidmouth or Cheltenham.

Here I was, facing a new life pattern, one of my deliberate choosing, one which I had dreamed of having for as long as I could remember, certainly from my very earliest days when we came over to France each summer for the cherished holidays which marked me for ever with a deep and undying love for the country. And long ago I had decided that one day, when the time was right,

I would seek out a place of my own there and stay for good.

The time was now, the place had been sought and found, and I was on the very brink of making the great change, so . . . all my preconceived and accepted ideas and notions must be set aside for they would not fit into the scheme of things, or into my new pattern of life which I hoped was stretching out ahead of me like an unwalked map. If I tried to fit them in, if I tried to adapt or bend them at this point of the journey, I'd be lost.

So. Calm down, Listen. Watch, try to understand what takes place, how things are done, how things are *not* done. Reason with it all, and, above all else, try to see the French point of view: for it is their country you are about to enter, and they know it far better than you do and how to make it work for them. After all, you are not starting negotiations to purchase a holiday caravan; you are negotiating for a new life. Yours. So you'd better take it all very seriously indeed. Even the logic. Just remember that second chances don't come so easily at forty-nine.

All this went through my head as I lay sleepless in my hotel bedroom the night before I was due to present myself at the local Notaire's office in a neighbouring village, to set my name to the deeds of the house and surrender my cheque, just wrestled from the Bank of England, which amounted to a great deal more than half my life savings. My bonnet, if not actually at this moment over the windmill, had been thrown high. Time to take things very seriously indeed: to remain calm, to be orderly.

Order restored, somewhat, I turned on my side and attempted sleep.

In a cutting wind, brilliant sunshine, and a thick tweed coat, I was outside the Notaire's office, with Forwood, at precisely five to nine the following morning. Loschetter and his wife Clair, who had now most agreeably taken over all the fussing legalities since she knew the ropes and spoke faultless English, were waiting, smiling and stamping fur-booted feet. As the village clock clanged the first stroke of nine, we entered the Notaire's bureau and all at once a sudden hush of sanctity and gravity descended about us like a pale shroud.

A shadowy room, wood-panelled. On one side, neat and tense in bentwood chairs, the owner and his representative all with dark suits, briefcases and heavy glasses; on the other, our bentwood chairs standing empty on thin legs like insects, waiting. Before us on a high podium behind a large desk, the Notaire, a youngish man with a framed photograph of an unsmiling President flanked by two furled tricolours and a wreath. On our entrance there was a scraping of chairs and the assembly rose in a rustle of blue suits and papers. A silent 'Good morning' was nodded and we eased into our seats. The atmosphere was extremely grave. A case of rape, perhaps? Or embezzlement?

No. The purchase of a house. I couldn't imagine why my mouth was suddenly so dry.

Needless to say, it all took a very, very long time indeed and I didn't understand a single word uttered. My sense of order and discipline started to slip. I became completely lost, and although Clair whispered the translations rapidly, I was none the wiser, for I was far out of my depth with the legalities; even in English. I only knew for certain that my offer had been accepted and that now, one hour later, they were still discussing the house and its twelve acres with as much intensity and attention to detail as if my offer had been for Versailles and its entire park. Furnished.

Clair suddenly touched my arm to attract my wandering attention.

'Now they will make the renouncement,' she said in a low voice.

The room was suddenly hushed. A crackle of papers, rustle of a coat, a chair scraped on the stone floor. A tall, white-haired, aged man, faded and wrinkled, as if he had been stored like an apple in an attic, rose unsteadily to his feet and, raising his right arm high above the silent group below him, renounced his rights to the house and the land which had been in his family's possession for over five hundred years, 'for all eternity'. Three times he repeated, slowly and deliberately, the words, 'Je renonce. Je renonce. Je renonce.' The room was still. He turned to look at me with a tired, kind, smile, nodded his head, and sat down carefully. I found it extremely moving.

Clair gave me a pen and, as I signed my name to the deeds, she handed my cheque in a sealed envelope to the old man's son, M. Claude, who was, or had been until that moment, the nominal owner.

Outside in the brilliant sunlight we suddenly came back to life. Hands were shaken, hats removed, and the ex-owner, he of the sequinned drums, suggested a glass of wine to warm us and to seal the deal in all amicability. We crossed the dusty square to the local bar in grateful acceptance. The deliberations had taken so long that the bar was almost full, and the heady scent of thick tobacco and pastis made me realise how badly I needed my glass of rouge, which arrived at the marble-topped table by the stove almost before I had had time to wedge myself into my chair.

'Well!' said Clair, spreading her hands to the glowing heat. 'Now you are the patron! You have your house at long last. Do you feel happy?'

'I feel extraordinary. I can hardly believe it after all the struggle and the worry . . . all I want to do is go there immediately and start measuring things.'

She looked at me with a gentle smile. 'Measure what things?'

'Oh, the rooms, the walls for pictures. I have really only seen the house twice, you know. Now I want to get down to things before I return to Rome.'

Clair lifted her glass of wine, raised it in a light toast and said, 'Ah, but that is not possible, you know.'

I didn't know.

'It is in the contract. You cannot visit the house just as you please.'   'But it is mine!'

'Yes, yours, but you cannot take possession until April.'

'Why?'

'It is in the contract. The family must not be disturbed and they will vacate in April, when they have found alternative accommodation. So you cannot visit it.'

'But this is madness!'

'It is in the contract.'

'But I *must* see it again. I have to go with your husband and decide on a hundred things . . . '

She shrugged gently. 'He cannot start to do anything for you until April. They will not permit it.'

'But it is *my* house!' I began to bleat like a sheep in desperation.

'You understand that the family do not know that their papa has sold the house. And the children will be unhappy. He wishes to break the news of the sale to them very gently, as a *fait accompli*, before he does anything else. There will be many tears, you know.'

'You mean he didn't tell them? They don't know that I own the place?'

Clair looked uncomfortable. 'No. They do not know yet. He felt it was wiser to do it this way. Now that it is done, it is done. It is all in the contract, you know. Did you read it carefully?'

Not carefully enough, I realised wretchedly. The ex-owner, Jean-Paul, was looking excessively sheepish during this exchange; although he did not understand a word of English, he very well understood my anguish and surprise. As if to try and mollify my anger he cautiously pushed a sheet of crumpled paper towards me, and murmured something under his breath to Clair.

'Ah! M. Claude has here a list of all the animals and birds which you will find on your land, is not that very thoughtful of him?'

'I would far rather know where the plugs and switches are, and where I can fit a new bathroom.'

'If you look at this list you will see how many splendid beasts you support. Look. There is a badger; you have pheasant . . . '

I looked at the list in crushed silence. Jean-Paul hastily went to get himself another glass of rouge. Numb with disappointment, I looked down the list.

Badgers indeed were there, partridge, pheasant and rabbits; black, I noted. The hoopoe and the golden oriole came every spring, the cuckoo arrived with the punctuality of a Mussolini train on 16th April, the nightingale a little later, and the swallows a week after. There was a fox in the oak wood at the back of the house, and wild flowers of bewildering species in abundance. I should never lack for water on the hill, for there were clear springs all over the land, and the olive trees numbered exactly four hundred.

But none of this could be mine until the arrival of the nightingale and the swallows. Or the cuckoo.

However, after a very lengthy, and sometimes heated discussion with M. Claude wringing his hands and shaking his long locks about his shoulders, it was finally agreed that I would be allowed to visit the house just one more time, in company with Loschetter or Clair, while his wife was away in Nice and the children were at school. In that time we were to make our final plans and decisions about the alterations, and the time laid down was very exact. From ten a.m. until eleven-thirty a.m. The children would be back at noon precisely to start lunch. One and a half hours to re-plan an entire house. Well: we did it. Order prevailed generally. The next morning we arrived at the house, attacked the problems, took a mass of photographs, and stole away like thieves as the first child, aged about six, wobbled up the track from school on his bicycle. Loschetter would start work sometime in April and I would return, all being well, in July: for 'Death in Venice' would fully occupy me until that time . . . and probably even longer. It was a tormenting thought. However, as Forwood wisely pointed out, the house was mine. Loschetter was very sensible, capable and fully understanding, and I had a very big job ahead of me on the film. When it was over the house would be ready, or ready enough, for me to move in in some kind of order. Meanwhile we had plans, measurements, many photographs, and we could spend our time, during the shooting of the film, making lists of the furniture, packed and stored somewhere in London, which we would require or reject. First things first. The house was secured, so now back to Rome and the demands of Visconti, Thomas Mann, and the ghostly shade of Von Aschenbach who was waiting tentatively in the shadows of my mind.

One morning in the middle of July, sitting alone, as was my habit throughout the making of the film, so that I could contain complete concentration, Forwood arrived at the door of my little beach hut on the Lido, with a telegram. It was from Loschetter to say, very simply, that the house was finished and the front door key was hanging on a nail behind the orange tree.

The film was, at last, slowly drawing to a close. In a week's time I knew that we should have finished the main shooting in Venice and would move up to Germany to shoot the opening shots of the film in some abandoned cemetery and, later, a railway station. This move would take at least a couple of days, which would be the first free days away from my alter ego, Von Aschenbach, that I had had since he had come to join me in early March. I resolved that we would use those two days by driving to the house to see what had been done and to make the final plans for the arrival of the furniture from England, for although the film had overrun its original schedule by many weeks, the light was clearly at the end of the tunnel and August, or the early part of that month, must see it finished.

Grudgingly, for he was appalled that I could allow any personal problems to come near me at such a time, Visconti allowed me to make the trip on the clear understanding that I should break the threads of my concentration for only forty-eight hours. I promised this faithfully, and we drove through the night a week later, to France, and on the morning of July 21st, in blinding heat, I found the front door key on its nail behind the orange tree and pushed open the heavy wooden door into the house.

And there it was. Just as I had always hoped it would be. Loschetter had been as good as his word. Inside, the whole house sparkled in a fresh coat of whitewash, the dingy khaki plaster had gone, the drums had gone, the canopied kitchen and the two crumbling stables were now transformed into a long, cool, elegant room, fifty feet in length, linked by gently irregular arches. Ancient tiles covered the once dirt and concrete floors, the stable door was a graceful window, the giant beams had been stripped, sanded and cloth-washed with white, the whole place was light, serene as if it had been thus for centuries.

On the floor above, Che Guevara had gone, along with the upright piano which had almost filled the small room; the black pit was less black under a coat of white paint, and a shining new cooker standing in the centre of the floor gave it an almost immediate feeling of space and light. But it was still too small, and I wondered how Antonia would manage when she arrived from Spain to 'settle me in', as she and Eduardo had promised. However, for the moment, that could wait. I went on up to the hay loft and found to my delight that it was now a set of three pleasant bedrooms and a bathroom. We were complete. I looked out of the round windows, which had been retained, and down across the olives and the huge untended vine. Hollyhocks in all colours nodded on tall spikes, lizards dozed, and Labo, the stray dog which I had found in Rome, ran about the tussocky grass far below, putting up rabbits. It was all exactly what I had hoped.

Downstairs, in the long white room, sitting on a box and drinking a beer from the bottle, I looked about me and wondered how it would look with all the furniture which was soon to be on its way from England. Would it fit? Would all the planning which had gone on over the months with lists and graph paper and detailed measurements of chairs and pictures have been a waste of time, or would every item slip comfortably into its allotted place? The room looked as if it would easily contain every stick which I had chosen to bring abroad.

Before I had left the last house in England, I had had a vast sorting-out of all my goods and possessions, knowing that never again, come what may, would I have a house of forty rooms; for this was the 'cutting down' period, the two suitcases and small flat plan. Except that the present house, small as it was, was certainly not a flat, and there were already rather more than the two allotted suitcases of my theory that from now on I must travel, so to speak, light. And live simply. A great auction had been held of all the surplus stuff. Books, furniture, paintings, glass, china and God only knows what else. For two days the housewives of Guildford and Godalming fought hysterically to outbid each other for items which ranged from a Minton tea set of sixty pieces to a wicker hamper containing two tin plates, a wooden towel rail and a hurricane lamp. The dealers arrived in heavy overcoats and picked through my dud Old Masters, carting several away in exchange for comfortable cheques, and the hysteria mounted as did the money. I was bemused, amused, and only saddened that I had been forced to part with so many books, some two thousand. But two thousand books bundled into boxes took up room, and there was, I felt certain, nowhere that they would fit in the new life somewhere then vaguely ahead of me. But I saved the best and the favourites, and planned to start again, from scratch, when I finally settled down. So what would arrive in the vans from England would be a very much cut down list of possessions, things which I had cherished for many years and which would fit into my new life-plan easily and comfortably.

But what of the people? The friends, the acquaintances, the figures who had decorated, embellished, enriched, filled out my life before? I had made no selection of them: there had been no auction of surplus-friends. Would they come all this way to join me in my long white room? Would there, as it were, be a Cast of Players to fill the Set which I was thoughtfully planning with my bottle of beer on this still, hot morning? Impossible to say at that stage. But of one thing I was quite certain: there would never again be any more Beel-Bendrose-Nore-Sundays. Twelve or sixteen people for luncheon, tea, and dinner. Those days were finished, and a good thing too — absurdly extravagant, tiring, and self-indulgent.

Twenty years of almost constant entertaining had become finally exhausting. There had been long weekends, from Friday to Monday, as well as the famous 'Sundays' and this, of course, could not be done without help, and help was 'Staff'. And staff were more people in the house, and more problems. Battles in the staff sitting-room, smoothing ruffled feelings between an hysterical parlour maid and a furious cook, allocating jobs and territory — who fed the dogs, laid the tables, ordered the food, turned down the beds, did the laundry, cleared the fires, brought in the logs, cleaned the brasses or ironed my shirts? There were also often serious problems to face in the staff room, which only a qualified psychiatrist could properly handle. What to do if three out of five people wanted to watch 'Come Dancing' on the TV, while the other two wanted to stay with 'Panorama'? Buy another television set. Simple. So one did. Many people preferred not to eat what we ate in the dining-room. Risotto Milanese, Coq au vin, Osso bucco, Lapin aux pruneaux, or even Bratwurst and cabbage; that sort of thing. I hasten to add that we did not only eat these continental delights, there were also English dishes like Steak and Kidney and enormous barons of beef and so on. But one had developed a liking for slightly more exotic dishes during one's travels, which were considered as 'muck-ups' or 'too spicy' by the staff sitting-room, so they had to have a separate menu. Days and nights of cottage pie, baked beans, fish pie, fish fingers, chemical sausages, eggs and bacon or horrendous 'fry-ups' of old Brussels sprouts and mashed potatoes drenched in margarine and fried until carbonized.

Of course it all meant a great deal more work, and a great deal more expense: at times it seemed that we subsidised the frozen food manufacturers, and the two big refrigerators were jam-packed with junk-muck that had been advertised nightly on the television. However, I tried to be scrupulously fair, and the problem was not daunting on condition that one realised that an early death from cholesterol poisoning was the staff room's personal choice. Not mine. Food therefore was a simple matter. Even I could manage to play Herod at the discussions on Friday nights when the week's menu was normally planned. But it all took time. One did not need the psychiatrist for that. There were darker problems which lurked about behind the green baize door.

One morning the housekeeper sobbed, in great distress, that the gardener's boy, all of sixteen and dim with it, had chased her round the kitchen table with the bread knife. She was doubly outraged because at the time she was wearing her best 'negligee'. There was the cook who had been in service with Queen Mary and who insisted on a personal maid for herself to bring up her morning tea and massage her legs which, she said were frail with years of standing at a stove just 'slaving'. She also, on one memorable occasion, ordered ninety-eight white pillow-cases from Harrods: for the staff bedrooms. I never knew why. Another cook was brutally shot in her large backside by a ricochetting bullet fired from a double-barrelled gun by her eight-year-old son(strictly forbidden to have a gun as he had already shot two of the cats during the summer) just two hours before a Christmas dinner at which we were to sit sixteen, and there was a Portuguese couple who threw enormous parties, in my absence, ate mountains of food, drank vast quantities of drink, and lay about all over the drawing-room in highly immodest positions, all of which were unpleasantly, and clearly, revealed in a scatter of Polaroid snapshots which one of them, dazed on Mouton Rothschild and Chivas Regal, had unwisely forgotten underneath a cushion.

Those were the rich and gaudy shades of life's brilliant pattern; and I knew, sitting in my long, white, empty room, that I wished for a less vivid and disturbing set of colours. Muted, simpler; patternless in fact.

Of course, there were glorious exceptions to these aberrations. The Zwickls from Vienna had stayed with me in complete harmony and love for ten years until the temptation offered by a millionaire in Palm Beach overcame their sensibilities and off they went. There was hiatus then, of course, but after the storms, which lasted a number of wearying years, Antonia and Eduardo arrived, bringing serenity and order, from Valencia, where they were now waiting patiently for my call to arrive in France, for they had decided generously, long before, to throw in their lot with me when I left England, and to wander about Europe with me until such time as I found the place in which I wanted to spend the rest of my life. And here I was, sitting in it, drinking my beer, remembering the past, and looking forward to a bright, clear, uncluttered, orderly future. But the friends? The Cast for the Set which lay before me . . . would they come back? The fare was expensive, the distance far, the house humble, there was little to do, no swimming-pool, no television, no English newspapers, no sea lapping a foot from the terrace. Hardly a terrace. Yet. A shepherd's house, up a goat track, and worst of all, no guest room. That would be the 'cruncher'; for no one could stay.

It was a 'cutting off' all right. A complete change of tempo and life. I was greatly interested to see how I would cope with it, let alone the curious group of well-loved friends who thought that I had taken leave of my senses anyway. Some would come back, out of curiosity, others might brave the trip from affection and, perhaps, pity, for I was broke now, to all intents and purposes, with a tight and limited budget ahead. But of one thing I was certain; my family, which I cherished above all, *would* arrive, and somehow if they passed it as sensible and sound, then I would know that all was well. And I was pretty sure that they would approve and that my father, in particular, would be delighted. He had approved of the idea from the very start although he had shown vague, if amused, doubts as to my ability to carry the plan through. But here I was, starting it. First move accomplished. In the high July sunlight I wandered round my acres feeling well satisfied, if a little astonished at my own temerity.

It was mostly what I call goat-land, that is to say, broom and thyme, coarse grass, jagged boulders with here and there boggy patches of brilliant green where little springs bubbled among wild watercress and bulrushes. And all about was the gnarled age of the olives, some as old as the house, others as young as one hundred years. Walnuts flourished, elms, and behind, rising high up the rocky hill, a wood of towering oaks. The house stood four square to the winds on a small plateau shouldered on three sides by the mountains which would protect it from the worst of winds, and facing down over the plain beyond which lay the sweep of the sea, Corsica, and beyond that, Africa. This land, I thought with happiness, would look after itself. I should have sheep to graze it, perhaps even goats, which are good at that sort of thing. We'd have chickens and ducks as well. I'd clear and dig the overgrown *potager* to the east, and grow leeks and potatoes, lettuce and radish, and maybe, because I couldn't quite see myself without them however tight the budget was to be, flowers for cutting. I had it all planned out, easily. Here there would never be acres of velvet lawn to cut, as there had been at Nore. No box hedges to trim, no roses (two hundred in the last rose-garden; to be pruned each March), no herbaceous borders to tend and dig, no gravel paths to rake and weed, no ponds and waterfalls, no fruit trees to prune and spray, no greenhouses to air and fumigate. It would be the simplest possible existence: a few pots of geraniums here and there, a scythe for the grass immediately about the house, and the little *potager* bursting with fresh vegetables, mint, chives, garlic and tarragon. There was already a great rosemary hedge around it, and a bay tree of incredible girth. We would be self-sufficient in time, with our own grapes and olives and water from the stone well, eggs and chickens and, perhaps, when the time came, our own mutton and lamb . . . I might even keep a pig. The orderly man *had* taken leave of his senses.

I was completely unaware at the time, of course, that I was suffering from almost total exhaustion. The five months of work on 'Death in Venice' had been the hardest I had ever known for stress and mental strain; daily I had struggled with a personality of my own invention who had overwhelmed me to such an extent that every single function I performed in my daily life was as he would have done. I was never without his influence at any time, even in sleep. Therefore on one single day in a completely different environment, with very different problems to face, with a mind and body briefly released from his demanding personality, I lost my head and sense of balance and, at the same time, my invaluable sense of order.

I was looking at my possessions that day, not through rose-tinted glasses, but through glasses of every known tint and hue in the spectrum. Nothing, I was to find, would be as I had thought and planned. But for the moment, that supremely happy moment, I was as confident as I could possibly be. Sure, brave, secure, without apprehension. What folly!

But that was all then. And I am, as I said earlier, doing what I should *not* do, looking back, or going back, which is madness, except that it is a joyful madness.

Satisfied, satiated, and a little giddy with so many pleasures, we locked the empty house, hung the key on the nail behind the orange tree, packed the dog into the car, and headed back to Italy.

The day before we had set off from Venice for the trip, Visconti had suddenly decided that he preferred a railway station in the port of Trieste to the one which he had originally chosen in Munich. It was closer to Venice, more rococo than the Munich one, and there was an extraordinary restaurant in the back room of an alimentari near the docks which he insisted I must not on any account miss. So to Trieste we drove, secure in the knowledge that within two or three weeks 'Death in Venice' must finish and the word could go out to the furniture vans in London that they should start the journey bearing all my worldly possessions to the shepherd's house up the goat track. I settled myself into my seat, and almost as soon as we had crossed the frontier at Ventimiglia, Von Aschenbach was once again plucking softly at my sleeve, a little resentful that for one day I had almost completely banished him; but so insistent, so strong was his personality, that it was he, and not I, who drove into Trieste in the lengthening shadows of that late afternoon.

TWO

I don't, at this moment, remember exactly who wrote 'The best-laid schemes o' mice an' men gang aft agley'. Or words to that effect. I rather think that it was Burns. But it really doesn't matter much now, for, happily, it never entered my head on that blazing August morning when Eduardo, Antonia, Forwood and I shuffled about in the shade of the trailing, unkempt, vine. (It was already hot at seven-thirty a.m.) Eduardo, as usual, had a cigarette hanging from his lower lip; Antonia, in fresh floral apron, flapped a brand new duster at flies; Forwood was messing about with the vine, and I stood staring down the track, willing the container vans with all the furniture to arrive from England.

We had come together the evening before at the Colombe d'Or; they from Valencia, Forwood and I and the dog from Bolzano, in northern Italy.

It had been their first glimpse of the house that morning at seven, and Antonia, with the grace and tact of so many Spanish women, professed that she found it all 'Lovely!' and that the black pit, which I had kept till last, 'wasn't *so* bad', and she'd make a kitchen out of it by nightfall.

I confess that I was a little startled to re-discover the bright new cooker in the centre of the floor, and even more surprised to find an enormous refrigerator gleaming in white enamel, high as a man, and very expensive, standing proudly in the middle of what would, I hoped, later be the dining-room, both like children awaiting confirmation. They seemed to me not to have any kind of connections: but since I know as much about electricity as I do about hang gliding, I put my surprise aside; in case it should turn to unease. I was really most orderly about everything. And nothing was to spoil the pleasure of this long-awaited event: the arrival of my goods and chattels from England after a year or more in storage.

We were not alone, the four of us. Under the lime tree, in a small group, two gendarmes, a man from Customs, and another who had arrived just moments before from Nice, and who was to represent the Beaux Arts. They stood together smoking and murmuring.

The gendarmes, I assume, were there to check that I was not smuggling hashish or worse in my wardrobes, and to check, minutely, each item against the inventory held in their hands. Each piece which entered France had to be accounted for. The chap from the Customs was there with a large pair of metal clippers to break the seal on the vans; the gentleman, who wore pince-nez, and stooped a little, there to check, against *his* inventory, the pictures, lest I should smuggle them out, or sell them. It was all most correct; the scent of Gitanes hung in the air and I rather longed for a cup of coffee.

But then, oh, blessed sight! They arrived. Gleaming yellow through the trees. Like elephants ambling slowly towards a water-hole, the two great container vans came up the track, thrashing against the low-hanging branches, nudging carelessly at the tree trunks on either side, rolling easily over the boulders and potholes, they came to a halt by the house as we moved towards them.

With that splendid over-importance all minor officials wear as easily as their shiny uniforms, the gentleman from Customs clambered on to the trucks, and with a great deal of unnecessary ceremony, clipped the steel wire seals which had, I suppose, been placed there in England.

'I wonder,' said Antonia, hands clasped in happy expectation like a child watching a conjuror, 'what will come out first?'

The doors swung wide and there, in crates and bundles and great disarray, lay the tumbled contents of my house. The vision we got that morning was one of wreckage. Total.

There is no point now, all these years later, in going into detail over the dismal and distressing sights which we stared at in disbelief. No point in remembering Antonia's anguished cries as one shattered piece of porcelain after another was carried in sacking cloth and laid in the sun; no point in remembering the life-size lead garden figure, smashed at the knees, and jammed, blind eyes to heaven, in the shards of what had been an elegant Carolian table, or the tea chest so lovingly packed, and upon which we got to work with care, certain that it would contain the best of a Meissen collection of wild birds. What it *did* contain, wrapped in yards of sticky paper, cotton wool, and newspaper, was fifty electric light bulbs of varying strengths. Intact. The Meissen parrots, both pairs, were smashed beyond repair, as were all the rest. And so it went on. Kitchen utensils spiked through oil paintings, every frame on every picture, chipped or worse; all the plates were bundled, loose, in old blankets and had rumbled and splintered themselves across the Channel. Only Antonia's sudden cries of woe as she discovered another piece in ruins broke the grim silence as we unloaded the wreckage.

We had managed to clear half the first container when one of the gendarmes suddenly folded his inventory, stuck it into his tunic, touched his cap politely to us and suggested, in a low voice tinged with sadness rather than scorn, that if the British really did want to join the Common Market, they'd better manage things better than this.

There wasn't much I could say to that.

He and his companion straddled their motorbikes and bounced down the track followed, very shortly afterwards, by the stooping gentleman from the Beaux-Arts who shook his head in despair at a painting which appeared to have been impaled on the prongs of a garden fork, and by the Customs man who said that he'd come back one day soon. If I'd been into drug smuggling that day I'd have made a hell of a killing.

But we went on doggedly, and wretchedly, unloading, for the vans had to be back in Nice that evening.

Antonia, sensible creature, collected some assorted cups and said she'd go and make coffee. I handed round beer, which we had bought in the village with some other bits and pieces to tide us through the day, and just as we were about to sling a rope round a large chest of drawers which we were going to haul up through one of the top windows, for we had suddenly discovered that nothing larger than a tea chest would ever be negotiated round the sharp corner on the lower stairs, Antonia called softly from an upper window; there was no electricity.

Anywhere.

Plugs we had; switches in abundance; but every wire in every ceiling had been neatly cut off, one millimetre in length, by the previous owner, and somewhere along the line the builders, who had striven so hard to break through the three-foot deep walls and open them up into graceful arches which I had wanted, had also severed the main cable. And plastered it tidily away. We had not the least idea where it could be. We hadn't got any coffee either.

It was August, the middle of the biggest French summer holiday. Not a hope of finding an electrician, let alone one who knew where the main cable might run. We continued unloading the vans as fast as possible, all thoughts of a refreshing bath banished, no comforting coffee, no light, and presumably no heat to cook a meal.

My splendid sense of orderliness was still with me. But badly fraying at the edges. I passed the now loathsome refrigerator constantly, and the idiot cooker, and carted pictures, blankets, chairs and God knows what else past them all day, placing each object exactly where we had planned they should go from the long evenings' work with graph paper and rulers. Everything, that is to say everything that was not smashed into small pieces, fitted into place eventually, and a sort-of house began to take shape. I felt rather comforted. At least we had all got there, even if not all of us were entirely unmarked or unscathed. And my comfort increased greatly when a perspiring Eduardo discovered a gas cylinder, half full, under the kitchen stairs. Triumph! All we needed now was a gas ring and a bit of rubber tubing and we'd have a hot meal that evening.

Which we did; sitting among the chaos of the long room, forking at bowls of hot tinned Cassoulet which we'd bought that morning, and admiring everything around us by the light of six candles someone had found rolling about in a drawer.

'Is a big adventure, no?' said Antonia, cheerfully drinking white wine from a cup. And that's exactly what it was: at least we had got our beds into place, found sheets, and the lavatories worked perfectly.

I decided that I'd think of the greater problems tomorrow.

There were to be rather more than I'd envisaged.

Somehow it all got settled, in a rough and ready kind of way, a few days later.

A cable was looped round the house like bunting, and the lights went on. The refrigerator and cooker took up their respective positions, and in time, we got some more or less hot water, and Antonia started to cook – her main problem being the re-discovery of her cooking utensils which were adrift in every conceivable part of the house. In spite of all the initial problems, the destruction of the collection of Meissen, a sudden and alarming feeling that one might have done the wrong thing and realised the error a mite too late, the search for coat hangers, wooden spoons, saucers, picture hooks, glue, and the dire efforts to deal with the one and only telephone in inadequate French, in spite of all these, and many more things, I wandered about in a state of mild euphoria.

On the other hand it could have been diagnosed as amnesia.

But after the last six months or more of living with Von Aschenbach, with his sadness, loneliness, fastidiousness, his cold precision, I did, quite honestly, feel a lifting of a tremendous burden. There is no other word for it. Cliché though it may well be. I had a lightness about me, which I recognised from having once possessed it many years before; there were sudden surges within of supreme joy and happiness, which caused me to skip like a goat (when no one was looking). They did not occur very often (they don't at forty-nine, after all) but when they did they were intense and glorious. I was released. Von Aschenbach had gone. For ever.

While others were busy dusting and polishing, sweeping and nailing, I would go with the dog, Labo, and walk about my rough land, pressing through bramble and broom, touching sun-hot boulders buried in thyme, caressing olive trees of vast girth and great age, drinking from the little springs which bubbled in mats of verdant green, marvelling that all this should, at last, be mine.

How could I possibly know, in this state of amnesia, for that is surely what it was I fear, that all I touched, saw and drank was not as it seemed? What would have happened to this sudden and new-found joy with which I was suffused had I been told that the four hundred olive trees of venerable age and impressive girth had been neglected for more than thirty years; and were slowly dying? That the sun-hot boulders, wreathed in their collars of thyme, were not boulders at all but parts of long-tumbled terrace walls? That the sparkling springs from which I drank so romantically came not from the bowels of Provence but from leaks in the giant reservoir, which held the water for Cannes, high in the hill behind me? That the bramble and the broom concealed acres of once-tilled land on which had grown jasmin, roses and artichokes?

What should I have done then?

I have no way of knowing because no one did. I found it all out painfully, for myself. By which time my amnesia had faded and reality had grabbed me by the throat.

After a week of sitting hunched in various armchairs eating our meals, it did, finally, dawn on me that a dining-table might be just the thing we needed. Why I had overlooked this vital item I cannot now remember. All I do recall is that the splendid Sutherland table, around which so many people had sat, at which so many discussions were held, decisions made, marriages repaired and, sometimes, broken, and which I had had for a great many years, was sold with all the rest of the 'excess baggage' at the auction in Guildford, as being unsuitable for a cottage.

So a table was the next, and indeed most pressing, item, plus an electric drill of some kind, since every nail one hammered into the stone walls did a tremendous U-bend or sprung, lethally, back into one's face. Therefore pictures stood stacked in rows everywhere, and Eduardo couldn't hang a shelf. Antonia ranged her modest supply of cooking implements in a cardboard box, and our clothes stayed, mouldering, in our suitcases.

So: a table and an electric drill.

The local antique shops were useless to me on my limited budget, and, in any case, mostly sold rather over-glazed bits of Louis-anything. Along the main road there was a rather raffish shop, however: it had its fair share of over-glaze and fake Sèvres, but also it had lower floors on which were crammed a great variety of goods. This seemed my best bet.

At first, the Madame inside took me to be an American, with my dreadful accent, and showed me, with a flinty eye, all that was most desirable to the well-heeled and ignorant. When it was explained that I was English merely, and poor, she shrugged, and led me down to the basement which was filled with, as far as I could see, broken bits and pieces, sagging, springless chairs, and an unattractive odour of decay. But, in the midst of this, I discovered a table. Big enough to sit eight, ten at a pinch; hefty, wooden, covered, at that moment, in tattered shards of dirty American oilcloth which had been nailed down its edges. It was, frankly, a pretty unattractive sight. And I made clear to Madame that I considered it so, in order to put her off any possible scent of interest she might be picking up. I could see, in the knowing eyes, under the imposing yellow wig, figures flicking through her cunning mind like those in a fruit machine. I sought other pieces of junk, poked about among terrible paintings, a wicker-work bedhead, a batch of cracked plates in a tin bath bearing the words 'Hotel', and finally, in as laconic a manner as possible, I asked her the price of the table.

She'd been yawning, so I caught her by surprise. She said suddenly: '600 Francs', which was a little under sixty pounds in those days, and I, pulling at a filthy strip of chequered oilcloth, asked her if it was made of pine.

'Oh yes!' she cried. 'It's all pine. I swear.'

I told her I'd think about it, because it was larger than I had wanted and I had a serious problem in my house with a dangerous, unnavigable, bend in the staircase. She shrugged, asked where I lived, and that was that.

A little before dawn, or so it seemed to me, the following morning, Antonia called up to my room from the terrace that there were a 'lady and a gentleman' with some wood for me.

It was the table.

Madame had made a determined effort to see that it would, no matter what, go round my unnavigable corner in the stairs by demolishing the thing. There it lay, in the back of her large shooting-brake, in about ten pieces, legs, stretchers, planks still a-flutter with torn strips of oilcloth.

I don't know why I didn't stop her. Perhaps because she was much taller than I, and the yellow wig gave her a majesty which unnerved me. In any case, she threw wide her arms, assuring me that the table would now fit perfectly.

Her 'gentleman' meanwhile carted pieces of lumber past a horrified Antonia, and the dining-room, for an hour or so, became a carpenter's shop while he re-pegged the bits, and hammered them home. Once up, it was perfectly clear that it would never be got down the stairs again unless an axe was used.

Madame, meanwhile, accepted coffee in an odd cup, and cast an acquisitive eye about the bits and pieces in the long arched room. She made me some not too bad offers, but I refused them all politely, saying that I was not allowed to sell anything on account of everything being listed on the Inventory. This she accepted, in a disagreeable way, and we went once more to the dining-room where it was obvious to all and sundry that the table was, indeed, a table and not a bundle of old sticks, but, more important, that it was far too low, and no chair would pass under it. This did not bother her in the very least. Holding out a plump palm for her six hundred francs, she assured me that tomorrow morning she would arrive with 'four little glass things, which you use under grand pianos. They will give you all the height you need. And I won't charge.' And left.

The table was a sorry sight; Antonia's face sorrier. With tears which she did not bother to conceal, she stripped the pieces of oilcloth away, revealing a wooden top covered in bottle-ring stains, and said that it was the very stupidest thing I had ever done. Eduardo said something useless to her like 'Cheer up, Cookie,' and started to sweep up shavings.

Order, my order, swept back. 'Now look here!' I said. 'I'm sick of eating crouched in armchairs and I wanted a pine table and here it is.'

Antonia looked at me heavy with reproach. 'If you eat from this table, sir,' she said, 'you will die instantly from stomach trouble. It is filthy. Filthy. All grease.'

For three solid hours we scrubbed the damned thing. I removed a full tin mug of rusty nails from the sides, we burned the oilcloth, and scrubbed the wood again and again with a very strong bleach. And when we sat down to supper we sat at a too-low table, sideways. But a table made from solid walnut.

Not pine.

Madame arrived the next morning, not early as she had promised, but just before luncheon, while we were applying the first coat of polish to her bit of treachery. She had not found the little glass things which you use under grand pianos, but had brought, instead, a length of old wood which she said I could have free, cut into blocks, and *le voilà*! And then she saw the table.

'It's not pine!'

'No.'

'It's *walnut*! Solid *walnut*!'

'So we have discovered.'

'You have cheated me! I gave it to you for nothing!'

'You swore it was pine.'

'How could I tell! Under all that filth.'

'How could I?'

She left in a rage, bouncing down the track so that not a shock-absorber could have remained intact.

A few months later she was found in her garage, headless, handless, footless, and run over five or six times by her own car. It was strongly rumoured in the village that she 'entertained' Arab youths from time to time, and this was the unpleasant result. The house and shop have remained empty and derelict ever since.

But I still have the table. On wooden blocks. Free.

September came: the heat abated, the grapes started to turn, wasps droned among the heavy bunches, the morning grass was silvered with dew, and the great French holiday was over. Which meant that people started coming up the track to get things sorted out generally.

Electricians arrived and wired us up so that probable electrocution was not always as inevitable as it seemed it might be, but they never found a trace of the cut main cable, which stays a mystery to this day.

Plumbers came, mercifully, so that we no longer had to fill the baths with the shower-spray, a form of entertainment I cannot recommend.

A very strong man came with an electric drill big enough to bore holes through a battleship, so that pictures got hung, and a less monastic atmosphere prevailed in the whitewashed rooms and passages, and carpenters arrived to put up shelves and cupboards, hooks and hangers, followed by the plasterers in newspaper hats (to keep the plaster out of their hair, but not out of the rooms themselves, to Antonia's vexation) and covered unsightly pipes and built bookcases, in old tile and brick, so that gradually we eased into a promising, bright, and rather more comfortable life without the hazard of falling headlong over piles of books. What with a table on which to eat, pictures at which to look, and baths which flowed full and hot from real turn-on taps, we felt pretty well off.

I bought another table, this time of metal, an old restaurant table, large enough to seat eight. It stood on the terrace, and there one ate, while poor Eduardo and Antonia sat hunched at a fold-down flap thing in the black pit and I made plans, on sheets and sheets of paper, to convert the present woodshed and the olive store above it, which abutted the house, into a self-contained flat for them. This gave me great pleasure, but seemed, oddly, to make them rather uneasy. I couldn't quite work out why, but put it down to exhaustion, from which, in one way and another, we were all suffering. In any case, I knew that they had promised to stay with me for six months, to get me settled in, and then they would return to Valencia where they had bought themselves a small flat. However, stubbornly optimistic, I felt certain that if I built them a perfectly splendid little house up here, with this amazing view, this soft air, and gave them land for a garden, well: perhaps they'd stay a bit longer. They had been wonderfully loyal and good in agreeing to come with me from England and stay where I stayed. Rome had enchanged them. Venice they had loathed deeply. Except for the fact that they could go to Mass at the drop of a hat, almost anywhere. And they had liked all the churches and the bells but disliked, with vehemence, the damp, the water, the drains, and the people. Since Venice is all water, drains, damp and people, they had a fairly miserable time of it. Apart, that is, from Mass.

But how, I wondered, could they not love this present situation as much as I? No damp, no drains — almost none we even needed — and no people for miles. And Mass practically on tap in the neighbouring villages.

At supper, on the tin table, moths flopping round the oil lamp, a soft wind rustling the vine above, the darkness beyond infinite, save for the distant lights of Grasse on one side, and the rope of diamonds which wound itself along the Corniche far across the bay on the other, I felt almost certain they would fall under the spell, as I had done. Given time . . .

'Do you think so?' I asked Forwood.

'Couldn't possibly say. All people are different,' he said. 'But one thing I do know for certain is that if we are only allowed, say, well, five years here, it'll have been worth it.'

The telephone suddenly rang: such an unusual occurrence in the house that for a moment I couldn't remember where it was, and panicked about in fear that it might stop ringing. It didn't, I found it, and it was my sister, Elizabeth, on a rather crackling line from Sussex, to say that our parents were safely on their way and should arrive at Cannes station early the next morning. Greatly elated, for I had not seen them for a year at least, I hurried up the stairs to the black pit to tell Eduardo who was stacking the supper plates and who told me that Antonia thought that very possibly she was seriously unwell.

Now I understood the unease I had detected.

Sudden shock usually spins me immediately into banalities.

'Eduardo! How do you know? Are you sure?'

'Not sure, no. But there is something . . . not so big, like this only; we knew in Rome.'

'In Rome! But that's months ago, why didn't you say then?'

Eduardo shook his head. 'We were not so certain, and you had the film before you, such a big job, so we waited. But now we have been to some doctors.'

'Where?'

'Here. In Grasse. Instead of doing our French lessons. They think maybe.'

'Then you must return home at once. Discuss this with your own doctors; you can't mess about with a thing like this in a language you can't even speak.'

'It is difficult, and people here have been very kind. But I agree.'

'Well, go downstairs and telephone Valencia and start getting things moving.'

Eduardo lit a cigarette nervously. 'It will take some time, to make appointments with the specialists, all thing like that, but I will do so, and we will go as soon as your parents leave.'

Antonia had, tactfully, stayed out of the way, but now she came into the black pit to accept my embrace of gratitude, and also my reprimands.

'It will be well, sir, you see. But please do not tell your parents, it will spoil all their holiday, and we shall go as soon as they do.'

So we agreed. Antonia and Eduardo knew, and loved, my parents well, for they had, as it happens, been 'broken in', or whatever the phrase is, by them while I was making some frightful film in Budapest, and with my enforced absence the four of them, and my ever-loyal secretary, had managed very well indeed in the large house in England. I knew that they wanted my parents to enjoy their short stay, and that it would, as Eduardo said, take him time to arrange appointments. So for the time being, and it would be no longer than a week, we would concentrate on the holiday only. Now that we *all* knew there was a problem made it a little easier to cope. A burden shared. After that . . . well, we'd have to wait and see.

The Flanders Express was dead on time the next morning at Cannes. My parents were suddenly there before me; incongruous in tweeds and Burberrys among the hustle of shorts and summer frocks.

'It was bitter in England, yesterday. Oh! It's all so beautiful, Ulric! Can you feel the sun? It hasn't been as hot as this all summer at home; mildew on the roses: the garden's a washout.'

They had little luggage, but I was glad to see that my father carried his old wooden paint-box and a small, folding easel.

'Oh yes! Couldn't leave this behind very well. You know, I never *did* get that green of the olives right in Rome. It's extraordinary!'

'Well, you've got four hundred specimens to choose from at the house, so it's just a matter of careful selection.'

'Good heavens! Four hundred. Take me ages. But of course this is Cézanne's light, isn't it? Maybe that'll help me.'

'Cézanne was a bit more towards the Var, some miles away really. This is Bonnard light. That do?'

My father slung his paint-box into the boot of the car. 'I'll settle for Bonnard,' he said.

The house was, as I had hoped, a great success, even roughly furnished as it was. My mother refused to take off her hat until she had seen every room, accompanied by a delighted Antonia, arm in arm, and my father begged, with eloquent signs of dire thirst, a beer immediately.

'It's a bit early, Pa. You sure?'

'Certain. A lovely glass of French beer. Stuff they're selling us in England really is piddle, you know. Awful muck.'

My mother called down from their bedroom. 'Ulric! Come up and look at the view, the mountains, you can see the sea and all the little boats.'

'I *am* looking at it, my dear,' he called, 'through a lovely glass of beer.'

We sat at the white tin table on the terrace, Labo leaping and squealing with pleasure at the remembrance of an old friend whom he had not seen since the far-off days of Villa Fratelli in Rome.

'Got a present for you, dog,' said my father. 'Where's my little hold-all? Get it for me, will you? All the presents are there.'

A ball for Labo and four sticks of sulphur to put in his water bowl, and worm powders, a tin of hair lacquer Antonia had asked for particularly, Players cigarettes for Eduardo, and a half-a-pound of wine gums for me.

'And those are the real ones. None of those squashy substitutes. Look!' he said holding one scarlet shape against the sun. 'There you are, 'PORT'. I don't know why 'SHERRY' is green all of a sudden, but I expect you'll find them just as good as they used to be. And here are some seeds: Canterbury bells, Shirley poppies, lupin, sweet peas, wall-flowers and foxgloves. Must have a few foxgloves somewhere.'

Looking out across my bouldered acres, where only teazle, thistle, broom and bramble seemed to flourish, I felt a sudden stab of panic. Had I gone absolutely mad? Made a gigantic error from which escape would be costly if not impossible? Could this long-deserted land ever be made to flourish again? Could it ever produce anything as ravishing as a foxglove? A Canterbury bell? At this tender moment of the day, just before noon, the September light spilling gold across the wilderness, it reminded me, with depressing clarity, of Chobham Heights, or, at best, a remote corner of the Shetlands.

During the last three weeks I had watched, with ever-increasing anxiety, the many workmen who dug deep into my earth in search of lost water mains, electric cables, and drains. My anxiety stemmed from the fact that everywhere they dug, the top soil, if that is what it could be called, lay ten inches deep only, and was limestone shale and dust. Below (for which they needed great picks and electric drills) it was solid rock, or as solid as made no difference. I was, after all, living on the side of a moderately high hill. Nothing, I was assured by one of the workmen, would flourish here without constant help. It was barren land fit only for the olive and the cypress, and in any case the Mistral, a particularly savage and unpredictable wind, blew straight down the Rhone Valley and hit the house dead centre. In the summer it scorched every leaf; in the winter it froze them.

I was in for a very agreeable time. Without Canterbury bells and foxgloves, it would seem.

'I'm sure you'll get round that somehow,' said my father. 'Things did grow here once, I imagine, and you have plenty of time on your hands to get things to rights, and of one fact I feel pretty certain; you haven't made a mistake in the house or the view. Magnificent! Just grow olives if the land beats you. I would.'

My father, as far as I knew, had never so much as lifted a spadeful of earth in his entire life. Except, perhaps, on one or two occasions when we had had to bury a pet cat or a dog. Even a goldfish in a matchbox. But otherwise he was strictly a non-gardener.

My mother's distress each time he constructed *another* small bridge over a drain, or sawed down large branches from a tree which he felt obstructed his view, was often acute, for it was she who gardened with Old Charley, or Nick, or Mr Pierce, or whoever would come up and do 'the heavy work'. My father took his easel and his paints and drifted away into well-deserved relaxation. However, he did enjoy constructing hideous little hump-backed bridges out of bricks and concrete, and was a fiend with a saw and an apple branch. But that is as far as he went, and although we could, indeed we did, *step* across the tiny little drains over which he spent such hours of labour bridging, and had to cart away his wretched branches to cut up for firewood or kindling when he had all but wrecked the orchard, no one said anything, even our mother, because we all knew, very well, that working at 'The Times', as he did, was a very demanding business. He deserved his relaxation.

His advice today, however, seemed very sound. If the land beat me, as I strongly suspected that it would, then I should concentrate on the olives. They'd been there for centuries bearing their crops and, apparently, flourishing. I should make them do the same for me. Exactly how, at that moment, I did not know. I had some hazy idea that it was a sort of Christ-like business: disciples, and loaves and fishes. Ageless somehow. Figures seemed to drift before me in flowing homespun, baskets on arm, bare feet treading beneath the venerable trees, culling the ripe fruits with slender Veronese hands. A Biblical style of life which had, in fact, existed long before that Book had even been written. Timelessness. Calm. Absolute rubbish: of course. Like so many of my fantasies. Had I been told then and there, that morning on the terrace, with my father swigging his French beer and swatting wasps, that my Biblical image would be cruelly shattered by the inescapable fact that the harvest took place in the four bitterest months of the year, December to March, that I'd spend my time, not wandering in homespun, bare foot, from burdened tree to burdened tree with a basket on my arm, but crouched on my knees in an anorak, sodden, frozen, fingers white with ice, gathering up the blasted little fruits one by one, mice-nibbled, worm-ridden, in a howling mistral, I might easily have caved in, moved to an hotel and pressed buttons for Room Service for the rest of my life.

As it was, thankfully, I was ignorant of the facts, and order wavered back; the great trees silver in the light reassured me of my dream, and my mother arrived on the terrace obviously delighted by what she had seen in the house, and the exceptional courage and determination of her eldest son. Or so I hoped.

'Well: I've seen it all. It's extraordinary. And how wonderfully all the old stuff from England fits. So awful about the Meissen birds, I could weep.'

'Well,' I said. 'There's a lot to do yet, but it's beginning to feel like a home, don't you think?'

'Oh yes! And when you've laid the carpets it'll be much more comfortable.'

'Oh. No carpets.'

She looked at me uneasily. 'No carpets? Just those rough tiles everywhere?'

'Just the tiles.'

'But not in the long room, surely?'

'Yes. It's that sort of house.'

'What sort of house? Ulric, open me a beer, darling, will you?'

'A shepherd's house. Simple. It stays that way.'

'With no carpets *at all*?'

'No.'

'The beautiful green one you had in the drawing-room in England?'

'Sold it.'

'I see,' she said, but clearly didn't. She sipped her beer. 'I think it'll be hell in the winter. With no carpets.'

'A bit of rush matting,' said my father suddenly. 'That would be all right. And some curtains of course.'

'Ah no. No curtains.'

'You *must* have some curtains,' he said in surprise. 'People looking in – awful.'

'Shutters.'

'You mean nothing in the bedrooms? Not even in the lavatories! You *must* have curtains in the lavs.'

'Why?'

'Well . . . ' he fidgeted a bit, stroked his nose with a finger. 'Rather inhibiting.'

'But who's to see you? Only trees, they won't inhibit you, will they?'

He shook his head. 'Well, Margaret, how will you feel? Blackbirds and so on peering at you. Fearful business.'

'It seems very strange to me,' said my mother and stared vaguely up into the vine.

'I've fixed a sort of curtain in your bedroom actually; you are in mine, I've moved into the little room Gareth is having as his. I've put up a big bedspread. Just stuck up with nails, but it'll keep out the early light anyway.'

'Well, that's a blessing,' said my father, and finished his beer.

That evening I found the upstairs lavatory window neatly covered with Tuesday's edition of *The Times*.

My father was a very stubborn man. I discovered, many years after, that he was known, by some of the more irreverent members of the staff of that journal, as CD; which, literally translated, meant 'Constant Dripping Wears Away the Stone'. That was Pa.

THREE

In 1892 Oscar Wilde wrote *Lady Windermere's Fan*, the first trains arrived at Johannesburg from Cape Town, Lottie Collins sang 'Ta-ra-ra-ra-boom-de-ay', and my father was born in a pleasant villa in what was then a small village outside Birmingham, called Perry Barr. I was born in a nursing home in Hampstead in 1921 and did not really get to know him until one blustery April day twenty-three years later. Perhaps I should say that I did not get his approbation until then, when I marched up the steps at Sandhurst Military College as a fully fledged, shining new young officer ready, and even willing, I rather think, to die for my King and Country. Only we were already calling both those things 'Democracy'.

It probably seems a long haul for approbation, or even getting to 'know' your own father, but that's how it went.

I had seemed, frankly, a dismal failure to him up until that time. His dream, as a stubborn man, from the moment that I drew breath in that Hampstead nursing home was that I should be trained, and trained hard, to follow him into the sanctity and majesty of 'The Times'. I was, however, just as stubborn as he, and nothing on earth was going to persuade me to climb upon that red brick altar in Printing House Square on which, my mother so often said sadly, he had sacrificed himself and his family.

Of course that part wasn't true. My mother had been an actress and rather preferred the twopenny coloured to the penny plain in speech.

However, that was to be my destiny. I resisted passively. Hopeless at school except at things like art, pottery, and bookbinding or metalwork, greenery-yallery bits of effort which would obviously be of no use whatsoever to a future in 'The Times', he sent me off to the Sun Engraving Works in Watford to learn all about photogravure, where all I managed to do, in the time I was there, was to see 'Snow White and the Seven Dwarfs' twelve times and make friends with a printer and his wife who bred budgerigars. Then, in final desperation, my stubborn father sent me to Chelsea Polytechnic to study art, since that was about the only fairly reasonable thing in which I had made an effort to excel.

This time things went slightly better: I was lazy; spent most of my time in the Royal Court Cinema or The Classic in the King's Road, but got excellent reports by doing *all* the term's work almost overnight. Among others, I had two splendid teachers, Henry Moore and Graham Sutherland, neither of whom saw in me the spark of actual genius: in fact many years later at luncheon in his house in Menton, Sutherland admitted that he felt certain I'd do 'something quite good'. But that it was certainly *not* to be in painting. However, I managed to ease my way towards theatrical design, in a slightly underhand manner, by being exceedingly pleasing to the lady who ran the Drama Society. My aim was in sight. The Theatre.

That's where I wanted to go, and where I was determined to get. My father was appalled. No job for a man, nor for a gentleman. No job, in fact, at all.

But in fairness, with the war looming just across the last peaceful cornfields of Europe, he sent me off with a pound a week in my pocket, for one year. In which time I had to have made my mark 'definitively' or, and here his persistence was so remarkable, do as he said and start from scratch again: as an office boy on his sacrificial altar.

Well: I made my mark 'definitively', in a very small way, in that year, and somewhat to my surprise he agreed that I could continue. Stubbornness had met stubbornness. But the war put waste to that agreement, as well as to many, many others. The fact that I had even managed to survive the Army did, I think, amaze him. That I should actually *enjoy* it astonished him.

That I was doing it, in fact, for him and for his long-sought approbation I don't think he ever knew, although from the moment that we met after my splendid parade, crisp in my new uniform, wearing the same Sam Browne belt that he had worn in his war, I knew him for the very first time as my father and he knew me as his son. It was a private, unemotional, extraordinarily deep feeling. And thankfully it was never lost. It would have been unthinkable to have failed him.

He viewed the years which followed the war, the years of my being a 'film star', with detached amusement, really hardly taking them seriously at all, although he was pleased that I was making what he called a 'go' of it and rather enjoyed the trappings and things which come with film success: trips abroad, fast cars, and the fact that he could now manage to afford a 'decent' red wine instead of the cheap stuff he had had to put up with before.

But at the very beginning I had not been at all certain that this would be so. The week in which my very first starring picture came out he dismayed me greatly.

There were posters everywhere, feet high sometimes, which pleased me in a rather smug way. Not very long ago I had been only a demobbed ex-officer hoping to get a job as a Prep School teacher, so the posters looked rather comforting, smothered, as they were, with my name in huge letters and that of my co-star, Kathleen Ryan.

One morning the telephone rang: it was my father. He sounded grave. Something, I felt certain, unpleasant had happened at home.

'I'm at the office.'

'Well yes, so I imagined. Nothing wrong at home, is there?'

'No. You've seen the posters about this film of yours, I suppose, stuck up everywhere?'

'Oh those. Well yes, actually, I have.'

'I just thought that I'd tell you that I have just come through Charing Cross Underground a few moments ago. There's a *mile* of them there, everywhere you look, place is simply littered with them.'

'Oh. I see . . . yes . . . '

'I suppose,' he said quietly, 'you realise that you have brought the family name down as low as you possibly could?' And rang off.

Things which distress me very much, but about which I can do absolutely nothing, I tend often to try and smother into oblivion: not a good fault, I agree, but then I have never been a militant for hopeless causes. There was nothing that I could do about my name. I had altered it to some degree, and it had been printed a number of times already in a couple of television plays and a stage play. Too late now to try and scrape it off the posters plastered over half of London. So, after an anguished hour of worry, I put it from my mind and tried to pretend that the unhappy conversation had never taken place. It was never referred to again by either of us until many years later in a restaurant in Madrid when, for some reason, I suddenly felt brave, or emboldened, enough by the years to repeat the story in his presence.

His amazement was a glory to behold. Normally a very shy and retiring man, it was unusual for him to show much feeling in public.

'But good gracious! My dear boy!' he cried. 'It was just a joke! Do you mean to say you've been fussing away about that all these years. It was just a silly little joke!'

'Well, it didn't feel like one at the time, I can tell you.'

'My dear boy. Listen. Charing Cross Station is the *deepest* station in London, on the whole Underground line, didn't you know? Good gracious me! I really think you had better order another bottle, don't you?'

I did as he suggested, and the unease which I had carried about with me for many years was all but lost in the general laughter: at my expense, naturally. But all but lost is what I mean. I was not absolutely sure: he was, I knew well, capable of being genially mischievous.

My mother, on the other hand, was absolutely without mischief. She was far too Scots honest for that, entirely without guile, naive at times, at others extremely shrewd, she blazed with courage, and called a stick a stick. Not that it always pleased people, and sometimes got her into trouble which she shrugged off cheerfully.

When she married my father she had been a modestly successful actress with a burning ambition. A year after their marriage my father had to insist, and he was pretty good at insisting as I had found out, that she either stayed married to him or went, alone and forever, to join the Lasky Players in Hollywood who, she said, had offered her a contract. Which I personally doubt. But she was a very beautiful creature and it could have been true. Anyway: she *believed* it to be so. All her life. She stayed with my father. And that was that.

But, if she couldn't be a Great Actress, she was damned certain that at least she would look like one. And she did. She had an amazing eye for colours, for fabric, for fashion, and for finding strange items of apparel in secondhand shops or, her favourite place of all, the Caledonian Market. There she would rescue bolts of strange cloth, mandarin robes, tarnished silver belts and buckles, feathers and flowers and, with a long-suffering Lally kneeling on the floor at her feet, mouth stuffed with pins, grumbling, 'Oh! Hold still, do! You'll have a wavy hem,' concoct ravishing outfits which, if not altogether *à la mode*, could not be ignored, and in which she looked magnificent.

I remember once, when I was about ten, walking with her in Hampstead High Street. She wore that day, and I vividly remember it to this, a black wide-brimmed sombrero hat, and an enormous black cloak which billowed behind her elegant stride. Someone on a bus shouted, 'Blimey! Look! Sandeman's Port!' and people turned to look. No one laughed. She was too splendid for that.

I was abashed that we, or rather that she, had caused a minor commotion. She was absolutely delighted, and strode ahead, eyes sparkling with pleasure, her modest moment of triumph seeming to envelop her like a second cloak.

For triumph, to her, it had been. No actress now: no chance of reaching out to be a Great Star; the Theatre and all its dreams had been denied her. But an audience had not. And by God! She was going to find an audience whenever, and wherever, she could, and if possible hold it. And this she always did, seeking it out, sometimes almost desperately, to the end of her days.

My father watched these dressing-up sessions, as he sometimes called them, with tolerant amusement. He was very proud of her, and loved her profoundly, never fully realizing, I think, the deeply buried frustration and resentment lodged in her heart like steel darts and which she was never to lose, or forget, all her life.

Tolerant and amused, proud too, he may have been, but for some of the more formal functions to which they were bidden, from the Opera to Ascot, he insisted that she wear something rather more conventional. Which was not an altogether simple matter on the modest salary which he earned from 'The Times'. In those days, it was considered that the paper was run by gentlemen for gentlemen, and gentlemen had, of course, private means. Except my unfortunate father, whose only expectation of a fortune had been squandered by *his* father, who had spent it all 'exploring the Amazon River'. Years before.

But a close, and devoted, friend of my mother's was Yvonne Arnaud, a French actress of great wit, charm and warmth, and possibly, apart from me later on, the closest link she was to have with the theatre. 'Aunt' Yvonne dressed only at Worth or Patou; wore those confections once, or at most twice, and then handed them on to Mamma. So propriety, and my father's anxious concern that perhaps his wife might turn up for a First Night of 'Carmen' at Covent Garden dressed as a bullfighter, was put to rest.

She may never have been, who can tell?, a Great Actress, but she was a wonderful wife and mother. Our childhood was, it seemed, always summer. She was gay, funny, beautiful and loved us. She cooked and gardened, dealt with wounds and bumps, bad school reports (mine always) and assisted at the births, and deaths, of countless guinea-pigs, rabbits, white mice and stick-insects. Nothing surprised her, everything which made us happy, within reason naturally, she provided. She sublimated all her hidden frustration in her children and her husband, who had been through a hideous war which, although he had not suffered any physical wounds, had left him with almost unbearable memories and griefs, which she alone could ease. Naturally, we were completely unaware of any hidden streams of distress. They were always kept strictly away from us, and life was as serene as it could be; there appeared no cause for any alarms anywhere. Beyond my appalling track record at anything academic.

And then the war. An upheaval of unimagined proportions, not only for us as a family, but for many thousands of others. My unfortunate younger brother was sent off to a Boarding School; my sister and I, in time, went into the Services; Lally had long since left to look after her parents; the big house was sold up; and my parents moved on their own into a glum little cottage some miles away.

My mother embraced the war with open arms. Joined every committee she could find; fitted gas-masks, learned how to set a fractured leg, and everything that the Red Cross ladies could teach her. She arranged accommodation for the lost refugees from London, planted row upon row of garlic, to add some flavour to the miserly rations, cared and tended my overworked father after his returns from London, and generally found herself so busy that there was no time to think, or for regret. In any case the most important thing of all was that she was needed.

And then the first Allied soldiers arrived in the area, the Free French, Canadian French, Canadians, and later the Americans. Life now took on a really glamorous hue for her. She was everyone's surrogate Mother: writing letters for the illiterate, cooking meals for the canteens, running an open house so that those who were lonely, bored, or had nowhere to go, could read a book in peace, talk if they wished, or bring out the millions of snapshots of wives and children 'back home'. She was vastly popular everywhere; not only because of the material things which she could supply, but because she was always gay, sparkling, laughing, warm and caring. Very unlike most of the tweedy ladies of the district who did their duty as a sort of moral right to King and Country: without the fun. My mother had a heart big enough for all. She now also had the one thing she most craved all her life: her audience.

And here it was; packed houses every night, adoring, applauding, avid for the stories she would tell about her years 'as an actress' which had driven us, her family, to the brink of insanity with repetition, but which all her lonely soldiers had not heard, and didn't mind, if they had, hearing again. She said, often enough, that she was only doing her bit for the War Effort. What she was also doing, and doing extremely well, was holding the stage. Dead centre. And there is not question in my mind that she absolutely adored every minute.

She was very proud that I had managed to achieve a Commission for myself, and every leave I had was a big event: a splendid, for her at least, showing-off of her son. What she was doing, and doing so well, she hoped that other women in her position would do for me in distant lands. Although, to be absolutely fair, one could hardly call Kent, Yorkshire, Northumberland and Cornwall 'distant lands'. But they were to come eventually, and her generosity *was* reciprocated by other 'mothers' from Normandy to Holland and much further East.

My father, overworked, exhausted, lacking sleep from the nightly raids on London which meant that he had to sleep in shelters or his office, wrote to me every single week. My mother wrote once or twice only in the six years. But always added a little scribbled footnote to his letters which, in a very little time, I learned by heart. It wasn't difficult. Short and to the point, it was always the same. 'Take care of your dear self, and come home soon. Daddy will have given you all the news. Much, much love, Ma.'

But I knew, or the actor in me knew, that she was working; very happy, fulfilled, and at last finding herself In Demand and, as she used to be billed on her early stage appearances before marriage, 'Always Applauded'.

But it finished. The War. The curtain came down and everyone went home.

There was no one left on my mother's lonely stage, not even her children, for my sister married as soon as she could, I left for London and a round of job seeking, and only my small brother remained to her, in Boarding School. My father was still wedded to his paper, helping to rebuild it.

What to do in a glum little cottage under the Downs all day? The sound of applause was fading fast. The lights were down. There was no one left who remembered, and no one to listen, once again, to the stories of My Career. Suddenly, with appalling swiftness it seemed, she, in her late forties only, still amazingly beautiful, vivacious and alive, was, to all intents and purposes, alone. She called it 'buried'. Only my father and my teenage brother now 'needed' her.

If it was finished for her, it was just beginning for me, and some of the pleasures, to be sure, she shared. Proud that I had made my way in a relatively short time, and that I was in 'her profession' and doing well, she enjoyed the periphery of my early career. But it wasn't really enough for her own ego, although she did quite like being known as my mother, and often made sure that people did so. She was about the only one in the family who enjoyed it: my sister got sick to death of her relationship to me, with perfect reason, and angrily said that she had her own identity; my younger brother decided that my career might jeopardise his own, for he, to my mild astonishment, decided, at a very early age, that he too would like to be in the movies and gave a heart-rending story to some tabloid which made it clear that he was 'in my shadow'. All bunk, of course, and it lasted a very short time before he went off to make a name for himself in another sphere, very successfully indeed.

With time, often too much now, on her hands, my mother joined the local village Drama Society and started producing and, on one memorable occasion, acting. But it didn't last. She simply could not be made to realize that the people who joined the company did so for relaxation after work, as a sort of social pleasure. She looked upon it as a mission. If someone missed a rehearsal through illness, a dental appointment, a lost bus, or a death in the family, she was furious. The Play was All. The company, however, didn't in all honesty think so, and why indeed should they? It was a pleasurable evening out for them in the local hall, with a nice coffee break, home-made biscuits, and a gentle exchange of gossip. Anyway, it was only for fun.

Not alas to my mother, who took it deadly seriously, upset the company, and finally withdrew angrily. And that was that.

On her fiftieth birthday, without warning her, I drove in the morning with some friends to the dark little cottage under the Downs. We arrived about eleven o'clock. The house seemed deserted, windows closed, no sign of life. She was in bed, curled up on her side, the curtains drawn. She lifted her head. Even in the gloom of the room her face was a wreck, and I saw that she had been weeping.

'Darling!' I said. 'What's the matter? Are you ill?'

'I'm fifty.' The voice was dead with despair.

'Nothing else?'

'Isn't that enough?' she said.

As a matter of fact she was fifty-one. But, fortunately, we none of us knew it at the time.

In under an hour she was dressed, made-up, radiant, and we all went off to Brighton, had lunch at English's, and bought pounds of sweets in the shops along the front, for it was also the day that they came off ration.

A day had been saved by great good fortune, but the acute despair and the depressions which came later, suddenly and alarmingly, were to remain for ever. However, I had taken warning. And from then onwards I did my best to involve her and my father in as many of my film activities as I could. She really wasn't very interested, however. The theatre was what she knew about and loved, not the cinema. And her happiest times were those spent at the Studio, when Stella and Biddy, or Iris and Pearl, took her off to the Hairdressing and Make-Up Departments to turn her into a Great Actress for a couple of hours. In the triple mirrors.

One night, after some long-forgotten premiere (to which I always invited them but to which my father would only go if he hadn't got to wear a black tie) she stood proudly beside me for the photographers' flash-lamps, a moment which she adored above all others.

'Was I all right?' I said. 'I think I just pulled it off, don't you?'

'You were marvellous, my darling,' she said, smiling and smiling. 'But of course, you see, you get it all from me.'

But that was all a long time ago; now here we were together in my new house in a strange land and she was over seventy: slim of figure, bright of eye, hardly one grey hair on her fine head. And she was bored.

We were reading, or at least my father and I were, the London papers which arrived a day late. She refused to read the 'damn' things because, she said, she was on holiday, and could read all she wanted to at home. The fact of the matter was that she kept on losing her reading glasses and just couldn't be bothered to find them. Anyway, all she cared about was how hot, or wet, or cold it was in Sussex. Unless there was a really spectacular murder. But they didn't seem to occur as often as she would have liked.

'You know,' she said suddenly, 'you were conceived in the Hotel Crillon, Paris.'

My father cleared his throat. 'Margaret really! What a thing to say! How *could* he know?'

'I'm just telling him, that's all. He's living in France. I wanted you to be born in Paris, too.'

I set my paper aside, recognising the signs of boredom; obliging. 'Why wasn't I, then?'

'Oh,' she waved a slender hand vaguely, 'that idiot Dr Morgan, mistimed it all.'

I knew my cues, knew too the following lines she'd speak. 'And so I was born in a nursing home in Hampstead?'

'In the nick of time,' she said swiftly. 'Just made it. Otherwise you'd have been born in a taxi. God! You gave me a hard time, I can tell you.'

I picked up my paper again and started to read.

She sighed deeply. 'Is this all you do up here in the evenings?'

'Well, it's not bad, Ma. Music, reading, peace.'

'Too bloody peaceful,' she said. 'I might just as well have stayed at home.'

Writing this, reading it back, sounds cruel. It is not meant to be, and she didn't, I knew, mean exactly what she said. But she *was* bored. All life that was not before 'an audience' was boring. That was the nub of the matter, and it never altered.

If I write here at length about my parents it is for one perfectly simple reason. I am half-and-half of each of them. I have inherited many of their faults and some of their virtues, naturally. To know the parents is to know, in part, the child. I recognise in myself today my father's stubbornness, his persistence, even his deep shyness and reticence. I also recognise, sadly, his particular form of selfishness, if you like, and the bitter depressions which, inherited by him from the aftermath of his frightful war, he handed down to me. Diluted, to be sure, but still very much there, and often a handicap. However, I trust that I have inherited his strange sense of order, for that he also had, and could not have existed without it: neither could I.

From my mother comes my easy boredom, my anxiety, some of the restlessness, all of the Theatre. I inherited her love for the theatre but never her passion or longing for an audience. I never even considered them, to be honest. Merely acknowledging that they were as much a part of the profession as the proscenium arch or the curtain. Of course I *knew* that one had to play to an audience: but as far as I was concerned they were just people who filled up the empty seats beyond my world. And the fewer there were of them the better I liked it: a sentiment which went entirely unshared by my companions, needless to say.

So there I was: the extravert and introvert mixed. The half-and-half. Clearly I was in the wrong job.

But it never occurred to me. I wanted to go into the theatre as a matter of course. It was as simple, as familiar, as unsurprising as breathing or walking. But I never, at any time, wanted the fame and adulation which is expected as a kind of essential in this career, I just wanted to act. I didn't much mind what, but to be there, to *do* it: the infinite excitement of re-representing someone else was overpowering, otherwise it was a stubborn, but passionless, love affair.

And then I discovered the cinema. Or it discovered me, to be truthful, and I was off. I loved, and I still do, the sheer mechanics of the cinema. Of working in a team, of learning from a team, of having, at the moment of greatest impact, no audience save the technicians who are assisting you towards that moment. They were, and always have been, the only audience I ever wanted, apart from the camera.

Forwood once said, 'You know, I think that he really would like to make four films a year which no one would ever come to see.' He was right. And often they didn't.

Of course, I had overlooked the fact that the cinema is money, and people have to come, otherwise no more cinema. So we had the audience all over again. But this was a subtly different one. I didn't have to witness their approval or disapproval: didn't have to hear the matinee tea-trays drop, the chocolates rustle, the drunk whistle from a box. I could be miles away while they were eating their peanuts and popcorn; I had done my work months before on a darkened set with my mates.

However, there were the dreadful premieres to which, while I was under contract, I was forced to submit myself. In agony I would go, in agony I would sit among them, in agony, but smiling (of course), I would leave. A dog returning to its vomit. A remark which once I made to my bosses with very unfortunate results. Of all the things I think I most detest about acting is the fact that one has to witness the spectacle of oneself doing it.

Now, of course, with television, it is harder than ever to avoid: but I do. I never watch a film of mine on what is called the Box: sometimes I have a look for ten minutes to see if the 'print' is all right, what the colour is like, if my work has become mannered (it often has) or whether I am doing too much with too little (constantly). But never for longer. What was, was. It's over and done, and I have no residual sentiments whatsoever for the quacking little figure on the screen.

The only times I have ever enjoyed seeing anything I was in have been in a private projection room, with the director and the team, and a packet of cigarettes. That was peak-time. And, as far as I was concerned, the finish. The job is over, done and put together, good, bad, or indifferent. But done with as much honour as possible. It was only then that one realised that the whole thing was geared towards that invisible, for most of the time, looming bulk. My mother's deepest pleasure: the audience.

I had been working away all this time in a Factory-Fantasy-land, absurdly overlooking the people for which this particular product was being produced. I suppose I really thought that it was only being done for me. Naturally, I learned otherwise.

Normally I detest September and dread October. I hate the slow decay, the fall of the leaf, the withering, the russet colours beloved by so many. I hate Michaelmas daisies, dahlias, and the mournfully urgent chiselling of the blackbird, the scent of bonfires and 'the days drawing in'.

But it seemed to me, on that brilliant September morning, that all these horrors might not occur here in Provence. Perhaps it wouldn't be autumn at all down here? Perhaps everything would sort-of just melt away, leaving no untidy traces of death behind to cart to towering rubbish heaps: but there was, even I had to admit, a certain charm in the turning of the grapes on the vine, and the soft yellowing of the leaves through which the still-hot sun filtered on to the lunch-table.

My father was wandering up the hill, hip-high in amber grasses and alien corn, the dog snuffling and routing in the track, like a pig snuffling truffles. I poured a cold beer.

'Golly! Just what I need. Gets jolly hot clambering up this hill.' He settled at the table, foam round his lips. 'Dog found a badger's sett right down at the bottom; you know you've got one, don't you?'

'Yes. Someone inside it too. Fresh droppings and a rabbit skin the other day.'

'Got to watch Labo. He was very excited, they could give him a hell of a fight, he wouldn't stand much of a chance with that wonky leg of his.'

'Four steel pins in it. Cost me a fortune, rotten animal.'

''Course,' said my father, wiping his mouth. 'He's really a slum dog, isn't he? Not his kind of smells up here. Rather be in the gutters somewhere. You know, by the way, I have a feeling that under all this brush and stuff you've got a lot of old walls. He put up a fat green lizard down there and I poked about, and I think those big boulders are really tumbled walls. You'll have a hell of a job with them, won't you?'

'No. It stays as it is. Wild, savage, I'm doing nothing. Maybe sheep one day.'

'But what *are* you going to do? I mean now that you've decided to chuck the cinema bit for a time? You can't just sit on your bottom.'

'Don't see why not.'

'You'd go mad. You've led a terrifically active life ever since the war, and even including the war; you can't just suddenly stop. Terribly bad for you. Bad for the system.'

'Well, I told you in Rome: I might have a go at a book. Childhood.'

'Oh well, that. Hmmm. I think you ought to have a look where I was this morning. I have a very shrewd feeling that this land was terraced once: and they are all there still. Splendid exercise for you, bringing it back to shape.'

'All I'm going to do is dig over the old *potager*, grow a few vegetables, if the land will cope, some flowers for picking, and stick a few tubs and pots about. Pot gardening, I'm really not into archaeology and all that. If there are walls there they can stay. It's been abandoned for nearly thirty years!'

'What about my seeds then? The Canterbury bells, and so on; a few lupins. I do think you'd find it pretty boring up here after a while with nothing to do.'

'Lots of natural springs about.'

'I know. Soaked my good shoes.' He peered at his feet.

'I might make a pond, have a few goldfish. Your feet really wet?'

'No. Ruined my shoes but not wet really. It was a little puddle, looking for the wretched lizard. What's that delicious smell coming from the kitchen?'

'Antonia's doing something heavily Spanish with rice and eggs. Garlic, I'd say.'

'Yum yum,' said my father. 'Margaret,' he said, as my mother came on to the terrace and took her place at the table. 'He's just said he's going to do nothing here. Just sit on his backside. You have a word with him: he ought to start a garden, try and reclaim the land. He can't just do nothing, don't you agree?'

'Who could ever make a garden out of this wilderness?' she said sensibly. 'You haven't the very least idea how hard it is.'

'All I want to do now,' I said, 'is nothing at all for a while. And I'm not going to start a whole new deal digging up old walls. I haven't the money for one thing.'

Forwood arrived with the wine. 'Four francs fifty in the village, Ulric. I don't know if it's drinkable.'

'Anything is drinkable in this lovely place.'

'I think it's tragic,' said my mother.

'What's tragic?' I said. You could never be absolutely certain which way she'd gone off on her own, or to where.

'Giving it all up. The theatre first, now the cinema. Tragic.'

'It's not for ever, darling. A year or two or so. I want a rest, sort things out.'

'I'd never have done such a thing. If I'd had your chances, my God! Just letting it all go and sitting up on this hill. Such a tragic waste.'

'It's a very pretty hill, and I've worked very hard for a long time: now I'm just going to wait until I'm ready again. If ever. I'm doing it my way now.'

My mother picked up her wine glass and made way for Eduardo who arrived with a large dish of saffron rice with eggs sitting in nests of home-made tomato sauce.

'Don't touch, Madame,' he said. 'Is very 'ot.'

'So arrogant,' said my mother sadly.

'Who is?' said my father, trying his wine. 'Not bad, this. A bit sharp, but perfectly all right.'

'He is. Your son. Arrogant.'

'Hardly surprising, with his blood,' said my father and winked at me.

'We're not an arrogant lot, are we?' I said, thinking of his humility and extreme good manners, his dislike of ostentation, travelling only ever third class, visiting his tailor once every five years, shopping for himself at Marks and Spencer. There was nothing arrogant about him, quite the reverse indeed. My mother might be a little more so: but in an 'actressy' way. She was not naturally arrogant at all.

I started serving lunch.

'No, not us, I suppose,' said my father. 'It probably missed us, your mother and I, but perhaps you have got a bit of it. No bad thing, properly used.'

'But where from, if not from you two?'

'Well,' said my father, cutting himself a slice of bread, 'your mother has the blood of the Buccleuchs on one side, and I've handed you down a bit of . . . '

'Oh Ulric!' cried my mother. 'It was all so long ago.'

'Still blood. Wrong side of the blankets, of course,' he said with a wide grin. 'Very good blankets, but still the wrong side.'

'But when, who, why did you never tell me this before?'

'No point really.'

'The wine's gone to his head,' said my mother.

'Oh come on, Pa! Tell me more.'

He shook his head, grinning cheerfully. 'No, no; no more. All done. That's it. You don't need to know anything else. Enough is enough. Maybe mother's right. The wine's gone to my head.' But he was smiling. 'I say,' he said. 'This is jolly good grub. Antonia really does cook marvellously.'

We ate for a little in silence, looking out across the rough land, down into the valley, across to the smudged ridge of the mountains.

'Anyway: whatever you say. I think it's tragic. Just tragic.'

'Oh, Mother! Do shut up.'

'I will *not* shut up! I'm never allowed an opinion of my own. Can't even open my mouth. Tragic, that's what it is. It breaks my heart.'

'Look, darling: I've only been here a month. I'm a new boy at school. Maybe I'll hate it and go belting back. I don't know. But I'm going to give it a damned good try.'

'Well, I suppose you know what you're doing,' said my mother, with a heavy sigh which clearly indicated her own opinion. 'It's beautiful, absolutely beautiful, but it's a long way away, you'll be forgotten. I mean, after all, when did the telephone last ring? Tell me that? Not since Daddy and I arrived over a week ago. Silence. I'd go mad! They'll forget, you see. But you must do as you want.'

'And so I shall.'

'Arrogant,' said my mother sweetly.

They left a couple of days later, brown, smiling, well: a little picnic of cold chicken and a bottle of a 'not too bad Beaujolais' in a basket, and as I watched the train pulling out of the station at Cannes in the evening light I felt a deep surge of regret. Having them to the house had, to me, been vitally important. I wanted them to be the first to stay there, and they had. I wanted the 'feel' of them about the place, the smell of his pipe tobacco in the long room, the sound of her busy feet clacking along the boards of the corridor, the sense of permanence they could bring, and did.

Like every other person I had forgotten, or chose not to remember, that mortal permanence is illusory. And that there is no such thing as 'forever'. Forever is just a measured length of time.

FOUR

On the morning after my parents' departure, Forwood drove Antonia and Eduardo down to the airport for their journey to Spain. They left with the bleak faces of people who are worried.

I was alone, suddenly, in my new, echoing, house. Not a tap dripped, no sound of gentle singing from the wash-house, no breath of wind. The vine hung still. No one slammed a door, rattled china, trod upon the stairs: the dog lay stretched as for dead in the shade.

It was a pause. Quite a long pause. Which, I confess, I had really not expected.

After the weeks of bustle and hustle, hanging things, unwrapping things, arranging things with other people about me, after the months of work 'inventing' Von Aschenbach, alone, so to speak, in the centre of a devoted team like a Queen Ant, of the years, in fact, of work, three or four films per year, more than twenty years of continual motion; after all that, here I was alone. And still. Sitting in the long arched room like someone who had missed the last train in a midnight station.

It was an oddly uncomfortable feeling. Rather as if one had suddenly slammed on the brakes in a speeding locomotive.

I had crashed to a stop.

To be sure, there had been a Past. There would be, I felt uneasily certain, a future, but at this present moment, momentum had ceased. I was an unwound clock. Timeless, silent, limbo.

I had wandered about the empty house, feeling an intruder, shy, in my own domain, of being caught peering into rooms which I knew, already, well.

Antonia and Eduardo's was stripped. Bare almost, as if they had never been. Would they, I wondered with anxiety, ever come back? Perhaps not. I'd be left on my own with only school French to help me.

Except Forwood, who had guided my career and work since 1939 and had volunteered, as his son Gareth was now a grown man of twenty-six and carving a way through his own particular theatre jungle, to join me in my exile. What else, he had reasoned, was there for him left to do? There was always the possibility that I *might* work one day again, and in any case I would need his help still, because every deed, clause and statement was firmly in his hands and head: he could also drive a car and I could not. He was in all degrees essential.

Perhaps, I thought, as I came down the stairs into the long room, my mother was right. It *was* too far away. 'Out of sight, out of mind'. I'd be forgotten. And it was quite true that, during their stay with me, the telephone had never rung. Not even a wrong number. Perhaps it never would again?

My fault. My decision.

The dog got up, shook himself into a scatter of legs and tail, stretched, yawned, curled round, lay down, slept.

Of course, if I was really desperate (was I?) I only had to pick up the crouching black telephone and speak to someone. About anything. Hear a voice. But my French, and spelling-out the London Telephone Exchanges phonetically, as one had to do then, was daunting indeed. Fremantle, Frobisher, Primrose were all so long, and the operators grew impatient and usually cut me off.

I should take my father's advice and go down to the bottom of the land and see just exactly how much brush and rubbish there was to clear away: perhaps have a look at the boulders which, he had assured me, were parts of long-fallen walls. This was the life, the life-site, the existence I had chosen: high time to get my backside out of the chair on which I now sat staring at the telephone, and go, in solitude and peace, to examine exactly what I had bought.

But if I *did*, supposing the telephone should ring? And I not be there to answer it?

'So what?' I said aloud to the empty room, alarming myself. 'If it did ring and you were at the bottom of the hill you'd never know. So what would it matter?'

'Well. I don't know. They might be calling from the airport . . . flights to Spain cancelled, you know.'

'Bunk. Excuses. Just admit you're in a funk.'

'Not really.'

'You don't think that this room will ever have people in it, do you? You think that you have severed all your ties, cut adrift, are floating into limbo.'

'Well, that's all right. It takes time. People will come, of course they will.'

'Certain?'

'No, not *certain*. But they will. It's early days. I mean, I have never really been absolutely on my own for years and years, it takes a bit of adjusting to. In all the other houses there was always someone around somewhere. Cleaning silver, ironing, watching TV, mowing lawns, peeling potatoes, that sort of thing: there was always a sort of 'life' about, a pulse beating.'

'You said that you wanted solitude, now you have it.'

'Yes.'

'You so hated the telephone in England that you took it off the hook.'

'I know.'

'And now you are sitting here willing the thing to ring.'

'I'm not. Absolutely not. I'm *glad* I'm here. This is what I wanted. I'm not going back on my word.'

'What you *are* doing, mate, is talking to yourself. First signs of melancholia or advanced senility, something. I'd get your ass out of this chair and go up to the kitchen and wash the breakfast cups, clean a lettuce for lunch, start to function as you should. Away with self-pity.'

Talking aloud to myself! Crikey! I rose from the chair in which I was slumped, my mood having slipped into total inertia and creeping depression, and made for the slate stairs and the kitchen.

A housewife. I'd become a bloody housewife, that's all. By my own choice. The telephone rang.

An Olympic spring across the polished room, cracking my shin against a table, hobbling in agony to reach the thing before it rang off, catching it just, I imagined, in time.

Joyful voices! Old chums of many years suddenly in Nice, travelling home to Uzès in the Gard. Could I give them a bed by any chance, just for a night or two? Wings to my heels, cracked shin forgotten, lark-gay, stripping down Antonia's beds, throwing on clean sheets, scurrying about; a happy lunatic.

Of course people would come to the long room!

Of course I wouldn't be forgotten!

The telephone *would* ring.

It already had.

I put out fresh towels, blew away a thin drift of Antonia's talcum powder on the dressing-table, and started to sing. Very loudly. My sense of order had returned.

Thus, Daphne and Xan Fielding were the very first of the old crowd of steady chums from the past to come to the house and start the slow, subtle application of a patina of life on it.

There was laughter; discussion and argument, long conversations round a log fire in the late evenings, for it had already become cool once the sun plummeted behind the hump of Le Bois de Marbrier, and long lazy relaxed picnic meals round the tin table on the terrace in the heat of the day, or the cool of the early mornings, when the dew sparkled the spiders' webs in the long grass and butterflies, peacocks, red admirals, swallowtails, attracted by the nectar of the ripening grapes, flopped from cluster to cluster under the rustling canopy of leaves.

I knew, of course, that the house must have witnessed many lives in the centuries in which it had been built. Quarrels and arguments, laughter and deaths, births and toil. During the war it had sheltered, because of its isolated position, groups of frightened Jewish children collected from all over, who had rested up within its thick walls and then been smuggled, in the night, down to the sea where silent fishing boats bore them away to the Spanish coast: their names, some of them, still scribbled in pencil on the woodshed walls. The house had been filled with life: but since my arrival everything seemed, indeed had been, swept away, cleared and whitewashed, literally, and the old ghosts had fled. It was essential that a new force came in among the long beams and tiled floors. For the moment, spruce, clear, glowing, it was also to some degree sterile and without memories. They had to be re-started: no easy thing to do, and not one done immediately. One could not impose memories instantly, as one had imposed 'age' on new plaster, they must develop. And the arrival of Daphne and Xan was just the start, the placing of a second layer upon the memory, already, of my parents' presence which had raised the curtain on my new beginning.

In the extreme pleasure of their company, with the pre-occupation of meals to plan, washing-up, laying the tin table, cutting wood for the occasional fire in the evening, clambering together over my rough acres which, Daphne said, reminded her 'quite amazingly of Crete' and on which Xan suggested that I had a herd of goats as soon as possible, who would deal with the thyme, the tussocks and the springing brambles, in all this I had completely forgotten the hunch-backed telephone until one afternoon, as we sat lethargically over the debris of a late luncheon planning how best to make wasp-traps, it rang. Shattering peace with an urgent bell.

Robin Fox, my agent, but more than that, a greatly valued friend, had fallen gravely ill just before I started work on the film in Venice. Months of uncertain news, of despair, rising hope, fearful operations and all the rest of the hideous things which accompany a desperate illness, followed.

He and his wife Angela had shared many holidays with me in various places from Padua to Rome to Hollywood and the awful Blue Room at Villa Fratelli, and when it was discovered that he was ill, we had made one of those rather wistful plans that when he was better (and we were all perfectly certain that such a thing was possible) he would come down to the new house high in the hills and convalesce in the calm and the peace, and above all, the purity of the mountain air. We called it 'The Plot'.

If, sometimes, I had an uneasy feeling that this 'plot' was really no more than a ploy to keep his morale from crumbling during the interminable months of his illness, I let that feeling evaporate immediately at the sound of Angela's voice on the telephone. High, clear, confident, happy even. Robin was in good shape, the doctors had sent him off, recommended strongly that he should take his long-promised trip to the South and convalescence. They were, could I believe it?, presently in Paris and would take the Blue Train that night and be at Cannes early next morning. Was it too short notice? Had we all got settled in? Had we a bed? Wasn't it simply marvellous?

It was. It was simply marvellous news, and I quickly explained my situation, but that I'd go immediately up to a very decent little inn five minutes away and get them a room until Daphne and Xan left, in a day or so I guessed, and then the house would be theirs. The long-hoped-for 'plot' was now, obviously, not a possibility but a fact. A day indeed for rejoicing, I thought, as we drove down to Cannes the next morning in the early sunlight.

But early rejoicing is nearly always a mistake: the Blue Train, when we got to the station, was seven hours late. And any kind of rejoicing which one whipped up again, seven hours later, was quickly shattered into fragmented distress at the sight of Robin lowering himself very slowly from his carriage, a gaunt, ashen, aged man, stooped now and only able to shuffle towards one, a desperate attempt at a smile of welcome on his stretched lips, eyes blazing in a once-familiar face now the texture and colour of crushed parchment. Angela, leading him carefully, had mustered a brilliant smile and, braver than the brave, embraced me closely, explaining that Robin had had food poisoning all night, from something he'd eaten at dinner, and that they hadn't had a wink of sleep, added to which the train was so appallingly late, just their luck, but here they were now and wasn't it marvellous?

Well.

No question of a bed in 'the decent little inn'. As soon as we got to the house Daphne and I re-made my bed, and chucked some sheets on Gareth's bed in the little room next door. I would sleep downstairs on one of the sofas. The house, as once I had hoped and once I had almost doubted it would ever be, was full again: but not perhaps in quite the way that I had planned. but then, as one knows, the best-laid schemes . . .

Robin, a man of very firm decisions, of courage and, like my father to some extent, stubborn to a degree, insisted that he be shown round the house before he would even hear our imploring suggestions that a fresh bed awaited him. Leaning heavily on Forwood's arm, he shuffled from room to room breathlessly, but with intense interest, recognising, with delight, pictures and furniture which he had known in very different surroundings; amazed at the panoramic view before him of valley and distant mountains, and generally expressing himself delighted with everything, he finally insisted on a cold beer: and got it. He swore he felt better already, just being where he was, and breathing the purity of the air. After his beer he allowed himself to be taken up to bed, assuring us all that after a good night's sleep, etcetera, etcetera.

But it was not a good night's sleep which Robin enjoyed in my small bedroom. Very early the next morning I found Angela in her dressing-gown, wandering about in the black pit distractedly looking for a tea pot, a kettle, a cup. He had been desperately ill all night and most of the time delirious. Did I know of a nice little Frog doctor locally, because his temperature was still well above the hundred mark.

There was no French doctor that I knew — we hadn't got that far in the settling process — but Forwood picked a name in the directory which had an address the closest to us and, by the grace of God, the doctor was there, would come to us immediately, and knew the house from the past.

Xan who was, thankfully, bi-lingual, said that he would do the translating, since not one of the assembled group could speak much more than menu French which would be of little use to a medical man. Tactfully he explained that he would have to know the medical background, so that he could give the doctor a clear idea of what treatment was needed.

Angela was sitting at the head of the tin table, the sunlight easing in and out of the thick vine above. She pushed her tea-cup from her slowly and, as it were, laid her cards completely on the table.

Robin had cancer, and one lung had been removed; he was here because his doctors knew that there was nothing more they could do : this he did not know. He had so longed to make the trip that they were convinced it was wiser that he make the appalling journey than lie in his bed without hope, for even in the very blackest hours there could, couldn't there?, be a tiny spark of hope? It was, she suggested, for that spark of hope that they had come. A spark which Dr Poteau, brisk, efficient, sympathetic and comforting, swiftly extinguished for me as I walked him back to his car later.

Only months, he said. And outlined his plan of campaign to get the temperature down. He handed me a sheaf, it seemed, of prescriptions, said he'd arrange for the local nurse to come in immediately, and always twice a day for injections, warned me that none of us must smoke in Robin's presence, have a cold or a cough. He even arranged, with the care and immediate understanding which he possesses, that his laundry woman would take in the bedding, because we would certainly have to change all the linen twice, if not three times, a day, and I didn't really look as if I could cope with that too. Had I ever washed a double-bed sheet? he asked, and laughed when I said no. I watched his car bump slowly down the track.

Well: I had wanted people to come to the house, I had wanted a 'pulse' to beat, wanted the house to be a house again, to have the patina of life and of memories. And here they were, just beginning to impose themselves. It was idiotic that I hadn't quite taken into account that this could start with something so brutally distressing.

But then, I hadn't taken a lot of things into account. Life was all learning and burning one's fingers: grief was an unavoidable ingredient of the patina I sought, why did I think otherwise?

In the days which followed, Angela and I divided the chores between us, Forwood did the marketing, and a cheerful, very efficient, nurse arrived every morning and evening. We whipped off sodden sheets, remade beds; Robin's temperature started to drop, and one morning, bright-eyed and determined, he demanded a glass of champagne. He was on the mend. So far as any mending could be done.

Daphne and Xan had driven off home, tactfully, and Eduardo telephoned from a distant part of Spain to say that Antonia was all right: there was nothing at all wrong, no need to worry, but she was weak and tired and they would stay away for a bit; if that was all right with me? It was fine with me. I told him I'd call when they should return.

As September started to ease towards October, as the sun sank earlier each evening, the dew became thicker every morning, the days still blazed; and Robin gained strength. Sometimes he was well enough to come down and eat on the terrace, even though walking was a hazard because he kept falling over, which, in a man of some height, elegance and enormous pride, was wounding to see, though we all laughed as we hurried to help him up. But the days became happier, Angela braver. There were times now when it felt almost like the past, when we had sat together so often in England or in Italy, discussing, arguing, reading bits to each other from newspapers or books, listening to music, being together. All perfectly all right. A time switch. Each evening, about six o'clock, Angela went to her room to 'preen a bit' as she called it, and would shortly re-appear fresh, crisp, groomed; pearls, a different dress, a cloud of scent about her. Immensely encouraging, and a swift reminder to oneself to change from the mucky garb of the day. It is something I have always admired tremendously in women, the extraordinary ability, which some possess, of being able to illuminate a room, lift morale, turn the edge of evening into an event, by nothing more, it would seem, than the changing of a skirt, a cotton dress, a quick brushing of the hair, a touch of scent, a stroke of lipstick all within, apparently, moments. Angela did this supremely well, charging the evenings with a brisk normality in which we all could function.

And then the mistral arrived.

I have lived here long enough now to know the warning signs: then I was quite unaware that there were any. I don't really think that I ever knew what a mistral was, except that it was a wind and blew sand into your eyes on the beach and sent the sea roaring. But just a wind, that's all.

The sudden appearance one morning of a shoal of slender cigar-shaped clouds drifting across the intensity of the late September sky gave me no cause for alarm. I accepted them as amusing and unusual and recommended everyone to come and admire them. We stood, that day, Robin supported by Angela, and watched with pleasure as the little silver zeppelins idled above us towards the sea. To us it was all a part of being 'abroad', and 'abroad' had a different sort of cloud; it also had a very different sort of wind, as we were shortly to discover.

First a zephyr. Nothing more. A breath which rustled suggestively, uneasily, in the vine and then went scurrying across the land whispering among the trees, swaying them, scattering fallen leaves across the terrace, sweeping dust into suddenly spiralling, eye-stinging, eddies. Then, gaining strength, it took off, and wrestled, tossing the trees like feather dusters, racing through the big oaks high behind the house with such force that they beat and swung, twisting, lurching, writhing, like a host of crazed Rackham witches, howling and rending.

Deck-chairs clattered, bowled over and over into the tossing scrubland, dustbins spun through the air and were lost to sight, shutters slammed, wrenched open, slammed again: dust and sticks, small branches, scatterings of grapes beat all about us until, unable to stand upright, we managed to drag Robin, and indeed ourselves, into the house.

Standing in bewildered disarray, the dog cowering in a far corner, I saw a large potted fern, recently bought, career past the open door and explode into smithereens as it crashed into the side of the stone laundry-tanks, the water in which foamed and boiled like small Atlantics. It was all very impressive. I wondered how many tiles there would be left on the roof as they clattered down to shatter on the stones below. Not many, was the obvious answer to that. The roaring and screaming was such that we had to shout to be heard, and I then remembered the elderly builder who had told me that when the mistral came it would hit the house dead centre. He was absolutely right.

The only one of us who really enjoyed it all was Robin: he begged to be helped out again, notwithstanding shards of singing tile whipping about like shrapnel, and hung on to the orange tree by the door with both arms round its straining trunk, his head thrown back, eyes closed, mouth wide, gulping in the roaring air as it buffeted and bullied him, and far across the valley, high up on the mountains ahead, clear in the wind-washed air, I saw smoke.

At first I thought that perhaps it was scudding cloud, but in a second I knew that it was smoke streaming away in the wind towards the sea, for at its base, in the brilliance of the scoured morning light, there was a sudden leap of vermilion light.

The fires had started.

By nightfall more than half the long mountain range before us was alight. Acres and acres of pine and scrub, of mimosa and oak, blazed. Silently we watched the sudden shafts of yellow fire streak upwards when a great tree caught and burned, or the sudden bursts of billowing smoke from a house. And then we waited, dry-mouthed, for the explosion we knew must follow as the gas-tanks burst asunder, barrelling tumbling flames high into the crimson sky.

By morning the fires had reached almost to the sea, and they burned unabated for three days, until suddenly the wind dropped, trailed lazily off to Africa, and left the devastated land smoking in great clouds which curled silently into the high copper sky from a ten-mile ridge of black dust and cinders; the once pure air acrid with ash and the scent of burnt wood and earth.

Aware of Dr Poteau's strict advice, we had, on the first night, arranged that if by chance the wind should change and blow towards us from the fires, we would get Robin down to the coast by ambulance. But the wind stayed on its course and never veered. For days the mountains were blotted out in the thick haze of dust and ash, and the sun smouldered wanly in the sky like an umber disc.

And then, after all that, I caught a cold. Nothing much; a cold. A head cold. But enough to alert us to fear. It was time for Robin to leave.

'You know,' he said on the morning he was flying to London, 'I'm going because I *want* to go, not because of the fire and the smoke, or because of your cold; not for those reasons.' He was sitting in a big armchair in the long room, a beer in his hand, which he could hardly hold but which he steadied from time to time with the other. 'I want to go because I'm not going to die in your house.'

'You're not going to die anyway.'

'I'm not frightened of that. Bloody angry at fifty-six, but not frightened. But I'm not going to die here, in your new house, and leave you that memory, you're starting a new life. You aren't going to start it with a death.'

At the airport, Angela pushed him through the barrier at International in a wheel-chair, he raised a hand, blew a kiss to the dog.

I never saw him again.

Dirk Bogarde

With the return of Eduardo and Antonia, relieved but 'flu-ridden though they were, a semblance of order returned to the dishevelled house, and I had the time, at last, to explore the land to which I had paid scant attention, apart from over-romantic delight. The fact that I actually owned twelve acres of France had seemed quite enough for me; what I did not know was anything about those acres in detail. So I set off. At close quarters, climbing and struggling through the wilderness, it was not greatly encouraging, and my father's ominous suggestion that the boulders were parts of long-fallen walls proved to be dismayingly correct.

The springs with which I had been so enchanted, the boggy areas of green watercress and rushes, the tiny rivulets which sparkled in the sun as they meandered down the hill among the myrtle, camphor and broom bushes were not, alas, quite what they seemed. So, call for expert advice.

A pleasant young man with thick-lensed spectacles, a box of many-coloured dyes in the back of his car, and heavy-duty wellingtons on his feet, arrived from the Water Department and, splashing about with the glee of a child in the soggy land, finally pronounced that it was flooded.

I suppose that I must have looked to him like a ventriloquist's doll, mouth agape, eyes glassy. For he explained, carefully and with infinite patience, that the many delicious springs and rivulets were not the result of Nature but were leaks from the reservoir buried deep in the hill above me, and that it was perfectly clear to him that my olives, to vulgarize Stevie Smith's immortal line, were not waving in the wind, but drowning. All four hundred of them. Their roots, he said gently, were deep in water and had been, by the apparent state of the land, for many years.

Gaining encouragement from my wooden-faced expression, he led me eagerly to the splendid stone beehive of a well which stood among the fig trees. Peering into the dark depths he assured me, with delight, that the water was doubtless polluted from the seepage of the septic tanks of the two houses on the top of the hill. To prove his point, and perhaps to try and alter my rigid expression of shock, he produced a phial of red dye from a pocket and dribbled it into my crystal well-water which immediately marbled into virulent shades of bile yellow.

His satisfaction was tremendous; his smile so warm and pleased that I shut my mouth abruptly, only to open it again when he asked, with enormous solicitude, if any of us had drunk from the well?

Fortunately, we hadn't.

'The solution?' he asked with a merry laugh. 'You must sue the Water Board for gross damage to agriculture.' Olives, he reminded me, were an extremely valuable crop. *Voilà!* Sue.

As my French was restricted to saying 'Good morning', 'Good-bye' and 'Thank you', I didn't really see that I should get far in legal terms. In any case, I had been in France for barely nine weeks . . . it seemed a bit cavalier to start sueing people right, left and centre, let alone the mighty force of the Cannes Water Board.

The only other alternative, he suggested, ploshing happily along with me through the bogs, was to drain the land thoroughly. There was no point, it seemed to me, in having four hundred slowly drowning olive trees. Everywhere I looked I received silent reproof. I would be crippled with shame at my neglect for the rest of time. We would drain the land.

So one day a caravan of assorted trucks, camionettes, cement mixers, jeeps and dusty cars of various makes, came crunching up the track. A small crane swung enormous concrete pipes high above one's head and stacked them roughly against the shaking trees. They were wide enough to crawl through and could have dealt, easily, I was certain, with the entire sewage output of Paris.

Men arrived among this agglomeration, speaking many varieties of languages: some French, some Italian, some Spanish and Portuguese, others Arab. The once-calm oasis, where my badgers shuffled through the evening dusk, where my pheasants stalked with jewelled crowns, now rang to the urgent cries of many nations, the clang and crash of metal, the grind and squeal of gears. It all looked remarkably like a lift-off at Cape Canaveral: with more hysteria.

The star performer, like all true stars, arrived a little later and immediately dominated the scene. A huge, shuddering, orange dragon, groaning, howling, screeching, bowed its jointed neck and, with shining pointed teeth, ripped the soil of centuries asunder, tossing boulders, scrub and small trees about in wanton fury, biting deep into my limestone shale and dust, gorging itself into insensibility by the lunch-break, which thankfully arrived at twelve noon precisely. When a great silence fell. The men went off to the village to feed, the machines lay still in the sun, stinking of hot oil and metal.

I wandered alone among the drowning olives wondering how on earth I should ever be able to afford all this activity, quickly realising that to worry now was far too late, for the land was gashed and riven, criss-crossed with deep trenches which only needed yards of barbed wire to give a very good impression of a 1914–18 battlefield painted by Paul Nash or Orpen.

In a small dell, near the house, there was a little pool, inhabited by mosquitoes, and this I had long ago decided would be the basis of a pond; for water is an essential part of living to my scenic life. And so I had started to enlarge the area, digging away silt and sludge so that the water, which clearly was from a *real* spring and not one of the dreadful leaks from above, would fill out and make a fitting habitat for golden orfe, even carp, a waterlily or two and perhaps yellow flags. I'd sit there in the long summer evenings under the trees, maybe plant a willow even, and contemplate the book which I could feel stirring somewhere in my head.

My dell-digging, or pond-digging, kept me occupied during the roar and crash of the activity all about me, and I laboured contentedly. The pool area grew daily wider, I dredged up bucket after bucket of silt and muck, and was constantly happy to see the water run clear, until one day I noticed a small twist of paper swirl past my legs. It was nothing more than a scrap, possibly thrown there by one of the Arabs who, instead of going to the village for their mid-day meal, lay in Biblical scatters together under the trees and ate informal picnics. A couple of days later, knee deep in my pond, horror struck me at the sight of another fragment of swirling paper which, this time, it was not possible to pretend had come from any Arab picnic. It was instantly recognisable as a shred of flower-patterned lavatory paper. I knew it extremely well.

The bespectacled gentleman with his box of dyes was summoned. Eagerly he scattered his phial over my future carp-pond, triumphantly he cried, '*voilà!*' as it marbled from red to odious yellow, anxiously he inquired if I had at any time taken this water to my lips. Head bowed, I admitted that I had.

We clambered up the muddy bank together and he hurried off with more phials of dye and rods and poles while I swallowed a quarter of a glass of neat brandy. Two hours later he found the leak with the triumph and awe of Lord Carnarvon at the tomb of Tutankhamen.

The run-off pipe from my own septic tank was broken. My pond was the site.

I decided to pack everything 'romantic' away, for the time being, and having been assured that I would not get typhoid, or worse, by Dr Poteau, packed my bags and left for London where I was to give a lecture at the National Film Theatre. Then, with my sister's invaluable help (women are so much less cowardly than men when it comes to fighting for their rights), I would go to the furniture depository where some of my goods still stood, uncared for and dusty, and demand some kind of justice for the destruction of all my Meissen birds and the rest of the things which had arrived that August morning in the container vans.

Elizabeth behaved splendidly: she went to war without quarter. In great dismay a huddle of the Company heard her out: grovelled with apologies which my sister turned aside as easily as if they had been scatters of confetti, and forced them to admit that 'our Mr Fellows' had been 'very unwell at the time of the move.'

'He wasn't 'unwell',' said my sister. 'He was *drunk*! I saw him drinking almost all day long out of the bottles on my brother's table in the drawing-room. He was just swigging it down. Sherry, whisky, cognac, even vodka on top! He could hardly stand by five in the evening. I mean, let us be *quite* honest, you only had to look at his face to know he'd been boozing for *years*.'

They paid up a very modest sum of money eventually, not enough by a long chalk to mend the Meissen, but just enough to prove their error and concede, very uncomfortably, that their Mr Fellows *did* have a 'weakness', but would I please not mention this problem to any newspapers: it would prove to be greatly embarrassing to the firm. They willingly agreed to transport all the remainder of my possessions, which were surplus to my needs in France, to anyone I cared to name within the United Kingdom. The only person I could think of immediately was Lally, who lived in a tied cottage in Essex and who might be happy to have some extra cupboards, lamps and things.

She was. Or would have been. However, her cottage must have been very modest, not to say small, for none of the stuff would fit. So the firm had a wasted journey, which pleased me greatly, and they had to hump the lot back to London.

More years ago than I care to remember now, Capucine and I sat in brilliant sunshine on the terrace of a small restaurant near La Napoule eating oysters with a bottle of champagne, and rosemary-grilled *rouget* netted from the sea below us. It was two days before Christmas and our inordinate delight in each other, as well as the brilliance of the morning and a plump mimosa bush singing with bees, has stayed in my mind always.

I have forgotten, to be sure, many of the things which followed in the years to come, but never that moment: and it fixed in my mind forever the fact that Christmas on the Riviera would always be as warm, as golden and as pleasurable as it was on that long-lost day.

But not so. The first Christmas on the hill was as brutal as it was unexpected. Two days before Christmas, Gareth Forwood (he had just arrived to join the 'family' for the celebration; if that's what it can be called) and I crunched over thin ice-fringed puddles, stamped frozen feet, crouched against the knifing wind which swung down from the hills, and in a grey light, as cheerless and bitter as remotest Sweden, went to admire the four big cypress trees which had recently been planted above the house. They had transformed the place splendidly from a Provençal kind of *Wuthering Heights* to a well-framed, friendly and welcoming abode. It was also, the local dustman who lived below told me, essential to have them. They kept off the Evil Eye, assured fecundity, and Faith, Hope and Charity.

I had planted the four, and they had cost a great deal of money; the eldest and tallest having reached the age of thirty years, the other three a more modest twenty. I was learning, very quickly, instant gardening. At a price.

Earlier in the morning in Rue d'Antibes in Cannes where we had gone to do the shopping, the first snowflakes fell and all the shopkeepers came running into the street in amazed delight at the sight, cupping them in their hands before they reached the pavements. It obviously gave them the greatest pleasure: it depressed me beyond words.

I hate Christmas. I hate its false good humour, its gluttony and greed, the idiot cries of 'Peace on Earth' and all the rest of it. In actual fact the French manage it a great deal better than most people, and it is for them a holy occasion as well as a gathering of the family. I do my level best always to ignore it: beyond the obligatory gifts to local tradesmen and the reluctant sending of a few cards to people 'abroad'.

But this year, because it was my first in the house and Antonia and Eduardo's last, for they were leaving for Spain and retirement on New Year's Day, I decided that we'd have the wretched turkey, which pleased Antonia, but no decoration of the place with holly and mistletoe; to her chagrin. The turkey would be my sole contribution to that hypocritical day.

Antonia, naturally, was surprised at my apparent meanness, but on the night, sitting at the head of the long walnut table, elegant in black velvet and a rope of pearls, with a couple of goodish bottles of wine and the candles burning steady in the warmth, she enjoyed herself as we all waited on her, perhaps inelegantly, but with affection. And then we all shared the washing-up and went down to the big fire in the long room.

Sitting in the light of the fire, listening to Mozart, a cognac at hand, the dogs snoring, we sat in peaceful comfort together, relaxed, warm, replete. What more, I wondered, could one wish?

Of course, it is possible that Labo, the Roman slum dog who had chosen me to be his lifetime companion, much against my will and better judgement initially, might well have wished that Forwood had stayed his hand when he had purchased an eight-week-old Boxer bitch to be company for him when I was away, as I often was in these early months, in London or Rome.

Days before a departure, without a word being said, a suitcase being handled, a drawer opened, Labo would know what was afoot and begin shaking from head to tail wretchedly, trailing one from room to room, afraid to leave one's side for fear that one would leave his. It was a very distressing business: something had to be done, and Forwood had done it.

She had come from a very chic pet shop in Cannes a few weeks before: no puppy bought in a chic Cannes pet shop, just before Christmas, can be a good buy. And she wasn't.

She arrived with a smudged-brown bunface, enormous pads, no pedigree of any sort, worms, and rickets from gross underfeeding. Labo found her instantly disagreeable, thieving, greedy, and over-demanding of our affections. He resented her bitterly: but she stayed; we called her Daisy, and here she lay, bloated with turkey pickings, velvet face crushed deep into Antonia's indulgent and caressing hands. With the music, perhaps also the wine and the cognac, I looked about me in the warm glow with deeply satisfied pleasure. Taking stock.

At least from where I sat it didn't look too bad to me. We had made it into this new life, and somehow I had the impression that things were going to be all right: the house was a real house after all. Not just an empty Set.

My father had always believed that Christmas, rather than New Year, was the time to do a little stock-taking; it was the time for looking back and checking up on your life's balance. He would sometimes alarm unprepared guests at his, or my, Christmas table, when he stood to propose his annual toast, 'To absent friends'. In some strange way he would charge it with a sense of finality. Instead of thinking of people one loved who might presently be in Kenya or California or merely London, S.W.3, one had a distinct impression, for some reason, of Kensal Green or, anyway, of cemeteries. Many a gay and laughing heart was chilled by this toast offered across the remains of the pudding and exploded cracker-papers, and it was often followed by a sudden and intense series of worried silences, bowed heads, and murmurs of assent.

A very cathedral-like atmosphere indeed: which didn't go at all well with the paper hats and champagne. However, it lasted but a moment, and Lally always said that it was 'just his little way'. He was reminding us all that there was a bit more to it than just a feast of food and wine and high spirits. A gentle warning perhaps, that we had, according to our ages, spent time . . .

Taking stock, as I now was doing, adding everything up in the last months, the extreme pleasures, the sadness, the shock surprises, the destruction of goods and chattels, of broken drains and lost electricity, of ruined wells and carp-ponds fed by a shattered septic tank, of too much money spent from too little an allowance, of rats in the roof, the terrible fires of September, and many more things besides. It might have seemed to be quite a lot for so short a time: but the happiness I now felt, induced by wine or Mozart or just the sense of ease and order at last, didn't seem to me to be too bad a total for such a sum.

And the fears that I had secretly entertained, at first, that I had made a frightful error, that I would be indeed forgotten, friendless, left a recluse five hundred metres up in a foreign land, had been unfounded. The reverse had been true, and even the hunch-backed telephone which once so unnerved me had grudgingly come to life, becoming, in time, almost as irritating as its predecessors in England. But it brought great consolations, not the least of them being the husky, impatient, for he hated telephones as much as I, voice of Visconti.

''Appy. Very 'appy,' he said one day in October. 'I have seen the first rough assembly of the film, and it is not so bad: not so bad at all.'

'Thank God for that!'

'Not God! Thank me,' he said. 'We have no music yet, but otherwise we have a film. You will come soon to Roma please, to see it, for I must take it to terrible Los Angeles to show the Americans. Like a poor student. Dio! They say to me, 'Sure, sure, Signore Visconti, *maybe* you have a fine film, but will they understand it in Kansas City?' What a remark. Bogarde! Where is this terrible place of which they are so afraid?'

'The Middle-West, I think.'

'Of China, is it? Pouff . . . they behave 'orrible to me as always. *Merde* to Kansas City! You will come soon?'

'After Christmas, Luchino, I have to see my dentist.'

'*Dentist*! You have so little finesse: no polish. You understand what I say? When I ask you to come to see *my* work you speak of a *dentist*! Dio mio . . . '

'As soon as possible, I promise.'

'You have the toothache, this is it?'

'Yes.'

'With so little sensitivity how can you know? Eyee . . . I must be patient: so all Roma must be patient until this dentist had done his work. Ecco! For your teeth we wait. We must. Ciao, Bogarde.'

Remembering this in the firelit room, I laughed suddenly at the pleasure of recollection. Daisy farted. We all laughed and carried her out to the terrace. Heavy snow was falling. We looked at each other in astonishment.

A very strange five months.

FIVE

The rough-cut, or rough-assembly of a film is just exactly that: rough.

It is inevitably a depressing affair to the uninitiated, and very often to those who are not. In general it looks like a bad set of home movies. Scenes are stuck together in sequence, so that a 'shape' is apparent, but there is no grading of light, of sound, of colour. There is no music track, there are no credits; not a single thing which looks, or feels, like cinema.

It is a scratchy, jerky business, best observed only by those with the strongest hearts and expert knowledge. Which is why many directors, rightly, refuse to let their actors see them. Actors, in general, have a great deal of ego. A bad rough-cut (and most of them are) is enough to send them wandering to the nearest river bank or whimpering round town that the film is 'frightful!' What they actually mean is that they were unsatisfied with their own presentation, profile, or performance.

The film, which is all-important, is forgotten.

The self-appointed intellectual film critics, and there are quite a number of these today, would probably sit through the whole business enthralled that they were in the know, as it were, and would certainly dub the result with their most often used words of approval: 'gritty' and 'grainy'.

And in this I could not fault them.

That's how I first saw 'Death in Venice' at three o'clock one afternoon in a cold projection theatre in Cinecittà Studios, Visconti sitting in a canvas chair surrounded by various members of his family, or such members as he deemed fit to witness the unveiling of his work, plus a few select members of the troupe.

There was a discreet flurry of princesses, a contessa or two, three or four actors who were *not* in the film but whom he had honoured because he knew that their sycophancy would be useful to him beyond the confines of the Studio. Men like Visconti always keep a little squadron of 'favoured' people, the pilot fishes round the whale. He knew he could count on them to talk, in the most favourable way, about the film from Milan, Rome and Naples, to Paris and London if need be. They never failed him. If they did, their fate was a slow death from social, and theatrical, suffocation.

I can't remember, today, just exactly how I felt that afternoon when the last image flickered through the projectors. Numb; I do remember. That the film had a great, and curious, power, that my own performance depressed me deeply, that it was very beautiful to watch. Not more than that.

However, Forwood correctly said that I was too close to the subject to be objective or dispassionate, and that on this occasion it was wiser to behave politely and say as little as one possibly could.

Which wasn't, after all, very difficult. I had nothing to say.

Visconti, a cigarette stuck permanently between his fine strong fingers, received the homage of his Court with Pope-like dignity, moving his head in a gentle nod here, bowing there, waving a vague cigaretted hand at a shadowed figure, and greeting me, eventually, with two paternal pats on the hand.

'Ah! Bogarde. Va bene? No toothache today? And not tomorrow! For tomorrow we must re-voice some lines. You noticed? A motorcycle in the gardens, and those damned motor boats on the canal, but it is very little. Just words here and there: so no toothache tomorrow, eh?'

'No toothache tomorrow, Luchino.'

As I turned to leave he suddenly halted me with my name.

'Bogarde!'

I stopped at the door.

'Bene?' he asked quietly.

'Bene,' I said. 'Molto bene.'

His eyes were grey, clear, direct. Very still. Making me an accomplice.

'Grazie!' he said quietly, and then turned to someone who had come to kneel at his side with a favour to ask, or a compliment to pay.

Leaving the Studios, my heart lifted a little: I knew that he was pleased with the work we had done, even if I was not particularly certain, or pleased, about my own contribution. And there was further confirmation of his pleasure later when we were all bidden to supper with him at Gigi Fazzi. A certain sign of his confidence and content.

In Forwood's diary for that afternoon, he has written of the film, 'tremendously impressive'.

That same evening I wrote a letter from the Hassler Hotel to an American woman in New England:

'*He* [Visconti] *gave us a splendid supper later at Gigi Fazzi, the latest "in" restaurant. A lot of noise, clattering of knives and forks, bowls of fettuccine, red wine flowing, a great deal of chattering and laughter. Why is it, do you suppose, that the Italians have fifty words to every one of ours? I could never learn to speak it, which annoyed V. very much.*

'*Anyway: it's all done now, and I am writing this in a rush so that I can get it off to you before I leave for work in the morning.*

'*I think that I have possibly failed in the film: a good "try", but I don't think that I have quite done it. My fault: not V.'s by any means. He says that he is very happy with my work, but I wonder? I have a nagging doubt. Sad. But I suppose that it had to happen one day. I have had a very good innings: it is just possible that I attempted too much this time. Oh well. What is it you say in your country? "That's the way the cookie crumbles?" Anyway: I did it. And I tried like hell.*'

In time the film was finally finished. Scored, dubbed and all the rest of it, and Visconti, who had amazingly managed to keep it to himself and his technicians and not show it to the American Money, as he called them, was finally forced to go to 'terrible Los Angeles' and show them what they had, in part, paid for.

It was a 'Full House' I was told, and when the lights went up in the Los Angeles projection room, there was not a sound, and no one moved. Visconti said that this encouraged him enormously: obviously they had been caught up in the great emotional finale of the film.

Not at all. Apparently they were stunned into horrified silence.

No one spoke. Some cleared their throats uneasily, one lit a cigar. A group of slumped nylon-suited men stared dully at the blank screen.

Feeling perhaps that someone ought to say something, anything, a nervous man in glasses, got to his feet.

'Well: I think the music is great. Just great. It's a terrific theme. Terrific! Who was it did your score, Signore Visconti?'

Grateful that anyone had shown the remotest interest in his film, Visconti said that the music had been written by Gustav Mahler.

'Just great!' said the nervous man. 'I think we should sign him.'

Much later, safely back in Rome, we laughed. But no one laughed that day; least of all Visconti.

It was finally decided that the film was 'un-American', and the subject matter very dangerous. It would never be a commercial project, and sure as eggs were eggs no one in Kansas City would know what the hell it was all about. It was even suggested with some tact but not much, that if the film were ever to be distributed in America it could be banned on the grounds of obscenity.

Visconti and Bob Edwards, his Associate Producer, came back to Europe with the film, so to speak, under their arms. In a state of great depression.

I, of course, was blithely unaware of all this, paddling about on the edge of my new pond, which I had got the orange-dragon to scoop out during all the drainage business. Life on the hill was calm and serene, ordered. A pleasant elderly couple, Henri and Marie, had arrived to take over from the departed Eduardo and Antonia, and I spent most of my time either in the pond, arranging rocks about in 'romantic' Salvatore Rosa cliffs and cascades, or hacking out the neglected *potager* so that a modest rose garden could be started. I was quite unaware that probable disaster was winging its way across the Atlantic.

The sun shone, the skies were clear, mine at any rate, and I was delightedly easing into my period of retreat with a smug pleasure and a varied set of garden tools.

In Rome the situation was quite different: Visconti remained at loggerheads with the Americans, refusing their suggested 'cuts' and even, it was rumoured, a new, and happy, ending.

'How,' Visconti had cried in despair, 'can I give Thomas Mann a happy ending? It is what he wrote, it is his conception, it is the story, it is sacrosanct!'

Although, at first, I was out of this struggle, Bob Edwards began to keep me in constant touch by telephone, and each week seemed to bring more evidence of a total deadlock. It appeared perfectly clear to us that the American Money wanted the film 'killed': this is something which has happened often before. I am told a 'loss' is often set against taxation.

However, Visconti threatened to make 'a great scandal in all the world papers if such a thing should happen' each time anyone in Los Angeles even reached for a telephone.

One evening Edwards called from Rome.

'Someone, how is it? John Julius Nor-wich? He's a lord or something, you know him? Well: he's started some fund to try and save Venice from sinking. It's called 'Venice in Peril' and he wants to have the film to run as a Charity First Night in London, very expensive seats, and the Queen has agreed to attend and has said that she will bring both her children. How about that!'

'When?'

'Soon as we can get things fixed up. We're working on March 1st, her first free night.'

The excellent John Julius Norwich, it would seem, had perhaps saved 'Death in Venice'. It would remain to be seen if his valiant efforts could save Venice itself.

The Queen, anyway, had graciously accepted, at pretty short notice, and, as Visconti said to Los Angeles, 'If you say it is "off", that you will not show it, then *you* will tell the Queen of England. Not I. I do not. *Never.*'

We were 'on'.

On January 19th I was telephoned from London to be told that 'we want you here about February 24th for pre-publicity on the movie. It opens March 1st, a Monday, so we want to try and get the week-end journals.'

I said that I was not at all certain that I would be there.

'But you *have* to be there!' said an exasperated male voice.

'Listen! I don't *have* to do a goddamned thing. I did the film. That's enough.'

Hearing, once again, the familiar, chivvying voice of the commercial cinema, knowing a little, but enough, of what Visconti and Edwards had had to deal with in 'terrible Los Angeles', I regrettably allowed anger to overrule good manners: it was an intrusion, that voice, into the calm, orderly, very satisfying form of life which I had elected to live.

Of course, I knew perfectly well that nothing on earth would make me betray Visconti in any way whatsoever. I'd support him through whatever hells were ahead, but I would never again allow myself to be *ordered* to do anything by the cinema. I had had years and years of it. Enough was enough. As far as I was concerned it was all over, for the time being. I'd only ever return on my terms. Never on theirs.

'We'll get back to you,' said the exasperated voice a little more calmly.

'I'll get back to you,' I said. 'If I have reason to,' and hung up.

I felt amazingly refreshed! Golly! When the worm turns . . .

I found Forwood digging away in the *potager*; sacks of peat and manure all about.

'It's definite, I gather. March 1st in London. Some Royal Charity thing.'

'Well: that's something. What did you say?'

'That I'd consider it.'

'Did you now. Well . . .' he thrust a spade into the earth. 'You'd better have a look at your old dinner jacket.'

'Why?'

'Moths.'

'The hell with it. There's plenty of time.'

The next evening Joseph Losey telephoned from London to say that Robin had died.

More than a year before all this, an advertisement had been placed in the papers in Stockholm, Oslo and Helsinki as well as Copenhagen, to the effect that a youth, aged between thirteen and fourteen, was being sought by Visconti to play an important role in his forthcoming film, 'Death in Venice'. The role of Tadzio.

Wrapped in furs, scarves, and wearing a huge fur hat with ear-flaps, he set off into the snowy wilderness of Scandinavia like a very chic Eskimo. He thought to be away at least a month. As it happened, the very first boy brought to his hotel in Stockholm by a hopeful grandmother was, in his opinion, the one and only person to play Tadzio. Nevertheless, he was honour-bound to follow on with the tour so as not to disappoint the hundreds of anxious parents who dragged their children to the interviews in the hopes of instant fame. However, he was certain of his choice, but went on with the tour anyway, though he saw no one who could even equal the boy, and on March 1st, 1970, Edwards telephoned in great excitement to say that Visconti had found his Tadzio and was starting the negotiations.

Exactly one year later, to the day, I stood in line with the boy awaiting the arrival of the Queen under an 'EXIT' sign in the Warner Cinema, London.

In physical respects Björn Andresen was the perfect Tadzio. He had an almost mystic beauty. On the other hand he had a healthy appetite for bubble gum, rock and roll, fast motorbikes and the darting-eyed girls whom he met, tightly jeaned, ruby of lips, playing the pin-tables in the local hotel bar on the Lido.

The last thing that Björn ever wanted, I am certain, was to be in movies.

What he did want was a Honda. The biggest and most powerful ever made. He spoke almost fluent English, but in that curious mutilated manner used by American disc jockeys. Which was perfectly reasonable, as he spent most of his time listening to the American Forces Network.

Thus, almost every other word was punctuated with 'Hey!' or 'I dig!' or 'crazy', or most often, 'man!'.

Fortunately, as Visconti said dryly, he would never be required to open his mouth as Tadzio, so that the 'enigmatic, mystic, illusion' which he appeared to have could be preserved. It was absolutely essential that it was; which was why he was never allowed to go into the sun, kick a football about with his companions, swim in the polluted sea, or do anything which might have given him the smallest degree of pleasure.

He suffered it all splendidly, even the governess, sent by the Swedish Government, with whom he had to spend any time that he was not required on Set working. The only time he had to himself was at week-ends, if we didn't work, when he went off to the pin-tables in the little bars along the Lido.

On many a Monday morning he arrived for work with eyes hooped in mourning, and a pallor which was neither enigmatic nor mystic but almost close to death with exhaustion.

'When did you get to bed, Björn?'

'Heck, man, I didn't go to bed, we danced and danced. It was groovy, man.'

'Well, get into make-up, for the love of God.'

And he'd go like a lamb to the slaughter. And fall asleep within ten seconds of his backside hitting the chair.

However, his manners were at all times impeccable, he was never late, and never once was he not ready for a 'scene'. He was unafraid of Visconti, even in a rage, and perhaps the only fault he really had was that of chewing away constantly at slabs of black bubble gum which he would blow into prodigious bubbles until they exploded all over his face; or yours if you were close enough.

We were not what you could call a rich company. By that I mean no one had vast film-star trailers with showers and TV: no one even *had* a trailer. We made up, and got dressed, in whatever school room, church, deserted palazzo, or cellar was nearest to the location we were using in the city. Sometimes we even did it all in small, noisy bars, dodging frantic waiters, deafened by shouts, and the hissing of the Espresso machines.

One night, early on in the production, we were all gathered together in a dank, abandoned chapel. Björn and I were dressed and ready (it didn't take either of us long). All round people were being laced into desperately tight corsets, having their hair teased, curled, waved and pinned up (Visconti insisted, rightly, that hair was living and he would never allow anyone to wear a wig: dead hair, he said, *was* dead; and that was that), while others were being painted and powdered. A little removed from us, as she almost always seemed to be in some curious way, Silvana Mangano sat in a chair doing a crossword. Her hair and make-up finished, but not yet in her costume. She wore a pair of slacks and a fur coat; quiet and contained.

'You know, man?' Björn was twisting his sailor cap thoughtfully in his hands. 'You know, she is just so beautiful. Don't you think so?'

'Yes, I do. The funny thing is, she doesn't. She thinks that she is plain.'
'You kid me! She thinks that? I think she is the most beautiful woman I have ever seen in my life, man.'
'Why don't you tell her? Or have you?'
'Tell her! Crazy, man, crazy.'
'I think that she is too. Why don't we go and tell her?'
He looked at me with astonishment. 'Tell her. She'd think we were nuts.'
'No she wouldn't. If you really feel that about her, that she is so beautiful, then I think it is your duty to tell her so. It's a very great compliment from a young man: I'll come with you.'
'You would?'
'Sure. We'll both go across and kneel . . . '
'Kneel!' He looked horrified, twisted his cap round and round. 'Kneel, man!'
'You can't make a statement of that kind to a woman if she is sitting and you are towering over her, and so we kneel.'
Which we did, one on either side of her chair. Silvana looked up without surprise.
'We are probably interrupting you . . . ' She waved my remark away lightly. 'But Björn has something which he wants to say to you.'
He was kneeling upright in his blue sailor suit, a tumble of fair hair round his shoulders, cap in his hand.
'I think that you are the most beautiful woman I have ever seen in all my life,' he said, and looked across at me.
'And I agree,' I said.
Silvana didn't move; a very small, warm smile. Then she put out her hand and touched his cheek.
'Thank you, Björn. You know you are kneeling in your new uniform?'
'I know.'
'Thank you,' she said gently. 'You are both mad. But thank you, thank you, really.'
Back in our chairs across the dingy chapel, Björn pushed his hair from his forehead. 'I think she liked that, she had tears,' he said. 'That was a very nice thing to do, man.'

Three or four evenings later, crossing the Piazza San Marco on the way to yet another make-up room, Björn came belting up behind me, scattering pigeons and some Japanese tourists with their cameras.
'Hey, man, I just read it.'
'You just read what?'
He fell into step beside me. 'The book. This film, I read it.'
'The book! Now look, for God's sake, you're not *supposed* to read it. It's strictly forbidden, no script, no book. You do just what Visconti tells you and no more.'
'I know that, man, but it's so crazy. Someone left a paperback in one of the rooms so I read it.'
'So you read it. And so what?'
'Hell, man, now I know who I *am*,' he said. 'I'm the Angel of Death, right?'
'In one,' I said.

So there we stood in the presentation line one year later. I was at one end, beside Visconti; at the other, the American Money and their frilly wives; somewhere in the centre, Björn and Silvana.
The Queen, followed by Princess Anne dressed in orange furnishing-fabric and ear-phones, came slowly along. I think that she murmured something to

the Americans (they did, after all, speak a form of English) but I am not certain that she said a word to anyone else. They were all Italians, so she nodded and smiled and came to Visconti, at whom she looked rather fixedly for some moments as if he were a cenotaph; wordless. She reached me and commented on how long the film had taken to make, and then wandered off with her daughter and a small posy to the auditorium.

It was over. Visconti watched her go with a sad smile.

'*Maladroit,*' he murmured, and shrugged.

It is tremendously sad that a Royal Occasion of this kind is inevitably plunged into a doomed kind of silence. No one laughs, dares to speak, cough even. No one can possibly enjoy it, most particularly the Queen herself who, as I know, is much more fun than the glumness of these occasions would lead one to suppose.

However, there it was. We were enormously grateful for her patronage; it would have been *extremely* pleasing had one of us been able to tell her.

The audience, too, is affected, and sits as lead: not daring to laugh, applaud, or even speak above a church whisper. So it is impossible to judge how anything is received. At the end we all rose as the Royal Party trailed up the centre aisle, and it was only when they had left the auditorium that people came alive and I found myself grabbed in a tight fist-hold by Moura Budberg, ebony cane in one hand, me clutched in the other, a flowing grey dress. Her eyes twinkling with mischief.

'Hello, my darling,' she said in her whispering Russian voice. 'It is marvellous, *very* marvellous, but it is *not* Mann!'

The reception was held at Burlington House, but by the time I had got there with my small party of five, the place was jammed, and all I could see was what appeared to be the entire audience, and it had been a very heavy turn out, crammed round small tables in candlelight. A harassed man at the door said it was full, so we all started down the elegant staircase again to try and eat elsewhere.

Leaning over the slender banister, one of the American Money, who looked like a bar tender in his evening dress, was talking to some of his associates. They were clearly worried.

'We open in Rome, Thursday – you be there?' he called as I was halfway down the stairs.

I said that I really didn't know at the moment.

In actual fact I knew very well indeed: it was just that no one had asked me to attend. Rome, when all was said and done, was Visconti's territory. No one was about to muddy his pitch there. He was to have it all to himself. And he did.

'Well, we'll talk about that tomorrow morning maybe,' said the American Money, busy biting the side of his thumb with ill-suppressed anxiety. 'You know,' he said, turning to his companions on the stairs, 'what I can't understand is how the Queen of England could bring her daughter to see a movie about an old man chasing a kid's ass . . . '

Outside in the courtyard snow was falling. We drove back in silence to the Connaught where, although it was long past dinner- or supper-time, the night porter, oh, blessed man!' made us pots of black coffee and two piled dishes of ham sandwiches which the six of us, for I had collected another lost soul unable to force her way into the candle-lit glory of the reception supper, ate with a couple of bottles of Krug, shoes and jackets cast aside, sitting on the floor of my sitting-room before a glowing fire.

We all agreed that by far the most moving, and regal, moment of the whole evening had been when John Julius's mother, Lady Diana Cooper, had made a deep, and graceful curtsey in the presence of her monarch.

Twenty-four hours later I was once more back at home on the hill.

The next day the film had its premiere in Rome to tremendous enthusiasm while I was busy on my hands and knees sealing the tiled floor of the long room with a fifty-fifty mixture of linseed oil and turpentine.

And the morning after that the household awoke to an astonishing sight. Eight inches of snow; an unfamiliar, unwanted, cold white world, in which the lanes were blocked by drifts, the olives were bowed with the excessive weight, and the cypress trees had turned into mutilated bottle brushes.

This was not at all what I had expected; but nothing that had happened to me since I had arrived in France was quite what I had expected. Crunching up through falling snow to the village with baskets and boots, I knew that if I had determined on a sense of order in life, as I had, there were to be a great many unexpected factors which would arrive to dismay me; but not to defeat me.

Fine words, those. But I was to be severely tried.

After the worst snow and ice seen for seventy, some said one hundred years, in the area, there had, one presumed, to be a thaw at some time.

And it came; warm winds blew in from Africa, the leadened sky swirled about and ran clear, the snow and the ice dissolved as one watched, and the land was left a ravaged, beaten, mire.

The damage was quickly revealed. And it was devastating. The orange trees had all been burnt away by ice, the great lemon tree, proud beside the house for more than fifty years by the size of its girth and height, stood dead in a tatter of frozen leaves and spiked twigs. Roses, so expensively bought, so carefully planted, were slimy and brown as a bar of chewing tobacco. Nothing which had impudently budded was spared. The ice had thawed, re-frozen, thawed again. The land was a sodden ruin, and the olives, whose slow death by drowning I had tried so hard to arrest, would take another four or five years before showing the signs of another death; the withering of their leaves. Fortunately for me. For if I had been aware of that at the time, as well as all the other disasters which stood wretchedly before me, I think I might have, possibly, slung the whole business in and gone off to the tropics.

But I didn't know. So it was a matter of starting again from scratch, something I have never found impossible to do: merely exhausting. Not daunting. So back to work again. The *potager*, in a short time, was re-planted, dead trees cut down, grass seed in quantities sown anywhere and everywhere, beds re-dug, and a fair semblance of order brought back to the land torn by drainage-trenches, trucks and bulldozers.

And then, quite suddenly, as happens in this oddest of climates, it was Spring. Almost overnight the whole area was clothed in tender green and starred about with a million wild anemones: hazed here and there with long drifts of grape hyacinths and violets, and a willow which I had planted by the pond hung golden in the still air; broom and bramble were in bud, and I bought a small plastic bag of goldfish from the local Monoprix and set them free to swim among my Salvator Rosa rocks, and awoke one brilliant morning to find that I had reached my half-century.

I was fifty.

I was not particularly surprised by this event: after all I had been expecting it for a number of years. Now that the moment had arrived it didn't seem to me that any fearful metamorphosis had taken place overnight. My hair had not instantly gone white: I was still able to hold my razor unassisted, the lines and bags scattered about my face had been with me for some time now, and were familiar: and even though the face which peered back at me from the steam-misted mirror was, without any doubt, that of a middle-aged man, the innermost heart, I knew, was still unnervingly that of a mildly retarded sixteen-year-old.

So much for being fifty.

Forwood called up from the terrace. 'Marie says it's mince, sprouts and mashed for lunch. Or would you rather go out somewhere? You won't be fifty again.'

So to the Colombe d'Or, lunch in the sun under the budding fig tree with Vivienne and Paddy Glenavy (Patrick Campbell), the former a very old friend from the early Ealing Studios days and now happily rediscovered as a close neighbour, Simone Signoret and Yves Montand and, later, James Baldwin who very sensibly suggested champagne for such a rare occasion.

A perfectly balanced table, a perfectly pleasant way of easing into one's second half. No standards had been lowered.

With the Cannes Film Festival only a few weeks away, I found myself in a curious situation.

From amongst the wealth of films being shown, 'Death in Venice' had been selected as the official Italian entry, and Joseph Losey's 'The Go-Between' as the British one.

I was inadvertently in competition with the director who had, perhaps, had the most effect on my cinema career. We had attended festivals together with our joint works in past years. But this time we would be rivals; a fact which neither of us took very seriously and which amused us in a wry sort of way. After all, the cinema was supposed to be international, so whether I was in an Italian movie or a British one didn't make much difference really. And anything and everything in the cinema was 'up for grabs', as they say: which eased my tremor of conscience. I had, I must confess, a very small, never expressed, hope that I might perhaps 'grab' a bit of something for myself this time. As usual, rumours had started wheeling about the Croisette like swifts on a summer evening, and one which came to my ears, and gave me a feeling of keen pleasure, was that I was 'definitely' up for the prize of Best Actor.

But this kind of thing happens every year at Cannes and no one really takes any notice; in any case I never win prizes. I'm not the sort that does.

However, it was a warming, if suppressed, idea.

Squashed, rather than suppressed, almost as soon as it had started to wander about in my subconscious, by a long, apologetic letter from Visconti saying that the film as the official Italian entry *had* to be shown in Italian. That is, dubbed. A rule of the Festival (now conveniently set aside during the last year or two) stated that any player who was dubbed in a film was not eligible to qualify for an award.

This was a rule with which I absolutely agreed: a dubbed performance is not a performance at all. An actor's voice is, in my opinion, more than seventy per cent of his work.

However, we had made the film originally in English, and although I had hardly ever opened my mouth during the thing, I had made a very careful effort to speak what words I had in English but with the cadence and nuance of German. The construction of each sentence was precisely planned, and I had followed Thomas Mann extremely closely. The thought of that dry, unsentimental prose being dubbed into Italian, which is a lyrical language at best and romantic at worst, depressed me very much.

Visconti agreed sadly the next day when I managed to get him on the telephone.

'It is tragic! I agreed to come to Cannes for the Festival with a copy of the film in the English tongue. *All* was arranged. All. We would have the subtitles in French. Va bene . . . I insisted on this out of respect for you, Bogarde! I want your voice to be heard in Cannes, in our film. All went so well . . . I controlled with Pasquale de Santis [who had photographed the film] every single frame so that it would be perfect: we made two copies. Ayee! Much work, you understand.'

'But what happened?'

'I have enemies, Bogarde. There was a protest made to the Italian Ministry that the film was Italian and must be submitted in its own tongue.'

'But we made it in English!'

'When I made *my* protest I was warned not to show the film in English because I would risk something worse. We could be banned!'

'Oh really . . . '

'Si, really. Now I must start all over again to do another two copies in Italian. So you will be speaking in Italian but not with your voice! What can I do? I can not revolt against a silly law and possibly risk something far worse . . . '

'Who are these enemies? You know them, of course?'

His voice was as dry and black as charcoal.

'I know. Certo, I know. So alas . . . '

So alas I was out of the running for an award, which angered me far less than the idea of all my careful preparation and 'German' of the text being sung by some Italian tenor. My anger stayed at a high point for a day or so, and then dispersed into a vague sense of disappointment. There was no point in whining on.

One thing cheered me considerably. Now that I had been eliminated from the competition, I was on neutral ground as far as Visconti and Losey were concerned. I could cheer them both on to the winning of the coveted Palme d'Or. For Best Film.

The American Money hit the roof with fury at the Italians' decision, and a terrible battle raged between Rome and Los Angeles: the Italians said that they were 'desolate' but the film *was* Italian, and must be dubbed; the American Money protested that it was made in English and must *not* be dubbed. Then the Italians brought up the heavy weapons and warned those concerned to keep out of the argument and stop resisting.

There was a slightly uncomfortable feeling of politics about, especially when it was very tactfully leaked from some quarter that 'the film was scheduled to win in any case'.

All very Italian.

But, to give them their due, the American Money fought on bitterly, and finally a compromise was reached. The film would be shown in English, as shot, to the Press, but the Gala Performance in the evening would be in Italian.

Under these circumstances, I agreed, therefore, to attend the Press showing, but not the Gala.

No one attempted to dissuade me. Everyone was very pleased with the turn of events and, after all, there could only be one loser, the actor.

At the same time that this unseemly business was taking place, another event, far more important than this, was also going on. The waiters and waitresses, indeed all the hotel staff, from top to bottom, decided to go on strike indefinitely, so that the chances of a Festival being held grew daily more and more remote. However, in the end someone gave in to someone else, as usual, and the strike was called off just in time.

Unfortunately, the rain was not.

It was the wettest Festival for years, bitterly cold, drenching, grey. Flags and bunting hung limp among the banners, the gutters raced with muddy water, and those who went to the movies did so in plastic macs and huddled under umbrellas. We might just as well have been in Manchester.

But on the day of our Press Show, God, as Lally sometimes said, leant out of Heaven, and cleared things up. The rain stopped, the sun came out, and when we reached the Palais des Festivals, Björn, myself and Visconti, the day was bright and there appeared, at first glance, to be a major revolution beginning on the steps of the building.

The place was jammed with a seething mob of jeans-clad youth, intent on forcing the doors in spite of the 'Complet' signs displayed everywhere.

The auditorium was packed to the roof. People sat in the aisles, on the stage, stood five deep at the back of the circle: the Press were outnumbered by hundreds. The majority of the audience was young. A very different kind from the one in London which, doomed by the presence of Royalty, and consisting in any case of elderly Diplomatic Corps, Social Figures, or just people whom John Julius had forced to part with a hefty bit of money to help save Venice, had offered no warmth and almost no signs of life.

This was very different: there was a surging atmosphere of excitement. The feeling that an 'event' was about to take place. I felt that if they hated it they could very easily throw rocks or bottles at the screen. It was not to be a passive crowd, and some of them had fought, and queued, for hours to secure a place.

Sitting between Visconti and Björn, I wondered if they would think that it *was* too slow: the music too obscure? Or, remembering the remark made by the American Money on the landing at Burlington House, perhaps they would send the whole thing up and laugh at the old man who was chasing . . .

But I put that thought aside quickly. It even distressed me to remember it. I sat back as the house-lights started to dim and a sudden hush fell over the packed place. They sat there in absolute silence: no one moved, coughed, crackled paper, turned a head. There was an incredible feeling of intense concentration until, at one specific moment, halfway through, when Von Aschenbach makes a silent decision to return from the railway station to his hotel on the Lido and confront his future, no matter what, the entire theatre exploded with a tremendous roar of spontaneous delight, and a thundering of applause and cheering which drowned the sound track and astonished the three of us by its force. It must have lasted only a few moments, though it seemed at the time, far longer, and then almost as suddenly as it had arrived it faded into intense silence once again. Somewhere I heard a girl sobbing.

I turned to Visconti and in a low whisper, much moved by what had happened, for I had never witnessed such a moment in a cinema before, nor since, I said, 'Luchino! I think we have won!' He turned his grey-cropped head briefly towards me, eyebrows arched in shaggy reproof. 'Certo!' he said, implying that I had been an idiot not to have realised that from the start.

We walked through a dense crowd of cheering people to the obligatory Press Reception. Visconti moved slowly, enjoying every second, one hand raised to the left, then to the right, a Benediction, or a monarch on a walkabout. Björn and I trailed him, pleased and relieved, moved by the hands which thrust to take ours, by the cries of 'Thank you!', the gentle thumps and pats as we moved among them, and by the flowers, some in battered bunches, others just single blooms, which were pressed upon us.

The news had spread all over Cannes. We were a triumph, and the world loved us.

Except for one important member of the official jury, who had *loathed* us, and let it be known in every bar or restaurant that he managed to visit in the course of his onerous duties.

Unfortunate. However, that didn't prevent the crowds from gathering for the gala that evening, and the reaction in the theatre, for an 'Italian dub' was every bit as exciting as the morning one.

I didn't know about all that, because I had gone up to the Colombe d'Or to dine with Losey and his wife, Patricia. Joe was uneasy and depressed about his own film, due to be shown in two days' time, and felt that it had no chance of winning, mainly because of our overwhelming success, but I did my best to lift his morale by reminding him of the chattering jury member who had spread his gospel of hate far and wide. There was no certainty, yet, that we had won. And that cheered him up for a time.

People started to telephone through from Cannes to tell me how the film had been received, and couldn't I be persuaded to come down, just to the reception?

I apologised politely and explained that, at the moment, I was extremely busy trying to encourage the Competition.

And the Competition won.

Just before noon on the day of the awards the news leaked out, whereupon Visconti quietly packed all his Vuitton luggage, checked out of his hotel, and went to the airport where he sat on his suitcases awaiting the next flight to Rome. Consternation reigned; officials flew about in harassed flocks, traced him and begged him to return, they had a special prize for him, and he must, they implored, be there to accept it. He sat as still as a block of granite; considering this.

Then reluctantly agreed. On condition that the prize was awarded at the very end of the evening, *after* the Palme d'Or.

I can't remember now what the prize was actually for: twenty-five years of the Cannes Festival, or his contribution over the years to the cinema. However, in the packed theatre that night no one seemed to care what it was for, just as long as he got it, and when the Best Film was announced, and Losey walked rather uncomfortably on to the stage, he was booed just as much as he was cheered. But the announcement that Visconti had won a 'special' prize brought the whole house to its feet, cheering and applauding.

He strode on to the stage, accepted, with the greatest grace, his award from Romy Schneider, bowed briefly to the cheering crowd, and left. He did not stand, as all the other winners chose to do, in a self-conscious line, embarrassedly holding their scrolls and scarlet boxes.

After the awards, the final film is run: usually pretty boring. And that year it was no exception, but Visconti insisted that we all sit through it as a mark of respect to the director. Fortunately I wasn't near him and managed to slip out and have a meal at the Blue Bar next door, returning only in time for the last few moments. Losey, we discovered, had taken his prize and left for his hotel, leaving the field wide open to Visconti, who took it . . . marching down the great staircase to thundering cheers and flashing cameras, clearly the winner: not only of the evening, but of the whole Festival. Romy and I followed him down, I holding his Burberry, she the prize, so that his hands were free to acknowledge his triumph with gentle gestures all about. It was the greatest fun. A perfect example of 'winner takes all'.

Afterwards an enormous supper party was given to end the Festival. The only person not present was Joe who had gone earlier without any farewell.

'He is not here, your Losey?' asked Visconti.

'No. He went home.'

'He has *la grippe*, perhaps?'

'Perhaps . . . '

'Poor man.'

'And this is the finish now, isn't it? Cinderella time?'

'I do not follow you, Bogarde.'

'I heard midnight striking. The Ball is over.'

'Oh no! Not over. Now we just begin. In Tokyo, in New York even, in Cape Town, in London, Rome and Paris . . . all over the world they will see our work. It is not yet finished! You must be pleased to go back to your shepherd's house with poor Poverino [Labo], it is as you wanted.'

'And you?'

'I? I start with Proust. Maybe three years' work, you know. It is complicato.'

'I may never see you again after tonight.'

He drew on his cigarette in its paper holder. 'Is possible. Si.'

'I mean . . . well, it's all breaking up, and you'll go and I'll go, and we may not ever come together again. Do you see?'

'Si, si. I see.' He stubbed his cigarette into a saucer.

'I feel rather bereft,' I said.

Visconti had no time for sentimentality: he was also curiously shy. Suddenly he got up, gathered his Italian clan around him, bowed over hands here and there, and started moving towards the big hall.

This is how it all ends, I thought. I was *very* sentimental: even if he wasn't. I remembered, sitting among the debris of the supper table, the long, long haul we had come together since the day, years ago it seemed now, that he had arrived at my villa in Rome for lunch and, after an enormous helping of Antonia's trifle, which he liked more than anything, he had pushed a wrapped packet across the table towards me. 'A present,' he had said. 'Not for anything . . . but perhaps for the pudding Inglese, certo . . . for that.'

It had been a paperback copy of *Death in Venice*.

Finale now, in a dispersing, laughing, supper party crowd at the Carlton.

He had almost reached the doors when he turned suddenly, looking about him with those steady grey eyes, bright beneath shaggy brows, and saw me.

'Bogarde!' He raised his hand and I went across to him. 'You have a dentist in Roma, you tell me?'

'Yes.'

'So. You telephone me one day, eh?' He patted my shoulder, turned into his group, turned back once more, waved, and was gone.

SIX

Illiterate 1. Unable to read or write. 2. Violating accepted standards in reading and writing. *Collins' Dictionary.*

I cannot, in all truth, be accused of the first, although I am well aware that I am guilty of the second part of the definition. This stems, of course, from an almost total lack of education.

My father's desperate efforts to try and alter this sorry situation were to no avail, as I have explained. I resisted placidly, peacefully and stubbornly all attempts at learning. Tutors were engaged; hopelessly shrugged shoulders, and left; I achieved the supreme accolade of determined non-education once by being rewarded with two marks out of a possible one hundred in Maths. It was pointless trying to explain to me, as a great many people did, that a sound knowledge of Algebra, Geometry, or Mathematics would assist me in the acquisition of a logical mind.

As far as I was concerned I had no need of a logical mind. I was absolutely certain that I already possessed one: so why waste time?

I made a strenuous effort to try and do my best only in those lessons which would cause me the least stress or strain. And there weren't many such.

Strangely enough, reading was one thing which I found fascinatingly simple and exciting to do, even though I could neither spell correctly nor punctuate; but that didn't bother me. I just ploughed on, only reading those books which were not 'difficult' or 'dull' or 'dense' (favourite words of mine at that time). Perhaps this was inherited from my mother who was, what she was pleased to call, an avid reader, devouring like a python anything set in her path by Michael Arlen, Ethel Mannin, Daphne du Maurier or Mary Webb etc.

And I swallowed them too. Whole.

These were splendidly easy books: and although my despairing father offered me the chances of reading Trollope, Collins, Thackeray, Hardy and Dickens, I scented the dust upon their pages and turned instead to the bright, well-spaced, simple, cheap romances best digested with a box of chocolates at one's side. Which is exactly what my mother did, most afternoons, lying in elegant splendour on her day-bed. Chewing and reading.

The result of all this was that I left school at sixteen, stuffed to the gills with Romance and Fuller's chocolate (metaphorically speaking), and lacking in almost any other kind of education whatsoever.

The main thing, as far as I was concerned, was that I could *read*. And reading was, in itself, Education. It was all that I could possibly need to assure me of a safe future in the profession which I had chosen long ago, to follow. The theatre. This was, perhaps, my first major failure in assessment.

The theatre was the one place where the reading of cheap, bright novels would *not* be quite enough. There was, I found out quickly, more to it all than that. Shakespeare, Shaw, Wilde, Congreve, Ibsen, Tchekov . . . oh! how appallingly difficult they were after the delights of *Rebecca*! With what relief I turned to Dodie Smith and Merton Hodge, with whom I felt far more comfortable.

I learned my Shakespeare (I realised wistfully that I had to if I was to follow in his profession) in much the same way as I had learned to take syrup of figs — by holding my nose, swallowing it all down, and then sweetening the dose with something by Agatha Christie, perhaps, or Dornford Yates: they caused me very little pain or trouble and wrote convenient, easily digested English, requiring no kind of dictionary at the side to aid me.

In time I spouted Shakespeare like a spiggot, without having much idea of what he was saying: from the Plays to the Sonnets; and about the only thing I wrestled from Wilde was his encouraging remark, 'The stage is the refuge of the too charming.' With which I heartily agreed.

Shaw left me glazed of eye: Ibsen and Tchekov were the Dead Sea Scrolls. However, Wilde's pleasing remark lent me encouragement, and leaning heavily on what I interpreted as his version of 'charm', I trod blithely into my theatre life unaware that I had the education of a mole and the assurance of Mont Blanc. I also had an unshakable belief, at that time, that I was God's gift to the theatre, so there was absolutely nothing for me to worry about at all.

It was exceedingly fortunate that after two short years of this tiresome behaviour I found myself in an ill-fitting battle-dress trying, with no success whatsoever, to come to terms with the absurd mysteries of the Morse Code in the Royal Corps of Signals.

However, I was not in the least bit cast down: it was not my fault that some idiot in Whitehall, or wherever it was, had sent me, of all people, to learn how to send the S.O.S.

They had picked the wrong man for the job: and that was their bad luck. Not mine. I muddled about generally: worked hard at the standard things which one was required to do, like throwing grenades, or forming fours, and polishing fire buckets, and discovered, with mild interest, that I was a deadly shot on the rifle range. I also turned out the very best kit inspection it was possible to see, arranged, within the very strict limits of regulations, with the precision and elegance of the fish counter at Harrods.

I was still, however, not doing very much to become a Signalman. That was quite beyond me; and bored me witless, even though, somewhere in the darker recesses of my mind, I knew that my life might one day depend on it.

There were, on the other hand, some extraordinary compensations in this idiotic, to me at any rate, army life.

Even though the days were crammed with the trivia, effort and exhaustion of training, there were long, wearying Sunday afternoons when Church Parade was over, and the interminable evenings of boredom once one had polished one's brasses and boots for Morning Parade.

I had brought with me, at my father's suggestions, a couple of books which would be my constant companions in these slack moments. For he had told me that, although much of his own war had been fright, a great deal more of it was lethal boredom. So I took, predictably, the *Oxford Book of Modern Verse* and a pocket edition of Shakespeare (to keep in touch, as it were), only to discover, in a relatively short time, that they became as heavy and dull as the majority of my hut mates. There was a limit to my patience with the 'hey-nonny-no's' and James Elroy Flecker and company.

And then, one evening, wandering about the hut begging a book which I could *read*, I found, to my amazed surprise, Auden.

I found Isherwood too: then Evelyn Waugh, Cyril Connolly, Emily Brontë, and even managed, with one finger pressed hard to every line, the negativity of

Ivy Compton-Burnett. There was Hemingway for the first time, and the rustic joys of John Surtees. I went through a catholic library with the voracity of a silver-fish.

Not all my hut mates were leaden and dull, lying on their bunks reading what my father always called 'housemaid's trash', or smoking lethargically like a host of opium eaters, occasionally scratching some unwashed portion of their bodies and farting genially. Some, and they were the ones who loaned me these wondrous volumes, actually read books.

A small reading group had been started in the dingy NAAFI, and we would sit around our two tables drinking thin beer or thinner cocoa just before Lights Out, discussing, arguing, even reading selected passages aloud (I rather fancied myself at this part, naturally), debating and questioning.

But I sat, for the most part, in silence: an unusual habit for me, for I knew only too well that I was woefully behind in this 'school', and that I had a great deal on which to catch up. I had a lot to learn, and, quite suddenly, I wanted to: so I stayed silent and listened.

I had realised, just in the nick of time, what I had so carelessly left aside; and although I had been a bit slow in starting the race, at least I was now among the runners.

If it had seemed to me that learning in civilian life was a chore and to be avoided at almost all costs (for my life had seemed to be so splendidly simple without it), I was now discovering that it mattered a great deal in the army. I was much surprised.

I had quietly become aware, for example, that my hut mates who lay about reading papers or just scratching, staring blankly into space and smoking, were, for the most part, not much good at anything else. They could argue indeed: and did almost constantly, about their 'rights' and what they would do when they got back to Civvy Street, but all of their arguments amounted to little sense and no awareness of life at all. They were the untrained minds.

Stupid on the rifle range, lethal chucking their grenades at Practice, clumbering about like heifers on the parade ground, brilliant at avoiding duties, and useful, 'nifty' one of them called it, with motor transport, they slouched through their lives complaining and protesting.

It was from their numbers, I had the wit to notice, that hastily assembled squads were issued with khaki shorts, pith helmets and a pass for embarkation leave: after which they were dispatched to Alexandria, Calcutta, and Bombay grumbling bitterly.

The reading group members were not.

This culling of the untrained minds alerted me, almost too late, but in time, to become aware of my own need for survival. Trying to keep up with the people I had selected to assist me was extremely hard with almost no educational background, but I struggled on determinedly. Often I fell. I wallowed and splashed about in ignorance, floundered and became lost a good deal of the time; but I was never afraid to ask questions, to seek help, to admit defeat, even to invite ridicule. Which never came.

The assistance I received in return for this humility and determination was constant, for the people who knew what *I* wanted to know were delighted to share their knowledge, patiently, calmly, cheerfully, setting me out on my rather rutted track, helping me to pick up the scattered pieces of my knowledge like so many fallen packets; they were clearly glad that I was trying to learn, and rewarded me handsomely.

Of course I knew very well that starting my Prep School education at the age of nineteen in a gloomy NAAFI was, facing things absolutely squarely, leaving things a trifle late; to say the least. Almost an afterthought indeed; but I threw whatever pride I might have had to the winds and got on with things.

I knew that there wasn't much chance, really, of repairing all the holes which negligence had made in the fabric of my life: I also knew that I would never quite recapture the squandered years. There could be, at this late stage of the game, no possibility of my weaving a good thick blanket to hide the tears and rents: all I could hope for now, and I was well aware of the fact, was some kind of rough and ready patchwork quilt which might, with any luck, help to distract a really discerning eye away from my grosser intellectual faults, and help to cloak the draughty holes which I could not hope now to fill, late starter that I was, but which I would continue to try to patch continuously.

A patchwork quilt, however, needs a good needlewoman. Which I was not.

And how could I know, at nineteen, with a long war ahead of me, that there were two such women, many miles apart, and many years away, who were old hands at 'patching', and who would come to my assistance quite unexpectedly?

In 1967, Mrs X, sitting under a hair dryer in her local Beauty Parlour in a small American town, idled through the pages of a cheap woman's magazine.

It was not her kind of reading matter at all, and she was just about to set it aside when a photograph of an unknown man standing on a daisied lawn before a house, stayed her astonished hand.

It was a fortunate moment: for it was to make a difference to her life and have a profound effect on mine.

I was the stranger in the photograph, and the house belonged to me. But it had once belonged to her, many years before. She knew every tile, timber and brick. It was the house in which she had spent the happiest years of her life and she had not set eyes on it, until that moment, since September 1939 when she and her husband, as Americans, had to leave England at the outbreak of the war.

She left the Beauty Parlour with the magazine; and having read the sorry little article which accompanied the photographic spread, she wrote to me, enclosing a small, sepia snapshot of the house as it had been when she had first found it, uncared for, crumbling, overgrown with nettles, in 1929.

It was a hesitant letter. She hoped that I would forgive a total stranger for making such an unwarranted intrusion, but the coincidence was so odd, and she wondered if the house had changed a great deal in the years . . . ?

It is not unusual for a film star to receive letters from total strangers: it is, in fact, the norm. My letters are usually replied to by a secretary and only very rarely by myself. And I do not write a second time.

But in this particular instance it seemed that we were not total strangers, for we both shared the common love for one particular house, and we both knew it intimately.

So I wrote back. And started a correspondence which was to last, unbroken, for five years, until her death in 1972.

At first I wrote formally about the changes in the house and the gardens over the years: I drew a map, in red ink, to show her where new tree plantings had taken place, or where paths now went, and where doors had been blocked up or windows re-opened, for there had been other tenants before me and since her.

March 18, '67. DB to Mrs X:

'. . . *mucking about below the wall where you said your pond had been. Ain't no pond there now, not even a shallow dip, I dug around and all I could find were a few bits of broken flower pot, some pebbles and two shards of blue-glazed terracotta. Anything you recognize? The big ash went years ago, there is a sort of Humpty Dumpty kind of depression . . . covered in thick meadow grass . . . '*

April 5th, '67. DB to Mrs X:
' . . . *I am very well aware that my syntax is 'all to hell' . . . so is my spelling and punctuation . . . relics of a mis-spent youth . . . Alicebright Lane was called after one Alice Bright . . . Gipsy girl who sold wild daffodils outside the pubs and was found 'drowned' in a horse trough in 1888. Want any more?'*

To begin with, our letters were formal in address, Dear Mrs, Dear Mr, but in a very short time these were dispensed with and we wrote to each other without any form of address. The letters became 'essays' rather than mere letters, and we had so much to say to each other, it seemed, that I started writing more than spasmodically, but at least once or twice a week; and she wrote to me every single day.

Gradually it emerged, though she never at any time *said* so, that she was alone, and that she was ill. The illness, I deduced for myself, was possibly grave, and the essays, letters, what you will, became a 'steadier' for her and gave her strength when,

' . . . *the pain gets really intolerable, which it does from time to time, but I get tremendous comfort from re-reading your letters and (I suppose I'm hinting?) when I get a new one . . . '*

Sometimes, due to pressure of my work, I was not able to write letters, and so I sent postcards. From 1968 onwards I sent one every day. Sometimes these postcards got 'bunched up' in various sorting offices for some unknown reasons and, when released, seemed to *'fly about my head like huge flocks of birds'*, which is why she called them 'starlings'.

At her death, five years of letters and 'starlings' were returned to me from America, according to the instructions which she left in her will. They were all neatly filed in paper folders. Some, for her own fun, she had 'corrected' in pencil, altering my spelling, correcting punctuation. The last item in the file for 1972 is a postcard (starling) of the local village church here. To my bitter regret I wrote:

21st April, '72
'*Up to the eyes with work. Don't give a damn to whom you leave my ruddy letters, Yale, Harvard or the British Museum, or try St Pancras. Do as you like, if it makes you feel better, I really don't care. Will write when I'm sorted out.'*

It, like all the others, was carefully dated in her fine handwriting with its arrival, and filed. She died that night, suddenly and alone.

I never met her. I never saw her. We never even spoke to each other. I had no idea of her age.

Late in our correspondence she once wrote:
' . . . *I did fall desperately in love when I was twelve. With the most stunning steward on the 'Lusitania' . . . '*

But I wonder?

All I know for certain is that she wrote like a joyous girl: and gave me five years of extraordinary pleasure and 'learning'.

In all that time I can't remember that we ever asked each other a personal or direct question; we both knew that we were 'the people of the letters' and left it at that. Gradually, like a puzzle taking shape, I learned that she had one child who was in Holy Orders, and a husband, whom she greatly loved once, in a nursing home, who was to die during our relationship, causing her bitter distress, for even though the marriage had fallen into decay and desolation, it had once been glowing and glorious. More than that I did not know, nor presumed to ask. That neither of us presumed upon the other was, I am certain, the core of our friendship.

And, after all, it is not an unusual one, two people meeting through letters: there have been many others like it before. But it is a once only business. It can *never* be repeated.

As far as I know, this correspondence was kept a complete secret from most of her friends, and she had a great many, except for three or four to whom she confessed, with some guilt lest they should laugh. Which, thankfully, they did not. The only person who was privy to the whole thing was her devoted, and adored, Polish maid, Anna, who couldn't really be prevented from seeing the long air-mail envelopes, which arrived so frequently, or the starlings, which she had to gather up and carry to her lady, as she called her. In time, Anna became bold enough to signal the arrival of these envelopes by placing a single red rose in a fluted vase on her mistress's miserly (because of a stringent diet) breakfast tray.

One red rose meant a letter. No rose, no letter.

April 2nd, '69. Mrs X to D.B.:

' . . . *got myself downstairs unaided, big deal! Awake from three am with the most hellish 'jangles', so found it an effort. Depression maybe; no rose on my tray. I guess I am a spoiled woman. Somewhere Anna was singing and came into the 'salon' bearing a great jar of the first forsythia, just beginning to break bud. 'You got forsythia!' she said. 'I didn't get a rose,' I said in my self-pitying voice (which you are spared!) 'Why don't you take a look at the electric light fittings in the kitchen?' she said.*

'*There, sellotaped to the wires, three glorious, beautiful letters! Red, white, and blue, strung like bunting: all from you. I was as 'high as the Flag on the Fourth of July', truly. Anna's delight at MY delight made us both laugh and the 'jangles' faded. She is SUCH a clever one . . .*'

As far as I know, other than these few, no one else ever knew, although she was to have some narrow escapes: after all, it is perfectly reasonable for a young boy or young girl to write to his or her favourite film star, or pop singer, but it could not be considered at all fitting behaviour, or even balanced behaviour, in a patrician lady associated closely with an extremely respected American University in a small town.

The least said about writing to film stars the better; especially as she had never really seen one outside the pages of her newspapers where, she said, they

'*seem a bit 'flashy' really, fighting waiters and getting drunk on Chat Shows on the Television . . . but I have never seen EITHER, so can't really judge. You SEEM all right . . . but in general they appear to me to be very shallow people, most often poorly bred so that sudden fame and riches must be desperately hard for them to deal with: so of course they don't. Oh! Lord! I am sounding DREADFULLY pompous, and you ARE a Fillum Star! I keep on forgetting . . .*'

In all the years, all I ever really knew of her background was that she had a British-French passport, was possibly Viennese, had travelled widely, and was now doing a job at the University which was

' . . . *well, you know: literature, books, research, cataloguing, writing. All that kind of thing. I'm, I suppose, a Book-Worm, deadly dull truthfully . . .* '

She lived in an old-for-America house on a quiet street in a pleasant garden (about which she knew a very great deal), surrounded by a picket fence; and her 'salon', as it amused her to call it, was

' . . . *stuffed with books and papers everywhere and has a pot-bellied window which sticks out over the street. Pretty ugly, but ugly-pretty, if you know what I mean . . .* '

All this was shaded by a huge white chestnut tree of great age, and a high bush of lilac.

The 'salon' seemed mainly to consist of writers, students, Deans and their wives and people from the University who '*come at all hours to pick my poor addled brains*'. In spite of almost constant pain, she was seldom able to say 'No' to any request for help from some unhappy student, a poet with pentameter problems, or a Dean's wife going through the change of life. She took all that came her way because she dreaded so

' . . . *the haul up stairs after they have all gone, my room so softly reflected in my beautiful Vauxhall glass mirror, the awful loneliness, and fear of pain coming on again and having to wait until the first light comes to start another day. The nights, even though I am now struggling with "Meeting Mrs Jenkins" by Richard Burton (I see no reason for its publication. Do you?) seem terribly long . . .* '

But it's all gone now. The pot-bellied window, the giant chestnut, the lilac and the little 'salon'. It's all a parking lot. And she is dead.

She was the first of my two 'needlewomen' and started in on the 'patching' almost from the start, or at least as soon as the direct formalities of writing to a stranger were mutually dropped.

One can't be taught to write, any more than one can be taught to act or to paint or play a piano or any other musical instrument. All that can be done for potential students is to offer the basic rules, advise, suggest, counsel, encourage and correct. The rest is entirely up to them, and if they have a spark, an ember so to speak, they might get through the tremendous seas of chance.

But the spark is not always present; and no amount of encouragement will kindle a dead ember into a flame, and the flame into a fire.

Fortunately for me, Mrs X seemed to think that, from the letters which I sent her, I had some kind of ember worth the fanning, and fan away she did. My appalling punctuation at first amused her, as did my spelling:

'*I don't see why you SHOULDN'T spell "cough" as "koff" . . . it's perfectly reasonable but ugly . . .*'

I carried on, explaining that she was bloody lucky to get letters from an overworked, illiterate movie star in the first place, and she correctly countered that it just seemed a waste not to do it 'properly'. My punctuation was so negligible that I simply resorted to dots, which drove her frantic; but as the years went by I was amused to see that she resorted to the beastly things herself:

'. . . *they do save time, somehow. However, it is not "literate" and that's what we should be trying to concentrate on . . .*'

Sometimes she would carefully correct an entire page of one of my letters, have it photocopied, and send it back for my thoughful examination. And sometimes I tried, but the efforts made her laugh so much that she decided that the best way to try and penetrate my thick head was by reading. Books were sent. We spent a fortune on books which flew to and fro across the Atlantic.

She was wise enough to realise that I wrote as I wrote: straight off with no set of rules to bog me down, and she much preferred the 'straight off' letters to the ones which I wrote with Fowler and the Oxford Dictionary. So I was let off the hook gleefully.

' . . . *do it all your way, I'm used to it now and would HATE the letters to be any other way, they are vivid, funny, alive. I see all you see, all you share with me, and that is more than enough for a grumpy University critter like me . . . it's no good stuffing you in a strait-jacket of correct literature-behaviour! I'd far rather you were able to wave your arms about, and shout freely. And that you certainly do!*'

The books were something else. We shared them constantly. I discovered that there were 'gaps' in her knowledge, much to my open delight and sent her books on people she had hardly, if ever, heard of, to my surprise, and on whom she feasted.

' . . . *finished reading your Margot Asquith autobiography and diaries. How good of you to alert me! I was in at the birth of "Puffin", and her theories of educating children. To confess to you the depth of my ignorance, I had suffered all these years under the illusion that she was of American birth! And used to cringe at some of the things she said and did as being vulgar Americanisms! . . .*'

' . . . *the book on Rupert Brook (Michael Hastings) saddened me. You are of course, wise enough to know that one can thoroughly like a book, and yet be critical. It struck me as really "mordant" . . . almost a cruel piece of work. I'm all for "debunking", but at the same time, I feel that we need myths. Ridiculous, isn't it?*'

' *B---- here today, barged in saying "There'll be a long wait, the Library (University) hasn't even heard of it!" And his eyes popped when he saw your copy (Cynthia Asquith's Diaries) lying on the table. Of course if you WILL pay air mail postage, which is almost the amount of the book! But oh! I AM grateful . . .*'

And here they all stand, the letters of a long time ago, packed tightly into fat box files. Each in its original envelope, hundred upon hundred, all marked carefully in pencil with the exact date of delivery, some with scribbled pencil notes concerning the information they hold. Or questions to be asked next day. '*Malamud's "The Fixer" offerd as film. He refused.*' Or '*Arrives Plaza Hotel, NYC.*' Or '*Has he read Connolly's "The Rock Pool"?*'

She, for her part, offered me writers I had never read, or set aside as 'too difficult' in the past: T. S. Eliot, Ezra Pound, Albert Camus, Robert Graves, James Joyce, Faulkner, and, early in 1967, Thomas Mann for the very first time. She 'introduced' me to a host of people I had little or no knowledge about: Zelda Fitzgerald, whom she had known; Gerald and Sara Murphy, who, many years later, were to 'spike off', as it were, my second novel; Leonard Woolf, and

Rilke, Theodore Roethke and so on. The 'patching' was very subtly beginning.
And I enjoyed it.

> ' . . . *absolutely no need to thank me. You make me feel like some ageing spinster-teacher,*
> *like the one in "The Corn is Green", and that isn't me at all. I have grown wondrous used*
> *to your intriguing spelling: at least it is real! Not like that idiot Dora Carrington whose*
> *spelling was pure affectation. I think everything she did was "affected". Except, perhaps,*
> *some of her painting . . . but your spelling is just downright 'iggorance' Sir! . . . '*

Needless to say, after a while, we both cheated on the strict set of rules I had
insisted upon, and which she had accepted (a bit reluctantly at first) that we
should never meet or speak, but must remain only correspondents. I had had
too many unpleasing encounters, in the past, with elderly ladies who wrote
packages of junk and would, as often as not, arrive unannounced and unwanted
at my house in their best C & A hats and coats with, for the sake of appearances,
some autograph book to sign. So I took particular care.

But eventually she managed to wheedle me into sending, against my better
judgement, a portrait-still so that she could *'take it into hospital when I go, next
month'*. It was a rough picture taken off-set, not a glossy, retouched thing, and of
course she didn't take it to hospital at all. She framed it in a neat shagreen frame
and foolishly stood it on a small table by her chair in her 'salon' hiding it, she
swore, every time an unexpected visitor arrived, under a book of Klee's works.
It gave her, she said *'a terrific sense of danger . . . very stimulating'*. I accepted this
'cheating' because, after all, she could see me, if she had so wished, on someone's
television, and I was, even in America, often to be found in illustrated
magazines, and if she enjoyed the vicarious thrill of hiding a picture under a
book, that was entirely her business.

In any case, I really couldn't take a hard line: I, faced with a telephone in my
suite in a New York hotel, and a little advanced in my wine, pressed the buttons
on the machine which I knew would ring a bell in the salon with its pot-belly. It
did. And the moment I heard the receiver lifted, I hung up; my hands shaking
with treachery.

If I take up five or six of my returned letters, spread them like a fan or a hand
of cards, they appear to be just what they are. Envelopes. They have no life,
only the postmarks hint of something more. Budapest, Rome, Crowborough,
Paris, New York, Lewes, Port Antonio, Sidi Bou Said, Venice . . . it is
impossible to believe that once their contents gave immeasurable happiness, or
that they even assisted to sustain a failing spirit, or gave me incalculable
pleasure.

What on earth do they contain, these spread envelopes, and the hundreds of
others stuffed into the files before me? What did I write about over all those
years to divert her and, I always hoped, to amuse her?

They seem to me now more like journals than essays or letters, and that is
what they eventually became, four to eight pages of close typing. (I never, or
seldom, wrote in hand because mine is illegible.)

I wrote of every day and that day's events, detailed accounts of every
conversation which might amuse her, and thus the voices of my parents, or
Losey, Visconti, Resnais or Cukor and so many others, spring vividly from the
paper, even now, so many years later. There was never any reason, when I
started to write my autobiography, to invent conversations; they are all here, in
the letters, verbatim, at least as far as I could recall them three or so hours later,
or perhaps next day.

But more than conversations, I wrote the most minute details of sights, sounds, of smells, and texture, light and colour, so that sitting alone in her salon or, as was so often the case latterly, lying alone in a hospital bed, she could share my world, and escape, if only metaphorically, for a time the sterility, the fear, the meandering odour of ether and polish.

It was her unyielding determination that I should write. And this was my homework and practice. She bullied and cajoled; I crumpled and gave in. Willingly. Looking at these bunches before me, I do rather wonder how on earth I managed to put out so much energy on top of the work which I was then doing for the cinema. But somehow I managed, because her daily letter became of paramount importance to me, because I knew, in some strange way, that I *had* to write, that I wanted to do so above all else, and the most important thing was that I had a recipient.

I could not have written all those hundreds and hundreds of pages without that: it would have seemed absolutely pointless to me, and my inherent laziness would have taken over. But I was kept alert, even though my emotions had been all but drained from me after a difficult, or even an easy, day of shooting. But I went on, because I knew that what I wrote was important. To one person.

And that person was my 'patcher', leading me on with tacit encouragement, fanning my vanity at the same time as she was pushing me towards taking the halting steps of a writer. '*Write anything that comes into your head,*' she once said, '*but write!*'

Before a particularly unpleasant operation on what remained of her poor mutilated body which we called the 'Banjo Belly' because of the amount of stitches an earlier operation had necessitated, she wrote:

'*Oh! Poor Banjo Belly . . . how I twang! And I can't scratch, sit up, can do nothing but lie here staring at this particularly uninspiring shiny-green paint on the ceiling, or scribble as I am now, notebook above head. Oh! Do send me something again soon, it seems days since your last letter. A delicious, idiotic, "puff"? Don't worry about spelling and so on, but don't make me laugh too much for fear I bust all these stitches and have to go through the dreadful cobbling business again. They have removed my poor little Contemplating Navel . . . somehow they seemed to take a tuck here and there. I am bereft. Write ANYTHING. About the vegetable garden NOW. This instant. Write about every stone, every shoot, every precious clod of English earth. Are there, oh COULD there be? any stray relics somewhere of my cherished Parma violets in the cold-frames which you recently discovered behind the "sagging greenhouse". No. Too long ago now . . .*'

And I wrote. And wrote.

Holding hands for comfort, really.

There came a time, as there had to come, when I decided to leave England for good and, therefore, the house which had been our common bond and which we had both, in different ways, loved so much. I wrote to break the news as gently as I possibly could, and my letter provoked a response which had nothing whatsoever to do with patching or learning or even teaching.

'*Coup de grace . . .* ' she wrote, '*if you leave the house. The little fringes of my heart that have never hurt when the whole heart ached, now feel pain at the very thought of the house without you.*

But c'est la vie . . . and its helps me not to care very much whether the surgeon's knife slips tomorrow or not: except that you do, I think, make it feel as though our silly literary 'amour' could still go on, even without the common bond. But please don't cast me off with the house . . . '

It is, alas, not possible to regulate the arrival of a letter, and this of mine, breaking such saddening news, had reached her at a cruelly inopportune time. A risk taken in correspondence liaisons.

My arrival in Rome, to live, provided more 'stuff' for letters, and although the house was never forgotten, we moved on into other things and the balance was kept, although now, of course, it was difficult to find books in English and we had to make do with those we already had.

I had never lived in a rented house in a foreign country before, never 'lived' abroad, never had had so little to occupy my days. Trips to the supermarkets and the street markets were tremendous treats, but they didn't exactly fill the day. And my days had hitherto always been filled. From five a.m., when I was called, to eight or nine in the evening when I would return home. Time started to lie heavy on my hands and I hated it. Never social as a person, I shunned invitations and turned to the rented, very uncared-for garden of Villa Fratelli, and dug about, planted annuals (for I had only a year's lease and wasn't there for permanence), got happily stupid on the Frascati wine, of which I drank far too much, and often found myself drifting about oblivious to the world, filled with wine, in my swimming-pool at seven in the evening.

A correction had to be made. My sense of order had completely vanished.

'I am amazed,' she wrote one day, *'that you actually SAW Virginia Woolf! And to think that you thought her a witch. Poor creature, so maligned, I feel, by Holroyd . . . but what can the truth be? And this person "Lally" is absolutely irresistible . . . did she let you both play with those village louts, what are their names? Reg and Perce . . . and marvellous Mrs Fluke! You made me laugh out loud about her. And I assure you, sir, I don't do that often! almost not ever!'*

I found a clue

Rather than clattering my trolly through SuperRomano in search of the day's shopping, or drifting, slightly drunkenly, in the warm shallows of my pool, I decided I'd rough something out for her: a longer kind of journal about childhood. At least it might keep me sober: which would be a very good thing indeed. Sudden idleness had almost brought me to a full-stop. My initiative had dried up entirely. Incentive had been dissolved by the sun and wine.

I set up the typewriter, bought a stack of paper, and started.

Heading the blank piece of paper (which in those days seemed to be friendly and inviting, but today fills me with dread and anxiety that it will remain in that condition, blank) with a rough and ready title, I started off on *The Canary Cage*. My intention, apart from trying to return to a strict life-routine and remain sober, was to amuse her, to write a story which would be far away from the cold sterility of a hospital room, and from the almost unbearable waiting for what she called, *'their dreaded prognosis'*.

It was a tough start, but gradually some kind of form emerged, not easily, with effort. For a time it seemed that I had swung an arc lamp on to a long-forgotten part of my life which lay discarded in the dark. My youth. A life so completely different from the one I now lived in a rented house on a Roman hill where once Constantine had pitched his camp on the eve of the battle of Milvio. It took me all of a week; a bit longer to correct, re-write, and make a fair copy which I could send her. And then I had to wait for the verdict. Drinking Frascati cheerfully, without guilt, because, I felt, I had done something.

The verdict, when it came, was daunting:

' . . . the first pages are okay-ish. I mean I see what you want; to recapture Time Lost.

But it doesn't start to 'grab' until you write from the point of view of the child. That's good. That's nice stuff. But it has a patronizing air about it when you merely write as you. Get back to the child's mind. Write from his point of view. Be twelve again! Bet you can . . .'

But I felt that I couldn't. '*FORCE memory!*' she counselled. But memory was dimmed by years of a war, the cinema, the struggle to survive, to create; childhood could not be forced back upwards from the darkness into which it had been thrust; but I struggled on bleakly trying to find the childmind, to 'be twelve again'. It was, I felt truthfully, hopeless.

I wrote one day:

'Alas! The years of innocence have sped away. Elizabeth and I, in those days, had never heard of cancer, a race was something which you ran, and either lost or won, communists were people who lived quite near China, and we didn't know where THAT was exactly. A Golliwog was a black doll in a striped weskit and fuzzy hair which you took up to bed as a comfort against the dark.

But we knew about Ouzles and Thrushes, and the difference between them, about cuckoo-spit and cowslips: roach and perch, about emptying what was politely known as "the night soil" or making ginger beer, and saw Virginia Woolf wandering along the banks of the Ouse and quite convinced ourselves that she was a real witch . . . and . . . and . . . oh hell! It's ALL GONE.

If only we could have that innocence back again . . .'

She replied, in an unsteady hand on a piece of paper torn, I imagine, from an old exercise book:

'Lovely letter of the 5th has just arrived. Clever you! Hand a bit shaky from the 'shot' they give you to steady your nerves before the Op. Idiots! I'll be going in soon, but before I do, I must say something important to you.

That Innocence of which you speak. You CAN have it back.

Write it for me. Please?'

I did. They were eventually the first three chapters of my first book, but by that time, as she had once warned me that she might, she had 'slipped away', and another needlewoman had come along to assist me with my patching. But that is still a long way ahead.

SEVEN

There was a Rover, badly parked, outside the village shop. On the back window-ledge, a set of Travel Scrabble, a dusty *Daily Telegraph*, a battered box of Kleenex. Spoor of the middle Middle-Class Briton abroad.

Inside, the shop was empty; except for Madame Raybaud who owned it, and two young women with a small boy. One woman in a crumpled Laura Ashley garment with puff-sleeves; the other, with the generous buttocks of a dray horse, was in shorts and a brief cotton halter, hair cut in a fringe, glasses, and flip-flop sandals. She was poking about among the bottles in the mineral-water section.

'Nothing here that *I* recognise as lemonade. Something called 'Pschittt'! Too funny; *really*, the French! Would Coca-Cola do?' she shouted. 'It's in litre bottles.'

The Laura Ashley one was down at the vegetable section thumping melons as if they had once betrayed her. 'Oh, get anything! And tomato juice for Giles' Bloody M . . . '

The small boy picked up a tin of peas and rolled it the length of the shop. It clattered to a stop at the check-out desk. Madame Raybaud looked down impassively, hands folded.

'Jason! I'll give you the hiding of your life! Put it back at once and do up your fly-buttons.'

The fat girl wandered slowly past me scanning the shelves murmuring, 'Tomato juice . . . tomato juice . . . tomato juice . . . ' like a whispered snatch of forgotten catechism: she saw me; wandered on uncertainly; stopped as if struck by an axe. Then she turned and hurried back to the vegetables, great breasts bouncing.

'It's *him!*' she said loudly.

'It's who?' said the Laura Ashley one.

For a moment there was a gobbling sound of smothered conversation, they both turned round and looked at me with distrust and hostility.

'Jason! Stop playing with yourself. I've told you before; you'll get stuck like it.'

'*Much* older than he looks on the screen, don't you think?' said the fat girl.

'Never watch him,' said the Laura Ashley, sorting angrily through the leeks. 'He's balding anyway.' There was a glint of triumph in her voice.

'And skinny,' said the fat girl, rattling the bottles in her basket. 'I do think it is quite extraordinary to come out dressed like that to do the shopping. I mean, *anyone* can see him. Filthy jeans . . . '

'No pride,' said the Laura Ashley woman. 'I imagine they just go native when they live down here. Give up . . . these melons are like rocks and the leeks are limp.'

'The Saxbys say he's frightfully stuck up.'

'Stuck together, more like it.'

'Well, poor thing. I've got the tomato juice; four tins enough? And the Coca-Cola, although I don't suppose it's the real thing: you know, English. Probably made here. French yuk. He's buying cheese now! Do we need cheese?'

The Laura Ashley girl suddenly reached out and caught the small boy a swift, stinging blow on the side of his head; he opened his mouth to scream, saw her hand raised in threat, closed it again sharply and pulled a row of tins off the lower shelves.

'I'll *kill* that child! What's got into you? You've been the very devil ever since we left Dover!' She shook him roughly, dropped her shopping list. 'Tins everywhere. Put them all back just as you found them, or else . . . '

'Jennifer! He's tired that's all. We all are,' said the fat girl.

At the check-out I paid my bill, asked for a loaf and a copy of *Nice Matin*. Madame Raybaud smiled.

'Anglais?' she murmured.

'Oui. Anglais.'

'Ahha.'

'He's paying his bill,' said the fat girl brightly, her voice carrying the entire length of the shop as, indeed, it had all the time. 'Bought bread. Do *we* need bread? Or would Ryvita do? I can't remember if we have bread left from yesterday. I mean, he's so much smaller than he looks on the screen, don't you think? So disappointing.'

'Oh! For God's sake shut up, Barbara!' said the Ashley girl angrily. 'Do shut up, and don't stare at him all the time. You know they *love* it!'

When Clair Loschetter had told me, at the very beginning, that the village was 'quite by-passed, it is almost undiscovered, you could say,' she was, to all intents and purposes, perfectly correct. It was well away from the main road, stood high on its hill, surrounded by acres of olive groves and terraces of orange trees, and looked down across the plain and the woods to the sea and the sprawl of Sodom and Gomorrah which edged it in the far distance.

But what Clair didn't know, or perhaps chose not to tell me, was that the local name was La Colline Anglaise. The English Hill.

It was littered with them, and many of them had found it long before Clair or I had ever set foot in the area, when the land, so far from the sea and 'quite by-passed', was a cheap place to retire to; and retire to it they had, in droves. To my consternation, my determined attempt to seek anonymity after years of living in a metaphorical goldfish bowl had failed, for here I was: surrounded by the voices of Tunbridge Wells, Godalming and Gerrards Cross, with a few Dutch, Americans and Germans thrown in for good measure.

They walked their 'doggies' every morning through the lanes, sought their day old *Telegraphs* and *Daily Mails* in the paper shop, lived in Walt-Disney-Provençal cottages in desperately cultivated gardens, threw noisy cocktail parties almost every Friday evening ('Our turn *next* week, remember, Phyllis!') and 'barked' (there is no other word for it) at each other in the local shops and called the French 'They' and 'Them'. Good-naturedly. Perfectly pleasant people.

I had obviously made another error in calculation. It vexed me greatly to think that I had hauled myself and my shattered possessions almost a thousand miles in a desperate search for privacy and peace, spent a small fortune on a half-ruined house, and had found myself almost full circle again: back where I had started. The Home Counties. In France.

However, my French neighbour assured me that things were far worse up in the Dordogne where practically every village, he said sadly, was a British Fort; and I did have a good deal of land about me for protection, and La Colline Anglaise was on the other side of our hill. So . . .

As long as I was careful I need not, I felt sure, become involved. For I had never played whist or bridge, been to a wine and cheese party, or run a stall for any charity. (To my shame.) I saw no reason why I should do so now: even if asked. Which was most unlikely, because although the English abroad can often seem noisy and sometimes appear to be overwhelmingly patronising and arrogant, they are, in fact, extremely shy and on occasions perfectly polite, but their peculiar class system (usually self-invented) would preclude them from dealing with 'Film People', who are unclassifiable, except as extroverts, and in consequence alarming.

The Working, or Labouring, Class and the Aristocratic Top have no such fears. They know precisely where they belong and are therefore quite secure: but the Middle Classes are not absolutely certain *what* they are, and for that reason anything which might unsettle them to any degree is best left alone for fear it could bring them all tumbling down from the comfortable, if uneasy, position in which they exist.

They distrust, intensely, anything which is different; and actors, painters, writers, even musicians, are of course different and to be approached with caution. Hence the reaction in the village shop from Jennifer and Barbara: a scene which was repeated a good number of times until I managed to rearrange my marketing hours, and although I became, in the end, perfectly used to the performance, it always saddened me, and made me feel like Dr Stiffkey sitting in his barrel on Blackpool Pier.

M. Marc, my local mason, came one morning to continue some job he was doing in the house. He was in a depressed mood, disinclined to talk: unusual in him, for he normally chattered like a magpie. This morning he did not. Fearing that perhaps his wife, who did my laundry, or one of his children was ill, I asked him if all was well at home.

He suddenly pulled off his cap and threw it on a table. 'It's finished!' he said, and his eyes were strangely bright.

'What is finished?'

'You didn't hear the radio last night?'

'No.'

He brushed his eyes roughly with his sleeve. 'She's *dead*! Josephine is *dead*! *Malheur*! The light has gone out, there is no more light!' He pulled on his cap and went about his business without another word.

Josephine Baker had died during the second performance of her new show in Paris: France was distraught over the death of an artist. And no one more so than M. Marc.

I wondered ruefully if it could have happened under the same circumstances, in England. We do not, in the most general terms, rate the arts very highly: even though we have produced so many men and women of unique brilliance in all its fields. For the average Briton, Sport is God. Art is pretty cissy. In Latin countries sport is equally revered: but an artist, be he painter, musician, dancer, writer, singer or actor, is treated with equal esteem and affection as is his sporting counterpart. Sometimes more. After all, they are all a part of the same game. Achievement. And no one chucks bottles at the referee.

In my first year in France I had not made up my mind, absolutely, to settle there. I had some vague idea, unexpressed clearly even to myself, that I might make it my base and wander, as a free spirit, from place to place, perhaps even take a small flat in Rome, a city which I loved.

But the tremendous amount of money, which I could not afford, and which I had spent on the restoration of the house, the clearing of the land and pruning of the drowning olive trees (they cost nearly five pounds a tree to save: and with 400 I had to do them in modest groups of ten or twelve when I could afford it) put any ideas of that nature, or little flats in Rome, however humble, right out of my head. I'd have to stay put. There wasn't anything spare for wandering abroad.

It was the habit that if you resided in France you could only stay unregistered for a period of three months. Now it is six. Some foreigners found it desirable, and easy, to slip across a neighbouring border, Italy or even Switzerland, for a day or so at the end of their three months, get their passports stamped on re-entry, and start another period of residence.

But once I had made up my mind to live for good in France, and not wander about, I found the uncertainty, and my sense of order, such as it was, would not permit me to join this country dance. I knew that I could not jig about to Italy or Switzerland every three months because the house, which contained all that I owned, would never really seem to be mine. Also I'd probably forget when my time was up. It seemed far too temporary a life and I wanted, above all things, to be settled. To this end, every three months (I marked the date on the kitchen calendar) I would go up to the Mairie in the village and sit in the ante-room on a bentwood chair with a clutch of foreign immigrants, mostly Arab, Spanish or Portuguese, and await my turn to go into the inner sanctum, where the Deputy Mayor sat at a cluttered desk, chain-smoking, and writing down, in immaculate copperplate, all one's particulars, which didn't amount to much anyway, on a small piece of grey paper which was one's permit to live in his country for another three months free of complications. It seemed, to me, easier, and pleasanter, than fleeing to a border like a fugitive. But in time the three-monthly haul up to the Mairie became a bit of a chore. I was more certain of my feelings now, less anxious to trail about, and wanted roots. So I decided to stay in France legally and for as long as they would allow me.

I had got fed up with the lurking sense of impermanence, I knew that I was fairly well known in the village and the neighbouring town and that, if anyone asked, it would be absurd to say that I didn't live in my house all the year round, winter and summer: I was too familiar locally for any kind of deceptions, however modest.

Another thing which forced this slightly dramatic decision was the almost constant inference in the British press that I was doing something illegal anyway. If a photograph was published of me in the cheaper papers the caption often contained a reference to the fact that I was a Tax Dodger, in much the same way that they might have said I was a member of the Great Train Robbery gang. I resented the implication bitterly.

The British Consul in Nice was a pleasant, florid man in a crumpled blue pin-striped suit and a service tie. About the walls of his fairly gloomy office above a shop and opposite a bar in a side street hung photographic relics of his more adventurous youth.

Motor torpedo boats, or something of that sort, cutting through rough seas, the flag streaming. They were framed in too-thin passe-partout and hung haphazardly on the butter-yellow walls.

He politely offered me the chair standing before his barren desk (or perhaps it was just tidy), listened carefully to what I had to say about becoming a resident, played thoughtfully with a ruler, lips pursed like a child at the breast.

'You're *quite* sure, are you?' he said uncertainly.

'Quite. So I wondered if perhaps you could recommend a local lawyer, I don't think that it is anything my London man can handle, I mean, he doesn't live here . . . '

'Quite.' He shrugged his shoulders once or twice before speaking again, eyes still on his ruler. 'Local?' he said finally. 'You did say local? Not easy. No. Not easy. Lawyers, I mean: it's a bit difficult.'

'Are there any British ones then? There must be a pretty large British population here in Nice: all those retired nannies and so on.'

He looked at me balefully. '*Nannies?*'

'Well, retired people living here. There are masses where I am.'

He cleared his throat uncomfortably, looked vaguely round his collection of motor boats. 'Couple of fellows here who are all right. British, I mean.'

'Could you perhaps recommend one to me?'

He looked at me for a moment, reached out and tore a sheet from a small, virginal memo pad, scribbled two names.

'And these are all right? They know all the rules and regulations? I mean, I *don't.* Haven't an idea, so I don't want to put a foot wrong, and I need the advice.'

He picked up his ruler. 'They're all right. Use one of them myself, s'matter of fact.'

'Ah! Could you tell me which one? I mean of the two? If *you* use him he's very likely the best bet.'

'Can't tell you that. Sorry. Find out for yourself. Not my business.' He dismissed me by opening a drawer under his desk and taking out a thin file which he rustled importantly.

I had obviously made a grave diplomatic blunder. I left with some relief. A couple of weeks later I filed my papers at the Mairie in the village requesting permission to become a Foreign Resident of the Alpes Maritimes. Six months later I got it.

The first two years at the house passed pleasantly enough; and slowly. Time didn't race away as it seems to now, when every second day is suddenly Saturday again. There was a great deal to be done on the land; and bit by bit a garden, of sorts, was wrenched from the shale and rock. Bales of peat, and tons of earth were brought in by truck, trees planted, the terrace made comfortable with chairs under the vine, and all the other terraces, once a wilderness of tussocky grass and bramble, were brought under control and mowed as smooth as they could be got.

I had inherited, from one of the early labouring teams, a lunatic Arab who spoke no known language, anyway to me, couldn't use a machine or sow a nasturtium, but was strong enough to lift rocks. He started off by re-building all the fallen walls, and erected a high stone pillar at the entrance to the track which he decorated with broken bits of red glass from someone's rear-light, and crowned, majestically, with a metal sign bearing the word 'Fiat' in gleaming letters. I managed to get this off before the cement set. Much to his sorrow. But between us, Forwood, Aziz, and myself working almost non-stop, the place suddenly began to emerge from its years of neglect; and in the second spring the scent of wallflowers and stocks reminded me that it was about time that my parents came back: to look and exclaim in pleasure. And, I hoped, to praise: for a great deal had been done since their last visit.

'Well,' my father sounded uncertain on the telephone, 'you've rather sprung it on us . . . but you *always* do that, I suppose. I'll have to ask Mother. She's not been too well, filthy cold all winter, and that fall shook her up a bit. It's all the train and the boat business. Rather tiring, you know, at our age.'

'You'll fly out. Much easier, far more comfortable, and quicker, too.'

It wasn't.

London airport was in chaos as usual, it was Easter, or just about to be, the plane was an hour late, and they had had a bumpy trip.

However, here they were on the terrace, a little wobbly from the journey, a little amazed by being here, surprised and praising, as I had hoped, at the changes which had taken place since their last visit two years before.

They looked a little frail. I noticed that my father's hands were not perfectly steady, but put this down to the exhausting journey they had made, and my mother walked much more slowly, taking her time to cross the polished tiles. 'Still no carpets . . . ' she murmured. But they both looked incredibly young, and she, trim and beautifully made up, a long ritual which took her a lot of time each morning, still had hardly one grey hair in her head, and moved her ringed hands graphically and vividly: an actress's hands, of which she was justly proud.

Sitting there in the warm March sun they were a splendidly handsome couple, and I felt an enormous lift of pleasure at their presence.

I opened a bottle of Krug: the cork popped, and flew upwards into the budding vine.

'Champagne!' said my father. 'I though you were bust?'

'The last of the Christmas stock. I am bust.'

'Well, not for me. You don't mind, do you? I'd rather have a glass of beer.'

'It's a celebration,' I said.

My mother took her glass eagerly. 'Just what I needed. The people in that airport! Really. It's steerage, all pushing and shoving. I could have died!'

My father opened his beer carefully, poured it so that the foam lay lightly on the top. 'Don't want to waste a drop. What's the celebration? Oh yes, you mean us?'

'And today I'm fifty-one. My birthday.'

My mother, who had almost finished her wine, set the glass on the table. 'I forgot! *Many* happy returns, darling. God! Fancy me forgetting that!'

'You've come a long way. Plenty of other things to remember, and anyway fifty-one isn't such a big deal.'

'Fifty-one,' she said, and drained the glass, holding it out for re-filling. 'My God! You gave me a time! Nearly eight pounds you were: I told you, didn't I, that you were conceived in Paris? This is going to kill you . . . '

'Now, Margaret,' said my father. 'We've been into all that.'

'Oh, I know! I know! But he was, and I wanted you to be born in France. Did you know *that*?'

I nodded obediently. The story was starting. I took up the bottle.

'But it was all mistimed or something, wasn't it?'

'*I* didn't mistime a thing. That idiot Dr . . . whatever his name was . . . Mortimer . . . or something.' I poured her another, modest flute of Krug.

'Dr Morgan,' said my father quietly, scraping the bowl of his pipe with the blade of his penknife.

'Morgan. That's who it was. No: *I* didn't make a mistake. He did. Idiot. I could have wept.'

'Well, it doesn't matter much really, does it?' I said.

'It did to me. Terribly. I was furious. Some awful nursing home in Hampstead.'

'But here I am! In France anyway, just as you wanted.'

I was keeping my patience because, although the stories were as familiar as my two hands, to lose patience, and I did quite often when they started, would have been insufferable at such a moment.

'Many happy returns,' said my father, putting his penknife away and taking up his beer. 'I must say, you look very well. I suppose it's all this air, the sun and the light . . . '

'Hard work, digging and mowing. Hay-cutting, I mean, it's hardly mowing. I'll show you the machine later on, it's enormous.'

My mother drained her glass and handed it to me. 'I'd like some more, while you're on your feet. My tiredness is going. Oh those people!' I poured her wine carefully.

'Ma, you'll get tiddly.'

'Who cares?' she said. 'My dear! My wallflowers aren't even in bud yet, just look at yours! And the camellia . . . oh, this is heaven,' she said, raising her face to the late March sun.

I caught my father's eye: he was smiling lightly, but there was a shadow of concern on his face. He winked at me, sipped his beer.

'Now then. Where's this doss house you're going to put us in? Not far, you said?'

'At the end of the road, it's very clean, comfortable . . . you've got the only self-contained suite. Won't have to go padding about corridors for a pee in the night.'

'Should hope not,' he said. 'We'd lose your mother. No sense of direction. Remember the "Queen Elizabeth"? We lost her for two hours . . . amazing woman.'

'I remember that!' said my mother. 'The *dear* "Queen Elizabeth". I met a charming woman in one of the corridors, a steward or something. From Ayrshire . . . I can't think why you were so worried. We had a wonderful talk, she was a dear soul.'

A little later I took them up to the small hotel where they were to sleep and have breakfast and from which, each morning, I would go to collect them at about ten and drive them back after supper. It seemed a sensible arrangement, and they were delighted with their room which had a splendid view down the valley, and a comfortable, modern bathroom.

'Only one thing,' said my father, vaguely picking the side of his nose, a sign that he had a slight doubt.

'What?'

'Well, these awful sausage things on the beds. I can't sleep with those, and I know Mother can't. Be a good boy and bring us up a couple of real pillows when you come to collect us, will you? About six o'clock, all right?'

'Yes. Unpack, have a bit of a rest and I'll bring you some proper pillows.'

My mother was singing in the bathroom: water ran.

'She's happy now she's here,' said my father. 'Had a bit of a job to persuade her to come, mind you. Seems to be giving up a bit. Everything is too much trouble; she is very emotional, you know. Your birthday and all that sort of thing. A long time, fifty-one years; and she's getting a bit shaky, won't walk much.' He folded his tobacco pouch, put it in his pocket. 'Fortunately I can get about, do the shopping and so on. She's not keen now . . . cooking and that sort of thing.' He leant across and touched my arm, 'So, be a good chap and don't snap at her, it's difficult sometimes, but it makes her so miserable.'

'I *don't* snap, Pa!'

'Oh yes you do! When she starts her 'stories', I know.' He was smiling.

'Well, we have heard them since birth, almost. I don't mean to snap.'

'Be patient then, perhaps I mean that? Let her have her say, she loves it. She won't read now, you know? I read to her; she likes that. I think.'

'Why won't she read?'

'Oh, can't be bothered. Loses her glasses. Concentration a bit fragile. She is seventy-three, you know. Got to remember that, amazing, she looks so much younger but . . . ' He sat on the edge of the bed, thumped it. The springs twanged. 'I think we'll be very comfortable here. With proper pillows, of course! Do you know? I spied a nice little bar when we came in? Might have a little drink before you collect us. I'm going to be eighty in June, you realise? So I feel a bit of self-indulgence is in order.'

At six o'clock Forwood drove me up to the hotel with a pair of pillows and a bunch of extra coat-hangers. The hotel seemed deserted. I went through into the small lobby and saw my mother lying at the foot of the stairs, an anxious group of people in holiday clothes standing round her, my father, with a waxen face trying to help her to sit, but as he touched her she screamed out, 'Don't! Don't! Oh don't, please!'

I pushed through the crowd; someone murmured that the steps were always dangerous. I knelt beside her, she lay on one side, a tumbled ruin of black lace and Chanel beads, her earrings had fallen off and her face was chalk white, eyes blazing with pain, her shoulder pressed high against her ear.

'The steps. I fell on the steps,' she said.

Somehow we got her into the car and drove, at snail's pace, because every rut and stone caused her to cry out in agony, to the house where a horrified Henri and Marie helped us to get her into the long room where I gave her a treble brandy neat, and Forwood called Dr Poteau.

'Double fracture or dislocation,' he said swiftly. 'Look, the upper arm bone is almost pushed into her ear. Dislocation, I think; the bone is out of the socket.' He started to dial an ambulance but I asked him if he had any morphia in his bag. He did and gave her an injection which would have calmed a raging bull.

There was no single ambulance in all the area, which could find the way to the house. The ultimate irony of my search for privacy, anonymity and peace. The only person who did know the way through the lanes was Maurice in the bar in the village who ran a taxi. He was free and on his way. Poteau called a clinic in Nice.

'Nice! Isn't there somewhere nearer? Nice is an hour away, and she's in terrible pain, and in a taxi . . . '

'It's the best place, St George's at Cimiez; they are waiting for her. You know,' he looked at my mother who sat slumped against the whitewashed wall on a low stool, the nearest we could get her into the room, 'it is grave. She may never use that arm again.'

It was a kind of living nightmare, the journey to the clinic. Forwood, my father and I sat crushed in the back, my mother in the sear beside Maurice, her head lolling; silent, sedated.

When we got into Nice it was dark and no one knew where the clinic was. We drove about desperately, winding down windows, asking for directions. No one knew, or if they did were uncertain, and we ended up lurching along unlighted roads in the middle of unfinished building estates.

Eventually we found St George's, an enormous new building, white marble, plate glass, more like a very expensive hotel than a clinic, and three-and-a-half hours after her fall my unfortunate mother was in the gentle, competent, hands of hurrying nurses, being wheeled down to the X-ray Department. My father, Forwood and I followed, as useless and out of place as skiers in a ballroom. I suddenly realised that I hadn't even changed, and was still wearing old jeans and a T-shirt.

Dr Fallacci, a tall, quiet man, came out of the Radio Room, a dripping X-ray plate in his rubber-gloved fingers. The damage was grave. A severe dislocation, a fracture, an operation and the chance that, as Poteau had said, she would never again be able to use her left arm. Did we, he asked politely, wish to have her bandaged and strapped up so that she could be flown back to England for treatment? She would have to fly out the next day, not a second later.

I translated this to my father, who spoke almost no French and who was standing apart in a fringe of shadow in the long corridor. He was holding, cupped in one hand, my mother's rings which I had helped one of the nurses to remove, with some kind of lubricant. They clinked and winked in the light as he turned them.

'I don't want her moved again,' he said. 'Can they do it here?'

They could and they did, with the greatest care and skill, and Dr Fallacci found, to his obvious delight, that he was able to manipulate the bones back into place without using surgery, and that the chances of my mother regaining full use of her arm were very possible. But that was all to come later.

After we had left the clinic that night to drive back to the house, we were not certain of anything: a decision had been made, we'd have to wait until the next day for a verdict.

'She was incredibly brave,' said Forwood suddenly. 'Not a word of complaint, didn't cry once.'

'She's very brave,' said my father.

'But she did cry,' I said. 'One time only: when I had to remove her wedding ring. She wept then.'

My father cleared his throat. 'Got them here, in my pocket. Curious thing . . . ' He patted his pocket vaguely: I heard the rings chink.

He was sitting on a fallen tree-trunk down beyond the cane-break: I could just see the top of his white head above the easel. Otherwise he was completely hidden by the canvas on which he was working. Daisy and Labo careened past him after some imaginary rabbit (they had long ago flushed them off the land, alas). He looked up as I came down through the tall grasses.

'You have come to tell me something dreatful,' he said. He always pronounced the second 'd' as 't' for some reason.

'No. Nothing dreadful. Just that lunch is in fifteen minutes and I called the clinic and Ma is in fine fettle and she can come out on Friday. Afternoon.'

He made no reply for a moment, stroked away with his brush at the canvas. 'She's all right, is she?'

'Sounded fine. She said she's been having a marvellous time with the nurses, telling them funny stories: in Glaswegian.'

'Oh, she would,' he said. 'She's wonderfully good with people; what on earth they can possibly make of her Scots accent I don't know, but she loves a crowd.'

'An audience?' I said.

'Yes. Very fond of audiences, your Ma. A performer, like you. She really comes to life with people to listen to her. She finds it pretty dull, you know, at home now.' He mixed a little yellow paint with a swift movement, loaded his brush, applied it to the canvas. 'These cane-things. More beige-green than yellow, wouldn't you say? I really shouldn't have married her.'

It was very still: then Labo barked.

'Mother? Shouldn't have married her?'

'Been kinder, really. She's missed the theatre and all that hurly-burly her whole life. I'm afraid it was all my fault. But I was very much in love with her.' He was painting with neat, tight strokes.

I moved round the easel, sat down on the trunk beside him. The dogs came lolloping up the hill, tongues hanging, foam flying.

'"Silly dogs, then,' he said. 'You'll give yourselves heart attacks.'

I looked up towards the house, Henri was turning the cushions on the terrace chairs, small clouds drifted towards the sea across the brilliant blue sky like fat cherubim.

'I don't think I ever knew two people who were more in love than you and Mother. I mean, that's what it seemed like. As children, Elizabeth and I were really pretty disgusted when you took each other's arms; touched. We called you the Lovers. Thought you were both terribly soppy.'

He started to clean his brush carefully on a piece of cloth. 'Oh, we managed. When you were young it wasn't so hard for her; lots of things going on, people about, she liked first nights at the theatre, going to stay at Hever, parties. People flattered her. She was very striking looking, I don't know how she managed to dress so well on the little I was able to give her: a wonderful mother to you and very loyal to me. I can't complain, she had the worst part of the bargain. Gave up such a lot, all her cronies. Theatre people; I didn't much like them, you know, I was happy pottering about, at the cottage; it was too lonely for her. She was bored most of the time away from London. No; she made the sacrifices, not I.'

'What do you mean, though, that you 'managed'? It's not really so, is it?'

He placed the cleaned brush into his paint-box, started to screw on the lid of the turpentine bottle. 'Yes it is. I was twenty-seven when we married: if I had had the money then that *you* had at that age, we would have been divorced in four months; but as it was, I didn't have the money; you know *The Times*? So we just muddled through.'

Henri's voice called down thinly from the terrace. 'Dix minutes, Messieurs!'

We collected the easel and the paint-box in silence; my father carried his wet canvas carefully up the hill behind me.

'You carry on,' he said. 'I'm not hurrying up this path: got a splendid thirst so I hope there is something very refreshing in the bar-cupboard. We've just got time, eh?'

'Yes. Yes, there is. All waiting for you,' I said. There was absolutely nothing else that I could say.

We never spoke of it again: I think that I was too frightened to talk of it, to question the shattering confession which he had made so casually, so calmly, down by the cane-break.

It was obvious then, that after all he *had* realised the deep current of frustration which ran beneath my mother's otherwise cheerful and ordered surface; it was equally obvious from his confession that this frustration had caused desperate pain to them both. I had had no idea that there had ever been a case of 'muddling through' in their lives which at least on the surface is all I suppose I ever took the trouble to see, and had seemed as stable and devoted as any marriage I had ever known.

But a tropical island, serene in a limpid sea, can suddenly explode into a Krakatoa; a stretch of golden sand, shimmering serenely in the sun, can pull you into its depths and drag you implacably to your death: without warning. Nothing, in short, is ever exactly what it seems. And a human relationship is perhaps the hardest to evaluate, and quite as treacherous as natural phenomena like sands and volcanoes, and causes just as much damage and pain. But, as I have said, things which distress me greatly and about which I can do nothing, I tend to smother into oblivion: and I did so that day. It was far too late, in all our lives, to make any changes or offer solutions, they could do no possible good. Habit had taken a tight hold; and habit, at least, can sometimes be comforting.

When my mother went into the clinic, I cleared everything from the little hotel with its three treacherous steps, and made my father comfortable in the little single bedroom at the house. For a week he broke all his habits and was content to potter about with his sketch-book and easel, read and listen to music in the evenings, or even, on occasions, help out with the garden work. He was perfectly happy. Indeed, he showed very little anxiety in my mother's situation, knowing, I suppose, that she was in good hands and well taken care of: he just enjoyed himself, by himself.

When I suggested that we would have to drive over to Nice and see her he was always agreeable, but not over so.

'Today? We must? Oh, very well, it's just that the light is perfect and I'm in the middle of a job. Might not quite recapture it if I let it go.'

But we went, and he sat uncomfortably on a wooden chair while my mother, in a frail voice filled with pleasure, told us how superb the food was, that she had a 'dear little half-bottle of wine' for each meal, and that the nurses were 'out of this world' and loved her stories. She was rested, not in pain, and only resented the heavy plaster which covered her damaged arm and shoulder. Dr Fallacci came in each day to see her, she said, and he loved her stories too.

'You must be having a whale of a time,' I said.

'Oh, I am! I am! I'm never allowed to open my mouth with you lot. I'm having a *wonderful* time.'

But the time ended when we collected her, finally, and brought her back to the house and a local *Maison de Repos*, which was not, perhaps, the most cheerful of places, but in which she could be given the treatment which she still needed. My father, rather silently, moved in with her but spent all his days up at the house. She was in bed for two weeks, and only allowed out for a short time, as she became stronger, on condition that she went to bed every afternoon. It was not what you might call a riotous holiday for anyone: and she firmly refused to walk an inch, terrified that she'd fall again.

'She *could* walk perfectly well,' said my father impatiently. 'But the other night she said it was 'all coming true'.'

'What is all coming true?' I asked.

'Oh, that damned woman at the Coxes' wedding, years ago in Brighton, don't you remember? She came up to your mother and said that she was a medium and that she could 'see' Mother's 'aura'. Apparently it was violet or purple or something, and the woman said that showed that Mother was a Tragedy Queen.'

'Well, she is rather, isn't she?' I wasn't taking it very seriously, for his sake.

'She also said that she'd lose the use of her legs and they'd have to be cut off! I ask you! What a thing to tell anyone, and especially at a wedding. Of course Mother believes every word. So now she is convinced that she fell because she is losing the use of her legs. Honestly! That bloody woman. They ought to lock up people like that, they cause so much damage. There's nothing wrong with her legs, we've had doctor after doctor, all say the same thing. Remember that doctor of yours in Rome when she couldn't walk?'

'Frank? Very well.'

'Said all she needed was a good kick up the backside. Well. I wouldn't have used quite those words, but *he* did.'

'She was furious. I remember.'

'Still wouldn't walk, though: would she? Oh, women!'

On the morning that they were to leave, finally, for London, my mother was sitting out on the terrace, a huge Dior scarf slung round her shoulders, in her broad-brimmed hat, and the trim jersey suit in which she had arrived four weeks before.

'Do I look all right?' she said.

'Smashing. Very 'chic' indeed.'

'My face all right?' She smiled up at me into the sun.

'Perfect. You are clever, once an actress, always an actress.'

'To the death,' she said. 'A hell of a job putting on your make-up with only one hand. My eyelashes all right? Not smudged?'

'Immaculate. Where's Pa?'

'I don't know. Went off with the dogs somewhere. Go and find him, you know what Ulric's like, we'll miss the 'plane. He drives me mad.'

'Hours for that. Don't worry.'

He was up at the end of the Long Walk under the cherry trees, looking out across the valley to the sea and the mountains. I walked towards him slowly, not wanting to disturb him, but he turned and raised a hand.

'Ma's getting into a fret. Thought you'd gone off somewhere with the dogs.'

'No. No, just having a look, that's all. Curious about Renoir, isn't it? Living in that house in the village, opposite the paper shop. And you didn't realise?'

'No, clever of you to spot the plaque-thing.'

'1900 to 1903, wasn't it? I made a note somewhere. Is it time we were moving? We're all packed.'

'In half an hour. Time for a little drink if you want one.'

'Well, not a bad idea.'

'Pa, no goodbyes at the airport, eh?'

'Lord, no!' He followed me down the grassy track to the house. 'I've said all mine.'

I turned in surprise. 'Said them?'

'To this,' he said, and nodded his head briefly towards the far mountains.

'Not goodbye! Au revoir, surely.'

'No. I don't think we'll be back, you know. I'll never get your mother to move out here again. We're getting on a bit now, and I think that she feels, well, safer in her own house, she really doesn't enjoy travelling much, and this fall business. Rather put the lid on things, I'm afraid. Bit of bad luck, that.'

'Well, next time she can stay with Elizabeth and George and you come out on your own, why not?'

'Oh no,' he said, kicking a forgotten dog-ball into the grass. 'I couldn't leave her. Anyway I've done a lot of work here this time, painting. I've got a mass of sketches, too, which I can work up, keep me busy all year. Oh, one thing you might do for me, that square in Le Rouret? Where they play *boules*, with all the plane trees round it?'

'Yes. What?'

'Could you send me a photograph of it? From the doorway of the bar? I never seemed to get the time to go there, so much here to paint. Will you?'

'Of course,' I said and followed him down to the terrace.

At the airport I pushed her wheelchair to the barrier at International.

'Can't come any further. Pa will have to take over.'

'Is this where we go?'

She looked splendidly defiant, the green silk scarf about her shoulders, concealing most of the plaster-cast and the empty jacket sleeve; the wide-brimmed hat.

'Someone will get you aboard, and Elizabeth and George are waiting at the other end: it'll be super. Home in a flash.' I stooped to kiss her.

'Goodbye, my darling. Give my love to the dogs, it's been a *wonderful* holiday.' The platitudes of farewell came easily to her lips.

My father was sorting his papers and passports.

'You won't need anything here, Pa, just the passports. Give Ma the boarding passes.'

'No, no, now don't you start bullying me. I like to have them all together like this, you see?' His hands were shaking.

I kissed him briefly on both cheeks. 'No goodbyes, remember?'

'No, off you go. We can manage now.'

I left them and walked away into the middle of the mall. He pushed the chair through the swing barrier. A shimmer of green silk, the broad-brimmed hat, his Burberry; small tweed cap.

Angela and Robin at the same barrier.

Two men in blazers hurried through, laughing, 'We've missed old Rodney . . . ' Obliterating my parents.

I suddenly had a lump in my throat. Forwood said, 'Well, that's that. I'm going up to the Post Office, coming?'

'No.' My voice was unsteady. 'See if there are any London papers. Meet you at the doors.'

The paper-stall was small and crammed, a good place to hide in, to compose oneself. In the far corner among the children's books, my back to the shop, I felt safe enough to let the sudden, unbidden, tears well. Idiotic to blub at fifty-one. I thumbed through some coloured pages, they blurred: I blinked. They cleared.

'I think it *is* him,' said a woman's voice.

'No. Couldn't be.'

'I think so, saw him come in.'

'Well, ask him then, silly! Don't stand there staring.'

'No. *You* ask him. Anyway, he won't mind us staring. They love it, you know.'

EIGHT

Forwood was showing, as usual, the greatest patience. 'Now; look at it this way. You have twelve eggs and use eight for an omelette. Right? How many eggs have you left?'

Oh Lord! I thought. Here we go again. Arithmetic.

'Ummmm. Four?'

'Right. Splendid! You see you *can* be quite bright if you put your mind to it: now then, supposing that the one hen you own . . . '

'One only?'

'One. Supposing that hen is 'off lay', that no more eggs are coming your way after you have used the last of your four. What then?'

'There won't be any more eggs.'

'Marvellous. You've got it.'

'Well. I try. I'm not as daft as you seem to think sometimes: what's all this rubbish about eggs and hens; non-laying hens, I mean?'

'Money. It's rather where you are, I'm afraid, after two years of 'off-laying'; if you follow me?'

'Oh yes. Yes, I follow you. So what am I supposed to do about it?'

He closed his note-book, collected the stack of bills together, put the top on his fountain pen. 'Start laying again,' he said. 'And soon. There are four eggs left.'

'You mean I'm the bloody hen?'

'That's exactly what I mean. Looking at this pile of stuff here, it occurs to me that you will be in need of a big basket of eggs. And pretty soon. And as you are the only hen you've got, as far as I know, you'd better start laying.'

In the two years since I had retreated, as opposed to retired as has so often been said, from the cinema after 'Death in Venice', there really hadn't been much corn, so to speak, to induce a hen to lay anything. Scripts had come in fair quantity; and they stood stacked in a slithery pile down in the cellar, which seemed to me the best place for them.

Depressingly, the work which I had done in the last film had resulted in my being firmly established, at least in the film-makers' minds, as an aging 'oddity', apparently willing to play a wide range of schoolmasters with secret lusts for their pupils, either boys or girls (it didn't really matter) or priests in flowing robes creeping about the Gothic corridors of suspect public schools hearing appalling confessions in the confessionals. That sort of thing. The only other variation was the spy thriller, and there was a pile of those too, in which I was variously asked to play Philby, Burgess or Maclean.

Here and there, lying among the suitcases and wine bottles, you could perhaps lay hands on an 'updated' version of, say, 'Dr Jekyll and Mr Hyde' or a brand new version of 'Rasputin, The Mad Monk'. There was also quite a number of 'Today Subjects' (as they were then called), which were concerned with 'bent' policemen, or rapist photographers who liked schoolgirls; and so it went on.

So much for Thomas Mann, Visconti, and the work which we had shared together so lovingly. Apparently, all it had done was to prove, without any shadow of a doubt, that I was now 'available for degenerate parts'. A saddening, chastening blow.

So I had bunged them all down in the cellar and got on with pruning, planting, mowing and sowing where the air was fresh and, at least, clean.

To be fair, there had been one or two, in the welter of muck, which were of higher quality; and Losey had offered me a subject at which I baulked only because of its politics and its over-simplified script; my reaction alarmed him until another actor, far more bankable than I, accepted it happily. So that was all right. And there were one or two dull things with splendid players like Deborah Kerr, Joanne Woodward and Peter Ustinov or Topol, and one even with Elizabeth Taylor, indeed; but none of them could tempt me away from the bucolic life into which I had entered that hot August day two years before. I was perfectly happy; for the time being.

However, I could see Forwood's point of view. I had to.

More money, by far, had been spent on the house than one had ever envisaged at the start. Not just in the reconstruction, which was modest, but on all the unexpected things which had occurred to make life expensive. Re-wiring the whole place for a start didn't cost pennies; and then the water-pipes were discovered to be made not of iron but of black lace, which leaked lakes into the limestone and shale, but made little impression in the bathrooms or the kitchen. So they had to be relaid, miles of them; the olives had to be 'pruned', the land drained, and so it went on.

Unfortunately, I had never been what is now known as a Superstar, a debased word coined, I think, in the 'seventies, and I had never, at any time, earned the kind of money they commanded; and got.

Fourteen years under contract to Rank, starting at a humble three thousand pounds a year and increasing, if they took up the yearly 'option' on your talent, modestly every year, did not make me a millionaire: although it did allow me to live very comfortably, with care.

A pound was a pound in those days of the 'fifties and 'sixties: and when I was 'loaned out' to other companies or even to Hollywood, Rank took a sharp share of the profits, and I got a pleasant percentage. However, I was not a greedy fellow. Until then I had never earned more than ten pounds a week, so I justly felt that as long as I could pay my way and save a bit for the old age which I hoped lay ahead, barring some unforeseen disaster, I was perfectly happy.

In any case, my total ignorance of money in any form prevented me from worrying, really. I never actually knew, to the figure, what I earned, was never permitted to have a cheque book, or sign cheques (for fear that I would hand them round like communion wafers) and almost never carried money in my pocket.

Sometimes, if I was unaccompanied at some event or even on a location, I was given a few pounds in order to buy cigarettes or a round of drinks, otherwise I never saw the stuff, and was happy in my ignorance.

The facts of life, that is to say money, which so bewildered me, were handled by Forwood and by the accountants and lawyers, trim in their black jackets and pin-striped pants, who saw to it that I was kept solvent, saved tax, and did not overspend. They were all good men and true, and I saw, and had, no reason to question them at any time.

The only things that I insisted upon were that I should never owe anyone a penny, not even the local greengrocer for a week, and that I need never take out a mortgage on, or for, anything. If that was needed then I went without. Debt had terrified me ever since the days when I had carted my money about with me in an old Oxo tin: I had always expected to go back to the beginning again, and start anew, and I was determined that when this happened I would be debtless. Bad enough to start off again, without owing money.

I think the only time I actually agreed to have anything on credit was for the television sets for the staff room: I was certain that such a vulgar 'toy' did not merit a purchase, and it was only many years later, when I came to France, that I had to change my point of view and buy one in a desperate effort to silence an extremely talkative guest who, literally, never drew breath for a week. I thought that it might shut her up in the evenings. But alas! It was, of necessity, all in French which she could not understand, so she went on talking: and the television gathered dust.

It was also many years later that I was persuaded to work in a film, which the French so aptly called a 'Khaki Melo', that is to say, a 'War Film', which was as stuffed with Superstars as the proverbial pie is with plums. They were all perfectly pleasant young men, some of whom earned, for just fourteen days work, more than double the amount of money I had earned in fourteen years in forty-plus movies, with Rank. If I had earned, for just one film out of the many I had made, what these young men got for a two-week stint in this single Epic, I wouldn't have been faced with the idiotic 'chicken and egg' analogy, and I could have secured the house and my old age, without worry.

But as it was, I hadn't got that sort of cash, had overspent at the beginning, and was now, it seemed, spending more on its maintenance and general upkeep. Quite simply, I hadn't got the wherewithal to do so.

So, in a very irritated way, I was forced to agree with myself that the glowing idea I had held of being able to do as I wished in security was all nonsense. I wasn't secure at all; and I'd have to go back to work again.

My ideals had been too high. And so, now, were prices in general.

But how many people ever realised that the vengeance of the Arabs would strike them to their very souls? I was not the only person who feverishly rustled about in the pages of a school atlas to find out exactly where these terrible new areas of danger really were. Most of them were unpronounceable; all of them inhospitable.

So I came to terms with things rapidly. The next reasonable script which arrived, if one ever should again, must be viewed with a little more care: unless it was about yet *another* demented priest or raving schoolmaster. Surely there *had* to be some kind of alternative?

Meanwhile all about me spring had made rapid advances towards summer. The skies had taken on a more intense blue, the grass was thick and green, and up on the Long Walk the cherry was exploding into blossom; and my pond, the pond which I had caused to be torn from the barren land where no pond had ever been before, was pulsing with life and mating-toads, who waltzed inelegantly together, stringing ropes of glossy black pearls among the budding water lilies. Creatures which had never existed on the hill arrived in quantities. Dragonflies of every shape and hue flicked and spun above the thrusting spears of water flags; wagtails, both the grey and the yellow, skipped and dipped from stone to stone. A fat, edible, frog quietly appeared and nestled himself into the sedge and water-mint on the island which I had built, by carting rocks down from the upper terraces, and the six goldfish, bought in a plastic bag from Monoprix, mated and now swept in brilliant shoals about the Salvator Rosa rocks (already, after only two years, romantically mossed) like the tails of comets. And the king of this man-made extravaganza was a large carp, brought in a bucket from the fishmonger in Grasse, nudging lazily in the mud, blowing little puffs about him, like an aging wrestler; his belly gleaming copper in the sun.

Of course I had altered the ecology. No question of that. But surely for the better? These creatures had never existed up here. Mint, brought by my father in his washbag, from Sussex, had never flourished in the dry shale, nor the high arum lilies which ringed the pond, or the bulrushes which had suddenly appeared, or the nettles, already starred with butterflies, or the whispering papyrus.

Of course it was for the better. And sitting under the giant olive tree on the bank, the early May sun hot on my back, my new water-world just below, I found it incredibly easy to set aside the nagging fear of a return to work. But it was, and now could only be, a 'setting aside'.

However, I felt calm and contented and considered myself to be exceptionally fortunate. Eggs or no eggs.

That kind of complacency usually meets with an unpleasant, sometimes even brutal, end. And mine did: in fact my rare moments of complacency always do; which is why I have moved through my life with more caution than most. I have never believed that anything I had could last; always aware that, at any moment, a door could be slammed in my face.

Six years of a fighting war, I suppose, had taught me that the only *certain* thing was the moment. Anything else you got was a bonus.

The postman came bumping up the track in his bright yellow van. We exchanged greetings, shook hands, admired the carp and agreed that, indeed, the day was brilliant. He handed me a small blue telegram, tipped his cap, accepted my coins for his trip up the long track, bumped away again, the dogs leaping and capering beside him to the gate.

It was a brief telegram, the postmistress's elegant handwriting spelling out a bleak message.

'Regret Inform You Mrs X Died Saturday Heart Attack'.

I did not know the signature; but I heard the slamming of a door somewhere along the corridor of my life, and the day, and quite a number of days which followed, lost its brilliance.

There was no one now to write for: no one to save up the bits and pieces of the day, the scents or sights, the grabbed fragments of conversation overheard, or conversations held. And my life, for a time, seemed strangely empty. I had to keep reminding myself that there was now no recipient for the scraps I collected to write down, to amuse or deflect: it was no good seeing something and saying, as I had done so often in the past five years, 'I must remember that. It'll make her laugh'. Or, '*That's* the colour a poppy ought to be; just like that, the sun burning through the scarlet petals, translucent. How can I describe it?' None of that was needed now, so I got on with the ordinary work on the land and dug, hoed, mowed daily. And a poppy became just a poppy; not something worth the noting and the careful setting down.

If my days were fully occupied with the problems of weeds, peat, fertiliser, white fly and general garden chores, my evenings were free, for there now was no letter to be written, and it was on one of these evenings, I can't remember exactly when, that I aimlessly pressed a button on the despised television set hidden away in a bookshelf, and was instantly transported into magic. It was an Italian film with French sub-titles, and I had tuned in somewhere in the middle.

But I stayed, uncomprehending of the words, visually amazed. I had never seen colours used like this; nor a camera moved with such fluency and authority. I hadn't seen costumes of such style, brilliance and simplicity. It was as if a giant fresco by Caravaggio had come to instant life at the touch of my aimless finger.

All, I regret to say, that I could understand of the work was that it was the story of Galileo; and that is as much as I could follow. But of one thing I was absolutely certain: the storyteller was a master, and I waited for the final credits with impatience. None of which I recognised until the last one, which was that of the director: Liliana Cavani.

Somewhere, far away at the back of my cluttered mind, I knew that I had seen this name before, and that it was very likely lying down in the cellar among the pile of discarded scripts: which it was indeed. Thicker than the Bible, badly typed and appallingly translated into American-English, there it was among the others in the slithery pack: damp, crushed, the gold-embossed letters faded but still legible. 'The Night Porter'.

By Liliana Cavani.

Standing in the cellar among the fallen scripts, flipping through the limp pages in my hand, I remembered that I had originally refused the thing because it was, yet again, about another degenerate, this time an SS officer in a concentration camp. I remembered that I had only 'skip' read it originally. Perhaps, now, I should give it a little more attention.

I re-read it that evening: the first part was fine, the middle a mess, the end a melodramatic mish-mash. Too many characters, too much dialogue, two stories jumbled up together where only one was necessary, but the point was that in the midst of this tumult of pages and words, buried like a nut in chocolate, there was a simple, moving, and exceptionally unusual story; and I liked it.

I telephoned Rome and spoke to Bob Edwards, Visconti's associate producer on 'Death in Venice'.

Yes, indeed, Cavani had made a film called 'Galileo', and yes she had written a script called 'The Night Porter' which he had submitted to me but which I had rejected. What could he do for me?

'Well: I've just re-read it, has she made it by this time?'

'No. She wrote it for you. Remember?'

'There's a hell of a lot wrong with it.'

'She knows that.'

'But there is a pretty good story somewhere way-down-there-at-the-bottom.'

'Thanks. She knows that too.'

'Is there a producer?'

'Yes. Me.'

'Would you like to come down here and talk about it one day?'

'I would indeed. Do I tell Lilly?'

I hesitated. Eggs and chickens. What the hell. 'Yes,' I said. 'Tell Miss Cavani.'

'Fine. If you want any, well, you know, references about her, call Luchino.'

'Visconti?'

'The same. She is one of his favoured few.'

Visconti, who had faded into the distance since our last meeting in Cannes, had embarked on what he wrote of in a letter as 'a small thing, about Ludwig of Bavaria. For [Helmut] Berger to play. But only a *little* film, nothing so much. While we work on the Proust.'

But in time, as was so often the case with him, the 'little thing' developed into a marathon and Proust was set aside. Indeed, strong rumour had it that Proust was no longer his, but Losey's, who had acquired the rights.

A telephone call, under these circumstances, must be handled with tact. He was, when I finally reached him at home one Sunday night, extremely affable and apparently pleased to hear me.

'And the Poverino? Poor creature, he is happy in France?'

'I think he prefers the gutters rather than the fields.'

'Certo. He is a city dog. You deny him his heritage. For years and years they have scavenged the streets of Italy. You will see him, Bogarde, even on the walls of Pompeii, you know this?'

'I know this. Luchino, Liliana Cavani . . . ?'

'Ah ha! So?'

'She has sent me a script.'

'You like?'

'Some of it. But she is . . . Do you think she is good?'

'Very good. You speak of 'Portiere della Notte', eh?'

'Yes. She sent it ages ago and I said no. Now I've re-read it.'

'And you must do it. It is very important to you.'

'Thank you. I was just picking your brains really.'

'Non capisco niente. But you must do it.'

'They will come to see me, there are many things to discuss. How does your film go?'

'Ach, very fatiguing, you know. So many problems, actors, costumes. I smoke one hundred cigarettes a day, you know this?'

'Madness. And Proust?'

There was a slight pause as if, perhaps, he had taken a sip of water.

'Proust? What of Proust?'

'Will you do it after 'Ludwig'?'

'Certo, but there is a lot to do, adapting, this you know: the Americans have now agreed to finance Olivier for Charlus because he has been made a Lord. It is so crazy.'

'I asked because there are rumours that Losey has acquired the rights. Did you know?'

The same pause again. When he spoke, his voice was gruff, impatient. 'Rumours! All Rome is full of rumours. It could not be true what you say, it could not be. Losey would have told me of this. He is a gentleman, so. You will give my compliments to Poverino?'

I called Bob Edwards again and said that if Cavani could agree to some hefty cuts in both dialogue and characters and reduce the story to just the simple one, of two people, I would do it.

He said that Cavani had been told of all this and was busy re-writing: he said also that he was very happy about my decision, and that she would be too. I said that I was.

And part of me was; the other part, the idle non-laying hen was not, but the die had been cast. I cheered up remarkably quickly when I remembered that it was quite possible that they wouldn't be able to lick a complex script into shape. I could still back out if things did not work.

Forwood was busy staking some delphiniums which had got battered about in a mild mistral the evening before. The air was soft and warm, the first crickets were singing. Now that I had, for the moment, committed myself to a film again, my good humour began to fail me at the thought of having to leave the calm and beauty of this place for which I had worked.

But calm and beauty cost money.

I remember Vivienne Glenavy saying that every time her husband had to go to London to do one of his television shows he was in such despair at leaving that he would walk round his garden embracing every olive tree the evening before departure.

That's exactly how I should feel when, and if, the time came for me to leave. Except that Paddy had thirty olive trees: I, four hundred. I'd have to pick just one token tree. But, with any luck, it wouldn't be for ages yet: if ever.

'That's that,' said Forwood, collecting a bundle of canes and twine. 'You been on the telephone all this time?'

'To Rome. Edwards and then Visconti.'

'I see. You've lost a case of Scotch and a case of vodka.'

'How?'

'That's what it'll have cost. Probably more.'

I followed him up to the house. 'You needn't worry. I got your message loud and clear.'

'Did you now?'

'Yes. I'm going to start "laying" again, I'm sorry to say.'

An aimless finger had pressed the button on an almost forgotten television set and had ended two years of perfect, if unheeding, peace and happiness. The thoughtless gesture had done more than that: it had re-opened a door which I had most deliberately closed, and now the furies, even though pleasant ones, were a-snapping and tugging at my heels.

Edwards arrived on the terrace one day in early July and Forwood and he started to rough out a draft contract: no one was losing much time it seemed, and the next day I signed it. Now there really *was* no going back. I was in, unless perhaps the script would prove to be unmendable.

Which, as I well knew, was always possible. We would start shooting in Rome and Vienna probably in January. It seemed comfortably far away.

Two days later, Yvonne Roux called from the Colombe d'Or to say that a distinguished French director called Henri Verneuil was staying there and wanted me to read a script. Could she give him my telephone number?

He arrived the next day, an energetic, bright-eyed, pipe-smoking gentleman who, once settled comfortably in a chair under the vine, outlined the whole of his considerably detailed script ('Le Serpent') which proved to be, yet again, another 'spy story based on the truth', in which I would be required to play (as I already guessed from the start of his monologue) Philby: or 'a kind of Philby'. He said that he had already signed Yul Brynner and Henry Fonda, and that everyone would be a star on this ambitious production.

The idea of working with Mr Fonda was, I had to admit, attractive. I would apparently have one 'marvellous scene with him: the most important in the film'. But they always are at the wooing stage of the game, so I didn't take much notice of that; however, the money for a mere fifteen days, five of them in

Munich, the rest in Paris, was really quite interesting under the present circumstances. And so was Mr Fonda.

I agreed to read the script, and give a speedy decision. Satisfied, he left in a flurry of pipes and pouches, assuring me that I must realise that he was an Armenian and that in Armenia every village had its own story-teller who would sit cross-legged in the market-place weaving tales of magic and beauty to enthralled audiences: that is all he was, he said with humility. Just an Armenian story-teller in the market-place; and he climbed into his expensive car and drove away.

Watching him go down the track, with great prudence, I realised that my re-opening of a once-closed door had now thrust upon me many things which I had hoped would stay out of sight for a long time to come: like opening the door of an, almost, forgotten attic; all the junk and jumble of the cinema was falling about my ears once again. Two films now, not just one. Not my intention at all.

'It never rains but what it pours,' Lally used to say, although it was obviously fate of some kind which had caused me to press the button on the TV set when an urgent replenishment of funds was so badly needed. Well. If I had to play yet another Mr Philby, or a degenerate officer in a concentration camp, then so be it: I would. I had no alternative, alas.

Summer had arrived with the cuckoo and the swallows, and the work on the land could not be neglected. Philbys or SS officers must be set aside for the moment, and the big chore, the mowing of the hay, had to be tackled without delay. One bright afternoon Forwood, thinking that his great rotary mower had jammed, stuck his hand under it to discover why: it hadn't, and sliced off the tops of his fingers.

Blood, bandages, Poteau.

Two days later the front page of the local paper carried a small story that Visconti had collapsed at dinner and been rushed to a clinic in a police car, as all Rome's ambulances were on strike. I tried to telephone to find out what had happened, but to get a call through to Rome, then or now, and to get any kind of response is as unlikely as meeting a pride of lions in Hyde Park.

However, the next evening Edwards got through to me: Visconti was in a clinic but it seemed at this stage of affairs just a matter of a complete fatigue, and he appeared to be in typical form, because, although it was being kept as secret as possible, some friend had managed to smuggle himself to the side of Visconti's bed, where he knelt in whispering hysterics.

'Oh God! Dear God! My brave Luchino, Luchino! Tell me, how are you?'
Visconti opened one slate-grey eye balefully.
'Better than you, my good friend,' he said.
'Oh dear God! Dear Mary! I thought that you were dying.'
'I shall know when my time comes,' said Visconti. 'It is not now and it will, in any case, not be before yours.'

So, if the story were true, we had high hopes that it was simply a matter of exhaustion after the marathon work he had done on 'Ludwig', 'the little thing', as he had called it only a short time ago. However, I couldn't help remembering one hundred cigarettes a day . . .

Edwards said that he would shortly bring Cavani down to see me, so that we could discuss the many problems which 'The Night Porter' posed. As she only spoke Italian, I was pretty certain that it would be a one-sided discussion, as all the Italian I could speak, put together, would hardly get me through a market, or even enable me to order a meal, with a very patient waiter, in a restaurant. There will be translators, said Edwards cheerfully.

I can't, at this moment, really remember what I expected Cavani to look like.

Certainly, because I have a literal mind, I expected someone dark, vivid, passionate and, in all probability, extremely noisy: with a great many gold bracelets and the fierceness and aggression of an Italian woman driver.

I did not expect Caravaggio, of course; but neither did I expect the shy, slender, fair-haired young woman who arrived with Edwards one evening, and a hustle of people who had come to discuss business and help to translate for us both. Translation, as it happened, was not needed; because for some reason we immediately established a strange kind of inner bond, based on mutual respect for each other's work. And so, while the others sat out on the terrace with a bandaged Forwood discussing contracts, dates, money and all the ugly paraphernalia which goes with the making of a movie, she and I sat alone in the long room with a bottle of wine and no common tongue.

And got on exceedingly well: in a hideous tumult of French, Italian and English. No one else might have understood us, but we understood each other completely, and it was only after a very short time that I knew, without any reservations, that I had been right in my first assumption that here was a master, and I wanted to work with her.

However, I realised that I could easily be drowned in the torrents of Italian with which she flooded me, so I firmly made my own points as best I could.

I said that there was far too much political polemic in the story.

She nodded agreeably and said that she *liked* the political polemic.

I said they wouldn't stand for much of that in America or England, which, as the film was being made in English, would constitute her main market.

She nodded cheerfully and said they'd have to.

I suggested that under all the welter of polemic there was just a very simple, very moving story of two people, a man and a woman who had come together in Hell, had discovered an extraordinary love there in the mud and the filth of the camp, rather like a tiny flower thrusting through the brutality and degradation of a battlefield.

I was rather pleased with this analogy, and she smiled brightly and said that that was the original story anyway, and that it was true.

She had been making a documentary for Italian TV on prison camps in, I think, Dachau. Bad weather had forced work to a halt. Sitting under an umbrella in the mud she saw a smartly dressed woman walking through the drenching rain carrying a sheaf of red roses, and she watched as the woman searched among the sites of the long-demolished huts where the prisoners had been held. In time she found the place for which she was looking, the brick angle, flush to the ground, of the hut foundations, and knelt there placing the roses on the spot, and remained, head bowed, in the rain for a few moments, then rose and walked away. With Cavani in pursuit.

With a woman's innate curiosity, and a film-maker's eye for the bizarre and equally for this tragic fragment of life, she hurried after the woman, who had obviously come to mourn her family (dead), who had died in that terrible place.

There had been no family. She was not Jewish. She came back, she said, every year on the anniversary of her lover's death. He was a member of the SS, she a girl who had been imprisoned for holding Socialist beliefs, and having a well-known Socialist father. The hut foundations, where she had placed her roses, was the site of the one in which she had been imprisoned; the day was the anniversary of the day on which her lover had been executed by the liberating Americans. She lived now in America but came back every year on that day. It was perfectly simply told, and unemotional. She left in the rain leaving Cavani with a story which haunted her for months.

What, she thought, would have happened if the SS man had *not* been killed?

Had escaped and gone to ground like so many of the others, and years later, in some unexpected place, at some unexpected time, the two had met again? What then? She wrote 'The Night Porter'.

But, I said, in the script the girl is definitely Jewish. In life this was not so. I was convinced that if we made the girl a Jewess, it would cause the bitterest offence in Jewish circles even to suggest that such a thing could possibly have happened.

But it did! Cavani said, thumping the table. A number of women, of all faiths, had fallen strangely in love with their gaolers. She discovered this, to her consternation, interviewing survivors of a number of women's camps while she was gathering her information for the documentary.

And *that's* the story! I said, the lovers. Not the political polemic, which is distracting and swamps the simplicity of the story.

Cavani was cracking a walnut. It was politics, after all, she mumbled through a mouthful of nut, which had brought the two together in the first place, didn't I agree? She grinned happily.

I could not disagree.

But I begged her to cut as much as she could, remove a lot of extra, tiresome characters, and concentrate on the essence of the thing. The SS man and the girl, and that she must be, as she was in life, Aryan. She shrugged a couple of times, cracked another walnut, shovelled the shells into an ashtray and used her only English word, reluctantly.

'Okay,' she said.

Cavani was young. Anyway, young enough to have missed the war about which she had known almost nothing, living in the safety and comfort of her family retreat in north Italy. There had always been butter on the table, she had never heard a bomb fall, the jug was always full of oil. Luxury; removal. She had only gradually become aware of the terrible things which she had been spared when she eventually went to university after everything was over; and the impact had been overwhelming. She began to make up for those protected years with a blinding dedication to the facts; none of which she was going to relinquish.

But she had, finally, said 'Okay'. I was greatly relieved.

The new script arrived in September. Pale blue. As slim, sleek, empty and dead as a gutted herring.

The rough, deeply felt, over-written script which I had retrieved from the cellar had been sent to the dry cleaners, and nothing remained of the fabric. I refused it, and said that we should continue working on the original; somehow we'd manage, although I was not at all sure how.

Meanwhile, the Armenian story-teller had sent his script. Highly polished, slick, fast-paced, unoriginal, it required me to do very little except stand about in a black raincoat looking enigmatic.

There were, however, two goodish scenes, one indeed with Mr Fonda, which didn't look as if it was going to tax either of us. But in the main it was, apart from the raincoat, what I call a 'cardigan and knitted tie' part, and I had hardly to open my mouth. Which suited me perfectly well. And, aware of the situation in my egg basket, I accepted my 'kind of Mr Philby' role; at least I had the necessary wardrobe.

So October found me sealed, literally, in a palatial suite in the Munich Hilton with unopenable windows looking out over the Englischer Garten, and with a spiral staircase leading up to a vast shelf on which stood what appeared to be the Bridal Bed. The central heating roared day and night.

No matter that each morning I awoke with a face like a boiled turbot; the whole thing was extremely luxurious, the work unexacting (Mr Brynner and Mr Fonda had not as yet joined our merry team) and it seemed to me a very good way of getting broken in again to playing for the cinema. I had been away for over two years, the longest I had ever been out of work, but it all came back smoothly, and five days later I was released from my chores in Munich and was free until work commenced again, for me anyway, in Paris on the giant set which M. Verneuil had erected. 'An exact copy,' he said proudly, 'of CIA Headquarters in Virginia.'

We left early one morning with Forwood at the wheel of his BMW just as the first frosts whitened the long alleys of the Englischer Garten. A few days before he had suggested that, on our journey back to France, we could perhaps make a small detour, of some two hundred kilometres, via Lake Como where the Visconti family had a country villa and where, at this moment, he was resting. It would be good manners, Forwood said, to do so.

I spent half a morning looking for some kind of gift to take, finally deciding on a large photographic book about Ludwig of Bavaria and his epoch. We arrived late in the afternoon at the splendid Hotel Villa d'Este, which I knew to be very near Visconti's villa, and which was 'supervised' by my old school friend from Convent days in Hampstead, Giovanna Govoni Salvadore. I felt certain that she'd get us in to the hotel somehow. And she did.

'But you'll *never* get into the villa. It's right next door to us, adjoining our land, and no one is allowed,' she said. 'But try . . . '

I telephoned the villa. A sombre-voiced man took my name and address and hung up. Half an hour later a telephone call, and this time a pleasant English-speaking woman's voice asked me if I could, please, identify myself, because the message I had left was not very clear. Who was I? I explained briefly.

'Ah, si, si. Goodbye,' she said, and rang off.

It was obviously not going to be easy; as Giovanna had said.

'Never mind. But I told you. He is guarded day and night and *no* one gets there. You come and have dinner tonight with Luca [her husband] and me. I'll show you what real Italian cooking should be. Not a pizza or a meat-ball in sight.'

In the hotel bar, where Luca had opened a bottle of champagne to celebrate our reunion, for Giovanna and I had hardly met since she was thirteen and I sixteen, when my father and I had managed to push her aboard the last boat leaving from England for France in the war hysteria of 1938, I was summoned to the telephone.

Visconti would see me. For only ten minutes because he was very tired. If I came immediately.

I can't remember much of the journey in detail, which was anyway very short. Only impressions come to my mind today.

Two fine lodges, a great iron gate being dragged open, Albino Coco, Visconti's First Assistant Director, there to meet us. We embraced warmly: 'For Papa you come?' he said, and immediately put a warning finger to his lips. I knew why. I had, years before, christened Visconti, strictly behind his back, 'Papa,' for he was the Father of his troupe and his actors. The troupe had been appalled at my levity, but in time they started to use the term, in hushed whispers, recognising it to be, as I meant it to be, a form of affectionate respect. But it was never, at any time, mentioned in his presence, and we took the greatest care to see that it never was. However, tonight the old word of endearment and respect had come from Albino's lips, not mine.

'He is okay, Albino?'

'Is okay, you see, but . . . ' he shrugged and we moved into the drive.

At the side of both lodges, servants standing in formal rows, their white aprons and pinafores glowing in the flickering fire from giant torches which continued all the way up the drive, held by liveried men at regular intervals. As we reached the house, Albino ran ahead and we turned into a great courtyard to be greeted on the steps of the villa by the housekeeper, who conducted us to Visconti.

A footman opened double doors. A high, shadowed room, shabby English-grand, books everywhere, a blazing log fire, dogs sprawled, chintz chairs, a pile of *Country Lifes*, a pleasant-looking woman in a worn armchair knitting: she smiled, nodded in greeting. Another, younger, in tweeds and cashmere sweater. On a small table, an abandoned game of Solitaire, and almost in the centre of the room, facing me as I entered, Visconti in a wheelchair, a tartan rug draped across his body.

'Ciao, Bogarde,' he said quietly, and I crossed the room with my gift, and kissed him on the head, a thing I would never have dared do before. He was grey. Shrunken. Small. The Lion, the Bull, the Emperor, was now an aged man hunched in a chair, his one good arm lying idle across his tartan lap.

'I have brought you a present,' I said.

He reached up slowly and took the book in his right hand. 'Kind. Very kind,' he said, and started tearing the coloured wrapping away like a child at a birthday. The paper fell in scraps at the foot of his chair. 'Ah si!' he grunted, holding the book close to his eyes. 'I know this.'

'You already *have* it! It's just come out this week in Munich!'

'I have it,' he grunted again. 'I have *everything* on Ludwig.' He pushed open a few pages, set it aside. 'you have come then from Munich?'

'This morning.'

'You have a dentista also in Munich?' There was just a glinting light of amusement in his eyes.

'No dentist. A film.'

'Is good, the film?'

'Just started. Fonda is in it.'

'Ah si. Is good, Fonda. And so you come here to see my photographs? Of 'Ludwig', is so?'

It wasn't, but it had to be so. Of all things I detest it is looking at books of other people's photographs.

'Forwood, you ring that little bell, we see the photographs. Very beautiful.'

A footman in house livery arrived, took his orders, left through the great doors.

'And the Poverino? Tell me now.' The tartan rug had slipped from his shoulders, his paralysed arm lay dead at his side. 'You see this damned thing, eh?' He lifted it with his right hand. 'Look. Is morto. Finito. I have to make exercises, but it will not work. Ah, ha! Finito, finito.'

Two footmen arrived with stacks of enormous red leather-bound albums. My heart sank.

For two hours we sat and looked at the, admittedly, glorious photographs of 'Ludwig'. Visconti grew less and less tired, less and less morose, more and more eager, the fine right hand caressing the photographs, pointing out overlooked detail, turning pages, dragging his paralysed arm across the springing covers to hold them down. The two women were watchful, but seemed pleased.

'Visconti,' I said at length, unable to face a sixth great album being placed upon my knees by a footman. 'We'll have to leave soon.'

'Why soon!' His voice was strong, the voice I once had known was there again.

'We've been here two hours. I have to dine at the Villa d'Este. You must dine too, it's almost nine-thirty.'

'I eat late, you know,' he said. 'But if you go, you go. Very well, va bene.'

He thanked me for the gift.

'You will come to Roma to see the first assembly, eh? Just a few people, private. Family only, you will come? And where is Charlotte [Rampling], someone tells me is married, is true, and a baby?'

'Yes, it's true.'

'If you speak to her, tell her she must also come. I tell you when.'

'I promise,' I said and stooped and kissed his head. He took my hand in his strong right one and held it for a moment, the grey eyes like chipped flints under the bushy brows, smiling at my audacity, knowing it for the homage which it was.

'Ciao, Bogarde, ciao, Forwood. You will drive safe.'

I turned briefly at the double doors and looked back. His head was lowered, chin to chest, the right hand possessively caressing the red leather binding of an album on his knees.

A week later, on the morning that I was setting off to Paris to join M. Verneuil on his vast set of CIA H.Q. in Virginia, I collected the mail from the tin box at the end of the track. I instantly recognized the handwriting on one small envelope, the sharp, staccato, and at the same time florid, handwriting of Visconti.

On a small piece of paper, probably from a message pad, he had written:

13 Oct. 72

Dear Bogarde,
Thank you for coming so far out of your way to see me: now that I am no longer of any use to you.
                    With very much love

He had signed it simply: *Papa.*

The CIA set was splendid and extremely impressive. Mr Brynner was exuberantly polite, and spent a great deal of his time amusing the crew with funny faces and varied tricks; which delighted them.

Mr Fonda was polite too, and highly professional, sitting silently in his chair with the day's script in a tidy little plastic envelope on his knee. He spoke only the lines of his part: otherwise he was to all intents and purposes mute.

I sat about aimlessly in my tweed jacket and knitted tie and listened, which was all that was required of me, and spoke to no one because, quite frankly, no one spoke to me. It was with some relief that my second week was over and I headed back to the house in the South.

The vine was turning fast, the grapes hung heavy, the sun warm, and green and yellow mantis climbed anxiously away from the path of the mower as the last of the hay was cut before winter. I resented that I had to go once again to Paris to finish off my piece in 'Le Serpent', but at the same time I was well aware that I had put a few more eggs into the basket and that there could be more to come in the New Year, because 'The Night Porter', it appeared, was almost definite.

One evening in the Lancaster in Paris, Forwood had had a sudden brilliant idea that we should play Charlotte Rampling as the girl. I had met her first on 'The Damned' some time before, and had been tremendously impressed by her work, and Visconti had said that one day, if she so wished it, she would be a star. He didn't make those remarks lightly. I knew, instinctively, that she was right for the girl.

I immediately telephoned Edwards, who was cautious but interested. So was Cavani. I had then called Charlotte in London and explained everything. Yes, she was interested; yes, she had a baby, but he wouldn't be a problem; and yes, she could be free to work in the early part of January. Was there a script?

'There is a script, it's a terrible mess, but I think you'll be able to see the nub of the story in the welter of polemic and junk, it's pretty marvellous. One snag though . . .'

Her voice was cool. 'What's the snag?'

'It's to the knuckle. It's not MGM or anything. There's no money.'

She laughed wearily. 'There never is, love, is there?'

But she had accepted a few days later. We were ready to go. With the old, original, black script.

So that last evening, mowing among the crawling mantis, I felt cheerful about things: I had gone back to 'laying', and although it hadn't exactly been the greatest joy, it hadn't been bad. I hadn't lost my touch, I thought; I'd done the best I could do with the material given me, and the future now held an exciting promise. I wanted to make 'The Night Porter', I wanted to work with Cavani, and I wanted, above all things, to work with Rampling. I'd got all three amazingly.

On the Blue Train that night, going up to Paris, I started to cut away at the pages of the old black script from the cellar, and the more I reduced it the more sure I became that we had an extraordinary film to make. Always supposing that Cavani would agree to my ruthlessness. I consoled myself that she couldn't speak or read English and that Charlotte and I would blind her with our magic. I felt dangerously confident.

We arrived in Paris the next morning, got to the Lancaster and ordered a huge breakfast, and I started to shave, when the telephone rang.

Nine-fifteen on a Sunday morning? M. Verneuil checking me in, I supposed.

I heard Forwood in his room talking, heard him call me: I turned off taps and, razor in hand, went through the sitting room to his room where he was sitting on the edge of the bed, his hand covering the mouthpiece of the receiver.

'What?'

'It's bad news, I'm afraid. Ulric's dead,' he said.

NINE

My brother's voice was calm, firm.

'Heart attack about six-thirty this morning. Been trying to reach you.'

'Train was late.'

'We're all here. George and Elizabeth drove up right away. Cilla [his wife] and I got here about an hour ago.'

'And Ma?'

'Marvellous. Wonderfully calm. Shock hasn't hit her yet.'

'Of course.'

'When can you get across?'

'When's the funeral?'

'Wednesday. We'll have to have an autopsy, just to be sure.'

'Of course. I don't know *when* I can get across. We start work tomorrow, I'm in every damned scene.'

The shaving soap was drying on my face, the tiny bubbles fizzing as they burst. I studied, with infinite care, every millimetre of the carpet between my feet, razor slack in my hand.'

'Well, it would help to know.'

'I'll call the film people today. But it's Sunday; they all go off to their little bungalows in Fontainebleau.'

Fortunately, M. Verneuil hadn't. He was, he said kindly, deeply sad, such a thing to happen! But of course I knew that tomorrow was the start of the big week with Henry Fonda and I was in every shot? Saturday was a day of rest. Sunday the last shooting day, my scene with Fonda; I knew that, of course? If I could get there *and back* on the Saturday . . . Otherwise. He was desolate, but of course the film . . .

My brother's voice was still calm and firm, and very reasonable. He knew, because he worked for television, that nothing short of a national disaster, and a big one at that, could possibly alter the 'schedule'. Personal affairs had no part in our job.

'Well, we'll try for Saturday. It's the gravediggers. Overtime, that sort of thing. I'll try for Saturday and you call if anything alters.'

'Nothing will. They have to get rid of Fonda by the end of the week. He costs.'

'Of course.'

'Saturday then?' said Elizabeth.

'Soon as I can, night ferry on Friday, be with you about ten. I can't make it before.'

'I know. Typical, isn't it? You go back to work after two whole years and the first week, Daddy . . . '

'Typical,' I said.

It was a grey, bitter Sunday in Paris. The Grands Boulevards deserted. A cat perhaps; a huddled figure with the morning paper, a sharp wind whipping the last November leaves, bowling them across the cobbles.

The whole length of the Champs Elysées down to the Rond Point was empty: fading into a grizzly mist, the traffic lights all the way down springing up; red, amber and green with no one to warn save a lone parked taxi. The whole world was suddenly a void.

I had a business luncheon at Lippe: no point in cancelling it and sitting staring at the wallpaper in the Lancaster. Heat, cooking smells, laughter; plates of cabbage and sausage, carafes of wine; my host assuring me earnestly that if I joined his firm I would never cease working, there was already something he had in mind with Audrey Hepburn.

In the privacy of the lavatory of the suite in the hotel I suddenly beat the white tiled wall with my fist and yelled, 'But why *him*?'

An absurdity.

Why not him? Everyone dies.

On Friday night there was a rail strike. There would be no ferry, but the train would go to Calais. We'd have to depend on British Rail after that. Calais at three-fifteen in the morning. A light drizzle, but hopeful news. A car ferry had been diverted from Dunkirk. We trailed aboard cold and tired.

At Dover at five-forty-five a.m. an officious little fellow in Customs called me over, examined every item in my handgrip; I had no other baggage and was travelling in a black suit which I had worn in the film. He was as tired, no doubt, as we, cap on the back of his head, cigarette stuck to his lower lip, shirt open at the neck, crumpled tie undone.

'I take it you're a resident of the UK?'

'No.'

'Staying with us long?' he was poking and prodding.

'No.'

'Come for a holiday?'

'No.'

He grew impatient. 'What have you come for, if I may ask?'

'To bury my father, if you will allow me to get there.'

'Well then . . . ' He closed the hand-grip, zipped it up. 'Got an autograph book here somewhere.' He fished about under the counter on which he had placed his foot, one knee bent in shiny blue serge. 'Sign it, will you? It's not for me actually; my sister. Big fan of yours. Or *was*. Don't see much of you these days, do we? For Lorraine. With an 'e'.'

The train was freezing and dirty.

'Didn't expect you lot,' said a steward. 'Supposed to be a strike. Take time to get the steam going.'

We sat huddled in our coats for an hour watching, through frost-ferns on the filthy windows, the residents of Dover starting a new day. A woman in a pink quilted dressing-gown, and curlers. A man in his vest, yawning, tugging open curtains, standing in thought picking his nose unawares: someone shaking a packet of Corn Flakes, taking up a milk bottle; a woman opening a back door and pushing a reluctant cat into the frost and the scrap-yard of a garden.

The train lurched suddenly, clanked, stuttered, a long hiss of steam. We started moving slowly past the ugly grey houses towards London.

An ancient English country church: centuries of candle wax, varnish, dust. Stone pillars, pine pews, flagged stone floor. A muted organ, rustling of clothing.

Gareth, Elizabeth and I in a line: left in solicitous solitude by the others who had come to mourn him with us. Friends from the village; from his favourite pub; from London. The Chesterfields of childhood were there too, and, most movingly, some of his companions from *The Times*.

My mother had stayed behind at the cottage with Cilla and Forwood. 'He's dead,' she had said. 'I don't want to see what happens. Please?'

They say that death diminishes, and it is so; at least it was that day. The coffin, of plain oak, carried by six bearers, shuffling past us along the flagstones, could not, I thought to my astonishment, contain my father's body.

So small, so humble; nothing to do with the man we had known and loved so well. But we were all there to bury him: so it must be.

For the first time, Elizabeth suddenly bowed her head and wept into a crumpled paper handkerchief. Not noisily, just hopelessly.

Gareth and I stood together stiffly upright, looking intently at the glass in the windows, the shine on the brass candlesticks; anything but the coffin.

And afterwards, in the gravediggers' pit, dug from the Sussex earth and flints, he was lowered carefully down on ropes, and as the first spade of frozen soil hit the coffin lid I heard no door slam, but the sound of bolts rammed home: a key turned.

And that was it. There was no more. We trailed in little groups up the path to the gate and the waiting cars: a woman said, 'Must rush, but I just had to come;

he was very much loved here, you know, in the village. We were all very fond of your father. A gentleman; not many left now. I've got to dash: just wanted you to know.' She hurried away, unchained her bike leaning by the gates and rode off into the November light.

There was champagne at the house, smoked salmon sandwiches: the room was jammed with people. My mother sat upright in a large armchair, smiling, hands outstretched in pleasure and gratitude, greeting people who had come so far for this occasion. She was groomed, elegant in black, easy, calm, extraordinarily composed. She was particularly moved to see, once again, his colleagues from *The Times*, and particularly his devoted secretary, Mr Greenwood, but at no time was there the slightest sign of grief or sadness; sorrow perhaps. That. But masked. She was behaving with incredible dignity and grace.

I realised that in some strange way she was 'on stage'; an audience had come to see her and she would not, under any circumstances, let them down. Or herself, her children or her husband. She had a 'Full House'.

This was no invalid who would not walk; no helpless creature enveloped in her chosen aura of Tragedy Queen. Quite the reverse of these things, her eyes were bright, her hands eager, caressing, her laughter soft. She was straight-backed, confident, putting each and every one of her guests at ease.

'Oh! My dear! How wonderful of you to have come . . . Ulric would have been *so* proud.'

What would happen later, when the curtain, so to speak, had fallen and this 'full house' had gone, I did not dare to imagine. But for the moment the performance was spellbinding and the room, instead of being muted by grief, was, to my joy, gradually, cautiously, filling with laughter. People were mourning my father as they should, with the pleasure in the remembering of him; not with sadness.

The atmosphere was almost that of a party, which he would have enjoyed greatly, not that of a wake, which he would have scorned.

Elizabeth looked as if she had scrubbed her face with a wire-brush. I hugged her tightly.

'Do I look really awful? I know I do. I tried not to, you know, I mean, cry. So silly, and he would have hated it. But it was that coffin. So titchy . . . '

'I know. Thank God Ma didn't come. Much better here.'

'Oh much! I think it might have killed her really: that little box; fifty-two years of a marriage, carried to that awful hole.'

'But she's in good form now. She does put up a bloody good show when she has to; it's what's called setting a good example.'

'Yes. She jolly well knows how to behave.'

'Sad about Lally.'

'Well, too far for her to come all that way, and it was a bit short notice, she's not getting younger either.'

'It's later on I worry about for Ma. After . . . '

'Not now,' said Elizabeth. 'Not today. Talk about that later. But not now.'

For some extraordinary reason Gareth and Elizabeth and I had never really thought that our father would be the first to die. We were almost convinced that Ma, who was growing ever frailer, losing her grip on life generally, caring less, having her 'little falls' rather too often, catching colds and so on, would be the first to go. And then, in an abstract way, we agreed that Pa would come to stay with one or the other of us. We even looked forward to the fact that he might, if the terrible day arrived.

I think that he had seemed to us permanent. A fixture in our lives, I can't imagine why, for it is patently idiotic to think in that way. Life is life, and short. But the human spirit is determined that it is immortal, and in some strange way I think we thought that he was.

The deep-rooted bitterness and despair in my mother had grown as she grew older; the years of disappointment, of long-quenched ambition, of smouldering fury at the frustration of her acting-life had started to emanate from her very body almost in the form of a corrosion. It was tangible now. You could, and did, touch it. And it was incurable.

On the other hand, Pa was like the cliché oak: flourishing, steady, no signs of malaise, of inner distresses, no signs even of aging. He had never been ill. Although he was the most secretive of men, he made no secret, whatsoever, of the fact that he loved life and all that it had to offer so, naturally, we were quite convinced that he must be the survivor.

But he had not been: he was not the stronger member of the partnership. He had gone. And that shock-wave was still to hit the three of us fair and square between the eyes.

'What about Christmas?' said Gareth quietly. 'We'll have to do something about that, it's not far off.'

'I'll speak to George and Elizabeth about it. Perhaps they'll bring her out to France, with the children. We'll have a non-Christmas.'

'Best idea. I'd have her with us but we're a big family now, I think she'd be far happier with a trip to make. Take her mind off things, keep her occupied, it's the first hump we have to face. When's your flight tonight?'

'Sevenish. I'd better start making my farewells.'

The next morning at eight-thirty, in the gilt and mirrored saloon of the Travellers' Club in Paris, I played my 'marvellous scene' with Mr Fonda. It was all very simple, easy, and Mr Fonda expert, although still oddly mute; however, it was finished by five o'clock. The next day, I had one more small piece to do and that was that. I caught the Blue Train back to Nice, fairly sure that my first screen work, after two years' absence, had not been disastrous, and that I had not lost my 'edge'. Some months later, when the film opened in London, Miss Dilys Powell in the *Sunday Times* wrote: 'Mr Bogarde, given too little to do, does far too much.' I never saw the thing; but I am absolutely certain that she was right. She always is.

A week later I was back in Sussex trying to help Elizabeth to sort out the papers and belongings in my father's studio, a small room up a flight of narrow and very steep stairs.

'I really can't imagine how he got up and down here every day; *I'm* puffed already.' She was leading the way. 'You know he had a terrible truss-thing. A hernia?'

'No. No, I didn't.'

'Said he did it heaving himself out of the sea on some rocks at Denia, when you were all there on some film. I can't remember what. Ruptured himself.'

'But he never said anything to me! Never a mention.'

'No. Well, he was secretive. Didn't give away things like that. I only found out years ago by accident.'

She pushed open the door. A strong, familiar smell of oil paint, linseed oil and turpentine.

'I've been burning a lot of stuff this week; bits and pieces. Of course, trusses don't bloody well burn.'

'Of course not. They're metal.'

'Awful things. And his teeth . . . ' She stopped herself quickly, hand to her eyes.

'Teeth? He didn't have false teeth?'

'A dear little plate. With two or three on one side. I wanted to get rid of all those things; shaving brushes, razor, well you know. Reminders. For Mummy.'

On the easel I remembered so well, a big unfinished canvas of Windover Hill, the hill sketched in, the sky a great expanse of blue and clouds. I'd forgotten how good he was at painting clouds.

Bottles; his paint-box open; the tubes neatly stacked. A dirty paint-cloth on a nail. His brushes standing stiffly in an old Tate and Lyle syrup tin, cleaned, erect, ready. Canvases stacked against the walls, a hard wooden chair, a cushion with the imprint of his body. On a low yellow-oak bookcase a long row of old box files marked 'Private'.

'We'd better get to work,' I said.

It was bad enough being in his empty studio, still so alive with him, but it was utterly wretched for the two of us rummaging through his private papers, the personal hoarding of eighty years of a life.

Papers and papers. Letters, hundreds, it seemed; from *The Times*, from J. M. Barrie, from Pavlova, from Munnings with a drawing of a little horse, letters of thanks for photographs which he had used in the paper from a hundred names which he had chosen to keep. Then his diaries, dating back to 1910, all in an unbreakable code and the smallest, neatest, writing. They meant nothing to us. Cyphers, figures. There were old newspapers printed in Flemish, a few school reports, some sketches which he had made in Italy during his war, and then we found his Will signed and dated in 1954: leaving everything he owned to his wife.

Everything was the house and contents. And he was overdrawn at the bank.

'Why? Why in God's name didn't he tell me?' I said in anguish.

'He wouldn't. You know that. But did you know about this?' Elizabeth held up a fat pile of bills and receipts from a firm of undertakers in a suburban town for the upkeep of his mother's grave. Paid up to date. We looked at each other in bewilderment.

Granny Grace!

We had hardly heard her name mentioned by him in our entire lives. And yet right up until the present moment he had been paying for the upkeep of her grave.

All we knew of Granny Grace was that she had died in 1917 while he was fighting in Passchendaele. There was a three-quarter portrait of her hanging on the stairs. A pale, smiling woman; head to one side, wearing a black velvet coat with sable collar, holding a closed fan in gloved hands, folded before her. She was one of three sisters, the eldest of whom, married to an eminent lawyer called Nutt, became our surrogate grandmother, the younger of whom, Rose, lived in a pleasant cottage in Sidcup, which was then, as far as I recall in the early twenties, still almost the country, waiting for the return of her husband who had been posted 'Missing' in 1915.

The house, I well remember, was kept ready for him, just as he had left it. His slippers were in the hearth, his pipe and tobacco jar on the table by his chair, his raincoat still hung on the back of the kitchen door. Each night Rose, or Great Aunt Rose as we called her, would unlock the front door, leave one small lamp burning, and fill a thermos with tea. 'Because, you see,' she said, 'it is very possible that he will come home quite late. One can't tell.'

But we knew very little at all about Granny Grace. She was not real as her sisters were; one had seen them and spoken to them and liked them well. She was unimaginable, a shadow. Never spoken of, a private part of my father's life.

Except that once, when I was about eight or nine, hunting about at the top of my mother's wardrobe where I knew she used often to hide early Christmas presents from us, I found, to my astonishment, a steel-mesh purse full of coppers and shillings which I knew instinctively must have belonged to her. I stole from it from time to time.

I had a feeling of guilt, but it never lasted very long. She was dead and I had never seen her. It didn't feel like stealing at all. My logic satisfied me perfectly.

'Well, one thing is absolutely certain,' I said. 'Ma is broke.'

For two days we sorted, sifted, packed and filed whatever seemed worth the keeping, and burned all the rest at the far end of the garden. I am certain that we made errors; it is impossible to sort through the hoardings of a man's lifetime in two single days, but we had to move quickly and cut away the undergrowth, so to speak, before we started the family discussion on what to do with Mamma, because something had to be done, and soon.

There was not the slightest possibility, now, of her being able to manage on her own again. For the last five years Pa had been her help, cook, cleaner, nurse and comforter. She was now bereft of all five: not just her husband. Her initiative had gone, she was lost and bewildered. I had feared that she might perhaps crumble the moment that the 'full house' had left, and this is exactly what she did.

In the week since the funeral, the bitter numbness of her grief bit deeply. She sat for most of the day, in her deep armchair, in black, chain-smoking, offering us no help whatsoever simply because she no longer knew how to.

'Darlings, you do as you like. Please! I don't care. I really don't care. I don't even know what Daddy did with all those papers and things; I've never seen them, he never told me, just burn them all, burn everything.'

We didn't, of course, and did our best to try and rekindle a spark of interest in her for some of the things which we considered must be salvaged.

'Gareth ought perhaps to have the diaries, don't you think? He's got all those sons, they may like to have them later.'

'As you like. I don't care.'

'And there are boxes and boxes of glass negatives. Some could be valuable. Records of things he did for *The Times* perhaps; of us even, family things; we can't just chuck them away.'

'I don't know about any glass negatives. I don't know what they can be, probably all old-fashioned stuff. Do what you want.'

And that is as far as we ever got.

Finally, Forwood called us all to attention and the family conference. Down to brass tacks. Very brass ones. No money. Alone. Helpless.

We talked about and around for far too long, deciding nothing, reaching no definite point of view, and finally Forwood, who listens a great deal before making any remark of importance, suggested that perhaps George and Elizabeth should move into the house, which they would buy from my mother at a reasonable price and then invest the money for her future. She would also, he reminded us, be certain to receive a decent pension from *The Times*, and my father's studio could be easily turned into a separate wing of the house, where she could be perfectly independent, still in her own surroundings, and among her family.

She agreed uninterestedly, and lit another cigarette. The possibility of her coming out to France to live with me had been firmly scotched. Too long a journey. Foreign people she couldn't understand; too many stone stairs in the house and, she added, shrewdly, too damn lonely. What was she expected to do when I 'went off making films all over the place?' She'd go *mad* there. So that was that.

Gareth had already a large and growing family and she wasn't keen on a lot of children, and anyway she would pose a dreadful burden for him. She didn't, under any circumstances, want to be a burden. That much she made clear. She insisted that she could stay on in the house. Alone. She'd manage somehow.

We all looked at poor George and Elizabeth who were obviously going to be the ones to face a sacrifice. Elizabeth loved her house by the sea, she loved her life there, but she bravely, if perhaps a little bleakly, agreed that it seemed to be the only possible solution.

'I don't know what else we can do, truthfully. She can't stay here on her own, that's certain.' She shrugged. Her arms wrapped round her knees, squatting on a low stool by the fire, shoulders hunched. 'We'll just have to try and see how it works out: it may. Nothing else for it really, is there?'

The next day I left for France feeling wretched and acutely aware that she and George had made an enormous personal sacrifice and knowing, even if she did not quite at this moment, that Elizabeth was now hopelessly trapped.

Before leaving the house I noticed, high up in a dark angle of the staircase, a small portrait of my mother, in chalk and wash. It had been drawn two years after I was born, and I had forgotten about it until that instant. I asked her if I might have it to take back to France with me.

She was suddenly alert, interested, eyes sparkling. 'Oh do! Darling, do. If you want it, take it. Ulric always hated it, that's why it was always hidden away in dark places. He didn't ever want to see it: but it's really terribly good, he was a wonderful artist, and it is so *like* me. Amazing.'

'Why did Pa hate it so much?'

'Because he was convinced that poor Hookway [the artist] was desperately in love with me, and Ulric was a very, very jealous man, I can tell you. It was all so silly. But *I* loved it, so it stayed: and you like it, so you have it. I want you to.' She took the slim oak-framed portrait in her hands. 'Yes. You take it. You won't stick it away in some corner. I wasn't bad-looking, was I? Really not so bad. I made the best of myself, your old Ma.'

When Liliana Cavani saw it hanging here in the long room, she went to it instantly. 'Who is?'

'My Mama. 1923.'

'Ah . . . si bella. Si bella,' she said, and then laughed softly shaking her head in amusement. 'Oh ho, oh ho!'

'Oh ho, oh ho! What?'

'La Malcontenta, no?' she said.

The sweet-sour stench of naked bodies huddled in a frightened mass in the huge tiled room with a filthy concrete floor. Overhead, glaring white lamps in metal shades. Bitterly cold: no heating except for one big gas burner which roared away uselessly, blowing little gasps of warm air into the freezing room.

Old men, young men, old women, children, young women. Hands folded across their bodies trying to conceal, in one hopeless gesture, their sex.

A woman, heavy-breasted, pregnant, a child of about two slung round her hips looking more naked even than the others because she wore a hat on her untidy hair; gay with two bows.

In the centre of the crowd, which was filing barefoot towards the trestles at which sat a number of black uniformed SS men and women who were taking down their particulars, Charlotte was as naked as the rest; and she was clearly distressed. Her distress was sudden, and nothing whatsoever to do with acting. Suddenly she broke away from the crowd and ran blindly to Maria, the

Wardrobe Mistress who had dressed me on both Visconti films and who now smothered her in a coat, clucking and whispering consolations.

Tears, which did not fall; her voice unsteady, fighting for control. 'That *hat*. Why did she keep her hat on? Everything else has been taken from her, why the hat: those bloody bows. Why?'

'Because that is what she did. Last relic of dignity, of self, of identity perhaps.'

'But it's true? It's not Lilly's idea?'

I found the large black folder of photographs from the archives which Liliana had collected together for just such a moment as this.

'No. It happened.'

The blurred photograph taken in Poland in 1943 was an exact replica of the scene before us. And the naked woman with the child round her hips, heavy-breasted, pregnant, wore a silly hat.

In Vught Camp, or perhaps in Belsen, I can't remember exactly which now (both were as terrible) I had wandered through huts piled high with the relics of human life: hair in mounds, higher than myself, from shaven heads. Whole rooms filled with artificial legs and arms; metal things with joints and a single shoe, or one gloved hand, worse somehow, a gloveless hand in polished wood with articulated fingers. Rooms full of false teeth, hearing-aids, spectacles rimmed in tortoiseshell or dull gold, glimmering in the light; an avalanche of dusty metal, glass and porcelain.

In one shed, apart from the others, a rack of women's evening-dresses on hangers, swinging gently in the April wind. Another rack of tail-coats, the white ties knotted round the hanger-hooks like dead worms; top hats; gold and silver dancing-shoes, patent leather ones in a neat row as if in an hotel corridor waiting for a valet.

Appliqued flowers, crushed cotton roses on a thin shoulder strap, sequins hanging by a single thread.

'Dutch Jews,' said my guide, an Estonian 'Kapo'* who had over-eagerly offered to show me the camp. He touched the shabby dresses with indifference. 'Is pretty, yah? They caught them at a big celebration. All.' He pronounced the letter 'c' like the word 'sea', in a hissing sibilant. Turning back the collar of one of the tail-coats, he twisted his head about, squinted, read the tailor's label. 'Is so. Yah. Dutch Jews. I remember. From Amsterdam.'

'And they kept these things like this? On hangers . . . '

'Oh! Excuse me, please. Oh yah. Always very tidy. For the concerts we had: many concerts for the guards at Christmas and other times. Also we have orchestra. Very fine, this orchestra. Jews are good musicians, but this you will know; so. But not all the peoples here were Jews, we had many kinds, Communists, Socialists, religious ones, homosexuals, many kinds, and we had good orchestra. Ah yah, all this we had.'

I am not absolutely certain of the camp, but I do remember the conversation with the 'Kapo'. I remember his shaved head, the striped suit of his prison garb, his over-eager smile, terrified, fawning, wanting to please. I gave him the 'unexpired portion' of my daily rations, a bully-beef sandwich and an apple. I could not eat. He touched the newspaper packet with his lips.

'So thank you. So thank you. I taught English, you know, to the young ladies of my city by the sea. Thank you, chentleman.' He was crying.

At twenty-four, the age I was then, deep shock stays registered for ever. An internal tattooing which is removable only by surgery; it cannot be conveniently sponged away by time.

---

* 'Kapo', the local word then for a 'Trusty' in the camps

Bombs, shrapnel, tracer-bullets in the night, even flame throwers, all the vile and ugly mechanics of war I had managed, over time, to accept, even the constant dead who *never* 'lay serene, peaceful, as in sleep' but were sprawled and chunked by metal shards in the hedges and cornfields. These too I had managed to deal with. After all, I was in a war, and these things are part of war, and young men have to get accustomed to them. Or go under. I had become accustomed to them: they came to me gradually.

But I could not, and I never have, become accustomed to the rack of evening-dresses, floating, twisting silently in the soft spring wind. Nor to the mounds of stinking hair, tumbled; or the angled legs and arms. They were something so horrifying that my mind could not even accept them at the time, and even when my 'Kapo' friend took me proudly to the long hut where the concerts were held, I still could not accept, though I saw the stage, the sagging red curtains, the rippled backcloth of a pretty Austrian lake with a white steamer crossing. It was only when I tripped over a scattered pile of tangled music stands in a drift of sheet music that I believed. And came to terms. The evidence before my eyes.

But coming to terms is not the same as becoming accustomed. That morning, in the bitter cold of the tiled room, among the naked people, the women with white hair and breasts as empty as old pockets, the hat with the bows, the smell of stripped bodies crowded together, Charlotte too had come to terms: suddenly.

Born long after the war, she had no conception of what had taken place in those camps. Reading about them is not the same; the written word does not, always, fully evoke the horror and the terror. But standing there, naked as the others, before a table lined with black uniforms, with the smell, with the shame, she understood.

When I first started in the cinema, in 1947, Mrs C. A. Lejeune was one of the most distinguished, and important, critics of the time. She and Dilys Powell were affectionately, and respectfully, known in the industry as 'The Girls'. They kept away from the junketing and the dreadfulness of the press parties, and their reviews were all their own work, unhindered by wheedling press agents or anxious film producers who always tried to buy good reviews by serving ghastly lunches and a constant flow of gin and tonics.

Mrs Lejeune and Miss Powell did not attend these orgies. But once I did meet the former, and her words stayed with me throughout my career. 'It is not my business,' she said, 'to know what troubles you had, what problems you had to overcome, what discomforts you endured making your film. My business is simply to judge the finished result: nothing more.'

She was absolutely right.

But movies aren't made the way we made them then, in the comparative comfort of a studio. Things have changed radically.

We had started the shooting of 'The Night Porter' on a freezing day in January in a condemned TB sanatorium out on the via Tuscolona, Rome. It was, like all Liliana's locations, brilliantly chosen; for it had all the atmosphere of a Death Camp, and the years and years of sadness, illness and despair which had filled it originally were distilled into the air like a vapour.

Walking, or perhaps I should say strutting, through the empty huts and wards, the long dim corridors and the decaying scraps of abandoned garden surrounding the place, in my fine black-and-silver uniform and high-peaked cap with its Death's Head insignia, cracking my boots with a thin silver-topped whip, I had no illusions at all that I was *not* the man I was supposed to be playing. I felt exactly right. I felt frightening; powerful; commanding. The uniform did that; at least externally. The internal struggle of the man himself was my own affair: but I found it much easier to become him than poor Von Aschenbach, although the role was to prove equally demanding and draining.

The uniform itself had a curious effect on the inmates of the camp. Perfectly ordinary paid-up members of their actors' union, they had been carefully chosen for their thinness, drabness, age and general feeling of decay. They scurried away as I walked past them or hid, crouching, in corners, huddled nervously; and the more that they huddled and scurried, the taller I stood, the wider I strode. It was an interesting experience.The SS uniform had been extremely well designed for the purpose it was to serve: fear.

I remember how small, weedy and insignificant Himmler had looked lying dead on the scratched parquet floor of a bourgeois villa in Lüneburg in 1945: his feet thrust into a pair of old army boots, a blanket roughly thrown over his naked chest and belly, his hairy shins sticking out at angles, like broom-sticks on a scarecrow. They hadn't even given him a pair of socks: and his tongue hung limply from thin lips like that of a dead dog.

And dead dog he was that day, without his splendid uniform which had once inspired so much fear and dread in so many people. It seemed, that morning, inconceivable that this runty little man could ever have inspired terror, or had the power, the authority, and the absolute control over people's lives that he did, for he looked, lying there in the thin spring sunlight, as if he could never have had the force to push a barrow or hold a begging-tin.

A British Corporal beside me kicked him lightly in the ribs. The boots shuddered, eyes glazed, half closed, the head rolled.

'Nasty little bastard, wasn't he? Did 'isself in with cyanide or something. They had a right old scrum trying to get it from him, but he just bit it, I reckon, got it down. No guts, this one hadn't.

But he had had incalculable power over life and death not so many weeks before.

The uniform did a great deal to assist him in his lethal tasks: there was no goodness in a man who wore it; and this the huddled Italian 'extras' knew only too well. They had known the Occupation; and the sight of that uniform on their streets. It was not easily forgotten.

If I had the wardrobe to help me with the performance, I still hadn't, quite, got the dialogue together; which was a little worrying.

Liliana and most of the crew had their scripts in Italian, Charlotte and I and the other actors had the English translation. This was literal; and being literal, far too long. Understatement is not an Italian virtue. Every day Charlotte and I would go through the script, cutting away and chipping at yards of over-explanation under the ever-darting, suspicious eyes of our director.

To help us all get through this effort, she had brought a splendid woman named Paola Tallerigo to join us as translator. Paola spoke every known language, as far as I could gather, and English fluently; her job, as go-between, was not an enviable one, but at least she got things wonderfully clear, and translated what I had to say to Liliana, and what she had to say to me. Constantly.

Charlotte spoke a little Italian, so her life was a bit easier, but it was Paola who held us all together and with the greatest tact. Each time I cut another chunk of dialogue Liliana, or Lilly as we now called her with affection, screamed as if stabbed, and shouted for Paola.

'What is he doing to page 56? He is cutting everything I have sweated writing!'

'He says he doesn't need so many words.'

'*I* say what he needs! I *wrote*; he butchers! I have things I want *said*!'

'There are simpler ways of saying things in English. It is a simpler language than ours. He will say what you want, don't worry.'

'Butcher! Will he say what I *intend*? Dio, Dio, I wrote what he kills!'

One day I managed to reduce almost half a page of dialogue to just the one word, 'No'.

Lilly stared at the offered page in stunned amazement. 'What does he do?' she said. 'He says one word. I say,' she thumped her own original script with a clenched fist, 'I say fifty, sixty words!'

'He says that 'No' is enough. You will see: in the playing.'

'It is my *polemic*!' Lilly cried furiously. 'He is ruining my argument!'

All this, I hasten to add, was done with the greatest good humour, although any stranger wandering on to our set could well have been excused for thinking that they had walked into a bitter battle in the life of the Borgias; but we knew what we were doing, we all trusted each other implicitly, and on the occasions when Lilly had thought, seriously, that I was wrong and she right, or that even Charlotte was wrong, she had watched the scene played and had come to understand that thoughts on film convey far more than words. And had given in gracefully. If sometimes grumpily.

In this odd manner of working, the only one we had, we came to terms with the script although it was often wearying and always exhausting. But it was, at the same time, exhilarating. I was back in full harness as a creating actor, and I honestly rather liked it.

It was far easier than mowing terraces: and much more stimulating.

After two weeks in the sanatorium, we moved into Cinecittà for a time and then out into the cruel world again. The cruel world was an empty villa built at the beginning of the centrury, which awaited the demolition teams. As soon as we had finished work it would be wrecked.

After a day or two of trying to exist in it, I didn't think this a bad idea at all. There was one working lavatory, with a cold tap for us all. It was arctic cold and damp. We ate, when we got the time to do so, in a small trattoria on a neighbouring corner.

For a dressing-room I had a vast empty room, in which the wallpaper had peeled in ugly strips, and somewhere above a pipe had burst, leaving a great fan of damp fungus on the wall. It was not over-generously furnished, with a chair, a table and a one-bar electric fire.

Charlotte was next door with her months-old child in a Moses basket on the floor, a double-barred fire, and an electric blower heater (which regularly blew up) to heat her freezing infant, and a small divan on which to lie.

All superstar stuff.

But we were happy together; all of us.

There is a strange moment, usually a couple of weeks into a production, when the crew, and everyone else, gets the feeling that what we are all doing is good: better than good, important. From that moment on, any sacrifice is made for the film, willingly.

However depressing the subject-matter of 'The Night Porter' might be, the atmosphere was one of radiant hope and secret excitement. Something quite marvellous and strange was happening on the screen, and we were all responsible. It is a greatly rewarding feeling: and it doesn't occur often enough for one to become over-sure, over-confident. It is too rare.

But, alas, if all looked well on the surface, and even more than well, things below were not so good. We were running out of money daily.

The film story of my life, it seems.

We finished all the work which we had to do in the 'Hotel' (which the hideous house had been transformed into by brilliant designers) at the end of March, and on the last evening of work an exhausted Bob Edwards came up to my freezing room and announced sadly that we had no more money: he had tried, begged, implored for the extra needed to take us to Vienna for the last important segments, to no avail. I could go back to France leaving the film unfinished.

I was so used to this situation (it happened to every film I had made which had been worth the making from 'Darling' to 'Death in Venice') that I accepted it as normal. There really wasn't much else to do. Back to the terraces.

In quiet despair we packed up, with three-quarters of the film finished, the last vital quarter to be shot in Vienna, abandoned. Anyway, for the time being. Charlotte was sitting in her room, humped in a chair, her hands wrapped round a big mug of coffee for warmth. Maria, with a face like granite, was packing up costumes in a corner.

'I mean, what's *happened*?' said Charlotte. 'Why have we run out of money suddenly?'

'Spent the budget, there isn't any more.'

'*How* have we spent the budget, for God's sake! It's been Economy Week every single week since we started. It's a small picture; we aren't making 'Ben Hur'.'

'Well, they won't give us any more. I don't think they like the subject anyway, and so we won't be able to finish it. Basta.'

Charlotte prodded her laughing infant with a loving finger.

'If we don't get the stuff in Vienna there isn't a picture anyway.'

'Perhaps that's what the money gentlemen know. Abandon the thing.'

'They'd do it on purpose? Scrap it all?'

'They've done it before in movies. Edwards says he's off to try elsewhere; he might succeed. He's determined.'

'Money!' said Charlotte. 'God. What they're paying me wouldn't keep a hamster for a week. I just don't see how we *could* have got into this state.'

Maria bundled up a pile of clothing, stamped across the room, opened the door with her foot, slammed it with a kick behind her.

'Everyone is so miserable. We were all so wonderfully happy, so sure, it was a feeling so terrific. Oh well!'

Lilly seemed a great deal less depressed than the rest of us (she possibly knew a little more than the crew or the players did) and smiled away agreeably through cascades of Italian.

'She says,' said Paola, translating carefully, 'that we must not lose faith, we must hold firm, we will fight them to the death and, ultimately, we shall win.'

'She's not on the bloody barricades now!' I said. 'How *can* we finish without any money?'

'Lilly says that when she has cut this film together, and we have a lot already, they will be so excited that someone will give us money, not much, but some. And some, you know, is quite a lot. It is a beautiful picture.'

And so I went off back to France, and Charlotte carried her Moses basket back to London. There wasn't any alternative.

A month later, in April, we were, amazingly, reassembled together in Vienna. Not one member of the crew had left to do another job, all had stayed, loyal and unpaid, so strong was their belief in the film, and waited: just as we had done.

And in pouring rain (not bitter cold this time) we finished the film as intended. Somehow, someone had got some extra money, as Paola had said; not much, very little in fact, but just enough to finish; with nothing left over or extra. So tight, indeed, was the budget for the final week in Austria, that we had a handful of extras only to fill the whole of the Volksoper. No mean task.

But Lilly, with careful camera angles, and by impressing members of the crew who were not immediately engaged, even Forwood, the publicist or the hairdresser, and any odd person who had wandered into the theatre, achieved an atmosphere of an 'All Sold Out' performance from Gallery to Stalls and Boxes.

Working in Vienna, the crucible, once, of Nazism in Austria, in my black SS uniform, was not going to be quite the same as it had been in Rome. Wearing it at all was a provocative thing to do in that particular city, so I spent all my time draped in coats and hid the cap in a box. We were shooting in the streets and it seemed tactful, and wiser, to keep a very low profile.

The night I most dreaded was left until the very last day of shooting. A small shot, but it was to be in the eastern sector, the Workers' Quarter, which was well known for its toughness and also for the monolithic blocks of flats, the Karl Marx Hof, to which people came from all over the world to admire the brilliance and advance of the design.

This was mainly a strong Communist area, one of the crew warned me thoughtfully, full of extremely rough people who would probably lynch me if they saw a swastika, let alone the hated SS uniform. His remark compounded my unease, so I sat wrapped up in a raincoat in a corner bar until the very last moment that I would be needed.

It had been arranged beforehand that I would be smuggled through the crowds, which were already gathering to watch, to a flat on the fourth floor from which Charlotte and I would make an exit, descend the concrete stairway, and so arrive on the street. I would be given a signal to start the action when the cameras were actually rolling so that no time would be lost. In lynching me, I supposed. Charlotte was perfectly all right because she was wearing a simple pink dress and long white socks; nothing provocative in those, except perhaps Charlotte herself.

These elaborate precautions had been taken so that I should have only a very few moments of vulnerability on the pavement below before getting into a car and driving off. Which was all the scene was about. I was terrified.

As the evening wore on, the crowds grew larger, attracted by the blazing arc lamps which lit the front of the monstrous block: children ran about screaming and laughing, clambering about the equipment, dancing in the light. There was a feeling of a circus in the air; and me skulking in the corner bar feeling exactly like a naked clown.

A polite, slightly uneasy, Austrian assistant came to collect me and hurry me through the seething mass outside the flats. We were nearly ready to 'go'. I had the cap well hidden under the raincoat; no one noticed the whip or boots because we were almost unobserved hurrying up the concrete stairs to the flat on the fourth floor, where an old lady, white hair in a knot, braids about her ears, shuffled down her hall to let us in, her face suffused with pleasure because she had been paid handsomely for the use of her apartment for just a few moments, and, as she said to the assistant, she lived all alone and it was much nicer than watching the television.

She smiled at me and 'Grüss Gotted' quite a lot, bobbing her head like a swallowing duck: I was shown her two canaries, a bad colour print of two exceedingly plain women and a very fat man on a mountain who were, she explained, her 'Kinder', and was offered coffee from a metal pot simmering on her spotless stove.

The Austrian assistant was leaning out over the balcony waiting for the signal from below for us to start moving down. Charlotte would be picked up half-way down the stairs. I stood clutching my raincoat about me, and the old lady kept saying that it was 'kalt' this winter, when the signal came to move.

I threw off the raincoat, adjusted my cap and belt, took up my whip, and the old lady gave a loud cry, the coffee pot held in one hand, her other hand to her cheek. Her eyes were wide, watery, pale blue.

She was not shocked. The eyes were surprised: pleased.

She replaced the coffee pot briskly, wiped her hands on her apron and came towards me quickly, speaking as she did so to the assistant. Then, standing before me, she put out her hand and stroked my arm smiling.

The assistant was acutely embarrassed. 'We have to go now, they are ready, but this woman says please to be so kind and shake her hand. She says that this thing . . . ' he indicated the uniform with a slight move of his finger ' . . . remembers her of the good old days. This is how you say in English, I think?'

I agreed and shook her hand. What else do you do?

The signal came up, 'Rolling!'. I left the little flat, the old woman nodding and smiling, hands clasped tightly.

'Camera!'

When Charlotte and I reached the blinding lights in the doorway below, there was a sudden, extraordinary, silence as I stood there in my glittering regalia and high-peaked cap: and then a great gasp of astonishment rose into the still air from a thousand throats.

My heart shamefully thudding, I supported Charlotte and started 'acting' the finding of the car keys. I knew that there were a number of hefty crew members strategically placed around to hustle us away if any trouble broke out — the only member of the police I had seen had been having a beer in the corner bar.

The gasp faded to an intense, excited, silence. I walked Charlotte across the width of the street, got her into the car. Someone started to applaud. A lone sound. Then it grew, others picked it up, it mounted in intensity, there was cheering and somewhere I heard a voice shout 'Sieg Heil!'. Another whipped across the crowd. 'Sieg Heil!' to an enormous roar of laughter and applause. 'Sieg Heil! Sieg Heil! Sieg Heil!'

I got into the car and drove off into the darkness beyond the arc lamps. The crowds were cheering and laughing, applauding. They 'killed' the lights. The laughter and cheers continued. The Sieg Heils rang in my ears.

'Probably a few drunks,' said Charlotte.

'I don't think so.'

'You take things so seriously! But do you *believe* it! It's amazing! They loved it. Just loved it!'

Not the 'acting' alas: the uniform.

Ten months after my father's death, on her own in the house for the first time while Elizabeth and George were lunching locally with friends, my mother drank the contents of every bottle on the drink-table, plus a crate of Light Ale, replaced all the stoppers neatly, and plunged headlong down the staircase which led to her bedroom, breaking almost every bone in her body: except her neck.

At the hospital they regretted that it would take forty-eight hours to 'dry' her out before they could operate.

The shock, which we had all expected, had finally struck her: and her purgatory began.

TEN

A trim, smug, Georgian house surrounded by green lawns still spiked with frost in the shadow it cast, on this brilliant January morning.

In the hall, polished wooden floors; rugs scattered; a brass bowl of dried grasses. Sunlight, the smell of furniture polish and Air-Wick. In a small room to the left, a little bar in a corner. Dubonnet, Cinzano, Booths gin, two bar-stools: a fire crackling.

'Oh yes!' said the matronly woman. 'She's waiting for you: very thrilled. Up the stairs, first landing, then up four more little ones and hers is the first door on the left. Just knock and go in, she'll be so pleased.'

As I started up, she said: 'You'll be four altogether for lunch, right?'

'Right. If it's no trouble?'

'None at all. Your sister, Mrs Goodings, did warn us.'

White paint shining, good quality fitted carpet, cleanliness. Almost, perhaps, a little spartan. I knocked at the door and she said, 'Come in.'

She was sitting on the edge of her bed, dressed, made up, hands folded in her lap. On her feet, heavy black lace-up shoes.

'Well then! Here I am.' I stooped to kiss her, and put the big bunch of daffodils I had brought on a small table.

'Darling, you shouldn't have spent all your money like that.'

'I could have got you some in pots, in bud. But I thought that these would be a bit easier.'

'Much. Lovely. I'll get Mrs . . . I can't remember her name, my mind's gone; anyway I'll ask for a vase. Or vause or vaze.'

I sat in a small chair opposite her.

'How do I look?' she said. A false smile; fingers pulling at the stuff of her skirt.

'You look marvellous! You've had a good rest.'

'You're telling me. Five weeks. And then all that ghastly physiotherapy.'

She had shrunk, she was old. Very sad. The fire had died, leaving nothing but a banked pile of greyish ash.

'It's not bad here, Ma. Really *very* pretty, the house . . . and it seems clean and all the rest.'

'Oh yes.' She brushed her skirt. 'It's clean. Hellish.'

'Oh come on! I mean this is very nice, this room. You've got all your little bits and pieces with you, I see.'

'Bits and pieces. Yes. Elizabeth did that.'

A photograph of my father, a heavy silver presentation cigar-box, a Staffordshire figure in a kilt; odds and ends from the house.

'You've got your Scotsman too.'

'Who?'

'The Staffordshire thing; behind you there.'

She turned without interest. 'Oh that. Bonnie Prince Charlie. Yes, he's here. Poor bugger.'

It was a figure of Macbeth, but we had never told her because she had invented him to be Bonnie Prince Charlie, and so that's how he stayed.

'Well,' she looked at me straight in the eyes, unsmiling. 'How do I look?'

'I really think you look marvellous. And you've done a terrific make-up job. Does it take ages now, I mean to do?' I was floundering.

'Oh yes, I still do my face. God knows why. No one ever comes, so why bother?'

'I've come.'

'That's your answer. Why I did my face.'

'Your hands are all right? I mean, after the fall?'

She looked at them lying in her lap as if someone had retrieved them for her. With vague surprise that she had lost them.

'That terrible fall. God. Yes. Oh yes. The hands are all right. They took my rings away. You see? No rings.'

'Why did they do that?'

She shrugged, looked across the pleasant room to the window. 'Don't know. Knuckles swollen up: something.'

'Well, we'll get them back.'

'Oh no! They won't go on now. My knuckles . . . '

'Ma, you said people didn't come.'

'I said what?'

'People didn't come to see you. But they do. Elizabeth comes every day . . . and Mrs Brown and Miss Smith, I mean people *do* come to see you, darling.'

'Who told you that?'

'Elizabeth. I mean a lot of people have come to see you here.'

'Some do. Some don't. It's too far out of the way. It doesn't matter.'

'Of course it matters! But it's not too far out of the way, Elizabeth is literally ten minutes distance, I mean you're not buried on the moors or something.'

She laughed dryly. 'I'm buried. Your father buried me for years in that cottage. All the way up that bloody hill to the village to catch a bus: then all the way down again when I got back. You don't know what it was like. Where's darling Tony?'

'Gone on to collect Elizabeth, for lunch.'

'Oh lovely! We're going to have lunch together, are we?' Without interest.

'Well, darling, I haven't come all this way just for a quick chat. And I need a drink. I saw a little bar-thing downstairs.'

'It doesn't open until twelve o'clock.'

'Not long to wait.'

'Where have you come from then?'

'Home. In France.'

'Oh yes. Dear France. I'm only allowed one small glass of wine with lunch now.'

'Well, perhaps today we could go one more, celebration?'

'Some celebration. I really look all right, do I?'

'Terrific. A bit of nail varnish perhaps, that super red you always wore.'

'They took it off in the hospital place. I had that terrible fall.'

'I know.'

'And I *have* got varnish on. You can't see it, it's natural.'

We had lost contact. She was shy, nervous, possibly ashamed. Dreading that I should ask her questions which she would be unable to answer, that might perhaps expose her to criticism, to being cautioned. Blamed.

I walked across to the tall Georgian windows and looked down into the gardens. Frost under the shrubbery, a donkey standing dozing in the sun, his breath puffing from his nostrils like a small, fat dragon.

'There's a donkey, did you know?'

'Donkey? Horses too, I see them from the window.'

'Don't you ever go out? You can, can't you?'

'In this weather?'

'No. But you can take a little walk?'

'Oh yes. I can take a little walk. Have to use that thing there. Impossible.'
There was a walking-frame in a corner.

'Well, we'll go out for a bit after lunch if you like. You could lean on my arm,
couldn't you?'

'That terrible fall. No, you go if you want to see the horses. Mrs . . . ' She
stopped, smoothed her hands together. 'I suppose that I've got to stay here for
ever?'

'No, not for ever.' I was lying, and she knew it. 'But it's not a bad place, is it?'

'Too many stairs. I'm terrified of the stairs.'

'Well, perhaps there's another room on the ground floor? I'll ask.'

'No, no. Don't interfere on my account. For God's sake. I'm all right.'

'Look, Ma. The main thing is that you are as happy as we can possibly make
you.'

She cut through my sentence harshly. 'Really you make me laugh! Happy!
Who is *we*, may I ask?'

'Elizabeth, Gareth and me.'

'Well, I'll be happy only when I get back to my own house. Not in this bloody
place.'

The conversation, such as it was, had edged again towards the topic I
dreaded most. Her return home.

There was no possibility that she could now. Without a nurse in constant
attendance; and there was no room in the cottage for a nurse. The blunt fact
was simply that she could no longer be left without supervision. She could not
be trusted, for one second, on her own, and she knew this deep down in her
canny Scottish way. She knew what had happened and why; and she knew
damned well that we, her children, knew.

I had written to the surgeon who had performed some kind of miracle on her
poor shattered body, asking him, in all our names, to explain to her, for we
could not, why she had had to suffer such terrible pain at the very beginning,
and what he had had to do before operating. But he had ignored my request, in
a cold, if polite, manner, and I had obviously made an ethical blunder in
requesting his help.

So it was up to me now, as the eldest, to try and get it over to her that for the
rest of her life she would have to be under constant watch and care. And that
Elizabeth, with a growing family and no help, could no longer cope.

But just at that moment I funked saying it outright: perhaps after lunch; after
a glass of beer or a stiff Scotch. Perhaps.

I pulled a small packet out of my pocket and threw it lightly into her lap.
'What's this?'

'It's so odd about your rings, I know how much you loved them.'

'I loved them.' She took the packet in her hands. 'Ulric lost them.'

'Daddy did?' The childhood word came out easily.

'In France. Somewhere. I had a terrible fall. You remember?'

'I remember, yes, you were staying with me. I've brought you some new
ones.'

She gave a little cry of pleasure for the very first time, her eyes, wide and
sparkling.

'For me? Oh darling, spending all your money on me.'

'Not very expensive; no diamonds.' I started to unwrap the jeweller's packing and tumbled three modest enamelled rings into her cupped hands. 'I just hope they'll fit.'

'My knuckles, you see?' She held them towards me. 'Swollen.'

'We'll try, give me your hand. Which for which finger? The green one on this hand, the red and gold?'

'Not near my wedding ring. Ulric lost that too, you know. It's a new one, this. He bought it for me. I was so sad, so sad.'

We got the rings on easily; she spread her fingers before her face, admiring them.

'I'm so happy! They are heaven! Heaven. You *are* a good boy, where did you get them?'

'In France. Cannes.'

'To tell people, you see. They ask and I like to know.'

'And this. Look! Scent! 'L'Air du Temps' . . . '

She clapped her hands with delight. 'I'm being so spoiled. Flowers, rings and scent.'

'Remember your favourite one? 'N'aimez que moi'? You can't get it any longer, but this is good for you, I think.'

'No, you can't get it. That was before you were born. In Paris. Ulric bought it.'

She was tearing off the bottle wrapping; from somewhere in the house a couple of dull sounds. a muffled gong hammer.

'The bar's open,' she said. 'It's nothing but rules and regulations in this place. I could die.'

I took the scent bottle from her, opened it, poured a little into the palm of her hand, she rubbed it carefully on to her wrists, took the bottle back, put some scent behind each ear, smiled at me, openly, easily, without constraint.

'How do I look? Do I smell all right? I can't smell a thing. Someone, I don't remember who it was, said that scent didn't stay with me, but tell me: all right?'

'You look ravishing and you smell marvellous. It suits you.'

'Time for my glass of wine. It's Spanish, but I like it.' She put out an arm. 'Help your old Ma. God! These good-woman shoes. But I feel safer in them, and anyway no one ever sees me. No one comes.'

We went out on to the landing; suddenly she stopped. 'My flowers! Put them in the washbasin in my room.'

'I'll take them down and ask for a vase.'

'No, no! It'll cause a fuss. The woman gets fussy just before serving lunch. Do as I say, fill the washbasin and stick them in there. I'll do them afterwards.' She followed me back into her room.

'When you've gone away,' she said.

A high-ceilinged room, sunlit. Tables round the walls, one or two in the centre, mostly single people. Perfectly silent except for a muted symphony of cutlery and the chink of china, a soft murmur now and again of conversation.

On each table a tin biscuit-box, little clusters of pill-bottles; when someone had finished eating they would play nervously with their napkin rings, turning them endlessly in a shrivelled hand, chewing thoughtfully, awaiting the next course served by a girl in a floral pinafore.

Our table was set well away from the main body of the room, in a window, 'so that you can be a bit private', the matronly woman had said. The sun lanced across the polished oak table, the dainty place mats, Views of Olde London, a small pot of daffodil heads in the centre. It was all very dainty.

'I wish they wouldn't do that,' said my mother.

'Do what?' said Elizabeth.

'These daffodils. Just their flowers stuck in a pot.'

'Heads, you mean?'

'I mean flowers. Heads. I don't know. But they should be long, lovely. Dirk brought me a huge bunch.'

'Well: they'd be too tall on a lunch-table, wouldn't they?'

'You think so?' She looked away across the room, humming under her breath, a habit she had when she no longer wished to pursue the conversation.

'I love your rings, terribly pretty.' Elizabeth crumbled a piece of bread.

'From France,' said my mother. 'He's a good boy to me.' The inference being that no one else was.

Forwood collected his glass with mine. 'I think I'd like another; Maggie dear?'

My mother turned suddenly, questioningly, as if she had been mentally miles away, another trick she had of pretending, or choosing, not to have heard the question.

'Another little glass of wine? I think we can swing two today, don't you? A sort of celebration,' he said.

She agreed, holding out her glass. 'The girl will come if you can get her: you aren't allowed in the bar during meals. Strictly forbidden. I don't know why.'

While Forwood was catching the eye of the girl in the floral pinafore and ordering the drinks, Elizabeth dragged her fork across the ugly plastic place-mat before her.

'When do you go back? To France, I mean?'

'Saturday.'

'Just a quick In and Out then?'

'To see Ma, and I had a blood test. It's clear; but I haven't been feeling absolutely terrific.'

'You look a bit thin: gaunt. You all right?' There was concern in her eyes; she still prodded the beastly table-mat.

'Fine. I have to go steady on the drink. No, I'm fine. And I wanted to buy a hand-fork and a trowel. Can't get them in France for some reason. Good wooden-handled ones.'

'What sort of a trowel?' My mother returned from wherever she had decided to go mentally.

'Just an ordinary garden trowel; with a wooden handle.'

'Extraordinary thing to come all this way for,' she said.

Two women in floral pinafores arrived, one with the drinks, the other with a tin tray and four plates.

'Roast lamb?' she said, waving the plate unsteadily.

My mother offered her wrist to Forwood. 'Can you smell me?'

He bent his head to her wrist. 'Yes, I can. It suits you.'

'Dirk brought it for me. From France.' She put her wrist across the table to Elizabeth. 'Can you smell it? I can't smell a thing.'

'Lovely, it's flowery; hyacinths, jasmin . . . '

My mother sniffed her own wrist. 'Floral scents aren't really me. I'm better with something heavier. I can't smell a thing.' She started to eat her roast lamb. 'Can't chew anything either. I'm a dead loss. That awful fall I had . . . '

'Well, anyway,' said Elizabeth, 'you look marvellous today.' And appealing to me she said, 'Doesn't she? Marvellous. Your lamb all right, Ma?'

'Yes. All right. I don't know why I bother: no one ever sees me. Who cares?'

We drove Elizabeth home through once-familiar lanes very little altered. A new house here, a copse grown thicker there; the land smiling, sharp, clear in the cold sunlight, the cottage (which I had always privately hated ever since my father had bought it as a row of three semi-derelict cottages set in the middle of the common, beetle-browed, sagging-roofed, viewless) shining with fresh white paint.

'Did you get a shock? Seeing her? She's had a terrible time.' Elizabeth was opening up the house.

'A bit. She's different. Of course. God knows how you've coped.'

'I'm glad *someone* does. Tea? Or too early?'

'Love a cup,' said Forwood.

'The thing is, she's convalescing, and getting grumpy. Quite normal, but a bit hard to deal with every day. And people have been wonderfully good about, you know, going over to see her. She was popular with people. Her friends and Daddy's here. Mind you,' she switched on the electric kettle, 'I know that they think that George and I have just moved in and packed her off to a home. She tells them so. It's jolly hard.'

'I know that. I, even, have had letters saying the same thing. In France, from the Old Brigade. I know,' I said.

'It's been damned difficult. And it's just not true. I suppose that you didn't say anything to her? About not coming back. About needing supervision and so on.'

'No. I couldn't. I mean, how could I? I'd just arrived there: but I think that she knows, deep down inside, I am sure she does. She's not a fool, whatever else she is. She knows.'

Elizabeth was setting cups on a tray. 'Can't find the sugar bowl. Can't find anything today.'

I looked round the pretty sitting-room. She had made a lot of changes: the heavy oak and plum velvet which my father strangely liked had gone, the walls were white and no longer dull cream, the thick curtains removed, light streamed in.

'It's much better, darling; what you and George have done, it's all opened up, looks much bigger, lighter, cheerful.'

Elizabeth came in with the teapot. 'She hates it. Naturally, I suppose. Every time I bring her over, once a week for lunch, she puts things back where she liked them. She keeps on calling it her house and it's not! George paid a proper price. If it wasn't for that she wouldn't be where she is, and warm and comfortable, even if it is a bit awful and prissy, but she couldn't afford it otherwise. And the hospital! I mean, really, it is no joke to be ill today, National Health or not. She doesn't really understand all that, you see: Daddy took care of the money; what there was of it. You can't tell her about the decimal point, or how much a pack of cigarettes costs. She just says she doesn't understand.'

'I'm afraid that Pa did her no good by taking over as he did.'

'Had to,' said Elizabeth, offering a tin of biscuits. 'No alternative. It started with that first 'little fall' when she broke her wrist, remember? And just went on from there. I know she *hates* where she is, but what else can we do?'

'Nothing. You've done enough. You've been a saint: both of you have, and I think she'll be better off in her new room. It's on the ground floor, no stairs, which she dreads.'

'You know it wasn't the first fall she had down these bloody stairs. It was the fifth, my dear. We just daren't risk it; I couldn't leave her here even to nip up to the village for a bottle of milk. You can't turn your back.'

'Well, Mrs Whatevershe's called was very pleasant, and the room downstairs is vacant so she can move in, or you can move her in, whenever you like.'

'It'll cost a bit.' Elizabeth poured herself another cup of tea. 'There's nothing to spare.'

'Well, we'll manage that somehow.'

'It might be a good idea,' said Forwood, 'if you got some of her personal stuff over there, her dressing-table, so on.'

'That's just what *I* thought,' said Elizabeth. 'George can take things over in the van, anything she wants. Pictures, china, things to make her feel that she's in a little flat and not in a hotel. I mean it *is* an hotel, you know? It's not a home, as she keeps telling everyone: she really is awful about that, but I suppose I do see what she means.'

'I just funked telling her the truth, which she knows anyway,' I said. 'Maybe when she starts to pick out the bits and pieces she wants for her 'flat' she'll realise it's for good. It's a dreadfully shabby way of saying it, *not* saying it, I mean; but I think it's the best way. She'll take it in gradually. To tell her right out would break her.'

'She's pretty tough,' said Elizabeth.

'Not as tough as that,' I said. 'I honestly think that she has given up for good. She's started to die.'

With 'The Night Porter' finally finished and ready to show, Bob Edwards flew off to California, as Visconti had done before, rather like a commercial traveller with a product to sell. The product, he felt, was pretty good: the few people who had seen it at private screenings had been enormously enthusiastic, and he felt we had a reasonable chance of making an acceptable deal.

He was wrong.

The reaction from the major company executives was one of stunned incomprehension; followed by charges of 'offensiveness', an 'insult to the Jewish faith' (although there was absolutely no Jewish connection anywhere in the context of the film), and 'obscenity'. Warner Bros, refreshingly, found it 'dull and uninteresting'.

I thought that 'obscenity' might perhaps have interested them, because obscenity always makes money, but this time they stuck to 'incomprehensible'; and that was that.

Of course what they had entirely failed to understand was all Lilly's bitter anti-Fascist 'polemic' and argument, and so they had just concentrated on the Love Story, and found it appalling, and the idea that a woman could fall in love with her gaoler completely unacceptable.

A brief cable from Bob said that the audiences at the screenings had been 'very enthusiastic' but that the executives remained . . . 'uncomprehending'. He wished me a Merry Christmas.

The New Year brought a ray of hope: if the Californians had loathed it the French had liked it; and what was more important, understood the political background as much as the romantic attachment. There was a very good chance that we would open the film in France before anywhere else.

The French, and the Italians, had been through the hideous and humiliating process of Occupation, and they knew very well the strange relationship which can, and did, exist between captive and conqueror. They were much closer to the facts. America was a long way off and no one had invaded them since Columbus, Cabot and Amerigo Vespucci. Who didn't linger there anyway. The millions who followed in their paths were of no consequence; except perhaps to the unfortunate Indians whose land it once had been.

However, there it was. We might have gained a foothold in the European

Market with France, but it was obvious that we had lost America. A serious blow.

One night there was a call from Los Angeles: Deena, an old and trusted writer friend who got herself about the town, and missed out on nothing.

"Happy New Year! I've seen your movie, at a private screening. And wow!'

'What do you mean, wow?'

'Well, it's strong stuff. I didn't know you were into soft porn, honey!'

'Soft porn? Deena!'

'Well, it sure as hell isn't Goldilocks.'

'Not supposed to be: and I gather we've bombed with the majors?'

'You'll sure as hell never do a deal with them; anti-Jewish, and *black*, *black*, *black*.'

'It isn't anti-Jewish. There isn't one frame in which a Jew appears or a Jew is mentioned. It's anti-Fascist, I give you that, but not anti-anything else.'

'That's what it looks like from here. You know in L.A. it is considered the Jew's prerogative to die in a concentration camp. It's stuck fast. You can't make them listen to anti-Fascist speeches with all that sex and stuff going on, and the lovey-dovey stuff, in a *camp*! Be reasonable!'

'There is hardly any stuff *in* the camp. It's afterwards that counts, the present.'

'Listen, the audience loved it, don't ask me why. I loved it, no, not loved it, I was shattered; but I've been around a bit, and you know some of it is a little melodramatic.'

'Where?'

There was a crackle of silence for a moment.

'Well, I can't really remember now; the speech on the cathedral roof in Vienna? I mean, that's going too far . . .'

'You mean the 'I'm proud I did what I did, and I'd do it all again, Heil Hitler' piece?'

'Exactly. Now come *on*.'

'We took it from the Austrian newspapers that very morning. It's from Eichmann's speech for the defence at his trial in Israel. Verbatim.'

Another crackle.

'Perhaps you should have put in sub-titles. I didn't know.'

'Well, we've made a deal with the French anyway: that's something.'

'Oh the French! All that sex, naturally. *Amour*.'

'Nothing to do with sex. With the Occupation, they know all about that.'

'Listen, I just called to say Happy New Year! I was shattered by the movie, and I am sorry you won't make a deal this side. No way. Not even with the soft-porn stuff.'

'There *is* no soft-porn stuff! It's all in the mind of the beholder, Deena.'

'Sure is, and you give them an eyeful. This call is costing me the earth.'

I wandered about the long room in despair. Soft porn? Sex and melodrama? Had I perhaps, and it was entirely possible, lost my head? Been away from the cinema for too long, not caught up on the current trends, made a mess of clipping the literal translation under Lilly's beady eye? Had we all really been having a happy time of self-indulgence? Been offensive? I couldn't answer the questions.

Perhaps the bucolic life I was enjoying had blunted my senses. I'd been out of touch for too long, lost my way as an actor; not just my sense of order. It was frighteningly possible that I had become like some of our kind in the profession who get stuck in the rut of self-satisfaction. Certain that they are right and that things are as they have always been, allowing no possible time for change, unaware that they are quietly, but deliberately, being moved from centre stage towards the Exit sign by younger, more dynamic and inventive players. I had seen it happen often enough. Had it now happened to me, all unawares?

Well: if it had, it would be better to pull out right away, draw a veil over the whole sorry mess, before I started shuffling off into playing cameo roles, or worse, featured bits, in a nightdress on some dusty location in Spain in 'inspirational' epics about the Holy Family.

Scripts of this sort had started to arrive in the tin mail-box at the end of the track, overtaking the Spy Thrillers and the Schoolmasters.

I'd better get out, and try and find something else to do. Laying my metaphorical eggs had been a disaster. They had got scrambled.

But, before I made such a definitive move, such a crippling move, indeed, I knew that I must have advice. I had no intention of trusting the verdict of the major company executives; they never knew anyway. Forwood was probably too close; I had lost my confidence and could no longer judge.

Someone absolutely independent, unbiased, must have a look at the film and tell me that I was wrong and should pack it in, or that I was right after all and should fight for it. A tough assignment, but I had an idea how to go about it.

Bob arrived back from California tired, dispirited, very downcast. I called him in Rome and suggested an unethical and dangerous plan. We should have a private screening in London for four or five selected critics whose only job would be to pass a verdict on the film. It would be secretly arranged, no one would know beyond those invited, and all they had to do was to write to me, as the instigator of the scheme if it came off, and say exactly what they thought. Under no circumstances would they be asked to review the film because, technically, the film was *not* a film (as no one had bought it) and it was not mine to show anyway. It belonged, as it stood, to the company in Italy who had made it; to write about it could have serious consequences for me.

Although their verdict would not be law, it would however be an invaluable indication of where we or, more to the point, *I* had gone wrong. After all, it was I who tuned into that television and re-started the wretched project.

Bob agreed. He was so weary, so disillusioned, and it seemed a reasonable idea, if unethical. However, he said, he was on his way to London immediately with the film anyway because Columbia wanted to have another look at it; just to make sure.

I chose four critics, three of whom had known me since my earliest days at Rank, and all of whom had consistently influenced and encouraged my career. These seemed to me the best people to give me a clear-eyed verdict. They were Dilys Powell of *The Sunday Times*, Margaret Hinxman, then of *The Sunday Telegraph*, Felix Barker of *The Evening News* and Alexander Walker of *The Evening Standard*.

Knowing them as I did, I was certain that they would be unbiased, honest, and certainly pull no punches, however devastating their verdicts might be. They were, above all things, devoted to their craft and to the cinema. As well as being highly professional people.

I would not be present, for that would be inhibiting, so I arranged with Theo Cowan, who had looked after all my publicity through the Rank years, and since, and who was a highly respected figure in the industry, to take charge for me. He started to work immediately. We had four days in which to set the whole thing up, for Bob could not keep the film out of Italy for very much longer.

To my relief, all my guests accepted, even at such short notice. Theo suggested, quite rightly, that four people sitting by themselves in an otherwise empty projection theatre would be pretty soulless. Projection theatres are at the best of times, and this was the worst of times. So he arranged to invite a handful of my friends to furnish the place, people who could be counted on not to talk, and to keep the whole affair quiet; he also added a small bar for a glass of wine at the end of the showing.

I felt extremely nervous. I had never done anything as underhand as this in my life, and I was very well aware that there is always a risk in doing something unorthodox in secret: somewhere along the line, there could be a disaster.

My heart lifted when Theo telephoned to say that the evening had been a minor triumph. People had been held in complete silence throughout the film, and had lingered a long time over their wine, discussing and talking about it: a very important sign. No one had actually sprinted from the building, no one had hissed or booed, although, he warned me, it was clear that Mr Walker had not liked the film at all. But that, I felt, was perfectly reasonable. Not everyone would. And after the general reaction from Los Angeles, the atmosphere at this special, private, showing was enormously encouraging. Perhaps the film would have a fighting chance after all? Maybe the three years which I had spent away from the screen had not, after all, impaired my work or my judgement?

All I could do now was wait, as patiently as possible, for the verdicts. They were bound to write in a day or so, and as the mail took so long, it would be at least a week before I would know anything. But six days later Theo telephoned to say that two of my guests, to my consternation, had gone into print and reviewed the film. While Mr Walker had slammed us with a scathing attack spread across two pages, Mr Barker, on the other hand, had been extra-ordinarily generous.

It was, of course, perfectly possible that the exceptionally private and sensitive nature of the screening had not been fully explained that evening. There very well might have been some 'human omission', so to speak, in the hustle of getting everything organized at such short notice. I do not know. In which case Mr Walker and Mr Barker were perfectly justified in going into print, and it was abundantly clear that the latter had done everything he could to draw attention to the fact that the film, in his opinion 'of extraordinary quality, terrifying but compulsive', was without a buyer. He had championed us in every way possible. But the fat was in the fire: the secret was out.

Meanwhile Columbia had rejected the enthusiastic recommendations of its London office, and turned the film down flat, and, in some dismay, Miss Powell and Miss Hinxman had no alternative but to follow their companions' lead and go into print themselves on the following Sunday, with the result that 'The Night Porter' was, to all intents and purposes, reviewed without having been sold to anyone, anywhere.

In contrast to Mr Walker's two-page spread of distaste and ridicule, the other reports (for, rightly, they stopped short of giving the film full reviews) were greatly comforting. Miss Powell praised both the film and the playing; Miss Hinxman compared Charlotte to Garbo; and Mr Barker proclaimed it, in a large headline, as 'The Classic You May Never See'.

Well, so much for that. Vindication. Four highly experienced critics had passed verdict on us publicly, and the verdict, of three of them, was favourable. Not a bad ratio.

Naturally there were distressing repercussions to my clumsy effort to save the film, or at least obtain a balanced judgement on it. As I had suspected, there was anger and disappointment from some of the critics who had not been privy to the event; but my almost abject letters of apology and explanation to them of the entire affair were handsomely accepted. A very unhappy experience, however. Very unorderly, and entirely my own fault.

This unexpected flurry of interest had other repercussions. The Americans immediately re-summonsed the film for another look; the London reviews could hardly be ignored. France made a definite deal, and the film, after all the months of trial and tribulation, opened in Paris in March to vast box-office business, even though the President, Georges Pompidou, died on the day we opened.

However, we had 'arrived', and in thirteen days in Paris 98,000 people went to see our scorned effort, and the readers of *Elle*, one of the most influential women's magazines in Europe, voted it the Film of the Month. As their ages ranged from sixteen to seventy, I felt that this must be a good sign: if you have the women behind you it is difficult to fail. The rest of the press was, generally, highly favourable, and the only bashing we really got was, predictably, from the *Herald Tribune* which was a certain indication of how we should be received in America if we ever got there.

So there we were.

For a while only: a few days after our triumphant success in Paris, the Italian censor banned the film in Italy. Lilly hit the roof and immediately went into battle. This was her affair, in her own country; there was nothing I could, or would, do to meddle further. She fought hard and won, in the meantime causing a tremendous scandal in the press, which was extremely useful publicity anyway, and with all the Women's Liberation groups behind her she stormed to glory, and the film finally opened in Italy in the major cities to unanimous press support and packed houses everywhere.

It closed the following day when all the prints were sequestered by the police.

Back to square one: even a 48-hour strike by the entire Italian film industry who had come out in sympathy with her, failed to budge the Police Chief from his verdict. Obscene.

And that, I thought to myself, is bloody well that. No more cinema, no more struggle and strife: I'd have to find something else to do to earn a living; this was just too much, and I was weary with the stresses and strains. Acting posed little, or no, problem, and could be greatly enjoyable. But all this clatter and banging was nothing to do with acting. It was politics, and I have always abhorred them.

'I'm not fighting anymore,' I said. 'You'll have to get your eggs elsewhere. I've got to try and do something else.'

'What'll you do?' asked Forwood reasonably. 'You can't do anything else.'

'I don't know. I really don't know. The only other thing I have been trained to do is be a soldier. Or paint, and I'm no good at that.'

'You wouldn't contemplate joining up again, would you? You're over-age now, and I honestly don't think you'd like it.'

'I have to find another way to earn a living. Have to.'

'Tough at your age.'

'Practically impossible, but this business is strictly for lunatics.'

That evening, Charlotte telephoned from Milan to say that she, Lilly and I were to be prosecuted by the Milan courts. For obscenity.

And that, I thought, really *is* that. I'm leaving. Order remained: but it was slightly pear-shaped. The frame had buckled.

I realised, perfectly well, that I had brought the whole thing on myself from the instant that I had fiddled with the neglected Television: that was my fault altogether, but what I could not come to terms with was the fact that after years and years of playing those wholesome, jolly, rollicking doctors, stiff-lipped soldiers, soul-eyed lovers who never, it seemed, got to bed with anyone and actually made it, I'd be summoned to a Court on charges of obscenity.

'But what in the name of heaven did we do that is obscene!' I said to Charlotte. 'I mean, we never undid a button, untied a bootlace . . . '

'Apparently it's what we did *without* undoing shoelaces and buttons that has made them all so up-tight. God knows why. Don't ask me.'

'But it's absolutely potty! We didn't do anything obscene! If Lilly had made us roll about naked on double beds, or if she'd used some of the archive pictures like the one of the people being hanged with a full orchestra playing the overture to the 'Magic Flute' behind them, I *could* understand. But she didn't; we didn't do anything remotely like that. I suppose it's a question of defining obscenity and a work of art? I mean, like Joyce, Lawrence, Epstein, hundreds of others. I mean, look at the lists throughout history.'

'*You* look at them, love,' said Charlotte. 'I'm leaving Milan tonight; just thought you'd like to know the latest news. Lilly is on her way to Cannes for the Festival, and Bob is in America again. Stay where you are; keep a low profile, my darling.'

Her advice seemed sound to me; but Lilly raged back into battle. Again, to tremendous publicity and championed everywhere, fought bravely, fiercely, and in the end victoriously. For the final outcome was that the Judge in Milan's High Court, the most powerful in Italy, pronounced 'The Night Porter' to be 'a work of art', and that meant that no one could lay a finger on it under any circumstances. We were saved at last.

But the relief was still soured by the bitterness of the whole silly business. Underlying all the banning and sequestering lay a distressing knowledge that, once again, politics had played a major, if not total, part in the scheme of things. The film was vehemently anti-Fascist and that, *not* obscenity, was what had caused the trouble.

Interested parties, and there were and are still a great number in Italy, had done all that they could to suppress the film, using the tritest excuse, as far removed from the real facts as possible. You cannot alter an entire nation's political belief overnight just by hanging its Dictator from a petrol pump. People slip into the shadows and wait. Lilly's attack on their beliefs had encouraged some of them back into action; but they had, fortunately, been foiled. For the time being at least.

She arrived here one evening, bright-eyed, victorious, bursting with ideas for her next effort, bringing with her an ecstatic review of the film by Edward Behr in *Newsweek*, which almost, but not quite, went to our heads, and the day before Visconti had telephone me to say that he agreed with the Milan Judge that the film *was* 'a masterpiece' and that we must go on fighting to get it shown in America and England.

But my heart had left the battlefield long since. I had had enough.

Down in the *potager*, wrenching about at the roots of a rosemary bush which had outgrown both its plot and itself, I realised that I had done the very same thing: outgrown the cinema and my place in it. However, if it *was* really the only way that I could earn a living then I'd have to try and adapt my feelings and plod on; but I was absolutely determined, after this experience, to wait until Disney made me an offer to play opposite a baby elephant, a pack of cuddly puppy dogs, or even a herd of bloody Bambi's. I'd even accept Mr Darling in 'Peter Pan'.

I was quite unaware that at that exact moment Forwood was starting negotiations for me to make a film in Austria. Playing, once again, Mr Philby. Or, anyway, 'a kind of Mr Philby'.

Some people never give up.

The happy furore which we had made in Europe, obscenity cases, vast publicity, law cases, police sequestration, and all the rest of it, finally crossed the Atlantic. The major company executives were still terrified of it, afraid of insulting a large part of the population and alienating their Jewish audiences, equally aware that there was the smell of profit around, but too frightened, in the final event, of losing their own heads. Heads roll faster, and more frequently, in Hollywood than they ever did in the French Revolution. So while they dithered and fretted, the film was sold under their noses to a gentleman called Joe Levine who was an old hand at picking up 'difficult' subjects.

I knew Mr Levine fairly well. He had originally made a fortune from a minor Italian film starring an American bodybuilder, and never looked back; came in at the eleventh hour and salvaged a sinking 'Darling . . . ' which netted him a lot more loot, and had since become a very rich and powerful operator.

We met from time to time at various functions in New York and London and, when he remembered who I was, he always promised to make me a World Star. But never quite got around to it. My face, apparently, didn't 'stick' with him. But he was always affable and did greatly entertaining tricks with dollar bills and dimes, for in his earlier days he had been a successful conjuror. It seemed to me that he was the ideal man to sell 'The Night Porter' in the States. He was known for his lavish publicity campaigns and could have sold sand to a bedouin.

Lilly and Charlotte were flown out in great style to New York to assist him. I was not invited because once again, I think, he had forgotten my face. But I was perfectly happy to remain where I was, well out of things. I'd done all I could at my end to support the film; now it was over to them.

They settled down to enormous publicity and a disastrous press led by a more than usually loathing Pauline Kael and a review in the *New York Times* which for savagery could have felled the Empire State Building with its blows.

But the public flocked to the cinema. Which made Bob, who had also gone out, so happy that he sent constant cables to tell me how many records we were breaking. Apparently daily.

Charlotte and Lilly were bruised but brave, and Charlotte only gave up when she discovered that the press receptions to which she was invited were jammed with Girlie magazines and coaxing photographers, whereupon she silently fled, after two days of humiliation, and was not heard of again.

Lilly, bemused, battered, a stranger in a strange city, found herself not very much in demand for interviews, for once the press have failed you in New York no one is anxious to meet you. Failure is contagious. So one doesn't touch for fear of contamination. No matter that the film was a raging success at the Box Office and that Mr Levine was smiling broadly, the Nero's of the press had given the thumbs down sign, and so Lilly too fled away.

Mr Levine, faced with the loss of his two main attractions, instantly remembered my face and insisted that I should fly out at once to fill the gaps.

'What happened to Charlotte and Lilly?' I asked.

'They just took off! I don't know why and we don't know where, and I've got a great campaign going! We're the hit of New York, and you gotta *get* here.'

Prudently, I called a journalist friend in New York. She was to the point.

'Don't budge. Stay just where you are. The press have belted the movie, it's a press disaster, and a terrific box-office success. If you got here now no journalist would give you a quarter inch. It's a damned shame because it's been sold as a porno-movie, and there's as much porn in it as there are snowflakes in Hades, and what's more it's good. It's really a *great* movie. But the damage has been done.'

Apparently the Press Show Luncheon was fairly odd. Tables draped in black vinyl, chains across every chair, black candles and book matches covered in fake leather embossed with boots and whips. A veritable sado-masochistic feast. Oh well . . .

However, despite the trials and tribulations which we had all endured in order to get 'The Night Porter' on to the screen, the struggles had been well worth it in the end. It made Charlotte a major star, confirmed Lilly as a director of great force and originality, and is now no longer considered as just a titillating piece of pornography but, as we had all hoped, a major film which is still being shown to this day.

If I hadn't tuned in, by sheer chance, to 'Galileo', gone down to the cellar to look among the slithery pile of slug-trailed scripts, if Lilly had lacked courage, if Charlotte had said 'No' . . . all ifs. Life is full of ifs: I suppose it's part of the fun.

I traced Lilly eventually to Rome and explained that I would not be going to New York. She pleaded that I must go and 'fight for the film, for its honour', but I read her two of the reviews which had come in the morning mail and reduced her to helpless weeping. With reviews like these there was nothing to fight for; except one's sanity.

London, a couple of weeks later, was not really very much better although we managed to do without the vinyl tablecloths and whips or chains, and the press were treated to a spectacularly lavish luncheon and a speech by Mr Levine in which he assured them all that very soon they would see, running about the 'streets of London Town', a fleet of motorbuses, one of which would bear his name, another that of his wife, one his children's, and one the name of his 'brand new grandchild'. These buses were going to take 'the poor little blind kiddies of London Town' to the seaside for a happy day.

None of us present was absolutely certain just what this gesture of quite astonishing generosity had to do with 'The Night Porter', and it didn't exactly bring forth a burst of thunderous applause from the weary press. Neither did the film the next day. Notices were mixed. Some excellent, some disaster.

However, at the luncheon, Lilly, lost in a babble of American and English spoken too rapidly for her to comprehend, buried behind, and under, vast floral arrangements, and choked by the smoke from eight-inch cigars, assumed cheerfully that all was well. Realizing her error the next morning when she had the newspapers read to her, she packed her bags and quietly returned to Rome, leaving me to do my final chore for the film before I, too, went into retreat.

I suppose that of all the things which I have been required to do as an actor, the television chat show has always been the worst. And I've had to do a number in the course of my career.

Banal, facetious, ill-lit and as mentally stimulating as the information on the back of a cigarette card, they are, however, apparently essential as a method of plugging whatever it is you have to sell. Or so I am always assured.

I was once flown out to New York especially to take part in a Johnny Carson show to plug a long-forgotten (and never-to-be-remembered) film. It was considered a tremendous 'scoop', and I dutifully went. Mr Carson, with an apricot face, a shiny blue suit of synthetic fabric, and small, darting eyes, received an hysterical reception from an audience composed entirely of US Marines on leave, and introduced his guests.

Miss Zsa Zsa Gabor adrift in chiffon and diamonds, myself, and a pleasant gentleman who knew all there was to know about chimpanzees.

Mr Carson got my name wrong, shook hands vaguely, pointed to a chair in which I might sit, and had a brief conversation with the chimpanzee expert who had, unfortunately, brought a live specimen of the breed along with him; which Mr Carson instantly gave me to hold for the entire programme, while he concentrated his confident charm lavishly on Miss Gabor. They had a ball together. So did the US Marines.

But if you had stooped to pick up a hairpin you'd have missed me; I can't believe that it helped the film, I don't remember that anyone mentioned its name, and I couldn't believe that a chat show could sell anything; apart from the interviewer's ego.

Russell Harty, I was assured, was not at all like that. He was different from all the others, had been to university, was intelligent, sharp, and no fool. I'd like him. I did.

We had a congenial luncheon at the Connaught, during which I did all the talking, leaving him little chance to open his mouth, apart from forking a mouthful of Sole Véronique into it, or sipping his Chablis. This was less rudeness on my part than incipient hysteria.

I had been giving interviews for five days solid. Eight to ten a day sometimes, and although I was much moved by the warmth and kindness which I received from all those who came to talk to me, I grew progressively more exhausted, haggard, and hoarse, and feared that I must soon be reaching the edge of lunacy.

Conscious that this luncheon, and the show which had to follow it later in the evening, would be the last effort I would have to make for 'The Night Porter', that the next day I would be on my way home to France, and that my host was sympathetic and interested, I relaxed: found a second wind, and chattered away like a demented parrot. Mr Harty gave no signs of minding. He listened courteously, even attentively, while I rattled away like an electric typewriter about everything from Hollywood to Belsen; with digressions in between. At the end of the meal he said that he would scrap his arranged programme for that evening and allow me to have the entire fifty minutes to myself on condition that I repeated the same dazzling virtuoso performance which he had just been forced to endure. To the letter. I accepted from sheer exhaustion.

It was, as it happened, a great deal more fun than sitting slumped behind Miss Gabor with an incontinent chimpanzee in my lap.

Mrs Norah Smallwood, a weekend guest of friends in the country, happened to switch on Mr Harty's programme. And stayed to watch.

My second 'needlewoman' had arrived.

ELEVEN

The mail strike which France had endured for seven long weeks finally ended; without having done anyone very much good, or harm; and every morning an exhausted postman trailed up the track to the house bearing bundles of accumulated letters bound in lengths of rope more suited to a hangman.

Personal mail was easily set aside by the particular 'code' I use, and then there were scurries of fan letters from Japan (where, it seemed, the young were taking 'A Tale of Two Cities' for their English exams, but had ducked reading the book and caught the movie version, which I had made in 1958, instead), appeals from earnest Reverends for the roofs of their churches or gifts for their tombola stalls, early Christmas cards and, naturally, bills.

Among the litter of Robins-in-the-Snow, stage-coaches and 'Snoopy' Santa Clauses, the ever-arriving bills and the fan mail ('I have seen every film you have ever made, and I love you. Please send me your photograph. Sandra. Age 10'), I one morning came across a letter addressed to me at the Connaught Hotel in London, and sent on by them. As it bore the 'code' and was therefore Personal, dated November 1st which made it just over a month old, for the date was now December 6th, I thought that I should open it before settling down to the Tombola Stalls and the anguished letters from Kyoto and Yokahama.

It was from a publisher. Chatto and Windus. Brief, ten lines in all. But ten interesting lines. It read, in part, as follows:

'*Dear Mr Bogarde,*
Several of us here saw your television appearance last week and were most impressed. Have you ever considered writing about your life? If so, on the strength of having heard you speak the other night, we have no hesitation in saying that we would be delighted to publish it . . . If the idea appeals to you at all . . . we should welcome an opportunity of discussing it in greater detail.'

It was signed in a generous, but firmly upright, hand: John Charlton. '*No hesitation in saying that we would be delighted to publish it.*'

That was fairly amazing! No one had said, or written, anything like that to me ever before: it was not something to take lightly. Pretty impressive. And Chatto and Windus themselves, I knew, were pretty impressive also.

But had they, perhaps, taken leave of their senses? Together with The Hogarth Press, their list of writers was formidable: Aldous Huxley, Henry Green, Virginia Woolf, Isaiah Berlin, Iris Murdoch, and even, I remembered, Freud, among others. Not to mention M. Proust himself.

There must be something wrong here. What on earth was a firm of such exalted reputation and grandeur doing making overtures, for that is surely what it was, to a film star? Perhaps they were going bust? It was always possible. And who was this upright fellow Charlton?

I took a look at the list of directors on the letter-heading, and yes indeed, there was a J. F. Charlton. I had been written to, not by a literary tout, but by one of the directors no less.

There were five of them; all with initials save one who declared proudly, with her full name, that she was female. The rest I assumed to be male. One of them had a slightly Alpine flavour, but the rest were unmistakably English in every way: Parsons, Smallwood, Trevelyan and Charlton.

Safe-sounding names. To be trusted absolutely. Like a list of bishops. Could anything be more sober and reliable?

But did bishops ever watch television? Did they know anything remotely about film stars? It seemed to me unlikely: but here was the letter of proof in my hand, that one had written, and that 'several of us here' had indeed seen television. Now Chatto and Windus were not merely Tom, Dick and Harry in publishing. They were far above the rubies.

I had lunched with many a Tom and a Dick, and not a few Harrys in my time: bland, charming, manicured, perfectly tailored, they would chat away happily over oysters and chicken pie, or roast beef and bread-and-butter pudding at the Connaught, and not come down to business until we had reached the coffee and liqueurs.

What would I say to writing my memoirs? Eh? After all, Brigitte Bardot, Ava

Gardner, Judy Garland; what? It was unfailing. And unfailingly tedious. 'A book about your film life . . . so *much* to tell, such a tremendous innings . . . so many *glamorous* people.'

There were one or two alternative suggestions, on occasions, that I should only write a little book about my craft. As if I were a weaver or potter, or beat pewter into bracelets. Educational stuff.

The problem was that I didn't know much about my 'craft', as they insisted on calling it, because being mainly an instinctive actor I didn't go by any absolute set of rules, preferring to make them up for myself as I went along. I could no more have set these down on paper, like the instructions on the back of a seed packet, than swim the channel, because I couldn't explain them even to myself. And if I couldn't do that, then how on earth could I write them down for a clamouring horde of hungry-to-be actors who wanted to know all?

Impossible.

'Nonsense!' cried the educational Toms and Dicks and Harrys, and immediately tried to prove how easy it was by sending me slim books written by distinguished players who had already done it before. It was always perfectly clear to me, after about two pages in, that they had been spoken to a tape recorder and had as much life as a smoked haddock and as much inspiration going for them as the Albert Memorial. What they did, they did supremely well: they crushed for ever any remote curiosity I might have had about acting as a craft. Or writing about it.

However, I tried to be absolutely fair at all times: and after listening to them all mutter away about the extraordinary career that I had had, the incredible amount of people I must have met, the enormous interest there would be for future actors in what I had to say, I would start my hesitant suggestions that I *would* like to write. One day. But that when I did it would not be about the cinema or the theatre as much as about my childhood, my family, and the countryside which I loved. The eager light died in the eyes behind the cigar smoke, and I usually ended up paying for the luncheon while they fussed about with credit cards and cheque books. It seemed only fair that I should pay, for after all they had gained nothing from their efforts to cajole me, so I might as well feed them. Lunch was over.

Of course it was always made perfectly clear, at the start, that there was nothing more than an interest being shown, nothing else was suggested; nothing outlined, it was simply a preliminary discussion and no offer, of course, was made. Which was hardly surprising, for I hadn't, as far as they knew, written so much as a baggage label in my life. And what they wanted really, when all was said and done, was a tell-all, rough-and-tumble, film-star book, including, one supposed, immodest chunks from my most flattering reviews, blow-by-blow accounts of my best acting-scenes and, most important of all of course, succulent pieces about Veronica Tishtush or Monica Mishmash: those would be *certain* to secure serial rights in the cheaper papers, and that could mean a great deal of money. They smiled enticingly; I shook my head.

So the lunches always ended amicably, if disappointedly, and I nodded to a waiter. Which saved all their fiddle-faddle with wallets and leaking fountain pens. Having rejected so many ideas, I thought it wiser to part as soon as possible. There was no use in prolonging the subject. It was tidier my way, and much more orderly. And no one ever complained. After all: the Connaught has the best restaurant in London.

Now, it seemed to me that the upright Mr Charlton might well be one more of these smooth, plump, manicured gentlemen; how could I possibly tell? And as I was just about to embark on my 'Mr Philby' role in the film which Forwood had started to negotiate some time before, I felt it wiser to reply to his letter out of simple good manners, and at that same time do my best to 'put him off': I felt almost sure that even so imposing a firm could only want from me exactly what all the others had wanted, either a slim book on my 'craft' or else, which seemed rather unlikely but which was always possible allowing for the problems which were besetting publishers, a rollicking film-star book full of hilarious anecdotes and tales of indiscretions written, of course, in the nicest possible way.

I wrote, immediately, to Mr Charlton, apologizing for the delay, thanking him for his kind comments on the Russell Harty show, and adding that I *was* writing, in a desultory fashion, a series of essays on some of the highlights of my life, but that I really didn't want to write a film-star book and that what I had to say had already been said; and much better. I added, as a further dampener, the news that I was almost immediately off to Vienna where I was to make a film and would be there until mid-March, and that what I had written so far was probably libellous.

I felt perfectly safe with this gentle refusal. Essays and so on would surely put him off, just as it had the Toms and Dicks and Harrys chumping cheerfully through cold chicken pie at the Connaught.

Quite unaware, of course, that behind Mr Charlton lurked the deceptively gentle-sounding female on the directors' list on the letter-heading: Norah Smallwood.

Satisfied that both honour and good manners had been saved, and that I would never hear from them again, particularly after my carefully planted suggestion of libel, I bundled up all my old cardigans and knitted ties and headed off to Vienna to start work on the film in which I would be required to play Mr Philby. Or rather, 'A kind of Mr Philby'. No one ever seemed quite certain. Least of all myself.

I was egg-laying again. So far the earlier results, I had to confess, had been moderately successful: 'Le Serpent' had allowed me to rip out the dreadful black pit and replace it with a splendid, gleaming kitchen. The struggles on 'The Night Porter' had produced a modest terrace at the back of the house at which meals could be taken during the summer heat; and this present effort, I hoped, would help to re-tile the roof of the house, since the original ones, which had lain there since 1641, had a heart-chilling tendency to zip away across the valley during every mistral, exposing both rats' nests and the bedrooms below, to the rains. It was time to secure them.

I had known the Chinese Suite in the Bristol Hotel, Vienna, for many years. I had lived in it, and almost died in it, trying to come to terms with playing a piano (thoughtfully supplied by Columbia Pictures) and the genius of Liszt for months. I had since made other films in and around the city, and the Chinese Suite, or the Red Room as I called it, was always my base, my home, my womb. A shelter from all the idiocies of filming and the people who make them.

Red flock paper, heavy, black, carved furniture. Chinese bowls and plates on every inch of wall; what-nots of alarming intricacy stuffed with smiling buddhas and bent, aged fishermen. Lace table-cloths and hard, over-stuffed, upright chairs under an enormous chandelier. The windows looked down on to the Ring and the Opera House on one side, on the other up the glittering length of Kärntnerstrasse. In the spring, with the windows wide open, a blackbird always nested on the top of the Opera House and sang until dusk swallowed the great bulk of the building and the lights sprang up along the Ring. Over all the years I had stayed in the Red Room, nothing had ever changed; not even the blackbird. Joseph Losey had once filled it with bowls of white cyclamen while he forced me to sit and read three scripts, one after the other, to advise him which one he should make. I suggested he made none of them; which he accepted with extreme good nature. Elizabeth and George and the children had come out for a Family Christmas, and all caught 'flu which put a damper on the festivities. I had played night and day on my beastly piano, with my despairing music coach shrieking out the beat. Capucine had had a mild form of hysterics in it from the sheer terror of starting her first film, and was only brought to her senses by a glass of vodka so strong that it would have dissolved a spoon; and Charlotte Rampling had gone from it one evening in furs and a snowfall to her very first Opera. The room, therefore, was full of memories. A secure place, a loved place, nothing unpleasant could intrude whatever the problems were, which I always tried to leave outside and never bring home.

I took no account, of course, of mail. That intruded, and could not be avoided. I had been there three days only when a letter arrived. From Mr Charlton.

He was certainly wasting no time. He was, he said, delighted to know that I was writing about some of the highlights of my life. He said that he felt very encouraged, brushed aside the problem of libel, which I had hoped would dissuade him, and said that 'we' (Who were they? All the directors, one wondered?) would be extremely happy to see what I had written so far because they would have a 'better notion of the terms that we would offer you if you would like us to draw up a contract'.

Mr Charlton was not giving up easily. Was not giving up at all, it appeared. He was, politely, using force. As I can only ever do one thing at a time, lacking as I do any form of co-ordination between left and right hand, I decided that I would have to write to him immediately and stop all this nonsense, for nonsense is what it seemed at the time.

I had to go off and 'be' my Mr Philby. This would take three months of work: I couldn't possibly deal with a publishing house which had either lost its head or gone into the red and needed a rib-tickling anecdotal film-star biography to save it. Ever since the amazing success of David Niven's book, every publisher, it was known, was trying to tap another gusher.

I wrote, that afternoon, a polite postcard saying that I was extremely busy on a film and would write again one day; 'when the dust has settled'. And hoped he'd take the hint.

It is strange, but I remember graphically, sitting down at the black carved desk in the corner of the Red Room, facing a painting of two Chinese ladies messing about in a boat, and scribbling this card urgently.

For some reason his letter, which was a long one, had filled me with a sense of unease and fear: I felt that I was possibly being forced into making a promise to do something which was far beyond my powers. I couldn't get caught up in something as complicated as writing, whatever it was, or on whatever scale. Although it had been the determined wish of Mrs X, and although I had felt it might be something I could have a shot at one day, she was no longer there to advise me or, more important, to correct me when I went wrong. The essays which I had mentioned were only that: exercises in writing to amuse myself. They wouldn't stand the cruel scrutiny of all those directors.

I was not about to attempt something in which I would fail, for if that happened at such an early stage, when I was only just playing about with an idea at the very back of my head that I might one day develop, I should be cast down and would lose all confidence and never try again.

I knew the length of my corridor: I was aware of the doors on either side, of the inevitable final one at the far end. But what I did not realise that afternoon in the Red Room was that a corridor is not necessarily one long walk in a perfectly straight line; there are corners there too.

And a corner is not for standing on only; you can turn left or right and alter your direction absolutely. With courage, support, and encouragement.

I know today what I did not know that afternoon, that Mr Charlton's letter had indicated a change of direction.

I mailed the postcard and put Chatto and Windus out of my mind while I concentrated on assuming the mantle of my cardiganed imaginary Mr Philby.

The film was certainly no Disney frolic with a pack of Bambis in a bluebell wood, and I was not playing Mr Darling. However, although it was a pretty ho-hum kind of story, the script was at least literate and at worst a re-tread of countless secret agent stories. But the Company was pleasant and I was working with Ava Gardner once again, and in Vienna. Those were two particular pleasures.

Ava and I had not worked together for fifteen years, when we had made a perfectly frightful film about a priest and a tart in Spain during the Civil War which, when it opened, apparently to ten Eskimos in North Alaska, closed the next day and sank without trace.

It was a sad blow to us both and also to our gentle, civilized writer-director, Nunnally Johnson who, after trying to battle with the Hollywood company who wanted the whole thing made pretty and glamorous ('A Man and a Girl in Blazing Madrid' kind of thing) threw his cap in the air and gave in; as both Ava and I had been forced to do. It is impossible now, and it was even more impossible then, to try and buck the studio system. We ploughed on in misery, and Nunnally was once heard to say that although he had ruined my career I was a really very nice guy, because I still talked to him.

Nothing to do with Nunnally or careers being ruined; but that was the tenor of the times; we were a dispirited, battered group, and parted, when the time came, with relief that it was all over.

But here we were again, Ava and I, reunited and full of that idiot optimism which all actors have to carry with them as part of their survival kit.

At least the film was peaceful: there was no polemic, this time; no arguments about Jew or Aryan, not a whiff of obscenity, and nothing that could possibly cause crowds to march in the streets as they had done in Germany when 'The Night Porter' finally opened there and Jews marched to demonstrate against the film for being anti-semitic while on the next night a large Arab contingent stormed the cinema protesting that the film was pro-Israeli.

This was going to be a good old-fashioned spy thriller, without any complications, and as such was surely going to be a relief. All I'd be required to do this time was act: I hoped. After a couple of halcyon weeks in Vienna we all set off for the location work.

For countless days, it seemed, we sailed up and down a frozen lake in Upper Austria in blizzards, chased about for endless nights in the very bowels of Schwechat Airport, or stood freezing to death in melting snow among mournful black fir-trees, desperate for the arrival of tea-urns and something hot to eat. When the tea arrived it was usually stone-cold. The sight of a pile of cold, boiled spaghetti on a sagging paper plate, a plastic cup of cooling milkless coffee on the upper deck of a listing lake-steamer in a biting wind is engraved on my mind for eternity.

Finally, one bitter day, I lost my head and my temper and raced back to the Unit Hotel in the motor-boat which came out daily to supply us with this congealing muck.

Snug in the hotel dining-room, just finishing what seemed to have been a splendid luncheon, puffing contentedly at their cheroots, the money looked up at me in some surprise, and went white to their collars when I demanded their presence in a less public place. I rather think they thought Ava had drowned and I had come to break the tragic news.

Crushed between the service door of the kitchen, the telephone booth, and the gentlemen's lavatory, I exploded.

I don't often lose my temper; about once every twenty years perhaps. But when I do, I am informed, it is a pretty spectacular business, not because I shout and rail or wave my arms about, but because I am deadly cool, brutally accurate, and the hundred minor, or major, faults which I have noticed about my victims over the years are suddenly, vividly, and with appalled dismay on their part, laid before their eyes. Naked, as a skinned rabbit.

I, the good-natured, understanding, co-operative, reasonable, orderly man, suddenly erupt like Mount Saint Helen's, and my flow of molten fury and dislike engulfs them. I strike so far below the belt that they are often severed from their feet.

It would be wrong to think that I leave these encounters with a manly stride, proud of my success in the worm-turning act: far from it. I am so unnerved and shattered that I manage, usually, to blast my targets, and stagger off in desperate need of a bed in a sanatorium; so much does my fury and anger exhaust me.

So, naturally, I am careful not to do it very often, and spend months, even years as I have said, holding firm. Storing up my bits of shrapnel. Not a very attractive part of my make-up, I agree.

This particular encounter, as it happened, didn't do much good. All that happened was that the coffee urn arrived at blood heat, and the food still stuck to the paper plates in hardening fat. Naturally, the weather, and the freezing conditions, were to blame, and all that could be done had been done.

Eventually, Ava finished her part, leaving a loving note for me filled with relief, and saying that she was not 'saying goodbye', but that London called to her 'quite desperately' and she was off.

I worked on in my knitted ties for a little longer until I too, thankfully, reached the end of my assignment and was free to leave the gloomy little town on the lake, the mournful fir-trees and melting snow, and fly home to clear skies and the swelling buds, heralding a warm spring. God knows why people always think that filming is a glamorous business.

Sadly, I was not to see the Red Room again: it passed, as so many other pleasant things have done, into the mists of time and memory.

Home, then, to capering dogs, a welcoming Henri and Marie, a neglected garden, and an ungathered olive crop, fallen into the wild anemones and bee orchis. At the pond a last pair of toads lurched about obscenely, the willow trailed greening ribbons, and the first leaves of the water lilies lay on the still surface like pink plates. There was a great deal to do before the sudden burst of summer, which in this climate seems to happen almost overnight.

And it promised to be a busy one, for now the house boasted a Guest Room, and people had already started booking.

The year before, Henri and Marie, getting on a little, and no longer wishing to continue working after years of labouring for other people, decided to retire, but promised that they would always come to care-take if I had to be away for any length of time. This suited me perfectly, and so the staff room was stripped out, re-carpeted, re-curtained, and Antonia's selection of pictures, tom tits in apple blossom, and autumnal views of Burnham Beeches, was replaced.

And I, once known as the Idol of the Odeons (sic), could be found daily in the bright new kitchen, up to the elbows in detergent, washing up burnt saucepans, scrubbing out the dog bowls, and doing all the jobs which had been done for me for over thirty years by other people. The pleasure of having the house to oneself far outweighed the mundanity of the daily chores: it also saved a good deal of money.

The trim, smug, Georgian house in which my mother was living had suddenly raised its prices to an alarming degree, and it was necessary to find an alternative place for her; and one in which she would be happier. This Elizabeth managed to do eventually, and Ma was installed in a big comfortable Edwardian house, set in attractive gardens, and had her own self-contained flat full of her own furniture and pictures, into which she seemed to settle very well.

Elizabeth, on the other hand, was exhausted. I telephoned every Sunday to keep a check on things, and every Sunday her voice was more and more dispirited and weary. She needed a break from obligation desperately, and now that Ma was settled, and in good hands, she found it possible to come out to stay, with the intention of just sleeping for days, or mucking about in the garden.

It was a brilliant spring, and the garden work went apace. She found that, after a day's complete rest in bed with a couple of books, the extreme tiredness, most of which was mental strain, had almost worn off, and together we planted and mowed and dug, trimmed the bay trees, and brought out all the terrace chairs.

'It's a funny business, isn't it? Growing up, I mean,' she said one morning while we were filling buckets from a great truck-load of earth which had been dumped at the back of the house and with which we were replenishing all the ornamental pots on the terrace, since my own mix of limestone, shale, peat and local earth dug, at great effort, from the *potager*, had produced nothing but spurge and chickweed. Naturally.

'Growing up? What do you mean, it's funny?'

'Well. I mean, take Ma. She looked after us and now it all goes in full circle and the children start having to look after her.'

'She's all right where she is now, isn't she?'

'Says she is. Difficult to tell really. But it's a terribly pretty place, very much like a private house, you know? Not impersonal. Big bowls of flowers everywhere, the rooms are awfully nice, and the man who runs it is charming. Ma took to him right away and he's told her she can do as much gardening as she wants to. Well, it isn't much, she pulls up a weed here and there, feeds the birds. But she's happy, yes, thank God, this time I think it'll work. She's even using a walking-stick now.'

'And the penny has dropped? About staying there?'

Elizabeth stuck her spade into the earth pile. 'I think so. Yes. But it's going to be a long haul. She still comes over to the house every week, for lunch. I take her out in the car twice a week, to all the old places we used to know as children: Lewes, Alfriston. She likes that: and we usually have lunch at 'The Five Bells'. They make a terrific fuss of her there, she and Pa went so often. She likes that best of all.'

'Doesn't leave you much time, for yourself I mean, does it?'

'No,' she laughed shortly. 'None. You know what she says every single time I arrive at the house? 'Well,' she says, 'and where have *you* been? Haven't seen you for weeks!' I could kill her sometimes, quite cheerfully. Oh well . . . '

'Well, as long as she's happy.'

'She thinks the people at the hotel are a better class. She hated the ones at the

other place. Not her type, she said. 'Nothing to say for themselves.' Fact is, they
got bored stiff with her stories, poor old love, and when *this* lot get bored she'll
say *they* aren't her 'type'. My dear,' she said half laughing, 'you and Gareth
simply don't know what it's like to be the daughter in a family, don't know at
all.'

She was right. Growing up was a bit funny. Here we were together, messing
about with buckets and earth, filling urns and pots, talking to each other as we
had in the days of childhood. Comfortable in each other's company, knowing it
so well, trusting it so deeply, relaxed, continuing. Aware that we knew each
other better than perhaps anyone else would ever do. Conscious of each other's
doubts, apprehensions, and private joys, which were not private between us,
because one flick of an eye, caught suddenly in a crowded place, amid laughter
or conversation, struck instant, private responses which no one else on earth
could ever share, and comforted us.

Here I was at fifty-five. No longer the skinny boy in plimsolls and baggy
shorts, and she no longer the thin child in a cotton dress and sandals skipping
high over the tussocks of grass in Great Meadow lest she be bitten by an adder:
the exteriors had altered, but the minds, and above all, the affection, had stayed
constant.

We remained the original children, on our own together; while all about us
had quite altered. Pa was dead; Ma in a private hotel with some of her personal
possessions and whatever memories she had chosen to retain; Forwood was now
a grandfather; my young brother had five children of varying ages; and Lally
was a widow with two children of her own to care for, although she was always
to refer to us as 'her children'. But at this moment, shovelling earth together
under the olive trees, it felt almost as if we had stopped the speed of time and had
gone back: an illusion. Time is not stoppable.

'Are you managing? I mean, without Henri and Marie? Running the house?'
she said suddenly.

'Yes. Very well really. I can't iron, though. Well: only tea-cloths and
napkins, square things, you know.'

'They're easy. Wait until you get to collars. And you can't separate the yolk
from the white of an egg: I saw you yesterday when you were doing the dogs'
dinners. You just bunged the whole lot in. Awful.'

'Oh! Come on! Now be fair. Not the shells.'

'No, not the shells. I'll show you how, it's easy. And they hate the white and
it's not good for them.'

'Well, I don't make too many mistakes, really. I mean, I know about mitring
sheets, and Harpic down the lav, and I'm really pretty good at washing up. I
learned it in the army, in the Tin Wash. I can gut and skin a rabbit, scale and
clean fish, and pull a chicken. What more do you want?'

'Can't boil a tin of soup, can you? I mean *in* the tin. And I just hope you know
how to cut out that little green bag in the chicken's inside: the gall-thing.'

'I do now.'

'Jolly well better. Perhaps you should have got married really: a nice wife
who would iron your collars and sew on buttons.'

'No thanks. Set in my ways now. I don't believe that marriages are made in
Heaven: they're made in a double bed, and when that wears off there's not
much left except habit, or duty.'

'What a dreadful thing to say!'

'I know. And I know more married people who are unhappy than unmarried
ones. It's all right for some, of course. If I'd become a schoolmaster after the
war, remember?, at Windlesham, things might have been different. But

marriage and acting don't work: I know, I just didn't want anyone to get in my way. Wanted it all for myself. No school fees and fret, no four-door saloon and a mortgage on a house in Barnes or somewhere.'

'Dreadfully selfish, honestly. And when you're old and grey, what then?'

'You'll come and look after me.'

'Silly fathead. Some hopes. I've got my own problems, thank you.'

'It's not easy, marriage, mate.'

She stuck her spade in the earth pile, brushed her hands on her jeans. 'No. It's not. I'm going up to get the salad and stuff out of the fridge,' she said.

And Forwood called down from the kitchen balcony to say that Alain Resnais wanted to speak to me on the telephone.

After seeing 'Last Year in Marienbad' and 'Hiroshima Mon Amour' I knew that, as an actor, life had nothing more magical to offer than to work with Alain Resnais. But I suppressed the idiocy of the idea almost as soon as I had thought of it; and never spoke of it to anyone lest they think that I had taken leave of my wits, for a sea separated us, literally, and I was certain that he would never have heard of me anyway and, in any case, being a Frenchman working in France, would be sure to use only the local product.

One evening in 1966, his wife, Florence Malraux, telephoned me from Paris and asked me, in perfect English but with a slight frill of uncertainty in her voice, if I had ever, perhaps, heard of her husband? When I said yes indeed that I had, she asked if one day I would have lunch with him? If I said 'Yes' he would come over from Paris right away; he hadn't telephoned himself, she added, because he was afraid that I would not know who he was, and was shy of being rebuffed. I said that I would be greatly happy to meet him anytime, anywhere, in London and when? She said, 'How about Thursday?' (which was two days later). And I said that I would be at the Connaught at twelve-thirty sharp.

He arrived, this tall, pale, grey-haired man, bundled up in a shabby raincoat, a red wool scarf round his neck, for comfort not politics, and slung over his shoulder an old airline bag with the letters BOAC peeling from the canvas.

Once he was unburdened, of all except the BOAC bag, to which he appeared permanently attached, we went into lunch. He spoke English impeccably, he knew every film I had ever made and wanted to know if I would perhaps be prepared to work with him? When I agreed without hesitation, he nodded contentedly, and sipped his Perrier. I asked him when this amazing event, at least for me, would take place. He said he was not absolutely certain; but perhaps in two years or three.

My heart slid.

He then asked, looking anxiously at his watch, what play in London I should recommend him to see; he only had the afternoon, for he was leaving for Paris that evening, and therefore the play must be a matinee.

'It's a quarter to two now,' I said. 'The matinees start, usually, at half-past two. Will you have time?'

'I will have time,' he said. 'I eat little.'

He had eaten a small omelette and salad, refused all wine, wiped his lips with his napkin and I dropped him off at Wyndham's Theatre, with ten minutes to spare, so that he could see Vanessa Redgrave in 'The Prime of Miss Jean Brodie'. And that was that.

But he did not forget me. In time to come two quite remarkable scripts, 'The Adventures of Henry Dickson' and one on the imprisonment of the Marquis de Sade, came my way. But although we battled hard together, no one would touch them as commercial subjects, and they lapsed into the dead-letter box finally. And tragically.

Both were too expensive to make, neither of us was safely 'bankable', and the conditions under which he was expected to make them, even at the preliminary stages, were so unacceptable that neither of us wanted to be a part of them. So they died. We had last met together in Venice at my house on the Giudecca during work on 'Death in Venice' to discuss the de Sade subject, but long before the shooting on 'Death' was finished, de Sade had folded, and the rest was silence.

Until this moment. Filling pots and urns, starting the terrace off for the summer. We went through the obligatory signals of greeting. How are you? How is Florence? I am well. It's so good to hear from you. Where are you now? And then he told me that a Swiss company had offered to finance him to make a film on two conditions: one that David Mercer, the English writer, should script it, and two, that I should star in it. Would I?

Naturally, unthinkingly, happily, I agreed. When?

In a year, maybe longer, about a year. There was no script, not even a subject. He just wanted to know my reaction before going any further; now that he knew it, he could put things in motion and would go to London for the first discussions with Mercer. He would, he assured me, keep me informed at all times on the development of the script.

Having battered through 'The Night Porter' and the film on the lake in Upper Austria, cutting lines, adding lines, re-writing, and all the rest of it, I knew I wanted no more of that. All I wanted to do was my job, to act. Nothing else. 'Just,' I said to M. Resnais, 'wind me up and point me in the right direction.' I am not certain that he understood exactly what I meant, but he got the point.

'I'll see the script only when it is completely finished and when you are certain that it is the film *you* want to make; and then I'll do it,' I said.

He seemed satisfied with the remark, but added that, just the same, when he and Mercer had worked out a story-line he'd send me a synopsis, to which I agreed. No harm in that.

'One thing, Alain, I beg you.'

'Which is what?'

'Well, if you are writing this for me, will you please give me some rage?'

'Rage?' He sounded startled. Rage in French also means Rabies.

'Anger. Fury. Let me rage somewhere, I'm sick to death of all the enigmatic, silent creatures I have been playing. I want *anger*.'

He agreed, I would have some 'rage' and a synopsis quite soon.

I went out on to the terrace into the early sun. At last, I thought, well into my fifties, it's going to happen. After a decade of waiting.

'Tea?' said Elizabeth, coming out with a tray and cups. 'I can't remember where you keep the biscuits; can't be bothered anyway.'

Forwood came walking slowly up the steps with a watering-can. 'What did Alain want? They down here or something? By the way, I've fed the dogs.'

'Wants me to do a film with him. This time it seems it might be definite.'

'How lovely!' said Elizabeth, pouring tea carefully into the Italian spode.

'When?' said Forwood.

'Next year. Anyway, a year's time.'

'A year!' Elizabeth cried. 'My God! Who knows where we'll all *be* in a year.'

In July the sky was white with heat: roses opened, bleached, and scattered crumpled petals across the cracked earth of the *potager* within the day. Lizards lay still on the hot stones of the terrace, golden eyes shut, only the gentle throb of their green-scaled bellies betraying that they lived.

Under the vine the shade was green, dark, cool; no breath of air. Occasionally a fat blue Provençal bee would drone past, swing about among the swelling grapes, soar up and away into the white afternoon; and down the hill, in the speckled shade of the olives, the summer guests lay in angular groups, knees bent upwards, arms thrown wide, heads to one side, inert; bodies by Stanley Spencer.

I had been foolish to believe that no one would ever come to this house, as I had on the very first day that I had taken the key from behind the orange tree and let myself into the long white room. Everyone had come, in time; and only one had considered me mad.

'Bumble' Dawson arrived on a summer's night, driven up the bumpy track by two over-tanned gentlemen in sailors' caps and striped shirts, in a white Rolls-Royce which looked as out of place, as it inched up the hill, as a double-decker bus. 'Bumble', a-flutter and a-swirling in printed voile, unsteady on high heels, bade them goodbye (for they were off to Monte Carlo for dinner) and reminded them to come back to collect her before midnight. They had crept down the track, wincing, one thought, with every bump, each caress against the pristine white coachwork from every unpruned bramble, thankful to get away.

'Bumble' had been a weekly guest at the Bendrose-Beel-Nore gatherings, and her arrival, a little disapproving, for she disliked the French and France, was a moment of charming emotion generally; and then she saw the house for the first time and was deeply shocked.

'This is *it*?' she had said. Her voice had a dying fall. 'I thought the servants perhaps . . . '

'No, this is it. All of it. Come and look.'

She was not impressed. Hated the 'things which fly about at night and bite' and shook her head sadly. 'The furniture looks so sad here. So out of place. It's simply not *you*. It's not your background. You'll never stay here . . . too lonely, too far away! Who'll ever come all this way, up that ghastly road and then that track. It's not *possible*, darling. You don't *fit*.'

But I did fit. And I did stay. And everyone else came up that ghastly road and the track, but 'Bumble', alas, never did again, and although we met at suppers in her elegant London flat, stuffed with china cats and tight satin settees, from which I constantly slid, she never mentioned the house, and died one New Year's morning in her bathroom at Castle Howard, where she was staying, in far more suitable surroundings.

In August the weather sometimes makes an abrupt and surprising change. At first the clouds appear, high above the crest of the hill, which grow as one watches into enormous hammer-heads, colouring from ice-white to deep copper; the birds are silent; the air still.

'There's going to be a storm,' someone will say with blinding obviousness, and we hurry about closing the shutters, dragging the cushions from the terrace chairs, gathering up the books and papers and all the symbols of a lazy summer day.

With the first, tremendous, zig-zag of lightning comes a gust of hot wind, as if hell has opened its doors for a brief moment, scattering the lizards, the first yellowing leaves on the vine, bending the last of the hollyhocks, ripping the flowers from the fuchsias in their pots, and sending wild scurries of dust and leaves spiralling high into the air; and then the rain roars in, beating down like steel beads, as everyone hurries to shelter in the house and the dogs flee, tails between legs, to the darkest corners of the long room. A cruel, and abrupt change of season, after which the weather will never quite be as hot again, for the first fingers of autumn have laid themselves upon the parched earth.

It can (and often does) rain for days; sometimes it clears away, racing in great black clouds down towards the coast, tumbling and rumbling to spend itself far out in the ocean. But in general it marks the end of summer on the hill and the arrival of cooler, moister, days.

September came treading with suggestive steps across the land, the evenings became cooler, the vine started to turn from vibrant green to pale yellow, the wasps arrived and every morning the grass was wet with the early dew, and the sun began to sink each evening a little earlier behind the big oak by the front gate as my summer-guests prepared to pack and head slowly home. The last of the holiday postcards had been sent: summer was over.

But for me September meant that Alain Resnais would soon be arriving. Bringing with him both Mercer's synopsis and a thousand photographs which, he had warned me, he had taken during his hunt for locations. In Providence, Rhode Island. Which meant, naturally enough, America.

This last piece of information about Rhode Island had, when I heard it, sent me into a mild state of depression. I knew that the film was to be a twelve to fourteen week business, and even though that was far too long by my standards to be away from the house, I had willingly, deliberately, insisted that I should have nothing whatsoever to do with the script, and only read it when it was quite finished. Of course, having an obvious mind, I had reasoned that as Resnais was French, and his film French, he would, of course, shoot in France. That seemed perfectly logical to me. But then I have such a depressingly literal mind; and it often kicks back at me. To my constant surprise.

I had forgotten that Resnais had once confessed that, among the main passions in his life, one was America, like most intellectual Frenchmen for some reason, and the other was ordering breakfast in bed at Claridge's in London. Pressing the bell in that hotel, he said, gave him profound pleasure. The breakfast 'arrives almost before you have removed your finger from the bell!'

However, of the two passions it was clear that Rhode Island had won over Claridge's. Which was a pity. The thought of spending all those weeks in America, so far away, was very depressing. I'd never be able to get home for a week-end.

If September had begun the dispersal of holidaymakers, it hadn't finished the job; some would linger on as the crowds departed, enjoying quieter, if cooler, beaches, less congested restaurants and roads, and on the first Sunday one telephoned.

'This is John Charlton speaking,' said a brisk voice.

Who the hell was John Charlton?

'I'm down here with the family, only a little way from you, I think. The other side of Grasse. I wondered if, perhaps, I could pop over one day; just for a few minutes? You *did* mention in your last letter that you had written some essays, if you remember?'

I remembered all right. Chatto and Windus. With its apparent list of Bishops, and a Nun.

My last letter had been written years, it seemed, ago. And the postcard scribbled from the Red Room in Vienna was supposed to have put them off, but had obviously been filed in 'pending' rather than thrown into a wastepaper basket; as I had hoped. But one couldn't be impolite: the man was only fifteen minutes away, and nothing could possibly be lost by seeing him for a glass of beer or a cup of tea, because my time, from April anyway, would be fully occupied, and I'd be far away in Rhode Island, America. I was perfectly safe now. We arranged a rendezvous at the house for a couple of days later, after five o'clock, he stipulated, because that's when everyone got back from the beach.

So after five it was.

What on earth, apart from a drink, could I offer the man? Certainly there were some essays; small bundles of ill-typed stuff, nothing which would interest him or the row of names on his letter-paper. For the most part they were enlarged versions of some of the things which once I had written to Mrs X in her hospital bed so long ago. A story about, for example, Visconti: of a morning's shopping in the Marché Forville in Cannes, of the wild flowers high in the back-country in April, of my days with Rank, of my first sight of a grass-snake devouring, alive, a slightly anxious toad. There was nothing here for those distinguished directors to look at with anything but a shrug.

The row of files which contained these pitiful pieces nudged those which contained all the returned letters to Mrs X. She had always encouraged me to try and edit them, had even offered to do so herself, for she was certain that they would make a book, apart, as she had said, from the fact that, '*books of letters are really very difficult to publish. No one seems to buy them except University people.*' So that didn't appear to me a very good idea. I *could* offer them perhaps, and that would be the end of that. Mr Charlton would finish his drink, thank me, and go on his way back to his family holiday.

And then, just as I was stuffing some of the letters back into a file dated 1972, three pieces of writing, stapled together and obviously not letters, slid to the floor. Chapters 1 to 3 of the tentatively titled book of childhood stories which I had started to write for her called *The Canary Cage*.

These will do, I thought; they are cleanly typed, stapled, self-contained. Essays in fact. He'd certainly not find them of any interest, like all the other Toms and Dicks and Harrys in the past. But I'd have at least kept my word, he'd have his wretched essays and a drink and that would be that, and the hundreds of letters which, after all, were extremely private, would remain where they were, in their files, unread by strangers' eyes. They were far too personal to be picked about by the directors of Chatto and Windus with all their initials.

John Charlton didn't look remotely like a director of an extremely august publishing house. A tall, lean, angular man with a strong nose and an absurdly boyish cockscomb of hair which sprang in a high curve from the back of his neat head, he seemed, in his flannels and plain tweed jacket, far more suited to a sports field blowing a whistle, perhaps, on the sideline, or shouting LBW! triumphantly to some unfortunate youth in cricket pads and gloves.

An illusion which he quickly dispelled.

I have an uncomfortable feeling now that I greeted him with some reserve and even vague hostility: I was fully aware that I had no need to fear anything, the essays would see to that, and also I had the safety-net of the Resnais film to sustain me. I can't remember what we talked about, but I do remember that I paddled about for quite a while avoiding the subjects of writing or books as if they were sea urchins, until he decided that we had had enough of pleasantries and reminded me why he had come.

'Well, yes: I have got a few bits of stuff, as I said. Really nothing much and I haven't written anything for ages: nothing which would interest you anyway.'

'Well, those of us who saw you on that television show were deeply impressed.'

'I was pretty exhausted. I'd been doing publicity all week and that was the final chore. I think I must have been hysterical. I do apologize.'

'Oh no! Not at all, don't apologize. It was first-rate, and we wondered if you felt that you could, perhaps, write about some of the things of which you spoke. If you felt that you could put it down, I can truthfully say that we would be more than happy to publish such a book.'

The man is going potty, I thought. How do I get out of this one? Perfectly simply, by using the same suggestions which I had used at all those Connaught luncheons with the bland, well-tailored, plump gentlemen, Tom and Dick and Harry.

'Well, the point is that I do want to write one day, and I *have* set down a few bits and pieces, but I honestly don't think they'd interest you.'

'How do you know until I have read them?' he said perfectly reasonably.

'But it wouldn't be a film star's autobiography, you know. All my films, full of randy jokes and who I slept with, that kind of thing.'

Mr Charlton looked calm. 'I don't think that we would want that kind of book,' he said.

Which caught me off guard.

'What I'm actually thinking of is a book about my early childhood with my sister and our nanny in Sussex.'

If that doesn't squash it, I thought, nothing will.

It didn't. Mr Charlton leant forward. "That sounds a bit more like it," he said. "As a matter of fact I'm a Sussex man myself. Have you got something written in that vein?"

"Yes," I said, fairly ungraciously, and handed him the three thin chapters of *The Canary Cage*.

He took them politely, flipped roughly through the pages. In his hand they looked suddenly not thin, but famished.

"The title is only a working title," I said; as if I knew what I was talking about.

"Might I take these back with me to the house? I'll send them back to you as soon as I have read them."

"That won't take you very long," I said with a laugh which I hoped was deprecating. But I agreed; said I had a carbon copy anyway, and after a few more moments of not very much, he left amid handshakes, and I watched him drive down the track with extreme care. And that, I thought, is that.

Two evenings later he telephoned to say that he had read the chapters and that he had enjoyed them thoroughly. Couldn't I be persuaded to carry on, and meanwhile he'd like to take what he had back to London for his colleagues to have a look at?

'Are you sure?'

'Perfectly sure. It could be a very charming book; I really think you ought to carry on. Really. Of course it's difficult to judge from just *three* chapters, but I am convinced you've got something very good there, you must write a little more, say another five or six, in the same style; exactly the same style.'

Praise, when it comes, often embarrasses me, and I don't handle compliments as well as I should. Judy Garland once told me that all one had to do was say, 'Thank you', or 'Thank you *so* much', or, if things persisted, 'You're *very* kind'; which helped me greatly. But encouragement is something absolutely different.

Encourage me and I will part the seas; if you want me to.

The morning after Mr Charlton's telephone call I bought two trestles, a thick piece of planking, took one of the chairs from the kitchen, and my typewriter, and locked myself in the old olive store above the woodshed and started to write.

I am still there today.

TWELVE

The quinces were already yellowing on the bough when Resnais arrived, bringing with him his wife Florence, a thousand photographs of the locations which he had chosen in and around Providence, Rhode Island, the second synopsis, and the first draft of the first two acts of the film. Which I politely declined to read until it was final and he had approved it fully.

The first synopsis had arrived in April. It was extremely detailed. The film was to be set in some city in the West: that is to say, the West as opposed to the East, but it must have nothing identifiable about it; it was not America, England, France or Germany, just vaguely in the West. We would start shooting in February 1976 for twelve weeks, eight in New England, the rest in Paris; the title was 'The Stadium'; and the provisional budget was set at a low 2,700,000 dollars.

We were a small company of seven. I was to be a barrister with a wife and a twenty-four-year-old daughter who was in love with a footballer whose brother was a soldier in a paramilitary unit. There was also a cancer research pathologist, male, and a female American journalist who was dying of leukaemia. We were about to be taken over by a military junta and, in bewilderment and disarray, herded into a football stadium from which, eventually, we were to be driven to an, obviously, unfortunate end just as a World Cup football match began under the new regime.

Not a lot of laughter there, I couldn't help thinking. And not a lot of the rage in my role, for which I had asked Resnais long before. Perhaps there would be in the complete script: this was after all nothing more than a synopsis and one couldn't be absolutely certain of anything. However, it was perfectly clear to me, even at such an early stage of events, that I was going to be exposed to a good deal of political-hype (little of which I should be able to understand) and that Mr Mercer had determined that his audience would be spared no kind of brutality, interrogation, torture or death.

But by September all that had changed radically.

Among the scattered photographs in the long room, I read the second synopsis, now called 'Providence', to find that I was still a barrister (rageless) with a wife but no daughter. She had faded away, along with most, but not quite all, of her footballer-lover and almost all of the cancer pathologist: the paramilitary brother remained in a different guise, as did the ailing American journalist, and I discovered, with a deeply-rooted sense of unease, that I had suddenly acquired an aged novelist father with a vicious tongue and a love of the bottle. I had a pretty shrewd idea that this could be a most commanding role: I've been an actor long enough to know about those rascally father parts with bottles and vicious tongues. They invariably take the picture.

Nervously, or perhaps I should say cautiously unnerved, I turned my attention to the photographs which had spilled about the room. Some were exceptionally interesting, some extraordinary; all conjured up a strange and unidentifiable place. But I became overwhelmed by the plethora of roots, tree trunks, boulders, rocks, oddly shaped houses, hideous streets, and in particular one exceedingly ugly house standing on a bare knoll high above the Hudson River. This was to be our main location, and Resnais was obviously as delighted with it as he had been with room-service in Claridge's. It had been photographed from every conceivable angle and still, to my mind anyway, looked like a mill owner's house in Ramsbottom, Lancashire.

I held my tongue: but I couldn't help feeling that all these items, so carefully recorded on large glossy prints, could have been found a lot nearer home, without us having to trail all the way across the Atlantic. However, Resnais was adamant; as he was about everything, with a quiet, still, polite, firmness which could not be budged. Providence, and a singularly unpleasing little town nearby, were to be our bases; so be it.

The photographs were collected up, the script and the synopses filed away, and I turned my uneasy mind to more pressing things: for this was September only. The film was still a long way off, and Resnais had promised that by the end of the year I would have the final, approved, script from him. I'd waited a decade for it, so four more months wouldn't make much difference and would give me time to get on with the job which now awaited me, daily, up in the olive store.

Encouraged by John Charlton's reaction to the first three chapters which he had read and taken off to London with him, and following his suggestion that I would have to write 'four or five' more before anyone could possibly say that a book was under way or not, I wrote and wrote daily, sending him each chapter immediately it was finished.

By the time that I had written three, or perhaps it was four, his letters became more encouraging and his use of the words 'we' and 'colleagues' more frequent. Obviously his were not the only eyes to scan my tumbled sheets: he was distributing my chapters like tracts all about the lofty halls of his firm for the bishops on the letter-paper to read; and from his remarks, which were extremely guarded, they appeared to like what they had read also. Which was comforting.

Once the name 'Norah Smallwood' appeared; in October. A throw-away reference in a PS reminding me that '*our Managing Director*' would welcome an opportunity of meeting me, should I be in London at any time, and reminding me that it was *she* who had first heard me talking about 'The Night Porter' on the television, '*which was the start of our* [his and my] *correspondence.*' This was the first *I* had heard of it.

I looked at the letter-heading and noted that the name of Mr Parsons was now no longer at the top, but that the nun among the bishops had slipped into his place. No nun this: rather the Reverend Mother. Or, to be accurate, Managing Director.

So, with an approving, I gathered, Managing Director behind me, I wrote on furiously, and by the time that I had completed six chapters, to universal approval, it became pleasingly apparent to me that, with luck, I might actually be writing a book, and that in that case I would be in need of literary advice, perhaps an agent, and most certainly a typist who could deal with my dire spelling and lack of punctuation, for I was still using dots when in doubt, and from the look of my pages I was in doubt most of the time.

Robin Fox's partner, Dennis van Thal, who still looked after whatever theatrical ventures came my way in England, had just such a person to hand in his own firm. His brother Herbert, or Bertie as he is called, was a literary agent, had been a publisher himself, written an impressive number of books, and was gentle, witty, unassuming and much respected in the publishing world. I liked him immediately. Fortunately, he liked me, and what he was given of my work to read: dots and all.

'Don't worry about the dots, dear boy,' he said. 'We'll get someone to clean them up in a trice. A couple of margins would be attractive, I think, easier to read. And then we'll sort out the paragraphing.'

And one afternoon at the Connaught he produced a slight, fair-haired girl, in a pale blue trouser suit, who took my mangled pages in capable hands and read fluently every single hieroglyphic with which each page was liberally covered. For it was not my practice, and still is not I regret to say, to retype my corrections. I prefer to write them all in afterwards, scribbling them over and about the page like lengths of bent wire, spiked with directional arrows, erasures, and far too many capital letters.

I was much impressed at the speed with which she managed to decipher this stuff, but she was as sure and calm as if she had written it all down herself, and Sally Betts became (and still is) the only person living who can make head or tail of my typescripts. She accepted the marathon job cheerfully.

So now I had a literary agent, a typist, and could, with extreme caution and a good deal of finger-crossing, murmur the magic phrase 'my publisher' to myself. Caution and finger-crossing were important: for there *was* no publisher as yet, just an interested one offering encouragement.

It is strange now to remember that, almost six months to the exact day that John Charlton had come to the house, in the middle of his family holiday, and faced my slightly hostile (or perhaps indifferent is better) reception and read my crumpled chapters from the file of letters which once had belonged to Mrs X, I completed an eighth chapter, and Bertie telephoned to say that Chatto and Windus had accepted the book. Half written.

He said that just to be published by Chatto was something which he himself had dreamed of for many years, and hoped that I was very proud.

More amazed than proud. Still half a book to finish and quite the hardest part. For it was obvious to me that after eight chapters of childhood and a continual summer sky, I had to make a change, otherwise the whole thing could slide down into a soggy mess. A different flavour, sharper, had to be injected, and Bertie agreed.

'Go on with what happened after that summer-childhood. The growing-up part. Never much fun, that. But you *can't* stay embalmed as twelve years old. Make a switch, dear boy. Won't be easy, but just knuckle down and try. Remember: you have half a damned good book already, a marvellous firm to publish it, so finish the job.'

Which, on February 24th 1976, assisted by all the bits and pieces which my father had collected for me in a large cigar box and which I had found in his studio during the clearing-out process after his death, at the trestle table in a howling draught in the olive store, I did. For a few moments I sat staring at the final page. Battered out a row of asterisks below the last line to indicate that I had finished, and realised that I had actually written a book.

I never expected to write another.

It would be unwise to think that this astonishing creative effort on my part had taken place in monk-like calm and serenity in the room above the wood shed. Far from it.

There were still the daily chores to deal with: the dustbins to lug down to the end of the track, logs to split, dogs to be fed, and the telephone never stopped ringing with urgent calls about 'Providence' which, like every film I had ever really wanted to make, was proving to be as difficult to get started as any. It was on and off with the amazing regularity of a conjuror's trick-hat. Resnais kept me always closely informed: sometimes filled with happy optimism, on other occasions as drab with despair as a potential suicide case.

Contracts, mine anyway, got altered. Billing was changed, dates were scrambled, even though the contract itself had already, months ago, been signed. And only the force and determination of my agent in Paris, Olga Horstig, and my own stubbornness, got things sorted out, although it meant that on two occasions I withdrew from the project altogether, causing a tremendous flurry and fuss but instant withdrawals of unacceptable alterations.

None of this had anything whatsoever to do with Resnais. He remained aloof from this as much as possible and proceeded with his wooing of Ellen Burstyn (who had just won the Oscar) to play my wife, John Gielgud to play my rascally old father, David Warner and the splendid Elaine Stritch; and by the end of October he had them all. It was a most impressive company of players. Resnais was to call us his quintet. A violin, a piano, a cello, a harp etc. Although I was never absolutely sure which instrument I was; perhaps a tin drum.

Through all these trials and tribulations I worked on at my summer recollections and slow approach to adolescence, grateful for the diversion, and comforted enormously by the fact that I was working towards an end-product which someone actually wanted and believed in. But it wasn't very easy: every day brought a new cry of disaster or joy from the 'Providence' company, culminating in Resnais' sudden decision, for reasons I no longer remember, to postpone the whole thing until April. So I had plenty of time to start on my 'revisions', another new word I learned from Bertie, which meant that one had to do a bit of re-writing here and there, but that the book, although finished and delivered, was still very much a part of my life. Thankfully; for with all the fizz and fuss about the wretched film, I think that without it I might very likely have finally pulled out in disenchantment. Which would have been a grave error.

In December I received the final draft script. I was the last member of the company to read it, as I had insisted. I remember that it arrived on a mild, wet day. The vine was bare against the low cloud scudding towards Corsica and the coast of Africa: far across the valley and beyond the mountains there was a thin saffron light over the Var. I sat alone in the long room and started to read.

It was a marathon. Page after page of dialogue, little of which I can truthfully say I understood. My earlier feeling that I should be subjected to a heavy exposure of political-hype seemed only too obvious; and my deep-rooted feeling of unease about the rascally old father with the vicious tongue was fully realised. It was a brilliantly placed role, and I knew that with John Gielgud playing it none of us would stand a chance. He'd pinch the picture. Which he did.

When I finished reading, two hours later, I knew three things were certain: I had lost the film for myself; I had no rage whatsoever; and I had to do it without question. What I was not certain about was whether it was a work of genius or one of pretentious rubbish. I secretly suspected that it was the latter; but I also knew instinctively that it was brilliant rubbish and would play, with the given company, as magic.

Forwood came down into the long room.

'Finished? What's it like?'

'Extraordinary. I'd be out of my skull if I said that I understood what the hell it's all about, but it's marvellous: quite marvellous.'

'And your part?'

'Enormous. All chat. Pages and pages. Big black chunks. I don't know what it means, it all sounds to me like a lot of intellectual twaddle: they all take themselves *so* seriously. I honestly don't think that much of it makes sense really, anyway to me. But then Shaw didn't always make sense when one analysed his stuff. Remember that big speech to the Doctors that Dubedat makes? *It's* all nonsense; always has been.'

'But you want to do it?'

'Oh yes! God yes! I'd be dotty not to: all my instincts say I must, but I can't really think why. It's a long, dull, barrister-part. No rage, as I asked, and a mass of chatter. A dull man: with a lot of intellectual nonsense to spout. I'll never be able to learn it.'

'You'll just have to work extra hard.'

'I'm getting a bit long in the tooth for learning. Anyway: I'm probably wrong. Remember I was brought up for years on a very simple diet. Boy Meets Girl . . . and even though I have a shrewd suspicion that they won't be actually beating down doors to see it in Preston, Cricklewood or Putney, I reckon that if it ever does get made it'll still be showing somewhere in a hundred years. A typical Resnais classic.'

'Which is what you wanted.'

'Which is what I wanted. Funny. I don't understand much of what I've read but what is really extraordinary is that I have a terrific lump in my throat. So there must be something working: something's got to me. I'm *very* moved. I wonder why?'

Outside on the terrace the last of the day was fading into night. Across the valley and the mountains the saffron light which had hung over the Var had died to a sullen, smouldering, crimson thread. I stood leaning against the iron trellis in the thin December rain, watching until it had gone.

The battle of the budget for 'Providence' was waged well into the New Year. I don't know what happened in Paris, Zurich or Geneva or wherever the action was, but just as I was starting on the last chapter of the book, Resnais called to say that he was going to postpone the entire project for a year, to give him time, I assumed, to get enough cash to enable him to cart us all off to the location work in Providence, Rhode Island.

That was the main stumbling-block. We didn't have enough money to go to America. Which didn't worry me in the very slightest, but obviously distressed him very much indeed, for the locations were an integral part of his film and its particular atmosphere. I remember begging him to reconsider this drastic action, and reminding him that he had a magnificent company ready and waiting, some of us for months in fact, and that if he disbanded us now it was almost certain that he would never be able to assemble us again in a year's time. I said that I was certain that the script was so strong, so magical, and the cast so perfectly balanced, that if needs be he ought to 'make it in a tent' and forget the locations. We were all ready and anxious to start; we were ready to begin the next day even.

I think that I had had my second whisky when I spoke to him that evening, and he listened in his usual, cautious, silence, saying nothing. In truth I hadn't left him very much of a chance to get a word in anyway. After I left the telephone I felt a surge of anxiety that I might perhaps have been discourteous, the very last thing that I would have wished to be to the director I wanted so much to work for, and for the rest of the evening I felt an anxious nagging of doubt. I had probably been extremely rude; but at least I had spoken, and I had meant everything that I said.

Two days later I was informed that we would be shooting the picture in Europe: America was out, and Resnais was going off to Belgium to inspect alternative locations.

The day after I finished the book, Olga called to say that the film was now firmly 'on', but that it would take time to find the new places in which to work and we wouldn't start shooting until the end of March or late April at the earliest. But we were 'on'. That was the main thing. I was delighted, now I had all the time I would need for the revisions which were to come.

And the drawings.

Mr Charlton had written one day suggesting that he '*felt more than ever that the book should have some illustrations. I had no idea when I raised the subject before that you yourself had had artistic training . . . and what distinguished tutors you had.*'

Graham Sutherland and Henry Moore, to be precise, but sadly the fact that they had tried to batter some 'artistic training' into my eighteen-year-old soul didn't mean much more than that. It didn't mean, by a long chalk, that I could actually draw. I could scribble, yes. But not much more.

However, as Mr Charlton and I now seemed to be joined at the hip, so to speak, and as I listened to his every word like a pupil at Plato's knee, followed his suggestions as much as I possibly could (well aware that there was another voice echoing his wishes), I decided that I'd better settle down in the time I now had free to do some free-line scribbles with which to decorate the book.

I was aware of the other voice, softly echoing his own, simply because the names Mrs Smallwood or, on occasions, Norah Smallwood, began to thread themselves through his letters like a scarlet ribbon weaving a pleasing pattern of managerial approval.

I was, frankly, enjoying myself tremendously. I had written a book. I was about to be published. I would do everything within my powers to assist them, so I put my long-unused pen to work recalling a myriad things which I had let lie buried in the dust of childhood and uneasy growing up. I remembered the privy, the pump, the cabbages in the cottage front garden, all the simple symbols of happiness, and fixed them on to paper to pleasure Mr Charlton.

I was always very pleased when I read in his letters that Mrs Smallwood had been 'delighted' with them also.

At the beginning of March, Resnais called to say that he had found his locations, and that we would start shooting in Brussels on April 20th; and a few evenings later Simone (Signoret) telephoned, just as I was sitting down to supper, to tell me that Luchino Visconti was dead.

I remember that all I could say was, 'Oh shit.' A hopeless, useless, despairing oath at such a moment, and a very few minutes later, Joseph Losey telephoned; in tears, to tell me the same wretched news.

I sat for a time in the long room alone and in silence. Firelight flickered; a log settled. The Emperor had gone, and with him much of the splendour of the cinema.

We had spoken together not long before: he had a cold, wheezed slightly. 'Is influenza. Is not serious, only annoying. I am thinking of *The Magic Mountain*, you remember we spoke of this?'

'Very well indeed.'

'You are interested to work with me again? Or are you still feeling distaste for my work?'

This was a direct, and sharp, reference to the fact that I had declined, a long time before, to play a character based on himself in a film which he had made as soon as he was given permission from his doctors. The set of the film was built on one level so that his chair could be wheeled easily from place to place, and was to be very lavish, but I had disliked the script and knew that I could not possibly play a role founded on himself. He was furious. And for a time I was banished; I didn't even get the usual card at Christmas, nor were messages sent by mutual friends, as had been the case before.

'Luchino! I have *never* felt distaste for your work. That is a terrible thing to say. I just didn't like the role in 'Conversation Piece'.'

'And you were right. You would not have been any good. Burt Lancaster was *much, much* better. He has brio!'

'Well . . . there you are! But 'Mountain' is something else, when would it be?'

'We have problems with the Germans about the rights. Always they make difficulties. But we will work this out. I must think if you are right for Peeperkorn or for Settembrini: I am not sure; perhaps Settembrini, we see. Now I go. I talk too much. We speak later. Ciao, Bogarde.'

But there was not to be a 'later', and sitting in the long room that evening I knew that another door had closed: softly; with a terribly final 'click!'. He would always be a major figure in my life even though, strangely, we hardly knew each other off the studio floor. Socially we met very occasionally: a Christmas party in his house in Rome; two days when he had come to my villa in the suburbs of the city, once bringing the book of *Death in Venice*. The fact that I could not, and would not, learn Italian irritated him to fury, for he thought that as I was a guest in his country, the least I could do was to pay it the compliment of speaking its language. When we spoke, which was not often, he would frequently force me to speak in French because, although he spoke English very well, he said that it fatigued him. The fact that I have a tin-ear as far as languages are concerned was of no consequence; he dismissed my excuses with an impatient wave of his hand.

But I know that he respected me, and I know that he knew how much I respected him. During the whole five months of work on 'Death' we were never far apart, and at all times extraordinarily close: without ever speaking, or very seldom.

Each day I was bidden to lunch with him at whatever location we were working, and each day it was I who sat on his right as he poured his olive oil on his garlicked *bruschetta* while I ate my usual small boiled sole and three potatoes: for any other kind of food repelled me. And this he understood completely; without words. He knew that I had brought Von Aschenbach to the table, not myself, and respected that fact above all other things. Forgiving even my lack of Italian, and my solitary, unsocial life which had surprised him, until he realised that I had to live in that manner in order to contain the intense concentration which I needed to give him the performance he wanted.

He had marvellously curious ways of expressing his pleasure in the work one did. I never heard him ever say 'Good' or 'Thank you' or 'Perfect' or any of the other cliché words a director will use to his actors. His thanks, if they came at all, came in a surprising, touching manner.

Once on 'Death' we were working at night in a tiny square in the centre of Venice. It was raining; it was cold. The little square had been scattered all about with the contents of stinking dustbins in order to give the impression of the squalor and muck that existed in the city in the middle of the cholera plague in 1910. In the centre of the square was a small, much-used, marble well-head, against which I had to lean, laugh, and slowly sink to the ground: laughing in hopeless misery and despair at the tragedy of life.

A simple enough shot, one might think. Except for the fact that I had only one white suit; and that meant that there could not possibly be a chance of doing a second shot if the first did not work. Lying in the rain, the filth, the mud, I'd be a ruin. The laughter, plus the bitterness, pain and disillusion which it must express, had to be absolutely correct. Otherwise the shot would be ruined as well as the suit, and we'd have to do it all over again the next night after the thing had been sent to the cleaners. It was a 'one off' job. And I was petrified.

So petrified that I mucked it up. The laughter was, Visconti said quietly, 'too aware, too knowing; too young, above all. You must laugh old. We go again.'

I had pulled myself up from the filth in which I had lain, and was suddenly surrounded by the entire troupe; cameraman, wardrobe, props, electricians, carpenters, everyone whispering 'Bravo! Bravo!' and smothering me in handfuls of white chalk-powder. The suit was clean again. We did a second shot which satisfied Visconti, and I heard him say, through the snot and tears which coursed down my face, mixing with the fine steady rain, 'D'accordo,' as he came across the filthy square to help me to my feet.

'Bogarde,' he said. 'I have something *incredible* to show you: look!'

With one arm around my shoulder he pointed to a tall, arched, pillared house across the little square, roped about with washing-lines, tilting against the night sky.

'You see! Only the Venetians know. It is not in the guidebooks. *We* share the secret, eh? Is the house of Marco Polo!'

Visconti had said, 'Thank you.'

We finally started shooting on 'Providence' on a bitterly cold day in an ugly, and extremely busy, street in Brussels. I was not 'called' but, as I always do, went down to see the first shot put in the can, and to wish the troupe, and the actors who are breaking the ice, good luck.

Ellen Burstyn I found in the make-up truck, reading a thick paperback on some form of psychology or other, dressed immaculately in her Yves St Laurent costume and looking just a little tense.

'Is it normal,' she asked, 'that on European movies a star doesn't get to have a trailer dressing-room?'

I admitted that it was so; but that there was a small bar across the street which had an area reserved for the players to relax in.

'I don't relax in small bars,' she said. 'Is it going to be that kind of a film?'

'It's that kind of a film.'

She returned to her book. 'Just as long as I know,' she said.

And it was that kind of a film. We shuttled about from Brussels to Antwerp and Louvain, taking in sundry squalid, and depressing, locations on the way, eventually ending up in a château, empty and deserted since the war, which was a kind of bastard French-Scottish baronial, turreted pile set in an immense and beautiful park some way out of Limoges, a peculiarly ugly industrial town.

By this time we had all started to settle down together: the troupe was marvellous, all hand-picked by Resnais himself. Ellen had very quickly come to terms with the sort of European movie she was in and threw in her not-inconsiderable lot happily with the rest of us; and Resnais himself, although seldom seen to smile much, was proving more and more to be the supreme example of an *auteur* director, and gave a very good impression of being happy: now that we had at last started and got under way.

Our close-knit group was joined at the château by John Gielgud, for his two-week stint on the film, bringing with him tremendous zest and pleasure and an inexhaustible fund of reminiscences. The Resnais quintet was, at last, complete.

If I had thought, at my first reading of it, that the script was difficult and at times obscure, the playing of it proved my point. It is one thing to read words, quite another to say them aloud. Mr Mercer's enormous blocks of dialogue were exceptionally difficult to learn but, more than that, they were extremely difficult to speak. The root of the trouble was that the verbosity lacked any form of rhythm, nor did it flow.

Although Resnais spoke impeccable English, and wrote it even better, his ear was still unsure and not quite in pitch with the poetry of our tongue. Which was hardly surprising, because there was none whatsoever in what we had to say: the players had to supply the poetry themselves, infusing the strange torrents of words with some kind of form, pace and, hardest of all, meaning. Because unless *we* believed incontrovertibly in what we were saying, no audience would.

Often, preparing at night for the work of the next day, I would discover that the removal, or even the substitution, of a word could make all the difference to a speech, but the script, as far as Resnais was concerned, was as sacred as the Turin Shroud, and although he would listen to my feverish explanations with the greatest politeness and attention, he would not budge, or permit an alteration unless I telephoned Mr Mercer himself and got his personal approval.

Since Mr Mercer lived at the time in Haifa, Israel, and we were stuck in a small village in central France with a distinctly uncertain telephone link even to the next village, to call him was, to say the least of it, difficult. It seemed to me a bit idiotic to telephone so far just for permission to alter a word like, say, 'because' to 'become' . But if, by any chance, one thought that one was being clever and simply left the offending word out of the speech during playing, Resnais would instantly notice the omission, and one would see him huddled over the sound recorder, ear-phones on his head, playing back the error, detecting it as he read the script. So it was wiser to telephone.

'For God's sake!' cried Mr Mercer one evening when we had finally tracked him down after a long day on the beach with his family. 'The script isn't sacrosanct! I'm not that kind of writer: change it about if you want to, if it's easier to play. I haven't written the Bible!'

'You have as far as this end is concerned.'

'Well, for God's sake, if something bugs you, alter it. I won't sue!' He was at all times trusting and generous.

But having to stand in the office of the little house which Florence and Resnais had rented near the château, while he sat upright, silent, unsmiling, calm, attentive, made me feel like a delinquent schoolboy in a headmaster's study while I yelled down the telephone to a very distant Mercer in Haifa asking permission to alter a word here and there to simplify a complicated sentence, or speech. But it happened very few times: it caused too much trouble. So one gave in, but fought on with the words.

John's arrival caused a different form of reverence. One which was well justified, although it fussed him greatly.

'I do wish they wouldn't keep *on* calling me Sirjohn,' he said one day. 'It's frightfully inhibiting. Couldn't you ask them, and Alain as well, just to call me 'John' as everyone else does on a film? It saves time, you see. Of course I have asked them not to but they still do. I know Alain thinks that it is disrespectful, but *do* please ask them.'

I promised that I would try. 'It'll be difficult. After all, you must realise that you are one of the greatest living actors in the English-speaking world, you are knighted, you have had a tremendous career . . . they *will* find it disrespectful. The French hold their great performers in high esteem.'

'Well, it's very nice of them: but be a dear, and do what you can.'

'It'll be almost impossible. But if you find it irritating . . . '

'Well, you see,' he said, 'I've always been lucky in having very un-sycophantic friends around me, who just say, 'Oh! Stick a crown on his head and shove him on.' It's *so* much more relaxing.'

In time he got his way: his very modesty, his generosity and warmth, made it possible; although I know that behind his back the troupe only ever referred to him as 'Sirjohn' . And that was that.

Shortly before he was to work, for the first time, Resnais suggested that I might have a little supper party and invite John to dine. I was staying in a small, isolated hotel some way out of town which had an excellent restaurant. Forwood arranged a perfect supper in a private room one evening for Resnais, Florence and John, whom we placed at the head of the table with Resnais at the other end; in this way he could observe his actor closely. Such was the entire nature of the exercise, and John caught on quickly, in spite of his asparagus, fresh river trout, and an excellent champagne.

He talked and talked, happily aware that he was holding the table and that no one would interrupt him. I don't know what Resnais knew before about Ellen Terry, Marie Tempest, Peggy Ashcroft, Edith Evans, or the third act of 'Lear' , but by the end of supper he should have known all that he ever needed to know. John's fund of stories, funny, and often gloriously irreverent, was limitless, and he was enjoying himself tremendously.

Once, while plates were being changed for another course, he leant across to me and murmured in a low voice: 'You've fixed all this up! I know. I'm under observation, aren't I?'

I confessed that it was true.

'Most unnerving,' he said, and started off again on a long, moving story about Eleanora Duse.

Resnais watched him with the rigid attention of a cat at a mouse-hole: it was a happy and extremely useful evening. We had all relaxed in John's company, and the first morning's work he did was comfortable and easy, and although Resnais found it difficult at first, he managed to drop the Sirjohn and called him simply, John.

Towards the end of work at the château, on June 3rd to be exact, Resnais had a birthday. The troupe decided to club together and get him a tape-recorder because he didn't own one, so we all put our offerings in a hat and someone went off to Lovely Limoges (as it had now become to us all) and bought the best model available. Which wasn't much of a deal. Nevertheless it would be the main offering from a devoted and loving troupe and actors.

There was one small problem. They felt that it was essential that the first voice to be recorded on the virgin tape should be John's. And that he should say, 'This is John Gielgud wishing you a happy birthday, Alain, on behalf of the troupe and actors of 'Providence'.' Or words to that effect. We all knew that Resnais was passionate about John's voice, indeed he had told me long before that he was determined to immortalize the splendour of the voice and the actor on film; which is what he was doing at the present moment. It seemed ironical that such a signal honour should come from France, and not his own country . . . however: Resnais did so.

The troupe left it to me to ask him to speak these lines on to the tape and dispatched me across the grassy terrace to where he was sitting doing *The Times* crossword. He heard me out politely and refused absolutely.

'But John, why? It's such a little thing.' I could see the troupe standing some way off watching anxiously.

'My dear boy,' he said. '*I'm* not the star of the film. You are. It's *your* job.'

'You *are* the star, for God's sake.'

He looked up with a grin. 'You have top billing. So *you* are.'

I walked back to a saddened troupe. 'He won't.'

Their disappointment was so obvious, so dejected did they look, that I decided to go back and have another try. I knelt beside John's chair in my most supplicatory manner, and spoke to him in a low voice. For the troupe had inched nearer anxiously.

'Now John, listen. They want Alain to hear your voice on the tape; for it to be the first sound recorded on the new machine. Their gift.'

He didn't even look up: shook his head, printed a word, deliberately, in the white spaces of his crossword.

I was desperate. 'John. Please. You probably have one of the most beautiful English-speaking voices in the world . . . '

He looked up over the top of his glasses. 'THE!' he said sharply.

And spoke the message.

That evening, before the presentation and the Troupe Feast (a whole sheep roasted in the orchard behind the house), he did his last shot in the film and the one which would, eventually, be the final shot of the entire picture. As night drew great dark clouds from the west, as the wind started to blow and cut with cold, he sat alone at a long table among the debris of his film-birthday-party, an aging, bitter man in solitude below the huge turreted house in which he lived and would shortly, one knew, die.

The table-cloth on the deserted, plate-littered table fluttered and bellied, a napkin was caught by the wind and whipped across the darkening terrace, his body crumpled slowly, his eyes rimmed with unshed tears, and then he reached for a bottle and poured himself unsteadily a glass of wine.

'Just time for one more,' he said, and night hurled black shadows across his face and the towered house and it was dark.

I knew, in that magical instant, why long ago I had said to Forwood after reading the script for the first time, 'There must be something working: something has got through to me. I am *very* moved.'

We broke up shortly afterwards: John went back to London, and the rest of us went on to do the major bulk of the film in the studios in Paris in the hottest summer for seventy-five years; some said one hundred.

In the simplest possible terms, 'Providence' was about one long night in the life of a dying novelist who, racked with pain, filled with drink and pills, is struggling to create a new work. Using the members of his family for his characters; muddled with the past, in terror of the future, filled with anger, spleen, and guilt, aware of swiftly approaching death.

This was the first two-thirds of the film; the final third (which we had all been busy working on) was the next morning, the day of his seventy-fifth birthday, and only then, in the sun and the brilliance of the day, when his sons and his daughter-in-law arrive to greet him and celebrate the occasion, did the film become 'real' .

The rest was all in his morbid, cruel imagination, and we, his family, were cruelly distorted puppets. It was this part which we now had to face in the Paris studios: the imagined section in which nothing was real, or true, at all. There was no sunlight in this part of the film, no light, except a cold one. Everything which we wore, touched, or through which we moved, was in sombre colours. Wedding rings were silver, not gold, our make-up was greenish-grey, the clothing dark, unmemorable; everything was, in fact, almost monochrome.

'Memory is colourless,' Resnais said. 'If you fill your car with petrol at a garage on the autoroute, what colours do you remember, *as colours*? Perhaps the overalls which the attendant wears? The petrol pump? Perhaps a door, a fallen leaf . . . nothing more; all the rest you will only remember without colour.'

Memory was a rather depressing place in which to work.

The playing in this long section, two-thirds of the film, had to be larger than life: for everything that we did or said was only in the aging novelist's mind, an imagination heightened by pain and pills and drink. This called for a particular 'style' in the acting, totally different from that which we had used in the summer garden and the sunlit reality. There it had been relatively easy; we were free, relaxed, laughing, real.

'How am I going to play this cold rage-less barrister my father has invented?' I asked Resnais. 'Obviously he is detested for some reason so I suppose that he must show detestable signs? Have I got that right?' I was never absolutely certain.

Resnais smiled his cool Breton smile, shrugged, spread his hands; inferring, in those eloquent movements, that it was up to me to work out.

I was very perplexed; but suddenly I hit on an idea that I should play the role for him in three different ways, and whichever performance of the role he liked, and thought correct, we would stick with.

'You could play it three different ways?'

'I think so. Let's try. I'll play it absolutely straight — cold, attacking barrister; then in the style of, well . . . Congreve, the Restoration comedies; and then I'll give you my impersonation of Rex Harrison being bloody. Which shall we try first?'

I think that it was really the only time that I saw Resnais laugh with pleasure. But he also considered the suggestion with care. He was undecided how it should be played himself.

We did the scene three times, as suggested. He thought the Rex Harrison effort was possibly going a little too far, although it was funny, and finally settled for the high style of Restoration to begin with, mixed with the cold, attacking barrister, and here and there he suggested that I might add a pinch, just a pinch, of Rex Harrison. Which when I did always broke him up, to such an extent that he once fell off a chair.

I had started to shape my character, bearing in mind at all times that I must carry with it echoes and traces of Gielgud's *own* personality. Like father, then like son.

The supper which we had at the hotel, when John was under close scrutiny by his director, had proved immeasurably useful to me also: for I was able to recall, when I needed them, many small mannerisms and characteristics of the man, with which I could flesh out my playing of his 'son' . And so, for some days, until the performance finally 'firmed' , I did two, or even three different interpretations of every scene, and left Resnais to choose the one which he preferred.

The *auteur* director at work.

It is the parrot cry of many actors, especially those with a mainly theatrical background, that a screen performance is 'manufactured in the cutting-room' , which is as idiotic a remark as it is ignorant, and equivalent to saying that Van Gogh or Vuillard painted pictures by numbers.

To be sure, a bad, poor, even appalling performance can be saved by a brilliant editor, and often is. God knows, I have seen enough dreadful performances in my time lifted to a higher plane than the actor would ever have dreamed of, or been able to perform by himself, by the judicious use of a pair of scissors; but it happens very seldom (it's easier to recast, and cheaper), and if the player has learned his film technique, which is essential, and his director knows exactly what he wants and how to obtain the results, there isn't anything an editor can do, one way or another, to 'manufacture a performance' of any importance, because that has already been done, and *fixed*, on the floor by the player himself through his thoughts and the force of his concentration.

A great many actors don't know that the camera actually photographs thought; which is a pity. For if there is 'no one at home' , so to speak, there won't be much on the screen in the final result, and no amount of work on the editor's part can magically paste together millions of scraps of film in the cutting-room and come forth with a *thinking* performance. It really doesn't work that way.

A very distinguished actor recently said in print that all the waiting about he had to do while filming dissolved his concentration to such an extent that in the end he was only able to play himself; rather than the intended character. A very sorry admission. Another, equally distinguished, complained that the nerve, energy and concentration needed to act were easily lost when 'simply' performing *before* a camera. I don't know what he meant by the word 'simply' ; I imagine he has had more luck than I, for the last thing I have ever found it to be is simple. And *performing* before a camera is what you don't do. You work to it. And beyond it.

However, they both used the word concentration, and that is the main key to cinema playing; without it you are lost, and the retaining of it, through thick and through thin, is essential, exhausting and sometimes so hard to contain that one is brought to the edge of madness. It is a lesson that many actors never learn. But you have got to have it, and the strength to hold it. Resnais perhaps had it to the highest degree: and he fired us all with his firm, quiet, determined force, and drove us hard.

Now that we knew the form of the film, the texture as it were, the quartet, Burstyn, Stritch, Warner and I, found the going a little easier; although the heat nearly killed us, and the work left little or no time for any form of relaxation, and we ran with sweat constantly (Ellen's hair going, literally, straight before my eyes on one exhausting day) under blazing lamps in the hottest summer known, we were all extraordinarily happy because there was a feeling in the parched and burning air that what we were doing was not only pleasing Resnais, with his pitiless demands for perfection, but that we were actually playing together as he had first requested we should, as a full, perfectly balanced, quartet. Or quintet: even though our main instrument, John, had performed his solo, and left us.

I saw the film, eventually, at a press screening in Paris. It was exactly, for me, the film I had always hoped to be a part of; for it did all that I ever desired a film to do. It disturbed, educated and illuminated, and above all it made me laugh, much to the anger of some of the French press who hissed at me furiously like geese, thinking, I suppose, that I was being irreverent.

It opened in New York to savage reviews from the Three Butchers of Broadway as they were, and probably still are, called, who took axe, cleaver and saw to our effort. But this produced an immediate and exciting backlash of dismay and rage from their more discerning colleagues, and others, who had been overwhelmed with pleasure, all of whom wrote reviews and personal messages which they sent to Resnais with permission to use them for publicity.

So the *New York Times*, which had damned us cruelly, carried enormous advertising bearing lavish words of praise from Susan Sontag, Judith Crist, Rex Reed, Liz Smith, Sidney Lumet, William Wolf and a great many others. It was a brave, moving and generous gesture, but it failed to save the picture in that strange city of paradoxes.

I don't suppose that it would have troubled the Butchers had we worn wigs and breeches, carried tricorn hats and simpered under our patches. Restoration

Comedy they might just have managed to cope with; especially in fancy dress. But not in a modern lounge suit. That became something quite else.

It has to be remembered that America is more a continent than a country: it takes over five weary hours to fly across it in a jet. It is an immigrant land, made up from every known race on the face of the earth.

The English language which was inherited from the earlier British settlers was, of necessity, rendered down to a simple mush, so that everyone from North to South, from East to West, could understand readily and simply. Instant recognition.

But in the simplification, the wit, the nuance, the irony and, perhaps above all, the *style* of the English language have been eliminated: they have no meaning for the vast majority of Americans. And the majority *is* vast. It is little wonder, therefore, that a film like 'Providence', based on these very essentials of speech, should founder as it did.

Resnais, who had been present at the New York opening, later said, with a wry smile, that perhaps he should have shown the film there in the French-dubbed version. With sub-titles. It would have made all the difference, and New York would then have understood the film better.

He proved his point some years later, with his next film, 'Mon Oncle d'Amérique', which opened to rave reviews, not only in New York but across the entire country. In French. With sub-titles.

In Paris, we were an overwhelming success, and the smash-hit of the season, with reviews of a kind which I have never seen before and probably never will again, going on to win seven Oscars (French) with embarrassing ease, including, justifiably, one for Mr Mercer from Haifa.

And so it was over.

The wait of a decade had been worth every minute and I had, at last, achieved what was perhaps my greatest ambition as an actor: to work with Alain Resnais. It was, I couldn't help thinking, a hell of a long way from being The Idol of the Odeons.

THIRTEEN

It was also, as it happened, the last major film I was to make. Three weeks after finishing work on 'Providence' I was on my way to Holland to play a small role in Richard Attenborough's epic war-film about the disaster of Arnhem.

My sense of order, at this point, had completely broken down. I had sworn never to play featured-bits, or slide off towards cameo-roles, but reversed that decision, unwisely as it was to turn out, by allowing myself to be persuaded into joining the massive band of superstars and lesser mortals who had been gathered together to recreate one of the most appalling defeats the British had had to suffer in the Second World War. One at which I had personally been present: not in the city, but just across the river. I am still not clear, even today, why I broke my rule. My valued friendship with Attenborough certainly had a great deal to do with it: he and his wife, Sheila, had been the only people to show a modicum of kindness and thought towards me during my fledgling days with

Rank, and I have never forgotten that kindness. Also I reasoned, I suppose, that it wouldn't take me long to do (it was a very small part) and would round off the summer's work admirably.

I took from the vast script the few pages in which my role appeared and, following Henry Fonda's trick on 'Le Serpent', stuck them into a plastic cover; this was lighter, and so made packing easier.

The set-up in a small town in Holland was quite different from the one in Lovely Limoges. No small troupe of intimate friends here. Rather a crew of some hundreds, all, apparently, aged about nineteen, all running, all wearing walkie-talkie sets which screamed and bleeped endlessly. Every player had his own private trailer dressing-room complete with flush lavatory, his name in large letters on the door, and a private servant (usually an out-of-work Dutch actor or student of drama hoping for a 'break', in the film about their own agony) to bring food, and run errands. I found it rather uncomfortable and uneasy.

There were trucks and trailers, generators and jeeps, an enormous 'Honeywaggon' (the Unit lavatory; neat little stalls in a row), luxury cars to ferry the superstars from their hotels in Amsterdam, two hours away, and at all times the wail and scream of the walkie-talkies bringing a surreal air of hysteria to the whole vast safari (for that is really what it looked like) through which, with his stick and an affable, even jovial, demeanour, stamped Mr Joe Levine, whose extravagantly budgeted production this was. Some said twenty-seven million dollars, others thought perhaps a little less, at twenty million odd; in any case Alain Resnais, the poet-director, could have made his film ten times over, and still had enough left for breakfast and room service at Claridge's.

Mr Levine's presence was there mainly to encourage everyone to finish on time and, if possible, under budget. We finished on time I know, because I was in the final shot: I have no idea what happened to his budget.

Alas! My performance caused an uproar when the film was finally shown. There were cries of fury and distress from the widow and family of the man I was representing, and anger was expressed, so I was reliably informed, from Windsor Castle to Clarence House. Letters were even written to *The Times* (of *all* papers) complaining of my interpretation. I was crushed with dismay.

I didn't see the film, so I am not qualified to make any comment, nor can I judge where, or if, I went wrong. I had known the officer I played, in Normandy and in Holland: the very last thing I would have dreamed of doing was to defame his character or reputation, but both of which I was told I had; God knows how.

Such distress did this cause me that I considered making an apology in the press and sending my salary to an army charity. It wasn't much, as it happened, but I was determined not to retain one farthing.

After thirty years of working in the cinema and sixty odd films, this was the harshest blow I had had to take. And it taught me, for the last time, never to go against my sense of order again. At least, in the cinema.

However, my hysteria simmered down after two trusted people had seen the film, at my request, and instructed me to make no apology but just shut up. My work, I was informed, was 'professional, straightforward, military and cold''. 'Which,' as one said, 'I suppose, is what Generals were meant to be.'

So that was a relief; but it took a long time to set aside. Forgetting, however, was different.

This unhappy business meant flying to and from Amsterdam for short spells of work from July until the final day of shooting, on October 6th, and it was extremely difficult to think of the book under these circumstances.

Finished even though it was, there was still a certain amount of work to do on it, not least corrections, which were sent by Mr Charlton, and extra scribbles for chapter headings or main page illustrations which he flattered me into providing. Not to mention the cover itself.

At first I had thought of using a fragment of Van Gogh's 'The Cornfield', but then realised it was an impertinent thing to do to use a master's work in which to wrap up the writing of an amateur; so I decided to have a shot at doing my own. It would all then be of a piece.

Throughout 'Providence' I had never lost contact with the book, even during the hardest and most trying times. I drew on hotel letter-paper whenever an idea came to me, and Mr Charlton kept me in touch with anything which he thought I should know; although he was very careful to leave me in tactful peace to get on with my proper work. But like all beginners, I constantly brooded on the things I had written and kept finding different, or better, ways to express myself, because I had been told that once the type was set up and the book in proof, corrections would be unwelcome – they take time and cost money. 'Print is not made from india rubber' Mr Charlton reminded me.

Thus I abandoned a number of ideas which I had let float about in my mind for the re-writing of certain paragraphs and even, in one instant, an entire chapter, and concentrated on ideas for the cover design, finally roughing out the one I thought would fit the subject well enough on the back of a page of one of the sheets torn from the Arnhem script during a flight from Amsterdam to Nice. I then got down to work with long-disused brushes and a box of paints on the trestles in the room above the wood shed.

Ignorant as I was about anything whatever to do with publishing or printing, I did a happy, colourful, design and sent it off to Chatto and Windus, only to discover that it was the wrong dimension, and would have to be done all over again. However, Mr Charlton (who now had become 'John' as I had become 'Dirk' during our lengthy correspondence, and also due to the fact that he had come all the way out to the house for twenty-four hours to discuss minor alterations in the work and to sift through the many photographs which I had assembled for him to choose from as illustrations for the final book) indicated that the cover design, though far too small, was 'excellent', and thus encouraged once again, I started from scratch with the correct dimensions; thoughtfully provided.

Sometime in late October, I can't be absolutely certain, he wrote an enthusiastic note about the new effort, and down at the bottom of his page I saw an odd block of red ink scratches which were obviously not from his clear, upright hand. These were spiked, angular, and quite unreadable.

I pondered over them for a very long time and finally came to the conclusion that whoever, or whatever, had penned these fascinating scraps was either 'sad' or 'mad' about the design.

A difference.

The only part of any kind of signature that I could make out was a probable letter 'N'.

On the telephone the next day, John assured me that the word *was* 'mad' and that the writer was Norah Smallwood. Overcome by this nod from the Top, I suddenly decided that I would draw her a small remembrance of Virginia Woolf as she had appeared to me in those distant days when I was an 'embalmed twelve' sitting by the River Ouse fishing, and she would sometimes walk along the river bank, singing to herself, carrying an enormous golf-umbrella. It was not for the book.

It was a personal gift of gratitude, modest though it was, to my, as yet, unseen needlewoman.

My sister-in-law, Cilla, on a wet camping holiday somewhere in northern France, with her two small children, once sent me a postcard on which she said that the holiday had had some benefits, in spite of rain and a series of minor accidents; she had been forced to learn a little more French than the phrase 'Help! My postillion has been struck by lightning!'

I took the old phrase for the title of my book, and here at last it was before me in 'proof'. A pale green paper-covered volume, which I held as tenderly, as proudly, as filled with awe as a mother with her first-born child.

The fact that I had to correct the thing didn't worry me at all: I sat and read it through three times right off in a daze of pleasure, and self-congratulation. I was absolutely amazed. I had written a book.

Naturally I hadn't the least idea how to go about the corrections, but bearing in mind John's firm edict that print was not india-rubber, I started off with a light heart and a red pencil.

And work began again in earnest. Not only on proof corrections.

October is a hellish month on the land here. The last terraces have to be mown and raked before winter, the grapes picked, a venture spiced with danger from a million wasps, and far more tedious than it is romantic; the beds made ready for the spring with wall-flowers and ten-week stock, the pots and urns emptied and cleaned and, finally and with regret, the terrace furniture put into store. Summer is over.

Azis, the crazed Arab who helped with some of the heavy work, had long since wandered off. Probably back to his village in Tunisia.

He had finished some of the walls, and kicked the smaller lawn-mower to pieces in a fit of violent rage which overtook him one blistering day during Ramadan. As he appeared to be spending most of the day with his head stuck under one of the garden taps I offered him, unwisely, a cold beer, not knowing if he was a faithful Muslim or not: he was not. He accepted the beer with grateful signs (we still had no common tongue) and shortly afterwards I found him jumping up and down on the top of the mower, screaming hysterically and calling on Allah, waving his arms about like a demented semaphore, so that any move towards him must prove dangerous, while the mower shook to pieces under his fandango until, with a hefty kick, he sent a bit flying in the direction of Mecca and went to sleep curled up under a tree. Although it had been entirely my fault, I felt that the time had come for us to part: however, the following week he didn't turn up, or the next, and was never seen again. Which was a relief: except that we were now minus one pair of hands and a strong back to do the heavy work. But the mowing went on, we grubbed up the big stones for the walls, and hacked away at the summer's growth of brambles and broom.

The book still simmered among this activity; corrections were finally done, the photographs chosen, and John telephoned from time to time to say that the paperback people were 'very interested', the Book Clubs 'excited', and that there was heavy interest being shown in publishing it in America.

I drew a firm line at this. Or tried to. I had no desire that my modest child should be thrown to the wolves there: I told John, whose voice, after I had refused to consider this suggestion, showed definite signs of distress for the first time since I had once blithely decided to re-write an entire chapter long after they had started setting. Normally calm and unruffled, he now betrayed slight tremors of anxiety.

America was a big market, he assured me, and begged me to re-think my decision. I pointed out, I thought rather sensibly, that the Americans would expect a very different book from the one I had written, full of film stars, confessions, and film-hype. They would expect an index bursting with glamour.

All that I could put in the index were some vague names which would mean nothing to them: perhaps Henry Moore would pass; but I really couldn't see them going a bundle on The Sun Engraving Works, Watford, or Cissie Waghorn. Could he?

I suppose it was the first time that I had realised that, like the cinema, publishing was 'business'. A sale was a sale, a profit and a loss the same as they were in my profession, where no one was actually employing one for anything other than money. But, even if the thought saddened me momentarily, I wriggled clear of depression by consoling myself with the thought that in publishing everyone was gentlemanly, calmer, more elegant. Nothing could be as ugly or deceitful as the cinema.

Could it?

Not with Chatto and Windus, Bertie assured me cheerfully, but there were some very dark corners in publishing, into which I must not stray. 'I know some who'd have your guts for garters, my dear,' he said brightly. 'You are with the best firm in town, with the best boss. I'd listen to her advice if I were you.

On the last day of October I was listening to another voice. A rather high, anxious one, which sounded on the telephone, as if it was coming from the middle of a bus-station. 'Hello? Hello?' it shouted, and I shouted back.

'My name is Tom Stoppard,' cried the voice. 'We haven't met.'

'No.'

'I'm at London airport.'

So I wasn't far out with the bus-station sounds.

'Oh, are you?'   'I've just got in from Munich.'

'Splendid!'

'I gather that you aren't making any more films; am I right?'

'No. Wrong. I'm not making any more crap.'

There was a short pause.

'I don't write crap,' he said crossly.

'I'm sorry. I wasn't talking of *your* work.'

'I've just written an adaptation of a Nabokov book, 'Despair', which Fassbinder is making in Germany and we both think that you would be marvellous for the leading character.'

'When do you start?'

'Oh . . . *I* don't know. Early next year. Can I send it to you; the first draft?'

'Well, I am supposed to be doing 'Under the Volcano' for the Mexican Government . . . but I don't know exactly when; anyway there are a lot of problems there. So do send your script if you are certain I'd be all right?'

'I'm certain and so is Fassbinder. I thought of you on the flight out and when I got to Munich they told me that you were his preferred choice, coincidence?'

'I've got a book coming out,' I said in a casual throwaway voice. 'In March. I don't want to miss that.'

'I think they'll probably start some time in April, anyway must go now, I'll send it tomorrow.'

He rang off. Stoppard, Nabokov, Fassbinder.

Not a bad package: and he had said 'leading character', not just 'a part'. The old surge of excitement welled up again: after all it *was* my job, and those three names were not easily dismissed.

The first draft of 'Despair' arrived a few days later with a hastily scribbled note attached to it explaining that there was still a lot to be done to it, begging me to wait until a final draft was ready, in December. Which, when it arrived, had enough exciting material in it to persuade me, for almost the first time, to go against Forwood's advice and accept. He didn't feel it would be the commercial success which my career needed at that moment.

I reasoned, I think very sensibly (all order restored), that my book would be out in March and that after the hullabaloo, if there was one, it wouldn't last more than a week; after which I would be left with absolutely nothing to do.

Nothing to create either theatrically or in written words. There would be a silence. A blank.

Far better, therefore, to have a project in mind and a script in hand, and the fascination of working with Fassbinder was overwhelming. If, as I felt certain in the deepest recesses of my heart, my days as a working actor of the kind I had been for twelve years were beginning to fade out, I was determined that they would not fade out on a cameo role.

At least I would go out above the title; a position to which I had grown accustomed ever since my first film in 1947. The only slight twist of doubt I had was that, if indeed it was to be my final film (and who could possibly tell?), it had a most unfortunate title for the closing of a career: 'Despair'.

But I accepted — the temptation was too strong: a new director, a new country to work in, a new type of role altogether. And quite apart from anything else it had become increasingly clear that the Mexican Government was unsettled; to say the least. So, R. W. Fassbinder.

In January I finished lagging all the outside water-pipes in the garden, and then went off to London to start the promotion for *Postillion*, rather bemused by the interest it had so far engendered. Little, I thought, do they know what they are in for. No True Confessions here, just a rural ride through a time which had gone for ever: but before I started work I insisted on going down to Sussex for the family reunion luncheon with Elizabeth and George.

Ma was there. Brought over from her flat in the comfortable Edwardian house a mile or two away. She was frailer than the last time I had seen her, but immaculate; sitting in what she insisted was 'her' chair by a blazing log-fire, a wide scarf about her shoulders, pinned by Capucine's gift, of many years before, a Chanel clip of false pearls and emeralds; the heavy black shoes.

'Well. And how do I look?'

'Marvellous. You look terrific, Ma.'

'I had my hair done especially. Elizabeth took me last week. Do you remember the brooch?'

'Of course I do. Cap gave it to you.'

She looked vaguely about the light, pretty room. 'Who?'

'Capucine. One Christmas. It's a Chanel original.'

'Oh yes. I know. I love it. I'm never without it.' She lit a cigarette, picked a piece of tobacco from her lip. 'Your brother's gone to America. Chicago,' she said, and put her lighter into the big black bag she always carried.

'I know. Very sensible. All those kids to educate: far more chances for them all in America.'

'He took all my furniture.'

'Darling! Not *all* your furniture: you know that. A few pieces only. And you told him that he could.'

'Well. I hate them being in America. Ulric's dressing-chest went too . . . and all my babies.'

'Ma dear. They *aren't* your babies, they're Gareth's.'

She stared at me with defiant hostility. '*I'm* his mother!'

'And he has a wife. They are not *your* babies. Anyway it'll be super for them there, it's a young country.'

She looked away, interest lost. 'I don't know,' she said. Then suddenly, as if remembering something, 'and why are you here all of a sudden?'

'My book. I've written a book, remember? About us all, years ago, at the cottage. I'm here to do the publicity stuff.'

'Will you be on television?'

'I think so . . . and the BBC.'

'I must know when. To tell the maids at the home, they like to know.'

'Ma darling, it is not a *home*, it's an *hotel*; that's quite different.'

'It's a home to me. So that's your answer. When's it coming out, this book?'

'March. Just before my birthday.'

'This room looks bare without the furniture.'

'I think it looks lovely: lighter. The things Gareth had, the wine-cupboard, the secretaire, were a bit heavy, weren't they?'

She smiled. 'Were they? *I* never thought so. Daddy and I liked them: I must be getting senile or something.'

I poured her a glass of wine.

'What's that? Not my stuff?'

'No. It's a Chablis. I brought it: no good?'

She savoured it for a moment. 'Personally I like a sweeter wine. That Spanish stuff suits me. I have a glass at night.' She set the glass down carefully on a small table. 'It helps me to sleep. So that I don't have to think. Where is this book then?'

'Oh. It won't be out until next month. You get the first copy, then Elizabeth, and one for Lally.'

She suddenly looked up sharply, stubbing out her cigarette. 'Why Lally?'

'Because she's in it. A lot of it.'

'I see.' She began to hum softly to herself, brushing imaginary dust from her arm.

Elizabeth came in from the kitchen, an oven-cloth in her hands. 'Just about ready. Guess· what? Boiled beef and dumplings!'

'Oh Lor' . . . your rotten·old dumplings. All soggy: and hard in the middle.'

'You are a beast. Quite vile. I bet you can't get them in your soppy old South of France.'

'No, thank God.'

'I'm simply not taking any notice of you. Ma? Ma, will you be warm enough in the dining-room?'

My mother started to ease herself out of her chair. 'I always *was*. It's a cold room. Ulric blocked in the fireplace. Useless to argue. I told him not to. Anyway: I have my scarf.' She raised an arm towards me for assistance. 'Help your old Ma: getting so stiff. I do if I sit for too long: but I can't walk much now. My legs. You remember when I was in the Munitions in the first war, we all had to volunteer, and I dropped a shell on my foot? An enormous thing . . . '

'Yes. I know.'

'Oh. Sorry you've been troubled. I've told you before. Well, I'm paying for it now, can't walk anywhere. Don't forget to tell me when you are going to be on the BBC or the television, I have to tell the maids at the . . . ' She stopped, and waved a slender hand vaguely in the air as we walked slowly together to the dining-room. 'The *hotel*. Is that right?'

'Absolutely right,' I said.

William IV Street is short and unexceptional, linking St Martin's Lane with the Strand. On one side stands the ugly bulk of Trafalgar Square Post Office, on the other, and directly opposite, the unremarkable building which has housed Chatto and Windus since 1936.

No strip lighting here, no drooping rubber-tree in the reception area: no reception area in fact. A step up from the pavement and one is in a sort of hallway; on the right a glass case in which George the telephonist sits, an amiable spider in a web of wires and plugs before the aging switchboard. A little beyond, an elderly lift, and a sagging staircase, offer transport to the higher realms of literature. The lift is lethal; a shuddering coffin which holds four crushed over-intimately together, hauled aloft by greasy cables and rumbling wheels. It very often doesn't work at all and sulks in its well. In any case it is usually wiser, and safer, to climb the wooden staircase, an inelegant structure, mottled with years of chipped paint-scars, one's feet clattering on the worn linoleum. There is a 'smell' of paper, of cardboard, of print, of dust: above all an atmosphere of work, and serious work at that.

It reminded me when I arrived there, that first morning, of *The Times* and Printing House Square, and I was strangely instantly secure in the familiar feeling of the place. The same sagging floors, scratched linoleum, narrow corridors, central-heating pipes strung about like macaroni, the coming and going, the rustle of papers, the grimed windows, the unlovely loveliness of it all. For an instant I had the impression that I had been here before: to ask my father for a loan, which I did often enough, receiving half-a-crown at the most, a florin at the least. And usually given to me by Mr Greenwood, his secretary, because, as my father would always say, 'Greenwood: I've only got a ten bob note . . . what have you got?' Mr Greenwood had inexhaustible pockets.

A fragment of memory induced so easily by an atmosphere I knew so well.

John had hurried along a corridor to greet me. 'Ah! There you are.'

'Not late, I hope? I hate to be late.'

'No. No. Absolutely on the dot.'

Rosalind Bell, the PR girl, joined us, looking, deceptively, like a Dickensian waif dressed at a Women's Institute stall. 'Everything all right yesterday? The interviews?'

'*The Spectator* was well-intentioned; there was a maddening woman from *The Observer* who had just sent her child off to its first Day School and kept telephoning the place to see if it was 'happy' . . .

'Had she got the proof copy? I sent her one?'

'Hadn't read it.'

Miss Bell almost shouted – for her. 'Hadn't read it! I've *told* them all . . . '

'Well, by the look of it she'd had a bash at the first two chapters. The rest was unthumbed, and she'd lost her biro.'

'I think,' said John, 'that Mrs Smallwood is waiting. Just round here a little.'

A half-open door and a crisp voice came ringing through. 'I thought I heard visitors!' The door flew open and there before me stood my second needle-woman, my 'patcher'. After all this time.

She was tall, very slender, elegant in a white silk blouse and coral-red wool skirt. In her hands she held two books, one bound in blue, one in yellow; she thrust them towards me.

'Which colour d'you like?' She left the books in my hands and turned back into her room. 'I'll get my jacket.'

I stood there in the corridor holding two copies of *A Postillion Struck by Lightning* and knew that nothing as wonderful could ever happen to me again. Norah Smallwood came out directly, shrugging on a jacket, a wide-brimmed

Herbert Johnson hat on her head.

She moved swiftly; sharp, brisk movements as if even going from point A to point B was using up time and had to be done as rapidly as possible.

'Have we got transport? It's the Garrick. We've booked for one o'clock.'

We hurried down the stairs behind her, John, Forwood, an American publisher's representative and scout, and a pleasant young woman in paperbacks, much as if the Garrick Club was a ship casting off to sail.

Mahogany, oak; I don't know now. An impression of a fireplace, high, sombre rooms, portraits everywhere, a hatrack, a porter and signing registers. A gathering of figures whose faces one remembers, actors or writers; the actors tightly clothed in lounge suits, sipping glasses of sherry in their double-breasted waistcoats; the writers, if that's what they were, less formal, more relaxed, the hand which did not hold a Guinness thrust into a pocket.

At lunch a long table. I beside my 'patcher' who had taken her place, naturally and with ease, at the head and ordered oxtail stew. There was wine; waitresses in black with white aprons, muted conversation from other tables, the shine of silver on the canopy of the carving-trolley, and I haven't the least idea about what we spoke.

Before me, high up on the wall, a full-length portrait of Gladys Cooper: a sudden jump of pleasure, a tug of familiarity again. My marmalade Aunt. Marmalade because, years ago, in her garden in Hollywood she had shown me a giant orange tree heavy with fruit.

'What to do with it all? Such a wicked shame to throw them all away.'

'Make some marmalade.'

'I can't boil an egg! Marmalade . . . '

And later, one evening sitting in her cluttered, comfortable, very English sitting-room in Napoli Drive, she handed me the first pot. It had a label. 'The Other Cooper's Marmalade'. Written in her huge, looping, generous handwriting.

And now there she was before me, coolly watching as they picked through the oxtail stew and spoke of American sales, paperback rights, and press promotions.

'I've written a book,' I wanted to say to her. 'All by myself. How about that?' Not quite by myself.

There was no portrait in this calm, high-ceilinged room of Mrs X from New England. No portraits of those who, so long ago in a dreary NAAFI, had welcomed me into their reading group and offered me unknown, unexpected, unbelievable treasure: Isherwood and Waugh, Surtees and the pale Brontës; Owen and the bewilderment of Wyndham Lewis and so many others.

No. I hadn't quite done it all by myself. There had been a little help from my friends; and from my second 'needlewoman' sitting reassuringly beside me now, alive, touchable, tangible, spooning up her apple pie.

'Scrumptious, isn't it?' she said suddenly.

'I'm having cheese.'

'You'll need a lot of strength in the next two days: there are masses of interviews laid on.'

Of course, the thing was, she didn't know that she was my 'needlewoman'; my 'patcher'. She didn't even know that I knew her voice had echoed quietly behind many of the letters which John, sitting opposite me, had written: didn't know, at this moment, that I was aware that she had watched a television chat show so many months ago and that I knew perfectly well that '*Several of us here* . . . ' was, in reality, only herself.

I looked up at my marmalade Aunt. 'I've got a hell of a lot of responsibility to this little group down here. Pray God I don't come a cropper and let them down: they seem confident; too confident. You once told me that you thrived on responsibility, absolutely loved it, you said. I wonder if I will too? It's a different kind of responsibility in the theatre or the cinema; this has become extraordinarily personal; I'll do my damnedest, even though half the time I don't understand a word they say. Wish me luck. Cross fingers?'

Suddenly, with courage gained, I leant across the table and told John, and the pleasant girl from paperbacks, almost the entire plot of a novel which I wanted to write. One day.

And did.

Elizabeth wrote immediately after she had received her advance copy of *Postillion*.

Cherry Tree Cottage. February 4th '77

' *. . . I LOVE IT DESPERATELY! Not because I am in it, and, may I add, you have made me much nicer than I ever was, and brighter.* (sic)

Was I as bossy as that!? . . . I long to talk to you about it all. What bliss to be taken back to one's happy, sunny, days even for twenty-four hours, and how lucky to be able to go there through a book.'

And Lally.

The Street, Steeple, Essex. March 10th '77

'*Dirk darling,*

The book sounds just right, don't change anything, I hope I shall always be "Lally" to you whatever happens, dear . . . it is a great day for me to know you still remember all the lovely times we had together. Take care of yourself, darling.'

My mother didn't write. This was not surprising because she wrote very occasionally and when she did her letters were sad. '*I've no news to tell you, people don't come to see me now because of the petrol.*'

I went to see her just before publication day. Her little flat in the Edwardian house was comfortable and warm, with a pleasant view across the lawns and gardens. It was furnished with 'bits and pieces' of her own. On the walls were some of my father's paintings of places which she had known with him and loved, Alfriston, Berwick, Firle Beacon; a portrait in chalk and wash of herself which someone else had done and which she treasured. Everywhere there were pots or jars of flowers and plants and, here and there, small piles of paperbacks, mostly by Barbara Cartland and Georgette Heyer.

'All paperbacks!' I said.

'Easier to read in bed. I can't hold a real book. I get them from the maids.'

'Where's mine?'

'Your what?'

'Book. *Postillion*?'

'Oh!' She began to twist her rings. A sign I recognised very well. 'Oh darling: yes. Of course. Your book. I gave it to one of the maids.'

'Ma!'

'Well . . . she's a dear soul and she has been so kind to me; wonderful. She saw it lying here and begged for it. They all know who you are, you see.'

'But you read it first, didn't you?'

The rings again.

'Looked at the pictures. God knows where you found some of them. There's *one* good one of me, with Elizabeth when she was in the WRENs. Daddy took it. But that terrible one of you both sitting on the stairs like a pair of slum children. Elizabeth looks as if she was knock-kneed.'

'Most people seem to like that one. But did you read nothing. Nothing?'

'It's heavy for me to hold in bed.' She reached out and took a cigarette from a paper packet, lit it. 'Anyway, it's all about children.'

'I know, darling, yours. Elizabeth and me.'

She put the lighter down, closed the cigarette packet carefully. 'Elizabeth tells me that these cost a fortune now. I can't think why. Taste of straw. Aunt Belle won't be very happy: with what you've written about her and that man she married; Duff.'

So she *had* read something. Aunt Belle was her elder sister and there had never been much love lost between the two.

'I've been a damned sight nicer about them than I needed. And changed all their names. You don't mind, do you? Not angry? About the Scottish part?'

'Good God, no! I had to come all the way up to get you away, if you remember; the most awful row.'

'I know. It's in the book.'

'She wanted to adopt you, did you know that? When you were born. She thought that I wouldn't be able to bring you up properly. Too flighty, she said. She didn't approve of me. The Scarlet Woman. An actress.'

'I'm jolly glad that you didn't let me go.'

'Narrow-minded, awful. *I* brought you up.'

'Marvellously.'

She tapped her cigarette deliberately on the edge of the ash-tray two or three times. 'Lally didn't: that's all I'm saying.'

'I know she didn't.'

'She's all over your book. Lally this and Lally that . . . I don't understand it.'

'It's all about the time when we were on holidays with her at the cottage. We had a wonderful time. You know what it's like. When the cat's away the mice will play, and when you and Daddy weren't there we ran riot . . . I mean that's all it is.'

'You don't mention Daddy and me at all.'

'I *do* darling! You just haven't read it so how can you tell? I wish you'd read it.'

'Oh, I will. I will. I've plenty of time. I've always got plenty of time. I could go mad.'

'Well . . . just as long as you aren't upset about your family in Scotland . . . the Aunts and Uncles. I've been very tactful, you'll see.'

'My dear boy! I'm not upset. Your father couldn't stand them. He wouldn't even go up there; he dreaded me suggesting it. I'm not upset.'

But the Scots family were. From the moment that *Postillion* was published they never wrote to, or contacted, my mother again. Punishing her cruelly for a fault of mine. Once, some years later, a gentler sister-in-law sent her a small calendar for Christmas. It was about the size of a postcard. The price, in pencil, was thirty pence. It had 'Views of Bonnie Scotland' on the cover and she pinned it on the wall at the foot of her bed: but we never spoke about them again. Although she had all their photographs in a frame beside her bed. It was the nearest they would ever be to her for the rest of her life.

I walked across the room to look at one of my father's paintings: trees, sun slanting through them; a road.

'That's down at the bottom of Great Meadow, isn't it?' I said.

'Somewhere. I don't know. I like it.'

'Anyway: you're coming up to lunch at the Connaught on Friday. Celebration lunch for the book.'

She stubbed out the cigarette. 'Darling Connaught. How am I getting there?'

'George is bringing you up by car. Friday, remember.'

'*I've* written a book,' she said suddenly.

'You haven't! God knows, we've been trying to get you to for ages: when?'

'Oh . . . someone came to help me. Suggestions. She was fascinated; encouraged me.'

'Remember Daphne Fielding?'

'No.'

'Well, she gave you a note-book once, with 'Maggie's Story' printed on the cover. Is that what you used? That what you've done? Your own story?'

'That's what I've done. It's not much. Tragic. The woman was fascinated. It's too far for me to go all the way to London now.'

'Don't be daft. You just have to get in the car and you'll be there in a flash.'

'I'm not keen.'

'I won't see you for ages if you don't. I'm off to Germany to make a film.'

'Oh. Is my hair all right?'

'You look lovely.'

Someone tapped gently at the door and said that lunch was ready.

I liked Rainer Werner Fassbinder the very moment that I saw him. Thickset, wordless as far as I could tell, his inscrutability increased by tin-rimmed glasses and a thin straggly moustache.

He sat at supper that first night at the Colombe d'Or listening intently to every word spoken, but never made a sound himself, reaching for what he wanted and eating bread as if he was starving. I was assured, by his pleasant producer who had come with him (as well as Mr Stoppard), that he would not speak English, so he would translate any problems we had with the script.

And there were quite a number.

It didn't take me long to realise that Fassbinder probably spoke fluent English, or if not, that he understood it perfectly: for he laughed often at our remarks, and shook his head in angry disagreement from time to time at a suggestion made, or else nodded happily in agreement. I couldn't help thinking that he must be pretty well aware of everything said: his mother, after all, I had been told, was official translator to Truman Capote or Tennessee Williams, so it was very likely that he spoke English himself. It was going to be a hell of a problem working together in an English-language film with no common tongue.

The next day everyone came up to the house to have lunch and 'iron out the bumps' in the script. We sat round the tin table, pencils poised, scripts before us, while Mr Stoppard feverishly re-wrote passages and then read them, eagerly, aloud, while Fassbinder shrugged from time to time, showing a marked indifference to what was going on, and frequently yawned.

It was perfectly clear to me, after half an hour of this, that he would make *his* version of 'Despair', when the time came, and do exactly what he wanted. Which is precisely what he did.

At one moment during this somewhat lethargic conference I said to him, in English, that I had a feeling that he and I had nothing more to say to each other, that we both understood each other very well, and knew that we would work together easily. He grunted something, grinned, nodded, and finally said, 'Ja'. So I took him into the long room where he spent the rest of the morning lying prone among a pile of old motor magazines while we still battled away 'ironing out the bumps', which were of no consequence to our director, who only appeared again when lunch was served.

His apparent refusal to speak English caused a good deal of confusion when we got to the studios in Munich; but I had been given a translator/interpreter through whom I had to make some form of contact with Fassbinder. His name was Ossie. German-English, born in Egypt, he had a fantastic ear for language and dialects. But he didn't find it easy on this assignment; nor did I.

I *knew* that I knew the man inside my director, but I was never going to be able to reach him, or give him a performance, under these circumstances. After two days of mistakes and misunderstandings, I took him aside and said that I was certain that he spoke English, perhaps only a little, but that unless he tried to speak to me in that tongue we would be lost. I'd pack it in.

He trod on a cigarette butt in his heavy motor-cycle boots, rubbed his eyes with a nicotined finger under the tin-rimmed lenses, and said, in English, that he would try. But he was shy of speaking before his Unit.

'For heaven's sake, Rainer, I'm shy too! Just because I made a movie almost before you were born doesn't make *me* any the less shy: nervous, terrified! I'm a foreigner on a completely foreign set. I know that I'm old enough to be your father, but that doesn't alter the fact that you are my director, the boss. I need your help if we are to get this film off the ground. And I can't contact you if I can't speak to you.'

He ground the squashed butt deeper into the floor.

'I can't go on trying to understand what you want through a translator; it just won't work, and we'll lose the picture. And it's much too good to lose. Please help me.'

Rainer never spoke German to me on the set again, leaving Ossie, who had fast been approaching a breakdown, thankfully relieved.

If Rainer had a fault it was that he found it completely impossible to concentrate, think, or create, in anything which remotely approximated to silence. He had to work in a vortex of sound: torrents of sound; it was something with which one quickly came to terms. Or perished.

From the moment that he roared up to the set (wherever it was) in his vastly expensive motor car, until the moment that he left, usually far later than the rest of us for he stayed on writing, planning, and setting up, in detailed drawings, his shots for the next day, he worked in a shuddering blast of music. Maria Callas at full pitch in both 'Tosca' and 'Norma'; sometimes, as a light relief, the entire score of 'Evita', which made the very air vibrate, on other occasions 'Der Rosenkavalier' over and over again.

A very different atmosphere to the saintly, cloistered, hush which had reigned at all times on 'Providence'.

But then this was a film about madness: perhaps it all helped.

One important problem, the first to arise after the discussion about what language to use between each other, was the fact that among a whole group of English-speaking Germans, plus my superb co-star from France, Andrea Ferreol, who had learned her English in a crash-course at Berlitz a couple of months before, my Home Counties accent simply wouldn't do. It sounded absurd in every possible way, I didn't fit in with anyone: I'd have to use an accent myself.

Ossie, now relieved of his main job as translator and interpreter, came to the rescue with a splendid Prussian one. Prussian, because I was playing a Russian émigré, and my German accent could not be that of Berlin, or Hamburg or Munich. The nearest accent that a Russian-trying-to-speak-German could have would be Prussian. Very complex. It was all extremely interesting: but when was I to learn it?

The fact was that I hadn't time to learn it: work had started, and I had to jump in with Ossie holding me, at a distance, like an anxious father with his infant in a swimming-pool.

We did it. God knows how, but we did. I made many errors at first, but these were gradually eliminated, and in time, in a remarkably little time in fact, I settled down as comfortably as a hen on her eggs, secure with the accent, secure in the role of poor, demented, Hermann.

In truth, the part of Hermann in 'Despair' was the nearest thing to a complete mental and physical take-over that I had endured since Von Aschenbach had eased silently into my existence: it is an extraordinary experience in every way. The actor has to empty himself of *self*, completely, and then encourage the stranger he is to be into the vacuum created.

It is not easy. But once caught, and it takes a time to do the catching, one's whole personality alters, and it is not at all understandable to 'civilians', as I call non-players, to comprehend. It is more of a mental alteration than a physical one, but sometimes in a bar, in a shop, at the reception desk of an hotel, even talking to Forwood at a meal, I would find that I was speaking, and more than that, behaving, exactly as my alter-ego would have done. This is not affectation: it is possession. But it is a curious experience for outsiders to observe.

Rainer's work was extraordinarily similar to that of Visconti's; despite their age difference, they both behaved, on set, in much the same manner. Both had an incredible knowledge of the camera: the first essential. Both knew how it could be made to function; they had the same feeling for movement on the screen, of the all-important (and often-neglected) 'pacing' of a film, from start to finish, of composition, of texture, and probably most of all they shared that strange ability to explore and probe into the very depths of the character which one had offered them.

They took what one gave and built upon it, layer upon layer of physical and mental strata, so that eventually, together, we could produce a man, entire. Plus soul.

Exhausting, exhilarating, rewarding and draining, finally. But that was the way that I liked my cinema. It was the only way I could really work.

Which was just as well, for we had a pretty rugged time. We started work in Interlaken, moved up to Munich, to Brunswick, Hamburg, Berlin and then came to our final location, a small town near Lübeck in the north, only about a mile from the Wall. There were no luxuries: as on 'Providence' so on 'Despair', we were a tightly knit group and worked like a band of travelling players – which, I suppose, is exactly what we were, after all. Andrea and I, and the rest of the cast, changed our costumes in the back of cars, in the corners of sheds, once in the back kitchens of a filthy Berlin restaurant where today's food lay on the floor amidst the debris of yesterday's, and the air was full of droning bluebottles. But we were all tremendously happy. That strange feeling that things were going better than well took hold of us all, and Rainer, I was told, had never been seen to laugh so much or show such evident signs of pleasure.

I finished my role three days before the film wound up, and Rainer decided that there would be a big farewell party in the little hotel in which we were all staying. It was pleasant, quiet, set on the edge of a vast lake, with a terrace overlooking the town beyond.

I was sitting in the last of the sun having a beer when Rainer came and joined me. This was unusual indeed. He always went off to his room with his close group of friends after work, and one seldom saw him again until the next morning on the set.

He refused a beer, lit a new cigarette from the butt of the old one which he spun into the still evening water of the lake.

'I come to thank you,' he said, 'for the Hermann you made possible for me: I hope it will be our Hermann, like his madness is a little bit our madness.'

He was smiling; extremely shy.

'I hope so too. I should be thanking you.'

'No! I thank. I thank you for the things I could learn from you, things I never learned before. I thank you that you showed me authority, without fear. Normally, you see, authority goes with fear; but you did show me a way how to combine authority with freedom.' He stopped and looked out across the lake. 'I knew that only theoretically; so far. It is one of the most important things for work and life.'

'I've been very happy working with you, you know that. I don't mind now if I never make another movie! You have spoiled me for any others.'

He grinned, rubbed his eye with a stubby finger, dropped the cigarette into the puddle of beer on the table.

'In life . . . ' he shrugged, crushed the cigarette ' . . . it is more likely there is more despair than anything else. But, and this is what *I* think, life is timeless and end is endless. And this means it is not so sad; like it seems.'

He rose suddenly. 'Danke,' he said, and walked quickly away.

People were calling from the bar, the evening had begun. Rainer didn't come to the party. I knew that he wouldn't. We had said farewell.

There is no question in my mind that 'Despair' should have been a major film: as it was, it became a critical success and a box-office failure for reasons which I cannot fully determine. A sort of Jacob's coat of a film: a curate's egg somehow. Whatever went wrong, and something did somewhere along the line, it was, however, an incredible, detailed, study of madness by a brilliant director.

And that, of course, might have been one of the faults. Madness embarrasses people to watch; it makes them uneasy and uncomfortable.

However, for better or worse we were chosen, many months ahead, to represent Germany at the Festival in Cannes. Perhaps being chosen so far ahead was an error, for I have a feeling that Rainer grew weary of his production and started to clip away at it with his scissors, thereby carrying the abstract motive too far.

Anyhow here I was, once again, representing a foreign film at Cannes. This time with a splendid Prussian accent; and what is more, once again I was tipped to win.

Well: I'd been through all that nonsense before, and although the rumours which drifted up from the coast became more than usually insistent, I set them aside and got on with more pressing concerns with which I had to occupy myself. My second book.

Postillion had jumped into the best-seller lists, gone into a second printing, and had been sold to paperback: I had not let my 'needlewoman' down after all, as I had feared, and with her encouragement had started off on *Snakes and Ladders*, which I finished in the year before 'Despair' came to Cannes. All I really had to do, apart from the usual proof correcting, was the cover design, and the end-papers, which I decided to do myself.

But the rumours persisted as the Festival wore on, and I was haunted by television teams who wanted interviews 'in depth', from Italy, France and Germany, which I gave: because it was easier to do them than to refuse. I was photographed, dutifully walking among my olive trees, playing with Labo and Daisy, and giving a series of pretty dull interviews. The atmosphere was pleasant and polite, there was a feeling that they were all interviewing the winner. One French team asked me to make a special speech in which I was to thank all those who had made it possible for me to win the most coveted prize at

Cannes, the Palme d'Or, and were sullen with dismay when I declined, politely, to do so.

The final day of the whole idiotic affair was unsettling, in spite of my apparent unconcern; and the telephone became an instrument of dread. At ten a.m. it rang, and I was informed, unofficially, that I had certainly won the prize. The jury would make the official announcement at noon.

It rang again at eleven. A journalist from a London paper wanted to know how it felt 'to win the most prestigious prize'. I told him I didn't know, and hung up.

Lunch was oddly difficult to swallow. I began to think, against all my orderly instincts and my better judgement, that this time maybe, perhaps maybe . . . and went up to see if I had a clean white shirt; with buttons intact. Just in case.

At two o'clock the jury were still deliberating, but would I stand by because, I was assured, it was almost certain that I had won; with Marcello Mastroianni a close second.

I looked out my dinner jacket. Held it up to the light for moth-holes. I was in good shape there: no holes.

In the kitchen, washing up and preparing the dogs' dinners, I allowed myself to toy with the idea of a modest little speech of thanks in French: which was very silly indeed, for at two-thirty exactly I was told that I had lost to an American actor, Jon Voight.

I hung up the suit, put the shirt in the drawer.

It had been a good try. I'd almost enjoyed the suspense; and I wasn't in the least ashamed of my work on the film because I knew that it was, in truth, the best screen performance I had ever given. That in itself was reward enough.

When 'Despair' eventually opened in New York to high critical acclaim and a box-office failure, Jack Kroll of *Newsweek* wrote of it: 'Bogarde is superb: you seldom see such a sustained, moment-by-moment characterization on screen. . . . It's a performance by one of the best movie actors ever, at the peak of his talent.' Which I really couldn't help thinking was pretty nice, and much more rewarding, to me, than a Palme d'Or.

Right or wrong, it made comforting reading; and reaching the peak of one's talent is, perhaps, no bad time to go out – for out I went, as things transpired.

Not from choice, for I have never at any time wished to abandon my chosen profession, but simply from a lack of acceptable material.

The cinema is often called The Seventh Art; and perhaps it is. Certainly men like Resnais, Losey, Visconti and Fassbinder are artists (or sadly, were, in two cases) but their work has always been a desperate struggle against Big Business.

No longer do the great Jewish dynasties hold power: the people who were, when all is said and done, the Picture People. Now the cinema is controlled by vast firms like Xerox, Gulf & Western, and many others who deal in anything from sanitary-ware to property development. These huge conglomerates, faceless, soulless, are concerned only with making a profit; never a work of art. The Picture People have grown old, been bought out, sent scurrying to retirement in Palm Springs or Palm Beach, dismayed, displaced, bewildered by the loss of the cinema they once knew and which has probably gone for ever.

The Seventh Art is now but a small part of Big Business.

And Television Rules! Okay?

A question of profit and loss.

It is pointless to be 'superb' in a commercial failure; and most of the films which I had deliberately chosen to make in the last few years were, by and large, just that. Or so I am always informed by the businessmen. The critics may have liked them extravagantly, but the distributors shy away from what they term 'A

Critic's Film', for it often means that the public will stay away. Which, in the mass, they do: and if you don't make money at the box-office you are not asked back to play again.

But I'd had a very good innings. Better than most. So what the hell?

FOURTEEN

And I was still creating, still inventing, still learning. To write.

I had reached a corner in my long corridor and made a deliberate change of direction, not a change of profession. It was simply an extension of the original job and there wasn't a STOP sign in sight. At least, as far as I could see.

Corners are not for hanging around at: they are for turning, for making a change; unless, of course, one loses heart and decides to lope off back the way one has come, which seems to me a very unadventurous thing to do.

Of course, the turning takes a bit of courage; the new way seems at first to be daunting and frightening after years of familiarity with the old, but there are some familiar facets along the new corridor.

The doors which had stood to the left and right of one before are repeated. There they stand: ajar, wide open, half-closed; filled with light, deep with sombre shades. But familiar. And there for the pushing open and discovery, perhaps, of very different contents, but they comfort one.

The final door, right down at the far end, is ever-present, just as before. You can't escape that, whichever way you decide to turn, so in the final analysis you might just as well take a risk in your journey, for that one door can never be avoided. It is there.

I have always been told that writing is a lonely, solitary, reclusive job. Very different, therefore, from acting, which is the absolute opposite. But even as a novice writer I have not found that to be true at all. It is neither lonely nor reclusive, and it is solitary only by virtue of the fact that one has to be alone and in silence in order to hear the voices which fill one's head. It is impossible to be lonely with so much conversation going on.

Some people, or so I am informed, can only write on a pad on their knees in a tumult of sound, or blasting music; others sit in a cell staring at blank walls so that the intensity of concentration is not broken.

Jane Austen apparently sat at a small table in the hall at the centre of the family house and wrote perfectly serenely, slipping her work discreetly under cover if she was disturbed; but this would not do for me.

I look out of my small window here above the woodshed, across the sloping tiled roof where lizards scuttle and chase, tails upraised in anger, and spiky geckos lie flat in the sun snapping at flies or bees. Beyond the sloping roof I can see the spires of four cypress trees, behind them a distant wood, beyond that the far hills. I see rain fall, sun blaze, snow pile, mist drift, the vine turn, the trees become bare in the wood, the hills stand stark and harsh against the light of winter.

But I am not distracted by these things, rather they comfort me; and although I am lost in time, secured against the outside world by a firmly closed door, I am never for one moment lonely.

How could I be?

The papers, letters, journals which one starts to research for work gradually fill the room with distant voices which grow ever louder the longer one reads. Voices drift out from all corners, from the ceiling, from the floor, from the shadowy shelves of reference books. Voices which one has loved, has laughed with, has even burst with fury at . . . but *voices*: and one is transported back to a past which becomes more vivid and alive than the present.

It is even stranger (and much noisier) when one is actually in the process of inventing people. It is then that the theatrical part of my life hastens to assist my writing-extension.

I sit, in a leather chair, and *talk* them into life. Ask them questions, work out with them how they lived, who they were, who they are going to be, what they will do, whom they will meet or couple with, and when they will die. I hear their laughter in my head, their accents in my ear: I know their sadness, their treachery, their kindness and their anxieties, for I have invented them all; and they are completely mine.

If anyone ever passed the door of this olive store, I reckon I'd be carted off as barking mad for talking to myself (it would seem) in different voices and dialects. For I play every scene I write, so as to be absolutely certain that the words are true and that the mood is correctly set. Dialogue can do this: and saves a lot of needless writers' explanation.

It is an extraordinary sensation, spending hours with my people. Exceptionally pleasant most of the time, irritating often; especially if a character takes off on his or her own path against my better judgement and I lose control of them. Then I rip them from the typewriter, screw them into a ball and chuck them away, insert a new sheet into the machine, and start again. 'Now, this time get it *right*!' I say. Of course I suppose it is all a form of lunacy (so is acting come to that) but certainly it is not lonely.

And with autobiography, long-forgotten voices from the past return, jogging the memory, sometimes pulling at the heart cruelly, so that one walks in a daze, only very slightly aware of the present.

Occasionally, when she has been staying here, Elizabeth, who knows me all too well, will say, 'Oh, he's off again. In one of his *moods*.' And of course she is right. Except that I am not in a mood in the terms which she means, I am mentally removed from the present with more than half of my mind far away. But I am not, for example, sulking. Just backtracking.

One of the things which makes writing magically different from acting is that I, and I alone, am responsible. In the theatre or in the cinema the actor is the interpreter of other people's words and work. His performance is directed by another: he has to balance his playing to other performances and other players, must at all times adjust, juggle, give way on occasion, so that he can find space for his own contribution to dazzle. If he can.

In the cinema there are a thousand technical things which he must take into account before he can even begin to offer a performance. The lights, the sound, the camera itself (a capricious beast to those whom it does not love) and there is focus, timing, other performers; a plethora of traps for the unwary.

But writing is your responsibility entirely. You are the writer of your script, the director of your play or film, the creator of your characters, you are every single technician, and you do all this quite alone. You are the boss, and for better or worse it is you who will have to carry the can in the end.

I have been surrounded at all times with advice, caution, suggestion, approval, and have been offered courage in abundance by my publishers, but I am perfectly well aware that what finally appears in print comes from my imagination, and it must be *I* who takes the rap. It's a solo performance all right; often nerve-racking.

At the beginning, I thought that one's Muse, for that is what I was always told it was called, just waited silently in the shadows, and all you had to do was to beckon her with one finger and she would arrive before you bearing a veritable cornucopia of riches in her arms.

A happy thought, but entirely false. At any rate in my case. *My* Muse sits slumped in the shadows, sulking. No amount of pleading, cajoling, tears, or begging and hand-wringing will drag her forth from her intense disinclination to assist me.

I have to go and grab her, wrestle with her, beat her about like a drunk, and force something from her grasp, however modest it might be. Mine holds no cornucopia of riches for me: a match-box at best, not more. And that is only offered resentfully. I have never been able to train her better: perhaps time will tell, but it is still a monstrous battle every single time I roll a sheet of paper into this machine. Sullen silence from my Muse. Anguished pleading from me as I stare in misery at the blank sheet before me.

Words, therefore, do not, as one kind woman in Australia wrote to me, 'pour from your pen'. They don't by a very long chalk. They are squeezed out one by one in sheer desperation, rather as one has to roll up and squeeze out the very last drops in an exhausted toothpast tube; and no pen is involved, I regret to say, nothing nearly so romantic. It all goes straight down, flat and hard, from the typewriter at the very start. Mainly because I have an inbuilt belief that I have not written anything unless I actually see it printed before my eyes, also because my handwriting, reminiscent of unravelled knitting, confuses even me half an hour later. I am quite unable to decipher what I have set down: this is a clear case of the hand being faster than the mind, I suppose. I try to go too fast too soon. But then I have always done that: in as orderly a fashion as I can.

After the surprise success of *Postillion*, I realised that I would have to make a firm set of rules in order to write properly; or to write at all. If I was to take the business seriously then I must perform it seriously.

So from eight-thirty a.m. until twelve-thirty I write. The afternoons are clear then for the many jobs which await me on the land, but in the evenings from six until seven I re-read the morning's work and try to correct it, if I do not altogether destroy it (which I do all too often) and start off again the next morning.

It seems to me that I write each book twice; rejecting, correcting, destroying, cutting, adding, polishing. It's a long business. Sometimes I manage to get eight hundred words written, at other times I am very lucky if I manage eighty, and it's an exhausting, empty day: all the fault of my sulking Muse. I obviously got a dud.

Anyway: a lonely, solitary, reclusive job, I was assured by many who knew far more than I did, and I had been prepared for it, but it had proved to be untrue as far as I was concerned.

What I was *not* prepared for when I started writing was the appalling act of promotion. I had no idea that this vulgarity existed; no idea that once the book was finished, bound, and tidy, you had to go trotting off and flog it. For even if the word is unattractive it is exactly what you have to do: just as if your effort was plastic table-ware, a new brand of soap, or a Born-again Christian tract. I was astonished that such a gentlemanly (or so it had seemed to me) profession could stoop so low. I was well aware that in the cinema one had to work hard to sell the product, and I had had a great deal of experience in doing so; but I didn't expect it to happen in publishing. It is, however, essential today.

And, alas! it is exactly the same procedure as the cinema. The same interviews, the same chat shows which will guarantee sales, although I am certain that the people who watch chat shows don't buy books (but that's neither here nor there) and the same personal appearances in provincial cities. And what is perhaps the worst of all, the signing-sessions in bookshops. Those are the 'crunchers': those really terrify me.

In the cinema at least I was always kept at a discreet distance from the audience. In writing I found, to my intense horror, that I was to be shoved right into its very arms. Stuck behind a desk or a table, with no way of escape, confronted far too closely by the people who had once been unseen, unheard, but who now were extremely visible, and vocal.

There one sat, pen in hand, selling one's wares like a pedlar at a fair.

'My dear, *do* look!' I heard a woman say in Harrods during one of these sessions. 'Look what he's doing now, for God's sake! *Selling* himself in public!'

The second-generation Harrods' voice cut through the book department like a rapier and pierced me to the depth of my quaking heart. My hand shook with anger, and someone got a very wobbly signature, but I couldn't possibly refute her remark: I was, as it happened, sitting only two feet away from the till, and every time we made a sale there was a shrill, chilling, 'Ting!' to prove her point.

My first signing session ever was at Hatchards bookshop for *Postillion*. Elizabeth, Forwood, and I drove from the Connaught in silence. My voice had gone; my throat was dry, my tongue had become inextricably involved with the roof of my mouth and stuck there as if held by Jumbo Glue. Terror gripped me at the mere idea of having, as an actor, to leave the safety of my proscenium arch or the confines of my cinema screen and face an audience from a distance of feet, or less, stuck behind a table. If there *was* an audience. I knew that I would have to sit there for an hour at least, a blotter before me, pen in hand and smile inanely at perfectly ordinary customers, who had only come in to purchase an atlas perhaps, or the latest bestseller, in the desperate hopes that just one of them might be persuaded to buy a copy of my own modest offering, much as if I was selling flags for a charity, rattling my tin anxiously.

We didn't, therefore, speak to each other as we drove through Berkeley Square, and it was only as we started the down-run towards Piccadilly that I managed to croak something to the effect that I wished that I was dead and what the hell had I got involved in this potty business for anyway; then we swung left into the wide thoroughfare and I heard Forwood mutter the word, 'Policemen'.

'Where are the policemen? Has there been an accident? A bomb!' I said, suddenly alerted to near panic.

'Can't quite tell yet if they are outside Hatchards or Fortnum and Mason.'

'Perhaps it's for the Queen. She's out shopping or something.'

'It's Hatchards,' said Elizabeth in a faint voice. She was as frightened as I was.

'What are they *doing*, for God's sake?'

'There's a queue, quite a big one too. And in this bitter wind . . . '

And there was.

And the morning was tremendous fun, warming, generous, extremely touching and fully rewarding. I enjoyed myself to the full, it wasn't any different from my role as an actor: signing books was a breeze of a performance, and the audience, for want of a better word, who had waited so patiently in the cold March wind, were extraordinarily friendly to play to. It was an altogether happy occasion, and we sold a lot of copies, which, naturally, made everyone full of glee.

'Don't sign names,' a discreet voice murmured in my ear. 'Just your signature.'

'But I *can't* just write my signature and nothing else!'

'Well, leave out the 'Best Wishes' part.'

'It's not possible!'

'It's a question of time. *And* sales,' said the discreet voice of authority resignedly.

But even though I insisted, and wrote the Maureens and Bettys and the Best Wishes as well, we had a record sale and everyone was smiling. A happy morning.

That evening I gave a small cocktail party to celebrate my new venture as a budding writer. The words which Mrs X had written with such firmness years ago came back to me in the midst of the pleasure and the laughter.

'*Force* memory!' she had insisted. And I had. And here we all were as a result.

The telephone rang. I clambered across small tables littered with glasses, olives, and bowls of scattered nuts. Charlotte Rampling from Paris.

'I wanted you to know. I've had a baby. He's six hours old and very beautiful.'

'Oh Char! How super!'

'We're going to call him David.'

'I've just had a baby today too; only it's got a slightly longer name.'

'Oh! Your book. It's out! I forgot: what next; another one?'

I looked about the crowded room and the smiling faces, sensed the sweet smell of success, of belief supported and proved. Forwood refilled Norah's glass, they were laughing.

'Yes. I think so,' I said.

What I didn't say was that I had already started on the first chapters of the next book. It would, I thought, be tempting fate to do so, and I'd done quite enought of that in the last few months.

'I think so, Char . . . but we'll just see how it goes. Cross your fingers?'

I had arrived at my mother's Edwardian hotel about half an hour late, a potted hoop of jasmin in one hand, a bag of trinkets and gifts in the other. Mr Brockway, the Manager, met me in the hall as I pushed open the front door, his pleasant, open face slightly tight with anxiety.

'Oh there you are! Good. She's got herself into a little state, nothing serious. I have been sitting with her. I think she thought that you'd had an accident . . . she's in her room, you know the way?'

I thanked him, asked him to tell my driver where to go for his lunch (for I knew no pubs in the area) and went down the corridor to her room.

She was sitting in a chair by the window, hands in her lap, her face puckered with distress, twisting her rings. Hyacinths in a pot, a jug of fading daffodils, a half-finished glass of wine beside her.

She bowed her head.

'Darling! I'm here . . . I'm sorry, we got lost. Came out of town the long way: Streatham, Purley . . . and then took the wrong lane here.'

She made a strange, low, shuddering sound.

'Don't cry! For heaven's sake . . . your mascara will run! Come on now, it's all right.'

She pulled herself together, sat upright, eyes wide, bright with unshed tears.

'I thought you weren't coming.'

'You *knew* I was . . . I'm late, I'm sorry.'

'I'm all right. I'm all right. Just worried. What's that?'

'Jasmin, you can plant it in the garden later.'

'From darling France.'

It wasn't. It was from Maida Vale, but there was no point in saying so.

'I'm dying for a drink, I've brought my own. Are you having one?'

'Yes . . . oh yes. I'm having one. My Spanish.'

I poured myself a stiff brandy and soda which I had brought with me in my hand-grip.'

'Where's your bottle? You've almost finished that glass.'

'It's here.' Her hands were still restless, twisting the rings constantly.

'Let me fill it up . . . where is it?'

'Here.'

In the wastepaper basket beside her chair.

'Why do you keep it in that?'

'The maids come in and out all the time.'

'But they know that you have a bottle a day! Why hide it, darling?'

'That's my business.'

I filled the glass: she took it eagerly, hands shaking a little, spilling some down her chin.

'Elizabeth brings you a crate of twelve every Saturday, doesn't she? I mean the maids know all that.'

'I keep it in my room now. It was in the kitchen and I had to *ask* them when I wanted a bottle. They stole it.'

'Oh Ma! Now come on . . . that's nonsense.'

'Tell me why, pray?' Her eyes were enormous, angry, brilliant. 'It's supposed to last me a week and I always run out by Thursday . . . now I keep it in here, hidden.'

'Well: I've brought you a few bits and pieces, and look! A copy of my very first novel! How about that? I'm a novelist now. My third book!'

'Lovely.' There was no interest. She screwed up her eyes. 'What's this, on the cover? I haven't got my glasses.'

'Bamboo, barbed wire, a butterfly. It's called *A Gentle Occupation*.'

She placed it carefully on the coffee-table before her, took up her glass and drained it.

'Lunch is at one. Punctually. Do you like my hair?'

'Super. It's softer-looking.'

'Had it done two weeks ago. I've combed it out. But it's going grey, isn't it?'

'No . . . pepper-and-saltish. Not grey, and after all you'll be eighty-one next month, I mean you ought to have a grey hair or two, surely?'

'You haven't.'

'One or two.'

'And you're about sixty. You take after my side of the family. My mother, Granny Nelson, had jet-black hair when she died; well into her eighties.'

'We're lucky. Sometimes they say I dye mine.'

'Who do?'

'Oh, the press.'

'Jealous,' she said, offering me her glass. 'Fill it up, will you, before lunch.'

'Will you take it in with you?''

'To lunch? With all those people looking on. Good God no.'

A high-ceilinged, sunny dining-room. Separate tables round the sides; at one end a table of four, a son and daughter visiting, low murmurs of conversation. I called out, 'Good morning' as I sat down. There was a small hush: 'Good morning,' they said, and continued murmuring and clinking cutlery.

A man at the table beside us finished his meal, pushed himself up with the aid of a white stick, adjusted a green plastic eye-shade over his forehead, and inched from the room in little shuffles.

'Cheerful, isn't it?' said my mother.

After lunch she refused to return to her room, so we went into the Residents' Drawing Room instead.

'I spend the whole bloody day in that place of mine, I want a change. No one ever comes in here after lunch, they all go to their rooms until supper time . . . at six.'

The drawing-room was large, light, lined with books, a long window with a window seat, an open fire, logs smouldering, a potted plant trailing on the mantelshelf. A television set in a corner.

'Do you come in here often? To watch TV or something?'

'If you are 'on' I do. But I can't work it; the button things. I had a friend who used to come and watch with me if you were 'on'; she was a dear soul. They took her away one night and she's dead. Cuckfield Hospital.'

Suddenly she laughed, a coarse, bitter sound. 'They'll all finish up there, the lot of them: in Cuckfield-bloody-Hospital.' She lit a cigarette with a flick of her lighter. 'I never thought that I'd have to end up here. It's all coming true, you see.'

'What's coming true?'

'That woman at the Cox's wedding, years ago; she saw my aura. Purple, violet. She said that I was a Tragedy Queen, that Ulric would die suddenly, that I'd be sent to a home . . . '

'Ma, for God's sake stop . . . it's all rubbish.'

She smiled, snapped the cigarette lighter a couple of times. 'This is really very interesting. You don't know *this* part.' She looked at me with defiance. 'She said that they would have to cut my legs off.'

'Why?'

'Oh . . . because of something the soldiers got in the trenches. Begins with a G.'

'Gangrene?'

'Gangrene.'

'It's all silly rubbish, you know: it's simply none of it true. Now look here, listen to me: I'll do anything you like, *anything* you want. Would you like to come back with me to France? Live there?'

'God! No. I'd never make the journey. Anyway, we'd fight all the time; we're too alike, you and I.'

'Would you like to move away from here then? To somewhere else, like Brighton; somewhere you could see a bit more of life. A town. Anywhere you say.'

'No, no. I'll stick it out here.'

'Would you like to go up to London, have a couple of weeks in the clinic, a real check-up, see what's what; would that be a good idea? A nice long rest in bed, lots of nurses and so on. Just to make sure you're all right, if you are worried.'

'*I'm* all right. Don't bother about me. I've had my day, I'll stick it out. I'm tough, God knows I've had to be, all my life.'

'You were walking almost normally today, all the way to the dining-room, and all the way back here. No stick, you didn't even need my arm, that's wonderful: and you *have* to walk, the doctors say so.'

'I walk all right. I walk.' She looked at me suddenly with a gleam of anger. 'I made a big effort for you today. You are my first-born, after all.' She threw the butt of her cigarette into the fire.

'I know that, and you really do look marvellous, the effort was well worth it. I haven't seen you look like this for ages and ages . . . you really look incredible.'

And she did. Straight-backed, elegant, perfectly groomed, the high bones in her face catching a slant of sunlight through the window, her eyes enormous. She looked ten years less than her age.

'I always tried hard to look my best for Daddy: I never wanted him to see me in an apron, you know. I had standards. I still have.'

'Do you talk to Daddy?'

She looked at me suddenly, with a sharp, swift turn of her head as if I had caught her out or tricked her.

'Talk to him? Where?'

'In your room. His photograph is on your dressing-chest.'

'Yes.' She pulled a curl of hair behind her ear. 'Yes, I talk to him. All the time, all the time.'

'What do you say to him, Ma? Tell me what you say?'

With neat, small movements she began to rearrange a string of beads around her neck, smoothed the long tie of her brown silk shirt. And then she looked across at me with wide, clear, calm eyes, her hands folded on her thigh, the cigarette lighter clasped in slender hands.

'Come back,' she said. 'That's what I say to him.'

I drove away, a couple of hours later, through the greening Sussex lanes in a state of grim depression to face what my Journal records as 'a gruelling week: almost *too* much in fact.'

In America I had done a number of promotional tours for various films; these were known in the business as Total Exposure, and started at eight in the morning until eight in the evening. Now and again, on the crammed schedule, I would notice a small bracketed 'SC' which, I was informed, stood for 'Shirt Change'; and that was the only break one got. What I was about to face was almost as bad. Publishing and the cinema were not so very far apart, after all. In both, one had to sell the product hard.

Work started the next morning with the BBC at eight-thirty and went on throughout the day with interviews on the hour, every hour: even lunch was an interview. But there was almost never time to change my shirt, a tie, or my jacket. The day came to a close with the Publishers' Party given in my honour, at which I remember shaking hands with Margaret Drabble dressed in snow boots and a brown woollen knitted hat, and then I got hurried to the Royal Command Performance where I shook hands with the Queen who was wearing white fox and emeralds: most of the day is a haze, and I just remember crawling into bed with a modest temperature and the firm conviction that I was beginning, at least a cold; at worst 'flu.

Which was all that I needed with five more days of 'selling' to go. At the same time, it might as well be confessed, I was not feeling particularly well anyway.

A few weeks before, the excellent Dr Poteau had managed (after two wearying years) to diagnose a very tiresome malady to which I had become victim, as an intestinal parasite, which he assured me I must have contracted through drinking unboiled water in southern Italy. (I hadn't been in southern Italy for years.) They could lie dormant for a long time, he said, and were tenacious, destructive, weakening and had shells: which made them extremely difficult to eradicate.

He prescribed a pill which was a brutal remedy and which, although it would surely destroy the beasts, was at the same time bringing me gradually to the edge of suicidal depression.

There was a very jolly added side-effect to all this: it was imperative that I should know exactly where to go, and how to get there speedily if, and when, disaster should strike; and with Dr Poteau's remedy one could never be certain. An altogether unnerving situation which necessitated a swift, and if humanly possible, discreet exit.

So I was hardly in the happiest state of mind to give interviews-in-depth, or really to enjoy the signal honour accorded me of a Foyle's Luncheon in the Blue Room at the Dorchester. I had a quick, to the point, chat with the Toast master just before we all sat down, who assured me that my worries were at an end because what I might need most was situated exactly behind my chair, at the Top Table, through the door into the kitchens. It was marked, he said, clearly MEN. 'Just one sign from you, Sir . . . ' he said, and I relaxed. Well: almost. I still had to make an exit.

Neither did the situation help me to enjoy the signing-session, this time once again, thankfully, at Hatchards Bookshop, where they tactfully sat me miles away from the degrading till and I managed to sign over six hundred copies, all of which carried Best Wishes and the personal names of the purchasers.

'You'd have sold over seven hundred if you'd left out the trimming: just written your signature.' said the quiet voice of authority sadly. '*Sales* and *time*, remember . . . '

However, everyone seemed perfectly satisfied, the customers were warm and relaxing, and I was aware that if I had had to leave the session, for a few moments, I knew exactly where to go.

Forwood was brilliant at doing his reconnaissance in this particular field, and during the rest of the Promotional Week the ravishing PRO, Miss Bell, who had four years before seemed to me as if she was dressed from a Women's Institute stall, so strangely assorted were her garments ('Jumble sales, flea markets, yes: but *never* the WI.' she had said firmly), quickly caught on to the problem with her usual efficiency and became as adept as he.

'Down on the left, second door, past the fire-extinguishers,' she would murmur as I, with outstretched hand, a welcoming smile, and a happy greeting on my dry lips would go to meet another interviewer, or radio disc jockey, secured by my knowledge and usually managing to overcome the problem, by forgetting it. Apart from my two loyal scouts, no one else, of course, knew anything. And fortunately there were no bolts from the blue; or anywhere else.

Perhaps the happiest, and most relaxing event of the whole week was my own dinner party at the Connaught at the end of the fourth day: I was, I confess, pretty well flaked-out by this time, but the arrival around the big table of Norah Smallwood, John and his wife Susan, Charlotte and her husband Jean-Michel Jarre who had flown in from Paris especially for the celebration, and Angela Fox, the friend of many years, filled me with comfort by their own, obvious, pleasure: and after almost thirty years of staying at the Connaught I naturally knew the lay-out; so anxiety faded in the security of that vital information.

It was a little more unnerving the next day in Oxford when Blackwells gave me a splendid luncheon at the Randolph Hotel; but I knew the Randolph of old, having played in the theatre next door, and made a couple of films in the city, and knew that Forwood and Ros ('Miss Bell' had long ago been discarded for the more familiar name) would be well prepared, and able to do a cover-up job should the need arise and it would be discovered that I had, suddenly, left the gathering.

On the sixth day we flew to Amsterdam in the greatest style. Everything had been arranged and organised with extreme efficiency by Quentin Hockliffe,

Chatto's Export Sales Director, reminding me of the times, years ago, when Betty Box and Ralph Thomas and I would tour the provinces promoting our films. I remember, distinctly, the extreme pleasure it gave me to feel the train slide slowly into the stations in Birmingham, Bristol, Manchester or wherever it might be; a sighing of steam, the compartment moving very gently along the platform until we absolutely, and *precisely*, stopped before the imposing figure of the Station Master, top-hatted, rose in buttonhole, who would then lead us proudly through his teeming domain to waiting cars, past rows of yelling teenagers waving hands, flowers and autograph books. I always managed to look back towards the engine and wave my thanks, receiving a salute back and a weary grin.

The Amsterdam trip was much the same, although done by air, and the day was one of extraordinary nostalgia and emotion. There, in the book shop, were gathered people who had come from all over Holland and whom I had known in the desperate days of our occupation of Java when we had liberated the civilian prison camps and released thousands of laughing, cheering, embracing skeletons from the Japanese.

Time had altered us: we were older, hair was white. At first I recognised no one; and then the photographs were produced. Brother officers I had forgotten. Myself aged twenty-four walking through a burning village. A laughing girl with a flower in her hair.

'That's me! Can you believe it? Annie . . . remember me? I'm a granny now!'

Programmes of the concerts which I had produced, my name indecently important across the top. 'Pip van den Bogaerde Presents: 'Curtain Up!' and we all laughed together.

'Oh, they were *funny* days! Of course you won't remember *us* after all this time, but we remember you.'

'I'm older too. And I *do* remember.'

'But we got through, didn't we? Most of us.'

'Remember Jenny? She was in your show, but she didn't make it home. Typhoid.'

'Bob stayed on for a time: but it was pretty hopeless. He's married now, in Breda.'

The conversations were limited; I had a job to do, and the press to meet.

Polite, crisp, interested, because *A Gentle Occupation* was apparently the first book written about that period and those people and their courage.

The Left was a little cool, inclined to disbelieve that the book was fiction; the Communists (humourless, young, bearded, leather-jacketed) aggressive and at pains to explain that the word 'terrorist', which I used, was incorrect. There had been *no* terrorists in Java, they insisted, only Freedom Fighters. They were indignant because, they said, it was the first time that the word had been publicly used in Holland, and it should be altered. Quite suddenly, at this conference, I was involved in Politics against my will, my modest novel became a tract; and cautiously abused. However, as all my interviewers at the session had been born many years after the events I had recorded, and had never, as far as I could gather, set a foot in the East Indies, I acceded to their insisting, refusing only to withdraw the word terrorist. It was pointless to argue. As I pointed out, all I had done was to write a fictional account of a tragic period which had cost us all many lives; I had not written a doctrine.

And then it was all over, the promotion campaign, and the next day I flew home to France, a bit haggard, down to eight and a half stone, but immeasurably happy all the same. I'd worked hard, as I should have done, and the book was selling. So that was all right.

A day or two later I discovered, to my mild surprise, that I was fifty-nine: an enormous pile of cards and telegrams confirmed this event, but I was far too tired to deal with them, I'd wait until I had settled down.

Walking with Labo, aging too, through the bright spring grasses, and the drifts of wild anemones, the sun warm on my back, the sea shining like a silver knife thrusting from the Estérel Mountains, I was curiously content: mainly because I was home again, but also because the fourteen months of solid slog which had produced *A Gentle Occupation* had not, it seemed, been in vain, and because a fourth book was already drifting about in my head: indeed I had taken the first completed chapter to Norah the day I arrived in London, and she had given me the green light to carry on. So . . . in a day or two, I'd be back at my trestles in the olive store talking to my new 'people'.

But for today, this first one of relaxation and peace in my paradise regained, I'd do nothing much. Just potter about: dead-head the spent narcissus in the rough grass under the willow; perhaps trim the pomegranate, already spiked with scarlet buds among its thorny branches, and simply enjoy the irreversible fact that I was fifty-nine.

At least I'd got there.

And according to my own peculiar brand of arithmetic and logic, I determined that *tomorrow*, and not today, would mark the start of my sixtieth year.

I was not to know that tomorrow would also bring me the news that Ma had died.

When the two great tent-poles fall, which have, for so long, supported the fabric above the circus of one's life, the guy-ropes fly away, the canvas billows down, and there is nothing left to do but crawl out from under, and go on one's way alone.

'A Show For All The Family!' is over.

EPILOGUE

They told me that flying at sixty-five thousand feet I would be able to see the curvature of the earth form Concorde.

But I don't. All that I can see is blue: an immensity of blue. Cornflower, to indigo, to darkest ink. Infinity.

I don't really want to see the curvature of the earth, to be perfectly honest; I am more than content with this view of infinty. I have long wondered what it looked like and now I know.

It is, quite simply, for ever.

I am so distanced in both mind and body that the earth is of no consequence.

Before me on this little table, in this most graceful, most elegant, most orderly of machines, my René Lalou hardly trembles in the crystal goblet, even though we are racing to New York at twice the speed of sound.

We left Paris a little over an hour ago: an amazing, heartlifting roar, and a tremendous upward, zooming, thrust; up, up, up, and away into this extraordinary cerulean atmosphere. Another change of direction.

We broke the sound barrier over Le Havre on Mach 1, and climbed higher and higher to reach Mach 2. It says so on the little illuminated panel ahead of me: otherwise I would never have known: naturally.

I am in limbo. An intermediate place between two extremes; perhaps the word 'condition' is more fitting. At any rate I find limbo exceptionally pleasing.

Today New York, tomorrow Los Angeles, after a lapse of some twelve years, to make a film with Glenda Jackson.

My first time before a camera for over four years. That'll be interesting: but it is a cardigan-and-knitted-tie role, so I may not find it too taxing. Unless I have lost the trick. Could it be so? Always possible after a long time away.

I wonder? I wonder too how Miss Jackson will be. We have never met.

I saw her standing in one of the doorways, as I wandered along my corridor, four books finished and behind me; nothing much else to do. She didn't beckon me, or solicit my favour. She didn't even move. But she was Lorelei; and I, like the bewitched sailors on the Rhine, found myself unable to resist. I am told that she is very dedicated to her work, and doesn't suffer fools gladly.

So here I am. I do hope it doesn't lead to destruction?

No one else on earth but she could have got me back to Los Angeles. Should I tell her that? It might please her; and she might smile kindly on me. I do hope so. I have no reason to suppose otherwise, of course, but one is always uncertain; even in limbo. When I come home I think that I'll put Actor/Author on my Immigration Form, that would be right and proper surely?

We are about to begin our descent to New York; the Captain has just said so. Quite soon we shall be down on the prosaic earth again: limbo will give way to Customs and Immigration, to passports and work permits and, I hope, an enormous Cadillac to bear me off to my hotel. I can't help feeling that it is all going to be a tremendously exciting adventure, but I shall not let it go to my head.

I'm an orderly man.

Often pinched by doubt . . .

Backcloth

This book is for Glenda Jackson
with my love.

SOURCES AND ACKNOWLEDGEMENTS

My principal sources have been the notebooks and diaries kept from 1940 until the present day, plus some letters to my father written between 1940 and 1946. I have also made use of material in many of the letters which I wrote over some years to 'Mrs X' in America. Her constant questioning and interest forced me to remember a great many details with which I attempted to amuse and distract her during her final illness.

All these letters, postcards, and some of the notebooks, will be destroyed after the final editing of this book, for I have no wish that they should perhaps fall into the hands of uncomprehending strangers.

They have served their purpose well.

I have made no efforts to correct these 'pieces', or to alter their 'style': they remain exactly as written at the time. In the diaries I have excised portions which were repetitive or of no interest to the progress of the book.

The spelling of all the place names in the section on Java is correct. These are how the towns were named in the years before Indonesian Independence.

Where necessary I have used, to avoid distress, pseudonyms.

I am particularly grateful to Hélène Bordes, *maître de conférences* at Limoges University, who when I had reached a particularly despairing period in my work threw, as it were, a 'plank' across the ravine and encouraged me to continue.

My gratitude, as always, to Mrs Sally Betts who, after ten years, still manages to cope effortlessly, it would seem, with the trials and tribulations which my untidy typescripts must cause her, and for making sense and order out of my many corrections and sudden additions.

D.V.d.B.

PART ONE

ONE

Memory: I scratch about like a hen in chaff.

The first thing that I can recall is light.

Pale, opaque green, white spots drifting. Near my right eye long black shapes curling down and tickling gently.

Years later when I reported this memory to my parents they confirmed it. There had, apparently, been an extraordinary pea-soup fog; it had snowed at the same time. My mother had lifted me up to observe the phenomenon; the black feathers which wreathed her hat irritated my eyes and I tried to pull them away. I was nine months old.

When I was two, I remember lying on my back on the lawn behind the house in St Georges Road. It was a brilliant day of high wind and scudding cloud. The tall house reeled away from me as the clouds whipped across the blue sky and I was afraid that it would fall down and crush me.

And later I saw our giant ginger cat – well, giant to me then – nailed alive to the tall wooden fence which separated us from an unfriendly neighbour. I remember my mother weeping: which frightened me far more than the sight of the dying cat for I had not yet learned to recognize cruelty or death, but I was recognizing pain and distress on a human face for the first time.

It would not be the last.

The house in St Georges Road was tall, ugly, built of grey-yellow bricks with a slate roof. It had the great advantage for my father, who was an artist, of a number of high-ceilinged rooms with a perfect north light. It also had a long narrow garden with ancient trees.

An Irish woman lived in the basement with two children and cleaned the house from time to time. She had once been a maid to the Chesterfields, who lived in a very grand house not far away called The Lodge.

Sometimes I would see her crouching on a landing with a mop or a brush. There was an almost constant smell of cooking from the basement, and my father said it was Irish stew because that's what the Irish ate.

I suppose that made sense to me – at least, I have remembered it.

My father was a prudent man, with little fortune, and he let off most of the rooms in the house to artist friends, so that (apart from the prevailing smell of Irish stew) the place reeked of turpentine and linseed oil, and the mixed scent of those two is the one that I remember best and with which, anywhere I go, if I smell it, I am instantly at ease, familiar and secure.

One of his lodgers was, in fact, an artists' model who had been left behind, in a rather careless manner, by an artist who had wandered off to Italy to paint. I knew her as Aunt Kitty.

Tiny, vivid, a shock of bright red hair brushed high up from her forehead, brilliant green eyes heavily lined with kohl, she was loving, warm and exceptionally noisy. For some reason, which I can no longer recall, I always seemed to see her carrying a tall glass of Russian tea in a silver holder. I never knew why – or even what it was, then; and I never asked. She just did.

She had a powder puff in a red leather bag which I found interesting, for it looked exactly like a fat little bun with an ivory ring in its middle. If you pulled the ring, out came the powder puff, of softest swansdown, and the powder never spilled. It smelled sweet and sickly. I liked it.

Her room was dark nearly all the time for she hated daylight, which, she said, gave her terrible headaches. So the room was lighted here and there with small lamps draped with coloured handkerchiefs; each had a stick of incense burning beside it. The handkerchiefs cast strange and beautiful patterns on the ceiling.

There was a gold and black striped divan. Cushions in profusion tumbled all about the floor for one to sit on or lie upon. She had no chairs. I found that exceptionally curious. As I did the polar bear rug with roaring head, fearful teeth, glassy eyes and a pink plaster tongue, and the tall jars stuffed with the feathers from peacocks' tails.

It was the most exciting room in the house. She also had a portable gramophone which stood on a table with a broken leg that she had supported with a pile of books. She would wind it up after each record, a cigarette hanging from her lips, hoop earrings swinging from her ears, dressed as I only ever remember her dressed: in long, rustling dressing-gowns, covered with flowers and blue-birds, bound around her waist with a wide tasselled sash. The tassels swung and danced as she moved.

On occasion she was distressed and wept hopelessly: then my mother had to go down to the scented room and comfort her. Sometimes, too, she was rather strange. Leaning across to caress my cheek, for example, she would quite often miss me and crash to the floor in a heap. I found this worrying at first. However, she usually laughed and dragged herself upright by holding on to the nearest piece of furniture.

She once told me, leaning close to my face, that she had had 'one over the eight', but I didn't know what she meant, and when I asked my father he bit his lower lip, a sign I knew to indicate anger, and said he didn't know.

But I was pretty certain that he did.

Her dazzling eyes, the henna'd hair frizzed out about the pale, oval face, the coarse laughter, the tassels and the peacocks' feathers are still, after so many years, before me – and remain indelibly a part of my life.

She offered me, in that crammed room, a sense of colour and beauty, and even, although I was almost unaware of it at the time, excitement. I was uncomprehending of nearly all that she said but I did realize that she was offering riches beyond price.

First had come light; after light, scent, originally of turpentine and linseed oil (hardly romantic one might think), and now I was shown colour and, above all, made aware of texture.

'Touch it!' she would say. 'Touch the silk, it's so beautiful. Do you know that a million little worms worked to make this single piece?'

I didn't, of course, but the idea fascinated me. That something so fine, so sheer, so glorious should come from 'a million little worms' filled me with amazement, and I liked worms from then on.

Sometimes she would go away, and when I asked Mrs O'Connell where she had gone to she would only reply, 'Avoyagin'.' Which was no help. My parents when questioned said that she had gone on her holidays. I had an instant vision of buckets and spades, shrimping nets and long stretches of sand with the tide far out. And in consequence, knowing that she would be having a lovely time, put her from my mind.

When she returned she came bearing amazing gifts. Silver rings for my mother, a basket of brilliant shells of all kinds and shapes for me, French cigarettes for my father who, I knew instinctively, liked them better than he liked Aunt Kitty.

She brought for herself rolls of coloured cloth. Silks, voiles, cottons of every hue and design. These she would throw about her room in armfuls, so that they fell and covered the ugly furniture, then with the cigarette hanging from her lip she would wind up the gramophone, drape a length of cloth about her body, and dance. Barefoot, her nails painted gold.

Mesmerized I would sit and watch the small feet with golden-tipped toes twist and spin among tumbles of brilliant silks and the spilled shells from my palm-leaf basket.

> 'And when I tell them
> How wonderful you are,
> They'll never believe me-e . . . '

She told me, winding up the gramophone for the second side of the record, that the silks had come across the sands of Araby on the backs of camels, that she had seen monkeys swing among the branches of jacaranda trees, and flights of scarlet birds sweep across opal skies.

I hadn't the least idea what she meant. But somewhere in my struggling mind the awareness was growing, from her words, that far beyond the confines of St Georges Road, West End Lane, Hampstead, lay a world of magic and beauty.

Once I heard my father say that one day Aunt Kitty wouldn't return from one of her 'voyages'.

And one day that's exactly what happened. She never came back again: the Ground Floor Front was locked. I asked where she had gone. My father said possibly into the belly of a crocodile. It distressed me for a whole morning.

Years later I was to discover that no crocodile had taken Aunt Kitty: she had gone off, perfectly willingly, with a rich sultan from the East Indies.

When her room was opened it was exactly as she had left it, she had taken nothing with her, not even the silks. There were the gramophone, the draped lamps, the gold-striped divan, the bear-skin and the little red leather powder puff wrapped in letter paper on which she had printed a message to my mother, begging her to keep it always as a remembrance of her.

And she did. For many years it lay at the bottom of her jewel case and sometimes I would take it out, with permission, pull the little ivory ring, release the swansdown puff and the strange, musky scent. Naturally, over years, the scent grew fainter and fainter until, finally, there was only a ghostly odour, and the swansdown puff grew thin, grey, and moulted. But Aunt Kitty remains in my mind today, as clear and as vibrant as she was in the days when she wound up her gramophone for me.

'We'll have a little dancy, ducky, shall we? Would that be lovely?'

> 'And when I tell them
> How wonderful you are,
> They'll never believe me-e . . . '

Sometime after Aunt Kitty had left us, my sister Elizabeth was born. I was taken off to Scotland by my maternal grandmother Nelson, a friendly, firm, warm, straight-backed woman in black, to keep me 'out of the way'. I can only remember a new tweed coat with a velvet collar, of which I was inordinately proud, a railway compartment and on my lap a round, black lacquered wicker basket, painted with pink roses, which contained my sandwiches for the journey. It is a fragment of memory; that's all there is, but I see it sharply.

When I returned to the ugly house in St Georges Road, an enormous pram, with wheels like dustbin lids, stood in the front drive and Mrs O'Connell said that I had a baby sister and that, if they weren't careful (they apparently being my parents), a cat would sit on the baby's face and smother it. Faithfully, I reported this piece of information and my squalling sister was draped in netting.

With another member in the family, my personal discipline was relaxed, and I was left free to wander from studio to studio, squashing tubes of paint, watching the 'uncles' (they were all called 'Uncle', the resident artists who rented my father's rooms) painting their canvases, and being as tiresome as any child of four could be in a cluttered room full of sights and smells and bottles.

Bottles had a great attraction for me. I wonder why? I can remember, very clearly, taking down a full bottle of Owbridges Lung Tonic and swallowing its contents. I liked the taste of, I suppose, laudanum or whatever the soothing drug was which it contained. Though I well remember performing this wicked act, the time following it is obliterated. I went into a coma for four days, and nothing, not even salt and water, mustard and water, or being given my father's pipe to smoke apparently made any impression on me. No one was able to accomplish the essential task of forcing me to vomit up my stolen delight. I lay as for dead, heavily drugged.

I recovered – and later drank a bottle of rose-water and glycerine to the dregs. I was thrashed for this by my father, who always did it rather badly and apologetically with one of his paintbrushes.

But it didn't stop me. I stole from every bottle set high on shelves or left, carelessly, standing about. The studios were forbidden territory. Not only did I squash the artists' paint tubes empty, I was obviously quite capable of scoffing their linseed oil and turpentine.

A 'handful' is what I was considered, and handfuls such as I had to be dealt with firmly.

But no one had much time to deal with me, so, apart from being locked out of all the uncles' rooms, I was pretty well left on my own to play about in the garden and feed my sister with pebbles or anything else which came to hand. And, of course, got another walloping. People simply didn't understand that I was being kind.

Some of these fragments I remember with intense clarity. Others less well. Memory, as far back as this, is rather like archaeology. Little scraps and shards are collected from the dust of time and put together to form a whole by dedicated people, in this case my parents, who filled in the sprawling design of my life at that early age, and made real the pattern.

Aunt Kitty's room, for example, I can only see as a vague, shadowy place, filled with sweet scents and the trembling shapes of feathers and handkerchiefs flickering high on the ceiling. And I remember the gold and black striped divan, for it was to become my own, many years later, when we moved to the cottage. Equally I remember the polar bear rug. It was the first time that I had dared to place a timid hand within the roaring mouth; for the simple reason that Aunt Kitty had assured me that it would not bite.

It didn't. I trusted her from then on implicitly.

I trusted everyone in sight. Unwisely.

I can remember the great spills of cloth, but not the stories of camels and Araby or the scarlet birds swooping across opal skies. These items were added by my parents much later, who had, doubtless, heard her recount them and she told stories all day long to enthral me. But I do remember the worms; and the million it took to make a tiny scrap of glowing material. However, most of those very early years are simply the shards and scraps. Vivid none the less.

But from five years old onwards I have almost total recall – although I rather think that Elizabeth, with a feminine mind, has a far greater memory for detail than I.

My father grew restless in the grey-yellow brick house and decided that he wanted to move out to a quieter area: he suffered from catarrh, and also from hideous nightmares which his experiences, a few years before, in the Somme and at Passchendaele had engendered.

These of course I knew nothing about. Sudden shouts in the night perhaps, I can remember those, and my mother's anxious, caring face the following morning as he set off to his work at *The Times*, where he had become Northcliffe's golden-boy, and the first Art Editor at an absurdly young age.

So we moved away from the grey street off West End Lane into a small, but pleasant, house among abandoned fields just outside Twickenham. It was the talk of the family, and of its friends, that the sale was a 'snip'. He had bought it extremely cheaply for some reason, and everyone was amazed. The reason was soon to become apparent.

But for the moment we had a muddy road running through fields before us which trickled off into a path between high summer grasses, elderberry bushes and past a great rubbish tip buried deep in a quarry.

Behind our house ran an immense rose-pink brick wall, and behind that lay a park of great beauty and a square, complacent Georgian house burrowing away among chestnuts and elms. The people who lived there were exceedingly pleasant, and had children of about our age, and there was a green paint-peeling wooden door in the wall through which we were allowed to enter and join them at play on their smooth lawns among the croquet hoops.

We also had a garden, but, naturally, far more modest, in which my mother started to grow herbs and exotic vegetables which were, at that time, not easy to find in England. We had a huge cherry tree, some apple trees at the far end and a mass of climbing roses. Nothing could have been a greater change from the long narrow garden near West End Lane and the continuous smell of Irish stew.

We, Elizabeth and I, were in a paradise: but as in Paradise itself there was a serpent.

One morning the dirt track in front of the house began shuddering with trucks and lorries of all descriptions; they droned and rumbled all day long, and when they left, in the late evening, we discovered the fields before us, and around us, stuck with scarlet wooden stakes and draped about with sagging ropes. My anguished father discovered, too late, that he had purchased his house in the exact centre of an enormous building development; which was the reason that it had been, as everyone said, 'so ridiculously' cheap. 'A snip.'

We were buried among bricks, lime, cement and piles of glossy scarlet tiles. The road was churned into a mud-slide and the windows rattled all day with thudding trucks.

Within a year the fields in front had yielded up a row of semi-detached villas, with bay windows and tudor gables, their roofs, as yet untiled, looking like the pale yellow bones of a smoked haddock.

My father was in despair.

I was fascinated by all the work and upheaval and spent as much of my time as I possibly could clambering about in the unfinished foundations of suburbia. Although the workmen were friendly, and seemed not to mind me being among them, there came a time when they shouted at me to 'bugger orf!', and once someone threw a half-brick which sent me scurrying.

Another time I got a hod-load of lime full in the face; rather like a custard pie. It was, of course, quite accidental, and all I can remember is that it burned appallingly and I fled, blinded, from the half-built house, screaming at the top of my lungs, across the battered field and the rutted road. My distracted mother could not understand what had happened, naturally, and I was unable to tell her because I was yelling. She washed my face and hair and tried to get me to explain what had occurred, to no avail.

At that moment, an enormous man burst into the kitchen, pulled me on to his lap, and licked, with naked tongue, the lime from my eyes. Had he not done so, I have been assured, I would in all probability have been blinded for good. Counselling my distraught mother to bathe my eyes with milk and not let me out of her sight ever again, he left. I wondered who he was, and have often thought of him with gratitude.

I only stopped going to the half-built houses because I was warned that I'd be given a thrashing I'd never forget if I did. So I wandered off up the little path towards the deep rubbish tip in the quarry. It was quieter there, no one came near, and I could explore the tumbled rubbish of Twickenham with complete freedom. Boxes and crates, broken chimney pots, old tin cans, a battered pram; pieces of wood, quantities of smashed tiles and earthen drainpipes. Nothing smelly.

I remained always just at the edge, for it was very deep, and I had a fear of falling in – which, one day, I did. Because I heard a kitten crying down at the bottom. Leaning too far over the slippery edge of broken tiles and chimney pots I slid rapidly to the bottom, found the kitten, a skinny creature which had managed to get out of a sack, leaving the dead bodies of its companions, and sat down cradling my find, confident that someone would collect me.

I had tried to clamber up but had found that impossible: each step I took up the jagged slope of rubbish sent me slithering backwards, and there was no possibility of climbing the, to me at that time anyway, sheer sides with a frantic kitten. So I just sat quietly.

Calling had no effect either, I was soon to discover, for my thin voice never reached the lip of the pit, and my wretched mother, who had quickly discovered my absence, passed and repassed my prison without having the very least idea that her first-born was sitting below among the debris. Eventually a search-party was formed from the builders and masons on the swiftly growing estate; I was discovered and dragged to the surface with the kitten. I think that my mother had been so frightened that she forgot to punish me or even scold, and I was permitted to keep the kitten, who grew into a fine creature which we called 'Minnehaha'. Unknowingly getting his sex wrong.

The little path through the grasses was not exactly out of bounds, although now the quarry was. But along the path a jungle of most attractive plants and grasses grew, and tiny green crickets scissored in the sun. I picked handfuls of bright black fruits from a small bush, ate them, and stuffed my unprotesting sister. Full. With deadly nightshade.

Both of us, this time, went into a coma. There had been a nurse and a doctor and enemas and thermometers and the moment I was well enough to do so I up-ended the nursery fire-guard, shoved my sister into it as a patient, and we played 'hospitals'. It was very exciting, but pretty dull without 'pills' or 'medicines'.

I consumed, because it was my 'turn' to be a patient, a full bottle of aspirin. Another coma.

My mother was told that nothing could be done – I had taken such a massive overdose that I'd either die or recover. All that she could do was lie with me, her hand on my heart, and if she felt the least change of rhythm she was to call the doctor instantly.

I slept like a lamb, my heart beating contentedly.

I do not think that I had suicidal tendencies. Certainly I had no murderous ones. Then. However, my parents decided that the time was ready for me to have some kind of supervision and discipline in life: I had been altogether far too spoiled.

To this effect, early one morning, my sister and I, peering down into the hall through the white-painted banisters from the upper landing, saw our mother (elegant even at that hour, in a coffee-lace morning-gown and boudoir cap) engaged in earnest conversation with a Girl Guide. The latter smart and upright as a ninepin. Trim in her uniform with a bright white lanyard at her shoulder, a whistle at her neck.

Miss Ellen Jane, of Walnut Cottages, Twickenham, had just entered our lives. She has stayed part of it ever since.

'Ellen is my given name,' she said. 'At home I'm called "Nelly", but you'd better call me "Nanny", that's what I'm supposed to be, and that's that. It's more fitting.'

Elizabeth couldn't come to grips with 'Nanny', so she compromised and called her 'Lally'; and that is what she has always been.

It was a curious feeling having someone literally 'in charge' of one at all hours of the day, and even night. I began to enjoy it quite. I lost any suicidal tendencies I might have had because all bottles, knives, pills or potions were removed from my reach, and I willingly gave in to this cheerful creature who would stand no nonsense, as she said (and clearly meant it), and who looked a little less daunting in her new uniform of blue cotton and long white apron with celluloid cuffs.

It was rather interesting, I found, to be forced to sit upright at table and not to 'slouch about'. To replace my napkin in its linen envelope, to stop swinging my legs, to ask permission to leave the table (and often be refused until we were all satisfied), to have to wash my hands every two minutes (so it seemed), and above all to be read to in bed – a great change from 'Gentle Jesus', which we had to mumble in a hideous monotone, kneeling, with one eye on *The Water Babies*. But perhaps most interesting of all was the morning journey to the lavatory, the details of which operation had to be reported in full. If they were unsatisfactory one was sent back again.

But after a while I became less interested. I am easily bored. The novelty wore off, and I began to resent the routine and having my neck examined each morning to make certain that I had, in fact, washed 'round the back'.

My sister didn't seem to have to undergo quite so many humiliations, I began to realize, and she was far more cosseted and fussed over because she was younger. And prettier. Jealousy started to sprout like a bean shoot in the darkness of my heart – it also began to show.

And that was the start.

Miss Harris and her sister ran a genteel school for young children in a square Victorian house overlooking the Green. In their back garden, down among the laurels, and where the teachers parked their bikes, there was a long tin shed, painted dark red; this was the kindergarten.

I landed up there.

A blackboard, a big iron stove, tables. I remember nothing else. I imagine that one was instructed in the very basics, but I never bothered to learn them. This has had serious consequences for me throughout my life.

Jealousy seething, anger mounting, I sat and thought only about Minnehaha or how best to build an aquarium, or when we would next go down to Teddington Lock with net and jam jar to fish for sticklebacks.

I simply didn't bother with Miss Harris and her silly kindergarten; my brain absolutely refused to see the connection between 'CAT' and 'MAT' and I frankly didn't give a damn which sat on which. As far as I was concerned it was a wasted morning.

My parents found it to be the same thing after one caustic report from Miss Harris herself: 'He doesn't try. Won't put himself out at all.'

He was not about to.

Stronger medicine was needed, and it was found in the form of a tall red building along the river, almost next door to Radnor Park. A convent-school a-flutter with smiling nuns.

I was captivated by their swirling grey habits, by the glitter and splendour of the modest, but theatrically ravishing, chapel, the flickering lamps beneath the statues of the Virgin Mary and Joseph. It went to my head in a trice and I fell passionately in love with convent life.

I liked, above all, our classroom, a high-ceilinged, white-painted room with great mirrored doors which reflected the river, the trees beyond and the boats; I worshipped Sister Veronica with her gentle hands and the modest mole from which sprouted, fascinatingly, a single hair, and Sister Marie Joseph who was fat, and bustled, and stood no nonsense, but taught me my catechism and let me come into the chapel whenever I felt the need, which was often.

Not to pray, you understand, but to drown in the splendours of lamps, candles, colours, a glowing Christ and the smell of something in the stuffy air which reminded me of Aunt Kitty.

The colours, the singing of the choir, the altarcloths shimmering with gold thread filled my heart and my head with delight. I was lost: and decided, there and then, to be a priest.

Religion, certainly the Catholic religion, was not taught in our house. My father was born into a strongly Catholic family, with a staunch Catholic convert mother, and it was as a Catholic, firm in his belief, that he went to war in 1914. His belief, like that of so many other young men of that time, was shattered on the Somme, in Passchendaele, and finally for all time when he pulled open the doors of a chapel, after the battle of Caparetto in Italy, and was smothered in the rotting corpses of soldiers and civilians who had been massacred and stuffed high to the roof.

'Jesus,' he once told me, many years after, 'does *not* have his eye on the sparrows. But you follow whatever faith you wish; it is your life, not mine.'

And so Elizabeth and I grew up and flourished in a vaguely ambiguous atmosphere. We were sent to the convent on the riverside, I was allowed to have my own altar, which I built with intense care in a corner of the nursery, and we mumbled our 'Gentle Jesus' and The Lord's Prayer without interference. We were left to make up our own minds about God and Jesus, Joseph and The Virgin Mary.

It was not a difficult process for me because I had fallen quite in love with everything that Catholic teaching had to offer. Without, of course, realizing that what I had *actually* fallen in love with was the Theatre. Not religion at all. The ritual, the singing, the light, the mystery, the glowing candles: all these were Theatre, and Theatre emerged from these things and engulfed me for the rest of my life. Learning my catechism was, after all, merely the prelude to learning my 'lines'.

Like my father before me, I laid aside my belief, not that it had ever been very strong to be sure, for ever in my war.

Whenever I make a declaration of this kind I am inevitably swamped with letters from well-meaning people, usually women, who want to convert me to 'believing' again. I am bombarded, literally, with religious books, usually American paperbacks, of all possible permutations and persuasions. One which turns up regularly is called *Wrestling with Christ*, which appears to be an enormous best-seller but fails to answer any of the questions which have concerned me over the years. I have absolutely no wish to wrestle with anyone – especially with Christ.

It is particularly hard to retain a shred of 'belief' standing in the middle of a battlefield, at the age of twenty-three, watching piles of dead, frequently mutilated, soldiers, their bellies bloated with the gases of decomposition, being bulldozed into a mass grave. I watched them tumble, spill, slither like old shirts in a spin-drier, and as I walked away, retching in the stench of death, I knew that, at last, I had come of age, and that I could never recover the happy platitudes of immortality and 'Jesus Loves You'.

Where I wondered, on another occasion when I tripped over a row of what I took to be dusty footballs, but which were, in fact, the maggot-ridden heads of a file of small children who had sought shelter from our *own* bombing in a French village, what ever happened to that loving, comforting phrase, 'Suffer Little Children to Come unto Me'?

Something was not quite right. It was not what I'd been taught, and my first, appalled, uncomprehending sight of a concentration camp, two of the women guards smiling brightly and wearing scarlet nail-varnish among the decaying mounds of bodies, shred whatever belief I had had to tatters and dispersed it in the winds of fact, and hideous truth.

I would always, however, say my prayers. I still do to this day. But it is a prayer to a greater force than the simpering plaster figures to which I prayed so ardently all those years ago.

However, to return to Twickenham and innocence: a priest I decided to be, and that was that. The fact that no one took my decision seriously, even beloved Sister Veronica herself, did not trouble me. I had time before me, and I was exceptionally happy.

There were other moments of happiness which I recall during the Twickenham years. Days on the river in a punt. My father in white flannels and shirt, poling us along, my mother lying among cushions, a Japanese parasol shielding her face from the sun, Layton and Johnstone on the portable gramophone, a picnic hamper among the bathing-towels, the smell of boat varnish, and the excitement of getting to one of the locks and watching the rise and fall of the water.

In Church Street there was a small toy-shop filled with treasures, and every Saturday I went there with my 'Saturday penny' (actually I was given two) to buy a celluloid animal from a huge cardboard box to add to my growing 'zoo'. I, the budding priest, thieved one or two occasionally when the elderly woman who ran the shop was not looking. Twopence only bought one creature. Sometimes the desire to have another was too great and wickedness overcame me. With horrifying facility.

I knew perfectly well, for Sister Veronica had told me, that if I had done some 'really bad' thing I could one day go to confession and all would be forgiven. Catholicism, I figured, was a convenient affair.

The General Strike was something which threw a mild spanner in the works of this halcyon life; no amount of prayer, and I did a good deal of it both at home and in the chapel, seemed to help. My father drove an omnibus in a tweed cap and plus-fours and my mother joined some ladies and handed out soup. Otherwise it had little effect on my life or Elizabeth's. We were still marched off to the lavatory each morning and I still had my neck examined to make certain I had not 'skimped things', as Lally said. The days were fairly calm apart from the fact that we saw less of our parents, who were busily engaged. But there was a vague sense of unease about, and I didn't much care for that.

I never have.

All around us the terrible red brick houses with Tudor gables continued to spring up: the deep quarry into which I had fallen, and in which I had found Minnehaha, was filled in and a road laid across it; the pale rose-pink wall which surrounded the splendid park behind us was demolished; the great trees were felled; the Georgian house lost its complacency and crumbled into dust beneath a huge metal ball swung on a chain, and a cinema, with Egyptian suggestions in its architecture, arose slowly on the site, the gently croquet-hooped lawns were buried under asphalt for a car park.

My father decided that it was time to leave.

The fields had gone and in their place we now had lamp-posts and neighbours whom we really had not expected. I minded less than my parents, who were sunk in gloom. For who, in their right minds, would purchase a house, pretty if shabby, surrounded by fences, gates and tudor gables? As a matter of fact, I found neighbours rather interesting.

Immediately opposite us a Mrs Rance had moved into the first of the houses to be finished. She was a small, thin woman, her hair in curlers under a hairnet; she spent a good deal of her time coming across the still muddy road to borrow a cup of sugar or a 'small jug of milk, I've run out dearie'.

Lally disliked her intensely. She knew *her* position and *her* class. Mrs Rance obviously did not, we gathered. But what made her interesting was that on one or two occasions she would come staggering to our front gate screaming and waving a blue glass bottle in the air; then she would fall down in a fit and our mother would have to telephone a doctor.

'Been at the iodine again,' said Lally with satisfaction. 'If she wants to do away with herself, and this is the third time she's tried it, why come and trouble innocent, law-abiding people, I'd very much like to know?'

I took a deep interest in Mrs Rance and her well-being, and with vague notions of the priesthood looming in my mind I felt impelled to go to her assistance, as she was often lying, writhing about, outside our front gate. But there was little chance of that with Lally. I was carted off to our nursery, or room, and as it looked out over the back garden and the cherry tree I never saw what happened to Mrs Rance. I can't remember seeing her ever again – maybe the iodine did the trick.

The next people to move in opposite were the Hammonds. A family of four, three boys and one girl called Jessie. Jessie was one year older than I was and I liked her because she had a small tent in their back garden, a wilderness still of rutted mud and cement dust, and invited me to come and play with her.

It made a change from my sister, because Jessie was really pretty daring. She showed me a secret box in which she kept cigarette butts, and we sucked away at these for a time; without, of course, lighting them. They made me feel sick. So she rustled about and produced another tin box, battered but secure, in which she had a hoard of rotten apples, bits of cake and a whole tin of baked beans, which, with an opener in the shape of a bull's-head (which I coveted instantly), we opened and ate cold, in handfuls.

I felt a little more sick, but felt better after a bit of mouldy cake. Then she pulled down her knickers and said that she would show me her 'thingy' on condition that I showed her mine. This surprised me slightly – we had only known each other for an afternoon. Also I was still feeling a certain unease in my stomach and anyway I'd seen Elizabeth naked in the bath every night, just as she, indeed, had seen me: so I was not fearfully interested for I could hardly believe that I was about to witness something extraordinary or amazing.

I complied willingly.

We regarded each other in silence, standing in a half crouch in the sagging tent. I was quite unamazed.

'My brothers have got one like yours,' she said.

'My sister has one the same as yours, so there.'

'Girls have to sit down if they want to have a pee-pee; it's easier for boys.'

'I think I'll go home now,' I said.

Later I was extremely sick, and couldn't eat supper, which alerted Lally to the fact that perhaps all was not well. She told my father that I had spent the afternoon with 'those dreadful people in the new houses. It's not fitting. They'll spoil his ways, and there is nothing that I can do on account of the fact that I have only one pair of hands and no eyes in the back of my head. He wanders.'

My father was a just and kind man; he followed my anxious mother down to my room and asked me what had happened that day. 'We only want to know what has made you so ill, and then we can get it set to rights,' he said reasonably.

So I told him in detail, from sucking cigarette butts to eating mouldy cake and cold tinned beans, and examining each other's 'thingys'.

He looked grim but said nothing; my mother took my temperature, found that it was normal; they said goodnight and went away.

A few weeks later we moved to Hampstead.

And that is that. The first seven years of my life recalled as faithfully as I can remember, aided by others who have filled in the gaps.

The years of innocence. These, I am told, are the impressionable years, the formative ones during which all the things which one discovers, or is shown, stay with one for the rest of life and, as it were, one is moulded. One sets like a jelly. Perhaps not quite the right word? Cement? That sounds too heavy. Moulded, or fixed, must suffice.

I discovered light and scent, and, through Aunt Kitty, was made aware of colour and texture. Enduring sensations for me all these years later.

I have, it would seem, left out a fifth most important one. Music.

Music was a constant part of my life in those years: my father's passion was music. Not always the kind that I particularly cared for, it must be said. His studio at the top of the house was filled with what I grew to know, and detest, as chamber music. It was the music to which he painted. We called it, naturally enough, 'po music', and I always had a vague idea that it was played in lavatories – for where else on earth could anyone be forced to sit still long enough to hear those sombre cellos and skinny violins?

But there was opera too. Great ballooning sounds soared through the house, voices swept us from corner to corner, subliminally reached us in sleep; we were aware of music from our earliest moments, and in time, as is right and proper, the sounds which were incomprehensible between four and seven years, for example, began to take their own forms and one responded, or did not, as the case might be.

At the convent, of course, there were songs of praise and sonorous organs and those too became a part of the whole pattern of one's existence.

Music was everywhere; but I agreed with Lally, fervently, when she said that she 'did like a nice tune, something you can hum. And you can't hum much of your father's music I can tell you. No tunes there.'

But, anyway, music.

Light, scent, colour, texture, music. I entered the next phase of life with a rich haul.

But I was equally alert to grief and distress. My mother's face and the nailed-up cat; Mrs Rance with her blue glass bottle writhing about in the dirt of the street. There were distressing things in life which had little to do with colour or music and texture, or any of those things, and pain took its place in the pattern, inevitably, for I would always remember my near-blinding and the intense bewilderment of pain without sight.

A warning, an alerting to things. Childhood was not all halcyon days.

Nevertheless, it was a radiantly happy one for me. For one thing, we were very close, and we loved each other. We also touched each other, and were emotionally demonstrative in public, this at a time when such a thing was not encouraged generally.

Nudity was perfectly normal, and all the natural functions were discussed openly. There were no sniggers, blushes, nudges or, later on, dirty jokes in corners of school playgrounds.

We knew, at an early age, all the facts of birth, had watched countless kittens, guinea pigs and white mice being born, and, on one momentous occasion, had even seen a foal dropped. There were no secrets there for us, which is very possibly why poor Jessie was such a 'dud' that day in her tent. I suppose it might have been a different thing had she possessed two or three anatomical necessities – or even one made of Meccano; but poor Jessie's 'thingy' was just like any other old 'thingy' as far as I was concerned, and I was splendidly unimpressed. I was also, at the time, we must remember, about to throw up.

Another thing which was of vital importance to those early years was the fact that our parents, and Lally too, *talked* to us. Which is not the same thing as being spoken to. By 'talked to' I mean that things were discussed, analysed, argued about (within reason), and that all questions were answered. No one said 'I don't know, dear', or 'Do go away, I'm busy', or 'Go and play'. We were encouraged at all times to observe, and were questioned on the things which we had seen: a sunset, a tree root, a full moon, a half moon, dust motes in a beam of sunlight, the colour of an apple, anything. Everything.

I was fortunate in speaking coherently at a very early age. It must have been pretty excruciating for people most of the time, especially the 'uncles' in their studios who had other things on their minds, but I questioned and I was always given an answer which would satisfy me. For the time.

Lally had the patience of Job, my mother, an ex-actress, had most enviable sources of invention, my father had a calm, considering and very deliberate sense of reason: from the three of them one attained interest and satisfaction. So, naturally, I found life at home far more stimulating than life in Miss Harris's tin shed down among the laurels, where everyone seemed to me to be very young and deadly dull. If I decided to ignore, absolutely, the very basics which the poor woman, and her wretched assistants, tried, despairingly, to drum into my head, that was entirely my choice.

I have already said that I get bored easily. Well, Miss Harris and her 'CAT' and 'MAT' business, or making Christmas decorations with flour-paste and strips of coloured paper, or shoving round pieces of wood into round holes in other pieces of wood, seemed to me to be the ultimate in idiocy and tedium. I was bored witless. No one answered my questions; or else they looked anxious if they did because, as my mother was told, some of the questions were considered 'not quite suitable' for a child of such 'tender years'.

So I packed it in. It was all a waste of time. I was quite wrong of course. It took me a long time to latch on to that fact, and much longer to catch up, as indeed I had to eventually.

I imagined that family love and family life were sufficient, but you can't do without 'the basics', alas. A little bit of learning *can* be a dangerous thing, but it doesn't come amiss if it is used sensibly. I wish that I could say that all this bounty and love turned me into a child of an adorable disposition. By all the rules it should have done.

But it did not.

As you have discovered, I was an embryonic, if not an actual, thief. You could also say that I was a drunk: if you consider rose-water and glycerine or Owbridges Lung Tonic. It's a moot point.

But, naturally, I did not consider thieving in the toy-shop in Church Street as a crime. The shop-keeper had far more celluloid animals than I did; she very probably didn't care for them as much as I. So I took from the rich to assist the poor. The poor, in this instance, being myself. I reckoned that it made perfect sense.

After all, it is a widely held belief even to this day.

'A giraffe!' said Lally. 'Goodness me. I didn't know we had a giraffe in your zoo.'

'Ummmm.'

'Now, when did you get that? I don't remember it, do I?'

'No. I don't know . . . '

'With Mummy was it? Perhaps with her, eh?'

'Well . . . ummm, well, you know . . . '

'No I do *not* know! What I *do* know is that a giraffe costs much more than your Saturday penny, that's what I know.'

'They cost fourpence. Because they are bigger.'

'So?'

'I took it. When she wasn't looking.'

'You thieved it!'

Dry-mouthed, tear-flecked, I was dragged by my mother to Church Street and the toy-shop, where I was forced to return the giraffe and, what was even worse, made to apologize to the woman before two strangers who happened to be present at the time.

The woman folded her arms slowly. I can see her now. 'You want me to call a copper, then?'

My heart ceased to beat.

'It is entirely up to you, Miss Pratt,' I heard my mother say as if I was far below ground at the end of a drain somewhere. 'You do as you see fit: you are the one from whom he stole.'

I couldn't believe it! Such heartlessness! My own mother! Prison!

'By the looks of him, I'd say he'd had a good fright, so I'll let him off this once. But I don't never want to see you in this shop again, my boy.'

I emerged from my drain. Enraged at the humiliation. Furious that I had been caught.

I never stole again. Without being absolutely certain that I'd get away with it. I pinched the 'tips' from under the plates when I was, briefly, a waiter; took bottles of milk from doorsteps on many a grey winter morning when, foodless, I went off to start the little boiler at the 'Q' Theatre, and like everyone else scrounged, or 'swanned' as we called it, in the army during the war. Very modestly indeed.

However, the scar made in the toy-shop that day remained, and remains. Once in 1945, in Germany, we were in urgent need of a coffee-pot – our old one had been hit by shell splinters – so I broke into a cottage on the edge of a wood to see if I could find a replacement. Which I did. A fine grey enamel one with blue flowers and a hinged lid.

All the time I was aware that eyes were watching me.

Guilt flooded. Church Street came back in the shattered cottage kitchen with the clarity of immediacy. I set the pot back on the dead stove and left, just in time to see the vague shadow of a woman dragging two small, terrified boys to safety behind a row of blackcurrant bushes.

My shame was as acute as, under the circumstances of a war of Occupation, it was absurd.

But, once upon a time, I had been as small as they were.

TWO

If Aunt Kitty was the first of my surrogate aunts, as she undoubtedly was, and the artists who crouched earnestly before their easels in the grey-yellow brick house in St Georges Road were my first surrogate uncles, they were not to be the last. I collected relations assiduously in much the same way that any other child collected birds' eggs, or coloured shells, cigarette cards and marbles.

However, I was extremely prudent: one has to be selective, and especially so with uncles and aunts. Children are instantly aware of, and alerted to, people who do not particularly like them, or who feel uneasy and discomforted by their presence. In much the same way that a dog senses this antipathy, so does a child, and he is careful to avoid them: they are not usually people one can trust. So I chose with caution. It was really not very difficult because I picked them only from the tight-knit group of my parents' friends, who were all considered to be 'rather good with children'.

Certainly they did not patronize, or dismiss, or talk down. They were often fun, and always patient with questions which I rattled at them with the speed of a sub-machine-gun, and on occasion they offered splendid gifts. That was a particularly important requirement. Rather like awarding stars to restaurants. Thus the aunts and uncles who where the most prodigal, or imaginative, were awarded the highest marks. But, generally, they were chosen to flesh out our exceptionally happy family life, and to rectify an apparently serious omission.

We had all the love that we could possibly require from our parents, and in the comforting presence of Lally. But what we seemed urgently to lack were kith and kin, as she called them. It worried me greatly even though, until it was mentioned one day in the ironing-room, it had not really occurred to me that kith and kin were necessary. We had moved away from the river-mud of beloved Twickenham, to the gravel hills of Hampstead, which I hated.

Twickenham, even though the trees and fields in which I had started to grow up were vanishing under bricks and pebbledash, still had a vague village charm about it, and the river provided constant magic. Just the muddy smell of it satisfied me, or the trailing lengths of willow on Eel Pie Island, the punts swinging idly about at their moorings in the boatyards, the lush grasses across the river in Ham Fields. All these gave me the (inaccurate) illusion of the country. Hampstead was far less attractive, and the late Edwardian house into which we moved was not a patch on the shabby, but embracing, house we had left behind. The Hampstead one had a long garden at the back with apple and pear trees and a monstrous castor oil plant, or bush, plus an abandoned patch at the far end, overgrown with docks and nettles, which was allocated to Elizabeth and me as our 'place'.

The house was solid and ugly, and, apart from an immense stained-glass window, staccato with bulrushes, dragonflies and waterlilies which I liked above all else, it was gloomy and unloving. Even though I was, after a couple of years, removed from the pink and white-daisied nursery which I shared with my sister, and given the precious privacy of a room of my own, I was always ill at ease there. Except in my room. Very small, but overlooking the back garden and the branches of a tall pear. I was allowed to choose my own wallpaper (blue-tits in wistaria), and rebuild my altar to Jesus in a corner, and grieved privately when the splendid stained-glass window, which rose from the first floor to the second landing in shimmering glory, was covered by long net curtains and thus banished from sight.

The only place left which had any relics of Twickenham-remembered was Lally's area – the ironing-room and her sewing-room – and we spent a good deal of time there with her. The rest of the house had taken on a strange formality, under my father's exuberant hand, which hindered our carefree existences.

We had a drawing-room now. Rose and black panels with gold Chinese dragons, and Aunt Kitty's black and gold striped divan. Immense cushions were strewn about the floor, and great bowls of philadelphus or peonies, according to the season, stood on low tables and blackamoor pedestals. It was out of bounds to us, except on Christmas Day. And as that only arrived once a year, we really hardly ever saw it.

So to Lally we gravitated willingly. To the room with the sheet-covered table, the comforting smell of warm linen and the curious damp scent of Robin starch. And while she cheerfully folded table napkins, pillowcases and our striped pyjamas we sang the songs which she had heard at the local cinema – still more or less forbidden to us, unless Charlie Chaplin or Jackie Coogan were in the film; but as I liked neither very much (Mr Chaplin never made me smile once, and often scared me out of my wits, and still, I regret to say, does; and Jackie Coogan I considered a bit soppy), I did not feel deprived in the least. Lally told us, in great detail, the story of every film she went to, and she went often, and sang us all the songs, la-la'ing when she couldn't remember the words.

My job in the ironing-room was to take the piles of warm ironing and stack them on the shelves in the linen cupboard, where Minnehaha spent a great deal of time when he was not lying stretched out under the castor oil bush like a Rousseau tiger. One day I had arranged the yellow damask table napkins tidily away when Lally set down her iron and sighed.

'Funerals,' she said. 'Sad business at the best of times, but yesterday's was sadder than many, I won't deny. I don't like them, not as a rule, not funerals. But I felt it was my duty so I just had to go. Poor Edna Stannard dead, with no kith and kin to see her off! All by herself.'

Unease pricked me.

'What's kith and kin?'

'Relations. Aunts and uncles, cousins. Family and all that, and so forth.'

'Well, we haven't many of those either. Do you *have* to have them?'

'It's usual,' said Lally, taking up her iron once more and spitting lightly on it to see if it fizzled. Which it did.

'What do you have to have them for?'

'Things like yesterday. Funerals . . . birthdays, holidays. All sorts of things. Nice to have your kith and kin about you. Your own flesh and blood.'

'Have you got them?'

''Course I have! There's brother Harold, and Ruby, and baby Dennis, and others – remember I told you? We had a lovely time together last Christmas with Mr and Mrs Jane (her parents), and a goose and a bottle of tonic wine, and brother Harold played "Come All Ye Faithful" on his clarinet. A *lovely* time we had.'

I was silent with mild dismay. I remembered our Christmas in the black and rose drawing-room. The tree in the corner, and all our 'uncles' and 'aunts' laughing and talking. Aunt Coggley, Uncle John, Aunt Celestia, Uncle Salmon, Uncle Bertie and Aunt Gladys . . . a host of kith and kin, but, I realized now, they were not *real*, they were just pretend ones. Ones whom Elizabeth and I had collected. They had nothing to do with our own flesh and blood. It was extremely disturbing.

'What's the matter now? Cat got your tongue, young man?'

'No. I was thinking, that's all.'

'Well I declare! We don't do very much of that; do we now?'

'We don't seem to have any kith and kin, do we? Not really. Only pretend ones, like Aunt Celestia, or Uncle Bertie . . .'

'What a lot of tommy-rot indeed! What about all your mother's family in Scotland then? They are your kith and kin and no arguing. Not to mention Granny Nutt.'

'But Granny Nutt isn't really our grandmother. She's our real grandmother's sister. Only she died, so Granny Nutt took her place, sort of.'

'Your English! I declare! Well, if you are a bit thin on your father's side, and no blame to him I hasten to add, you've got plenty on your mother's side, nine in family she was, so don't you start getting into one of your moods about no kith and kin, goodness-me-today! You've got more than I have, and hand over that bundle of handkerchiefs, if it won't break your arm.'

She was right, of course. But however much I considered the truth of what she said, I simply couldn't put it all together or reconcile myself to an enormous tribe of Scots relations glowering away in the gloomy north. I had only been there, to my knowledge, once in my life when my sister was born, and that was five or six years ago. Apart from a hazy memory of my straight-backed, black-garbed Granny Nelson, and a white-haired man who sat alone with a small dog by the big stove in the kitchen (who was, I was told, my grandfather: banished for some unspeakable misdemeanours), I remembered little else.

Apart from the fact that I had to put pepper and salt on my porridge. I remembered *that* with shock. But no face came back to me, no suggestion of 'nine in family'. I suppose that the sheer distance between us all, and the fact that none of them sallied forth, or ventured south, made them impossible to visualize. I had therefore dismissed them swiftly. In a few years' time they were to swamp me; but as yet, in the happy warmth of the ironing-room, I was blithely unaware of unhappiness ahead. However, I decided, there and then, that kith and kin must be collected diligently from now on. I had no intention of dying suddenly and finding no one loving and kind at my graveside. That was absolutely out of the question.

Granny Nutt (Nutt because she had married a jovial solicitor of that name) was of 'the blood'. That could not be denied because she was my father's aunt. She was also 'good with children' in a rather timid way; but she was all we had as 'family' so we made do with her, and managed very well. She was a small creature, with fine bones and brown eyes, her hair piled tidily on top, fixed by a tortoiseshell-pin through a neat bun, a black velvet ribbon round her throat, silver buckles on her shoes.

We often went to her pretty house by the river at Hampton, where her husband, the jovial solicitor, tended an immaculate garden. We had polite tea, with a good many different kinds of sandwiches and cakes, after which we were allowed to explore Uncle Arthur's domain. I remember that it was desperately ordered, trim and uninteresting, except for a stone bird-bath, a rustic summerhouse and the river Thames which formed the boundary at the far end. This always attracted me, and Uncle Arthur admitted that it was 'Extremely useful. All I have to do when I have finished weeding, or cutting the lawn, is to bung the whole lot over the hedge into the water. The tide bears it all away to the sea. Most useful.'

Apart from the teas and the Thames, which were pleasing, there arrived, every Christmas and on each of our birthdays, a very respectable postal order from our surrogate grandmother. I have an uncomfortable feeling today that Elizabeth and I accepted her for these yearly spasmodic bursts of generosity instead of any deep-felt love of 'family', or loyalty to blood. We really didn't know what those meant, anyway, but we did know what a postal order meant.

Granny Nutt was warm and gentle, and Uncle Arthur patient. He taught us to play croquet on his smooth lawns, which bored us witless, but seemed to amuse him. And I played attentively; pretending passion almost, because I felt certain that to do so could remind him, when the time was due, that our postal orders might be bumped up a bit. Surely he would say to his wife, at the end of our visit: 'Charming children! Most interested and enthusiastic about croquet. Perfect manners; they even allowed me to win a couple of games. I think that perhaps at Christmas we could increase the amount from seven and sixpence to, say *ten* shillings, don't you?'

Of course he never said anything of the sort. The postal orders stuck implacably at seven and sixpence for all time, and I can't even be certain that he wasn't as bored as we were with his wretched game, even though we did, on occasion, let him win deliberately. To no avail.

But Granny Nutt was our only tangible piece of kith and kin, of blood, I now realized. One moved with caution therefore.

I last saw her in the early fifties sitting on a metal chair in the front garden of a hideous hotel in Bournemouth to which she had retreated at the death of Uncle Arthur. Upright still, a furled umbrella tightly held in gloved hands, a toque with a stiff black feather, her skirts, even then, to the ground, the velvet ribbon round her throat, silver buckles – or were they steel? – on her shoes. I kissed her goodbye – I was off to London – and I can still recall the light scent of her cologne, the tickle of the spiky fur collar on her coat.

'It was so good of you to come and see me. So good . . . '

'I'll send you a postcard from Abbeville, when I get there next month.'

She barely smiled, nodded, clasped the umbrella to her knees.

'I would imagine that it would be difficult for you to send it *before* you got there, wouldn't it? But please do. I shall so look forward to it.'

'I will. I promise.'

'I can't think why you want to go to that sad, sad place in France.'

'To see the war graves and the old battlefields.'

'Your father had a most unpleasant time there, you know? And Grace, your grandmother, died while he was fighting there in 1916. He was left quite an orphan.'

'I know.'

'I'm getting old and repeating myself. A fault in solitary people. You'll place some flowers, won't you, on a grave?'

'A grave?'

'I shall set you an errand. Will you do it for me? Place them on one of the Unknowns. There are very many. They are forgotten easily: known only to God. Put some flowers on one, will you? For me?'

I said that I would and drove away to London, leaving my kith and kin, the nearest and, finally, dearest, sitting on her tin chair in the thin spring Bournemouth light. She died before I remembered to send the card from Abbeville to tell her that I had indeed put some wild flowers on an unknown grave, and that I had kept my word.

So although I did have the Nutts for real kith and kin (Uncle Arthur just scraped in because, after all, he was not of the blood), the pretend uncles and aunts were always the more amusing and gave infinitely more pleasure. This was mainly so because they had been hand-picked, so to speak, and had had to undergo extremely stringent tests before they could be elevated to the august ranks of the chosen. Also, they were younger.

These tests were naturally changed conveniently from person to person, but in the main they were basic, and remained the same. First of all a prospective mourner had to like children. That was the essential, and main, requirement.

They must not patronize, ignore, or belittle. They had to have the vitally important qualities of humour and, above all, laughter. Without those they couldn't possibly be accepted. They must also like animals: if they couldn't quite *adore* them as I did, then they had to show, at least, a warm interest and not, as some, pale with terror at the sight of a harvest mouse, or cry out in horror at the presence of a cheerful old toad or even, silliest of all, a harmless bat.

People like that simply couldn't pass. It was not essential, but of course greatly to be desired, for them to come fishing for efts or sticklebacks, or even to assist at the delivery of a family of white rats or a litter of rabbits, but it was perfectly all right if they merely showed interest in the business, and more so if they offered (as many did rather than actually look at the messy business) a piece of silver money with which to defray the cost of feeding them, or for the purchase of a larger cage or a better aquarium in which to house them.

But it was not absolutely essential. Laughter and kindness was all that really mattered, for after all I was making sure that there would be a cheerful assortment of loving kith and kin at my graveside. I had no intention of being sent off quite alone like poor Edna Stannard. My parents and Lally, I was certain, would be *far* too distressed at my demise to do more than just stand sobbing. I wanted jollity and love at such a moment, and people to comfort the bereft members of my family.

I had it all arranged.

How easy it was in those distant days! How simple life, or even, on this occasion, death, appeared to be.

Now that I am well down my personal corridor, I have made firm rules that there will be absolutely no one to mourn my going: no flowers, no music, no loving pretend aunts and uncles – they've all gone already anyway. When I go, I go as I came in; if I'm lucky. Quietly, and alone, and absolutely without fuss. During the intervening years I have learned a great deal – but then, in the crystal-clear days of early childhood, nothing had as yet cast any ugly shadows across my path.

The shadows were to come of course; but fortunately one doesn't know that at eight or nine, and I, for one, lived in Cloud-cuckoo-land, unaware of mortality in its true sense. Except that it came to white mice or goldfish. And Edna Stannard.

I have said that we were seldom permitted to go into the rose and black panelled drawing-room, but that is not strictly true. Certainly Christmas Day was the time when we were given absolute freedom among the blackamoor pedestals and fat scattered cushions.

But there were evenings too, during the year, when, dressed in our best, we were allowed to come down to join our parents in welcoming their guests for half an hour. This happened really fairly often, because they entertained a good deal, and it was on these formal occasions that I would spy out a possible member for kith and kin. It was a useful pastime. While handing round olives, or little biscuits, and cheese straws, in my white silk shirt, grey flannel shorts and patent leather pumps with shiny buckles, I sized up likely mourners for the churchyard.

Aunt Coggley was the very first member of the chosen: Irish, with a long nose and beautiful hands clustered with rings, she laughed with a warm, private sound and did her very best to teach me the basics of spelling at which I was, and still am, appallingly bad.

'There is no "e" at the end of "potato", darling. You keep sticking in "e's" where there are none. Try again, and how many "s's" are there in "necessary"?'

I would struggle to please her, because she was so nice, but I still, to this day, shove in 'e's' with the abandon of a best man throwing rice at a wedding, and scatter 's's' about like salt. But I can still hear her patient voice in mild reprimand every time that I do so.

Uncle Bertie was jolly, fat and also Irish. He was a highly considered surgeon at the Ear, Nose and Throat Hospital, and so he had double uses. He was always full of cheer and delightedly dressed up as Father Christmas every year. He also removed my tonsils and adenoids perfectly, assuring me that it was most unlikely that I should die in the process. I did not. His stock was therefore gilt-edged.

Aunt Celestia I chose because she was extremely interesting and often went mad. From time to time she was sent away to a home where, she told me, they did quite terrible things to her with electric shocks. Celestia was short, with grey cropped hair and hands like a bricklayer's. She was a sculptor and potter of some renown, and smoked by holding the packet in one hand and lighting a new cigarette from the butt of the old one as soon as it had burnt her fingers. Which were amber-coloured, as was the long streak which ran through her boy's hair. She used to give me the dead butts, wet at the end, to put in the fire.

'Don't put them in ashtrays, boy,' she would say. 'They'll start counting them, and then they'll try to stop me. But I do need my nicotine, you see.'

I didn't, and burnt the stubs secretly, in the fire, once holding a hot, and smelly, handful for a long time while she told me, in a low, whispering voice, full of conspiratorial laughter, how she had unscrewed the keyhole cover from the door of her room at the home, and swallowed it.

'There!' she said triumphantly. 'Wasn't that a sensible thing to do?'

'Was it?'

'Of course it was, boy! Then, you see, they had to take me to a *real* hospital and I was able to prove that I wasn't mad at all!' Her voice was like gravel shaken in a box.

'How did you unscrew the keyhole thing?'

'A nail file. Had it in the lining of my handbag. You must always carry a nail file about with you; can't ever be sure when you'll need it. And of course,' she added, lighting a new cigarette from the wet, glowing butt, coughing a good deal, 'of course you can always stick it in their eyes, the nurses, when they get unpleasant. Here's another butt! Off to the fire, heigh ho! *What* a good fellow you are!'

No patronage from Aunt Celestia; she took one splendidly into her confidence and made one feel extremely important.

But it was, perhaps, Uncle Salmon who had almost the biggest effect on my life at that time. He was something very important at *The Times.* Foreign News Editor? I forget. A big, burly, tweedy man, who smoked a stubby pipe and enjoyed his claret. It was he who, one evening, suggested to my father that we should take over the lease which he held on a ramshackle cottage in the middle of the Sussex Downs. He had lived in it, at weekends, for some years, but the place was too isolated for him finally, and he was moving to another cottage near Hailsham. The rent was seven and six a week, there was a well, no electric light or telephone, an outside privy, and nothing but sheep and larks to disturb the peace.

'Excellent place for the children, they can go wild there. Most important to do that in your early years, Ulric. They shouldn't be cooped up in Town all day.'

We took the cottage, which altered all our lives in various ways.

Uncle Salmon came down to stay during our first weeks there, bringing with him a case of excellent claret and a tortoise for Elizabeth and me. We called it George; after the donor, although his name was William.

However, Uncle Salmon was warmly accepted to see me off at the graveside: there would have been no better uncle for the job.

But of all the aunts and uncles, the one who had the profoundest effect on the whole of my life was Aunt Yvonne.

I chose her from the group of friends who were closest, and therefore more frequently met, to my parents. She was Belgian (but insisted on being French), and an actress of great renown. She had all the right qualifications for a mourner: she was exceedingly pretty in a plump, sparkling-eyed way, she laughed a great deal, she never condescended, she adored children, supplied extravagant and greatly imaginative presents regularly, was curious and interested in slow-worms, lizards and my jar of snails – which, she assured me, were delicious baked in garlic and butter – taught my mother how to cook, and, eventually, introduced me to the theatre one afternoon in Glasgow when I had gone to see her in a matinée of a play she was touring.

For thirty glorious minutes I was on a real stage in a real theatre, and almost from that moment I set aside the idea of graveyards and mourners, of kith and kin, of practically everything except a blinding determination to become an actor myself one day: in the then quite short corridor of my life, Yvonne Arnaud took me by an eager hand and pushed me, willingly, through the door which was to lead me towards the theatre and my future. I never looked back.

But I am looking back now, so many years later, with amused wryness. What nonsense it all was.

How seriously I searched for kith and kin to mourn my departure from a life which I had hardly begun! But how well I chose; for many of them added enormously to that life, not only to the pleasure of living it, but to my awareness of what it actually means to *be* alive.

In those smugly happy early years I thought, if I thought at all, that nothing would change. But of course it did, inevitably, and caught me on the hop. Idling my way through life with the complacency of a well-fed cat, avoiding any kind of responsibility to anyone but myself, wandering through my schooling with the uninterest of a sloth, I was disagreeably shocked when, at the age of thirteen, a completely unexpected brother was born, throwing me into a turmoil of appalled jealousy and almost speechless self-pity, and my sister and the rest of the family into twittering delight. I had not planned on this hideous arrival. It was unthinkable; and because of that I literally *hadn't* thought. Fatal error.

Suddenly I, and my self-centred little existence, were brutally set aside (as I saw it at that time). Within days a whole raft of carefully cherished aunts and uncles turned, as one, with happy cries of joy and welcome to the red, wrinkled creature howling up in the daisied nursery.

To my stricken dismay Aunt Celestia, my closest friend, the one for whom I had toiled so hard to hide the soggy evidence of her shameful vice, even went so far as to design, and make personally, a magnificent silver christening goblet for the intruder. I was horrified at the treachery.

In the rose-pink and black panelled drawing-room my brother, carried by an adoring Lally, was the centre of an admiring crowd (of the very people whom I had personally chosen for my *own*!) and, swathed in a billow of lace and fine wool, bubbled and smirked as they drank his health in champagne from a traitor's-cup, fashioned by the disloyal hands of my cherished, up until then, Aunt Celestia.

It was almost more than I could bear. My mourners had reneged on me! But worse was to follow.

My real kith and kin, my mother's 'family of nine', were still glowering away in the dark north: spectral figures of my future doom, unremembered, unloved, hovering in the gathering gloom of Scotland and my own suffocating misery. Shortly I was thrust among them. Bewildered, astonished; an astounded stranger. The apparent object of this vile action, being sent far away to join exactly what I had always felt bereft of since Lally's conversation in the ironing-room, was school.

As I had long ago detested poor Miss Harris and her teachers in Twickenham, so I had idled or ignored the excellent facilities offered me in Hampstead to improve my mind. I had even drifted in a haze of happy, and determined, ignorance through the veined hands of a black-booted and wing-collared tutor. In a stifling room in a mouldering villa in Willow Road. To no avail.

So, a good Scots education was deemed essential. No slacking; nose to the grindstone; hard slog.

To soften the blow, for after all my parents were not monsters and I adored them even if they had deliberately upset my house of cards, and because I had already reached the advanced age of thirteen (too old it was felt to hurl me into boarding school), the evil deed was to be made more palatable, if that word can possibly be applied to such a measure, by sending me to my real kith and kin. Kith and kin who would cherish, console, counsel, feed, and water me while I worked away at logarithms, algebra and the Divine Right of Kings.

I found that real kith and kin were very different indeed to my carefully hand-picked assortment of happy, carefree aunts and uncles in the south who had no blood ties whatsoever. These were creatures of happiness and gaiety. Now I was surrounded by serious, flannelled, kind, restrained, unlaughing, colourless – to me at any rate – people who played bridge and tennis, went weekly to church (a long walk each Sunday), and visited the ageing members of the family on regular days each month.

There was never, at any time, music in the houses of my kith and kin. For that one was hauled, reverently, to a concert hall. And then very rarely: it was expensive.

Aunt Kitty's colours, scents, textures, simply did not exist in the porridge-and-beige 'living-rooms' (as they were called, as opposed to 'drawing-rooms'), and the nearest I ever got to 'flights of scarlet birds swooping across opal skies' were flocks of moulting pigeons feathering through the drizzling rain above the oily cobbles of Glasgow's streets. 'Imagination and breathless wonders' were occasionally suggested by dreary performances every year of the D'Oyly Carte Operatic Company. The tragedy was that, by the time they reached Glasgow, most of the lustre seemed to have faded, and there was precious little 'breathless wonder' to be seen.

My aunt and uncle, with whom at that time I lodged, had a deep affection for the Company. They knew every show and song by heart, and never missed a chance to see them *all* when they came to town. Seats were booked, for the entire season, months ahead. It was a deathly business, I thought.

Nightly I sat in sullen despair, unmoved, uncomprehending; hating the pouting, the winking, the gymnastic movement, the posturing and the words. Few of which I could understand, however loudly they were sung. 'Poor Wandering One' or 'The Lord High Executioner' were nothing in comparison to the songs to which my mother and Aunt Coggley danced the Charleston, with beads and skirts flying:

> 'Who's wonderful! Who's marvellous!
> Miss Annabel Lee!'

Of all the shows, I think that perhaps I disliked *The Mikado* most. I can't remember how many times I had to sit through it, numb with misery. I only know that today the merest echo of 'Titwillow' is enough to fill me with terror and a sense of dreadful claustrophobia. Everything comes instantly back: the Circle Stalls, the shabby red plush, the gradual, terrifying dimming of the great chandelier above me, and the image of Uncle Duff doubled up with gleeful laughter at those bloody three-little-girls-from-school, the tears coursing down his cheeks and the side of his nose, until he would reach for my aunt's handkerchief (never his own, I wonder why?) to dry them. Hiccuping with pleasure. 'Titwillow' had them both rocking with refined delight.

'Yon's a comical song!' Uncle Duff would say. 'A very comical song, I tell ye . . . '

I hated 'Titwillow'. I still do.

And then back on the tramcar to the shabby suburb where, owing to straitened circumstances caused by the Depression, we now lived in the porridge-beige house: antimacassars on each chair, framed covers of *Nash's Magazine* on the walls, and lazy-daisy-worked table-centres.

With cocoa and biscuits before bed.

It is strange, looking back from here, that these Special Treats, for that is what they were known as, never, for one moment, kindled the remotest desire within me for the theatre. I was unmoved. I, who had written my own plays from the age of five, who had dressed up as an actor at the drop of a hat, and recited pages of home-made poetry to silently suffering kith and kin in the south, was left absolutely cold by D'Oyly Carte and his Company.

If I seem to be ungenerous, and I do, then I can only say that I am. There was great kindness on offer from my real kith and kin on all sides; they did everything possible to make my life tolerable, amusing, instructive and pleasing. Within the strict limits, of course, of what was tolerable, amusing, instructive and pleasing to themselves. They couldn't move out of the restricting frame of their traditional behaviour, and the appalling regularity of their lives depressed me beyond bearing.

Of course it was understood that I was 'difficult' because I had come from a 'Bohemian background', as they called it. After all, my mother smoked, wore lipstick and nail-varnish ('It's *not* suitable,' my aunt would say distantly, but she wouldn't explain what *was* suitable), and went so far as to dance the Charleston. What, I wondered, was so awful about the Bohemians? In the dictionary I discovered that Bohemians came, reasonably enough, from somewhere called Bohemia. Which didn't seem to me half as bad as, for example, coming from Bishopbriggs. In any case I had not the remotest idea where Bohemia was, or what they did when they were there. I *had* noted an added line in the dictionary which said something about 'unconventional behaviour', but 'unconventional' was too long a word to look up, and my interest, hard to hold at the best of times, had already flagged.

As far as I was concerned, if the life I had been living was Bohemian, then it was absolutely splendid. At least it was a life filled with pleasurable surprises, omitting of course the distressing, and unexpected, arrival of my unfortunate brother, but we didn't live a *single* day in which *every* moment was planned down to the last fragment; I never knew precisely what would happen on the third Sunday in the month, or the last day of the week, or four Tuesdays ahead. Anything could happen, and did. All was wondrously unplanned, and free.

Among my real kith and kin, every single hour, day, week, month had been fully organized in advance, and nothing ever changed anything. I knew exactly what I would eat for my lunch and supper days ahead – the menu would never alter. Mince and sprouts; cod and parsley sauce; finnan haddie and mashed potatoes; black pudding; and so on, all the way through until we got to mince and sprouts again. Usually on Wednesday.

I knew, weekly, to whom I would be taken to Sunday tea. Some aged friend, 'under the weather a wee bittie', or a crumbling member of the kith and kin, and I recall, with numbed awe, those crammed tables piled about with plates of oatcakes, potato pancakes, drop scones and God knows what else, at which they glutted, talking all the while about gallstones, gall-bladders or Aunt Teenie's enemas. I was forced to listen. One was not permitted to leave the feast.

Friday, without fail, was bridge night. The small green-baize table was set up (we ate early for this occasion), pencils were sharpened, score-cards put out, the cards reverently placed in the centre. My aunt wore her 'good blue'. It was during the very first session that I discovered exactly what a bridge roll was, because it was my job, at half-time, to serve them, along with paper napkins, while the tea was poured. Glossy, tasteless, doughy cigars stuffed with fish paste and cress. I found the discovery less than interesting. Merely curious.

On Sunday we walked to church. Two miles there, two miles back, before the terrible teas later.

In the beginning, when it had been explained to me that church parade was absolutely obligatory every Sunday, I felt exceptionally happy. Memories of Sister Veronica, of a smiling Christ, of the heady smell of incense and the mysterious ritual of the Holy Water, crowded back, and I was certain that I would feel less strange and lost among the familiar splendours of crimson and gold, and soaring organ music.

Ah, but no! No. This was not the Church to which I had turned with such joy and passion, and devotion. Here all was sombre and cold. Ash and charcoal. We apologized for our sins (I never knew what sins any of the congregation could have possibly committed, so dull a lot were they) and begged forgiveness repeatedly. It seemed to me that the Scots were very much aware of wickedness and redemption, but no one ever, as far as I could understand things, worshipped Jesus or God or the Holy Ghost or anyone else with whom I had been familiar.

What on earth, I wondered, was there to forgive them for in this sterile, spartan, ordered life? No one *did* anything! I was fully aware that I had, up until then, committed no sin: even masturbation had long since ceased. The effort of trying to conceal a twopenny tin of Vaseline had proved too difficult: I knew that all the drawers and cupboards in my room were 'tidied up' every single Saturday; so I took a vow of celibacy. The only sin to which I could possibly make a claim was that of peeing out of the carriage windows in Queen Street tunnel on the way back from school. But it hardly seemed worth mentioning in the harsh, whitewashed church, among the black overcoats and the tweed-and-fitch costumes of the congregation humped forward in repentance.

So I took no part in the proceedings except to kneel, stand, or sit. And when I did pray it was to a very different Jesus: whom once I had loved, and to whom I had built glittering, if modest, altars. If, for the time being, he had deserted me, I had absolutely no doubt that he'd come back and rescue me. I have always been optimistic. To the point of being unrealistic.

However, I had to wait a good time for rescue: I eventually returned to my Bohemian family, and my abandoned life among them, triumphantly un-tutored, but strong, when I was almost sixteen.

They were, I know, the three most important years of my life, the horseshoe-on-the-anvil ones. I could not have done without them. In that time I was forced to reconsider who and what I was. I had never, to be sure, given it much thought: only that I was a pleasant enough fellow, happy, obliging and fond of everyone, or nearly everyone, I met. Causing no trouble that I knew of, and wishing none. It was a simple pattern.

But in the bosom of my real kith and kin I began to realize that to survive I must alter the pattern of behaviour drastically. Being happy and obliging and fond of everyone was a sign of weakness. It was, in fact, considered 'cissie' to behave like that. A boy had to be strong, play games, speak when spoken to, and never idle around with poetry or books, keep frogs and tadpoles, or play the piano. Having a personal opinion was considered impolite, and to ask questions would only make one 'impertinent' or imply disrespect for one's elders.

So I began to construct a private world of my own.

I worked at creating this world of a 'loner' harder than I had ever worked at anything in my life before – which was, one must admit, about time.

I avoided my schoolmates, few of whom liked me because I was a Sassenach and spoke with a 'posh' accent. So I withdrew from their company as often as I could. In time I learned, in self-defence, to speak as they did, with the same ugly accent, so that when I *had* to be a part of their group my failure as a person was not quite so apparent, but this accent brought horrified criticism from my uncle, who said that it was 'vulgar' and was not to be used in his house. I thought that this was rather unfair as it was he who had recommended the school to which I was sent, and he ought, I thought, to have known that it was a fairly tough one. Rather than join my fellows, therefore, I spent most of my time alone, or else walking dogs for the neighbours. For which I often got a sixpence or a cup-cake. Solitude became desirable in this world, and I sought it.

I started to isolate myself from people, and to build a strong protecting shell against loneliness and despair, both of which could have been my constant companions had I been weak enough to allow them to come too close. I sometimes felt, cheerfully, that I was rather like a hermit crab. Tight in his borrowed shell, like the ones I had scrabbled about for in rock-pools at Cuckmere Haven in the happier days. I was safe from predators; and by predators I meant everyone I met.

There were, of course, times when I was able to leave, for a short time, my self-imposed shell protection, certainly at holiday times when, to my aching relief, I was allowed to return to the south and my family. But I went back into the shell the moment my train left Euston Station for Glasgow, and settled there until the next holiday.

There was, I have to admit, one aunt whom I loved very much. Tall, once pretty, now harassed and impoverished, living in a mean flat with two children and the remains of a 'disastrous marriage', who, it appeared, played whist all day. With her I felt quite secure. We talked about music and about books, she allowed me to play her piano, an out-of-tune upright, jammed into the too small sitting-room, and did not think it ridiculous when, one autumn, I found a red admiral butterfly which I kept in a jam jar in one of her cupboards and fed on jam spread on the tip of my finger. She was as delighted as I that we managed to rear it through a bitter winter and release it in the early sun of the following spring. A triumph indeed! We were both very proud. No need of a shell, therefore, with this splendid woman.

And then there was the time when Aunt Yvonne, my pretend member of kith and kin, arrived in the city with her play. I played truant and raced to the theatre as if she was a life-raft rather than a famous actress: it was at that time that I found my life *could* be altered, and that the theatre was to be my future.

So there were vital compensations, and I made do with the rest of my existence until the time came for it to end; at least, that episode of it. The years were really not harsh. It was simply that I was, as I have said before, an astounded stranger set among people with utterly different standards of behaviour and of living: we simply couldn't understand each other; that's all it truthfully was. We couldn't come to terms or make any compromises. I was the guest, it was up to me to conform to their ways, so I did. But I never compromised.

The hermit crab idea worked very well for us all. I was quiet, well-behaved, polite, and worked, as best I could, at my lessons: I caused no trouble, sat at the dreadful teas, handed round the bridge rolls, walked peacefully to church, helped with the washing-up, and did my best with D'Oyly Carte and Co. All the time I was watching, observing, noting down every little thing which I saw or heard in my more-or-less silent existence: for future use.

It was a vastly important change in my life: I, who had heeded little around me before, was now suddenly obsessed with storing up sights and sounds, and people too, for that matter. I had notebbooks filled with coded scribbles (coded because of the Saturday 'tidying'). There was nothing about this new development in me that I was about to give away. I was determined to bring all my treasures with me when the time came, intact. It was impossible to write letters to my family, with any truth, for they were always vetted by my uncle, to ensure that they were correctly spelled . . . and punctuated. So.

But no one discovered the notebooks.

In two years I had discovered the intense joy of observing, recording, and writing. I had also discovered the theatre and planned my future. The third, and thankfully last, year was spent in polishing everything up so that I would be ready to amaze my Bohemian world when the time came for me to regain it.

This was much harder to do than I had expected. Three years of offering bridge rolls and paper napkins, of playing constant truant from the unloved school, peeing out of carriage windows, and playing endless games of solitaire in silent rooms while my elders and betters knitted or read the *Glasgow Herald*, hardly prepared me for the sophistication of the Chelsea Polytechnic, to which I was almost instantly despatched, in the Kings Road, Chelsea.

This was, I hasten to add, a very different street to the tacky, glittery place it is today, but even then it was pretty startling after the glumness of Renfrew Street or the dainty refinement of Kelvinside. I was woefully ignorant of everything that happened in the Kings Road, knew nothing of the speech patterns, nothing of the patterns of behaviour, and was overwhelmed by sudden independence.

There were no members of kith or kin here: either of the blood or merely pretend. They had long since vanished, with the last of my childhood. It was a question of starting off again and relearning. A new existence beckoned – and this was a way of life which I had deliberately sought; it was a road which I hoped (in secret for I did not speak of it aloud to my anxious, almost hopeless, parents) would lead me towards the theatre. Eventually.

I knew that I had years of lost time to make up, and set about doing exactly that.

The still-sharp memories of Aunt Kitty and her ground-floor-front room, sweet with the scent of incense, her bright silk kimonos, the spills of cushions, the thick fur of the polar bear rug, raced back and embraced me in many a peeling painted house in Worlds End where students lived in shabby rooms and gathered together (each of us bringing a quart bottle of beer, two if we could afford it) for parties on Saturday nights.

If Aunt Kitty's incense was overwhelmed by the greasy smells of fishy newspaper which had wrapped up twopence worth of fish and chips, or the sour smell of sweat, in these scrofulous habitations, then I hardly noticed. The essence was the same.

There was music, laughter, texture and colour. We lived our lives among these things, they were essentially a part of the work we were trying to accomplish. Or thought that we were trying to accomplish.

The Sunday mornings afterwards were, perhaps, a let-down.

Smelly, stale, snoring people lying in untidy heaps like discarded clothing from a charity sale, crumpled paper, stacked canvases, jars full of browning, cigarette butts (a shade here of wicked Aunt Celestia, but no fire in which to burn them) and empty bottles lying about like tumbled skittles.

But I was absolutely convinced that what I was seeing about me represented Life, with a capital 'L', and my heart beat like that of a soaring lark's.

This innocence could not, of course, last long. The vow of celibacy which I had taken in the yellow-oak bedroom of my uncle's house was, mentally, set aside. It was abruptly broken by an avid girl with earphones and breasts like filled hot-water bottles, who raped me expertly on the floor of her studio in front of the gas fire and sent me reeling on my way.

I'd arrived!

Although I was, privately, a little irritated that she, and not I, had made the majestic move (and *that* while I was afloat on light ale), it did not diminish the slight swagger which I attempted to use on my daily walk to catch the No. 11 bus to Victoria. But I don't think that anyone noticed this subtle demonstration of my manhood: certainly no one did at home.

From then on, as well as doing my best to design book-covers, shade spheres and pottery jugs (for perspective), and come to terms with the exceptionally complicated human form in life class, I also determinedly set out to be a predator, eyeing every wretched girl with a slavering regard, which I earnestly hoped was suggestive. I didn't get far.

Young women were not as 'easy' then to snare, morals were still, even in the Kings Road, morals, and nothing much happened beyond a smeary kiss in the locker corridors, or a hasty, inept fumble and grope in the Classic cinema.

'Stop it! Oh *do* stop! I'm trying to see what's happening.'

'I love you.'

'Isn't she marvellous! So *svelte* . . . '

'I love you.'

We hissed at each other like adders in the back row of the half-empty afternoon performance. My yearning was desperate.

'What *are* you doing! Stop it! Stop fidgeting!'

'Please, Anthea, let me. Be a sport . . . '

'Stop it! Just stop. It's disgusting.'

'Anthea . . . '

'Ow! That hurt! You're pinching me. People will notice.'

'You are so marvellous, please let me, please . . . '

'Stop it! You're too rough and anyway I've got my knickers on.'

I sulked back to Victoria Station vanquished. Ruined, having spent the last of my weekly allowance on the back stalls. I was very worried. I seemed to be rebuffed by every girl I hauled off to the back stalls with a bar of Toblerone chocolate to watch Bette Davis or George Brent.

Could it be that I had bad breath? I cupped my hands about my mouth and huffed and puffed trying to trace any unpleasant odour. I scraped my teeth to points brushing them with the sharp-tasting Euthymol toothpaste, which almost took the roof off my mouth at the same time. I had no pimples; no dandruff; or acne. I was skinny, I had to admit that, but not all girls liked muscular men, and surely it was apparent that if anyone had kicked sand in my face I'd have fought back? Not *all* skinny men were weaklings. Perhaps I was unattractive? Too boyish? Not rich enough? Always a possibility: I had to manage on a pound a week which, even in those distant days, was pretty tight.

Perhaps they were frightened that I'd give them a baby? That must be the reason for such reluctance. My spirits rose: I was potent! They feared me! But there was something you could do *not* to have a baby, and yet still be allowed the delirium of the search, pursuit and capture. I was certain of it.

I couldn't quite remember what it was.

To my father then, one weekend. The Father and Son discussion which both he and I had always avoided from shyness. We were walking up through the orchard to an oak where the terrier, Rogan, had possibly found a badgers' sett. My father carried a pitchfork, for some reason.

'If you make a mistake, there is always the possibility that you could end up in serious trouble,' he said. 'What if the girl became pregnant?'

'Well, actually that's really why I wanted to talk to you.'

'It's a difficult subject. And today's Sunday.'

I was uncertain why Sunday had anything to do with it.

'Well, the thing is that, of course, I know all about babies. I've known about them all my life. Where they come from. How. So on.'

'Good,' said my father. 'I can't think why that dog keeps on yelping.'

'But what I want to know is what do you have to do so that you *don't* have them?'

'He's probably cornered some wretched cat.'

'Can you tell me? What not to do?'

'Well, it's obvious, isn't it? Don't go too far. You are sixteen and a half, you really ought to know by this time.'

'I didn't have much of a chance in Scotland. They're very funny up there.'

'Well, for heaven's sake, don't get some wretched girl into trouble.'

'I don't want to. That's the whole *point*. Why I'm asking you. I mean it's only fun.'

'Fun can be bloody expensive.'

'Pa, I know there is something one can do.'

'I don't suppose you bothered with that blue book I gave you last year? It's all in there. Simple. Diagrams, everything.'

'I couldn't understand it. And how do you not go "too far"?'

'He's still howling away, it can't be a badger . . . a cat up the tree. Have a word with Dr Lovell. He's a good chap, he'll put you right.'

'But I'm not ill!'

My father turned suddenly, the pitchfork over his shoulder.

'You haven't got clap, have you? Is that it?'

I was frozen with shock.

'What's clap?'

'I'll give Lovell a call, ask him to come down for a drink. You can explain it to him then. He's a good chap. Sensible. He'd better have a look at you.'

'But I'm not ill! I told you. I haven't got whatever it is . . . I only want to know how not to have babies, that's all, Pa!'

'Oh for God's sake! I thought your mother had explained all this, years ago. It's her job. I've got enough on my hands with *The Times*.'

I followed him on up the orchard to the oak in perplexed silence. At the tree, the terrier, shuddering and slavering, howling at something in the high branches.

'I knew it couldn't be the badgers. They cleared off ages ago. It's a damned cat.'

'When will you call Dr Lovell then?'

My father cleared his throat a couple of times. 'As soon as we go back to the house.'

We turned and started back down the path.

'Thank you. Could you tell him what it's about, I mean before he comes? It's a bit embarrassing.'

Perhaps I did have clap? What was it? Could you get clap from just kissing a girl or having a bit of a fumble? My mouth was dry.

'That's all it is, is it?'

'Yes. That's all.'

'I mean, be frank. You haven't got someone into trouble have you?'

'God! No!'

'It's rather a liability. Starting a family at sixteen and a half. I'd have said.'

'No. No . . . I haven't. Just . . . about how not to. That's all.'

'I'll ask him in for a drink. He's a good chap.'

We walked on in silence, the dog still yelping far away among the trees. The *last* thing I wanted to do was to start a family, I thought. Families are all very well but they mean kith and kin.

And I'd had quite enough of them to last me a lifetime.

THREE

In the first sixteen years of my life I had, by my reckoning anyway, thirteen years of childhood. Which, when all is said and done, wasn't so bad really. From thirteen onwards, an early thriteen too, I was forced into adolescence.

In very much the same way that rhubarb is forced. A flowerpot is placed over the first tender shoots and the stems left to struggle, lightless, leaves uncurling like tight yellow fists, striking up wan, pink, unexposed to the elements.

By the time I had reached sixteen this is really what I felt like. Forced rhubarb. Pink, tender: suitable for tarts and puddings and not much cop in jam – in my opinion anyway. The sturdy, crunchy, healthy green plant has much more bite to it than the pallid forced stuff. Alas! I was the latter, not the former.

In my notebook, now rather torn and battered, for 1934, I see that I have headed the first page 'The Anthracite Years'. I can't, for the life of me at this moment, really think what I meant by this pretentious phrase. I imagine that it was written in hindsight, for precious little of it is in the code I had to use against prying eyes, but I know that it referred to the long, to me then, years I spent in the north. It was meant to imply, I would think, the drabness and blackness, or bleakness anyway, of my life there.

Rather inaccurate as it happens: anthracite is a sharp, glittering substance. Black indeed, but it looks rather like jet. Not dusty and drab like, for example, coke. But at thirteen, if I was thirteen, and I can't be certain because there is no written date beyond the year, and I am not absolutely certain that even *that* is quite accurate, life did seem to me to be grimly, unrelentingly grey.

Perhaps, on the other hand, I used the word 'anthracite' on account of the stove in the sitting-room, which was fed with the stuff from a hod which stood on a neat piece of folded newspaper at its side. (So that no 'mess' would be made.) Was I using the stove and the hod as a symbol for the years? Or was I referring to the 'tips', or 'bingies', as they were called then, which peaked across the ruined countryside surrounding our wretched suburb? I can't be at all sure.

What I am certain of is that those three years caused an extraordinary personality change in me. I was perfectly aware of it even at the time. Far from my 'Bohemian' life, isolated by speech, custom and behaviour, I was forced to assume immediate defence mechanisms: my solitary life (for in spite of being in the heart of my maternal family I never joined them) forced me to become my only friend and partner.

To be sure, I joined in with my cousins as often as I had to; I entered into the gloomy existence of my elders and, as they would have it, betters. But I was always a little way apart, looking at myself, aware of another person who politely and pleasantly went through the motions of meek acceptance.

However, in the heart of me I never accepted at all. I stayed separate. Watching and, as I have said, keeping notes on the, to me, curious behaviour of my relations.

In time I almost grew to enjoy this forced separation from self; I enjoyed being the 'loner', although as far as I was aware there was no such word for that in those days. But the happiest times I ever spent were by myself, or walking those damned dogs across the tussocky, grimy fields among the 'bingies', the detritus of some long worked-out pit.

Instead of sharing everything in an extrovert manner, as I had done before, with my sister, Lally and my parents, I burrowed deeply into a secret life, writing my notes, thinking my own thoughts, and paying far too much attention to myself. The perfect example of an introvert. This has remained with me all my life.

After those years of solitary existence in the midst of an alien community, I rebuffed any advances whatsoever towards the shell I had built around me. The hermit crab syndrome was firmly fixed, and I only quit that shell as I grew older, to find another, more suited to my size. But still a shell. I dreaded, and I still do, possession.

No one was allowed to come too close. I staved off all-comers with a quiet, determined strength. It puzzled a great many people then – it does to this day. I share – up to a point. Not beyond that point. And the limit is fixed by myself. So far and no further. I make the rules in this game of self-preservation. After all, it's my life.

Those first thirteen glorious years of childhood ended almost at the moment that I reached Queen Street Station, Glasgow, and, without my properly being aware of it, adolescence began. Or *had* to begin.

To be firmly crushed, a foot on a beetle, nearly six years later when my call-up papers arrived one morning; and with very little ceremony, in fact absolutely none at all, I bade it goodbye to commence manhood.

It is little wonder to me that I have made some peculiar errors throughout my life, for I have constantly tripped myself by falling into the holes which I have made in my snatched experience. I've always been as green as a frog: I have no one to blame for that except myself, and I do not. I am my 'onlie begetter'.

It is no wonder then that at sixteen, and in the Chelsea Polytechnic, I lost my head to some degree, but never absolutely my 'shell'. The temptations which were strewn across my path were extraordinary. Freedom itself was amazing! Even, at times, alarming.

I often wonder, today, watching a bus-load of Russian tourists plodding through the glittering streets of Cannes in their solid shoes, floral prints and thick suits, what they can possibly be thinking, deep down in their Slavic hearts, as they are confronted by so much bounty, beauty and luxury around them. Very much the same, I would say, as I felt when I got my release from Scotland, School, and Kith and Kin. An hysterical, numb bewilderment.

But perhaps they don't. Perhaps they see it all as vulgar decadence. Perhaps I am merely being romantic – a fault of 'the loner'.

However, I took off, in a cautious way, and even though the excellent Dr Lovell gave me, at my father's urgent request, the 'low-down' (as he had called it) on my sexual proclivity, he only succeeded in dousing desire, failing absolutely to extinguish lust. He was, I recall, distressed that I should spend my time with what he called 'those louche young women in Chelsea'. Although I wasn't absolutely sure what 'louche' meant, I got a pretty good idea. He suggested, in vain, poor man, that I should spend more of my time with 'clean, healthy girls' and actually named a mutual acquaintance in the area as an example. To my horror.

Pam Wimborne looked like a younger version of my Scottish aunts. Neat, scrubbed, tweed skirts, flat-heeled shoes, pursed lips, a kirby-grip in her hair. She played a daunting game of tennis, and used words like 'actually' or 'frightfully' all the time, and everything she encountered in life was either 'top hole' or 'too ghastly for words'. She had the sex appeal of a vegetable marrow and was destined, I knew instinctively, to grow to look like one in the years ahead. Quite apart from all these unhappy faults, she was what I privately called 'a broody'. That is to say she was ready to settle down, and lay. Possession!

So Pam Wimborne was out, and I returned to my louche ladies in Worlds End. They hadn't the least intention of settling and spawning. Sex, to most of them, was as casual and as intimate as a handshake in a crowded room. It suited me very well indeed.

But naturally the summer holidays from the Poly were rather long, and it was during this period of time that I was at my most vulnerable. There were any amount of 'broodies' in my part of the world; all cheerfully ready to own me. Or so I liked to think. I was always a little too certain of my irresistibility.

It seemed that one only had to go out with a girl for a few cycle rides in a week, to walk through Rotherfield Woods twice, or go to the cinema in Haywards Heath for their families to start to vibrate with interest about one's intentions. Mine were perfectly clear to me; theirs, the girls', were perfectly clear to them. But we were poles apart – as I was frequently to discover.

If one of them expressed mild interest in, say, nature generally, I would have ready, almost at hand, a fascinating colony of ants in Rotherfield Woods. In those woods I knew that the bracken was dense, shoulder high and secluded. One lady (by courtesy of the Gas Light and Coke Company, where she worked) so overwhelmed me with her physical splendours that I made desperate plans to go and see ants' nests daily. But she had little interest in ants or their habits. She also pointed out, on the only occasion that I managed actually to lure her in their direction, that she was wearing (as if I was not alert to the fact; slavering almost) a new white pleated skirt, that she wanted no sort of 'funny business', if that is what I had in mind, and that in any case bracken stained things green, and it would never come out. She added that she didn't give a fig for ants and *hated* nature.

So I gave up and returned to the difficult task of building a studio up in our orchard where I had a vivarium full of grass snakes and tree-frogs (which were devoured by the snakes with amazing speed), a marionette theatre, four bound volumes of *Theatre World*, a heap of windfall apples in a box and a number of *Health and Efficiency* magazines hidden beneath the floorboards.

Thwarted, I turned to Veronica. She was gentle, pink and white, with glasses and an obsession for nature. That is to say of *Field and Wood* variety. She was also enraptured by the idea of my poetry, and listened with the patience of a pyramid while I droned away at the plays which I wrote with effortless ease. She said that she felt she had a mission in life to encourage my mind towards 'more intellectual thinking'. (She could, she once said, feel 'the latent stirring'. Of what, I wondered.) Little did she realize that trying to do that was the equal of sweeping up fallen leaves in a gale. But she persisted, sweetly.

Her family, after a spell of this overt intimacy, grew restless. Knowing smiles and nods were the order of the day. I was pressed to stay for meals whenever I cared. A cottage on their estate was suddenly taken in hand, repaired, retiled, repointed, the modest garden tilled. A nest for another 'broody'!

The day that she arrived on her cycle, a thick wallpaper sample book strapped to her pillion, I knew that I would be lost if I so much as flipped open a single page. I could already see that some were slipped with 'markers', ready for my approbation. I dumped Veronica.

The Chelsea Poly opened up again, and I hurled myself into its custody and the arms of my louche ladies in Markham Street, Sydney Street and Jubilee Place. It was much easier, and armed with Dr Lovell's grudging recipe for 'prevention' I felt safe.

Thus, in 1937 and 1938 I drifted pleasantly enough through life on my own particular voyage of self-discovery, retaining at all times my shell, striving to keep intact the anonymity which I had found so useful in the Anthracite Years. It was an excellent shield against hurt or involvement. I let time trickle through my fingers like sand, scattering it recklessly about for my own pleasures. A reprehensible state of affairs.

Living in a cosmopolitan world, like the Chelsea Poly, did not of course mean that I could be totally unaware of the world around me. I knew, in a vague, shimmering way, that unpleasant events were taking place. They were difficult even for me to escape completely, but I don't think that I ever considered, for a single moment, that the dreams which I was so busy dreaming, and stringing around my head, would be scattered by these unpleasant things and left fluttering in the gutter like old bus-tickets in a matter of months.

I had always taken great comfort that there would never be another war. My father had said, over and over again, that his generation had fought so that our generation would be brought up in bucolic peace and serenity. Naturally, as I trusted the quiet wisdom of my father (even if I didn't go along with his ideas on my education), I believed him implicitly. It suited me very well to do so.

Until something went badly wrong in Spain. A civil war had started in the year before I left the gloomy school in the north. I was only aware of this, in truth, because a number of red flags and clenched fists became apparent among the Bunsen burners and retort stands in physics class. (Why are scientists, I wonder, so political?) Some people sang the Internationale in distant corners of the playground, and it was reliably rumoured that three of the masters had volunteered to go and fight.

But for whom, and exactly why, I had not the least idea. I went on contentedly throwing dreadful little bowls and jugs on my potter's wheel in art class. It was, as far as I was concerned, all a matter of alarums and excursions: very Shakespearian.

Of course, I had heard that there was a place called Italy and another called Abyssinia. But both were a long way from Glasgow, and even when Hitler marched into the Rhineland, which was closer, I was as unperturbed as the majority of my fellow citizens, only a few of whom shook their heads gravely and muttered worriedly. I was safely armed with the promise from my father that there would never be another war which could possibly affect me or any member of my beloved family. Foreigners could do as they pleased, but whatever they did couldn't possibly affect us. This brilliant reasoning, which I maintained determinedly until I reached sixteen, gave me tremendous comfort.

I had been more moved by the sight of some collected aunts and uncles sitting motionless round a bakelite wireless set while the King of England abdicated his duties in order to marry the woman he loved. I thought it both romantic and proper; if that's how he felt. I almost sympathized with my mournful aunts, now sitting twisting their handkerchiefs in sodden grief, but I was far more distressed, personally, at the destruction of the Crystal Palace by fire earlier in the year.

So, you see, I *was* aware. Here and there. The hermit crab did not just hide away in his shell and rock-pool; he ventured, occasionally, abroad. However, on my release from the fastness and dourness of the north, I spread my downy wings and flopped about; a fledgling sparrow rather than an eagle. I moved with caution. Which is sensible if you don't know what the hell the world into which you have fallen is all about.

Chelsea led, eventually, to the theatre in the three short years I had of glowing freedom, and there I grew my feathers. Slowly, to be sure, but feathers of a kind. They were hardly strong enough to keep me aloft, but did enable me to get from one lower branch to another without undue panic. I scrambled about avidly. A hermit crab and a fledgling was, is indeed, a strange mix.

But at all times I avoided any form of possession; I was as determined to keep my freedom as a nun her vows. I was equally not to *be* possessive either: an odd fact which has often surprised me when I have considered it. For I have, of course, a sense of *possession*, but *not* of possessiveness. I think that I have never really expected to have anything for long. The Anthracite Years led me to expect nothing to last. It has stood me in good stead all my life: I am romantic to a foolish degree as a man. I will blub easily at a perfect phrase in a letter, a passage which I consider beautiful in a book, an instrument brilliantly played, the sight of wind across a field of standing corn, or Kathleen Ferrier singing 'Blow the Wind Southerly'.

But that is where romanticism ends. With perfection.

There were, I have to confess, a couple of times when romance did blind me to all thoughts of sense and reason. I found myself engaged to my leading lady in a small local rep theatre where we worked. I was never absolutely certain how this happened. Where did my hermit crab shell go? How could I have been tempted from it for long enough to be, literally, caught? I have no idea.

At the time the Germans were overrunning Europe. The retreat from Dunkirk had just taken place. Bombs fell nightly on familiar places. Was it that? Did I lose my cool and control simply because of war hysteria? It is impossible, all these years later, to remember. Perhaps, and it is quite possible, I was simply in love with her, and with the army looming at my side, so to speak, military service was beyond avoidance. (I had tried to be a conscientious objector, at her suggestion, but found that the questions which were asked at a tribunal at High Wycombe were so idiotic that I simply had to abandon her idea.) With the beckoning terror before me, I suppose that I decided, as so many did, to marry before I was thrust into oblivion. She found an engagement ring, and we called it all off after a couple of months when she discovered, to her consternation (and delight), an American pilot in the Eagle Squadron, who offered her the world. Instantly.

So that didn't last long; neither did my distress. I had become involved with another actress who danced better than she acted, and that's not saying much. But she had a splendid body, and did extraordinary things with a long cigarette holder in a skin-tight satin evening dress to Ravel's *Bolero* twice nightly.

One afternoon, ashen and almost plain, she arrived at my digs, in a prim house in Fellows Road, Swiss Cottage, to say that she was pregnant. My immediate reaction was one of gibbering terror.

We were sitting uncomfortably in the large dining-room of the house. Ladies were never admitted to the rooms; Miss Haley, the owner, saw to that. Any meetings were therefore permitted only in the long, drab room, smelling of stale food and sauce bottles, sitting in chairs around the vast table at which we, the lodgers, ate our meals. It was an all-male household, apart, that is, from the owner, who served the food at the head of the table with the dedication and awe of a high priestess at an altar.

'Aren't you going to say something?' said Velma (not her name – she may well be a grandmother today).

'How do you know?'

'I'm late.'

'But it's not possible! I mean . . . well, how? We didn't DO anything.'

'I'm late; that's what I know. And there was that time in the Green Room . . . '

'It *can't* be my fault!'

'Then whose is it, I would like to know? All these insinuations . . . '

In a large, sunny room on the second floor at the back, William Wightman had his quarters. I had known him for some years. Older than myself by fourteen or so years, he had been my first counsellor when I made my entry into the theatre. A tall, calm gentleman, with a private income and an immaculate sense of good grooming, he was as unlike an actor (which he was) as anyone could be, and Miss Haley had taken him as a lodger because he, as she said, 'set a tone and has a beautiful speaking voice'. Also, with a private income, he was pretty safe: you couldn't count on bank clerks, or solicitors and school teachers (who made up her regular clientele), for their fortunes ebbed and flowed. She demanded security. William Wightman gave her that.

So pleased was she to have him in her Best-Second-Back that she permitted herself to be persuaded, by him, to take me as a lodger, in a small room at the top of the house, because, he assured her, I didn't behave like 'an actor', although I was gainfully employed at a nearby theatre. So I had a room in which, years before, some wretched kitchen maid must have existed, with a square sink at one end and a narrow window at the other. There was a bed, to be sure, and a midget dressing-table with three drawers. Nothing else. But I was grateful for its spartan comfort, even though I had to hang my best, and only, suit on a hanger from a hook behind the door, and keep my scripts and books in the sink.

Wightman was a wise man, calm, as I have said, unruffled, reasonable, who offered considered, logical advice when asked. He was exactly who I needed at this disastrous moment.

'Hello!' he said affably when he opened his door. 'How nice to see you. Have you come for a cup of tea, the kettle's just on the boil.'

'Something terrible has happened.'

'Oh dear. I *am* sorry. Just let me put off the gas-ring and then you can tell me with no fear of the kettle boiling dry. Such a business.' He turned off the gas-ring and bade me sit down. 'Now. What is this all about?'

'Well, you remember Velma? In the Revue?'

He thought for a moment, fingertips pressed together beneath his chin. 'Ah yes! The girl who danced *Rhapsody in Blue*. Very striking.'

'She also dances the *Bolero*.'

'Most energetic,' said Wightman.

'And she's downstairs in the dining-room and says that she is pregnant.'

'In the dining-room here?'

'Yes. And she's going to have a baby.'

'Splendid! How nice for her. I do hope she's pleased, she was an arresting looking girl.'

'She's not pleased. She says it's my fault.'

There was a taut silence; Wightman removed his fingers from under his chin. 'Yours?'

'She says so.'

'Could it be?'

'I don't know . . . '

'But I mean, what I should say is, are you . . . were you . . . did you. Is it *true*?'

'No! I don't think so.'

'"Think" is perhaps not the word we want today. Do you KNOW?'

'No. I *don't* know. But I'm pretty sure. I mean . . . yes . . . I think so.'

Mr Wightman leant back in his easy chair. 'This is very grave.'

'I know! I know!'

'A serious matter; and you have come to ask my advice. Therefore I shall have to ask you serious questions. You don't seem to me to be at all certain.'

'But I am!'

He leant forward, his face lightly flushed with concern. 'Have you impregnated this luckless girl?' he said.

I stared at him. I'd frankly never heard the word before but understood, in a haze of fright, what he meant.

'No! Dr Lovell has told me exactly what . . . '

Mr Wightman waved an impatient hand crossly at my haggard face. 'Have you made "advances" to Velma?'

'Well, sort of.'

'Have you told her that you love her? That you wish to marry her?'

'No!' I cried in despair. '*Never.*'

He rose imposingly. (He was over six feet tall.) 'I shall go down and have a word with her now. You go up to your room and don't come down until I call you. We must get to the bottom of this business.' He carefully locked his door behind us and I went up the creaking stairs to my attic with its sink and single bed.

It seemed days before I heard his voice calling me to descend. The door of his room was open, he was bending down relighting the gas-ring under the kettle.

'Tea,' he said. 'Tea is essential. And I have some oatmeal biscuits here. Chocolate-covered. Sit down.'

I did as I was told, hands clutching my knees.

'Velma has left,' he said, taking his place in his chair. 'She was *very* distressed indeed and doesn't want to see you ever again.'

'What happened?' My voice sounded as shrill as a penny flute.

'She had made a slight mistake in, er, um . . . she has made an error in her dates. She is not actually due to have her, umm, well, it is not normally due until about the 28th. She got things a little muddled, it seems.'

'Thank God! I knew it couldn't be me . . . I knew it . . . '

'But I *do* feel that you have behaved in a most regrettable manner to the poor young woman.'

'How? What have I done?'

'You have, I understand, suggested that your family is very rich. Is that so?'

'Well . . . not really. I mean . . . '

'I rather think that you have.'

'Not *terribly* rich.'

'And did you, by chance, refer to the fact that you are in all truth a . . . a baron?'

'I might have done.'

'Neither thing was exactly true. Was it?'

'Well I *could* be a baron – my father told me. We have a splendid coat of arms and so on . . . '

'Which doesn't necessarily make you a noble.'

The kettle started to steam, and the lid wobbled about. Mr Wightman (I was too downcast even to think of him as plain William, or Bill, as he was always called) rose and made the tea with care and precision, found a tin box of biscuits, placed all, with two cups, on the table in the window, and sat down.

'I fear that you have led the unfortunate Velma on with a lot of fairy-tales. In a time like this, when everything is upside down, bombs are falling, and the future is most uncertain, young women, especially one on her own, look for security. I fear that you gave her a false impression of that. Here is your tea, milk it yourself, and there is a bowl of sugar on the top of the little cupboard there.'

'I'm very sorry.'

'So was Velma. And wretched.'

'I'm sure that you behaved very kindly; thank you.'

Mr Wightman stirred his tea steadily. 'I merely behaved in a gentlemanly manner. Which is more, I'm afraid, than you can claim. I think that it is time that you came to terms with life, and with yourself. You are no longer a callow youth – or should not be. Shortly you will be joining the services and going to battle with the Hun, and behaviour of this kind will not be tolerated. I don't think that you precisely *lied*, but you did exaggerate; and exaggeration will get you into serious trouble in life. Poor Velma! She was quite distressed.'

My hands, I discovered, were shaking so much that I slopped tea over the ugly table and had to wipe it up with the sleeve of my pullover.

'Mind you,' said Mr Wightman watching this clumsy operation calmly. 'Mind you, if anything should go, ummm, go wrong, so to speak, in the region of the 28th, you could be in a fearful pickle.'

'Oh God!'

'Ah yes. Just so. Not out of the wood yet,' he said and reached for a biscuit.

The next weeks were hell. I spent them in a state of suspended terror and dread. My whole life, I realized nightly in my narrow bed with bombs hurling down outside, the sink rattling, and the ack-ack guns on Primrose Hill showering the slate roof, inches above my head, with chunks of red-hot steel, could be ruined. I would be a possessed man! With no freedom left, no chance of living my life according to my own pattern. I'd have to marry the girl, be a father, and go to work on the Underground to some hellish office. If anyone would take me.

I never heard from Velma again. And terror gave way to a lethargic relief. I went back to my shell for a time. But I had learned a lesson. I made a vow never to sail so close to the wind ever again. It is foolish, to say the very least, to strike out for the wilder shores of love unless you can swim. And I could not.

So I paddled about in the shallows, until the day came for me to be shunted off, like some stray goods-wagon, on to the main line to the war. Which took care of a great many problems.

It may seem, in this tightly condensed segment of my life, that I had behaved in a highly irresponsible manner. This you could think: and you could be right. But in fact all it was, I am certain, was a sudden, extraordinary liberation of suppressed emotion. After the damped-down existence of the Anthracite Years I let freedom of thought and action go to my head. In much the same way that a tightly corked bottle, when opened, explodes in a cascade of foam and bubbles. To be sure, I spilled a good deal more than I drank, if I may continue with the analogy, but it was harmless and, save for a near-disaster with Velma of the *Bolero*, caused no one any grief.

In the uneasy months before my call-up I kept myself occupied as hard as I possibly could to avoid any kind of involvement emotionally; I do not wish to give the impression that, added to all my earlier faults, I had now become an inchoate lecher, but my interest never waned and had to be controlled by sheer exhaustion.

To this end I worked myself to the bone, waiting at tables in a dingy restaurant in Bear Street near Leicester Square, washing shop windows, those which had not been blown out by blast, playing in the theatre at night and, after that, going on to a subterranean drinking-club to do a perfectly appalling 'act' (which I personally thought at the time was rather good, but was, I have been since told, extremely embarrassing). All this was good for me, in that I had not the least shred of energy, or interest finally, to do anything foolhardy.

It was desperate medicine, but it worked, and by the time I had reached my nineteenth birthday and was ordered to report immediately to Catterick Camp in Yorkshire to be trained as a signalman (God knows why), I arrived there sensibly unattached. A new, very different phase of life began. The callow youth, like so many other callow youths, was off to war, to 'do battle with the Hun'.

In the early stages, this consisted of having the Morse code forced into me like castor oil, shooting at tin targets (at which I seemed to be rather good), and chucking hand-grenades all over the Yorkshire Moors. It was not very strenuous or desperately serious, as far as I could see. Not a shadow of the Hun came near as we polished boots, whitewashed coal, cleaned our rifles, and generally found ourselves drifting into a controlled, boring existence. But this didn't last for very long. It was Initial Training. More was to follow.

I had not, to my infinite surprise, been in the least unhappy or surprised by this new, dreary existence. I enjoyed the route marches, the target practices, even the communal life. This might appear to be a strange admission for one who was determined to stay aloof and apart from the crowd. But a crowd is one of the perfect places in which to be alone. I quite enjoyed the warmth of the companionship around me, but went through those first weeks' training as if I had been lobotomized: all I had to do, I was certain, was the best that I could. No more could be expected of me; if I did my best, then life would just continue on its dull, but undemanding, way, and I'd be perfectly secure. Oh! How often I have been wrong in life!

The army, however, wanted me to do a great deal better, and give much more than I was presently offering, so to my dismay, for I had quite settled down into my own unexacting existence, I was hauled out of complacency and bundled off, without the least ceremony at all, to a mud-bog of a camp in Kent where killing the enemy was the main lesson taught – quite apart from killing off what were called 'the slackers'. It was tacitly understood that I was such.

This new existence had absolutely nothing whatsoever to do with life in the dullness, if comparative safety, of Catterick Camp with its greasy NAAFI. In Kent we were wet. And remained wet. The tin huts in which we lived ran with water and there were puddles on the concrete floor which were to remain a permanent hazard to anyone foolhardy enough to crawl out of his bunk in the dark. Which was at least every dawn, and often during the sodden nights to find the latrines. We were cold, muddy and frightened out of our wits. Now the shadow of the Hun was dark indeed.

Around this squalid clearing in a chestnut wood there were assault courses of such devilish invention that I never imagined, for one moment, that I would survive. Death faced me at every instant. Rivers had to be crossed on slippery ropes, sagging low into the racing water so that one got even wetter than ever. Quarries had to be scaled while live bullets whined about one's writhing body, particularly in the direction of one's nether quarters. (The sergeants took intense pleasure in firing rounds at one's backside, missing only by millimetres, to encourage one to climb higher and faster.) There were obstacle courses to follow these pleasantries: tunnels of rusty barbed wire; twelve-foot-high walls of mud-spattered tree trunks to scale; wide water-filled ditches to be jumped. (Should one miss the leap and fall into the muddy water, impalement on a thick wooden spike was probable, rather than possible.)

During this obscene – sweating, sobbing, staggering, gasping – canter, the staff threw fiendishly painful, if not quite lethal, explosives around like children on Guy Fawkes Night, and finally, when this was all over, for in time one reached the last of the obstacles and staggered wearily into what once had been a sweet Kentish meadow, there came the shrieked order to 'Fix bayonets!'

This final piece of gaiety brought the Hun extremely near. Huge, swollen, sagging sacks hanging on a gibbet-like construction of beams were attacked with fixed bayonets to shrill screams from the instructors to 'Thrust! In! twist! Withdraw! Get the next bastard!' The word 'Twist', roared at full pitch, was to remind one that one's blade must not get tangled up with a rib or stuck in a breast-bone. Should this unfortunate error take place, you'd be trapped, held fast, and unable to get on to 'kill the next bastard'. He'd very likely kill you; or his friends might. Even I could see the wisdom of that.

But my first attempt at the swollen sacks was rather a mess, which was perfectly reasonable, as each sack (to our slack-jawed amazement) was stuffed with the rotting entrails of cattle, sheep and pigs. The stench was remarkable, and the slithering mess of putrid muck which burst from every thrust one made induced retching and revulsion – the great gobs of jellied blood which spattered one's face weren't particularly pleasant either.

Valiant conscripts keeled over quietly before their swinging 'victims' in a dead faint and got booted hard in their backsides by the instructors. This had no effect on them whatsoever. The 'lily-livered half-wits', as the unfortunate men lying prone in the mud with ashen faces were screamed at, lay as for dead.

This rather barbaric practice of stuffing the sacks with entrails was, I think, eventually stopped. It caused far too many failures among the cadets, and the sacks were decorously filled with sawdust. Which wasn't nearly as much fun for the instructors.

I got through, to my utter amazement, simply because I was petrified that I might not; which would have meant that I would have been 'Returned to Unit', bundled into a draft, and sent to die in North Africa or anywhere else considered in need of replacements.

Another thing came to my rescue, apart from sheer terror, and that was that I had been brought up as a 'country boy'. Most of the others came from towns and cities and had never, as I had, skinned and gutted a rabbit, drawn a fowl, or cleaned a fish. Entrails to me were very ordinary things indeed; I'd first learned to gut a rabbit, for example, at the age of eight. It was a perfectly normal part of my life.

So indeed were mud and rain, swollen rivers and climbing trees. All country stuff. For city dwellers this was a much harder task. A bank clerk, the man in insurance, the shop assistant did not have the enormous advantages which I did.

So by a miracle of endeavour and terror combined, I got through the traps and snares set in the Kentish camp, even though I was unable to swim and suffered desperately, at times, from vertigo. It was suggested that it would 'make men of us' at the end, and that, of course, meant that we should be able to 'do battle with the Hun'.

I suppose that I must have cheated my way through to victory by giving a 'performance'. I screamed and yelled (as commanded) like a crazed Red Indian (this was supposed to instil the fear of God into the most stubborn Hun). I stabbed sack after sack with apparent relish (aware that this item was almost at the end of the course), worried my skinny frame through yards of barbed wire like a ferret, all with a stretched leer of blind panic on my face.

Which no one noticed because it was covered in mud and guts from the sacks. The fear of failure was far greater than the fear of the course. I survived.

There was no residue at all now of Aunt Kitty: of silks and scents and texture; there were no remembrances of Jessie Hammond and her sorry 'thingy', no recall of kith and kin, of Lally and my loving parents, not even a shadow of thought for the Anthracite Years, although they had helped so much to give me the force and determination to survive; and the ambitious lecher had been calmed completely by sheer exhaustion, plus bromide in the breakfast tea-mugs.

At night, in the water-running hut, I would clean my rifle and myself, and when that was done crawl into my bunk with a copy of Surtees or Trollope, and read until lights out, oblivious to anything except the fact that I had managed to survive another day, and that a new one would break to tempt my cunning and resolve all over again.

But I was perfectly contented. I was on my own. And surprisingly fully in charge. The hermit crab had survived intact. There was nothing whatsoever to worry about – except myself.

That's how I liked it.

Not very long ago, a young journalist was interviewing me for a book I had written about a part of my war which took place in the East Indies (*A Gentle Occupation*). He was finding trouble, he said, because he could not 'identify' with the people in the book, the place or the situations. Perfectly reasonable. He was twenty-one; the war had been over for years, I was nearly three times his age. I tried to explain that the title was ironic. This had absolutely no effect on his pleasant, unfinished face at all. I went on, in some degree of desperation I admit, explaining to him that he had no conception of war and would, I sincerely hoped, never have to go through the experience. As if from a distant cloud I could hear my father's voice, many years before, saying the very same thing.

'I honestly don't think that you should worry about this book. It's not your scene, as you say, and it is impossible to explain. War *is*. It's as simple as that. So why don't we just leave it alone?'

'No . . . no I can't do that! I mean, I was fascinated by the book, but I just couldn't believe it. That things like that could have happened.'

I was tempted to suggest to him that there were a number of 'wars' raging about the world at that very minute, but it would have been unfair to have done so because he was a young journalist working for a glossy paper, not a war-correspondent.

'Well, these things do happen, the book is a work of fiction but only up to a point; I would be very distressed if you had to go through a war simply to "identify" with a novel.'

'But tell me,' he said suddenly and urgently, his fork pointing at my chest. 'Do you think that a man has to go through a war to . . . er . . . to crack his balls?'

The baldness of the question didn't trouble me. My reply to it did. What should I say? What, in truth, did I feel? Was it true or false? He settled my dilemma by prodding me earnestly in the chest with his fork and repeating the remark.

'Frankly, yes,' I said. 'Or at least, it was right for me.'

He looked around the restaurant. 'Oh Christ!' he said.

'A war finds one out, I'm afraid. The wheat from the chaff business. But I honestly don't think that it is *essential*; we haven't had a war in Europe, and I am not counting Ireland in this argument, for nearly forty years and it seems to me that your generation is doing perfectly well without one.'

'I am not so sure,' he said. 'Not sure at all. I begin to wonder if people of my age, or a bit older, would even go to fight in a war anyway.' (The Falklands war had not at this time taken place.)

I eased myself out of the conversation and managed to change the subject. But his question has remained in my mind ever since.

I went to Catterick Camp at nineteen; I came out of the war, almost physically unscathed, unlike a great many others, five months before my twenty-sixth birthday, and in those years I had, at last, come of age and grown up. Nothing in life could ever now be the same, and was not. I had managed to get through and I had even, I am ashamed to admit, enjoyed it.

But I was lucky. My war in Europe was not a particularly comfortable one – I didn't sit about in an office – but I wasn't, on the other hand, maimed, and never personally had to kill a man. Although I know that by remote control, that is by selecting targets for bombing, I was responsible for a great deal of death and destruction. At twenty-three.

I felt no burden of guilt. We were at war and that excuse excused all else. Strangely, it wasn't always the tough-guys who made it; the skinny ones like me, who got sand kicked in their faces by the brawny brigade, often fared better. Perhaps because we were physically at such a disadvantage and *had* to struggle harder to survive?

Bingham-Summers was a case in point. A big, ruddy-faced bully, with a hearty moustache, whose greatest pleasure was to force those of us whom he considered 'drips and Nancy Boys' to play an obscenely stupid drinking game called Cardinal Huff, or Puff, I forget which, determined that he would drink us under the table while he maintained his sobriety and, therefore, his manhood. He landed on the beach on D-Day, dragged himself ashore with a green face (everyone was seasick anyway that morning), dug himself a deep slit-trench, and stayed in it for some days, refusing to come out for any reason whatever. Food was, reluctantly, lowered down to him on a rope, and eventually he was removed by force, screaming and fighting, strapped to a stretcher, and flown back to England. You couldn't, as Lally had so often said, 'tell from the outside'.

The Prawn, as we called him, was on the other hand as wispy a fellow as you could meet. Elegant, fragile apparently, he always changed into his pyjamas (even though at that time we slept in slit-trenches), and wandered about during some fierce night strafing in a Liberty silk dressing-gown crying wearily above the din: 'Oh! darlings! Do stop being so *boring*! You can't see a thing, and it's frightfully late. Pack it in, for God's sake!' Our morale soared at his ridiculous performance. However absurd he may have sounded, he was as strong as an oak and as unyielding. Later we heard that he had got the MC for destroying, single-handed, a persistent machine-gun post which had caused considerable casualties, by lobbing a grenade into the position from a distance of three yards. He lost his arm. But his only comment was that the Germans were so damned pig-headed that he had been forced to take some action. 'They killed a lot of my friends, you know. It simply wouldn't do.'

The strangest people survived, while others went to the wall. There was no knowing who was who until the guns went off for real.

On 15 July 1944 I wrote my first long letter to my father:

. . . We are in an apple orchard (cider apples, I suppose?) and the farmer is pissed off with us because we have flattened his cornfield for the airstrip and dug slit-trenches all among his ruddy trees.

We are supposed to be the brave Liberating Allies but you'd hardly know that from his sullen face and angry shouts. No one takes any notice of him, of course, we just shrug and wave him away, his wife, an old crone in black, shakes her fist.

You learn something different every day! Life is very interesting indeed. I now discover that tin-hats are not for wearing on your head, they are too heavy and fall off when you run fast, but they are used to protect your private parts when lying on your truckle bed (if lucky!) or over your bum should you make a turn face-down. Very useful idea. Why didn't I think of that before? If you cop one in the head you're a goner anyway, but you wouldn't have much of a life without your privvies!

I feel, at last, pretty well grown up. About time, you'll say. I can hear you! I used to think that being grown up was tearing about Sussex in Buster's red MG with Cissie Waghorn and being terribly sophisticated drinking lagers in Road-Houses whipping down to Brighton. But it isn't that at all, is it? I'm terribly glad that at last I am coming to terms with it all now: a great relief after all the years I have spent TRYING TO.

I never asked for the life which you and Ma gave me. That was your own decision after all, wasn't it? We none of us actually ASK for our lives, but once we are given it, golly! we hang on to it like grim death and take all kinds of precautions, fair and foul, to preserve it, and it takes a bit of a blow-up like this to show just how much it all means to one. Life is pretty cheap here. I mean to keep mine for as long as I possibly can: I'm enjoying it, thanks!

'Coming to terms with it all now,' I wrote!
There was still a long way to go.

PART TWO

FOUR

I am almost twenty-six.

I'm standing on a platform at Guildford station in a thick fog.

I have just been demobilized.

I have a railway warrant, my ID card, a pocket of small change, fifty Singapore dollars, a 1,000 yen note taken from a dead Japanese, six campaign medals, a cardboard box with my cardboard demob suit and, somewhere on the platform, upended like a bit of Stonehenge, the tin uniform trunk I bought in Calcutta.

All my worldly goods.

Nothing else.

The army has just informed me that I owe them eight hundred pounds because they have been overpaying me for the last two years.

As if that was my fault. As if I had been keeping accounts in the Far East.

I don't know quite how I will be able to pay this back; or when.

They sounded irritated; I suppose that I flustered about.

I have not been back in England since I left for France in 1944.

It is now the fag-end of 1946, and Guildford station offers me not the slightest cheer, or hope.

Delight, which I am supposed to be feeling on demobilization, is drowned in the gloom, and all that I feel is a sense of enormous loss. An incredible unhappiness. All the more incredible because I am on my way home.

The war is finally over.

It's been over for these people on the platform for quite a time: we are rediscovering peace again and I am finding the sensation disturbing.

The mist drifts, veers, wavers. Up the line a blurred pink light changes suddenly to wan green.

A splot of pale colour on grey, damp paper.

The London train is due.

Somewhere a trolley trundles about among the shapeless figures hunched in the pewter light.

A porter is singing. It's an old song; probably an old habit. It isn't funny:

'Pardon me, boy, is that the Chattanooga choo-choo . . .'

I wanted to stay in the army.

I tried to for a time. But an army without a war is as pointless as a car without gas, a party without guests, a bomb without explosives.

And when the war finished, with the great white light over Nagasaki, younger men than I had arrived in bragging good health, with a faint air of superiority, to patronize those of us who had worked to earn the ribbons on our chests.

Which didn't amount to much, really. Endeavour, experience. We were none the less proud of them.

We were called the veterans. With a thin vein of sarcasm in the voices. We called them the newcomers, white-knees, because under the flapping, brand-new, starched shorts, their knees, untouched by any tropical sun, looked like dimpled dough.

I think that we resented their freshness, their superiority as 'new' over 'used'. Foolish no doubt; it was hardly their fault that they had not been old enough to come out earlier. But we resented them all the same, so I packed it in, and came back.

They would always remain 'young'. We *knew*. They did not – and never would, even though there were still a few scraps and scrapings of war left to tidy away.

And we who had known could never be quite the same again.

On D-Day plus four, on the beach at Arromanches, there was a single left leg in an elegant boot, laced above the ankle, drifting around lazily among clumps of weed, a tangle of webbing belts and half a *Reader's Digest*.

Not really a leg. A foot and a shin. No knee cap. No thigh.

The flesh which protruded from the ripped uniform trouser was bleached white by sea-water, trailing little frills of shredded muscle like tiny tentacles.

'The tide brings them around, all these bits and pieces. Funny thing. Yankees. From up the coast at "Omaha". Strong currents about, you don't want to go in for a dip here.'

I didn't.

As I clambered back up the beach through tangles of wire and broken ammunition boxes, gulls wheeled out of the sun like Stukas, feathered on to the rippled sand, stalked towards the bobbing leg with arrogant, watchful eyes, prodded at the elegant boot.

A bell starts clanging, and through the grey the London train surges slowly towards us. The porter is still singing:

'So, Chattanooga choo-choo, won't you choo-choo me home?'

'You had a varied war, really,' my father said. 'In our war we just sat in one bloody place for months, in the mud, moving forward or backward now and again.'

Mine was varied all right. I had no complaints on that score. I got about.

'I expect you were pretty scared sometimes, weren't you?' said Elizabeth.

'Some of the time. We all were, we expected that.'

What I had not expected was that almost the first thing I would have to do in action was assist in the delivery of a child.

That's the odd thing about wars. Everything gets so mixed up.

There was quite a lot of stuff flying about, the road was chalk-white in the sun, barred by the shadows of pollarded elms; my driver muttered: 'Screw this for a lark!' and pulled the jeep into the shelter of a barn wall.

We clambered out and sat in a clump of nettles. It is always wiser to move away from a vehicle, if you can, on account of the petrol tank exploding if the thing gets hit.

A mortar landed in the middle of the road some distance away, sending up a shower of metal, stones and smoke; we crouched low, our faces in the nettles.

'They don't sting if you really grab them,' I said.

'You're kidding.'

Another mortar crumped somewhere behind us; a slithering of tiles from the barn roof, a stink of cordite on the still morning air, and a woman's voice calling.

We looked up in surprise. I had thought that all the civilians had cleared from the area; but obviously not.

She was old, that is to say she was at least forty, in black, with a white and red floral apron, and a man's hat on her head.

Another mortar went over us.

The woman came towards us in a half crouch, running along the side of the barn, her hands open, fingers wide, arms outstretched.

It is impossible to recall at this moment exactly what she said as she reached us; it was in French, naturally, and Norman French at that, and my French was almost limited anyway to 'Oui' and 'Non' and, sometimes, 'Merci beaucoup'. But by signs, and her pulling at my arm, I understood that she wanted me to follow her, so I did.

The barn was part of a farm complex, built round a courtyard. The house was a ruin, tiles, bricks and three dead goats with their legs in the air were scattered about.

Still talking – she hadn't drawn breath since she had grabbed me – the woman pulled me into the barn, where, in the light filtering through the smashed roof, I saw a perfect nativity scene.

A pregnant woman on a pile of hay, another woman kneeling at her side, two dogs cowering. The elder woman spoke rapidly: I understood the word 'anglais' and felt her finger jabbing at my shoulder, to indicate my rank apparently. Then she pulled me towards the two others and got me to kneel at the head of the younger woman lying on the hay who was in labour, and forced my hands on to her shoulders.

I understood what I had to do: hold the writhing, moaning woman down while the two elder ones got on with the job.

I didn't watch much.

The girl screamed and shouted so loudly that I didn't even hear if any more mortars were flying around, and in any case, at that particular moment, I didn't very much care if they were. My cap had fallen off, and the girl under my hands was strong and difficult to hold.

The baby was born amidst screams and sobs, grunts and cries, shouted words of constant encouragement (I imagine) from the two midwives, and an appalling stench of warm excreta. I held my breath for as long, and as often, as I could, and stared into the trampled hay at my knees.

In her struggles the girl's dress, or blouse, or whatever it was, had ripped away and one heavy, milky breast swung loose; her right hand clenched and unclenched; a glint of a wedding ring in the thin sunlight.

It's as difficult and painful to arrive in, I remember thinking, as it is to leave this world.

The midwives grabbed and pulled things about, the girl began moaning, and then was still, all except her head which rolled from side to side, eyes wide like a frightened cow; then she yelled: 'Yeeee! Yeeee!', and one of the women slumped the pulpy scarlet head of a new-born child on to the sweaty white breast of its mother, the umbilical cord wriggling down her body like a length of spent elastic.

I found my cap and went to the door for a breath of clean air.

The mortars had stopped; on the other hand the child had started to cry.

It never occurred to me to wonder about its kith and kin: I didn't think about my own then either.

Everything in my past had been erased from the blackboard of my mind. I thought only of the present moment, and the present moment was all that we really had in Normandy that summer.

All the things which had once seemed to be so important to me, and to my existence, had been ploughed like stubble into the square, hedge-framed fields which were now my life: I walked over memory with heavy boots.

The woman in the man's hat joined me. We looked up at the sky.

There was no sound except for the rattle and clatter of tank-tracks some distance away.

She crouched, pulling me with her, and we scuttled across the cluttered courtyard to the ruined house. There was a vermilion geranium in a pot on a windowsill tangled in a torn lace curtain: gaudy as a whore at a wedding.

Inside an overwhelming smell of dust and soot. Half the room above had crashed down into the kitchen, spilling bricks and lengths of timber across the long wooden table, scattering the chairs like startled witnesses to an accident. At the far end of the room there was a wide fireplace, a tall iron stove with a tin chimney, a long shelf above it on which an avalanche of rubble and dust had fallen among some candlesticks and a plaster figure of the Madonna.

The woman scrabbled about, dislodging pieces of mortar and stone, and finding what she wanted she came across to me, wiping the object carefully on her red and white overall.

She held it out to me in work-cracked hands, blood still packed round her broken fingernails.

A shaft of sunlight which probed through the hole above us glinted on a small glass sphere set on a white china base.

She offered it to me again with impatient upward little jerks.

In the globe a swirl of glass strands. Red, orange, blue.

Like the marbles with which I had once played long, long ago, before the Anthracite Years, at school in Hampstead.

Moving in her agitated hands, winking in the sunlight, they sparked a lost memory. I understood that this was a gift, for she thrust it into my hands impatiently, nodding with some kind of smile: half frightened, half tender. Then she turned and hurried from the house.

I've still got the globe. It's a cheap thing, the sort of prize you win at a country fair.

It is on my dressing chest. I suppose the baby, if it still lives, is forty years old.

'What was that all about, then? Yells and screams.'

I swung into the jeep beside him, the globe in my hand.

'I've just had a baby,' I said.

'You never!'

We pulled away from the barn wall and drove back to Saint-Sulpice and the airstrip.

'My face is still bloody itchy,' he said.

'It's the nettles; so is mine.'

'It's a funny old war, this,' said my driver.

He was driving slowly so as not to raise dust from the white road.

'The mortars have stopped,' I said.

'We wouldn't be on this road if they hadn't, bet your bloody life. They're just over the ridge up there, in the wood.'

I looked at the glass globe lying in my lap. In the long grasses at the verge of the road lay two bodies in British uniform. On their backs, helmets on their chests, a gag of flies across their mouths, two rough crosses made from twigs at their heads.

'You deliver it, then? The baby?'

'Helped. There were two women there.'

'That sort of thing', said my driver turning left at a narrow crossroads, 'just makes me puke. I don't know how you could do it.' He cleared his throat noisily. 'Sir,' he added as an afterthought.

From the early spring of 1944 until the end of the war in Europe in May 1945, Flt/Lt Christopher Greaves and I were joined at the hip as air photographic interpreters attached to 39 Wing of the Canadian Royal Air Force. I really don't remember where we were 'paired off', probably at Odiham airfield, but there we were, an unlikely couple in many ways, but as immutable as Laurel and Hardy, Huntley and Palmer, or Rolls and Royce.

Chris was senior to me by some years, had already had distinguished service in the RAF in Malta, survived the siege, contracted polio, and constantly fell in love with his nurses: he was, later, to marry one and raise a large family. But after Malta, and convalescence, he was stuck with me.

We had a truck which served as our 'office', with a couple of desks and lamps and not much else. In this, plus a jeep, we drove across Europe in the wake of our Forward Recce Squadron who took the photographs.

Being determined young men with great ambitions the pilots had their airstrip as near the front as they possibly could be, dragging us, in consequence, along with them; for we had to be on hand for every sortie flown, ready to interpret.

I have often wondered, and did at the time, how Chris put up with me for so long. We were stuck together in that truck for hours and hours on end, and even when we did manage to get a break, usually when the weather was too bad for flying, we went off into the shattered countryside contentedly and painted. We never had a dispute or row, and remained together in work and in the snatched moments of leisure. We were a good team.

As I have said, the leisure was pretty nearly always in bad weather, which is why the great majority of my paintings had lowering skies, pouring rain and acres of mud and puddles. I never got to paint a sunny day – I rather doubt if I could have done so even if such a day had presented itself. I preferred 'mournful' light.

Chris was a professional artist; I only had the sparse training which I had gleaned at Chelsea Poly in between bouts of fumbling passion at the Classic cinema. But together we painted almost the entire campaign in Normandy, and were made Unofficial War Artists: our work belonged to the Air Ministry and was only returned to us after the German surrender.

At first, after the landings, there wasn't much time for painting anything. The early weeks were, to say the least of it, bewildering, on occasions unnerving. But as the Allied thrust got under way we started to settle in, knowing that we were there to stay until the end which, I was convinced, had to be in Berlin.

On the fortieth anniversary of D-Day, Chris telephoned from his home in the West Country.

'I don't know if you've been looking at telly today?' he said. 'Have you? Do you get that kind of thing in France?'

'All of it. I tuned in for ten minutes and stayed right through until the end.'

'Amazing, wasn't it? What about Mrs Reagan in that awful coat and NO hat! I mean, can you imagine a woman going to a memorial service without a HAT? Damned discourteous, I thought.'

'Oh well . . . it was all a long time ago, Chris.'

'Seemed just like last week to me, but then I'm getting ancient, I suppose. But you know, Pip, it was damned dangerous, wasn't it? If I'd have known how bloody awful it was going to be I'd never have gone!'

Fortunately for us both we neither of us thought much of the danger at the time. Perhaps sheer youth takes care of that emotion, I don't know.

And Chris, who did most of the driving while I navigated, did some extremely dangerous things on our 'off days'. Driving along a wide stretch of open road along a ridge above the still-occupied town of Caen, shells fell behind and ahead of us, sending up ugly bursts of smoke and shrapnel.

'They're getting closer each time,' I said.

Chris was bent over the wheel of the jeep like a crouching charioteer, his cap had fallen off, his glasses glittered in the wet light.

'Bracketing us,' he said through clenched teeth.

One shell to the back, another to the front, each time the range was slightly altered. And they came nearer and nearer. It was extremely uncomfortable.

'Playing silly buggers.'

'So are we. Can't we get off this road?'

'You should know, you've got the map. I've got enough to do.'

There was no turn-off; the map shook and flapped, and was impossible to read. I only knew that when the shell behind us and the shell ahead of us landed simultaneously in the one place, we'd be dead centre.

The spectacle, to the Germans below the ridge, must have been amusing – although they are not a race noted for their humour.

But a single jeep belting along a dead straight road, silhouetted against the sky, as if the hounds of hell were after it, obviously proved an irresistible target for 'bracketing'.

A hawthorn hedge on the right of the road suddenly, providentially, was there and Chris swung into a field behind its sparse shelter of thorn and torn leaves.

We crawled out; lay flat in the crushed corn.

The Germans went on 'playing silly buggers' for about twenty minutes and then, mercifully, decided to give up. I couldn't help wondering, with each splintering crash, why they bothered to waste so much ammunition on so meagre and unimportant a target. Perhaps they thought we were Churchill? But in any case the German is always a very thorough creature.

Anyway, they stopped.

In the silence which followed the cease-fire, we crouched our way back to the jeep, inching across the trampled corn.

A group of Canadian soldiers suddenly rose as one man from a high-hedged bank, rifles cocked, mouths open in surprise.

'Where did you come from? For Chrissakes that's Jerry territory!'

'An error in map reading,' said Chris.

'I couldn't read the blasted map bucketing along like that with God knows what flying about. I honestly don't see the point in taking unnecessary risks, Chris, we've got quite enough to take without inventing more.'

'Rubbish.' Chris crammed on his cap and restarted the engine. 'A nice little country run. No need to get fidgety, old boy.'

So I shut up. It was all kids' stuff anyway. *Boys' Own Paper* nonsense.

Nothing to it. And we were still all in one piece.

Bigger and better things were ahead.

Two nights later we all stood in the shelter of the trees in the orchard, rocking and stumbling into each other, as wave after wave of giant bombers roared low over our heads and ripped the heart out of Caen.

We held on to each other, or the scaly trunks of trees. Showers of leaves and tiny apples shook around us as the earth rippled beneath our feet with the shock of the bombs which thundered down three kilometres away. The air trembled and rolled with the sound as if a thousand drums were beating a gigantic tattoo, and the night was drenched in noise, drowning speech or even coherent thought.

We stood, heads bowed, eyes screwed up against the onslaught, grabbing about for support, like men drowning.

Ahead, through the trees, the whole skyline north of Caen was ablaze with white light, the clear night sky columned with enormous clouds of smoke and earth which barrelled upwards lit from the fires below, appearing to support a vast canopy of crimson cloud above the blazing town. A monstrous cathedral of flame.

With each shuddering blast, which seemed to suck the air upwards and leave us gasping for breath, the trees, in the light of the explosions, doubled themselves as leaping shadows, zig-zagging against the dancing shapes of the tents. In the midst of the fury, a cow, maddened with terror, crashed among us trailing a broken rope at its neck, bellowing with fear, until it tripped in the guy-ropes and crashed to the ground under a sagging canopy of once-taut canvas.

There were no more Germans along the ridge road at Carpiquet to play at 'silly buggers' with a lone jeep: by the next day Caen had fallen and the battle for Normandy was almost over.

It was no time at all, I reckoned, for hermit crabs. All that, with so much else which I had devised for my personal protection, was cautiously set aside. Self-preservation and anonymity were, however, still uppermost in my mind. However, the former now took first place to the latter.

Strangely, I discovered in the first two months of battle that, though I was, indeed, often dry-mouthed with fear (or perhaps fright is a less craven word), at the same time the inbuilt eye of the observer was as alert as ever: I was curious, anxious to see, to experience, to be aware of the extraordinary things which were taking place about me.

And, in the letters to my father, to whom I wrote every week at least, if not twice a week, I was still 'keeping notes', just as I had done a thousand years ago in the Anthracite Years.

There was plenty of scope.

August that year, according to the letters which he had kept for me, appears to have been like a childhood summer: that is to say, eternal sunshine, cloudless, hot and clear.

The sky was always blue, that strange intense blue of northern France, sea-washed, wind-cleansed, limitless, criss-crossed with lazy scrawls of vapour trails like the idle scribbles of a child in a crayoning-book.

In the orchards the shade lay heavy beneath the trees, spiked here and there with emerald blades of grass and clumps of campion.

But everywhere the land was still. There was no birdsong.

Sometimes a bee would drone up and away, or a grasshopper scissor in the crushed weeds of the chalky soil, and then fall silent as if the effort had been too much, in the still heat, or as if, perhaps, reproved that there was no response in the ominous quiet.

No rabbits scuttled in the hedgerows, the corn stood high, ripe, heavy in the ear, unharvested, and in the meadows cows lay on their sides, stiff-legged, like milking stools, bellies bloated with gas.

Sometimes one of them would explode with a sound like a heavy sigh, dispersing memories of a lost childhood in the sickly stench of decay.

Death was monarch of that summer landscape: only the bee and the grasshopper gave a signal of life, or suggested that it existed. The familiar had become unfamiliar and frightening. A world had stopped and one waited uneasily to see if it would start again: a clock to be rewound in an empty room.

But that comforting tick-tock of normality, of the life pulse, had been provisionally arrested. In some cases it had been stopped for good, for a little further back, towards the beaches, they were burying those who would remain forever in silence.

There was plenty of noise back there: of gears grinding, engines roaring, tracks rattling, metal groaning.

At the edge of an elm-fringed meadow, I stood against a tree watching, curiously unmoved, the extraordinary ballet between machines and corpses, which proved conclusively that the human body was nothing but a fragile, useless container without the life force.

For some reason it had never fully occurred to me before: I had seen a good number of dead men and had, as a normal reaction, felt a stab of pity, a creep of fear that perhaps it could be me next time, but I had become accustomed to them and got on with my own living.

But that afternoon in the shade of the elms I stood watching the bulldozers (a new toy to us then) shovelling up the piles of dead very much as spoiled fruit is swept into heaps after a market-day, and with as little care. Shuddering, wrenching, jerking, stinking of hot oil in the high sun, they swivelled slowly about with open jaws ripping at the earth to form deep pits, and then, nudging and grabbing at the shreds and pieces, rotting, bloody, unidentifiable, which heavy trucks had let slither from raised tail-boards in tumbled heaps of arms and legs, they tossed them into the pits.

Back and forth they droned and crunched, swinging about with casual ease, manoeuvred by cheerful young men, masked against the stench and flies, arms burned black by the August sun.

'Tidying up,' said someone with me. 'One day they will turn this meadow into a war cemetery. Rows and rows of crosses and neat little walks; perhaps they'll erect a fine granite monument, a flagstaff will carry a proud flag to be lowered at the Last Post, they'll plant those bloody yew trees, and relatives will walk in silence through the toy-town precision and order, looking for their dead.'

I remember what he said, because I wrote it all down later, but I can't remember who he was.

Fairly typical of me, I fear.

The words stayed with me for the simple reason that they moved me more than the things which I was observing. The dead lying there in putrid heaps among the sorrel and buttercups didn't move me at all: they were no more than torn, tattered, bloody bundles. The soul had sped; there could only be regret for those who had loved the individual bodies in this seeping mass: for everyone there had once belonged to someone. That was the sadness.

The absolute anonymity of mass death had dulled grief.

The silence didn't last long – silence in war never does. One gets to discover that very early on.

The ominous stillness which had reproved both grasshopper and bee simply preceded a gigantic storm: Caen fell, the Germans began their terrible retreat to the east. The battle for Normandy was over.

I use the word 'terrible' advisedly, for the retreat, estimated at that time to be composed of at least 300,000 men plus vehicles and arms, crammed the dusty high-hedged roads and lanes, even the cart tracks through fields and orchards, in a desperate attempt to reach the ferries across the river Seine: the Allied armies surrounded them on three sides. We knew that all the main bridges had been blown, so it appeared evident to us that we contained the entire German fighting force in one enormous killing-ground. Tanks and trucks, horse-drawn limbers, staff cars, private cars, farm carts and all kinds of tracked vehicles, anything in fact which could move, inched along the jammed lanes and roads in slow convoys of death.

Unable to turn back, to turn left or right, they had no alternative but to go ahead to the river, providing undefended, easy targets for Allied aircraft which homed down on them as they crawled along and blasted them to destruction: ravening wolves with cornered prey.

By 21 August it was over.

Across the shattered farms, the smouldering cornfields, the smoking ruins in the twisting lanes, smoke drifted lazily in the heat and once again the frightening silence came down over a landscape of shattering carnage.

Those of us in the middle of things really thought that a colossal victory had been achieved. The Germans had been destroyed along with their weapons. There could be nothing left of them to fight, the Russians were about to invade their homeland, surely now victory was ours and the war would finish before the end of the summer?

We were wrong. The people who are in the middle are nearly always wrong. The canvas of war is far too great to comprehend as one single picture. We only knew a very limited part – and even that part was not as it seemed. Gradually we began to realize that the war was not over, that it was going to go on, that the Germans were still fighting, still highly armed, stubborn and tougher than they had been before. Slowly 'a colossal victory' faded from our minds and we accepted the fact that something must have gone a little bit wrong in our jubilant assessment of an early peace.

It had indeed gone wrong. But it was only some years later, when the generals who had squabbled, quarrelled, and bickered all the way through the campaign began to write their autobiographies, that one learned that, far from a victory, the retreat had been a catastrophe.

By that time it was far too late for thousands of men to worry.

They were laid out in neat rows under white crosses.

What had happened, quite simply, is that the Allied generals, by disagreeing among themselves, had left the back door open to the killing-ground permitting thousands of Germans, and their arms, to escape and live to fight another day.

But we didn't know it, fortunately, at the time.

Standing in the aftermath of violent death is a numbing experience: the air about one feels torn, ripped and stretched. The cries of panic and pain, of rending metal, though long since dispersed into the atmosphere, still seem to echo in the stillness which drums in one's ears.

On the main road from Falaise to Trun, one of the main escape routes which we *did* manage to block, among the charred and twisted remains of exploded steel, dead horses indescribably chunked by flying shrapnel, eyes wide in terror, yellow teeth bared in frozen fear, still-smouldering tanks, the torn, bullet-ripped cars and the charred corpses huddled in the burned grass, it was perfectly clear that all that I had been taught in the past about Hell and damnation had been absolutely wrong.

Hell and damnation were not some hell-fire alive with dancing horned devils armed with toasting-forks. Nothing which Sister Veronica or Sister Marie Joseph had told me was true. Clearly they had got it all wrong in those early, happy Twickenham days. Hell and damnation were here, on this once peaceful country road, and I was right in the middle of it all.

My boots were loud on the gravel, oily smoke meandered slowly from

smouldering tyres. Blackened bodies, caught when the petrol tanks of the trucks
and cars had exploded, grinned up at me from crisped faces with startling white
teeth, fists clenched in charcoaled agony.

Down the road in a haze of smoke stood a small boy of about seven; in his
hand a tin can with a twisted wire handle.

I walked towards him and he turned quickly, then scrambled up the bank
where a woman was bending over a body in the black grass, a hammer and
chisel in her hand.

The boy tugged at her skirts, she stood upright, stared at me shading her eyes
with the flat of her hand, then she shrugged, cuffed the boy gently, and bent
again to her task.

Hammering gold teeth from the grinning dead.

The boy raised the tin for me to see. It was almost a third full of bloody
nuggets and bits of bridge-work.

Waste not, want not.

In the ditch below us a staff car lay tilted on its side, the bodywork riddled
with bullet holes in a precise line as if a riveter had been at work rather than a
machine-gun from a low flying plane.

A woman was slumped in the back seat, a silver fox fur at her feet, her silk
dress blood-soaked, a flowered turban drunkenly squint on her red head. A
faceless man in the uniform of the SS lay across her thighs.

I kicked one of her shoes lying in the road, a wedge-heeled cork-soled scrap of
coloured cloth.

The woman with the hammer shouted down, 'Sale Boche! Eh? Col-
laboratrice . . . c'est plein des femmes comme ça! Sale Boche!'

I walked back to me jeep. My driver was sitting in his seat smoking.

'Where do they all come from?'

'Who?'

'Those blokes . . . wandering about having a good old loot. They just go
through the pockets, get the wallets, pinch the bits of jewellery. There's a squad
of women civilians in all this lot. Gives you a bit of a turn seeing dead women in
this sort of set-up.

Here and there, pulling at the blackened corpses, wrenching open the doors
of the bullet-riddled cars, a few elderly peasants clambered about the wreckage
collecting anything of value. God knew where they had come from – every
building nearby was destroyed, but like the woman on the bank with the boy,
they had come to scavenge what they could.

As we drove away the first bulldozers began to arrive to clear the road. I
didn't speak: the sight of the dead girl with the red hair had distressed me
profoundly.

I was prepared for people to be dead in uniform, but my simple mind would
not come to terms with the sight of a dead woman in a silk dress on a battlefield.
That didn't seem to be right. They hadn't warned us about *that* on the assault
course in Kent.

We had to pull aside to let a bulldozer grind past; I looked back and saw an
old man dancing a little jig. In a fox fur cape.

Chris was kneeling on the grass before a five-gallon petrol can, sleeves rolled
to his elbows, kneading a shapeless mass like a baker.

'What on earth are you doing?'

'Don't come near!' he yelled. 'If you light a cigarette we'll be blown to
smithereens.'

'I'm not smoking. What are you doing?'

'Cleaning my uniform. Absolutely filthy.'

'So is mine.'

He dredged up a sodden battledress jacket. The smell of petrol was overwhelming.

'Just look at it! Black! Filthy!'

'Is there any particular reason why you want to clean the thing now?'

He looked up at me, dunked the jacket again, did a bit more kneading.

'Thought we might go to Paris,' he said. 'Can't arrive looking like a tramp.'

'But it's not fallen yet . . . they're still fighting.'

'Well, as soon as it stops. Couple of days' time. Seems fitting.'

'But it's forbidden to the British. Only the Free French and the Yanks.'

'Which is damned unfair, we've got every right to be there too, why not?'

On the morning of 26 August, almost before it was light, we set off in the jeep with the unexpired-portions-of-the daily-ration, a painted paper Union Jack, which Chris had made and stuck on the windscreen, and a fairly taciturn driver who didn't drink.

'He's essential,' said Chris. 'Teetotaller. We aren't; and liberating Paris should mean a couple of glasses here and there. Got to get back in one piece.'

We liberated Paris: a celebration of the heart in an atmosphere of exploding gaiety and joy.

Driving back to the airstrip, just as evening nudged the edge of nightfall, I realized how wise Chris had been to bring a teetotal driver with us.

We'd never have got back without him.

Teetotal and taciturn he was; indeed he had hardly moved a limb, nor once smiled all day, among the tumultuous crowds of cheering and laughing people. His only comment, which almost brought us to complete sobriety, was: 'These French haven't got no control. Know what I mean? All over you before you can lift a finger to say bugger off – not so much as an "Excuse me". Bloody liberty! Foreigners! What can you expect?'

But he drove safely back through the dark while Chris and I assured each other solemnly that we had spent a really *most* agreeable day. A very agreeable day indeed. Probably the most agreeable day we'd had since the landings. *Certainly* so. A *splendid* day. We decided, after a mumbling silence, that we ought to liberate another city as soon as one became available.

We had our wish granted a week or so later when Brussels fell, and the unexpired-portion-of-the-daily-ration, wrapped in a sheet of the *Daily Mirror*, proved to be a great success in an expensive restaurant on rue Neuve, where our two tins of bully-beef were presented to the room at large on a giant silver salver, sliced as thin as a paper handkerchief, garnished with tomato and cucumber rings, and offered, at our request, to the elderly clientele who accepted with well-fed, but graceful, bows and nods.

The black market, it would appear, didn't run to bully-beef. Yet.

That was early September – ahead lay another city awaiting liberation.

This time we failed disastrously.

There was to be no liberation for Arnhem.

Another catastrophe.

I (seconded to an infantry division) sat in the mud and ice during a long, bitter winter just across the river while the Dutch starved to death on the other side.

This time the catastrophe was obvious. We had no need of the books the generals might later write to explain things. We saw it happen before our eyes, unwilling witnesses to a shattering disaster.

The euphoria of Paris and Brussels drained away. The tough times were back. It was just as well that I was aware of that fact for there was worse to come.

In April, as the last of the snows melted in the larch forests like strips of soiled bandage, we came to Belsen and the first concentration camp: a hideous 'liberation' this time which erased for ever the erroneous idea we had had that 'Jerry is really just the same as us'.

No way was he.

The war ended, for Christopher and me, not as I had somehow always thought it might, triumphantly in Berlin, but while we were sitting on a pile of logs in a pine forest near Lüneberg Heath, drinking coffee in tin mugs.

'Well, old dear,' said Chris. 'That's it. All done; all over.'

I had never felt so useless in my life.

In a letter to my father dated 7 May 1945, I wrote:

. . . It is the strangest feeling imaginable to know that it is over: one just idles about. There are no 'sorties' being flown so no work. And there won't be need of us, *or* our work, from now on. There is a weird vacuum: for so many months now it has been a fourteen or sixteen (sometimes twenty-four) hour day of strain and anxiety. All gone now. The in-built fear that someone somewhere might take a shot at you, or drop a bomb on you, has evaporated. There are still hazards about. Mines, and a band of zealots called Werewolves who are determined to fight on, but, apart from stringing piano wire across the roads thus decapitating one or two unfortunate blokes driving jeeps or motorcycles, they don't amount to much and most of them are kids anyway; about fifteen or so. So we don't worry much.

Jodle apparently capitulated to Ike today in Rheims, and if that is so, that's that. I don't know quite what will happen to me now, it's been a bit sudden in some ways, but I expect I'll be given UK leave and then get shipped off to the Far East. There is still a war there. One sometimes forgets! It'll suit me in a way. I think I'll have a serious try at staying on with the Army: if I survive the next lot of course! I've enjoyed the companionship and the unexpected lack of responsibility. The Army, as far as it can, DOES take care of you, and I'm not at all certain now that I would ever be able to settle down among civilians again. I've got my books, a tent, a servant and a jeep. I honestly don't think I could be happier! But time will tell, it's very early days after all, and I *do* need a job to do. Maybe the planning for the fall of Singapore? It's in the air . . .

They swooped low, swung upwards in a spiralling loop, spun down, and scattered into glossy leaves of a banyan tree, screeching and squabbling as they settled to roost. Aunt Kitty's flights of scarlet birds across an opal sky.

These weren't scarlet – just ordinary green parrots – but the sky was opal, the high monsoon clouds were rising against the darkening sky, washed in carmine, orange, blue and green.

Over the verandah of the Mess, which had once been Tagore's house, peacocks planed down as gracefully and silently as hang-gliders to settle on the crumbling dome of a little temple buried in long grasses, marigolds and zinnias. They preened, bobbed, and fluttered their tails like foppish fans. Raindrops from the last heavy fall edged the leaves of the Canna lilies like diamonds.

Somewhere, from the very back of memory, these sights were somehow familiar. Even to the monkeys who swung through the jacaranda trees baring yellow teeth in hideous grins, defecating in anger.

In the bazaar, across the compound, the sense of texture and scent which she had offered me all those years ago was mine in abundance: silks, cottons, linen, trembling voiles, blazing everywhere in colours far too brilliant for any northern light; and the scents of coriander, mace, clove and nutmeg, of flour and damp hemp, ghee, camel dung and patchouli, swamped the senses.

As the light failed, the wail of flutes and the tapping of drums mixed with the cries of the merchants and beggars, and the high laughter of children trailing kites.

A different world to the one I had left a few months ago, arriving as a Draft of One, to cross India and begin, as I had expected, to join the planning of Operation 'Zipper'.

Only there was no planning because the monsoon had arrived with me; and that meant no flights and no flights meant no sorties and so, workless, one idled through the humid days.

'Difficult to say what they'll do with you,' said Scotty rattling the ice-cubes in his gin-sling. 'No telling really. Once we start off again, after the rains, we might get a clue – you'll probably be sent down to one of the Divisions, I shouldn't wonder. The bloody Japs have got their backs to the wall but they fight like hell.'

'So I have been told.'

'Sub-human, the buggers. For God's sake don't think otherwise. Monstrous people. Don't get taken prisoner. Take your cyanide pill instead.'

Remembering Belsen I said: 'The Germans weren't actually Fairy Twinkle Toes.'

'These are worse. Unfathomable. Savages. Bound four of our chaps with bailing wire into a tidy bundle, head to feet, doused them with petrol and set 'em alight. Alive.'

'Christ!'

'*He* wasn't around at the time; they've no pity, no mercy.' He drained his drink, tipped the melting ice-cubes into a potted palm. 'Should be exterminated like the vermin they are.' He got to his feet, pulled down the skirt of his bush-jacket.

'Want the other half of that?'

I followed him into the Mess.

Three nights later we heard that the bomb had been dropped on Hiroshima.

In the silence which greeted the news in the crowded, still Mess, someone said: 'God Almighty! Now look what we've done, let the bloody genie out of the bottle, we'll never get it back in, never.'

Just for good measure they dropped another on Nagasaki three days after, and a week later the Japanese capitulated. The war was finally over.

If I had felt absolutely useless when Germany had surrendered, I felt worse now. There wasn't a war to fight and I wanted to stay on in the army: I was deeply thankful that I would not have to face the Japanese in battle – everything I had been told by the old hands had horrified me into incomprehension of so barbaric an enemy – but I consoled myself further by my awareness that there would be much to do in the areas which they had occupied and ravaged and in which they had spread their dreadful gospel of hate and vengeance.

Someday someone would send for me.

But they didn't: I was forgotten for the time being. The army had other things to do apart from worrying about one lone captain who wanted to stay on.

In the atmosphere of euphoria and exotic laziness, among the sights and sounds and scents, I drifted into an affair with a woman some years older than myself.

Nan was no starry-eyed girl. Quite the opposite: she knew very well, instinctively, that I was cautious, evasive, unwilling to be trapped. Afraid of possession.

So she played her cards supremely well, encouraging me to read, to write my dire poems, even (time was so heavy on our hands) to write a play, which she carefully typed out for me in the evenings in the now deserted office. She encouraged, flattered, suggested a brilliant future in civilian life, and almost convinced me that I should not remain with my regiment and stay in the army.

She never once, in all the plans which she laid for my future, included herself. Far too clever for that, she was certain that in a matter of time I would come to depend on her for so much that I should find it impossible to break the bond which she was carefully forging.

And the bond, at that time, was strong: we were inseparable, and she was fun. We danced at the Club almost every evening, spent all our time together, rode mules into Sikkim on a three-week trek which I planned could take us to Tibet because I had a great passion to see Lhasa. We never got to Tibet – that was forbidden territory – but at least we saw Everest and lay hand in hand under the stars and the deodars.

As far as our companions were concerned we were 'paired'. I think that Nan believed so too.

I did not. At nights, lying in the noisy darkness beneath my mosquito net, her body heavy in sleep beside me, the scent of 'Je Reviens' on her throat and shoulders, I felt a wrench of panic that I was entering a maze from which there could, decently, be no escape. My love for her was provisional only. I hadn't the remotest idea how to escape from an intense affair which I had helped create only to ease the tedium of my boredom and idleness, and which was now beginning to overwhelm me.

But the army had not forgotten me.

After three months, I was despatched to Java where, Scotty informed me with some degree of relish, they were 'having a hell of a time with a bloody civil war; the Japs surrendered to the Indonesians and *they* won't give the guns back to the Dutch! You'll have a very jolly time, old boy.'

Nan came down to Kidderpore Docks to see me off on the LST which was to carry me across the Equator.

'It seems very small to cross the Indian Ocean in,' she said. 'A walnut shell.'

'It is.'

'LST 3033. At least I know what you're in and where you are going.'

'Yes . . . keep your ears open; in case the fishes get me.'

'And you'll write? Remember, after the 27th of next month write to my sister's place. Ladbroke Grove. She'll keep them for me.'

'I will. As soon as I'm settled in.'

Somewhere among the jostling, feverish crowds on the quayside, someone shouted: 'Quit India! Quit India!'; others joined in waving clenched fists in the air at no one in particular.

'You'd better get away, they are starting to get restless. Bloody Congress, bloody Gandhi. Don't get stuck, go now.'

'I will. The gharri's there. Ladbroke Grove, remember?'

'After the 27th.'

I watched her walking straight-backed, but with a slight limp – the strap on her sandal had snapped. She carried it in one hand.

I knew that she wouldn't look back, and she did not.

The bond had been broken.

I turned away as the engine started up, a dull throbbing shuddering up through the metal deck. I went below as a Draft of One: for Java.

At Guildford station carriage doors are slamming. A woman with an anxious look and a paper carrier-bag hurries past the compartment, and the singing porter rattles his empty trolley to the door. Stands there looking up, smiling, waiting for his tip. I fumble among assorted coins.

'All on board. Your gear. Heavy. Full of loot, eh?'

'The Japanese Crown Jewels, that's all.' I give him half a crown.

'Demobbed are you? Happiest day of your life, I reckon.'

'You reckon wrong.'

'Ah.' His eyes narrow, slide across my medal ribbons, badges of rank. 'Singapore, was you? On your trunk. Bombay. All that?'

'All that. And more.'

'Saw you had a nice tan. Expect you'll miss the sunshine. Ta,' he says and goes off singing.

'Until I tell her that I'll never roam,
'So, Chattanooga choo-choo, won't you choo-choo me home?'

But that came much later.

FIVE

We had crossed the equator in the early hours of the morning; I had set my tin alarm clock for 3.00 a.m. and went up on deck to watch. Some well-meaning idiot at the bar in Raffles Hotel the day before had assured me that there really was a visible line in the sea, and I had laughed, naturally; but none the less set an alarm clock.

To make sure.

And there was. Or so it pleased me to think.

Stars blazed from a jet sky and a half-moon appeared to cast a strange rippling line across the water: it was exactly as if two tides were meeting, riffling together, merging, shimmering in the heavy swell. It satisfied me, leaning over the thin iron rail of the ship.

I liked the idea, even though I knew perfectly well that it could only be an illusion. But then so much of my life in the last two or three years had seemed to be an illusion that one more wasn't going to upset my particular apple-cart. I accepted the line for a 'line', and that was that. I had, after all, *seen* a strange joining of the waters, like the interlocking of fingers, and that is how I would always remember it, and do.

Our snub-nosed LST cut through the phosphorescent waters with an elegant curl of white foam tumbling the wake behind us in folds of gold and silver. Apart from the throb of engines far below my feet, and the soft creaking of a metal stanchion, there was no other sound except the swish and swirl of the sea against the hull.

I felt strangely alone, exceedingly rich, drenched in these sights and gentle sounds with no one in the world to share them, and no one to shatter the beauty by comment and the banality of human speech. That kind of beauty needs no underlining.

It just is. Perfect, complete, rare, unshareable.

Far away to starboard a tiny light flashed with the regularity of a metronome. A lighthouse on the coast of Sumatra, brighter even than the stars.

We slid across the 'visible' line through the glittering night, with the Southern Cross tilted high above, into equatorial waters.

I had come a long way from Great Meadow and the Cottage, from the mud-scented delights of the river at Twickenham, from the grey conformity of the Anthracite years which had been, after all, the anvil on which my strength, such as it was, had been forged.

I knew that tomorrow all this glory would be memory, which is probably why I spent so much time on that deck memorizing it for ever, imprinting it on my mind so that wherever I went, whatever became of me, as long as I should be breathing and aware, I could remember and in remembering be enriched once again.

My short stay in Singapore during the last two days had heightened my sense of awareness, re-reminding me that life is at best ephemeral, at worst too easily lost and rubbished into oblivion: tomorrow, I knew, I should land on a strange island, wrenched by strife, anguish, bitterness and blind hatred, to take my part as a 'policeman', nothing else, in the bloody shaping of its future.

It seemed to me at the time a pretty daunting enterprise, and unworkable, which so it proved to be eventually, but I had no sense of fear then, or the remotest apprehension: it was a job which I should enjoy somehow, even though I would be forbidden to fire a shot in anger, even to protect myself.

I knew, of course, that it was almost impossible, indeed it *was* impossible, to try and impose law and order on a country hell-bent in ridding itself of colonial rule. I'd seen a good deal of that already in India with the rioting of the Congress Party. If the wretched island to which I was presently on my way wanted its Dutch rulers out, there was nothing, I knew, that anyone, however well-meaning and however imbued with a sense of order and control, could do to stop the surging masses, hysterical with slogans and blood-lust.

In Calcutta one afternoon I had seen the kind of fury that lay just beneath the surface of apparent orderliness when a Hindu youth of about sixteen jumped a food queue and was, there and then, hacked limb from limb in the busy street. There was no quarter, no mercy, no possibility of law or order, no reasoning.

Nan had grabbed my cap and buried her face, trying at the same time to cover her ears so that the screams could, at least, be muffled.

No one tried to help; but then, no one ever did.

We stood trapped in the seething, screaming crowd.

The youth's trunk lay bloodily in the gutter, head savagely battered, hair matted, eyes staring wide in surprise among an incongruous litter of old confetti and orange peel.

It was a fairly common occurrence in those days; mob violence was only a skin's-depth away, and incidents such as this were just the lid rattling on the boiling pot.

Caught in such a situation, the wisest thing to do was to try to ease oneself away as discreetly and quietly as possible; *never* push or hurry; walk slowly.

Capless, I led a weeping Nan through the shouting crowd; her long hair had fallen about her face and shoulders in an untidy cascade, and this probably helped our departure, for we were unrecognizable as officers of His Majesty's detested services by the jostling, screaming horde with its foam-frilled lips.

In India we knew that the fuse was short, the mechanism ticking, the bomb gigantic. When we left, as leave we knew we must, a tidal wave of hatred, violence and heedless frenzy would sweep the great continent, and Hindu and Muslim would only stop to catch their breaths when the killings were done.

The Indian Christians, and the terrified Eurasians, knew this equally well, and begged constantly for help, to be allowed to leave with us when we went, but no one gave a fig for them frankly; no one even bothered to do anything about them.

When we left we'd lower all the flags and quit, and then, as someone said in the Mess one night: 'We'll let the inmates run the bloody asylum, sort it out among themselves – they won't be able to, of course, but let the buggers try if that's what they want.'

It was a sentiment frequently expressed by a great number of men in the army who had come out from Britain to hold India against a Japanese invasion.

It was a negative approach of course – but then India induces negativity.

Standing on the deck that night, now so long ago, I remember being very glad that I had left the country at last; I knew that the official war was over, that the Japanese had surrendered, and that I had chucked my cyanide pill into the sea long since. *That* fact comforted me very much indeed.

I was sailing to a new job as a 'policeman', and if that was the role I had to play, so be it – it was a great deal better than having to fight the Japs, for I knew that if that had been my fate I could never have survived.

I felt pretty certain (wrongly of course) that it would be a fairly peaceful affair; I'd be there to assist in collecting the lost POWs and the Dutch internees (that had been my briefing in Calcutta) and help get them safely home. Nothing to it really – almost a Red Cross job.

So there I stood against the rail, filled with contentment by the splendour of the night all about me, and a feeling that the worst was over, and that I had survived: so far.

I waited until the first thin thread of scarlet day split the night on the portside horizon, beyond Borneo. I was linked with my earliest memories; for these were Aunt Kitty's islands and already, in my imagination, they were half familiar.

I thought.

It is true that defeat has an odour.

It meandered through the paint-peeling streets of Singapore like a slowly dispersing marsh gas, lying in pockets here and there, loitering in rooms and corridors, bitter, clinging, sickening.

We docked in Keppel harbour: rusted cranes, a half-sunken steamer, ruined warehouses with hollow, bullet-pocked façades. Military trucks, piles of stores, oil drums, a Union Jack hanging limply from a pole. It was five weeks after the Japanese surrender.

Beyond the wrecked buildings, which lined the dockyard like a row of rotten teeth, the towers, palms and pinnacles of the city struck hard against the intensity of the blue sky; sampans criss-crossed the oily waters like waterboatmen, and birds, strange to me, mewed and cried, swooping low above the churning wake of our LST.

The day was already hot and humid when I set off through the dockyard to go and see the city which had 'died' so ignominiously in the February of 1942.

A whitewashed bastard Tunbridge Wells – with palm trees.

Domed, arched, turreted, pillared, apparently empty.

Miss Havisham's wedding cake crumbling in defeat and cobwebs after three and a half years of Japanese occupation.

On the Singapore River Chinese life, however went its way in a tidy explosion of activity.

Sampans jammed the muddy waters like the tumble of a thousand dominoes spilled along the winding fringes of the riverbanks.

In Chinatown proper, washing hung from every window and balcony, or from bamboo poles thrust out across the narrow streets; shutters were bleached by years of sun and tropical rains, some had never been opened, others hung like lolling tongues. On the shops, Chinese lettering danced and sprang in scarlet strokes in the brilliant light, and rickshaws and bicycles bounced over the pot-holes in the twisting alleys, tinny bells furiously ringing, weaving through crowds of laughing, playing children, as innocent as butterfly swarms.

Among this cheerful chaos, ramshackle stalls were piled with all kinds of goods, from dried mushrooms and rice to Japanese whiskey and scrawny hens bunched alive, hanging by their legs looking anxious. Everywhere there was the cloying smell of frying oil and dried fish, heavy on the morning air, but above all there was activity and life.

The European quarter was different.

A deserted Sunday afternoon lethargy. Some military personnel here and there, jeeps and trucks revving up, turning, tail-boards clattering noisily in the almost deserted streets, Robinsons Department Store (the Harrods of the East, they said) had been struck by bombs and stared in sullen shock across the silent street with empty eyes: sockets in a scabbed, decaying face.

The city smelled of drains, damp and desolation. The mustiness of a long-closed room. My booted footsteps cracked back in echo in the stillness.

In Raffles Place there was a small parked Austin car with rusted chrome and a flat tyre, and two Chinese men in flip-flops carrying a bamboo ladder.

Far above, in the dazzle of the morning sky, kites planed and swung, coasting in the currents of higher air.

Beyond the cricket club grounds, rutted and worn, St Andrew's Cathedral crouched in abandoned grace surrounded by a filigree of jacaranda and flame trees, as alien and out of place as a swan on the Ganges, and all around the pompous pillared buildings, heavy with swagged stone urns and proticos, stood silent, vacant, blind – their Colonial grandeur humbled as if they too, like the occupants who had been forced to leave them, had also 'lost face'.

I hitched a lift on a truck to Tanglin Barracks and the Club; we drove through wincingly genteel suburbs, past gable-beamed and pebbledashed houses with names like 'Fairholm' and 'The Paddocks', buried now in bougainvillaea and flame trees, the jungle already weaving lianas through shattered verandahs, and thrusting bamboo thickets across long-forgotten lawns and rose gardens.

Some had been used as desperate, hopeless strong-points in a lost battle. Blackened shells, incongruous chimney stacks striking up through charred beams, latticed windows swinging urgently in the stiff breeze which rustled the sword-like spikes of the palms. Some stood in an almost pristine state of suburban elegance, and these, my companions told me, had been used as Happy Homes for the Japanese rank and file; but the sounds of feminine laughter and the whisper of silken kimonos had dispersed into the air as surely as the 'thwack!' and 'thwock!' of tennis balls on the overgrown courts of the 'unconquerable' memsahibs.

In the almost empty bar of the Tanglin Club a friendly Australian ex-POW came over and offered to 'buy you a round, okeydoke?'

Ronnie had a long face and no teeth. 'Rifle butt; I answered back.' His skin was drum-taut over angular bones, his joints, elbows and knees were swollen like melons on arms and legs as thick as drinking-straws, his new jungle green uniform hung on his tall, bony frame like a tent.

'Been here since '42. We arrived just as the bloody place folded up. Great bit of timing. Shoved us up into the rubber and said: "Dig defences", but there

weren't any shovels and the English bastard who owned the plantation said
we'd be fined if we so much as laid a finger on one of his fuckin' trees. I ask you!
The bloody Japs were up the road. Fined! Christ! This was the island that *no one*
could touch. It was impregnable. Took me a day to work out what that word
meant and by the time I had it didn't bloody matter anymore, it didn't apply.
The Empire the sun never sets on they all said. Trouble was they didn't know a
fuckin' sunset when they saw one.'

'I thought you had all be repatriated?'

'Yah, we've nearly all gone. I go Wednesday and I tell you one thing, cobber,
I won't be coming back, never want to see this sodding country ever again. I just
survived, by the grace of God, and next time they can stuff their bleeding
Empire.'

'I think they have.'

'I think so too. Good on 'em. When did you land?'

I told him and signalled for the unsmiling Malayan boy in his white jacket
and ordered another round.

'Timed it really nice. All over bar the shouting, right? You know there's one
thing saved our bacon: those bombs. If you lot had tried an invasion, know
what the Japs were going to do? Kill all their prisoners – men, women, kids . . .
mind you, they'd been doing their best to do it for nearly four years, but that's
what we heard. Wipe us all out. The day they dropped that bomb was the best
day that I can remember.'

He spoke quietly, in a tired level voice; there was no anger left in him. 'Only
thing is,' he said, pushing his empty glass round in circles on the table, 'only
thing I say is, they should have dropped twenty more, wiped the bastards off the
face of the earth, because you know why? One day they'll try it again; betcha.
All jammed on to those fuckin' little islands. Breeding like rats, they'll be falling
off the edges soon, and then what? Plenty of room in Australia, it's dead *empty*.
Get me?'

I got him. I was unshocked. The quietness of his voice and the authority with
which he spoke of terrible things defused argument.

'Well, not for a while,' I said.

The boy came back with two bottles of Tiger beer and set them on the table.
Ronnie began to refill his glass, his hands shook slightly.

'Maybe. Not for a while,' he said. 'If I'm talkin' funny it's because of no teeth,
sorry, mate. You stuck here long? Singapore?'

'Leave for Java, day after tomorrow.'

'Good on you. No place to stay: they're all so bloody ashamed here. Lost face
you see, and the Malays and Chinks *know* it. Doesn't do to "lose face", it isn't
forgotten. Never in front of the natives.'

He sipped his beer for a moment in silence. Put his glass down. 'The men are
all right, not too bad, the civvies, I mean. It's the bloody women, they are the
worst, they ran this place. They didn't come here with smiling faces, they came
here as bloody rulers. Do this! Get that! Rule Britannia! Christ!'

A small boy with a rubber inner-tube round his middle clambered out of the
swimming-pool beside us and came across to the table, his wet hair dripping.
He wiped his nose on the back of his hand, pointed to a small dish of rice-
cookies.

'Can I have those?'

I pushed the dish towards him and he took a handful, without thanks.

A pale, blonde woman, at the far end of the pool, lying on a li-lo, suddenly sat
up in her bathing costume, one arm across her breasts. She wasn't bad, long
hair, a drawn face, thin, looking angry and embarrassed all at the same time.

'Jeremy!' she called. 'Jeremy! Come here, I told you not to. They're *soldiers*, come back at once.' A voice as harsh as a cane striking steel: meant for us to hear.

The boy swivelled slowly on his heels and went back to her pushing cookies into his mouth. She said something to him, slapped the cookies out of his hand, lay back.

Ronnie shrugged, sipped his beer. 'See what I mean? Really got a complex, all of them.'

Not all of them however: Mrs McCrombie hadn't any complexes what-soever, at least as far as I could see. If she had, then she hid them quite admirably.

She was sitting on the lawns of Raffles Hotel in a Lloyd Loom chair, wearing a man's khaki shirt and khaki slacks, a red ribbon tied about her short, iron-grey hair, face as wrinkled as a winter apple, eyes as sharp and blue as sapphires, and she smiled a lot.

She was, I suppose, then, about sixty-five or so (old in my youthful opinion). Her husband, David, who had survived the ordeal of Changi Jail, had gone up-country to see what, if anything, remained of the rubber plantations of which he was once the manager, and she had settled for a readjustment to life with friends in a small flat in the city after four years in Syme Road Camp.

'Frankly,' she said, 'I hope he *doesn't* find anything worth saving up there. He's most terribly conscientious of course, but I really have a *terrific* hankering for home – home's in Dorset. Near Corfe, do y'know it?'

'Very well. My father used to paint there a lot.'

'Artist, was he? Oh, we had masses of them. I expect you knew the Greyhound pub then?'

'Lord, yes! Smiths crisps and ice cream soda; shandy when I got bigger.'

'The crisps,' she said, 'with those little twists of salt in blue paper.'

For a moment I realized that I had lost her, she had drifted away, her eyes looking beyond the staff cars and manoeuvring trucks on the carriage drive of the hotel.

Unseeing; a tiny smile trembling.

Suddenly she rubbed her forehead nervously, almost with irritation, adjusted the red ribbon, smiled back at me.

'Sorry. I went off somewhere. It was all such a dreadful muddle here, you know. People *do* behave in the oddest ways in times of trouble. I mean to say, here in this place, they were dancing and playing tennis just as if nothing was happening! The Japs had crossed the Causeway, and we'd pulled out of the naval base leaving it quite undamaged! David saw it. Everything intact. It was madness.'

'Did they really come across on bicycles, the Japs?'

'Oh yes! That's quite, quite true. Hundreds of the blighters spinning along on those dreadful little Japanese bikes. Can you imagine? *We* couldn't. No one here did – we never thought of that, naturally. Bikes! They are, of course, the *most* ingenious people – quite caught us on the hop.' She laughed suddenly, like a dry cough. 'Hop!' she said. 'That's what they did, and that's what we were doing, or they were doing. Dancing. Tennis. Funny. Do you know a dance tune, something called, was it "Deep Purple"?'

'Oh yes. Yes I know that.'

'I hate it,' she said.

A stiff breeze from the sea wrestled with the traveller's trees stuck along the edges of the lawn, snapped the Union Jack on its pole above the façade.

She looked up at it.

'Nice to see it back again.' She folded her arms on the table top. 'We had to kill the dogs. I think that was almost the worst thing really.'

'The dogs?'

'Well, when we realized that it was the end, David and I knew what we had to do; he got the Humber out and we took the dogs to the vet.' She leant forward, her hands cupping her face.

'They thought they were going for "walkies". You know? They adored the car an'all. But of course everyone else had the same idea at the same time. There was a queue of cars simply miles long; people walking too; weeping. So many dogs. All kinds. Tongues hanging out, pulling at their leashes, some being dragged. They were anxious, aware of our grief. Dogs are; did you know? They sense one's anxiety, one's fear, one's distress. Of course you got the odd Jack Russell behaving badly, snarling and jumping at everyone. Terror I imagine – most of them knew what was happening. I know that mine did. Barney was trembling from head to foot, and Rollo, he was David's dog, just stayed close to him, his head jammed tight against his master. He never moved from him. Never.'

She cleared her throat, placed her arms on the table top again. 'Poor people. The vets were dead with exhaustion. Collies, spaniels, Airedales, pekes, all kinds . . . so many – but we simply had to do it; had to.' She sat back in the Lloyd Loom chair and when she spoke again her voice was firm and brisk.

'*You* don't want to hear all these awful things! Too depressing – all in the past now anyway. Gosh!' she said, her eyes sparkling. 'We *were* glad that you all got here when you did! I don't think that we could have managed for very much longer really, things were getting pretty grim. We *were* glad! Oh goodness yes!'

'I'm afraid I wasn't here for the Liberation. I'm on my way down to Java, I only got in yesterday.'

'Well. You know what I mean, don't you? All of you, so young and fresh, so strong; we really never thought it possible towards the very end. There *was* a rumour that they would kill us all. Too many mouths to feed and what to do with us if you had invaded, you know? And then that bomb was dropped; after that it was different. But before, in the dreadful days, goodness what muddles! No one knew what to do, and when the *Repulse* and the poor *Prince of Wales* went down, that was pretty well that. No navy, no air force to speak of, and the Japs were so *much* stronger than we were, thousands of them swarming all over the place. We hadn't a chance. Just caved in, I'm afraid.'

She laughed shortly. Pushed the ribbon about on her forehead. 'Not *really* the sort of thing to tell one's grandchildren, is it?'

Long, long after the disaster of the Falaise Gap in Normandy, we learned just what had happened there; and long after my meeting with Mrs McCrombie, and long after I had stood miserably in the fog on Guildford station, I discovered what had actually happened in Singapore, and why the British were so deeply shamed and, as Ronnie had told me, 'lost face'.

Lieutenant General Yamashita, commanding the Japanese forces at that time, was outnumbered by three to one, short of supplies and exhausted. If he had had to hold on and face a counter-attack, he admitted later, he would have lost, and the greatest military disaster in history, as it has since been called, would never have occurred.

But no one knew at the time. And there was no thought of a counter-attack.

Hindsight is a woeful word.

So, as in Normandy, as in Malaya. Those in the middle of things didn't know. Bickering, squabbling, incompetence, absurd snobbery and idiotic arrogance caused the deaths of thousands of men and lost the British their Empire –

perhaps not immediately, but the chocks had been kicked away and the ship of state, so to speak, was on the move down the slipway to disaster.

I have always thought that it would have been comforting to think that Mrs McCrombie, and others like her, would never learn the true facts; but if she survived I suppose that, inevitably, she did.

But thousands upon thousands would never know - would never realize that it had all been in vain finally. There are no learned revelations for the dead.

Near the District Commissioner's tennis court in Kohima there is a modest memorial to all those who died in that campaign. It carries a simple message, four lines long:

> When you go home
> Tell them of us and say
> For your tomorrow
> We gave our today.

Who goes now to Lohima?

After I had done my stint as a 'policeman' in Java, I returned once again to Singapore and Tanglin Barracks, waiting for a berth back to England and repatriation.

Many changes had taken place since my first visit. The streets were busy again; Orchard Road was jammed with trucks, cars and rickshaws; ENSA was installed; there were scores of tatty little restaurants 'In Bounds to HM Forces'; people were dancing again at The Happy World; Raffles Hotel stated, on a discreet card, that 'If you are wearing HM Uniform you are not welcome'; and there was a subtle, understated, segregation of Singapore civilians and military personnel in the Tanglin Club, part of which had been commandeered as an Officers Club, where the dough-kneed newcomers (with one Defence Medal up) sat about in their over-starched shorts drinking Tiger beer and gin-slings, talking too loudly; and in the city, Kelly and Walshe's splendid bookshop had opened up again with new deliveries of books from America and Britain.

It was there that I went to find something to read on the long seven-week voyage home. I found just what I needed: a copy of *Gone With the Wind*. As I put out my hand to take it, a neatly gloved woman's hand reached towards it at the same moment.

I instantly withdrew mine, and offered her the book politely.

She was a middle-aged woman, straight-backed, grey-haired, in a blue tussore suit and a blue straw hat, a handbag in the crook of her elbow.

I can see her in this room now – at this very moment.

She turned abruptly away from me, and calling down the entire length of the shop, to a startled assistant, she said: 'Boy! Tell this officer that if he wishes to address me, to do so through you.'

Not everything had changed in Singapore.

Major-General Douglas Hawthorn, DSO, was not standing with open arms to greet me as we docked at Tandjoeng Priok. To be perfectly fair he had no idea that I was coming to join his Division.

No one else had either, for that matter.

The place was swarming with people of all kinds and colours, with tanks and trucks, with perspiring coolies, with running Japanese in little squads, naked save for their boots, peaked caps and flapping loin-cloths, with jeeps jolting over the rubbled concrete, with turbaned Indians and tall, bony British military police in crisp green uniforms and gleaming white lanyards. A bewildering crowd scene overwhelmed by the acrid stink of burning rubber and the more subtle, and far harder to identify individually, scent of spices.

With my tin trunk, portable typewriter and a canvas suitcase I stood abandoned in the midst of carnival. Unwanted, unplaced, unexpected.

A military policeman, with a ginger moustache and the disdain of a llama, led me to the office where, he said, with no degree of certainty: 'Someone will sort it out for you.'

The office was sweltering, even at this early hour, and a pallid corporal, with skin as translucent and as pale as a potato shoot, wearily looked up from some files.

'Any idea where they are? Your people?'

'None. I was sent down from Calcutta; told to report to 23 Indian Div. HQ.'

'Could be anywhere. I'm new myself. Calcutta, did you say?'

'Yes.'

'Long way, sir.'

'Long enough.'

'You come in on 3033, did you?'

'I did. She's unloading over there.'

'Dicey trip.'

'Oh. Why dicey?'

'Submarines, sir.' He was rustling papers. 'They say that there are Jap subs all over the place and that some of them don't know, or won't believe, there's been a surrender. Could have been nasty, if you see what I mean.'

'Very. I can't swim.'

He looked up sharply, a paper in his hand. 'Not much point in swimming. That sea is stiff with sharks.' He went to his telephone. 'Got some "gen" here, we won't be long now.'

Two hours later I was still sitting on my tin trunk, wreathed in the fumes of rubber smoke and spices; but any thoughts of Aunt Kitty's magical islands in the Indian Ocean had long been dispersed.

The subaltern who finally arrived helped me load my gear, and started off through the swarming crowds. He was disinclined to talk, but offered the excuse that he had been on night duty, was bushed, and that no one knew I was coming.

As if I hadn't realized this with blinding clarity some hours before.

The sky grew darker as we got nearer the City, the sun floated, an aluminium disc, behind the heavy pall of smoke which hung above the distant buildings like a wavering canopy.

The traffic was intense, the subaltern's driving alarming, the roads pot-holed, swarming with dogs and children, rickshaws and bicycles, sagging electric light cables and heavy trucks pushing through heedlessly; he suggested that I hold on tight.

'Extremists,' he said suddenly, indicating the billowing cloud of smoke under which we now were weaving an intricate, and near-suicidal, path. 'They hit a rubberstore last night, got the oil depot the night before, hacked thirty internees to bits near Bekassi, and you'd better watch out for landmines – *and* grenades. They chuck them about like ping-pong balls, all in the name of freedom. It's not like Margate.'

I wondered why on earth he would have thought I might think it was. But said nothing. I was dispirited enough without this generous information.

A small villa in a suburban street, standing in a long-abandoned quarter-acre was where I finally landed. This was 'A' Mess. It said so on a piece of cardboard nailed to a pole in the front garden.

In a prim, almost empty little room, with sun-rotted lace curtains at the bay window, a picture of a windmill and a canal on one wall, and a rusty tin garden table against another, a silent, but grinning, Gurkha with an embarrassment of gold teeth unpacked my kit, erected my camp bed and mosquito net, and indicated that his name was Goa.

As far as I could comprehend, for we had no common tongue, and it was only by his pointing to himself with his finger and repeating an incomprehensible string of words that I was able to isolate, phonetically, an assumed name, Goa.

Goa he remained for the rest of my tour of duty, and I came to love him dearly. When the time arrived, eventually, for me to leave Java, Goa smuggled himself, and his kit, into my transport to the docks and pleaded to be allowed to come with me to England. He was splendidly smart, his brasses gleamed, his belt was blanco'd, his boots shone, his tears streamed down his cheeks.

By this time, a year later, we had invented a strange form of language which we used together. Anyone listening to us would not have understood a word, but we did. Which is, after all, what mattered.

'No, Goa. No – *Sahib go*. Not possible Goa go.'

For a moment he looked at me in stubborn silence.

'Goa stay along Pip-sahib. Stay along.'

'Pip-sahib go along Britain. *Tikh hai?*'

He suddenly fumbled in the pocket of his battledress jacket and brought out a worn and tattered piece of card. Stuck on it was a photograph of King George and Queen Elizabeth cut from a magazine.

He held it out to me, then turned it towards himself at arm's length, drew himself to attention, and saluted.

'Goa, go. Look-see burra sahib. Burra, burra sahib Brit-inn. Okay?'

'*Not* okay. Not good. Goa not go. Goa rest along Division. Is *duty*. *Tikh hai?*'

He looked at me with such bewildered pain and distress that I felt a lump rise in my throat as large as a fist.

Our 'language' was far too limited to explain why he could not come with me to see his King.

He stood perfectly still, then replaced the piece of card, never once taking his eyes from mine, rebuttoned his pocket, moved one pace back, slammed to attention in his brilliantly polished boots, saluted, turned on his heel, hoisted his kitbag over one shoulder, and was lost in the jostling crowd pushing about the foot of the gang-plank.

He'd gone. And I never saw him again.

He had been 'allotted' to me temporarily, at first, because he was considered to be hot-tempered, difficult, stubborn – and he was all these things, but we grew fond of each other and respected each other. In some strange way we made a pattern of life together which worked well: he retained his pride at all times while serving as my batman-driver, which must have been difficult for him because he was a fierce, brave fighting man, and it was never his wish to be a servant.

No one else was anxious to have him for the simple reason that he had removed the head of his last officer, neatly, with a single swipe of his *kukri* while the man was asleep. Apparently there was good reason for this extravagant act, for the officer had, in some way which was never fully explained to me, insulted Goa, his bravery, his religion and his race. The whole ugly affair had been hushed up and dealt with discreetly within the Division, for it was well known that Goa was a fair and fearless man, and had shown incredible bravery and courage in battle from Imphal onwards.

The story may, indeed, have been apocryphal, but I accepted it as true. It was far more interesting.

He was proud, funny, devoted to the Division, kind and at all times passionately loyal to his King. He was, I imagine, in his early forties and had a wife and three sons in the hills of Nepal and I can only hope that he got back to them safely in the end.

And forgave me for leaving him behind.

There is a profound difference between being 'alone' and 'lonely'.

I was both for the first few days after my arrival in the Division, stuck in one or other of the three bleak little villas which constituted 'A' Mess. My brother officers were perfectly civil at all times, but there was a clear feeling that I was an outsider among a group of people who had fought together, and suffered heavy casualties doing so, in bitter and costly battles up on the Assam-Burma border, which they had secured against the Japanese.

I knew nothing of their war, they knew nothing of mine in Europe. I spoke English only, no Urdu or Malayan. We had absolutely nothing in common. The problems which they found in Java were not what they had expected at all. It was by no means (as *I* had cheerfully thought on my LST) simply a matter of being a 'policeman' and shunting POWs and Dutch internees back to Singapore and doing, as I had been told earlier, a simple Red Cross job.

It was far graver than that.

The Indonesians wanted to be rid of the Dutch, and freedom from colonial rule: they were determined to get it at all costs, and the costs were awesomely heavy.

Fully armed, by the surrendered Japanese, they harassed the Division at every turn. It is all familiar today – but then, forty years ago, it was a frightening and new manifestation.

Many Indonesians felt that independence would be a disaster too soon, and wanted the protection of their Dutch masters; the main body, however, were determined on complete freedom now, and the main body was the Mass.

Every building was covered with patriotic graffiti screaming for 'Bloodshed or Freedom!', and the blood flowed.

Nightly the explosion of bombs planted by 'extremists' (as they then were called) rocked the city. Machine-guns stuttered and chattered on the deserted suburban streets around the perimeter, fires drenched the starry nights with orange and crimson light, and the crump and crash of mortars and grenades was a familiar sound at any time of the day or night.

There was a lot of Japanese ammunition about, which they had thoughtfully handed around, and a lot of people only too ready and willing to use it against the hated, suppressive colonialists.

This included the unfortunate British, there only to do a humanitarian job before returning home after a long and cruel war. The Division had sustained heavy losses in Burma, and were still to suffer a thousand and a half more casualties before repatriation came in what, they honestly thought, was someone else's affair.

So really it was little wonder that I wandered about feeling like a leper with his bell. I didn't fit, had not been expected, no one knew what to do with me, and quite frankly had neither the interest nor inclination to suggest anything I could do; they were much too preoccupied with the bloody job in hand, which had taken them by surprise as much as it had taken me. No one had expected such an involvement. However, my irritation and despair grew daily.

I had crossed the Indian Ocean in, as Nan had suggested, a walnut shell, and had arrived, if not absolutely breathless with eagerness to die, at least with a willingness to do any job I could to help. But it seemed to me, in my over-sensitive state, that I was politely rebuffed at every turn and could very well moulder sadly away, forgotten in this distressing existence.

So, I sat about in the prim little room, writing letters to my parents and filling in my journal, or in the messroom in the villa next door. I watched Goa cleaning my brasses, my boots and his *kukri*, read month-old copies of *Punch* or *The Field*, and sometimes looked through the modest, two-sheet, Divisional paper, *The Fighting Cock* (which was the Division's insignia). It contained local news: '28 MURDERED IN DOWNED DAKOTA', and foreign news lifted from radio reports: 'VIDKUN QUISLING GETS DEATH!'; there were a crossword puzzle, sports results (local) and, perhaps most important of all as it was to turn out for me, a correspondence column which aired Divisional moans and complaints: 'CIGAR-ETTE SHORTAGE AT YMCA!'

Lally had always said that the Good Lord helps those who help themselves. I decided to give her advice a try and one morning, after a week of this mournful, useless, isolated and lonely existence, I sat down at the tin garden table in my dreary little room and typed a stingingly bitter letter of suppressed anger and complaint, threw all caution to the wind, and sent it to *The Fighting Cock*.

To my absolute astonishment it was published the next day under a banner headline: 'WHY THE BOYCOTT?'

Which was not what I had intended.

Suffused with embarrassment, I thought it prudent to keep to my wretched little room and skip lunch in the Mess that day.

Lally had been right, as it happened.

My life was changed overnight.

Within twenty-four hours I had been given an empty office right alongside that of *The Fighting Cock* itself, stuck up my trade-plate on the door – APIS – got hold of a desk and two chairs, opened up my portable typewriter (looted in Hamburg), and settled down to a new, if slightly apprehensive, existence.

There was just one small problem.

No one needed a photographic interpreter. Which is what I was. There were no reconnaissance planes nearer than Singapore; no one was flying photo-graphic sorties anyway because they were all too occupied in flying out the POWs and internees.

What, then, should I do? Having made such an unseemly fuss, and drawn attention to myself in a perfectly reprehensible manner, I knew that I had to try and justify myself. I did the only thing I knew how to do under the circumstances: I wrote reams of stories, articles, poems and God only knows what other bits of trivia and bombarded the office next door with them.

My talents were pretty limited, but this was the only way I knew in which to try and join my new Division – it was a case of desperation.

To my intense relief a number of 'pieces' were accepted (the genial editor later admitted that he was short of 'stuff') and in time I started to do so well that I began to write under two separate names: 'Icarus' and 'Bantam'. I can think of no good reason for choosing either name – perhaps I didn't? It is very probable that they were chosen for me. 'Icarus' was supposed to be fairly heavy and have some political comment or content.

One might have called it 'The Leader' if one had been unwise. Heaven knows what it was really: it certainly wasn't political, for I have the political, and historical, knowledge of an aphid, and there was hardly any 'comment', but somehow it passed muster, and by pinching bits and pieces here and there from radio transcripts of foreign news I managed to get by reasonably enough.

'Bantam' was altogether a much lighter exercise, dealing with anything and everything, and in particular large chunks of 'nostalgia' relating to Suffolk fields, Sussex Downs and so on. 'Icarus' and 'Bantam' and I took off.

By this curious method, using *The Fighting Cock* and my Hamburg typewriter as a sort of Trojan horse, I invaded Troy – or, to be accurate, 23rd Indian Division. I was very proud indeed. I had never, in my life, been fully integrated into a fighting Division before. Within a year of landing at Tandjoeng Priok, wreathed in rubber smoke and the scent of spices, I had joined Radio Batavia as an English Announcer, produced an ambitious (and quite unoriginal) revue with which we reopened the Concordia Hall in Bandoeng, fallen seriously (and fruitlessly, as it turned out) in love with my cool lady interpreter-secretary, become editor of *The Fighting Cock*, assuming full power, and, in an act of amazing generosity and patience on his part, become the ADC to Major-General Hawthorn, DSO, CB, and Commander of Java.

You really couldn't say I hadn't tried.

And very grateful I was that in looking after myself the Good Lord had showered me with such amazing bounty.

If life is (as I think it is) a long corridor lined with many doors and turnings, then that first miserable week in 'A' Mess had found me standing at a fearsome crossing. Which way to go? Hopelessness had almost swamped me.

Backwards was impossible (3033 had long since returned to Calcutta anyway). The way ahead was dark with alarming shadows; the turnings left and right were just the same, but did have the advantage of a few glimmers of light along the way – not very many, but just enough to keep the last vestiges of courage flickering in the draught of uncertainty and trepidation.

Hopelessness, at twenty-four, is something one does not submit to for long, so I made my brave turn, wrote my letter of outrage and complaint, drew notice to myself (ill-mannered to be sure, but essential at that time), and with the opportunity which its publication offered me I got down to the job with the only tools I had to hand, the modest gifts which I had acquired directly from my almost forgotten life years before in the theatre.

There was to be a party in 'A' Mess. Someone was going home on repatriation. Any excuse for a party would do in those ugly days.

The General had said that he would attend. Throwing the Mess President and his committee into a state of despairing hysteria. The dank villa was simply that: a dank villa. With trestle tables and board floors.

I offered to decorate it, and did so, with lavish, if inaccurate, murals of the Eiffel Tower, the Place de la Concorde, the Arc de Triomphe and groups of naked ladies whom I stuck all over the place at little café tables under Parisian parasols. From a distance of forty years I find it hard to believe that I could have managed to create an 'Oo! La! La!' feeling of 'Gay Paree' in that awful house, but I do know that I rid it, to some extent anyway, of the ponderous gloom, which at all times prevailed, of a Harley Street waiting-room swamped with the smell of stale curry and fried spam.

The General seemed impressed.

Tall, imposing, no nonsense and a sharp eye.

'You do this business?'

'Sir.'

'Ah. Gather you write for *The Cock*?'

'Sir.'

'Journalist were you? In civvy life?'

'An actor, sir.'

'Oh Christ!'

'Sir.'

'Well, it takes all kinds, I suppose.'

'Sir.'

'Know where I can pump ship?'

'Sir.'

'In Europe, were you? France, Germany?'

'Sir.'

They were dancing 'The Lambeth Walk' with a great deal of laughter and shouts of 'Oi!'.

'Bloody whirling dervishes,' he said.

'Sir.'

He followed me up the stairs to the only lavatory, its door decorated with a moderately indecent lady in suspender belt and long gloves, at which he stared for a few silent moments, snorted, and then pushed inside.

I was waiting for him, hands correctly clasped behind me, feet apart, at ease in the right manner, when he returned.

He grunted, rearranged his bush jacket, flicked a fingernail in the direction of my chest as he retied the stock at his throat.

'Five ribbons up, I see. Action?'

'Sir.'

'Arranged all this fandango too?'

'Helped, sir.'

'And her on the door, ummm?'

'Sir.'

He regarded me from beneath shaggy brows for a long moment, pulled his lower lip down with his finger and thumb, then started down the stairs.

I followed him dutifully.

'Know how to sit a table?'

I thought that he had said 'Know how to sit at table', so I said 'Sir' again.

He turned at the foot of the stairs under a giant bunch of inflated condoms which floated above his head in a festive manner; I'd painted faces on them.

'Know any *other* words?'

'Sir?'

'Any other words? Apart from "Sir"?'

'I beg your pardon, sir . . . I was minding my P's and Q's. You are my first general.'

He grinned suddenly. 'I may well be your last.'

'Yes, sir.'

'Apart from all your other talents, lavishly displayed here, I take it then that you have never performed the functions of an ADC?'

'Yes, sir. I have.'

'Have! For whom, if you are not familiar with my rank?'

'Brigadier Wade. North Grampians, sir.'

'Brigadier! Bloody Brigadier! What the hell was *he* doing with an ADC? Brigadiers don't HAVE ADCs, for God's sake!'

'Well, he had me, sir. More of a dogsbody, really, than anything else. Map reading, fixing his appointments, the cars, all kinds of arrangements . . . that sort of thing . . . '

'I KNOW what an ADC is supposed to do. And sitting a table?'

Then I knew what he had meant. At my first effort, two years before, at sitting a table, I had got myself into a muddle about who sat where according to rank and age and the rest of it. We were in a commandeered hotel in Worthing, and the linchpin of the whole evening was a tiresome, but important, ageing

Lieutenant-General vaguely connected to the Royal Family. His ADC had advised me, by message, that his General was stone deaf in the right ear and that his only passion was stag-hunting. Which was a great help. Brigadier Wade advised me to sit on his right-hand side and encourage him to talk about stags, and not to interrupt beyond murmurs of awe and respect.

'If you do that he'll tell me after dinner what a damned good talker you are,' he said. Which is precisely what happened.

So sitting a table, I knew, was important.

'I *can* sit a table, sir. We did a lot of entertaining in the Brigade.'

The general grunted, pulled off the folded stock at his throat. 'Too bloody hot for this. What's your name?'

I told him; he looked baffled. '*All* of it?'

'Yes, sir.'

'Something shorter? What brings you to heel?'

'Pip, sir.'

'Pretty silly as well. All right!' He handed me his sweat-sodden stock, ran a large hand through thinning hair. 'Pip, hop off and get me something cool to drink. A John Collins with plenty of ice. And don't lose that!'

He turned about and strode through the leaping and barking 'Lambeth Walk' dancers leaving me with his sweaty stock which I held with the reverence due only to a fragment of the Turin Shroud.

A few days later I was informed that I was to pack up my belongings and move down to a small villa next door to the General's house in Box Laan.

I was 'on trial' as an ADC.

If the news astonished me, it absolutely overwhelmed Goa.

'It's not sure,' I said, shaking my head to emphasize the possibility.

'*Stay* along him,' said Goa. It was an order, not a request.

Even if the promotion was only temporary, and he seemed determined that it would not be so, his position was greatly enhanced in the Division. For a whole day all one could see of him was a furious polishing, and the blinding flash of golden teeth as he prepared our kit, his *kukri* and a cheap brass photograph frame with a picture of his wife and three small boys.

The batman-driver to the General's ADC was perfectly permissible, in his eyes, and socially he could go no higher; it was a fitting job for a fighting Gurkha.

We moved to the shabby little villa which had one large room downstairs, two bedrooms up and three giggling Malayan girls who were there to clean and cook. Goa arranged his belongings in the garage and was well content, especially when he discovered my pea-green Buick coupé, commandeered from the Transport Pool because we were short of military transport.

He set his hat at a slight angle and drove as arrogantly as if he had Mountbatten in the back.

Things had changed indeed.

We had only one enemy, it seemed, and that was the General's own batman, who was an Indian and who disliked us both on sight; he spent a good deal of his time peering through the shutters on my verandah, or looking across the weedy, bamboo'd garden from their house to mine, through binoculars. It irritated me but I realized instantly that my irritation must never show in front of Goa; fortunately it did not, and his *kukri* remained in its belt round his waist, the Indian batman kept his head, and I, owing entirely to the boundless patience and forbearance of Major-General Hawthorn, managed to keep mine. And my job.

A week earlier life had seemed pretty bleak – the corridor frighteningly long, dark and confusing – but I had found the courage to make a decisive turn at the right moment, and managed to keep on track, mainly because I was determined not to fail, but also because, many years before, in my father's study, I had taught myself to type, with two fingers and a thumb, on his black, upright Underwood.

SIX

The transport skidded to an abrupt halt as the first mortar hit a truck some way ahead in the convoy.

It exploded in a ball of smoke and fire.

We were some miles out of Soekaboemi on the road from Batavia, going up to Bandoeng in the hills.

The convoy commander came running through the oily smoke, waving his hands above his head.

'Road-block! Looks as if they'll make a fight for it, take cover!' He ran on waving and shouting.

I knew the drill and left the car like a rocket, throwing myself into a narrow drainage ditch running alongside a banana plantation. I pressed myself into the earth as if I could have pulled it around me like a blanket.

The hermit crab: shell-less.

I lay rigidly still for a few moments. Up on the road I heard feet running, distant shouts, rapid bursts of machine-gun fire, then silence. I looked up and saw, with some embarrassment, Goa walking casually from the car, his rifle held aloft. He slid down the side of the bank into the ditch and knelt upright, close to my prone body. He was humming mindlessly, nodded cheerfully when I moved my head to look at him.

Grinning at my unseemly haste.

There was another splintering crash somewhere on the right, but I couldn't see what was happening because my hands had instantly covered my head and were pressing it deep into prickly grass and smelly mud. However, I could hear the ripping noise of hot metal fragments whipping through the frilly banana leaves, and the 'clonks' which they made as they hit the bodywork of the trucks and cars on the road.

For a few moments there was absolute stillness; no feet ran on the rough road, no one was shouting, no shots were fired. It was the stillness of a held breath. Inches from my face, in the murky shade of a broad-leaved plant, a large frog with amber eyes and pulsing throat sat staring at me unblinkingly.

I looked up again cautiously and was gratified to see that Goa, for all his enviable cool, was also buried face down in the mud, hands over his head, hat lying beside him.

For an instant I thought that he might have been hit by the hot metal shards, but even as I tentatively made a move with my hand to touch him, he looked up suddenly, hands over his ears, grinning gold.

Another mortar sailed cross and exploded on the far side of the road. Steel rattled against the transport and the air was thick with cordite and smoke. We ducked again, and I stared at the frog, which had not budged, as a spiral of torn leaves and twigs pattered down about us. A fourth mortar crumped down somewhere up the road, towards the rear of the convoy. They had got our range; I was grateful that I had pitched into the right ditch. Goa grunted, and his grin had gone.

I hated, at that moment, with a consuming hatred, the idiot Major in Calcutta who had summonsed me to my briefing on 'what to do in Java'. He had a red-veined nose, a bushy moustache, little, plump, over-manicured hands which he held before him, delicately clasped together, like a sleek, trim, fat hamster.

It was fairly clear that he had never left Calcutta throughout his tour of duty except, perhaps, to 'take a spot of leave' up in Simla or Darjeeling; he'd probably never even left the fussy office in which we sat under the clickety-clack of his ceiling fan, and he knew as much about Java as I did.

A desk-wallah. India was littered with his kind: they usually ended up with an OBE and a bungalow in Camberley or Cranleigh.

'It'll be pretty cushy, you know. You won't fire a single shot,' he had said, the plump little fingers folding and unfolding like a sea-anemone. '*Not* even in self defence, got that? Consider yourself a policeman, nothing more. Behave with caution and restraint at all times. It is not our quarrel. That's a Dutch problem. It's their look-out not ours, let them sort it out. If they are going through a revolution it's got nothing to do with us. All *we* do is maintain order and get the POWs out and home.'

How, I remember wondering, does one 'maintain order' during a revolution without firing a shot. By waving white flags and saying 'Excuse me'?

He saw my look of doubt, which he instantly took for silent insubordination.

'Now, look here! The Supremo doesn't want us to make any *ripples*, get it? Least said, soonest mended, that sort of thing. Just do our job and get out. Leave the Dutch to do the tidying up, it's their affair, not ours, remember that. Any more questions?'

I hadn't asked any.

'Where do I report to? And to whom?'

He briskly told me, handed me a sheet of paper. My Movement Order.

'What do I do when I get there? Am I still Air Photographic?'

He looked at his watch, buttoned a pocket, reached for his cap and cane on the desk beside him. It was time for 'tiffin' at the Saturday Club.

'No idea. You'll soon find out. Replacement, I'd imagine, frankly. We're having quite a lot of casualties, I hear. Quite a rumpty-tum down there.'

Hardly to be wondered at if one was unable to fire a shot; even in self-defence. All his instructions went overboard the very instant, almost, that I set foot on the dockside at Tandjoeng Priok anyway.

During the war in Europe I had never had to use my revolver, which was probably just as well. It had rested comfortably in its holster at my hip, uncleaned and dusty, and was never drawn in anger or fear. In any case, it aimed low, so that when I fired it, as I sometimes did for practice so to speak, it kicked up scatters of gravel at the foot of the target, but did no other damage whatsoever.

Frankly I was far better off with a .303 rifle, but these were not issued to officers.

However, in Java things were different. I quickly learned that my revolver had to be clean, and brilliantly oiled, at all times – and loaded. At the start of my duties, in the first couple of weeks, I even slept with the thing beside my pillow; in a constant state of dread that perhaps I had not applied the safety-catch and that I should be found one morning by Goa like a suicide.

But in time one settled down to life with a loaded gun quite easily, and eventually, as the immediate sense of unrest and preparedness began to slacken and Batavia came more and more under our control, and the 'extremists' pulled out to positions beyond the city, my revolver remained in its holster, clean, ready but unloaded, and even though I took it nightly into my bed like a teddy bear it was attached to its belt, and the bullets were in the pouch.

I fortunately never had to use it.

However, the nights, and often the days, were spasmodically interrupted by sudden bursts of rifle fire, of grenades exploding, and all military dumps or public buildings were still irresistible targets for the restless, angry 'extremists' and supporters who smuggled themselves through the road-blocks into town with ease. And we fired back: chucked grenades, strafed suspicious positions, bombed strong-points, and generally gave as good as we received.

So much for the Supremo's desire that we should not make ripples. We did not.

We made waves.

So much for the hamster-Major in Calcutta sweating it out for his OBE.

He wasn't lying face downwards in a stinking ditch beneath a cluster of rapidly shredding banana trees.

From a distance came the sound of heavy-machine-gun fire, followed by the urgent crackle of small-arms. The machine-guns made a good deal of noise; and then everything stopped again and the silence fell.

I sat up and saw Goa scraping mud out of the buckles of his gaiters with a piece of twig. Another rattle of small-arms fire, this time irregular and further off, as if they were pulling back; I put on my cap and crawled up the side of the bank to look along the road.

Smoke drifted from the truck which had been hit at the beginning of the attack, there was no immediate sign of human life; and then one or two cautious heads appeared along the edge of the ditch, alert, expecting another mortar. All seemed calm; I started to walk along the road, Goa hard at my heels.

There wasn't much to see: the burning truck, a scatter of metal, some charred cloth. Someone gave orders for a half-track to move down and try to nudge the truck into the side of the road so that the convoy could proceed, and I almost tripped over the shapeless lump under a blanket which had been the driver. His five passengers had been carried down to one of the ambulances which were travelling with us.

'Funny really,' said the Scots MO. 'The bastards usually go for the ambulances first thing. They must have misjudged it this time: just a short, sharp, wee attack.' There were bright splashes of blood on the road at his feet; he slammed the doors of the ambulance.

'Buggers,' he said.

The convoy commander came fussing down the line of transport. 'Must get a move on. Come along, don't all stand about . . . we've got to make the harbouring area before dusk and the day's going fast. Come along now! Everybody on the move . . . jump to it, that's the ticket!'

A nanny: we knew that we had to make the harbouring area before dusk, and that he was a man under strain repeating phrases automatically, a reflex action.

As I turned to go back to my vehicle I saw two men start to drag the body of the driver towards the second of the ambulances, an arm fell free of the shrouding blanket, trailing a dark hand in the dust.

His day had gone already.

Windscreens which had been shattered by mortar splinters were smashed out, people began to clamber on board, motors revved up, doors slammed.

Goa had gone ahead and was standing by the staff car adjusting his belt and humming.

'Think you'd better go up to Bandoeng with the advance party,' the General had said. 'Scout around for a decent billet for me. We'll be up there until the place is settled, so make sure we are comfortable and protected, and not in the middle of everyone else. Find a good house, get a lift with the BM of XX Brigade, he's a decent feller, show you the ropes.'

And so there I was, on the Bandoeng convoy with a taciturn Major in a staff car and 'extremists' all over the place.

We started up; ahead one of the half-tracks pulled out into the road and courageously took the lead. We passed the still smouldering truck lying forlornly in the ditch.

It was not what you might call a race for the harbouring area: our pace was that of an ambling camel, and there was a good reason for this – we had to follow the half-track, and the half-track driver had to keep his eyes open for mines which the 'extremists' laid like molehills anywhere and everywhere on the winding road. They were thorough but not very expert, so that the mines were fairly easy to see – as long as the light was right and you hadn't already hit one.

It was not a comfortable, or relaxing, journey and the Major from XX Brigade was an Indian Army regular and disinclined to talk, unless one knew all about horses; but I didn't, so we sat in silence until he took out a mouth organ and, knocking the fluff and dust from it against his knee, began to drone mournfully through a selection of Ivor Novello melodies.

At least that's what he said they were, but I was hard put to recognize much of Mr Novello's music, since he played in one key only with astonishing monotony.

As we climbed, the land fell gently away to the vast chequerboard of the plains, criss-crossed with dykes and raised banks, squared with paddyfields, stands of sugarcane and banana plantations. The water in the paddies glinted in the fading sun and melted away into the far distance in varying shades of blue. From the palest petrol haze to violet and darkest indigo. Beyond, and high above, a shadowy fretwork against the lavender sky, the mountains hung flat-topped with slumbering volcanoes.

It was not really a landscape of the heart: that, for me, was in Sussex, with its soft green woods, and clustered villages, its chalk-scarred downs, and curving fields of plough, creamy with clay, regular as corduroy; its gently winding rivers and streams rippling towards the sea through fields of buttercups and meadowsweet, its crow-crowded elms along the hedgerows, its white roads cutting through high hawthorn banks under a sky wide, clear and as blue as flax. A far cry from this land beyond the staff car windows.

Clusters of coco-palms stuck up like feather dusters at the edges of burned and abandoned *kampongs*. Sago-palms stood in neat groves, with kanari trees here and there, and flowering bushes of brilliant colour which I had never seen before. But there was no sign of life anywhere. Everyone had fled, and the land lay still, idle, untended.

No white ibex on the dykes, no water buffalo pulling slowly through the paddy fields, no children running; a dead landscape.

Sometimes a flock of pigeons, or a swoop of bronze-green parakeets, would fly in skimming bounds from a tree to tree quarrelling and chattering, and once I thought that I saw a black pig swerve from the roadside and blunder away into the bushes; otherwise everything was still, deserted, and the silence of apprehension fell across the lush, green, watery land like a vapour.

The BM of XX Brigade stopped playing, shook the spittle from his mouth organ on to the floor at our feet.

'"Shine through My Dreams",' he announced gruffly. 'Rather good, what?'

'Fine. Yes. Good.'

'Got a bit lost somewhere there in the middle; difficult part. But I don't think you noticed, eh? I covered it up pretty well. All by ear, you know? I've got the record if you'd care to hear it one day?'

I was slightly surprised that he should have asked, but thanked him anyway. He started sucking and blowing again. Paused. Grunted. Thumped the instrument hard against the heel of his hand, started off once more.

Goa turned and grinned at me, wagging his head in silent dismay. The moaning sound in the closed car was almost insupportable, and my anxiety began to increase as the light faded gently across the empty land.

We passed a European house set back from the road, the red-tiled roof sagging, fans of black smoke scorched above each window, the shadows beginning to deepen in a thick grove of high bamboo, swaying lightly against the darkening sky.

At least I had the consolation, I thought, that whatever happened next I could at least fire a shot to defend myself. The idiot hamster-Major loomed before me, my hatred blurring his plump, porcine face: all that I clearly remembered of him was his fussy little hands.

Then we all careened to a stop, against the ambulance in front, as a burst of firing broke out once again.

The mouth organ, mercifully, stopped; we leapt out of the car and took cover in the bamboos and a giant datura, heavy with white trumpet flowers.

The firing continued for about twenty minutes, but there were no mortars, and we just crouched where we were, revolvers in hand, Goa kneeling with his rifle at the ready. I thought this was a pretty stupid way of setting out to find the General a house. In time the firing stopped; my knuckles, I noticed to my surprise, were shining white over the butt of my gun. I pushed it into its holster and pretended that I was not shaking.

With a little careful manoeuvring, and rough handling, we managed to disengage ourselves from the back of the ambulance; there was not much damage – one door was stove in, and we'd lost a headlamp and dented the radiator. One of the wounded, jolted cruelly by the sudden lurching halt, began to cry out in pain. A high, sharp, howl: 'Ieeeee! Ieeeeee!' I ran, crouching, along the line of trucks to find the MO.

The shaking, which had surprised me, had also shamed and angered me: it was no way to behave. Running down the open road restored my confidence. If I got hit it wouldn't be while crouching in trembling timidity.

'I think they've scarpered,' said the MO, as a medical orderly clambered into the damaged ambulance with a first-aid sack. 'No one hurt; we were lucky. The shots went wild.'

We eventually got everything sorted out and moved off again at camel's pace, alert, listening for any signs of another ambush; but there were none, and we reached the harbouring area just as night was falling without further incident.

It had been, by and large, a quiet day: only two, short 'wee attacks' as the MO had said earlier.

'I don't know where the bloody RAF got to,' said the BM of XX Brigade. '*Supposed* to patrol this road with a convoy on it . . . I suppose we weren't large enough for them. So damned choosy . . . *Never* there when you need them. I think that I must have dropped my mouth organ.' He was patting his jacket anxiously. 'Have you seen it?'

'No. Probably fell out of your pocket back there in the bamboo.'

'How *could* it! It was in my ruddy hand when we stopped – have a look on the floor, or under the seat, will you . . . '

We found it and he put it into his pocket, buttoned the flap firmly.

'Be absolutely lost without this. Terribly important. Good for morale, what?' He fortunately didn't wait for my reply, but turned to collect his map-case and papers.

A quiet trip, with only minor incidents. One dead and five wounded.

The Bandoeng convoy was often far more costly. We had, in truth, been lucky.

In October, seventeen vehicles, carrying civilians and POWs, were attacked: the convoy commander was killed, two hundred women and children were taken off by the 'extremists' and never seen again.

By that standard, today wasn't much to write home about.

So I didn't bother; however, two days later we got a three-line mention in *The Fighting Cock* under 'Local Events', followed by a glowing report of a hockey match between Div. HQ and 24th Indian Field Ambulance.

There was no score on either side.

If the General's house bore a striking resemblance to the Hoover factory on the Western Avenue I was unaware of it at the time. I don't think that I had ever seen the Hoover factory then: it wasn't until some years later, driving past it on my way to work at Pinewood Studios, that I would feel a sudden pull of memory, and remember the house in Bandoeng. Set on the edge of a high escarpment, overlooking the plains below and the heat-hazed mountain range in the distance, approached by a long tree-lined avenue, across an immensity of weedy grass, long since scabbed with seedling bushes and trees and tufts of whippy cane, it stood in concrete splendour. Compact as a set of shoeboxes, surmounted by a high, square tower (which contained the water tanks), a roof garden with pergolas, arched-trellis bowers and a flag-pole.

Exactly what I felt the General would like: and fitting for his position as the Commander of Java. A 'decent billet' in fact.

Once upon a time it had been white, striking hard against the deep blue of the sky, a dazzle of neo-Bauhaus (plus Chinese) elevations which would have shocked Gropius but delighted me by the audacity of its Sino-Teutonic mix.

It had been built, I was informed, for a Chinese merchant who prudently fled before the Japanese arrived, and it had been left empty during the Occupation. It was now mouldering slowly away in abandoned decay. I was convinced that it could be restored to its former glory, that the General would like it, and, above all, that I could get the job done.

The site was superb; so was the swimming-pool, hacked out of the cliff-face below, which hung over the plain like an enormous turquoise bidet. During the barren years only nature had been bountiful, creeping across the once-trim lawns, the gravel drives and paths, invading the oval lily-pool before the house, mossing the iron fountain which might have been a Giacometti, but which was not, and smothering the flagged path which led down, across the grass, to a hidden guest pavilion, drowned now by bougainvillaea, a giant datura and a tall grove of bamboos, each as thick as a shin, which I instantly coveted for myself. The whole set-up was perfect.

I could be near the General, but not too near; we would be self-contained, easy to protect and 'not in the middle of everything else', as he had instructed.

I stood, I well remember, in the still heat of the afternoon and watched butterflies as large as saucers flap about the datura with indolent grace, saw birds of astonishing brilliance, and found, under the branches of a giant banyan tree behind the pavilion, clusters of flying foxes hanging like old raincoats, in the diluted light which filtered through the leathery leaves.

There was a familiar scent of wet dog: musty, damp, animal. They watched me with eyes as bright as cut steel: motionless, ears pricked, wings folded about them like the ribs of an umbrella.

Umbrellas, raincoats, wet dogs: the half-remembered sights and smells of distant childhood.

A signal was despatched to the General to say that his house had been found but that a certain amount of work must be done to it before his arrival. The next day I had delivered to me, at seven in the morning, fifty Japanese prisoners accompanied by a sullen officer who never stopped saluting. A tiresome, and automatic, gesture which he, fortunately, discarded.

The General had made his orders on the treatment of surrendered Japanese perfectly clear. They were to clean the streets, and perform all menial tasks required; the officers were to work with the men; they were to double to and from their labours at all times, and if they were some distance from their place of work, which might therefore restrict their hours of effort, they had to start doubling earlier. They stood to attention in five rows of ten, the officer stiff beside them, arms at his sides. Through a Tamil, who spoke some Japanese and had once been their prisoner and cruelly tortured, instructions were given, and their work began.

The house was stripped down and scrubbed, lawns were cleared and mown (with garden shears and pairs of scissors), bushes and canes were hacked up, the avenue of trees pruned and trimmed, the gravel drive weeded inch by agonizing inch, the lily-pool and the swimming-pool restored to their former glory, and two Dutch cannons which flanked the iron gates of the main entrance to the estate were rediscovered beneath years of smothering vegetation and burnished to such a brilliance that they shone like silver and one could easily read the year in which they were cast: 1709.

It took them, in all, I suppose, about fourteen days: at the double.

Which made the General impatient.

They were frighteningly thorough, swarming across the grounds clipping and pruning, uprooting, scrubbing, weeding, raking; pouring with sweat.

I watched them, half embarrassed, half loathing.

Naked, except for their loin-cloths and cotton peaked caps, wearing rubber boots with a curiously separated big toe, they received no quarter from seven in the morning until dusk fell, only being permitted one half-hour in which to rest, drink, and eat a handful of rice and a piece of boiled fish.

As the light began to fade in the sky, just before the sudden hush of sudden night, they were collected together and marched away by their sullen officer: at the double.

It was always a moment of supreme relief to me when they went. I disliked walking among them, being near, smelling the odour of sweat and straining flesh. If I approached them they would instantly cease work and spring upright, nodding and bowing, standing stiffly to attention, or else, which was even worse, they would cringe in humiliating servility, hissing all the while like demented geese, eyes dulled with defeat, mouths wide in grins as fixed as in rigor mortis.

Ugly, abject little men these, who had ridden their bikes across the Causeway and defeated the greatest bastion in the East, who had spread like bubonic plague from China to the borders of India, swamped Burma, Siam, Malaya and the Philippines, who had killed savagely, tortured brutally without a shred of compassion, bound their prisoners like cord-wood and burned them alive, beheaded them, buried them still living, imprisoned men, women and children under conditions, as I had seen, which defied even the most depraved of imaginations, force-marched the defeated to Burma to build an impossible railway where they met their deaths in thousands from disease and deliberate starvation.

How then could I have compassion?

Standing in the blaze of noon watching them at work, their nimble, expert fingers frantically combing the gravel paths for a blade of grass, a crumpled leaf, sweat running into eyes half closed with exhaustion, dribble looping at their chins from slack lips and parched mouths, I could feel no shred of pity.

Embarrassment, after the first two days, drained away: only loathing remained. Superimposed over the vision of these grovelling, bow-legged creatures sweating in the equatorial sun, another vision ran through my mind like an unbroken loop of film, repeating itself continuously. I could see, almost more clearly than the ape-like figures before me, the Circle Stalls, the shabby red plush, the lights dimming in the great chandelier above, and hear, with acutely remembered despair, the words of the song I had so detested long ago:

> 'On a tree by a river
> A little tom-tit,
> Sang, "Willow,
> Titwillow,
> Titwillow . . . "'

The Dutch were proud of Bandoeng, with good reason.

A pleasant town of wide tree-lined boulevards, elegant public buildings and a fine hotel called The Savoy, it was set in the cool hills, some two hundred miles from Batavia, surrounded by neat suburbs of expensive villas and bungalows.

It was also completely surrounded by the 'extremists' who occupied a neighbouring hilltop suburb, or garden city, called Lembang, from which they were able to dominate the entire town and lob mortar bombs and shells indiscriminately into the streets whenever the fancy took them. Which was almost every day.

Making life complicated and dangerous for everyone; and everyone consisted of two brigades, Divisional HQ, plus 45,000 internees and POWs who had fled the camps and hoped to find safety and repatriation.

It was surrounded, under siege and bursting at the seams.

The only way in or out of the town was by road, hence the convoys and the constant patrolling of the RAF, or by air from the one airfield down on the plain at Andir, which we hung on to with grim determination and a constant casualty list.

It is a fact of life that things reach a peak, level out, and then seem to spill away. One is often taken unawares: it happens gently.

Bandoeng was for me the peak: it seemed that I had settled at last into a routine military life. Pleasant accommodation, a good job, a decent boss, *The Fighting Cock* to set up again, plus the fact that suddenly air photographs began to arrive (pretty late but, still, they arrived) from Singapore and now the sign on my office door read 'APIS' coupled with the name of the newspaper in large letters, and the word 'Editor' in becomingly more modest ones below.

The original, genial, editor had been left behind in Batavia to continue with his regular duties, and somehow it fell to my lot to take over his job. Along with the duties of an ADC. I was far from the lost, useless and ignored leper of some months before; there was almost too much to do now.

General Hawthorn was a fighting general; he believed, unlike some of his ilk, that he should be 'up front with the men' and as close to the fighting as possible. He took me along with him.

'Useful, Pip. See how things are at first hand, can't abide second-hand reports, get it all down in the paper as it happens. Be an eye-witness!'

An eye-witness, willy nilly, I became.

He had liked his house; he walked through the high marble rooms in heavy silence. A silence broken only by the crack of his boots on the floor, and the squeal of steel heel-tips as he swivelled around looking at the funishings which I had coliected from among the looted stuff stored by the Japanese in the go-downs by the railway. A fairly theatrical flourish: dressing the set. My held breath was freed by his nods of bemused approval.

'Good stuff. Well done,' and then he had turned and fixed me with his cold blue eyes. 'And where's my golf course?' he said.

My own humble abode caused him to snort with indignation: I had made an error in showing it to him, that was perfectly clear. Although far from pretentious, it was pleasant, with carved teakwood chairs and a large glass coffee table supported by nothing less than an aquarium, bejewelled with tiny fish caught in the river far below.

'Don't think that you are going to sit here on your arse playing a bloody banjo all day,' he said. 'You've got a job to do. *Agreed* to it – I don't want that forgotten!'

It was never forgotten, and there was never time to 'play a bloody banjo' all day, whatever that may have meant, because quite apart from the newspaper, which took up a great deal of time, the drawing of new maps of the town and surrounding area, pin-pointing from the air photographs gun emplacements, road-blocks, tank-traps, and so on, the 'extremists' saw to it that we were fully occupied by what were euphemistically known as 'incidents'.

They were not particularly agreeable affairs.

The Chinese suffered the most at first: their villages were put to the torch with sickening regularity, their people massacred without pity. The indolent, easy-going Indonesians were blind with hatred and bitter, bigoted vengeance towards their more industrious, and therefore more prosperous, neighbours, and burnt and pillaged without restraint.

Through blazing *kampongs*, in the scorching heat from burning bamboo and rattan, among bodies hacked to bits and left to roast and blister in fiery embers, the General and his staff walked in impotent anger. He grew progressively infuriated – I grew progressively more sickened by the sweet stench of decay and roasting flesh which clung to one's hair and clothing and which not even constant washing or bathing would eliminate. But there was little that we could ever do: the 'extremists' melted like wraiths into the sheltering landscape as the victors.

Once I saw what, at first, I took to be the body of a child lying in the swirling smoke and drifting ashes. It moved slightly, a limb twitched, an almost shapeless huddle attempted desperately to rise.

Not a child. A large cat chained to a flaming bamboo post, half dead, but clearly also partly alive. I took it back to the pavilion where, swaddled in bandages, it slowly recovered, nursed by myself and an amused, if reluctant, Goa, until one day, when the bandages were finally removed, a strange beast of extreme beauty stood weakly before us. Not a domestic cat this, a much larger creature with new-growing fur, like a lynx, tufts to its ears, and pads and claws of considerable size.

For some reason, which now I do not remember, it was named 'Ursula'. Although it was quite distinctly male. Although I have forgotten why we named it so absurdly, I did remember a giant ginger cat crucified to a garden fence, when I had seen pain and distress on a human face for the first time. I was to see it again and again in this strange, wasteful and vicious war.

After the Chinese it was the turn of the wretched Dutch colonials. Some, just released from the camps, imprudently made their way back to their homes in the outlying suburbs, trying with what remained of their looted belongings to restart their lives, only to lose them in acts of hysterical hatred and violence.

In a small villa, standing in what had once been a neat garden plot, smothered in a rampant, florid Dorothy Perkins rose, with a stubby palm standing in a circular grass-bed before two ugly little bow windows, just like any other suburban house in Eindhoven or Deventer, two elderly people lay sprawled in their blood, hacked to death by knives and machetes. The woman was lying in the kitchen, on her back, faded blue eyes staring wide with terror, a flowered skirt pulled high above thighs the colour of cold boiled macaroni, mottled with bruises and sores. She had put up a desperate fight, her hands shredded by the knives, her blood sprayed in elegant arcs across the tiled walls. The man lay face downwards in the sitting room, his balding head almost severed from his body, among a tumble of chairs, broken china and scattered gramophone records.

Above us the roof was burning, tiles cracked and exploded in the heat, and printed in crude capital letters across the damp-paper-peeling wall the jeering words: 'TIRENT IMPERLIST!'

The familiar, mindless slogan which was repeated wherever we came across an 'extremist incident' of this type.

This was to be the last of the many events of its kind I was to see: it was in fact the last straw for General Hawthorn.

Three days later an assault was launched on the hill-top estate of Lembang, which fell without very much resistance, and not long after the whole area south of the railway, which had harboured the main body of the 'extremist' group, and their guns and mortars, was cleared. The airfield was secured, and gradually some semblance of law and order was restored to the besieged town and a tremulous normality began to spread.

Shops and restaurants cautiously opened on Bragaweg, the main boulevard among the rubble and ruins of the buildings which had suffered during the bombing and shelling, and people began to start the job of clearing up. The internees, drawn, haggard, at the edge of starvation, were flown out to Batavia, and although there were still furious clashes in the villages along the main convoy route the town gradually eased back to an almost peacetime calm. I no longer slept with my revolver like a comforting, if angular, teddy bear, but kept it close at all times.

The peak had been reached, the levelling out began slowly, things began spilling away, bit by bit.

Little things at first.

Goa was stricken and lay moaning on his bed in the garage of the pavilion with a high fever.

Appendicitis was diagnosed and he was hurried to casualty and replaced by a grim, unsmiling, unspeaking Gurkha called Kim, who found being a 'servant', even to the General's ADC, much below his dignity. He made it perfectly clear, from the start, that all he intended to do was to call me at 5.30

a.m. with a mug of tea, roll up my mosquito net, pull up the bed, clean any boots or belts or cap badges, and clear off.

Until the next day, when the same routine took place. In silence.

I took my meals down in 'A' Mess, the pavilion began to lose its attractions under fine coatings of dust, the fish died in the aquarium, the water became as thick as asparagus soup, and Ursula got fed only because I managed to scrounge bits and pieces from the Mess cooks.

My interpreter-secretary, Harri, complained daily that the place was beginning to show distinct signs of neglect.

'I haven't time to *dust* bloody furniture!'

'Well, give me something to do it with and I'll try. And we must throw the dead fish away, they smell.'

Harri was ravishingly beautiful: long legs, long hair, long neck – a sort of Modigliani creature; she detested housework and wasn't very good at it anyway.

'How long does it *take* to have an appendicitis?'

'Oh, I don't know. About three weeks . . . something like that.'

'Perhaps you ought to move back to "A" Mess . . . until Goa is better? Ummmm?'

'I can't take Ursula to "A" Mess, for God's sake!'

'So you keep in this place, this silly place, just for a wild cat?'

'I *like* this silly place; I *like* to be on my own. Not in "A" Mess.'

'You could be murdered by extremists, they can get into this house easily, all on one floor. Aren't you afraid?'

'Yes.'

'Well!'

'I stay here. I like it here. The grounds are patrolled day and night, and things are quiet now.'

She would begin humming under her breath, a sure sign of irritation, tossing her hair over her shoulders, thumping the cushions on the teakwood chairs with such force that dust spiralled up in clouds to resettle gently on the furniture which she had already made a brave attempt at dusting.

'Things are changing. You will see,' she said.

'What things are changing?'

'Ah ha! Things. You should look carefully. People are going away; new people are coming. The white-faces from Holland, the new boys. Soon you will all go, back on your repatriation, the Dutch army will take over.'

'You are so bloody sure! I suppose you've seen it all written in your loony old Tarot cards . . . '

'Oh! You are in a mood. I hate you in a mood. You are impolite. I will not speak to you while you are in your mood. You cannot see what is evident.'

But I could see. And I had seen; and the fact that she was reminding me that we would all be leaving disturbed and distressed me: I had no wish to leave.

And so we bickered, like any other couple who have become physically and mentally close to each other, affectionately aware of each other's frailties and weaknesses. I had, for some time, convinced myself that I was deeply, permanently and irrevocably in love with her.

She put this notion of mine carefully aside, refusing to acknowledge it, accepting it merely as an emotional reflex which every man suffered during a war. She never for one moment, I know, took me as seriously as I took myself. She would smile shyly, shaking her head slowly from side to side as if she had heard it all long ago and many times, that she found it touching but just a little wearying.

However, she always listened to me tolerantly and let me argue: with myself. I knew hardly anything about her, for she never offered information about herself or her past life. I knew only fragments which, like stalks of corn in a harvest field, I gleaned diligently.

But they didn't amount so much: I couldn't have made a quarter of a loaf from them. She once said that she was 'diluted Dutch', and when I pressed her, in laughter, for an explanation she flushed and said that she had a maternal grandmother who was Indonesian but a 'pure Dutch father: he was tall and very fine to look at'. Although this combination gave her great elegance and grace I knew, instinctively, that it distressed her profoundly.

I didn't even know exactly where she lived, or if her family had survived the Occupation. From some scattered corn-stalks I deduced that they had not; but I never asked, and she refused to speak more of them. I knew that she had a 'pleasant room with a nice Chinese family' in the Chinese Quarter but I was never allowed to go there with her, and when I dropped her off from work sometimes, at her insistence it was always vaguely some streets away from the house where she lived. She was determined to keep her private life apart from her life with me, and the Division. Harri was a 'loner' in every way. Something which I understood perfectly.

'You tell me that you do not like to be possessed, or to possess! Neither do I. So that is why we are beautifully matched. We understand each other very well,' she said.

But sometimes I was not altogether certain that we did.

'People, you know, Pip, always want to know too much about each other, and when they do, then they get bored with them and throw them away like an apple core. Finished! It is much more *enviable* to be like us; isn't it?'

I would agree because I was unable always to follow her logic. Her attitude to me, as the months went by, was at all times generous, loving, warm, lightly mocking, affectionate, sometimes half impatient, half amused, but always tolerant of my gaucheness and my sudden enormous leaps of enthusiasm or deep plunges into black depressions.

She managed me very well, and we laughed together, and, more important perhaps, we were capable of spending long periods of time with each other in complete, comforting silence, without need of speech.

A contentment.

Sometimes she would sit hunched forward, her elbows on her knees, chin in her hands, hair tumbled across her eyes any old way, looking unblinkingly into space. And when I asked her where she had 'gone' to, or of what she was thinking, she would suddenly laugh, as if caught hiding, pull her hair behind her shoulders, and shrug.

'Oh. Thinking. Thinking of a million things.'

'Was I among them? The million things?'

'No! Goodness no! Sea shells. Sea shells on a beach that I know. Thousands of tiny shells, the sand so white, the water so clear, little fishes darting like arrowheads, so swift, so sure. No pain anywhere, no fear. All peace.'

'I know those shells.'

'You do? So many different kinds.'

'Some like emerald snails? Like vermilion fans? Like long cases to keep your spectacles in? I know, I had some once in a basket, it was made of palm leaves.'

'From where?'

'From here. Somewhere near here. When I was very small.'

'Pink shells, tiny as the nails on the hand of a new-born baby, delicate, small as small, transparent; starting to die.'

'To die?'

'A new-born baby commences to die from the moment that it leaves the womb, didn't you know that? We are only alive in the womb. When we leave it we begin the process of death.'

I would laugh because I didn't, then, comprehend what she meant, and she would laugh with me, to oblige my ignorance.

'You are mad, woman!'

'I am mad, yes. How good! Mad people are sometimes happy, I think.' And she would fall silent once more, thinking again. Back to her shells.

I was intrigued by these silences, by her laughter which was rich and full-throated with delight, and which did not arrive often. I liked her distance, her reticence, her sense of the idiotic and ridiculous; her mischievous grins which, I knew, would never be explained to me. Above all, perhaps, I admired, as well as loved, her coolness and her bravery, for we had been caught together in ugly situations from time to time during the worst of the shelling and she never faltered in her courage.

She spoke perfect English, French and Malayan and, because she had been a prisoner of the Japanese (shut in a lightless cell for one year as a punishment for some 'conduct which was anti-Nippon' as she said), she also spoke a little of their hideous tongue.

Unlike Nan she never, at any time, spoke of a future: as far as she was concerned there was no future, only the present, living moment. There was certainly to be no future for us: Harri was not, by any manner of means, a 'broody'. She had absolutely no intention of nesting anywhere, and certainly not in England.

'I would die there! My goodness me, yes! I would *die*, you know. And you would have to see me wearing shoes and stockings and terrible big coats; maybe even a hat! And you would be very bored of me, you know, because I would be weeping and sighing for this high blue sky, for the scent of spices, for the millions of shells on my white sand. And I would always have a cold, which would be very unattractive.' I let her chatter away, for I was quietly convinced that when the time came, the ultimate moment of choice, to stay or to come away, she would come with me.

I may have a modest ego, but it has a loud voice.

In this instance, however, it did not prevail.

When the time came, the ultimate choice, she was far more stubborn than I, partly because she knew exactly what she wanted from life and I, at that time a newly minted twenty-five, did not.

In any case, I lost out.

A letter to my father: Batavia, 24 June 1946.

. . . only hope that this reaches you in time to cancel the Air Mail Edition [of *The Times*, which he had sent me weekly]. I shall be on my way back to the UK in a matter of weeks now, end of August certainly, and the OM [the General] is on his way back for some conferences at the WO [War Office] so there won't be anyone left here to appreciate the paper! The other chaps, in any case, riffle through it and *only* read the bloody Sports pages!

I know that I should be feeling elated and terrifically happy at the thought of coming back, like the others here, but, frankly, I rather dread it. I'm not being the ungrateful son, believe me! I long to see you and Ma again, but I have got terribly habituated to this sort of life, Army life I mean, and especially with this Division.

But there we are. We all pull out of here in November, I gather, for the job is done and there seems to be no need for us now: India is being handed back to the Indians and I expect after that they'll *all* start clamouring for Independence, just as they did here: so there won't be any need of the Army because there won't be an Empire to run. We'll feel the draught when the time comes! The sun is really setting! God knows what I'll do in UK. It's a gloomy prospect, but there is no point in trying to hang on in the Army as I thought. But what do ex-Officers DO? No one wants to bother about ex-Service people, once we've won the blasted battles for the stay-at-homes they forget all about us. Look what they've done to Churchill, for God's sake! Surely the most dishonourable, ungrateful, behaviour ever given to a Leader. There is still the prospect of that prep-school in Surrey that X suggested I might go to, but I really don't think I'm up to being a teacher yet! I've only just started learning myself.

I won't, by the way, be bringing the cat with me. Which may or may not be a relief to you all! He was ready to be brought down from Bandoeng last week, but got wind of the cage I had had built for him, and jumped through the windows and sat staring at me balefully from a safe distance. They eventually caught him, bribed him with a chicken, got him caged safely to bring him down on the Rear Convoy (I had to fly down here) but they ran into an ambush fifty miles from here and in the banging and crashing he managed to escape and fled into the forest.

So that is that. I mind very much: but perhaps it is better that he returns to the wild, as long as some gun-happy Indo doesn't shoot him for 'sport'. Oh well . . . Batavia is hot and noisy, changed a lot in the months: it's heaving with traffic and people, and is almost back to normal. There are even tea-dances at the Hotel des Indes with 'dancing to The Pickler Brothers Dance Band'! Dear God . . .

I never mentioned Harri, it seems in the letters that have survived from that time. Not a whisper of her name.

A week or so before I was due to sail to Singapore she just disappeared, and, although I eventually managed to trace the exact house in the Chinese Quarter where she had her room, no one would admit that she had existed, or that they could speak English. They nodded and smiled, arms folded, impassive faces shaded by their wide coolie hats. I couldn't very well storm the house, and all the shutters were tightly closed. The place seemed deserted, the gate into the bamboo-fenced yard wired up. So I left.

The day before I was due to sail, clearing up the office, taking down the maps and emptying the files, I discovered, set at the far edge of my desk, a blue cut-glass bowl which I had never seen before. It wasn't very big, just big enough to hold three vivid sunflower heads.

There was a folded note stuck under the base; it read:

'These two colours go well together. Adieu.'

'Adieu' sounds far more final than 'Goodbye'.

A farewell party was given for me in 'A' Mess that evening; a lot of farewell parties were taking place in those days, for men were beginning to gather like October swallows, awaiting repatriation and the long, happy voyage home. I got pretty drunk on Japanese White Horse whiskey sitting in a deep, plush armchair under a pepper tree in the garden.

We had stripped out the main rooms of the house to make more room for the dancing. The garden, in consequence, looked like a village fête jumble sale. I sat maundering away under red and orange fairy-lights strung in the trees, and bored everyone witless who would listen to my sad story about being the odd man out and not wanting to go home at all, but to stay on. Naturally everyone thought I was as high as a kite, which I almost was, and took no notice.

I moaned away to myself in sullen despair, the 'loner' suddenly alone in a crowd.

The laughter and the scratchy music from the wind-up gramophone only compounded my misery. I was sober enough to realize that the evening was almost over-happy, that people were laughing and talking with an edge of hysteria to their voices: an hysteria born of relief that the end was in sight, that the fighting had stopped (as far as they were concerned anyway), that a new life was about to begin – and they had got through.

Some were taking their new wives with them; laughing, sparkling-eyed girls who had worked for us in the offices at HQ, but who had only the vaguest idea of what England or Europe might be like, and who would have to face the grey north, and new habits and customs in places like Swindon, Manchester, Macclesfield or Croydon. I didn't, at that moment, envy them.

No high blue skies there. No scent of spices. No million little shells scattered along the white sandy beaches . . .

A group of three came wandering towards me, arms round each other's necks, glasses in unsteady hands; they stood swaying cheerfully, their voices unmatched, unsteady, loud with drunken happiness.

> 'Oh! *When* there isn't a girl about,
> You do feel lonely . . .
> When there isn't a girl about,
> You're on your only . . .
> Absolutely on the shelf with
> Nothing to do but play with yourself . . . '

One of them leant forward and patted my head, I ducked his hands, and they laughed, turned and roared back into the dancers . . .

> 'When there isn't a girl . . . AROOOOUND!'

We sailed in the *Oranje* for Singapore on the evening tide. I was completely sober by that time, but wore dark glasses to conceal the massive hangover which was still apparent in the hoops of mourning under my eyes.

I had said an unsteady, almost gruff, farewell to the General earlier in the day, and was wretched as he himself seemed to be.

'Did a good job, Pip, thanks. I put you through it rather, didn't I? But you came through damned well . . . really very grateful. Good luck.'

I had saluted, about-turned, left his room.

Standing at the foot of the gangplank, saying a last farewell to those who had come down to send me off, we talked lamely together; the usual useless words used at departures.

'Give my love to the Albert Memorial when you see it, if *it's* still there, eh?'

'Be on my way in a month. If you would just telephone Suzanna when you get time? I did give you the number?'

'Yes . . . you did.'

'You have got it? Speedwell 2345?'

'Got it, Bobbie.'

I looked past the jostling soldiers, sailors in their whites, the hurrying, laughing girls in batik sarongs, calling and waving up at people on the upper decks.

Gulls swung and swooped about the ship.

She might, possibly, have come down.

Perhaps standing quietly in the shadows by the go-downs?

She'd be bound to wave, if she was there.

But I saw no sudden turn of a familiar head, no long hair swinging in the evening light, no white shirt, no grey cotton skirt – her 'uniform' almost – no slender arm raised in farewell.

I shook hands all round, turned to mount the gangplank. Then I saw Goa.

A postcard to my father dated Singapore, 2 September 1946.

This is THE Raffles. Need I say more? When I get home and have my letters published (!) I shall use this as an illustration. Off to lunch with some old friends I re-met here. It's torrid, dull, I am hotter than a snowball in hell. Must away to have a shower. Have only been able to draw $\frac{1}{4}$ of my month's pay! So you'll have to forget silk and gold, all I can possibly bring back as a present is myself! I'm awfully sorry . . .

Seven weeks later, in the fog on Guildford station, it was all over.

The mist drifted, veered, wavered. Up the line a blurred pink light changed suddenly to wan green.

A splot of colour on grey, damp paper.

The London train was due.

PART THREE

SEVEN

In New York, yesterday's snow hillocked down the length of Park Avenue in varying shades of soot, charcoal and pewter. The sky was zinc-coloured, when you could see it, the giant buildings melting into low cloud and a heavy flurry of fresh snow.

The doorman heaved the last of our baggage into the trunk of the car, slammed it, accepted my ten-dollar bill, and, turning away, said: 'Have a nice day.' I almost thanked him. But remembered that the phrase was as impersonal and uncaring as a belch.

At Kennedy Airport the — Building was high, spacious, surgically clean, almost empty at this early hour in the morning. Cold, functional; glass and cement. A candy store with journals and Snoopy toys, a self-service restaurant, the check-in desks, two signs baldly marked 'Men' and 'Women'.

No social niceties here. From the shoulder.

The check-in clerk was polite, efficient, middle-aged and smiling. He arranged a window seat, stowed the bags, handed me the boarding cards.

'Super-Executive Service,' he said admiringly, as if I had made it socially or won a cup. 'You go right up there, along to that gallery, you see? Then you ring the bell at the door of the Super-Executive Class lounge and they'll take real good care of you, so have a nice day, now.'

Two tall steel doors set into a steel wall. A tiny, discreet bell at the side. I pressed it and the doors opened silently into a cavern of simulated leather armchairs, each attached to a telephone for the last-minute business calls executives always make, a jungle of glossy green plants, a small bar already, even at 8.30 a.m., in full swing, a mixed smell of hot coffee and Bloody Marys. There was a scatter of elegant women in New York black; inelegant men in shirt sleeves, braces yanking up plaid trousers two inches above their shoes.

Bells were ringing, deals were made, a woman took a crushed Yorkshire terrier from a bag, rearranged its bow, kissed it, stuck it back again.

At a small reception desk beside the doors, an obese woman in a careful wig, net-covered and sparkling with rhinestones, was stapling papers.

'Your Cards, please.' She didn't look up through her lozenge-shaped glasses. I offered the boarding cards and our tickets.

'I said Cards,' she said with a flick of impatience and began dialling a number on one of the telephones squatting before her like a hatching of multicoloured toads.

'What card? I'm sorry . . . '

'Super-Executive Class. Helen? Helen, honey, do you have news yet on Mrs Aronovich? She didn't show yet? Oh. You don't? Well, maybe she didn't make it, the snow, traffic . . . I'll get back to you.'

'I'm afraid I haven't got a Super-Executive Card,' I said.

The obese woman replaced her receiver patiently. 'Then you can't come in here. You do not have the right.'

'But I'm *flying* Super-Executive Class. The check-in clerk told me . . . '

'That's not my problem, what the clerk told you. If you don't have the Card you don't belong here.' She was busy looking through a list of numbers in a notebook. 'You haven't done the mileage. Right?' She started to dial briskly. 'It stands to reason. Okay? Oh, Joanne? Joanne, don't bother about Mrs Aronovich. If she makes it just before we board that'll be just fine. Sure, I'll take care of her. If she checks in with you before I see her, call me? Sure thing . . . '

She hung up; and looked at me; for the first time. 'I'm sorry. You don't have our Card, so you don't have the mileage.' She took a pencil and scratched the back of her head under the wig, then folded her hands together like a pair of stuffed gloves. 'If you want to stay here it'll be eighty-five dollars. That's the fee. Right?'

I began to collect my hand baggage, my manager, Forwood, lifted the briefcase and his coat. The woman picked up the telephone again and started to dial with the pencil.

'Have a nice day,' she said.

Down in self-service, among the glitter of stainless steel and cellophaned packets, we sat at a long empty table, bare save for a bottle of ketchup and a jar of mustard, drinking weak coffee in half-pint paper cups. The only other people present in this impersonal, lifeless, sterile world sat across the way; they were elderly, tired. The woman wore a shabby cloth coat and a brown woollen hat like an inverted pudding basin. She wept quietly into a paper handkerchief.

The man, huddled in a crumpled raincoat, touched her hand from time to time across the table, murmuring to her in a pleading voice in Polish. She kept shaking her head, wiping her eyes, staring blearily at an unopened plastic-wrapped sandwich on the table before her.

It was a sorry change from yesterday's splendour of the flight from Paris on Concorde.

But that was already a different world; and very far away.

On board a squad of hostesses waiting to greet one. Cosmetic smiles, severely cut uniforms, double-breasted jackets, skirts shiny at the seats, crisp collars and ties. A bevy of minor matrons. Name-badges over the heart informed one that we had a 'Margie', a 'Barbie', a 'Tracey' and a 'Cindy', who was, she assured me while taking my coat, 'All yours for the trip; hope it makes you happy?'

The shabby suburbs of New York swung away and tilted far below, rapidly lost to sight in low cloud and flurries of driving snow.

'And now,' said Cindy, handing me a fairly grubby card, 'here's the lunch menu. You take a look at it and I'll be right back . . . '

The lunch menu had *Dinner* printed quite distinctly at the top. Not a bad one either: Hors-d'Oeuvres, Cornish Game Hen and Wild Rice, a Maine Lobster, Prime Beef 'Texan Style'. A comforting wine list: Château-Lafite, a white Bordeaux, Moët et Chandon.

It would do, I thought. At the bottom of the card there was a small print of the Arc de Triomphe. Beneath this, elegant script suggested that '*When In Paris, It's "The Holland-House-Hotel"! Right In The Heart Of The City Of Light!*'

The date in the far right-hand corner was three days before.

'I have a distinct feeling,' I said to Forwood, 'that we are presently returning to France.'

He looked over the top of his glasses. 'Why?'

'It's the 16th today, but this menu is for the dinner on the 13th.'

'Ohmygod!' cried Cindy. 'They screwed it! This is the Eastern flight menu for Paris, France. We're Domestic today!'

A fuss of blue-clad women hit the Super-Executive cabin like a hockey team without sticks. Suddenly a butch lady, who could quite possibly have been the referee, broke away from the menu-retrieving throng and pushed her way up the aisle swinging a narrow basket holding three upright bottles. The sign over her left breast stated that she was 'Mary-Jo'.

'Red,' she announced, handing me a plastic beaker. 'Or do you want the white, or the champagne?' From the shoulder all right.

I asked for champagne: it was warm, sweet and Californian. I took a careful look at the bottles while she filled Forwood's beaker.

'You know, this isn't *French*? You really shouldn't call it champagne,' I said with residual charm.

'We do *here*,' she replied. Without any.

'It might be wiser not to argue,' said Forwood quietly. 'I'd do it their way, or else they'll get annoyed. When in Rome . . . '

'I wish to God I were.'

Somewhere over Maryland the menus got sorted out and Cindy spent much of her time on her knees before two gentlemen in the seats in front of us. She was being very attentive – she had no option, as neither of her passengers could speak, or read, a word of English and came, it would appear, from Korea or Vietnam. Or maybe just Hong Kong.

The nodding heads, the flashing gold in the teeth, the smooth, flat Piaget watches on each immaculately cuffed wrist, eyes slitted by the fixed smile, gave them away as the Inscrutable East. And rich with it. Unhappily they decided, with many a nod and a leer, to have 'Prime Rib of Beef Carved Before You', which meant that Cindy had to crouch on the floor with a knife and fork and a chunk of meat on a wooden board, hacking away and muttering 'goddammits' each time a piece of Prime Rib slid to the blue nylon carpet. She stood before me a few moments later, wiping her hands on a cloth.

'You want the Appetizer, right?'

I didn't, particularly. I wasn't even hungry, but I had been so overwhelmed by her performance with the Prime Rib that I agreed meekly.

Not to do so seemed churlish.

It was, when it arrived and was set on the pull-down table, a small roll of rubbery substance in a diluted tomato sauce; it swung idly around in its plastic bowl like a specimen in medical class.

It had no recognizable taste whatsoever; Forwood watched me curiously without touching his.

'So? Can you cut it?'

'Just. I think it's fish. There is a faint, lingering flavour of synthetic fish, nothing more. Perhaps formaldehyde . . . '

Forwood placed his fork on the little table beside his untouched dish. 'Never eat fish of any kind on a flight. Imagine two hundred people with diarrhoea.'

I imagined them and ate no more.

'Fish!' Cindy was wide-eyed with surprise. 'What do you mean, fish?'

'Well . . . that's what it tasted like. I don't think I'll bother.'

She took up the soiled menu and read it rapidly. 'The Appetizer is chicken. It says so, right here. Chicken.'

'Quite the fishiest chicken I've ever eaten.'

She looked at me with hostility. 'You're funny!' she said, collected the two dishes, and went away.

I didn't see her again, at least not with food, which was probably just as well. If I did happen to catch her eye during the flight, she turned quickly away with a toss of her head. An insulted hostess, who had been 'all yours for the trip', cruelly rebuffed.

Mary-Jo eased past me a couple of times, doing her best to ignore me, but failing when confronted with my outstretched arm and the plastic beaker thrust almost into her stomach. She refilled my beaker reluctantly each time, but did her best, like Cindy, to keep her distance, and if it hadn't been for the Koreans, or whatever they were, in the seats in front I'd very likely have crossed America parched as well as starved. They drank like desert survivors.

The heart of the Middle West lay 35,000 feet below us, stretching away into a haze of light and infinity. It lay as chequered and as flat as a giant's tablecloth: not a curve, not a wood or forest, no winding river, no hedgerows, no irregularity – everything at right angles, with, here and there, a small cluster of buildings round a farm, a tree for shade, drowning in an immensity of space.

It was clear to see that the people who lived in this vast area of land and sky could never adjust to confinement of any kind: during the war American prisoners from this wide land curled up in their prison camp bunks, their faces to the walls, and died in sleep. One understood perfectly well why: the lack of space, of sky and wind, of distance, did the killing.

But even from so many thousand feet above, the monotony appalled one; there were hours and hours of it to cover before Kansas gave way to Colorado.

Across the aisle a tall, balding man sat bolt upright, fists clenched, safety-belt buckled, stiff with apprehension, still wearing his galoshes which he had omitted to, or dared not, remove. He had been in this state ever since take-off, during which he uttered high piercing cries, like those of a bird trapped in a net, his eyes tightly shut. He watched the activity in the cabin with glazed terror, wincing in anguish at the smell of the food, the pouring of Mary-Jo's bottles, at the masticating gentlemen from Korea eating their Prime Ribs with the relish of starving cannibals; and now and again, exhausted by the smells and sights around him, he stifled moans of despair, and stared ahead of him at the back of the seat in front, but he never once relaxed his clenched fists or slumped into exhausted repose. During the whole length of the dire in-flight movie he, very sensibly, looked at his knees, occasionally closing his eyes in misery.

As we began to reach the two hundred square miles of housing density which constitutes the city of Los Angeles, he suddenly made a surprising, and desperate, lunge towards Mary-Jo, fumbled for a plastic beaker, and indicated, with animal grunts of distress, his need for refreshment.

'You want red, white or the champagne?' said Mary-Jo, but he rolled his eyes in agony, so she shrugged and filled his glass, and turned to me, the empty bottle clasped by its neck in her strong fist like a hanged cat.

'You want to see this label, real good? Napa Valley C-H-A-M-P-A-G-N-E from California. It is the greatest place in the whole wide world for wine, just let me tell you. We even shipped our vines right across to you Europeans when yours all got the pest: right? We saved Europe one more time. So when you lift a glass of your fancy stuff over there, just you remember that it is *Californian* wine you are drinking.' She dumped the empty bottle into the basket.

'I'll remember,' I said.

'You just do that,' said Mary-Jo triumphantly, and stamped down to the galley.

'There seem to be some contradictions in her argument,' said Forwood. 'But let it pass, we're coming in to land, I think.'

Below, the scrubby desert, grey-pink in the afternoon sun, began to disappear under the hideous agglomeration of back-to-back ticky-tacky houses each with its own blue square, rectangular, oval, kidney or circular shaped swimming-pool.

The 'Fasten Seat Belts' sign flashed up. The man across the aisle groaned, let his plastic beaker fall from a now nerveless hand; his chin sank to his chest, his eyes closed.

The two Koreans looked intently at their Piaget watches, compared times, nodded approvingly: we began our slow descent to International Airport.

The Call from the Coast.

For millions upon millions of actors, singers, dancers, musicians and anyone even remotely concerned with entertainment, or having the least pretensions to being in Show Business, the Call to Hollywood is the burning, enduring dream. From New York to Tacoma, from London to Paris, Berlin, Amsterdam, perhaps even Moscow and Leningrad, certainly, as I know, in Bombay and Sydney, they wait: longingly, yearningly.

Even my own mother, in the year that she was married, heard the Call for which she had waited so long, only to be forced to let it go unheeded when, packing with alacrity, she was halted in euphoria by a bewildered, and extremely stubborn, husband. Her heart was broken, and the searing wound of disappointment never fully healed; she carried the scar all her life, and we, as her family, endured it for all of ours.

Once upon a time(I don't know if they still stand today), there were rows of wooden posts all along the beach from Santa Monica to Malibu, each with a telephone attached, so that out-of-work actors lying supine in the smoggy sun might call 'in' to their agents to see if the great moment had arrived for them, or pray hourly that the post might ring with the Call.

I never heard that it did.

Hollywood, where after all the commercial cinema began in a barn in an orange orchard on a dusty road which became Sunset Boulevard, the street of dreams and shattered illusions, is still the Mecca for actors all over the world. The dream is absolute, it is almost never lost; the tragedy being that while some *are* called, very, very few are chosen.

Yet the myth persists. Fame and fortune, in that order, lie at every corner, on every street and parking-lot, in every drug-store or greasy-spoon 'Ethnic' restaurant.

They know, with blinding faith, that one day the Call will come; they are certain that they will be ready to take it, and after that the rest will be plain sailing. Patience and determination will pay off with their name in lights, a star on the door of the dressing-room, a swimming-pool and servants, a Cadillac, furs, orchids, Dom Perignon for breakfast, their name in the papers, adulation in the streets, and as much cocaine as they can possibly sniff.

They know, without any doubt, that it has happened before: a ruby has been found in the mud, diamonds in the shale, gold in the desert – why, then, should it not happen for them? The player is admirable in his optimism, courage and tenacity. And of course it *has* happened – someone has been 'spotted' on a bar stool, washing down a car, driving a truck, crossing the screen in a crowd scene, selling shirts in a department store – certainly it has happened, or happened *once*; so it can happen again.

What is forgotten, or overlooked, is that when they do reach the mountain peak of fame and glory, it is the staying there which is the toughest part: it tears the nails, breaks the back, destroys the soul, empties the bottles, kills illusion, and can finally erase the last shreds of reality and personal dignity. The slide down is bitter, and no one waves goodbye for there are thousands eagerly waiting to take the vacated seat, and in the hysteria of the rush the loser is crushed by the weight of numbers, callous with ambition. Some, a lucky few, manage to survive – but it is a brutal, often dishonourable, battle.

At the end of the war with Japan, Hollywood came 'shopping' to replenish its local talent with fresh blood from Europe. Britain was the main market-place because of the language. Conveniently, people spoke English. In a short time Hollywood and its major studios stripped the British studios of many of their top players.

James Mason, Deborah Kerr, Stewart Granger, Jean Simmons, Michael Wilding and others found that the Call was irresistible.

After years of wartime privations they were ready and eager to bask in the sun, to dive into the swimming-pools, to accept the vast salaries offered, to enjoy the peace and the plenty of California, not to mention the vigorous, exciting, highly skilled industry which had exploded with astonishing power during the years of war and had cornered the world market – now their talents would be spread far and wide, not just confined to a weary, battered, strike-torn Britain sliding into socialism and bleak with continuing restrictions.

Who could possibly blame them? Mecca had never beckoned so enticingly, nor so successfully.

So they left, but in leaving they made space for newcomers to fill.

I was one of the lucky ones.

The Call first came for me early in 1947 when I least expected it. I had no yearnings in that direction and hadn't even considered that it might be a fact of life.

What was a fact of life at the time was that I still owed the army some eight hundred pounds in back-pay, and hadn't the least hope of paying the debt. I had managed to secure a few jobs in television, at that time just starting up again after the war, and eager to employ anyone who would work. The pay then, as now, was not going to make me rich, but it did enable me to put down a deposit for the rent of a one-room flat in Hasker Street, and with all my wealth contained in a large Oxo tin, my demob suit kept ready for 'interviews' (the trousers pressed nightly beneath my mattress), and on a steady diet of Weetabix and Kraft cheese I was beginning to face up to the realities of peacetime.

Without, it must be confessed, a great deal of enthusiasm.

However, owing to one appearance in a television play I was approached by a major Hollywood studio, at that time 'shopping' among the left-overs in London, and told by a bird-like, bright-eyed, tough middle-aged woman that the 'world could be your oyster', as she put it graphically, on the one condition that I placed myself entirely in their hands and worked myself to death. If I signed the contract which she had before her on her desk in a splendid office on Piccadilly, I would be required to move – directly to Mexico, or perhaps it was New Mexico, I wasn't certain then and still am not, where I would learn Spanish. After three years 'under wraps' and, presumably, with a perfect knowledge of the language, I would be 'reimported to the States' under the name of Roderigo Something-or-other, given a house in Pacific Palisades and a car (I remember that this was to be a Volkswagen to emphasize my foreignness), and gradually, through small parts at first, I would be 'built into a major star . . . if only you let us do the whole construction deal, and give us your trust. We *know*; don't forget that . . . we've been building stars since Noah left the ark.'

'Who would I be in the end?' I remember asking.

'Our major import from South America. We've got English, French and a German, and a South American is important for that particular market.'

'What *part* of South America?'

She looked irritated suddenly. 'I don't know what *part*. How do I know?

That's not my job. My job is to get you signed. I guess it depends on the kind of accent you acquire. But you get to speak Spanish: not Portuguese, that's a no-go market . . . we stick with Spanish.'

'And what else?'

'Well . . . ' She looked suddenly shy, for the first time, tapped her writing-pad with a pen, smoothed out the 'regular, seven years plus options contract' awaiting my signature. 'Well, we have to see how it goes, right? If you make the grade; what impact you have on screen. We have ways of finding that out, naturally. *If* you make the grade. If you *are* star potential for an audience in, say, San Diego or maybe even in Dallas, if they like the "sneaks" we'll screen, we'll really go to town.' She looked up at me, her black eyes slightly hooded.

'And then what?' I said.

'Then you get married. You'll see the contract list of the girls we have and all you have to do is pick the one you really like and we'll fix the rest.'

'Oh.'

The hooded eyes suddenly opened wide with a glint of panic. 'You aren't *already* married?'

'No.'

'That's great. Fancy-free.' She sat back in relief.

I tried to explain, as politely as I could, that I did not wish to go and live in Mexico or even in New Mexico, I didn't want to learn Spanish, be 'under wraps' for three years, or marry a lady on the studio contract list.

'Listen.' She picked up the contract, struck it crossly with the back of her hand. 'This is a great opportunity for you! We have literally queues of people waiting for this chance – thousands. The studio takes all the risks, not you! We pay you all the time you are studying, we pay you *all the time*! You can have the world if you want it. As long as everything works out right. The marriage doesn't have to bother you one bit. It's routine, that's all. You get to choose the girl, we have a slow build-up of publicity, then a fun marriage and lots of publicity, so you get well covered world-wide – maybe you could even go to Europe for the honeymoon . . . and that's all. Nothing to it.'

'But it's still marriage.'

'Sure it's marriage. We are an honourable studio, for God's sake! But you don't have to stay married, you can split after a year or two . . . if that's the way it goes, you just have to put a face on things. Think of Louella and Hedda! Think of the gossip if you were single! You'd be ruined, so would the studio. It would lose you, the money, the *time* and its reputation. You want that?'

'I don't want any of it.'

'But what have you got to lose?' she said in exasperation. 'Who are you, anyway?'

Who indeed?

An out-of-work, 26-year-old ex-Captain, saddled with a burdensome debt for having had the extreme privilege of serving his country in the cause of democracy. That's who I was.

Walking through Green Park in a heavy snowfall, I realized that my demob shoes were leaking, that my feet were both wet and freezing, but also, which was far more important, that I was not about to be shipped off to Mexico, learn Spanish, drive a Volkswagen, or marry anyone on a studio list.

I had made that perfectly clear.

I was, when all was said and done, still my own master, even if the money in my Oxo tin rattled mockingly like the sound of distant maracas.

There were to be other Calls during the years which lay ahead of me, but they were ignored, except for two which proved to be minor disasters and convinced me that to be a biggish fish in a small pond was a great deal better than being a dead fish in an ocean. Each time the Call sounded I said 'No', and the money always doubled alarmingly – but I stuck to my last and made do with a more modest, but far happier, life.

However, here I presently was, coming in to land at Los Angeles for the first time in twelve years, perfectly well aware that I had heeded the Call yet again but that this time things would be different.

Why does one always think that 'this time it'll be different'? I suppose because one never finishes learning in life.

But I had considered the script with care; the star was Glenda Jackson, whom I greatly admired and with whom I wanted to work very much, the director a young and brilliant Englishman, Anthony Harvey; the money was reasonable, the time absolutely right.

January is a brutal month here on the land. Los Angeles would be no bad place to spend three weeks of the winter, it was time I heaved myself out of my comfortable rut and went out into the world again. I might even enjoy it; I was pretty sure I'd be happy: the idea of working on a good script with a superb actress pulled me out of apathy, rekindled the old excitements and challenges, filled me with eager curiosity about working in Hollywood once again now that I had reached the sensible, balanced age of sixty and could, I hoped, cope with any problems which might come my way – what, I thought, as we made a perfect touch-down and trundled along the runway, could possibly go wrong?

Plenty could – and plenty did.

Anthony Harvey sprawled comfortably on the over-stuffed settee in my hotel suite.

'*Thrilling!* That you are here at last. Really *marvellous*, quite thrilling: it all begins to feel real. Glenda won't be in for a couple of days; her father died suddenly, you knew that?'

I said that I knew that, but that I had decided not to wait about in New York but get across to California, lose my jet lag, and begin to feel my way around again.

'Marvellous! Absolutely thrilling, *thrilling*. And we are shooting the whole thing on film, not tape – so don't think of television, think of cinema! It'll be TV in the US, but a real movie in Europe and the rest of the world. We must not even consider that it's a television film. Cinema, remember it's *cinema!*'

Perhaps our very first error.

The story, at this stage called *Pat and Roald*, was the true history of the appalling tragedy which struck the writer Roald Dahl and his actress wife, Patricia Neal. During work on a film in Hollywood she had suffered a massive stroke and had become, to all intents and purposes, a vegetable.

Only Dahl's determined, desperate cajoling, bullying and fighting got her through and brought her back to life, eventually.

They had been friends and neighbours of mine when I had lived in Amersham, and when the subject had first been offered to me I immediately telephoned them to ask if they had agreed to the film being made and had accepted myself and Glenda to portray them. They were shattered that a film was to be made of their private life, but they had no option other than to let the project go ahead: a book had been written, with their permission, about the whole tragedy and thus they were, as they were firmly reminded, in the 'public domain'. The film rights of the book had been sold and they were helpless, and powerless, to stop the film.

However, they seemed relieved that Glenda and I were playing them – at least we were serious players – and Roald was reasonably pleased with Robert

Anderson's very sympathetic and un-Hollywood script: they generously gave us their blessing.

'We won't look much like you,' I told Roald. 'But at least we'll do our damnedest to honour you both and to keep any sensationalism out, that'll be our main job. But the script is good, that's why I even considered such an impertinence.'

'Don't, for God's sake, let them tart you up in Savile Row suits,' he said. 'I'm not that kind of chap . . . you know that.'

I knew that, and assured him that I would cart all my old jackets, flannels, cardigans and knitted ties out to Hollywood, and if I couldn't actually look like him (he was to begin with over a foot taller than me), I'd try to 'represent' him satisfactorily. He very kindly offered to 'jot down some things I remember from that time, things I said and did, which might help you'. And I had left for America with a fairly clear conscience.

The cardigans and knitted ties were now spread over the suite for Harvey's, and the wardrobe master's, approbation, when the telephone rang. Harvey answered it: there was a brief pause and then he erupted into roaring fury.

The room shook, the wardrobe master stood stunned, I sat crouched in a chair, stiff with alarm, the storm roared and rumbled and reached tremendous crescendos of rage. Then he slammed down the receiver, his face crimson with anger. Shaking, he crashed back on to the settee, his head buried in his hands. We waited in silence for him to recover.

'What's wrong? Glenda . . . ?'

His voice was muffled by clenched fists when he spoke. 'No. No. The script. The script. Our glorious script! It's too long!'

'Too long? How can it be too long? It's the script we all agreed to shoot, isn't it?'

'It was, it was. That was the script girl. She's just read it through with a stop-watch, timed it to the tenth of a second. It's thirty minutes too long!'

'But how *can* it be? We start in three days . . . why didn't they know that long ago? Why only today?'

'They only hired the script girl today . . . '

'How can the script girl possibly time a scene which we haven't even played yet!'

He looked up with a haggard face. 'As it stands it won't fit the time slots for the commercials, it'll run over.'

'But you said we were shooting a film . . . not a television film.'

He shook his head wearily. 'They are making cuts. Making cuts. It's too long.'

We looked at each other in despair. I knew, and Harvey and Forwood knew, exactly what this meant. We would be getting rewrites every day on pink, yellow and green pages, the script would be hacked to bits to fit the commercial breaks. Although I had never made a film for commercial television I knew perfectly well that it was far more important to sell hair-spray, shampoo, deodorants or aspirin than to sell the film, and that under these present circumstances we couldn't hope to make a main feature film at all: we would be forced by the sponsors (a new, and dreadful, word to add to our vocabularies) to bow to their selling time. All ideas of a movie, the bait on the hook which we had all so naïvely swallowed, must be set aside.

I had only been back in Hollywood for two hours and nothing, it seemed, had changed one jot since I had left it twelve years before – it was the same old place: the town of deceptions.

Forwood broke the silence which prevailed, the wardrobe master continued quietly folding away my shirts and ties.

'I think it probably *is* a bit too long. It might be good to have a few cuts . . . if they are carefully done. I shouldn't give up hope yet . . . '

'But WILL they be carefully done?' cried Harvey in despair. 'Thirty minutes is thirty minutes, a hell of a long time on the screen.'

'Well . . . ' said Forwood with his customary reasonableness. 'If they cut it about to such an extent that it is no longer the script which Dirk and Miss Jackson agreed to shoot, then they can, I imagine, pull out.'

My heart sank: more battles ahead. Perhaps I had made a dreadful mistake after all; I should have stayed quietly in France and got on with writing. I really had no appetite for any more film fun. I'd had years of that form of exhaustion.

'Let us wait until Miss Jackson gets here,' said Forwood. 'She'll have something to say about this, I feel certain.'

When Glenda eventually arrived she was far too exhausted to say anything after a gruelling flight from Birmingham, via London, directly over the Pole to Los Angeles. She came down to my suite the night that she arrived in a pink candlewick house-coat; she said it was her dressing-gown and did I mind? I didn't; and perhaps it was. Her face was white with fatigue, her eyes pulled through to the very back of her head like upholstery buttons, but all her faculties were splendidly intact. It was our very first meeting – we had never even spoken on a telephone together – and it was a miraculous, instant joining.

My failing courage soared; with this person at my side I'd be able to fight all the bloody sponsors, producers and script girls.

I thought that I passed muster as well, for as she was walking down the hotel corridor with her small entourage after a happy, and even relaxing, hour in the suite I heard her say: 'Well, he *seems* all right, doesn't he?'

I felt braver than a lion.

I needed all the courage I could use during the next three weeks. The first two days were fairly calm: we settled down to work on location in an elegant house out in Pasadena, where the main body of the filming was to be done. This necessitated getting up at 5.00 a.m. in order to get out to the location and begin shooting at 7.30 a.m.; we worked through, with half an hour for lunch on the spot, until seven-thirty in the evening. A tough schedule.

There was no let-up; Glenda and I were, apart from three children, the two main characters and were in every scene – those which remained of the once-rich script, which was treated rather like a chicken carcass: defleshed of much of its 'meat', crushed, beaten to fragments, and stuck in the stockpot. From the tattered remains of Anderson's work we retrieved as much as we possibly could that was nourishing, and Harvey, true to his word, shot the whole thing as a film, in long takes, with low-key lighting and a sense of 'documentary work' rather than glossy Hollywood.

Screams and cries from the Office.

The results, after five days' shooting, were deemed to be too dark and 'unseeable'. Harvey's 'gritty' and 'grainy' method (these two words were his favourites, apart from 'thrilling') caused tremendous concern and alarm.

Fine, it was argued, for a big screen in the cinema, but hopeless on a small screen twenty inches in width. The sponsors couldn't see anything when they looked at their sets, but were entranced when they saw the material projected on the big screen. Which was precisely what Harvey had intended. A movie, not a TV film.

We came unstuck: everyone came unstuck. While the performances were genuinely praised, the lighting was considered disaster. Fire the cameraman, fire *everyone*, then get lots of 'run by's', that is to say establishing shots of the locations, 'so that they'll know where they are when they see it in the Middle West'.

How *they* saw, understood, empathized in the Middle West was the key to everything. No one really cared all that much what anyone thought on the West Coast or even on the East Coast: the people who lived down on the giant's tablecloth, over which I had so recently flown, were the arbiters of all taste.

They were the people who would buy the goods which we advertised on television. They were the profit. If they should grow restless, become bewildered, bored or disturbed, and turned, in consequence, to another channel, the loss to the sponsors would be incalculable – come what may, we had to keep their attention; therefore, if they couldn't 'see' us they would turn the switch and no one would buy the deodorants, the sliced bread, the shampoo, the lavatory paper ('So Soft, So Soft, Softer Than A Sigh. So Kind To Your Skin'!) or the aspirin.

In order to hold this vast audience, and it was vast indeed, things had to be simple, people must be able to 'identify' easily with everything they saw, above all they must be 'involved', and it stands to reason that you can't be involved if you can neither see nor hear.

A turn of a knob on a television set is as lethal to commercial television as a button pressed in the death chamber.

So, flood the film with plenty of light – no half-tones or shadows – so that people will see. Use simple words which they will understand, have no subtleties in playing that get in the way of 'the direct approach', have no pauses for thinking – there isn't time for thinking, and pauses can make an audience restless, anxious or bored – and as a further added restriction the name of the Lord must never at any time be used in vain. No 'My God's!' or 'Goddammits!' No God at all.

As most of our story was set in a hospital, concerned a massive brain haemorrhage, and necessitated a good many incomprehensible medical terms and distressing sights (Glenda spent half the picture lying flat on her back, bandaged like a mummy with tubes up her nose and stuck into her arms, only able to communicate by animal grunts and cries), we were on a pretty sticky wicket from the start. But we stuck firmly, determinedly, to our intentions, in spite of daily screams and thumping fists and the repeated demands that everyone should be sacked. Except for Glenda and myself, who were constantly lavishly praised, even though, apparently, no one could see what we were doing.

It was a battle for banality against quality, and it raged unabated. People were frequently fired, removed from the set by physical force in the very middle of shooting a scene, something I had never witnessed in over thirty years of film making (but there is always a first time), and the crew, with good reason, grew more nervous and despondent; and each day brought a flutter of coloured pages indicating scenes 'cut' or 'trimmed'. None of this made for a happy atmosphere, but Glenda and I hung on grimly. We were passionate in our work together and had no intention of throwing in the sponge. Or towel.

We all knew, from the work on the set and the support from the whole crew, that we were salvaging something from the tottering edifice, enough at least to make a reasonable, if compromised, movie.

Harvey stuck doggedly to his original plan of a cinema film: we worked long and exhausting hours, sometimes shooting as much as ten or twelve pages in a single day, where the norm in my experience was never much more that a page or two at the most, so that what we actually got *on* to film could serve as a main feature film for theatrical release in Europe and the rest of the world, but could be cut about for television and the Middle West, the theory being that when it was completed eventually there would be enough footage in reserve for the cinema.

That was the theory; it was exceedingly hard to make it fact.

There was never any possibility of Glenda and me pulling out, as Forwood had once envisaged – we were too deep in, too fond of the loyal crew who were bending backwards to help us achieve what we all wanted so much, too involved, anyway, with the original story and the excitement of playing together. There were some heavy-hearted evenings in our hotel restaurant in Pasadena when we sat, exhausted and drained, before plates of dreary little fish in breadcrumbs, known as sand-dabs, which were about the only thing on the menu which we could eat in our exhaustion, wondering how we could manage to survive the next day – seeking, at all times, acceptable compromises for television; and for ourselves. Not easy.

One evening the telephone rang in my rather tatty suite (it was like cheap digs in Newcastle). Forwood answered it, fully expecting it to be another member of the crew who had reached breaking-point calling to apologize for quitting. This had happened two or three times already, and always caused me keen distress, but it was Tessa Dahl, the eldest of the Dahl children, who had been extremely hostile to the whole idea of a film about her parents' private grief, and about the invasion of her family's privacy.

I was certain that she would have something disturbing to say; we had never met or spoken before – doubtless she had bad news of some kind.

But she had not. She said that she had been cajoled and persuaded to see a good piece of the completed filming in the hope, perhaps, that she would publicly change her objections to the making of the film and might therefore provide some useful and 'positive' comments for publicity.

But she had made no sound during the projection, nor did she move a muscle, contenting herself with a polite, but noncommittal, 'Thank you', and leaving the theatre in silence. She immediately telephoned her mother, then staying in Martha's Vineyard, to tell her that what she had seen had overwhelmed her and that she now whole-heartedly approved. Her mother, Miss Neal, suggested that perhaps she should call the actors concerned and tell *them*; so she called me.

'It's really all right?' Relief suddenly gave me new strength.

'It's more that that. It's fantastic, really wonderful. If you want to know I went along to have a laugh – but I couldn't. I thought that I'd be able to send the whole thing up as a bit of terrible Hollywood schmaltz, but I was simply stunned. I wanted to burst into tears, only I knew that I was under observation, that they were waiting for a good response from me to leak to the Press – you know what I mean: "Tessa Dahl Sobs At True-To-Life Movie", that kind of thing?'

'That kind of thing. I know.'

'So I didn't move. I just sat there. It was tough; but amazing. I was only twelve when that all took place; I didn't really fully understand what was happening, but now, because of you and Miss Jackson, I know just how wonderful my parents were, how terribly brave, how hard Roald fought to get my mother through – I'm so grateful, will you tell Miss Jackson that I think she is magnificent?'

'Well . . . why not tell her yourself. She's in this hotel . . . '

'No. I can't do that. I'm too ashamed. I made a fuss about this film being made, I didn't want her to play my mother, I didn't think that *she* was beautiful enough, but she is. She IS my mother.'

Tessa Dahl saved the film from disaster, that is to say she saved us all from moral collapse. It had not been far off, but her encouragement was tremendous: we got a new wind, new courage, new strength and we fought even harder than before, which was just as well because the battle got tougher; Tessa became our talisman. If Tessa Dahl thought that we had got things right, and she ought to know, then to hell with the Middle West.

Eventually, with half the film safely 'in the can', we finished work late one night in a heavy desert mist, everyone streaming with flue caught, we all were quite certain, from the redundant hospital in which we had been working and which had been stripped clear of everything except germs.

I got bronchitis in the last three days and lost my voice completely: stuffed with cortisone, in order to shrink the vocal cords in a hurry, I managed to croak my way to the final shot. Glenda survived intact – she is not the sort of person to succumb to anything trivial – and we all said sad farewells in the swirling fog.

The second half of the film was to be shot in England, but not until the summer, when Glenda had completed the run of a new play, *Rose*, which she was taking to Broadway. The film was put on ice until June, the American crew were miserable that they would not be able to finish the job, and we were equally saddened that they were to be left behind after the tremendous encouragement which they had given us, determined to get us through the disasters. Never, indeed, have so few owed so much to so many.

The Teamsters – the truck drivers and car drivers – members of the toughest union in America, had become our greatest supporters, admiring the way we worked and the determination to stick it out no matter what. On that final evening they made a presentation to Glenda, myself and Forwood of three pearl-handled revolvers, in the form of cigarette lighters, as a token of their regard. We were very much moved.

With heavy hearts, in spite of all the problems, we went our separate ways, Glenda to New York, I to France to await the Call, not to the Coast this time, but to England and a rose-embowered cottage in Hertfordshire for the second half of the film when Glenda was free.

To England in June: a new director in Anthony Page (Harvey had other commitments in America to which he was bound), a little less hectic atmosphere and continual help from Roald Dahl, who wrote copious notes for me on a great many things about which he had forgotten, or perhaps banished from his mind during that desperate time, which were immeasurably useful.

Glenda worked daily with a voice therapist who helped her to invent a manner of speech which, while comprehensible, suggested the inarticulate manner of speaking which a victim of a paralysing stroke would use; it was distressing but appallingly real, and we finished on a dull, wet English summer evening, comforted by the fact that we had made a film as authentic as possible to its origins.

It opened in America (as *The Patricia Neal Story*) in December to quite sensational reviews. Glenda and I were praised extravagantly; so were Harvey, Page and Bob Anderson. The telephone rang almost daily with calls for interviews from newspapers and journals, some as far apart as Quebec, Hawaii, Florida and New York. It was prime-time coast-to-coast, and the movie of the year on television.

Or so you'd think.

We finally reached the peak of euphoria when it was rumoured that Glenda and I were each nominated for an Emmy, the television equivalent of the cinema's Oscar, and, perhaps best of all, news came that it was all such a success, the Press had been so enthusiastic in their praise, that the movie version, re-titled *Miracle of Love* (well, you can't have everything) was being hurried into Los Angeles cinemas to qualify for the Oscars in April.

I sat about up here in the olive store where I work, bemused and happy, reading through plays and stories in a search for something else for Glenda and me to do together because everyone insisted that we 'were a really great team' and we both wanted to get on with something else while the iron was hot, so to speak.

But the iron cooled rapidly.

The ratings came in. I don't exactly remember what they were, but they weren't any good: not 50 per cent, not enough to make us a success or to make us a smash hit. The Middle West, that giant's tablecloth, had turned off after about fifteen minutes to look in at a popular series called *Hart to Hart* which starred Robert Wagner, whose wife, Natalie Wood, had died tragically in a drowning accident only a few days before. The Middle West, it was suggested, was curious to 'see how Bob looked after the tragedy; how he was taking things'.

The fact that the sequence of *Hart to Hart* was probably made some time before Natalie died, and that Robert looked just fine and was managing very well indeed, made no difference.

The Middle West stayed with the show and we lost out, on the ratings. Then I understood the colossal power of television to make or break.

The telephone stopped ringing, no one got an Emmy, and the movie version, if it ever really existed, slipped quietly into oblivion.

Was it honestly as simple as that? Was more than half the population of America really so concerned about poor Robert Wagner? Or was our film, perhaps, too painful, too distressing, too 'gritty' and 'grainy'? Did the hospital, bandages, drip-feeds and inarticulate speech put them off? Was I too bullying or too British? The imponderable questions remain imponderable: only the harsh facts of the ratings provided the glaring truth – we'd flopped.

But there was never the least feeling, in my mind, of doubt or regret, that I might perhaps have made a false move in pushing wide the open door in my corridor which led directly to Los Angeles and the cinema again. I had enjoyed the experience enormously, learned a great deal, and even if a lot had been hellish much more had been sheer delight.

The greatest pleasure, without question, had been working with Glenda Jackson – it was one of the highest peaks in my career as an actor – as strong as teak, as pliable as plasticine, as professional and dedicated as any actress I had ever worked with. We joined together seamlessly, and the work we did was stimulating and exciting – it didn't really matter what happened left and right of us: when we were together, united in a scene, we were absolutely isolated by performance.

We hardly discussed the roles we were playing – there was no need. We knew who we were, and matched each other's emotions and responses exactly. There was never any heavy breathing, head beating or 'anguishing', as they call it, about 'motivation' or 'who' and 'how': we'd got that together long before the cameras rolled.

Sometimes I know that our set behaviour bewildered the crew, obviously used to a different style of playing: we'd sit around on the set, waiting to be called to work, talking and laughing, discussing books or music, people we knew, places we had been, anything and everything; none of it profound or deep, just light, easy – to the onlooker perhaps even casual.

And then we would go directly into a scene of almost Shakespearian tragedy, dark, desperate, wrenching: which often brought tears, and applause, from the crew. A response which astonished Miss Jackson.

'But why? What's the matter with them all? I mean: REALLY!'

There was nothing wrong with them: they were just not accustomed to this form of playing; the (apparently) instant leap from one world to another caught them quite by surprise, they were at a loss to know how we had performed this act.

What in fact surprised them, truthfully, was the sudden release of 'actor's energy'. A different thing altogether from mere 'energy', which is physical. 'Actor's energy' is both mental and physical, it is the life force behind a performance; without it a performance can be adequate, acceptable: but lacking in lustre. Nothing is worse than a dull actor – far better to be a bad one: at least a bad actor may have some interest but a dull one has absolutely nothing.

Many actors have 'actor's energy', but most don't know that they have, or how to use it, and spend a good deal of their ordinary energy frittering it away. It must be cherished like chastity, guarded, husbanded, kept gleaming and bright, and the only possible way to do that is by concentration. Concentration so intense, so hard, so deep that it causes almost physical pain. Sitting on the side-line, chatting about, say, Proust, or perhaps China, or the best way to make corned beef hash, we would none the less be concentrating subliminally on holding the 'actor's energy' so intensely that I swear had someone touched us they would have found that our bodies were tense and trembling as if we had the palsy.

The physical and mental release after playing a scene perfectly, or as near perfectly as one can try to achieve, is so draining that it often feels as if one has just played an exhausting game of squash.

Sweaty, breathless, weak-kneed, drained, limp from effort spent. And, really, that's how good playing should be: like an exhilarating game of squash.

It seldom is.

But when it is, an audience will react instantly; the experience disturbs, excites, and involves them completely.

As Tessa Dahl had seen for herself, Glenda had the uncanny power, as some of our great actresses in the past have had, of being able to transform herself from a shaven-headed, inarticulate, shambling vegetable-woman into a creature of glowing beauty. It never ceased to amaze and move me to watch this happen. It occurred before one's eyes, not through tricks of make-up or lighting. It was instant and extraordinary and came directly from the gut, the repository of nearly all an 'actor's energy'.

No one can possibly be taught how to do this, there are no short-cuts, it doesn't come free in the actors' acting kit; it is a far from liberal gift, based on absolute truth and complete belief in the person one has become, and on concentration. 'Being' and 'believing' unshakeably are the essentials for the cameras – not 'pretending', as is so often supposed.

The camera, with its cruel lens, can often shatter the most carefully prepared performance. If there is no belief or truth behind the work it is photographing, the whole thing goes for nothing. No lustre, no impact.

It is therefore not so surprising that the crew members were moved to applaud; it was an instinctive reaction of a group of people identifying instantly with what they saw before them; they had been removed from the immediate world and transposed to a higher plane of experience. They were observers no longer; they were *sharing*.

Which is, after all, exactly what acting is about, and always has been.

It was not so surprising either that, after a full day's work at high pitch, there were never glamorous parties or suppers in the evenings: there was absolutely no residual energy left, 'actor's' or the other, for that kind of frivolity. The batteries had to be recharged come what may, so that 'delivery' was assured for the next day; even if the recharging took place before a plate of breadcrumbed sand-dabs in a dreary hotel dining-room.

But sand-dabs notwithstanding, and all the rest of the miseries right and left, it had been a wise decision to push open the door in the corridor; even if the film had tragically been lost, I had gained immeasurably in many other ways.

It was eventually shown on British television one New Year's Eve by a commerical station who apparently decided that New Year's Eve was a perfect time to get rid of it.

There would be no one at home to watch it, and no one was, as far as I could ever find out.

They were all extremely occupied in their own personal revels or pushing each other into the fountains in Trafalgar Square.

It was a bitter blow to us – but that was that.

It all might never have happened.

I have always firmly believed in taking one hurdle at a time in life.

And taking it with caution.

I see no point in trying to clear them all at one go: the whole lot can so easily fall and bring one crashing helplessly down among them. Far wiser to take it slowly than to break one's neck at the very start (you usually get there in the end); in any case, I have such feeble co-ordination that I can only ever really manage one thing at a time anyway – so it's a case of *force majeure*.

The first hurdle, in this instance, was the Hollywood shoot. Apparently I had cleared it and survived. The next hurdle, the English shoot, was so far ahead in time that I really could pay it no heed, and sitting in the calm splendour of an Air France jumbo jet I had absolutely no desire to try. Here there was no Cindy with her chicken Appetizer, no Mary-Jo with her three-bottle basket, no petrified traveller across the aisle jammed into his galoshes, just peace, and a caring young woman in a silk dress replenishing my glass with discretion and skill.

I was going home to France at last.

We roared out into the night skies from International Airport, leaving the city far below in a slight drizzle, a myriad of winking lights for as far as the eye could possibly see: green, crimson, blue and gold, a casket of jewels strewn far and wide as if by a wilful child. We swung over the Pacific and climbed high above a lone lightship rocking gently on the swell, its beacon lamp bobbing idly, an incandescent lollipop, then we banked sharply and turned inland towards the dark immensity of America.

It was the last I saw of Los Angeles.

Wheezing and coughing, croaking like a tree-frog with acute bronchitis, stuffed to the gills with cortisone, I was none the less comfortable and relaxed at last, relieved that the first leap had been accomplished.

My work seemed not to have suffered from the four-year lay-off since *Despair*, which pleased me, so the more minor hurdles, ones which I could almost step over really, could now be considered under the soothing influences of wine and a moderately high temperature.

At home the proof copy of my second novel was awaiting my urgent attention, and there was a cover design to plan. Norah Smallwood, my publisher, had written to say that she felt it should be 'something as gay and filled with sunlight as a child's painting. Perhaps we could consider a kind of *faux* Dufy? Think it over.' So I thought it over, mulling it about for a while.

But then the pond was ready for mucking out, the waterlilies were ready for dividing, there were new roses to get in before the end of the month – we can plant late in Provence – and somewhere, pinching my blurring consciousness like a too-tight shoe, the first lines for the opening chapter of a new book were arranging and rearranging themselves in different patterns.

I managed to get the opening line fixed in my head before I fell asleep. It was not the full line, only the first five words in fact, but five important ones none the less:

'I am an orderly man.'

That seemed to me a good start: the other ninety-five thousand could follow on later.

When I was just a bit less tired.

One thing at a time.

EIGHT

When Aunt Kitty went 'a-voyagin'', as Mrs O'Connell often told me, I don't suppose that she minded – it is far more than probable that she liked it, for the First Floor Front of my father's house was pretty gloomy. I didn't find it so, at three or four, but she was, it would appear to me now, in constant search of somewhere better. And she found it, of course, in the islands where the beaches were of white sand glittering with a million tiny shells.

However, that is *one* thing I did not learn from her.

The best part of 'a-voyagin'' for me is always coming home. The supreme moment, I suppose, is when the taxi from the airport turns into the track towards the house, winds up through the terraces and the olives, a dog capering in welcome, the sun, on this particular occasion, shining hard on the frost patches under the walls, gleaming on the water of the pond, throwing the shadows of the cypress trees across the smooth grass at the back of the house like long pencils.

Then the car stops, the doors slam, the luggage is humped from the boot, greetings are called to Henri and Marie (who have been guarding the house in my absence), the dog arrives breathless with delight, a stone carried in his mouth as a welcoming gift.

I'm home again.

I do not immediately enter the house but, fatigue temporarily dispersed, eyes sharpened by the brilliant winter light, go to take stock of my land; to see what has happened to my private world since I left a month ago. Forwood deals with the trivia of household problems within, and I walk over crisp, springy grass, breathing clean air into lungs still foul with the soot of cities and the haze of paraffin from the flights.

Nothing very much seems to have happened anywhere.

In February spring is only about to begin, the land stirs slowly, almost reluctantly, as one does waking from a deep, relaxing sleep.

The daffodils under the willow are thick with fat green buds which thrust from scattered tufts, like green-gloved hands, among the rough grass, brown with last year's leaves; there are lambstails on the hazel, clumps of arabis sit white in the sunlight, tight snowballs on the gravel and in the cracks of the terrace, the first primavera and pansies fill the pots and tubs which in the summer will dazzle with scarlet geraniums and the brilliance of lobelia, a much despised plant used mainly as bordering in public gardens but which here riot in azure glory from May to November.

Otherwise the land is still sere and ice-burned: a few cautious anemones indicate where the drifts will later spread across the terraces, scillas cluster in the shelter of the stone walls, braving the frost, the first celandine, down by the cess-pit run-out, look like green enamel buttons scattered on the banks of the ditch, and the early coltsfoot star the rough ground by the bonfire site, bold on their single stems.

Above, the sky is achingly blue – in the summer it is white with heat, but in winter the mistral washes the air, the winds are sharp and cutting, and the hills are revealed in sharp clarity, every rock and fissure, every crag and boulder, every stunted pine holding hard to the barren limestone. The silence is so intense that the hurdy-gurdy noise made by the guinea-fowl down at the Miels' farm comes up clear and distinct; so do the sheep bells tonkle-tonkling somewhere down beyond the wood.

It is still here. So still that summer guests complain that they cannot sleep because of the silence.

The silence of childhood; of the ramshackle cottage on the Downs which Uncle Salmon long ago offered us as a second home, and which became, for me and for Elizabeth, merely 'home'. Nothing else. Everywhere else was 'the other place'. And so I had come full circle, to the stillness, the sheep bells, much as I had heard them on Windover Hill, the guinea-fowl gobbling as they did at Court Farm, the wind wuthering in last summer's dead grasses.

After Los Angeles, New York and, more recently, Paris, the silence sings for me and I am once again 'within my skin'.

Down by the pond, which I had had bulldozed years before out of the shale and rock, the fish lie still; a pair of toads tumble lazily together in the ugly waltz of copulation and a lone hen-toad threads her ropes of eggs in long slippery strands among the brown stalks of the water-iris, as busy as a basket-weaver.

Below her, in the crystal water, the first bronze buds of the water-lilies have begun pushing through the silt. Elizabeth brought a root of these for me from her pond in her garden at Angmering. She wrapped a chunk in damp paper and stuck it in her wash-bag. Now, after more than a decade, the chunk has increased alarmingly and the dividing of the roots will have to begin before the pond is smothered with the big green plates which these tender bronze buds will become by April, if I don't get into the water pretty soon.

Life is starting again: no doubt of that.

Another season is about to commence and I am here to see it. After sixty years each spring which arrives is a glorious bounty, and is not to be taken for granted. Standing under the giant olive at the edge of the pond I am suffused with contentment and relief; until I remember that this new season will once again deny me the sight of my father clambering up the hill, easel under his arm, canvas in one hand, whistling to the dogs, coming up for his lunchtime beer.

My mother's feet will not be heard clacking across the tiled floors which she so disliked. 'How you can *live* without carpets I simply don't know! *So* uncomfortable.' Her idle humming won't be heard under the vine when we open the wine, and Labo and Daisy were not leaping beside the taxi as we came up just now – and never will again.

This season will be without some familiars.

Daisy died just before Christmas, a not very good boxer bought on impulse from a pet-shop in Cannes, and Labo, who sought me out fourteen years before in Rome, a slum dog riddled with worms, his foreleg smashed to pulp, insisting on my company, had apologetically haemorrhaged while I was washing up just before I had left for Los Angeles, and died in my arms.

Fourteen years of a shared life lay buried under a rosemary bush in the *potager*. He would not be present when I lugged the lily roots from the pond this time. It was a particular job which he enjoyed for it entailed smells and muck and, as often as not, a bite at a gasping fish which I sometimes, accidentally, chucked out with the silt.

He was a street dog and hated the country. Smells were all. He really only liked filth.

Once he had caught and killed a pullet (chicken was his favourite food) and I had tied the stinking carcass round his neck as a punishment. He was killing them off daily after all; something had to be done. He ate the lot with relish.

Visconti called him 'Poverino', which in English means 'poor little fellow'. Poor little fellow, my foot.

He was as sly and deceitful as a pickpocket, and I loved him with all my heart.

Fourteen years of life; and over a decade with Daisy. The deaths of the dogs were the hair-cracks in the fabric of my complacency, but, as is usual with hair-cracks, their warning was not immediately apparent.

Forwood called from the terrace, and as I turned to walk back up the slope from the pond I suddenly noticed that all the shutters were closed on the house, save for the one pair over the room where Henri and Marie took their meals; this was quite unusual.

'All right?' I knew that my voice carried uncertainty.

'No. Not at *all* all right. Henri's ill. Very ill. We'll have to get him home right away.'

'What's happened?'

'I don't know. How do *I* know? Marie says he's been getting slowly worse ever since they arrived. The doctor has been, they don't know what's wrong.'

Henri and Marie had come to run the house, wash and cook, during my first three years; they had suggested that they were much younger than in fact they were, but loved dogs, were loyal, and had splendid references; I finally retired them to a small flat with a balcony down in the valley. They came to 'mind the house' whenever I left it, enjoying what they called a 'little holiday in the clean air of the hill', but this time when they had arrived it was clear that Henri was unwell.

He was vague, stumbled a bit, was slow to recognize words. Marie, indomitable as ever, swore that 'the change of air will do him good, the doctors have said so'. Nothing would persuade her otherwise.

The decline had been swift.

He sat slumped in his armchair, chin on his chest, hands in his lap, as if for dead. Somehow, I don't honestly remember quite how, Forwood and I half dragged, half carried his dead weight down the stairs and into the car; Marie had packed and stood watching in silence.

Henri moaned softly to himself: 'Oh God! My God! What has become of me, what has become of me?'

We drove to their flat. The strong neighbour who lived opposite was out, so we had to carry him up two flights of stairs, his arms trailing, head lolling, then Marie called a doctor and begged us to return, for we had left the house untended. We drove back through the lanes, too tired, too sad, to talk. The late sun starting its slide down behind the mountains, the sky fading from blue to lavender, from lavender to saffron.

At the gates to the track the new boxer, Bendo, a replacement for lost loves, hurried up beside the car, leaping the low stone walls, turning back from time to time to be assured that we were following, and when he was certain his anxiety gave way to pleasure and he tore off to find a stone as a welcoming gift.

It was a rough homecoming.

In May the water-lilies sat among their green plates like shining porcelain cups, as well spaced and set about as a nursery tea-table: the winter-work had been justified, and in time.

On the terrace, the roses which I had managed to plant into their pots before the end of March were already fat with buds; the orange tree by the front door was beginning to scent the mornings with its bridal blossoms; wallflowers and columbine had invaded every rough corner; the wistaria hung presumptuous purple tassels round the window of the olive store; and Henri died.

The funeral was in his local village church. There were no relations, no children, no one close, for they had no one.

I picked a bunch of roses from the garden and we drove down to their village and waited in the early morning – it was not yet nine o'clock – at the square. The church bell began to toll for the dead, that solemn, rather tinny, deliberate Clong! Clong! Clong!

A girl hurried into the baker's and hurried out again with the breakfast bread, a small boy rode across the cobbles on his bicycle, lifting his small rump from the saddle with each shuddering bump as he hit the kerbstones.

The hearse swung into the square, wine-dark, flowerless.

We watched the coffin being carted, with not much delicacy, into the dark door of the ancient church; there was no sign of Marie.

A few people, perhaps five or six, straggled in behind Henri, neighbours from the flats; all women.

Inside, the church was cold, dusty, dim, neglected. The village was predominantly a Communist community and the Mayor was allowing the church to decay deliberately, 'phasing out' religion.

I sat at the back, near the door, on the hard wooden bench.

The tiled floor was cracked, the walls, scaling with wet crumbling plaster; there was a smell of damp wool, leather from the bindings of mildewed prayer books scattered here and there, of varnish and rust. On the walls, grimy marble plaques set into the mouldering frescoes of the Stations of the Cross. Christ had lost his head in the *Scourging at the Pillar* and his feet and shins in the *Crucifixion*.

On one plaque, a name, a date – 1916 – a place – Verdun.

On another, three Italian-sounding names; their ages, between twenty and thirty-one; a date – May 1943.

Deportation. Buchenwald. Germany.

Neglected reminders of the agonies of France which had reached down even to this small place.

There was a scattering of people now among the pews, perhaps not more than twelve of us, plus Henri in his wooden box (pine, because it was cheaper) on bare trestles standing before the shabby altar, two candles guttering in the wind from the open doors, an altarcloth, plain as a winding sheet flapping and rippling like laundry on a clothesline.

Beside me on the wall a glass bead wreath hung crookedly, the words '*Ave Maria*' worked in dusty violet silk; beside it, a headless saint, hand raised in a fingerless blessing; and the iron pipes, which once must have provided some form of heating in this cheerless place, had long since cracked and leaked emerald moss in broad fans across the crumbling stonework.

The bell continued to Clong! Clong! Clong! somewhere above us; I took the bunch of garden roses and placed them on the coffin, about where, I judged, his chest must be.

People turned, looked over their shoulders, coughed, nodded, returned to their glazed study of the guttering candles.

Henri, with his silly chuckle, his boyish good humour, his love of beasts and birds, his pride for the land from which he had sprung, his extreme clumsiness, his 'moods', his terrible slurping when he took his soup, his pleasure in, and knowledge of, his tiny cellar with its modest rack of bottles, his relish in a piece of good Saint-Nectaire cheese – all these things, and the mortal remains of him, were bundled up in a shoddy box before us, under a clanging bell.

'Oh God! Oh my God! What has become of me?' he had sobbed as we carted him down the stairs.

Well, this is what had become of him, boxed up under the bells and a bunch of Grand'mère Jenny roses.

There was a shuffle of sound behind us and Marie, leaning heavily on the arm of the neighbour across the hall, came down the cracked-tiled aisle, as the priest came through a little door by the altar, youngish, in a white surplice with neat lace cuffs, a small book in his hands.

He waited before Henri, rocking gently on his heels, lips pursed, as Marie was led, rather than shown, to the front pew.

She was bowed, no longer upright now, wearing a blue wraparound cardigan which I had brought her once from Marks and Spencer's, a grey stuff skirt with a drooping hem, elastic stockings. On her feet, beige plastic sandals from Monoprix; on her head a widow's cap in cheap black lace.

A short service, the priest laconic; there were no acolytes to swing his censer so he did it, almost irritably, himself. Little puffs of smoke meandered in the damp air.

We were on short means here – very different from the chapel at the convent in Twickenham, the glitter and the glory, the soaring organ music and the flying Christ, the viridian and crimson, the rustle and bustle of Sister Veronica's grey habit, the clatter of her rosary, the overwhelming scent of the incense which, once, long ago, I had been permitted to swing in its silver censer, puffed with pride and reverence.

I'd like to have done it for Henri, even though I knew it was all nonsense, that it really didn't matter and that it could no longer comfort him now. That dead is dead, and that bodies are bundled and tumbled by bulldozers, left to rot in tiered bunks in Buchenwald, exploded into bloody fragments in Verdun, or bound, doused with petrol, and burned alive beneath frangipani trees.

Henri, I reckoned, was neat and tidy where he was.

When the service was over, Marie was assisted by her neighbour and began the cruel walk, past her husband of fifty years, towards the open doors. Her face was gaunt, wrenched with tearless grief, ashen with cheap powder, her lips a startling scarlet weal.

A lipstick, as far as she was concerned, was red. And red was red.

As she drew abreast of Forwood and me sitting in the gloom, she half raised her head for a moment, and saw us.

She smiled the smallest smile of gratitude, suddenly stood tall, removed her arm gently from that of her neighbour, and walked out into the sunlit square, the rough wind teasing her widow's cap.

They shouldered Henri out of the church, the roses wobbling dangerously so that I removed them and when he had been rolled into the wine-dark hearse replaced them on his chest. They drove him out of the square, down the road to the new cemetery. And, as far as we were concerned, that was that.

Dead is dead when all is said and done. And all had been said, and all had been done. If a door had shut quietly behind me in the corridor, I confess that I was not immediately aware of the fact: it is sometimes just as well that we do not hear the closing, and the turning of the key.

I remember, driving home that morning, thinking how wretched it was that Forwood and I were the only kith and kin that they had had. Finally your life ends and you are left with only your last employers as mourners, apart, that is, from a handful of kindly neighbours.

However, my own desperate search for kith and kin to attend my funeral had finally come to nothing.

Aunt 'Coggley' Chesterfield, who had tried to teach me to spell: 'There is no "e" at the end of "potato", darling. You keep sticking "e's" where there are none. How many "s's" are there in "necessary"?'

Uncle Bertie, who had removed my tonsils and who swore to keep me alive while so doing; his laughing wife, Aunt Gladys, pink of nails, blond marcelled hair, silk stockings on elegant legs; and Aunt Celestia with her nicotined fingers and damp cigarette butts; Uncle Salmon, who had given me 'George', the tortoise, and opened a new world for me through an ancient cottage in a Great Meadow; Aunt Yvonne, who had, literally, pushed me on to a stage for the first time in my life; and Granny Nutt, and garden-proud Uncle Arthur whom I let beat me at croquet.

And my parents.

All of them had gone long before I had had need of them to mourn me. But they had not altogether gone, and Henri, I was pretty certain, was now about to jostle his way among them on to the backcloth of my life before which I performed my modest show with those of the cast who remained: Elizabeth and George, my brother Gareth, his wife Cilla and their family, Forwood and, without question, the ever-constant Lally.

She was still 'on stage' with us.

Valiant, strong, brave of heart, and of soul, she had sent me a picture postcard of a palm tree from Torquay a few days before.

Here for my little annual holiday, dear, with my nice friend Mrs Hutchings who can drive a car. So that's good, isn't it? Coolish at the moment but it'll cheer up because I have brought my bathing-costume. May have a dip after tea-time, the water is hot in the hotel pool! Whatever next!

Remembering her card, the day was suddenly brighter; I no longer heard the Clong! Clong! of the bell.

But I hadn't heard the closing of the door either.

After Henri and Marie had, reluctantly, been retired, Soledad came to do 'two hours a day, six days a week'. She was a sturdy, bright-eyed young woman, who arrived on her *moto*, a two-year-old daughter strapped into a seat behind.

She looked about the house, in silence. The principal reason for this being that she was a Spanish immigrant and spoke almost no French. However, she made it clear that she would not work in a house where there were women; I assured her that she would not be troubled by her own sex and she agreed to try it out, for a month.

That was in 1972, and she is still here today.

The giddy idea that two men could run, single (or is it double?)-handed a house and twelve acres very soon faded in a scurry of irritation and helplessness. I can't cook an egg; and practically not even boil water – Forwood agreed to do the cooking (he was good at cauliflower cheese and could grill a chicken). I was to be the scullion, preparing the vegetables and doing the washing-up.

I frequently thought that I had got the worst of the deal.

Madame Bruna, the mason's wife, did the 'heavy laundry' and I stuck the teacloths and underpants in bushels of Persil and hung them on the line.

It really wasn't very satisfactory: cauliflower cheese becomes wearisome, and I got bored cleaning the oven, and the land, of necessity, became neglected. So Soledad was engaged, and after she had decided to remain and take things in hand she was called 'Lady', and 'Lady' she has remained.

I reckon that she is known right across the world now, from San Francisco to Delhi, for as soon as it was possible we stripped out the staff flat, converted it into a guest suite, and opened, what seemed to us all, a small *pension*. Suspicious, at first, of strangers in 'her' house, she quickly warmed to their odd habits and over the years became as indispensable to them as she is to me.

Although there was hardly any common language (after all this time she is far more fluent in French) she managed very well, and most especially with Elizabeth, to whom she became devoted.

Without a single word in common, they would screech together, laughing and whooping in some strange form of invented Esperanto, and when I was away for a long seven months working on two films, back-to-back, Elizabeth and George came to mind the house and Lady and she became even closer, especially as Lady was pregnant and had little 'turns' from time to time. She eventually had a rather severe one and was sent home on her *moto*, bouncing down the track, her crash-helmet rocking, blue smoke spurting from the noisy exhaust, and an hour later gave birth to a son – almost on her kitchen floor.

She was back at work, up the track on the *moto*, three days later, earning Elizabeth's undying admiration and affection.

And so it was; a household had formed that was altogether satisfactory, held together by Lady, who took the teacloths and underpants, and sundry other pieces of washing, and did it all properly.

Like rinsing them.

Perhaps, apart from Elizabeth, her favourite guest in Tart's Parlour, as it became known because it was a smother of English chintz (fat roses and lilac), pink shaded lamps and an elegant Eugénie chair, buttoned tightly and braided in silk, was Norah Smallwood, who came to stay every year with a leg, foot or an arm in plaster, for she was accident prone and very frail, and Lady enjoyed the shocks and surprises which accompanied Norah on her visits.

I first saw her sometime in the early seventies in the pages of a glossy magazine in an article on 'Women in Power' or 'The Silent Geniuses', or some other idiotic editorial heading. It was a small photograph of this, I gathered, elusive, mysterious, extraordinary woman, who almost single-handed, it implied, ran Chatto and Windus, the publishers. I was suitably impressed because, though small, it was a photograph of great elegance. Norah appeared to be swaddled in a sea of silk cushions. She had a fine patrician head, a slightly mocking smile (she detested the Press and loathed being photographed), an air of luxury and, distinctly, breeding.

It was well known, even to me, that Chatto and Windus were *the* publishers, the most respected, the ones with the most impressive 'list' of authors, the most desired by all writers. If Chatto accepted you it was the highest accolade; whether you were accepted or not depended entirely on this woman. She had the power of life and death, as it were, over a book, and she very seldom made an error.

It was not in her nature to do so.

The next time I saw her, some years later, was standing at the door of her own office, slim, tall, chic in a white silk shirt and a coral wool skirt, her white hair set and groomed, a tiny pearl in each ear, her eyes sparkling, her voice and movements brisk and unfussy. In her hands she held two copies of the first book of mine which she had agreed to publish, and she demanded, in a firm voice, which colour binding I preferred? the blue or the yellow?

I was too overcome by the sight of my own book, in whatever colour of binding, to properly answer her, so she chivvied me off to the Garrick Club for luncheon. I was pretty overcome by her as well. Awed is a good word.

We had reached, by this time, the Christian name level. Although it still slightly embarrassed me to call her 'Norah' she obviously had no compunction in calling me by mine. We had written letters to each other during the writing of the book, but only in the latter stages. At first the letters were signed by someone other, and only when we got down to selecting drawings (mine) and photographs, and when I had, in some way, 'proved' myself to her, did she finally sign her own letters; and, in time, she dropped the 'Smallwood' and signed herself simply 'N'.

Our first meeting, at the Garrick, seemed to satisfy her that I did not eat peas with my knife, talk about the cinema, or pick my nose at table. Her relief was frankly obvious: she had no knowledge of an actor's life and feared, I'm certain, that I might be swathed in chinchilla, smoking 'hash'. That I wore a sober suit and tie, had washed behind my ears, and spoke the Queen's English (even though I found it difficult to write it correctly) reassured her, and we began to relax together; I think that our friendship was finally sealed at the supper party which I gave at the Connaught on the day of publication.

It was a carefully seated table; I had ordered what she called a 'scrumptious supper' (of six courses) and a splendid claret with which she could find no fault. My training as an ADC, and understanding of 'sitting a table', had paid off admirably.

Norah, a corking snob in many amusing ways, was agreeably impressed by 'her writer'.

Once, some years later, when I had the temerity to suggest that perhaps she was 'a bit of a snob', she had smiled at me wistfully, touched a pearl in her ear, twisted it thoughtfully – an old habit of hers.

'Well. I don't really know. I've never thought much about it. I know that people *think* I am; but if it means that I only tolerate the very best in things, you know, like . . . well, Colette, perfectly fried eggs and bacon, an Auden poem, Sienna in the autumn, the best of *anything* . . . then I suppose that I am. I can't abide mediocrity, ugliness, cheapness . . . I can't bear slackness in word, deed, writing, or in people. Behaviour is terribly important to me. Grace, good manners, kindness, a striving to attain, to be better. If that's being a snob then I suppose that I must be – and I so *detest* "snobs"!'

Her first visit to the house here was curious for many reasons.

Lady had bashed herself into a state of near exhaustion polishing the floors my mother so detested, the house was filled with flowers, white and green for the white-and-green room. Tart's Parlour shone with hours of waxing, the pillows were plump and fat and daisy-scattered. The view from the windows, across the wooded hill to the valley and the sea, and the ragged line of the Estérel range, soft against the sky, caught Norah's voluble breath and stilled it. She stood in silence, filled with joy at the beauty before her.

In the evening we sat around the burning logs in the stove, and began to 'discover' each other. She admired bits and pieces in the room, and then apologized for so doing.

'But *do*! It's splendid that you admire the Portuguese dishes . . . '

'My father always said that one must NEVER admire anything in anyone's house, that it was the height of bad manners, just as it was to speak of the food at a meal . . . '

'Your father sounds very strict, Norah? Surely to admire one's host's choice is a compliment?'

'Not to my father. It was an impertinence.'

Later, a glass of framboise clutched in her arthritic hands, she spoke about 'fillums', as she called them, slightly disparagingly.

'I never go, you know . . . oh, I used to years ago, with the Bloomsburys for fun. We used to go and see all those rubbishy things made by a man called Cecil Someone.'

'B. de Mille?'

'*Cecil*. I don't remember the "B." . . . Perhaps. But we used to sit and laugh like anything at all the ghastly mistakes. You know, the Bible all the wrong way round, and silly ladies with sillier faces speaking Yankee in Egypt and Palestine or wherever.'

'They gave a lot of people a great deal of pleasure.'

'I suppose so,' she sighed. 'I wish they would read instead of looking at all that nonsense; can't be good for them.'

'Have you never seen a French film? *Un Carnet de bal? La Règle du jeu? Casque d'or?*'

'Oh yes . . . sometimes I got taken along by one of my writers to the Curzon, and we saw a foreign fillum . . . they were MUCH better. Much. Intelligent, too. Oh, quite different. I loved *them*. But really the cinema and that awful television thing are such utter rubbish.'

'There are sometimes good things to watch.'

'I never do. Unless forced.'

'You were watching television when you saw me.'

'Oh! Absolute fluke. My hosts were glued to the damned box all day watching sport and when they put the thing on AGAIN after dinner to watch something they called "replay" I nearly went mad; so I got up and turned the button to see if there was ANYTHING other than a crowd of men kicking a ball about, and I got your programme, talking to that nice man.'

'And I'm very grateful indeed. It's because of that desperate gesture that I wrote a book and we are here together tonight, isn't it?'

'Correct. But it was a fluke, a lucky fluke, but that's all.'

I refilled her glass.

'I'll sleep tonight,' she said. 'I never sleep, these wretched hands keep me awake. You've noticed them, of course? Like seal's flippers. I did have pretty hands, I was very vain. My punishment, I suppose.'

'Are they frightfully painful?'

'Frightfully. I'm stuffed with pills all day. Don't do much good. A glass of wine or a stiff whisky does much better. If you see me wearing my table napkin wrapped round my fist, take no notice. It's just pain.'

'You are wearing one now.'

She looked at it in surprise.

'So I am. Brought it down from dinner I suppose. It was pretty hellish for a while. Now.' She changed the subject briskly. 'I *did* see a really splendid fillum some time ago, I think the young Graham Greene forced me. A fillum of a novella of Thomas Mann's . . . of course I was very suspicious, you know how they always fudge that sort of thing, but it was quite magical, absolutely wonderful . . . not *quite* Thomas Mann. The director person had stuck in some outside stuff, but it all seemed to work. Now that was one fillum I saw three times! *Death In Venice.* Did you see it? Do you get those kind of fillums here in France?'

'I was in it,' I said.

There was a long, still silence; a log settled.

'*Death In Venice?*'

'Yes . . . Thomas Mann.'

She unwrapped the table napkin, looked into her glass, wrapped the napkin round her poor, knobbled fist again.

'But what were you? There was only an old man and a rather beautiful youth . . . '

'The old man. I played von Aschenbach.'

Norah's eyes were steady with disbelief.

'I saw it three times.'

'And each time it was me.'

'Well . . . ' She shook her head. 'It didn't look the LEAST bit like you,' she said.

This first visit was a test-case. Friday to Sunday was all that she would spare. She was not about to take a risk and find herself perhaps trapped in marble jaccuzis, swimming-pools, Le Corbusier chairs and, perhaps worst of all, wall-to-wall television.

She wasn't; and relaxed gratefully.

Her real reason for coming, apart from testing the ground, was to collect the finished, and edited, typescript of my second book, and to ensure that I did a cover design for her to take back to the office for Monday morning.

A rather hefty demand which, fortunately, I was able to manage.

'I know', she said tartly, 'that there are only supposed to be twenty-four hours in a day, of course, but I manage to make mine last thirty-six at least.'

And she seriously expected lesser mortals to behave in the same way; even with twelve acres to tend and tables to lay and food to buy, dogs to feed, and all the rest of the trivia of life. Having 'discovered' me, helped me to write, encouraged me to work until I dropped, she would not take slackness, as she called it, as any kind of excuse.

The ground tested, and found acceptable, the food tasted, and declared 'scrumptious', the knowledge that she need not trouble to conceal the agonizing pain which she suffered practically all the time, the delight in what she called 'conversation' after dinner on the terrace, or by the fire, the fact that there was so much to discuss and plan and that she had taken my new career, for that is what it was beginning to seem to be now, firmly in hand, brought her to the house every year and, now that she knew its pattern, she stayed longer and was a demanding, but wonderfully rewarding, guest.

She was also a fearsome responsibility.

Her poor skin was as thin as tissue paper from all the drugs which she had to take to lessen her pain. The least knock, scratch or bump, even the touch of a leaf, could cause instant, and alarming, bleeding which nothing would staunch until the wound healed, and every time she went off into the garden, heavily gloved, with secateurs and a box, to potter about deadheading whatever caught her knowing gardener's eye, my heart was in my mouth. But the light songs she sang, trailing sweetly across the lawn, or from behind the bay hedges, gave me infinite pleasure, and usually reassured me that she had not come to grief.

One morning I took her breakfast into her bedroom. She was, as she always was, wide awake, sitting up among her pillows, looking through the open windows to the hills.

'Didn't sleep?'

'Until three. Never after three, the pills wear off. Anyway, it's getting light by five, so I open the window and breathe in this delicious air. It's like being on top of a mountain.'

'You almost are. It's four hundred metres high here.'

'I wish the bed was.'

'The bed was what?'

'Higher. You see, lying here I just *can't* see the hills . . . come and sit where I am; by the pillow. You see? The bed is too low, or the window too high; something.'

'What should I do, Norah?'

'Well . . . would it cost a frightful lot to *lower* the windows?'

'Frightful. The wall is a metre thick, it's been like that for 400 years.'

'Pity. Never mind. It would be nice, but very spoiled of me. Is that fresh orange juice?'

'Pressed by myself. As promised.'

'I loathe that tinned stuff; how good you are.'

Two months later I bought a pair of brass beds, copies of those in the Paris Ritz. They were higher; and the next time she came she lay in delighted glory, looking at the hills, the sea, down to the vineyards in the valley, frail and content among her pillows. It was well worth it to me.

We were neither of us, of course, unaware that in the world of publishing there were murmurs of dissent, even derision. I was teacher's pet, and the fact that my name as a film star had helped to get my work on to the best-seller lists did not please those who were still struggling to get published at all.

'Of course,' someone once said to her, 'we know that you are biased, Bogarde can do no wrong in your eyes. It's dangerous, you know.'

Norah's reply was sharp and to the point. 'He's making money for the firm, that's all I care about.'

Her personal judgement was being questioned, and she would not accept that. Her judgement, as far as she was concerned, had been justified. I did my best for the rest of my time with her to honour that belief.

Lady gave a soft cry of despair when I told her that Henri had died. Her hands went to her face to cover instant, rather facile, tears.

'And Marie?'

'Very sad, and very lonely.'

'Better that she dies too, poor thing.'

'Oh I don't think so . . . in some ways it might be almost a release for her now, and she has no intention of giving up. She's coming to lunch on Tuesday.'

'And when is the big party, for the Festival?'

'On Wednesday. There will be fifty people at least.'

She threw her duster into the air and caught it; inexpertly. 'Where will you put fifty people?'

'At tables under the olive trees – it is May after all.'

'And if it rains? It always rains for the Film Festival.'

'It won't.'

It didn't. The rains, which indeed had been looming over Cannes all week, suddenly veered away, and the day broke brilliant with sunshine for the party to

honour David Puttnam, his director Hugh Hudson, his actors and their various
appendages for *Chariots of Fire*, which had been the British entry the night
before.

We'd borrowed trestle tables and little folding iron chairs from the mayor
and set them up under the trees among the buttercups. Scrubbed wood, peeling
green slatted chairs, dappled sun: very informal, very Renoir, very, I chose to
believe, French.

Madame Rolles, a formidable lady from Alsace, did the catering (someone
said that it was 'criminally over-catered', but this wasn't going to be a bridge
roll affair) and her son, resplendent in white coat and tall chef's hat, served an
apparently never-ending, and starving, crowd of laughing, relaxed people.

Everyone had turned up except one who declined because, he said, he was
not going to be 'patronized by a bloody film star'. His absence, however, was
hardly noticed; which might have irked him.

No sooner had the tables and chairs been folded down and carted back to the
village for the next Old Folke's Supper than Lady was up in Tart's Parlour
scrubbing the white carpet and polishing the wood in preparation for Madame
Petit-Bois's (the nearest she could get to 'Smallwood') yearly arrival.

This year Norah hobbled in. Ugly bandages on her elegant, crane-slender
legs: the result of a careless collision with a coffee table some weeks before. So,
sticks and footstools again, and the village nurse daily to dress the wounds and
to complain to me, privately, that 'Madame is dehydrated! She is all skin and
bone! She has no fluid in her! You must make her drink water, litres and litres of
water, or she'll die . . . '

Trying to force Norah to drink litres of water was about as absurd as trying to
force an elephant into a barrel.

'Silly woman! She's mad! I *detest* water. I drink lots of my wine, lots of lovely
tea. Dehydrated! Absolute bosh!'

'I only passed on a piece of medical information and advice.'

'Stuff! Now . . . ' She changed the subject swiftly, for she detested talking of
her ailments, thinking, I suppose, that if they were not discussed they would go
away. 'Now . . . what have you written? Anything to show me? Should be.'

I handed her the first chapter of *An Orderly Man*, which made her laugh and
which she accepted 'as a start'.

'When can you get down to things? I'd say pretty soon frankly. That
wretched fillum Festival is over now, so there is nothing in your way, is there?'

I looked across the terrace down to the acres of mown, unraked hay, thought
of the weeds flourishing in the *potager*, the gutter which had to be painted, the
pots which had to be fed and watered, the small bunches of grapes already
forming on the vine above our heads, which had to be removed before they grew
too large and their weight brought down the iron trellis.

Nothing in my way but work.

'I'll start, surely, when I get back from England next month. I've still got half
the film with Glenda Jackson to finish, remember.'

She took up her wine and sighed with impatience. 'That dratted fillum. They
do get so in the way.'

'Three weeks, that's all. Then I'll be back at work, I promise you. But I've got
to earn a little loot, you know, darling: books don't exactly match the movies in
money, unless you are a Frederick Forsyth or a Dick Francis, and I ain't either,
as you know.'

She knew perfectly well: she was scrupulously fair, but not over-indulgent, as
far as money was concerned; she didn't believe in cosseting, as she called it, her
writers and, sadly, her ideas of money were based strictly on pre-war standards.

'I think that you may well do comfortably with *Voices* (*Voices in the Garden*). I think it's your best novel so far really: the Meringue-hats will go for it, but I'm not certain about the Young. It's a book about class, you see, and the Young have rather dismissed class; such a pity . . . they won't understand "your people", I'm afraid. Don't believe that they exist. All this business of "identification". Really it's *too* boring.'

'Well. Let's wait until September, when it hits the shops. Then we'll get an idea. And this time no publicity, no promotions in Bradford or Birmingham, above all no chat shows. Never again.'

She took a sip from her wine, eased her leg on the footstool. 'You may regret it, you know, it made a lot of difference to the last three books.'

But I knew, in spite of her undoubted concern, that she was secretly relieved. A true Scot, the last bill for my expenses at the Connaught during promotion had caused her to rock slightly on her Ferragamo heels with horror.

'My dear! This is a year's salary for some people!' she had cried. 'Couldn't you take a *room* next time? With friends? You must have lots of friends in London who would be delighted to let you have a *room* somewhere.'

I had argued that I simply couldn't do promotional tours of the punishing variety which she, in part, had organized and which she was almost insistent that I should do, even though I might bleed to death in the doing of them. Reluctantly, she was convinced that I had to have hotel service to fulfil my job and help sell her wares, as well as my own. But it always rankled.

'Norah! Think of the money you'll save this time. All you have to do is take a little advertising in one or two of the better papers and sit back and see what happens. No Connaught bills, no car hire, no trains, no planes . . . easy.'

'Do you know the cost of a "little advertising" in the better papers today?' A fat Provençal blue bee swooped in under the vine, she ducked, it swung out into the breathless morning. 'I'd like to get this' – she wagged the chapter at me – 'on board as soon as you can manage really. I'd like to have it "in the house" at least by, well . . . let's say March. Can you try?'

'I can. Certainly. You're pushing me a bit – you've always said "Take your time" and "Don't hurry". Why the pressure?'

She placed the chapter on the table beside her, the wine glass on top, lay back, closed her eyes.

'I think that perhaps I'd better tell you something. I wasn't going to, but . . .,

'Something not very good, is that it?'

'Well, not very good for me. No. I think I'm going to pull out of the firm in March. Retire me'self.'

I sat mute with surprise. This. Of all things.

'I've been there a long time, you know. William IV Street. Not getting any younger either, and this pain is really pretty fearsome.' She opened her eyes wide, looking up into the leaves above; not at me. 'I think that it's spreading, the arthritis. Into my hips . . . and perhaps my legs . . . a frightful nuisance but there we are. Time for someone younger to take over the ship, frankly.'

I was so stupefied with shock that I could think only in banalities. 'Have you someone in mind? You must have?'

'Oh yes. I've been thinking about it for a long time. I'm a woman, but I managed to run that firm pretty well for a long, long time. I'd like another woman to take it on. I've got my eye on her. Very bright, clever, sharp, very, very ambitious, tough as anything and strong. Just as I was when I was young. Lots of guts: I had those too. Keep this to yourself, it wouldn't do to let it out yet.'

'I'm unlikely to telephone the *News of the World*.'

'The *Bookseller* would appreciate it much more, my dear, I assure you!'

'No fear . . . '

'So if you can get this . . . what's it to be called? *An Orderly Man*.' She squinted at the chapter, held it to the light. 'Good title. Don't change it. Have it under way so that I can get it all set up and "in the house" before I . . . ' She placed the pages back on the table, lay back. 'By March anyway. On board by March. Try?'

'I'll try. Promise.'

Nurse Humery's car turned into the track below in a cloud of pale dust.

'Here's nurse. The bandages all in your room?'

'All ready,' she said. 'What a bore it all is, really.'

I knew the anguish that this decision had cost her: the restless, pain-filled nights which forced her to reach such a conclusion, the rage against her body which had given up so long before her brilliant, sharp, inquisitive mind, the cruelty of forcing her own retirement.

Chatto without Norah was unthinkable, even to me who had been with the firm for only a few years; she was the core of it, the heartbeat, the very life; she had seemed to be as permanent, as solid, as dominating and unshakeable as Nelson's Column beyond her office windows, and the fact that she was, after all, merely human and full of all the human frailties we know I had overlooked.

As I walked across the grass to meet Nurse Humery, I heard, this time quite distinctly, the whispering creak of hinges swinging uncertainly in the wind of change which was riffling along the corridor, and I resolved, there and then, to get down to work on the new book as soon as I humanly could so that she should have it 'in the house', and in her hands, before she closed her door.

Although Henri's death, and the uneasy awareness of Norah's possible retirement, were not exactly hurdles over which I 'could almost step', for they had come harshly and out of left-field, so to speak, I had somehow managed to take them in a clean leap without coming to absolute grief in a tumble of emotions: somehow I was given extra strength for the unsuspected effort and got over.

The main hurdle, and one which I had expected for a long time, and not without trepidation, was the English shoot; but that, as I have said, went pretty well, all things considered, and although it was a pretty high hurdle, and dangerous, that too was cleared, mainly owing to Glenda, who slipped effortlessly back into her role of 'Patricia Neal' after a three-month absence on Broadway just as if she had never been away, and held my hand tightly.

Mainly, too, because of the excellent British crew who, smaller than the giant one which we had used in Hollywood, nevertheless, coped smoothly with, to them, a brand-new production, and who were far less liable to 'fuss' or intimidation.

'I wanna rostrum!'

'Okay, guv. Rostrum it'll be.'

'A ten-foot, maybe twelve-foot rostrum. You got that?'

'We have, guv.'

'And set it right here! Right where I'm bloody well standing. Here! See?'

'Got it, guv.'

'What's that tree thing?'

'A tree? Nah, guv, not a tree. It's a *bush*. A rose bush.'

'What kinda rose bush. Special?'

'Very, guv. Oh, very special.'

'We can't clear it away? It's in shot. Right in shot! I want the camera right on top of this rostrum and I wanna pan it right down this road-place and that fuckin' rose bush is right there in the way. Get rid of it.'

'It's a *Tudor* rose, guv. Can't move it. Heritage. All that.'

'Tudor? That is?'

'Elizabethan. Real English.'

'That so? Well . . . Hey! Mike? That's a Tudor rose, right? So *linger* on it when we pan across, right? Atmosphere. Then speed up and catch the car as it passes, you got that?'

One dog rose was spared for another English summer.

Whereas in Los Angeles everyone on the set seemed to be forced to 'jog' everywhere, even while eating their tuna sandwiches, the British just took their time, in the traditional British manner, and in spite of constant shrill screams from the Office caused by uncomprehending exasperation (for they did not fully understand the way that the British work, and why, indeed, should they?) everyone had their bacon sandwiches, their tea-break, their sit-down lunch-break, and another tea-break at four o'clock, with a 'snack' coming up about five-thirty. It was reckoned by the Office that we lost two hours' work a day, which I am certain is a grave exaggeration, but where time is money, exaggeration becomes truth. We worked to union rules, which in consequence made for a calmer, less frenetic, happier atmosphere. After a few days everyone got sorted out and settled down, and in spite of inclement weather we crammed in the work (all those bacon sandwiches for energy) and sometimes shot until last light at about eight-thirty in the evening.

And then, suddenly, it was all over. No slow wind-down, no gentle easing of the stress, just a cheerful call: 'Okay, boys . . . that's it. It's a wrap. Thank you one-and-all.'

Together, after we had shed 'Roald' and 'Pat', and sent their garments off to wardrobe for packing, Glenda and I sat in the grounds of a hospital near Wendover in my trailer, a Guinness for a 'strengthener' on the formica table between us, before we attempted the long journey back through the traffic to town.

We looked pinched and tired, and we were. Listless; and we were.

When a player has been wound up to a high pitch of emotionalism for any length of time the sudden ending of work comes as a physical, and mental, shock. One is drained suddenly: the adrenalin is still flowing but now there is no need for it, no receptacle in which to store it, so that it seeps and dribbles away leaving one weak and void.

A stoked-up engine, boiler roaring, steam billowing; stuck at the buffers.

'Well.' Glenda started to collect her hand-grip, a book, a half-eaten apple. 'That's it. Off we go, that journey back to Blackheath in all this traffic is just what I don't need. At this time of night.'

'You shouldn't live at the end of the world.'

'It's got a lovely garden. You should come and see my garden.'

'I feel I've been shooting for months.'

'Three weeks, love. I mean it hasn't been all *that* long.'

'Feels like it. I wonder if they'll pay us?'

'Pay us. What do you mean?'

'It seems to me that I don't get fully paid for the movies I make, I can't think why.'

'You got paid for the first half, didn't you?'

'Yes. And expenses. Expenses on this side too, but there's a deferment, and deferments have a habit of not getting paid.'

'Well I've been paid all I'm owed. So they tell me.'

'For the whole deal?'

'I don't know! You *are* suspicious! Listen to you!'

'I still haven't had my deferment for *Death in Venice*. I got twelve thousand quid for that and not a sou extra. We're still in debt, five million or something, and the movie only cost about *two*, so I don't know . . . you have to believe what they tell you because no one is bright enough to work it out. Including me.'

'As far as I'm concerned, I'm paid. That's all I know.'

'I've got a written guarantee that they'll pay me for this piece of the action. Signed and sealed it is.'

'Fancy. I haven't got anything as grand as that.'

'Forwood fixed it up in L.A. My contract wasn't exactly "in order", as they say.'

'Wasn't it?'

'Was yours?'

'Never saw it. I imagine so.'

'Be sure, then. It's not much good "imagining" 150,000 dollars. I need it now.'

I wasn't far wrong, and I didn't get it right away. At the time of writing (July 1985) there is still a modest 50,000 dollars owing and the roof has had to wait – it hasn't really been dealt with since 1641. It's about time something was done.

But, one thing at a time.

There was a book to be written.

My Muse had wandered off again in the most maddening way: she does this frequently now, leaving me sitting here in the olive store staring glumly across the sloping tiled roof of the woodshed towards the three cypress trees (there were four, but one was torn away during a particularly fierce mistral), the little wooded hill beyond and a tall stump of an olive, straight, sturdy, as unbranched as a Doric column. It is fourteen feet high and has been peasant-pruned. By that I mean that it had simply been ruthlessly cut to promote new growth; olives are pruned every twenty or so years.

Usually M. André, who is a magician with olives, and cares for their beauty as much as I do, clips away gently, cutting out the dead wood, always leaving the basic shape of the tree standing in trimmed, lace-like splendour. He never savages them, but, alas, he retired a few years ago and no longer comes.

The stump of which I write was butchered years ago, and has never put out more than a collar of leaves half-way down its trunk, the top of which is as round and smooth as a breadboard. This is the direct result of peasant-pruning: they care not a fig for the aesthetic splendour of their trees, but only for the harvest. Which is absolutely understandable. And the trunks, which they hack down, fetch a vast price on the market, where the wood is used for hideous pepper-mills, salad bowls, cheeseboards, egg-timers and sundry bits of tourist kitsch. So pruning means harvest; it also means money.

My neighbours on the west boundary (alas! I have neighbours now to the left and right of me) had their grove savaged to such an extent that the land resembles Passchendaele. They have been assured, naturally enough, that 'in three years, the trees will be just as they were; but healthier'. I know that nature has an amazing capacity to heal: but how she can possibly regrow in three years limbs which took perhaps twenty or fifty, even eighty years to evolve beats me.

And of course it doesn't happen like that at all: what *does* happen is that, though the trees never fully recover from the savaging, they do, eventually, start to look like moulting feather dusters, and then, about three years or so later, the gnarled trunks resemble rows of broccoli staggering up the hill. Of course, in years to come, they will *appear* to be trees again. But, frankly, who has so much time left to await the miracle?

As I sat looking at my mutilated column I noticed a movement on the breadboard top. Sitting in the late sun, preening and brushing, upright on his hind legs, so that he could give full attention to his toilet, was a fat, bright-eyed vine-rat washing his cream-yellow weskit. I don't know the real name for this species; we call them vine-rats simply because they forage among the grapes and don't resemble at all those scaly tailed, ugly black rats of the streets and markets. This breed has a fair pelt, enormous round ears, bright eyes, a yellow blaze on its chest and coral-pink feet. It is altogether pleasing to look at in the warmth of September as it rustles through the vine overhead searching out the ripest 'framboise' or dusty-green 'muscats', and causes no revulsion in the timidest heart; it's more like a squirrel than a rat, anyway.

There he was, occupied in the sun, grooming himself with such intensity that he was unaware of the weasel which was creeping up the olive stump. A red streak of danger, arrow head, tail flat to the bark, hidden from the rat by the frill of leaves which wreathed the column a foot or so below him.

Then the sudden dreadful fury of the two tumbling, writhing forms. A horrifying dance of death on the breadboard: red and cream rolled together in turmoil, the squeals of the rat, perfectly audible from my vantage point, the looping, writhing, leeching shape of the weasel gripping tightly to the creamy throat of his victim, until it suddenly went limp, blood spilled like scattered rubies, and the weasel dragged his prey, jerking now in death, down through the collar of leaves into the long grass at the foot of the stump and out of sight.

I watched this fandango of sudden destruction mercifully unaware that in actual fact I was like the preening rat in the sunlight, all unsuspecting. I did not know then that weasel-time would creep up on me suddenly and bring an end to my tranquillity. I suppose that I thought the peaceful, easy life could go on for ever, really. That nothing now could mar the simplicity which I had worked to achieve.

It has always been a failing of mine: I really should have learned by this time. Shadows would fall across the childhood fields, and the hermit crab would be forced from his too tight, far too snug, shell, to become as vulnerable as a sprat on a griddle.

But for the moment, for that caught instant watching from the olive store window, I was unaware, and the shadows of the future, when they fell, fell lightly.

At first.

NINE

They arrived uninvited and unwanted, just in time for tea.

Margaret, whom I knew, and her friend, whom I did not know, nor wished to know, but who radiated relentless charm and an overpowering determination to be instantly friendly and overtly familiar.

Not my style at all.

Uninvited guests are a particular hate; 'dropping in' something which I find personally unforgivable. But when it happens, and it doesn't frankly happen all that often, one is forced to put on a performance and 'pretend' goodwill; good manners usually ease the moment.

'I *knew* that you'd be furious,' Margaret said in a low murmur. 'But Netta is very tough indeed. When she wants something she goes at it until she gets it: we were passing the house and I just happened, unthinkingly, to say that it was yours and she simply insisted that we came up the track. I do feel *awful*. Really.'

Silently I decided to buy a padlock, aloud I said that it really didn't matter, I wasn't actually working at that hour, that it wasn't her fault (of course it was, the idiot: why not just drive on?), but there were only biscuits, no cake, for tea.

Netta Wynn-Gough, broad of hip, and teeth, tall, scrubbed-faced, came up gaily on to the terrace: she had gone off on her own to 'have a look round the place', with Bendo.

'We, that is my husband and I, Derry – he's Navy, and NOT "wavy" I might add – were offered this place simply years ago, long before you bought it, but it was quite hopeless. A wreck. And the price my dear! Quite potty! The land had gone to hell, there was a car on blocks in one of the rooms, and no telephone! There was nothing one could do with it: *nothing.*'

She named a price far in excess of anything I had paid and announced that I must show her 'simply everything'. I'm *so* curious!'

Well, I didn't as it happened; I managed to avoid that tour, and we had an uneasy tea with supermarket biscuits while Mrs Wynn-Gough chattered on endlessly about what *she* would have done with the garden if it had been hers, and spoke of all the plants I *should* have planted, using only their Latin names, which irritated me because I don't know the Latin names for anything.

'I do see,' she said cheerfully, 'that it is a perfect place for a "recluse", I mean, no one could possibly find it unless they were in a helicopter.'

'You weren't in a helicopter.'

'Ah, no!' she said, with what I suppose she imagined was a roguish smile. 'But sweet Margaret here knew the way, so that was splendid, and I was *so* interested to see how you lived up here in your stronghold.'

'Well . . . it really isn't a stronghold, exactly. There is no moat, no drawbridge, no portcullis, I don't pour boiling oil on people from the ramparts, and, as far as I know, I'm not a recluse. I don't live in a cave exactly.'

Suddenly all eight items seemed instantly desirable.

'Well, shall we say a hermit crab then? People in the neighbourhood say you are,' she said with stunning tact.

'I don't go about in the neighbourhood so I can't understand why people should say that.'

'Just because you *don't* go out! No one ever sees you, do they?'

'I really haven't the least idea: I've spent most of my adult life being stared at by strange people so that I have cultivated deaf ears and a sort of blind eye, it's the only way that I can survive.'

'What I find so extremely odd,' she continued remorselessly, 'is that an actor, of all people, should try to be a hermit crab anyway! It's so contradictory. I mean you all love showing off on the stage and so on. Wallowing in all that adoration and those awful fans. I mean to say, it's not like a hermit crab at all, is it? If a hermit crab did that sort of thing, you know, went about showing off, he'd be eaten alive in no time, wouldn't he?'

She appeared not to realize that she was as voracious as a killer shark herself.

The crassness of her conversation, if that is what she considered it to be, was wearying: it was quite obvious that she had never seen the house before in her life, with or without non-wavy Derry. It had never been for sale before I bought it, it was not a ruin, no car had stood on blocks, and she had, as she had let slip, forced poor unwilling Margaret, now sitting in abject silence, to bring her up because Margaret knew the way and had made a careless remark.

Sheer curiosity had spoiled an afternoon.

The 'hermit crab' part of her conversation was boringly familiar: I always get it, and the 'recluse' and the 'stronghold' bits, too.

I admit to the hermit crab, as you are well aware, but she did not know of the Anthracite Years and the reasons which had forced me to fashion my cover. Neither are people like Mrs Wynn-Gough remotely aware that most actors are hermit crabs by nature. The pulpy flesh within being the true creature, the 'shell' the role which they play on (and sometimes off) the stage or the screen.

An actor is entirely his own instrument. Whereas a painter has canvas, paint and brush to come between himself and his observers, the musician his violin, cello, piano and, at a pinch, his electric guitar, the writer his pen and his selectivity, an actor has only himself to set before an audience: naked and available, even if he be festooned with Falstaff's padding or an astounding variety of putty noses and padded hump-backs.

Discarding his protective shell he is, indeed, completely vulnerable to the sharks who will as often as not eat him alive 'in no time'.

But then those are the rules of the game: he is therefore forced to grow a shell. The almost desperate determination to avoid the Netta Wynn-Goughs of this world, and their ilk – the mundane, the dull, the envious and resentful, the unfulfilled and untalented (and they seem to me to be legion) – literally forces one to become what *they* choose to call a 'recluse' out of sheer self-preservation.

And all that this really means, in the final analysis, is that one tries to avoid direct contact with them as much as is possible for they exhaust, demand, give nothing in return, are supremely self-satisfied, unaware, complacent and patronizing, and, apart from all these little peccadilloes, they are (worst of all things) *boring*. They almost force one to concede that Sir Walter A. Raleigh, who died in 1922, was bang on target when he wrote:

> I wish I loved the Human Race;
> I wish I loved its silly face;
> I wish I liked the way it walks;
> I wish I liked the way it talks;
> And when I'm introduced to one
> I wish I thought *What Jolly Fun!*

At the car, Mrs Wynn-Gough laughed a happy laugh.

'Well, now that I've managed to winkle you out, so to speak, we won't take "No" for an answer, you must come along to us for a glass of sherry on Friday: we have open house every Friday; lots of terribly amusing people, and Derry will be *so* curious to meet you. He encouraged concert parties like anything during the war when we were in Mombasa. You'll have lots to talk about: just let me have your telephone number and I'll give you a tinkle on Thursday to give you directions up to our place.'

I stared at her in glassy silence.

'I really don't remember it, I'm afraid.'

'Your telephone number!'

'Quite forgotten it.'

'I see,' she said, getting into the car. 'A recluse – and rude with it.'

She seemed unaware, as they always are, that she had been pretty bloody rude herself.

I didn't bother to tell her that I can't stick sherry either.

Within my acres up here on the hill I normally have no need of the carapace which I have carefully assembled about me over the years. I am free, in my own little rock-pool as it were, and, apart from the unexpected and unwanted arrivals of outside predators, I feel perfectly safe and relaxed.

The hairline cracks in my complacency, such as the deaths of the dogs, don't for the moment alarm me, for I was almost unaware of them. However, shadows are things which one can see creeping across the landscape; you can't duck those, cannot be unaware. They show.

During the first few years up here, life had been pretty well serene, give or take minor ailments, household disasters and the havoc caused to the land by the unpredictability of the weather at such a height, just below the snowline. The land then was all unfenced, the fox and the badger free to roam at will from field to field as they had always done; but in time changes began to take place which I could not possibly ignore.

The peasants in the valley gradually began to sell off their land and their old houses, moving into the high-rise blocks nearer the town. The jasmine fields, the *rose de mai* and the vineyards were gradually abandoned to thistle and burdock, and one now seldom saw, in the early mornings, before the sun was too high, industrious figures culling the blossoms in the fields below.

It was a harsh life, however romantic it may have appeared from a distance, and now that the essences were made synthetically, and the rose petals were cheaper to import from Turkey, the peasant who had toiled for centuries on his land in the valley found it was less back-breaking, better paid and far more comfortable to work at the check-outs in Monoprix or Carrefour, to attend the petrol pumps in the many new garages, or to work on the big building-sites which were starting to ring the town: you couldn't ignore them either.

Splendid Edwardian villas were torn down and in their places huge blocks of flats, looking like slabs of marzipan cake, rose high above the butchered trees of ancient gardens. The old peasant houses were abandoned, sold to rich Dutch, Danish and German buyers who stripped them out, tarted them up, and laid out lawns and 'patios' where once chickens and ducks had prodded and poked about in dusty yards. The jasmine fields, the fields of *rose de mai*, the artichokes and the vines fell into the hands of speculative builders from London, Paris and Düsseldorf (and almost everywhere else) and were smothered with neo-Provençal villas, each with its swimming-pool, standard lamp-post, wishing-well and barbecue chimney.

The gentle days were torn asunder by the groan and whine of machinery ripping out the new foundations and the song of Provence, if there ever had been one, was no longer that of the golden oriole, the blackbird or the nightingale, but of the cement mixer and the bulldozer.

Times were changing – and changing rapidly; as Madame Miel said sadly one morning when I took down the kitchen refuse for her goats: 'You can't turn your back for a week here now! It happens so quickly, and they are destroying the very things they all come down here to enjoy! The silence and the beauty! The world is crazy.'

Crazy indeed: suburbia was spreading all about us.

Each new villa had, naturally enough, at least two cars to sit in the garages, or to jam the narrow lanes; each villa, of necessity, had an Alsatian or a fierce

Dobermann pinscher to guard the hideous property from intruders. The Alsatians and the Dobermanns roamed the terraces at will, fouled the land, savaged the dogs, and scattered the fox and the badger to distant places up in the hills.

The birds began to leave, too: for the hedges and sheltering brush were destroyed, and crazy-paving or chain-link fences took their place; a nightingale, for example, will only nest in thick scrub three, or less, metres from the ground . . . there was no room for the nightingales. Transistor radios and lawn mowers took over.

The time came, therefore, when I, with a heavy heart, was forced to fence in the land and erect a high wooden gate at the foot of the old track. The ugly chain-link fencing glittered all around me like barbed wire, but it did, at least keep out the Alsatians and the Dobermanns as well as the *folles*, as we called them; these were strange women who found their way up the track in high heels (in the heat of July even), see-through dresses and black frilly underwear, who claimed that they were either 'journalists' or else that we had had imagined assignations in the past or, at least, hoped-for ones in the future. Lady got fed up with locking herself in the house against their abuse but I was always given warning of their unwelcome approach in good time to hide like a criminal.

It was altogether very tiresome, but the fence and the gate did give me some chance of privacy, and thus the 'recluse' became, over the years, far more of a recluse than he had ever wished to be: the first shadows had begun to fall.

In time, however, the fence was smothered with bramble, rust and old-man's beard and was hardly noticeable, the ugly villas were screened by 400 olive trees and a desperate planting of bamboos and poplars along the lower border of the land, and although I felt that I was in a cage, after the freedom to come and go at will, it was an acceptable cage, and, like everything else in life, one grew accustomed to new routines: like locking the gate with padlocks.

For centuries there had been a short-cut through the land down to the lower road and the little chapel on the hill opposite, and this short-cut I insisted must remain, so a gate was built at the top of the hill for Madame Miel to get down to her farm from the village without taking a two-kilometre trudge; and the three old ladies, who tended the chapel, could still make their way, bent in black with broad straw hats in the summer, and knitted caps in winter, to their duties, which consisted of getting the chapel prepared for Easter and Christmas Eve services, clearing out the swallows' nests, and decking the modest altar with wild flowers in old baked-bean cans, and seeing to it generally that the place was cared for.

Time caught us all out eventually.

One by one the old ladies in black died off, the penitents' chapel, consecrated in 1189, crumbled quietly into decay and, in a few months, became only a silent relic frequented by village wooers in the spring and summer, or by hunters in winter who, unable to find anything much to shoot, now shot each other, and lit fires for warmth on the cracked tiles of the chapel floor below the abandoned altar.

Madam Miel began to find the haul up to, and down from, the village too much of an effort, gate or no gate, and securing a tinny 'deux-chevaux' for herself drove, with excruciating caution, round the lanes to her farm; so the gate at the top of the land was locked for ever and the large padlock, and widelinked chain which held it, fused into a rusty lump: a warrior's head by Elisabeth Frink.

From the end of September until the beginning of May the telephone seldom rings, and no one comes, welcome or unwelcome, until the sudden little burst of short-life, which is Christmas.

This lasts only a couple of days in France and is a holy celebration more than a five-day bloat, as it has now become in England, and after it is over everything sinks back into deep winter torpor, the snow falls, ice sheets the pond, bitter winds rattle the shutters and howl under the roof tiles; evenings by a blazing log-stove are long and it seems almost impossible to remember that one had ever walked barefoot across too-hot tiles on the terrace, or sat exhausted with heat under the dense green of the grape-hung vine, grateful for the stillness and the coolth.

Then the spring arrives and the 'recluse' raises the portcullis, lowers the drawbridge, and welcomes the cherished invaders who arrive with the swallow, and the cuckoo.

The house is filled with laughter, conversation, music and sunlight.

Sheets are changed like minds, towels replaced, soap replenished in the bathroom, Tart's Parlour is littered with coathangers, tumbles of suitcases, shoes and other people's clothing.

In the kitchen, there is food that has been carted up from the car in prodigious quantities, wine and beer fill the fridges, ice is made; bowls and jars are crammed with flowers, dishes brim with peaches, apricots, cherries and nectarines, according to the month, and down on the iron rail by the old circular water-tank which once watered the long-lost vineyard the swimming-pool towels flutter like circus banners.

The water-tank is about thirty feet in circumference and six deep; every year I clear it of rotting leaves and water-boatmen and paint it a virulent blue, and it serves very well as a swimming-hole. It is called, with some affection, the Hippo Pool, because all that one can really do in it is wallow.

Essential in the blistering heat of July and August.

From where we sit, sprawl, stand, or lean from windows, the world all below is still strangely very much as it looked when the little chapel was consecrated. The hills have not altered, the land holds its contours, the new villas are more or less hidden, or covered with plumbago and wistaria, even the dreadful modern industrial city, lying in the plain like a pile of discarded pink and white shoeboxes, twelve storeys high, takes on an almost romantic aspect hazed as it is in the glaze of the heat, glowing in the firefly-nights like an Aladdin's Cave.

The fox and the badger have returned, through the holes I left in the fence, at the entrance or exit of their trails; the little owl, the hoopoe, the golden oriole and the nightingale are back too, because my fenced-in area is now an official and registered refuge both for them and for myself; the nightingale, in early June, sings hard in his thicket down by the cess-pit outlet, frogs agree with each other in the pond, '*Quaite, Quite, Quaite, Quite*', a genteel bickering in the still evenings presaging, perhaps, rain tomorrow.

There isn't much that I can complain of for the present.

In late August the thunder-heads begin to rise silently above the hills, the cicadas chatter frantically in the crackly bark of the olives, dragonflies swing and zig-zag over the rushes in the pond, the grass lies dry, golden, crisp as straw. On the vine the grapes have swollen, red and amber-green, gorged on by wasps and the dreaded *frelon*, one sting from which can send you to your doctor, two to the local hospital – and three (so I am assured by the local dustman, who has lived here for seventy years) will kill a horse.

It is wise, therefore, to be prudent in August under the vine.

In the evenings the sun begins its slow decline into dusk just a little earlier. Summer is almost spent.

Down on the trampled beaches the holiday-makers start to pack up the sun umbrellas, tanning lotions, beach balls and beach bags, lash the rubber dinghies to the roof-racks of their cars, and begin the weary bumper-to-bumper journey back to the grey cities of the north.

Trains are crammed with travellers standing in the corridors waving forlorn handkerchiefs in farewell to the deceptively clear blue sea as they speed along the coast to turn inland up the Rhone Valley, until – perhaps? – next year

It must seem a very long time to wait.

In the neo-Provençal villas the shutters go up, the burglar alarms are set, the Alsatians and Dobermanns are crated and despatched home, the garden furniture is stacked under cover for the winter ahead, and the narrow lanes, all at once, become quiet again, and as they were.

There are sudden flash-storms which break the stifling air: swift, wrecking winds which tear the last of the plants in the terrace pots to shreds and scatter the petals of geranium, nicotiana, petunia and roses like cheap confetti across the wind-driven tiles; and then the rain comes – drenching the crisp, baked grass, cooling the fading evenings – and, quite suddenly it always seems, the house is strangely quiet; rooms which echoed with laughter and argument are still – so still that standing alone in the middle of the Long Room one can hear, perfectly distinctly, the drip! drip! of a tap in the guest bathroom.

Everyone has gone.

Down by the Hippo Pool a tumbled bathing towel: yachts and seagulls gaily scrambled.

A pair of sunglasses forgotten under the mulberry tree, bum-dents on the fat upholstery of the terrace chairs: the marks left by a body which has now become only memory, no longer vibrantly physical.

It induces a feeling as strange and as unsettling as that of finding, in the washing-machine, a lipsticked glass and realizing with an acute sense of loss that the person who drank from it last is now already perhaps in New York, San Francisco or London: worlds away. Has there ever been laughter here? Did we talk? Did someone sing, argue about a play, a book or Francis Bacon? Was there life? Did ideas form? Was theory disproved? Was there Mozart, Bach or Gershwin?

Where are the voices which soared with joy as bodies jumped into the Hippo Pool? The cries of pleasure from nephews and nieces, Brock, Rupert, Sarah and Mark, from Rosalind and Nicholas, Penelope and Roddy, Kathleen, Capucine, Glenda, or Elizabeth and George? All gone now, spread through the waves of time, lapping at the edge of memory like a lazy sea, flip-flopping on the sandy beach of a lost summer.

This was negative thinking: negativity, like tears, never does anyone any good, and I had a book to write.

And a secret to keep.

Norah's decision, if such it really was, to 'pull out in March' weighed as heavily with me as bricks in the pockets of a drowning man.

In that early May, when last she had been here, I had taken in her breakfast as usual and found her standing at the open window of Tart's Parlour, her thin nightgown fluttering in the morning breeze, the little silk scarf which she always wore about her shoulders pulled tight in anxious, crippled hands; her head bowed.

'What is it? Norah! What's wrong?'

'A magpie! Down there on the grass.' Her face was taut with distress.

'Dearest Norah! The place is *full* of magpies, all the birds are back again . . . the place is full of magpies: you could call it *Domaine des pies* . . . '

'What's that?' Eyes sharp.

'Oh . . . literally translated: "The Domain of the Magpies".'

She shuddered visibly, pulled the scarf tighter round her shoulders. 'I *must* see another. I simply *must*. Not one; never just *one!*'

'Well, look out again, I bet you'll see fifty . . . '

'I wouldn't dare. I'm flying back to London today . . . and you know the rhyme I suppose?'

'No.'

She crossed the room on bare feet; settled into her Ritz-copy bed again. 'You *do* spoil me. Scrumptious croissants. Black cherry jam . . . '

'What rhyme?'

'This *is* fresh orange, isn't it?'

'You know it is . . . '

She was fiddling with a tea cup and strainer and didn't look up. 'The rhyme? Oh, there are many versions; the one I hate is:

> 'One for sorrow.
> Two for mirth.
> Three for a death.
> Four a birth.
> Five for silver.
> Six for gold.
> Seven for a secret . . . '

She looked up at me quickly, a half smile, tea strainer pointed at my heart.

> 'Ne'er to be told!'

'I promise. I may be dim-witted, you know, but I can keep a secret, I spent years of a war keeping them.'

'Can't imagine how they trusted you.'

'There are six magpies strutting their stuff down on the grass now.'

'Six. That's for gold, isn't it? So that's all right. Except that *you* saw them, not me.'

'You were too chicken.'

'I assume that's American slang for "cowardly"? Well, I was . . . but it'll bring *you* luck, anyway.'

Standing on the deserted terrace, the evening light dying, the cypress trees black against the distant hills, I wondered what on earth I would do without her advice. Who would help me over the high hurdles of writing which I felt unable to leap? Who would assist with the essential 'patching', with the 'needlework' which my unskilled hands and brain would need? Who now would encourage, cajole, bully, sometimes praise, and always lift a flagging morale? I was pretty certain that I would never be able to manage on my own.

The light had almost gone, I started to gather up the garden cushions and cart them into shelter.

It was still only the end of August: I had just seven months.

My moment of vivid panic faded with the last of the light. I reminded myself to go up and turn off the dripping tap in the empty guest room.

Before they were playing 'Jingle Bells' and 'Holy Night' in Monoprix I had completed the first four chapters of the book (*An Orderly Man*) and mailed them to Norah, who accepted them without alteration (she never altered anything I ever wrote – but had a hell of a time with my paragraphing and punctuation) and asked, rather plaintively, when the next ten would be ready. 'It's difficult, you know, to judge a book on only four chapters, but this does "feel" good. If you don't have those beers at lunch I am certain that you could write all afternoon, you follow?'

It had been a bone of contention between us that I could write, clear and fresh, only in the morning, but that after twelve-thirty I was drained, and needed my glass . . . after which all afternoon work was dulled, and in any case the land had to be tended, so the book waited until my head cleared, the hay was mown, and I could go back to the olive store at five-thirty in the afternoon to correct and revise and, as often as not, rewrite. And I was damned if I would break this rule even though I sometimes thought that she was right.

By mid-March, just before she retired from William IV Street, she had ten complete chapters on her desk and the book, lacking only two, was securely 'in the house'. She was greatly pleased and liked it, bullying gently for the final two.

It had been a struggle to get as far as I had; not only because of winter work on the land but because, to my growing consternation, I realized gradually that Forwood was not in his usual good form: something was wrong, and something, he finally confessed, had been wrong ever since we were doing the English shoot the year before. He had said nothing about this at the time because, as always, the 'film comes first' and even though I was sometimes aware, during the shooting, that he was more tired than normal, less interested generally, I put it down to sheer boredom and pushed any nagging fears behind the bastion of work.

'I just haven't any strength now; I suppose it's age?' he said one morning while I was having my beer.

'Better see Poteau. Let him check you over.'

'I think I might.'

The last thing that Forwood ever considered was going to a doctor. This acceptance was a certain sign that all was not as it should be, and the hairline cracks of complacency widened; if he was concerned about himself I had cause to worry. But I was not, at that time, particularly alarmed.

I was sixty-one now; we were no longer the same people who had arrived on a hot July morning more than twelve years before; people grew old, strength did give out. Together we had worked the twelve acres of terraced hillside in all weathers, mowing, raking, carting, burning, tending the trees, the terrace and the lawns which had been created around the house from the tussocky, abandoned land, and were now as green and smooth as baize.

Apart from a couple of wandering Arabs who had carted boulders and rocks about and rebuilt the fallen walls of the terraces, the rest was entirely up to us to manage. It was hard work by any standards; it was also back-breaking, and the fact that it was impossible to leave the place untended for so much as a week, let alone a month, kept work at a constant peak of activity; only in the dark months of winter was there any respite, which is why I started to try and write a book in the first place: it filled in the time.

But now we had a Socialist government in France, a great deal of New Broom Sweeping went on, and one of the first things swept away were the wandering Arabs who, for a pocketful of francs, and a few bottles of iced water during Ramadan, would sweat their guts out carting rocks about and generally doing the heavy work. Everything had to be regularized: no more moonlighting, no more under-the-counter francs according to the hours and the work done.

I could no longer afford the prices charged by the local 'experts'; nor could I afford their social security stamp money.

So twelve acres of land were entirely in the hands of two elderly gentlemen, and with only *one* pair of hands I knew that the land could be lost.

It was something we had often discussed in the past. At forty-nine I was optimistic, or fat-headed enough (have it which way you wish), to think that although the time *would* come when so much land could not be handled, when it would become a kind of albatross about our necks, it wouldn't be for a while.

It would happen 'one day'. No shadows then. Just 'one day . . . '

Well, it seemed that 'one day' had arrived, or if not it was snapping at my heels like a chivvying hound.

So, blood tests were taken which proved negative, pills prescribed which proved useless; and although nothing 'unpleasant' was discovered, Forwood felt not the least bit better, a warning light had flickered on to remind us, if we had forgotten, that we were mortal, and that twelve acres of land were already too much to handle.

But tension, to some extent, had been relieved, and I battled on with the final chapters, the afternoon work was eased a good deal, and I did a 'bit extra', leaving Forwood to cope with lighter work and lighter machines.

In May again Norah arrived in Tart's Parlour for the holiday which we had planned she would have to help ease the hurt of her retirement from Chatto – it was something which she had kept in mind during her bleak last weeks in the shabby little office in William IV Street which had been so particularly her own – but she arrived in pretty good spirits (the break had really not quite hit her) to correct and edit the now completed typescript of *An Orderly Man*, the last book we would do together.

'I had hoped to hang on until you'd got six under your belt: a nice round figure, don't you think? However, five isn't such a bad record, so I can't complain . . . and you are on time, and Iris [Murdoch] is almost ready with hers so at least I go out, as they say, with two damn good books, and I'm still on the letter-paper, somewhere. Down at the bottom as a "consultant" or something. Doesn't mean a thing of course, but it's better than being scrapped absolutely. Now,' – she took up her typescript, pencil in hand – 'you've used the word "sagging" in four places on one page . . . delete three, I suggest?'

We worked together through the warm spring days on the terrace, she gay, alert, relentless, arguing, bargaining, snapping sometimes, as she always did when she was 'editing'. It was fun, exhausting, instructive, and we 'put the book to bed', so to speak, in three days of intensive work, whipping out extraneous words, reparagraphing, deleting pieces which, although they delighted me, alarmed her by their threats of libel. But the book was finished and in her hands. As she had wanted.

One evening, while I was lighting the stove, she suddenly said: 'Is Forwood quite all right?'

'No. Not really. I don't know what's wrong, but something is . . . and now that this is all finished, the book, I think we'd better get over to London and get him looked at. Do you know a first-rate chap? I've been away since '68. Out of touch.'

Naturally, with her many medical problems, she did: and fixed an appointment.

From then on it was a gentle slide: all the way down. Weaseltime was creeping up the tree-trunk, and I was caught almost, but not quite, unaware.

To London, then, and the diagnosis of 'a very slight form of Parkinson's: it's NOT Parkinson's, you understand, but related. It can *all* be dealt with by a very good pill.'

And, to our joint relief, it was: one hurdle over.

The second, as in all good races, was not far beyond; paces only.
A hernia.

Dr Poteau had been long retired by this time so new advice in the area had to be sought. It is far easier to discuss one's symptoms in one's own tongue – having mastered, almost, the vocabulary needed to deal with plumbers, electricians or cess-pit cleaners and the intense complications of the French tax system was not enough. Medical terms are bewildering in any language, describing one's ailments subtle and very complicated, especially in French where a simple word like *fatigue* can, when incorrectly applied, cover anything from 'weariness' to 'a stout pair of walking shoes', and *fatiguer*, different by only one letter, *could* mean that you are boring someone witless or merely tossing a salad. You have to be careful. Errors must be avoided at all costs. One must make the greatest efforts to speak precisely and, even more to the point perhaps, listen with extreme care and attention.

The hernia was diagnosed by a new young doctor Forwood approached one morning in the village shop. He had only recently arrived in the area, had a very pretty, pregnant wife, and rented a pleasant house at the end of the lane. He also spoke excellent English. A young doctor, and an English-speaking one at that, seemed to be the very best solution to many problems: he would know the latest drugs and potions, and would be fresh from training and up to date in his methods.

Just what was required.

Patrick and Solange became very good friends; they were decorative, amusing, young above all, and excellent company, and Patrick, perhaps not perfectly trained in the bedside manner yet, but gentle anyway, spread confidence all about him.

For a little while things seemed to go on an up-stroke.

Okay, a 'form of Parkinson's' and a 'very mild hernia' were boring, and caused problems, but they could be coped with.

I started the mowers. Forwood pushed them around. We got used to it in a short time because we had to do so: I couldn't take on all the mowing myself and write a book. I carried in the heavy stuff from the shopping expeditions, and took the dustbins down to the wooden gate at the end of the track: with patience and understanding, all would be well.

And was: until Forwood started to lose weight rather too rapidly.

In the Long Room one morning Patrick said the word one least wanted to hear.

'Cancer.'

At this stage it was only a 'possibility'; at any stage it was undesirable.

So, more tests and X-rays at the local, excellent, clinic, and after a number of anxious days of waiting a negative report. *Not* cancer, as feared, merely a 'polyp in the lower intestine'.

Anxiety falls away like armour-plating, leaving one light-headed and light in body. There is no great euphoria, I have discovered – one has been too frightened, too exhausted, too tensed for that. There is just a slow, calming spread of relief, and no one gives champagne parties to celebrate. You simply thank whatever Fate may be in charge of you and get on with the life which has, apparently, been returned.

In the middle of all this a film, in the form of a book, had arrived for Glenda and me to make together: we liked it, and were assured that there was enough money, that a good script would be forthcoming, plus director, and that we would start shooting in the January of the following year. I had gone ahead with discussions because until we were quite certain of the medical facts it seemed foolish not to – it was also good for morale to have an alternative thread of thought, even if the thread, at the time, was exceptionally slender. I also started a new book based mostly on the trip I had made to Hollywood a year earlier when I was able to go, for the first time ever, to places into which I had never ventured before, simply because on my first visits to Hollywood those areas were considered either 'unsafe', 'black' or 'unsmart'. One didn't go, I wasn't taken. So I never got to them. On this last trip things had changed a little, and I went off and discovered an area of Los Angeles (and a forgotten cast of lost Europeans living there) which I had never come across before. I discovered a strange bigotry, hatred, hysteria and racial intolerance which was new and disquieting. To lose the chance of writing it up seemed foolish, especially as it is essential to try and exist normally during a period of excessive stress.

Barium meals, blood tests, X-rays and all the rest took their places sensibly in my mind as I started to plot and plan and work out a construction line for the new book.

The land foundered . . . if land can do such a thing – the grass grew longer, the walls became slightly ragged, the energy behind the extreme effort required to maintain it was low, to say the least – but on the surface, to the unobservant eye, it looked not very different. Just a bit blowsy. Not yet neglected, but not quite cared for with passionate love.

There wasn't much strength left over to give it that now.

Things could have been a great deal worse, it had to be faced. A new film ahead of me, a new book, in a new 'style', well on its way, and as soon as we got to London in January the polyp, which naturally was ever-present in the darkest recesses of the mind, would be 'nicked out', as Patrick had so eloquently said, and everything would be back to normal again. Or as near normal as we now could ever be, give or take a 'mild hernia' and a 'very slight form of Parkinson's'.

The fact that the first script of the new film was a disaster didn't cause me a great deal of surprise, or Glenda for that matter, who is hard to surprise, anyway – and we were assured that a new writer would be brought in, that the money was still all there, and that a splendid director had been chosen whom we would both like very much. (We did, as it happened, greatly. But he was whipped off the project to do a far bigger job, just before the end of the year.)

However, after more than sixty films I was pretty well undismayed, and still – idiotically – trusting, and rather gratified to think that I had already got six chapters of the new book finished and ready to take to London in January when the film – surely? – must go as planned.

The night before I was due to leave, packing a large suitcase for the three months' shoot, with a wretched Bendo hanging around, hounding – or is it really 'dogging'? – one's footsteps, aware that something unpleasant for him was in the air, the telephone rang to say not to come over, there *was* money for the film – but there *wasn't*. What does one make of that kind of inane remark? You either have the money or you haven't, especially one week away from shooting, and with Glenda already half-way through fittings for her wardrobe.

I was more concerned, frankly, with getting to London and seeing that Forwood had his polyp removed.

So we left anyway; the whole thing, at my end – guardians for the house, accommodation booked at the Connaught, appointments made for hospitals and doctors, and so on – was all too firmly arranged: I couldn't pull out, even had I wanted to. In some odd way I felt secretly convinced that as soon as we got to England things would fall into place somehow.

And they did.
But not quite as I had expected.

I was fidgeting through a battered copy of *Country Life* in the waiting-room of the London Clinic: a small dreary room, chairs round the sides, a table with old magazines and a sad-eyed Pakistani lady sitting opposite me.

I don't know what month the *Country Life* was, I don't even remember what year it was, but I do remember a church, a river and daffodils on the cover: the trivial detail which imprints itself on the mind when one waits for a medical diagnosis.

Suddenly, a whisper of starched overalls, a woman at my side, half kneeling, her hand on my arm. She was small, dark; a gleam of glass beads at her throat, the edge of a flowered print showing at her neck.

'Now *please*! Don't be distressed, don't panic!'

I closed *Country Life* carefully: I had not the slightest intention of doing either.

'It's bad news,' she said, quite unnecessarily.

I got up and replaced *Country Life* among the pile of tattered magazines on the table.

The Pakistani lady placed her hands together, bowed her head towards me with a sweet smile of sympathy; I said: 'Thank you', and turned to the overalled woman hovering at my side impatiently.

'If you'll come along with me? I'm afraid that Mr Forwood is rather, ummm, rather upset.'

Mr Forwood was, apparently, quite the opposite: he was lying on an inspection bed, in a short blue paper shift, a cup of tea and a biscuit in one hand, his other comfortably behind his head, smiling wryly.

'Well then,' he said.

'What's up?'

There was a tall, pleasant-looking young doctor in the small room and a red-haired nurse.

'Well, apparently it's a bit more than *just* a polyp . . . not quite as simple,' said Forwood.

'The sooner it's dealt with, surgically, the better,' said the young doctor. 'He'll be a lot better without it, I assure you.'

The nurse smiled kindly, took Forwood's empty cup, and she and the doctor left.

For a moment we looked at each other in silence; somewhere in the street below a car blew an impatient horn three or four times.

'Go and have a word with him, will you? While I get dressed? They took photographs, I think, and I'm not certain that he's told me all I'd like to know. You have a word, will you? Try and find out. They are all so secretive – after all it is *my* bloody polyp . . . or whatever it is.'

In the hall outside, men were repairing the ceiling, there were dust sheets draped everywhere, and perfectly ordinary, healthy people clambered about on step-ladders repairing pipes or electric wiring, banging and joking, pulling things about.

The young rugger-bugger doctor was extremely pleasant; he was drinking a mug of coffee when I reached him behind a cluttered desk.

'I think that Mr Forwood is a bit uncertain about what he's actually *got* – I'm pretty good at disinformation, if that worries you . . . but if you could perhaps let me know?'

The doctor picked up a small bundle of Polaroid photographs.

'Help yourself. Take your pick. But take a look at this one first: may give you some idea.'

A black photograph with, dead centre, a sulphur yellow blaze of vicious light. An evil starburst brilliant, flaring; deathly.

'Well, not a polyp,' I said.

He shook his head. 'No. Not a polyp, I'm afraid.'

'Odd. Everyone has checked the X-rays – the French doctors, the London doctor . . . '

'Doesn't always show up on an X-ray. Easy to miss.'

'How long can it wait?'

'*Not* long. A day or so . . . soon as possible, frankly. Sorry, it's bloody bad luck.'

An immense sense of calm swamped me.

Now that I knew for sure, now that the weeks of uncertainty and strain were ended, dissolved instantly by the blatant, brutal, vicious yellow blaze in my hand, I knew exactly what to do and how to do it. I was grateful, also, that we were in London and not sitting, all unaware, up on the hill miles from anywhere: now at least there was a chance.

If you have a chance you can deal with anything. Or try.

'Well, what did he say?' Forwood and I were walking down to the street, rather than talking together in the lift with others around us.

'Didn't really say much, honestly. I saw the photographs . . . looks to me like a sort of abscess-thing. Obviously the sooner it's removed the better – no wonder you've been feeling so wretched for so long.'

No wonder.

Four days later he was filling in his rank, name and number, and various other military details requested, on a buff form in a small grey room in the King Edward VII Hospital for Officers, naming his son Gareth next of kin, but giving me full authority to take charge.

Gareth and I walked down Marylebone High Street in the bitter winter Sunday, across a deserted Oxford Street towards the Connaught.

'I'd better tell you quite frankly that it is cancer – Pa doesn't know that *yet*, but he's not an idiot,' I said.

'Is it malignant?'

'Don't know. Can't say. But the photograph I saw was not friendly. That's all I can tell you at this moment.'

'So it's a matter of crossing fingers?'

'That's it. In one.'

At the Connaught I stripped out Forwood's room and repacked his suitcase; couldn't afford that now, it would be at least a six-week haul, and severe, stringent economies had to be made immediately.

The film had collapsed like a wet paper bag the week before – so had the money, my expenses and its director.

With an intestinal 'problem' . . .

The week before – how far away it seemed.

It had started reasonably well: London was arctic, the plane on time, the luggage intact; the Connaught suite (modest because I was there to do a modest film, with matching expenses) crammed with spring flowers, and gift-wrapped bottles to welcome one back, not just to London, but to the start of a new film after some years away.

It was all very jolly and comforting.

I started work almost immediately, with costume fittings at Berman's, who had dressed me for a great many films and plays for more than thirty years, and discovered, to my pleasure, that according to Phillip Link, my cutter, I had only put on two inches round the waist in all the years.

'Beer bloat' Norah would have called it. Rightly perhaps.

I chose a selection of shabby suits and tattered shirts, old shoes and battered hats (it was a battered-hat, shabby-suit part), and although there was always a faintly queasy feeling that there *was* no money to make the film we carried on in that idiotic way film-people do, confident that all was well, certain that, whatever happened, we were bound to start work on the appointed day: too much had already been set up to pull back now.

Glenda liked her costumes, her wigs and almost everything else; except the script: which was, after five rewrites, still a mess. A curate's egg: bits good, bits bad. We were fairly convinced that we would get it all together eventually, 'on the floor'. That fatal phrase which has been used so often in the cinema and brought so many films to grief. You can't (or very seldom can) get it right 'on the floor'. It doesn't work that way. But we always hope it will; it's a survival complex.

We had a new, exuberant, determined director who threw optimism about him like a happy reveller with a sack of confetti at *mardi gras*. We were smothered in his confidence and happiness. If *he* felt like this, why, then, should not we?

For some reason we didn't. Unease lay just below the surface like a quicksand, but I have made so many films under these same circumstances that I was not dismayed. I'd walked planks across quicksands more often than most players – I was sure I could do so again, conveniently forgetting that I had often slipped neatly off, and drowned.

I confess that I did have a slight gut twinge when I overheard someone suggest, at Berman's, that my costumes should 'not be altered or refitted for the time being'. We were only days from the start.

A pretty clear suggestion that the money *wasn't* there, and was far from secure; but I battered along with the happy director daily, up in the little suite among the spring flowers, trying to wrestle the script into some kind of shape.

There were, of course, other pleasures.

Suppers and luncheons, visits to the cinema and the theatre – things I missed in France, where all the films were dubbed and there was no theatre; anyway, in my town.

I went to Drury Lane to see *The Pirates of Penzance* in a new American version, desperately hoping that the hideous theatre ghost of the Anthracite Years in Glasgow would be laid for ever: and it was.

I went to see *ET* in a cinema whose audience was obviously on the verge of acute starvation, for they crammed themselves with food, to right and left of me, from the start of the advertising to the end of the main credits; and beyond. They slurped tomato soup through paper straws from half-pint plastic cartons; removed onion rings with fastidious fingers from their McDonald's, scattered them under the seats and over my shoes.

'Too many onions,' a woman in thick glasses and an Aran-knit sweater said.

'Probably horse, not beef, anyway,' said her companion.

'Eric! You've put me off . . . you *are* rotten . . . '

Finally, ten minutes into the film, they threw their litter under the seats, and crunched and crumpled it under their feet.

'Eric! Hanky, dear,' she said.

They started to clean up.

Did Mr Spielberg know that this was the audience for whom he was making his film? Why, in the name of sanity, was I making one myself if this is how our work was now accepted? They shut up after a while, and finally, in floods of tears, held on to each other like survivors on the raft of the Medusa, sobbing helplessly.

A perfect example, if example was needed, of a Television-Trained Audience. Contempt and indifference, and then facile emotion. A frightening new breed; anyway to me.

No wonder people had stopped going to the cinema. It was no longer a pleasure. Who wants to watch a film in a litter of plastic, and the stench of fat-saturated foods?

But there were happier compensations to this cinematic gluttony. Norah, in her pretty flat in Vincent Square, was definitely one of them.

Brown bread and butter, scones and honey, Earl Grey's tea, a blazing fire, the plane trees in the square whipped by a sleety wind and the first bound copy of *An Orderly Man* in my hands.

'And the six chapters of the new book are *werry, werry* good,' she said, stretched out in her deep armchair in orange slacks and an Italian sweater.

'Werry good.' Sometimes, when she was making a strong point, she used 'W' instead of 'V' and it never ceased to amuse me, and impress me, because I knew that her emphasis was indicative of her enthusiasm.

'I just wish the firm were going to print it. It seems terrible to me. A neat *six* books . . . it would have been perfect. *I'd* have said "Yes" in a shot.'

'Well the firm [Chatto] haven't exactly invited me to stay: I haven't had a letter, or heard a word from them, in the year since you retired, so I feel it's better I go elsewhere. If I'm lucky.'

'But surely John? You've been writing to John, surely?'

'Oh yes. Of course . . . but only about *Orderly Man* . . . business, that's all.'

'What's your *agent* . . .' – she paused heavily on the word – ' . . . going to do: she's a nice gel, very tough, very competent, you're in good hands, so I suppose she's got plans for this?'

'Pat [Kavanagh] is going to auction it. Next week.'

Norah sat bolt upright staring at me as if I had kicked her cat or vomited on the carpet before her.

'Auction it! It isn't even finished! You're a chapter short! You can't auction – *filthy* word – an unfinished book! It's madness.'

'Well . . . that's what's happening. Sorry. You asked and I've told you. I'm on my own now, I have to do as I'm advised by Pat and I reckon she knows what she's up to.'

'A pretty gel, *very* bright indeed, but to auction an unfinished book seems to me to be verging on insanity. When can you finish it?'

'It's blocked out. I know where I'm going. I'll get down to work as soon as the film is over and I'm back home. April . . . sometime about then.'

Norah sighed resignedly, offered me another scone, put a log on the fire. 'Things are changing' was all she said. 'I suppose I'll never come into the twentieth century, will I?'

I walked through the gathering dusk from Victoria, up across Green Park, where years ago I had scuffed my way through deep snow in wet shoes having refused fame and fortune in Hollywood, back to the modest suite in the hotel and the smell of white hyacinths which Joseph Losey had sent with 'Welcome! Next time it's with me.'

We had tried to work together for years, but there was always the same old problem. Money. We were neither of us any use to the 'box office', in fact we were famously known as 'risks'. So there wasn't much point in any 'next time' – I was certain there never would be, and there never was, alas. But the hyacinths and his thought comforted me.

Forwood was on the telephone when I arrived, replaced the receiver.

'They've fixed an appointment for the polyp business on the 8th . . . so we'll have to hang on until then, film or no film, and go back about the 10th . . . all right with you? I mean, if the film folds, that is?'

'What I'll do is accept the National Film Theatre Lecture. They have offered to pay my expenses here for two or three days, so if the film goes down the drain we can still hang on here until the 8th . . . it won't cost us much that way.'

Glenda came to lunch the next morning, uncertain, on edge, feeling, I could detect even before she said so, pretty certain that there was no money for the film and, what's more, that there never had been or would be. We ate an expensive lunch in light gloom, and when I saw her to her car in Mount Street to drive back to Blackheath she made me promise that if I heard any news I'd call her instantly. I promised.

I had only just got back to the hotel and up into the suite when the phone rang to say that our exuberant, optimistic, happy director had collapsed and been taken to the London Clinic with 'abdominal complications, probably serious'.

Glenda, by that time, could only have been going through Grosvenor Square . . . there was no point in calling her in Blackheath for at least half an hour or more.

Forwood and I sat in a fairly dejected mood. No money – we had expected that; but a 'probably' serious illness for a much respected and liked director was something else. What could that mean, now?

Agents and producers arrived; the suite was filled with fretful, worried executives. Yes, they *had*, finally, got the money, but the director was ill . . . and the production would have to be delayed until April at least. Maybe longer, depending on the seriousness of his illness. Would we postpone, Glenda and I?

Glenda, when I finally reached her, listened in silence and then, with a resigned sigh, agreed. We'd delay until April.

But I knew in my heart that the stuffing had gone out of us both.

The film had now been put on the 'back boiler', so to speak, but it was equally true to say that we had gone off the boil.

It had all dragged on too long: the 'on-off' business of the money had lowered our enthusiasm. Trying to raise a million pounds to cover the *entire* cost of one film, including our salaries, the sets and costumes, the crew, locations and our now unhappy director had irritated and depressed me.

I knew, very well, that some players received two or three times that amount as their salaries alone in dollars for playing almost supporting roles in some turgid war or Bible extravaganzas. To have to haul about, almost with a begging bowl it seemed, from company to company and, indeed, country to country (for they had tried to raise money even in Los Angeles), to finance a film in which someone of Glenda's stature was to play, infuriated me.

The fact that I was 'box office poison' because of the 'intellectual films' which I had made, and which did not attract a mass audience, did not faze me. I had made those films from choice, and I'd had a pretty good run for whatever money they earned me, which wasn't very much; but to think that the two of us, so recently apparently nominated (even if we didn't win them) for the Emmies in the States, praised for 'the two best performances of the year' in New York, and generally swamped with hysterically enthusiastic hype, couldn't get ourselves hired to make a small, amusing *British* movie filled me with despair.

Even though the scripts had been a problem, the book from which they were written was excellent, and there *could*, in time, have been an acceptable screenplay. More despairing indeed even than that was the unhappy fact that there *still* was no money, in spite of firm assurances to the contrary, but it seemed that the sudden collapse of our bustling director had come at an opportune moment: it gave everyone more time to go on looking for elusive funds.

Shortly after this, the pound fell so low against the dollar that it was essential that Glenda and I had our contracts completely redrawn; the deal we had agreed, months ago now, made no sense at all.

So, as far as we were concerned, the film was off for good. I determined that, for the few days left to me in London while we awaited Forwood's operation, I'd fill in the time by seeing some shows, meeting old friends, ordering books from Hatchards for the long winter evenings ahead, do my National Film Theatre Lecture and an 'in-depth' interview for the BBC, and then, when all that was over, clear off back to sanity and peace up on the hill, leaving the miseries and uncertainties behind.

Just chalk it up to experience, and forget about movies from now on in. I'd return to the olive store, bruised, but intact.

Three days later I was sitting in the waiting room of the London Clinic fidgeting through an old copy of *Country Life* . . .

TEN

DIARY

MONDAY, FEB. 14TH '83.

Walk to Edward VII in bitter cold. Buy champagne-splits, toothbrush, soap. F. wants a bath. No soap provided, apparently.

Back to Connaught: interview with rather smooth young man, pleasant, and possibly friendly, but won't know, as usual, until I see his piece printed. Many a slip between Interview and Article. Take the risk because it is for *The Times*.

F. asked for a print or picture to have on wall of his rather spartan room. Wants a 'Country scene: fields and things, summery: something I can tell myself stories about while I'm lying here. You understand?' I do. But where to go? Probably Medici tomorrow.

National Film Theatre Lecture. Theo Cowan collects me early at four-thirty. Show sold out with no advertising, which pleases me, but am still terrified. Good audience, clever, alert, good reception as far as I can make out, on stage for two and a quarter hours, which seems quite long, but as always am far too nervous to register anything.

Norah there, John Charlton and wife Susan, Olga (my French agent) comes from Paris, Margaret Hinxman, Gareth F. and many others. All have drinks in gloomy black Refreshment Room, but feel happy all went well. Olga Horstig Primuz amazed, and moved, by the long clip shown from *Neal Story* which closed show. She can't imagine why it has never been shown as a film; it looks fantastic on Big Screen.

I can't imagine why either. Ho hum.

TUESDAY, FEB. 15TH '83.

Hospital late, 10.45 a.m. because of incoming calls anxious about F. Amazing how news gets about. But comforting so many people care.

Walk to Medici. Fairly hopeless really. Flower prints, Burmese ladies, Chinese horses, and masses of Rowland Hilders. Finally unearth print of *A Somerset Field* for five quid.

Hospital staff wonderfully kind and helpful. Sister Hilda Ford and I stick print on wall at foot of F.'s bed with some kind of awful sticky chewing-gum stuff I've never seen before. She assures me that it won't mark wall or print.

Elizabeth calls in afternoon.

'Do you want me to come up to town? Bit of company?'

Worry about her own family obligations in Sussex.

Say 'Yes'.

'Good. If you'd said "No" I don't think I would ever have spoken to you again. I'll stay at Sarah's [her daughter] flat.'

Walk back to hospital in evening. Taxi fares too much, and exercise will do me good. Fairly safe from recognition. If people don't *expect* to see you in a place they don't see you. Simple. Passing Miss Selfridge, however, a whole window, it appeared, of young women started screaming and waving and jumping up and down. Maybe they thought I was someone else? Will buy tweed cap at Purdey's tomorrow for safety.

Watch an hour of dire television. God! They say the French are bad. Bed ten-thirty with this diary.

WEDNESDAY, 16TH FEB. '83.

D-Day for F.

Pat Kavanagh calls early to say she has made very satisfactory deal for *West of Sunset* minus its last chapter. Slightly overcome, but very cheered, couldn't have happened at a better time. All I have to do is finish final chapter: they say they will wait until May-June. They'll be lucky.

Elizabeth arrives 12.30 a.m. Brings mimosa for F. to 'remind him of home', it instantly goes into tight black balls in the heat of his room, but is a very kind thought. We wait with F. until his pre-med injection at two-thirty.

Sally Betts [my typist] suggests I write final chapter in hotel while I am stuck there: says she knows my handwriting after all these years and can easily cope. A very generous offer, but I don't see myself making the effort to.

Hospital at 6.30 p.m., sit in library and wait for 'Prognosis'. Read one sentence of the book I have brought with me fifty or a hundred times.

Surgeon extremely pleasant, kind, serious, aware. Get full details. Malignant growth. But certain, almost, that he has removed it 'cleanly' and nothing has spread. If all goes well he suggests that F. will be mowing and 'doing all those chores he dislikes in the garden' in a year. *If.*

Wait in F.'s room until he is brought down from Recovery (8.15 p.m.) Very pleasant matron offers me coffee or tea and biscuits. I decline. She says: 'You *do* know what to expect in here, don't you?'

I assure her that I do. Pretty good at hospitals after five hospital films (the *Doctor* series) in a row, plus *The Patricia Neal Story.*

F. zonked out, very small in large wheeled bed, lots of tubes and bottles, drips and feeds and saline solutions or whatever they are. Help nurses (all young and super) to hang bottles and untangle tubes. They say no point really in hanging about because he'll be 'out' for hours yet.

Take my overcoat and in passing foot of his bed raise my voice in full theatrical projection. 'Well. No good hanging about, Sister. I'll be off now.' F. suddenly opens his eyes, smiles, zonks out again.

Call Gareth F. and reassure him as far as I can, call Margot Lowe (F.s oldest and closest friend) in San Francisco. She says: 'You need money, or you need me? I'll get the next plane out, be with you tomorrow.' Am very touched, tell her I'll call when I know more details. At moment we just wait.

I think that nurses should be paid a thousand pounds a day.

THURSDAY, FEB. 17TH.

Hospital at 10.30 a.m. F. very doped but aware. Discomfort, prefers sleep.

I go with Elizabeth and Sarah to Covent Garden Market. Elizabeth so proud of new Market you'd think she built it herself. But a market is a market. Kitsch, pottery mugs, second-hand clothes, Japanese junk, tinny jewellery . . . but fun anyway, and not *like* London.

Drinks and sandwiches at The Globe. Super Victorian pub almost unchanged; jammed. A Guinness at ten bob rocked me slightly! Walk back to Connaught taking in the National Gallery. Elizabeth ravished by the Sargents: particularly the family group of the Sitwells. Lots of Impressionists I'd forgotten were here. Amazed, and very curious, at the amount of young people present. Punks, rockers, red hair, green hair, Mohican hair, shaved heads, but all informed, sensible, interested. Hopeful signs? Buy a dozen postcards of Vuillard's *La Cheminée*.

Hospital: F. okay, fed up with physiotherapist who thumps him all the time to try to get rid of some phlegm in his lungs, residue of the cold he arrived with; otherwise all well.

FRIDAY, FEB. 18TH.

Walk to hospital. Reckon I'm saving between £8-12 a day. Easy walk and pleasant. First snowdrops in Manchester Square and a blackbird singing this evening from some scaffolding. Dear Sir: Is this a record?

Woman at crossing in Oxford Street waiting for the lights says: 'Excuse me, were you Dirk Bogarde?' I say no, sorry. Not me. Perhaps it's the Purdey cap?

Tea this afternoon Norah. Crumpets and roaring fire. She has cut her hand on a rusty nail in a piece of firewood. Oh, Lor' . . .

SATURDAY, FEB. 19TH.

Dull. Bitter. Walk to hospital. F. stronger, more alert. Buy enormous tin of candies for the nurses, all of whom are incredibly kind and caring. Nurses should get two thousand pounds a day. Not one. Cold starting, I think. Bugger.

Lunch Elizabeth and Sarah at very noisy restaurant (their choice not mine) at end of Kings Road. Ear-splitting noise, plates crashing on tiled floor, food fairly oily, masses of Sloane Rangers, 'Hooray Henrys' plus 'Hooray Henriettas', with too many children, all shouting and eating pasta. Proof they've all 'done' Italy at some time, I suppose. Rupert [nephew] and pretty girl, Portia, arrive for coffee. Three bottles of wine. Elizabeth insists on paying with her Barclaycard. Never had one in her life before . . . showing off! Cost a bomb too, silly girl.

Rupert drives me back to Connaught in clapped-out car, very fast, very expert, a really super chap, at least six foot four. Where does he get the height in our family of 'ordinary measure'?

F.'s room massed with flowers like a mobster's funeral parlour. Remove most into the corridor, he'll suffocate. Stay longer than normal: a good sign.

Boaty Boatwright, Diana Hammond, Kathleen Tynan call from N.Y. A lot of love flying around.

Meet Kathleen Sutherland in Hall. Sad, growing old. She was so vivid and glamorous when she taught me fashion design at Chelsea Poly in '37-38. Misses Graham terribly and says she is just waiting to join him. Why did he have to go first?

No answer to that.

MONDAY, FEB. 21ST.

Hospital gives way this a.m. to TV. I do live-by-satellite interview with some chap on a chat show in Australia.

'Why do you do those awful chat shows, you always swore Never Again,' someone asks.

For £500 is why.

Telephones from Charlotte [Rampling], Rosalind [Bowlby], Glenda, [Jill] Melford and others offering meals, drinks, comfort, affection. Grateful and glad.

F. off his 'drips' and, more to the point, the hated cathoda (or however you spell it). Take him walk up and down corridor, first time out of bed: corridor crammed with crawling ladies and gentlemen in dressing-gowns with nurses at their elbows. A little like the Promenade Deck on the *Queen Elizabeth* but not as much fun.

Terrific improvement, however; last Wednesday was Op-Day.

We will have to return [to London] every six months for 'checks'. A slight blow. I am anxious to get home, try to finish chapter, and begin to sell up the house. It seems clear that the future must be nearer help. Not London, I hope. Maybe Paris. But whatever, it's farewell to the hill. Sod it.

F. could come out on Sunday for 'a couple of hours only'.

TUESDAY, FEB. 22ND.

Still freezing. Hospital early, but take taxi because I'm a bit late. Driver flatly refuses my fare, 'Because you have given me and my wife so much pleasure for so many years.' I'm very touched: there are some really splendid people in this town, it's just the people they vote in who are such sods. Sign his autograph book for 'Mavis'.

Forwood stronger, but still pretty fragile. Says that on the lunch menu today he could have 'African Beef Stew'.

What can it possibly be? Elephant, buffalo, giraffe? The mind is dazzled.

WEDNESDAY, FEB. 23RD.

In local shop for fresh fruit. At counter elderly man, frail hair combed like membranes over bald head, regards me with worry and distinct unease. I look at the broccoli avoiding his gaze. Recognition, I can see, is struggling hard while he chooses my Comice pears. Calls younger assistant (28?) arranging pyramid of wilting cauliflowers.

'Is it HIM?' asks Membrane-Hair.

Younger one looks at me with intensity of a scanner. I continue to look at broccoli and Golden Delicious.

'Nah,' says younger man. 'Might have been, years ago, but *not* now.'

Chastened I take pears and go to check-out; hear sudden cry behind me: 'Yeah! It *was* him!'

Make for Davies Street quickly. Age! Oh, Lord!

THURSDAY, FEB. 24TH.

Clear out mass of dead flowers into sluice room. Nurses rather pushed this morning so offer to help F. bath. A bit of a struggle, but quite funny, and stitches are out, clean as a whistle, which is why bath permitted.

Lunch with Charlotte at Claridge's. Pretty suite, very glamorous, terrible food. Charlotte lovely, cool, superbly dressed, calm. A pleasant lunch therefore, the food, with such elegance beside one, doesn't seem to matter.

Am amused, in retrospect, that the only person who has not recognized me in London, in one form or another, is the concierge at Claridge's.

SATURDAY, FEB. 26TH.

Lunch with Molly Daubeny in her elegant house in Victoria. Buy vast bunch of expensive freesias and have super lunch (smoked salmon and turbot cooked by my hostess) in exchange. A loving friend for almost forty years: it's important to keep your friends, thank God I have.

James Fox, amazingly, comes to dinner in evening. First time we have met since '67. Unchanged, a little more adult (but there was room for that) and a moustache which makes him look like a Camberley subaltern. He swears it's for a film. I hope so.

SUNDAY, FEB. 27TH.

Car to hospital to collect F. All nurses, and most of staff it would appear, on steps to wish him well.

Drive him back at four-thirty. Weary, but pleased that tomorrow he'll be out for good. Best day for a very long time indeed.

MONDAY, FEB. 28TH.

Last day of this fretful month. Buy framed prints (*Hay Wain*, etc.) for hospital rooms, with matron's approval . . . leave hospital in flurry of affection from nurses. F. clearly very well liked, *and* admired, in Ward 1.

Flowers galore at Connaught. From Sheila Attenborough, Daph Fielding, Melford, Forwood family, among others. He rests in the afternoon, I go to Royal Academy to see Cimabue Crucifix. (Okay if you like relics, I suppose.)

We discuss, gently, prospect of selling up in France. It is suggested that we might have to come back to England. Many hurdles to jump before that.

WEDNESDAY, MARCH 2ND.

Hounded practically all day by Press who want statement on David Niven (ill in the Wellington). I don't know David Niven, and wouldn't speak to Press anyway even if I did. Strange race, journalists, strange country; hounding a dying man to the grave.

THURSDAY MARCH 3RD.

Walk with F. very, very slowly 'round the block' (Grosvenor Square). But he's stronger. I walk all afternoon round the Serpentine. Brisk, sunny day. Masses of people about, not one English voice among them. It's like Central Park.

SATURDAY, MARCH 5TH.

Day of triumph! F. walks round Serpentine with strength and a stick and enjoys the air, the Brent geese, and the snowdrops in the Dell.

SUNDAY, MARCH 6TH.

To Royal Avenue to see Joseph Losey. Old, gross, weary and worried. He offered two suggestions for possible movies we could make but both are dreadful. He doesn't know what to do next and misses Paris (where he had been living for some years) bitterly.

'No one knows who I am here any more. They *all* do in Paris. And I know who everyone is there. London is different; it's changed entirely; new trends and new faces. I'm a stranger *again*.' A terrible sadness.

I think of myself and my probable return to this strange, to me too, city, and dread the thought, so tune out. Joe suddenly wonders if we could make *Lotte in Weimar* with Peggy Ashcroft and a script by Harold [Pinter], but I suggest that Harold probably a bit too busy and famous for us now. However, agree, because he looks so miserable, but am forced to ask 'When?' to which he, naturally, can give no answer.

MONDAY, MARCH 14TH.

Elizabeth and George arrive to accompany us to airport and home. She will do the housekeeping, George the land which has been neglected for so long. I'll need help. Wheelchair, stick and the rest of the paraphernalia. Forwood valiant and brave; anyway, it's better than walking at terrible Heathrow. I push him and no Press near because we are flying Air France. So that's a relief. Flight on time, easy, specified seats (booked in advance . . . why *can't* you on 'The World's Favourite Airline', BA?) and land at Nice about four. Fine spring rain, car waiting, arranged by Arnold (my ex stand-in for many years) and we drive home with anxious, and not very good, driver who is terrified of the narrow lanes, sounding horn at every bend.

Marie-Christine [guardian] has meal ready for evening, house spotless, flowers in Long Room. All smells of strong 'shag' (her husband rolls his own cigs) but all serene. Bendo slightly hysterical. Settle F. and then discover that I have left his suitcase down at the airport. Typical. I'm so bloody *capable*. But we are back at home.

For the time being, at least.

In June, when the big fig-tree down at the end of the track was breaking leaf, the roses in the pond-bed were at their peak, and the neglected terraces flowed with lush green grass, moving in the morning air just as I remember that it did years ago in Great Meadow before the hay harvest, I put the house on the market discreetly (even Lady didn't know), and sold it twenty-four hours later to a pleasant Belgian couple with two children and another on the way.

It was, they said, exactly what they wanted: no changes, no alterations, everything to be left just as it was. They even suggested that I simply pack the clothes and personal pieces and pictures and leave the place to them, as it stood.

This I had to refuse: it had taken years to collect all the clutter together which made it so, apparently, attractive to them, and I might need it again somewhere else. It was agreed that they could take possession in September-October.

We'd have a final summer on the hill.

The following week was spent with the firm in Cannes who had moved us in on that fateful day long ago (fateful because the English packers in London had smashed practically every piece to bits), and would now crate us up and move us to their depot in Paris until I knew where I wanted to settle.

I had absolutely no idea where to go: I only knew that a six-monthly medical check, and the possibility that something might go wrong at any time, meant that I had to be within an hour, if possible, of London at all times. It is no delight to be seriously ill, or ill at all, in a foreign language, and although I knew from experience that there were splendid hospitals, and excellent doctors, in Nice, Nice was almost as far away in the end as London.

How could I close up the house and just leave it? The place was seething with wandering Yugoslavs, Arabs and out-of-work youths who would have stripped the place bare in a few hours for drug money, and there was no one near enough to notice if they did. What would happen to the wretched dog? Couldn't cart him to an hotel in Nice . . . How could I, who had hardly ever thought for myself, deal with so many problems? No 'recluse' was I now: the hermit crab was suddenly shell-less – you can't take full charge of your life skulking away in protective camouflage.

I'd been spoiled over the years by Forwood, who shielded me from anything which might remotely disturb the work I was doing for the cinema. Every bill, contract, script, family problem, household worry, letter or tax demand had been in his capable hands.

Now there was no cinema – that door in the corridor had swung shut it would appear – the door which had opened into the world of writing cast the only light down the unnerving length, filled with worrying shadows. But it did leave me enough light to see which way to walk, which was just as well, frankly, because now, all of a sudden, I was Leader.

Although, as I have said, I have always had a reasonable sense of 'possessions' I have never believed in 'possessiveness', so that once I had made the unhappy decision to sell it was firm and definite and there was to be no looking back. It had been a good time – probably the best time of my adult life – and it had come at the right moment. If it had to end now, then so be it: I really couldn't complain, everything has to come to an end someday, however much we believe in 'ever after' and all that rubbish with which the frail human consoles himself by reiterating from childhood to tomb – which, as the song says, 'Isn't so long a stay'. And, in any case, I have never believed that anything can last – this was the one useful legacy, I suppose, apart from strength, which I gained from the Anthracite Years – so I am seldom taken by surprise.

I had, however, not quite reckoned on the effect this positive action of mine might have on a sick man.

While I was hustling about planning what to take and what to leave, what garden furniture to dump, what statue to remove, how a skip could be got to the house so that I could strip the olive store of the junk which I had accumulated over the years – while in fact I was trying to work out how the hell to clear from a place which I loved with all my being, I had overlooked the main cause of the upheaval.

Forwood grew more and more silent, more crumpled, greyer by the day. I had hardly noticed, so involved was I.

He said little – we had after all discussed this move logically and in detail for some months – but the psychological effect on him was disturbing. It reached a point one morning when, sitting under the vine for a breather (I had begun to sort out books in the olive store), he suddenly said: 'Are you *sure* that we are doing the right thing? Where shall we go from here? An hotel in Paris? To London and the greyness? I mean, if we tried *hard*, couldn't we manage to stick it out here? Do what we could with the land, let the rest slide, but try and hang on?'

The same afternoon I called off the sale, to the consternation of the unhappy Belgian family, and settled for a tougher existence, determined that whatever the risks were which I would have to face I'd face them here, on the hill.

Forwood began to recover almost immediately; it was strange to watch. So, I must confess, did I, for I had no idea where we would settle – there had been the floating plan of an hotel or an apartment in Paris (half an hour, give or take a bit, to London) or even, in final despair, renting a small house somewhere in the Chelsea area, while the furniture gathered dust once again in a warehouse.

I knew perfectly well that a 'small house somewhere in the Chelsea area' would cost me more than I had in the bank and would finally kill me off with claustrophobia, having lived for so long at an altitude of 400 metres with a green mountain-top beyond the kitchen sink and the whole of the Estérel range outside my bedroom windows.

So we stayed.

Naturally the hard work on the land had to be curtailed: two strong men with big machines, and far fewer years than I, dealt with the waving grasses on the terraces, while I worked the easier stuff around the house, and Forwood, with care, managed his lawns and long walks; and although the place would never again be 'impeccable', as it was once called locally, it was tidy, safe from fire and tended.

Somehow we'd manage.

I went back to work, finished off the missing chapter of the new book, mailed it to Sally, and started to plan the cover for my new publishers.

Things were, almost, back to normal again, or at least one did one's best to make it seem so.

It was the only way to play the game after all.

DIARY

SATURDAY, DECEMBER 31ST '83

Misty morning with light sun later. Gentle, and soft. Attenboroughs for supper to see the end of this disturbing, and almost disastrous, year.

The end of a year in which F. might have copped it but didn't; owing to care and wonderful skill. October 'check' (his first since op.) was successful all round.

An Orderly Man made the best-seller lists, I did a couple of episodes of one hour each in a marathon twelve-week French-Japanese 'cultural' TV series, *History through the Louvre*, with Charlotte [Rampling]. We won't measure up to K. Clark, but it was fun in an exhausting way. Weeks of homework on ancient Greek and Roman sculpture, plus the Flemish School of painters. *West of Sunset* ready for publication in March, and the land has not, as I so feared, reverted to 'savage heath' after all: we have managed to cope very well and had a bumper (200 kilo) olive crop, so that's not bad.

Another year ahead now. Orwell's 1984. Well, face it with high hopes and flying flags. To show my trust have started new novel (am I *really* quite neurotic?) and had timid try at start of autobiography four. Like novel, so far, best. Have to keep working somehow, and with No Cinema I am stuck with writing. I should be so lucky. At least I am pushing like a soap salesman at every door, along the corridor: I may well be astonished by what I find; but, as Colette says: 'To be astonished is one of the surest ways of NOT growing old too quickly.'

I'll go along with that.

There was astonishment all right.

In January I was summonsed down to Cannes and, in an imposing suite in the Carlton Hotel, invited to become President of the next Film Festival.

My first reaction, as always, was blind panic, my second to thank them and to ask for twenty-four hours to 'check my dates'. I had to keep the 'six-monthly medicals' in mind.

I telephoned Olga Horstig Primuz in Paris, who cried: 'Accept immediately! It is a great honour, actors are seldom asked to be President!'

I then called Losey in London, for he had been President once and could, if he felt like it, help me. I was not altogether certain what the President's duties were.

'Why you? For God's sake!'

'I don't know why me: probably scraping the barrel.'

'They must be.'

'I gather you are in one of your "mean" moods?'

'Just weary. It's a terrible job. *Terrible*, Dirkel.'

'Can you give me any helpful suggestions?'

'Say no.'

'Well I might say yes: I might like it.'

'You'll hate it. No one could *like* it. But insist on a private car and driver at all times for yourself, a suite of rooms – NOT a bedroom – and a translator to be at your side night and day if needed.

'Thanks. Did you hold your Jury meetings in French?'

'Did I hell! That's why you'll need the translator.'

'I think I'll manage.'

'Have a translator any way. Insist. He'll get you out of all the shit that hits the fan, and plenty will.'

'You've been a great help, Joe. I'm jam-packed with confidence.'

'Don't think that it's just a question of going to the movies three times a day and having fun. It's bloody hard work. Take pens and notepads, make your notes after *every* screening – otherwise you'll forget whether it's Sunday or last July. Any idea what films they'll shove in?'

'No. Nothing firm yet . . . there is talk of, *perhaps, Under the Volcano.*'

There was a silence from Joe.

Some years ago we had had a series of discussions about me playing the Consul for him, and I had been bitterly distressed when he, behind my back and without telling me at *any* time, decided to play a Celtic actor known for his extravagances and with whom Joe had become infatuated. I was 'dumped', and we did not speak to each other for some years. Then the breach healed: he lost the film anyway, and the rights reverted to the Mexican Government, who asked me to play the Consul. Without Joe. I accepted; but there were, shall we say, script and director problems, so that faded away too. No skin off anyone's nose finally.

'Well,' said Joe. 'That should make you happy.'

'What are you doing next?'

'I am doing a film with a lot of naked ladies in a Turkish bath.'

'Well, that should keep *you* happy.'

His laughter was tired, beaten, joyless.

'Turn down the President's job, Dirkel . . . it'll kill you.'

I accepted it.

'We want you to try and restore the dignity to the Festival which it has sadly lost over the last few years' I was told at my first 'briefing'.

A difficult job indeed. Joe's words were in my ear: 'Why you? For God's sake!'

The Festival had fallen on sad times. Once a glamorous occasion, it had now become a rather tacky affair, a film market attracting a host of unattractive customers, porno films, bums and tits, dope and drugs. The glamour had begun to fade, and the big stars, such as there were, stayed away. And, what was far more to the point, the film-makers kept their best films out of the Festival – its increasing (perhaps apocryphal) reputation for splitting the vote, juggling of the Jury votes, and general under-the-bar-counter chicanery to suit individual interests had frightened off many serious studios and directors. The American market wanted value for the money which they had lavishly poured into the coffers of Cannes in the past. It was openly suggested to me that a 'good film' had no chance of winning unless, as the saying went, a 'wallet was placed on the table'.

I felt rather like a member of the Salvation Army: I was in for a battle to save lost souls indeed. How to restore dignity to a crumbling Festival?

With a good Jury, honour and the discipline of a British Sergeant-Major? Perhaps it could work that way?

One other part of my briefing alarmed me.

The Jury was not to vote for anything overtly political. No emotional hysteria as there had been for Wajda's *Man of Iron*. Whoever went to see *that*? We were to choose films which would please a Family Audience, not ones which would appeal to 'a few students and a handful of *faux* intellectuals. Family Entertainment for all the world markets'.

My heart sank. Shades of the old Rank days. I began to think that I was not the right man for the job, for I had long ago deserted 'Family Entertainment', and catered, with the work I did, solely it would seem for precisely those 'few students and a handful of *faux* intellectuals'.

However, my Jury, when the time came in May, was superb. Serious, caring, no one at all frivolous. I began to assume my Sergeant-Major figure and we attended the first solemn meeting, in a heavily guarded room, sitting at a long table with bottle of mineral water, notepads and sharpened pencils, as if we were at a summit meeting. Secrecy, we were informed, was the key to the whole business. Not a word must be leaked out at any time. The Press must be avoided by all Jury members, and the final results of our deliberations would be announced by the President, only, on the last night of the Festival from the stage of the Palais where it would be sent round the world via Eurovision. This was part of the new formula to 'save the reputation of the Festival'. Before, the world Press had always had the results 'leaked' to them so that they could reach their readers with the news well in advance. Now they'd have to wait (breathlessly, it was assumed) for the last night and the first announcement.

All very well so far: secrecy was to be paramount, we all nodded and agreed and swore to be as monks and nuns, and take our vows.

But I had discovered, quite by chance, that the chic, and pleasant, woman who was there to translate for those members of the Jury who had no French, and who would be present at *all* our meetings and *all* our deliberations, was married to an American executive who represented two major American companies and was presently in town.

It seemed to me wiser, without impugning the undoubted integrity of the lady, to have someone with us who had nothing whatsoever to do with the cinema or the Festival. I asked for a teacher from the Berlitz School of Languages, or anyone else they could find, who would be impartial. A young lady, who translated for lawyers and doctors in the town, was found. She stayed with us for the whole two weeks.

It was my first (unpopular) stand against any 'errors'.

It was not to be the last.

We worked hard; we debated long hours locked in private rooms, haggled, discussed, argued, and finally, sometimes just before midnight, got our results ready. They were, at all times, a majority vote: that is to say seven or eight out of the possible ten. And there was no split vote at any time: if that seemed to be happening I insisted that we sat on and went over it all again until we had one clear, majority agreement.

Our results, on Best Actor and Best Actress, threw Authority into confusion. It was appalled, demanded who the players were, even asked what films they had appeared in. Since each and every film had been selected by themselves I felt that they really should know, and we stuck even more firmly to our decisions. They were official; they *had* to accept.

The last day's voting, for all the films, the Hommage and the coveted Palme d'Or, took place in a heavily guarded villa some way out of Cannes. We had outriders and police cars with flashing blue lights everywhere, and were locked in the villa all day until our results were ready to Authority.

We eventually reached our decisions just after six in the evening – the announcements were to be made, on the stage for the television and to the packed audience, by seven-thirty. We still had to change into dinner jackets and get back into town: there was little time left.

Authority arrived to hear our results. I read them out in a firm, clear voice. There was a horrified silence.

'What about the American films? There are no American awards?'

'No, none.'

Consternation and dismay. We sat perfectly silent at our huge round table.

'For *The Bounty*? There is nothing? It is not *possible!*'

'No votes at all.'

'For *Under the Volcano*?'

'Alas, I'm sorry . . . '

'You have not read the rules correctly, Mr President!'

I nearly, very nearly, took a punch at the speaker.

'I have read the rules correctly. We have followed them *precisely*. These are our considered and unanimous judgements.'

'You think that this . . . "*Paris, Texas*" is Family Entertainment?'

'We think that it was the best film submitted to us for judgement for the Palme d'Or.'

'And the Hommage! Why to Satyajit Ray? He is not here in Cannes!'

'No. He's in hospital in India with a serious heart complaint. This Hommage is to him for all the films, and entertainment, which he has given the world.'

'You *can't* do that! What about John Huston?'

'Nothing for John Huston.'

'You must give *him* the Hommage . . . '

'We have already given the Hommage to Ray.'

'Huston is here, in Cannes. He has come especially for the Festival, he has given us *Under the Volcano*! He is a very old man, he has travelled many, many thousands of miles, six thousand miles he has travelled to be with us. *Six thousand!*'

I sat mute, staring at my pile of votes; at the list which I would have to read out in less than an hour.

Suddenly a member of the Jury said, in a voice flat with hours of discussion, his pencil pointing at the heart of Authority: 'Listen: you do *not* win the fucking Palme d'Or for *travelling!*'

Astonishment indeed. But the verdict of the audience was tremendous, the applause and cheers for every one of our decisions was deafening – we grinned at each other with exhausted, happy relief.

We had, we hoped, restored a little dignity to the Festival. Only one compromise. No 'wallets on the table', all above board and honourable.

At the lavish supper which always ends the Festival in the pillared halls of the Carlton Hotel, the Jury and I sat together like a happy, weary group of schoolchildren.

Exams over, holidays ahead.

Madame Anne-Marie Dupuy, the formidable, enchanting and tireless Mayor of Cannes, came to thank us for our 'splendid work' on behalf of her city, and just one courteous member of Authority added his congratulations, suggesting that the evening had been a triumph.

Early the next morning I stood on the rain-drenched balcony of my hotel as a team of gardeners ripped out the wallflowers and primulas from the flowerbeds below and replaced them with fuchsias, petunias and geranium. Instant-Gardening for the Summer Season.

The Festival was over.

As I left to drive home in the rain a card from Olga was handed to me by the doorman.

It was quite simple, very gratifying.

SATURDAY.

Mon cher Président:
I am sorry to have seen so little of you . . . but work is WORK, and I have the impression that you have done a *wonderful* job . . .

There was no note of any kind from Authority – and there never was to be any note, not even to say 'Adieu!'

I had a shrewd feeling, somehow, that I would never be asked back.

Four weeks later, Patricia Losey, Joe's wife, telephoned one morning to say that he was dying. It was very sudden: a matter of days not weeks.

I was not, in some curious way, surprised. Perhaps I had subconsciously expected the news: his extreme sadness, weariness, disillusion and disenchantment were acute to a distressing degree the last time we had met and discussed, almost hopelessly, the possibility of doing *Lotte in Weimar*.

I telephoned at noon the next day, on a sudden impulse, to inquire how he was. His secretary, Victoria Bacon, answered: 'Well; have a word with Patricia . . . she'd like to talk to you.'

'I don't want to trouble her really; you can tell me . . . '

'No, honestly . . . Patricia is right here; we're just having a mug of coffee together –' She broke off suddenly.

There was a sound of scuffling, a door slammed, something fell.

Victoria was back on the line, her voice quick, alert. 'Call you back,' she said and hung up.

She returned my call in twenty minutes.

'He's gone,' she said. 'Isn't it strange? Just as you telephoned they called down for Patricia and she was with him. It's so odd that it should have been you. Do you think it could have been telepathy or something?'

It could have been – I don't honestly know. All I do know is that I had a strange compulsion to call at that precise moment – I could easily have waited until the evening. But knowing Joe as well as I did it would not have surprised me if, somewhere along the wavelengths, he had summonsed me: and I had obeyed.

We had known each other for over thirty years, thirty years of an 'imperfect friendship', imperfect only in that neither of us really *fully* understood the other and didn't trouble to do so. What we knew we liked well enough, admired and even loved, so that was sufficient.

I didn't know, or care, what his politics were. He laughed at me for my ignorance, and upbraided me for being a-political: 'It shows that you have no *real* thinking brain,' he used to say cheerfully. He didn't even like my life-style, although he greatly enjoyed some of the benefits which it brought him. He disliked 'servants' and 'aristocrats', as he called them, but made use of both at all times when he could. The 'aristocrats' he despised, just as he did 'servants'.

He was often distressingly rude to waiters, and maids, my own staff and anyone whom he considered to be 'subservient'; on the other hand, he was unable to do without them and enjoyed luxury to a disgraceful extent, expecting at all times only the best. He was jealous of people, courageous, he envied, was affectionate, caustic, rude, and quite capable of being devious if it so suited him. As I well knew. But whatever the faults, there were glorious compensations and nothing, finally, ever managed to break the deep affection, and respect, which we had for each other.

So. Joe had gone; Visconti, the Emperor, had gone; Cukor, who had perhaps taught me more about screen acting than any other director – he too had gone; and Fassbinder, the gentle, sometimes astonishing, genius-victim of a troubled and tortured childhood, had killed himself in his crummy flat. He too had, alas, gone.

It seemed to me that June morning, kicking a pebble down the track for a leaping Bendo, that the 'gathering' had begun.

As I walked into the ward I could see her, down at the far end on the right. She was lying half out of the bed, head down, arms trailing on the floor.

The bed beside her, where an ashen girl had lain unconscious for the last five days, was empty, the blankets neatly folded at its foot.

I called her name as I reached the empty bed and she looked up instantly, raised her arms, as thin as broom-sticks, to embrace me.

I leant towards her and kissed her forehead.

She smelled sour: the wound at her stomach had seeped through the dressings and soiled her nightdress.

'Darling!' she said. 'How lovely. I *knew* you'd come; get that chair and sit down.'

'What were you doing down there? Brushing the floor?'

'Resting. Getting the blood to my hands, what blood there is. I think they've drained it all away, I'm so feeble.'

She smiled weakly, her eyes sunken, hair straight, lustreless, grey: only the two little pearl earrings appeared to have life in the dull light of the ward. The woman in the far bed, a cheery person in glasses, nodded towards me with a bright smile, went on reading the *Sun*.

'She's *very* nice,' said Norah. 'They all know who you are now, of course; impossible to pretend it isn't a fillum star who comes to see me: aren't they extraordinary?'

'Where's your neighbour, the girl?'

'Oh. They took her away last night. Died, I suppose. That's the trouble with a public ward, you know everything that goes on, disagreeable business.'

'Well it's your fault. You insisted on National Health, not private.'

'Too expensive! Anyway . . . I hardly had any choice this time, darling, it was a near thing.'

Just before I had left France for the September 'medical check', Rosalind had telephoned to say that Norah had collapsed with a perforated bowel and had been rushed to hospital. They thought, at the time, that she was 'stable and all right'.

We had planned to dine together the night that I arrived in London, but instead she had telephoned the hotel and asked me to go and see her as soon as I could.

'Are you allowed visitors already?'

'I'm in a little curtained cubicle thing . . . you can come any time.' Her voice was frail, but the old Norah was lurking just below the surface.

She didn't, considering the seriousness of her operation, look too bad; she was bright-eyed, weak, but greedy for the smoked salmon sandwiches which I had brought her and which she ate almost before I could unwrap them.

'You are good to me! And fresh orange juice in a champagne bottle! How delicious.'

'Especially pressed at the Connaught. There must be a full pint there.'

'What a business it's all been.'

'What happened, for heaven's sake? You sounded absolutely splendid when I spoke to you on Tuesday.'

'I *was*! So odd. Then this terrible thing happened. I'm *werry, werry* lucky you know. They say they got me just in time. I was on the brink! Don't you love the way doctors speak? "On the brink"! *Honestly* . . . did you bring the photographs of the garden you promised me?'

She leafed through them with professional skill, admiring the roses and the lilies, the view of the pond and the yellow iris, one I'd especially taken for her of the view from Tart's Parlour and had had enlarged.

'Oh! How lovely! How I wish I were there . . . '

'How long, do you suppose, you'll have to be stuck here?'

'About a week . . . I hope. Then back again in six weeks for another operation which I simply dread. My guts, you see,' she said with a grim smile, eating away at her smoked salmon sandwich, the size of a postage stamp, 'are in a bag by my side, so for God's sake don't sit on the bed, will you?'

The elegant, fastidious, patrician creature with her guts in a bag at her side in a public ward.

'They are wonderfully kind to me. Nurses are marvellous. But I don't KNOW any of them, you see? As soon as you get used to one she's whisked off somewhere else or goes on 'leave'. It's disconcerting really. And all the young doctors are different every morning. Keep asking my name and what's wrong with me. Unsettling.'

'When you get out, then what?'

'Ah, that's the problem. I can't go back to the flat: all those stairs! So I think I'll go down to Betty in Kent . . . she spoils me marvellously, and I can have a tiny apartment to myself and the local nurse can come in . . . we'll manage.'

But it was not to be like that.

I went to the hospital every day and one afternoon discovered that she was no longer in the little cubicle, but in a different ward, on a different floor, and was looking a great deal less well. It was a busy ward and very full. As I arrived they were wheeling an ashen-faced girl towards the bed beside her, putting up screens; there was quiet bustle and rustle everywhere.

Norah smiled, as she always did when she saw me. 'There you are at last,' she said.

'Moved you?' I said, sitting beside her, my back to the bedmaking behind.

'And you found me. I was, apparently, in the wrong place. They want me in a ward so that they "can keep their eye on me". *Too* silly . . . no one seems to bother much anyway.'

The table across the foot of her bed was crammed with jars of flowers of all sorts, a few from gardens, others from expensive shops looking like hotel arrangements. The water in some was scummy, the flowers wilting, there was a faint smell of decay.

'They really have so much to do, poor creatures, they can't go around changing the water in my flowers . . . I don't like to ask them: they get quite snappish, you know.'

'How are you today. Mouldy?'

'I *look* mouldy, you mean? I feel bloody, frankly. Something's gone wrong.'

'What's gone wrong?'

She did look 'mouldy' and untidy and distressed.

'Well. One of the nurses, I don't know which one, gave me a purgative. I mean, can you beat it? A purgative with my guts where they are?'

'But why?'

'I don't know why. I complained to one of the interns this morning and he was very rude. Wagged his finger at me and said: "You *do* carry on, old girl" . . . I was so angry.'

'Well, I suppose they are rushed off their feet here . . . it's pretty well crammed.'

They had finished with the ashen-faced girl, removed the screens; she lay rigid beneath tight sheets and blankets, her feet poking up under them, like a Crusader's wife on a tomb.

'I hadn't been "carrying on" as he said, I simply told him that I had had the most dreadful time all night, terrible pain . . . I simply couldn't help myself . . . I had no control . . . '

'You are still in pain?'

'Yes. Fearful gripes . . . I don't know.' She brushed her hair helplessly with the back of her hand. 'Anyway, the intern went away, read my chart thing of course at the end of the bed, and then came back in a fearful state and said I should NEVER have been given the whatever it was. I ask you! I knew it was wrong . . . anyone would know. He was very apologetic . . . but the damage has been done. I feel *awful*.'

A tall, rather hefty nurse arrived at the bedside, the menu list in her hand. 'Tomorrow's lunch . . . what do you feel like, dear? Want to look or shall I give you a few suggestions?'

'I feel like death, frankly; give me a few suggestions.'

'Well, there's soup, three kinds: spring vegetable, mushroom or tomato . . . '

'I really don't want anything . . . just some bouillon. Or Bovril? Is there Bovril?'

'You must eat, dear,' said the nurse, and looking across the bed at me she said: 'She's being *very* naughty, you know. Simply won't eat, and that won't get us well and strong will it? I'll come back in a couple of ticks; think it over. There's a good girl.'

Norah looked at her receding back as she went down to other beds. 'They treat one like a monstrous child. Maddening. I really CAN'T eat custard and prunes or boiled cod and spinach . . . I can't eat anything.'

'Shall I nip out and get you some smoked salmon sandwiches, very tiny, thin, from the Connaught? It wouldn't take a moment really, the car is waiting.'

She shook her head wearily on the crumpled pillows. 'I can't eat, darling . . . I'd rather you stayed, don't go . . . stay with me. How's Forwood?'

'He's okay . . . the tests are all negative.'

'Thank God for that. I am glad. Do tell him . . . give him my love. All my love.'

'I wish to goodness you'd let me try and get you into Edward VII . . . '

'No . . . no . . . don't fuss about me. Of course I *could* go there: widow of a serving officer . . . but I don't think I could face the moving about. It would mean an ambulance and so on . . . '

'Let me try?'

But she refused point blank. The stuffing, as she said bitterly, with that odd twist of black humour which surfaced from time to time, had 'gone out of her'.

'Anyway,' she said, 'so many of my friends would have to be told, they all come to see me here . . . it would be frightfully difficult to tell everyone I'd changed and then, of course, there might not be a free bed.'

I could see that she was still playing, vaguely, with the idea of a move.

'I could call your friends . . . it wouldn't take long.'

'Take years! I have so many, they really are too good. Jerry, and Betty, Laurens, Iris, Grania, Amanda, dear Christopher . . . so many.'

'Too many. Sister says that you have far too many friends and that they exhaust you.'

'She's quite, quite wrong. They are my lifeline.'

I started to get up, she grabbed my arm urgently.

'Don't go! Stay . . . can't you stay a little longer?'

'The car's waiting. I've got to go all the way out to Twickenham.'

'Twickenham? What delightful friends do you have in Twickenham with whom I cannot compete?'

'It's a sort of, I know you hate the phrase, but it's a "sort of" memorial service for Joseph Losey. He hated all that rubbish in churches, ageing knights reading eulogies about him who had never even been to see his films. So we're having an end of film party for him on one of the stages at the studios, where he was most happy. Everyone is coming. Just to have a drink and a sandwich, to remember him.'

Norah was silent, she twisted one of her pearls. 'It's a splendid idea. Much better. Will you come tomorrow?'

'I'll come tomorrow, promise. No smoked salmon; sure?'

She smiled a sweet, lost, tired smile . . . as frail as a thread of fading light. 'No smoked salmon, darling. Kiss, though?'

As I walked through the long ward, two people were coming towards her with a large bunch of flowers, looking around at the beds.

'Ah! said the man. 'There she is . . . right at the end.'

It was the next day that I saw her from the door of the ward half hanging out of the bed, the thin arms trailing on the floor, her head down. The deterioration had been extraordinary overnight: I was alarmed and distressed by the haggard face, the circles under her eyes, the sunken look, but we had talked and she smiled a little and I got over the hump of the moment of shock.

'I wonder if you'd be an angel . . . there's an envelope there, on the table under the flowers somewhere . . . I haven't been able to read any of my letters. People write but I'm too exhausted to read them. But the envelope . . . a long one . . . not square . . . can you find it for me?'

I found the envelope under a jar of dying asters: a list of pencilled names scribbled down its length.

'Here you are; but let me get your pillows right, they are all squint and squashed.'

'They don't have time, you see.'

I pulled her gently towards me, she lay against my body as I leaned over the bed as light as a fledgling sparrow. I turned the pillows, restacked them, plumped them up, eased her back.

'There you are. Better?'

'Much. There's a pencil somewhere . . . I'm being a bother . . . a blue one, can you find it?'

'What are you up to? Making a will, or a shopping list?'

'Not a will . . . not that. Did it ages ago, but there are some people I perhaps forgot. I want the flat stripped out and auctioned; everything. Except my pictures and a few little bits and pieces. So I make a note of the names of the people I want to go and choose something before they chuck the lot out . . . you know how lawyers are, so slow, takes them ages to do anything. Just something to remind them of me.'

'Norah! Really . . . you've got plenty of time for that, come on now.'

'Must do it while I remember, they take so long, the lawyers . . . must see it in print. Amanda. I must remember my Amanda, she's been a saint . . . ' She wrote slowly, in her clumsy hands, the blue pencil wobbling with effort. 'Just a tiny remembrance, that's all.' She handed me the envelope and the pencil. 'Put them back under the flowers, will you. Then I'll know where they are. They will come and tidy everything up every minute of the day. There's a Philippino gel, a real devil. Everything goes into her waste-bucket.'

She lay back on the pillows as transparent as egg-white on a windscreen. 'You go tomorrow?'

'On the nine fifty-five Air France.'

'Lucky old you. I wish . . . I wish . . . ' She looked out of the big windows at the far end of the ward. 'When do you come back, then? Next "check" I suppose? Six months?'

I lied easily. 'There's a fillum on the way. Script's not right yet but I've said that I'll come over in October . . . about four weeks . . . and see how things are going.'

'Oh! October! Autumn . . . your hated month. All those dreadful colours you dislike so much.'

'Bonfire colours. Awful. I'll be able to come down to Kent to see you.'

'All the trees will be russet . . . like my hair used to be. Years ago . . . '

'In October, then . . . '

She turned suddenly and took my hand. 'You didn't tell me about the Losey thing at Twickenham. The memorial business. Was it fun?'

'Great fun. Everyone, well, nearly everyone, came. Lots of champagne, sandwiches . . . '

'If they ever had one of those terrible things for me . . . memorial services, you promise me faithfully that you'd never go, would you? Without me?' She was smiling lightly.

'I promise. Not unless you are by my side.'

She laughed, turned back to the windows.

'It's raining. Don't get wet.'

'I'll be back. In about four weeks. All right?'

'Lovely. Simply lovely.'

I leant down and kissed her on the lips.

'You know, I do happen to love you, very much indeed.'

She pressed my hand with both of hers, her eyes suddenly alive, bright with pleasure.

'I think that I *do* know that,' she said. 'I've got that on board.'

I walked quickly out of the ward and I didn't look back; or ever see her again.

I'm almost sixty-five.

I'm sitting on the platform, stage left, of the Younger Hall in St Andrew's University, Scotland.

I am shortly to be awarded an Honorary Degree of Letters.

Why? You may well ask; it'll raise a few eyebrows. It already has.

I don't give a fig about that.

I'm wearing a fine black satin cassock with wide cuffs. All down the front there are bright yellow buttons; these designate 'The Arts'.

I'm scared to death. I am not used to any form of academic life, and never expected to become a part of its rituals.

We were 'robed' a little time ago. A cheerful affair, like a changing room at a football match. Dons and tutors and graduands struggling into their gowns and hoods, the new boys, like me, being assisted by uniformed gentlemen of charm and distinction, who know exactly, after years of experience, just how one should be correctly dressed. And buttoned.

White bow-tie, the dark suit I bought to wear in Cannes for the Festival, a beating heart. You can hide that with clothing – but you can't stop it thudding under your shirt.

Then the procession. We walked in solemn state, two abreast, I too dry-mouthed to do more than smile weakly, led by liveried gentlemen carrying on high trophies and emblems of gold and silver. Tremendously serious, very moving, humbling.

Through proud crowds of singing parents and family members, mouthing the Latin words of the Gaudeamus, and then past the serried rows of singing students, all, I hoped, as anxious as I felt.

And so I sit up here, on the stage, so to speak, a captive audience below me. I can think a bit: there is nothing that I have to do for the moment.

All these young, unlined faces before me! Life has not yet printed its cruel map upon them, on their brows and cheeks, nor pulled down the corners of their mouths, creased their eyes, thinned their hair.

How I envy them their youth; how proud I am that I am there among them. I'm well aware that they have been sweating out their hearts for three or four years to reach this supreme moment in their lives, while I have idled through without the least thought of academic reward.

It's funny, sitting here in my leather chair, gowned like a clown with my yellow buttons, that when I was first asked to accept this honour, and it's an honour I never dreamed of, I thought it was a student hoax.

'No hoax indeed!' the Secretary of the Senate scribbled in his own hand in reply to my cautious acceptance.

I remember (sitting here, watching the Chancellor take his place at the 'altar') that I, puffed with pride, telephoned Norah with the news and only stopped when I had got to 821 of the code: she had died three weeks before.

I hung up, and looked out of the olive store windows to the oaks turning russet on the chapel hill. She'd have been 'werry' pleased, I think, that I am to be honoured by Scotland's most ancient university, founded in 1411; thirty years before Joan of Arc was burned at the stake in Rouen, and many, many years before Columbus discovered America. It's pretty clear to me that they don't chuck honours and degrees about like ping-pong balls. Which makes my situation all the more astonishing.

It would have pleased her, too, because it would have proved that her 'judgement' was not at fault, and that was something about which she minded greatly. Her life was books, words and her writers – she cared for little else. She always insisted that she 'published writers' as well as publishing books, and she at all times loved, bullied, cajoled, supported the people who came within her world. She gave beginners encouragement, often a start, always a chance, and by a sudden switch of a television button she had given me mine.

It would appear, therefore, from this wondrous moment, in this softly rustling hall, that her judgement had not been misplaced: her 'writer' had been accepted. It might have amused her, wryly, that while she had received her doctorate from, what they call here, a 'municipal university', I will get mine from so ancient and hallowed a place. But I never knew her to be envious or resentful of anything.

I'm thinking all this to stop rising panic: I hope that I appear laid-back and cool.

They are calling on the first degree students. The Chancellor stands tall and splendid in black and silver, John Knox's cap in his hand.

I wish that Pa and Ma were here.

She'd have cried beautifully, with enormous care, so that her mascara didn't run. Pa, I reckon, would have scratched his head in amused bewilderment thinking of all the money he had spent in the past to try and educate me against my will.

Look where ignorance has got me today, Pa!

I'd like Forwood to have been here too: after over forty years of care and counsel he'd have been pleased as punch, but the journey, and the standing about, and all the social business would have been a bit too much for him; however, I'm not entirely alone – Rosalind has come with me to be my 'minder'. I'm really not absolutely used to doing it all for myself. Yet.

I can see her, right up there in the front row of the packed gallery. Very pretty, blonde. Very straight-backed, very proud, very much a 'Smallwood product', for she was trained by Norah and became one of her 'gels'. So it's fitting that she is with me here today: a direct link with the past and this extraordinary moment. She started work with me on my first book at Chatto's; now she brings me ineffable comfort.

A linking indeed.

I know that behind me, in ranks rising high to the ceiling of this splendid hall, sit the dignitaries of the university in their varied cassocks, gowns and caps, but I know equally well that behind them, far, far away, and only in my mind's eye, is the backcloth massed with the faces and figures of the people who brought me here, providing the support I need for the modest performance, without words, which I shall shortly be required to make.

When I kneel before the Chancellor, as soon I shall, I will know that they are all about me, watching somewhere in the cosmic atmosphere.

DIARY

FRIDAY MORNING, JULY 5TH '85.

It's 3.35 a.m. and I can sleep no longer. They say that as one grows older one needs less sleep. Perhaps it's true?

I'm writing this at the oval table in the bow window of my opulent suite in Rusacks Hotel overlooking the 18th hole of the oldest golf course in the world. It is already quite light. I had forgotten how short the nights are here.

I've got two fat armchairs, settee, coffee table with a wobbly leg, a vitrine full of tarnished silver cups for long-forgotten matches played on that course below, a vase of dried leaves and grasses on the mantelpiece, the colour of mashed turnips, a large, dark print of anemones in a bowl, parchment lampshades hanging high on the ceiling.

There is a thick sea-mist and I cannot see the waves, only hear them sighing lazily along the beach, and only then when I open the windows. Close them because it is bitterly cold.

Last night was fun. Graduation Dinner with tables at herring-bone angles, a piper to play us in. Me at top table with silver candelabra, apricot roses, crystal and silver. Very elegant, rich apparently, established. Scowling scholastic faces in heavy gilt frames on the panelled walls, stained glass, speeches, a loving cup passed from one to another. Altogether moving, ancient and perfect. Kindness has overwhelmed me all day.

Later the graduation Ball, in a giant chiffon-draped marquee on the lawns. A Tissot painting. Girls in long dresses and tartan sashes, some of the men in the kilt, the rest in tails with white buttonholes. Everyone young and gay, and alive, and I an unbelieving part of it all.

Walked home to Rusacks with Rosalind through a silent St Andrews. I suppose, after so many centuries, the town takes all this in its stride? I can't, quite, yet.

This morning – or was it yesterday morning? – a television man said: 'Doctor van den Bogarde, would you move a wee bittie to your right . . . you're too far apart for the camera.'

I turned in surprise to see which of my relatives it could have been.

I *am* a mutt. I'll get used to it.

Perhaps back to bed: it's so damned cold my fingers are white.

Across the brilliant green of the 18th sacred hole, coming wanly through the mist, a young couple, she in a long dress trailing a negligent scarf, he in crumpled tails. They are wandering slowly, her head on his shoulder, through the meandering spume and fine rain, arms around each other.

In no hurry. Life before them. Or is it only breakfast? Which they are serving at four o'clock.

No matter: a new day has begun and it is as beautiful a way to see it start as any I can imagine.

A billow of mist rolls in from the ocean, drowning the ancient Club House, swirling across the pampered green below, dimming the light about me.

The tarnished cups in the vitrine look like lead; the chairs, the settee, the wobbly-legged coffee table become dark looming shapes, like fat scattered cushions; and the dried grasses on the mantelpiece are ghostly, still, spiky as sticks of incense; the lamps above me hang in shadow, shrouded in the gloom.

It's *very* cold; back, I think, now to bed. The maid is bringing tea at eight o'clock.

Perhaps, in that ethereal light, if I had heard the distant whisper of a scratchy wind-up gramophone, the rustle of a silk kimono, the clinging scent from a small leather powder puff, I might well have been persuaded that I was back where it had all begun for me: in Aunt Kitty's room.